MISSION LEGACIES

The American Society of Missiology Series, in collaboration with Orbis Books, seeks to publish scholarly works of high merit and wide interest on numerous aspects of Missiology – the study of mission. Able presentations on new and creative approaches to the practice and understanding of mission will receive close attention.

Previously published in
The American Society of Missiology Series

American Society of Missiology Series, No. 19

MISSION LEGACIES

Biographical Studies of Leaders
of the Modern Missionary Movement

EDITED BY

Gerald H. Anderson

Robert T. Coote

Norman A. Horner

James M. Phillips

ORBIS BOOKS

Maryknoll, New York 10545

The Catholic Foreign Mission Society of America (Maryknoll) recruits and trains people for overseas missionary service. Through Orbis Books, Maryknoll aims to foster the international dialogue that is essential to mission. The books published, however, reflect the opinions of their authors and are not meant to represent the official position of the society.

Library of Congress Cataloging-in-Publication Data

Mission legacies : biographical studies of leaders of the modern
missionary movement / edited by Gerald H. Anderson . . . [et al.].
   p. cm.
 Articles originally published in the International bulletin of
missionary research
 Includes index.
 ISBN 0-88344-964-1
 1. Missionaries – Biography. I. Anderson, Gerald H.
BV3700.M55 1994
266′.0092′2 – dc20
 [B]   94-16771
                                          CIP

Contents

PART TWO: AFRICA

PART FIVE: THEOLOGIANS AND HISTORIANS

Preface to the Series

The purpose of the American Society of Missiology (ASM) Series is to publish – without regard for disciplinary, national, or denominational boundaries – scholarly works of high quality and wide interest on missiological themes from the entire spectrum of scholarly pursuits relevant to Christian Mission, which is always the focus of books in the Series.

By "Mission" is meant the effort to effect passage over the boundary between faith in Jesus Christ and its absence. In this understanding of mission, the basic functions of Christian proclamation, dialogue, witness, service, worship, liberation, and nurture are of special concern. And in that context questions arise, including, How does the transition from one cultural context to another influence the shape and interaction between these dynamic functions, especially in regard to the cultural and religious plurality that comprise the global context of Christian mission?

The promotion of scholarly dialogue among missiologists and among missiologists and scholars in other fields of inquiry may involve the publication of views that some missiologists cannot accept, and with which members of the Editorial Committee do not agree. Manuscripts published in the Series reflect the opinions of their authors and are not understood to represent the position of the American Society of Missiology or of the Editorial Committee. Selection is guided by such criteria as intrinsic worth, readability, and accessibility to a range of interested persons and not merely to experts or specialists.

The ASM Series Editorial Committee
James A. Scherer, Chair
Mary Motte, FMM
Charles Taber

Contributors

Catherine B. Allen is president of the Women's Department of the Baptist World Alliance, a voluntary post for the years 1990-95. She served on the staff of Woman's Missionary Union, Southern Baptist Convention, 1964-89, and on the staff of Samford University, 1989-92.

R. Pierce Beaver was professor emeritus of Missions at the University of Chicago Divinity School when he died in 1987. He had been director of the Missionary Research Library (1948-1955), and director of the Overseas Ministries Study Center (1973-1976).

Clinton Bennett is lecturer in Study of Religions at Westminster College, Oxford, England.

John C. Bennett is director of the Theological Resource Center of Overseas Council for Theological Education and Missions, Inc., Greenwood, Indiana.

Kathleen Bliss did educational work in India (1932-39), was editor of *The Christian News Letter* (1945-49), and lecturer in religious studies at the University of Sussex (1967-72). She died in 1989.

J. Jermain Bodine, formerly assistant director of the Duncan Black Macdonald Center in Hartford, Connecticut, and bibliographical research consultant and supervisor of library resources at the Hartford Seminary Foundation, is pastor of the Stratham Community Church in Stratham, New Hampshire.

William H. Brackney is principal and professor of Historical Theology at McMaster Divinity College, McMaster University in Hamilton, Ontario.

Eleanor Brown, now retired, served as a missionary educational worker with the Church Missionary Society in Kenya. After returning to England she was a member and then the head of St. Julian's Community in Sussex.

David Bundy is librarian and associate professor of Church History at Christian Theological Seminary, Indianapolis, Indiana.

Paul Rowntree Clifford, now retired, was president of Selly Oak Colleges in Birmingham, England, and served for many years as treasurer of the International Association for Mission Studies.

Ralph R. Covell is retired from Denver Theological Seminary, where he was professor of missions and dean of the faculty.

Hugo H. Culpepper, now retired, was senior professor of Christian Missions and World Religions at the Southern Baptist Theological Seminary, Louisville, Kentucky.

F.W. Dillistone taught in theological seminaries in Canada and the United States, then became dean of Liverpool, England, and later chaplain of Oriel College, Oxford. He died in 1993.

Ruth Franzén holds a doctorate in church history from the University of Helsinki, Finland, where she is a teacher and researcher.

Hans-Werner Gensichen, now retired, was professor of the History of Religions and Missiology at Heidelberg University, Germany.

Arthur F. Glasser is dean emeritus, School of World Mission, Fuller Theological Seminary, Pasadena, California.

Winfried Glüer is East Asia secretary of the Association of Churches and Missions in South West Germany.

H. McKennie Goodpasture is professor of Christian Missions at Union Theological Seminary in Richmond, Virginia.

Peter G. Gowing, an American missionary serving under the United Church Board for World Ministries, was director of the Dansalan Research Center, Marawi City, Philippines. He died in 1983.

Carol Graham was an Anglican missionary in India from 1927, with interruptions during World War II, to 1960. She died in 1989.

Willi Henkel, O.M.I., is director of the Pontifical Missionary Library and editor of the *Bibliografia Missionaria*, Rome.

Libertus A. Hoedemaker is lecturer in Missions and Ecumenics at the State University of Groningen in the Netherlands.

W. Richey Hogg, now retired, was professor of World Christianity at Perkins School of Theology, Southern Methodist University, Dallas, Texas.

C. Howard Hopkins is professor emeritus of History at Rider College in Philadelphia, Pennsylvania.

Lydia Huffman Hoyle teaches in the Department of Religion, Georgetown College, Georgetown, Kentucky.

Everett N. Hunt, Jr., is professor of the History of Missions in the E. Stanley Jones School of World Mission and Evangelism, Asbury Theological Seminary, Wilmore, Kentucky.

George G. Hunter III is dean and Beeson Professor of Evangelism and Church Growth in the E. Stanley Jones School of World Mission and Evangelism, Asbury Theological Seminary, Wilmore, Kentucky.

Eleanor M. Jackson is a lecturer in Religious Studies at St. Martin's College, Lancaster, England.

Ernst Jäschke, a pastor emeritus in Erlangen, German, was a missionary in East Africa and Papau New Guinea and served as executive secretary of the Leipzig Lutheran Mission.

R. Park Johnson, retired mission executive of the Presbyterian Church (U.S.A.) in the Middle East, worked in Iran, Lebanon, Pakistan, and Nepal.

J. Herbert Kane was professor of Missions, Trinity Evangelical Divinity School, Deerfield, Illinois. He died in 1988.

Hans Kasdorf, formerly professor of World Mission, Mennonite Brethren Biblical Seminary in Fresno, California, is professor emeritus, Freie Theologische Akademie in Giessen, Germany.

Creighton Lacy, now retired, was professor of World Christianity in the Divinity School of Duke University, Durham, North Carolina, is professor emeritus, Freie Theologische Akademie in Giessen, Germany.

Michael A. Laird is senior lecturer in Modern History, University of Portsmouth, England.

Christopher Lamb, in Coventry, England, is secretary for Inter-faith Relations for the Board of Missions (Church of England) and the Council of Churches for Great Britain and Ireland.

Charles Henry Long, an Episcopal priest, is editor and director of Forward Movement Publications in Cincinnati, Ohio.

F. Dean Lueking is pastor of Grace Lutheran Church, River Forest, Illinois.

Louis J. Luzbetak, S.V.D., now retired, was editor of *Anthropos: International Review of Ethnology and Linguistics* and served on the staff of the Vatican's Pontifical Council for Culture.

Joseph Masson, S.J., professor at the Gregorian University in Rome since 1958, also serves as Pontifical Consultant to the Congregation for Evangelization of Peoples (Propaganda Fide) and to the Secretariat for Non-Christians.

James K. Mathews, a bishop of the United Methodist Church, now retired, went to India as a missionary in 1938 and later was an administrator for the Board of Missions of the Methodist Church.

Gerald E. McGraw is director of the School of Bible and Theology and Fuller E. Callaway Professor of Biblical Studies at Toccoa Falls College, Toccoa Falls, Georgia.

Josef Metzler, O.M.I., taught mission history for more than thirty years at the Papal University Urbaniana, Rome, and was archivist of Propaganda Fide. Since 1984 he has been prefect of the Vatican Archives.

Karl E. Müller, S.V.D., is the former director of the Society of the Divine Word missiological institute in Sankt Augustine, Germany.

Olav Guttorm Myklebust is professor emeritus of Missiology in the Free Faculty of Theology, Oslo.

Lesslie Newbigin, now retired in London, was for many years a missionary and bishop of the Church of South India in Madras.

James A. Patterson is associate professor of Church History and chair of the Department, Mid-America Baptist Seminary, Memphis, Tennessee.

Dana L. Robert is associate professor of International Mission at Boston University School of Theology.

Andrew C. Ross is senior lecturer in the History of Missions and deputy director of the Centre for the Study of Christianity in the Non-Western World, University of Edinburgh, Scotland.

Anne Rowthorn has been a lecturer at Hartford Seminary and a member of the Standing Commission on World Mission of the General Convention of the Episcopal Church.

Gerold Schwarz is study director at a Gymnasium in Esslingen, Germany.

John T. Seamands, now retired, was professor of Christian Missions at Asbury Theological Seminary, Wilmore, Kentucky.

David A. Shank, now retired, was a missionary of the Mennonite Board of Missions (Elkhart, Indiana) serving as a Bible teacher with Independent churches in West Africa, based in Abidjan, Côte d'Ivoire.

Eric J. Sharpe has been professor of Religious Studies in the University of Sydney, Australia, since 1977.

Wilbert R. Shenk is director of Mission Training Centre and associate professor of Missions, Associated Mennonite Biblical Seminary, Elkhart, Indiana.

A. Christopher Smith is program officer (for non-Western Christianity and cross-cultural Christian partnership) in the Religion Program of the Pew Charitable Trusts, Philadelphia.

Marc R. Spindler is director of the Department of Missiology, Interuniversity Institute for Missiological and Ecumenical Research, Leiden, Netherlands, and professor of Missiology and Ecumenics at the State University of Leiden.

Vivienne Stacey has worked in Pakistan under the Bible and Medical Missionary Fellowship since 1954.

Richard W. Taylor, a Methodist missionary in India for thirty-three years, was on the staff of the Christian Institute for the Study of Religion and Society. He died in 1988.

Notto R. Thelle served as a missionary in Japan (1969-1985) and is currently professor of Missiology and Ecumenics at the Theological Faculty of Oslo University.

Jack Thompson is lecturer in Mission Studies at the Centre for the Study of Christianity in the Non-Western World at New College, University of Edinburgh, Scotland.

Edvard Torjesen, now retired, served forty years as a missionary with TEAM in China and Taiwan among aboriginal peoples and in North America and Europe.

J. van den Berg is professor emeritus of Church History at the State University of Leiden, Netherlands.

Andrew F. Walls is director of the Centre for the Study of Christianity in the Non-Western World, New College, University of Edinburgh, Scotland.

Darrell L. Whiteman is professor of Cultural Anthropology in the E. Stanley Jones School of World Mission and Evangelism, Asbury Theological Seminary, Wilmore, Kentucky.

Jean-Paul Wiest is research director of the Maryknoll Society History Program, Maryknoll, New York.

Dorothy Clarke Wilson, now retired in Orono, Maine is the author of numerous biographies. In addition to *Dr. Ida*, she has written *Apostle of Sight*, the story of Dr. Victor Rambo, surgeon to India's blind; *Granny Brand*, the story of Evelyn Brand, Paul Brand's mother; *Palace of Healing*, the story of Dr. Clara Swain, first missionary woman doctor; *Take My Hands*, the story of Dr. Mary Verghese, a paraplegic Indian doctor; and *Ten Fingers for God*, a biography of Dr. Paul Brand, pioneer in surgery and rehabilitation for leprosy patients.

Introduction

In 1792, when a cobbler in Northamptonshire, England, issued a call for world mission, almost ninety percent of the world Christian community shared his racial identity: Caucasian. The cobbler – William Carey – also reflected a geographical reality: Three out of every four Christians in the world resided in Europe and North America.

Largely as a result of mission from the West, and the growth of the churches of the non-Western world, the profile of global Christianity changed dramatically in the next two hundred years. Numerically the church mushroomed from 200 million souls in A.D. 1800 to nearly two billion in the final decade of the twentieth century.

Not surprisingly, as non-Western Christianity has grown, the Caucasian Christian community, in its ratio to the world church, has declined – from ninety percent in 1800 to less than fifty percent of the total two centuries later. And the Christians of Western Europe and North America no longer account for almost three-quarters of the world Christian community but only thirty-five percent. (Data provided by David B. Barrett, editor of the *World Christian Encyclopedia*.) This fundamental shift of the Christian heartland from the West to Africa, Asia, and other Third World regions was envisioned and promoted by a vast cadre of Christians, people who from the outset were motivated by a global vision of the kingdom of God.

Mission Legacies preserves the stories of a selection of nineteenth- and twentieth-century pioneers of mission, men and women, Protestant and Catholic, who played creative roles in turning that global vision into global reality. Here, students of world Christianity can gain insight into the spiritual and human dynamics that produced the modern Christian missionary movement.

Most of the personalities in this collection are products of Western European and North American churches. The disproportion of white faces in the story of Christian mission will ultimately be rectified as a result of the initiatives of people like Carey. Carey's own story is retold here, respectfully stripped of its idealized aura. Also found here is the story of Gustav Warneck, the "father" of scholarly mission studies. Who would have guessed that the great German scholar traced his spiritual awakening to a crusade by an American "deeper life" evangelist? Or who would have linked Joe Oldham, coordinating secretary of the Edinburgh 1910 World Missionary Conference and founding editor of the *International Review of Missions*, with a circle of friends like Michael Polanyi and Karl Mannheim? Readers unfamiliar with Catholic mission history will enjoy discovering the "missionary pope," Pius XI, one of the first to see the importance of the scientific study of culture in the service of Christian mission. Wonderfully human vignettes run through these sketches, such as E. Stanley Jones running from the room in confusion as his Indian wrap-around garment loses its moorings.

One is struck by the frequency of cross reference, provided quite accidentally. (The authors of these essays wrote independently of one another.) Familiar names crop up time and again. One is also struck by the deep and steady commitment to Christ that resonates throughout these chapters. There is also an impressive unity despite differences of century, national origin, and church tradition – testimony to the superintending inspiration of the Lord of mission.

Mission Legacies is divided into several generic categories: "Promoters and Interpreters," beginning with Charles Simeon; "Theologians and Historians," beginning with Gustav Warneck; "Theorists and Strategists," beginning with William Taylor; and "Administrators," beginning with Henry Venn. In addition, there are three regional groupings: Africa, China, and Southern Asia. Perhaps a future volume will provide additional stories of mission leaders associated with North Africa, the Middle East, Northeast Asia, the Pacific, and Latin America.

The editors of *Mission Legacies* are, or have been, senior staff members of the Overseas Ministries Study Center (OMSC), where several generations of missionaries and overseas national church leaders have spent their furloughs or study leaves. Formerly located in Ventnor, New Jersey, OMSC relocated in 1987 to New Haven, Connecticut. More than a few of the chapters of this volume were researched at the Day Missions Library of Yale University Divinity School, within a five-minute walk of OMSC's front door.

The chapters of this volume first appeared in the *International Bulletin of Missionary Research*, published since 1977 by OMSC. The value of the series was signaled in the mid-1980s when the Associated Church Press twice presented an Award of Merit to the *International Bulletin*, recognizing in particular the mission legacy series for excellence.

The chapter assignments were made in a serendipitous fashion over a period of nearly twenty years, as the editors identified contemporary scholars with the necessary expertise to share particular biographical profiles. A product of this informal editorial approach is the underrepresentation of women and of individuals from the Two-Thirds World (six of each). As world mission scholarship matures and probes more deeply into the Great Story, we may expect the gallery of mission leaders to be drawn from all ranks of the global church.

Mission Legacies provides an authentic starting point for understanding in human terms the dynamic that produced today's global church. Here are some of the pioneers that led and inspired the movement that gave a new face to world Christianity.

Part One

PROMOTERS
and
INTERPRETERS

Charles Simeon

Thomas Fowell Buxton

Adoniram Judson Gordon

Arthur Tappan Pierson

A.B. Simpson

Fredrik Franson

Pius XI

Helen B. Montgomery

Lucy W. Peabody

Robert P. Wilder

John R. Mott

William Owen Carver

Ruth Rouse

Friedrich Schwager

Florence Allshorn

W.A. Visser 't Hooft

Charles Simeon
1759-1836

Church Loyalist and Mission Innovator

John C. Bennett

As the vicar of Holy Trinity Church, Cambridge, and a fellow of King's College, Charles Simeon (1759-1836) was arguably the foremost evangelical clergyman in the Church of England during the late eighteenth and early nineteenth centuries. Well known for pressing evangelicals to observe the discipline and order of the established church, he also contributed significantly to the development of the nineteenth-century British missionary movement, a markedly voluntary phenomenon. Reconciling the tension between his regular Anglican churchmanship and the voluntaryism of evangelical missionary efforts is key to understanding Simeon's mission legacy.[1]

Seeds of 1759

In the birth records of England in 1759 are the names of four men who were to have significant effect on the evangelical Anglican share of the British missionary movement.[2] Most prominent of the four was the younger William Pitt, made prime minister at the age of twenty-five in 1783. Pitt was no evangelical, but he created a political and economic climate that was conducive to the developing British Empire and the missionary movement that would be connected with it.[3] Only slightly less noticeable, and of far more direct influence, was William Wilberforce. His vision for a Christian nation and his evangelical agenda in Parliament – supported by Pitt at key points – cleared the way for missionary activity in British India and beyond.[4] John Venn, later rector of Clapham, was also born in 1759. Venn was the leading clerical light of Wilberforce's "Clapham Saints" and a prime architect of the Society for Missions to Africa and the East, soon after renamed the Church Missionary Society. The fourth person was Charles Simeon.

The future vicar of Holy Trinity Church was born at Reading on September 24, 1759, into the family of Richard Simeon, a wealthy landowner and businessman. His mother, Elizabeth Hutton, descended from a clan that boasted two archbishops of York. Simeon's elder brother, Richard John, was a master in Chancery until his untimely death in 1782. His younger sibling, Edward, became a successful London merchant and a director of the Bank of England.[5]

Simeon entered Eton at the age of seven. Later in life he characterized the school as "so profligate . . . [that he] should be tempted even to murder his own son" rather than submit him to the same experience.[6] Simeon found the spiritual climate of Cambridge, when he entered as a King's Scholar in 1779, to be little better than what he had left behind at Eton.[7] Like many first- and second-generation evangelicals, Simeon's faith was not shaped by the institutional process; rather he was *mentored* in the faith. The autobiographical account of his spiritual pilgrimage begins with an encounter with the Scriptures and continues through a series of relationships with a number of the leading lights of the evangelical movement, including John Newton and the elder Henry Venn.[8] The efficacy and value of the evangelical mentoring process was etched into Simeon's worldview and played an important role in shaping his missionary agenda.

Following his evangelical conversion on Easter 1779, Simeon decided to pursue the Christian ministry. He took his degree in May of 1783 and was made a fellow of King's and ordained deacon in the same month. Simeon spent the summer as honorary curate to Christopher Atkinson at St. Edward's Church in Cambridge. When the parish minister of Holy Trinity Church died unexpectedly that autumn, Simeon's father sought the post for his son. After a squabble between the bishop and the congregation, who favored another candidate, Simeon was made vicar and preached his first sermon in the pulpit of Holy Trinity Church in November. It was, however, not a happy beginning:

> The disappointment which the parish felt [because of my appointment] proved very unfavorable to my ministry. The people almost universally put locks on their pews, and would neither come to church, nor suffer others to do so . . . I put in there a number of forms, and erected in vacant places, at my own expense, some open seats; but the churchwardens pulled them down, and cast them out of the church. To visit the parishioners in their own houses was impracticable; for they were so imbittered against me, that there was scarcely one that would admit me into his house.[9]

With Simeon's Sunday morning service under boycott, and pastoral ministry largely impossible, Simeon decided to establish a Sunday evening lecture. This, too, the church wardens prevented by locking the church doors. Nevertheless, Simeon persevered. He took priest's orders the following September (1783), eventually made peace with his parishioners, and became an evangelical fixture in the parish, his college, and the university for the next half-century.

White Knight of Evangelicalism?

In the one and a half centuries since his death in 1836, Charles Simeon has been the focus of a host of funeral sermons, one memoir, two full biographies, more than ten "remembrances," and at least a half dozen thematic assessments.[10] Throughout these treatments Simeon is regularly characterized as an evangelical *and* a committed churchman. Indeed, the most common impression associated with Simeon's name has always been his twin loyalty to the evangelical cause and the established church.

Smyth's *Simeon and Church Order* (1940), the definitive work to date on his churchmanship, speaks of Simeon's "steadying influence" on evangelicalism in the established church. According to Smyth, Simeon addressed the two most significant internal problems confronting evangelical Anglicans at the outset of the nineteenth century: the need for adherence to church order, and the means for continuity in parish leadership.[11] Simeon applied himself to the former issue by tutoring his Cambridge students in conformity to church discipline. He attended to the latter concern through innovations in clerical patronage. Elliot-Binns, in *The Early Evangelicals* (1953), seconds Smyth in noting the "parochial terms" in which Simeon expressed his evangelicalism.[12] Even Ford K.

Brown, in *Fathers of the Victorians* (1961), acknowledges the quality of Simeon's churchmanship, despite his disaffection with Simeon's evangelical agenda.[13]

With the weight of a century of uniform historical opinion pressing upon them, Pollard and Hennell concluded that Charles Simeon, more than any other, was instrumental in retaining the commitment of second- and third-generation evangelicals to the Church of England.[14] Thus, Charles Simeon, "the complete Anglican,"[15] emerges from British ecclesiastical history as the white knight of second-generation evangelical churchmen.

In Search of Charles Simeon

To label Charles Simeon of Cambridge as an evangelical and churchman cannot be incorrect. It is, however, an incomplete description of the man, his worldview, and his work. His complexity becomes especially apparent when his involvement in the British missionary movement is considered.

First, though we have in Simeon an Anglican clergyman with a fundamental concern for ecclesiastical order, he nevertheless championed the formation of a voluntary missionary society – the Church Missionary Society (CMS). Moreover, Simeon knew that the CMS would be governed exclusively by evangelical churchmen, that it would operate independently of the hierarchy of the established church, and that it would compete with the church's existing missionary societies.[16] This was Simeon the voluntaryist.

Second, in Simeon we have an evangelical clergyman and founder of an evangelical missionary society who insisted on the submission of that society and its missionaries to the hierarchy of the established church. Simeon urged the CMS to subject itself to the Church of England, although its power structure had become known for its ambivalence, if not opposition, to the missionary agenda. This was Simeon the churchman.

Third, in Simeon we have a university figure who, although endeavoring to impart missionary vision to the established church, and aiding the creation of voluntary missionary societies for churchmen, failed to direct a sizable number of students toward missionary service through either channel. Instead, Simeon encouraged large numbers of "his" missionary candidates to seek employment as chaplains with the British East India Company and then used his influence with the company's Court of Directors to secure the appointments.[17] This was Simeon the mentor and patron.

These interconnected and contradictory developments were not the product of ordinary evangelicalism and Anglican churchmanship. Such conflicting outcomes were made possible by a certain toleration for paradox.[18] Indeed, the closer one looks at Charles Simeon and his missionary agenda, the less predictable he appears.

Simeon's Missionary Agenda

The roots of Charles Simeon's evangelicalism, his commitment to Anglican order, and his penchant for the exercise of patronage merged in their effect on the British missionary movement. The net result was an agenda for promoting Christian mission with three interacting centers of gravity: churchmanship, voluntaryism, and personal patronage. The churchman in Simeon, the activist in Simeon, and the mentor-patron in Simeon found appropriate roles in the missionary movement. True to paradoxical form, Simeon also argued for the supremacy of each aspect of his work. The interplay between the three facets of Simeon's missionary agenda is apparent in a brief chronology of his chief mission-related efforts.

1787. From the outset of his ministry Charles Simeon championed Christian mission as the appointed means for the global proclamation of the universal grace of God in Christ. An opportunity to apply his support for missionary work arose in 1787. In that year Simeon undertook the promotion of a "missionary establishment" in Bengal under East India Company patronage.[19] However, he was surprised and disappointed by the opposition of the company and Parliament to the plan.

1797. By 1797 Simeon was openly encouraging voluntary effort for Christian mission. However, he had discovered that he could not expect Anglicans to support the "undenominational" (London) Missionary Society (LMS), and he would not ask his evangelical colleagues to limit their backing to the SPCK and the SPG. An alternative society for evangelical churchmen had become necessary.

1799. For two years Simeon had crisscrossed England from the Midlands to Cornwall in support of an evangelical missionary society for the established church. During his travels to numerous clerical meetings Simeon had become impatient with the reluctance of his evangelical colleagues to take definite action. Consider Simeon's plea to the Eclectic Society at its meeting on March 18: *"What can we do? – When shall we do it? – How shall we do it? . . .* We cannot join the [London] Missionary Society; yet I bless God that they have stood forth. We must now stand forth. We require something more than resolutions – something ostensible – something held up to the public. Many draw back because we do not stand forth. – *When shall we do it?* Directly: not a moment to be lost. We have been dreaming these four years, while all England, all Europe has been awake."[20] Simeon's spirits were greatly lifted by the creation of the CMS the following month.

1800. With the founding of the CMS, Simeon's concerns turned to recruiting candidates for missionary service. Simeon discouraged volunteers per se, that is, those who stepped forward from personal enthusiasm or vocational despair: "When a man asks me about a call to be a Missionary, I answer very differently from many others. I tell him that if he feels his mind to be strongly bent on it, he ought to take that as a reason for suspecting and carefully examining whether it is not self rather than God which is leading him to the work. The man that does good as a Missionary is he who . . . says, 'Here am I; do what seemeth good unto thee: send me.'"[21] Simeon advocated a sending strategy in which God, via a mentor, discovers missionary potential, shapes it, and channels the candidate toward a sphere of activity, perhaps through an appointment arranged by the mentor.

1804. By the end of the CMS's first half-decade, Simeon had become concerned over the unwillingness of most university students to consider missionary service.[22] Owing to the pioneering work of the Dissenting societies (e.g., the Baptists and the LMS), missionaries had developed a reputation as artisans and schoolteachers. University graduates found little to recommend these vocations.[23] Moreover, Simeon had become frustrated with the establishment's restrictions on missionary work in India. His relationship with the CMS also became strained by his unsuccessful efforts to recruit missionaries for the society. Simeon began to search for alternatives to missionary service with a voluntary society. His connection with David Brown and Charles Grant, dating back to 1787, proved to be formative.

1805. Simeon gave serious thought to an alternative channel for missionary activity. East India Company chaplaincies – a respectable vocation for university graduates – would allow Simeon to send his best students to India while avoiding the establishment's restrictions on missionaries per se. From 1805 to 1820, Simeon encouraged more than three dozen of his students to apply for India Company chaplaincies. With the support of Grant, twenty-one of Simeon's disciples made successful applications. It is significant that more than half of this activity occurred after the 1813 renewal of the India Company's charter lifted most of the restrictions on missionary access to India. Simeon's indirect influence in India, through "his" chaplains, extended far beyond his death in 1836.

1809. The alternatives to the CMS continued to emerge for Simeon. He began to give serious attention to a moderate form of millenarianism and, as a result, developed an enthusiasm for the conversion of the Jewish people. Simeon came to believe that Jewish converts would become a strategic means to evangelize traditionally non-Christian societies. This conviction, combined with continued difficulties in recruiting and placing missionaries, motivated Simeon to participate in the work of the London Society for Propagating Christianity Amongst the Jews (LSPCJ).[24] Simeon's most significant contribution to the LSPCJ was its reorganization in 1814 as a society governed by churchmen.

1814. With the creation of the Calcutta episcopate in 1813, Charles Simeon had anticipated a close and profitable relationship between the CMS and the bishop of Calcutta. However, Simeon became concerned for the CMS's commitment to church order when the society balked at the submission of its missionaries in India to the new bishop. The General Committee of the Society had become suspicious of T.F. Middleton from the first notice of his appointment in 1814. Middleton was no evangelical. The society would not instruct its missionaries to submit to the bishop until he licensed them. In turn, Middleton refused to license the missionaries because he was unsure of their loyalty.[25] Problems of this sort plagued the CMS's work in India until the 1840s. In contrast, Simeon consistently urged proper cooperation between the CMS and the bishop of Calcutta. Simeon's influence in the matter was also indirectly exerted through his former students who were then chaplains in India.

1818. Although the CMS's ecclesiastical policies and practices troubled Simeon and strained his relationship with the society, he did not abandon the CMS. He regularly encouraged his Cambridge congregation to subscribe to the society.[26] Moreover, Simeon supported the development of auxiliary Church Missionary Associations (CMAs) from the inception of the plan in 1813. However, Simeon delayed his backing for the Cambridge association until 1818. He had deferred his support for a local CMS auxiliary because of continued trouble between the society and Middleton and the residual tensions in the town from the founding of the Bible Society's auxiliary in 1812.

The 1820s. During the closing decade and a half of his life, Simeon did not fail to continue to mentor and influence second- and third-generation leaders for the evangelical Anglican missionary movement. Consider, for example, his relationship with Henry Venn, the distinguished honorary secretary of the CMS, and Daniel Wilson, the evangelical bishop of Calcutta. By means of his influence on the two men, Simeon indirectly helped the CMS to strike a balance between its ecclesiastical and missionary priorities. Venn and Wilson made peace between the society and the Calcutta episcopate in 1838.[27] Charles Simeon is, perhaps, owed some of the credit for the achievement of this "Concordat." Although it was an indirect product of his efforts, it serves as a fitting reminder of the evangelical Anglican who strove for balance between churchmanship, voluntaryism, and individualism in the first decades of the British missionary movement.

Legacy of Charles Simeon

As has been suggested in the main body of this article, Charles Simeon approached his missionary agenda as a voluntaryist and a mentor-patron. His intense efforts on behalf of the formation of the Society for Missions to Africa and the East, later renamed the Church Missionary Society, highlight his willingness to rely on voluntary means in order to forward the missionary agenda. Simeon's role in the creation of the CMS established him as a voluntaryist to no lesser extent than Wilberforce and the Clapham Saints. When the CMS became a less fruitful channel for his missionary patronage, Simeon turned to the East India Company as an alternative, demonstrating the independent spirit of his patronage. It is certainly true that Simeon's work in support of the CMS and his partnership with Grant in appointing EIC chaplains were consistent with his evangelical commitment, but this fact does nothing to lessen the tension between his missionary activities and his churchmanship.

The standard secondary sources on Charles Simeon, such as those by Smyth, Pollard and Hennell, and Hopkins, do not attempt to resolve this tension. Simeon's missionary agenda is not the major consideration in these accounts of his life and work. The fact that Simeon's involvement with the CMS had greatly diminished by 1804 may have caused these authors to connect his embrace of the CMS's voluntary principles with the other irregularities of his early years. Moreover, the limited emphasis on Simeon's missionary efforts in these studies is consistent with their ecclesiastical (versus missionary) focus. However, it would be a mistake to relegate Simeon's missionary concerns to the periphery of his agenda. The frequency with which missionary affairs were addressed in Simeon's correspondence, sermons, autobiography, and Carus's *Memoirs* suggests that the global progress of the Gospel was a central concern to Charles Simeon.

The voluntaryism and independence of action that is inherent in Simeon's missionary agenda stand in contrast with his churchmanship. Nevertheless, the Cambridge minister's reputation as a regular churchman was well deserved. The reality is that Simeon's pragmatism and tolerance of paradox made room for these divergent agendas. Recognizing this tension is the key to understanding Charles Simeon's legacy for the British missionary movement in the early nineteenth century.

Notes

1. Portions of this article are based on the author's "Charles Simeon and the Evangelical Anglican Missionary Movement: A Study of Voluntaryism and Church-Mission Tensions" (Ph.D. diss., University of Edinburgh, 1992) and also appear in "Voluntary Initiative and Church Order: Competing Values in the Missionary Agenda of Charles Simeon," *Bulletin of the Scottish Institute of Missionary Studies* N.S. 6-7 (1990-91), pp. 1-15.

2. The term "evangelical(s)" is used in this article to refer to evangelicals in the Church of England. This was common usage at the time. Evangelical Nonconformists were no less "evangelical," but they were unable to escape the label "Dissenters."

3. For a discussion of the connection between the British Empire and the missionary movement, see Max Warren's *Social History and Christian Missions* (London: SCM Press, 1967).

4. William Wilberforce's notion of a Christian nation and its impact on his worldview may be seen in his *Practical view of the prevailing religious system of professed Christians in the higher and middle classes in this country contrasted with real Christianity* (London, 1797). This work may be the clearest example of evangelical thought at the time. For a good account of the life of Wilberforce, see John Pollock's *Wilberforce* (Tring, Herts: Lion Press, 1977).

5. See J. Williamson's *Brief memoir of the Rev. C. Simeon* . . . (London, 1848), pp. 6-7, for a concise summary of the Simeon family vitals.

6. Henry Venn quoting Simeon in a letter to a friend, September 18, 1782, in W. Carus, *Memoirs of the life of the Rev. Charles Simeon, M.A., Late Senior Fellow of King's College and Minister of Trinity Church, Cambridge,* 3rd ed. (London, 1848), p. 28. Simeon never had opportunity to carry out his threat: he remained a bachelor.

7. See Bennett, "Simeon," p. 150, for Simeon's views on the spirituality he found at Cambridge.

8. Carus, *Memoirs*, pp. 15ff. A thorough summary from many sources is provided in Bennett, "Simeon," pp. 44ff. and 122ff.

9. Carus, *Memoirs*, p. 39.

10. A summary of these works may be found in Bennett, "Simeon," pp. 406ff.

11. C.H.E. Smyth, *Simeon and Church Order: A Study of the Origins of the Evangelical Revival in Cambridge in the Eighteenth Century* (Cambridge: Cambridge Univ. Press, 1940), pp. 250, 255.

12. L. Elliott-Binns, *The Early Evangelicals: A Religious and Social Study* (London: Lutterworth Press, 1953), p. 284.

13. Ford K. Brown, *Fathers of the Victorians: The Age of Wilberforce* (Cambridge: Cambridge Univ. Press, 1961), p. 289. Brown is highly critical of what he perceived as subversive efforts by "evangelical missionaries to the Gentile world in England," namely, the "proselyting" of orthodox Anglican laity into the evangelical camp (p. 271).

14. A. Pollard and M. Hennell, eds., *Charles Simeon (1759-1836): Essays Written in Commemoration of His Bicentenary by Members of the Evangelical Fellowship for Theological Literature* (London: SPCK, 1964), p. 26.

15. H.E. Hopkins, *Charles Simeon of Cambridge* (London: Hodder & Stoughton, 1977), p. 181.

16. A chief complaint against the CMS was its inherent competition with the Society for Promoting Christian Knowledge (SPCK) and the Society for the Propagation of the Gospel in Foreign Parts (SPG).

17. Simeon's missionary expectations for India Company chaplains are considered in depth in Bennett, "Simeon," chapter 6, "The Missionary Agenda by Other Means," pp. 291ff. Simeon saw "his" chaplains as hardly less missionary than those he might send to India with the CMS. This is readily apparent in his correspondence with Charles Grant (senior), a member of the company's Court of Directors from 1794 to 1816 and Simeon's chief ally in securing chaplaincy appointments for more than two dozen men. In one sequence of letters Simeon discussed the expected impact of the "native schools" proposed by chaplain Thomas Thomason – one of Simeon's men – on the progress of the missionary task in India. See Simeon to Grant, March 15 and December 17, 1814; and July 1 and August 5, 1815 (Simeon MSS, Ridley Hall, Cambridge).

18. D.M. Rosman has observed that a tolerance of paradox was a mark of nineteenth-century evangelical expediency ("Evangelicals and Culture in England, 1790-1833" [Ph.D. diss., Keele University, 1979], p.19). The argument is valid, but it is an incomplete explanation for Simeon's ability to embrace contrasting values. Simeon genuinely believed that the Scriptures affirm principles that appear to be contradictory. For this reason he did not fear to do the same. One paradox in particular stands out in connection with Simeon's name: On biblical grounds Simeon spoke of himself as a Calvinist, as an Arminian, and as neither of these. See Bennett, "Simeon," pp. 19ff.

19. I.e., the September 1787 "Plan for a missionary establishment in Bengal and Behar," as proposed from Calcutta by David Brown, William Chambers, Charles Grant, and George Udny (Simeon MSS).

20. Carus, *Memoirs*, pp. 125-26; see also J.H. Pratt, ed., *Eclectic Notes . . .* , 2nd ed. (London, 1865), p. 99.

21. Brown, *Fathers*, p. 208.

22. "Not one of them says, 'Here I am, send me'" (Simeon to Thomas Scott, August 22, 1800, CMS Archives, University of Birmingham, G/AC 3; also cited in C. Hole, *The Early History of the Church Missionary Society* [London, 1896], p. 62).

23. This problem had become apparent to Melville Horne a decade earlier. See Horne's *Letters on missions addressed to the Protestant ministers of the British churches* (London, 1794; reprint, Andover, 1815), p. 32 and throughout.

24. For a complete summary of Simeon's efforts in aid of Jewish evangelism, see J.B. Cartwright, *Love to the Jewish nation: A sermon preached at the Episcopal Jews' Chapel, Bethnal Green, London, on Sunday morning, November 27th, 1836, on the occasion of the death of the Rev. Charles Simeon* (London, 1836), pp. 31-43.

25. There is evidence to suggest that Middleton refrained from licensing any missionaries, whether CMS or SPCK, until he could license all of them, and that more than a legal technicality hindered him vis-à-vis the CMS. See Bennett, "Simeon," chapters 4 and 5, where this important example of church-mission tension is considered in some detail.

26. For example, the first parochial collection on behalf of the CMS was taken at Holy Trinity Church in 1804. See Hole, *Early History*, p. 96.

27. In 1836, Daniel Wilson proposed four "rules" to guide the bishop of Calcutta in his relationship with the CMS's clerical missionaries in India: (1) determine the missionary's fitness for licensing, (2) approve the stationing of the missionary, (3) superintend his ecclesiastical work (versus his missionary work), but (4) receive regular reports from the society on the missionary work of the clergyman (Wilson to the CMS General Committee, June 9, 1836, CMS Archives, University of Birmingham, CI 1/08/4). "Appendix II" to the thirty-ninth *Report* of the CMS, drafted by Henry Venn in 1838, reflected the acceptance of Wilson's proposal. These principles were formalized in Venn's "Concordat" of July 1841, incorporating them into "Law 32" of the society. With the publication of the new regulations, the archbishops of Canterbury and York and the bishop of London finally consented to serve the CMS as vice-patrons. (See W. Shenk, "Henry Venn as Missionary Theorist and Administrator" [Ph.D. diss., University of Aberdeen, 1978], pp. 242-53.)

Selected Bibliography

Works by Charles Simeon

1802 *A sermon preached at the parish church of St. Andrew by the Wardrobe and St. Anne, Blackfriars . . . June 8, 1802, before the Society for Missions to Africa and the East . . . being their second anniversary . . .* London.

1816 (ed.) *Memorial sketches of the Rev. David Brown: With a selection of his sermons preached at Calcutta.* London.

1821 *The conversion of the Jews, or, Our duty and encouragement to promote it: Two discourses preached before the University of Cambridge, on February 18th, and 20th, 1821.* London.

1837 *Substance of an address . . . in behalf of the London Society for Promoting Christianity Amongst the Jews, on . . . October the 27th, 1834: Communicated as a letter to the Rev. J.B. Cartwright, M.A., Secretary of the Society.* London.

1845 *Horae homileticae, or Discourses digested into one continued series, and forming a commentary upon every book of the Old and New Testament . . .* 7th ed. 21 vols., with indexes by T.H. Horne. London.

1959 *Let Wisdom Judge: University Addresses and Sermon Outlines by Charles Simeon.* Edited with an introduction by A. Pollard. London: SPCK.

Works about Charles Simeon

Balda, W.D. "Spheres of Influence: Simeon's Trust and Its Implications for Evangelical Patronage." Ph.D. diss., Cambridge University, 1981.

Bennett, J.C. "Charles Simeon and the Evangelical Anglican Missionary Movement: A Study of Voluntaryism and Church-Mission Tensions." Ph.D. diss., University of Edinburgh, 1992.

Brown, A.W. *Recollections of the conversation parties of the Rev. Charles Simeon, M.A., Senior Fellow of King's College, and Perpetual Curate of Trinity Church, Cambridge.* London, 1863.

Carus, W. *Memoirs of the life of the Rev. Charles Simeon, M.A., Late Senior Fellow of King's College and Minister of Trinity Church, Cambridge.* 3rd ed. London, 1848.

Hopkins, H.E. *Charles Simeon of Cambridge.* London: Hodder & Stoughton, 1977.

Moule, H.C.G. *Charles Simeon.* London, 1892.

Pollard, A., and M. Hennell, eds. *Charles Simeon (1759-1836): Essays Written in Commemoration of His Bicentenary by Members of the Evangelical Fellowship for Theological Literature.* London: SPCK, 1964.

Smyth, C.H.E. *Simeon and Church Order: A Study of the Origins of the Evangelical Revival in Cambridge in the Eighteenth Century.* The Birkbeck Lectures for 1937-38. Cambridge: Cambridge Univ. Press, 1940.

Thomas Fowell Buxton
1786-1844

Missions and the Remedy for African Slavery

Andrew F. Walls

Perhaps the most striking of all the monuments and memorials that adorn St. George Cathedral in Freetown, Sierra Leone, is a bust commemorating a person who never set foot there. It was set up by Africans in memory of Sir Thomas Fowell Buxton, described in the language of the times as "the Friend of the Negro."

Thomas Fowell Buxton[1] – he ordinarily used his second name – was born in 1786, the eldest son of a country gentleman. For a long while he combined a business career with managing his estate. He was brought up under both Anglican and Quaker influences and experienced evangelical conversion through the influence of Josiah Pratt, secretary of the Church Missionary Society. He married into a great Quaker family, the Gurneys (Elizabeth Fry, the prison reformer, was a sister-in-law). In 1818 he became member of Parliament for Weymouth, which he represented until defeated in the election of 1837. Serious illness, increasing in later years, punctuated his public activity; he died in 1844, aged fifty-seven.

An Evangelical in Politics

Buxton was a public man by duty more than liking. An effective, but not a brilliant, speaker, he never enjoyed the rough-and-tumble of politics and believed that "good woodcock shooting is a preferable thing to glory."[2] He never held an appointive government office and was not regarded as a reliable party man either in religion or in politics.

Three concerns dominated Buxton's public life. The first involved reform of the penal code (in particular reducing the number of offenses which carried the death penalty) and conditions in prisons. This early career built up a lifelong habit of thorough research and mastery of detail.

His second concern was the treatment of non-Western peoples under British rule. Beginning with the issue of *sati* (widow burning) in India, he was soon absorbed by British dealings with the indigenous peoples of South Africa. Then came wider questions of the effects of Western colonization on the land-rights and way of life of the indigenous residents.

The third concern was slavery. In 1821 the aging Wilberforce asked Buxton to assume the parliamentary leadership of the antislavery cause. Buxton inherited a major project: to gain

11

emancipation for all the slaves within the British dominions. He achieved this long-sought goal only to find it imposed new tasks: ensuring that the act was implemented and getting rid of the apprenticeship system, which was the price exacted for emancipation in the West Indies. It led Buxton to his great dream for Africa, his famous book, and the disaster that brought him horror, heartbreak, and premature death.

These matters kept Buxton in public life when he longed for his estate and the woodcock. His selection of issues sprang directly from his evangelical vision. "Whatever I have done in my life for Africa," he wrote to Josiah Pratt, his old minister, "the seeds of it were sown in my heart, in Wheeler Street chapel."[3]

Evangelicalism was about "real," as distinct from "formal," or "nominal" Christianity. This is instanced in the title of Wilberforce's celebrated book, *A Practical View of the Prevailing Religious System of Professed Christians in the Higher and Middle Classes in this country, contrasted with Real Christianity.* "Real Christianity," following on the knowledge of sin and the consciousness of forgiveness in Christ, involved a life of ongoing devotion and practical duty. It had an inescapable social aspect, for the whole of society was assumedly, if far from really, Christian. The path of duty thus involved showing society the true implications of the profession it made. Buxton consistently grounded his arguments in the professedly Christian nature of British society.

Buxton was prepared to demonstrate statistically the sheer wastefulness and commercial inefficiency of the slave trade. Self-interest, however, was never a sufficient reason to evade a moral imperative:

> When I come to humanity, justice and the duties of Christian men, I stand upon a rock . . . Without doubt it is the duty of Great Britain to employ the influence and strength which God has given her, in raising Africa from the dust, and enabling her, out of her own resources, to beat down Slavery and the Slave Trade.[4]

In all of this, Buxton stands in the British evangelical mainstream. From its beginnings the Protestant missionary movement was linked with opposition to slavery. West African and West Indian experience demonstrated the hostility to missions of traders and planters alike. But Wilberforce and his Clapham Sect associates did not conduct the abolition campaign on the basis of moral and religious proclamation alone. The slave trade was an economic institution, upheld by political sanction; to win reversal of that sanction entailed winning the economic argument.[5] In such matters Buxton is very much Wilberforce's "heir at law"; his campaigns use the methods of Clapham.

The Campaign against Slavery

When Buxton assumed the leadership of the anti-slavery movement in 1821, the British slave trade had been illegal for fourteen years, and Britain was officially committed to inhibiting slave trading by other nations. But slavery itself was intact in most of the British Caribbean. The island of Mauritius also had it in a particularly brutal form; its legality protected all sorts of indignities and cruelties in South Africa and elsewhere. Few now defended slavery as beneficent; it was commoner to regard it as an unfortunate necessity. But there were strong vested interests, and even more complacency. Many held that things could not be as bad as the campaigners for emancipation declared. Successive governments had their own agendas, and Buxton's priorities, even when applauded in principle, did not rank high there.

Part of Buxton's task was thus the assiduous collection and systematic presentation of facts. His workload was prodigious: the Mauritius case brought on a heart attack. He had to employ parliamentary procedures skillfully; would the appointment of a committee be a useful way of examining evidence, or simply a means of delaying action? He had to maintain pressure to the annoyance of government and party managers, to put his friendships under strain. And he had to build up a body of informed opinion outside the House, and especially among committed Christians. Missionaries played a key part in his campaigns and supplied much of his evidence. The evident hostility of the planters toward them and the sufferings of West Indian believers demonstrated the true nature of the case:

> The religious public has, at last, taken the field. The [planters] have done us good service. They have of late flogged slaves in Jamaica for praying, and imprisoned the missionaries, and they have given the nation to understand that preaching and praying are offenses not to be tolerated in a slave colony. That is right – it exhibits slavery in its true colors.[6]

After twelve years of motions, divisions, and commissions, the House of Commons in 1833 approved the emancipation of all slaves within the British dominions, Buxton presenting a national petition bearing so many pages of signatures that it needed four people to carry it. But the price of government sponsorship of the legislation was a clause binding slaves in the West Indies to a transitional period of apprenticeship to their former masters. The clause split the abolition movement. Buxton, fearing to lose the whole measure, conceded apprenticeship in return for a government guarantee of complete emancipation at the end of the transition. (He afterward concluded that this was a misjudgment.) After the passing of the emancipation act he constantly called for the review or reduction of apprenticeship. He demonstrated – again with missionary evidence – that the emancipated people had behaved with dignity and responsibility, their former owners with spite and tyranny. When apprenticeship was formally ended in 1838, Buxton was no longer in Parliament. He attended the debate as a visitor and was ejected for cheering.[7]

"Aborigines' Rights"

Buxton's campaign against slavery ran alongside a series of interventions on other colonial issues, until "aborigines' rights" became his main political concern. Once more, a missionary was at the center of the matter. John Philip, superintendent of the London Missionary Society at the Cape of Good Hope, championed the indigenous Khoi ("Hottentots" in the contemporary phrase) against abuses by whites.[8] By raising the Khoi question in Parliament in 1828, Buxton helped to secure the decision that Khoi in the Cape were on the same legal footing as whites – a decision with long-term consequences. But larger questions were arising in South Africa, as whites seized land or cattle beyond the colony's frontiers. Buxton secured a parliamentary motion recognizing the principle of African peoples' right to their own land; its pious language may have blinded some members to the implications of the statement they were approving. Briefed by Philip, Buxton raised the conduct of the frontier war of 1835 against the Xhosa. To his delight, the government handed back "the territory we lately stole." Buxton wrote:

> The hand of the proud oppressor in Africa has been, under Providence, arrested . . . Only think how delighted must our savage friends be, and with what feelings must they have viewed our retreating army . . . This is, indeed, a noble victory of right over might.[9]

The Cape question led Buxton to demand a parliamentary committee to investigate the treatment of indigenous peoples in British overseas settlements. Buxton was the committee chairman and the principal drafter of its report. Philip gave evidence, bringing also a Xhosa chief and a Khoi spokesman to do so as well. The secretaries of the three main missionary societies testified to the trail of violence, land robbery, rape, disease, and alcoholism left by the white settlement. The committee, calling for watchfulness against white exploitation of indigenous peoples everywhere, declared:

Europeans have entered their borders uninvited, and, when there, have not only acted as if they were undoubted lords of the soil, but have punished the natives if they have evinced a desire to live in their own country.[10]

The tone of the 1837 report of the Select Committee on Aborigines contrasts with modern generalizations about nineteenth-century opinion, and indeed with developments later in the century. Yet it represents the overseas policy desired by the evangelical, humanitarian, and missionary interests that Buxton embodied.

Buxton desired to see "aboriginal peoples" in secure possession of their lands, able to deal with Westerners on equal terms. He believed their happiness, however, would best be furthered by the spread of Christianity and "civilization." The condemnation of the British presence overseas was that it inhibited, rather than furthered, the spread of Christianity and civilization.

"The African Slave Trade and its Remedy"

These ideas lie behind Buxton's last great adventure, the project that consumed and eventually broke him.

As emancipation became realizable, it became evident that the slave trade itself, far from being abolished, was not even reduced. The sufferings of the victims were worse than ever. Diplomacy and naval patrols were manifestly incapable of stopping it on their own. There was still a transatlantic demand for slaves and a demand in Africa for manufactured goods that was supplied primarily by the slave trade.

Buxton determined to confront slavery at the economic level: to cut off its source of supply by providing a more profitable alternative. "The real remedy, the true ransom for Africa, will be found in her fertile soil." The redemption of Africa could be effected by calling out her own resources.[11]

After he lost his parliamentary seat in 1837, Buxton incorporated his researches in a book that eventually appeared as *The African Slave Trade and its Remedy*.[12] It examines the current statistics and context of the slave trade by means of standard sources and especially official papers. It concludes that in 1837 and 1838, more slaves were crossing the Atlantic than when Wilberforce began his campaign fifty years earlier. The related raiding, marketing, passage, and landing murdered seven out of every ten slaves taken. The depopulation of Africa was proceeding at the rate of half a million people per year. The slave trade deprived Africa of all possible benefits of civilization and inhibited Christian preaching.

> Were this obstacle removed, Africa would present the finest field for the labors of Christian missionaries which the world has yet seen . . . [T]here is in the Negro race a capacity for receiving the Gospel beyond most other heathen nations.[13]

The West owed restitution to Africa for the desolation it had inflicted upon it. Africa had a right to Britain's best blessings, the Christian faith and that corpus of intellectual and technical achievement implied in "civilization," but it could receive them only with the destruction of the slave trade.

Buxton proposed to strangle the slave trade by the development of African agriculture. The West could stimulate that development by maintaining regular trade, buying African agricultural products, and selling the consumer goods so obviously welcome in Africa. The paths of Christianity, commerce, and civilization thus crossed. Only Christianity could cure Africa's ills or foster civilization there; but commerce – in which Africans, holding the rich resources of their land, would be equal partners – could open the way.

> Let missionaries and schoolmasters, the plough and the spade, go together, and agriculture will flourish; the avenues to legitimate commerce will be opened; confidence between man

and man will be inspired; whilst civilization will advance as the natural effect, and Christianity operate as the proximate cause of this happy change.[14]

Buxton saw Africans as the evangelists and civilizers of Africa, with Sierra Leone and the West Indies providing an independent, educated mission force. In human as in economic terms, his vision was the liberation of Africa, under the leading of Providence, out of her own resources.

In 1840 European knowledge of inland Africa was very sketchy. Buxton saw the great rivers of Africa as highways. He proposed that the British government should commission an expedition to the Niger, concluding treaties with African rulers promising regular steamer trade in return for an embargo on slave selling, and investigating the possibilities for agricultural, commercial, and technological development.

The Niger Expedition

The political climate was unusually favorable. The government accepted the proposal. Buxton received the honor of a baronetcy. The expedition was prepared with elaborate care: specially designed ships, high-quality commanders, hand-picked crews, a team of agricultural and scientific experts. The Church Missionary Society was invited to send observers. The Prince Consort inspected the vessels and presided at a vast public meeting. In Sierra Leone a company of interpreters and auxiliaries joined the vessels, people who had once been taken as slaves from the areas the expedition was to visit.

In mid-August 1841 the expedition entered one of the mouths of the Niger. Early in October the last of its ships was limping back, its commander prostrated by fever, the cabins crammed with sick and dying, the geologist working the engines with the aid of a textbook. Those seven weeks cost forty-one European lives.[15]

It was the end of publicly sponsored schemes for the redemption of Africa. Satirists had a field day.[16] Buxton, discredited and heartbroken, died little more than two years after the disaster.

Buxton and the Christian Significance of Africa

In assessing the legacy of Buxton it is well to begin with this, his greatest failure.

Buxton himself did not believe that the disaster invalidated the argument of *The African Slave Trade and its Remedy*: "We know how the evil is to be cured; that it is to be done by native agency; by colored ministers of the Gospel. Africa is to be delivered by her own sons!"[17]

The Niger Expedition helped to concentrate minds on what missions had long agreed in principle: the key to the evangelization of Africa was the preparation of an African mission force. Not a single African member of the expedition had even been seriously ill. Sierra Leone's Christian community, which had come from all over West Africa after being uprooted by the slave trade, was the nucleus of a missionary force, already equipped with the necessary languages. One of the expedition's missionary observers was the Yoruba ex-captive and future Christian bishop, Samuel Ajayi Crowther; his outstanding qualities showed the potential available in Sierra Leone.

The few years following the Niger Expedition saw unprecedented expansion in African missions. Missions were established further inland than before; there was more investment in African education, more trust in Africans as missionaries. The Church Missionary Society opened its Yoruba mission with Crowther as an ordained member of a mission party containing other Sierra Leoneans. His later ministry was spent with a Sierra Leonean staff, evangelizing the area through which the Niger Expedition sailed, or had meant to sail. Against all the early evidence, Africa became the most productive field of mission endeavor. Buxton had grasped the Christian significance of Africa ahead of most of his contemporaries.

As for the West Indies, his book was read there, and Caribbean Christians were so stirred by it that they moved for a mission to Africa. The Calabar Mission, later a proud boast of Scottish churchmen, began rather against the advice of prudent Edinburgh. Its original membership, white and black, ordained and lay, came from Jamaica, on the initiative of a Jamaican presbytery. It was one of a series of Caribbean initiatives, now largely forgotten, but traceable to the legacy of Buxton.[18]

Mid-century missions worked on Buxtonian principles. The Yoruba Mission party took Sierra Leonean builders and carpenters (who were also catechists and teachers) and introduced machinery and printing and newspapers as well as churches and schools. They inhibited the growth of a slaving economy by showing that cotton growing was a viable substitute.[19]

Two of the best-known names in mid-century missions are true heirs of Buxton. Henry Venn became a secretary of the Church Missionary Society (of which Buxton was a vice president) during the Niger Expedition period. In his practical, evangelical vision, missionaries were asked to report on seeds and soils; mission supporters might be asked for machinery, or specialist advice, or the services of their firm to import Yoruba cotton. Buxton had foreseen the African evangelization of Africa; Venn spelled out the formula of a self-governing, self-supporting, self-propagating church with both godly African bishops and skilled African mechanics. A self-governing church needed leaders on a par with missionaries; a self-supporting church needed a viable economic base.[20]

The whole life of David Livingstone (who as a missionary candidate was at the Niger Expedition sendoff) embodies Buxton principles. He shared Buxton's belief in the efficacy of legitimate commerce to displace the slave trade, and even his mistaken predilection for rivers as the key to Africa. He knew at first hand the colonial abuses that roused Buxton. He shared Buxton's active hatred of slavery and his belief in African dignity. His famous words at Cambridge in 1857, "I go back to Africa to try to make an open path for commerce and Christianity," can only be understood with Buxton's work in mind.[21]

The Inheritance

In less than fifty years from Buxton's death virtually the whole of Africa was divided between the Western powers, and monopoly companies took their pleasure with great tracts of the continent. Neither in concept nor in deed was this the legacy of Buxton. Buxton loathed what was done in most existing colonies, and sought no empire, political or commercial. He looked for a free partnership in which Africa and the West would share economic benefits, technological resources, a common discourse of ideas, and deep-rooted Christian faith:

> I firmly believe that, if commercial countries consulted only their true interests . . . they would make the most resolute and persevering attempts to raise up Africa – not to divide her broad territory amongst them, nor to enslave her people, but in order to elevate her into something like an equality with themselves, for their reciprocal benefit.[22]

Buxton gave shape and direction to ideas accepted in the Christian constituency of his time. He was certainly not an original theologian; he used the standard evangelical expressions of his day. That faith involved the application of the Gospel to all of life and all the world. He would have been puzzled by a phrase like "holistic mission" and bewildered by some modern debates about it. But whenever someone today raises in Christ's name a voice on behalf of the voiceless; or seeks in that name to bless a people with better crops, or renew land ravaged by warfare; to build free and open relationships with people despised or exploited, or to demonstrate to their own nation its responsibility for another's sufferings – Fowell Buxton was there first.

Notes

1. Buxton's descendants reflect another form of his legacy. Several were distinguished figures in anti-slavery and social reform. Others (including his grandson Barclay Fowell Buxton in Japan and his great-grandson Alfred Barclay Buxton in Congo and Ethiopia) played an important part in mission developments. The family relationships by marriage – Barclays, Grubbs, Hookers, Studds – would provide a map of a large sector of the British evangelical world.
2. Charles Buxton, ed., *Memoirs of Sir Thomas Fowell Buxton, Baronet* (London, 1848; Philadelphia, 1849), p. 139.
3. Ibid., p. 46.
4. Thomas F. Buxton, *The African Slave Trade and its Remedy* (London: Murray, 1839-40; repr. 6, Frank Cass, London, 1867), p. 529.
5. See especially Roger Anstey, *The Atlantic Slave Trade and British Abolition* (London: Macmillan, 1975).
6. Buxton to John Philip, November 10, 1830, *Memoirs*, p. 209.
7. Buxton to Mrs. Upcher, May 23, 1838, *Memoirs*, p. 364.
8. On Philip, see A.C. Ross, *John Philip (1775-1851): Missions, Race and Politics in South Africa* (Aberdeen University Press, 1986), and Philip's own rumbustious *Researches in South Africa; Illustrating the civil, moral, and religious condition of the native tribes* (London, 1838).
9. T.F. Buxton to Miss Gurney, March 18, 1837, *Memoirs* pp. 314ff.
10. *Aborigines' Report*, Select Committee on Aborigines, 1837, p. 4.
11. Charles Buxton, *Memoirs*, p. 365.
12. The book has a complex publishing history, since there was a private circulation version for government ministers, separate publication of part one, and revisions of it thereafter. See the preface to the Cass reprint. References here are to the second edition, 1840.
13. T.F. Buxton, *African Slave Trade*, p. 8.
14. Ibid., p. 511.
15. There are accounts of the expedition in William Allen and T.R.H. Thomson, *Narrative of the Expedition sent by Her Majesty's Government to the River Niger in 1841* (London, 1848), and *Journals of the Rev James Frederick Schön and Mr Samuel Crowther who accompanied the expedition up the Niger . . .* (London, 1842).
16. See the ludicrous scheme for a coffee colony at "Borrioboola-Gha, on the left bank of the Niger," in Dickens's *Bleak House*.
17. *Memoirs*, p. 471.
18. An account by a participant in Hope Masterton Waddell, *Twenty-nine years in the West Indies and Central Africa* (London, 1863).
19. Accounts in S.O. Biobaku, *The Egba and Their Neighbours* (Oxford: Clarendon Press, 1975), and J.F. Ade Ayayi, *Christian Missions in Nigeria: The Making of a New Élite* (London: Longmans, 1965).
20. On Venn, see W.R. Shenk, *Henry Venn – Missionary Statesman* (Maryknoll, N.Y.: Orbis Books, 1983). A good example of Venn's Buxtonian thought is his *West African Colonies* (London, 1865).
21. David Livingstone, *Cambridge Lectures . . .* (Cambridge, 1858), p. 24. On the connection between Buxton, Venn, and Livingstone, see further Andrew F. Walls, "The Legacy of David Livingstone," *International Bulletin of Missionary Research* 11, no. 3 (July 1987): 125-29 (also pp. 140-47 in this volume).
22. T.F. Buxton, *African Slave Trade*, p. 525.

Bibliography

Buxton's only major writing is *The African Slave Trade and its Remedy*. London: Murray, 1839-40. Reprinted by Frank Cass, London, 1967. Various speeches, pamphlets, and contributions to the *Anti-Slavery Reporter* were published but have not been collected.

Anstey, R. "The Pattern of British Abolitionism in the Eighteenth and Nineteenth Centuries." In *Anti-slavery, Religion and Reform*, ed. by C. Bolt and S. Drescher. Folkestone: Dawson, 1980.

Buxton, Charles, ed. *Memoirs of Sir Thomas Fowell Buxton, Baronet*. London, 1848; Philadelphia, 1849. It gives generous selections of Buxton's correspondence. A modern scholarly study is needed.

Drescher, S. *Econocide: British Slavery and the Slave Trade in the Era of Abolition*. Pittsburgh: Univ. of Pittsburgh Press, 1977.

Report of the Parliamentary Select Committee on Aboriginal Tribes (British Settlements). Reprinted with comments by the Aborigines Protection Society, London, 1837.

Adoniram Judson Gordon

1836-1895

Educator, Preacher, and Promoter of Missions

Dana L. Robert

In April 1986, Gordon College and Gordon-Conwell Seminary celebrated the sesquicentennial of Adoniram Judson Gordon's birth. The extensive celebration reminded the theological world of A.J. Gordon's legacy. As educator, pastor, and foremost American Baptist of the late nineteenth century, Gordon shaped a generation of Christian workers who witnessed to the world for Jesus Christ. In the success of Gordon College and of Gordon-Conwell Seminary, a leading evangelical theological school, the memory of A.J. Gordon is kept alive.

But A.J. Gordon's legacy cannot be confined to the two schools that bear his name. With eschatological urgency, Gordon spent the last ten years of his life promoting world evangelization. His high view of Scripture and of the Holy Spirit dominated his mission theory. As member and then chairman of the Executive Committee of the American Baptist Missionary Union, Gordon orchestrated an era of expansion for Baptist missions. Gordon's pastorate at the Clarendon Street Church in Boston catapulted the church into the leading Baptist fund-raiser and promoter of missions in New England. Co-worker of Dwight L. Moody, Gordon was one of the most influential American evangelical mission theorists of the late nineteenth century.

Background and Pastorates

Some might argue that Gordon was foreordained for mission work. Born April 19, 1836, to Baptist parents, he was named Adoniram Judson Gordon after the pioneer American Baptist missionary, Adoniram Judson. His father, John Calvin Gordon, ran a family woolen mill in the hills of New Hampshire. A.J. Gordon grew up working in the mill and playing with friends until his conversion at age fifteen or sixteen. The conversion experience convinced him that he wanted to be a minister and that he needed to pay attention to schooling, hitherto a low priority. Walking thirty-four miles in a suit of homespun, baggage in hand, Gordon began his high school education.

In 1856 Gordon entered Brown University. Following graduation from Brown, Gordon completed his theological course at Newton Theological School (now the Baptist half of Andover-Newton Theological Seminary).[1] An average student but promising preacher, Gordon was called to the Jamaica Plain Baptist Church in West Roxbury, Massachusetts, in 1863. Settling into his pastorate, Gordon married Maria Hale, fathered several children, and enjoyed a successful six years as a suburban pastor. Portraits of him reveal a square-set man with a prominent jaw and large, bright eyes.

After two years of entreaty from the Clarendon Street Church of Boston, A.J. Gordon reluctantly accepted a pastorate there in 1869. He labored at Clarendon Street Baptist for twenty-five years, until his death in 1895. The congregation was "fashionable" and was not in total sympathy with Gordon's commitment to missions and his concomitant hatred of "ecclesiastical extravagance" such as paid choirs, Easter flowers, and elaborate architecture.[2] But a paradigmatic event in the life of the church occurred in 1877 when Dwight L. Moody brought his first successful American crusade to Boston. Moody arrived fresh from revival tours through Great Britain, Brooklyn, Philadelphia, and Chicago that had made his name a household word. He erected a huge tent within 300 feet of Clarendon Church and began several months of revival services. Clarendon Church was the site of the overflow and after-meetings. The church members began to minister to those in need, and nearly thirty reformed alcoholics had joined the church by the end of the crusade.[3]

The Moody revivals inaugurated a new period in the history of the Clarendon Street Church. In his spiritual autobiography, *How Christ Came to Church, the Pastor's Dream,* Gordon reflected on the missionary outreach of Clarendon Church. Missions to Jews and to the Chinese in Boston, outdoor preaching, rescue work among women, and an industrial home for men all dated from the spiritual vitality engendered by the Moody revivals. Work with converted alcoholics made the church members realize how difficult it was to be "spiritual" if one were homeless and unemployed. Consequently, Gordon began the Boston Industrial Temporary Home as a shelter for the unemployed, often alcoholic, homeless men. In exchange for work at a woodpile that provided fuel for Boston's poor, the homeless received food and lodging. Despite financial and other difficulties, the industrial home became a fixture of Boston social service in the late nineteenth century.[4] The attendance of alcoholics at church services led the Clarendon Street Church to substitute grape juice for wine in the communion service. Despite the disapproval of his evangelical Republican friends, Gordon became a political prohibitionist and joined the Prohibition Party in 1884. Frances Willard, president of the Women's Christian Temperance Union, was one of his friends and supporters.

Clarendon Street Church's vision of mission was global as well as local in scope. The church repeatedly surpassed itself in raising money for Baptist foreign missions. In a year of special need for the American Baptists, the church raised $20,000 for foreign missions. A.J. Gordon credited his church's sacrificial activity to neither careful budgeting nor planning, but to the Holy Spirit:

> The Holy Ghost, the present Christ, has been given to be the administrator of the church; and . . . in these days of endless organizations and multiplied secular machinery, he will surprise us by showing what he will do if we will give him unhindered liberty of action in his own house.[5]

His connection with Dwight Moody in 1877 changed the life of A.J. Gordon as well as that of the Clarendon Street Church. Gordon became a regular speaker at Moody's Northfield conferences. For several summers when Moody was absent, Gordon took charge of the conferences. Gordon was one of the major speakers during the Northfield Bible Conference at Mount Hermon School in 1886 when the "Mount Hermon 100" volunteered to become foreign missionaries. The 100 young college volunteers were the core group of the Student Volunteer Movement that sent thousands of college graduates to the mission field. Many of the earliest volunteers looked to A.J. Gordon as their spiritual mentor.

While at Clarendon Street Church, A. J. Gordon developed a reputation as a spiritual leader in demand both in print and in the pulpit. His first book, published in 1872, was *In Christ,* on the spiritual identity between Jesus Christ and the believer. Other works on spirituality and theology included *Ecce Venit – Behold He Cometh* (1889), *Risen with Christ* (1895), *The Two-fold Life* (1883), *The Ministry of Healing* (1882), *How Christ Came to Church* (1895), and his most famous book, *The Ministry of the Spirit* (1894). With A.T. Pierson, friend and mission theorist, Gordon wrote and edited *The Coronation Hymnal* (1894). Gordon's most famous hymn was the music to "My Jesus, I Love Thee," now a standard in Protestant hymnals.

Wider Mission Work

In 1888 Dr. and Mrs. Gordon sailed to England to attend the Centenary Conference, convened to mark roughly 100 years of Protestant missionary work. The Centenary Conference was the most representative Anglo-American missions conference to date, and 139 mission societies from around the world sent representatives.[6] At the conference, A.J. Gordon gained an international reputation as apologist for the missionary enterprise. Euphoric rhetoric about Christian civilization and Anglo-American superiority rang at the Centenary Conference. But Gordon found the high-flown phrases to be inadequate. Because the conference talked about mission but did not take action, he met afterward with other dissatisfied evangelicals such as A.T. Pierson, J. Hudson Taylor, George Post, and H.G. Guinness to pass resolutions condemning the British opium trade, the liquor trade, and licensed prostitution in British India.

Following the historic conference, the Gordons and the A.T. Piersons set off for a European vacation. While in Rome, they received an urgent invitation from Scottish ministers in Edinburgh to hold a missionary meeting for university students. The success of the ensuing campaign was such that an interdenominational committee of Scots begged the Americans to conduct a missionary crusade throughout all of Scotland. Not since the Moody-Sankey revivals of 1875-76 were the Scottish Christians so aroused. The mission tour of Gordon and Pierson was a huge success that inspired increased contributions and numerous young Scots to volunteer for foreign missions.

A.J. Gordon returned to Boston from Scotland to find that he had been elected chairman of the Executive Committee of the American Baptist Missionary Union (ABMU). The chairmanship entailed weekly meetings and virtual responsibility for all missions of the American Baptists. The Executive Committee created policy for and administered the missions. It decided which missions would be opened, and it appointed missionaries and fixed their salaries. The ultimate responsibility for Baptist missions had come to rest with A.J. Gordon.

Gordon had served on the Executive Committee since 1871. He played a key role in the expansion of American Baptist missions to Africa. All eyes had turned to Africa in 1871 when Henry M. Stanley of the *New York Herald* searched through the jungles for the missionary explorer David Livingstone. The explorations of Livingstone and Stanley had proved that the "Dark Continent" was in fact penetrable, and mission societies and European governments rushed into the interior. In 1876 the Rev. and Mrs. H. Grattan Guinness, prominent English Baptists, started the Livingstone Inland Mission along the Congo River. One of the earliest Protestant missions to Africa, by 1884 the Livingstone Inland Mission had sent fifty missionaries, opened seven mission stations, spent $150,000, and reduced the Ki-Kongo language to writing; it also owned a steamboat named the *Henry Reed*.

The work of the Livingstone Inland Mission grew too large for the Guinnesses, and in 1883 they proposed that the American Baptist Missionary Union take it over as their Congo Mission. The ABMU had already passed general resolutions in favor of opening an African mission, and they had surveyed the coastline of Africa to find a suitable location. The Guinnesses' offer forced the issue of African missions for the American Baptists. Though the Missionary Union adopted the mission in 1884, many Baptists continued to raise their voices against it. Many feared the death rate in the Congo, volunteers were in short supply, and Baptists doubted that the Missionary Union, already hard-pressed for funds, could raise enough money for the risky venture.

A.J. Gordon lobbied incessantly for the Congo Mission and was in large part responsible for its acceptance by American Baptists. In 1886 he accompanied around the northeast the first Congo missionary to visit the United States, and Gordon arranged for him to speak to influential groups of Baptists. Among his literary works to promote the mission, Gordon wrote a pamphlet, "The Ship *Jesus*," that swayed popular opinion. In "The Ship *Jesus*" Gordon played upon American guilt over African slavery – slavery that had first come to American shores on a slave-ship named *Jesus*. Now that Afro-Americans were Christians, Gordon argued, the hand of the Lord was revealed. It was American responsibility to ensure that Afro-Americans could return to the Congo to convert their brethren: the ship *Jesus* was ready to go back to Africa. Gordon argued that Americans owed it to Africa to support missions there because their forefathers had enslaved Africa's inhabitants. "Next to the disgrace of having for centuries taken the wages of Africa's unrequited toil, will be the disgrace of refusing to refund those wages for Africa's redemption as God now calls for them."[7] Every American who had grown rich from the work of slaves or from the industries spawned by the Civil War now owed something to every African. "The ship '*Jesus*' is ready to sail; the mariners are eager to depart; what will you do to furnish the outfit?" asked Gordon of American Baptists.[8]

In August 1886 a revival broke out at the Banza Manteke Station of the Congo Mission. Within a few weeks, a thousand Africans became Christians. Upon hearing that the new Baptists needed a chapel, the Clarendon Street Church raised $2,500 and sent a complete prefabricated chapel by steamship. The African Christians divided the chapel into 700 loads and carried it piece by piece on their heads over sixty miles.[9] The faith of A.J. Gordon in the Congo Mission had been vindicated, and its future was now secure.

Gordon remained as chairman of the Executive Committee of the ABMU until his death in 1895. He guided the Missionary Union through its centenary celebration of the Baptist missionary William Carey in 1892. Introducing a resolution against "so-called Christian nations" sending liquor into the Congo Valley, he supported the Congo Mission through thick and thin.[10] Gordon oversaw a shift in the fortunes of Baptist missions from a time when volunteers were scarce to one in which student volunteers flooded the agency. In 1891 he added regular editorial responsibilities for missions when he became associate editor of the *Missionary Review of the World,* the leading nondenominational missions journal of the day.

Mission Theory

A.J. Gordon's mission theory was an outgrowth of his premillennial theology. Early in his ministerial career, Gordon became convinced of a premillennial interpretation of Scripture; he was a proponent of the theological movement that culminated in dispensationalism and fundamentalism in the early twentieth century. Gordon was a participant in the Niagara Conference for Bible Study, and his name appeared on the call for the first American prophetic conference in 1878.[11]

In 1878 Gordon founded the *Watchword,* a monthly journal "devoted to the advocacy of the Primitive Faith, the Primitive Hope, and the Primitive Charity." The *Watchword* was to help believers "looking for that blessed hope, and the glorious appearing of the great God and our Saviour Jesus Christ."[12] With his editorship of the *Watchword* and his leadership in the prophetic and Bible conference movements, A.J. Gordon was one of the most important premillennialists in American theology.

Men like Gordon who were both premillennialists and missions advocates were forced to defend their unpopular doctrines from denominational executives who charged that premillennialism "cut the nerve of all missionary and evangelistic enterprises."[13] To many critics, belief in the imminent, physical return of Jesus Christ threatened the optimistic tone of much of nineteenth-century Protestantism and thus undercut Christian progress through education and social reform. Gordon defended the doctrine in the *Watchword,* notably in an article entitled "Pre-millennialism and Missions." In the article, Gordon argued that when one expected the physical and literal return of Jesus Christ before the millennium, the thousand years of peace foretold in the Book of Revelation, then one was an even more ardent advocate of missions than a person who did not hold the belief.

Gordon pointed out in "Pre-millennialism and Missions" that of the fifty-four graduates of Princeton Seminary in 1864, the only eight who became foreign missionaries were the eight who believed in the premillennial return of Jesus Christ.[14] The difference between the premillennialist and others was that the premillennialist put all mission emphasis on preaching the Gospel. In addition, Gordon argued, "The purpose of preaching the gospel in the present dispensation of the Spirit, as set forth in Scripture, is the gathering out of an elect body called the Church."[15] Such an "out-gathering" of the elect from all nations was a necessary prelude to Jesus' second coming. Premillennial emphasis on the evangelization of the world, therefore, focused on preaching the Gospel to the whole world so that Jesus would return soon. Premillennialists believed that their theological position was the most plain and true interpretation of infallible Scripture. They believed it to be the faith of the early church and was thus a large reason for Christian expansion in the first centuries after Christ.

For A.J. Gordon, the focus of premillennial mission theory was the preaching of the Gospel throughout the world so that the elect would be gathered into God's church and Jesus would return. The corollary of such a burning zeal for "preaching the word" was a de-emphasis on Christian civilization and its fruits. On the theoretical level, premillennial mission theory flew in the face of the optimistic, civilizing missionary crusade of the late nineteenth century – the imperial era of Christian missions. A.J. Gordon was a trenchant critic of "Christian civilization." He did not believe that the world was slowly improving under the force of Christian progress. Rather, society was approaching the low spiritual level of Sodom and Gomorrah as it waited for Jesus' return.[16]

In an article "Education and Missions," Gordon spoke out of his premillennial mission theory when he attacked one of missions' most treasured institutions – higher education. Gordon quoted approvingly from Gustav Warneck's *Mission and Culture*:

> We look in vain, in the history of the ancient and the modern mission, for examples of the heathen being slowly prepared, to and through culture, for the acceptance of Christianity; while conversely there is no lack of examples that the systematic way through civilization to evangelization has been not only a circuitous but a wrong way.[17]

Because of the innate sinfulness of culture and of human beings, Gordon believed that higher education was a barrier to Christian conversion. It undercut faith in the supernatural. Gordon pointed to critical scholarship to argue that higher education was pushing miracles, prophecy, prayer, and regeneration out of theology.[18]

In "The Missionary's Shoes," Gordon opposed mission theories that led to Christian civilization and colonization rather than to the preaching of the Gospel:

> Concerning industrial and mechanical forerunners of the Gospel we may speak with equal emphasis. So ingrained is the notion that what has been called "a propaedeutic dispensation of civilization" must prepare the way for Christianity, that colonization has not infrequently been proposed as a John the Baptist to evangelization.[19]

Gordon underscored the hypocrisy of a modern "Christian" civilization marked by whiskey and guns:

How little apprehension of the subject does an eminent writer on the evidences of Christianity exhibit in saying that "The wisest modern missionaries admit that they must civilize heathen nations in order to make Christian institutions permanent." No! not the sandals of law, of education, or of social science for the missionary of the Apostolic school; but "feet shod with the preparation of the Gospel of peace."[20]

In his premillennial opposition to Christian civilization, A.J. Gordon went against much of the mission theory of the imperial era of Christian missions. In his separation of Christianity and culture, Gordon was a somewhat sophisticated social critic. But in his theology, Gordon was an ardent supernaturalist. He condemned civilizing theologies of Christian mission because he felt they left little room for preaching the word "so that the end may come." Gordon's most famous exposition of mission theory centered upon the supernatural element in Christianity. His book *The Holy Spirit in Missions*, the Graves mission lectures for 1892, remains the central statement of his mission theory.

Gordon argued in *The Holy Spirit in Missions* that the Holy Spirit had revealed and supervised the program of missions from the days of the apostles through the present: "The Holy Ghost is omnipresent in the great body of Christ; and omniscient in His oversight of the vast work of that body in evangelizing the world."[21] The Holy Spirit revealed the program for world missions to James at the Council of Jerusalem. First, following Israel's rejection of Christ after his first advent, there would be elective redemption from the nations of the world. The responsibility of the church would be to plant witnessing churches in every nation of the world from which the Holy Spirit could gather out the elect. The second stage of the Holy Spirit's plan for missions would occur in the "latter days." Then Israel would be restored in its relationship with God, and universal redemption would follow.

A.J. Gordon believed that the world was near the end of the first stage of the Holy Spirit's plan for missions. As the recent successes for Christianity showed, the elect of all nations were being gathered out. The Holy Ghost was in active operation redeeming individuals around the world. In the context of the eschatological countdown of the "dispensation of the Holy Spirit," Gordon reduced the primary purpose of missions to one thing: the preaching of the Gospel. He stated in *The Holy Spirit in Missions:* "The Word of God carried by the man of God is the simplest statement of the missionary method."[22]

In his quest to get the Word of God to as many people as possible in a short amount of time, Gordon believed in the decentralization of missions. In the *Missionary Review of the World* in 1892, Gordon wrote that "how to distribute responsibility for the work of evangelizing the world is the great problem to be solved in the present 'crisis of missions.' "[23] Though Gordon did not question the indispensability of the denominational mission boards, he believed that they created certain dangers, such as the centralization of responsibility into a few hands and undesirable uniformity in mission method. If only every local church could act as its own mission society, then the burden of mission work would be spread equitably among Christians and the work would be accomplished much faster. As a Baptist who believed in congregational polity, Gordon had little fear of a divided Christendom. Rather, he believed that decentralization of missions was the most efficient use of church resources:

I believe that God designed to lay the burden of the whole world upon every church, that every church might thus find out that it has a whole Christ with whom to bear that burden. Then would it not only pray and give, but it would go and send of its own instead of depending on a central bureau to attend to all this.[24]

One implication of Gordon's position on decentralization was to support the new "faith missions" springing up in the late nineteenth century.[25] Although he was head of the Executive Committee of the American Baptist Missionary Union, a denominational agency, Gordon supported the multiplication of mission-sending agencies. Faith missions such as the China Inland Mission and the International Missionary Alliance were more theologically compatible with Gordon's thought than were some denominational organs: faith missions seemed to rely on the Holy Spirit in a direct and prayerful way. Premillennial theology like that of Gordon was a hallmark of the faith missions. Above all, the independent faith missions tended to stress "preaching the word" over the civilizing functions of missions.

A.J. Gordon's fervency for evangelistic missions was perhaps best expressed in his address to the American Baptist Missionary Union in 1893:

> The church which is not a missionary church will be a missing church during the next fifty years, its candle of consecration put out, if not its candlestick removed out of its place. As ministers and churches of Jesus Christ, our self-preservation is conditioned on our obedience to the great commission. Now it is: Preach or perish! Evangelize or fossilize! Be a saving church, with girded loins and burning lamp, carrying a lost world on the heart day and night; or be a secularized church, lying on the heart of this present evil world, and allowing it to gird you and carry you whithersoever it will. Which shall it be?[26]

Missionary Training School

In 1889 A.J. Gordon opened the Boston Missionary Institute. The purpose of the school was to train laypersons in evangelistic methods and urban rescue work, using only the Bible as a textbook, so that they could go into the "harvest fields" and work as lay missionaries. The school was designed for those who had neither the time, money, nor opportunity to receive a seminary education, but who had a call from God to do mission work. Gordon believed that bureaucratic requirements of Greek, Hebrew, systematic theology, and ordination unnecessarily limited the numbers of missionaries needed for mission work.

In 1884 the ABMU had accepted the Livingstone Inland Mission from the Rev. H.G. Guinness; but by 1889 the American Baptists had still provided no missionaries for the Congo Mission. Guinness was distressed at the lack of progress, so he traveled to the United States to investigate the situation. Upon meeting with Gordon, Guinness suggested that Gordon begin a missionary training school to provide recruits for the Congo Mission. Guinness successfully operated his own missionary institute in London. Gordon consulted with Baptists in Boston, engaged Baptist pastor Frederick L. Chapell to organize the school, and classes began on October 3, 1889.[27]

Nothing A.J. Gordon did stirred more controversy than opening the training school. Bitter criticism poured in from Baptists and from the religious press. Gordon was accused of doctrinal fanaticism and of abetting "short-cut" routes to the ministry. Opponents of the training school attacked Gordon's premillennialism and lamented that "short-cut" schools were spreading the doctrine.[28]

Gordon defended the training of lay missioners in the press, notably in his article "Short-Cut Methods."[29] He felt that his school was commanded him by God so that "eleventh hour" laborers would be plentiful in God's vineyard. Gordon did not intend for the training school to compete with college or seminary training. He encouraged those persons qualified to attend seminary to do so. But for those not so fortunate, "we will give the best practical and biblical instruction we can."[30] The school had ample precedent in the Moody Bible Institute, Guinness's Missionary Training Institute, and other schools founded in the late nineteenth century to accommodate the increasing numbers of laypersons interested in becoming missionaries.

The missionary training school took much of Gordon's energy in the last years of his life. After two years in operation, the school moved to the Clarendon Street Church. A residence home for female students and missionaries was opened next door to Gordon's house. The teaching staff consisted mostly of part-time visiting instructors, and financial need was a way of life for a new school that charged no tuition. Gordon donated all of his salary as associate editor of the *Missionary Review of the World* to the training school. Despite no advertising budget, no money and only word-of-mouth publicity, students from many places, drawn to Gordon's zeal for missions, entered the school. By the time of Gordon's death in 1895, the school had graduated twenty-five foreign missionaries, fifteen ministers, twenty evangelistic workers, twenty home missionaries, and fifteen persons into higher theological education.[31]

One of the most notable features of the Boston Missionary Training School was the preponderance of women. Because women were often denied seminary training and had heavy family obligations, the missionary training or Bible school was often the only theological educational avenue open to them. A.J. Gordon's support of women's right to preach, prophesy, and teach men in the church was reflected in the student composition of the school. There was even talk at one point of making Gordon's training school into a female school only.

In the context of defending women's rights to be missionary evangelists, Gordon wrote a biblical defense of an expanded role for women in the church based on examination of the seemingly most negative Pauline injunctions against female leadership roles. "The Ministry of Women" appeared in the *Missionary Review of the World* in 1894. In his article, Gordon argued that the spiritual equality under the current dispensation of the Holy Spirit gave women "equal warrant with man's for telling out the Gospel of the grace of God."[32] Through Greek exegesis of assorted Pauline passages, Gordon pointed to places where Scripture had been deliberately mistranslated in order to limit women's sphere. Though stopping short of arguing for the ordination of women, Gordon showed in Scripture that women acted as deacons, teachers, and even as apostles.

One significance of "The Ministry of Women" was that Gordon's "fundamentalistic" zealotry for every word of Scripture led to a more progressive role for women in the church. A generation of women responded to Gordon's concern for the theological training of laywomen and registered for courses in the Boston Missionary Training School. Gordon believed in the full utilization of women as missionaries. The need for workers to harvest God's fields in the eleventh hour extended also to women. In the political arena, A.J. Gordon fully supported the suffrage movement and believed that women should be enfranchised and given equality under the law.

After A.J. Gordon died in February 1895, the name of the Boston Missionary Training School was changed to the Gordon Bible and Missionary Training School. Gordon's close friend A.T. Pierson became the second president. Over the years, the nature of the school changed, and it became a Bible college. In 1927 Gordon College of Theology and Missions received the power to grant higher degrees, and the Gordon Divinity School came into being as the graduate department of the college. In 1970 the two departments split.

Today Gordon College, a four-year liberal arts college, and Gordon-Conwell Theological Seminary stand a few miles apart north of Boston, the city where A.J. Gordon spent most of his career. Gordon-Conwell students keep alive some of Gordon's legacy as they work with immigrants in Boston. Gordon College has recently reinstituted a minor in missions. It is thus recapturing a bit of the time when its sole purpose, under A.J. Gordon, was to train missionaries.

Conclusion

Because of A.J. Gordon's stature among conservative Protestants, many are eager to claim that they now wear his mantle. As with any popular historical figure, different groups of people embrace diverse parts of his legacy. To some, Gordon was the fundamentalist par excellence, a premillennial dispensationalist who promoted quick missionary training and faith missions. A modern-day fundamentalist might cynically inquire whether Gordon College and Gordon-Conwell accurately reflect Gordon's intentions of providing a quick educational alternative for those who could neither afford nor qualify for a higher education.

On the other hand, more moderate evangelicals point with pride to the way in which Gordon, though holding premillennialist views, was able to keep the goodwill of American Baptists and others who despised his theology. Though jealous for the "truth," Gordon was a model of working within denominational structures for the sake of the mission of the church. After his death, the American Baptist Missionary Union under President Augustus Strong honored Gordon for bringing to them a greater awareness of the role of the Holy Spirit in Christian life and missions. Moderate evangelicals also appreciate the high opinion Gordon held of women in the church. His relatively liberal and yet scriptural voice of the apostolate of women is a high point in evangelical history.

Part of the secret of Gordon's ability to maintain friendships across theological barriers was his warm personality. People may have disagreed with what he said, but they continued to like him as a person. Another secret to his enduring popularity is that Gordon died in 1895. If he had lived another ten years, he would have been involved in even more bitter theological debate as the fundamentalist-modernist controversy heated up. Evidence suggests that Gordon was about to begin a free-lance career as a fundamentalist Bible teacher at the time he died. If Gordon had lived another ten years, he also would have seen the day in which his theology of the Holy Spirit was used to justify Pentecostalism, a movement he probably would have rejected.

While he lived, however, A.J. Gordon showed that unity for missions could transcend theological and institutional boundaries. His ecumenism and his refusal to separate social justice from evangelism are legacies of which all evangelical Christians can be proud. With his training institute, Gordon encouraged anyone who felt called to mission work – the poor, women, students, and members of ethnic groups. Gordon's was a leading voice for foreign missions, but he spent much of his time in an inner-city ministry; he refused to separate home and foreign missions. For us today, A.J. Gordon's legacy is one that defies stereotypes. He worked where he saw the Spirit leading – not where narrow theological parties thought he should go.

Notes

1. Gordon served as a trustee of Brown University for fourteen years and as a trustee of Newton Theological School for twenty-seven years.

2. See A.J. Gordon, "Missionary Money – Quality and Quantity, part 2," *Watchword* 13 (1891): 284-88.

3. Ernest B. Gordon, *Adoniram Judson Gordon: A Biography* (New York: Fleming H. Revell, 1896), p. 100.

4. See T.D. Roberts, *Means & Ways; or, Practical Methods in Christian Work*, with an Introduction by A.J. Gordon (Boston: James H. Earle, 1893).

5. A.J. Gordon, *How Christ Came to Church, the Pastor's Dream, a Spiritual Autobiography*, with Life-Story by A.T. Pierson (Philadelphia: American Baptist Publication Society, 1895), p. 68.

6. William Richey Hogg, *Ecumenical Foundations: A History of the International Missionary Council and Its Nineteenth-Century Background* (New York: Harper & Bros., 1952), p. 42. Also see Thomas A. Askew, "The 1888 London Centenary Missions Conference: Ecumenical Disappointment or American Missions Coming of Age?" *International Bulletin of Missionary Research* 18, no. 3 (1994): 113-18.

7. A.J. Gordon, "The Ship *Jesus*," Red-Letter Series, no. 1 (Boston: American Baptist Missionary Union, [1885]), p. 7.

8. Ibid., p. 10.

9. Robert G. Torbet, *Venture of Faith: The Story of the American Baptist Foreign Mission Society and the Woman's American Baptist Foreign Mission Society, 1814-1954*, with a Foreword by Jesse R. Wilson (Philadelphia: Judson Press, 1955), p. 323.

10. American Baptist Missionary Union, *73rd Annual Report* (n.p., 1887), p. 27.

11. The Niagara and prophetic conferences were late nineteenth-century gatherings for "fundamentalist" Bible study. The meetings promoted premillennial dispensationalist theology, biblical exegesis, and prophecy.

12. *Watchword* 1 (October 1878): 1.

13. A.J. Gordon, "Pre-millennialism and Missions," *Watchword* 8 (April 1886): 30.

14. Ibid., p. 32.

15. Ibid., p. 30.

16. Ibid., p. 31.

17. Quoted in A.J. Gordon, "Education and Missions, part 1," *Missionary Review of the World,* August 1893, p. 585.

18. Ibid., p. 587.

19. A.J. Gordon, "The Missionary's Shoes," *Missionary Review of the World,* April 1891, p. 291.

20. Ibid., p. 292.

21. A.J. Gordon, *The Holy Spirit in Missions* (New York: Fleming H. Revell, 1893), p. 217.

22. Ibid., p. 121.

23. A.J. Gordon, "Decentralization in Missions," *Missionary Review of the World,* July 1892, p. 492.

24. E.B. Gordon, *Adoniram Judson Gordon,* p. 248.

25. See A.J. Gordon, "The Overflow of Missions," *Missionary Review of the World,* March 1893.

26. A.J. Gordon, "The Missionary Outlook for the New Century, no. 2," *Watchword* 14 (1892): 201.

27. See Nathan R. Wood, *A School of Christ* (Boston: Halliday Lithograph Corp., 1953).

28. George Gerald Houghton, "The Contributions of Adoniram Judson Gordon to American Christianity" (Th.D. diss., Dallas Theological Seminary, 1970), p. 200.

29. Ibid., p. 201.

30. E.B. Gordon, *Adoniram Judson Gordon,* p. 272.

31. F.L. Chapell, "Dr. Gordon & the Training School," *Watchword* 17 (February-March 1895): 62.

32. A.J. Gordon, "The Ministry of Women," *Missionary Review of the World* (December 1894), p. 911.

Selected Bibliography

Works by A.J. Gordon

1885 "The Ship *Jesus.*" *Red-Letter Series,* no. 1. Boston: American Baptist Missionary Union.

1891 "The Holy Spirit in Missions." In *Report of the First International Convention of the Student Volunteer Movement for Foreign Missions (Cleveland, Ohio, 1891).* Boston: T.O. Metcalf.

1893 *The Holy Spirit in Missions.* New York: Fleming H. Revell, 1893.

Articles on Missions in the Following Periodicals:

The Watchword (editor 1878-95).

The Missionary Review of the World (associate editor 1891-95).

The Baptist Missionary Magazine.

Sermons, addresses, and other articles available at the Archives, Winn Library, Gordon College.

Works about A.J. Gordon

American Baptist Missionary Union. *Annual Reports* 1871-95.

Gordon, Ernest B. *Adoniram Judson Gordon: A Biography.* New York: Fleming H. Revell, 1896.

Houghton, George Gerald. "The Contributions of Adoniram Judson Gordon to American Christianity." Th.D. diss., Dallas Theological Seminary, 1970.

Russell, C. Allyn. "Adoniram Judson Gordon: Nineteenth-Century Fundamentalist." *American Baptist Quarterly,* March 1985.

Seville, George H. "A.J. Gordon's Zeal for Foreign Missions." *Sunday School Times,* March 30, 1958.

Wood, Nathan R. *A School of Christ.* Boston: Halliday Lithograph Corp., 1953.

Arthur Tappan Pierson

1837-1911

Evangelizing the World in This Generation

Dana L. Robert

When the Rev. Dr. Arthur T. Pierson died in 1911, the missionary movement lost a man who had edited the interdenominational *Missionary Review of the World* for twenty-four years, written over fifty books, and spoken at hundreds of major mission and Bible conferences in the Western hemisphere. His protégé, Robert E. Speer, memorialized Pierson as the greatest popularizer of missions of the age, a man who had revolutionized missionary literature.[1] In 1886 at a Princeton University revival, Pierson had brought Speer to Christianity and then in 1891 suggested him for a secretaryship with the Presbyterian Board of Foreign Missions. Comrade of A. J. Gordon, J. Hudson Taylor, Charles Haddon Spurgeon, and Dwight L. Moody, Pierson participated in the great evangelical movements of the era. He originated and promoted the watchword of the Student Volunteer Movement, "The evangelization of the world in this generation." The churches of which he was pastor included the Metropolitan Tabernacle in London and Bethany, the institutional church in Philadelphia.

Though a self-styled conservative Presbyterian, Pierson's influence was astonishingly broad. Living in the generation preceding the division between ecumenical and evangelical parties within Protestantism, Pierson's legacy extends to both camps. On one hand, he supported the established denominational mission boards with promotional tours and publicity. He insisted that missions were the work of the whole church, calling repeatedly for a world missions conference and a world federation of churches. He was a delegate to the World Conference on Missions in London, 1888, and he addressed the great Ecumenical Conference on Foreign Missions in New York City, 1900. On the other hand, he defined evangelization as "bringing the gospel into contact with unsaved souls,"[2] stressing the presentation of the gospel message to individuals over building up indigenous churches, or social, or educational aspects of evangelism. He helped to create faith missions such as the Africa Inland Mission. Believing in an infallible Bible and the premillennial return of Jesus Christ, Arthur T. Pierson preached a divine mandate for the missionary enterprise.

Early Career

A native New Yorker, Pierson was born in 1837 in an apartment above the Chatham Street Chapel. His father was confidential clerk for the famous evangelical merchant and abolitionist Arthur

Tappan and named his son after his boss. A.T. Pierson never outgrew his childhood abhorrence of slavery; during his later years, he opposed southern convict-leasing and colonial exploitation of natives. He attended Hamilton College in upstate New York. Phi Beta Kappa, prize orator, and language scholar, he there perfected the Greek and Hebrew that he used daily in his study of Scripture. In New York City, Pierson became one of the first 100 members of the city Young Men's Christian Association. A passion for YMCA work lasted his lifetime. He received the first of several special experiences of the Holy Spirit during the urban revivals of 1857. His seminary classmate, George E. Post, decided on a missionary career in 1858, and though Pierson agonized, he chose regular parish work over a foreign missionary career. Pierson was graduated from Union Theological Seminary in 1860 and was shortly thereafter ordained an evangelist in the Presbyterian Church.

Marrying Sarah Benedict and taking a job with the First Congregational Church of Binghamton, New York, Pierson settled into a highly successful career as a parish minister. Renowned for his pulpit oratory, he also was a prolific writer, publishing hundreds of poems, journalistic articles, and sermons. After three years in Binghamton and six at a larger Presbyterian church in Waterford, New York, the Fort Street Presbyterian Church of Detroit, Michigan, extended him a call, which he accepted, in 1869.

Pierson remained at the Fort Street Church for fourteen years, becoming ever more prominent as a pulpit power and a leading Presbyterian. The Fort Street Church had a large, elite congregation of wealthy Presbyterians, rented pews, and a building that was one of the landmarks of Detroit. The church grew rapidly under Pierson's leadership, and he instituted monthly prayer for missions and eventually, five separate missionary bands, one of which supported its own missionary. He became so famous for Bible study that he led a weekly Bible Class and Teachers' Institute for all the Sunday school teachers in Detroit. Committed to city mission work, he helped to found both the Presbyterian Alliance to help struggling churches in Detroit, and the Tappan Presbyterian Association at the University of Michigan in Ann Arbor.

Though powerful, busy, and immersed in Scripture, Pierson was unhappy with his own level of spiritual consecration. From the stately pulpit of his prominent church, he could not reach either the urban poor of Detroit or the non-Christian multitudes of the mission field. His biblical conscience left him guilt-ridden with his own comfortably worldly response to Matthew 28:19, "Go therefore and make disciples of all nations." Several events led him to turn his back on an upper-class ministry and to fulfill his ordination vows as an evangelist and then as a mission theorist. First, in 1874, the revival team of Major D.W. Whittle and P.P. Bliss conducted a Detroit campaign for six weeks. Struck by their simple gospel style, Pierson housed the evangelist in his own home for a month. He became increasingly restless at his own ambition for literary fame, and after a year-long struggle renounced his ambition and recommitted himself to spreading the good news to the unsaved.

A deep peace filled Pierson's heart, and he permanently changed his preaching style from a literary one to an extemporaneous biblical exposition. Feeling himself on the verge of a crisis in his ministry, he decided to pray with members of his church about his desire to save souls. At a Friday evening prayer meeting, March 24, 1876, Pierson met with sixty or seventy of his parishioners, citing the promises of God to answer prayer and praying that any obstacles between the Fort Street Church and the evangelization of the masses would be removed. Unknown to them, while the congregation prayed, the costly church edifice was burning down. By the next day, the entire church was in ashes with the exception of Pierson's Bible notes, even though the desk in which they were stored had been completely destroyed. Seeing the burning of Fort Street Presbyterian as the answer to prayer, the church hired the local opera house, where Pierson held open evangelistic services for sixty-three weeks.[3] During this time, hundreds of people were converted under his revival preaching. When the leading men of Fort Street Church rebuilt their building and reinstituted a pew rental system, Pierson felt that the church was turning its back on the unevangelized poor. Believing that the purpose of the church's existence on earth was to evangelize in obedience to Christ's command, he felt that God no longer wanted him at the Fort Street Church.

Pierson resigned in 1882 in order to take a church in Indianapolis, which promised to help him reach the poor unchurched of the city. Wooed by John Wanamaker and dissatisfied with the Indianapolis job, in July of 1883, Pierson began a six-year pastorate at Bethany Church in Philadelphia. Bethany began as a Sunday school founded by Wanamaker, who was a business man, philanthropist, evangelical, and the postmaster-general under President Benjamin Harrison. By 1883 it had several thousand participants, mostly working-class folk from urban Philadelphia. Wanamaker and Pierson were united in their vision of an aggressive, urban institutional church. Bethany held classes on all subjects, conducted city evangelism, established chapels for the poor, formed temperance and mission societies, and left its door wide open all winter for the needy. Here, at last, Pierson had found "a church for the people"[4] whose commitment to city evangelism matched his own and whose personal support enabled him to launch a second career as a spokesman for the American missionary enterprise.

Mission Theory and Career

The American missionary movement of the 1880s and 1890s must be seen in connection with an immigrant America. Arthur Pierson and many others of his generation saw the problems of urban America to be the obverse side of problems of the non-Christian world. What both the poor immigrants who crowded into American cities and the heathen of foreign lands needed was the Gospel, and the obligation of the more fortunate American Christian was to save both by proclaiming Jesus Christ to all people. Only changing people's hearts could alleviate urban social problems such as poverty and intemperance. Pierson believed Christianity to be the only base from which world problems such as slavery and the oppression of women could be attacked successfully. This belief in the intimate linkage between world problems and American social problems and the single solution to both caused Pierson as early as 1881 to call, in print, for a united Protestantism to fight on all fronts at once. Pierson was a lifetime supporter of the Evangelical Alliance, which consisted of Protestants united for evangelism and for solving social problems. He sought to apply the model of the Evangelical Alliance to foreign missions. In 1885 at a Northfield Bible conference sponsored by evangelist Dwight L. Moody, Pierson called for an ecumenical council of evangelical churches to plan a worldwide missionary campaign. The conference ratified the call, signed by Pierson, Moody, A.J. Gordon, George Pentecost, William Ashmore, J.E.K. Studd, and others.

By 1885 Pierson's reputation as an advocate of the worldwide mission of the church was established. Inspired by his pastor's repeated sermons and articles on the missionary obligation of all Christians, John Wanamaker offered him $1,000 to lead a Christian colony to a foreign mission field. With seven volunteers, Pierson set forth a proposal for a Christian industrial colony, before the Presbytery of Philadelphia, in a paper called "The Problem of Missions." He felt that a Christian colony would provide an example of Christian life to non-Christians, as well as teach them industrial trades and help them to be self-sufficient. The Presbytery reached no conclusive action on Pierson's proposal, and the colony was never launched.

Although he never went out as a foreign missionary, it was not because Pierson was unwilling to go. Repeatedly, God seemed to call him to promote missions at home and to struggle with "home base" issues. He stated in *The Problem of Missions* in 1885: "For twenty years, by tongue and pen, I have sought to spread knowledge of facts, and fan the fires of intelligent zeal; my own heart has meanwhile been strangely drawn out to the work, and I have bent all my energies to the solution of the question, how to secure a large increase of money, and especially of the working force in the foreign field."[5]

In 1886 Pierson published the major promotional book of the missionary era. *The Crisis of Missions; or, The Voice Out of the Cloud*, a masterful balance of crisp reasoning and emotional appeal, captured the attention of Christians everywhere and directed it to the foreign-mission fields. It begins by asking the question, Why missions now? Pierson argues that God's plans for the evangelization of the world are being confirmed by history, and he relentlessly marches through the mission history of the world to show that doors to missions have been opening everywhere – in Japan, China, India, Africa and South America. "Current events are God's own commentary on his Word," he writes.[6] Then Pierson presents as immediate the crisis of missions, the turning point of history, the awesome combination of opportunity and responsibility for world evangelization:

> Never, since Christ committed a world's evangelization to His servants, have such open doors of opportunity, such providential removal of barriers and subsidence of obstacles, such general preparation for the universal and immediate dissemination of the gospel, and such triumphs of grace in the work of missions, supplied such inspiration to angelic zeal and seraphic devotion; but it may well be doubted whether there has ever been greater risk of losing the opportunity. We are in peril of practical apostasy, with respect to this stewardship of the gospel, this obligation to a lost world.[7]

To Pierson, missions reveal God's providence and action in history, and human duty to God demands cooperation with his plans.

In the last part of the book, Pierson outlines the reasons for the crisis of missions: the apathy of the church and "spiritual Darwinism," which sees Christianity as only a stage in the evolution of religion. He exhorts Christians to support missions before the time God has allotted for them has run out. Pierson suggests things that Christians should do to expedite contact with non-Christians. Individual churches should support individual missionaries, shorter and more practical training (i.e., Bible schools) should be provided for prospective missionaries, and a world council for missions should meet regularly to organize the missionary enterprise. *The Crisis of Missions* ends with a copy of the call for a world council promulgated at Northfield in 1885.

Pierson spoke again at Northfield in 1886, this time on "The Bible and Prophecy" at Moody's first YMCA student conference. At the request of Robert Wilder, Pierson held an extra missionary meeting, there speaking in terms of "the evangelization of the world in this generation," soon to become the slogan of the Student Volunteer Movement. Thanks to Wilder, Pierson, and a few others, missionary interest quickened at Northfield, and 100 men dedicated themselves to missionary careers. The "Mount Hermon 100" became the nucleus of the Student Volunteer Movement (SVM). By the time of Pierson's death in 1911, over 5,000 American student volunteers had sailed overseas as foreign missionaries. Among the students at the Northfield conference was John R. Mott, who was impressed by Pierson's challenge, "All shall go, and shall go to all."[8] Mott, later head of the SVM, the YMCA, and honorary president of the World Council of Churches, credited Pierson with inventing the Volunteer watchword and promoted it in his own book *The Evangelization of the World in This Generation*.

Pierson supported the Student Volunteer Movement throughout his career. He spoke at the first and second quadrennial conferences of the SVM and at the Liverpool quadrennial in 1896 of the Student Volunteer Mission Union, the British equivalent of the SVM. He continued to lead various Northfield Bible studies almost up to his death. Though he was the acknowledged author of the influential watchword, Pierson's use of the slogan differed from that of Mott. Through extensive

Bible study after a chance meeting with George Müller of Bristol in 1878, Pierson became a premillennialist. He largely kept his controversial premillennialism out of his speeches and articles, but it underlay his mission theory. He did not wish to divide the church over the issue of the second coming of Jesus Christ, but he defended the doctrine when attacked or when he was asked to explain his position by fellow premillennialists, such as the Bible students who met yearly for Niagara conferences.

For Pierson, "the evangelization of the world in this generation" and "the crisis of missions" referred to the theory that the second coming of Jesus Christ was imminent, and believers needed to spread the Gospel both to expedite the second coming and to "gather in" the church. He did not believe that the world would be converted to Christianity before Christ returned but that, with proper zeal and organization, Christianity could be proclaimed throughout the world within a generation. Pierson's urgency and enthusiasm for the missionary enterprise were directly related to his millennial hopes. With his friend A.J. Gordon, Pierson subscribed to the view that, through evangelization, the *ecclesia,* or elect church, would be gathered in before the second coming.

Pierson's premillennialism was attacked by postmillennialists as pessimistic and as cutting the nerve of missions. But Pierson defended the doctrine as being the basis of missions in the early church and as the basis of his and Gordon's missionary interest. He expounded his premillenarian mission theory in an essay "Our Lord's Second Coming as a Motive to World-Wide Evangelism," delivered in 1886. The imminence of the Lord's coming encourages activity and discourages indolence or time-consuming doctrinal controversy. The hope of the Lord's coming provides the reward of salvation for missionary activity; it makes disciples unselfish and opposed to material returns gained from missionary activity. Christians are responsible for contact with non-Christians, but only God is responsible for actual conversions; therefore, discouragement over small results is illogical. "Thus, while premillennialism is charged with cutting the nerve and sinew of Foreign Missions, it in fact supplies their perpetual incentive and inspiration in teaching us that duty is ours; results, God's."[9]

Critics agreed that schools, churches, and other marks of social progress are superfluous if the imminence of Jesus' return be taken literally. Pierson considered this to be a travesty of his position. After all, Jesus said to occupy the world until he came. Jesus meant for Christians to take their social responsibilities seriously. In an editorial in the *Missionary Review* of November 1892, Pierson argued against a negative reading of his premillennialism.

Dr. Gordon and myself firmly believe that "preaching the Gospel as a witness among all nations" means setting up churches, schools, a sanctified press, medical missions, and, in fact, all the institutions which are the fruit of Christianity and constitute *part of its witness*; but that our Lord's purpose and plan are that we should not wait in any one field for the full results of our sowing to appear in a thoroughly converted community before we press on to regions beyond. Missions begin in evangelization, but have *everything* to do with Christian education, and the printing press, and the organization of churches, and the training of a native pastorate.[10]

Pierson's literary output was huge. The most frequent forum for his opinions was the *Missionary Review of the World*. He began to edit the journal in 1887 and continued until his death. A monthly interdenominational missions journal, the *Missionary Review* contained original articles, abstracts of foreign articles, statistics, and news from every mission field in the world. A body of editors, including the Methodist president of the International Missionary Union, J.T. Gracey, the English Baptist F.B. Meyer, and the American Baptist A.J. Gordon, sifted through over 500 articles and letters each month to compile material for the journal. The *Missionary Review* published articles on missions and politics, mission anthropology, mission history, mission biography, and analysis of a different mission field every month. It contained both popular and technical articles and was the major organ of ecumenical church events in the late nineteenth century.

Pierson's other missionary writings include *The Miracles of Missions* (1891-1901), a series on missionary history; *The Divine Enterprise of Missions*, the Graves lectures for 1891; and *Forward Movements of the Last Half Century* (1900), a unique chronicling of various Christian spiritual and social movements. Missionary biography was one of his talents, and his best biography was of his friend Müller, *George Müller of Bristol* (1899), the rescuer of English orphans.

In 1888, Pierson attended the World's Conference for Foreign Missions in London as a delegate-at-large. His speaking ability so captivated the audience that the Free Church of Scotland and the United Presbyterians pressed him to make a promotional tour of Scotland on behalf of foreign missions. Co-speaker with his close friend A.J. Gordon, Pierson's triumphant tour of Scotland began an association with British evangelicalism that kept him in Britain one-fourth of the time for the rest of his life. With no means of financial support for his evangelism, Pierson nevertheless resigned from Bethany Church in order to be a free evangelist of foreign missions. This was a step of great faith, for he had a wife and seven children. In 1889 he returned to Scotland for a second promotional tour, where he was selected as Duff Lecturer by the Duff Foundation established by the missionary Alexander Duff. Missionary lectureships were a forerunner of seminary professorships in missions and world Christianity, and they encouraged academic work in mission studies. In the 1890s, Pierson spoke at meetings for many great British mission organizations, including the Baptist Missionary Society, various Mildmay missions, the Society for Furtherance of the Gospel among Heathen (Moravians), the London Missionary Society, and the Church Missionary Society (CMS).

Despite his widespread ecumenical activity, Pierson remained a loyal supporter of the Presbyterian Board of Foreign Missions. He conducted several tours on behalf of the Presbyterian Board, and he felt the Presbyterian polity to be the best form of church government. In principle Pierson supported denominational mission boards, but he did not hesitate to criticize them for their bureaucracy and the slowness by which candidates were trained and sent to the mission field. In the early 1890s, when the Presbyterian mission force faced retrenchment due to financial difficulty, Pierson was a forceful voice for increased funding and for missionary volunteers.

Pierson's support for mainstream mission organizations did not preclude his supporting extra-ecclesial "faith missions." His impatience with mission bureaucracy led him to encourage groups that could get missionaries into the field quickly, such as the China Inland Mission. A close friend of the founder, J. Hudson Taylor, Pierson admired the CIM for the spirit of prayer rather than overreliance on business methods that underlay its activities. He was a frequent speaker at CIM meetings and hosted Hudson Taylor on his trips to America. In 1895, Pierson helped to organize the Africa Inland Mission, another nondenominational faith mission. Though wary of despotism, which could occur in faith missions dependent upon one person rather than a mission board, Pierson supported reputable faith missions because of their efficiency and spirituality.

Later Career: Biblical and Spiritual Work

In the 1890s A.T. Pierson was at the height of his career as a mission advocate and conference speaker in both the United States and Great Britain. In late 1891 the ailing Charles Haddon Spurgeon of the Metropolitan Tabernacle in London asked Pierson to take his pulpit while he left for a rest cure. Pierson agreed and preached so well that revival occurred at the tabernacle, despite the absence of the famous and beloved pastor. When Spurgeon died in 1892, Pierson preached his funeral sermon and was left as minister of one of the then largest Baptist churches in the world. Not being a Baptist, Pierson could not and would not continue indefinitely as the preacher, even though a majority of the congregation favored offering him the job. From England Pierson had to write several letters to his presbytery denying rumors that he had become a Baptist. Public speculation and controversy over Pierson's future at the Metropolitan Tabernacle embarrassed him; and though he refused to take a permanent job as preacher, jealous supporters of other candidates for the position attacked him in the public press.

Pierson continued his rounds of lecturing and writing, preaching in long stretches at the tabernacle. But the strain of public controversy, constant travel, and late middle age began to wear him down. Economic recession, retrenchment of foreign missions, and world events such as the massacre of Armenians and advancements in weaponry depressed him. Doctrines of universalism and optimistic views of human nature, the theological liberalism of the World's Parliament of Religions in 1893, and higher criticism all seemed to deny the need for Christianity. The cruelest blow of the decade occurred when his best friend and co-worker, A.J. Gordon, died on February 2, 1895. That night Pierson wrote in his diary, "Gordon died today at midnight and the change it makes in my life is unutterable. Of all men on this side he was dearest to me, my counselor in everything – no difference of opinion in anything important and perfect sympathy of heart and action."[11] After Gordon's death, Pierson assumed the presidency of Gordon's Missionary Training School, a position he held until 1901. The Gordon Training School, a Bible school like that of Dwight Moody, later became Gordon College of Wenham, Massachusetts.

In the year before Gordon's death, Pierson's many discussions with the American Baptists had convinced him of the scriptural validity of believer's baptism. He did not want to leave the Presbyterian Church, or to become a Baptist and thereby disfellowship all who adhered to infant baptism. But exactly one year after Gordon's death, while in England on a lecture tour, Pierson felt that he had postponed obedience to God's commands and was immersed in a private ceremony. The public outcry nearly wrecked his lecture tour, for many thought that he was plotting to obtain the permanent position at the Metropolitan Tabernacle. Despite Pierson's pleas that he wanted to remain a Presbyterian and that he deplored the exclusivist policies of the Baptists, the Presbytery of Philadelphia removed him from the Presbyterian Church. Pierson never joined another denomination, and he continued to worship at a Presbyterian church for the rest of his life.

Throughout the difficult years of the 1890s, Pierson held firmly to an infallible Bible. He engaged in daily Bible study, and he often presented the results of his study at conferences, in articles, and in the fourteen books he wrote specifically on Bible study. In the final ten years of his life, Pierson became as famous in Bible study as he was in missions. He gave three major courses of Bible lectures at Exeter Hall in London under the sponsorship of the YMCA. He taught at the Moody Bible Institute, and his final work of biblical scholarship was as original editor of the Scofield Reference Bible, first published in 1909. Pierson's dispensational premillennialism was the result of his many years of Bible study, his belief that the Bible was an internally coherent and consistent system of theology, and that higher criticism undermined the validity of the Word of God.

Beginning in 1897, Keswick conferences on the deepening of spiritual life dominated Pierson's spirituality. Always a man with tremendous faith in prayer, Pierson began to attend and to lead Bible readings at Keswick conferences in Great Britain. The Keswick theology stressed the believer's absolute surrender to God. Enduements of power from the Holy Spirit enabled the believer to live a holy life in God's service. The holiness teaching of the Keswick conventions combined belief in the plenary inspiration of the Bible with deep faith in the activity of the Holy Spirit. Pierson viewed Keswick piety as biblical and as a tremendous impetus to mission service. Though the interdenominational Keswick conventions were not missionary societies per se, they supported missionaries who were of Keswick views within the established societies. Several missionary bishops of the CMS came out of Keswick conventions. The Keswick meetings also aided missionaries by sending assistants to them to conduct sessions for their spiritual renewal.

Bible and Keswick work were in addition to, not in place of, Pierson's missionary activity. He addressed the Ecumenical Missionary Conference in New York in 1900. He continued to edit and to write for the *Missionary Review*, despite hands crippled with arthritis. He provided solid support from the pages of the *Missionary Review* for the young ecumenical movement – the Edinburgh Conference of 1910, its continuation committee chaired by John Mott, and the Laymen's Missionary Movement. In 1910 Pierson celebrated the jubilee of his ordination to the ministry and his golden wedding anniversary. Much to his happiness, the 1910 General Assembly of the Presbyterian Church saluted him in gratitude for the service he had given to the world extension of God's kingdom. At the end of the year he attempted to fulfill a lifelong dream by touring various foreign mission fields. Though in ill health, his desire to inspect personally the missions he loved was so great that his family permitted him to go to Japan, carrying a set of fifty questions for a poll of missionaries. While visiting his daughter, a missionary in Japan, he became too ill to continue, and he returned to the United States. Arthur T. Pierson died in his Brooklyn home on June 3, 1911, at the age of seventy-four.

The Legacy

The most important part of Arthur T. Pierson's legacy was the fervent supporters he made for foreign missions. John R. Mott, ecumenical statesman; Robert Speer, secretary of the Presbyterian Board; Samuel Zwemer, missionary to Arabia; and Henry Frost, American secretary of the China Inland Mission, traced their initial "conversion" to foreign missions all or in part to the words of Pierson. Pierson's correspondence with missionaries such as Henry Jessup of Lebanon and J. Hudson Taylor of China gave them much encouragement. In the *Missionary Review*, Pierson published their ideas and supported their plans. The years that Pierson spent in Great Britain stirred up great enthusiasm for foreign missions, and older missionaries still recall reading his books in their youth. Pierson's contributions to mission literature and statistics were a great help to local pastors as they sought to interest their congregations in foreign missions. His legacy was strikingly demonstrated in that all seven of his children became either home or foreign missionaries for all or part of their lives.

Many of Pierson's ideas have endured, though some have vanished as the outworn prejudices of an earlier era. For instance, Pierson's anti-Catholicism and his parochial view of the "degraded heathen and their needs" have largely disappeared. His vision of a worldwide Protestantism united for missions and social services still exists. His premillennial urgency and the slogan "the evangelization of the world in this generation" still survive in conservative mission circles.[12] His goal of evangelizing unreached peoples is that of the Wycliffe Bible Translators and of the United States Center for World Mission, directed by Ralph Winter. Schools such as Gordon-Conwell Seminary and the Moody Bible Institute reflect Pierson's legacy, as does the Inter-Varsity Christian Fellowship.

Pierson's reputation today rests partly on the *Missionary Review of the World* and partly on the fact that he was a man of prayer. Ultimately, he wanted to resolve doctrinal differences in prayer, and he prayed before every speech and for all evangelical enterprises. He went where he believed God wanted him to go, even at the risk of public scandal, unpopularity, or personal loss. By his devotional works Pierson is now remembered, and books such as *George Müller of Bristol, In Christ Jesus,* and *The Acts of the Holy Spirit* are still in print.

Notes

1. Robert E. Speer, "As a Missionary Advocate," *Missionary Review of the World*, August 1911, p. 580.

2. Pierson, "The Crisis in Cities," *Missionary Review of the World*, November 1889, p. 830.

3. For Pierson's account of these occurrences, see his pamphlet *The Pillar of Fire: To the Brethren in the Ministry of Christ* (n.p., March 1880).

4. Pierson, "Estrangement of the Masses from the Church," in *Problems of American Civilization; Their Practical Solution the Pressing Christian Duty of Today* (New York: Baker & Taylor Co., 1888), p. 59.

5. Pierson, *The Problem of Missions and Its Solution* (n.p., June 1, 1885), p. 9.

6. Pierson, *The Crisis of Missions; or, The Voice Out of the Cloud* (New York: Robert Carter & Bros., 1886), p. 23.

7. Ibid., p. 273.

8. C. Howard Hopkins, *John R. Mott* (Grand Rapids, Mich.: Wm. B. Eerdmans Publishing Co., 1979), p. 27.

9. Pierson, *Our Lord's Second Coming as a Motive to World-Wide Evangelism* (n.p., John Wanamaker, 1886).

10. Pierson, "The Improvement of the *Review*," *Missionary Review of the World*, November 1892, p. 864.

11. Pierson, quoted in Delavan L. Pierson, *Arthur T. Pierson* (New York: Fleming H. Revell, 1912), p. 261.

12. See Denton Lotz, "'The Evangelization of the World in This Generation': The Resurgence of a Missionary Idea Among the Conservative Evangelicals" (Ph.D. diss., Hamburg, 1970).

Selected Bibliography

Works by Arthur T. Pierson

N.d. *Free Churches*. N.p.

1884 "God's Hand in Missions." In *Memoirs of Rev. David Brainerd*, ed. by J.M. Sherwood, pp. liii-lxxx. New York: Funk & Wagnalls Co.

1885 *The Problem of Missions and Its Solution*. N.p.

1886 *The Crisis of Missions; or, The Voice out of the Cloud*. New York: Robert Carter & Bros.

N.d. *Our Lord's Second Coming as a Motive to World-Wide Evangelism: An Essay delivered before the Prophetic Conference, Chicago, November 1886*. N.p.: John Wanamaker.

1887 *Evangelistic Work in Principle and Practice*. New York: Baker & Taylor Co.

1887-1911 *Missionary Review of the World*. Editor and contributor.

1891 *The Divine Enterprise of Missions*. New York: Baker & Taylor Co.

1891-1901 *The Miracles of Missions; or, The Modern Marvels in the History of the Missionary Enterprise*. New York: Funk & Wagnalls Co.

1895 *The New Acts of the Apostles; or, The Marvels of Modern Missions*. Duff Lectures, February and March 1893. Introduction by Rev. Andrew Thomson. New York: Baker & Taylor Co.

1897 "The Hon. Ion Keith-Falconer, Pioneer in Arabia." In *The Picket Line of Missions. Sketches of the Advanced Guard*, pp. 117-48. Introduction by Bishop W.X. Ninde. New York: Eaton & Mains.

1897 *Seven Years in Sierra Leone: The Story of the Work of William A.B. Johnson*. CMS 1816-23, Regent's Town, Sierra Leone. New York: Fleming H. Revell.

1901 *The Modern Mission Century Viewed as a Cycle of Divine Working: A Review of the Missions of the Nineteenth Century with Reference to the Superintending Providence of God*. New York: Baker & Taylor Co.

1905 *Forward Movements of the Last Half Century*. New York: Funk & Wagnalls Co.

Works about Arthur T. Pierson

The Christian (pseudonym). *A Weekly Record of Christian Life, Christian Testimony, and Christian Work*. London: Morgan & Scott, 1888-1911.

Ferguson, Michael T. "Arthur Tappan Pierson: A Reinterpretation." M.A. thesis, Graduate Theological Union, Berkeley, California, May 1978.

Maclean, J. Kennedy. *Dr. Pierson and His Message*. New York: Association Press, 1911.

Pierson, Delavan L. *Arthur T. Pierson*. New York: Fleming H. Revell, 1912.

Robert, Dana L. "Arthur T. Pierson and Forward Movements of Late Nineteenth-Century Evangelicalism." Ph.D. diss., Yale University, 1984.

A.B. Simpson

1843-1919

From Home Missions to a World Missionary Movement

Gerald E. McGraw

Where should a pastor locate if his highest priorities for the 1880s included missionary promotion and the evangelizing of unreached masses? From what American port did overseas missionaries sail? To what harbor were nearly a million immigrants arriving annually to seek a new life? The answer, obviously, was New York City, which was both the haven for new settlers and the hub of missionary departures, arrivals, and information.

Yearning to spread the Gospel abroad as well as to neglected people nearer, an innovative middle-aged Louisville clergyman known for captivating preaching, Albert Benjamin Simpson (1843-1919), began a pastorate at Manhattan's Thirteenth Street Presbyterian Church on December 9, 1876, the dawn of a decade when American urban population increased by 50 percent. Two months later Simpson launched the *Gospel in All Lands*, North America's first illustrated missionary magazine.

It is difficult to imagine a more vivid contrast than the disparity between the serenity of the isolated, rural Prince Edward Island of Simpson's birth and the teeming New York commercial metropolis where his major ministry would occur. Albert was born of Scottish Presbyterian ancestry on December 15, 1843. At age three and a half, he was transplanted by his stern, religious family to a farm near Chatham in southwestern Ontario.

What influences ignited his missionary zeal? With fervent desire but Calvinistic submission, his godly mother Jane had prayed before Albert's birth for a son who should become a minister or missionary if God willed and the child was so inclined.[1] Jane and her husband, James, a Presbyterian elder, had gained a concern for missions through their pastor at Cavendish, Prince Edward Island, John Geddie, who would in 1846 sail for the New Hebrides as one of Canada's first foreign missionaries. When Geddie had baptized young Albert, in his prayer he had also dedicated him to the ministry or to missionary service.[2] In his teenage years, Simpson sensed a call to preach. Subsequently, amid physical, emotional, and spiritual stresses he found assurance of personal salvation after reading Walter Marshall's *Gospel Mystery of Sanctification*. He studied classics in high school and with tutors, taught school, and entered Knox College in Toronto for college and seminary.

On furlough twenty-one years after baptizing the lad, Geddie inquired from Albert's father the whereabouts of the boy he had dedicated. Upon learning that he was serving as pastor of Knox Presbyterian Church in Hamilton, Ontario, Geddie immediately visited Albert.[3] "Towards the end of his own life and ministry Simpson recognized Geddie as probably the strongest influence that led him into active participation in foreign missions," notes Daryl Cartmel.[4] Simpson evidenced missionary interest while at college and in his Hamilton pastorate. His call to the pulpit of Louisville's Chestnut Street Presbyterian Church came after he preached a guest sermon in a New York church while in that city as one of 516 delegates attending the Sixth General Conference of the Evangelical Alliance, an interdenominational organization promoting Christian unity and cooperative efforts. At this conference he heard convincing papers on methods of reaching the unevangelized overseas. After he returned home, the *Hamilton Spectator* reported, "An excellent sermon was preached last evening in this church by the Rev. A.B. Simpson on the 'Lessons of the Evangelical Alliance.'"[5]

Sensing a lack of personal cleansing and anointing for service, in the early days of his Louisville pastorate Simpson found as the solution the Holy Spirit's empowering.[6] The new dynamic impelled him to unite quarreling Louisville churches in a highly successful 1875 city-wide crusade, led by Major D.W. Whittle and P.P. Bliss. As Simpson beheld throngs entering the fold in this campaign, he determined to guide his congregation to minister to its community in less conventional ways with a more aggressive, popular, evangelistic approach. Stirred by missionary fervor at a Believers' Conference at Watkins Glen, New York, in 1878, Simpson next visited friends near Chicago, where a vivid dream aroused him to missionary commitment. All the world's Christians sat in a vast hall while multitudes of anguished "heathen" – mostly Chinese – occupied the platform, wringing their hands. Awakening, Simpson responded, "Yes, Lord, I will go." Finding no open door, however, he eventually concluded that his missionary call meant that he must toil for world evangelism as enthusiastically as if he were permitted to venture overseas as a resident foreign missionary. This driving conviction led him to New York, where the time seemed ripe for launching a nonsectarian monthly periodical chock-full of factual material on every conceivable missionary effort. Sparkling with geographical and cultural data, a typical monthly issue would specialize in a given continent or major field. Mission leaders lauded it. Dr. J.M. Reid, secretary of the Board of Missions of the Methodist Episcopal Church, called it "the best Missionary Magazine in the world for general purposes," and Dr. S.H. Kellog, Allegheny Seminary professor, wrote, "It is far beyond anything in the missionary line published in this country." Most issues of the *Gospel in All Lands* survive at the A.B. Simpson Historical Library at the international headquarters of the Christian and Missionary Alliance, Colorado Springs, Colorado.[7]

Although he had energetically served that traditional Thirteenth Street parish for two years, at the same time he kept pursuing cross-cultural ministries in public halls and on the streets. Reputed to constitute the metropolis's most wealthy, fashionable parish, his congregation refused to welcome hundreds of Italian immigrants he was winning to Christ. Consequently, despite the remonstrating of his denominational colleagues, the wonder of the press, and the criticism of his loyal wife, Margaret, Simpson forsook a comfortable salary to become, as he explained, an evangelist who would remain on the scene to follow up his converts and who refused to trust anyone but God for his support. Urging his Presbyterian fold to remain with their own worthwhile work, Simpson soon attracted followers from many denominational backgrounds to a new independent ministry, which he eventually formed into a local church, the Gospel Tabernacle. Within ten years, his movement would include a membership all over the United States and Canada, supporting twenty-four missionaries in Asia, Africa, the Middle East, and Central America.

Concurrently with the commencing of his new Manhattan enterprise, in January 1882 Simpson began publishing a new magazine, *The Word, the Work and the World*, which included Bible teaching and articles urging bold outreach – both local and overseas. (As a result of a collapse of his health in 1880, Simpson had turned over responsibility for the *Gospel in All Lands* to a Methodist publisher, Eugene R. Smith.) Organizing the Missionary Union for the Evangelization of the World as early as March 1883, the Gospel Tabernacle by November 1884 had already sent five male missionaries to the Congo.[8] Due to hostile traders, disease, and death, the Congo mission quickly failed,[9] but the bravery and faith of the original missionaries later inspired others.

His new periodical's first issue contained the probing question: "Has the time arrived when the Christians of America should be asked to unite in forming a new missionary organization for the special purpose of evangelizing, within the present generation, the unoccupied fields of the world?"[10] When he shared this ambition with W.E. Blackstone, the latter replied that such an interdenominational movement should have Simpson rather than himself for its founder.[11] In an 1886 sermon on the final day of Simpson's first Old Orchard, Maine, summer convention, Blackstone suggested the formation of a movement to evangelize Tibet, supposedly heathendom's final outpost. The result was the formation of two societies a year later at the July 30-August 9, 1887, Old Orchard Convention. While the Christian Alliance comprised a home base committed to proclaiming the Word in North America, the Evangelical Missionary Alliance constituted a foreign mission board. In recognition of Canadian participation, the latter society soon became the International Missionary Alliance. Since the two alliances resembled two arms of one body, they merged ten years later to form the Christian and Missionary Alliance, an interdenominational movement to promote overseas and homeland missions. As the society grew and more organization became inevitable, it finally accepted denominational status more than half a century after Simpson's death.[12]

Simpson's Philosophy of Mission

Simpson's philosophy of mission majored on a person rather than a creed. Advocating Trinitarian views, Simpson nevertheless saw Jesus Christ, the Redeemer, as constituting the center, source, motive, goal, and dynamic for Christian living. Missions, then, must focus upon Christ, the one who died to create the Gospel to be proclaimed. Even as missions should expound Christ's message, please Christ, and glorify Christ, so also the fullness of Christ provided the power to equip missionaries for their work. Instead of formulating one's own objectives for service, the Christian worker must see the Lord's purposes for the world.[13] Thus Simpson's philosophy concerned a *world view*, which sought to ascertain a divine perspective on the needs of the world and the solutions Christ advocated. Since Christ was as concerned about a lost soul in New York as about a lost soul in Shanghai, Simpson advocated home missions as well as foreign missions. He comprehended the entire worldwide task as Christ-centered work. Celebrating the centennial of William Carey's ordination, Simpson approvingly quoted the dying Carey: "Mr. Duff, you have been speaking about Dr. Carey; when I am gone, say nothing about Dr. Carey – speak of Dr. Carey's Savior."[14]

Christ-centered work should build on Christ-centered doctrine. Missions, for Simpson, involved the proclamation of a message centering in the Lord Jesus Christ. Four doctrinal distinctives underlie his philosophy of mission. Although numbers of his contemporaries underscored these same emphases, it was Simpson who popularly codified the message as the Fourfold Gospel: Christ as savior, sanctifier, healer, and coming king. Believing that apart from Christ people remained eternally doomed, he considered evangelization – not education or social or medical relief – as mission's prime essential. The majority of the world lacked an opportunity for salvation.[15] Overseas candidates needed to experience Christ as sanctifier for power to present the Gospel convincingly, live the Gospel exemplarily, and lead converts to mature Christian behavior. "All missionary enterprise must have its source in deeper spiritual life."[16] Learning of Christ as healer in Maine in 1881, Simpson was himself suddenly spared from anticipated death from a diagnosed heart condition. Although he resisted making divine healing the whole of the Gospel, experience and Scripture taught him that it constituted a part of the Gospel to be communicated overseas. Faith would see God confirm his Word with healing signs.[17]

Simpson's philosophy of mission flowed from two major eschatological streams. Frequently recurring themes in his missiological literature include premillennialism and the dependence of Christ's imminent return on missionary endeavor. Converted himself from the postmillennialism so common in his times, Simpson allowed postmillenarians to join the Alliance but called mission policy "foolish and short-sighted" when Christian workers aimed to establish an earthly millennium through proclamation. He held that the Jerusalem Council had proclaimed the divine intent for world evangelism in the present age. Citing Acts 15:14-16, he complained: "If the church had ever kept this in view she would have saved herself the waste of much vain effort and bitter disappointment in her attempts to build up a permanent earthly institution and create on earth a kingdom without the King."[18] For him, the divine purpose for the present age includes not world conversion but the selecting of a people from among all nations to be Christ's bride. Christ will return to receive that bride only after the nations have heard the message. Quoting Matthew 24:14, he explained the relationship of world mission to the eschatological countdown: "The widespread aggressive missionary movement of our times is one of the most significant signs of the end . . . It is the one last condition preceding His advent – the door which we can turn."[19]

Urgency marked his philosophy of mission. Regardless of current events, Simpson would have said that "it is a tremendous emergency . . . because of the insistence of the Master's command and commission about it." Moreover, world needs called for immediate action. Faith became electrified at the 1891 summer conventions. Planners had earmarked for foreign missions only the final Tuesday of the Round Lake convention near Albany, New York. An early morning Bible study speaker that day concluded by suggesting the propriety of sending the Gospel to every creature within the coming decade. Although the statement was not profound, virtually the entire audience arose to assure their concurrence. Later that day, admitting that she had been first aroused to serious effort for missions, one of Simpson's convention staff members gave her jewels, estimated as worth $250, for missions. Others of the audience of only a hundred people, responded in joyous spontaneity with money or jewelry, so that they contributed enough to support four workers for a year. Two young men also surrendered themselves for overseas service. A month later when Old Orchard convened, the momentum from Round Lake seemed present from the start. Thousands attended, and members of the convocation pledged support for forty-five missionaries. Later, in his article "One Hundred Foreign Missionaries," Simpson commented that after eighteen centuries of comparative inactivity, "within a single generation, China, Japan, Africa and Turkey have been thrown open to missionaries without restriction," so that at the time of this mighty upsurge of missionary renewal at summer conventions, "there is scarcely a region beneath the sky which might not now be claimed for Christ, if the church were ready, and the men and means at hand." Although he had begun that year asking for funds to send ten new missionaries overseas, the response of the summer of 1891 was such that he ended the year by consecrating a hundred new missionaries, thereby demonstrating the movement's abundant zeal.[20]

Even aside from the aforementioned eschatological urgency, Simpson saw each generation as rapidly passing away with no one to minister to them except the current generation. Two articles, "The Great Commission," and "Eloquent Figures for the Cause of Missions," published in 1890 and 1892, respectively, form clear examples of how Simpson visualized the urgent need and resources for missions, making statistics live. Like the Student Volunteer Movement, he urged the evangelization of the world in his generation. In 1892 he was estimating that twenty thousand missionaries could complete the task before the century ended.[21]

On the very day that Simpson and his associates organized the Evangelical Missionary Alliance, in a Monday morning Old Orchard sermon, he charged that "the Church is failing and coming short in her work. She is not making the work of foreign missions her chief business, as Christ meant it should be. The apostles gave their best men to it, but the Church today is playing at it."[22] Seeing the church's feeble efforts as futile amid pressing needs, Simpson often pleaded for sacrifice.[23] Such pleas, as already noted, sometimes evoked gifts of jewelry in the offering plates. Somewhat embarrassing Simpson, such spectacular events attracted the press, with some newspapers publishing exaggerated reports.[24]

An additional feature in Simpson's philosophy, dating from the 1875 Louisville crusade, was cooperation. Assiduously avoiding the promotion of a schism at the Thirteenth Street church, Simpson found his resignation painful. When he commenced independent meetings, he avoided assembling at times in conflict with established churches, since he wanted to unite church people for world evangelism instead of drawing them out of one denomination into another. He later described his intent for his original Missionary Alliance thus: "Its scope shall be universal, and its character and spirit catholic and unsectarian and it will seek to unite Christians of all evangelical denominations in its work." Moreover, he affirmed a willingness to send workers overseas "without regard to their denominational preferences." He saw the demands of the world mission as urging the discarding of denominational barriers. In an April 1890 sermon in the Gospel Tabernacle, Simpson noted that "the churches of the mission field are growing weary of denominational names and finding the necessity of presenting to the colossal wall of heathenism the mighty front of the united Church of Christ." Cartmel has researched Simpson's attitude toward various interchurch actions and conferences, including his critical but positive commendation of the Edinburgh Conference of 1910, his approval of a plan to merge Presbyterians and Congregationalists in South India, his support for the Student Volunteer Movement, and his transfer of a China mission station to the Reformed Presbyterian mission. Eschewing lengthy involved creeds, he shared a common heritage with evangelicals, receiving members who ascribed to belief in the Trinity, verbal inspiration, vicarious atonement, eternal salvation, and eternal punishment. He saw other world religions as satanic counterfeits.[25]

Simplicity characterized Simpson's approach. If one can treat a matter directly, why create a cumbersome process? Instead of erecting institutional barriers against missionary preparation and selection, a mission should adopt open policies that encourage involvement in mission. Instead of introducing complexity overseas, missionaries should suggest simple church government – not imposed but natural. Instead of adopting complex doctrinal formulations that polarize, Simpson held that unity results from starting with a few distinctive points about Christ on which many will readily concur. Although one should not regard the essentials of historic faith as inconsequential, he or she should concentrate on great truths rather than on moot points where honest thinkers have long disagreed.

Methodology

Simpson traced Jesus' major directions from the instructions to the Twelve (Matt. 10), the Seventy (Luke 10), and so forth. Since the Seventy were to pray for additional workers and to precede Christ's own coming, Simpson described them as "the pioneers of the mighty army who were to succeed them in the coming ages." His chapter "The New Testament Pattern of Missions" explores specific directives.[26]

Several additional methods deserve mention. Believing in pioneer missions, Simpson sought out inaccessible neglected areas rather than areas already reached by another mission. Thus the aim expressed in the Evangelical Missionary Alliance constitution asserts the objective of carrying the Gospel to all nations but "with special reference to the needs of the destitute and unoccupied fields."[27]

In addition, he advocated planning, preparation, and field research prior to overseas advance. Preaching held a vital place in spreading the Gospel. After converts made a decision, instruction, discipling, and follow-up required priority attention.

Simpson repeatedly taught that the responsibility for missions lies with all Christians rather than with a select number of called ones whose circumstances permit overseas service. Someone must support missionaries with generous finances and intercession. Frugal economy, responsibility, and care characterized his fiscal policies. Although all Alliance missionaries served sacrificially, the 1890s provide a starting example of economical operation. Seeking earnestly for missionaries for North China, Simpson agreed to appoint forty-five from a pool of two hundred volunteers from Sweden who had expressed a willingness to live on an allowance of $200 per year. Twenty-one of these missionaries and fifteen children lost their lives in the Boxer Rebellion.

Overseas churches should work diligently toward self-support to release funds for dispatching additional missionary pioneers. All efforts should build toward indigenous operation. Originally advocating a self-sustaining mission concept in which missionaries earned their own support on the field through secular pursuits, Simpson forsook the plan when it proved impractical. Instead of paying workers a salary, however, he adopted a support concept that involved allocating living allowances based on individual field needs. While the faith principle must underlie the entire missionary enterprise, yet he believed that personnel would be wasting time and resources by raising their own support. Annual conventions where Bible teaching abounded and furloughing missionaries reported on their work constituted the very core of the early Alliance movement. In addition to national, district, and state conventions, every Alliance branch and affiliated independent churches conducted conventions. The missionary cause raised support by appealing to those in attendance to sign a pledge card to commit themselves to God alone to give to missions in the ensuing year. This dignified method of instilling regular giving remains as the lifeblood of missionary support more than a century after the Alliance's inception.[28]

Simpson's Many Roles

Although he ventured overseas on several tours, Simpson never served as a resident overseas missionary. Instead, his contemporaries saw him as a missionary planner, organizer, and promoter with keen leadership skills. People whom he mobilized for action were attracted by his winsome personality, spiritual warmth, candor, and sincerity.

He should be characterized as a pragmatist in the sense that he appreciated practical action more than theory. As a missions promoter, he depicted the feasibility of world evangelization within a few years if God's people would heed his call to all-out action. As a theological writer and professor, he disdained theology for its own sake, preferring to speak of great truths. As an educator, he expressed dissatisfaction with the common lengthy courses of study that equipped potential workers with a classical education in the humanities but lacked training in desperately needed skills.

Having urged the founding of missionary training colleges as early as 1880, Simpson arose to his own challenge. With no desire to replace existing colleges or theological seminaries for students who could attend them, he nevertheless perceived that he could mobilize many lay people for evangelism overseas or in the metropolis nearby if they had some basic training. Simpson believed the world's oldest Bible college to be the Chrischona in Basel, Switzerland, although he mentioned similar schools in Germany, Sweden, and Denmark as well as England. Following the lead of Henry Grattan Guinness's successful East London Institute, the Mildmay organization's Zenana training school in London, and the China Inland Mission's school for Chinese work, Simpson in 1882 founded the New York Missionary Training College, North America's earliest surviving Bible college (now Nyack College), the forerunner of hundreds of such colleges in North America. In contrast to the usual missionary education of his day, Simpson called for a speedier, more action-centered training for "light infantry" missionary workers. Nyack currently maintains a strong emphasis on missionary and ministerial preparation through its graduate division, Alliance Theological Seminary.

Delighting in pulpit ministry, from his graduation and marriage at age twenty-one until his death, Simpson continuously served pastorates. For years he conducted on Fridays the largest weekday religious service in New York City. In addition to serving as chief administrator of his college and of his Alliance movement, he took time to pen 101 books and 300 hymns and to edit at least one periodical continuously from 1880 through 1919. He claimed that "there is no more effective instrumentality today for awakening missionary interest for summoning the workers to the harvest field than the printed page and the consecrated pen."[29] He composed an abundance of articles and editorials on religious subjects. Sensing the multiplicity of his project, the *New York Times* asserted that "there was almost no end to Mr. Simpson's religious activities."[30]

Tensions

Simpson wrestled with several tensions in his life and ministry. Several which he encountered at great formative transition points in his ministry appear to have found resolution in his thinking, but a few likely clung to him through the years.

Many religions consider a saint as a holy person withdrawn from distractions and spending his or her life enjoying beatific communion with God. A missionary, to the contrary, as a divine messenger reaches out to lost and suffering people. In scrutinizing his biography, one senses that Simpson at times pondered the two contrasting roles. When on one occasion he sequestered himself away, intending to remain alone until he received a fresh spiritual enduement, he read after a few days the Great Commission in context, which convinced him that the divine empowering would only be available as a person obeyed the charge to go into the world to minister to the needy. As a promoter of Christ-likeness and a revered example of his teaching, Simpson yet avoided the temptation of isolating himself from his mission. Certainly Simpson appeared as no recluse; his holiness transcended contemplative monasticism. Pouring himself out in constant ministries, he promoted relief work to the destitute, sponsored rescue missions for the dissolute, operated Berachah as a healing home for the suffering, and engaged in bold evangelistic ventures to the unsaved. In so doing, he proved the validity of his statement in an 1894 article: "This great commission is backed up by a mighty promise, pledging all the needed power for its accomplishment," for Matthew 28:18 accompanies Matthew 28:19.[31]

Another ongoing tension concerns liberalism versus conservatism. Although Simpson never seemed to share the struggles of his contemporaries on issues like scriptural inspiration, the literalness of the virgin birth and of Christ's resurrection, or evolution versus fiat creation, yet he was a liberal innovator both in relation to what he called "neglected truths" and in evangelistic and service methods. Thus, Simpson disparages "conservative" churches unresponsive to his innovative ideas of evangelizing immigrants, abandoning pew rents, or ministering divine healing. He did not hesitate to use women on his platforms and boards and wrote of the Holy Spirit as portraying feminine qualities within the Godhead. Although he valiantly defended the historic Protestant heritage in works like *The Old Faith and the New Gospels*, he lacked patience with traditionalist rigidity – especially when it proved intolerant of the Fourfold Gospel or loath to plunge into vigorous world evangelization.

Whereas the roots of Simpson's theology grew out of traditional Calvinism, in time his position moderated. In fact, he found that "neglected truths" he had been uncovering deviated from his traditional seminary education. In addition, as he worked with Arminians as well as Calvinists, he appreciated the fact that truth often seemed to lie somewhere between extremes. Preferring to concentrate on Christ the unifier rather than on doctrine (a source of division), he sought to work with earnest people in both camps. The resulting doctrinal tension seems to surface at various points in his writings. Never choosing to renounce the revered Reformed heritage, he nevertheless supplemented it with new insights he believed to be biblical.

More quickly resolved in his thinking were such tensions as the relation between traditional education and practical training. Although he profited highly from his own classical and advanced education, he believed that the times called for urgent action by trained irregulars to supplement the inadequate quantity of highly educated (but sometimes inadequately trained) missionaries and pastors. In view of unfulfilled needs, one must not limit involvement in Christian work to men who have completed traditional college and seminary preparation. Consequently, in addition to opening his pioneer Bible college, he supported additional Bible colleges springing up throughout the continent and opened Bible schools overseas for nationals. Simpson, nonetheless, employed a number of highly educated professors in his training college.

In his earliest pastorate, Simpson defended traditional ministerial methodology, spurning novel approaches. Thus, one can discern a radical contrast between Simpson's composed, traditional ministry in Hamilton and the vigorous whirl of aggressive evangelism that characterized his New York work and much of his Louisville service.

Similarly, the years at Thirteenth Street Presbyterian Church bring into sharp focus the tension he himself was experiencing as a clergyman serving a staid parish and at the same time a zealous evangelist and editor bent on rescuing both lost immigrants in New York and unevangelized nations abroad.

Weaknesses

Some writers have discovered inconsistencies in Simpson's life and work. In his striving for practicality, Simpson sometimes ventured impracticably. Tending to dream like a visionary, some of his ideas proved dismal failures. Undaunted, he would look for a more workable program. Never chained to his own past starts, he maintained a flexibility that could always see new horizons.

Some have charged Simpson with forgetting that charity begins at home. Amid domestic discord, he first dragged his family to the nation's metropolis and later launched out from the ordered ministry of his denomination and its comfortable salary to become an unsupported independent preacher. Much grief resulted from these decisions. Some have pointed out that Mrs. Simpson's qualms about rearing children in the wicked urban setting proved founded. Like various other leaders of his time, he tended to neglect his natural family to enlarge and edify the family of God.

Probably the deepest criticisms of Simpson have surrounded his more distinctive and successful innovations. Critics viewed the Bible college as a dangerous educational short-cut; they distrusted his nontheological approach, his departure from the regular work of denominational ministry – which allegedly cheapened the Gospel – and his doctrinal emphases on divine healing, premillennialism, and sanctification. Traditionalists sometimes regarded his view of sanctification as unnecessarily requiring an artificial two-stage approach or as requiring too much sanctification prior to death; he conceived of sanctification as a preparation for living as well as for dying. Others withdrew from his movement because he considered it extremism to insist that all who have been baptized with the Holy Spirit must speak in tongues as the evidence. When three non-Alliance

Y.M.C.A. new missionaries died from untreated disease in Sudan, some writers heaped harsh criticism on Simpson, who had allegedly influenced their views toward a simple lifestyle and toward divine healing.[32] Always urging Alliance missionaries to make their own choices on use or refusal of medication, Simpson sought to build faith without living presumptively or inviting charges of extremism.

In conclusion, the *New York Times* called him "one of the leading . . . executives in foreign missionary work," and the *Sunday School Times* estimated that "he probably had no superior in missionary appeal."[33] Simpson's contribution to missions has proven to be noteworthy. Besides influencing many other missions and individual missionary statesmen, he fathered a "sending" organization that has demonstrated its viability in pioneering, sacrifice, evangelism, and church growth. Regarded by the Bible college movement as its founder, he instigated a kind of institution that has contributed to the education of some seventy-five percent of current evangelical missionaries.[34] Various churches and missions have learned from his plan of the missionary convention and the missionary pledge. His cooperative spirit and his sense of the urgency of the missionary task deserve emulation.

Notes

1. A.W. Tozer, *Wingspread: Albert B. Simpson – A Study in Spiritual Altitude*, centenary ed. (Harrisburg: Christian Publications, 1943), p. 12.

2. Daryl Westwood Cartmel, "Mission Policy and Program of A.B. Simpson" (M.A. thesis, Kennedy School of Missions of Hartford Seminary Foundation, 1962), pp. 1-4.

3. A.E. Thompson, *The Life of A.B. Simpson*, official authorized ed. (Brooklyn: Christian Alliance Pub. Co., 1920), p. 118.

4. Cartmel, "Mission Policy," p. 14.

5. See editorials, articles, and sermons in the *Hamilton Spectator*, October 9, 14, 17, 20, 1873; Thompson, *Life*, p. 51; Cartmel, "Mission Policy," p. 16.

6. Gerald E. McGraw, "The Doctrine of Sanctification in the Published Writings of Albert Benjamin Simpson" (Ph.D. diss., New York University, 1986), pp. 144-88.

7. "Kind Notice of Our Magazine," *Gospel in All Lands*, July 1880, back cover.

8. H.M. Shuman in Robert B. Ekvall, *After Fifty Years: A Record of God's Working Through the Christian and Missionary Alliance* (Harrisburg: Christian Publications, 1939), p. 17.

9. Robert L. Niklaus, John S. Sawin, and Samuel J. Stoesz, *All for Jesus: God at Work in the Christian and Missionary Alliance over One Hundred Years* (Camp Hill, Pa.: Christian Publications, 1986), pp. 57-60.

10. [A.B. Simpson], "A New Missionary Movement," *The Word, the Work and the World*, January 1882, pp. 33-34.

11. A.B. Simpson, "Introduction," in George P. Pardington, *Twenty-Five Wonderful Years* (New York: Christian Alliance Pub. Co., 1914), p. 6; A.B. Simpson, "Appii Forum," *Alliance Weekly*, November 10, 1917, pp. 82-83.

12. Niklaus, Sawin, and Stoesz, *All for Jesus*, pp. 70-76, 99, 229-30.

13. A.B. Simpson, "Consecrated Service," *Word, Work and World*, September 1886, p. 172.

14. [A.B. Simpson], "William Carey," *Word, Work and World*, September 1886, p. 25.

15. [A.B. Simpson], "Eloquent Figures for the Cause of Missions," *Christian Alliance and Missionary Weekly*, July 15, 1892, p. 44.

16. A.B. Simpson, "Aggressive Christianity," *Christian and Missionary Alliance*, September 23, 1899, p. 260.

17. T.V. Thomas with Ken Draper, "A.B. Simpson and World Evangelization," in David F. Hartzfeld and Charles Nienkirchen, eds., *The Birth of a Vision* (Beaverlodge, Alberta: Horizon House, 1986), pp. 203, 206.

18. A.B. Simpson, *The Challenge of Missions* (New York: Christian Alliance Pub. Co., 1926), p. 47.

19. A.B. Simpson, "Having Understanding of the Times," *Word, Work and World*, October 1886, p. 222.

20. A.B. Simpson, "One Hundred Foreign Missionaries," *Christian Alliance and Missionary Weekly*, August 7, 1891, p. 93; Niklaus, Sawin, and Stoesz, *All for Jesus*, pp. 89-93.

21. A.B. Simpson, "Redeeming the Time," *Evangelical Christian*, January 1912, p. 11; A.B. Simpson, "The Great Commission," *Christian Alliance and Missionary Weekly*, May 15, 1890, pp. 306-11; [Simpson], "Eloquent Figures," pp. 43-46; Cartmel, "Mission Policy," pp. 90, 152-54.

22. A.B. Simpson, "Mission Work," Supplement to *Word, Work and World*, August 1887, p. 106.

23. A.B. Simpson, "The Scriptural Principles of Missionary Work," *Christian Alliance and Foreign Missionary Weekly*, August 24, 1894, p. 172.

24. McGraw, "The Doctrine of Sanctification," pp. 103-4, 580-81.

25. Simpson, "The Great Commission," p. 310; Cartmel, "Mission Policy," pp. 61-62, 175-79.

26. A.B. Simpson, *Missionary Messages*, with an Introduction by Walter M. Turnbull (New York: Christian Alliance Pub Co., 1925), pp. 19-38.

27. *Christian Alliance Year Book*, 1888, p. 52.

28. Hartzfeld and Nienkirchen, *The Birth of a Vision*, pp. 208-11, 217-18; Simpson, *Missionary Messages*, pp. 68, 127-30.

29. Simpson, *Missionary Messages*, pp. 45-46.

30. "Rev. A.B. Simpson, Evangelist, Dies," *New York Times*, October 30, 1919, p. 13.

31. Daniel Joseph Evaritt, "The Social Aspects of the Ministry and Writings of Albert B. Simpson" (M.A. thesis, Drew University, 1980); Simpson, "Scriptural Principles," pp. 172-75.

32. Cartmel, "Mission Policy," pp. 64-68.

33. "Rev. A.B. Simpson, Evangelist, Dies," p. 13; Frederic H. Senft, "A.B. Simpson's Spirit-Given Gifts," *Sunday School Times*, November 29, 1919, p. 696.

34. Kenneth Gangel, "The Bible College: Past, Present, and Future," *Christianity Today*, November 7, 1980, p. 1325.

Selected Bibliography

Books by A.B. Simpson

1886 *The King's Business*. New York: Word, Work & World Pub. Co. Of its twenty chapters, seven appeared in 1900 and 1966 editions as *Service for the King*.

1888 *The Four-Fold Gospel*. New York: Word, Work & World Pub. Co.

1888-1920s Christ in the Bible series. 26+vols. Harrisburg: Christian Publications and publishing predecessors. See Sawin's chart in Hartzfeld and Nienkirchen, *The Birth of a Vision* (Beaverlodge, Alberta: Horizon House, 1986), pp. 282-84, for details on this set of five commentaries, prepared as college class lectures, and more than twenty sermon collections.

1892 *A Great Missionary Movement*. New York: Christian Alliance Pub. Co.

1893 *Larger Outlooks on Missionary Lands*. New York: Christian Alliance Pub. Co. Published following a round-the-world tour.

1894 *Millennial Chimes: A Collection of Poems*. New York: Christian Alliance Pub. Co. Twenty-three missions poems in a collection of sixty-two.

[1896] *Paul – the Ideal Man and Model Missionary*, New York: Christian Alliance Pub. Co.

1899 *Providence and Missions*. New York: Christian Alliance Pub. Co.

1900 *The Story of the Christian and Missionary Alliance*. Nyack, N.Y.: Alliance Press. Besides recounting origins, this unsigned promotional work attributed to Simpson spends fifty-six pages on seven overseas missionary areas.

1925 *Missionary Messages*. New York: Christian Alliance Pub. Co. Posthumously published collection of sermons preached 1892-1913.

1926 *The Challenge of Missions*. New York: Christian Alliance Pub. Co. Posthumously published collection of sermons preached 1897-1910.

Periodicals as Sources of Missions Articles by A.B. Simpson

Gospel in All Lands (editor 1880-81).
Work and the World (editor 1882).
The Word, the Work, and the World (editor 1882).
Word, Work and World (editor 1883-87).
Christian Alliance (editor 1887-89).
Christian Alliance and Missionary Weekly (editor 1889-93).
Christian Alliance and Foreign Missionary Weekly (editor 1894-97).
Christian and Missionary Alliance (editor 1897-1911).
Living Truths (editor 1902-1907).
Alliance Weekly (editor 1911-19). Later called *Alliance Witness* and since the centennial now *Alliance Life*.

Works about A.B. Simpson

Annual Reports, International Missionary Alliance and The Christian and Missionary Alliance, 1892-1919.

Cartmel, Daryl Westwood. "Mission Policy and Program of A.B. Simpson," M.A. thesis, Kennedy School of Missions of Hartford Seminary Foundation, 1962.

Ekvall, Robert B. *After Fifty Years: A Record of God's Working through the Christian and Missionary Alliance*. Harrisburg: Christian Publications, 1939.

Evaritt, Daniel Joseph. "The Social Aspects of the Ministry and Writings of Albert B. Simpson." M.A. thesis, Drew University, 1980.

Hartzfeld, David F., and Charles Nienkirchen, eds. *The Birth of a Vision: Essays on the Ministry and Thought of Albert B. Simpson. His Dominion*, Supplement no. 1. Beaverlodge, Alberta: Horizon House, 1986. Centennial essays by faculty members of Canadian Theological Seminary and Canadian Bible College, including "The Missionary Eschatology of A.B. Simpson," by Franklin Pyles; "A.B. Simpson and World Evangelization," by T.V. Thomas with Ken Draper; "A B. Simpson and the Tensions in the Preparation of Missionaries," by Jacob P. Klassen; "Early Alliance Missions in China," by Paul L. King; and eight additional chapters.

McGraw, Gerald E. "The Doctrine of Sanctification in the Published Writings of Albert Benjamin Simpson." Ph.D. diss., New York University, 1986. Ann Arbor: University Microfilms. In Simpson's thought, sanctification provides the dynamic for effective missions.

McKaig, C. Donald. "The Educational Philosophy of A.B. Simpson, Founder of the Christian and Missionary Alliance." Ph.D. diss., New York University, 1948.

_____, ed. "Simpson Scrapbook." Nyack, N.Y.: By the Author, 1971. An unpublished collection by a Nyack College professor.

Niklaus, Robert L., John S. Sawin and Samuel J. Stoesz, *All for Jesus: God at Work in the Christian and Missionary Alliance over One Hundred Years*. Camp Hill, Pa.: Christian Publications, 1986. A well-researched history by an editor, an archivist, and a seminary professor.

Pardington, George P. *Twenty-Five Wonderful Years*. Introduction by A.B. Simpson. New York: Christian Alliance Pub. Co., 1914. This early history by a well-educated early Nyack College professor was brought back into print in the 1980s as a part of a forty-eight-volume facsimile reprint series, "The Higher Christian Life," edited by Donald W. Dayton and issued by Garland Publishing.

Reynolds, Lindsay. *Footprints: The Beginnings of the Christian and Missionary Alliance in Canada*. Toronto: Christian and Missionary Alliance in Canada, 1982. Much attention to early periodicals and newspaper accounts in a history researched and written by a chemical engineer.

Sawin, John S. "Missionary Sermons by A.B. Simpson." Unpublished Manual. Nyack, N.Y.: [The Christian and Missionary Alliance], 1983. Including both chronological and alphabetical listings and an introduction, this valuable work contains a brief paper entitled "The Missiology of A.B. Simpson." Several Sawin manuals like this one, a handwritten Simpson diary and other primary sources, early missionary memorabilia, Simpson books and periodicals, and a number of theses and dissertations on Simpson are preserved in the A.B. Simpson Historical Library at the denominational headquarters, Colorado Springs, Colo.

Thompson, A.E. *The Life of A.B. Simpson*. Official authorized ed. Brooklyn: Christian Alliance Pub. Co., 1920. Although the official edition by a Canadian missionary to Palestine contained additional chapters by other authors whose work does not remain in print, all the Thompson material survives in a current edition entitled *A.B. Simpson: His Life and Work*.

Tozer, A.W. *Wingspread: Albert B. Simpson – A Study in Spiritual Altitude*. Centenary ed. Harrisburg: Christian Publications, 1943.

Wilson, Ernest Gerald. "The Christian and Missionary Alliance: Developments and Modifications of Its Original Objectives." Ph.D. diss., New York University, 1984. Ann Arbor: University Microfilms.

Fredrik Franson

1852–1908

Reaching Peoples Who Still Have Not Heard

Edvard Torjesen

Fredrik Franson (1852-1908) was a true fruit of the nineteenth-century evangelical awakening. He also became one of its great missionary evangelists.

Five of the seven churches that Franson helped to found in Utah, Colorado, and Nebraska during 1880 are still continuing. Fifteen missionary societies and church denominations, whose founding or early history he significantly influenced, also still continue. They are headquartered in nine different countries of Europe, North America, and Asia.

These missions have been meeting occasionally since 1980 for consultations on evangelical missiology. Their fifth such consultation was held in Japan in 1991 on the invitation of the Domei Church Association. This association in that year reached its 100th anniversary. It is the eleventh of these "Franson related" missions to pass its centennial.

A Little-Known Personal History

The question may well be asked, How could a man who made such durable contributions to the mission of the church in so many countries around the world be as overlooked in church and mission historiography as Franson has been? Professor Emanuel Linderholm, a church historian at Uppsala University, was already disturbed by this omission in 1925. He wrote:

> Already in the 1870s Franson had set his religious perspectives for life. He had already then become a typical representative of the 19th century American revivalism in Finney's and Moody's spirit. He is reminiscent of both of them, combining Moody's love with Finney's sternness . . . Yet, how and by what paths he arrived at all this, I do not know.[1]

Linderholm's predicament has been that of other historiographers as well. It has also been a predicament for missiologists. Without a knowledge of the factors that conditioned Franson's life and ministry, how could they understand his legacy?

Franson arrived in the United States as an immigrant from Sweden at age seventeen. In February 1877, four months short of his twenty-fifth birthday, he set out as an interdenominational evangelist on the American frontier.

From the start this young evangelist was compelled by a clear and well-focused vision of Christ. He lived by the motto Constant, Conscious Fellowship with Jesus. He was well read and informed on current issues. He was current on the evangelical discussions of the day. His knowledge of the Bible was thorough and immense. He applied this knowledge rigorously to himself and to his preaching. His life and ministry reflected a true and ready expectation of Christ's imminent return. He also carefully obeyed the scriptural injunction, "Do not go beyond what is written" (1 Cor. 4:6, NIV).

Franson's Spiritual Roots

What were the factors that had conditioned this development in Fredrik Franson's life? Briefly, they were his responses to cues from four sets of impinging influences. These were the Swedish American spiritual awakening; his personal spiritual crisis and its resolution; nurture through his local home church; and nurture through the Moody campaigns.

Cues from the Swedish American Spiritual Awakening

Fredrik Franson was born in Sweden in June 1852. His father and mother were both active in the local "Rosenian" pietist awakening (named after Carl Olof Rosenius). This awakening was the Swedish counterpart to the Evangelical Awakening, the spiritual renewal movement that surged through Protestant churches in different parts of the world all through the nineteenth century.

On the worldwide scale, this awakening distinguished itself by its emphasis on (1) the Bible; (2) evangelism and personal conversion; (3) the oneness of all God's children; (4) holiness; and (5) missions. These factors also characterized the Rosenian movement in Sweden. However, the Rosenian movement was further characterized by its emphasis on the following "in Christ" relationships: (1) the "truth in Christ," as found in God's Word alone; (2) every believer's "new life in Christ," a concomitant of justification; (3) all believers' "oneness and freedom in Christ," each conditioned by the other; (4) every believer's "gifts and calling in Christ;" and, after Franson, (5) the "hope in Christ," conditioning every believer's outlook on and mission in the world.

Franson's Spiritual Crisis and Its Resolution

Fredrik's parents were godly, capable and hard-working. Frans, the father, built a house for his family that still stands today. Fredrik was the eighth of ten children. However, the family also experienced grief. Three children died before Fredrik was born. Then in 1857 the father died, as did an infant sister and an older brother. The mother, Maria, at forty was left a widow with five children, ages three to twelve. Fredrik was five. Two years later she remarried. The children, however, all grew up with the surname Franson, after their father.

Maria must have early seen some unusual promise in Fredrik. She saw to it that he got as good a primary schooling as then was possible. When Fredrik got to middle school, he completed the four-year course in three. He passed the high school entrance exam in 1867. In his freshman year he got A's in Greek and Latin and B's in German, math, theology, and Swedish. However, tragedy again struck. In 1868, because of the economic depression, the three older children found it necessary to emigrate to America. Fredrik at the end of his freshman year had to drop out of school. In May 1869 the parents with the younger children (now three of them) also emigrated to America. For the next two years they lived in a dug-out shelter on the Nebraska prairie.

In the first year Fredrik took sick with fevers and chills. He also fell into a deep spiritual depression and was unable to believe in God. Not until after his twentieth birthday – and after long hours of prayer and faithful counseling by his mother – was he able to believe God's Word and put his trust in Jesus for salvation. In the resolution of this crisis, Romans 10:8 became especially meaningful to him. He began to study the Bible. The vision of Christ began to come into focus in his soul. He also read Christian study materials. However, he did not share his faith with anyone except his mother.

That was still the situation a year and a half later, when in January 1874 an awakening began to spread through the little Swedish Baptist Church in their settlement. One day, when a lady from their church came to visit and asked Franson about his spiritual condition, he suddenly realized what a shame it was that he had not let anyone know he was a believer. He determined that that evening he would get up in the church and tell everyone what Christ had done for him. He did, and immediately "the fear disappeared." As he himself testified, "That was because God was my strength, and he blessed the testimony."

Nurture through the Local Home Church

Franson now came under the spiritual nurture of this local Baptist church. This turned out to be healthy fare indeed. He soon became active as a layman. The church could then begin to draw on his skills and gifts. A pastor from a neighboring settlement took him along on his evangelistic circuit. Soon the church also began to include Franson in its delegations to various interchurch conferences. In some of these conferences he was selected to serve as recording secretary.

Nurture through the Moody Campaigns

In October 1875 a totally different period of learning began. That month Dwight L. Moody, after returning from his campaigns in England, began his North America big city campaigns at Brooklyn, New York. Franson went east to work in and to learn from these campaigns. The campaigns climaxed with the Chicago campaign that continued from October 10, 1876 to January 16, 1877. The next month Franson headed out in full-time evangelistic ministry.

During his sixteen-month apprenticeship in the Moody campaigns Franson came into touch with the heartbeat of the Anglo-American revival movement. He experienced interdenominational cooperation on an evangelical basis. He discovered the use and the biblical basis of aggressive evangelism. He also learned that God honors his Word, that the Holy Spirit empowers for service, that it is the preaching of Christ that counts, that sins need to be addressed and condemned, but that, at the same time, good news also needs to be proclaimed to the sinner.

Franson also became familiar with the biblical expositions underlying the expectation of Christ's soon (and premillennial) return, an expectation that had begun to take hold at this time in both the Anglo-American and German-American awakening movements. This expectation – the "hope in Christ" – now also conditioned Franson's outlook on and mission in the world. He also learned that it is crucial for Christian workers to keep themselves in a constant, conscious fellowship with the Lord. This lesson was to emerge as more important to Franson than any technique or method. Looking back five years later, he wrote, "Fellowship *with* Jesus and work *for* Jesus are two preoccupations that we can never assess too highly." To Franson it was unthinkable to *work* for Jesus without also keeping oneself in a constant conscious *fellowship* with him.

Fredrik Franson's public ministry lasted thirty-one and a half years. During these years he kept himself constantly alert to new situations and opportunities. His perspectives and his ministry never stopped developing.

Franson's ministry on the American frontier showed early the following dual thrust: aggressive evangelism for local church growth and mobilization of the local church for its evangelistic mission. In Minnesota, Swedish Baptist churches as well as churches of the Mission and Ansgar synods – both Lutheran and both Rosenian – experienced significant growth through his ministry. On the western frontier, two Presbyterian churches resulted in Utah, an independent evangelical church in Denver, and four such churches in Nebraska. During a four-month ministry in Illinois that followed, Franson shared in conferences on New Testament ecclesiology and eschatology.

Three premises in Franson's ecclesiology at this time became significant cues for the Evangelical Free Church movement that emerged from 1884 to 1885. These premises were (1) the polity we see applied by the churches in the New Testament is the standard for church polity also today; (2) each local church has an evangelistic mission in the world, for which the church needs to mobilize itself, including all of its individual members; and (3) the church is Christ's Bride on earth. The expectation of Christ's imminent return conditions our outlook on and our mission in the world. "The time is short" (1 Cor. 7:29).

Widening Horizons of Mission

In June 1881, a few days before his twenty-ninth birthday, Fredrik Franson arrived in Sweden. His mission: to so preach the Gospel that as many people as possible in the land of his birth should come to faith in Christ and have the assurance of salvation. In this mission he was singularly successful.

However, the Lord soon began to direct Franson's attention toward peoples that still had not heard the Gospel. Through the 1882 "May Meetings" in London his eyes were opened to the tremendous strategy and planning involved in bringing the Gospel to the various people groups around the world, and he began to apply these insights. Through his campaigns in Norway in 1883, and in Denmark in 1884-85, both the Norwegian Mission Covenant Church and the Danish Mission Covenant Church came into being. In 1884 Franson conducted four trial evangelist training courses. These courses proved fruitful. He soon incorporated such courses in his regular ministry.

Franson's vision, however, was still being refocused. He heard a message in 1884 by Professor Theodor Christlieb, a Bonn University theologian, at the Evangelical Alliance International Conference in Copenhagen. Through that message Franson heard God's call to Germany. Despite the readjustments which this necessitated, he arrived in Germany in June 1885. After seven months of fruitful but not easy ministry, he went on to Switzerland. He studied French, and soon he shared in French-language meetings. He then moved on to France. Here for five months he worked with various local Protestant churches and evangelistic missions, a distinct minority in France. Working with these missions and local churches, Franson learned in a new way the reality of the unfinished task still facing the church.

Moving into Italy and to Egypt, then to Palestine and Lebanon, and up along the coast of Turkey to Constantinople, Franson got a further hands-on experience of what was involved in communicating the Gospel to people of different cultures. In Constantinople, however, he met still another world: Armenians, Bulgarians, Serbs, Romanians, Jews from many nations, Greeks and Turks; and to the northeast, the millions of Russians, with many other nationalities among them.

Franson responded with characteristic enthusiasm to each opportunity; however, his attention was becoming increasingly focused on the masses in societies all around the world that still needed to hear the Gospel. When in July 1887 he finally arrived in East Prussia, he articulated his goal for the future as follows: "To be able to do something on a larger scale to help the masses of people who are rushing into perdition." He was then thirty-five years old.

Franson spent the next twenty-one years of his life implementing this goal. First he thought through various forms of specialized evangelism that held promise of achieving this goal. He then rigorously applied this evangelism. One type of personal evangelism that he identified as crucial was counseling with concerned individuals in "after-meetings," which directly followed public meetings.

A second form of specialized evangelism that he now put into use was special-purpose evangelist training courses. In 1888 he conducted such specialized courses in Norway, Finland, and Sweden, each course focusing specifically on the training of laypersons for evangelism in remote and unreached communities. In each country a large number of course participants moved out into this type of evangelism, both at home and abroad. The following six organizations particularly benefited: in Norway, the Norwegian Mission Covenant Church, the Evangelical Orient Mission, and the East Africa Free Mission; in Denmark, the Danish Mission Covenant Church; in Finland, the Finnish Mission Covenant; and, in Sweden, the Holiness Union.

In February 1889 Franson, together with Emanuel Olsson, began his long-planned Germany campaign at Berlin. They met much resistance, and progress was slow. In August, however, Franson was able to visit Barmen where he first had served in 1885. He sensed surges of revival, and an evangelist training course was scheduled for November. In the meetings that then ensued, God added his "times of refreshing" (Acts 4:19). The results were that a large number of people turned to the Lord and several of the course participants volunteered to go as missionaries to China. Through this revival the German Alliance Mission came into being. Also, Franson saw the cue for a new thrust in his own ministry: the mobilization of the church for special-purpose missions around the world.

On September 7, 1890, Fredrik Franson landed in New York. On October 14 he began an evangelist training course at Brooklyn, with the announced purpose of selecting and sending missionaries to China. He conducted similar courses in Chicago, Minneapolis, and Omaha. About two hundred Scandinavian young persons attended. From those who offered themselves Franson selected fifty. By February 5, 1891, all these were on their way to China, each supported by one or more local churches. Franson then also organized this whole undertaking as a new mission, The Scandinavian Alliance Mission of North America (today TEAM – The Evangelical Alliance Mission).

Over the eleven-year period from 1890 to 1901, Franson's ministry influenced significantly the founding or early history of the following ten missions: The Evangelical Alliance Mission (1890); Swiss Alliance Mission (1890); North China Mission of the C&MA (1893); Mongolia Branch of the Evangelical East Asia Mission (1897); Himalaya Mission of the Finnish Free Church (1898); China Mission of the Norwegian Mission Covenant Church (1899); the "Borken" Fellowship Deaconess Home of Marburg Mission (1899); Swedish Alliance Mission (1900); Women's Mission Association of the Finnish Free Church (1900); and Norwegian Missionary Alliance (1901).

From 1894 to 1895 Franson visited mission fields in Asia. He spent seven months in India, two months in Japan, and seven months in China. A total of 149 missionaries were then serving on these fields with missions he helped to get started. Franson visited and entered into the work of nearly every one of these missionaries. In each country he also studied the history and culture of the peoples, as well as the work of other missions.

In 1902 Franson set out on an evangelistic and missiological study tour, which in six years took him around the world. Among his ministries: organizing a Scandinavian church in Norsewood, New Zealand; setting up a seamen's home in Sydney, Australia; inter-mission evangelistic campaigns in South China; a six-month ministry in Japan; nurturing the first revival surges in Korea; thirteen months of cooperative ministries in North, West, and Coastal China; people movements in Burma and India; revivals in Turkey, which greatly influenced the emerging Armenian Spiritual Brotherhood; sixteen months of varied evangelism in South Africa; and nine months of interethnic orientation and cooperative ministries in the countries of Latin America.

When Franson landed in Mexico, he had personally evangelized among peoples in most parts of the world. He had gathered a unique body of missiological data from mission work throughout the world. Before leaving Mexico, he wrote an overview of his missiological findings. The title (as translated from Swedish) was *Five Different Methods of Missionary Work in Non-Christian Societies.*

On June 5, 1908, Franson crossed the border into the United States. His plan was to have some rest and then give himself to work among youth. The Lord, however, had other plans. He called Franson to his eternal rest on August 2, 1908. He was fifty-six years old. He had expended himself fully for the Lord.

Conclusion

How can we summarize the legacy of Fredrik Franson? He may be remembered best for these highlights of his ministry:

1. Reinforcement of, and his consistent and rigorous responses to the cues of, the Evangelical Awakening.

2. Special emphasis on "constant, conscious fellowship with Jesus," along with his other emphases on the message and programs.

3. Relating himself positively to all individuals and societies.

4. The dual thrust in his early strategy: evangelism with the local church as its goal, and the local church with evangelism as its goal.

5. The dual thrust in his later strategy: mobilization of the church for special-purpose missions around the world, and the continuing reinforcement of evangelism, church renewal, and mission engagement.

6. Two of Franson's characteristic statements: "That which is Biblical is everywhere appropriate, for all countries and all peoples"; and "I have been occupying myself with a country's history, geography and politics mainly because of their effects on the cause of God's kingdom."

Note

1. Emanuel Linderholm, *Pingströrelsen i Sverige* (The Pentecostal movement in Sweden), (Stockholm: Bonnier, 1925), p. 21.

Bibliography

Works by Fredrik Franson

1879 "Bidrag till lösning af den inwecklade samfunds-och församlingsfråga" (A contribution to the complicated denominational and local church question). *Chicago-Bladet,* May 23.
1880-81 "Den bibliska församlingsordningen" (Biblical church polity). *Chicago-Bladet,* December 17, 24, and 31, 1880, and January 5, 1881.
1887 *Die Nacversammlungen, betrachted im Lichte der Bibel* (After-meetings considered in the light of the Bible). Zinten (East Prussia): By the author.
1890 *Weissagende Töchter* (Prophesying daughters). Emden: Anton Gerhard.
1909 "Fem olika missionsmetoder på hednamarken" (Five different missionary methods in non-Christian societies). In *Missionar F. Fransons Testamente* (Missionary F. Franson's testament). Edited by Efraim Sandblom. Jönköping: Skandinaviska Allianmissionens Forlag.

Works about Fredrik Franson

Christensen, John. *Verdensmisjonaeren F. Franson* (World missionary F. Franson). Oslo: Det Norske Misjonsforbunds Forlag, 1927.
Grauer, O.C. *Fredrik Franson: An Evangelist and Missionary in World-Wide Service.* Chicago: Scandinavian Alliance Mission, 1938-40.
Kmitta, August. "Missionar Franson" (Missionary Franson). *Gemeinschaftsbote* (Elbing, West Prussia), June 10-July 22, 1917, Nos. 23-29.

Larsen, Emil. *Brydninger: Kirkelige og frikirkelige i sidste halvdel av det 19. århundrede med saerligt henblik pa Fredrik Franson's besög i Danmark 1884-85* (Surges: official and free church in the last half of the nineteenth century, focusing on Fredrik Franson's Denmark visit, 1884-85). Copenhagen: Tro & Liv, 1965.

Linge, Karl. *Fredrik Franson: En man sänd av Gud* (Fredrik Franson: A man sent from God). Jönköping: Svenska alliansmissionen, 1951.

Princell, Josephine. *Missionär Fredrik Fransons lif och verksamhet* (Missionary Fredrik Franson's life and work). Chicago: Chicago-Bladet Publishing Co., 1909.

Torjesen, Edvard Paul. "Fredrik Franson (1852-1908)." *Evangelikale Missiology* (Korntal, Germany), 4/1988.

_____. "Fredrik Franson, der Mann mit dem Gehorsam aus Glauben" (Fredrik Franson, the man with the obedience that came from faith). *SAM-Bote* (Winterthur, Switzerland), Jan/Feb-Nov/Dec, 1989, Nos. 1-6.

_____. *"A Study of Fredrik Franson: The Development and Impact of His Ecclesiology, Missiology, and World-wide Evangelism."* Diss., International College, Los Angeles. Ann Arbor, Michigan: UMI, 1985. Publication No. LD00851.

Pius XI

1857–1939

The Missionary Pope

Josef Metzler, O.M.I.

Pope Pius XI was born Achille Ratti, May 31, 1857, in Desio near Milan. Growing up in the milieu of the aspiring industrial middle class of Lombardi, he felt the impact of the modern rush for social and economic prosperity.[1] After excelling in his course in the humanities at Milan's state college and completing two years in the Milan seminary, at twenty-two years of age he entered the Lombard College in Rome. For three years he studied church history, theology, and philosophy and received his degree in all three. On December 20, 1879, he was ordained priest in the Lateran Basilica.

Early Years in Parish and Academic Ministry

In 1882 he returned to Milan. After serving for a short time as the administrator of a parish, he was assigned to teach "sacred eloquence" (homiletics) and a dogma course in the major seminary. After teaching for five years, he joined the staff of the Ambrosian Library and from that time onward was engaged in intensive academic research and writing. He published *Guida sommaria per il visitatore della Biblioteca Ambrosiana e delle collezioni annesse* (Brief visitor's guide to the Ambrosian Library and its related collections) (Milan, 1907) and numerous works on the history of the church in Milan as well as on Charles Borromeo and other subjects.[2] In 1907 he was appointed director of the Ambrosian Library and also papal domestic prelate.

When Franz Ehrle, S.J., resigned his post in 1911 as prefect of the Vatican Library, Pius X appointed Achille Ratti as vice-prefect; and, in 1914, as prefect. Monsignor Ratti was uprooted from his scholarly library routine on April 25, 1918, when Benedict XV appointed him apostolic visitor to Poland.[3] This new ecclesiastico-political and diplomatic task he performed skillfully and tactfully. Because of his knowledge of languages (German, French, Spanish, English) and his repeated journeys into Germany, Switzerland, and England, he was well prepared for this new assignment. His apostolic travels and visits took him through the whole of Poland and the Baltic States. After Poland achieved political independence in 1919, the pope appointed him apostolic nuncio and titular archbishop. However, his additional appointment as head commissioner for Silesia, East and West Prussia put him into diplomatic conflict both with Poland and with Germany. The pope freed him from this delicate situation by appointing him archbishop of Milan, and he raised him to membership in the College of Cardinals on June 13, 1921. His tenure as chief shepherd in Milan lasted for only a few months. Benedict XV died on January 22, 1922, and on February 6, Ratti emerged from the conclave as Pius XI.

Besides the traditional measures taken as pope for the promotion of the Gospel, his international relationships with states and peoples are of particular significance. The concluding of the Lateran Pact and the concordat with Italy, whereby after nearly sixty years the "Roman Question" was finally solved, clarified and underlined the church's spiritual role. The religious and pastoral tasks of the papacy manifestly came to the foreground, its temporal and political interests faded into the background, and the Roman Curia enjoyed as never before a universal moral esteem.[4]

Pius XI and Mission Science

Modern scholarly study of missions owes its foundations to Gustav Warneck (1834-1910), who in 1874 founded the *Allgemeine Missionszeitschrift* and in 1896 became the first professor of missions in Halle. His activities and publications in mission studies wielded their influence and became the norm for the founding of a Catholic science of missions. In his 1919 encyclical *Maximum illud*, Benedict XV had outlined a concept of missionary formation in sacred and profane sciences, and he asked that a center of mission studies be established in the Collegio Urbano in Rome.[5] Cardinal Willem van Rossum, prefect of the Sacred Congregation "de Propaganda Fide" (1918-32), immediately went to work to establish an academic chair for mission studies.

Pius XI took up these ideas right from the outset of his pontificate. Adopting the motto "Pax Christi in Regno Christi," the pope proclaimed 1925, 1929, and 1933 Holy Years. His lively concern for missions, and his bent for speedy execution, became evident when he gave orders that a missions exhibit, featuring a missions library, be organized in the Vatican for the 1925 Holy Year.[6] He selected a splendid location for the exhibit, the great courtyard of the Pigna, adjacent to the new wing of the museums. Vicars and prefects apostolic were asked to send mission books and maps to the exhibit.[7]

Close to 30,000 volumes, in all languages, arrived in Rome for the Vatican Missionary Exhibition, and experts from all over the world were invited to Rome to assist in its preparation. Among them was Father Robert Streit, O.M.I., already known in Rome for the publication of the first volumes of the monumental *Bibliotheca Missionum*. No one seemed better prepared to organize the library section, which was meant to display the literary and scholarly work of Catholic missionaries and missiologists. The pope followed Streit's work with special interest. When he visited the exhibition for the first time, he went directly to the library, where he paused to examine the collections grouped according to the origin of the volumes. When he came to open other pavilions, he stopped again in the library to inspect the new collections and documents that had recently arrived. "Whenever he would come to the exhibition in the quiet hours," recalls Father Streit, "he would never fail to come to the library to see how the work was progressing."[8]

"The importance," he said on the day of inauguration, "given to the scientific and literary section proclaims that even in holiness, hardships and sacrifices are not sufficient; neither is empiricism, but knowledge is necessary in order that fruit may be gathered from these hardships and sacrifices. Just as today in industry, commerce, and the more material occupations of life there is a search for scientific guidelines, so these must not be lacking in the missionary field."[9]

At the close of the Missionary Exhibition, which the pope compared to "a vast book," Pius XI expressed the desire that this "book" might always be open in Rome, "where the real center of propulsion and diffusion of all the missions is . . . where it will be ever available to all." Thus was founded the Missionary Museum at the Lateran (now in the Vatican Museum). With the same purpose in mind, he also decided that the literary section of the exhibition should remain in Rome as the Pontifical Missionary Library in order to make it a center for missiological research on the very site of the offices of Propaganda Fide. Father Robert Streit was named the first head librarian.[10]

That was a decisive step on the way to carrying out the mission science plans of the pope. Because of the prodding of Benedict XV from 1920 onward, missionary science courses were given in the theology faculty of the Athenaeum (today University) Urbanianum of Propaganda Fide. Finally, in 1933 Pius XI established in the same Athenaeum the Institutum Missionale Scientificum. The previous year the Jesuits had expanded their Gregorian University in Rome with a faculty of mission sciences.

The Mission Program of Pius XI

The missionary encyclical *Rerum Ecclesiae* of February 28, 1926,[11] is of the greatest importance in Pius XI's missionary program. In it are expressed in all their fullness "his broad outlook, his creative energy, the nobility of his heart burning with love for Christ."[12] In the modern missionary literature, *Rerum Ecclesiae* must be numbered among the church's basic documents. "Converting the pagans is an obligation of charity toward God and neighbor and binds all the faithful, especially the clergy and ecclesiastical superiors."[13] The pope thus strongly admonished the faithful to be more fruitful in their missionary activity. They were summoned to more insistent and constant prayer for missions and for missionary vocations. The bishops were exhorted to promote missionary vocations and not to fear a lessening of priestly vocations for their dioceses. The Pontifical Works for the Propagation of the Faith were recommended. To vicars and prefects apostolic, the pope strongly recommended the formation of an indigenous clergy and the establishment of new diocesan seminaries. Local priests were not to be employed in subordinate services only but ought to be educated to assume the direction of the missions so that the foreign missionaries could devote themselves to new tasks in other territories. Formation of local clergy was indispensable both because indigenous leaders know better the languages and customs of mission areas and because they run less danger of being expelled in case of war or internal upheavals.

The pope then asked that native persons of both sexes be admitted into the already-existing religious congregations and that they be helped to found new ones in conformity with local conditions and with the way native peoples think. The contemplative life must especially be furthered in missions, both because of its intrinsic value and because it corresponds to the natural dispositions of various peoples in mission lands. The number of catechists too ought to be increased. The encyclical concludes with some practical advice concerning the external organization of the church in mission lands and the development of schools of higher learning.

Pius XI's missionary program thus embraced the whole work of the evangelization of peoples, including the faithful of the established churches and the new churches. The pope reminded all the faithful, especially clergy and bishops, of their duty to collaborate and cooperate effectively in the world's evangelization, for all are responsible for the missions. Pius XI especially insisted that bishops were responsible for the missionary activity of the entire church.

In spite of the centuries-old tradition of the church and repeated reminders from the pontiffs and the decrees and instructions of Propaganda Fide, the problem of native clergy was far from solved. Pius XI tackled this problem and asked for an energetic and radical solution. He was aware that the contemporary world was moving at a rapid pace and that if the church failed to solve the problem of native clergy, it would be left behind. From the very outset Propaganda Fide had struggled against the interference of the colonial powers in mission affairs and had done its best to encourage the development of autonomous local churches. Now, after the First World War, the era of political colonialism was winding down, even though not all the powers were convinced of that.

Pius XI, a far-seeing man, was preparing the future of the church in the new countries that were nearing their time of independence.

Carrying Out the Mission Program

Already in 1926, the year the mission encyclical appeared, Pius XI took the first steps to achieve the missionary aims he had set for himself. He wrote the apostolic letter *Ab ipsis pontificatus primordiis* on June 15, 1926, which was addressed to the vicars and prefects apostolic of the missionary church in China.[14] In it the pope condemned missionary involvement in political activities, referring to recent dreadful consequences, and stressed the purely spiritual character of missions. He also warned against setting up barriers between the foreign and native clergies. He expressed joy that it had been possible in a short while to hand over several mission territories to the Chinese clergy and hinted that soon some Chinese priests would be ordained bishops. The pope also spoke about the French Protectorate in China. He stressed that if the church tolerated the exercise by foreign powers of a certain protectorate over the church in a foreign land, it was only inasmuch as it recognized the right of each state to protect its citizens all over the world.

The indication of an imminent ordination of Chinese bishops brought great joy in the whole Catholic world, but especially in China. The actual deed was not long in coming. Cardinal van Rossum informed the pope that a Chinese priest had just been named to the post of vicar apostolic, with all the episcopal dignity. Pius XI was not only pleased but also immediately declared himself ready to ordain personally the first Chinese bishop in the modern era. The episcopal ordination was to take place in the autumn of 1926.

The pope's readiness to ordain personally the first Chinese bishop prompted a flurry of activity both in Rome and in China. Not one but several Chinese episcopal candidates were to be presented to the pope.

Two Chinese prefects apostolic already in office were named bishops, and three new vicariates apostolic with Chinese ordinaries were established. Thereby six Chinese bishops were at hand for the solemn consecration in Rome on October 28, 1926. Pius XI had chosen this date because he himself had received episcopal ordination on October 28 in 1919.[15]

This event caused a sensation across the world. Celso Costantini, the apostolic delegate to China who had come to Rome with these bishops, compared it to an electric current that aroused the missions in China to new life and a new direction.

A year later in Rome, on October 30, 1927, on the feast of Christ the King, Pius XI ordained the first Japanese bishop; and on June 11, 1933, the first Vietnamese bishop. He would also have liked to ordain the first bishops from Africa in the modern era. This privilege, however, was reserved for his successor.

In the mid-1930s, Pius XI addressed another exceptionally important item, namely, the inculturation of the Christian message. This was particularly urgent in China in order to counter the accusation that Christianity was a foreign religion, serving only to spread Western culture and a Western mentality. Inevitably, the issue of inculturation revived the "Chinese rites" question.

The first step in this regard was taken in 1935 in Manchukuo. The vicars apostolic of this new state, which had been established out of five Chinese provinces in 1932 by Japan against China's will, witnessed a revival of the old Confucius cult. Pondering earlier Roman decisions against the Chinese rites which honored Confucius and the ancestors, they alerted Rome about this matter. In a letter of December 3, 1934, Cardinal Pietro Fumasoni-Biondi, prefect of Propaganda Fide since 1933, encouraged them to study this delicate question and to submit concrete criteria that would enable Propaganda Fide to come up with practical guidelines.

On March 25, 1935, the vicars apostolic submitted the requested data. They had consulted local authorities about the contemporary meaning of the Confucius cult. The Manchukuo government's reply was unmistakably clear: it was only a matter of a civil honor with no religious significance. Thereupon, with Pius XI's authorization, Propaganda Fide addressed the famous letter of May 28, 1935, to the bishops of Manchukuo.[16] It contains the following determinations: Missionaries should take care that the government's declaration regarding the civil character of the Confucius cult become known among the people. It was permissible in Catholic schools to display Confucius's picture and to pay him the state-prescribed homage. Because of the danger of confusion with religious devotion, Christian believers should not set up altars or burn candles before this image. Material contributions in honor of Confucius, but no "offerings," could be tolerated. Christians could also contribute money for the building and renovation of Confucian temples if this was included in the common taxes levied by the state. It was also permitted that Christians could participate in local burial ceremonies conducted as an expression of honor and gratitude toward the deceased person.

Pius XI emphasized that these decisions should be given due publicity throughout the whole of China. The result, as anticipated and desired by the pope, was that one after the other of the vicars apostolic in China reported to Rome that Christians were no longer attributing any religious significance to the Chinese rites. Therefore, they asked, could the same measures allowed in Manchukuo be granted in other areas as well? Such requests were granted. Finally, on December 8, 1939, the pope authorized Propaganda Fide to provide the following principles for the whole of China:

1. Catholics are allowed to take part in expressions of honor made before images and plaques of Confucius in Confucian memorial places or in schools.

2. It is permissible in Catholic schools to put up the picture of Confucius, or a plaque bearing his name, and to greet it with a bow of one's head.

3. Catholic teachers and students, who are ordered thereto, may take part in public ceremonies in honor of Confucius, insofar as such ceremonies can be considered purely civil.

4. Bowing the head and other civil signs of honor before the dead or their images or tombplates bearing only the inscription of the name are allowed and permissible.[17]

Conclusion

By means of all these historic measures, Pius XI gave testimony to his conviction that spreading Christ's message and the evangelizing of peoples was to be the first and highest aim of his pontificate. Other measures and decisions in regard to this aim were also taken; they can only be listed here.

In the first year of his pontificate, in regard to the three hundredth anniversary of the establishing of Propaganda Fide and the one hundredth anniversary of the founding of the (French) Society for the Propaganda of the Faith (Lyons, 1822), he took advantage of the occasion to summon all Catholics to zealous missionary cooperation along with prayer and sacrifice. In the same year he declared that the Society for the Propagation of the Faith, the Society of Saint Peter the Apostle (to provide spiritual and material assistance for the clergy in mission countries), and the Society of the Holy Childhood (Catholic children helping children in the mission countries) were now pontifical societies.[18] By this measure he gave new impulse to the missionary cooperation of the faithful on the home front.

The pope promoted the training of a native clergy and requested foreign mission superiors to prepare native priests to take over the leadership of the church. He expressed his special good will to the native seminarians in the Collegio Urbano in Rome. He provided the college with a new location on the Janiculum, and in 1931 he established the Ethiopian College in the Vatican. In 1927 the Agenzia Internazionale Fides was founded to inform the faithful on the home front about mission activities.[19] World Mission Sunday was also established.[20] In 1937 Pius XI laid plans for an exhibit of religious art from missions. Delayed by the Second World War, it became a reality only during the 1950 Holy Year.

An important step in carrying out his mission program was also the setting up of apostolic delegations in the mission countries. They were meant to help bring uniformity into missionary methods; later they were changed into nunciatures with diplomatic status. This happened in China in 1922, where the French Protectorate was to be terminated, as well as in South Africa (1922), French Indochina (1925), the Belgian Congo (1929), British East and West Africa (1930), and Italian East Africa (1937).

A rich literature on Pius XI as pope of missions underlines among other things the importance of this pope for missions on the home front, for missionary science and research, and for the promotion of the spread of the faith in all parts of the world. The fact that during his pontificate some 200 new mission sees were established and that 40 of these were given over to native ecclesiastical superiors speaks eloquently of the missionary legacy of Pius XI. He died on February 10, 1939, after a pontificate of seventeen years, which was fruitful for the entire church and especially for the Christian world mission.

Notes

1. Josef Schmidlin, *Papstgeschichte der neuesten Zeit*, vol. 4: *Papsttum und Päpste im XX. Jahrhundert. Pius XI (1922-1939)* (New York, 1939), pp. 5-6.
2. Ibid., p. 9.
3. Cf. Ottavio Cavalleri, "L'Archvio di Mons. Achille Ratti. Vistatore Apostolico e Nunzio a Varsavia (1918-1921). Inventario." In *Appendice le Istruzioni e la Relazione finale* (Vatican City, 1990).
4. Karl Bihlmeyer and Hermann Tüchle, *Kirchengeschichte*, pt. 3: *Die Neuzeit und die neueste Zeit* (Paderborn, 1956), p. 493.
5. *Acta Apostolicae Sedis* (1919), p. 448.
6. Cf. Josef Metzler, O.M.I., "The Pontifical Missionary Library 'De Propaganda Fide,'" in *De Archivis et Bibliothecis Missionibus atque Scientiae Missionum inservientibus* (Rome, 1968), pp. 347-60.
7. "Norme per l'invio dei libri destinati all'Esposizione Missionaria Vaticana dell'Anno Santo 1925," *Esposizione Missionaria dell'Anno Santo 1925. Bollettino Ufficiale* (Rome) 1, no. 1 (February 1924): 375.
8. Robert Streit, O.M.I., "Papst Pius XI. und die Missionswissenschaft," *Die katholischen Missionen* (M. Gladbach) 57 (1929): 215.
9. *Cronistoria dell'Anno Santo 1925* (Rome, 1928), pp. 117-18.
10. Since 1972 Willi Henkel, O.M.I., has been head librarian. In 1979 the Missionary Library was unified with the Urbanian University Library, and Henkel became head librarian of both.
11. *Acta Apostolicae Sedis* (1926), pp. 65-83.
12. Johannes Dindinger, O.M.I., in *Guida delle Missioni Cattoliche* (Rome, 1934), p. 19.
13. *Rerum Ecclesiae* (Feb. 26, 1928), par. 5.
14. *Acta Apostolicae Sedis* (1926), pp. 303-7.
15. Ibid., pp. 432-33.
16. *Sylloge praecipuorum documentorum recentium Summorum Pontificum et S. Congregationis de Propaganda Fide* (Typis Polyglottis Vaticanis, 1939), pp. 479-82.
17. *Acta Apostolicae Sedis* (1940), pp. 24-26. For other publications, see *Bibliotheca Missionum* 14, no. 3 (1960): 336-37.
18. *Sylloge*, pp. 672-82 ("Romanorum Pontificum").
19. Ibid., pp. 717-18.
20. A Sunday dedicated to the idea of mission, with prayers for the success of the missionary effort.

Bibliography

Bierbaum, Max,. *Das Papsttum: Leben und Werk Pius XI.* Cologne, 1937. See esp. "Die katholische Weltmission," pp. 125-62.

Brou, Alexandre, S.J. "L'oeuvre missionnaire de S.S. Pie XI (1922-1929)." *Etudes Tom.* (Paris) 201 (1929): 202-15.

Bruehl, C. "Pius XI and the Missions." *Homiletic and Pastoral Review* (New York) 39 (1939): 1257-67.

Burke, Francis J., S.J. *Pius XI, Pope of the Missions.* New York, 1929.

Carminati, Franco. *L'Opera di Pio XI per le Missioni.* Rome, 1929.

Gúrpide, Pablo. "Pio XI, el Pontífice de las Misiones y del Oriente." *Illuminare* (Vitoria) 9 (1931): 151-57; 10 (1932): 33-37, 209-16; 11 (1933): 41-45.

Hughes, Philip. *Pope Pius the Eleventh.* London, 1938. See esp. "The Foreign Missions," pp. 150-62.

Lavarenne, J. *L'oeuvre missionnaire de Pie XI.* Lyons, 1935.

Ledrus, Michel, S.J. "La doctrine missionnaire de S.S. Pie XI." *Nouvelle Revue Théologique* (Paris and Tournai) 56 (1929): 481-94.

Lima Vidal, Joâo Evangelista de. "A Obra da Propagação de Fé e o Santo Padre Pio XI." *Anais de Propagação de Fé* (Lisbon) 6 (1935): 246-55.

Martindale, Cyril C., S.J. *The Call of the Missions.* London, 1939. See esp. "Pius XI – Pope of the Missions," pp. 10-20.

Olichon, Armand. *Pie XI et les Missions.* Paris, 1928.

Ortiz de Urbina, Ignacio. "Pio XI, las Misiones y la Unión de las iglesias." *Razón y Fe* (Madrid) 87 (1929): 42-53.

Peters, Joseph. "Die Neuordnung des Missionshilfswesens durch Pius XI." *Die katholischen Missionen* (M. Gladbach) 59 (1931): 40-44, 126-31, 212-18, 246-51, 274-79, 344-49.

Pinedo, Ignacio F. de, S.J. "Pio XI y las Misiones." *El Siglo de las Misiones* (Bilbao) 21 (1934): 36-39, 65-69.

Streit, Robert, O.M.I. "Unser Missionspapst Pius XI." *Priester und Mission* (Aachen) 13 (1929): 7-16.

Tragella, Giovanni Battista, P.I.M.E. *Pio XI, Papa Missionario.* Milan, 1930.

Helen B. Montgomery
1861–1934
Lucy W. Peabody
1861–1949

Jesus Christ, the Great Emancipator of Women

William H. Brackney

The missionary enterprise is more than the involvement of persons directly engaged in evangelical ministries. It is also the educational, promotional, and spiritual work that provides support for preaching, healing, and social witness. In North America in the early nineteenth century a "benevolent empire"[1] of agencies assumed leadership for the support of missions. Prominent among these, from the very first, were women's organizations.[2] In the last quarter of that century, there was a coalescing of "women's work for women" that may be directly attributed to singularly gifted leaders. Two of those leaders were Helen Barrett Montgomery and Lucy Waterbury Peabody, who left a joint legacy of publication, promotion, and prayer on behalf of women across denominational lines and particularly among Baptists.

Helen Barrett Montgomery – "A College Woman"

Helen Barrett was born July 31, 1861, in Kingsville, Ohio, the eldest of two daughters and a son born to Adoniram Judson Barrett and Emily B. Barrows. Owing to her father's job as a school-teacher, the family moved to western New York, then characterized religiously as the "Burned-Over District."[3] Her childhood was spent in Lowville, New York, a village north of Albany; most of her adult life was spent in the city of Rochester. By her own admission, her father was a dominant influence on her development.[4]

A.J. Barrett was heir to a long line of Baptists, hence his being named in honor of the pioneer Baptist missionary to Burma, Adoniram Judson (1788-1850). Deeply devoted to education, Barrett taught in several academies as a self-trained person with a keen interest in the classics. Later in his career, and at great personal sacrifice, he attended the newly formed University of Rochester. In 1872 he responded to a call to Christian ministry and entered Rochester Theological Seminary. Rochester was a newer, pro-revival school under the aegis of the young and gifted theologian

Augustus Hopkins Strong (1836-1921).[5] Barrett, his wife, and three children knew the seminary faculty intimately, and he prospered in the student body. In 1876 upon graduation he became minister at Lake Avenue Baptist Church in Rochester, which became a prestigious congregation in the city's Baptist community. There he remained a beloved pastor until his sudden death in 1889 following an extended overseas tour. Helen later compiled a memorial book to her father and she helped to establish the Barrett Bible Class at Lake Avenue in his honor, which she taught personally for over four decades.[6]

Like her father, Helen sought a good education and pursued literature and classics at Wellesley College. Following her graduation from Wellesley in 1884, she took an M.A. degree at Brown University. Of her collegiate studies she said, "I knew what it was to be a poor girl in college, and I have as my richest possession the memory of four years that were the inspiration of my life. I believe in education with all my heart and soul . . . I am told that I am a college woman. Yes, I am."[7]

Helen was a superior student and took high commendation to her first position as principal at Wellesley Preparatory School in Philadelphia in 1887. Her time in Philadelphia was brief for she soon married a wealthy industrialist named William A. Montgomery (1854-1930), seven years her senior. The couple decided to move to Helen's hometown, Rochester, New York, where William continued his business interests.[8] She was remembered by friends in the 1880s as a tall, graceful, attractive woman who commanded attention in every gathering.

Early in their marriage, William Montgomery pledged to Helen his support for her far-reaching interests in civic life and Christian mission. This proved to be a considerable commitment of funds for travel and support of missionary work around the world, plus sharing his spouse for extended periods of time with speaking tours and administrative assignments. Montgomery busied himself with building a thriving subsidiary company to what became the General Motors Corporation; he was also on the board of trustees of Rochester Theological Seminary and served as chairman during the period when merger negotiations with Colgate Theological Seminary were completed. With Helen's encouragement, William quietly contributed the funds for construction of the new president's home, later named Montgomery House.[9] Together with their adopted daughter, Edith, the couple lived in a modest home in Rochester, choosing to give much of their income to missions.

From 1890 to 1900 Helen divided her time between parental care for daughter Edith and a growing interest in civic and institutional life in Rochester. It would prove to be good experience for her later career in Christian endeavor. In 1893 at the urging of her friend Susan B. Anthony (1820-1906), she helped to form the Women's Educational and Industrial Union to assist women in self-improvement and working conditions. This was to be a persistent interest throughout her life. Her stake in the women's movement amounted to a massive educational campaign:

> The greatest foes that menace the womanhood of America are the pagan ideals that are coming to dominate our theaters and social life. Luxury, easy divorce, indolence, and indulgence can make American women sources of temptation and objects of contempt like their sisters in the buried civilizations of the past.[10]

She took on two projects that brought her much attention in the city press. In the late 1890s she chaired a committee to open a women's college at the University of Rochester (a Baptist-related institution) and raised $100,000 to launch the program. In 1899 she became the first woman to be elected to the Rochester City School Board, thereafter spending a decade advocating manual training, vacation classes (summer school), art education and teacher training programs, especially for women. A sympathetic editor in Rochester's principal newspaper remarked that Helen had "more than a woman's tender heart and fine tact; . . . she has breadth of mind, earnestness of purpose, energy of execution, and high ideals."[11] An elementary school in the city was later named in her honor.[12]

Active in the Lake Avenue Baptist Church, which licensed her to the ministry, and in the regional Monroe County Baptist Association of churches, Helen began to expand her religious horizons. Lucy Peabody recalled that their debut as platform speakers occurred at the 1887 Monroe Baptist Association meeting in Penfield, New York, where they both nervously anticipated speeches on behalf of missionary work.[13] From that time on Helen was frequently in demand at Baptist and then ecumenical meetings where she organized support for women's mission organizations and overseas projects. In 1914 she was elected the first president of the newly unified (east and west) Woman's American Baptist Foreign Mission Society (WABFMS), following similar roles in the predecessor state and regional bodies among Northern Baptists. Except for the year she served as president of the Northern Baptist Convention, Helen was the uncontested presidential choice for the WABFMS for a decade. She wrote countless editorials, filled pulpits, and presided over meetings that sought to organize women's work in local church circles, associational bands, and in a national network.

Lucy Peabody, Mission Administrator

A few months older than Helen Barrett Montgomery, Lucy Whitehead McGill was born in Belmont, Kansas, March 2, 1861, the daughter of John and Sarah Hart McGill. Like Helen, Lucy was raised in a Christian home in Rochester, New York. She was graduated from high school in that city and, as an "eclectic student," attended classes at the University of Rochester, which was then closed to women degree candidates. At age twenty she partly realized her Christian ambitions by marrying Norman Mather Waterbury. The couple had met at Lucy's church, East Avenue Baptist, while Norman was a student at Rochester Theological Seminary and Lucy taught at the Rochester School for the Deaf. In 1881 Norman (with Lucy) was appointed a missionary to India by the American Baptist Missionary Union and they took up residence as Telugu specialists at Madras.[14] After five and a half years' work, Norman Waterbury died in India; Lucy and two of their three children, Norma Rose and Howard Ernst, returned to the United States, first to Rochester and then to Boston.[15]

The Woman's Baptist Foreign Mission Society of the East soon recognized Lucy's considerable administrative skills and appointed her in 1887 to the position of home secretary, a post she filled in Boston, Massachusetts. This allowed her to provide adequately for her children; she spent over eighteen years in the position. During this period she took charge of the Society's literature production and edited the popular *Helping Hand* and *Everyland* juvenile missions papers. Part of her responsibilities also included recruitment of new female candidates and the supervision of children's education. Her official photographs portray her as a person of medium stature with an intense but pleasant disposition.

In 1906 Lucy resigned her secretaryship to marry Henry Wayland Peabody of Beverly, Massachusetts. Peabody was a wealthy Salem import/export merchant twenty-three years her elder. The couple had met during Henry's service on the board of the American Baptist Missionary Union. Henry promised faithful support for his spouse's mission interests, which accorded with his own philanthropic pursuits. He died, however, in 1908, leaving her again a widow. She spent several months compiling a biography[16] of her late husband and then returned to active mission work.

Serving Together

The Central Committee on the United Study of Foreign Missions provided the structural context for an important component of the joint legacy of Helen Montgomery and Lucy Peabody. Beginning in 1900 as a committee of the New York Ecumenical Missionary Conference, and sponsored by the Woman's Union Missionary Society, the committee drew together from across the United States representatives of all the women's missionary efforts.

Its purpose was to coordinate information about the needs of Christian women worldwide and to provide publications and educational events that would rouse women to the missionary cause.[17] Commencing with $25.00 capital, and Lucy and Helen in its membership, the committee produced a steady flow of two study books per year for twenty-seven years (publishing a total of four million volumes), earning it Pierce Beaver's assessment as the most successful publisher of mission books.[18] In addition, annual summer conferences were developed at Northfield (Mass.), Chautauqua (N.Y.), Chambersburg (Pa.), and Winona Lake (Ind.), where missionary speakers had close exposure to vacationing laypersons. Lucy was chair of the committee and Helen was its most popular author, providing a dozen books and a million copies to its ministry. Helen's best-known book, *Western Women in Eastern Lands* (1910), sold over 100,000 copies.[19]

Lucy and Helen also shared in the development of the International Jubilee of Woman's Missions, which occurred in 1910. Helen had originally proposed the idea in her book *Western Women,* and she was one of the major promoters. Lucy later described the year of activities of the jubilee as

a spontaneous uprising of the womanhood of the United States against the entire conception of society as a selfish, sectional, material paganism. To everything that is involved in militarism, oppression, violence; here was a pointblank answer – arrangements for the care of mothers, for the upbringing of children, for the kindly progress of the community under the influence of Christ.[20]

Helen made a whirlwind coast-to-coast speaking tour, at one point delivering 197 addresses in a two-month period! Everywhere she challenged the "privileged educated woman of leisure to form a great sisterhood of service and league of love."

A second important achievement in the legacy of Helen and Lucy was their firsthand awareness as missionary educators and promoters of overseas work. For Lucy, of course, this knowledge stemmed from her own missionary experience in India in the 1880s; Helen had looked forward to an extended trip since her father's European tour in 1888. When John R. Mott announced a meeting in 1913 of the International Missionary Council in Amsterdam, Holland, Helen and Lucy decided to make an around-the-world tour. Accompanied by their daughters (recent college graduates), the two women journeyed from London to Tokyo in just over six months, November 1913 to April 1914.[21] In Amsterdam, they enjoyed a personal interview with Queen Wilhelmina, who received special editions of Helen's books. From Holland they traveled through Central Europe to the Middle East.

Throughout Asia Helen assessed the needs and possibilities for women's education. At Vellore, the two Americans conversed extensively with the famed Ida S. Scudder, who gave to Helen a plan for village education, girls' high schools, and a medical college for Indian girls. In Burma they visited sites associated with the three Judson wives of a former generation, and in South China they focused on the work of the William Ashmores, Baptist missionaries known to them from Rochester days. Finally, in Japan the great Christian statesman Nitobe appealed to the women for a Japanese women's college. In her literary account of the trip in India, Helen wrote,

Here is the situation: the evil conditions of society, the oversexing and under-moralizing of life make it undesirable and dangerous to subject girls to the temptations of attending classes with men in government colleges. Christian schools for girls are multiplying rapidly and increasing in size daily. They must have trained Indian teachers, since it is impossible to secure a large enough missionary teaching force, and even were it possible, it would not be desirable.[22]

In the years following their famous tour, the names Montgomery and Peabody became synonymous with women's work and overseas Christian education. Seven schools in India, China, and Japan benefited from either Helen and Lucy's personal advice or fund-raising efforts.

Helen reached the pinnacle of her public life as president of the Northern Baptist Convention in 1921-1922, while Lucy took an active interest in missionary work in Philippines and a new American missionary organization. They corresponded frequently, pressed much the same social concerns agenda, and met together from time to time at their summer residences in Florida.

Both Helen and Lucy early on realized that Baptist women could not accomplish their worthy goals alone. They engaged in the ecumenical sphere at every logical point. From her work with the Central Committee and the Jubilee celebrations, Helen gained a wide collegiality with American and international Christian leaders, including such well-known people as Isabella Thoburn, an American Methodist in India; Abbie Child, a Congregationalist secretary; and John R. Mott of the International Missionary Council. Lucy, too, served on countless cooperative bodies such as the International Committee on Educational Missionary Work, as vice president of the Foreign Missions Conference of North America, the Education Committee at Edinburgh in 1910, and the Federation of Woman's Boards of Foreign Missions.[23]

Perhaps their outstanding ecumenical accomplishment, though, was their coordination of what would become a World Day of Prayer. One biographer thinks that Lucy and Helen came up with the proposal as early as 1890. Certainly the idea crystallized for the two women as they traveled in the Orient and met with leaders who consistently requested prayer for their common tasks. Upon their return in 1914 the Federation of Woman's Boards of Foreign Missions adopted a resolution for a "Day of Prayer for the Women of the World."[24]

Convention President

By 1920 Helen Barrett Montgomery at almost sixty had proven vividly that there was power and purpose in the women's missionary enterprise. At the Northern Baptist Convention (NBC) meeting at Des Moines in 1921, she proudly brought forth the results of a "Jubilee" financial campaign among the Baptist women's societies – over $450,000; at the same session she was elected the first woman president of a national Protestant denomination.[25] In her presidential address in 1922, she responded to the organized "fundamentalists" in the convention by reminding delegates that they were trustees of great Baptist principles including soul competence (the capacity of the individual to approach God without human intermediary), voluntary cooperation, and world evangelization. She criticized confessionalism, defended denominational promotion, and called for a renewed commitment to the convention's goal of one hundred million dollars for the Northern Baptist "New World Movement." President Montgomery was especially vocal in her support of academic freedom in Baptist schools, a point of bitter contention for the Fundamental Fellowship.[26]

Following a year of speaking engagements as NBC president, Helen was set free to return to her first loves, overseas women's work and her enlarged writing ministries. She traveled abroad to address the Baptist World Alliance on the role and work of women and she continued to raise funds for institutional projects. In Czechoslovakia and Burma she dedicated "Peabody-Montgomery Homes" for convalescing women patients; elsewhere she raised money for women's colleges in India and China, in several cases inducing the Rockefeller family to make substantial matching grants. The social historian follows with interest Helen's (and Lucy's) support for the Volstead Act during Prohibition – Helen applied her missionary strategies to organizing public opinion of women on the issue through the religious press.[27]

Perhaps Helen's greatest literary achievement came in 1924 when Judson Press published her *Centenary Translation of the New Testament*, the first ever completed by a woman scholar. Using suggestions from D.L. Moody (1837-1899) and A.T. Robertson (1863-1934), plus her own fresh nuances, Helen produced a superior translation in the eyes of important critics.[28] Proceeds from the sale of the translation went directly to mission projects.

Mission President

Lucy Peabody followed a somewhat different course from Helen's in the 1920s. Lucy was drawn into the moderate wing of the Northern Baptist fundamentalist movement and she campaigned heavily for certain issues. Her daughter Norma had married an American Baptist medical missionary, Raphael C. Thomas (1874-1956), who was the administrator of the Baptist Hospital at Jaro, Iloilo, Philippines. A disagreement over personnel issues ensued between the Thomases and the board, eventuating in Raphael's resignation in 1927. Lucy used her considerable influence and organizational skills to help start a new, independent "historically Baptist" agency, the Association of Baptists for Evangelism in the Orient. Their plan was to continue an evangelism-based ministry in the Philippines.[29] Under heavy lobbying from convention loyalists, who several times tried to induce her to return to mainstream mission work, Lucy defended her separation as a necessary response to the rigid control of the mission board:

> After more than forty years' association with the American Baptist Foreign Mission Society and the woman's board, it was not easy for the writer to separate from them . . . Our missionaries are a noble company, with few exceptions. Authority vested in a small group in a small mission with bureaucratic control at home and wrong dispositions account for the acute situation in the Philippines. Add to this undue emphasis on the minor work of education and neglect of Bible-trained evangelists and pastors and you have a mission that has lost its way.[30]

In 1927 Lucy Peabody actually walked out of the Northern Baptist Convention meetings at Chicago and resigned from all of her Convention responsibilities.

Even in the new doctrinally orthodox mission organization, Lucy could not avoid difficulties. Following the lead of the Thomases (who became the senior missionaries of the new association), Lucy contended with dispensationalists on the board and in the Philippines. Her postmillennial position was ultimately marginalized by a doctrinal statement that was "premillennial, Baptist, fundamental, faith mission."[31] Yet another troublesome issue was the "matriarchal" leadership of Mrs. Peabody; a significant number of supportive pastors and some of the missionaries were opposed to female leadership. After seven years as founder and president of the Association of Baptists for Evangelism in the Orient, Lucy relinquished her position. In her letter of resignation she wrote,

> My major reasons for resigning are the propriety and wisdom of electing a man to fill this important office since it deals with churches and pastors, as well as with questions which properly belong to masculine leadership in the church.[32]

After 1934 Lucy reduced her involvement in mission work to writing, editing, and support services on behalf of missionary personnel.

Women in Christian Mission

In the half century of their joint involvement in Christian mission, Helen and Lucy persisted in creating a firm theological basis for a globally emerging womanhood. Both argued that in the New Testament women found a new sense of value: "Jesus Christ is the great Emancipator of women," wrote Helen. Further,

> He alone among the founders of the great religions of the world looked upon men and women with level eyes seeing not their differences, but their oneness, their humanity . . .

In the mind of the Founder of Christianity there is no area of religious privilege fenced off for the exclusive use of men.[33]

Lucy went on to list areas of achievement in the church which women could naturally pursue. These included caretakers of children, teachers, doctors, nurses and organizational directors. In a broader context, Lucy also believed that women are responsible for conditions in their communities, the religious life of churches, and for public decency and morality, as illustrated in amusements, the press, and literature.[34]

Helen and Lucy agreed that "so democratic a body as the Baptists should be among the first to further and to recognize the emancipation of women." Helen was in fact much less tolerant of paternalism than Lucy. She was wary of denominational proposals to merge women's mission agencies with the larger male-dominated boards because, she reasoned, women would soon become fund-raisers for men. Helen seriously questioned whether men – particularly Baptist men – were prepared to work with women unless the women were subordinate to the men. She argued that the "caste of sex" could be broken by a laymen's missionary movement parallel to women's work.[35]

In their twilight years, Lucy Peabody and Helen Montgomery continued to write "from under the orange blossoms," as Lucy put it,[36] on their cherished concern. Helen lent her name to several fund-raising projects in mission and in the mid-1920s Lucy became a major advocate and board member with her close friend, Marguerite T. Doane (1868-1954), of the Houses of Fellowship, later to become the Overseas Ministries Study Center.[37]

Both women also believed that the sphere of Christian womanhood was larger than the church, for, as Helen wrote, "some women should be selected in each circle whose duty it will be to keep watch on the course of state and national legislation, to circulate petitions."[38] Close to the progressive Republican political tradition, Lucy and Helen opposed military conflict, gambling, child labor abuse, and exploitation of women. Both women idealized international disarmament in the "treaty of Bethlehem," by which they meant that the angelic declaration at Christ's birth should have an impact on foreign policy.[39]

Lucy and Helen found, however, that the 1930s were a different era both for women and social activism, from the prewar years of triumph. Helen, still vigorous, with dark hair at seventy-three, died October 18, 1934. Lucy survived her to age eighty-eight; she died on February 26, 1949.

The enduring legacy of Helen Barrett Montgomery and Lucy Waterbury Peabody lies not in the positions they each held in the mission enterprise, or in their roles in the tumultuous battles of the 1920s, nor even in the many dollars each raised. Rather, their legacy was a burden for the international plight of women and the power of concerted action by women in being faithful to the Great Commission.

Notes

1. The term "benevolent empire" is found in several secondary sources; see especially Winthrop S. Hudson, *Religion in America: An Historical Account of the Development of American Religious Life* (New York: Scribners, 1973), pp. 153ff; Charles I. Foster, *An Errand of Mercy: The Evangelical United Front* (Chapel Hill: Univ. of North Carolina Press, 1954).

2. The story of perhaps the first such organization among the Baptists is Albert L. Vail, *Mary Webb and the Mother Society* (Philadelphia: American Baptist Publication Society, 1914).

3. This unique region was a virtual "psychic highway" in the nineteenth century. See Whitney R. Cross, *The Burned-Over District: The Social and Intellectual History of Enthusiastic Religion in Western New York, 1800-1850* (Ithaca: Cornell Univ. Press, 1950).

4. In her autobiography, Helen reminisced, "To this child, God always looked like her father" (Helen Barrett Montgomery, *Helen Barrett Montgomery: From Campus to World Citizenship* [New York: Revell, 1940], p. 22; hereafter cited as *HBM*).

5. Jesse L. Rosenberger, *Rochester: The Making of a University* (Rochester: Rochester Univ. Press, 1927); Howard D. Williams, *A History of Colgate University, 1819-1969* (New York; Van Nostrand, 1969), pp. 106-39.

6. Helen B. Montgomery, *In Memoriam: A. Judson Barrett, Born April 1, 1832. Died October 20, 1889* (Rochester: H.L. Wilson, n.d.).

7. *HBM*, p. 87.

8. Originally William made his fortune in the shoe business. Later in Rochester he bankrolled an unknown inventor who perfected an electric starter for automobiles. From this beginning came Rochester Products, Inc. (*HBM*, pp. 95-96); Winthrop S. Hudson, "Helen Barrett Montgomery," in *Notable American Women, 1607-1950: A Biographical Dictionary*, Edward T. James, ed. (Cambridge, Mass.: Belknap Press, 1971), 3: 566-68.

9. Montgomery was chairman of the Rochester Theological Seminary Board 1928-1930 and spearheaded the reunification of the two schools which enjoyed a common parent in Hamilton Literary and Theological Institution. The merged seminaries were called Colgate Rochester Divinity School, for which a new campus was constructed in 1929-30 on Mt. Hope in Rochester.

10. Helen Barrett Montgomery, "Women and the New World Movement," *Watchman-Examiner*, April 15, 1920, p. 503.

11. *Rochester Democrat and Chronicle*, November 5, 1899.

12. City School Number 50, located at 301 Seneca Avenue and known as Helen Barrett Montgomery Elementary School, was opened in 1956.

13. *Minutes of the Monroe Baptist Association*, 1887. The story is also told in Louise A. Cattan, *Lamps Are for Lighting: The Story of Helen Barrett Montgomery and Lucy W. Peabody* (Grand Rapids, Mich.: Wm. B. Eerdmans Publishing Co., 1982).

14. The ABMU, later known as the American Baptist Foreign Mission Society, did not appoint women and yet expected male missionaries to find a suitable spouse. Lucy, therefore, was technically not a missionary!

15. One of their children, a daughter, died on the return journey. Lucy briefly taught school in Rochester in 1886-87.

16. Lucy's anonymous biography was entitled *Henry W. Peabody: Merchant* (West Medford, Mass.: M.H. Leavis, 1909).

17. Ruth A. Tucker, in *Guardians of the Great Commission: The Story of Women in Modern Missions* (Grand Rapids, Mich.: Zondervan Publishing Co., 1988), p. 108, gives a very brief account.

18. R. Pierce Beaver, *American Protestant Women in World Mission: A History of the First Feminist Movement in North America* (Grand Rapids, Mich.: Wm. B. Eerdmans Publishing Co., 1968, 1982), pp. 155-65.

19. *HBM*, p. 124.

20. Ruth Lowrie, *Story of the Jubilee, 1860-1910* (New York: Central Committee, 1910); *HBM*, p. 123; Tucker, *Guardians*, p. 109, contains a photograph of the executive committee.

21. Norma Waterbury wrote a popular account of the trip under the title *Around the World with Jack and Janet* (Medford, Mass.: Central Committee, 1915).

22. Helen Barrett Montgomery, *The King's Highway: A Study of Present Conditions on the Foreign Field* (New York: Central Committee, 1915), p. 73.

23. Margaret Tustin O'Hara, "Lucy W. Peabody: An Appreciation," *Watchman-Examiner*, August 11, 1921, p. 1008.

24. Compare Susan T. Laws, "Lucy W. Peabody," *Watchman- Examiner*, March 17, 1949, p. 251, and *HBM*, p. 134.

25. *Yearbook of the Northern Baptist Convention*, 1921, p. 47.

26. Helen Barrett Montgomery, "The Tasks That Confront Us," *The Baptist*, June 17, 1922, pp. 625-26. While the Interchurch World Movement experienced severe difficulties, Northern Baptists continued to support the cooperative effort and their own "New World Movement" campaign. See *Annual of the Northern Baptist Convention*, 1920 (Philadelphia: American Baptist Publishing Society, 1920), pp. 122-23.

27. Helen Barrett Montgomery, "Civic Opportunities of Christian Women," *The Baptist*, August 28, 1920, p. 1073, and *The Baptist*, 1922, pp. 396, 468. On Lucy's involvement with Prohibition, see Cattan, *Lamps Are for Lighting*, p. 113.

28. Henry C. Vedder, "Translating the New Testament," *The Baptist*, April 11, 1925, p. 312; June 27, 1925, p. 617; *Watchman-Examiner*, June 26, 1924.

29. Mrs. Henry W. Peabody, "Reply to the Statement of the American Baptist Foreign Mission Society in the *Watchman-Examiner* of June 6," *Watchman-Examiner*, June 13, 1929, pp. 759-61.

30. Ibid., p. 761.

31. Harold T. Commons, *Heritage and Harvest: The History of the Association for World Evangelism, Inc.* (Cherry Hill, N.J.: The Association, 1981), pp. 5-15.

32. Quoted in ibid., p. 36.

33. Helen Barrett Montgomery, "The New Opportunity for Baptist Women," *The Baptist*, August 25, 1923, pp. 944-45.

34. Lucy W. Peabody, "Women's Place in the World," *Missions*, January 30, 1920, pp. 216-17; Lucy W. Peabody, *A Wider World for Women* (New York: Revell, 1936), p. 109.

35. Quoted in Beaver, *American Protestant Women*, p. 183.

36. Lucy W. Peabody, "Under the Orange Blossoms," *Watchman-Examiner*, April 26, p. 1934. Lucy whimsically referred to the plan to merge the women's societies with the male-dominated societies as "the New Deal." She was no Rooseveltian!

37. This friendship had started in Baptist women's missionary work in the Northern Convention. In 1927 Doane joined Peabody as a major supporter of the Association of Baptists for Evangelism in the Orient. See Robert T. Coote, *Six Decades of Renewal for Mission: A History of the Overseas Ministries Study Center Formerly Known as the "Houses of Fellowship," Established by the Family of William Howard Doane* (Ventnor, N.J.: Overseas Ministries Study Center, 1982), pp. 11-16.

38. Montgomery, "Civic Opportunities," p. 1073.

39. Peabody, *A Wider World*, pp. 57-63.

Selected Bibliography

Works by Helen B. Montgomery

1910 *Western Women in Eastern Lands.* Medford, Mass.: Central Committee.
1915 *The King's Highway: A Study of Present Conditions on the Foreign Field.* New York: Central Committee.
1924 *Centenary Translation of the New Testament.* Philadelphia: American Baptist Publication Society.
1929 *From Jerusalem to Jerusalem.* Cambridge, Mass.: Central Committee.
1932 *The Preaching Value of Missions.* Philadelphia: Judson Press.
1940 *Helen Barrett Montgomery: From Campus to World Citizenship.* New York: Revell.

Works by Lucy W. Peabody

1936 *A Wider World for Women.* New York: Revell.
1937 *Just like You: Stories of Children of Everyland.* Boston: M.H. Leavis.

Works about Montgomery and Peabody

Beaver, R. Pierce. *American Protestant Women in World Mission: A History of the First Feminist Movement in North America.* Grand Rapids, Mich.: Wm. B. Eerdmans Publishing Co., 1980. First ed. (1968) published under the title *All Loves Excelling.*
Cattan, Louise A. *Lamps Are for Lighting: The Story of Helen Barrett Montgomery and Lucy W. Peabody.* Grand Rapids, Mich.: Wm. B. Eerdmans Publishing Co., 1972.
O'Hara, Margaret T. "Lucy W. Peabody: An Appreciation." *Watchman-Examiner*, August 11, 1921.
Peabody, Lucy W. "Helen Barrett Montgomery" *Watchman- Examiner*, November 1, 1934.
Tucker, Ruth A. *Guardians of the Great Commission: The Story of Women in Modern Missions.* Grand Rapids, Mich.: Zondervan Publishing Co., 1988.
Waterbury, Norma. *Around the World with Jack and Janet.* Medford, Mass.: Central Committee, 1915.

Robert P. Wilder

1863–1938

Recruiting Students for World Mission

James A. Patterson

O ver a century ago, the Student Volunteer Movement for Foreign Missions dramatically jolted the lethargic Protestant churches of America toward new levels of missionary enthusiasm and action. This energetic organization supplied denominational mission boards with a steady stream of fresh recruits well into the 1920s. In addition, the SVM spawned a new generation of highly motivated and effective leaders, who infused the missionary enterprise with an optimistic, even triumphalistic vision for world evangelization previously unmatched in American Protestantism.

Robert Parmelee Wilder (August 2, 1863-March 28, 1938) probably exemplified this early SVM spirit as well as any other pioneer, but his contributions have been largely overshadowed by the more visible exploits of mission giants like John R. Mott and Robert E. Speer. In fact, a recent volume by Harvard historian William R. Hutchison virtually relegates Wilder to a secondary role in the shaping of foreign missions during the late nineteenth and early twentieth centuries.[1] Unfortunately, Wilder's career has been the victim of scholarly bypass; an assessment of his significance and impact is overdue.

Missionary Vocation from Childhood

In 1863, Robert Wilder was born in Kolhapur, India, the fifth and last child of his missionary parents, Royal Gould and Eliza Jane Wilder. The elder Wilders had served in the subcontinent since 1846, originally under the American Board of Commissioners for Foreign Missions (ABCFM). But Royal Wilder, a New School Presbyterian, battled with ABCFM administrators like Rufus Anderson over educational policies, which led to his dismissal in 1860. The Wilders then labored as independents in Kolhapur for a decade, after which they affiliated with the Board of Foreign Missions of the Presbyterian Church in the USA. His nurture in a missionary home had a profound impact on young Robert and he pledged himself to missionary service when he joined his father's church at the age of ten.[2]

Royal Wilder's poor health forced a family move to Princeton, New Jersey, in 1875. In 1878, he launched a new journal dedicated to the promotion of foreign missions, the *Missionary Review of the World*, which he edited for almost ten years. Meanwhile, Robert attended Princeton

Preparatory School and Williston Seminary (Easthampton, Massachusetts) before starting his undergraduate career at Princeton in 1881.[3] During these years, father and son shared common commitment to the validity and urgency of the missionary task.

His collegiate experience at Princeton decidedly reaffirmed Wilder's already well-established conviction of a missionary calling. In 1883, he participated in an Inter-Seminary Missionary Alliance meeting in Hartford, Connecticut, and he returned from the conference with a renewed desire to stir missionary interest on the Princeton campus. To that end, he was instrumental in the formation of the Princeton Foreign Missionary Society in the fall of 1883. Royal Wilder opened his home to this new group and frequently challenged the students to consider their roles in world evangelization. Several members of the Princeton "band" signed a statement of intent "to go to the unevangelized portions of the world," a pledge very similar to one popularized later by the SVM.[4]

Wilder postponed his senior year at Princeton because of physical problems and even worked for three months on a cattle ranch in Nebraska to restore his health. Following his subsequent graduation in 1886, he headed to Mount Hermon, Massachusetts, where the famed revivalist Dwight L. Moody was conducting a summer Bible conference for collegians. Wilder, Presbyterian minister Arthur T. Pierson, and others managed to bring a considerable missions emphasis to this student gathering, including the climatic "Meeting of the Ten Nations," during which Wilder spoke for India and reminded his audience of the great needs overseas. Before the conference ended, exactly one hundred students had signed the Princeton pledge for missionary service, thus laying the groundwork for what was soon to become the Student Volunteer Movement.[5]

For the next five years, Wilder made significant contributions of time and energy to the burgeoning SVM. During this period, he valiantly persevered through occasional bouts of illness, the death of his father, and the return of his mother and sister Grace to the mission field in India. Wilder visited several college campuses on recruiting tours, maintained SVM records, and somehow kept up his theological studies at Union Seminary in New York. He especially succeeded in persuading college students to embrace the missionary cause and he was personally responsible for bringing future notables like Robert Speer and Samuel Zwemer into the Student Volunteer fold.[6] Wilder also emerged as one of the foremost advocates of the SVM pledge, "We are willing and desirous, God permitting, to become foreign missionaries." In a special SVM pamphlet, he outlined the necessity, meaning, and use of the pledge, concluding that it was "the Keystone of the arch" of the SVM. At the first SVM convention in 1891, he led a discussion of the pledge and steadfastly resisted any attempts to change its wording. Perhaps his strongest argument was the fact that, in the five years since Mount Hermon, 6,000 volunteers had been enlisted.[7] At that point in SVM history, Wilder had done more than anyone else to boost the young movement to that level.

In 1891, Wilder finished his studies at Union Seminary and was appointed by the Presbyterian Board of Foreign Missions for student work in India. However, he delayed his passage to India in order to spend more than a year visiting students in Great Britain and Scandinavia. Armed with letters of reference from such dignitaries as Moody, Union professor Philip Schaff, Boston clergyman-educator A.J. Gordon and former Princeton president James McCosh, among others, Wilder arrived in England with the goal of organizing an SVM counterpart in the British universities. After his tour of several campuses and a special conference at Edinburgh in 1892, the stage was set for what became the Student Volunteer Missionary Union of Great Britain and Ireland. In addition to his organizing endeavors, Wilder also continued his pattern of personally persuading students to become missionaries, such as Glasgow's Donald Fraser, a onetime agnostic.[8]

Ministry in Four Continents

In Norway, Wilder met Helene Olssön and, after several months of courtship, they were married in September of 1892. The newlyweds soon left Europe for India, where they initiated their ministry to students, first in Calcutta and later in Poona. Wilder employed several methods for reaching educated Indians, including lectures to large groups and literature distribution. However, he usually preferred the personal and low-key approach of "private interviews," which were more appropriate to the cultural context and more in line with his unique gifts.[9]

The Wilders departed from India in 1897 in response to John R. Mott's request that Wilder take a temporary assignment as an SVM traveling secretary for seminaries in the United States. Mott, by now a leader in the SVM and the YMCA, believed that Wilder could help to strengthen both organizations but apparently did not anticipate the minor crisis his offer would create with the Presbyterian Board of Foreign Missions. The board hesitantly granted Wilder a leave to pursue his SVM duties, but this evidently placed strains on his relationships with some administrators.[10]

Before the Wilders returned to India in 1899, Robert quietly resigned from the Presbyterian Board to assume a new position as traveling secretary for the Indian YMCA. This job proved to be physically and mentally draining for Wilder and caused him to be away from his family for long stretches. The pressures of climate, travel, and poor health forced Wilder to take a leave of absence in 1902, most of which was spent in Norway. In 1903, he decided to resign his YMCA post and end his work in India. Several more months of recuperation in Switzerland and Norway followed.[11]

In 1904, Wilder received an invitation from Tissington Tatlow, general secretary of the Student Christian Movement (SCM), to tour British universities much as he had done in 1891-1892. Wilder's ministry to students, carried out in 1905, was impressive enough to bring an offer from the SCM in 1906 for a position as traveling secretary based in London.[12] Wilder remained in British university work for the next ten years and placed a special emphasis on evangelism. In addition, the SCM generously shared his services with the World's Student Christian Federation; this arrangement allowed Wilder opportunities to visit campuses in many areas of continental Europe, at least until World War I broke out in 1914. During the war, he served briefly as a foreign student secretary for the British SCM.[13]

Another appeal from John R. Mott brought the Wilders back to the United States in 1916. Robert accepted an appointment as secretary of the Religious Work Department of the International Committee of the YMCA, which involved administrative, evangelistic, and conference responsibilities. The entrance of the United States into World War I in 1917 generated new demands on the YMCA, and Wilder assisted with special programs designed for servicemen. He enjoyed a relatively smooth transition from student to military audiences, helped by an updated version of the old SVM commitment card: "I pledge my allegiance to the Lord Jesus Christ as my Savior and King and by God's help will fight His battles for victory of His Kingdom."[14] Apparently he discerned continuities in recruiting efforts for missionary and national crusades.

In the postwar years, Wilder returned to his first love, the SVM. He began an eight-year stint as general secretary in 1919, never expecting that this would prove to be the most difficult period of his career. Wilder fondly treasured the original SVM spirit, particularly as it was expressed in the slogan, "The Evangelization of the World in This Generation."[15] But he quickly discovered that this goal failed to motivate many in the student generation of the 1920s. The first hints of trouble appeared at the SVM quadrennial convention held at Des Moines, Iowa, in early 1920. Students pushed aggressively for a greater role within the SVM and for a more explicit commitment to international peace and social justice. Wilder, reflecting a concern shared by other SVM pioneers, bravely attempted to maintain a strong focus on evangelism: "Whether a man goes out as an agricultural missionary or as a medical missionary, all the work in the strictest sense of the term should be evangelistic, and we have the opportunity to make it evangelistic."[16] Wilder attempted to accommodate himself to some of the students' postwar agendas, but he consistently refused to compromise on the SVM's founding vision.

Not long after the Des Moines gathering, Mott stepped down from the SVM Executive Committee, leaving Wilder with added fund-raising burdens. Publicly Wilder maintained an optimistic posture as he interpreted and defended the direction of the movement, often with obvious conviction.[17] But he was also well aware of the decline in missionary recruits and that many SVM members were questioning more traditional views on evangelism and the relationship between Christianity and other religions. He must have sensed that he was fighting a losing battle against the liberal drift in the SVM, so he relinquished his job in 1927 to accept a much different assignment overseas.[18] This decision, no doubt an agonizing one, effectively ended his association with a missionary agency that had been so close to his heart for over forty years.

For his last full-time position, Wilder moved to Cairo, Egypt, to become the executive secretary of the Christian Council for Western Asia and Northern Africa, which was shortly renamed the Near East Christian Council. For six years (1927-1933), he engaged in ecumenical activities designed to create more unity and cooperation among Christian churches where Islam was a dominant force. He traveled extensively in the region, published several pamphlets, and edited the *News Bulletin,* the official organ of the Near East Council. But lingering health problems caused Wilder to halt his active missionary service at the age of seventy.[19]

Wilder spent his retirement with his wife in her native Norway. However, he was still in demand as a speaker and he continued to promote the cause of missions in Norway, France and Great Britain. In the last setting, his campus tours in 1935 came under the auspices of the British Inter-Varsity Fellowship of Evangelical Unions, a conservative group that was known for its emphasis on piety and marked zeal for missions. Wilder possibly identified the IVF as a more legitimate heir of the early SVM tradition than the increasingly liberal British SCM. His published reminiscences of the early generation of SVM, which contained more than a hint of nostalgia, served to demonstrate the substantial gap between Wilder's original dreams and the realities of ecumenical student movements in the 1930s. His minor part in the SVM convention at Indianapolis in 1936 hardly disguised his disappointment with an organization that barely imitated what it had been in the heady years immediately after the Mount Hermon conference of 1886.[20]

The speaking, writing, and family endeavors of Wilder's retirement years gradually diminished as his health, which was never strong, again wavered and finally claimed his life in 1938. He was buried in Oslo as many surviving stalwarts of his generation, including Mott, Speer, and Zwemer, mourned his death and hailed his influence on the world missionary enterprise.[21] Their tributes were fitting reminders of a consecrated and courageous missionary career, during which Wilder ministered on four continents and served over half a dozen religious organizations.

A Self-Effacing Pioneer

In evaluating Wilder's unique impact on missions, it is important to rescue him from the shadows cast by statesmen like Speer and Mott. Over the years, Wilder performed a much different function in the missionary movement and was not as well recognized or appreciated as some of his former colleagues in the early SVM. Whereas Mott and Speer were primarily mission executives based in the United States, Wilder was essentially a field missionary with only one lengthy period (1916-1927) in North America apart from his schooling. Additionally, Mott and Speer were widely known in American Protestant circles through their prolific writings and their frequent participation in missionary conferences at home and abroad. In contrast, Wilder found writing to be a laborious chore that sometimes interfered with his more urgent missionary tasks. Thus he delayed some major writing projects until retirement, and even then some of his efforts were simply compilations of addresses given during his more active years.[22] Wilder's overseas appointments also prevented him from accepting some speaking engagements at missionary meetings in the United States, such as those sponsored by the Foreign Missions Conference of North America, at which he rarely appeared. Finally, Wilder's quiet, almost self-effacing style of ministry was hardly designed to attract attention to himself. Unlike Mott in particular, Wilder seemed content to operate outside the boardrooms and crowded assembly halls.

Wilder's lengthy involvement in the student world constitutes his most significant contribution to the missionary impulse of the late nineteenth and early twentieth centuries. Sherwood Eddy, another product of the SVM glory years, aptly targeted Wilder's formative role in the collegiate agency:

> Although the time was ripe and the occasion ideal, humanly speaking, the Student Volunteer Movement would not have come into being without Robert Wilder. The movement was the result of Wilder's vision, Moody's spiritual drive, and Mott's organizing genius.[23]

Indeed, it was Wilder who channeled the raw enthusiasm of Mount Hermon into something durable, not only because he was a visionary, but also because he threw himself into the recruitment efforts and personal work that sustained the SVM in its initial stages. Across the Atlantic, Wilder similarly combined his idealism with practical skills to help build student movements in Europe. Few exceeded Wilder's fervor in advancing the movement, its pledge, or its ambitious motto. Few were more disappointed when the SVM derailed in the 1920s. Although the SVM eventually died as an organization, it could be argued that Wilder himself, in the 1930s, passed the SVM torch to Inter-Varsity Fellowship and thus indirectly to the Student Foreign Missions Fellowship and the Urbana triennial missionary conventions.[24]

Of course, Wilder's involvement with students was not an end in itself but rather a means to help fulfill the controlling passion of his life, "The Evangelization of the World in This Generation." He not only guided the early SVM to accept this lofty goal but also remained one of its most faithful exemplars. Even after some mission thinkers had discarded the watchword as unrealistic or outmoded, Wilder continued to uphold its relevance, arguing in retirement that "everyone should have the opportunity to hear the Gospel and to accept Christ in our generation."[25] He perhaps defined the evangelistic task more carefully in his later years but that did not weaken his loyalty to it. In fact, his disillusionment with SVM trends in the 1920s and 1930s was largely due to the dimmed vision for evangelism on the part of many students.

Undergirding Wilder's abiding devotion to world evangelization was an equally firm conviction about the need for student volunteers and missionary personnel to nurture vigorous spiritual disciplines. Wilder grew up in a home where prayer permeated family activities. Later he structured the meetings of the Princeton Foreign Missionary Society to allow for considerable periods of group prayer. As his career progressed, Wilder consistently spoke and wrote about the essential role of Bible study and prayer in the life of the Christian worker. His extensive experience in student ministry produced several practical pamphlets designed to outline the elements of a dynamic spiritual life. It is clear in these pieces that Wilder was sharing sincerely from his own pilgrimage of faith.[26]

On a related matter, Wilder identified the modern age as a dispensation of the Holy Spirit; few of his contemporaries in mainline Protestantism were as eager to link the Holy Spirit to missions as he was. His starting point was the controversial view that the filling of the Spirit was both a crisis and a process subsequent to conversion. This second work of grace endued the believer with the spiritual power required for a life of "Christ-controlled" service. Wilder was not a Pentecostal, as his cautious instruction on the gift of tongues reveals. But he obviously found his Presbyterian roots too confining on this issue and instead appropriated the doctrinal precepts of Moody and Gordon, which had so molded the ethos of the early SVM.[27] For Wilder, effective missionary outreach was absolutely dependent on the consecrating work of the Holy Spirit. His unceasing efforts to improve the overall spiritual tone of the missionary enterprise were unassailable, even if some questioned his teaching on Spirit baptism.

In the final analysis, Robert Wilder left his mark in ways that are difficult to measure by the standards normally applied to the missionary leaders of his generation. He was neither a brilliant mission theorist nor an innovative strategist. He is not remembered as an orator who overwhelmed audiences with his eloquence and his published writings are not voluminous or especially profound. Yet Wilder grasped better than most of his contemporaries the real essence of servanthood and discipleship. Through a life of humble and sacrificial service, he faithfully persevered, despite chronic physical problems, in his overarching commitment to world evangelization. Thus he modeled qualities that are vital and relevant in any missionary era.

Notes

1. William R. Hutchison, *Errand to the World: American Protestant Thought and Foreign Missions* (Chicago: University of Chicago Press, 1987). Compare the listings in the index for Wilder with those for Mott and Speer.

2. On Wilder's parents and his early years, see Ruth E. Braisted, *In This Generation: The Story of Robert Wilder* (New York: Friendship Press, 1941), pp. 1-11; Matthew Hugh Kelleher, "Robert Wilder and the American Foreign Missionary Movement" (Ph.D. diss., St. Louis: St. Louis University, 1974), pp. 11-14; and Robert A. Schneider, "Royal G. Wilder: New School Missionary in the ABCFM, 1846-1871," *American Presbyterians: Journal of Presbyterian History* 64 (Summer 1986); 73-82. For the elder Wilder's views on educational missions, see Royal Gould Wilder, *Mission Schools in India of the American Board of Commissioners for Foreign Missions* (New York: A.D.F. Randolph; and Boston: Crocker and Brewster, 1861).

3. On the family move to Princeton, see Braisted, *In This Generation*, pp. 11-14.

4. On the Princeton Foreign Missionary Society, see Robert P. Wilder, *The Student Volunteer Movement for Foreign Missions: Some Personal Reminiscences of Its Origin and Early History* (New York: Student Volunteer Movement, 1935), pp. 7-12.

5. Ibid., pp. 14-17.

6. Ibid., pp. 19-51; Robert Speer's diary entries for March 26-28, 1887, the Papers of Robert E. Speer, Princeton Theological Seminary, Princeton, N.J.; and J. Christy Wilson, "The Legacy of Samuel M. Zwemer," *International Bulletin of Missionary Research* 10 (July 1986): 117.

7. Wilder, *The Pledge of the Student Volunteer Movement for Foreign Missions* (New York: Student Volunteer Movement for Foreign Missions, 1890), and *Report of the First International Convention of the Student Volunteer Movement for Foreign Missions, Cleveland, Ohio, February 26-March 1, 1891* (Boston: T.O. Metcalf and Company, 1891), pp. 33-36.

8. Wilder, *The Great Commission, the Missionary Response of the Student Volunteer Movements in North America and Europe: Some Personal Reminiscences* (London: Oliphants, 1936), pp. 64-83. For Fraser's comments on Wilder's impact, see Tissington Tatlow, *The Story of the Student Christian Movement of Great Britain and Ireland* (London: Student Christian Movement Press, 1933), p. 24. For the reference letters, see correspondence files for 1891 in the Robert Parmelee Wilder Papers, Yale Divinity School, New Haven, Conn.

9. Wilder, *Christian Service Among Educated Bengalese* (Lahore: Civil and Military Gazette Press, 1895), pp. 5-12, and "The Educated Classes of India," *Missionary Review of the World* 21 (December 1898): 901-3.

10. See correspondence files for 1897-1898 in Wilder Papers, esp. Benjamin Labaree to Mott, May 5, 1897; Labaree to Wilder, June 29, 1897; and F.F. Ellinwood to Wilder, September 13, 1897.

11. Braisted, *In This Generation*, pp. 87-129, and Kelleher, "Robert Wilder and the American Foreign Missionary Movement," pp. 58-60. The Wilder family eventually grew to four daughters, including Robert's biographer, Ruth Braisted. See *In This Generation*, pp. 132-34.

12. Tatlow to Wilder, January 16 and March 15, 1906, Wilder Papers.

13. Braisted, *In This Generation*, pp. 87-129; Jan Willem Gunning, "Mr. Mott and Mr. Wilder in the Dutch Universities," *Student World* 5 (April 1912): 50-58; and Wilder, "A Recent Tour in South-Eastern Europe," *Student World* 7 (July 1914): 92-101.

14. Quoted in Kelleher, "Robert Wilder and the American Foreign Missionary Movement," p. 68. See also Braisted, *In This Generation*, pp. 143-47.

15. For an earlier defense of this motto, see Wilder, "The Evangelization of the World," *Northfield Echoes* 6 (1899): 162-70.

16. Wilder, "The Need of Men with a Life Purpose," *North American Students and World Advance.* Addresses delivered at the 8th International Convention of the SVMFM, Des Moines, Iowa, December 31, 1919–January 4, 1920, ed. Burton St. John (New York: SVMFM, 1920), p. 311. On student resentment toward Wilder, see C. Howard Hopkins, *John R. Mott, 1865-1955: A Biography* (Grand Rapids: Wm. B. Eerdmans Publishing Company, 1979), p. 568.

17. See Wilder, "Has the Missionary Motive Changed?" *Missionary Review of the World* 48 (December 1925): 931-35; "The Ninth Quadrennial Convention of the Student Volunteer Movement," *Foreign Missions Conference of North America.* Report of the 31st Conference, Atlantic City, N.J., January 8-11, 1924, ed. Fennell P. Turner and Frank Knight Sanders (New York: Foreign Missions Conference, 1924), pp. 239-42; and *The Spirit of God in the Colleges: Being an Account of the Present Position of the Student Volunteer Movement* (New York: SVM, 1924).

18. On Wilder's frustration with the SVM in the 1920s, see Joseph L. Cumming. "The Student Volunteer Movement for Foreign Missions: Its Seeds and Precedents, Its Origins and Early History, Its Growth and Decline" (B.A. thesis, Princeton University, 1982), pp. 176-87; and Kelleher, "Robert Wilder and the American Foreign Missionary Movement," pp. 84-111.

19. On the Near East Council years, see Braisted, *In This Generation,* pp. 169-93, and Wilder, "Some Achievements Toward Unity in the Near East," *Diocesan Review,* January 15, 1932, pp. 8-12.

20. For his SVM reminiscences, see Wilder, *The Student Volunteer Movement for Foreign Missions* and *The Great Commission,* both published in retirement. On his negative evaluation of student movements in the 1930s, see Kelleher, "Robert Wilder and the American Foreign Missionary Movement," pp. 115-19.

21. "A Man Who Stirred the World: Testimonies to Robert P. Wilder," *Missionary Review of the World* 61 (May 1938): 226-29. On Wilder's retirement, see Braisted, *In This Generation,* pp. 195-205.

22. See, for example, Wilder, *Christ and the Student World* (New York: Fleming H. Revell, 1935). On his reluctance to write, see Braisted, *In This Generation,* p. 201.

23. Sherwood Eddy, *Pathfinders of the World Missionary Crusade* (New York/Nashville: Abingdon-Cokesbury Press, 1945), p. 41.

24. Mott apparently was disturbed over Wilder's association with IVF, viewing it as a conservative shift. See Hopkins, *John R. Mott,* p. 632.

25. Wilder, *Christ and the Student World,* p. 79.

26. Wilder, *Bible Study for Personal Spiritual Growth* (London: Inter-Varsity Fellowship of Evangelical Unions, n.d.); *How to Use the Morning Quiet Time* (New York: Association Press, 1917); *Prayer* (Cairo: Nile Mission Press, 1933); and *United Intercession* (London: SCM, 1914).

27. See Wilder, *Studies on the Holy Spirit,* 2d ed. (London: SCM, 1913), esp. pp. 12, 18, and 31. On the influence of Moody and Gordon, see Wilder, "Power from on High," in *A Spiritual Awakening Among India's Students: Addresses of Six Conferences* (Madras: Addison and Company, 1896), pp. 26-27. Kelleher further suggests the contributions of John MacNeil and James Elder Cummings to Wilder's theology of the Holy Spirit. See "Robert Wilder and the American Foreign Missionary Movement," pp. 50-52.

Selected Bibliography

Unpublished Materials

The Robert Parmelee Wilder Papers are Manuscript Group Number 38, Yale Divinity School Library, Archives and Manuscripts, Yale Divinity School, New Haven, Conn.

Works by Robert P. Wilder
Books

1895 *Christian Service Among Educated Bengalese.* Lahore: Civil and Military Gazette Press.
1913 *Studies on the Holy Spirit.* 2d ed. London: Student Christian Movement.
1935 *Christ and the Student World.* New York: Fleming H. Revell.
1936 *The Great Commission, the Missionary Response of the Student Volunteer Movements in North America and Europe: Some Personal Reminiscences.* London: Oliphants.

Pamphlets

N.d. *Association Movement Among Theological Students.* New York: International Committee of the YMCA.
N.d. *Bible Study for Personal Spiritual Growth.* London: Inter-Varsity Fellowship of Evangelical Unions.

N.d. *Guidance*. Cairo: Nile Mission Press.
N.d. *The Plan and Organization for a Young Men's Christian Association Among Theological Students*. New York: International Committee of Young Men's Christian Association.
N.d. *Sin*. Calcutta: Santal Mission Press.
1890 *The Pledge of the Student Volunteer Movements for Foreign Missions*. New York: SVMFM.
1896 *An Appeal for India*. Calcutta: Student Volunteer Movement of India and Ceylon.
1899 *Among India's Students*. New York: Fleming H. Revell.
1901 *The Cannots of Character and Destiny*. Surat: Irish Presbyterian Mission Press.
1906 *The Bible and Foreign Missions*. 8th ed. Coventry, England: Curtis and Beamish.
1914 *United Intercession*. London: SCM.
1917 *How to Use the Morning Quiet Time*. New York: Association Press.
1919 *Report of the Activities of the Religious Work Bureau of the War Work Council of the YMCA to the Cooperating Committee of the Churches*. N.p.
1924 *The Spirit of God in the Colleges: Being an Account of the Present Position of the Student Volunteer Movement*. New York: SVM.
1933 *Prayer*. Cairo: Nile Mission Press.
1935 *The Student Volunteer Movement for Foreign Missions: Some Personal Reminiscences of Its Origin and Early History*. New York: SVM.

Addresses and Articles in

Diocesan Review
The East and the West
Intercollegian
Missionary Review of the World
Northfield Echoes
SVM Bulletin
SVM Quadrennial Convention reports
Student World
Young Men of India

Works about Robert P. Wilder

Braisted, Ruth E. *In This Generation: The Story of Robert P. Wilder*. New York: Friendship Press, 1941.
Eddy, G. Sherwood. "Robert Wilder and the Student Volunteer Movement." In *Pathfinders of the World Missionary Crusade*, pp. 40-48. New York/Nashville: Abingdon-Cokesbury Press, 1945.
Kelleher, Matthew Hugh. "Robert Wilder and the American Foreign Missionary Movement." Ph.D. diss., St. Louis University, 1974.
"A Man Who Stirred the Student World: Testimonies to Robert P. Wilder." *Missionary Review of the World* 61 (May 1938): 226-29.
Pierson, Delavan. "Robert Wilder and His Vision of White Harvest Fields." *Sunday School Times* 80 (April 23, 1938): 299-300.

John R. Mott

1865–1955

Architect of World Mission and Unity

C. Howard Hopkins

John R. Mott, 1865-1955, was the leading Protestant ecumenical and missionary statesman of the world during the first half of the twentieth century. He was not only the figure around whom much thought and action toward comity and ecumenism tended to revolve, but may rightly be called the "father" of the World Council of Churches.

The Man and His Career

Born in southern New York State a few weeks after the close of the Civil War, Mott was raised in what came to be the prosperous corn belt of northern Iowa. He and his three sisters grew up in an advanced, warm, small-town, devoted Methodist home. He attended Upper Iowa University, a Methodist school not far from home, as a preparatory and college student, transferring to Cornell University as a sophomore. As president of the Cornell University Christian Association, he built it into the largest and most active student YMCA – a preparation for his career. Upon graduation in 1888 he took a one-year assignment as traveling secretary with the Inter-collegiate YMCA. He was an immediate success: as evangelist to and organizer of students, charisma emerged at once; people he had never met sent contributions; he early revealed an uncanny facility to appraise men, whom he drew into the movement as leaders; and such were his administrative and diplomatic gifts that the student groups grew by leaps and bounds. What he would do after that first year really never came up. The organization and growth of the Student Volunteer Movement (SVM) was the most dramatic development of these early professional years.

In 1891 Mott married Leila Ada White, a graduate of Wooster College, then teaching English. The two became a remarkable team, traveling the world together; Leila Mott was her husband's critic, editor, and even secretary when needed. Their family of two boys and two girls grew up in Montclair, New Jersey, whence Mott commuted to his New York office; all of them made distinguished contributions to the medical/socially oriented professions. The climax of every year for Mott and his family was the summer in "the Canadian woods" northeast of Montreal, where Mott threw off his official personality, dressed in old clothes, read aloud, played and clowned with the children, fished, swam, and luxuriated in leisure and companionship.

The formation of the World's Student Christian Federation (WSCF) in 1895 was Mott's most creative achievement. He then moved onto the world scene by journeying around the globe, accompanied by Leila, to expand and consolidate the federation. This twenty-month tour established his reputation as a missionary statesman, since the prime targets for federation membership were the students of the mission colleges. Mott had already, somewhat inadvertently, become the leading American YMCA advocate of the expansion of that organization to foreign countries, and soon after his return that YMCA portfolio was added to his duties as head of the student department. In 1901-2 he made another world tour for the SVM, WSCF, YMCA, and missions, and in 1903 went again to Australia and New Zealand. He went to Europe every year, occasionally twice or three times, staying from two weeks to nine months.

From the very beginning of his secretaryship, Mott cultivated the executives of the mission boards; he was present at the founding in 1893 of what became the Foreign Missions Conference of North America and was a force in it for more than half a century. This brought him into a strategic position, together with J.H. Oldham, in the planning and leadership of the epochal Edinburgh missionary conference of 1910; he was responsible for its being a working conference, chaired its Commission I and the full conference itself, and played a large part in securing representatives of the younger churches and encouraging them to express themselves. His chairmanship was the high point of his career up to that time, and he was the logical choice to head the conference's Continuation Committee. He took the conference message to churches around the world in 1912-13.

Plans for a world missions body were frustrated by World War I, but throughout it Mott kept in close touch with Oldham, and the two with missions authorities, including the Germans. Mott made several trips to Europe during the conflict; when the Continuation Committee could no longer function, he, Oldham, and others formed an Emergency Committee that rendered heroic service on behalf of German and other orphaned missions and made significant representations to the peace conferees at Versailles in 1919.

In the meantime Mott had become general secretary of the YMCAs of the United States. When America entered the war, he offered President Woodrow Wilson (a warm personal friend who had begged him to become American minister to China in 1913) the service of the associations for functions comparable to the present-day USO. In 1917 Wilson appointed Mott to the Root Mission to Russia; he became its best reporter to the president and appears to have been Wilson's most trusted adviser on Russia, to the extent that earlier evaluations of the Root Mission and of Wilson's policies toward Bolshevik Russia must be reviewed by historians. Although this was a secular and diplomatic assignment, characteristic of most of the activities with which Mott was preoccupied during the war, he used the Root Mission to extend the ecumenical network to the Russian Orthodox Church, conferring for hours with its high procurator and inviting the Orthodox to participate in a Faith and Order conference.

In 1920 Mott relinquished the leadership of the Student Volunteer Movement and of the World's Student Christian Federation, although he continued to attend and address the SVM quadrennial conferences and remained on as chairman of the federation until 1928. The International Missionary Council, of which he was chairman, came into being in 1921. In 1926 he took on the presidency of the World's Alliance of YMCAs, which he converted from a Geneva club to a world body with an aggressive purpose and program; he devoted his remarkable continuing energies to these last two for two more decades. In 1946 Mott shared the Nobel Peace Prize with Emily Greene Balch. He died in 1955, a few months short of ninety years, and was buried in the Washington Cathedral.

The Sources of Mott's Ecumenism

John Mott's ideal of a community transcending denomination, race, nation, and geography was formed in his youth. The home background in Methodism, his first boyhood conversion under a

Quaker Bible teacher/YMCA evangelist, the profound influence of Dwight L. Moody, the biographies of evangelists – Wesley, Matthew Simpson, William Taylor, Charles G. Finney – all emphasized the evangelical tendency to disregard denominational and confessional lines. But the unique and cardinal influence in this direction was that of perfectionist Holiness, a movement then largely within Methodism, which was to result in controversy and schism. Unaware of these trends, Mott pursued the "second blessing" or "entire sanctification" promised by Holiness, achieving it his first winter in Ithaca, having joined a warm Methodist congregation that fostered his Holiness bent. The periodicals he read – they had been on the family reading table back in Iowa – stressed "unity in diversity" and spoke of the universal Christian church. Holiness was the base for Mott's mature thought on race, ecumenism, and the social gospel.

At least four other factors molded Mott's viewpoint: the Bible, the practice of prayer, his continent-wide and world-circling travel among the colleges and universities, and his preparation for this by extensive reading. Probably the most repeated phrase in his vocabulary was "that we may fulfill the prayer of our Lord 'that they all may be one.'" As the Motts toured the Holy Land on horseback in 1895, they reported that their Bibles "became new in the Land"; they were conscious of history and deeply moved by an unseen presence. Mott not only prayed, he practiced the presence of God in his daily life, believing that whatever he was able to accomplish was due to prayer. In spite of the popular image of him as the great religious entrepreneur, many remember him chiefly as a man of prayer. Unlike other contemporary evangelists, as he traveled the world he read voraciously for background not only in current affairs but in history and culture; as a result Mott grew from a somewhat provincial American into a citizen of the world and as such was welcomed on campuses from Berkeley to Oxford to Sydney.

An evangelical liberal, he early embraced the social gospel – a favorite phrase was "the whole gospel" – and was in the forefront of those who grasped its relevance to missions. He wrote more than a dozen books, most of them concerned with missions and the ecumenical outreach, all of which were widely read and some translated into several foreign languages. His output of pamphlets, articles, reports, and forewords to others' books was limitless. Although they are no longer read, they reflect concern for living issues that reveal their author as a contemporary to any age.

The Young Men's Christian Association as Fellowship and Power Base

The YMCA of the late nineteenth century was aggressively evangelical and evangelistic. As an undergraduate, Mott came increasingly into a dynamic relationship to this laymen's organization and he made it, rather than a denomination, the vehicle of his drive toward Christian unity. For a time at Cornell he worked at a frenzied pace to fit himself for the pastoral ministry, but consistently put off the Greek course required by theological seminaries.

Through the "Y" Mott met and came into intimate partnership with Dwight L. Moody. He made the Paris Basis of the YMCA, the model ecumenical statement of modern times, his own. The fraternal aspect of the associations had great appeal: in it at the age of twenty-three he already worked with men of power and influence, and as his own leadership grew he in turn attracted many to it. Nor did he limit himself or its outreach to Protestants. Against considerable opposition he not only approved but urged the recruitment of Roman Catholic members to YMCAs in Catholic countries and the same with the Orthodox; this policy also applied to the selection and training of secretaries. Mott would have been delighted with the spirit of Vatican Council II, but such rapport was impossible in his time.

The YMCA, to which Mott gave himself, served a worldwide community of students and an urban clientele in the major cities at home and abroad; it was a fellowship of activists motivated by the desire, as the Paris Basis put it, to be Christ's disciples "in their faith and in their life." Some

of Mott's colleagues deprecated his "YMCA mind" – lay rather than clerical or ecclesiastical stance
– and he was perhaps a bit unappreciative of the role of women in the ecumenical movement, in
spite of his own marriage partnership and the generosity of several women who made his key
projects possible.

The Student Volunteer Movement for Foreign Missions

As one of the "Mount Hermon Hundred" Volunteers of 1886, Mott contributed significantly to the
plans laid that summer for the spread of the missionary challenge among the colleges of Canada
and the United States. One of his first assignments upon becoming college secretary two years later
was the chairmanship of the joint YM-YWCA committee charged with domesticating this explosive
movement into the intercollegiate organizations: it became the missionary department of the student
YM-YWCAs, and for three decades Mott inspired, funded, and directed it, making it coeducational
in spite of the male chauvinism of the YMCA leadership. He did not invent its motto, "The
evangelization of the world in this generation," but he made it his own. The SVM became the
dynamic of the intercollegiate bodies; Mott invented and administered its great quadrennial
conventions and lived to count 20,000 volunteers sent to the fields of the world, numbers of whom
confessed that "he changed my life."

Not satisfied that the movement be solely a sending agency, he organized SVMs in most foreign
countries, both to focus youthful attention on missions and to enlist converts to work in their own
nations; he also encouraged SVM alumni on the field to guide their nationals at work and to enthuse
volunteers back home. Thus rising generations of young Christians, who would make up a
substantial segment of the "younger" churches as they moved into positions of leadership, were
made aware of the universality of both church and mission.

The World's Student Christian Federation

The WSCF embodied Mott's dream of a union of the Christian students of all nations. It was
characteristic of him that he should go to them to enlist them in the cause. Although he described
that epochal first tour in a book called *Strategic Points in the World's Conquest* (the points were
the colleges), the constituent members of the new world fellowship were equals; from the beginning
the Asian movements and their representatives played strategic roles. This was another lay
movement that included women. Its motto, "That they all may be one," became an ecumenical
rallying cry. The places Mott chose for its meetings demonstrated his sense of timing and of history:
the 1907 conference in Tokyo was the first international body ever to meet in Japan, and possibly
in Asia. In 1911 Mott took the federation to Constantinople, heart of the Orthodox world, where it
was blessed by the ecumenical patriarch. Miraculously, rather than being destroyed by World War
I, it expanded to render welfare services to thousands of students in uniform; there is at least one
instance of a soldier's calling out, "Does anyone know John Mott?" as a means of establishing
fellowship.

Approaching the Orthodox Churches

It was at first the fellowship of the YMCA into which Mott invited the leaders of Orthodox churches.
This is an almost forgotten saga that began in 1897 when he met the great Russian Orthodox
missionary bishop, Nikolai, in Tokyo. The two men were instinctively drawn to one another. Thus
began for Mott a lifelong love affair with Orthodoxy, enhanced by the music of the church and by
its central emphasis upon the Resurrection, which was also the cardinal point of Mott's faith. In
1911 Mott visited almost every Orthodox bishop, archbishop, and patriarch between Vienna and
Jerusalem, and in the 1920s repeated this gesture several times; on more than one occasion the
ecclesiastics he assembled had never met one another.

The International Missionary Council

As he began to lose touch with the post-World War I student generation, Mott gradually shifted his major thrust from the student world to missions and the parent YMCAs. After much prayer and diplomacy directed toward reconciliation with the Germans by Mott, Oldham, and their colleagues, the International Missionary Council (IMC) was organized in 1921. As its chairman and symbol, Mott circled the Pacific in preparation for its Jerusalem conference of 1928, then took that conference's message around the world the next year. He played a somewhat less significant role at Madras-Tambaram a decade later. He was an important agent in the formation of some thirty national councils of churches in as many countries. A last bit of advice to colleagues in the IMC was to beware lest it be swallowed too soon by the World Council of Churches.

The World Council of Churches

Mott took part in each of the movements that culminated in the WCC; his influence in them was pervasive. He had known Bishop Charles Brent of Faith and Order several years before Edinburgh 1910, which was the immediate source of Brent's inspiration. On his 1911 tour of Eastern Europe and the Near East, Mott sought to bring the Orthodox into that fellowship. He went to its Lausanne Conference of 1927 but was forced to leave because of illness. On the Life and Work side, his lifelong friendship with Archbishop Nathan Söderblom began in 1891 when the two young men were spontaneously attracted to one another at the Northfield (Massachusetts) student conference; over the years they kept in touch and met many times.

During the preparatory conference for Oxford 1937, at Westfield College, Pastor Marc Boegner of France, William Temple, William Adams Brown, H.-L. Henriod, and Willem A. Visser 't Hooft met in Mott's room each morning for prayer. Boegner declared that Mott's influence on the conference was "tremendous." The jibe that ecumenical meetings of the period seemed to be WSCF alumni gatherings was literally true. During the organizing phases of the World Council, Mott was one of six provisional presidents, then became honorary president upon its formal establishment, a symbolic recognition.

The Legacy

Mott's major contributions are implicit in the foregoing, and I shall not attempt to enumerate them. If Kenneth Scott Latourette's statement that "the ecumenical movement was in large part the outgrowth of the missionary movement" is true, Mott's legacy, as Hans-Ruedi Weber said of the Asian churches' debt to Mott, is "incalculable." It varies with country or organization, and may be measured not only in the cooperative bodies he fostered, but in the fact that he encouraged, nourished, and regarded as equals the rising lay and clerical leaders of churches and Christian bodies everywhere. This was apparent as early as the first world trip of 1895-1897.

Mott was unique. He is remembered as evangelist, man of prayer, leader, advocate of comity, builder of organizations, friend, chief, chairman, speaker, coach, executive, author, editor, fund-raiser, traveler. His influence lives not only in world bodies such as the WCC and the World's Alliance of YMCAs, but in the profound effect he exerted upon individuals of several generations who volunteered their contributions to the evangelization, the betterment, the unity of the world in their time.

In old age Mott was given standing ovations by tens of thousands of young people in post-World War II Germany because, as Bishop Hans Lilje put it, they were convinced that "he loves us." Soichi Saito, a Japanese colleague, called Mott "father of the young people of the world." Although the two organizations that were the chief objects of his early labor and love – the SVM and the WSCF – no longer exist as he knew them, his instinct for students and young people was sound. He chose his associates with insight and trusted them to build indigenous entities to serve their own place and time. There would of course have been an ecumenical movement without Mott, but as J.H. Oldham once remarked, it would have been a very different thing.

Perhaps the unique feature of his genius was an unusual combination of spiritual insight and leadership with hardheaded administrative ability. A hero to thousands, he was also trusted by businessmen and philanthropists, and was sought out for his organizational acumen. Yet to him the directing of organizations was secondary, really only a means to the main business of evangelism, mission, the ecumenical thrust. Asked to say a word at what proved to be his last public appearance, he declared, "while life lasts, I am an evangelist."

Selected Bibliography

From the beginning of his responsibility for the Student Volunteer Movement, Mott worked to make its library and collection of resource materials the most comprehensive available. The materials collected by Charles H. Fahs, whom Mott had trained for the job, on the world tour with Mott in 1912-13, became the nucleus for the Missionary Research Library (MRL), established with Rockefeller funding in 1914, under Fahs's lifelong direction. Mott's belief in the value of research was further realized during the 1920s through the Institute of Social and Religious Research, and in the 1930s by the Department of Social and Industrial Research of the International Missionary Council.

Well before the close of his active career, Mott gave his comprehensive archives of the WSCF to the Yale University Divinity School Library. He later added his personal papers; the residual files retained at his death also went to Yale, thanks to the concern of the librarian, Raymond P. Morris. During my research for his biography, personal and family materials were added, as were copies of his massive correspondence related to each of the organizations he served – the IMC from originals at the MRL, World YMCA and later WSCF at Geneva. The Library of the American YMCA at 291 Broadway, New York, N.Y. 10007, is the only large Mott archive of which I am aware whose materials are not duplicated in the Yale Collection.

Works by John R. Mott

1897 *Strategic Points in the World's Conquest.* New York and Chicago: Fleming H. Revell Co.
1900 *The Evangelization of the World in This Generation.* New York: SVM.
1902 *Christians of Reality.* Shanghai: YMCA of China.
1904 *The Pastor and Modern Missions.* New York: SVM.
1908 *The Future Leadership of the Church.* New York: SVM.
1910 *The Decisive Hour of Christian Missions.* New York: SVM.
1914 *The Present World Situation.* New York: SVM.
1920 *The World's Student Christian Federation.* N.p.: WSCF.
1923 *Confronting Young Men with the Living Christ.* New York: Association Press.
1931 *The Present-day Summons to the World Mission of Christianity.* Nashville, Tenn.: Cokesbury Press.
1932 *Liberating the Lay Forces of Christianity.* New York: Macmillan Co.
1939 *Five Decades and a Forward View.* New York and London: Harper & Bros.
1944 *The Larger Evangelism.* New York and Nashville: Abingdon-Cokesbury Press.
1946-47 *Addresses and Papers*, 6 vols., New York: Association Press.

Works about John R. Mott

Fisher, Galen M. *John R. Mott, Architect of Cooperation and Unity.* New York: Association Press, 1952.
Hopkins, C. Howard. "John R. Mott." *Dictionary of American Biography. Supplement Five, 1951-1955,* pp. 506-8. New York: Charles Scribner's Sons, 1977.
_____. *John R. Mott, 1865-1955, a Biography.* Grand Rapids, Mich.: Wm. B. Eerdmans Publishing Co., 1980.
Hopkins, C. Howard, and John W. Long. "American Jews and the Root Mission to Russia in 1917: Some New Evidence." *American Jewish History* 69, no. 3 (March 1980): 342-54.
_____. "The Church and the Russian Revolution: Conversations of John R. Mott with Orthodox Church Leaders, June-July, 1917." *St. Vladimir's Theological Quarterly* 20, no. 3 (1976): 161-80.
Mackie, Robert. *Layman Extraordinary: John R. Mott, 1865-1955.* New York: Association Press, 1965.
Mathews, Basil. *John R. Mott. World Citizen.* New York and London: Harper & Bros., 1934.
Wegener, Günther S. *John Mott: Weltbürger und Christ.* Wuppertal: Aussaat Verlag, 1965.
Woods, Roger D. "The World of Thought of John R. Mott." Ph.D. diss., University of Iowa, 1965.

William Owen Carver

1868–1954

Mentor of Southern Baptist Missionaries

Hugo H. Culpepper

The oldest *continuing* department of missions in America was established at the Southern Baptist Theological Seminary in Louisville, Kentucky, by W.O. Carver in 1899.[1] He had begun his theological education at this institution in October 1891. After two years of study, he taught in a college for one and half years. In January 1895 Carver resumed his seminary studies and was graduated in the spring of 1896 with both the Th.M. and Th.D. degrees.[2] His doctorate was in New Testament. During his final year as a seminary student he was also tutor in New Testament.

Carver began teaching missions in the spring of 1897. Two years earlier, H.H. Harris had come to the faculty from Richmond College where he was a longtime professor. He also had been president of the Foreign Mission Board of the Southern Baptist Convention for thirty years. Although Harris was professor of Biblical Introduction and Polemics, he offered a voluntary class in the history and practice of missions.[3] This prepared the way with faculty and students for what was to come in a few years. During Harris's terminal illness, Carver took over the class and completed the spring semester. He continued to teach the course as an elective for two more years. In 1899 the Department of Comparative Religion and Missions was established. It was approved by trustee vote in 1900.[4]

During Carver's long tenure as a faculty member (1896-1943), he made a unique contribution to his students by sharing with them his understanding of "missions in the plan of the ages." Many would agree with the writer that the most profound and life-shaping conviction gained in the seminary was that there is "a purpose of the ages which God made in Christ Jesus" (Eph. 3:11), as interpreted and applied by W.O. Carver. This was his supreme legacy. As a result of his lifelong teaching, writing, and speaking from this perspective, he strengthened the foundations for missions in his denomination and beyond. He developed a theology of mission that is still determinative for those who will work carefully through his thought as recorded in his extensive writings.

Carver's Roots

William Owen Carver (April 10, 1868–May 24, 1954) was reared on a fifty-seven-acre farm between Nashville and Lebanon, Tennessee. His father was a Confederate veteran who had been wounded four times and lost most of his left arm during the war. He was a man of strong character and hard work who held the respect of his children. The last time the writer was with Carver, in May 1953, he remarked in the midst of our conversation, "My father taught me to think for myself." This explains his independent, creative thinking. Life was a struggle during the Reconstruction period for his mother. "Once, I saw her, after milking the cow, slip as she climbed a fence where a gate should have been and spill the pail of milk. She wept, and it stabbed my heart."[5] He was the oldest of ten children who survived his mother. The oldest girl had died earlier. "Eleven children in twenty such years! No wonder she died. How did she carry on so long? And she did it with a brave, uncomplaining, even a victorious and conquering faith. How tired she must have been!"[6] She, who died when Carver was nineteen, had planted and nurtured the seed of a deep spirituality in him. He was always devoted to her memory. "Never for one day have I seen why and how it can be right for a mother to be thus taken. I trust in the dark and wait for light. Certainly, God had no direct part in her taking."[7]

"Education is never essentially a matter of schools or of the formal mechanisms by which it is encouraged and promoted. Education is the growth of personality in an environment . . . Every truly educated person is self-educated . . . Our ultimate environment is God."[8] Carver had no recollection of learning to read. He was told that he learned to read by the age of two, forgot how, and learned again. His public-school education seemed to be limited by poorly prepared teachers but he overcame this by personal application to the textbooks, excelling in mathematics, Latin and physics. When he was eighteen he entered Richmond College (now the University of Richmond in Virginia) as a ministerial student and registered for the full M.A. degree program. His college experience was normal, almost typical, consisting of study, extracurricular activity, social involvement, and student preaching. However, he was a devoted student who made the most of his opportunity for learning from books and teachers. He regarded Dr. H.H. Harris as one of the greatest teachers of his generation and the greatest teacher he ever had.[9] The larger setting of his seminary education was indicated in the first paragraph of this article. He had no easy time financially. Pastorates in small churches provided opportunities for service in ministry, experience in preaching, and some financial support. Probably his favorite seminary professor was Dr. W.H. Whitsitt, the one man on the faculty at that time who had formal studies in Germany (two years in Berlin and Leipzig).[10]

The Scholar

From early in his life Carver had manifested an aptitude for scholarship. After long years of study his scholarship was to be characterized by originality of insight, breadth of interests, and depth of understanding. One of the writer's colleagues on the faculty remarked recently that he considered Dr. Carver to be the greatest scholar this institution has produced. He is remembered as the faculty member most able to walk into any classroom on a moment's notice and do a creditable job of teaching any discipline in the curriculum. However, he had a far more modest self-image:

> While I had from 1895, when I began as a tutor, been nominally associated with only the two departments, New Testament and Homiletics, then with Comparative Religion and Missions, as a matter of fact I was from time to time asked to undertake work in other departments. I really became a sort of handy-man, teaching for longer or shorter periods in Theology, Biblical Introduction, Ecclesiology, indeed in the whole range of the curriculum except for Hebrew in which I even met classes now and then. Through the years I continued to share emergency demands, especially during the period of the first World War when I had to share with others almost all of Dr. Mullins' teaching load [in Theology]. Scattering my energies over such wide range, I was able to maintain a rather comprehensive interest

along with a limited knowledge of the entire theological field. *But the price of this was that I never was able to become an actual expert and authority even in my own chosen field.* While I made real progress here I never felt that I deserved the tribute which was too often paid to me by Southern Baptists as "the best informed man in missions in America" or "in the world." I knew that these gracious brethren were very little acquainted with the actual authorities in the field of missions and especially in the field of comparative religion.[11]

The Writer

Carver was the author of twenty-one published books, as well as a steady stream of articles in denominational magazines and scholarly journals. For twelve years he wrote a column in *The Commission,* the monthly publication of the Foreign Mission Board of the Southern Baptist Convention. As a teacher he did not have a popular style and was not interested in seeking popularity, just as he "never was nor desired to be a popular preacher,"[12] although "all through the years opportunities to enter the pastoral ministry continued to come to me and reassure me."[13]

As both teacher and writer, Carver's thought was too complex to permit, at least for him, ease of expression in a simple style. His sentences were long and involved.[14] He lost most students along the way in the course of an hour's lecture. For those who followed his thinking, it was often brilliant and even scintillating. In the spring of 1939 the writer was a student speaker for a prayer meeting at the Walnut Street Baptist Church, where Dr. Carver was a longtime member. Since he was having some trouble with his eyes at the time, he asked the writer to drive his car for him that night. When we returned to the seminary campus, we continued our conversation for a time while parked under the maple trees. Since the faculty was having a periodic curriculum restudy, he asked what was the most difficult course I had during the three years about to be completed. The reply was that if by "difficult" was meant sheer mental exertion (rather than time-consuming – which would have indicated the second year of Hebrew), then "that missions course" was the most difficult; "by the time one untangles the long sentences, organizes the material, and masters it, he is exhausted." The author of the book *The Course of Christian Missions* cleared his throat and said, "I think I know what you mean."

Much of Carver's publishing was situational in the sense that material, prepared for lectures in and also out of classes, was published on request. He wrote a total of eight books on missions. The most important and most influential of all his books, in respect to his life contribution and reputation, was *Missions in the Plan of the Ages.* It was published for forty years, beginning in 1909, by Fleming H. Revell Company. When it was dropped without warning or notice, the Broadman Press took over the publication and sales increased to the highest level (in 1955) since the book was first published. In 1908, after the book had been written from class notes while the author was in Switzerland on a sabbatical leave, the final copy was wrapped for mailing in London on Carver's way back to the United States. On the way to the post office, Dr. and Mrs. Carver got off a city bus to shop briefly. In the store they discovered that the only copy of the manuscript in existence had been left on the bus. They waited for the bus to make its circuit, anxiety increasing all the while. Finally, Mrs. Carver recognized the driver after many buses had passed. He had discovered the package, had it sitting by his feet, and promptly returned it.[15] Carver wrote with reference to this book: "I count it as one of God's great gifts to me that I was able to write this book which has served so many thousands in gaining a new orientation with reference to the core of the Bible as well as emphasizing the true and only basis of world Christianity."[16]

In the writer's judgment the best written of all of Carver's books is *Missions and Modern Thought,* published by Macmillan in 1910. The book that was most widely circulated (73,000 copies) of all his books was *All the World in All the Word,* written in 1918 at the request of the

Women's Missionary Union and published by the Baptist Sunday School Board. It was still in use after thirty-five years. The author received no royalty on the book. *The Course of Christian Missions* (1932), which Carver said was his most laborious task in writing,[17] is still valuable when read as a whole for the purpose of understanding the author's philosophy of missions as reflected by his interpretation of mission history. The best expression of Carver's ability to "read the signs of the time" and to relate God's redemptive movement to its contemporary world setting is *Christian Missions in Today's World*, published by Harper & Brothers in 1942. *God and Man in Missions* (Broadman Press, 1944) gives the clearest expression of Carver's view of missions to be found anywhere. Perhaps its lucidity is to be explained by the fact it was prepared and used for Vesper Hour addresses to young people at Ridgecrest (N.C.) Baptist Assembly. There was an urgent demand for the material to be published. Dr. John L. Hill, book editor of the Baptist Sunday School Board, said this was the best of Carver's publications.[18] After having recognized the merits of the books mentioned above, and all the others not included, the writer considers Carver's magnum opus to be *The Glory of God in the Christian Calling* (Broadman Press, 1949), written when the author was eighty-one! This is a study of the Ephesian epistle, which Carver had studied exhaustively from the time he began his work in the seminary. It expounds the biblical base in terms of theological understanding of the missionary movement. Carver saw the church as essentially the body of Christ in the whole world on mission through the churches. Both church and Christians were continuations of the incarnation of Jesus Christ through whom God is being glorified (i.e., manifested as he *is* in the full character of his being). Carver wrote, "I came to recognize this Epistle as the climax of the interpretation and understanding of God's revelation of himself in Jesus Christ and therefore of God's purpose in Christianity and in all history."[19]

The Theologian

In a graduate seminar in the philosophy of religion during the 1939-40 session, Carver said his daughter characterized him as being a theological liberal and a social conservative. He did not differ with the description. On another occasion in a seminar, Carver said that Wilhelm Herrmann was the theologian who had most influenced his thinking. During most of Carver's career as a teacher, missions was a required course with three semester hours of credit. The first month of each semester of this course was given to the biblical basis of missions. The last three months was a study of the history of missions. The student had a choice between the two other courses that Carver taught, each for two semester hours: comparative religion, and Christian and current thought. (In addition, he offered graduate seminars in all three areas: missions, comparative religion, and philosophy of religion.) The most influential books on his thinking, judging by his emphasis in requiring his graduate students to study them in the philosophy of religion seminar, were A.M. Fairbairn, *The Philosophy of the Christian Religion;* John Oman, *The Natural and the Supernatural;* Eugene William Lyman, *The Meaning and Truth of Religion;* John Baillie, *The Interpretation of Religion;* William Temple, *Nature, Man and God;* John Macmurray, *The Clue to History;* C.H. Dodd, *The Bible Today* (for its view of revelation). It is not surprising that he was not enthusiastic about neo-orthodox thought, since it was the earlier theologians who had most influenced his thinking. He regarded philosophical idealism as more congenial with religious values than any other philosophy, although Temple's dialectical realism influenced him greatly. All his theological and philosophical understanding was subjected to his convictions gained from the independent study of the Bible.

Comparative Religion

Early in his career Carver revealed a spirit of openness toward values reflected in other religious traditions. "Religion is man's God-consciousness, together with the theories and practices by which man gives expression to his God-consciousness . . . If we should define religion as we conceive it in ideal it would be the participation by the creature in the life of the Creator, however one might define the terms *creature* and *Creator*."[20] However, he held to what would today be called the fulfillment view as to the relation of Christianity to other religions. But his spirit of openness kept him on the left edge of the fulfillment view. "Christianity does not, and has no need to, deny all revelation and divine guidance in the origination and the development of other religions. Rather does it assert this, and rests its own hope of a successful evangelism upon the fact . . . The Bible recognizes revelation outside that of its own prophets . . . One must refrain from the universal negation of God's revealing presence in the 'heathen' religions. It is because God is in them, and more *fully* in Christianity, that Christianity has a mission to the other religions."[21] Carver's thinking continued as he critically evaluated such books as Hocking's Commission of Appraisal, *Re-thinking Missions;* Baker's *Christian Missions and a New World Culture*; Buck's *Christianity Tested;* Kraemer's *The Christian Message in a Non-Christian World;* White's *A Working Faith for the World*; and Hocking's *Living Religions and a World Faith.*[22] He saw clearly "that a friendly appraisal of all religions as ways in which men seek their deepest satisfactions in worshipful relation to the Highest Powers has become the accepted view and is a necessary condition for progress in world community."[23] At this point, the reader is reminded of the later views of Wilfred Cantwell Smith. However, Carver continued, "That there are dangers here for superficial thinking and for shallow and ineffective syncretism should be obvious. The danger of cultivating religious indifference is even more serious."[24] He apparently had the Kraemer/Hocking debate in mind when he wrote, "Already there is a strong movement toward rethinking the principles to be followed in the interpretation of the history and the relations of religions."[25] While Carver considered Kraemer's work classical,[26] he was inclined to agree with Hocking's view of "reconception." "Reconception is Hocking's term for what *must be* the process by which Christianity will become the religion of humanity."[27] Both Hocking and Carver expected that Christian conversions would result from reconception. Carver wrote:

> The sympathetic reconception of their Christianity by the missionaries will help Christians to reconceive the elements of other religions. Thereby there will be mutual help in reconceiving religion as such. Thus it becomes a process of finding God's full and expanding revelation and redemption. If in Christ Jesus we have "manifested all the fullness of redeeming Deity in bodily form," then in Christianity will be found the resources for redeeming humanity unto a true world community. Christianity will not then compete with other religions, it will enable their followers to transcend them. And this it will do as actual Christianity itself is cleaned and made comprehensive of the grace and the righteousness of God.[28]

The writer always shall regret that Carver is not with us today to react to the increasing volume of literature concerning religious pluralism. His honest mind would have made a contribution. In the spring of 1940 the writer confronted the question of universalism, as a soteriological and eschatological doctrine, for the first time while reading in the library William Temple's *Nature, Man and God.* On the way to lunch, in the hall he met up with Carver, who was then his professor in a graduate seminar on the philosophy of religion. The student asked the professor what he thought about universalism. As they walked down the hall, paused at length in the professor's office, and continued the conversation on campus at the point their path separated, Carver talked for more than an hour, giving his student a private lecture on the pros and cons of the question. He concluded by saying, "I shall have to wait until I am on the other side of the veil [of death] to know the answer to your question." The student's reaction was a growth experience: uncertainty as to universalism did *not* cut the nerve of mission motivation for Carver, whose life had been devoted to missions (he was then seventy-two years old); for him, the glory of God was the motive – the imperative was to make God known as he is!

Missiologist

Carver's legacy as a missiologist may be summed up in what he considered to be Paul's God-given insight as best expressed in Ephesians: *the Christian's calling is to be God's heritage for God's glory* (cf. Eph. 4:1). There are numerous verses in Ephesians in which the King James Version mistakenly translates "inheritance" as being "our inheritance." W.O. Carver's translation,[29] when compared with the King James, corrects this and rightly makes the point that "we are God's heritage."

	Carver's translation:	*King James translation:*
1:11	in him in whom we were made a heritage	in whom also we have obtained an inheritance
1:14	who is [thereby] a pledge of our being [God's] heritage	which is the earnest of our inheritance
1:18	what is his [God's] hope [in the people and plan] of his calling	what is the hope of his calling
4:4	you were called in [God's] one hope of your calling	ye are called in one hope of your calling

The classic example of Carver's understanding of Paul's thought at this point is Colossians 1:27, which he translated "Christ in you, the hope of [God's] glory."[30] Carver said in his classes that he was hesitant to express this interpretation for many years after it first came to him. Finally, he dared to express it boldly: "The calling of the Christian and the church is to be the continuation of the incarnation of Jesus Christ!" The writer will never forget the dramatic effect these words had upon his understanding of what Christianity is – and is not. In his judgment, this understanding is the greatest contribution W.O. Carver made to missiology in a long and productive life. It is not too much to say that the words "the continuation of the incarnation of Jesus Christ" were branded upon the minds and hearts of many student generations in the course of Carver's fifty-odd years of teaching. His exposition of Ephesians 3:1-13 gives the clearest statement of his understanding at this point.[31]

God has a mission in our world. It is *his* mission. He has entrusted it to the church, which is his heritage, for his purpose. The mission of the church is to *glorify God* by leading persons to come to *know* him experientially through faith in Jesus Christ. In turn, these persons become his heritage and serve as his agents to make himself known. In the words of William Temple:

> The true aim of the soul is not its own salvation; to make that the chief aim is to insure its perdition (cf. Matt. 16:25); for it is to fix the soul on itself as central. The true aim of the soul is to glorify God; in pursuing that aim it will attain to salvation unawares. No one who is convinced of his own salvation is yet even safe, let alone "saved." Salvation is the state of him who has ceased to be interested whether he is saved or not, provided that what takes the place of that supreme self-interest is not a lower form of self-interest but the glory of God.[32]

It was the conviction of W.O. Carver that "the earth *will be* filled with the *knowledge* of the *glory* of the Lord, as the waters cover the sea" (Hab. 2:14, NASB).

Notes

1. Olav Guttorm Myklebust, *The Study of Missions in Theological Education,* 2 vols. (Oslo: Forlaget Land og Kirke, 1955), 1:376f. Cf. W.O. Carver, "Recollections and Information from Other Sources Concerning

the Southern Baptist Theological Seminary" (Louisville, Ky.; an unpublished typed monograph of 137 pages, in the noncirculating manuscripts shelves of the seminary library, prepared between 1952 and 1954, during the last two years of his long life, by W.O. Carver at the request of the faculty as background material for a centennial history of the seminary to be published in 1959), p. 61. The first chair of missions was founded at Cumberland University in 1884 by Claiborne H. Bell but was dropped in 1909 when he died. Cf. Myklebust, *The Study of Missions*, 1:375. Apparently Carver was not aware of this, although it was in his home state. In his book *The Course of Christian Missions* (New York: Fleming H. Revell Company, 1932), p. 312, he wrote, "The Southern Baptist Theological Seminary established such a professorship in 1899, *the first in America*, but followed by others."

2. J.B. Weatherspoon, "A Teacher of Preachers," in William Owen Carver, *Out of His Treasure: Unfinished Memoirs* (Nashville, Tenn.: Broadman Press, 1956), p.129.

3. Ibid., p. 132.

4. Myklebust, *The Study of Missions*, 1:376; Carver, "Recollections," pp. 60f.; and Carver, *The Course of Christian Missions*, p. 312.

5. Carver, *Memoirs*, p. 9

6. Ibid.

7. Ibid.

8. Ibid., pp. 15f.

9. Ibid., p. 132.

10. Ibid., p. 129.

11. Carver, "Recollections," pp. 62f.

12. Carver, *Memoirs*, p. 57.

13. Ibid.

14. Ibid., p. 93.

15. Ibid., p. 110.

16. Ibid., p. 111.

17. Ibid., p. 114.

18. Ibid.

19. Ibid., p. 119.

20. Carver, *Missions and Modern Thought* (New York: Macmillan Company, 1910), p. 122.

21. Ibid., p. 140.

22. Carver, *Christian Missions in Today's World* (New York: Harper & Brothers, 1942), p. 44.

23. Ibid., p. 138.

24. Ibid.

25. Ibid., p. 139.

26. Carver, "The Function of the Church in the Marketing of World Order," p. 17 of chap. 4 (an unfinished manuscript for a book left at the time of his death).

27. Carver, *Christian Missions in Today's World*, p. 145 (italics added).

28. Ibid., pp. 147f.

29. Carver, *The Glory of God in the Christian Calling* (Nashville: Tenn.: Broadman Press, 1949), pp. 220-23, 228f.

30. The writer remembers Carver's customary and frequent emphasis of this understanding of Col. 1:27 in his classes forty years ago.

31. Cf. Carver, *The Glory of God in the Christian Calling*, pp. 43-61, 125-35, 201-3. Also cf. Hugo H. Culpepper, "Ephesians – A Manifesto for the Mission of the Church," *Review and Expositor* 76, no. 4 (Fall 1979), for a fuller exposition of this view of Carver's missiology.

32. William Temple, *Nature, Man, and God* (London: Macmillan and Co., 1935), pp. 390f.

Selected Bibliography

Works by W.O. Carver

1898 *Mission and the Kingdom of Heaven: The Inaugural Address of William Owen Carver, Th.D.* Louisville, Ky.: John P. Morton and Company, Prentess. Delivered on October 1, 1898.

1901 *History of the New Salem Baptist Church, Nelson County, Kentucky.* N.p.

1907 *Baptist Opportunity.* Philadelphia: American Baptist Publication Society.

1909 *Missions in the Plan of the Ages: Bible Studies in Missions.* New York: Fleming H. Revell Company.

1910 *Missions and Modern Thought.* New York: Macmillan Company.

1916 *The Acts of the Apostles.* Nashville, Tenn.: Broadman Press.

1918 *All the World in All the Word.* Nashville, Tenn.: Sunday School Board, Southern Baptist Convention.
1921 *The Bible a Missionary Message.* New York: Fleming H. Revell Company.
1926 *The Self-Interpretation of Jesus.* Nashville: Tenn.: Sunday School Board, Southern Baptist Convention.
1928 *Thou When Thou Prayest.* Nashville: Tenn.: Sunday School Board, Southern Baptist Convention.
1932 *The Course of Christian Missions.* New York: Fleming H. Revell Company.
1933 *How the New Testament Came to Be Written.* New York: Fleming H. Revell Company.
1934 *The Rediscovery of the Spirit.* New York: Fleming H. Revell Company.
1935 *The Furtherance of the Gospel.* Nashville, Tenn.: Sunday School Board, Southern Baptist Convention.
1940 *Sabbath Observance.* Nashville, Tenn.: Broadman Press.
1942 *Christian Missions in Today's World.* New York: Harper & Brothers.
1942 *If Two Agree.* Nashville, Tenn.: Broadman Press.
1944 *God and Man in Missions.* Nashville, Tenn.: Broadman Press.
1946 *Why They Wrote the New Testament.* Nashville, Tenn.: Sunday School Board, Southern Baptist Convention.
1949 *The Glory of God in the Christian Calling: A Study of the Ephesian Epistle.* Nashville, Tenn.: Broadman Press.
1954 "Recollections and Information from Other Sources Concerning the Southern Baptist Theological Seminary." Louisville, Ky.; unpublished manuscript in the seminary library.
N.d. "The Function of the Church in the Making of World Order." Louisville, Ky.; unfinished manuscript in the seminary library.
1956 *Out of His Treasure: Unfinished Memoirs.* Nashville, Tenn.: Broadman Press.

Works about W.O. Carver

Ellis, Curtis Ray. "The Missionary Philosophy of William Owen Carver." Nashville, Tenn.: Historical Commission, Southern Baptist Convention, 1969. Microfilm copy of a thesis, New Orleans Baptist Theological Seminary, 1968.
Forehand, Robert Vernon. "A Study of Religion and Culture as Reflected in the Thought and Career of William Owen Carver." Th.D. diss., Southern Baptist Theological Seminary, Louisville, Ky., 1972.
Smith, William Cheney, Jr. "A Critical Investigation of the Ecclesiological Thought of William Owen Carver." Th.D. diss., Southern Baptist Theological Seminary, Louisville, Ky., 1962.

Ruth Rouse

1872–1956

Missionary, Student Evangelist, Ecumenical Pioneer

Ruth Franzén

One of the pioneers in women's history asks us whether women are noteworthy only when their achievements fall into categories of achievement set up for men![1] Regardless of how one answers this question, it is undoubtedly time to attempt to explore the role of women in both the modern missionary movement and the ecumenical movement. One who deserves an honorable place in this history is Ruth Rouse (1872-1956), missionary, evangelist, and pioneer in reaching students in countless universities and colleges around the world.

A picture taken in 1908 of the officers of the World's Student Christian Federation (WSCF) shows three men and one woman: Ruth Rouse, then thirty-six years old. The intelligent expression behind the glasses typical of the period reflects good powers of observation. Her long dark hair put under a huge hat suggests that she did not assume the posture of a radical feminist, in spite of her pioneering role. A certain aristocratic elegance that was regarded as the right and proper thing in those years indicates that the tall slender woman in a fashionable skirt reaching down to her feet was well aware of the significance of appearing as a lady. Symbolically the picture suggests the framework of Ruth Rouse's life work. With her fellow workers she shared an interest in all branches of the burgeoning student and missionary movement of the period. Nevertheless her contribution was very special, a woman pioneering among pioneer women, in a society dominated by men. The picture shows her together with John R. Mott, Karl Fries, and Walton W. Seton; the first two were internationally known Christian workers. She was highly trusted by these men, with whom she had a good, long-lasting, fruitful cooperation.

George Woodford Rouse and his wife W.G. (née) MacDonald, the parents of Ruth Rouse, represented devout evangelical traditions, her father coming from an English family chiefly associated with the Plymouth Brethren and her mother being a Scottish Baptist. When Ruth was born, in 1872, they lived in Clapham Park, a London suburb. A layman leading seaside services from the Children's Special Service Mission was instrumental in helping the tall, sporty youngster fight her conversion through when she was nearly eighteen. After that Ruth was baptized in the church of her childhood, the Metropolitan Tabernacle, where Charles H. Spurgeon preached to thousands every Sunday until his death in 1892.[2] That same year Ruth joined the Church of England.

Both the work of the Children's Special Service Mission, based in the Church of England, and Spurgeon's preaching represented a type of interdenominational, or rather undenominational, evangelicalism emphasizing vital religion, not doctrine.

Cambridge, and a Life Purpose

In an age when a pious, Victorian, middle-class girl was supposed to stay at home and wait for a suitable suitor, Ruth had parents unprejudiced enough to send their daughter to some of the best schools available – first Notting Hill High School and then Bedford College in London. Later they also let her have her own way when she wanted to study at Girton College, Cambridge. This was one of the first colleges for women and one of the most prestigious ones, with the same standards as the best colleges for men. (The women students took their degree examinations in exactly the same way as men, but Cambridge University did not give women the titles of their degrees until 1923, and not until 1948 were they given membership of the university.)[3]

After studying for the normal three years, Ruth Rouse passed her tripos in classics. In preparation for a missionary career in India, she then studied Sanskrit one year at the British Museum in London.

In 1892 during Ruth Rouse's second year at Girton College, Robert P. Wilder visited Cambridge. He was the son of missionaries and himself on his way to take up a missionary career in India. This gentle and modest young man of prayer had been instrumental in starting the rapidly growing Student Volunteer Movement (SVM). He was one of the foremost advocates of the SVM pledge "willing and desirous, God permitting, to become foreign missionaries."[4] Wilder distributed declaration cards in Cambridge, and one of those who promptly signed a card was Ruth's friend and schoolmate Agnes de Selincourt. Ruth also took one, but she was unable to make a decision to sign it. About two years later, after much agonizing uncertainty and self-searching, she was finally able to take the decisive step, trusting not herself but God. She later told how Paul's sentence had flashed through her mind: "I know whom I have believed, and am persuaded that he is able to keep that which I have committed unto him against that day." Wilmina Rowland, who had several interviews with Ruth Rouse more than forty years later, writes:

> Suddenly it came to Ruth that what she could commit to Christ's keeping could be a purpose as well as anything else. A decision in his keeping, would be inviolable; there need be no fear of changing it. That intuition broke the back of her indecision. At once she signed the declaration. Never again was there the slightest uncertainty in her mind that the purpose of God for her was worldwide and missionary, nor the faintest thought of changing her purpose to follow that will for her life. Her indecision in other matters still continued for a time, but from this moment she began to "grow up."[5]

During the early nineties there was a great interest in religious matters in Cambridge, with many of the young students later becoming legendary for their enthusiasm and zeal, including Theodore Woods, G.T. Manley, Douglas Thornton, and Louis Byrde. University missions and open-air meetings were arranged using mature and experienced speakers. Many of the prominent evangelists and missionaries of the day were heard, men like Sir Arthur Blackwood, Wilson Carlile, Lord Radstock, E.A. Stuart, J.E.K. Studd, and Douglas Hooper. The morning watch and Bible study were essential parts of the students' active religious life, the center being prayer. Ruth Rouse and Agnes de Selincourt were the backbone of the daily Girton Prayer Meeting.[6]

Beginning a Life of World Travel

Ruth Rouse started her first paid job in 1895 as the editor of the *Student Volunteer* for one year. As a traveling secretary among women students during the following year, she shared her time between the Student Volunteer Missionary Union (SVMU), the Inter-Collegiate Christian Union, and the Missionary Settlement for University Women at Bombay. The last organization had been founded to secure women students' contributions to missionary work among the Parsees in India. Ruth and her friend Agnes de Selincourt were instrumental in the planning and implementation of this project from the outset.[7]

Miss Rouse (as she was generally referred to in an age characterized by the spare use of Christian names) went to her first student conference in the summer of 1894 at Keswick. There she met for the first time the Americans Robert E. Speer and John R. Mott. The latter was to become her most influential and much-admired fellow worker for about a quarter of a century. She belonged to the small group of young Britons who undertook to arrange the first International Students' Missionary Conference; the famous Liverpool Conference was held in January 1896, attended by more than seven hundred students.[8] These student conferences were marked by youthful earnestness, missionary enthusiasm, and prayerfulness. Later in life she attended innumerable conferences, both national and international, including the Edinburgh World Missionary Conference in 1910 and the World Council of Churches' first assembly in Amsterdam in 1948.

The Liverpool conference decided to adopt the watchword of the American SVM: "The evangelization of the world in this generation." Ruth Rouse was also one of ten signers (among them were also G.T. Manley, J.H. Oldham, and D.M. Thornton) of a memorial to the church urging it to accept this watchword as its missionary policy.[9] To their disappointment, no church adopted the watchword.

Ruth Rouse made her first tour abroad in 1897, as a traveling secretary visiting all the Scandinavian countries, including Finland, which in those years was attached to Russia, though as a rather autonomous part named the Grand Duchy of Finland. From these years on, Ruth took a never-ceasing interest in the evangelization of the student world, giving her time and energy especially to the work among women students in all parts of the world.

An appeal from John R. Mott brought her to North America for eighteen months in 1897-99. She served as a Student Volunteer secretary and then as a College Young Women's Christian Association secretary in both Canada and the United States. She was introduced to the movement in America pressing for the higher education for women; she came to know that this movement was pioneered by women of strong Christian conviction and purpose. She herself summed up the benefits of this period for her further career:

> An unbelievable opportunity was mine – a most direct preparation for work in the Federation. Not only did I learn to understand the varied and widespread work of the national Y.W.C.A. and Y.M.C.A. movements – a valuable training for cooperation – but along my own line I visited at least 100 universities and colleges, women's colleges and co-educational, denominational and State institutions, mostly in the East and Middle West. I attended and helped to work up delegations to the Quadrennial Student Volunteer Convention at Cleveland, February, 1898; I was present at summer student conferences, both men's and women's.[10]

John R. Mott and the WSCF

Her own contribution was to direct the attention of the national leaders of the YMCA to the student field, to help them understand the importance of their student departments, and to make valuable links with some new, very important colleges. She tried to cover the enormous area, visiting all types of colleges, from Bryn Mawr – the queen of colleges, "with a course fully as stiff as Harvard" – to small, denominational, coeducational colleges. By placing her side by side with many celebrities in foreign missions, C. Howard Hopkins in his biography of Mott gives her a fine tribute:

At no point was Mott's talent as a judge of men – and women – better displayed than in his selection of the traveling staff for the SVM. During his absence in 1895-97, Henry W. Luce, Horace T. Pitkin, and G. Sherwood Eddy, all Yale men, went on the road for short assignments before "sailing" to their mission posts. Others to make names for themselves were Harlan P. Beach, Fletcher S. Brockman, Robert R. Gailey, Robert E. Lewis, J. Ross Stevenson, Fennell P. Turner, S. Earl Taylor, Fred Field Goodsell, and Ruth Rouse.[11]

After attending the Cleveland Convention (2,214 delegates from 458 institutions) Ruth Rouse was offered a post by the YWCA as international student secretary among women. She did not accept it, however, as she felt it to be in conflict with her call to India. Still this invitation demonstrated the direction of her mission in life.[12]

In a very strict sense, Ruth Rouse's missionary career was a short one, from December 1899 to the end of 1901, when she had to leave India because of ill health. Sharing her time between the Missionary Settlement for University Women and the YWCA, she had a large and difficult field – from settlement work in Bombay during the years of the bubonic plague to developing and organizing Christian work among schoolgirls and women students in the whole of South India.

Ruth Rouse saw the need for radical improvement in the position of Indian women, and like many other Western women, she hoped for a cultural transformation through a Christian, and Western, influence. In her early years she was hardly aware of any problematic links between colonialism and British missions. In her later writings she still summed up the missionary motive in the words "saved to serve the world."[13]

In 1903 while on convalescent leave in England, Ruth Rouse was asked by Mott to visit Holland, Germany, Finland, and Russia "in order to study the religious conditions of women students, to seek to lead them to Christ and to promote Christian work among them." The arrangement was officially sanctioned in 1905 when she was appointed traveling secretary of the World's Student Christian Federation. In his characteristic manner Mott had taken care of the only serious objection to her appointment by securing means for her salary and expenses from Grace Dodge, a wealthy American lady deeply dedicated to Christian work among young women.[14]

Her personal qualities made Ruth Rouse an ideal traveling secretary. A sense of adventure was part of her constitution. She liked traveling and slept well anywhere; she had considerable ability as a speaker and was in her element doing personal work.[15] Being British, female, and a member of the Church of England, she was a perfect balance in the WSCF for Mott, the American Methodist, who in his turn received a gifted and loyal fellow worker.

Ruth Rouse, independent and capable in her own right, nevertheless admired Mott and his businesslike efficiency very much. Their relation as fellow workers seems to have been a happy one, based on mutual respect. Mott had the rare ability to trust and inspire his fellow workers, and obviously he had a high opinion of women's intellectual capacity and judgment. His own marriage created a unique husband-and-wife team as well.[16] In spite of all this, Mott was, as Howard Hopkins puts it, "a bit unappreciative of the role of women in the ecumenical movement."[17] Especially later in life Mott seems to have taken for granted the capacity and generosity of those capable women.

During Ruth's nineteen years as a WSCF secretary she visited sixty-five different countries, many of them several times. Opposition was not lacking, and her apologetic abilities were often put to test. Her steady aim was to "get a foothold in any group of women students, however few."[18] She early became accustomed to the aggressive type of woman student who reacted sharply against everything old and established. Probably her most fruitful method of work could be called evangelism by friendship. Furthermore, she had an outstanding ability of finding capable young students and training them for leadership. To all these she reached out in personal friendship, to which her vast correspondence bears ample witness.

Ecumenical Contributions

Ruth Rouse was animated by an ecumenical spirit. She was both a promoter and a product of the WSCF as the "experimental laboratory of ecumenism," which to her meant, according to her fellow worker and friend Suzanne Bidgrain, "the experience of fellowship in faith with all those who worshiped the Lord to whom her life was dedicated." She was herself gradually molded by her service within the student work, so that to numberless women students she became the embodiment of the WSCF. Her very existence made it impossible to "look at things from a purely racial, national, and confessional point of view."[19] By conviction both she and Mott tried, and usually succeeded, to avoid all controversies, whether theological or political.[20]

During World War I and afterward Ruth Rouse, together with J.H. Oldham, Karl Fries, and others, did much to eliminate differences and bring mutual understanding within the WSCF as well as between the missionary organizations of the opposite sides. Her most outstanding contribution to the relief of suffering and the restoration of international friendship was the launching of the cooperative undertaking of students known as the European Student Relief. Through her vision of the need and the opportunity to act "in the name and spirit of Christ," the WSCF decided to start a campaign to concentrate the energies of the students of many nations upon the relief of their needy comrades in other places of the world. Founded in 1925, the project grew into an independent university organization.[21] During World War II the organization continued its struggle to meet the needs of students.

Another field where the impact of Ruth Rouse was felt over an even longer period was the YWCA. From 1906 to 1946 she was a member of the World Executive Committee and its president from 1938 to 1946. The work of the YWCA and of the WSCF was correlated in such a way that the experience of each could help the other. Through her profound understanding and deep sympathy with both movements, she was able to help to make their cooperation more fruitful.[22]

Ruth Rouse's worldwide pioneering among students vitalized the missionary interest in many countries over three decades. Later (1925-39) she served the missionary cause in her own country as educational secretary of the Missionary Council of the National Assembly of the Church of England. This was certainly no easy task, as many types of conflicts affected this body.

At least one more important element of the legacy of Ruth Rouse must be mentioned: she was a good writer. Throughout her whole life she produced articles for several different national and international papers and magazines. In addition to her many other duties, she found time to write pamphlets and books. She started her career as editor of the *Student Volunteer*, and after retirement she took up a new career as historiographer of the WSCF and the ecumenical movement. To her, the ecumenical urge, a yearning for the reunion of all Christians, was an essential part of her Christian faith.

Like so many of the educated women who were her contemporaries, Ruth Rouse never married. Her opinion of marriage as a refuge in which one is "sheltered and cared for and happy" invites further analysis.[23] She was always careful that her private life should not cause rumors. Consequently we should not be surprised that no sources have been preserved that tell us the reason why she did not marry; we are left to guess. Certainly she would have refused to compromise her ideal of marriage if no appropriate suitor appeared. However, we must keep in mind that attitudes toward marriage were not easy for a professional woman of Ruth Rouse's generation, who first had to struggle her way to college, then to a professional identity. Female role models were usually all single women. Most educated women of this generation seem to have thought that marriage was a vocation incompatible with a career, not to mention with the opinions of a prospective husband.[24] Ruth Rouse might well have decided not to marry because of her ambition to "work out her missionary purpose" in worldwide service.[25] Still she had her own dependents. When she left her office as traveling secretary of the WSCF, an important factor was her need to take care of her aging mother, with whom she shared her home in England.

A "Female John R. Mott"

Ruth Rouse has sometimes been referred to a female John R. Mott.[26] In some sense this hits the nail on the head. She had the same zeal for evangelization and the same ability to inspire students. Like him, she is remembered as an evangelist, person of prayer, leader, advocate of comity, friend, speaker, executive, author, editor, fund-raiser, and traveler.[27] Influenced by Mott's optimism, she still seems to have been critical and reflective. Although she was not perhaps so contemplative as J.H. Oldham, she appears to have had a similar mediating effect. Furthermore, it must be remembered that she was born in a time when ideas of gender differences deemed women to be in a position of inferiority. Thus her starting point was different from that of her male colleagues. Also, working as a pioneer woman among pioneer women made her contribution different.

Though old and retired, Ruth Rouse was still very influential when she undertook one of her final jobs. She helped, rather unofficially, to arrange the archives of the WSCF and of John R. Mott in the library of the Yale University Divinity School. According to Robert C. Mackie, then general secretary of the WSCF, she was able to remove from Mott's papers some correspondence "which it would have done no good for posterity to discover."[28] Of course, to a researcher this is not altogether a cause of rejoicing. However, the incident illustrates the relationship between those two pioneers in a brilliant way and mirrors Ruth Rouse's manifold and far-reaching influence. This brings us back to the point where we started: the historian's still-unsolved problem of how to judge the contribution of women. Except for her work in the World's YWCA, Ruth Rouse did not chair large conferences as did John R. Mott. Neither did she shine as an administrator of genius in the same way as J.H. Oldham. Nonetheless she combined these same gifts with a third: the ability to do personal work.

When the women's portion of the ecumenical movement's history as well as their contribution to the nineteenth- and twentieth-century history of Christian mission have been properly evaluated, Ruth Rouse will have her obvious and unthreatened place in both. She will hold it abreast of such well-known males as Wilder, Mott, Speer, and Oldham – not primarily as a philosopher and thinker, but as one who heard the missionary call and worked out her missionary purpose. She saw the unique opportunities of her time and acted upon them.

Notes

1. Gerda Lerner, *The Majority Finds Its Past: Placing Women in History* (New York: Oxford Univ. Press, 1979), p. 13.

2. On Spurgeon, see W.Y. Fullerton, *Charles H. Spurgeon: London's Most Popular Preacher* (Chicago: Moody Press, 1966). On CSSM, see G.R. Balleine, *A History of the Evangelical Party in the Church of England* (London: Church Book Room Press, 1951), pp. 196-98.

3. Deborah Gorham, *The Victorian Girl and the Feminine Ideal* (Bloomington: Indiana Univ. Press, 1982); Martha Vicinius, ed., *A Widening Sphere: Changing Roles of Victorian Women* (Bloomington: Indiana Univ. Press, 1977). On higher education for women and Girton College, see Barbara Stephen, *Emily Davies and Girton College* (London: Constable, 1927); Rita McWilliams-Tullberg, *Women at Cambridge: A Men's University – Though of a Mixed Type* (London: Victor Gallanz, 1975).

4. On Wilder, see Ruth E. Braisted, *In This Generation: The Story of Robert P. Wilder* (New York: Friendship Press, 1941); James A. Patterson, "The Legacy of Robert P. Wilder," *International Bulletin of Missionary Research* 15 (January 1991): 26-32. On the start of the SVMU of Great Britain and Ireland, see H.W. Oldham, *The Student Christian Movement of Great Britain and Ireland: Its Origin, Development,*

and Present Position (London: BCCU, 1899); Robert P. Wilder, *The Great Commission: The Missionary Response of the Student Volunteer Movements in North America and Europe: Some Personal Reminiscences* (London: Oliphants, 1936), pp. 72-83; Tissington Tatlow, *The Story of the Student Christian Movement of Great Britain and Ireland* (London: SCM Press, 1933), pp. 22-35.

5. Wilmina Rowland, "The Contribution of Ruth Rouse to the World's Student Christian Federation" (M.A. thesis, Yale, 1936), pp. 58-59.

6. Ruth Rouse, "Agnes de Selincourt: Born 1872. Died 1917," *Student Movement*, October 1917; J. C. Pollock, *A Cambridge Movement* (London: John Murray, 1953), pp. 112-37; Rowland, "Contribution of Ruth Rouse," p. 58.

7. ICCU Minutes, 1895-96, Selly Oak Colleges Central Library, Birmingham, England; Tatlow, *Student Christian Movement*, pp. 57-58.

8. Oldham, *Student Christian Movement*, pp. 46-54.

9. *Memorial of the SVMU to the Church of Christ in Britain* (London: SVMU, n.d.).

10. Ruth Rouse, *The World's Student Christian Federation: A History of the First Thirty Years* (London: SCM Press, 1948), p. 117.

11. C. Howard Hopkins, *John R. Mott, 1865-1955: A Biography* (Grand Rapids: Wm. B. Eerdmans Publishing Co., 1979), pp. 225-26. See also Anna V. Rice, *A History of the World's Young Women's Christian Association* (New York: Women's Press, 1947), p. 83.

12. Rowland, "Contribution of Ruth Rouse," p. 95.

13. Ruth Rouse, "The Missionary Motive," *International Review Of Missions* 25 (1936): 250-58. For general discussion, see Andrew F. Walls, "The British," *International Bulletin of Missionary Research* 6 (April 1982): 60-64; Patricia R. Hill, *The World Their Household: The American Women's Foreign Mission Movement and Cultural Transformation, 1870-1920* (Ann Arbor: Univ. of Michigan Press, 1985).

14. Karl Fries to Ruth Rouse, March 9, 1904, Fries Papers, Uppsala University Library, Uppsala; Rouse, *World's Student Christian Federation*, pp. 102-3; Robert D. Cross, "Dodge Grace Hoadley," in *Notable American Women, 1607-1950: A Biographical Dictionary*, vol.1, ed. Edward T. James, Janet Wilson, and Paul S. Boyer (Cambridge: Harvard Univ. Press, 1974).

15. F.W.S. O'Neill, quoted in Rowland, "Contribution of Ruth Rouse," p. 70.

16. Hopkins, *John R. Mott*, p. 95.

17. C. Howard Hopkins, "The Legacy of John R. Mott," *International Bulletin of Missionary Research* 5 (April 1981): 71.

18. Rouse, *World's Student Christian Federation*, pp. 11-118.

19. Suzanne Bidgrain, "Ruth Rouse (1872-1956)," *Student World* 50 (1957): 73-75.

20. On Mott, see e.g. Hopkins, *John R. Mott*, pp. 631-33.

21. Ruth Rouse, *Rebuilding Europe: The Student Chapter in Post-War Reconstruction*, with a Foreword by John R. Mott (London: Student Christian Movement, 1925).

22. Rice, *History*, pp. 148-50.

23. Ruth Rouse to Helmi Gulin, May 16, 1920, Gulin Papers, Finnish National Archives, Helsinki.

24. On these and other tensions and ambiguities imposed on this generation of women who wanted careers, see Joyce Antler, "The Educated Women and Professionalization: The Struggle for a New Feminine Identity, 1890-1920" (Ph.D. diss., State University of New York, 1977).

25. Rouse, *World's Student Christian Federation*, pp. 111-23.

26. Karl Fries, *Mina minnen* (Stockholm, 1939), p. 100.

27. Hopkins, "Legacy of John R. Mott," p. 72.

28. Robert C. Mackie to Clarence Shedd, May 9, 1945, World Student Christian Federation Archives, World Council of Churches Library, Geneva.

Selected Bibliography

Major Works by Ruth Rouse

1906 *Studies in the Epistle to the Philippians*. London: SCM.
1917 *Christian Experience and Psychological Processes: With Special Reference to the Phenomenon of Autosuggestion*. Coauthor H. Crichton Miller, M.D. London: SCM Press.
1925 *Rebuilding Europe: The Student Chapter in Post-War Reconstruction*. London: SCM Press.
1948 *The World's Student Christian Federation: A History of the First Thirty Years*. London: SCM Press.
1954 *A History of the Ecumenical Movement, 1517-1948*. Edited by Ruth Rouse and Stephen Charles Neill. London: SPCK.

Pamphlets and Reports by Ruth Rouse

N.d. *Women Students in India.* London: Missionary Settlement of University Women.

1913 *The Missionary Motive.* London: SCM Press.

1905 "Auszüge aus einem Bericht über die Arbeit des Christlichen Studenten-Weltbundes unter studierenden Frauen." In *Bericht von der Konferenz des Christlichen Studenten-Weltbundes zu Zeist in Holland,* pp. 133-51. Halle: Christlicher Student-Weltbund.

1909 "Women's Work in the World's Student Christian Federation." In *Report of the Conference of the World's Student Christian Federation Held at Oxford, England,* pp. 255-73. WSCF.

1914 "Report on the Women's Work of the Federation." In *Religious Forces in the Universities of the World: Four Years of Progress in the World's Student Christian Federation,* pp. 47-74. WSCF.

N.d. *Christ and the Student World: A Review of the World's Student Christian Federation, 1920-21.* London: SCM.

N.d. *Under Heaven One Family: A Review of the World's Student Christian Federation, 1921-22.* WSCF.

N.d. *Quo Vadis: A Review of the World's Student Christian Federation, 1922-23.* London: WSCF.

N.d. *John R. Mott: An Appreciation.* Geneva: WSCF.

1935 *God Has a Purpose: An Outline of the History of Missions and of Missionary Method.* London: SCM Press.

Published Addresses in:

1896 *Make Jesus King: Report of the International Students' Missionary Conference, Liverpool.* London: SVMU.

1898 *The Student Missionary Appeal: Addresses at the International Convention of the Student Volunteer Movement for Foreign Missions, Cleveland, Ohio, 1898.* New York: SVMFM.

1913 *Fourth Biennial Convention, Richmond, Virginia, 1913.* New York: National Board of the YWCA of the USA.

1937 *God Speaks to This Generation: Report of the British U.C.M. Quadrennial Conference, Birmingham, 1937.* London: SCM Press.

Articles in:

Association Monthly
Church Missionary Review
Church Overseas
East and West Review
Evangel, Journal of the Young Women's Christian Association in the U.S.A.
Federation News (editor 1921-24)
Intercollegian
International Review of Missions
Student Movement
Student Relief Series (editor 1920-24)
Student Service Bulletin (editor 1920-22)
Student Volunteer, London
Student Volunteer, New York
Student World
World's Y.W.C.A. Quarterly

Unpublished Materials

Karl Fries Papers. Handskriftssamlingen (Manuscripts), Uppsala University Library, Uppsala.

Helmi Forsman Gulin Papers. Forsman Koskinen Suku 12, Finnish National Archives, Helsinki.

Student Christian Movement of Great Britain Archives. Selly Oak Colleges Central Library, Birmingham, England.

Lydia Wahlström Papers. Royal Swedish Library, Stockholm.

World Student Christian Federation Archives. World Council of Churches Library, Geneva (mostly related to the years after 1924).

World Student Christian Federation Collection. Manuscript Record Group 46, Archives and Manuscript, Yale Divinity School Library, New Heaven, Conn. (related to the period 1895-1924).

Works about Ruth Rouse

Bidgrain, Suzanne, "Ruth Rouse (1872-1956)." *Student World* 50 (First Quarter 1957): 73-77.
Rowland, Wilmina. "The Contribution of Ruth Rouse to the World's Student Christian Federation." M.A. thesis, Yale University, 1937.

Friedrich Schwager

1876–1929

Trailblazing for Catholic Missions and Mission Education

Karl Müller, S.V.D.

On March 19, 1912, Friedrich Schwager, member of the Roman Catholic missionary order Society of the Divine Word (S.V.D.), wrote to his superior general: "If you, Reverend Father, so severely criticize the evil consequences of 'education,' you surely do not wish to condemn the best possible formation and utilization of the intellectual faculties bestowed on us by God but are warning against the overestimation of a one-sided intellectualism."[1]

This statement sums up the concern for which Schwager untiringly worked and fought all his life. He was convinced that poorly trained missionaries are "at the mercy of the agitation of the free-thinking, social democratic and immoral tendencies," whereas good education "teaches them to form independent opinions" and thus makes them "intellectually robust." In this connection he recalls the "marvelous progress" of recent times, the "abolition of slavery, of witch hunting officially sanctioned by the popes, torture, the great civil insecurity of the Middle Ages – furthermore, the great positive achievements of charitable work, official social policy, and the natural sciences."[2]

Early Training

Friedrich Schwager was born on March 28, 1876, in Altenhagen, in the parish of Hagen, in Westphalia, Germany, where his father was a teacher. After attending the primary school, he continued his studies at a local church school and at the age of thirteen entered the new Mission House in Steyl, Holland, to prepare for the priestly and missionary life. Despite a rather poor state of health, he effortlessly completed the necessary courses and displayed a special interest in missions. His superior described him as a "perfectly well-behaved, reliable pupil."[3] From Steyl he went to St. Gabriel's Mission Seminary in Mödling, near Vienna, where he completed upper secondary classes and philosophical and theological studies. In addition to some practical mission courses he took mission studies and mission history and was one of the best students in his class. He was ordained on February 25, 1899. St. Gabriel's, which had a teaching staff of high standing (it included among others the geologist Damian Kreichgauer and Stephan Richarz and the ethnologist Wilhelm Schmidt), awakened in Schwager a life-long fascinating for science.

The Young Priest

Schwager's first appointment was not the China mission, for which he had a "great inclination,"[4] but the secondary school in Steyl. As was then customary, the young teacher had to be competent in all subjects. In the course of time Schwager taught German, French, natural history, geography, arithmetic, mission history, world history, and Italian; from 1904, because of other responsibilities, only mission studies and German; and from the autumn semester of 1906, only mission studies.

From the very beginning Arnold Janssen (1837-1909), the founder of the missionary society to which Schwager belonged, placed great trust in the young priest. He asked him to write up reports about difficult problems. In 1900 he gave him the job of editing the *Kleiner Herz-Jesu Bote* (later renamed *Steyler Missionsbote*), the official organ of the "Steyl Missionaries." Schwager left his own mark on the publication. Immediately he introduced the section entitled "From the Church's Life," in which he often addressed controversial ecclesiastical and social issues. This section soon included non-European countries, not only S.V.D. missions but also continents and countries such as Africa, Assam, Nepal, China, Japan, Peru, and others. Consequently what began as a very simple publication for popular consumption developed into a missionary magazine that also appealed to an educated readership.

Through his editorial activities Schwager himself became well versed in "mission studies." "The four-volume work *Die katholische Heidenmission der Gegenwart im Zusammenhang mit ihrer grossen Vergangenheit* (The Catholic pagan missions of the present in connection with their great past), the fruit of his research at this time, became a widely quoted work in the developing Catholic discipline of missiology. On the occasion of the publication of the fourth volume, *Vorderindien und Britisch-Hinterindien*, we read in the *Steyler Missionsbote*: "This work, up to now the only comprehensive description of all the Indian missions, provides every friend of the missions with a handy compendium, and at such a very reasonable price (90 pfennigs) is within the reach of every pocket."[5]

Launching a Catholic Missiological Review

By 1908 Schwager was contemplating a Catholic missiological review, somewhat like the Protestant *Allgemeine Zeitschrift für Missionswissenschaft* published by Gustav Warneck.[6] Considering his poor state of health and convinced that a university professor rather than a religious priest would be more suited for this task, he turned to Professor M. Meinertz of Münster University,[7] who had made a name for himself in missionary circles through his work *Jesus und die Heidenmission*.[8] Meinertz in turn suggested the young lecturer Josef Schmidlin, who in the winter semester of 1909-10 taught modern mission history.[9] Schwager had to use some persuasion to get Schmidlin to agree. But in the end Schmidlin said yes and took up the project with his characteristic energy.[10] Schwager moved to Münster and helped Schmidlin as much as he could. On September 14, 1910, Schmidlin wrote to the S.V.D. superior general: "I can frankly say that more than anybody else it was a priest of your society, the very judicious and active Friedrich Schwager, who encouraged me to tackle missiology on a wider scale, and in particular to found a missiological review."[11]

The first number of *Zeitschrift für Missionswissenschaft* (published quarterly) came off the press March 1, 1911. Schwager was a member of the editing and managing committees, and he was listed on the title page as one of the fifteen professors and representatives of religious orders serving as coeditors. In the first year of publication he introduced a series entitled "Missionary Panorama" beginning with "The Present Situation of the Catholic Pagan Missions" and "Japan and

Korea"; he also wrote "Suggestions About Catholic Mission Statistics" and a book review. In the second year he contributed 104 out of a total of 354 pages. In subsequent years Schwager wrote, in addition to extensive "missionary panoramas," a number of programmatic essays under such tiles as "The Educational Activity in the Catholic Missions" (1913), "Expectations of the Geographic Sciences Addressed to Missionaries" (1913), "The Importance of a Work Ethic for the Advancement of the Primitive Masses" (1914), and "Catholic Missionary Activity and National Propaganda" (1916).

Schmidlin was delighted that the review was so well received – in 1912 there were 900 subscribers, and in 1913 more than 1,000.[12] Two years after its founding, on the occasion of the 150th anniversary of the Aschendorff Publishing House, he wrote that this could be ascribed "in the first place to the faithful help of our friends and collaborators, among whom must be mentioned Father Schwager and Father Streit in particular."[13] Laurenz Kilger, O.S.B., looking back on the first five years of the review, felt that these texts were "the most important and the most promising ever written in the field of missiology." In this connection he mentioned Schwager and Streit as the "most active pioneers of the movement."[14] From its sixth year, only Schwager and Streit were mentioned as coeditors.

New Missionary Movement

Schwager contributed directly to almost every initiative made on behalf of the new missionary movement in Germany ushered in by the 1909 Katholikentag (Catholic congress) in Breslau. He attended the meetings of the Missionary Committee formed subsequent to the Katholikentag. He was a member of the commission of experts for the compilation of the mission bibliography. He acted as secretary of the conference of editors of the *Zeitschrift für Missionswissenschaft.* He exercised influence on the conference of missionary superiors. Early in 1911 he spent time in Rome working in archives. He promoted the idea of a school for catechists for the German diaspora. He was elected for important committee work at the first general meeting of the International Institute for Missiological Research. At the missionary conference of the diocesan clergy of the diocese of Münster (1912), he gave the keynote lecture. Pointing out the interaction of church in the homeland and mission he declared: "Today in France those Catholics who were the staunchest friends of the missions are the most faithful supporters of the pauperized French clergy."[15] He advocated a professorship for Wilhelm Schmidt in Münster. He recommended the opening of a mission house for Czech youth. He passionately promoted the missiological formation of the clergy. The founding of the League for the Cultural Endeavors of the Catholic Missions was his initiative. He gave lectures at the Colonial Institute in Hamburg and spoke at the jubilee celebrations of the Catholic Union of Teachers in Essen.

Despite all these external activities he spent much time at his desk. He wrote letters, made suggestions, voiced his opinions, worked out plans, wrote up reports. He contributed regular reports about the missionary movement and missionary literature for the review *Theologie und Glaube* in Paderborn. In 1912 he wrote nine reviews for the *Zeitschrift für Missionswissenschaft,* the following year eleven, and in 1914 again eleven. On top of all this he still found time to write books.

As mentioned above, the work that established his reputation was *Die katholische Heidenmission der Gegenwart im Zusammenhang mit ihrer grossen Vergangenheit* (Steyl, 1907-9). It dealt with the missionary movement in the home countries (vol. 1), in Africa (vol. 2), in the Orient (vol. 3), and in India and British colonies in Southeast Asia (vol. 4). The review of this work in *Bibliotheca Missionum* emphasizes that the author does not confine himself to a description of the mere facts of past and present but everywhere searches for the strands linking the more recent with the distant past: "Particularly striking is the author's more profound conception of mission history. Besides, Schwager was the first to attempt to describe the missionary movement in the home countries."[16] The book was very widely read. Undoubtedly Friedrich Schwager was the ideal compiler of the "missionary panoramas" in the *Zeitschrift für Missionswissenschaft*.

When Arnold Janssen, founder of the Divine Word Missionaries, died, Schwager wrote his biography (1910). It would be surprising if everything had always gone smoothly between two such independent and energetic characters as Janssen and Schwager, but the relationship between the two men was characterized by mutual respect. About a year before Janssen's death Schwager wrote: "In the course of the past year my relationship to Father General has changed; I understand him better now and really respect him."[17] Referring to the biography, Robert Streit remarked: "It was filial piety and respect that created this biography and enables us to come close to the personality of the greatest promoter of missions in the home countries and gives us an insight into this Pauline soul aflame with missionary zeal.[18] Here too Schwager sets the personality of Janssen and the history of his foundation within the framework of the religious, ideological, political, social, and missionary movements of the time.

Educating for Missions

Promoting interest in missions in schools was a matter of consuming interest for Schwager. As an aid for teachers of religion, in 1912 he published *Die katholische Heidenmission im Schulunterricht* (Teaching about Catholic missions in schools). This met a long-felt need for Catholics; Protestants had the twelfth edition of Warneck's epoch-making work *Die Mission in der Schule* (Gütersloh: Bertelsmann, 1909). The idea behind Schwager's book was to present mission as an educational *principle* constituting a leitmotiv coloring all branches of religious instruction, even such subjects as history and geography. He admirably succeeded in bringing out the missionary dimensions of the various fields and illustrating them with concrete examples from the missions. His aim was not just to impart knowledge about mission; he wanted to foster love and theologically founded zeal for the missionary cause. The *Magazin für Pädagogik* wrote: "If anybody is competent to write about this so neglected field of learning, then it is Father Schwager, a name familiar to us from the 'Katholikentag' in Aachen. Missionary interest must be fostered among the people, and the only effective way to do this is through the school and church."[19]

Regarding women, both Janssen and Schwager were ahead of their times. Janssen maintained contact with the most mission-minded women of his time and founded two missionary congregations of women. Schwager wrote the booklet *Frauennot und Frauenhilfe in den Missionsländern* on the problems of women in mission countries as "an appeal to all Catholic women" (1914; Eng. trans., 1915). After the war, he wrote the biography of Emilie Huch, who dedicated her whole life to the poor and afflicted and rendered great service by supporting the foundation of the S.V.D. Holy Cross Mission House in Silesia. Alfons Väth, S.J., wrote of this woman: "Her zeal for souls embraced the whole world. She deserves a place of honor as a pioneer of the missionary idea in Germany. With the whole-hearted support of her husband, the publisher Franz Huch, this great promoter of the missions spent all her time and energy to help 'missionaries at the front.' "[20] More than most of his contemporaries, Schwager recognized the "unworthy situation of women" in particular in the Asian and African countries and worked for the dignity of women and against polygamy, the dissolution of marriage, and the killing of baby girls. He promoted the education of girls, the employment of nuns in the schools, and the spiritual formation of local women teachers. For a man of his time it was only logical to support also the Society for the Propagation of the Faith and the Society of the Holy Childhood, the "Africa Association," the St. Peter Claver Society, and the Missionary Association of Catholic Women.

Just before the war he published *Die brennendste Missionsfrage der Gegenwart. Die Lage der katholischen Missionen in Asien* (1914; Eng. trans., 1915). In writing this, he was able to draw from his vast store of knowledge about the missionary world. What strikes us most of all about this book is his treatment of Protestant missions. It was natural that the new Catholic missiology in many respects either drew from or polemicized against the "older sister," Protestant missiology. From the very start Schwager had read Protestant authors. In *Brennendste Missionsfrage* he did not criticize or polemicize, however. On the contrary, he saw a real challenge for Catholics in the vitality, single-mindedness, imaginativeness, spirit of sacrifice, and successes of Protestant missions: "This situation must no longer continue, and it will not continue as soon as the Catholic people in all countries recognizes the important and critical situations of our missions." And, "When we objectively consider the presence of the Protestants and the prospects of the Catholic missions, the anticipation of what threatens us should spur all Catholics to make the greatest possible efforts."[21] Obviously Schwager did not exactly like the Protestants, but this is genuine admiration, certainly not a polemic determined by prejudice.

The Postwar Period

Though the war years were less fruitful from a literary point of view, Schwager nevertheless let no grass grow under his feet. He concerned himself with the problem of the world war and nationalism. He condemned nationalistic war propaganda. He organized a missiological course for the secular clergy in Cologne (Sept. 5-7, 1916).[22] Schwager would not have been true to himself if he had steered clear of the embarrassing wrangle between Schmidlin and the Franziskus-Xaverius-Verein (Society for the Propagation of the Faith, Aachen). Like all the congregations, he opposed the monopolization attempts of that association, but he also came into conflict with Schmidlin, since he saw in him an obstacle to unity. Schmidlin sensed Schwager's mistrust and wrote to the S.V.D. superior general: "After all I have learnt about the very odd behavior of Father Schwager in recent times I cannot but conclude that he too is one of these agitators." This was no news to the superior general; Schwager had often complained to him about Schmidlin – always adding, however, "Please keep this to yourself – it might reach Schmidlin's ears!"[23]

One reason for his reserve toward Schmidlin was that Schwager was getting more and more involved in the discussions of the German Conference of Superiors. This body was working for reconciliation and, for the sake of peace, rejected some of Schmidlin's suggestions, much to the latter's consternation. His wrath was particularly directed at Schwager, who since 1918 was in actual practice and, since July 23, 1919, officially the general secretary of the conference. Schwager was aware of the dilemma inherent in his official position but had to make a choice: "When Schmidlin harms the common interest of the orders, I must at least be free to make suggestions in this respect to the Conference of Superiors, and insofar as his behavior makes it necessary pass on the information."[24]

A matter of great concern to all missionary circles in Germany, in particular to the missionary orders, was the return of German missionaries interned or expelled as a result of the war. These included 318 priests, 296 seminarians and brothers, and 326 nuns. As far as the orders were concerned, this was mainly the responsibility of the general secretary. He spoke at the conferences of superiors, sent telegrams, drew up petitions to the Holy Father and the cardinal prefect of Propaganda Fide, wrote to the superiors general and procurators general in Rome, made approaches to influential cardinals of the victorious powers, wrote to the Peace Conference in Paris, and appealed to the German and Austrian bishops to send as many telegrams as possible to the pope "in order to save the Austrian and German missions." On May 5, 1919, he wrote to his superior general: "My one and only worry now is saving the missions."[25] On the occasion of the second postwar conference of superiors (July 23, 1919), the chairman mentioned the "comprehensive, untiring activity of Father Schwager."[26] The S.V.D. superior general, however, felt he should try to put a brake on Schwager: "For the time being the Germans in Rome should keep a very low profile."[27]

In 1923 the question of transferring the general secretariat to Berlin from Sankt Augustin where Schwager lived came up. Though Schwager had always committed himself tirelessly to the interests of the secretariat – among other things by carefully preparing the mission course in Düsseldorf (1920), participating in the first World Congress of the Missionary Union of the Clergy in Rome (June 1-3, 1922), lecturing at national and international congresses (Vienna, Utrecht) – he was unable to go along with the transfer to Berlin. On January 27, 1923, he submitted his resignation. As reason, he mentioned his state of health, especially his nerves, which "simply forced" him "to drop all external activities for a long time, perhaps for ever."[28]

Move to the United States

From 1923, at which time he was residing at the S.V.D. Mission Seminary at Sankt Augustin near Bonn, we hear little about Schwager. On August 4, he was in Techny, Illinois, to participate in a mission conference of American students. Here he remained. He envisioned a missiological review in the United States. For health reasons he could not produce it himself, but he set his hopes on a young American confrere who was just beginning his training in the Society of the Divine Word. He formally requested a transfer to the North American province. Once again he became active in matters relating to mission and the society, giving missiological lectures in Techny and suggesting the inauguration of a chair of missiology in Washington.

Unfortunately, the idea of a missiological review was doomed to failure; the local superiors showed no interest. He was bitterly disappointed.

Declining an invitation from Sankt Augustin to return to Germany, he came to the decision to leave the S.V.D. and the Catholic Church and join the German Congregationalists in the United States. He communicated this to the superior general on January 11, 1925, and on January 24 took the actual step. In a letter to his friend Father Grendel, later superior general, he stated: "I cannot express how much it hurts me to cause such pain to you and others. But deep down I am completely at peace with myself, even if tears run down my cheeks as I write these lines."[29] Settling down in Redfield, South Dakota, he supported himself by working in the library of Redfield College. On April 18, 1925, he married. He died four years later, May 8, 1929, at the age of fifty-three.

There has been much speculation about the reasons why Schwager acted as he did – his overwrought nerves, his disappointments, his contact with Protestant literature, and so forth. But who can know what is going on in another person's mind? He himself wrote to Bruno Hagspiel, S.V.D.: "If they ask you again about my 'apostasy' tell them that though I have changed churches I have not changed my attitude to God and the Savior and that now I pray more and better. If I had done otherwise I would have sinned and lost my soul. Don't you think that a person who follows his conscience and, in order not to play the hypocrite, abandons a secure existence even though he is sick, deserves respect? He has no need to 'expiate' for taking such a step."[30]

Notes

1. Archives Generalate S.V.D., Rome (hereafter AG), D8.
2. Ibid.
3. W. Wegener to A. Janssen, September 23, 1889 (AG – A. Janssen 67.520).
4. End of June 1899 (AG – A. Janssen 69.610).
5. *Steyler Missionsbote* 36 (1908-9): 186.
6. This was a genuinely scholarly review of missions, first published in 1874. The monthly *Die Katholischen Missionen*, founded in 1873, contained solid missionary information but was not a scholarly publication in the strict sense of the term.

7. Meinertz was born in Braunsberg, East Prussia, in 1880. After a time of lecturing in Braunsberg, in 1908 he was appointed as successor to Prof. August Bludau in Münster. Even before he moved to Münster, Schwager corresponded with him about the founding of the review. See M. Meinertz, *Begegnungen in meinem Leben* (Münster, 1956).

8. *Jesus und die Heidenmission* (Münster: Aschendorffsche Verlagsbuchhandlung, 1908) was a biblical-theological study.

9. See K. Müller, *Josef Schmidlin (1876-1944). Papsthistoriker und Begründer der katholischen Missionswissenschaft* (Nettetal: Steyler Verlag – Wort und Werk, 1989), p. 69 n. 15.

10. See J. Schmidlin, "Was wir wollen," *Zeitschrift für Missionswissenschaft* (Münster; hereafter *ZM*) 1 (1911): 1-10.

11. AG – Missionswissenschaft.

12. *ZM* 6 (1916): 6, 3.

13. *ZM* 3 (1913): 70. From the start Robert Streit, who made a lasting name for himself through the *Bibliotheca Missionum*, was a comrade-in-arms and collaborator of the young movement of Catholic missiology.

14. *ZM* 6 (1916): 6, 3.

15. "Die pastoralen Mittel zur Hebung des heimsischen Missionssinnes," *ZM* 2 (1912): 282.

16. *Bibliotheca Missionum*, vol. 1, 2nd ed. (Rome: Herder, 1963), no. 2019.

17. AG – A. Janssen 64.650.

18. R. Streit, *Die katholische deutsche Missionsliteratur* (Aachen: Xaverius-Verlag, 1925), 2:151.

19. Quoted from the jacket of the book *Frauennot und Frauenhilfe in den Missionsländern*.

20. *Die katholischen Missionen* 48 (1919-20): 184.

21. *Brennendste Missionsfrage*, pp. 128, 66.

22. Cf. J. Schmidlin (ed.), *Missionswissenschaftlicher Kursus in Köln für den deutschen Klerus vom 5. bis 7. September 1916* (Münster: Aschendroff Verlag, 1916).

23. Schmidlin to Superior General Blum, December 23, 1918 (AG – Superiorenkonferenz).

24. Schwager to the Superior General, July 2, 1919 (AG – Superiorenkonferenz). Cf. Müller, *Schmidlin*, p. 213.

25. AG – Schwager.

26. AG – Superiorenkonferenz.

27. P. Blum to Schwager, October 23, 1919 (AG – Superiorenkonferenz).

28. AG – Superiorenkonferenz.

29. Letter of February 11, 1925 (AG – Schwager).

30. Schwager to B. Hagspiel, October 14, 1925 (AG – Schwager).

Selected Bibliography

Works by Friedrich Schwager

For a complete list of articles, reports, reviews, and book reports, see Karl Müller, *Friedrich Schwager. Pionier katholischer Missionswissenschaft* (Nettetal: Steyler Verlag – Wort und Werk, 1984), pp. 202-7.

1902 *Die katholische Mission in Südschantung.* Frankfurter Zeitgemässe Broschüren, 21/7. Hamm in Westfalen: Breer & Thiemann.

1907-9 *Die katholische Heidenmission der Gegenwart im Zusammenhang mit ihrer grossen Vergangenheit.* Vol. 1, *Das hiematliche Missionswesen* (1907); vol. 2, *Die Mission im afrikanischen Weltteil* (1908); vol. 3, *Die Orientmission* (1908); vol. 4, *Vorderindien und Britisch-Hinterindien* (1909). Steyl, Netherlands.

1910 *Arnold Janssen, Stifter und erster General der Steyler Missionsgesellschaft.* Frankfurter Zeitgemässe Broschüren, 30/1-2. Hamm in Westfalen: Breer & Thiemann.

1912 *Die katholische Heidenmission im Schulunterricht. Hilfsbuch für Katecheten und Lehrer.* Steyl. 2d ed., 1913.

1912 *Die Kulturtätigkeit der katholischen Missionen, besonders in den Jahren 1910 und 1911.* Essen: G.D. Baedeker. Offprint from *Jahrbuch über die deutschen Kolonien* 5.

1914 *Arnold Janssen, Founder and First Superior General of the Society of the Divine Word: A Sketch of His Life and Work.* Translated by Francis J. Tschan, A.M. Techny, Ill.

1914 *Die brennendste Missionsfrage der Gegenwart. Die Lage der katholische Missionen in Asien.* Steyl.

1914 *Frauennot und Frauenhilfe in den Missionsländern. Ein Weckruf an die katholische Frauenwelt.* Steyl.

1914 *The World Mission of the Catholic Church. A Text Book for the Teachers of Our Parochial Schools, Colleges, and Academies. First Book.* Techny.

1915 *The Most Vital Mission Problem of the Day.* Translated by Agatho Rolf, O.F.M.Cap. Techny.

1915 *Woman's Misery and Woman's Aid in Foreign Missions. An Appeal to Our Catholic Women.* Techny.

1919 *De Missie bij het Onderwijs. Handboek voor Priesters en Onderwijzers.* Nijmegen.

1920 *Der Düsseldorfer Missionskursus für Missionare und Ordenspriester, 7.-14. Oktober 1919. Vorträge, Aussprachen und Beschlüsse des Missionskurus.* Aachen: Xaverius-Verlag.

1920 *Emilie Huch. Ein Frauenbildnis aus dem neunzehnten Jahrhundert.* Aachen: Xaverius-Verlag.

Works about Friedrich Schwager

Müller, Karl Friedrich. *Friedrich Schwager (1876-1929): Pionier katholischer Missionswissenschaft.* Studia Instituti Missiologici S.V.D. 34. Nettetal: Steyler Verlag – Wort und Werk, 1984.

_____. *Josef Schmidlin (1876-1944). Papsthistoriker und Begründer der katholischen Missionswissenschaft.* Studia Instituti Missiologici S.V.D. 47. Nettetal: Steyler Verlag – Wort und Werk 1989. 441pp.

Florence Allshorn

1888–1950

We Are Made to Love as Stars Are Made to Shine

Eleanor Brown

Florence Allshorn? Who was she? . . . She seems hardly to belong in this gallery of missionary statesmen, writers, influential figures in the international church scene: this Englishwoman who was known to only a comparatively small circle, who wrote nothing for publication, who was only directly involved in the missionary enterprise for the twenty years between 1920 and 1940.

Yet J. H. Oldham, who must have met most of the outstanding missionary leaders of his day in his work for the International Missionary Council and the World Council of Churches, could say that of all of them Florence Allshorn was "one of the most remarkable": she "saw further than most into the meaning of the missionary task and the nature of its demands." Who then was this woman who made such an impact on men like Oldham and William Paton, secretary of the International Missionary Council who said of her: "I think she has the greatest spiritual insight of anyone I have ever known"?

Early Life

Allshorn's life had very inauspicious beginnings. She was only three when first her doctor father and then her mother died, and she and her two brothers were brought up in Sheffield, England, by a governess, a kind but undemonstrative lady of strict religious outlook. It was a home without brightness, stifling to a child with a naturally lively, beauty-loving temperament. Her brothers went away to boarding-school, and Florence had a lonely and cramped adolescence. This hard early experience gave her much sympathy later on with people who had been deprived of a happy home life, but it also gave her confidence in human courage and resilience. "You don't give people credit for enough courage," she would say to someone who was handing out enervating sympathy.

Florence's promising beginning at the Sheffield School of Art was cut short by serious eye trouble. After a rest of six months in almost complete darkness her sight improved enough for her to take a four-year course in domestic science, from which she emerged with a first-class diploma. She used to say later, in her training of missionaries, that she thought the disciplines of art and homecraft were especially valuable in that they taught one really to *look* at things (and people) appreciatively and objectively, and to express one's seeing practically.

The first influence to draw her into a living relationship with the church was that of Dr. Gresford-Jones (afterward bishop of Uganda), who came to work in Sheffield. He and his wife recognized at once in Florence an unusual potential, which in the warmth of their friendship quickly flowered into vivid life. She worked with them on the cathedral staff, enlivening factory girls and Sunday-school teachers alike. Forty years later one of them wrote of her, "She inspired every girl with her intense love of beauty, not only to look at, but beauty of mind and thought; and everything we did had to be of the very best."

At some time in these years she "fell in love with Christ's way of seeing things," as she sometimes put it, in a new way. In her letters to friends there comes a note of passionate longing for "the one supreme thing." "I'm not content with goodness and niceness and duty, which I've struggled for. Now I want Him." And with a prescient note: "I'm so troubled about not loving enough. I feel as if I'm not awake yet . . . I used to think that being nice to people and feeling nice was loving people. But it isn't, it isn't. Love is the most immense unselfishness and it's so big I've never touched it. I hope I shall have enough courage to *want* it even."

Uganda

In 1920 Florence was accepted by the Church Missionary Society for service in Uganda, and at the age of thirty-two found herself in charge of a girls' boarding-school at Iganga in Busoga country; they spoke no English and at the beginning she spoke no Luganda. The climate of Busoga is exceptionally unhealthy: in the early days Bishop Tucker had written of it that all nature seemed to be suffering from limpness and lack of energy. Seven young missionaries had been sent to Iganga in as many years, but none had stayed. The trouble was not only the climate but the temperament of their senior missionary, who had struggled on heroically but at considerable cost to herself and to anyone who tried to live with her.

The crucial battle of Florence's life, which was fought and won during the following years, is best told in her own words, written in letters to a close friend:

I need God so much here. Everything is so difficult. There is so much "ungoodness" in everything. I keep reminding myself that I am here for Christ and that all the wild and miserable things as well as the holy and calm ones must beat through me if I am to be used at all. And I thank God that I am here and that it is not easy. I always wanted that.

Florence Allshorn was a born educator in the true sense and, in the few years she was at Iganga, brought the school to a point that was described in the Phelps-Stokes Report on education as "first-rate." She discerned the potential for growth in her apparently slow and lethargic pupils, and could write, "It is a work fascinating in the extreme, full of hope always." Underneath the hard but rewarding work in the school, however, Florence was aware all the time of a basic failure, a failure in personal relationship that was undermining all that was being taught.

My colleague is a dear in some ways, but the matter of fact is that Iganga is a hopeless sort of place. My colleague has stuck it; it just happens not to have affected her health, but it has absolutely rotted her nerves, and she has the most dreadful fits of temper. Sometimes she doesn't speak at all for two days. Just now we've finished up three weeks with never a decent word or smile! [And then, typically:] I'm sure it isn't the right thing just to leave her to it.

She was almost in despair. The children were fully aware that the atmosphere was wrong; words about the love and power of Christ sounded hollow. She had come to the crisis of her life. What followed is told in her own words:

One day the old African matron came to me when I was sitting on the verandah crying my eyes out. She sat at my feet and after a time she said: "I have been on this station for fifteen years and I have seen you come out, all of you saying you have brought us a Savior, but I have never seen this situation saved yet." It brought me to my senses with a bang. I was the problem for myself. I knew enough of Jesus Christ to know that the enemy was the one to be loved before you could call yourself His follower, and I prayed, in great ignorance as to what it was, that this same love might be in me, and I prayed as I have never prayed before in my life for that one thing. Slowly things rightened. Whereas before she had been going about upsetting everybody with long deep dreadful moods, and I had been going to my school depressed and lifeless, both of us found our way to lighten each other. She had a great generosity and I must have been a cruel burden to her, worn out as she was. But I did see that as we two drew together in a new relationship the whole character of the work of the station altered . . . The children felt it and began to share in it, and to do little brave unselfish things that they had never done before.

For a whole year Florence read 1 Corinthians 13 every day. Though she rarely spoke of this experience again, her later teaching of missionary students was founded on it, and in a talk given on the eve of her last illness, the hard-won truth is in every sentence:

To love a human being means to accept him, to love him as he is. If you wait to love him till he has got rid of his faults, till he is different, you are only loving an idea. He is as he is now; I can only love a person by allowing myself to be disturbed by him as he is. I must accept the pain of seeing him with hopefulness and expectancy.

To the end of her life she accepted the pain of seeing with hopefulness, suffering frustration and disappointment often, but never denying her central belief that "we are made to love as the stars are made to shine."

Training of Missionaries

When Florence returned to England on leave at the end of four grueling years, she was found to have a cavity in one lung. Having lost her mother and her much-loved brother through tuberculosis, it felt like a death sentence. But she had a strong faith that, as she said, "God is with life, and sickness is the enemy." She refused an operation, which would have meant living with one lung, and set her purpose toward healing. In one of her later talks she referred to this experience:

Faith is not an easy thing to come by. You are fortunate if you have been ill enough to think that only faith will save you. Then you have to have it, when your body is saying the opposite. You can gull yourself about the soul, not the body. To believe that God is stronger than the enemy and he has looked on you, His creation, and said, "It is very good."

After a winter in Switzerland and a year in a curious little colony of "dropouts" in the Sussex countryside – a year of bohemian existence that she found fascinating and freeing – Florence Allshorn was sufficiently recovered to work again, though she had to contend with precarious health for the rest of her life. At this point the Church Missionary Society (CMS) invited her to fill a temporary gap in one of their two small training colleges for women missionaries. The CMS did not know what the "temporary appointment" was going to mean. In the next eleven years Florence was to effect a quiet revolution in the whole concept of missionary training, a revolution whose effects have been spreading ever since, and which has changed the attitudes of people who never knew her. This was partly because she brought a completely fresh mind to the situation. She had never had missionary training herself; she was not greatly interested in church controversies or parties; her Christianity was founded more on her personal experience than on family influences. She had no academic qualifications for the post, only a quick and penetrating intelligence, wide reading, and a natural grasp of the essentials in a given situation. Above all she had learned in a hard school the meaning of those three words so often emptily used in Christian teaching: Faith, Hope, and Love. Armed with these not-always-available qualifications for a trainer of missionaries, she threw herself into her new work.

To begin with, Allshorn's unorthodox approach alarmed the more conservative elements in the CMS, and it was probably only because some of the secretaries recognized her rare qualities that she was allowed to continue. Suspicions gradually died down as those persons who were worried by her "liberal" ideas at one moment found themselves challenged at the next by her single-minded devotion to Christ. When the two colleges were amalgamated in 1934, she was appointed principal of the combined institution.

Allshorn's quiet revolution was not primarily in changes in the curriculum, but in her conception of what was the essential purpose of the training. She enlisted the help of excellent lecturers and broadened the range of speakers on topics of the day; she developed the practical training – all things that are a usual part of training. Underlying all this was her burning conviction that the prime necessity was for the Christian witness to be *real*. Her years in Africa has shown her the inadequacy of conventional religion up against the reality of conflicting personal relationships. This was by no means only a projection of her own experience. Her clear eyes had made her aware of what she called "the silent disasters" that went on in many missionary lives underneath all the hard work and the building up of successful institutions: the loss of vision, the hardening of attitudes, the acceptance of mediocre standards.

Florence Allshorn's first aim was to develop in her students some real experience in holding together belief and action, theory and practice. Far more important to her than any technical or academic training (though she valued both) was that they should be growing in their love for God and their capacity to live with their fellow students. She considered doctrine to be "of such importance that it must not be separated from the rest of the programme. Its position in this training is that it is related directly to the total experience of each person. The truths we know and teach must be 'proved upon the pulses.'" So pious words in chapel followed by complacent or contemptuous attitudes in conversation would meet her quick challenge; lofty sentiments about beauty would be held up against sloppy standards of practical work; new insights into the great Christian truths emerged from discussion of some small-seeming argument or breakdown in the common life.

For many of Allshorn's students it was a revelation of the wholeness of life. Everything was to come under the discipline of Christ's two great commandments; but within that discipline there was a sense of freedom to learn, to grow, to take risks, to rebel, to have fun. Florence's deep seriousness about basic issues was balanced by an irrepressible gaiety. As one of her friends said, unlike the self-conscious obedience that in many of us drains life of color, "her obedience put the color into life, and enabled others to see a new world, informed by beauty and light." "Religion to me really is *a song*," she said one day. She was an artist rather than a moralist in her approach to people, and she had the patience of an artist as well as the artist's care for perfection. "I do feel that Protestantism works too much on a subconscious feeling of suspicion – possibly because it is so concerned with sin – that it loses the vision of the lovely thing a human soul really is."

It was just because of the possibilities Florence Allshorn saw in the young women coming into training that she was able to confront head-on not their own weaknesses but what she felt to be the unfaced failures of the mission field. "I believe our great trouble is that we won't stir up courage to look at *failure*." In her only published article, "Corporate Life on a Mission Station," she set out forcefully what she saw the failure to be:

The failures amongst missionaries are those who have lost the forward vital impulse, the life of the Spirit, because they have never got through their own spiritual, personal and social problems. This may be due either to the fact that they were the wrong kind to send out – people whose spiritual life was unreal – or because they have become caught in the cog of the mechanical routine of too much work, and have become exhausted and unable to deal with their problems. Failing to find success in their spiritual and mental life they are seeking it by putting almost all their vitality into "the job." But womanhood may not do that. Womanhood means more than a bright vision of success in a job; it means patience and longsuffering and the deepening of gentlenesses; it means going down into deep places.

In this article, much of which is relevant fifty years later, she goes on to speak of how, in training, the emotional life of the student has been left to take care of itself – "this queer hinterland where there huddle the anxieties, timidities, antagonisms, self-deceptions, which somehow our spiritual life does not go deep enough to touch." Florence was considerably ahead of her time in getting all the help she could from psychology, and some of the books that are now considered classics were on her shelves soon after they appeared. But what she read only confirmed her growing conviction that any deep change in a person needs time. She was finding as the years went on that the year allotted to missionary training was only the first stage of a process. "You really cannot do much in the initial training," she wrote to a colleague. "They have not come to the end of themselves; you can only gently try to make them more real."

The first furlough was crucial: watching her own students coming home after what was often a very testing first tour, Florence saw that as well as those who seemed satisfied with their life and service, there were "those who had gone out on a big spiritual adventure, but rather immature in Christ and found they could not cope." For these especially it was necessary to have time for quiet thought and for guidance from someone further on, for regripping their vision in a deeper way.

But what was happening (what still happens) was that they were being plunged into a succession of courses, conferences, and meetings at which they had to give a "good" picture of their work, all conspiring to mask the things that were troubling them; so that often they returned to the same situation no further along, more likely than ever to be dominated by obvious needs, and to stop growing – in Florence's eyes the only real defeat.

With her usual incisiveness Florence Allshorn wrote in a memorandum:

> Some very clear thinking has to be done about what is real vocation. If they go out primarily to do medical work then obviously the first claim on their time when they come home is the renewal of their medical knowledge, and consultation with doctors who can help them. If they go out *primarily* as ambassadors for Christ, then surely the first claim on their time and energies is this period of readjustment to Him and fresh vision of Him. and nothing must be allowed to take its place.

Toward Community

It was largely her awareness of this need which led Florence Allshorn to resign from the Church Missionary Society training and to launch into the final, the hardest, and the most creative adventure of her life: the founding of St. Julian's Community in Sussex. She expressed some first thoughts about this in a letter to her old students:

> I want to do something where I can still go on serving you with what I have of experience and real caring for you. I have a dream of a house in some lovely quiet place where you could come and be quiet and rest and read and talk – where things could be refreshed and recreated before you went off on your new courses . . . Also for Church people at home who go on and on and on in the same rut.

Beneath this thought was another, which was pressing increasingly on Florence Allshorn's attention, and which was to become the dominant aim of the St. Julian's experiment. For some time she, like many others, had believed that the Christian witness needed by the twentieth-century world was not so much that of outstanding individuals as of groups committed to working together. She saw also that, while this was happening to a certain degree, there was almost always a sticking point, where human conflicts became too strong, and the group foundered or retreated to a diluted "putting up with each other," which in reality signaled defeat. She felt the need of a center where some would make the attempt to break past the point at which most people draw back.

The story of that attempt is told in Oldham's biography, *Florence Allshorn and the Story of St. Julian's*. Nothing illustrates more powerfully Florence's unique blend of originality, single-minded devotion to an ideal, and clear-eyed realism than the bringing of her purpose into being. In the darkest years of World War II, with little money and against active dissuasion from her advisers, she gathered three companions to begin a dual enterprise: to make a place of physical and spiritual refreshment for hard-pressed men and women, and to discover at depth the meaning of love in relationship. It seemed an exciting adventure as they hunted for a place in which to begin, and as they settled into an inconvenient but rent-free house in the lovely Surrey countryside.

They wrote together later:

We were very green, and did not realize the deep selflessness that was required of everyone. We were overburdened with self-centredness to an extent that we only began to realize when we got going. What kept us together was not that we immediately got on together. We did not. What carried us together was that we had said that we would not leave if we found ourselves in a bad patch, and that we would not accept defeat.

They were all people who had previously got on quite well with others in ordinary relationships; but now, living at very close quarters with none of the usual escape routes, and determined not to make "easy adjustment at a surface level," they were thrust down to a much deeper level, the level of conflicting wills and temperaments, which is so often the arena of human disaster. They had to get beyond "the sticking point," "the check that comes in human relationships," as Florence put it. "At times it seemed intolerable," one of the group wrote later.

We know hate and malice and that dreadful desire to hit back hard if we have been hurt . . . Such deep resentment, perhaps, that one knew that one could not forgive, and yet saying everyday the Lord's Prayer . . . When people talk about starting communities we look at each other. They seem to us like people starting for the North Pole without even knowing that they need a warm coat.

Through all the difficulties the four held together, gradually becoming a real community united in a common purpose and in a growing experience of "the peace which lies at the other side of conflict." From the beginning the house was filled with people of all sorts, both individuals and groups, grateful for an oasis of peace and order in the harshness of wartime Britain, and also looking for help in their own relationships. The community began to discover that, in a way they hardly understood, their guests seemed to find renewed strength and fresh vision just when their own struggles were most acute. This gave them confidence that they were being led in the right way, untried as it was.

Within three years the experiment was sufficiently established for a Trust to be formed and a larger house to be bought on a mortgage. The community grew to eight and then twelve, and launched into the running of a farm and the beginning of a children's house. This was accomplished during the exigencies of the war and of the drab war-weary period that followed it. Those of us who came to stay at St. Julian's Community can still remember the sense of vitality, of gaiety of spirit that met us, as well as the warmth of hospitality and the ordered beauty of the house and garden, somehow achieved in those penurious years: a quality of living that communicated the hope and grace of God much more effectively than words.

By the end of the decade the lovely old house at Barns Green was becoming too cramped for its purpose, and at the beginning of 1950 the community moved to its present location at Colham, near Horsham in Sussex, a spacious house, with outbuildings and cottages, in beautiful grounds looking out over a lake and wide fields, to the South Downs. It was a brave and risky act of faith, fraught with financial difficulties, but has proved to be a most blessed one for the community and the thousands of people who have visited it since then, not only for rest and quiet but to work alongside the community, learning from them and with them.

Florence was undaunted as one seemingly insuperable obstacle after another was surmounted. When the move to Sussex was finally accomplished, she wrote to a friend in Africa: "You'll love this place when you come home. It could be a lovely place for God's children for a hundred years." But Florence was not well; in May she developed an acutely irritating skin rash, which was finally diagnosed as Hodgkin's disease, and after some weeks of very painful illness she died on July 3, 1950. She was sixty-two.

It was a desolating shock to the community and all the friends for whom Florence Allshorn had been a strength, a challenge, and a light. Many thought that St. Julian's could hardly continue without her. But Florence had the ability, often lacking in strong personalities, to inspire rather than control; and because the inspiration came through her from beyond herself, from the Master she loved, it did not die with her. Many of the experiments in communal living that were made in the postwar years have passed into oblivion. But the strong foundations that were laid at much cost by Florence and her companions have enabled St. Julian's Community to live and grow, through the years since her death, as a center of refreshment and re-creation for men and women of many walks of life and varying religious allegiances, or of none. Many things have altered in those years, in response to changing needs and new insights; most of the present community never knew Florence "in the flesh," but they still keep steadfast in their living witness to "the peace that lies on the other side of conflict" and to the healing alchemy of love.

In Florence's last address, given when she was already ill, she spoke of something she had "proved upon the pulses":

> It is a hard way, but everyone who has known this "losing your life to find it" tells us how, as the mind and desire go the way of self-naughting more simply and readily with practice, you do know that you are living in a new and fresh world: that at the root of you, instead of the old unease, the old feeling of guilt, the lovelessness, there is a content happy shining, whatever comes. If God is love, and we were made to love as the stars were made to shine, then every creature is desirous of finding this disinterested love.

This faith lived out within a small company is the legacy of Florence Allshorn to all those who were and are willing to receive it.

Bibliography

Although Florence Allshorn wrote nothing specifically for publication, some of her writings have been published.

Allshorn, Florence, "Corporate Life on a Mission Station." *International Review of Missions* 23 (October 1934): 497-511. An address given at a Church Missionary Society Conference, also published as a separate pamphlet.

_____. *The Notebooks of Florence Allshorn.* Selected and Arranged by a Member of St. Julian's Community. London: SCM Press, 1957.

Oldham, J.H. *Florence Allshorn and the Story of St. Julian's.* London: SCM Press, 1957.

Potts, Margaret I. *St. Julian's: An Experiment in Two Continents.* London: SCM Press, 1968.

W.A. Visser 't Hooft

1900–1985

"No Other Name"

Lesslie Newbigin

Willem Adolf Visser 't Hooft (Wim to all friends and colleagues) is widely remembered and honored as the first general secretary and (in large measure) the architect of the World Council of Churches. It is less often remembered that his central passion from beginning to end of his active life was for the missionary faithfulness of the church.

Visser 't Hooft was born in 1900 in Harlem in the Netherlands into a distinguished family. His grandfather was a judge, and his father a lawyer. In the "Declaration" made at his ordination he said: "The home in which I was brought up was one in which there were firm moral beliefs but where Christianity was something very undefined." As a schoolboy he read voraciously and was soon a master of Latin, Greek, English, French, and German. The minister who prepared him for confirmation was a Hegelian much given to religious speculation, and (according to his own testimony) Wim "was on the verge of becoming a syncretist." But other influences, three in particular, were to turn him in another direction.

Early, Critical Influence

The first was the Dutch Student Christian Movement, which introduced him to Christianity not as a matter of speculation but as a personal call from the Lord Jesus Christ with the challenge to give his life to him. The second was his meeting, as a student, with John R. Mott. As a young YMCA secretary, he recalled how Mott "captivated me by his massive faith and the breadth of his vision." Forty years later Visser 't Hooft was still reminding students of "the common obligation of all churches to finish the unfinished task of the evangelization of the world." The third event that shaped the whole of the rest of his career was his encounter with Karl Barth in the *Epistle to the Romans*. His theological training had introduced him to a range of critical, historical, sociological, and philosophical questions about religion but had not helped him to find a clear standpoint, a criterion of truth. Barth did that for him. "This was a man who proclaimed the death of all the little comfortable gods and spoke again of the living God of the Bible . . . This was the message for which I had been waiting."[1]

In 1924 Visser 't Hooft completed his theological studies, married Henrietta Boddaert, and moved to Geneva to work for the YMCA in its newly established department for boys' work. From this point onward, Geneva was to be his home as he was called in succession to the leadership of the World's Student Christian Federation and the World Council of Churches. Their family – a daughter and two sons – were to be born and grow up in Geneva, and it was there that Wim lived in very active retirement till his death in 1985.

From Mott, Visser 't Hooft had caught the vision and the passion of a world mission, to bring the Gospel to every nation. From Barth he had learned to distinguish that Gospel as the very word of the living God from the mish-mash of religious and philosophical ideas that formed so much of the "Christianity" of Europe. In his early years in Geneva he came under the influence of J.H. Oldham – the creative mind behind the Edinburgh Conference of 1910 and the International Missionary Council. Oldham had become convinced that the most formidable adversary confronting the Gospel was no longer to be found among the world religions, which had occupied the attention of the Edinburgh Conference, but in the secularism that had overwhelmed the old Christendom and was beginning to take over the rest of the world; the Jerusalem conference of 1928 had this in the center of its attention but gave the suggestion that the world religions might be regarded as in some sense allies in confronting this new adversary.

Contending with the Syncretism of the West

For Visser 't Hooft, intellectually fired by Barth, this was no way forward. Oldham did not find in the missionary agencies the vision to recognize and deal with this new situation. He sought support in the Life and Work movement, which had flowed from the Stockholm Conference of 1925. Visser 't Hooft became one of Oldham's allies. He never ceased to demonstrate his commitment to the enterprise of "foreign missions," as many of his writings and speeches show, but he also saw that this enterprise had been corrupted by the fact that Western churches were hopelessly compromised by syncretism. They had allowed the Gospel to be confused with European culture, with all kinds of philosophy and with ideologies such as democracy in the Anglo-Saxon world and nationalism in Europe. To use one of his favorite images, the voice of the one Good Shepherd was either drowned out or confused by other voices.

From his position as general secretary of the World's Student Christian Federation, Wim was in touch with the ablest young people in all parts of the world, and he used his position to issue an unrelenting challenge to the coming generation to give their absolute allegiance to Christ and to him alone. His first major work of Christian apologetic was entitled *None Other Gods*. The West, he argued, owes its spiritual substance to Christianity, but there is no longer a "Christian West." There is a syncretistic mix of Christianity and pagan beliefs. The churches are deeply compromised. Now, he wrote, "Everything depends on the existence among Christians of a deep consciousness of the peculiar mission of Christianity. And it is precisely in such times that the Christian Church should re-affirm the sovereignty of its Lord over all life."[2]

When he first visited the United States he found the same syncretism but with a different form of paganism, in which "democracy was identified with the Kingdom of God" because (as Americans seemed to think) "God is found as individuals find themselves in the great cooperative enterprise of human progress."[3] He found the same syncretism in the famous "Laymen's Report on Foreign Missions," which he discussed in a scathing article in *The Student World* under the title "Spineless Mission."

As the clamor of the pagan ideologies became louder, Visser 't Hooft saw the calling of Christian students more clearly. "There are two decisive questions for us Christians to face today: are we witnesses, and thus forcing men to make their own choices for or against the call of God?

And, is our witness to Jesus Christ so clear that no one can mistake it for the voice of one or other of the new deities?"[4] It must now be clear that "the normal task of a Christian is to share in the evangelistic task of the Church."[5]

Championing the Witness of Unity

The corollary of this passionate concern that the word of the Gospel should be set free from its entanglement with the many words of men was an equally passionate concern for the unity of Christians. How can the world hear the voice of the Good Shepherd if the church consistently ignores it and insists on dividing into separate flocks whose respective identities are defined by nationalist or by some other human and cultural commitment? How can churches which find their identity more in their nationhood than in the Gospel possibly be faithful witnesses to the Gospel?

In a powerful address delivered in the early years of the war to the Basel Mission, entitled "Mission als ökumenische Tat," he affirmed that the freedom of the Gospel is only truly acknowledged when the church is free to be truly the *Una Sancta*, free from its compromising alliances with national cultures. Its unity must be a tension-filled unity that can include great cultural diversity in an overriding allegiance to the one Lord.[6] Speaking to a Western-based missionary society, he reminded his hearers that missionaries in non-Western societies will have a true discernment of the dangers of syncretism only if they have first been liberated from the syncretism endemic in the national churches of Europe. Only as the church is one across national frontiers can it witness to the royal freedom of the Gospel. At that moment, Visser 't Hooft could point to a fine illustration of his theme. The "Orphaned Missions" program of the International Missionary Council was enabling Christians to support the missionary work of those with whom they were at war.

But the link between world mission and Christian unity was, for Visser 't Hooft, something that worked in both directions. If authentic missionary witness required unity, it was also true that unity required active missionary commitment. The unique and universal lordship of Christ is obscured when a church is content to live within the frontiers of its own society. Foreign missions have therefore a permanent role in the life of any church that wishes to give faithful witness to the universal lordship of Christ. They are a necessary safeguard against the perennial temptation of the church to allow the Gospel to be domesticated within the life of a nation. And so, to a decidedly skeptical audience at the WSCF Conference in Strasbourg (1960), Visser 't Hooft affirmed his belief that "foreign missions reflect the truly cosmic character of the lordship of Christ. Every church which is able to do so must, therefore, take part in this form of specific witness to the universality of the Gospel."[7] The mission is indeed the mission of the entire *Una Sancta,* but this does not mean the end of "foreign missions," and neither "world development" nor "interchurch aid" can replace them.

This conviction was brought out most sharply at a WSCF meeting in 1949, when Visser 't Hooft was challenged by the young K.H. Ting, who asked: "Why go to faraway places? Is the task of evangelism not the task of the local church?" Visser 't Hooft replied: "Why not?" and he did not hesitate to draw a tough conclusion.

If there is a country where a Christian church has been planted, a relatively new church, and that church says "We want to do the job ourselves" (it is clear that it cannot do so) – what happens? I do not think that any church has the right to close the door to any part of the world. The rest of the Christian world will have to talk with that church and force the door. That is true for all churches in all parts of the world. Missions is a responsibility, a world-wide responsibility for the total Christian evangelization of the world, which goes beyond inter-church aid.[8]

This very tough stance had to be considered in a different context when Visser 't Hooft, as secretary of the WCC, had to deal with the bitter complaints of the Orthodox churches of the Middle East against the activities of Protestant missions from the Anglo-Saxon world who were recruiting members from the Orthodox fold. And, in another context, he was deeply concerned with the problem of religious liberty as it affected the minority Protestant churches in Roman Catholic countries.

While adamant about the permanent necessity of foreign missions, Visser 't Hooft was well aware of the factors that have made foreign missionaries the object of severe and justified criticism. He saw the root of the trouble in the syncretism of Western Christianity, which led missionaries into being the agents of cultural colonialism rather them simply witnesses of the Gospel. While unrelenting in his attack on the relativism that invaded a syncretistic European Christianity, he was compelled to wrestle with the question of religious liberty, especially during the years of the Second Vatican Council. Evangelism needs a measure of religious freedom and therefore religious pluralism, or at least religious plurality, while the Christian missionary must proclaim the total lordship of Jesus over all life. Its raison d'être is to bring all men and women to Christ.[9] Nevertheless Visser 't Hooft was able to see positive possibilities in pluralism. "Pluralism, rightly understood, creates for the Church a situation in which it is less in danger of falsifying its own nature, and in which it is better able to manifest its true calling. Pluralism provides the Church with a God-given opportunity to live according to its own inherent spiritual law . . . The church is in the right place, the normal position when, according to Pascal, it is supported only by God."[10] True evangelism will be distinguished from proselytism by the fact that when the authentic voice of the Good Shepherd is heard, those who hear it will seek to be one flock.

Visser 't Hooft's intellectual and spiritual formation was obviously in the European context. His book *The Kingship of Christ*, published in 1948, was primarily concerned with issues in the life of the Western and particularly European churches. It was a powerful affirmation of the sovereignty of Christ over the worlds of politics and economics and the whole of public life. The same year saw the inauguration of the World Council of Churches (in process of formation since 1939), and from that time onward he was necessarily drawn much more deeply into the problems of the churches of Asia, Africa, and Latin America. He recognized their need to develop their thought and life in contexts very different from that of Europe. His acute awareness of the syncretism that infected the European churches made him cautious in welcoming moves toward "indigenous" theologies in Asia. He took as a model for the proper relation of the missionary to the indigenous culture his friend Hendrik Kraemer's work in Indonesia. "He [Kraemer] considers that the real missionary is one who is completely bound to the Gospel, but who, precisely for the sake of the Gospel, seeks to enter as fully as possible into the spiritual life of the people to whom he is sent."[11] He wanted the churches of Asia and those of the West to enter into a life of mutual correction, a life in which there would be tension between different cultural expressions of the Gospel but in which all would profit by the correction offered by others. All this presupposes, of course, the absolute supremacy of the one Good Shepherd.

He is clear that the Christian message is not to be formulated as an answer to the questions that people (in any society) ask.

The foundation of Christianity is a question asked by God. On the first page of the Bible God calls Adam: Adam, where art thou? and the story of God's dealing with men is, as it were, a constant echo of this first call. In Christ's life we find again and again that he overrules the questions put to him by a new, a more decisive question, namely that of their relationship to God and to himself. The turning points of his dealings with his disciples are questions: "But who do you say that I am?" "Simon, lovest thou me?" To be a Christian is to take those questions more seriously than any other, to see one's whole life as an attempt to answer the call which is implied.[12]

Achieving Authentic Accommodation

Visser 't Hooft gave reasons for rejecting the term "indigenization." "Contextualization" is a word coined only in 1972 after the period of his active involvement. He preferred the term "accommodation." How, he asked, and by what criteria are we to test proposals for "accommodation"? He listed four. First, does this new presentation interpret the Gospel in the light of the Bible as a whole, or does it take only those bits of the whole canon that can be fitted easily into the new frame? Does it recognize that the New Testament is radically misunderstood if it is taken apart from the Old? Second, does the new presentation tell the great deeds of God? The Bible is not a book of religion but the history of God's mighty acts. In every culture this history must be told. Third, does the message in its new form make clear that the Gospel is concerned with the personal encounter with the living God and with the formation of a community based on this encounter? If this does not happen, if there is a compromise with impersonal ideas of God, then the church becomes the sugar, not the salt, of the world.[13] Fourth, does the message in its new form fill the local cultural or religious concepts (which have to be used) with biblical substance and so revolutionize them? Is the accommodation, in Kraemer's phrase, "subversive fulfilment" that fills old words and concepts with new biblical meaning?[14] He quotes as supreme examples the ways in which Paul and John, in bringing the Gospel from its Hebrew origins into the world of Greek thought, use Greek words but fill them with a new meaning that is determined by the history of God's doings in and for Israel. If this "subversive fulfilment" does not take place, the result can only be confusion.

Alert as he always was to the danger of syncretism, Visser 't Hooft had no doubt about the necessity of expressing the Gospel in terms of the local culture. He was horrified to find the East Asia Christian Conference singing the hymns of Moody and Sankey (and D.T. Niles's EACC hymnal was the result of his wrathful explosion), but he was always most aware of the syncretism of Western Christianity and insisted that the Western churches needed the correction that could come from other local theologies. But he insisted that this mutual correction would take place only if the dialogue between the churches was conducted on the basis of the absolute supremacy of the Bible as the norm by which all theologies were to be tested.

Visser 't Hooft saw that this potentially fruitful dialogue between Eastern and Western churches was complicated by the fact that all societies were being increasingly dominated by the science, technology, and political ideas originating in the West. So there is a special burden of responsibility resting on the Western churches. They have not themselves learned to face the problems created by the kind of civilization that they have helped to export to the rest of the world. Christians in Europe are therefore on a missionary frontier.

> European culture has become a debate between three forces: Christianity, scientific rationalism and neo-pagan vitalism. For a long time it had seemed that scientific rationalism would take the lead. But recently the picture has changed. The atomic threat, the terrible pollution, the lack of meaningful perspectives which the technocratic civilization has brought, have led to the growth of a new irrationalism . . . The lay-preachers of paganism in the period between the two world-wars, D.H. Lawrence and Hermann Hesse, are more widely read than before.[15]

Visser 't Hooft was going against the stream, and he knew it. He comments sarcastically on Bishop John Robinson's attempt to enlist D.H. Lawrence as an ally of Christianity and asks what Lawrence would have had to write to convince the bishop that he was not. He saw Europe sinking still deeper into the mire of relativism. His book *No Other Name*, published in 1963, was one more powerful statement of the uniqueness, the decisiveness, and the finality of Jesus Christ. In the same year he addressed the Mexico Conference of the WCC's Commission on World Mission and Evangelism under the title "Mission as the Test of Faith." "Faith is tested in various ways," he said, "but there is no more decisive test than the one concerning the translation of faith into missionary witness. A central question in the great examination is: Are you ready in all circumstances to proclaim that Christ is the Lord?"[16] The test of the real faith of a church is its obedience to the call for missionary obedience among all the nations. He quotes a range of the most influential thinkers of our time to show their total rejection of the Christian faith. The world, he says, is simply doing its job; we have no reason to be surprised. So let the church do its job with a single attention to its one sovereign Lord.

Notes

1. *Memoirs* (1973), pp. 15-16.
2. *None Other Gods*, p. 110.
3. Ibid., p. 19.
4. *The Student World* 26, no. 4 (1933): 361.
5. Ibid., 27, no. 4 (1934): 191.
6. "Mission als Oekumenische Tat," *Evang. Missions-Magazin*, September 1941, p. 138.
7. *The Student World*, 54, nos. 1-2 (1961), p. 34.
8. WSCF Missionary Consultation, Rolle, 1949, typescript in WCC archives, pp. 7-8.
9. *Ecumenical Review* 18 (April 1966): 144.
10. Ibid., p. 145.
11. Introductory note in *From Mission Field to Independent Church*, by Hendrik Kraemer (1958), p. 8.
12. *None Other Gods*, p. 126.
13. "Accommodation, True or False," *South East Asia Journal of Theology* 8, no. 3 (January 1967): 9.
14. Ibid., p. 10.
15. *International Review of Mission* 66 (October 1977): 355.
16. *Witness in Six Continents*, Ronald Kenneth Orchard, ed. (London: Edinburgh House Press, 1964), pp. 21-22.

Selected Bibliography

Works by W.A. Visser 't Hooft

1933 *Le Catholicisme non-Romain*. Paris: Cahiers de Foi et Vie. English trans., *Anglo-Catholicism and Orthodoxy: A Protestant View*. London: SCM Press.
1937 *None Other Gods*. London: SCM Press.
1948 *The Kingship of Christ: An Interpretation of Recent European Theology*. New York: Harper.
1953 *The Meaning of Ecumenical*. London: SCM Press.
1956 *The Renewal of the Church*. Philadelphia: Westminster Press; and London: SCM Press.
1959 *The Pressure of Our Common Calling*. New York: Doubleday.
1963 *No Other Name: The Choice Between Syncretism and Christian Universalism*. London: SCM Press.
1973 *Memoirs*. London: SCM Press; and Philadelphia: Westminster Press. 2nd ed. Geneva: WCC, 1987.
1982 *The Fatherhood of God in an Age of Emancipation*. Geneva: WCC.
1982 *The Genesis and Formation of the World Council of Churches*. Geneva: WCC.

Visser 't Hooft's papers are in the archives of the World Council of Churches, Geneva, where there is also a full list of his books and articles, numbering about 1,275 items.

Works about W.A. Visser 't Hooft

Van der Bent, Ans J., ed. *Voices of Unity: Essays in Honour of Willem Adolf Visser 't Hooft on the Occasion of His Eightieth Birthday*. Geneva: WCC, 1981.
Chirgwin, A.M. *These I Have Known: William Temple, William Paton, W.A. Visser 't Hooft, Martin Niemöller*. London: London Missionary Society, 1964.
Gerard, F. "The Concept of Renewal in the Thought of W.A. Visser 't Hooft." Ph.D. diss., Hartford Seminary Foundation, 1969.
Mulder, D.C. "'None Other Gods' – 'No Other Name.'" *Ecumenical Review* 38, no. 2 (April 1986): 209-15.
Nelson, J. Robert, ed. *No Man Is Alien: Essays on the Unity of Mankind*. Leiden: Brill, 1971.

Part Two

AFRICA

John Philip

Samuel Ajayi Crowther

David Livingstone

H.P.S. Schreuder

William Wadé Harris

Donald Fraser

Bruno Gutmann

John Philip

1775–1851

Standing for Autonomy and Racial Equality

Andrew C. Ross

In 1819 the Reverend Doctor John Philip, a tall, dark, strongly built Scots Congregationalist minister, began a career as resident director of the London Missionary Society (LMS) in South Africa. It was a career that would make him the missionary, in addition to David Livingstone, that any South African, white or black, could name. Indeed Philip has become so much part of the South African historical memory that Prime Minister Johannes Strydom could use his name as an immediately recognizable symbol. When, in 1955, he warned missionaries and other clergy not to imitate Fr. Trevor Huddleston, he told them not to "do a Philip."

The Scottish Years

John Philip was born in Kirkaldy, Scotland, on April 14, 1775, the son of a handloom weaver. At that time Scotland was going through a period of far-reaching economic and social change. Having survived for centuries as a poor agrarian society with a small urban periphery, after 1760 it was rapidly transformed to a comparatively wealthy society with a developing urban sector. Like the vast majority of the handloom weavers of the time, John's father was both literate and able to sustain his family comfortably above the poverty line.

Although his parents were members of the Church of Scotland, when John was converted as a young man, he became a member of an Independent chapel. He was converted during the evangelistic campaigns of the brothers Robert and James Haldane, whose efforts created many Independent chapels, some of which went on to form the Congregational Union and others to swell the ranks of the Scottish Baptists.

John became first a clerk, and then the manager, of a new spinning mill in Dundee, but this transition from artisan to middle-class status soon ended when he resigned in a dispute with the owners over child labor and inadequate wage rates. He was not back as a weaver for long when, in 1799, he went off to Hoxton, the Congregationalist academy of England, to train for the ministry. At the end of his three-year course at Hoxton, Philip went as the assistant minister of the congregation at Newbury, Berkshire. He was there for barely two years when he received a call from Belmont Church of Aberdeen. This was one of the oldest of the congregations that later formed the Congregational Union of Scotland.

Philip very quickly established himself as the leading evangelical preacher in the northeast of Scotland. He was in great demand in Church of Scotland kirks that were ministered to by members of the "popular party" as well as in Seceder kirks and Independent chapels. He was particularly effective in reaching young people, and in the university town of Aberdeen he always had round him a strong body of young women and men. He made his manse a meeting place for these young people and organized a series of Bible studies for them each year. These were conducted in a manner very different from what was usual at that time. In the first place, young women were encouraged to attend. Equally striking was his encouragement of the members to initiate topics themselves and to propound their own ideas. "It was customary for members of the class to propound questions, or to state difficulties arising in the course of Bible study. After hearing various opinions expressed by members it was no uncommon thing for Dr. Philip to turn to Miss Paul, before solving the crux himself and ask, 'Well, Margaret, what have you to say to this?' "[1] This was in a day when preacher and professor alike were used to being solo performers from pulpit or rostrum, from whence they pronounced on all matters with unchallenged magisterial authority.

In 1809 Philip married Jane Ross, who not only became a loving mother and powerful influence on the three daughters and four sons she bore him but also was his secretary and personal assistant throughout their life together in South Africa. Without any of the opposition that would certainly have occurred in the later nineteenth century, Jane simply took over the LMS office when John was away on one of the many long and arduous tours he undertook in South Africa. In addition, from 1830 until her death in 1847, she was, in her own right, the official agent of the Paris Evangelical Mission in South Africa.

The attitude toward women was typical, in the first half of the century, of the tradition of evangelicalism to which he belonged. It was that of Finneyite revivalism in America, which made Oberlin a coeducational institution where the first women were trained for the ministry in mainstream Protestantism. Again Philip's evangelicalism was like that of the Finneyite movement in his lack of concern for the classic differences between the denominations. In Scotland Philip was one of the main propagandists for the LMS, with its message aimed at bringing about in the individual a warm personal faith in Jesus as Savior, and a commitment to spreading this good news about redemption from the power of sin and death to all humankind, scorning denominational difference as a hindrance to the task.

> Our design is not to send Presbyterianism, Independency, Episcopacy, or any other form of Church Order and Government about which there may be differences of opinion among serious Persons, but the Glorious Gospel of the blessed God to the Heathen: and that it should be left (as it ever ought to be left) to the minds of the Persons whom God may call into the fellowship of His Son from among them to assume for themselves such form of Church Government as to them shall appear most agreeable to the Word of God.[2]

Called to South Africa

Although an ardent supporter of the LMS, Philip had not seen his ministry as lying with them. However, in the second decade of the nineteenth century, the work of the LMS in South Africa, within the Colony of the Cape of Good Hope and among the tribes beyond its frontiers, was in disarray. The solution to these problems, the board of directors decided, was to send two of their number to review the work and recommend reforms, and for one to remain as resident director to ensure that the reforms were carried out. Two Scots were chosen to perform this task, John Campbell and John Philip, with Philip designated to become the resident director. Philip's congregation in

Aberdeen was very loath to let him go. It took a great deal of persuasion and diplomacy on the part of the LMS board before they released him at last, albeit still grudgingly.

Together with his wife, Jane, and their four children, Mary, Elizabeth, William, and John, the new resident director of the society arrived in Cape Town in 1819. A further three children, Durrant, Margaret, and Wilberforce, were born in South Africa. William and Durrant went on to become ministers of Coloured congregations in South Africa,[3] while Elizabeth married John Fairbairn, her father's friend and ally, the editor of South Africa's first newspaper, the *Cape Commercial Advertiser.*

Fairbairn's paper was the vehicle for liberal political opinion in South Africa for all his long tenure of the editorship, and he, together with his father-in-law and Andries Stockenstrom, can be seen as the founding fathers of South African liberalism. Without them there would not have been the non-racial franchise for the Cape Parliament, which lasted from 1852 until 1910, when it disappeared with the creation of the Union of South Africa.

South Africa: The First Phase

The South Africa to which Philip came was divided into two. First there was the colony. It had been ruled by the Netherlands East India Company until the Napoleonic Wars, then by the Batavian Republic, and in 1815, by the British, whose authority was made permanent by the Treaty of Vienna. Ninety percent of the white inhabitants were what the British have traditionally referred to as the Dutch or the Boers, people who prefer to be called Afrikaners.[4] The first sizable influx of British settlers arrived in a mass emigration scheme in 1820, which brought the white population to about forty thousand persons.

The indigenous population of the colony were the Khoi, referred to by Afrikaner and Briton as Hottentots and some as Bastaards, since many were of mixed Khoi-white ancestry. The colony also contained slaves, whose number, at about twenty-four thousand, was roughly equal to that of the Khoi. They were mainly from Madagascar, Angola, and Mozambique, though there was a distinct group from Indonesia known locally as Malays.

The other division of South Africa was the area to the north and east of the colonial frontiers. To the east were the Xhosa people, who, by 1819, had effectively halted what once had appeared to be the inexorable advance of the Afrikaner cattle herders. To the north were many Tswana and Sotho groupings, with a major center of power at the court of Moshweshwe of the Sotho. There was also a small Griqua state that, by 1819, was already on the way to becoming a "Christian" state. The Griqua were people drawn from many tribes, including runaway slaves and white Dutch army deserters, who had come to accept the leadership of two Christian Bastaard families. They had been welded into one community, with the church and school as its center.

Upon his arrival in the Cape, Philip immediately started to get the affairs of the LMS in order and build better relations with the English governor and his staff. So successful was he that the governor appointed him to head the relief committee set up to aid the 1820 British settlers who were in grave distress after two successive bad harvests. These good relations soon ended, however, when Philip stood by his fellow Scots John Fairbairn and Thomas Pringle,[5] in their struggle for the freedom of the press in South Africa. Worse was to follow. At least in the matter of the press, British settlers and some Afrikaners were on his side. But this was not to be so when he began to take up the issue of the status of the Khoi and other "free persons of colour." Philip was content to leave the issue of slavery to Buxton and the Anti-Slavery Society in London,[6] where alone abolition could be achieved. However, he had come soon to see that abolition was of little use if the slaves were to be freed only to join the Coloureds in their de facto slavery. In 1811 and 1812 the British had passed laws that gave the Khoi and other "free persons of colour" legal recognition as people. (They had had absolutely no existence in law under the Netherlands East India Company.) However, the British laws in effect placed upon every "free person of colour" the need to be the servant or dependent of some white. Of these laws Philip wrote, "There is no tyranny so cruel (says Montesquieu) as that which is exercised under the pretext of law, and under the colour of justice; when wretches are, so to speak, drowned on the very plank to which they clung for safety."[7] The Coloureds were subject to many impositions that did not apply to whites, impositions that, as Philip came to believe, were deliberately created to provide a cheap labor pool for white farmers and traders. Such an imposition was the corvee. Philip complained of its effects in checking the attempts of some of the Christians at the mission stations to improve themselves. "If a Hottentot, possessing one wagon by which he is able to earn 76 dollars by one journey to Grahamstown, is liable to be dragged from his employment to serve for 4/- a day, the people liable to such exactions, labour under oppression."[8] Having campaigned vigorously but unsuccessfully for change, in 1826 he returned to the United Kingdom determined to enlist evangelical political groups in his cause – in particular, the Anti-Slavery Society.

He and Thomas Fowell Buxton became close friends, and Buxton encouraged him to write a book about the situation. This was published in 1828, the passionately Christian and radically egalitarian *Researches in South Africa*. In the campaign they waged together, Buxton and Philip gained a tremendous victory in Parliament.[9] In a series of complicated maneuvers in Parliament and at the Cape, it became mandatory in the colony for all His Majesty's subjects to share the same civil rights. This, in effect, meant that Coloureds (as well as Xhosa and Tswana people when some were incorporated into the colony later) could buy land anywhere, buy a house in any part of town, and, when the vote came (in 1852), qualify for it in exactly the same way as whites. It meant equal pay for equal work, at least some integrated schools, and many other things peculiar to the colony, all of which began to disappear once the Union of South Africa of 1910 was consummated.

The Tribes beyond the Frontier

On his return to the Cape, Philip became the focus of much bitter feeling on the part of Afrikaners and British settlers. This was made worse when he went again to the United Kingdom, taking with him several Coloured and Xhosa Christians to give evidence before the Aborigines Committee.[10] Undeterred, he continued, on his return to the Cape, to supervise the missions of the society, traveling thousands of miles by oxcart, touching the whole colony and also visiting the Xhosa, Sotho, and Griqua beyond the frontier.

In the case of the peoples beyond the frontier, his approach was radically different from that which he adopted toward people within the colony. His constant plea was for more and more missionaries and honest traders to go and live among them, but equally for the government to prevent any encroachment by whites who sought permanent possession of the land. This policy has led some modern writers to insist that he was a forerunner of the doctrine of apartheid. In fact he had a two-pronged policy. On one hand, he sought integration within the area where whites owned most of the land and the European economy had taken over. On the other hand, where this had not taken place, he wished African societies to be left autonomous. Working within those African societies, missionaries and traders (what Livingstone called Christianity and commerce) would, he believed, help trigger spontaneous change and development of societies both Christian and African. He believed that this had happened already among the Griqua and was about to happen among the Basotho. After visiting the court of Moshweshwe, he wrote to Buxton,

> Moshesh the king of the Basutos, of whom James Backhouse and George Washington Walker give some account, is one of the most extraordinary men I ever met with, and I had almost said a miracle of a man, when his circumstances in Africa are taken into considera-
> tion, and the French mission among his people, present one of the loveliest pictures under

heaven. Have I been permitted to visit that country, and to see the heavenly vision I have seen, merely to witness it and then be obliged to say it has fled forever![11]

Why he feared that it had fled was that the Basotho, and all other peoples beyond the frontier of the colony, were threatened by the massive exodus of the Boers from the colony known as the Great Trek.[12] Philip fought hard to persuade the British government not to allow this kind of settler expansion, but he failed completely, as the creation of Natal and the independent states of the Orange Free State and the Transvaal made only too clear.

Was John Philip primarily a social reformer? He would have been bewildered by the accusation. Everything he did was part of his service of the gospel message. His political work, which annoyed so many of the powerful, stole the headlines. Yet it was no more important than any other aspect of what he saw as his one task.

Every bit as important as his attempts to make the British government of South Africa the "regular and good government" that God demands was his persistent advocacy of what he called "native agency" as the key to the evangelization of Africa and his equally insistent attempts to persuade more and more missionary societies to come to southern Africa.

Just as the all-pervasive influence of new race theories affected British colonial policy increasingly after 1840, so, at first gradually, then with increasing pace after the coming of full-blown social Darwinism, the policy of missionary societies was affected also. (The most glaring illustration is seen in the tragic story of Bishop Ajayi Crowther, not to be succeeded by another African bishop in the Anglican Communion till the mid-twentieth century.)

Before this philosophy created the crippling perception of the African evangelist as inevitably the missionary's assistant, Philip insisted that only Africans could convert Africa and that an African ministry for an autonomous church must be created as rapidly as possible.

His attempt to bring more societies to come to work in South Africa achieved greater success. The Glasgow Missionary Society (an associate society of the LMS) came and created Lovedale, the most important single educational foundation open to Africans in southern Africa until it was destroyed by the Bantu Education Act of 1953. Philip went to France and persuaded the Paris Evangelical Mission to send missionaries to work with Moshweshwe and his Sotho people, with extraordinary results. The Rheineschen Missionsgesellschaft and the American Board were two other organizations brought to South Africa by Philip.

John Philip's last years were darkened by a great deal of sadness in his private life and by a sense of defeat over issues central to his life's work. In July 1845, his son William, pastor of the Coloured congregation at Hankey in the eastern Cape, was drowned along with Philip's grandson, Johnny Fairbairn. Then in October 1847, his beloved wife and comrade, Jane, died; his misery was added to when, a few weeks later, one of his granddaughters was killed in an accident. At the same time he felt, correctly, that the directors of the LMS in London no longer trusted his judgment or saw the problems of South Africa as he did. In addition he felt that so many missionaries of the LMS and of other societies no longer had a commitment to human equality.

In 1850 Philip retired from active service and went to live in the Coloured community of Hankey, where another of his sons was a pastor. He died there on August 27, 1851, and was buried by his beloved Coloured people in what was, until the abolition of the apartheid laws in 1991, a Coloured graveyard.

Troublemaker or Prophet?

Among twentieth-century writers in Britain and South Africa, John Philip has provoked as sharp hostility as he did in his lifetime among British settlers and the Afrikaner herders. Even the entry in the modern evangelical *New International Dictionary of the Christian Church* says of him, "His aggressive and intolerant manner did harm, as did his unwillingness to admit mistakes and his unsympathetic attitude towards colonists." Wealth, land, and the support of the British authorities were on the side of the colonists who had stolen the people's land; what was Philip supposed to do? The Coloured people inside the colony, and the Griqua, Sotho, and Xhosa beyond, had a very different view of him, symbolically proclaimed by his grave, which is in what was, under apartheid laws, a Coloured graveyard in a Coloured township.

Another picture of him in contrast with the negative was given by the young Eugene Casalis of the Paris Mission. He wrote about his arrival in South Africa:

> Dr. Philip received us with a kindness truly paternal. He was entertaining at this time several missionaries, coming, one from the interior of Africa, others from India and Madagascar.
>
> We were struck from the first hour with the heartiness and good humour which reigned at his table. I had rarely heard men laugh so heartily. This shocked us a little at first, being still full of the emotions of a first arrival. Young recruits, we were entering the camp with a solemnity perhaps a little exaggerated.[13]

John Philip has been honored by some in South Africa as the founding father of South African liberalism. This he was to a degree, but it was an incidental product of his devout evangelical claim of the sovereignty of God over all life. Today urgent debates go on about the priority of personal evangelism versus the seeking of justice for the oppressed. Philip saw no conflict between those two, which for him were but two faces of the same coin.

He saw that the African church had to be African. Fully 150 years before the "Apartheid is a heresy" decision of the World Alliance of Reformed Churches, he saw with utter clarity that discrimination was contrary to the Word of God.

Notes

1. John Bulloch, *Centenary Memorials of the First Congregational Church in Aberdeen* (Aberdeen: James Murray, 1898), p. 59.
2. Minutes of the Meeting of the Board of Directors, May 9, 1796, LMS Archives.
3. The Cape Coloureds are the descendants of Khoi, slaves, and many offspring produced in the eighteenth and early nineteenth century, when concubinage was common and interracial marriage not unknown. By the late 1840s they were one community whose language was what is now Afrikaans.
4. Afrikaners are the descendants of the farmers who settled in the Cape; some were Dutch, others were indentured German soldiers of the Netherlands East India Company, and still others were Huguenot refugees (hence names such as Malan, Retief, and deKlerk).
5. Thomas Pringle was a Scottish settler who came in 1820 and the first South African poet. He later became secretary of the Anti-Slavery Society.
6. For Thomas Fowell Buxton, see pages 11-17 in this volume.
7. John Philip, *Researches in South Africa*, 1:177.
8. File 215, letter 125, LMS Archives.
9. See A.C. Ross, *John Philip: Missions, Race, and Politics in South Africa* (Aberdeen: Aberdeen Univ. Press, 1986), pp. 102-11; *British Parliamentary Papers* 7 (1836): 538.
10. The Select Committee on Aborigines (British Settlements).
11. Philip to Buxton, November 22, 1842, SA Odds, box 3, folder 5, LMS Archives.
12. Between 1836 and 1840 about one-third of the Afrikaner people left the colony in an organized emigration, a form of "rebellion by removal" against British rule.
13. Eugene Casalis, *My Life in Basutoland* (London: Religious Tract Society, 1889), p. 66.

Selected Bibliography

Works of John Philip

Apart from the massive collections of his letters and reports in the LMS Archives housed in the School of Oriental and African Studies, London, there are three printed sources for Philip's ideas. The first is his book, published in 1828 and photographically reproduced as *Researches in South Africa* (New York: Negro Univ. Press, 1968). The second is his long letter to the American Board, published in the *Missionary Herald* of November 1833. The third source is the page upon page of evidence given by him to the Aborigines Committee, *British Parliamentary Papers* 7 (1836): 538.

Works about John Philip

Macmillan, W.M. *Bantu, Boer, and Briton.* Oxford: Oxford Univ. Press, 1963.

_____. *The Cape Colour Question.* London: Faber and Gwyer, 1927.

Philip, Robert. *The Elijah of South Africa.* London: John Snow, 1851.

Ross, A.C. *John Philip: Missions, Race, and Politics in South Africa.* Aberdeen: Aberdeen Univ. Press, 1986.

Samuel Ajayi Crowther

1807–1891

Foremost African Christian of the Nineteenth Century

Andrew F. Walls

S amuel Adjai[1] Crowther was probably the most widely known African Christian of the nineteenth century. His life spanned the greater part of it – he was born in its first decade and died in the last. He lived through a transformation of relations between Africa and the rest of the world and a parallel transformation in the Christian situation in Africa. By the time of his death the bright confidence in an African church led by Africans, a reality that he seemed to embody in himself, had dimmed. Today things look very different. It seems a good time to consider the legacy of Crowther.

Slavery and Liberation

The story begins with the birth of a boy called Ajayi in the town of Osogun in Yorubaland in what is now Western Nigeria, in or about the year 1807. In later years the story was told that a diviner had indicated that Ajayi was not to enter any of the cults of the orisa, the divinities of the Yoruba pantheon, because he was to be a servant of Olorun,[2] the God of heaven.[3] He grew up in dangerous times. Both the breakup of the old Yoruba empire of Oyo, and the effect of the great Islamic jihads, which were establishing a new Fulani empire to the north, meant chaos for the Yoruba states. Warfare and raiding became endemic. Besides all the trauma of divided families and transplantation that African slavery could bring, the raids fed a still worse evil: the European traders at the coast. These maintained a trade in slaves, illegal but still richly profitable, across the Atlantic.

When Crowther was about thirteen, Osogun was raided, apparently by a combination of Fulani and Oyo Muslims. Crowther twice recorded his memories of the event, vividly recalling the desolation of burning houses, the horror of capture and roping by the neck, the slaughter of those unfit to travel, the distress of being torn from relatives. Ajayi changed hands six times, before being sold to Portuguese traders for the transatlantic market.

The colony of Sierra Leone had been founded by a coalition of anti-slavery interests, mostly evangelical Christian in inspiration and belonging to the circle associated with William Wilberforce and the "Clapham Sect." It was intended from the beginning as a Christian settlement, free from slavery and the slave trade. The first permanent element in the population was a group of former slaves from the New World. Following the abolition of the slave trade by the British Parliament in 1807 and the subsequent treaties with other nations to outlaw the traffic, Sierra Leone achieved a new importance. It was a base for the naval squadron that searched vessels to find if they were carrying slaves. It was also the place where slaves were brought if any were found aboard. The Portuguese ship on which Ajayi was taken as a slave was intercepted by the British naval squadron in April 1822, and he, like thousands of other uprooted, disorientated people from inland Africa, was put ashore in Sierra Leone.

By this time, Sierra Leone was becoming a Christian community. It was one of the few early successes of the missionary movement, though the Christian public at large was probably less conscious of the success than of the appalling mortality of missionaries in what became known as the White Man's Grave. To all appearances the whole way of life of Sierra Leone – clothing, buildings, language, education, religion, even names – closely followed Western models. These were people of diverse origins whose cohesion and original identity were now beyond recall. They accepted the combination of Christian faith and Western lifestyle that Sierra Leone offered, a combination already represented in the oldest inhabitants of the colony, the settled slaves from the New World.

Such was the setting in which young Ajayi now found himself. We know little of his early years there. Later he wrote that

about the third year of my liberation from the slavery of man, I was convinced of another worse state of slavery, namely, that of sin and Satan. It pleased the Lord to open my heart . . . I was admitted into the visible Church of Christ here on earth as a soldier to fight manfully under his banner against our spiritual enemies.[4]

He was baptized by the Reverend John Raban, of the (Anglican) Church Missionary Society, taking the name Samuel Crowther, after a member of that society's home committee. Mr. Crowther was an eminent clergyman; his young namesake was to make the name far more celebrated.

Crowther had spent those early years in Sierra Leone at school, getting an English education, adding carpentry to his traditional weaving and agricultural skills. In 1827 the Church Missionary Society decided, for the sake of Sierra Leone's future Christian leadership, to provide education to a higher level than the colony's modest schools had given. The resultant "Christian Institution" developed as Fourah Bay College, which eventually offered the first university education in tropical Africa. Crowther was one of its first students.

The Loom of Language

This period marked the beginning of the work that was to form one of the most abiding parts of Crowther's legacy. He continued to have contact with Raban, who had baptized him; and Raban was one of the few missionaries in Sierra Leone to take African languages seriously. To many of his colleagues the priority was to teach English, which would render the African languages unnecessary. Raban realized that such policy was a dead end; he also realized that Yoruba, Crowther's mother tongue, was a major language. (Yoruba had not been prominent in the early years of Sierra Leone, but the political circumstances that had led to young Ajayi's captivity were to bring many other Yoruba to the colony.) Crowther became an informant for Raban, who between 1828 and 1830 published three little books about Yoruba; and almost certainly he also assisted another pioneer African linguist, the Quaker educationist Hannah Kilham.

Crowther was appointed a schoolmaster of the mission, serving in the new villages created to receive "liberated Africans" from the slave ships. A schoolmaster was an evangelist; in Sierra Leone church and school were inseparable. We get glimpses of an eager, vigorous young man who, at least at first, was highly confrontational in his encounters with representatives of Islam and the old religions in Africa. In later life he valued the lessons of this apprenticeship – the futility of abuse, the need to build personal relationships, and the ability to listen patiently.

Crowther began study of the Temne language, which suggests a missionary vision toward the hinterland of Sierra Leone. But he also worked systematically at his own language, as far as the equipment to hand allowed.

Transformation of the Scene

Two developments now opened a new chapter for Crowther and for Sierra Leone Christianity. One was a new link with Yorubaland. Enterprising liberated Africans, banding together and buying confiscated slave ships, began trading far afield from Freetown. Some of Yoruba origin found their way back to their homeland. They settled there, but kept the Sierra Leone connections and the ways of life of Christian Freetown. The second development was the Niger Expedition of 1841, the brief flowering of the humanitarian vision for Africa of Sir Thomas Fowell Buxton.[5] This investigative mission, intended to prepare the way for an alliance of "Christianity, commerce and civilization" that would destroy the slave trade and bring peace and prosperity to the Niger, relied heavily on Sierra Leone for interpreters and other helpers. The missionary society representatives also came from Sierra Leone. One was J.F. Schön, a German missionary who had striven with languages of the Niger, learning from liberated Africans in Sierra Leone. The other was Crowther.

Crowther's services to the disaster-stricken expedition were invaluable. Schön cited them as evidence of his thesis that the key to the evangelization of inland Africa lay in Sierra Leone. Sierra Leone had Christians such as Crowther to form the task force; it had among the liberated Africans brought there from the slave ships a vast language laboratory for the study of all the languages of West Africa, as well as a source of native speakers as missionaries; and in the institution at Fourah Bay it had a base for study and training.

The Niger Expedition had shown Crowther's qualities, and he was brought to England for study and ordination. The latter was of exceptional significance. Anglican ordination could be received only from a bishop, and there was no bishop nearer than London. Here then, in 1843, began Sierra Leone's indigenous ministry.[6]

Here, too, began Crowther's literary career, with the publication of *Yoruba Vocabulary*, including an account of grammatical structure, surely the first such work by a native speaker of an African language.

The Yoruba Mission

Meanwhile, the new connection between Sierra Leone and Yorubaland had convinced the CMS of the timeliness of a mission to the Yoruba. There had been no opportunity to train that African mission force foreseen by Schön and Crowther in their report on the Niger Expedition, but at least in Crowther there was one ordained Yoruba missionary available. Thus, after an initial reconnaissance by Henry Townsend, an English missionary from Sierra Leone, a mission party went to Abeokuta, the state of the Egba section of the Yoruba people. It was headed by Townsend, Crowther, and a German missionary, C.A. Gollmer, with a large group of Sierra Leoneans from the liberated Yoruba community. These included carpenters and builders who were also teachers and catechists. The mission intended to demonstrate a whole new way of life, of which the church and the school and the well-built house were all a part. They were establishing Sierra Leone in Yorubaland. The Sierra Leone trader-immigrants, the people who had first brought Abeokuta to the attention of the mission, became the nucleus of the new Christian community.

The CMS Yoruba mission is a story in itself. How the mission, working on Buxton's principles, introduced the growing and processing of cotton and arranged for its export, thereby keeping

Abeokuta out of the slave economy; how the missionaries identified with Abeokuta under invasion and reaped their reward afterward; how the CMS mobilized Christian opinion to influence the British government on behalf of Abeokuta; and the toils into which the mission fell amid inter-Yoruba and colonial conflicts, have been well told elsewhere.[7] Crowther came to London in 1851 to present the cause of Abeokuta. He saw government ministers; he had an interview with the Queen and Prince Albert; he spoke at meetings all over the country, invariably to great effect. This grave, eloquent, well-informed black clergyman was the most impressive tribute to the effect of the missionary movement that most British people had seen; and Henry Venn, the CMS secretary who organized the visit, believed that it was Crowther who finally moved the government to action.

But the missionaries' day-to-day activities lay in commending the Gospel and nourishing the infant church. There was a particularly moving incident for Crowther, when he was reunited with the mother and sister from whom he had been separated when the raiders took them more than twenty years earlier. They were among the first in Abeokuta to be baptized.

In Sierra Leone the church had used English in its worship. The new mission worked in Yoruba, with the advantage of native speakers in Crowther and his family and in most of the auxiliaries, and with Crowther's book to assist the Europeans. Townsend, an excellent practical linguist, even edited a Yoruba newspaper. But the most demanding activity was Bible translation.

The significance of the Yoruba version has not always been observed. It was not the first translation into an African language; but, insofar as Crowther was the leading influence in its production, it was the first by a native speaker. Early missionary translations naturally relied heavily on native speakers as informants and guides; but in no earlier case was a native speaker able to judge and act on an equal footing with the European.

Crowther insisted that the translation should indicate tone – a new departure. In vocabulary and style he sought to get behind colloquial speech by listening to the elders, by noting significant words that emerged in his discussions with Muslims or specialists in the old religion. Over the years, wherever he was, he noted words, proverbs, forms of speech. One of his hardest blows was the loss of the notes of eleven years of such observations, and some manuscript translations, when his house burned down in 1862.

Written Yoruba was the product of missionary committee work, Crowther interacting with his European colleagues on matters of orthography. Henry Venn engaged the best linguistic expertise available in Europe – not only Schön and the society's regular linguistic adviser, Professor Samuel Lee of Cambridge, but the great German philologist Lepsius. The outcome may be seen in the durability of the Yoruba version of the Scriptures to which Crowther was the chief contributor and in the vigorous vernacular literature in Yoruba that has grown up.

New Niger Expeditions and a Mission to the Niger

In 1854 the merchant McGregor Laird sponsored a new Niger expedition, on principles similar to the first, but with a happier outcome. The CMS sent Crowther on this expedition. It revived the vision he had seen in 1841 – a chain of missionary operations hundreds of miles along the Niger, into the heart of the continent. He urged a beginning at Onitsha, in Igboland.

The opportunity was not long in coming. In 1857, he and J.C. Taylor, a Sierra Leonean clergyman of liberated Igbo parentage, joined Laird's next expedition to the Niger. Taylor opened the Igbo mission at Onitsha; Crowther went upriver. Shipwrecked, and stranded for months, be began to study the Nupe language and surveyed openings to the Nupe and Hausa peoples. The Niger Mission had begun.

Henry Venn soon made a formal structure for it. But it was a mission on a new principle. Crowther led a mission force consisting entirely of Africans. Sierra Leone, as he and Schön had foreseen so long ago, was now evangelizing inland Africa.

For nearly half a century that tiny country sent a stream of missionaries, ordained and lay, to the Niger territories. The area was vast and diverse: Muslim emirates in the north, ocean-trading city-states in the Delta, the vast Igbo populations in between. It is cruel that the missionary contribution of Sierra Leone has been persistently overlooked, and even denied.[8]

It is possible here to consider only three aspects of a remarkable story. Two have been somewhat neglected.

More Legacy in Language

One of these is the continued contribution to language study and translation. Crowther himself wrote the first book on Igbo.[9] He begged Schön, now serving an English parish, to complete his Hausa dictionary. He sent one of his missionaries to study Hausa with Schön. Most of his Sierra Leone staff, unlike people of his own generation, were not native speakers of the languages of the areas they served. The great Sierra Leone language laboratory was closing down; English and the common language, Krio, took over from the languages of the liberated. Add to this the limited education of many Niger missionaries, and their record of translation and publication is remarkable.

The Engagement with Islam

Crowther's Niger Mission also represents the first sustained missionary engagement with African Islam in modern times. In the Upper Niger areas in Crowther's time, Islam, largely accepted by the chiefs, was working slowly through the population in coexistence with the old religion. From his early experiences in Sierra Leone, Crowther understood how Islamic practice could merge with traditional views of power. He found a demand for Arabic Bibles, but was cautious about supplying them unless he could be sure they would not be used for charms. His insight was justified later, when the young European missionaries who succeeded him wrote out passages of Scripture on request, pleased at such a means of Scripture distribution. They stirred up the anger of Muslim clerics – not because they were circulating Christian Scriptures, but because they were giving them free, thus undercutting the trade in quranic charms. In discussion with Muslims, Crowther sought common ground and found it at the nexus of Qur'an and Bible: Christ as the great prophet, his miraculous birth, Gabriel as the messenger of God. He enjoyed courteous and friendly relations with Muslim rulers, and his writings trace various discussions with rulers, courts, and clerics, recording the questions raised by Muslims, and his own answers, the latter as far as possible in the words of Scripture: "After many years' experience, I have found that the Bible, the sword of the Spirit, must fight its own battle, by the guidance of the Holy Spirit."[10]

Christians should of course defend Trinitarian doctrine, but let them do so mindful of the horror-stricken cry of the Qur'an, "Is it possible that Thou dost teach that Thou and Thy Mother are two Gods?" In other words, Christians must show that the things that the Muslims fear as blasphemous are no part of Christian doctrine.

Crowther, though no great scholar or Arabist, developed an approach to Islam in its African setting that reflected the patience and the readiness to listen that marked his entire missionary method. Avoiding denunciation and allegations of false prophecy, it worked by acceptance of what the Qur'an says of Christ, and an effective knowledge of the Bible. Crowther looked to the future with hope; the average African Christian knew the Bible much better than the average African Muslim knew the Qur'an. And he pondered the fact that the Muslim rule of faith was expressed in Arabic, the Christian in Hausa, or Nupe or Yoruba. The result was different understandings of how the faith was to be applied in life.

The Indigenization of the Episcopate

The best-known aspect of Crowther's later career is also the most controversial: his representation of the indigenous church principle. We have seen that he was the first ordained minister of his church in his place. It was the policy of Henry Venn, then newly at the helm of the CMS, to strengthen the indigenous ministry. More and more Africans were ordained, some for the Yoruba mission. And Venn wanted well-educated, well-trained African clergy; such people as Crowther's son Dandeson (who became archdeacon) and his son-in-law T.B. Macaulay (who became principal of Lagos Grammar School) were better educated than many of the homespun English missionaries.

Venn sought self-governing, self-supporting, self-propagating churches with a fully indigenous pastorate. In Anglican terms, this meant indigenous bishops. The missionary role was a temporary one; once a church was established, the missionary should move on. The birth of the church brought the euthanasia of the mission. With the growth of the Yoruba church, Venn sought to get these principles applied in Yorubaland. Even the best European missionaries thought this impractical, the hobbyhorse of a doctrinaire home-based administrator.

As we have seen, Venn made a new sphere of leadership for Crowther, the outstanding indigenous minister in West Africa. But he went further, and in 1864 secured the consecration of Crowther as bishop of "the countries of Western Africa beyond the limits of the Queen's dominions," a title reflecting some constraints imposed by Crowther's European colleagues and the peculiarities of the relationship of the Church of England to the Crown. Crowther, a genuinely humble man, resisted; Venn would take no refusal.

In one sense, the new diocese represented the triumph of the three-self principle and the indigenization of the episcopate. But it reflected a compromise, rather than the full expression of those principles. It was, after all, essentially a *mission*, drawing most of its clergy not from natives of the soil but from Sierra Leone. Its ministry was "native" only in the sense of not being European. Three-self principles required it to be self-supporting; this meant meager resources, missionaries who got no home leave, and the need to present education as a salable product.

The story of the later years of the Niger mission has often been told and variously interpreted. It still raises passions and causes bitterness.[11] There is no need here to recount more than the essentials: that questions arose about the lives of some of the missionaries; that European missionaries were brought into the mission, and then took it over, brushing aside the old bishop (he was over eighty) and suspending or dismissing his staff. In 1891 Crowther, a desolate, broken man, suffered a stroke; on the last day of the year, he died. A European bishop was appointed to succeed him. The self-governing church and the indigenization of the episcopate were abandoned.

Contemporary mission accounts all praise Crowther's personal integrity, graciousness, and godliness. In the Yoruba mission, blessed with many strong, not to say prickly, personalities, his influence had been irenic. In Britain he was recognized as a cooperative and effective platform speaker. (A CMS official remembered Crowther's being called on to give a conference address on "Mission and Women" and holding his audience spellbound.) Yet the same sources not only declared Crowther "a weak bishop" but drew the moral that "the African race" lacked the capacity to rule.

European thought about Africa had changed since the time of Buxton; the Western powers were now in Africa to govern. Missionary thought about Africa had changed since the days of Henry Venn; there were plenty of keen, young Englishmen to extend the mission and order the church; a self-governing church now seemed to matter much less. And evangelical religion had changed since Crowther's conversion; it had become more individualistic and more otherworldly. A young English missionary was distressed that the old bishop who preached so splendidly on the blood of Christ could urge on a chief the advantages of having a school and make no reference to the future life.[12] This story illustrates in brief the two evangelical itineraries: the short route via Keswick, and the long one via the White Man's Grave, the Niger Expedition and the courts of Muslim rulers of the north.

There were some unexpected legacies even from the last sad days. One section of the Niger mission, that in the Niger Delta, was financially self-supporting. Declining the European takeover, it long maintained a separate existence under Crowther's son, Archdeacon Dandeson Crowther, within the Anglican Communion but outside the CMS. It grew at a phenomenal rate, becoming so self-propagating that it ceased to be self-supporting.[13]

Other voices called for direct schism; the refusal to appoint an African successor to Crowther, despite the manifest availability of outstanding African clergy, marks an important point in the history of African Independent churches.[14] The treatment of Crowther, and still more the question of his successor, gave a focus for the incipient nationalist movement of which E.W. Blyden was the most eloquent spokesman.[15] Crowther thus has his own modern place in the martyrology of African nationalism.

But the majority of Christians, including those natural successors of Crowther who were passed over or, worse, suffered denigration or abuse, took no such course. They simply waited. Crowther was the outstanding representative of a whole body of West African church leaders who came to the fore in the pre-Imperial age and were superseded in the Imperial. But the Imperial age itself was to be only an episode. The legacy of Samuel Ajayi Crowther, the humble, devout exponent of a Christian faith that was essentially African and essentially missionary, has passed to the whole vast church of Africa and thus to the whole vast church of Christ.

Notes

1. Crowther himself spelled his Yoruba name (which he employed as a second name) thus. The modern spelling is Ajayi, and this spelling is commonly used today, especially by Nigerian writers.

2. On the relation of the orisa to Olorun, see E.B. Idowu, *Olódùmarè: God in Yoruba Belief* (London: Longmans, 1962). Idowu argues that Olorun is never called an orisa, nor classed among them.

3. The story is representative of hundreds that show the God of the Bible active in the African past through such prophecies of the Christian future of Africa.

4. Walls, "A Second Narrative of Samuel Ajayi Crowther's Early Life," *Bulletin of the Society for African History* 2 (1965): 14.

5. On Buxton, see pages 11-17, above.

6. Crowther was not the first African to receive Anglican ordination. As early as 1765, Philip Quaque, from Cape Coast in what is now Ghana, who had been brought to England as a boy, was appointed chaplain to the British trading settlement at Cape Coast. He died in 1816. Crowther had never heard of him until he went ashore at Cape Coast en route to the Niger in 1841 and saw a memorial tablet. See Jesse Page, *The Black Bishop* (London: Hodder and Stoughton, 1908), p. 53.

7. Especially by J.F.A. Ajayi, *Christian Missions in Nigeria: 1841-1891* (London: Longmans, 1965). See also S.O. Biobaku, *The Egba and Their Neighbours: 1842-1874* (Oxford: Clarendon Press, 1957).

8. Repeated, for instance, by Stephen Neill, *Christian Missions,* Pelican History of the Church (Harmondsworth: Penguin Books, 1964), p. 306, who said, "It is only to be regretted that its Christianity has not proved expansive." In fact, few countries can claim so *much* expansion in proportion to the numbers of the Christian population.

9. See P.E.H. Hair, *The Early Study of Nigerian Languages* (Cambridge: Cambridge Univ. Press, 1967), p. 82, for an assessment. See Stephen Neill, *Christian Missions* (pp. 377f.), for the common impression of the linguistic incompetence of Crowther and the Niger missionaries. Hair's careful catalog of their translations in the languages of the Lower Niger, as well as his descriptions of Crowther's linguistic surveys in the Upper Niger, show how misleading this is.

10. Crowther, *Experiences with Heathens and Mohammedans in West Africa* (London, 1892), p. 28.

11. See E.A. Ayandele, *The Missionary Impact on Modern Nigeria: 1842-1914* (London: Longmans, 1966), for a representative modern African view. Neill (*Christian Missions,* p. 377) reflects the traditional "missionary" view. Ajayi, *Christian Missions in Nigeria,* sets the context, and G.O.M. Tasie notes some

neglected factors in his *Christian Missionary Enterprise in the Niger Delta: 1864-1918* (Leiden: Brill, 1978).

12. Ajayi, *Christian Missions in Nigeria*, p. 218.

13. For the story, see Tasie, *Christian Missionary Enterprise in the Niger Delta*. See also Jehu J. Hanciles, "Dandeson Coates Crowther and the Niger Delta Pastorate: Blazing Torch or Flickering Flame?" *International Bulletin of Missionary Research* 18, no. 4 (1994): 166-72.

14. See J.B. Webster, *The African Churches among the Yoruba* (Oxford: Clarendon Press, 1964).

15. See, for instance, H.R. Lynch, *Edward Wilmot Blyden* (London: Oxford Univ. Press, 1967).

Selected Bibliography

Works by S.A. Crowther (other than translations and linguistic works)

1843 (with J.F. Schön) *Journal of an Expedition up the Niger in 1841*. London.

1855 *Journal of an Expedition up the Niger and Tshadda Rivers*. London.

1859 (with J.C. Taylor) *The Gospel on the Banks of the Niger . . . .* London. Reprint, London: Dawsons, 1968.

1965 (by A.F. Walls) "A Second Narrative of Samuel Ajayi Crowther's Early Life," *Bulletin of the Society for African Church History* 2: 5-14. An autobiographical fragment.

Works about S.A. Crowther

Ajayi, J.F.A. *Christian Missions in Nigeria: 1841-1891*. London: Longmans, 1965.

_____. "How Yoruba Was Reduced to Writing," *Odu: Journal of Yoruba Studies* (1961): 49-58.

Ayandele, E.A. *The Missionary Impact on Modern Nigeria: 1842-1914*. London: Longmans, 1966.

Hair, P.E.H. *The Early Study of Nigerian Languages*. Cambridge: Cambridge Univ. Press, 1967.

Mackenzie, P.R. *Inter-religious Encounters in Nigeria. S.A. Crowther's Attitude to African Traditional Religion and Islam*. Leicester: Leicester Univ. Press, 1976.

Page, Jesse, *The Black Bishop*. London: Hodder and Stoughton, 1908. Still the fullest biography, though limited in value.

Shenk, W.R. *Henry Venn: Missionary Statesman*. Maryknoll, N.Y.: Orbis Books, 1983.

Tasie, G.O.M. *Christian Missionary Enterprise in the Niger Delta, 1864-1918*. Leiden: Brill, 1978.

Walls, A.F. "Black Europeans, White Africans." In D. Baker (ed.), *Religious Motivation: Biographical and Sociological Problems of the Church Historian*, pp. 339-48. Studies in Church History, Cambridge: Cambridge Univ. Press, 1978.

David Livingstone

1813–1873

Awakening the Western World to Africa

Andrew F. Walls

If any "man in the street" – at least, in any British street – were asked at any time in the last century to name a Christian missionary, it is likely that he would name David Livingstone. This might indeed be the only missionary name he could think of. Somehow Livingstone has come to stand as the representative missionary, the missionary par excellence. Yet he was hardly a *typical* missionary. Of his thirty years in Africa not much over a third was spent in the service of a missionary society, and even then his independence of action was untypical, his relations with missionary colleagues and directors often brittle. His fame as an explorer, his zeal in scientific investigation, his widely canvassed views on European commerce and settlement in Africa, his service in government appointments, his activity against the Arab slave trade – all have raised in many minds the doubt whether or not missionary vocation was the primary factor in his career.

There is no doubt, however, of Livingstone's own views on this subject. He always thought of himself as a missionary, always believed that his exploratory and scientific work had missionary relevance, always thought of the social and political implications of his work as missionary too. We must therefore consider Livingstone in relation to the whole development of the modern missionary movement and its perceptions of the missionary task.

Evangelical Milieu of the Mid-Nineteenth Century

Livingstone's African career covers the middle years of the nineteenth century, from 1841 to 1873. It is not insignificant that this period is almost co-extensive with the secretariat of Henry Venn at the Church Missionary Society. Despite the obvious differences of upbringing and churchmanship, and their different spheres of operation, there is a remarkable similarity between the two men in their view of the missionary task and their understanding of its relation to human society. The period of their activity began as missions had become accepted in the public mind as a beneficent operation, and established in all church thinking as a necessary one. No longer, as in earlier days, were missionaries assumed to be fanatics, sectarians, or subversives, nor were missions as uncertain of any solid, practical results. When Livingstone and Venn died, a new missionary period was dawning in which a tidal wave of eager young people and a host of new agencies would seek the evangelization of the world. When Livingstone and Venn began their work, a new consciousness of Africa was dawning in Britain, the first industrial nation, conscious as it was of a need for new raw materials and markets, and of a surplus population; but official policy recoiled from expensive commitments and acquisitions of territory overseas. When their work was ended, the high imperial period was already at hand, when the Western powers would divide Africa among them and establish their hegemony over the rest of the world. They began their mission in a society where energetic Christian commitment was associated with strong sentiment against slavery and in favor of humanitarian causes, and where evangelical values counted in the nation as never before or since. At their end, the whole intellectual foundation of Christianity was being doubted where once it had been taken for granted, and a chorus of diverse voices would shortly call in question the whole validity of missions even as they reached their peak of activity. Livingstone, like Venn, represents a sturdy, confident evangelicalism, secure in its place in national life, sure of its right and duty to influence public and government opinion, and, for all its emphasis on personal regeneration and personal religion, looking to the transformation of society as a normal fruit of Christian activity.

David Livingston (the "e" was added later) was born in 1813 in Blantyre, Lanarkshire, Scotland. The family was of Highland origin, and an incidental remark by Livingstone that at times within his family tradition "the Highlanders ... were much like the Cape Caffres"[1] reflects a consciousness seen in other nineteenth-century Scots missionaries that the African present had much in common with the recent past of Scotland. The family was poor, but valued learning. David worked in a cotton-spinning factory from the age of ten, and at the factory school laid the foundation of a sound, though never a learned, education. His home was devout after the best model of traditional Scottish Calvinism, but he had no inclination for scholastic theology, and his intellectual curiosity and interest in science raised fears of his departing from the faith. Many major figures of the period were converted through reading Wilberforce's *Practical View*; Livingstone was punished for *refusing* to read it. He did, however, read the works of Thomas Dick (1774-1847), which proclaimed the harmony of science and faith, and the evangelical experience of conversion followed. His interest in China was kindled through the writing of Karl Gutzlaff, and he determined to serve in China as a medical missionary, a designation then newly developed with China specifically in mind. Factory work paid well enough to enable him to devote part of the year to the study of medicine, Greek and divinity in Glasgow, and to qualify in 1840 as a medical practitioner. In the meantime he had been accepted by the London Missionary Society, to which he was attracted by its nondenominational character. He was, however, quite prepared to dispense with any missionary society: "It was not quite agreeable to one accustomed to work his own way to become in a measure dependent on others. And I would not have been much put about though my offer had been rejected."[2]

When he became available for service, China was closed by the Opium War, and Livingstone found himself en route for South Africa. He arrived in 1841, the year that the British government sought to implement the ideas of Sir Thomas Fowell Buxton for extinguishing the slave trade by the dispatch of an expedition to the Niger.

African missions at this time were confined to a series of points along the west coast and a line of "stations" stretching inland from the Cape of Good Hope. European knowledge of the rest of the continent was very limited. The Portuguese, it is true, claimed enormous tracts of the southeast, but there was considerable doubt how far they could control them; and the same applied to the East African empire of the Sultans of Zanzibar, who exported slaves and ivory in quantity and imported goods from India. The mouths of the Niger, Congo, and Zambesi were all charted, but their upper reaches were unknown. The Niger Expedition of 1841 was the most ambitious expression of a favorite idea of the time that the rivers of Africa were highways to its interior.

Increasing knowledge about Africa was linked in some minds with the war against the slave trade. Militant opposition to the slave trade had been mobilized by the "Clapham" group of evangelicals of whom William Wilberforce was the best known. Buxton, Wilberforce's parliamentary heir, and like him an earnest evangelical, worked for the emancipation of the slaves in the British dominions in 1834; but he became aware that the abolition of the slave trade, Wilberforce's greatest parliamentary achievement, had not had its intended effect. There were actually *more* slaves being transported across the Atlantic in 1839 than were in 1807 when the Abolition Act was passed. The slave trade and the wars it engendered were depopulating Africa. Buxton returned to an old Clapham theme, the relevance of economic arguments to moral issues; and the outcome was his "New Africa Policy." According to this, "the real remedy, the true ransom for Africa, will be found in her fertile soil." African agricultural development would undercut the slave trade at its source, by providing much more profitable access to the Western manufactured goods that Africans clearly wanted. The slave trade, demonstrably the enemy of a Christian enterprise in Africa, could be extinguished by calling forth Africa's own resources; and by this means agricultural development and enhanced trade would help to produce conditions in which Christianity would spread. Such developments would in turn lead to literacy and thus to printing, to new technologies in Africa, to roads and transport, to new forms of civil organization – in fact, to "civilization." Christianity, commerce, and civilization had interests in common and could unashamedly support one another. Their united effect would be to improve the life and prosperity of Africans, stem the loss of population, and shrivel up the more violent institutions of African society.

The Niger Expedition was a failure on a scale to preclude any future attempts by government to implement the New Africa Policy. But in missionary circles the underlying ideas remained potent, coupled with the belief that the eventual evangelization of inland Africa would be effected by Africans. Livingstone broadly shared these views. He detested slavery, which he met at firsthand in South Africa and later in its Arab form in East Africa. He was anxious that Christianity should break out of its narrow geographical confines and penetrate the interior. But such penetration required safe lines of communication, incompatible with the conditions of the slave trade and with endemic war. This could be secured only by regular trade of a kind welcome to interior peoples. If this could be accompanied by the spread of Christian influences, a new moral climate would exclude slavery and soften other features of African life. There was a further need for exploration: healthy locations for mission stations were necessary to avoid the devastations of missionary life that had marked West Africa. From these locations, with good communications, an African agency would bring the Gospel to all areas. To "open up" Africa was thus a prerequisite for its evangelization, and it is in this context that we must see Livingstone's famous words to the universities of Oxford and Cambridge: "I go back to Africa to make an open path for commerce and Christianity; do you carry out the work which I have begun."[3] And in line with the ideas of the time much of his effort was directed to the quest of riverine "highways to the interior" – investigations, often frustrating, of the Zambesi, the Rovuma, and the Shiré.

Opening Up Inland Africa

Livingstone began his work at Kuruman, the showpiece station of the London Missionary Society (LMS), already famous through the work and writings of Robert Moffat. He was anxious to realize in practice what most missionaries recognized as a principle, but one of future application: rapid expansion into new territory and the delivery of the responsibility for evangelization to "native agents," that is, African Christians. The population around Kuruman was too sparse for these aims, and Livingstone believed that in any case the neighboring people had been conditioned against the Gospel by evil-living or oppressive whites, and that missionary work was always open to impediments from Boers who had moved out of Cape Colony following the abolition of slavery there. In these circumstances Christianity could be seen only in terms of a series of restrictions on liberty, especially in the matter of polygamy. Accordingly, we find Livingstone making a 350-mile journey within his first year at Kuruman. During it he made contact with Sgkoma, head of the ruling house of Khama of the Ngwato people, a family whose support was later to be vital to Christian progress in the whole of the Tswana-speaking area of southern Africa.

By 1843, Livingstone had formed a station of his own, with the Kgotla people, by 1845 he had moved to the Kwena people. By now he was married to Moffat's daughter Mary, but neither marriage nor the birth of their children made him sedentary. Indeed, Mary and the children often accompanied him on increasingly long journeys across the Kalahari desert. In the course of one of these in 1849 he made his first major contribution to geographical knowledge, the identification of Lake Ngami.

The year 1852 marks a watershed. As if to prove his point about the fragility of mission work in the area, his Kwena station, Kolobeng, was destroyed by the Boers. It also became desirable for his family to return to Britain. Livingstone accompanied them to Cape Town and then began the greatest of all his journeys. Its object was to find centers from which to reach substantial African populations, centers with healthy situations, good communications, and out of reach of the Boers. Livingstone had no illusions that the people of such areas were already "hungry for the gospel" – he reacted sharply against such language as pious fiction. But he expected them to be free from white contamination and thus without the disabilities to conversion of those further south. They would, moreover, immediately recognize the value of missionaries, attracting trade contacts and discouraging aggressors. Any understanding of deeper matters must spring out of that basis of human acceptance. Such realism is characteristic of missions in the pre-imperial period when missionaries had right of access only on terms set by African peoples.

From Cape Town, Livingstone moved up across what is now Botswana and renewed contact, made on a former journey, with the Kololo people. Some of these came with him along the Upper Zambesi and then right across Angola to the coast. Here he could have had a passage home to his family, but he had promised that his Kololo companions would return. He therefore went back with them, and then moved east, across modern Zambia (locating Victoria Falls in the process) and then through Mozambique until in May 1856, having walked across Africa, he arrived near the mouth of the Zambesi.

His journey had taken four years. He had found locations that met his criteria for mission centers, one, especially promising, with the Kololo and one with the Ndebele. He still believed in the community of interest of Christianity, commerce, and civilization, and his journey seemed to open new possibilities for the progress of all three. The Zambesi basin, in particular, had immense potential for agricultural development. It was now a principal source of slaves, a traffic that the introduction of plantation co-ops could undermine. The key to this was the riverine highway of the Zambesi.

The journey made him a celebrity. He had kept in touch with the scientific world, and his contributions to knowledge were applauded. He produced an excellent book, *Missionary Travels and Researches*, which made his activities known to a wider audience. He convinced his own society, the LMS, to open Kololo and Ndebele missions, and to appoint him to the leadership of the former. Established churchmen in the ancient English universities responded enthusiastically and formed the Universities' Mission to Central Africa (UMCA) to follow up some of the openings he had made. Merchants in Manchester caught at the idea of African cotton to replace American (a blow, Livingstone judged, at American slavery). Even the British government was convinced, at least to the extent of commissioning an investigation of the Lower Zambesi to survey sites for possible settlement and agricultural development along with the necessary communications. Livingstone's acceptance of the leadership of this expedition (and his consequent resignation from the missionary society, foregoing the opportunity to commence the Kololo mission) has to be seen in the light of his conviction that the Christian future of inland Africa was tied in with the whole complex of issues that his first great journey had revealed.

If the great walk across Africa from 1852 to 1856 represents the high point of Livingstone's career, the Zambesi Expedition, from 1858 to 1863, is probably its lowest. He was in charge of European colleagues, to whom he denied the trust and openness he commonly displayed to Africans. Personal relations went sour. Mary Livingstone came out to join him, and died soon afterward.

The first mission party of the new UMCA, under its bishop, C.F. Mackenzie (the event had been the occasion for zealous High Churchmen to assert the theory of the necessity of the bishop to the church), accepted Livingstone's guidance and assistance. But soon Mackenzie and others were dead, and the mission abandoned its situation in the Shiré highlands (and with it, for the moment, the Livingstone principle of missions) for the coast. The Portuguese, alerted by the publicity surrounding Livingstone's earlier journeys, refused free trade on the Zambesi. All attempts to find an alternative river route failed, which reduced the value of the most solid geographical achievement of the expedition. This was the identification of an area that would support agricultural development; it was the future Malawi.

The government recalled the expedition. Livingstone's next journey, though little noticed, was perhaps as extraordinary as any; he sailed his little Zambesi River boat himself, all the way from Mozambique to Bombay, to clear up the expedition's affairs. His views as to the future of Christianity and commerce in Africa were unchanged; but neither missions nor government would lend such a ready ear as before. His renown as a geographer was undiminished and the Royal Geographical Society invited him to investigate the interrelations of the upper reaches of the Nile, the Zambesi, and the Congo rivers. But he did not want to be a mere geographer; he wanted geographical knowledge to issue in Christian action. His sense of the horror of the slave trade – "that open sore of Africa" as he called it – was heightened. It seemed that the governments of Christian nations were determined to preserve the traffic; Portugal protected it, Britain did nothing to stop it but talk. Bitterest of all was the knowledge that in the circumstances his own explorations had simply opened new routes for slave traders.

In due course, the remit given by the Royal Geographical Society was widened to allow other sponsors (including the British government, which gave him an unpaid status as consul) and additional objects. He was not only to investigate river systems but to "open Africa to civilizing influences," especially missions and healthy commerce. He followed this remit from January 1866 to his death at Chitambo's village (now Ilala, Zambia) on May 1, 1873. In the meantime he covered immense tracts of what are now the republics of Mozambique, Malawi, Zambia, Tanzania, and Zaire. For the last four years of the journey he was very ill, desperately short of supplies, often in deep depression, sure that he was forgotten, but still convinced of his duty to persevere, refusing opportunities to return. He was often humiliatingly dependent on the Arab traders, a principal part of whose trade he wished to destroy. Of Europeans, only one, H.M. Stanley, saw him alive. The last journey of all was symbolic; his body was carried by his African companions through eight months of danger and toil to the coast. His heart was buried in Africa; his corpse in Westminster Abbey.

Judged by his own objectives, Livingstone had little to show at the time of his death. Those inland mission centers staffed by African evangelists, which he had dreamed of in the 1850s, were long in coming. The missions had not taken up his challenge in his terms with regard to Central Africa; or, as it seemed to him, they had given up. His assurances of the prospects of commerce and "civilization" in Africa met only occasional or tepid response. The British government, which alone could exercise power in the area for moral and beneficent ends, was leaving the field to the baleful influence of Portuguese and Arabs, perpetuating the curse of slavery, inhibiting the only forces that could undermine it.

True, within two decades the situation looked very different. The Central African mission of his own LMS recovered from its discouraging start (though by this time the Kololo, of whom he had hoped so much, hardly counted for anything). The Church of Scotland and the Free Church of Scotland began missions in Malawi, explicitly linked with his name, and, in his spirit, combining with Christian preaching and teaching agriculture and industrial technology as well as academic education. The UMCA, the High Anglican mission, which owed its inspiration to the very nonsectarian Scots Independent, renewed and developed its inland work. Livingstone's name inspired others in the new age of missions. The British presence was extended across East and Central Africa in a way of which Livingstone never dreamed. The lands that he traversed now all have large Christian communities, and Livingstone is in a real sense the pioneer of Central African Christianity. There were trading companies in regions of the lakes; European settlement (which at one time he thought might be the seedcorn of Christian presence and acceptable orderly technological and commercial change) came to some parts of the region. But the world had changed, and the effects were far from his dream of Christian civilization and shared prosperity.

Evaluating Livingstone's Legacy

But this is too narrow a frame on which to consider the legacy of Livingstone. Not for nothing is he remembered as the representative missionary of his time. His stature (not greatly damaged by modern biographers who have brought out the faults and limitations unmarked in earlier hero worship) was that of the missionary of his period writ large. His ideas and ideals were fully compatible with the central missionary thought of that period; once more the comparison with Venn comes to mind. But we must remember what that period was. It was one in which a missionary could become a national figure. In the British public mind, missions could embody national ideals, high endeavor, justice, generosity, self-sacrifice; they did not typify the zeal of a minority, as in earlier times, or the religious and educational aspect of the imperial presence, as in a later period. By the same token, the missionary movement, still holding firmly to evangelical doctrine and experience, felt an obligation to transform society abroad, and to influence government at home. Abroad, the missionary presence was small, and looking to the future; and in Africa, before the massive acquisitions of territory by the Western powers from the 1880s onward, this could only be seen in terms of persuading African peoples. At home, the missionary movement sought to lead, rather than to follow, national policy. The idea of mission based on personal conversion and personal piety alone belongs most characteristically to the imperial period.

The Western world awoke to Africa, and to much of the world, through the voices and writings of missionaries. Livingstone, like his father-in-law, Robert Moffat, and several other noted contemporary missionaries, wrote well and spoke powerfully. The missionary societies of the day created an informed readership and audience that could influence and at times change public opinion. By any reckoning, Livingstone is one of the outstanding explorers of the nineteenth century, and as a scientific observer hard to equal. (His commentaries on African life and belief are strangely sparse, though often revealing when they come, as in the famous abstract of dialogues with the rainmaker.)[4] In this he is representative of others of his generation of missionaries who opened new frontiers of knowledge for the West, pioneered new disciplines in linguistics, comparative literature, Oriental-history studies, ethnography, the history of religions. Yet – and this is also characteristic of the period – Livingstone's contributions to knowledge were all made in the context of a missionary purpose. As he put it, "The end of the geographical feat is but the beginning of the Missionary enterprise." He added, "I take the latter term in its most extended signification, and include every effort made for the amelioration of our race, the promotion of all those means by which God in His providence is working, and bringing all his dealing with man to a glorious consummation."

The missionary task as seen by Livingstone and Venn and their fellows is marked, not by an attempt at balance between a message of personal salvation and one of social renewal (a division they would have found hard to understand), but by the acknowledgment that the very presence of missions in a society had social implications. It is therefore fair to inquire what was the eventual social legacy to Africa of Livingstone and the missions of his day; and immediately one is conscious of some ambiguity. Undoubtedly he is, on one side, the herald of the coming imperial order. He took British power for granted; he desired that it should be used for moral ends. The presence of other incomers to Africa – Boers, Portuguese, Arabs – he saw as largely malevolent. He thought of white settlement – always, he insisted, with the right type of settler – as able to bring about beneficial economic transformation. He died before the annexations of the Western powers, or the realities of the white settlement that came about, brought a wholly new situation.

Yet equally Livingstone is a pioneer of modern independent Africa. His life and writings show a respect for Africans and African personality unusual at the time, and his confidence never wavered in African capacities and in the common humanity of African and European. His missionary principles gave the primacy to Africans in the work of evangelizing Africa. His later career was dominated by the desire to root alien oppression out of Africa. There is a real truth behind the title of one of the popular biographies – *Livingstone the Liberator* – by J.I. Macnair, published in 1940.

If Livingstone is a herald of imperialism, he is also more importantly and permanently a herald of African independence. In this, too, he is typical of the missionary movement of his day. In some respects it led the way to the empires. But, more than any other force of Western origin, it pointed beyond them.

Notes

1. Livingstone, *Missionary Travels and Researches in South Africa* (New York: Harper & Bros., 1858), p. 2.
2. Ibid., p. 6.
3. William Monk, ed., *Dr. Livingstone's Cambridge Lectures* (Cambridge: Deighton, Bell & Co., 1860), p. 168.
4. Livingstone, *Missionary Travels*, pp. 25ff.

Selected Bibliography

Bibliography of David Livingstone

Clendennan, G.W., and I.C. Cunningham. *David Livingstone: A Catalogue of Documents*. Edinburgh: National Library of Scotland for David Livingstone Documentation Project, 1979; Supplement, 1986.
Lloyd, B.W., J. Lashbrook, and T.A. Simons. *A Bibliography of Published Works by and about David Livingstone, 1843-1975*. Cape Town: Univ. of Cape Town Libraries, 1978.

Works by David Livingstone

1858 *Missionary Travels and Researches in South Africa; including a Sketch of Sixteen Years Residence in the Interior of Africa* . . . New York: Harper & Bros.
1860 *Dr. Livingstone's Cambridge Lectures*. Ed. William Monk. Cambridge: Deighton, Bell & Co. 2nd ed., 1960.
1866 (with Charles Livingstone) *Narrative of an Expedition to the Zambesi and Its Tributaries*. New York: Harper & Bros.

Journals and Correspondence of David Livingstone

David Livingstone: Family Letters, 1841-1856. 2 vols. Ed. I. Schapera. London: Chatto & Windus, 1959.
Livingstone's Missionary Correspondence, 1841-1856. Ed. I. Schapera. London: Chatto & Windus, 1961.

David Livingstone: South African Papers, 1849-1853. Ed. I. Schapera. Cape Town: Van Riebeck Society, 1974.

Livingstone's Private Journals, 1851-1853. Ed. I. Schapera. London: Chatto & Windus, 1960.

Livingstone's African Journal, 1853-1856. 2 vols. Ed. I. Schapera. London: Chatto & Windus, 1963.

The Zambesi Expedition of David Livingstone [1858-1863]. 2 vols. Ed. J.P.R. Wallis, in Oppenheimer Series. London: Chatto & Windus, 1956.

The Zambesi Doctors: David Livingstone's Letters to John Kirk, 1858-1872. Ed. R. Foskett. Edinburgh: Edinburgh Univ. Press, 1964.

Works about David Livingstone

Blaikie, W.G. *Present Life of David Livingstone.* New York: Revell, 1880. Verbose and hagiographical, but still valuable.

Chadwick, O. *Mackenzie's Grave.* London: Hodder & Stoughton, 1959. On the first UMCA party and its relations with Livingstone.

David Livingstone and the Rovuma: A Notebook [1862-1863]. Ed. G. Shepperson. Edinburgh: Edinburgh Univ. Press, 1965.

Debenham, F. *The Road to Ilala: David Livingstone's Pilgrimage.* London: Longman, 1955. By a geographer.

Gelfand, M. *Livingstone the Doctor, His Life and Travels: A Study in Medical History.* Oxford: Blackwells, 1957.

Jeal, Tim. *Livingstone.* London: Heinemann, 1973.

The Last Journals of David Livingstone, in Central Africa, from 1865 to his Death . . . Continued by a Narrative Obtained by His Faithful Servants Chumah and Susi. 2 vols. Ed. H. Waller. Hartford, Conn.: R.W. Bliss & Co., 1875.

The Matabele Mission: A Selection from the Correspondence of John and Emily Moffat, Livingstone and Others, 1858-1878. Ed. J.P.R. Wallis, in Oppenheimer Series. London: Chatto & Windus, 1945.

Pachai, B., ed. *Livingstone: Man of Africa: Memorial Essays, 1873-1973.* London: Longman, 1973.

Seaver, George. *David Livingstone: His Life and Letters.* London: Lutterworth; and New York: Harper & Row, 1959.

Stanley, H.M. *How I Found Livingstone.* New York: Scribner, 1874.

H.P.S. Schreuder

1817–1882

Friend of Mpande the Zulu Chief

Olav Guttorm Myklebust

When in 1882 H.P.S. Schreuder died in Natal, South Africa, Josiah Tyler, the veteran American missionary, in an article in the leading paper of the colony, hailed him as "the most remarkable missionary we have had in South Africa."[1] Tyler was not the only one among Schreuder's colleagues and contemporaries to speak of him in such generous terms. Thus John W. Colenso, the Anglican bishop, called him "one of the most experienced, devoted and learned missionaries among the Kafirs."[2] Similar descriptions, by representatives of different churches, could be quoted.[3] In the light of appraisals such as these it is somewhat surprising that most works on the history of missions have little, if anything, to say about the man whose legacy is the subject of this article.[4]

Friend and Linguist of South Africa

Born in 1817 in Sogndal, Norway, Hans Paludan Smith Schreuder, the son of a solicitor, passed his theological examinations at the University of Christiania (now Oslo) with highest distinction. In a treatise bearing the significant title "A Few Words to the Church of Norway on Christian Obligation to be Concerned about the Salvation of Non-Christian Fellow Men," he gave a closely reasoned exposition of the biblical basis of the missionary enterprise.[5] Because the churches in Europe had largely become static and introverted bodies, and also because of the individualistic and undenominational character of the evangelical awakening (to which the modern missionary movement is so deeply indebted), "the friends of missions" could express their concern only by forming independent organizations for the purpose. Schreuder saw clearly the danger of a separation between "church" and "mission." In the course of events, however, the two came to mean different things – a fact described by a competent missiologist as "one of the great calamities of missionary history."[6]

Schreuder's treatise aroused considerable interest, and as a result there was set up in Christiania a committee to enable him, in accordance with a call he had long felt, to go as a missionary to South Africa. When later in the same year (1842) the Norwegian Missionary Society was founded in Stavanger, Schreuder became its first missionary. On New Year's Day 1844 he arrived at Port Natal (Durban). Acting on the advice of Robert Moffat, he made his way northward into the country and became the pioneer of the Christian mission north of the Tugela River much in the same manner as Moffat had become the pioneer of the Christian mission north of the Orange River. The two had much in common. To mention only one thing, both won to an amazing degree the esteem of the people among whom they served. Schreuder's friendship with Mpande, the Zulu chief, was an event just as remarkable as Moffat's friendship with Mzilikazi, the Matabele chief. Schreuder was, to all intents and purpose, the prime minister of King Mpande until the latter's death.[7]

While not the first messenger of the Gospel to enter Kwa Zulu (Zululand), Schreuder was the first permanent resident missionary in that area. After two unsuccessful attempts to obtain from the king permission to settle in his country, and after an abortive attempt to establish a mission in Hong Kong, Schreuder founded in the British colony of Natal, as a base for future operations in Kwa Zulu, the first station, Umpumulo (1850). As a result of Schreuder's skill in healing the king, who had asked his help in a case of illness, access to the land was at last secured. In the early 1850s stations were founded at Empangeni and Entumeni. In the following decades, thanks to the arrival of new missionaries, there were established, under Schreuder's leadership, ten more stations. Due to a variety of causes – political unrest, the king's refusal to allow his people to become Christians, and so forth – progress for many years was very slow. Not until 1858 did the first baptism take place. In Schreuder's lifetime the number of converts never exceeded 300.

Schreuder also introduced two more Lutheran missions in Kwa Zulu, the (German) Hermannsburg Mission and the Church of Sweden Mission. After his consecration in 1866 as "Bishop of the Mission Field of the Church of Norway," Schreuder became the founder of the Norwegian mission in Madagascar. In 1873, because of a controversy with the home board over new administrative measures, he severed his connection with the Norwegian Mission Society. Supported by a new agency named "The Church of Norway Mission established by Schreuder," he carried on the work at Entumeni, the piece of land presented to him in the early 1850s by King Mpande in recognition of his services. He also began a new mission at Untunjambili in Natal.

Schreuder is the author of the first complete grammar of the Zulu language.[8] According to C.M. Doke, "the treatment of the various phenomena in this work is masterful." The work "bears the mark of real pioneer achievement."[9] Like other students of Bantu languages in the middle decades of the nineteenth century, Schreuder had learned from W.B. Boyce's *Grammar of the Kafir Language*.[10] However, Schreuder's own *Grammar* is the fruit of original and independent research. His phonetic approach to the language was much more detailed. In the numbering of noun classes he created his own method by distinguishing between no less than thirteen classes (a method later followed by Bleek and Meinhof for their comparative work). In his orthography he was far in advance of his time, for instance, by inventing special symbols for special sounds. Bishop Colenso, too, himself a linguist of no mean order, had a high opinion of Schreuder's *Grammar*, which he describes as "the work of an excellent missionary and an able philologist."[11]

Schreuder translated parts of the New Testament and of the Psalms into Zulu, but, sadly enough, he never had the opportunity to concentrate on the task of Bible translation. "It has been a matter of regret," writes J. Tyler, "that he did not devote his thorough scholarship and superior knowledge of the Isizulu to a translation of the Scriptures into that language."[12] Mention should also be made of his translation of Luther's *Small Catechism* and of the order of service as used in the Church of Norway.

Throughout his missionary career Schreuder was a keen student of the religion, history, institutions, and customs of the Zulu people as well as of the plant and animal life of their country. Due to the fact that he wrote in Norwegian, his research on these subjects, like that on the language, did not receive the attention it deserved.

Because of Schreuder's friendship with King Mpande, and also because of the trust placed in him by the British, Schreuder was able on several occasions to remove misunderstandings and to prevent clashes between the two races.[13] Under Cetshwayo, Mpande's son and successor, relations became more strained. It was his wish, Cetshwayo declared, that the missionaries should leave the country. On the other hand, he had the ambition of obtaining from the British recognition of himself as the rightful leader of his people. He therefore sought the advice of Schreuder, who agreed to approach the government of Natal in the matter. As a result Theophilus Shepstone, the secretary for native affairs, in 1873 formally installed Cetshwayo as king of the Zulus. An important part of the ceremony was the full assent given by the king to the introduction of new laws, the first of which was that the indiscriminate shedding of blood should cease.[14]

In the difficult years following the installation, Schreuder acted as an intermediary between the Zulu king and the British authorities in Natal. In the war that eventually broke out he offered his services, in the interest of peace, to Zulus and British alike. But when Sir Garnet Wolseley, the commander-in-chief of the British forces, wanted him to act as a spy, Schreuder flatly refused. What he wished, he said, was the destruction, not of Cetshwayo's person, but of his reign of terror only. He offered to go himself to the king and, through a personal interview, to make him realize the futility of further resistance. Schreuder supported Zulu independence, but he also saw clearly that in the new situation this could not be maintained.[15]

Schreuder was by no means an "imperialist." Unlike the English missionaries, who had entered Kwa Zulu at the recommendation of the Natal government, he consistently acted on the principle that missionary work should be carried out without the support of secular authorities. Not until the dramatic events just referred to did he make use of the letters of recommendation with which Lord Stanley, then secretary of state for the colonies, in 1843 had furnished him – letters to the governors of Her Majesty's colonies in South Africa requesting them to "lend their aid toward an object, in which all Christian nations have a common interest." Schreuder's sole object in making use of these documents was to secure for the missions, in connection with the reorganization of the administration of the country in 1879, their freedom and integrity. In these efforts, however, he was bitterly disappointed.[16] It is evident that Sir Garnet was willing to accept help from Schreuder only if by such help he could achieve his own purposes: "Bishop Schreuder left this morning . . . I am glad to get rid of him: he was of no use and I distrusted his judgment."[17]

In contrast to the traditional presentation of him as a self-centered and autocratic churchman, Schreuder can best be described as a simple, sincere believer and a humble servant of the Lord. He combined the strength of the giant with the tenderness of the child. He was essentially an evangelist, and as such he also took seriously the social and political realities of the milieu in which he worked. Genuine piety, moral integrity, independent judgment, rare intellectual gifts, a very high standard of consecration, and unswerving loyalty to the missionary cause – these were his chief characteristics.

In 1858 Schreuder married Emilie Löventhal, who for twenty years, under conditions both primitive and insecure, shared his toil and zeal. Mention should also be made of their faithful fellow laborer Johanne Vedeler, who, two years before Bishop Schreuder's death, became his second wife. Of neither marriage were there any children.

Schreuder's Principles of Mission

Schreuder's missionary thinking is dominated by what for lack of a better term may be called "the concept of wholeness." Of the total reality of the Christian faith, to which this concept refers, four aspects can be distinguished, though of necessity the distinction is for the purpose of analysis only.[18]

1. The finality of the Gospel. To be a Christian is, in Schreuder's words, "to love the Lord and the gospel of his grace, which is to be proclaimed throughout the whole world." By faith in Christ we are called to be witnesses of his redemptive purpose for all people. The Christian mission is participation in the mission of Christ.

More specifically, the source and secret of mission is the stupendous fact that God was in Christ reconciling the world unto himself (2 Cor. 5:19). The obligation to make God as revealed in Christ known everywhere corresponds closely with the uniqueness of the event. Message and mission are indissolubly connected.

Fully identifying himself with the biblical and historic Christian faith, Schreuder necessarily became a fearless opponent of Bishop Colenso. Along with the vast majority of churchmen and missionaries of his day, he was unable to accept Colenso's interpretation of Christianity as a true exposition of the authentic Christian faith.[19] Colenso's approach was essentially that of the scientist. In his theology, however, one misses the emphasis on the uniqueness and urgency of the apostolic message of God's saving acts in Christ for sinful people. The cardinal doctrine of the Gospel, he maintained, is "the Fatherly Relation to us of the Faithful Creator."[20]

2. The centrality of the church. The church, Schreuder insisted, is no mere addendum to individual Christians. On the contrary, it is the element in which the Christian lives and moves and has his being. In his own words, "The individual exists only as part of the whole, and he is called to labor for and along with the whole."

The Great Commission, as understood by Schreuder, is the unshakable and unalterable basis, not primarily of the preaching of the Gospel throughout the world, but of the ministry of preaching as such.[21] The church communicates, through the means of grace entrusted to it by the Lord of the church, Christ's salvation both among its members and to those outside.

Schreuder was not able to endorse the commonly held view that mission is essentially a voluntary activity and that, accordingly, the mission society is its proper agent. Mission, he maintained, is a concern not of a group of interested individuals only but of the church. It is a task in which the total membership of the church shares. Mission is not a specialized activity but, in Schreuder's own words, "a duty incumbent upon the Church and so upon its individual members."

That the missionary enterprise can have no autonomous existence apart from the church does not necessarily mean that, institutionally speaking, the church must be its own missionary society. The Church of Norway of Schreuder's day, a state church of the most rigorous kind, did not possess the organs needed for identifying itself with the task of world evangelization as one church through one missionary agency. What Schreuder advocated, and insisted on, was "the manifestation of the missionary enterprise *in toto* as belonging to the entire Norwegian Lutheran Church, i.e., both as regards doctrine and order."

There is no objection to the church's fulfilling its missionary obedience through an ad hoc organization, provided this organization conceives of its task as a task of the church. Schreuder's view can best be described as *churchly* mission. While consistently regarding himself as a representative of the Church of Norway, he welcomed the establishment of missionary associations and spoke eloquently of the enthusiasm of "the friends of missions." Not only that, but as a missionary he himself successively served with "independent" agencies – at first with a committee, then with a society, and again with a committee.

3. The catholicity of the faith. Although a Lutheran churchman of strong convictions, Schreuder placed his own work as a missionary in its true context of the entire church's obedience to mission. Far from absolutizing his own confession, he emphasized the need for cultivating in all churches, on the basis of the authority of the Scriptures, a sense of oneness. As a "good" Lutheran he looked upon the Lutheran church, not as a separate entity, but as a confessional movement within the total body of Christ. He prayed for the blessing of God upon his people and his work "in every area where the church is established." He rejoiced in the fact of ecumenicity: "to have fellowship with God's children near and far away."

Schreuder strictly adhered to the apostolic principle "not to build on foundations laid by others" (Rom. 15:20), and he expected others to act likewise. The mission is, primarily and fundamentally, the mission of the church of Christ. Missionaries should seek not their own glory but the glory of God. They should gather not for themselves but for God. The task is "first to further the Kingdom of God; second, to extend our own church and mission."

It is to be regretted that Schreuder's comprehensive and well thought-out plan for the evangelization of Kwa Zulu, through the combined efforts of Lutheran and Anglican forces, was rejected. His plea for comity and cooperation, too, fell on deaf ears. In Kwa Zulu, as elsewhere, the absence of consultation among the missions led to proselytism and confusion. Even among missions belonging to the same church family, the sense of mutual responsibility was, to say the least, very weak. In particular, relations between the Norwegian mission and the English mission became strained. Not only did the latter establish itself at a place at which Schreuder already had obtained from the king permission to settle, but the English mission also maintained that it was not in a position to regard efforts on its part as superfluous, because the Church of Norway, in its judgment, had no genuine episcopate.[22]

It was Schreuder's wish, as he put it in a letter to Bishop Colenso, to see Kwa Zulu "filled with the preaching of the pure Gospel," but he did not believe that this could be accompanied "by promiscuously intermixing stations of different societies." He hoped that new missions, before establishing themselves in the land, "first had tried to come to some friendly understanding with" the Norwegian Missionary Society, which has had "the arduous task of opening, under God's good providence, this country for Christian missionaries."[23]

4. The totality of the task. The urgency and vastness of the task that the church faces in the unevangelized regions of the world was, of course, fully appreciated by Schreuder. "Expansiveness," his own word, is of the essence of the mission. Yet he refused to restrict the missionary enterprise to Africa and Asia. "Foreign missions" comprise but a part of the church's total missionary responsibility. By its very nature Christian witness is directed both to the immediate environment and to the world at large.

According to Schreuder, the point of departure for the Christian mission is not the geographical area in which the church exercises its ministry of reconciliation but that ministry itself, which is the proclamation of the Gospel. The strengthening of faith in the countries of the Christian West is in itself a task of primary importance, but it is also of immense relevance to the missionary cause among the peoples of non-Christian continents.

"As Christians," Schreuder writes, "we should confidently praise, exalt and commend the wonderful works of this glorious Gospel among the children of men, among those who are far away and among those who are near at hand." And again: "God's true friends of mission do not neglect the home, i.e. the home of the heart, the home of the house, the home of the village, the home of the town – for the home of the heathen outer-world. Such neglect is in itself a negation of the life of faith. It is contrary to God's ordinance and so excluded from his blessing."

Schreuder's theology of mission is surprisingly modern. Its basic ideas, notably what we have called "the concept of wholeness," are largely identical with the views held by leading missiologists and mission administrators in the second third of the twentieth century. The agreement is the more remarkable since, in this period, the biblical and theological basis of the mission has had more attention paid to it than ever before.[24]

Notes

The following abbreviations are used in the Notes and the Bibliography:
ABCFM American Board of Commissioners for Foreign Missions
CNMS Church of Norway Mission established by Schreuder
NMS Norwegian Missionary Society

1. *Natal Mercury* (Durban), Feb. 17, 1882. Cf. ibid., Feb. 1, 1882: "In memoriam." The *Natal Witness* (Pietermaritzburg), too, bore "high testimony to the heroic work which that devoted missionary accomplished during the years he sojourned here" (Feb. 4, 1882). See also letters to the secretary of the ABCFM: by J. Tyler, Sept. 12, 1866; by N. Adams, May 24, 1845; and by A. Grout, Feb. 20, 1850 (ABCFM archives.)

2. W.H.I. Bleek, on behalf of Bishop Colenso, to Schreuder, Jan. 19, 1856 (NMS archives), J.W. Colenso, *Ten Weeks in Natal* (Cambridge: Macmillan & Co, 1855), p. 15.

3. E.g., J. Stewart, *Dawn in the Dark Continent*, 2nd ed. (Edinburgh: Oliphant, Anderson & Ferrier, 1906), p. 260.

4. In Stephen Neill, *A History of Christian Missions* (Hammondsworth, England: Penguin Books, 1964), the name of Schreuder is conspicuous by its absence. A notable exception is C.P. Groves, *The Planting of Christianity in Africa*, 4 vols. (London: Lutterworth Press, 1954), 2: 144ff., 265ff. The presentation of Schreuder, and of the Norwegian mission in South Africa as a whole, is based upon a summary in English, prepared at Groves's request, by the present writer.

5. Schreuder, *Nogle ord til Norges kirke*. As a vindication of the missionary cause, this treatise, published in Christiania in February 1842, holds a unique place within the Lutheran family of churches. In contrast to W. Carey's *Enquiry*, the approach is not historical and practical, but biblical and theological.

6. Lesslie Newbigin: *One Body, One Gospel, One World* (London and New York: International Missionary Council, 1958), p. 26. Cf. Neill, *A History of Christian Missions*, p. 512.

7. J. Tyler in *Natal Mercury*, Feb. 17, 1882; N. Etherington, *Preachers, Peasants, and Politics in Southeast Africa, 1835-1880* (London: Royal Historical Society, 1978), pp. 75-77, 86.

8. Schreuder, *Grammatik for Zulu-sproget*, a publication of the University of Christiania.

9. C.M. Doke, for many years professor of Bantu languages in Witwatersrand University, Johannesburg, South Africa, in a *Norsk Tidsskrift for Misjon* (Oslo), article on Schreuder's contribution to Zulu grammar (1950; pp. 222-26). The references are to the author's English manuscript. The phrases used are largely those of the author.

10. The first edition of this work appeared in 1834. The term "Kafir," as used here, denotes "Xhosa."

11. Colenso, *Ten Weeks in Natal*, p. 15. Cf. Colenso's *An Elementary Grammar of the Zulu-Kafir Language* (London, 1855), p. 39. Schreuder's elementary reading book, too, was much appreciated by Colenso (W.H.I. Bleek, on behalf of Bishop Colenso, to Schreuder, Pietermaritzburg, Jan. 19, 1856; NMS archives).

12. J. Tyler in *Natal Mercury*, Feb. 17, 1882. A. Grout, too, was greatly impressed by Schreuder's linguistic abilities; see his letter to the secretary of the ABCFM, Feb. 20, 1850 (ABCFM archives). For a recent assessment by an expert on African languages and African Bible translations, see E. Dammann, "Zum Todestage des evangelischen Missionsbischofs H.P.S. Schreuder," *Zeitschrift für Missionswissenschaft und Religionswissenschaft*, 1982, pp. 220-25, especially p. 224. See also E. Dammann, "Die Bedeutung von H.P.S. Schreuder für die Zulu," *Afrika und Übersee*, 1984, pp. 1-14.

13. See note 7, above.

14. Schreuder to Sir Evelyn Wood, Her Majesty's High Commissioner for Southeast Africa, July 30, 1881 (CNMS archives), trans. *Missionsblad* (CNMS, Christiania), 1881, pp. 161-84. See Accounts and Papers (12), Colonies and British Possessions, 1875, vol. 53, C 1137 (British Museum, London).

15. N. Etherington, *Preachers, Peasants, and Politics*, pp. 34f.; cf. N. Etherington, "Social Theory and the Study of Christian Missions in Africa: A South African Case Study," *Africa*, 1977, p. 36.

16. Schreuder to Sir Evelyn Wood, July 30, 1881 (CNMS archives); Accounts and Papers (12), Colonies and British Possessions, 1878-79, vol. 53, C 2308, 2316 (British Museum, London); J.W. Colenso, *Digest upon Zulu Affairs, 1879-83* (Bishopstowe, Natal, 1879-83), 1: 361ff., 642ff. Important materials including correspondence between Schreuder and Sir Garnet Wolseley in CNMS archives. *Sir Garnet Wolseley's South African Diaries (Natal)1875* and *Sir Garnet Wolseley's South African Journal 1879-80*, both edited by A. Preston (Cape Town: A.A. Balkema, 1971, 1973), refer to Schreuder in uncomplimentary terms. This is not surprising, however, as the general was a man rather difficult to deal with. According to the editor, his manner of business was autocratic and arbitrary, and his assessment of individuals uniformly uncharitable (*Diaries*, pp. 15ff.; *Journal*, p. 8).

17. *Wolseley's Journal*, p. 98.

18. The précis of Schreuder's theology of mission that follows is drawn from his published writings, but chiefly from his letters, reports, sermons, etc., in the NMS and CNMS archives.
19. Schreuder to H. Knolleke (London), March 27, 1863 (NMS archives). Colenso's gospel being deprived of its real content, his mission, consequently was only a "quasi-mission" (Schreuder's own description).
20. On Colenso as a "teacher of the modern school," see his "On Missions to the Zulus in Natal and Zululand" (reprinted from the *Social Science Review*, London, 1865, for private circulation); G.W. Cox, *The Life of Bishop Colenso*, 2 vols. (London: W. Ridway, 1888), 1: 156, 280ff.; C. Gray, ed., *Life of Robert Gray*, 2 vols. (London: Rivingtons, 1876), 2: 93ff., 104, 395. For a fresh appraisal, from a liberal point of view, see B.P. Hinchliff, *John Williams Colenso* (London and Edinburgh: Th. Nelson & Sons, 1964).
21. *Nogle ord til Norges kirke*, pp. 13f.
22. *Colonial Church Chronicle and Missionary Journal* (London), 1868, pp. 74ff.
23. Schreuder to John W. Colenso, Oct. 10, 1859 (NMS archives). The English is Schreuder's own.
24. For our purpose here it is sufficient to mention the names of Kraemer, W. Andersen, Newbigin, and Vicedom, and the reports of the conferences at Tambaram, Whitby, Willingen, Ghana, and New Delhi.

Selected Bibliography
Works by H.P.S. Schreuder

1842 *Nogle ord til Norges kirke* (A few words to the Church of Norway). Christiania: Guldberg & Dzwonkowski.
1848 *Laesebog i Zulu-sproget* (A Zulu-language reader). Cape Town.
1850 *Grammatik for Zulu-sproget* (A Zulu-language grammar). Christiania: W.C. Fabritius.
1860 *Psalmebog i Zulu-sproget* (A Zulu-language Hymnbook). Umpumulo, Natal.
1871 *Udtog af Alter-Bogen* (Selections from the Service Book). Translated into Zulu. Umpumulo, Natal.
1872 *Alter-Bogen: Collecter, Epistler og Evangelier* (The Service Book: Collects, Epistles and Gospels). Translated into Zulu. Umpumulo, Natal.
1874 *Dr. M. Luthers Lille Katekisme*. (Dr. M. Luther's Small Catechism). Translated into Zulu. Umpumulo, Natal.

Works about H.P.S. Schreuder

Aktstykker til belysning af forholdet mellem Biskop Schreuder og det Norske Missionsselskab (Documents concerning the relationship between Bishop Schreuder and the Norwegian Missionary Society). Stavanger: L.C. Kielland, 1876.
Beretning om Missionspræst Schreuders ordination til biskop over den Norske Missionsmark (On Rev. H.P.S. Schreuder's consecration as bishop of the mission field of the Church of Norway). Stavanger: NMS, 1868.
Myklebust, O.G. *H.P.S. Schreuder: Kirke og misjon* (H.P.S. Schreuder: Church and Mission). Oslo: Gyldendal Norsk Forlag, 1980. A reevaluation of Schreuder's work and thought, based primarily on unpublished letters, reports, etc. in the NMS and CNMS archives.
_____. "Det norske misjonsselskaps historie i Sør-Afrika" (History of the Norwegian Missionary Society in South Africa), in *Det norske misjonsselkaps historie i hundre år* (Centenary history of the NMS). 3: 5-187. Stavanger: NMS/Dreyer, 1949.
Nome, J. *Demringstid: Fra misjonsinteresse til misjonsselskaps* (From missionary interest to missionary society). Stavanger: NMS, 1942.
_____. "Det norske misjonsselskaps historie i norsk kirkeliv" (History of the Norwegian Missionary Society in Norwegian church life), in *Det norske misjonsselskaps historie i hundre år* (Centenary history of the NMS), vols. 1 and 2. Stavanger: Dreyer, 1943.
Statement of the Right of the Norwegian Church Mission Established by Schreuder to the Entumeni Station in the Zulu Reserve. Christiania: A.W. Brøgger, 1886.

William Wadé Harris

ca. 1860–1929

God Made His Soul a Soul of Fire

David A. Shank

In 1911 Monsignor Jules Moury, vicar apostolic in charge of the Roman Catholic mission in the Ivory Coast, frankly despaired of the future of the church in the neglected French colony. The priests of the Missions Africains de Lyon had arrived on the Gulf of Guinea in 1895 and after more than fifteen years with the help of brothers and sisters from two orders had expended a number of lives and much charity to build a chain of eight major stations along the eastern coast of the Ivory Coast. But they had yielded a slim harvest of only 2,000 baptized souls, and the tribal peoples along the coast were clearly not turning to the Light of Christ.

By contrast, three years later in his annual report of 1914, Moury was almost lyrical: "Space is lacking here for exposing the external means which Divine Providence has used for the accomplishment of His merciful designs. I must thus limit myself to exposing the effects. These effects – it's a whole people who, having destroyed its fetishes, invades our churches en masse, requesting Holy Baptism."[1]

The means that Divine Providence had used was the Glebo prophet William Wadé Harris, who had left Cape Palmas, Liberia, on July 27, 1913, and headed east across the Cavally River, which separated Liberia and the Ivory Coast, in obedience – as he maintained – to Christ's commission in Matthew 28:19. Accompanied by two women disciples – excellent singers playing calabash rattles – he visited village after village, calling the coastal people to abandon and destroy their "fetishes," to turn to the one true and living God, to be baptized and forgiven by the Savior; he then taught them to follow the commandments of God, to live in peace, and organized them for prayer and worship of God in their own languages, music, and dance, to await the "white man with the Book" and the new times that were to come.

In 1926, when missionary methods and their effectiveness were discussed at the international conference at Le Zoute, Belgium, Dr. Edwin W. Smith, former missionary to Rhodesia, wryly remarked:

> The man who should have talked at Le Zoute about preaching to Africans is the prophet Harris who flashed like a meteor through part of West Africa a few years ago. Africa's most successful evangelist, he gathered in a few months a host of converts exceeding in

number the total church membership of all the missions in Nyasaland now after fifty years of work. What was his method?[2]

At the time of Smith's writing, the prophet's legacy was still a recent and almost unbelievable fact in Western missionary experience and literature: more than 100,000 tribal Africans baptized within eighteen months, with many of them ready to be taught by the "white man with the Book" ten years after the event. It is not altogether inappropriate to take a new look at the prophet and his mission, described quite recently by one Catholic historian as "the most extraordinarily successful one man evangelical crusade that Africa has ever known."[3] In earlier years C.P. Groves[4] had pointed to "three notable missionary figures" during World War I in French Africa: Charles de Foucauld in the Sahara, Albert Schweitzer in the rain forests of Gabon, and the prophet Harris evangelizing the pagan tribes of the Ivory Coast. The first two are well known through their writings, their work, and much that has been written about them by their interpreters. But of the African Harris, who left no writings except a half-dozen short dictated messages, the legacy is written only in the historical consequences of his work and ministry; the perspective of seven decades is most helpful in understanding it.

Who Was William Wadé Harris?

In the immediate wake of his ministry of 1913-14, Harris's work was cursorily dismissed by the Catholic missionaries as that of an unscrupulous charlatan carrying out a "Protestant plot" against the mission. In the Gold Coast, Methodist missionaries and African pastors were divided in their appreciation of the man about whom they knew practically nothing, save that he had earlier related to the Methodist church in Liberia. The 1924 arrival in the Ivory Coast of the English Wesleyan Methodist missionaries and their assumption of Harris's succession made them the major source for knowledge of the man. Research in recent years has filled in many gaps of information and understanding, and we now have a fuller understanding of the man behind the prophet.[5]

Until the age of twelve years, Wadé (who was born around 1860) lived in a traditional Glebo village on the littoral east of Cape Palmas, Liberia. Son of a "heathen father," he claimed to be "born Methodist," indicating that it was at a time when conversion meant leaving the "heathen village" for the Christian village on the other side of the lagoon at Half-Graway. Wadé's mother quite exceptionally lived her life of faith in the midst of traditional family life with its sacrifices, divination, witchcraft, and the influences of the "country doctor." The other major exposure to Christianity during this traditional period was the common but ineffective evangelistic foray into the village by Episcopalian missioners.

A second period, with intense exposure to "civilization," came during his adolescence. This included six years with his maternal uncle, the Rev. John C. Lowrie, who took him as a pupil and apprentice into his Methodist pastor-schoolmaster's home in Sinoe, among the immigrant Liberians, outside Glebo territory and outside the influences of traditional life. Lowrie was a former slave, converted and educated at Freetown, and was a remarkable preacher as well as teacher. He baptized Wadé, no doubt gave him the name of William Harris, and taught him to read and write both Glebo and English. Though unconverted during this period, Harris was marked permanently by Lowrie's faith, piety, discipline, and biblical culture as well as his role in society as a man of the Bible. This period concluded with four trips by Harris as a *kroo-boy* (a crew member, sometimes of Kroo ethnic background) on British and German merchant vessels going to Lagos and Gabon, and a stint as headman of *kroo-boys* working in the gold mines inland from Axim in the Gold Coast.

During a time of revival in Harper at Cape Palmas, when he was about twenty-one years of age, Harris was converted in the Methodist church under the summons from Revelation 2:5 ("Remember from whence thou art fallen and repent") by the Liberian preacher Rev. Mr.

Thompson. "The Holy Ghost came upon me. The very year of my conversion I started preaching," he reported many years later. This new Christian period was marked by his Christian marriage in 1885 to Rose Farr, the daughter of Episcopalian catechist John Farr, from the Christian village of Half-Graway. Harris, a stonemason, built their home in the village, and it bore all the marks of a "civilized Christian": sheet-iron roof, second story, shuttered windows, fireplace, and so forth. In 1888 he was confirmed in the Episcopal church by the first Liberian bishop, Samuel D. Ferguson. At the time, the Methodist church was weakening and was chiefly Liberian, while the Episcopal church was financially strong and worked especially among the Glebo. Indeed, Harris later was to condemn his action, taken "for money." But with additional schooling, and a breakthrough in 1892 when the tribe agreed to observe the Sabbath (the bishop called it "the sharp edge of our Gospel wedge"), Harris was appointed assistant teacher and catechist to his native village.

In a context of upward mobility with "civilization and Christianity," Harris was to be a regularly paid agent of the Episcopalian structures for more than fifteen years, until the end of 1908. First a simple catechist, then charged with a village Sunday school, he became a lay reader and eventually a junior warden in his church; in the school he moved from assistant teacher to teacher and thence to head of the small boarding school where his father-in-law and brother-in-law had preceded him. Outside the mission and church circles, he became official government interpreter in 1899 and enjoyed the prestige of go-between for local Liberian officials and the indigenous Glebo populations.

Tragically this whole period was marked by intensive conflict between indigenous and immigrant Americanized blacks. If at the beginning Harris was committed to the "civilizing" pressures of the Episcopal church and the foreign patterns of the Liberian republic, it is also quite clear that halfway through the period a major shift in his loyalties was starting to take place. In 1903 he was temporarily suspended as head of the school and then reinstated in 1905, but his sympathies were very clearly in favor of the Glebo people against the Liberian regime, which was fully supported by the bishop despite its unreadiness to assimilate fully the "Glebo dogs."

Two important patterns of thought were at work in Harris during this evolution. The highly influential Dr. Edward Blyden, born in the Virgin Islands and prominent in Liberia – the best-educated and most articulate black of that period – constantly belabored the ineffectiveness and cultural imperialism of Western missions and firmly promoted an autonomous pan-African church; at the same time he was convinced that the political salvation of Liberia could come only by way of a British protectorate. And in Cape Palmas, Blyden's friend, the secessionist priest Samuel Seton, had created already in 1887 a separatist "Christ church" under the influence of the United States religious leader Charles T. Russell, founder of the group later to be known as Jehovah's Witnesses, whose apocalyptic writings were flooding the region despite the opposition of Bishop Samuel Ferguson.

During the last half of 1908, calling himself the "secretary of the Graway people," Harris engaged in threats and violence and the use of the occult in order to manipulate local Glebo chiefs in favor of the British, against the republic. In February 1909, when a coup d'état involving Blyden failed in Monrovia, co-conspirator Harris – at the risk of his life – was flying the Union Jack at Cape Palmas in expectation of the immediate British takeover for which he had labored. His arrest, imprisonment at Harper (Cape Palmas), Liberia, trial, and condemnation for treason led to a $500 fine and a two-year prison term, for which he was paroled after making monetary payment for all the penalties against him. But he had lost his job with the Episcopal church and with the Liberian authorities for whom he had worked for nine years.

Defying the terms of his parole, William Harris preached vigorously against the Liberian regime, helping to stir up and arm the local population. When war broke out in January 1910, he was back in prison, no doubt for nonrespect of his parole. The war, won by Liberian troops supported by a United States warship, was a complete debacle for the Glebo – fleeing population, plundered villages, fines, forced resettlement – and the most expensive war the young republic had conducted. Harris was in prison, despondent over the turn of events, and it was there around June 1910 that his prophetic future was determined.

The Vocation of the Prophet Harris

A trance-visitation of the angel Gabriel in a wave of light was to William Wadé Harris like a second conversion. During three appearances, he was told that he was to be prophet of the last times; he was to abandon his civilized clothing, including his patent leather shoes, and don a white robe: he was to destroy fetishes, beginning with his own; he was to preach Christian baptism. His wife would die after giving him six shillings to provide for his travel anywhere; though he was not thereafter to have a church marriage, he believed God would give him others to help him in his mission. He then received in a great wave of light an anointing from God where the Spirit came down like water on his head – three times. "It was like ice on my head and all my skin," he later reported.

The Gold Coast barrister Casely Hayford spoke with the prophet at great length in Axim, in July 1914, and was deeply impressed.

> Of his call he speaks with awe. It seems as if God made the soul of Harris a soul of fire . . .
> He has learnt the lesson of those whose lips have been touched by live coal from the altar
> to sink himself in God . . . When we are crossed in ordinary life we never forgive. When
> God crosses our path and twists our purposes unto his own, he can make a mere bamboo
> cross a power unto the reclaiming of souls. God has crossed the path of this humble Glebo
> man and he has had the sense to yield. He has suffered his will to be twisted out of shape
> and so he carries about the symbol of the cross.[6]

The man who in 1908 used whatever violent or occult means were at his disposal to achieve the political autonomy of his people was said to have reported six and a half years later: "I am a prophet above all religions and freed from the control of men. I depend only upon God through the intermediary of the Angel Gabriel who initiated me to my mission of modern last times – of the era of peace about which St. John speaks in the 20th chapter of Revelation, peace of a thousand years whose arrival is at hand."[7]

The young man who had begun his civilized Christian faith and ministry together at the age of twenty-one had compromised it "for money," for a future that led him finally into the morass of political duplicity and manipulation and the way of occult violence for achieving the liberation of his people. Stopped suddenly by events he had helped to precipitate, he was turned back, as it were, to his original task of preaching, but turned forward in absolute confidence of the coming peaceful kingdom of Christ. "Christ must reign," he insisted. "I am his prophet." But this time it was also as a liberated African to fellow Africans rather than as a "civilized" person to the barbarians.

Convinced through Russellite influences that Christ was soon to bring in the kingdom of peace, Harris predicted World War I as a judgment on the civilized world, and then announced a difficult period of seven years, before everything was to be transformed in the reign of Christ. Seeing himself as the Elijah of Malachi 4, he felt he had appeared before the great and dreadful day of the Lord in order to prepare the people for the coming kingdom of peace, during which he was to be the judge responsible for West Africa. His mission was to prepare his constituency through preaching of repentance and baptism and peace, so the Lord would know his own. He had renounced political machination and violence but not a political vision; rather, he had reordered its character and its means and was committed to advance through preaching what would come through the Lord's own doing. He saw as his marching order Christ's Great Commission in Matthew 28:19-20.

Except for his identification with Elijah, the seven-year dating of the arrival of the kingdom, and his own judgeship in it (none of which he imposed upon others), Harris had been caught up in the very un-African eschatological dynamics of New Testament messianism and its spirit, with which he was mightily empowered. The politician Casely Hayford insisted:

> You come to him with a heart full of bitterness, and when he is finished with you all the bitterness is gone out of your soul . . . Why, he calls upon the living God. He calms, under God, the troubled soul. He casts out strife. He allays bitterness. He brings joy and lightness of soul to the despairing. This thing must be of God. He attaches no importance to himself . . . He is the soul of humility.[8]

Twenty years ago, when the historian Gordon Haliburton visited village after village in the Ivory Coast seeking out the old men who could tell him about their memories of the prophet Harris, more than once he was told, "He taught us to live in peace."

Harris's Mission

After his liberation from prison in June 1910, Harris immediately began his prophetic ministry. Briefly reimprisoned, then released, he went up and down the Liberian coast preaching repentance and baptism with apparently only a limited success prior to his Ivory Coast and Gold Coast adventures. There, dressed in a white cassock and turban with a cross-topped staff in one hand and a Bible and baptismal bowl in the other, he cut a striking and original figure as he attacked the local spiritual powers, disarming their practitioners often in a contest where he proved to be the most powerful. In response all the village people would bring their religious artifacts to be burned; then they would kneel for baptism while grasping the cross, and receive a tap of confirmation with the prophet's Bible. The prophet then taught the Ten Commandments, the Lord's Prayer, and on occasion the Apostle's Creed. Migrant Methodist clerks from Sierra Leone and the Gold Coast working in coastal commercial activity were stirred up to follow through with the ministry. Elsewhere the prophet instructed each village to build a simple place of worship, and he would name twelve apostles to govern the new religious community. Where there was a Catholic mission, or the very rare congregation of foreign Methodists, he encouraged people to go there to be taught by men of God. His ministry was accompanied by remarkable healings and strange wonders: the burning of a ship when *kroo-boy* laborers were not discharged from Sunday work; the deaths in rapid succession of the administrator who chased him out of the French colony into the Gold Coast, and of his sergeant who had beaten the prophet; the falling of a church tower after a Catholic priest had dismissed him haughtily; the sudden deaths of those who were baptized but had only hidden, not destroyed, their fetishes. As the rumors of Harris's power and wonders preceded him, masses of people were prepared for his coming and sought him out. In the western Gold Coast, the British administrator could scarcely believe the moral and sanitary transformation that had taken place in villages that he knew so well.

Despite his having been arrested and imprisoned three times in the Ivory Coast, the prophet returned there from the Gold Coast because he felt that God had commanded him to do so. The masses flocked to him in Grand Bassam and Bingerville where again his baptizing was often accompanied by spectacular exorcism and healing. World War I had been declared in early August 1914, and in the French colony missionary priests and colonial administrators answered the call to arms. A religio-political movement was under way that was controlled neither by the Catholic mission nor by the French administration. Harris and his three women were arrested, imprisoned, severely beaten and, a month later (January 1915), expelled by the same authorities who had earlier recognized their public utility. The prophet had, in fact, preached submission to authorities under God's law, denounced alcohol abuse, and had clearly affected the moral climate of the populations by his denunciation of adultery. Back in Liberia in early 1915, one of his singers, the young widow

Helen Valentine, died as a result of the beatings she had received during her mission with the prophet.

Eight times Harris attempted to return to the Ivory Coast but was always stopped by the colonial authorities. But he went up and down the Liberian coast with his mission, often penetrating into the interior where missionaries had never gone. He went to Sierra Leone three times on foot: in 1917, 1919, and 1921. His ministry in Liberia, even if it gave problems to the Methodist missionary Walter B. Williams because of their differences over polygamous marriage, nevertheless provoked a mass "revival movement" in 1915 and the years following. Harris did not denounce polygamy but accepted it as a fact of African life, and this led to continuing problems with the Methodist groups and others.

In 1925 the prophet suffered a stroke, from which he only partially recovered; yet he continued his pilgrim ministry in the interior. When he was visited in 1926 by missionary Pierre Benoit from the Methodist mission, he had just returned from a mission where he had baptized over 500 people. Benoit's contact grew out of the 1924 discovery by British Methodists of the fruits of Harris's labors in the Ivory Coast, which opened a new chapter in missionary history: admitting the facts, accepting the responsibility for the legacy of the "Harrist Protestants," restructuring and absorbing them, teaching and disciplining them. Not all the baptized accepted the new Methodist government of their church life, and Benoit brought back from the aging prophet a Methodist-inspired "testament" to clinch the succession and urge the hesitant into the Methodist fold.

In 1927 the prophet received in his Spring Hill home a delegation of Adjukrou leaders from the Ivory Coast for counsel about accepting Methodist control, and Harris supported the latter against the traditionalist "prophet" Aké. But in December 1928 Harris received another delegation from the Ivory Coast complaining of Methodist disciplines in family and finance. At this final meeting the prophet clearly indicated his disappointment with the Methodist controls and charged a young Ebrié chorister, Jonas Ahui, from the village congregation at Petit Bassam to "begin again." Harris dictated a message to Ahui's father, the village chief, who had been puzzled about how to respond to the missionary presence. To the village chief, the prophet asserted the validity of polygamy if God's law was followed, and denounced the taking of money for religious services performed. Harris was eager to return to the Ivory Coast but could not, for he was "about to go home." But he predicted a new war for France, warned about going to Europe, and referred again to Malachi 4. "If you say you are for God you have to suffer many tribulations. Never give up your God . . . You must always have God before you. It is he who will guide you in all temptation: do not forsake or leave your God to save your life . . . I am yours in Christ."

In April 1929 the prophet died at close to seventy years of age, worn out and in total poverty. It is said that the simple Christian funeral in the village of Spring Hill was presided over by the local Episcopalian minister. Five of his six children, and numerous grandchildren, survived Harris. Today, an improvised but whitewashed cement "tombstone" in the Spring Hill village cemetery bears the crude hand-engraved epitaph: "In loving memory of Propha Wadé Harris born —— died in the year 1928 June 15 Erected by one Abraham Kwang in the year 1968." The local word is that where before there had been only a simple marker, a man from Ghana had made the cement tomb marker out of respect and homage for the prophet who years earlier had raised up his mother three days after her death.

The Legacy

It should be pointed out as a preface to a summary of the Harris legacy that, when compared to other African prophets and their movements, his impact was exceptional: in its massive inter-tribal and inter-colonial character; in its precedence to or major contribution to missionary Christianity; in Harris's initial positive attitude to both British and French colonial regimes, despite his preprophetic negative approach to the black Liberian regime. These unique features condition the legacy in unusual ways.

Harris's work brought about a massive break with the external practices of traditional African religions all along the coast: disappearance of a variety of "taboos" about days and places; disappearance of lascivious dance; the "taming" of traditional festivals; disappearance of huts for isolating women during their menstrual periods; transformation of burial and funeral practices. Ten years after the passage of Harris, the English missionaries observed the great differences between the Ivory Coast and Dahomey or Togo, which they knew so well. It was described in 1922 by the colonial administrator Captain Paul Marty as a "religious fact, almost unbelievable, which has upset all the ideas we had about black societies of the Coast – so primitive, so rustic – and which with our occupation and as a consequence of it will be the most important political and social event of ten centuries of history, past, present or future of the maritime Ivory Coast."[9]

There was created a new indigenous lay religious movement covering a dozen ethnic groups and involving new patterns of unity in the midst of diversity: one God, one theocentric law (the Ten Commandments), one day (Sunday), one book (the Bible), one symbol (the cross), one baptism (break with "fetishes"), one place of worship, one institution (church leadership by "twelve apostles"). Here prayer, including the "Our Father," and transformed traditional song and dance replaced sacrifice and fetish worship. Although different from European Protestantism and Catholicism, it was fed by foreign African lay Christians and constituted a reality so substantial that for Catholic missionaries in 1921 it "threatened" to make of the Ivory Coast a "Protestant nation."

There was a "take-off" of the Catholic mission along the Guinea coast. By 1923 the Ivory Coast church counted 13,000 members and over 10,000 catechumens. The official report of 1925 recognized Harris as the instrument given "to operate the salvation of the Ivory Coast – or at least to begin it." Father Bedal of Korhogo in the north lamented the fact that Harris had not got there to facilitate the evangelization of the Senufo. In Ghana, where there had been no baptized Catholics in Apollonia in 1914, there were in 1920 twenty-six principal stations and thirty-six secondary ones with 5,200 members and 15,400 catechumens. Roman Catholic missionary George Fischer spoke of the "divine fire lit by the grace of the divine Master," but he made no mention of Harris. In Liberia where the Catholic mission had only rebegun in 1906, its prefect, Father Jean Ogé, wrote in 1920 that "the missions are going ahead by leaps and bounds . . . due to the former teaching of the famous prophet Harris. The pagans, deprived of their old gods, stream to our churches and ask for religious instruction."[10]

There was a major breakthrough for Protestant missions. In Ghana the Methodist church was confronted with more than 8,000 people in the Axim area requesting church membership, with village after village requesting catechists and schools. In the Ivory Coast, the 1924 arrival of the British Wesleyans led within sixteen months to the reorganization of more than 160 chapels with more than 32,000 actual names on church registers. The "testament" brought back from Harris in 1926 increased that constituency. In 1927, in response to the Harris impact, the French Baptist Mission Biblique began its work in the southwest. The arrival in 1929 of the Christian and Missionary Alliance from the United States, eager to work with the fruit of Harris's labors, led to their activities in the central Ivory Coast. These constitute three of the major Protestant churches today.

There came about a stimulation of a mass movement into the established Protestant churches in Liberia. The Methodist Episcopal church wrote officially in 1916 of

the great revival movement among the natives with which God has blessed us. But for this our membership could not have made the advance it has. And yet we could not gather into the church all who professed conversion because we had not sufficient number of missionaries to instruct and train them. Many however went into other churches and were not lost to Christianity. Literally thousands, largely young people, have been swept into the kingdom of God.[11]

Dr. Frederick A. Price described it as a "real tidal wave of religious enthusiasm which swept hundreds of people into the Christian church . . . It was nothing else but Pentecost in Africa." But he also pointed out that because of their refusal to abandon polygamy, countless numbers were also refused by the churches, obviously in contradiction to Harris's understanding and preaching.

Many of these people may be members of the invisible church of Christ even though we cannot admit them into full membership in the local assembly . . . One remarkable feature about this great movement was the fact that tribes which seemed the most difficult to approach now became the most responsive to the preaching of the Gospel . . . The revival fire soon spread from one end of the coastline to the other and certain sections of the interior shared the wonderful experience of getting in touch with Christ.[12]

There was also the creation of the Église Harrist (Harrist Church) in the Ivory Coast, in 1931, as a result of the 1928 visit of the Ebrié leader Jonas Ahui, who was consecrated by the prophet, given his cross and Bible and the last written message from Harris. The church is today an important interethnic religious reality of perhaps 200,000 adherents, including communities in Ghana and Liberia. All seven weekly services (three on Sunday) are in the local languages and bear the distinct Harris stamp: strong anti-fetish accent on one God; prayer as a replacement for sacrifice; use of traditional music and dance; use of cross, Bible, calabash, and baptismal bowl as liturgical instruments; liturgical vestments following the model of Harris; traditional marriage practices, with preachers having only one wife; government by "twelve apostles"; self-supporting preachers chosen from within the local congregation. Ahui continued as spiritual head of the church until his death in 1992.

There was a growth of "prophetism" – a kind of third way between traditional religion and the mission-planted churches. The phenomenon has occurred constantly since Harris's time in areas touched by his influence: in Dida country by Makwi, almost parallel with Harris; by Aké among the Adjukru and Abbey in the 1920s; by the prophetess Marie Lalou and the Déima movement following the 1940s, along the northern edge of the areas influenced by Harris; Adaï among the Dida in the 1940s; Papa Nouveau among the Alladian in the 1950s; Josué Edjro among the Adjukru in the 1960s; Albert Atcho, from within the Harrist tradition, serving all of the lagoon peoples. Although Harris is a partial inspiration for the phenomenon, none of these leaders had the authentic Christocentrism of the prototype. Though the movements maintain a certain continuity, there is also a constant movement from them into Christ-centered communities. In Ghana, the prophet-healing accents of the Church of the Twelve Apostles places it somewhat in the same lineage, dating back to two of Harris's actual disciples, Grace Thanni, who accompanied Harris from the Gold Coast, and John Nackabah.

A further result of the grassroots religious shift – coupled with the failures of the missions and churches to follow through (lack of staff, Western piety and disciplines, refusal to recognize polygamy) with the élan of Harris – is found among the many post-Harris autonomous "spiritual" churches of Ghana and Liberia in an evolving popular African Christianity.

An openness to modernity is striking. The opposition of the coastal peoples to the education of their children by the Western colonial schools was broken by Harris, who insisted: "Send your children to school." In September 1915, less than a year after Harris's arrest at the initiative of Lieutenant-Governor Angoulvant, the latter wrote:

At Jacqueville [on the Alladian coast where Harris ministered] the excellent upkeep of the village struck me again. But what I noticed most was the enthusiasm with which the children came to the school which I had just opened. And the great desire that they show for instruction once they have a trained and zealous master like the one I sent them. No school has ever had such success. And it was the chief of Jacqueville himself who furnished the building free of charge until the administration can furnish one.[13]

Those children and the many who followed in numerous other places were among the first cadres of an independent Ivory Coast in 1960: ministers of state, ambassadors, legislative deputies, directors of societies, and so forth.

There was a general climate of peace and cooperative submission along with a deep inner rejection of colonialism with its brutal "pacification" prior to Harris and its conscription and forced labor after Harris. The climate, nourished by the important new autonomous religious grassroots, constituted a particular kind of nationalism, which led to "independence *with* France" under President Felix Houphouet-Boigny and made a significant contribution to the base of the modern-day so-called miracle of the Ivory Coast.[14] More than one well-informed observer has noted the relationship between the impact of Harris and the contemporary scene in the Ivory Coast, characterized by the African accents of hospitality and dialogue and by an absence of social and political violence. The president himself, in an early address to the national assembly, indicated his own awareness of the heritage from Harris that had preceded his own work.

Observations about Harris's Missionary Strategy

In the measure that Harris had a very simple message, insisted on an African church, exploited indigenous values and structures, and respected traditional family structures, one could say that his strategy of African evangelization and church planting was very much that advocated by Blyden, the erstwhile Presbyterian minister who had given up his ministry and his hope for Western missions while retaining his faith in Christ and in the "God of Africa." At one point in his thought, Blyden felt that Christianity in its initial impact upon "heathenism" should be quite similar to Islam in its simplicity of message, symbols, and ritual and in its adaptability to Africa. After an initial implantation, faith could deepen through Christ into a fuller understanding of the African God; even Islam itself could be such a stage forward to the fullness of the Gospel. It was a strategy not unlike that of the present-day Church Growth school with its terminology of "discipling" and "perfecting."[15] However, beyond Blyden the sophisticate, Harris understood that the issue was not just that of simplicity, but rather, of power. Indeed, many have insisted upon a break with the old powers as a crucial factor in evangelism in Africa. Islam has often effected that break but has not yet fulfilled in any massive way Blyden's hope for it in Africa. Harris in a similar way with Christocentric hope, symbolism, and congregation fulfilled the strategy from two points of view. First, Christianity in the lower Ivory Coast is rooted in African soil and it is African Christianity despite heavy Wesleyan Methodist and Roman Catholic overlays. Second, as Capt. Paul Marty observed in 1922, where Harris had left his mark Islam would probably have no appeal. The important presence of Islam in the lower Ivory Coast is due not to its influence among the coastal populations but to the massive immigrations to the prosperous south from upper Ivory Coast and countries to the north, especially under the effects of French colonialism.

The new dimension in Harris's strategy was the administration of baptism immediately following the shift growing out of the power-confrontation; this was to keep people from returning to the old powers – a preventive measure. It was Trinitarian Christian baptism even if the people did not grasp that meaning. Father Joseph Hartz at Grand Bassam wrote: "One day I asked him not to baptise. He therefore brought hundreds of people to me to baptise myself. Upon my request to wait until instruction should have made of these people's souls capable of grasping the character of Baptism, he answered me, 'God will do that.' "[16] If one were to critique the strategy, positively or negatively, it must be done at this point.

In the measure that Harris accented the Sunday Sabbath-keeping as a continued sign of a break with the past, introduced prayer as a replacement for sacrifices, used the Bible in the chapel as a replacement for the collective fetish of the village, introduced new festivals to replace the old, he was simply carrying out a standard Episcopalian pattern that he had seen and practiced among his own people in the Cape Palmas area.[17] The new dimension in the strategy was the maintenance of the traditional music with a transformation of the words, rather than the introduction of a new and foreign hymnology, though his own favorites included "Lo, he comes on clouds descending," "Guide me, O thou great Jehovah," and "What a friend we have in Jesus." The use of calabash and dance was a part of that strategy, despite the ambiguities implicit in their maintenance. But it was crucial for a people in a tradition of orality, and Harris did not see literacy as a prerequisite to faith.

Harris's strong awareness and expression of the power of the Holy Spirit and the Spirit's gifts (foresight, prediction, healing, exorcism, tongues, trance-visitations, empowerment of the word, wonders) was an appropriation of his own, of an important biblical and apostolic reality, which had been nurtured by a deep biblical culture begun under the influence of the Methodist John C. Lowrie. But with Harris the expression of those powers had its own African color and shape for which he had no other visual prototypes than the traditional "country doctors."

In the measure that he was driven by an eschatological urgency, confirmed by the "Armageddon" of World War I, and had himself become the point of power-confrontation in a major messianic breakthrough orientated to a kingdom of peace, Harris was involved in a quite un-African strategy influenced by the Russellite writings on the kingdom of God and the need for an Elijah-people to proclaim and live it faithfully until the end, despite opposition from political or ecclesiastical powers. The Protestant missionary milieux he had known had shielded him from this New Testament virus, which he caught from the sectarians.

Indeed, the Harris strategy, like the legacy, was a synthesis of many strands. But the legacy, unlike the strategy, has not maintained the central dynamic.

Notes

1. Archives of the Société des Missions Africaines (Rome), 12/804.07:28:761, 1914.

2. Edwin W.S. Smith, *The Christian Mission in Africa* (London and New York: International Missionary Council, 1926), p. 42.

3. Adrian Hastings, *African Christianity* (London and Dublin: Geoffrey Chapman, 1976), p. 10.

4. C.P. Groves, *The Planting of Christianity in Africa* (London: Lutterworth Press, 1958), 4: 41.

5. See David A. Shank, "A Prophet of Modern Times; The Thought of William Wadé Harris." 3 vols. (Ph.D. diss., University of Aberdeen, 1980).

6. Casely Hayford, *William Waddy Harris: The West African Reformer* (London: C.M. Phillips, 1915), pp. 16-17.

7. Translation from G. van Bulck, "Le prophète Harris vu par lui-même (Côte d'Ivoire 1914)," in *Devant les sectes non-chrétiennes* (Louvain: XXXème Semaine de Missiologie, 1961), pp. 120-24.

8. Hayford, *William Waddy Harris*, pp. 16-17.

9. Paul Marty, *Études sur l'Islam en Côte d'Ivoire* (Paris: Éditions Ernest Leroux, 1922), p. 13.

10. Quoted in E.M. Hogan, *Catholic Missionaries and Liberia* (Cork, Ireland: Cork Univ. Press, 1981), p. 103.

11. *Liberian Conference Blue Book* [Liberian Methodist Church] (Monrovia: College of West Africa Press, 1916), pp. 7f.

12. Frederick A. Price, *Liberian Odyssey* (New York: Pageant Press, 1954), pp. 142-48.

13. *L'Indépendant de la Côte d'Ivoire* [newspaper published at Grant Bassam, Ivory Coast] 137, Sept. 7, 1915.

14. This is discussed in E. Amos-Djoro, "Les églises harristes et le nationalisme ivoirien," *Le mois en Afrique* 5 (1966): 26-47.

15. The comparison of church growth theory and practice with the ministry of Harris has received attention in J. Stanley Friesen, "The Significance of Indigenous Movements for the Study of Church Growth," in *The Challenge of Church Growth,* ed. Wilbert R. Shenk (Elkhart, Ind.: Institute of Mennonite Studies, 1973).

16. See van Bulck, "Le prophète Harris," pp. 120-24.

17. The differences among community conversion, individual conversions through the Word, and individual conversions through the Holy Spirit power signs, in each of their social manifestations in the Ivory Coast, have been very carefully studied by Charles-Daniel Maire, "Dynamique sociale des mutations religieuses: Expansions des protestantismes en Côte d'Ivoire", unpublished memoir at Paris/Sorbonne, E.P.H.E., 1975.

Bibliography

Friesen, J. Stanley. "The Significance of Indigenous Movements for the Study of Church Growth." In *The Challenge of Church Growth,* ed. Wilbert R. Shenk. Elkhart. Ind.: Institute of Mennonite Studies, 1973.

Haliburton, Gordon Mackay. *The Prophet Harris.* London: Longmans, 1973.

Hayford, Casely. *William Waddy Harris: The West African Reformer.* London: C.M. Phillips, 1915.

Shank, David A. *Prophet Harris, the "Black Elijah" of West Africa.* Leiden: E.J. Brill, 1994.

Van Bulck, G. "Le prophète Harris, vu par lui-même." In *Devant les sectes non-chrétiennes.* Louvain: XXXème Semaine de Missiologie, 1961.

Walker, Sheila Suzanne. "Christianity African Style: The Harrist Church of the Ivory Coast." Ph.D. diss., University of Chicago, 1976.

_____. "The Message as the Medium: The Harrist Churches of the Ivory Coast and Ghana." In *African Christianity: Patterns of Religious Continuity,* ed. George Bond et al. New York: Academic Press, 1979.

_____. *The Religious Revolution in the Ivory Coast: The Prophet Harris and His Church.* Chapel Hill: Univ. of North Carolina Press, 1983.

Donald Fraser

1870–1933

God's Love and Forgiveness in African Terms

Jack Thompson

Deep in the bush of Malawi, Central Africa, on the edge of what is still the small village of Embangweni, stands a simple stone cross, inscribed with the words "In memory of Donald Fraser and Jonathan Chirwa." Here, side by side, in what was the chief's cattle kraal – the place of burial for those held in particular esteem among the cattle-herding Ngoni people – lie the Scottish missionary and his Malawian colleague. Fraser died in Scotland on August 20, 1933, following an operation for the removal of his gall bladder. He was cremated, and his ashes were brought back to Malawi by his wife for burial at the place of his missionary service. The positioning of the graves bears witness both to the respect with which the Ngoni people regarded Fraser and to the affection that he himself had for those among whom he worked.

Today Donald Fraser is not widely known outside Malawi and Scotland. Yet in his day he was both active missionary and internationally known mission strategist, friend and colleague of men like John R. Mott and Joseph H. Oldham, and many of his insights into both the theory and practice of mission remain valid, and valuable, for us today.

Early Development in Leadership

Donald Fraser was born on June 1, 1870, the fourth of eight children, at Lochgilphead in Argyllshire, Scotland, where his father, William, was the local Free Church of Scotland minister. Donald entered Glasgow University in 1886, at the age of sixteen but left without completing his M.A. to enter the Free Church Hall and study for the ministry.[1] In 1891, while attending the Keswick Convention for the first time, he had a deep religious experience that he later described as "the wonder of forgiveness."[2]

Three years later he had perhaps an even more important experience during a student conference at Keswick attended by many who were later to become important figures in the missionary movement, including Joseph Oldham, Temple Gairdner, and Douglas Thornton. Following a speech by the young American Robert E. Speer on the "watchword" of the American Student Volunteer Movement – "The Evangelization of the World in This Generation" – Fraser was so affected that he spent the night in prayer and meditation at the nearby Castlerigg Stone Circle. One of his colleagues later remarked, "After that we all felt the prophetic touch of leadership was upon Donald Fraser."[3] By this time Fraser had already helped to found the Student Volunteer Movement in Britain, having invited Robert P. Wilder to visit Britain in 1892.[4] As a result of a series of meetings in both England and Scotland, the Student Volunteer Missionary Union of Great Britain and Ireland was founded in Edinburgh in April 1892, and in 1893 Fraser became traveling secretary for the British SVM.

In 1894 Fraser visited the conference of the American SVM at Detroit, where he discussed with John R. Mott the desirability of creating a world student body. The discussions were renewed at the Keswick student convention of 1895, when Mott and Luther Wishard were both present.[5] In August of the same year the World Student Christian Federation was formed at a meeting at Vadstena in Sweden, and though Fraser was not present at its inauguration, his part in bringing it about was substantial.

In January 1896 the British SVM held a major conference at Liverpool with the theme "Make Jesus King." Fraser was chairman of this conference, which was attended by over seven hundred delegates. In the 1890s the sight of a young man of twenty-five chairing a huge conference of this sort with verve and efficiency made a deep impression. Among the decisions of the conference was one to adopt the American SVM watchword.[6]

By this time Fraser had already applied to the Free Church of Scotland to go to Malawi (then British Central Africa) as a missionary. Before leaving for Africa in June 1896, Fraser undertook a tour of six European countries on behalf of the SVM, and on his way out to Malawi he stopped in South Africa, where he undertook a three-month tour of universities and colleges to promote and encourage the movement there. He also visited Lovedale, the great center of Free Church of Scotland educational work in Cape Province, from which several local evangelists had gone to work in Malawi.

In the early 1890s, then, Fraser's impact on the student world in Britain, Europe, and South Africa was significant. Tissington Tatlow wrote that Donald Fraser "left his mark permanently on the [British] movement."[7] These early years of involvement in the SVM were also important in quite different ways for Fraser's future missionary career. First, they meant that he arrived in Malawi, not as a raw recruit, to be molded and shaped by the existing policies of the mission, but as an experienced and respected leader. Second, the ecumenical and international contacts that he had already made before he began his missionary career undoubtedly broadened his theological outlook, affecting the way in which he reflected on mission and put it into practice. The two points taken together meant that from the very beginning he was able to develop policies that were often distinct from, and occasionally at odds with, those of his missionary colleagues.

Mission and Innovation among the Ngoni

In January 1897, following his South African tour, Fraser arrived in northern Malawi, where he was to work with the Livingstonia Mission. This mission had been set up in 1874 in memory of David Livingstone, and though associated primarily with the Free (from 1900 United Free) Church of Scotland, it was technically an independent organization. It had begun its work in Malawi in 1875 at Cape Maclear, at the southern end of Lake Malawi, but by the time Fraser arrived the Livingstonia Mission was working predominantly in the north of the country, among the Tumbuka, Tonga, and Ngoni peoples.

Fraser was allocated to work with the Ngoni, a tribe related to both the modern Zulu and Xhosa nations of South Africa. The Ngoni had migrated from South Africa northward during the *mfecane* (the time of troubles), which had led to the rise of the Zulu leader Shaka.[8] They are normally characterized (if not caricatured) as a warlike people resistant to the Christian Gospel. By the time of Fraser's arrival various factors had combined to change that, and within a few years thousands were to seek baptism.

The policies followed by Fraser encouraged this trend. They did not initiate it, as Fraser himself was aware; but it would be fair to say that his policies were often closer to the priorities and concerns of the Ngoni themselves than were those of some of his missionary colleagues, and that they struck a chord of responsiveness.

One preeminent example of this was Fraser's use of large sacramental conventions as a mission strategy. In the Scottish highland tradition in which he was brought up, the tradition of the Communion season was well known. Here people gathered from a wide area for a week of services and teaching that culminated in the celebration of the Lord's Supper. Fraser based his African conventions on this tradition but added baptism to Communion as the essential ingredients of the occasion.[9]

When he held his first such convention at Ekwendeni in May 1898, about 4,000 people attended, although at the time there were less than 400 baptized Ngoni Christians. The following year the occasion was even bigger, with well over 6,000 attending, and 309 adults and 148 children were baptized. So big was the gathering that temporary grass huts (*misasa*) had to be erected to accommodate the visitors, leading some of Fraser's colleagues to compare the occasion to the Hebrew Feast of Tabernacles.[10] There is little doubt that the real attraction for the Ngoni was that it reminded them of their traditional feast, the *incwala,* or feast of the firstfruits. This was a national festival that had died out during the long migration from the south, but the memory obviously remained and was meaningful.

Fraser's use of these large conventions, against the wishes of some of his missionary colleagues who considered them too emotional, was part of his general sympathy for African culture. Many years later he wrote:

> I fear the Evangel which de-nationalizes, which refuses to recognize the power of the Gospel to purify what is not essentially wrong, and which preaches first through prohibitions, rather than by the attraction of what is positive . . . We come not to destroy distinctive nationality, but to fulfil what men have searched after gropingly; and for the enrichment of the world to retain and purify all that is not evil.
>
> If our presentation of the Gospel puts its emphasis on the prohibition of social practices which are not essentially evil, we are apt to arouse an antagonism of nationality when we should have made it our greatest ally.[11]

Fraser's attitude toward African culture may also be seen in his encouragement of indigenous music. The Ngoni were a very musical people, with a rich tradition of praise songs to the chief, as well as wedding, hunting, and war songs. Earlier missionaries had thought these inappropriate for Christian use, though William Koyi, one of the black African evangelists who had come from Lovedale in South Africa to work at Livingstonia, had introduced Zulu hymns to the Ngoni.[12]

The process of Ngoni Christian hymn composition was already under way when Fraser arrived. His contribution lay in the way in which he encouraged and channeled the tradition. He did so primarily in connection with the sacramental conventions, by holding hymn-writing competitions each year. On occasion there were as many as fifty new compositions submitted. Sometimes these were new Christian words set to traditional Ngoni tunes; on other occasions both tune and words were new, but in traditional style. At their best these hymns were not only sung but danced (though in a restrained way very different from Ngoni war dances).[13]

Before long these Ngoni hymns were being translated into the other languages used in the mission area. When, in 1910, a new hymnbook was being compiled by the Livingstonia Mission,

Fraser's membership on the working committee ensured that many Ngoni hymns were included. The best of these also found their way into other hymnbooks in different parts of Malawi and, more recently, into some international and ecumenical collections of hymns.[14]

In general it could be argued that Fraser was much more trusting of and encouraging toward the local Christians in his area than most of his colleagues. This can be seen in several ways – his practice of baptizing Africans relatively soon after their conversion, his encouragement of women in leadership roles, and his devolution of at least some missionary powers to local Christians through a system of subsessions.

By the time Fraser arrived in Malawi, a fairly rigid system of hearers and catechumens classes had already been established, which meant, in practice, that the period between confession of faith and baptism might (and usually did) last several years. While accepting the system in principle, Fraser administered it much more flexibly than many of his colleagues.[15]

As the Ngoni church grew, ways needed to be found for ministering to the large numbers of women converts. As early as 1901 Fraser proposed in the presbytery the organization and training of an order of deaconesses.[16] At this period the presbytery was largely dominated by white male missionaries. No action was taken on Fraser's proposal, so in the same year he instituted an order of women known locally as *balalakazi* (women elders). Since the presbytery did not recognize the right of women to be elders for a further thirty-five years, the *balalakazi* remained an unofficial grouping; in practice, however, these women fulfilled the functions of elders in the local church and mirrored similar female groupings in traditional Ngoni society.[17] Here, as elsewhere, Fraser succeeded because he worked with rather than against the traditional values of the Ngoni people.

Moving toward Indigenous Control

By the early years of the twentieth century, missionaries like Fraser were responsible for thousands of Christians spread over vast areas. The presbyterian system operated by the Scottish missionaries meant that groups of elders could meet officially only when presided over by an ordained minister. Since at this period there were no African ordained ministers in the mission, this tradition effectively centralized power in the hands of the European missionaries. Once again, Fraser bypassed the system by creating a completely new structure, known locally as *masessioni ghachoko* (subsessions). These were, effectively, groups of local Christians, presided over by an evangelist, who oversaw the work of the church in their own areas. Major decisions still had to be referred to the main session, presided over by Fraser, but the system did give local Christians at least some effective control of their own communities.[18]

Fraser's missionary career lasted from 1896 until 1925 (though he had several long periods in Scotland between these dates, organizing missionary campaigns in 1906 and 1921-22, and serving as moderator of the United Free Church in 1922-23). Throughout his missionary service Fraser wrote regularly on a wide range of subjects. He authored six books and wrote innumerable articles for church and mission publications. Running through all of these works is an unusual combination of evangelical fervor, on the one hand, and sympathy for African culture and political advance, on the other. This combination can be seen most clearly in Fraser's views on mission education, where he championed the idea of the vernacular village school, which he saw primarily as an evangelical agency but also as a means of self-sufficiency for the African masses. He was particularly concerned that Africans should not be educated simply to meet the needs of European colonists and traders. In a hard-hitting letter written to R.F. Gaunt, the newly appointed colonial director of education for Nyasaland (Malawi) in 1927, Fraser wrote: "Education must necessarily arouse discontent with poor conditions and the restlessness of the awakening natural consciousness. Some might think you desire to create an African who will be content with the position given to him and never be a trouble to Government." He went on to outline his own ideas of the kind of social effects education should produce: "The small trades and industries will be in the hands of the natives and not of Greeks, Indians or Chinese . . . A man should not finish his apprenticeship in an industry without knowing how to conduct his trade in his community, not as a servant of the European but as his own master."[19]

Contributions of a Veteran Evangelist

Throughout his missionary career Fraser had been in regular correspondence with men such as Mott and Oldham. With Oldham in particular he had a long-standing and close relationship, dating back to their early days together in the SVMU and continuing, for example, in 1906, when Fraser asked Oldham to become secretary of the Mission Study Movement that he was launching in Scotland.[20] Undoubtedly, however, it was in the 1920s that Fraser's influence as a mission strategist (both in Scotland and on the international scene) was greatest.

During the 1920s, he was successively director of the Scottish Churches' Missionary campaign of 1921-22 and moderator of the United Free Church of Scotland in 1922-23. He also, through speaking engagements at student conferences, had a considerable influence on a younger generation of missionaries and missiologists such as Stephen Neill and J.W.C. Dougall.[21]

Throughout his time in Africa Fraser was supported and upheld by his wife, Agnes, a medical doctor whom he had married in 1901 and who, among many distinctions in her own right, wrote Fraser's biography soon after he died. She then returned as a medical missionary to the newly formed Copperbelt Mission in Zambia. They had four children – Violet, George, Catherine, and Donald, Jr.

His missionary career ended, as it had begun, with the chairmanship of a major mission conference. Before leaving for Africa in 1896 he had chaired the Liverpool Conference of the Student Volunteer Missionary Union; in 1926, shortly after his final return from Africa, he was chairman of the Le Zoute conference on "The Christian Mission in Africa."[22] That he was asked to fill the chair at such a prestigious conference is, in itself, an indication of the esteem in which he was held by the international mission community.

Le Zoute was a difficult conference, caught between two worlds in several senses of the term. Some delegates thought it too biased toward the educational fashion of adaptation, popularized in the 1920s by the Phelps-Stokes commissions, and the ideas of Jesse Jones.[23] Others felt it was too biased toward education, with not enough emphasis on evangelization. Like Edinburgh 1910 (and in spite of all that had happened in between), it was predominantly a Caucasian conference, with only about four black Africans present. Writers such as Edwin Smith and Roland Allen were quite critical of several of the viewpoints expressed at Le Zoute, Allen, for example, arguing that the conference largely ignored the concerns of the local church.[24]

Fraser's particular contributions to Le Zoute came in the area of evangelism. In addition to his overall chairmanship, he also chaired the sectional meeting on "Evangelism and the Church." In preparation for this he had begun writing a major article, "The Evangelistic Approach to the African," before he left Malawi in 1925.[25] Fraser was always an evangelist at heart, and this article, which was one of the conference papers, represents his mature thinking on the nature of the missionary task after thirty years of practical missionary work.

Among the points made by Fraser in the article were the following: the danger of presenting Christianity in a Europeanized or denominational form, the importance of the missionary's character as a force for change, the need to relate Christian doctrines such as the atonement to historical African concepts of humanity and God and to accept African customs that were not essentially anti-Christian, the desirability of using African music in worship, and the missionary need to recognize the importance of dreams and visions in the religious life of Africa.[26] Such a list does not seem out of date even now, nearly seventy years later.

Yet, in spite of his contributions to international missionary thinking on such issues as evangelism and education, Fraser was, first and foremost, a practical missionary. Let us end where we began, with the stone cross linking Jonathan Chirwa and Donald Fraser. In 1916 Chirwa, one of the first Malawians to be ordained to the Presbyterian ministry, was posted to a remote station in what is now Zambia. There he committed adultery, which he returned to confess to Fraser.[27] The presbytery suspended him from his ministry and church membership, and there was a strong body of missionary opinion that was opposed in principle to reinstatement. Fraser, however, was convinced of the sincerity of Chirwa's repentance and, together with strong elements in the Ngoni church, fought for seven years to have him reinstated.[28] Finally in 1924, and against the wishes of the senior missionaries Laws and MacAlpine, the presbytery voted to reinstate Chirwa, and he became one of the most beloved and respected of early Malawian clergy.[29]

For Fraser, mission was essentially about the love and forgiveness of God, which he amply demonstrated in his own life and service.

Notes

1. Agnes R. Fraser, *Donald Fraser of Livingstonia* (London: Hodder & Stoughton, 1934), pp 12-13.
2. Article by Fraser in *The Student Movement* 15 (1912): 150, quoted in Tissington Tatlow, *The Story of the Student Christian Movement of Great Britain and Ireland* (London: SCM Press, 1933), p. 24.
3. Ruth Rouse, *The World's Student Christian Federation* (London: SCM Press, 1948), pp. 95-97.
4. Tatlow, *Story of SCM*, p. 24.
5. Rouse, *World's SCF*, pp. 52, 56, 57 and 62.
6. *Make Jesus King: The Report of the International Students' Missionary Conference, Liverpool, January 1-5, 1896* (London: Student Volunteer Missionary Union, [1896]).
7. Tatlow, *Story of SCM*, p. 63.
8. Earlier generations of historians had, on the whole, seen the rise of Shaka as a *cause* of the *mfecane*. It is now generally accepted that the causes were much more widespread – including overpopulation and famine – and that the rise of Shaka was a *result* of this process.
9. A full discussion of Fraser's sacramental conventions and their significance can be found in T.J. Thompson, "Fraser and the Ngoni: A Study of the Growth of Christianity Among the Ngoni of Northern Malawi, 1878-1933, with Special Reference to the Work of Donald Fraser" (Ph.D. diss., Univ. of Edinburgh, 1980), pp. 124-34.
10. *Free Church of Scotland Monthly*, September 1899; and *Aurora* 3 (June 1899).
11. Donald Fraser, "The Evangelistic Approach to the African," *International Review of Missions* 15 (1926): 438-49.
12. Letter from William Koyi, dated February 1883, in *Free Church of Scotland Monthly*, August 1883, p. 241.
13. *United Free Church of Scotland Missionary Record*, March 1902, p. 166.
14. See, for example, *Free to Serve: Hymns from Africa*, collected by Tom Colvin (Glasgow: Iona Community, 1970).
15. Thompson, "Fraser and the Ngoni," pp. 189-93.
16. North Livingstonia Presbytery Minutes, May 27, 1901, National Archives of Malawi.
17. Margaret Read, "The Ngoni and Adjustments to Social Change" (unpublished typescript in *Read Papers*, London School of Economics).
18. Middle Rukuru (Mariba) Session Minute Book, National Archives of Malawi.
19. Fraser to R.F. Gaunt, May 25, 1927, "Nyasaland Education," Box 1209, International Missionary Council Archives, School of Oriental and African Studies, London.
20. J.W.C. Dougall, "J.H. Oldham," *International Review of Mission* 59 (January 1970): 8-22.
21. Stephen Neil, personal communication, July 21, 1972; and J.W.C. Dougall, personal interview, November 30, 1977.
22. Edwin W. Smith, *The Christian Mission in Africa: A Study Based on the Work of the International Conference at Le Zoute* (London: International Missionary Council, 1926).

23. Two Phelps-Stokes commissions visited West and Central Africa in the mid-1920s. Considerable controversy surrounds the question of whether their interest in the concept of educational adaptation was inherently racist, aimed at limiting rather than expanding African educational opportunities. For detailed discussion of these points, see K.J. King, *Pan-Africanism and Education* (Oxford: Clarendon Press, 1971).

24. Smith, *Christian Mission;* and Roland Allen, *Le Zoute: A Critical Review of the Christian Mission in Africa* (London: World Dominion Press, 1927).

25. Donald Fraser, 1925 notebook, vol. 5, ms. 8981, National Library of Scotland, Edinburgh.

26. Fraser,"Evangelistic Approach."

27. Agnes Fraser, *Donald Fraser,* p. 231.

28. Jack Thompson, "An Independent Church Which Never Was: The Case of Jonathan Chirwa," in *Exploring New Religious Movements: Essays in Honour of Harold W. Turner,* ed. A.F. Walls and Wilbert R. Shenk (Elkhart, Ind.: Mission Focus, 1990), pp. 107-18.

29. W.H. Watson, personal communication, October 8, 1974; and Helen Taylor, personal interview, January 16, 1974.

Selected Bibliography

Works by Donald Fraser

1901 "The Zulu of Nyasaland: Their Manners and Customs." *Proceedings of the Philosophical Society of Glasgow* 32.

1911 *The Future of Africa.* London: Student Volunteer Missionary Union.

1913 "The Growth of the Church in the Mission Field." *International Review of Missions* 2.

1914 *Winning a Primitive People.* London: Seeley Service.

1915 *Livingstonia: The Story of Our Mission.* Edinburgh: United Free Church of Scotland.

1921 "The Church and Games in Africa." *International Review of Missions* 10.

1922 "The Scottish Churches' Missionary Campaign." *International Review of Missions* 11.

1923 *African Idylls.* London: Seeley Service.

1925 *The Autobiography of an African.* London: Seeley Service.

1926 "The Evangelistic Approach to the African." *International Review of Missions* 15.

1927 *The New Africa.* London: Church Missionary Society.

Works about Donald Fraser

Fraser, Agnes R. *Donald Fraser of Livingstonia.* London: Hodder & Stoughton, 1934.

McCracken, John. *Politics and Christianity in Malawi, 1875-1940.* Cambridge: Cambridge Univ. Press, 1977.

Thompson, T. Jack. *Christianity in Northern Malawi: Missionary Methods and Ngoni Culture.* Leiden: Brill, 1995.

_____. "Fraser and the Ngoni: A Study of the Growth of Christianity Among the Ngoni of Northern Malawi, 1878-1933, with Special Reference to the Work of Donald Fraser." Ph.D. diss., Univ. of Edinburgh, 1980.

_____. "An Independent Church Which Never Was: The Case of Jonathan Chirwa." In *Exploring New Religious Movements: Essays in Honour of Harold W. Turner,* ed. A.F. Walls and Wilbert R. Shenk. Elkhart, Ind.: Mission Focus, 1990, pp. 107-18.

Bruno Gutmann

1876–1966

Building on Clan, Neighborhood, and Age Groups

Ernst Jäschke

Johannes Christiaan Hoekendijk's doctoral dissertation *Kerk en Volk in de Duitse Zending-swetenschap,*[1] published in 1948, may be regarded in missiological circles as a definitive statement on the "organic folk unit" mission method. When Bruno Gutmann, one of the most remarkable representatives of that missiological school, passed away on December 17, 1966, a very important period in German missiology came to an end. Gutmann's concepts need to be taken seriously, especially in the light of recent developments in the Third World.[2]

For a true picture of Gutmann, one must consider his family background. He says of himself, "My paternal and maternal grandparents were farmers. My father came from the Meissen plains [German Saxony], where my grandfather had a farm. My mother came from the Erzgebirge ranges, where her father, Weichelt, was a small landholder."[3] It is in these rural origins that we find the roots of Gutmann's emphasis on ties to the soil, the source of his great love for animals, and his deep understanding of family relationships.

In his praise of God's creation, Gutmann was a gifted poet. He never tired of glorifying the Creator's greatness; nature in its manifold forms was, for him – a descendant of farmers – an ever new manifestation of God the Creator himself. Thus we find in Gutmann a theologian who regularly emphasized the first article of the Christian Creed.

Bruno Gutmann was born on July 4, 1876, in Dresden (Saxony). He says, "My youth was overshadowed by various misfortunes in the family."[4] His father lost part of his share of the inheritance by not finding a buyer for the house he had built on the outskirts of Dresden. His pious mother died on May 6, 1882, when Bruno was only five years of age, and he grew up with his grandparents. "Already at the age of eleven," he writes, "I had to contribute to the family finances with earnings from employment at the local factory after school. I worked at the factory for one year and received as wages every fortnight one taler [$1.50], which I handed over to my grandmother."[5] So in his childhood, he experienced both mutual assistance and strong family ties. We can thus understand his appreciation of clan relationships throughout his life's work.

Gutmann grew up at a time in which the welfare state was unknown. The family regulated its own affairs, as is still the case in agricultural societies. He encountered the same basic understandings among the African small landholders and, to a far greater extent than any European before him, he studied the origins of mutual assistance in their clan and family life and sought to make those relationships fruitful in the missionary task. To a certain extent the family as Gutmann experienced it corresponded to that described in Wilhelm Richl's 1854 publication, *Die Familie*.[6] But, of course, as a child he had already seen the decline of family stability in western Europe and the growth of the social and economic problems of the emerging twentieth century. He continues:

> After I left school at about fourteen years of age, I was apprenticed to the municipal administration in Pieschen, where I remained until I entered the seminary of the Leipzig Lutheran Mission . . . The incentive for my desire to serve in the mission came through my membership in the YMCA, so I began to study Latin, shorthand, and other subjects in evening classes at Dresden. It was during this time that I received many spiritual impulses from the active congregational life of those days.[7]

From 1895 to 1901 he entered upon an intensive and methodical course of studies to prepare for the theological examination and mission work abroad. During this time the theologians of the Erlangen School of Neo-Lutheranism, who were also the leading theologians in Leipzig, had a strong influence on confessionalistic Lutheran theology. The young student was also greatly influenced by Karl Graul, director of the Leipzig Mission from 1844 to 1860.[8]

During his years at Leipzig Gutmann came under the influence of the philosopher and psychologist Professor Wilhelm Wundt (1832-1920).[9] The Christian Socialist movement led by Pastor Friedrich Naumann and Pastor Adolf Stoecker, two men who influenced many young theologians, had an influence on Gutmann too. Throughout his lifetime, Gutmann remained faithful to Naumann's thoughts and was at times mistakenly accused of consenting to the "blood-and-soil theology" of National Socialism. Since it was my privilege to be associated with him during those years, I know from many conversations how remote that was from his thoughts. His beliefs and convictions were at all times based on Holy Scripture, on Luther's *Small Catechism* and the other confessions of the Lutheran Church.

In 1902, following his examination and a one-year vicarage at Vohenstrauss in Bavaria, the Kirchenrat D. Theol. Bard ordained Gutmann and seven other missionaries in Leipzig, on the occasion of the Leipzig Mission's anniversary. Gutmann, who had actually been preparing for service in India, was sent instead to East Africa.

Bruno Gutmann, Herrmann Fokken, and a medical doctor named Ploetze reached their African field on August 9, 1902. Gutmann was assigned to the Mission-Senior Althaus at Mamba in the then German East Africa Colony. Following an introductory period on the eastern slopes of Mount Kilimanjaro, he was transferred to the western Kilimanjaro area. After two years at Machame, he was entrusted with founding a new station called Masama in the lower Machame region. Martin Küchler says of this period in Gutmann's life:

> Gutmann dedicates himself fully to this task, giving his best. He places greater emphasis on winning the hearts of the Chagga people than on raising buildings. They find him not only a keen observer of their customs, mores and character, but also a faithful and energetic advocate of their laws and rights which he defends, if necessary, against European planters and administrative officials. Weakness and self-indulgence are foreign to his nature.[10]

For health reasons he returned to Germany in 1908, where he published his first major literary work, *Dichten und Denken der Chagganeger: Beiträge zur ostafrikanischen Volkskunde* (Thoughts and Endeavors of the Chagga People – Contributions to East African Ethnology).[11]

A short time after his return to Masama he was called to take over Old Moshi station, a congregation in middle Chagga, and from then on his life's work was closely associated with Old

Moshi and its people. He stayed there, with brief interruptions, until 1938. The Moshi people still think of him as their spiritual father, missionary, and apostle. With this assignment the most creative period of this gifted missionary's life began. He published twenty-three books, some of them more than six hundred pages in length, and 476 articles in various periodicals, annuals, collected works, and duplicated circulars.[12] The Theological Faculty of the University of Erlangen awarded him an honorary Doctorate of Theology in 1924, and two years later the University of Würzburg granted him the Doctorate of Law in recognition of his book *Chagga Law*.

In August 1920 Gutmann, along with the other German missionaries, was deported in accordance with "Mission Paragraph" 418 of the Treaty of Versailles. For a time he stayed in Berlin, but he was finally able to locate a home in Ehingen, a village in Franconia, where as a "rustic" he quickly put down roots. The ensuing period of waiting for permission to return to East Africa was filled with literary work. Earlier (in 1914) he had published his *Volksbuch der Wachagga* (Chapbook of the Wachagga), a collection of legends, tales, fables and anecdotes that he had heard among the Chaggas. This book, including its sensitive preface and profound introduction, had attracted attention far beyond missionary circles. Martin Küchler writes:

Gutmann's knowledge of these people has penetrated to an unusual depth. It is significant and programmatical for his subsequent scientific work when Gutmann says, "The so called primitive races are not childish organisms and easily manageable as some believe. Not only does the spirit of past generations live within them, but extinct cultures also smoulder within their souls. Would, therefore, that in addition to bringing in the disintegrating influences of our civilization, the colonial powers might come up soon, and with increasing emphasis, with constructive and considerate development programs, so that the indestructible life forces do not flare up unexpectedly like flames from a ruined structure, but that they be engaged creatively and effectively in indigenous forms for service in the total community."[13]

Küchler adds:

For Gutmann this was not a mere abstract theory. He strove to actualize it in the daily activities of his congregational work. This is characteristic of him and a factor to be taken into consideration in an estimation of his life's work. Whatever he advocates he practices, seeking to test its efficacy. He does not manipulate his congregation as a great performer plays his instrument to demonstrate his mastery and skill, but rather desires to make the congregation able and willing to undertake its own independent action as a serving organism. What he has found in the deep-rooted relationships of the Chaggas he seeks to utilize, in conjunction with the structures derived from the gospel for the benefit of the Christian congregation.[14]

Some significant publications during the enforced interim were *Das Chaggaland und seine Christen* (Chaggaland and Its Christians) and *Gemeindeaufbau aus dem Evangelium* (Congregational Nurture from the Gospel), 1925.[15] The latter, a programmatical work on mission theory, with the subtitle "Fundamental Principles for Mission and Church at Home," brought him recognition as an authority in the field of missiology. This book, although not easy to read, occasioned vigorous discussion in following years and led the author to defend his position in numerous articles, to clarify the questions, and to attempt to elucidate the basic principles of the book.[16] His last book, *Afrikaner-Europäer*, includes a bibliography of his works published between 1905 and 1966.[17]

Gutmann's Anthropological Insights

The starting point for Gutmann's theological thought is a basic consideration of people in their relationship to the world and to other human beings. He is primarily concerned with the so-called modern person, whom he sees as an individual misunderstanding himself or herself and the real purpose of one's life.[18]

Through his work on the slopes of Mount Kilimanjaro, Gutmann came into contact with a people whose community life was still intact. Civilization had penetrated to a limited extent only, and had not yet begun its destructive work. This stable relationship among people, these national, organic, social, and kinship units in Africa were the point of departure of his missionary activity. They were the basis for his reflection on both secular and theological problems at home and in the overseas mission of the church. With a wealth of illustrations from such basic human structures, *urtümliche Bindungen* as he calls them, Gutmann's slogan in his own practice and in all his publications was "back to the primordial ties."[19]

The three primordial ties Gutmann encountered in Africa – *clan, neighborhood,* and *age group* – were then in such pristine clarity that he thought he had found in them an approach for the Gospel in constructing Christian congregations. Indeed, those three relationships are still to be found everywhere in the world. Recent research has shown that even in the large cities of the Western world, with their extreme individualism, the primordial ties continue to play an important part. For Gutmann they were the absolute basis of true Christian life: in the power of God, it is the primordial ties through which people become true human beings, capable of receiving Christ. And the spiritual and ethical attitudes that bring inner unity to the human race, despite the most pronounced outward diversity, are developed in those same relationships. He was mindful in all his research of what he conceived to be the major task of mission: the struggle to preserve the values of the communal structure intact. From such ethnological perceptions he drew conclusions that made him a pioneer in missiology and enabled him to participate in the movement of culture criticism in his homeland.[20]

Despite universal concerns, the practical issue of building up the congregation was Gutmann's predominant effort throughout his entire stay in Africa. With forceful singlemindedness he concentrated on the one problem that was central in German missio-theological thought from the time of Karl Graul to World War II: utilizing indigenous structures in building up the national church.

All of Gutmann's utterances rest on his basic anthropological conviction that a man is to be addressed not as an individual but as a member of an organic whole. Thus Gutmann embraces Wilhelm Wundt's contention that individualism is to be overcome and the community, in all of its originality and independence, to be acknowledged. The individual in the community, the individual through the community, the individual for the community – this is the keynote of Gutmann's ethnology, ecclesiology, and missionary activity. With the organic-natural relationship man is called to freedom by God. The phenomenon of conscience, as he observed it ethnologically, also points in this direction: Conscience is the organ of equilibrium of the soul, which requires only minor resiliency so long as its bearer, living in an inclusive community, is unvariedly and uniformly governed by its impulses and life rhythm.[21]

Decisive, in his view, was the Chagga system of *relationships* between relatives, regulated to the last detail and assuring help and protection to the individual. The pedagogic and social duties of each member toward one's children, nieces and nephews, parents, and siblings are defined by age-old traditions. In the examination of the bride and groom at the wedding, or in the customs surrounding baptism, for example, Gutmann sought to strengthen the existing system of relationships and put it to work for a Christian understanding of family life within the congregation.

The *clan* in Chagga life is a comprehensive entity, based on biological relationships, which obliges all members to maintain both internal and external solidarity. The disappearance of the chieftainship, however, threatens the entire institution with disintegration. In places where the clan organization as such has deteriorated, the *neighborhood* may provide the necessary substitute.[22] "Neighborhood" is a highly important term in African culture. It is not to be understood as a merely geographical term, referring simply to people living in close proximity to one another. "Neighborhood" in African understanding is "neighborliness," a relationship of friendship and mutual assistance. To have a neighbor is to have a helper on whom one can rely in all circumstances and with whom one enjoys fellowship. There is a reciprocity of assistance and protection. Gutmann described the organization that developed in their social order under the supervisors of the canals which, fed from the Kilimanjaro glaciers and forest region, irrigate the Chagga gardens. He attempted to employ the same kind of structure in providing for church elders in each congregational neighborhood to organize meetings and to settle matters of church discipline.

Young boys in the neighborhoods, encouraged by their elders, begin to establish bonds of mutual relationships in their games. These bonds are later sealed in tribal initiation ceremonies, when the boys are assigned places in the overall organization. The entire male Chagga population is thus organized for war and peace in easily activated *age fellowships.* Gutmann adapted this traditional system in baptismal and confirmation classes, relating each group of two or three young people with a young man or woman a few years older for mutual assistance throughout their lives. This *Schildschaft,* or Fellowship of the Shields, came to have great significance in the lives of the youth and of the congregation as a whole.

The entire life of every Chagga is based upon unhesitating recognition of his or her place in this age-old social structure of the tribe – a triple relationship according to clan, neighborhood and age group:

Two considerations regarding these ethnological observations of Gutmann are of crucial importance:

1. He accords them a universal validity – beyond the purely African context. The three sociological points of reference as analyzed in East Africa – blood, soil and age – shape the basic, though varying, forms of every human community.

2. Without this arrangement healthy human life is not possible, according to Gutmann.[23]

It was Gutmann's main sociological contention that a people is composed not of individuals but of the units named above, and that the dissolution of these units signifies national death. For Gutmann this was a theological as well as a sociological observation. He was concerned with religious anthropology.

The social forms recognized by Gutmann reflect the will of the Creator, hence he calls them "ties in conformity with creation, or primordial ties," for whose absolute validity he passionately contends.

The structural pattern of all human social life, as delineated by Gutmann, now has a mortal enemy – civilization. This brings uprooting, proletarization, isolation, displacement of human by material values. Money becomes a substitute for brother and neighbor, dehumanizing and dissolving all mutual obligations.[24]

There is only one remedy to restore the health of a people: "Return to God's Way," as the title of one of his books puts it. In other words, "Make a determined effort to rebuild or reactivate what remains of the basic cells of the indigenous community." Salvation is to be found not in organization – the mere aggregation of like-minded individuals – but in the preservation of the living organism which the Creator provided.

As a young and inexperienced missionary, with imperfect knowledge of the Chagga language, I became Gutmann's successor at Easter time in 1938. I do not know how I could have managed the task of pastor to this congregation, scattered over a large area and numbering about 5,500 souls, had it not been carefully organized down to the last Christian farmstead. About 20,000 people lived in the whole middle Chagga area. The congregation was divided into neighborhoods, each with its own elders. A district, composed of several neighborhoods, was presided over by a church elder who came to be called District Elder. He served as mediator only if a neighborhood was unable to settle its own disputes, most of which were easily regulated without his involvement. Each neighborhood recognized its obligation to care for the poor and the sick and to reclaim lost members. In such tasks as community work, road building, schools, churches, and housing for teachers and evangelists, these neighborhoods were making remarkable progress long before the government inaugurated and implemented its policy of "community services."

Fathers and godfathers together brought their children for baptismal registration on Friday evenings, accompanied by the neighborhood elders. This provided a rich opportunity for instruction in the meaning of baptism. Matters of church discipline were regulated in the neighborhoods, where people knew one another so well that deception was hardly possible, and the missionary's counsel was sought only in the most difficult cases. The sharing of mutual concerns between church elder and missionary pastor was a source of blessing to the congregation.

Since the effectiveness of such a system depends to some extent upon the personality and personal qualifications of the leaders, there were naturally some failures. Nevertheless, a congregation organized into neighborhoods – especially into a *Volkskirche* – can perform its services much better than an atomized congregation of individuals. Such neighborhood organizations help to explain the fact that the African countries are not yet, and show no signs of soon becoming, welfare states. A well-functioning neighborhood, even when its services are imperfect, helps to provide for the poor and the aged. Saint Paul's injunction, "Bear ye one another's burdens" (Gal. 6:2), was not forgotten in the discussions of problems at congregational meetings.

Whatever criticisms may be made of Gutmann's exegesis in claiming a biblical basis for his sociological observations, it cannot be maintained that the congregational structure he advocated is either unbiblical or antibiblical.[25]

The Legacy of Gutmann

What is the significance of Bruno Gutmann's legacy for the African indigenous church? The Chagga tribe, along with all other Africans, will find untold treasures of ethnological material about their forefathers, customs, and faith in his five hundred publications. Such superb monuments of Chagga culture as *Stammeslehren der Chagga* (his corpus of Chagga law or Chagga tribal precepts) witness to the extremely high standard of African tribal culture, often hopelessly underestimated because its manifestations were undivulged to white people and largely unrecorded before they fell prey to the onslaught of a new age. Gutmann's writings can provide valuable aid in the present struggle of Africans for a new identity.

Gutmann was a master of the Chagga language and something of a poet. He produced a hymnbook for the congregation and, in 1938, a translation of the New Testament, fruits of thirty years of language study. A diligent foreigner can learn the grammar and vocabulary of a Bantu language, but few Europeans are capable of mastering its wealth of imagery. Gutmann was one who did have a command of the metaphorical nuances. I once asked Nahum Mrema, a teacher, whether the people were able to understand the Kichagga spoken by Gutmann. Nahum laughed aloud and replied, "Gutmann? He knows Kichagga better than all the rest of us put together." My question arose from the fact that Gutmann's German writings and lectures were phrased in a manner difficult for Germans themselves to understand, the reason so few of them have been translated.

Gutmann was a dedicated missionary. I heard him remark on several occasions, not entirely without pride, "I have never been a parish pastor, but I am thankful that I have been able to remain a missionary all my life." Following the example of Saint Paul in 1 Corinthians 9:20, 22-23, he wanted to become a Mchagga (an accepted member of the Chagga tribe); and he was able to achieve it in a relatively short lifespan only because he dedicated himself so completely to the Moshi people. In this self-limitation – he did not even learn to speak Kiswahili well – lies the root of his greatness. Precisely because of his intensive involvement with a single tribe in East Africa, he was able to understand and love them as no other European did.

Gutmann's preaching and writing were focused on presenting Christ to people of animistic faith, revealing to them that the "Lord of Heaven" in whom they unknowingly believed is the father of Jesus Christ. Among a people already in the throes of civilization's invasion upon their traditional lifestyle, his missionary method was to utilize the ancient relationships of clan, neighborhood, and age groups as divine gifts and vehicles for the propagation of the Gospel. In the process he brought new missionary incentives to both his home church and the African church. The evidence of his effectiveness is that today the entire population of Old Moshi is baptized.

As I have already suggested, Gutmann's sociological insights have a contemporary significance and a wider application than we once thought. Some of his critics maintain that primordial ties reflect only a certain historical stage in the development of a people, during which they play an important role, but after which they are less relevant. Recent studies, however, affirm the continuing importance of extended-family ties in Western city life. See, for example, the North American study *Kinship in Urban Setting*, published by Bert N. Adams in 1968. In *Mitteilungen* (March 1972), a "German research fellowship" reports that in a representative cross-section of people in Hamburg, 48 percent viewed their relationship to relatives as "very important"; 41 percent saw it as "important"; and only 11 percent considered it "unimportant." Thus the primordial ties are still significant to missionary strategy – not merely in Africa but everywhere, even though they may be more stable in a rural environment than elsewhere.

Gutmann has been criticized for the two-kingdom concept in his writing. In response to this criticism, we must insist that his theological ideas were rooted in Luther's doctrines and catechisms, that he was trained at Leipzig University, and that he was in full accord with the leading theologians of his time. To that extent he was a product of his own day and, as such, he should not be singled out for criticism at this point.

The problem of "creation orders," prominent in German theological discussions in the 1920s and 1930s, arose in part through Gutmann's writings. Werner Elert includes marriage and family among such orders. He calls them *Seinsgefüge,* the texture of existence or structure of being. In *Die Familie der Gegenwart,* René König says that they are older than human culture itself, being found even among the higher animals.[26] These relationships share the result of the fall in all humankind, and are therefore subject to abuse and sometimes destruction. Yet I agree with Gutmann's insistence that they can be sanctified along with the whole created order in Jesus Christ, and that they are a seedbed of fertile ground for the Gospel.

Bruno Gutmann was an original thinker. We are indebted to him for initiating much of the modern interest in examining the structure of the Christian congregation and the ways in which it can, in the here and now, reflect the coming kingdom of God.

Notes

1. J.C. Hoekendijk, *Kirche und Volk in der deutschen Missionswissenschaft,* edited and adapted by Walter Pollmann (Munich: Christian Kaiser Verlag, 1967).

2. An important work on Gutmann's anthropology is J.C. Winter, *Bruno Gutmann, 1876-1966* (Oxford: Clarendon Press, 1979). Complete bibliography of Gutmann's writings is in Ernst Jäschke, ed., *Bruno Gutmann Afrikaner-Europäer in nächstenschaftlicher Entsprechung* (Stuttgart: Ev. Verlagswerk, 1966), pp. 215ff. See also Ernst Jäschke, *Bruno Gutmann: His Life, His Thoughts, His Work. An Early Attempt at a Theology in an African Context* (Erlangen: Verlag der Evang.-Luth. Mission, 1985).

3. Gutmann's personal notes in typescript. Erlangen, Verlag der Evang. Luth. Mission, 1965.

4. Ibid.

5. Ibid.

6. Wilhelm Riehl, *Die Familie* (Stuttgart, 1854). Cf. Max Horkheimer, *Studien über Autorität und Familie* (Paris, 1936), pp. 49f., where we read: "Die Familie besorgt als eine der wichtigsten erzieherischen Mächte die Reproduktion der menschlichen Charaktere, wie sie das gesellschaftliche Leben effordert und gibt ihnen zum grossen Teil die unerlässliche Fähigkeit zu dem besonders gearteten autoritären Verhalten von dem der Bestand der bürgerlichen Ordnung in hohem Masse abhängt."

7. Gutmann's personal notes.

8. See "Karl Graul," in Stephen Neill, N.P. Moritzen, and Ernst Schrupp, eds. *Brockhaus Lexikon zur Weltmission* (Wuppertal: Verlag R.Brockhaus; and Erlangen: Verlag Evang. Luth. Mission, 1965); J.C. Hoekendijk, *Kirche und Volk*, pp. 71-75, 139-71; cf. Neill and Moritzen, *Geschichte der christlichen Mission* (Erlangen: Verlag der Evang. Luth. Mission, 1964), pp. 366ff., a translation of *Christian Missions* (Harmondsworth, Middlesex: Penguin Books, 1964).

9. Wilhelm Wundt, professor of inductive philosophy at the University of Leipzig, organized his course on socially conditioned processes, or phenomena of the human psyche, chiefly in the volumes of his *Psychology of Nations.* Language, art, myths, religions, society, law, culture, and history, the divisions of this series, are themes that recur throughout Gutmann's writings. A theological dictionary, *Die Religion in Geschichte und Gegenwart* (RGG), 5: 2052, says that Wundt's work "does not receive due attention from the theologians. This is especially true of his *Ethics* and the last volume of his *Psychology of Nations.* He is the moral philosopher of the collective will. It is he who asserted that the relationship of community to individual existence is the problem of problems, and he did not try to solve it collectivistically."

10. Martin Küchler, *D. Dr. Bruno Gutmann: Lebenslauf und Würdigung der Lebensarbeit D. Dr. Bruno Gutmanns* (Erlangen, 1951), a pamphlet published in honor of Gutmann's seventy-fifth birthday.

11. *Dichten und Denken der Chagganeger: Beiträge zur ostafrikanischen Volkskunde* (Leipzig: Verlag der Evang. Luth. Mission, 1909).

12. See bibliography in Jäschke, *Bruno Gutmann*, pp. 215ff.

13. Preface of *Volksbuch der Wachagga*, pp. 19f.

14. M. Küchler, *Dr. Bruno Gutmann*, p. 7.

15. Both books published in Leipzig.

16. See especially his *Christusleib und Nächstenschaft* (Feuchtwangen: Frankenverlag, 1931).

17. See Jäschke, *Bruno Gutmann*, bibliography.

18. Preface of *Dichten und Denken.*

19. Ibid., and Peter Beyerhaus, *Die Selbständigkeit der jungen Kirchen als Missionarisches Problem* (Wuppertal/Barmen: Verlag der Rheinischen Missions-Gesellschaft, 1959), p. 90.

20. Beyerhaus, *Selbständigkeit*, p. 88.

21. Ibid., p. 89.

22. Ernst Jäschke, unpublished manuscript, "Bruno Gutmann: His Work, His Thoughts, and His Life" (230 pages), pp. 15-16, 53-55.

23. Beyerhaus, *Selbständigkeit*, p. 90.

24. Ibid.

25. Walter Holsten, *Das Evangelium und die Völker. Beiträge zur Geschichte und Theorie der Mission* (Berlin/Friedenau: Buchhandlung der Gossnerschen Mission, 1939), essay on Bruno Gutmann's exegesis, pp. 89ff.

26. René König, *Die Familie der Gegenwart* (Munich: Becksche Schwarze Reihe, 1977), vol. 116, pp. 9, 13.

Part Three

CHINA

W.A.P. Martin

John Livingston Nevius

J. Hudson Taylor

Charlotte (Lottie) Moon

Karl Ludvig Reichelt

T.C. Chao

Francis X. Ford, M.M.

W.A.P. Martin

1827–1916

Promoting the Gospel through Education and Science

Ralph R. Covell

What is the most appropriate role for a missionary to take as he or she enters another culture in Christian witness? One that best fits the person's gifts? The one understood best by the receptor culture? A role that affords the best relationships with the country's leaders? A religious vocation? A secular position? These important questions and answers were debated long before the twentieth century. William Alexander Parsons Martin's life and ministry in China gave them special significance.

W.A.P. Martin, born in 1827 into the family of a pioneer Presbyterian preacher on the American frontier, graduated from the University of Indiana in 1846 and from Albany Theological Seminary (later moved to Chicago and renamed McCormick Theological Seminary) in 1849. Caring for the "last preparatory measure," a quasi-requirement of the Board of Foreign Missions of the Presbyterian Church, he married Jan VanSant a mere ten days before sailing for China on November 23, 1849. Four sons were born to them in China: Pascal, Winfred, Newell, and Claude.

"Foremost American in China"

His first field of service was in Ningbo, one of the five treaty ports opened to foreign residence by the Treaty of Nanjing in 1842. During ten years of general missionary service in this South China port city, Martin involved himself in two major events of Chinese history. First, he went on public record to advocate to his government in four newspaper articles that it should support the Taiping Heavenly Kingdom, a large-scale revolt against the reigning Manchu government. Second, he participated actively in the American delegation that produced the Treaty of Tientsin, the second of the unequal treaties between China and the Western powers, which opened up the entire country to traders, diplomats, and missionaries.

After a short transition period of one year in Shanghai, Martin moved to Beijing in 1863 and, with an interruption of only three or four years, remained there until his death in 1916 at the age of eighty-nine. His work was complex and filled with many activities, both inside and outside of the institutional missionary enterprise, that related to religion, education, law, science, government, and reform.

During this period of sixty-six years in his adopted country, Martin earned the plaudits of both Chinese and American officials. The Chinese government granted him the rank of mandarin of the third class in 1885 and of the second class in 1898. He was a personal friend to the highest-ranking Chinese government officials. Three American universities awarded him honorary doctorates for his contribution to China-American relations. John W. Foster, secretary of state under President Benjamin Harrison, stated that either Martin or the Englishman Robert Hart deserved to be ranked "the most distinguished and useful foreigner in China" in the generation preceding the Boxer Rebellion.[1] Charles Denby, U.S. minister to China in the early 1900s, called him the "foremost American in China."[2] In a day of great missionaries in China, Martin stood out.

With such recognition among his contemporaries, why is Martin a "no-name missionary" in both Protestant and Catholic missionary circles today? He had hoped for exactly the opposite. In his will was a specific provision that Arthur Smith, a close friend, write his biography. Martin had amassed a large number of personal papers, published and unpublished writings, diaries, and other memorabilia to assist Smith in this task. At Martin's death, his third son, Newell, came to Beijing to settle his father's considerable business affairs. He picked up all of the materials that his father had prepared for Smith, and that is the last that anyone has heard about them! Apparently Smith, and later potential biographers, waited to no avail for these materials to be found. Only with these documents, they evidently reasoned, could an adequate biography be written of this significant missionary figure.[3]

Impact of "Origin of the Heavenly Doctrine"

Why was Martin so highly respected both by missionary and nonmissionary colleagues? They recognized his ability to communicate the Christian faith in a cogent manner in the Chinese context. At the 1907 centennial of the Protestant missionary enterprise, Martin's Chinese book *Tiandao Suyuan* (Origin of the heavenly doctrine) was recognized as the single best Christian book of the century. Written by Martin in 1854 and printed in nearly forty editions over the next sixty years, this book was organized into three sections on natural law, evidences of Christianity, and revealed theology. It was used in the language study program for new missionaries who came to China and in theological schools for the instruction of Christian preachers. No other book had as much impact for Christianity on Chinese officials, with whom Martin had such extensive contact.

The section on natural law, although indebted to the current philosophical system of "common sense" as revealed in a book like William Paley's *Natural Theology*, fit well with the Chinese concept of natural law. Martin appealed constantly to the Chinese ideas of *tian* (heaven) and a moral universe, in which heaven's purposes (*ming*) and way (*dao*) could be seen in the created world and in the human mind and body. Only as people lived in conformity to heaven, which he interpreted as God, would their lives be fulfilled. From this apologetic beginning, very similar to the great book *The True Meaning of the Lord of Heaven* written by the Jesuit Matteo Ricci 250 years earlier, Martin presented the whole realm of Christian truth to lead his readers to faith in Jesus Christ.

Not all of Martin's efforts took place within such a specific religious context. With a renaissance-type mind, he wished to claim international law, popular scientific truth, and liberal arts education as a means of clearing away the underbrush of Chinese superstition in preparation for planting the Gospel seed. All of these "might wing the arrow, but religion should be its point."[4]

During a three-year period (1872-75), he served as editor of *Peking Magazine*, an illustrated monthly that included news, popular scientific truth, and general observations about the progress in modernization made by China's neighbors and other more distant countries. From this platform, as a kind of "secular missionary," he stated that the goal of the magazine was:

> By the introduction of modern science and liberal thought to endeavor to overthrow those ancient superstitions which constitute most formidable barriers in the way of material and social improvement.[5]

He debunked the Chinese concept that Haley's comet or Venus passing by the sun in 1874 could represent evil omens for China but not for the rest of the world. He gave numerous examples of how human beings could investigate and control natural phenomena, because they "wear heaven on their head and tread upon earth as their footstool," a popular Chinese proverb. Nature was predictable, he affirmed, and this meant that *tiandao*, the heavenly way, punished evil, protected from danger, and rewarded good. Pompeii's destruction came from *tiandao*, because it was such a licentious city.[6]

During his early years in Beijing, Martin was convinced that Chinese officials needed some knowledge of Western law in their international relations. Otherwise, he contended, they would not know how to act as they moved into the modern world and entered the family of nations. Ready at hand as a suitable textbook for him to translate was Henry Wheaton's well-known treatise of 1836, *Elements of International Law*. Martin remarked of this first effort of translation:

> I was led to undertake it, without the suggestion of anyone, but providentially I doubt not, as a work which might bring this atheistic government to the recognition of God and his Eternal Justice; and perhaps impart to them something of the Spirit of Christianity.[7]

This work, for which Martin was provided a room and translation help by the Chinese government, was distributed throughout China and to the Japanese government, where it was warmly welcomed as Japan's first introduction to this subject. The Presbyterian Foreign Mission Board was not certain that Martin's six-month's work on this project was really missionary work. He curtly replied to its inquiry that this translation "will not stand second in influence to the translation of the Bible."[8] He was beginning to see his role not merely as a proclaimer of religious truth but also as a "pioneer of progress," a contributor to the development of his adopted country. Because there was some link between Christianity and civilization, the arrow of modernization would reach its religious mark.

From Missionary to "Pioneer of Modern State Education"

Because of his serving as an interpreter in the American delegation in 1858, his translating Wheaton, and his general availability as an adviser to the American legation in Beijing, his fame grew among the Chinese as well as in the diplomatic world. Consequently, government officials asked him to take part in the *Tong Wen Guan*, a new school they had started to train interpreters for diplomatic service. At the beginning of his work at the school, Martin only taught English for two hours a day. When the school was expanded two years later, he was asked to become principal and to serve as professor of international law and political economy. In order to fulfill these added responsibilities, he resigned from his mission society in 1869.

Why would Martin give priority to this position over that of being a "real" missionary? First, he saw this opportunity as a continuance of his missionary career – he would be able to influence the "leading minds of the nation." Second, he wished to reform China's ancient educational system, and he felt that a government-sponsored school, with an expanded curriculum of liberal arts subjects, was one of the best ways to do this. Third, he believed that to work as a teacher in a school under government auspices was one of the best roles for a foreigner who wished to help in the modernization of China. At a time right after the U.S. Civil War, when his own mission board was struggling financially, it did not hurt that Martin's salary was ten times greater than what he was receiving as a missionary.

And why did the Chinese government, very conservative at this time, wish to invite an outsider to direct its school? Like Matteo Ricci earlier, Martin was a "foreign expert," and the Chinese government has always been ready to use such people for its own purposes. Martin served at this school for nearly thirty years, and when, in the last two or three years of the nineteenth century, it led to the founding of the Imperial University of Beijing, Martin became the administrator of the foreign faculty. Many of the graduates of the *Tong Wen Guan* became interpreters or accepted diplomatic positions. The school also contributed to the modernization of China at a time when its leaders were just beginning to get interested in this subject. Whether it influenced many students to accept the Christian faith is more questionable. The Chinese nation and its people were glad to take science and education from the West, but they wished to preserve the Chinese cultural "essence," and this had little room for the Gospel. Martin may not have hoped for actual conversions, but only that, under his direction, it would be "less anti-Christian than it would otherwise be."[9]

A fulfilling task that grew directly out of his administrative position in the *Tong Wen Guan* was his appointment in 1880 by the Chinese government to tour several foreign countries and report back on their educational systems. This trip, taking him to Japan, the United States, England, France, Germany, Switzerland, and Italy over a two-year period (1880-82), led him to emphasize the need for nations to learn from each other and to stress the value of comparative educational statistics.[10] This educational venture, his work with the *Tong Wen Guan*, his later relationships with the Imperial University of Beijing, and his short tenure with a school established by Zhang Zhihdong, governor-general of Hunan-Hubei, in Wu Chang in central China in the post-Boxer period, make it appropriate of think of Martin as the "pioneer of modern state education in China."[11]

Missionary schools run by Calvin Mateer and D.Z. Sheffield were equally innovative but were unrelated to the state. John C. Ferguson and D.C. Tenney developed the "most thorough and well-equipped government colleges" in the pre-Boxer period at Nanyang University (1897) and Tientsin University (1895) respectively, but they followed a trail that Martin had blazed thirty years earlier.[12]

Shortly before he began his work with the *Tong Wen Guan*, Martin found himself pressed into duty as a mediator and/or interpreter in many political events. For example, when the Chinese government appointed Anson Burlingame, formerly American minister to China, to be a minister plenipotentiary on their behalf as he returned to the United States, Martin defended this action in six long articles that he wrote in the *New York Times* under the pseudonym "Perry Plus."[13]

All of Martin's varied activities in science, international law, and education had one aim – to win China to the Christian faith. More than other missionaries, he made good use of his pen to relate the Gospel to all levels of Chinese people. Otherwise his missionary methodology was not unusual or particularly creative. More important to him than specific methodology was a flexible attitude toward Chinese religions and the ancestral cult.

"Confucius *plus* Christ"

While not tolerant of the errors of Mahayana Buddhism, he felt that its belief in the immortality of the soul and a divine being made it a better preparation for the Christian faith than the materialism of Daoism or the agnosticism of the current Confucianism. He believed that Confucianism at its best was an ethical philosophy "consonant with the spirit of Christianity."[14] Its five basic relationships, he contended, were rooted in the very nature of human beings and lacked only the "last link with Heaven" to complete them.[15] Therefore, the solution for new converts was "Confucius *plus* Christ," and never "Confucius *or* Christ."[16]

His views on the Christian attitude toward the ancestral rites were more controversial. These ceremonies are a complex of four activities: burial, the ritual in the home, annual sacrifices at the grave, and annual services in the ancestral hall. Martin did not wish to advocate anything that smacked of idolatry. He rejected outright, however, both the possibility and the wisdom of abolishing a cult with such cohesive power in society.[17] He first presented his views publicly at the General Missionary Conference in Shanghai in 1890. His views reflect many modern insights used by agents of change confronting adverse institutions. First he rejected both the form and function of patently idolatrous elements that recognize the deceased as tutelary deities. Second, he modified both the form and function of certain "announcements" so that they would not be regarded as prayers, but as mere expressions of natural affection. Third, he accepted both the form and function of kneeling and bowing, affirming that while these actions might be idolatrous in certain contexts, they definitely were not in others.[18]

In the heated discussion following the presentation of this paper, Hudson Taylor, whom Martin once said had "erred in leading his followers to make war on ancestral worship, instead of seeking to reform it,"[19] led nearly everyone in the assembly to stand in expression of their dissent from Martin's views. Only Timothy Richard and Gilbert Reid affirmed their support, while many, according to Martin, stated privately that they concurred with the general sentiment of his paper.[20]

Martin's strategy in adopting these relatively tolerant views was to work for mass conversions in China. How might this happen? First, baptism should precede inquiry and catechism, rather than following them. Second, "whole families, entire clans, villages or districts" should be admitted to baptism as soon as they "committed themselves to a better doctrine, however imperfectly it might be apprehended." Third, the catalyst for this would be the conversion of the head of the family or clan. Fourth, teaching and training, having gained a much larger audience, would follow rather than precede baptism, and this would eliminate many false motives. Fifth, the rapidly growing number of converts would "exert an irresistible influence on the community to which they belong."[21]

The Dashing of Great Expectations

During the Boxer Rebellion in North China, Martin and many of his colleagues were penned up in the siege in the British legation. This was the disappointment of his career. He tells of his meeting with Robert Hart, inspector-general of Chinese customs:

> As we looked each other in the face, we could not help blushing for shame at the thought that our life-long services had been so little valued. The man who had nursed their Customs revenue from three to thirty millions, the Chinese were trying to butcher; while from my thirty years' teaching of international law they had learned that the lives of Ambassadors were not to be held sacred.[22]

John Fairbank once commented that we are often disappointed in China because we expect too much from her. Martin's direct proclamation of the Christian faith in China had its results – nothing great, but probably more than that of other missionaries in its total impact. His hopes that he could wed Eastern knowledge with the Christian faith and produce a modern China ready both to become Christian and to join the "family of nations" by 1900 were hopeless fantasies. But his optimism, a product of the nineteenth century, was shared by most of his colleagues, even though they did not labor so strenuously to achieve such progress.

Following a short period in Zhang Zhihdong's school in Wu Chang, Martin was appointed in 1906 as an honorary missionary with no salary by the Board of Foreign Missions of the Presbyterian Church. He kept himself busy preaching, teaching, writing, interacting with Chinese officials, and doing whatever came to hand as a "self-supporting professor of things-in-general."[23] At his death in Beijing in 1916, he had served longer in China as an adult missionary than any other person, before or since.

In his eulogy for Martin in the *Missionary Review of the World,* Arthur Brown commented appropriately that his was a "life of extraordinary length, marked by extraordinary powers, filled with extraordinary labors, and crowned with extraordinary achievements."[24]

Notes

1. John W. Foster,"An Appreciation of Dr. W.A.P. Martin," in *Indiana University Alumni Quarterly,* 1917, p. 134.

2. Ibid., pp. 134-35.

3. The author of this article has written the only biography of Martin in English, entitled *W.A.P. Martin: Pioneer of Progress in China* (Washington, D.C.: Christian University Press, 1978). In this article I refer to the original primary sources used for this book and only rarely to the book itself.

4. Martin, "Western Science as Auxiliary to the Spread of the Gospel," *Missionary Review of the World,* n.s., 10 (October 1887): 773.

5. *First Annual Report* of the Society for the Diffusion of Useful Knowledge in China, published in *North China Herald,* January 29, 1874, p. 89.

6. Martin, "Flying Machines Measure the Weather," *Peking Magazine,* III, p. 23, "The City of Naples," II, p. 19.

7. China Letters (CL) 7, Peking, Martin to Presbyterian Board, no. 44, October 1, 1863.

8. CL 7, Martin to Board, no. 46, November 23, 1863.

9. CL 10, Peking, Martin to Board, no. 169, December 1, 1869. For more detail on the *Tong Wen Guan,* see Covell, *Martin,* pp. 169-98.

10. The report of this journey was published in Martin's Chinese work *Xixueh Kaolue* (A resume of Western education), which is no longer available. See also "Notices of Recent Publications," *Chinese Recorder* 14 (September-October 1883): 332. No indication exists that his report influenced the educational policies of the Chinese government.

11. Robert E. Lewis, *The Educational Conquest of the Far East* (New York: F.H. Revell Co., 1903), p. 173.

12. Ibid.

13. See the articles in the following issues of the *New York Times:* October 23, 26, 28; November 3, 9, 20, 1868. Each article is entitled "The Chinese Embassy."

14. Martin, *The Lore of Cathay* (1912), p. 221.

15. Ibid., p. 212.

16. Ibid., pp. 247-48.

17. Martin, *Hanlin Papers,* 2d ser. (1894), p. 341.

18. Ibid., pp. 343-46.

19. Martin, *Cycle of Cathay* (1900), p. 214.

20. Martin, *Hanlin Papers,* 2d ser., p. 355; *Records of the General Conference of Protestant Missionaries in China, 1890* (Shanghai, 1891), p. 59.

21. Martin, "Conversions En Masse," *Chinese Recorder* 40 (November 1909): 625-27.

22. Martin, *Siege in Peking* (1900), p. 97.

23. Arthur Smith, "The Nestor of Protestant Missionaries in China," *Chinese Recorder* 41 (April 1910): 289.

24. "Rev. W.A.P. Martin, D.D., of China," *Missionary Review of the World* 40 (March 1917): 195-201.

Selected Bibliography

Major Works by W.A.P. Martin

1880 *Hanlin Papers; or, Essays on the Intellectual Life of the Chinese.* 1st ser.
1894 *Chinese Legends and Other Poems.* Shanghai: Kelly and Walsh.
1894 *Hanlin Papers,* 2d ser. Shanghai: Kelly and Walsh.
1900 *Cycle of Cathay.* 3d ed. New York: Fleming H. Revell.
1900 *Siege in Peking.* New York: Fleming H. Revell.
1907 *The Awakening of China.* New York: Doubleday, Page.

1909 *Tiandao Hejiao* (Christianity and other creeds). Tungchow: North China Tract Society.

1912 *The Lore of Cathay.* 2d ed. New York: Fleming H. Revell.

1912 *Tiandao Suyuan* (Evidences of Christianity). Rev. ed. Taibei: Wenchuan Publishing Company.

Works about W.A.P. Martin

Covell, Ralph. *W.A.P. Martin: Pioneer of Progress in China.* Washington, D.C.: Christian University Press, 1978.

Duus, Peter. "Science and Salvation in China: The Life and Mission of William Alexander P. Martin, 1827-1916." A.B. Honors thesis, Harvard University, 1955.

Farquhar, Norma. "W.A.P. Martin and the Westernization of China." M.A. thesis, Indiana University, 1954.

John Livingston Nevius
1829–1893

Pioneer of Three-Self Principles in Asia

Everett N. Hunt, Jr.

John Livingston Nevius served for forty years as a Presbyterian missionary in China. An itinerant missionary with great appreciation for the Chinese, their language and culture, he was committed to winning converts and discipling them in systematic Bible study.

Though a missionary in China, Nevius may be best known for his influence on Protestant beginnings in Korea where the pioneer Presbyterian missionaries adopted his church planting concepts.[1] It is doubtful that the method originated with Nevius,[2] but without question it was formative in Protestant beginnings in Korea.

Formative Years

John L. Nevius was born March 4, 1829, in Seneca County, New York, where his family attended the Presbyterian Church of Ovid. His father, of Dutch descent, died when John was only eighteen months old and his brother, Reuben, was four. Sometime later, when his mother remarried, the family went to live for a year in New England. John stayed behind, however, and lived with his grandparents.[3] As a teenager John lived with his grandparents a second time and attended the Dutch Reformed Church of Ovid, where his grandfather was a member.

He spent seven years at Ovid Academy and then entered Union College, Schenectady, New York, in September, 1845, as a sophomore; John was not yet sixteen years old. In the winter of 1846-47 he left college to teach, then returned and graduated in 1848.

John's first mention of his future wife, Helen Coan, is in a letter to his brother written October 15, 1848, but there is little evidence of serious life purpose. In a letter to Reuben, John recalls their mother saying that "our education and all our plans for the future have been with a view to our entering the ministry." John confesses, "We have thus far fooled away our time. If we are ever to do anything in this world, we must begin living on a new system."

"It was a bitter trial to his mother," Helen recorded later in her biography of Nevius, "that neither of her sons had avowed his intention of living a Christian life." When John decided to go south "to seek his fortune," his mother said, "John, if you were going away to be a missionary to the heathen, and I should never see you again in this world, *that* I could bear; but *this* I cannot."

190

John sailed from New York for Georgia the last of October, 1849. He began keeping a journal there in which he reflected on his duty to God: "I have always thought that when I should make the slightest change toward a religious life, I should not stop short of a thorough reformation." But the only advance he made was "some slight idea of the sinfulness of my nature and my utter weakness." Finally, John wrote his mother confessing what she had wanted to hear for so long: "I know that I am not capable, of myself, of the first holy thought or aspiration; that I am indebted for everything to God . . . I find that to serve him is a great work – vastly greater than I first imagined."

To Reuben John wrote, "My pride and self importance kept me from God. The Holy Spirit was . . . taking the things of Christ and showing them to me. In a word, I am changed . . . I now feel my utter inability to take the first step in the Christian life without divine aid . . . My only hope is in God's mercy through faith in the Lord Jesus Christ."

Thirteen months after arriving in Georgia, John decided to enter the ministry. Influenced by friends, he chose Princeton Theological Seminary. He left Columbus for Princeton December 4, 1850, and found it hard to change from teaching to studying. "I wish I might run the Christian course without needing the lash," he wrote in his journal.

While at Princeton John adopted several rules to regulate his life, the first dated December 29, 1850, and the last, April 17, 1851. A sample suggests the tone of them all:

3. To keep my mind impressed with the idea that I am living for God and heaven.

4. To make it my object in my studies to become a useful, rather than a learned man.

5. To look forward to my future life as a continual warfare, and endeavor every day to gain by the help of God, a victory over some evil propensity of my heart.

6. Trusting the future entirely to God with full confidence, and exercising humble submission to all his righteous will, to pray that he will direct me in the course which will best promote his glory, and enable me every day to spend my time so as best to prepare myself for the station which he has allotted for me.

11. To cultivate assiduously a kind feeling toward and a pleasing manner in intercourse with everyone.

Included were rules for worship, checks against covetousness, envy and jealousy, rules concerning sleep, exercise and food, use of time, Bible study, procrastination, conversation, and one of special note:

16. Every Saturday night to eat sparingly or nothing at all, and spend a part of the evening in looking over these rules, seeing how far I have transgressed them, how much I can improve them and myself by them; and in preparation for the Sabbath.

His journal entry for January 6, 1851, a month after his arrival at Princeton, reads, "I have now an object in life – the glory of God and the salvation of my own soul, and the souls of others." The week following his first Communion at Princeton, John heard a missionary challenge that interested him.

Call to Missions

In the summer of 1852 John and Helen began to develop a deeper relationship. She writes, "It was then that we exchanged brotherly and sisterly friendship of long standing for something much dearer." September 1852 began his last year of seminary and an intensifying correspondence between John and his "Nell" in which he reflected on his studies at Princeton and their future ministry together. He recommended books for her to read, suggested how she should study the

Bible, and confessed problems he was still working on, such as indifference to the feelings of others, plus pride and selfishness.

When Walter Lowrie, Corresponding Secretary of the Presbyterian Board of Foreign Missions, visited Princeton, John felt stirred once again to consider a life in missions. "I shall not be hasty," he wrote. "I shall wait for more information about other lands, and for the leadings of God's providence with regard to places at home as well as abroad . . . I want to know where my duty lies. There I shall be successful; there I shall be happy."

Finally, on March 29, 1853, he announced to Helen, "It is my purpose now, if I do not meet with providential hindrances, to be a missionary to Siam or China . . . I am not enthusiastic, but I can heartily thank God, if he has called me to this work, for the privilege of engaging in it; and I only regret that I cannot bring to it a stronger body, a better furnished mind, and a more devoted heart."

Matters moved quickly when Helen consented to join him. John applied to the Board of Missions, requesting assignment to Ningbo, China. Accepted by the board on April 18, six days later he was ordained by the presbytery.

John and Helen were married at Helen's home in Seneca County, New York, June 15, 1853. Helen's father did not prevent the marriage, but he did not approve her marrying a missionary, especially one going to China.

The Neviuses sailed from Boston September 19, 1853, on the *Bombay,* which Helen described as "an old India trader, neither comfortable, nor indeed seaworthy; though, of that fact, we were, at the time, fortunately not aware." They spent six months on board ship in a room three and one half feet wide and not quite six feet long.

The Neviuses arrived in Ningbo in spring 1854, little more than a decade after the signing of the Treaty of Nanking, which ended the first Opium War and allowed foreign presence in five treaty ports: Canton, Amoy, Foochow, Ningbo, and Shanghai.

Shortly after their arrival, the Neviuses began to study Chinese. Both had facility with the language and, according to Helen, enjoyed their study. After eight or nine months, Nevius shared in chapel in an informal way, and in about a year was carrying a normal load of preaching and teaching in Chinese.

Helen was not well and in 1856, just three years after their arrival, she returned to the States for a year and a half. Meanwhile Nevius itinerated, wrote articles on China for new missionaries, and a simplified catechism for Chinese inquirers. Helen returned in 1858, but because it was a time of constant rebel activity, the Neviuses went to Japan to spend eight months with the Hepburns, Presbyterian missionaries there.

Nevius's Ministry Pattern

On May 18, 1861, because of political upheavals and the severity of the weather at Ningbo, the Neviuses moved their mission activity to Chefoo in Shantung Province. During this time Nevius continued to itinerate. He attempted to visit twice a year all the churches assigned to his care for instruction, discipline, and encouragement as well as evangelism. Between the spring and fall tours, Nevius invited church leaders to his home in Chefoo for advanced Bible instruction.

From 1861 to 1864, he wrote tracts and discussed with other missionaries the needs for a theological school and for new methods of outreach. Cholera broke out in 1864. This, along with renewed rebel activity, drove the Neviuses south and for a time back to America.

After three and a half years at home, the Neviuses returned to China in 1869 where John accepted an assignment to teach in the new theological school at Hangchow. After a year of teaching and after the Tientsin massacre in 1870, the Neviuses requested reassignment to Chefoo, where they built a house and lived their remaining twenty-two years in China. They followed moderate living standards, neither trying to "go native" nor remaining stiffly Western.

From 1872 to 1881 Nevius maintained an active schedule of itineration in Shantung Province. He traveled on horseback as far as 300 miles south and 200 miles west of Chefoo, keeping in touch with sixty preaching points.

In 1877 a severe famine struck and Nevius became involved in famine relief, an effort rewarded by increased credibility for his Gospel preaching among the people. But Helen's health was still not good. They were forced to return to the States, Helen in 1879 and John a year later.

Returning to China again in 1882, Nevius resumed his itineration and maintained it for the next eight years or so. From January to April or May, usually with another missionary, he preached, taught, visited, baptized, counseled, and pastored. From June till August, thirty to forty men came from rural areas to the Nevius home where they spent five hours each day in systematic Bible study. Then from September to December Nevius traveled again.

In 1889, the second general missionary conference of China convened in Shanghai and Nevius was invited to speak on his missionary methods. When the Neviuses left for furlough in June of that year, they were invited to stop over in Korea to share his method with Presbyterian missionaries there.

The Neviuses returned to Chefoo in 1892 ready to resume normal work. On the eve of his fall itineration, October 19, 1893, a heart attack felled John at age sixty-four.

What Is the Nevius Plan?

John Nevius's plan of mission work evolved over a lifetime of ministry. Of it he says, "The plans and methods made use of in bringing the truth to bear upon the minds of the heathen are various, and may and should be changed and modified according to the different conditions and circumstances."[4]

He considered the "primary and ultimate work of the missionary" to be "that of preaching the Gospel," while also acknowledging the need to meet physical needs. Preaching he defined as "every possible mode of presenting Christian truth."[5] Nevius guarded against following a universal pattern for mission work. "Some . . . seem to regard the heathen as all belonging to the same class, and conforming to one type; while in fact they differ widely, each nation having a marked individuality of its own."[6]

Nevius held unique views on the use of the Bible. He suggested it was never intended to be distributed among the heathen as a means of bringing them to the truth. He stressed that "it is principally by the instrumentality of the living teacher that God will save them that are lost." Only when they develop a knowledge of Christ, will the Spirit unlock the mysteries of Scripture to them.[7]

Nevius did not minimize the importance of the Bible but rather emphasized that "the Bible should accompany and follow the labors of the missionary, rather than precede them." The church's messengers must introduce Christ's truth "among the natives first and principally by oral instruction in their mother tongues; by acts of kindness and sympathy; by lives embodying and illustrating the Gospel which they preach."[8]

The Nevius Plan in Korea

The first two weeks of instruction Nevius gave the young Presbyterian missionaries in Korea in 1889 formed and focused their work. The Korea mission considered Nevius's suggestions so important that they adopted them as mission policy and gave all new missionaries a copy of his booklet, requiring them to pass an examination on it.

The most extensive work dealing with the Nevius Plan was *The Korean Church and the Nevius Methods*, written by a Presbyterian missionary to Korea, C.A. Clark. Clark summarizes the Nevius Plan:

I. Missionary personal evangelism through wide itineration,

II. Self-propagation: every believer a teacher of someone, and a learner from someone else better fitted; every individual and group seeking by the "layering method" to extend the work,

III. Self-government: every group under its chosen unpaid leaders; circuits under their own paid helpers, will later yield to pastors; circuit meetings to train the people for later district, provincial and national leadership,

IV. Self-support: with all chapels provided by the believers; each group, as soon as founded, beginning to pay towards the circuit helper's salary; even schools to receive but partial subsidy, and that only when being founded; no pastors of single churches provided by foreign funds,

V. Systematic Bible study for every believer under his group leader and circuit helper; and for every leader and helper in the Bible Classes,

VI. Strict discipline enforced by Bible penalties,

VII. Co-operation and union with other bodies, or at least territorial division,

VIII. Non-interference in lawsuits or any such matters,

IX. General helpfulness where possible in the economic life problems of the people.[9]

Nevius contrasted his method to former patterns: The former depended largely on paid "native agency," while the latter minimized such agency. Both sought the establishment of independent, self-reliant churches; but the old system did so by the use of foreign funds to foster and stimulate church growth in the first stage of their development, gradually discontinuing the use of such funds, while the new system applied principles of independence and self-reliance from the beginning.[10]

Nevius stressed the training of converts. This training could be best accomplished by the convert continuing in his normal place and putting his faith into practice. When he has grown he would then be recognized as fit for positions of responsibility.

Nevius emphasized teaching over preaching. His four-part outline for Sunday observance included teaching a simple Bible story. He stressed local leadership and encouraged informal arrangements, using the home and furniture provided by the group itself, rather than formal church buildings and furnishings.

The Nevius Plan called for a structured local group:

We have found it necessary, in order to systematize and unify our work, to establish rules and regulations, which have been put in our chapels as placards. Most of these are now embodied in the new edition of *The Manual for Inquirers*. This Manual, the Catechism, and the Gospels, are the books which I place in the hands of every inquirer, and little more is needed for years in the way of textbooks for those who have not previously learned to read.[11]

The Manual contains "general directions for Scripture studies; forms of prayer; the Apostles Creed; and select passages of Scripture, to be committed to memory." He offers a selection of Scripture stories and parables, with directions as to how they should be recited and explained.

Next follow "Rules for the Organization and Direction of Stations; Duties of Leaders and Rules for their guidance; a system of forms for keeping station records of attendance and studies; Form of Church Covenant; Scripture Lessons for Preparing for Baptism; the same for preparing for the Lord's Supper; Order of Exercises for Church Service and Directions for spending Sunday; a Short Scripture Catechism . . . enforcing the duty of giving; and a short essay on the duty of every Christian to make known the Gospel to others." Specially prepared questions were included to facilitate the teaching and examination of learners. Sometimes a selection of common hymns was bound up with the volume.[12]

Nevius recommended for all church members six types of study, "Learning to read, memorizing Scripture, reading Scripture in course, telling Scripture stories, learning the meaning of Scripture, and reviews of former exercises."[13]

The missionaries' role was to visit the area for examinations, general instructions, and direction. He found that it was necessary to have the local group send potential leaders for a six-week to two-month advanced Bible Training School. This program included secular subjects as well, and Mrs. Nevius taught music, "with singular assiduity and success."

The Nevius Plan evolved as each stage presented itself with an underlying principle always at work: it should never be other than the natural meeting of the peoples' own needs on their time schedule and within their financial capability. He recognized that these Bible School classes would eventually lead to theological education, but he was in no hurry to introduce such a program.

Discipline formed a part of the plan. Nevius wrote,

We regard the administration of discipline as indispensable to the growth and prosperity of our work, and attention to it claims a large portion of our time and thoughts. We administer discipline as directed by the Scriptures . . . first, by exhortation and admonition, followed if necessary by a formal trial and suspension; varying from a few months to one or two years, in failure of reformation, by excommunication.[14]

Nevius handled discipline himself, thus the importance of missionary itineration. He tried to visit each place at least twice a year, and discipline always formed a part of his visit.

Though the Nevius Plan was adopted and put into practice by the Presbyterian missionaries in Korea, Nevius's colleagues in Shantung Province were not so enthusiastic.

His most severe critic was Dr. Calvin Mateer, who did not favor Nevius's concept of workers supported by the local congregation instead of receiving a salary from the mission. Mateer, known to be a stubborn man, seems to have resented this newly arrived missionary trying to alter the old ways of doing things.

The greatest tribute to John L. Nevius is that the Nevius Plan is the most frequently cited factor in the outstanding growth of the Korean church.

Notes

1. On the use of the Nevius method in Korea, see Allen D. Clark, *A History of the Church in Korea* (Seoul: The Christian Literature Society of Korea, 1971); Everett N. Hunt, Jr., *Protestant Pioneers in Korea* (Maryknoll, N.Y.: Orbis Books, 1980); and Roy E. Shearer, *Wildfire: Church Growth in Korea* (Grand Rapids, Mich.: William B. Eerdmans Publishing Company, 1966).

2. Similar concepts of missionary activity were promoted by Henry Venn of the British Church Missionary Society and by Rufus Anderson of the American Board of Commissioners for Foreign Missions. See Max Warren, *To Apply the Gospel* (Grand Rapids, Mich.: William B. Eerdmans Publishing Company, 1971), and R. Pierce Beaver, *To Advance the Gospel* (Grand Rapids, Mich.: William B. Eerdmans Publishing Company, 1967).

3. Biographical information is taken from either Helen S. Coan Nevius, *The Life of John Livingston Nevius* (New York: Fleming H. Revell, 1895), or her *Our Life in China* (New York: Robert Carter and Brothers, 1869).

4. John L. Nevius, *China and the Chinese* (Philadelphia: Presbyterian Board of Publication, 1882), pp. 346-47.

5. Ibid., p. 358.

6. Ibid., p. 359.

7. Ibid., p. 367.

8. Ibid., p. 369.

9. Charles Allen Clark, *The Korean Church and the Nevius Methods* (New York: Fleming H. Revell, 1928), pp. 241-42.

10. John L. Nevius, *The Planting and Development of Missionary Churches,* 4th ed. (Grand Rapids, Mich., 1958), p. 8. First published as *Methods of Mission Work,* 1886.

11. Ibid., p. 38.

12. Ibid.

13. Ibid., p. 39.

14. Ibid., pp. 48 and 49.

Selected Bibliography

Works by John L. Nevius

1869 *China and the Chinese.* New York: Harper & Brothers, Publishers.

1886 *The Planting and Development of Missionary Churches.* 4th ed. Grand Rapids, Mich., 1958. First published as *Methods of Mission Work.*

1896 *Demon Possession and Allied Themes.* 2d ed. New York: Fleming H. Revell.

Works about John L. Nevius

Nevius, Helen S. Coan. *The Life of John Livingston Nevius.* New York: Fleming H. Revell, 1895.

_____. *Our Life in China.* New York: Robert Carter and Brothers, 1869.

Selected Works about Nevius's Missionary Method

Beyerhaus, Peter, and Henry Lefever. *The Responsible Church and the Foreign Mission.* Grand Rapids: Mich.: Wm. B. Eerdmans Publishing Co., 1964.

Clark, Allen D. *A History of the Church in Korea.* Seoul, Korea: The Christian Literature Society of Korea, 1971.

Clark, Charles Allen. *The Korean Church and the Nevius Method.* New York: Fleming H. Revell, n.d. Reprinted, Seoul, Korea: The Christian Literature Society, 1937.

Hunt, Everett N., Jr. *Protestant Pioneers in Korea.* Maryknoll, N.Y.: Orbis Books, 1980.

Shearer, Roy E. *Wildfire: Church Growth in Korea.* Grand Rapids, Mich.: Wm. B. Eerdmans Publishing Co., 1966.

J. Hudson Taylor

1832–1905

Founder of the China Inland Mission

J. Herbert Kane

One of the greatest names in mission among evangelical circles is that of Hudson Taylor. He was a spiritual giant who built an enduring enterprise by faith and prayer.[1] He believed in influencing people through God by prayer alone, and demonstrated to the Christian world that it is no vain thing to trust in the living God. The secret of Hudson Taylor's life and ministry may be summed up in four simple propositions: "There is a living God. He has spoken in His Word. He means what he says. And He is willing and able to perform what He has promised."[2]

Hudson Taylor was born into a devout Methodist family in Barnsley, Yorkshire, England, on May 21, 1832. Even before his birth, his parents dedicated him to the Lord. While still a youth he decided he wanted to be a missionary to China. At seventeen years of age he experienced a quiet but rather unusual conversion, not unlike that of John Wesley, which resulted in a full assurance of salvation that never left him.[3]

To prepare himself for missionary service, Taylor studied medicine and surgery in Hull and later in London. Upon moving to London, he chose to "live by faith" in modest quarters in a rundown part of town, subsisting on brown bread and apples, reasoning that if he could not "eat bitterness" in London he would not survive in China. In his spare time he devoured everything he could find on China, studied the Chinese language, brushed up on his Latin, and tackled Hebrew and Greek.

In 1853 Taylor sailed for China under the auspices of the Chinese Evangelization Society (CES), whose leading missionary, Karl Gutzlaff, had created something of a sensation in Europe by his widespread travels along the coast of China. His influence on Hudson Taylor was profound. "Gutzlaff's courage, originality, adventurousness, adaptability to Chinese customs, his principles and methods left a deep impression on the young man who was to follow him. When Hudson Taylor reached China, his actions and attitudes suggest that he was emulating Gutzlaff, albeit subconsciously."[4]

Hudson Taylor's early years in Shanghai and Ningbo were marked by difficulty and distress, much of it occasioned by his own mission, described by Stephen Neill as "curiously incompetent."[5] When the CES failed to meet his meager support of $400 a year, he was obliged, from time to time, to depend on the hospitality of others – a very humiliating experience for such a sensitive, conscientious person. In addition, from the beginning his manner and lifestyle led others to think of him as brash, venturesome, and something of a maverick. His decision to shave his head, grow a pigtail, and wear Chinese dress scandalized the foreign community.[6] Even some of his fellow missionaries considered him a crackpot. In 1857, after much soul-searching, he resigned from the CES so that, in his words, he could "live by faith."[7]

Launching a Mission to Inland China

After several years of arduous toil in Ningbo, Taylor suffered a breakdown in health. He returned to England in 1860, shortly after the Treaties of Tientsin opened inland China to Western merchants and missionaries. During his six-year stay in England, he became increasingly burdened for the eleven provinces of inland China that were without a single missionary. He offered his services to several mission boards, but none of them had the necessary resources to support such an uncertain venture. Consequently, he had to launch out on his own.

On a Sunday in June 1865, unable to bear the sight of hundreds of smug Christians in Brighton enjoying the consolation of a Sunday morning service while 400 million people were perishing in China, he left the service and made his way to a deserted beach. There, in an agony of soul, he surrendered to the will of God, and the China Inland Mission (CIM) was born. On the flyleaf of his Bible he wrote: "Prayed for twenty-four willing, skillful laborers at Brighton, June 25, 1865."[8]

When Hudson Taylor arrived in China in 1866 with a group of inexperienced missionaries, with no denomination behind them and no visible means of support, his closest friends questioned his sanity. When these raw recruits, including single women, were sent upcountry far beyond the protection of the foreign gunboats, where they faced the hostility of the superstitious peasantry egged on by the scholar/gentry class, the incredulity knew no bounds. Everyone predicted disaster; but it did not happen. With no weapon but truth and no banner but love, those young workers, two by two, penetrated the interior of China against incredible hardship and opposition.

By 1882 all but three of the eleven closed provinces had resident missionaries. From time to time special calls went out for more workers: 70 in 1881; 100 in 1888; and 200 in the depth of the depression in 1931-32. In each instance the goal was reached. Eventually the CIM grew to be the largest mission in China, with almost 1,400 Western workers and a church membership of over 100,000.[9] All of this was the result, under God, of one man's vision and passion. Kenneth Scott Latourette wrote: "Hudson Taylor was, if measured by the movement which he called into being, one of the greatest missionaries of all time, and was certainly, judged by the results of his efforts, one of the four or five most influential foreigners who came to China in the nineteenth century for any purpose, religious or secular."[10]

The influence of Hudson Taylor went far beyond China and the CIM. He is widely regarded as the father of the faith-mission movement,[11] which today embraces over 30,000 missionaries in well over 500 mission societies in all parts of the world. Many of the so-called faith missions based in England and North America adopted the principles and policies laid down by Taylor. To the present they are popularly known as "faith" missions, though they themselves would be the first to deny that they have any monopoly on faith. In North America eighty-five of these missions are members of the Interdenominational Foreign Mission Association with headquarters in Wheaton, Illinois. An even larger number of faith missions remain completely independent, without membership in any association.[12]

Taylor's periodic visits to the homelands included – besides England – Canada, the United States, Australia, Scandinavia, and several European countries. Everywhere he was in great demand as speaker and missionary statesman. His message was always the same: the speedy evangelization of the most populous nation on earth.

An Ecumenical and Generous Spirit

Faith missions have sometimes been dismissed as "sects." But Hudson Taylor was anything but sectarian. On his world tours he appealed to missionary-minded people in all denominations and urged them to support more actively their own programs, with their gifts and especially with their prayers. In China he managed to hold together hundreds of workers from most of the major denominations. The first bishop of West China, W.W. Cassels, was a member of the CIM. Hudson Taylor attended and addressed the General Missionary Conference in Shanghai in 1890, which called for a thousand workers for China in the next five years. In Europe and North America he moved freely in ecumenical circles, attending the great missionary conferences in London and New York, where his powerful ministry was always appreciated. In the United States he shared the platform with such ecumenical leaders as Dwight L. Moody, A.T. Pierson, John R. Mott, Robert Wilder, and Robert Speer, among others.

One of Hudson Taylor's outstanding characteristics was his humility. He had no desire to build an empire or to make a name for himself. Indeed, he was constantly bemoaning his own lack of faith, hardness of heart, and general unfitness for the enormous task thrust upon him. It grieved him deeply when people spoke of him as a "great leader." His one ambition was to be well pleasing to God. On one occasion in a large Presbyterian church in Melbourne he was introduced as "our illustrious guest." Taylor quietly began his address by saying: "Dear friends, I am the little servant of an illustrious Master."[13] Sherwood Eddy, who heard him speak at the Detroit Convention of the Student Volunteer Movement in 1894, said: "He was one of the purest, humblest, most sensitive souls I ever knew, fervent in prayer, mighty in faith, his whole life dedicated to the single object of doing the will of God. I felt myself in the presence of a man who had received a Kingdom which could not be shaken, without or within."[14]

Hudson Taylor was also marked by a broad and generous spirit. His first concern, naturally, was for the welfare of his own workers; but he was more interested in the evangelization of China than in the growth of his own mission. He eschewed rivalry and deplored competition. Deliberately avoiding the "occupied" cities near the coast, he sent his workers to the "unoccupied" regions of inland China.

Even though China was Taylor's first love – on one occasion he said that if he had a thousand lives he would give them all to China – he was equally glad when workers were called to other parts of the world. In his thoughts and prayers he embraced the whole household of faith. He knew what it was to rejoice with those who rejoice and to weep with those who weep. He was genuinely interested in the success of others, and was pleased when their work prospered. One reason he refused to appeal for money was his concern that in so doing he might siphon off funds from the established missions and thereby hurt their work. Not without reason has Ralph Winter described the CIM as "the most cooperative servant organization yet to appear."[15]

Nowhere was Taylor's generous spirit more clearly seen than in his handling of the Boxer indemnities. Following the Boxer Rebellion in 1900 the Western powers forced a prostrate China to compensate the missions for their losses. Although the CIM suffered heavier losses than any other Protestant mission, Hudson Taylor refused to submit any claims or to accept any compensation.[16] He considered such demands contrary to the spirit of love as exemplified in the Gospel of Christ.

A Man Ahead of His Time

In many respects Hudson Taylor was a man far ahead of his time. Nowhere was the unholy alliance between the Gospel and the gunboat closer than in China; yet in the heyday of Western imperialism, when others were waving the flag and demanding the protection guaranteed to them by the "unequal treaties," Taylor saw the evils of the colonial system and instructed his workers to look to their Heavenly Father, not to the foreign gunboats, for protection. CIM workers were expected to take joyfully the despoiling of their goods (Heb. 10:34) and not to seek compensation. When riots broke out, as frequently they did upcountry, the missionaries could request protection from the local authorities, but not from the foreign consuls.

When Hudson Taylor and a group of CIM workers were almost killed in a riot in Yangchow in 1868, the British authorities in China, looking for an excuse to settle old scores, dispatched a flotilla of gunboats up the Yangtze River to Nanking and a company of marines to Yangchow -- all against the expressed principles of Hudson Taylor. To make matters worse, the whole ugly affair was debated in the House of Commons and reported in *The Times* (London), resulting in a clamor for punitive action against China, on the one hand, and the recall of the missionaries, on the other. Though he was helpless to do anything about the situation, Taylor was sick at heart over the developments.

Nor was Hudson Taylor content to remain silent about the infamous opium trade. As editor for many years of *China's Millions*, he carried on a running battle with his own government over the evils of the nefarious trade. Closely allied with Taylor in this crusade was Benjamin Broomhall, general secretary of the CIM, a co-founder with James L. Maxwell of the Christian Union for the Severance of the Connection of the British Empire with the Opium Traffic. For years, Broomhall was editor of *National Righteousness*, the official organ of the antiopium campaign.

Realizing the vast untapped potential in the churches at home, Hudson Taylor appealed for recruits having "little formal education." What China needed, in the mid-nineteenth century, he believed, was evangelists, not scholars and theologians. Later on, when the Bible school movement got under way in the 1880s, many of the recruits came from that source. For many years humble Bible school graduates formed the backbone of the mission. Many of them made excellent missionaries, learning to read, write, and speak Chinese with commendable fluency and accuracy.[17] The women, as well as the men, were required to enroll in the stiff language course prescribed by the mission.

As might be expected, these men and women were most effective in reaching members of the lower classes. As a result, the CIM-related churches were composed mostly of the peasants and artisans found in such large numbers in inland China. The mission supported a number of Bible schools, but no colleges or seminaries. The mission did, however, have some outstanding linguists. F.W. Baller's *Primer* and R.H. Mathews's *Chinese-English Dictionary* were used far beyond the boundaries of the CIM.[18] Moreover, the mission had its own Chinese hymnal and two language schools for new workers – one for the women, in Yangchow, and the other for men, in Anking.

Through the years the mission has been blessed with a goodly number of fine writers: Mrs. Howard Taylor,[19] Marshall Broomhall, Isobel Kuhn, Phyllis Thompson, Leslie T. Lyall, A.J. Broomhall, Henry W. Frost, Robert H. Glover, J. Oswald Sanders, and others. *China's Millions*, first published in 1875 and for many years edited by Hudson Taylor, is one of the oldest house organs of its kind.[20] Altogether the mission has produced 550 books, scores of booklets, film strips, field reports, and one full-length film on Hudson Taylor.[21]

Hudson Taylor never claimed to be a missionary statesman; but he was a good administrator, ran a tight ship, and almost single-handedly opened inland China to the Gospel. From first to last he was an evangelist, primarily interested in the "salvation of souls." Schools and hospitals were opened and maintained, but they were of secondary importance. He believed that 400 million Chinese were lost in sin and darkness and would perish eternally without a saving knowledge of Christ. To this end he gave all his time, thought, energy, and prayer. His burden for the spiritual welfare of the Middle Kingdom was expressed eloquently and passionately in his book *China: Its Spiritual Need and Claims*, which did for China what William Carey's *Enquiry* did for the world.

Taylor was not greatly concerned about the *kind* of churches raised up. Each pioneer missionary was free to establish denominational polity – Congregational, Presbyterian, or Episcopal; but once established, denominational policy could not be changed by later missionaries – only by the churches themselves.[22] He had no desire to build another denomination; consequently the churches were never organized into a national body. This was perhaps his greatest weakness.

Another unique feature of the CIM was the fact that headquarters was located in China, not in the homeland. It made sense to Hudson Taylor to have the directorate as close as possible to the scene of action, rather than having the work directed by remote control from London, Philadelphia, or Toronto. Moreover, the members of the directorate were all missionaries with several decades of service behind them. Missionary work in inland China in the nineteenth century was a difficult and delicate operation and required the oversight of men with experience as well as wisdom. A weakness of this arrangement was the failure to recruit Chinese leaders to serve on the directorate; but the CIM was not alone in this. Very few missions in those early days had national figures in positions of leadership.

The fact that the CIM had all its work and workers in one country made it comparatively easy to locate the directorate overseas. However, the practice was continued when, following the mass evacuation of China, the mission branched out into ten countries of Asia in the early 1950s. Since then international headquarters has been located in Singapore.

In the mainline denominations married women were not required to function as missionaries, though some of them did. They were primarily homemakers for their husbands; and when children came along, they assumed responsibility for their education at home. Not so with the CIM. All women, married and single, were missionaries in their own right, were required to learn the language, and were expected, within reason, to carry their share of the work. To make this possible Hudson Taylor in 1881 established a school in the coastal city of Chefoo. All parents were required to send their children to the Chefoo School for twelve years of education. Children went home to be with their parents over the long Christmas vacation. Parents spent their summer vacation in Chefoo. In this way they managed to keep in touch with their children. Missionaries working on the borders of Tibet and other remote areas were able to see their children only once every three years.

The Chefoo School grew to be the largest and most sought-after school of its kind in China. The curriculum, based on the British system, was heavily weighted in favor of classical courses designed to prepare the graduates for entrance into Oxford or Cambridge University. A large number of graduates went on to college in the various home countries. Business people and members of the diplomatic corps vied with one another for the few vacancies at Chefoo. The most illustrated graduate was Henry R. Luce, co-founder of *Time* newsmagazine.[23]

CIM missionaries were a very diverse group. Hudson Taylor drew his recruits not only from all the major denominations in Great Britain but also from the other English-speaking countries as well as from Germany, Switzerland, and Scandinavia. Workers from continental Europe were members of a dozen associate missions, each with its own home council, support base, and recruiting system. In China they were all part of the large CIM family, working under the direction of CIM superintendents. For all practical purposes they were considered CIMers. That this large, international, heterogeneous group of active, strong-minded missionaries could achieve and maintain a high degree of harmony over a long period of time was a tribute to the wise, gentle, but forceful leadership of Hudson Taylor.

Building on the Faithfulness of God

Taylor was a firm believer in the faithfulness of God. Indeed, it was the cornerstone of his whole theology. Accordingly, he insisted on living by faith, which to him meant looking to God alone to furnish the personnel and the money needed to maintain the operation. On more than one occasion he said that God's work carried on in God's way would never lack God's supply. CIM workers were exhorted to look to God, not the mission, to meet their daily needs.

Taylor adamantly refused to go into debt even when funds were low. He argued that if his ways pleased the Lord, God would meet all needs according to his promise in Philippians 4:19. If funds were withheld, that was a sign of God's disapproval. In that case, the project was delayed or canceled. Available funds were used first to pay outstanding bills; the missionaries shared what was left over. During times when funds were low, all felt the pinch from the latest recruit to the general director. This practice not only kept the missionaries on their knees, it also made for a strong esprit de corps in the entire CIM family. To this day the mission adheres to this twofold policy – no indebtedness and no solicitation of funds.[24]

It would be a mistake to imagine that Hudson Taylor was a spiritual giant whose inner life was completely free of conflict. Following the Yangchow riot, funds fell off, opposition increased, and difficulties multiplied until Taylor was discouraged to the point of despair. Writing to his sister he said: "My mind has been greatly exercised for six or eight months past, feeling the need personally and for our mission of more holiness, life, power in our souls. I prayed, agonized, fasted, strove, made resolutions, read the Word more diligently, sought more time for meditation – but all without avail."[25] About that time (1875), as Hudson Taylor reports it, a sentence in a letter from a fellow missionary was "used to remove the scales from my eyes and the Spirit revealed to me the truth of our *oneness with Jesus* as I had never known it before."[26] Later, when recounting the experience to a friend, Taylor exclaimed, "God has made me a new man!"[27]

This experience, as life-changing as his earlier conversion, enabled Taylor for another thirty years to bear the enormous burdens of a rapidly growing mission by casting them on the Lord (1 Pet. 5:7). Never again was he in danger of giving way to despair. Even the horrendous losses of the Boxer Year of 1900 failed to rob him of his peace of mind. He had learned to trust God.

Arthur F. Glasser, for many years a member of the CIM, said of Hudson Taylor: "He was ambitious without being proud . . . He was biblical without being bigoted . . . He was Catholic without being superficial . . . He was charismatic without being selfish."[28] By all odds, Hudson Taylor was one of the truly great missionaries of the nineteenth century.

Notes

1. Hudson Taylor's life bears comparison with that of George Muller, his lifelong friend. Taylor learned much concerning the life of faith from Muller; and Muller, in spite of vast responsibilities of his own, gave periodically and generously to the work of the China Inland Mission.

2. Leslie T. Lyall, *A Passion for the Impossible* (London: Hodder and Stoughton, 1965), Preface.

3. While his mother was in another city praying for his conversion, Hudson Taylor picked up a tract, thinking to read the story and skip the moral, and was struck by the phrase "the finished work of Christ," which came home to him in full force and with new meaning.

4. Marshall Broomhall, *Barbarians at the Gates* (London: Hodder and Stoughton, 1981), p. 180.

5. Stephen Neill, *A History of Christian Missions* (Baltimore: Penguin Books, 1964), p. 333.

6. The pigtail worn by Chinese men was a sign of the Chinese subjugation to the Manchus over a period of 300 years, which ended with Sun Yat-sen's revolution of 1911.

7. Taylor left the CES without any bitterness on his part.

8. Taylor wanted two missionaries for each of the eleven closed provinces and two for Mongolia.

9. Following the mass evacuation of China in the early 1950s, the membership dropped to around 250. As one by one other countries of East Asia were entered, the membership climbed back to 950, where it stands today.

10. Kenneth Scott Latourette, *History of Christian Missions in China* (New York: Macmillan, 1929), p. 259.

11. There were faith missions before the CIM, but none of them had the growth and impact of the CIM.

12. Some of these, such as Wycliffe Bible Translators, New Tribes Mission, Christian Missions in Many Lands, and Baptist Mid-Missions, have thousands of members on their rolls.

13. Dr. and Mrs. Howard Taylor, *Hudson Taylor and the China Inland Mission: The Growth of a Work of God* (London: China Inland Mission, 1918), p. 493.

14. Sherwood Eddy, *Pathfinders of the World Missionary Crusade* (New York: Abingdon-Cokesbury, 1945), p. 194.

15. Ralph D. Winter and Steven C. Hawthorne, *Perspectives on the World Christian Movement* (Pasadena, Calif.: William Carey Library, 1981), p. 172.

16. The CIM lost fifty-eight adults and twenty-one children at the hands of the Boxers.

17. In the author's China days (1935-50) Ray Frame was the best Chinese speaker in the mission. He was a graduate of Prairie Bible Institute, Three Hills, Alberta.

18. During World War II, when the United States was preparing to send GIs to the China theater of the war, Harvard University republished Mathews's *Dictionary* for use in its crash course in Chinese.

19. Dr. and Mrs. Howard Taylor's two volumes on the life and ministry of Hudson Taylor constitute the "official" biography of Taylor. The volumes went through eighteen editions and appeared in many European and other languages, but are now out of print. A one-volume condensation, by Phyllis Thompson, was published by Moody Press in 1965. The title is *Hudson Taylor: God's Man in China*.

20. Since the CIM is no longer working in China, the name of the magazine was changed to *East Asia's Millions*, to reflect the wider outreach of the mission. In 1965 the name of the mission was changed to the Overseas Missionary Fellowship.

21. The film was granted the 1981 Film of the Year Award by the Christian Film Distributors Association.

22. Missionaries from the same denominational background were usually placed together in the same province. The Anglicans were sent to Szechuan in West China, where the CIM-related churches were part of the worldwide Anglican Communion.

23. To commemorate the school's centennial, the mission published a book by Sheila Miller, *Pigtails, Petticoats, and the Old School Tie* (London: China Inland Mission, 1981).

24. This practice, regarded by many as archaic, still appears to be effective. *Proving God* (London: China Inland Mission, 1956), by Phyllis Thompson, traces the financial experiences of the mission over a period of ninety years.

25. Mrs. Howard Taylor, *Hudson Taylor's Spiritual Secret* (London: China Inland Mission, 1932), p. 113.

26. Ibid., p. 114.

27. Ibid., p. 110.

28. Thompson, *Hudson Taylor: God's Man in China*, Preface.

Selected Bibliography

Works by Hudson Taylor

1865 *China: Its Spiritual Need and Claims*. London: China Inland Mission.
1875 *A Retrospect*. London: China Inland Mission.
1895 *After Thirty Years*. London: Morgan & Scott and China Inland Mission.

Works about Hudson Taylor

Armerding, Hudson T. "China Inland Mission and Some Aspects of Its Work." Ph.D. diss., University of Chicago, 1948.

Bacon, Daniel W. "The Influence of Hudson Taylor on the Faith Mission Movement." D. Miss. diss., Trinity Evangelical Divinity School, Deerfield, Ill., 1983.

Broomhall, A.J. *Hudson Taylor and China's Open Century*. Book 1: *Barbarians at the Gates* (1981). Book 2: *Over the Treaty Wall* (1982). Book 3: *If I Had a Thousand Lives* (1982). All published by London: Hodder and Stoughton, and Overseas Missionary Fellowship. [Ed. note: Four more volumes have come off the press to complete the series.]

Broomhall, Marshall. *Hudson Taylor: The Man Who Believed God*. London: Hodder and Stoughton, 1929.
_____. *Hudson Taylor's Legacy*. London: Hodder and Stoughton, 1931.
_____. *The Jubilee Story of the China Inland Mission*. London: Morgan and Scott, 1915.
_____, ed. *In Memoriam – J. Hudson Taylor*. Morgan and Scott, 1905.

Hudson Taylor. Film produced by Ken Anderson Films, Warsaw, Ind., 1981.

Lyall, Leslie T.A. *Passion for the Impossible: The Continuing Story of the Mission Hudson Taylor Began*. London: Hodder and Stoughton, 1965.

Pollock, John. *Hudson Taylor and Maria: Pioneers in China*. New York: McGraw-Hill Book Company, 1962.

Taylor, Dr. and Mrs. Howard. *Hudson Taylor in Early Years: The Growth of a Soul*. London: China Inland Mission and Religious Tract Society, 1911.

_____. *Hudson Taylor and the China Inland Mission: The Growth of a Work of God*. London: China Inland Mission and Religious Tract Society, 1918.

Taylor, Mrs. Howard. *Hudson Taylor's Spiritual Secret*. London: China Inland Mission, 1932.

Charlotte (Lottie) Moon
1840–1912

Demonstrating "No Greater Love"

Catherine B. Allen

L ike many other missionaries, Lottie Moon left a legacy that paved the way for succeeding generations. But unlike any other missionary, Miss Moon left a legacy that largely *paid* the way for the growth of the largest missionary force of any evangelical or Protestant denomination.

When she died in 1912 after nearly forty years in China, she left an estate of approximately $250 and a battered trunk of personal effects. She also left a shining name, a spotless record, and a sterling idea for fund-raising. The Woman's Missionary Union (WMU) of the Southern Baptist Convention (SBC) shaped these legacies into the most magnetic collection plate in mission history.

The Lottie Moon Christmas Offering for Foreign Missions is the largest source of funding for the SBC's overseas missions, involving almost four thousand missionaries. By 1992 the cumulative total of the offering was nearly $1.3 billion. With more than $80 million raised in the 1992 collection, the Lottie Moon Christmas Offering is thought to be the largest annual offering collected by Christians.[1]

After a century of intensive scrutiny by researchers, four-foot three-inch Lottie Moon continues to stand tall in estimation. She has become a cultural icon with wide name recognition in the southern United States. Southern Baptists have taken her name around the world, with Baptists in many countries contributing to the offering bearing Lottie's name.

Best Educated Woman of the South

The Lottie Moon story always begins with a touch of nostalgia for old Virginia.[2] Charlotte Digges Moon was born in December 1840 near Scottsville, Albermarle County, Virginia. She grew up on the "Road of the Presidents" at a family estate called Viewmont. Her maternal uncle, Dr. James Barclay, bought the nearby Monticello mansion after Thomas Jefferson died. Then as one of the early followers of Alexander Campbell, in 1850 he went to Jerusalem as the first missionary of the Disciples of Christ.

As a child, "Lottie" (as she was known) earned a reputation for mischief and intelligence. She was initially hostile to the religion of her devout Baptist parents, pillars of the Scottsville Baptist Church. She may have been influenced more by a highly independent older sister, Orianna. Orianna

Moon went away to study at Troy Female Seminary in New York, caught the early winds of the feminist movement, and was one of the first two southern women to earn medical degrees. Orianna graduated from Female Medical College of Pennsylvania in 1857.

Lottie's girlhood seemed similarly marked with higher intellect and greater potential than society would allow her to exercise. After studying with tutors on the plantation, she was sent for formal schooling at the Baptist-related girls institute, which became Hollins College, near Roanoke, Virginia.

By the time she graduated from Hollins, Virginia Baptists had organized a woman's college that was to be equivalent in quality to the males-only University of Virginia. Lottie enrolled in this new school in Charlottesville, known as Albermarle Female Institute, in 1857. Her professors included Crawford Howell Toy, who later became the fifth faculty member of Southern Baptist Theological Seminary. He would be branded a heretic and banished to distinction as Harvard University's professor of Semitic languages. Toy and Moon maintained a friendship, and they may have come to the point of an engagement by 1881, but the specifics of their private lives cannot now be documented. Under Toy's tutelage, Lottie studied Greek, Hebrew, and Latin. She became fluent in Spanish and French. In 1861, just as the guns of Civil War were beginning to sound, Lottie and four other young women were awarded master of arts degrees. These were thought to be the first masters degrees awarded women of the South or in the South.

Lottie took away from school a new life and vision as a Christian. During a student revival in 1858, she went to a prayer meeting to scoff but left to pray all night. John A. Broadus, who soon became one of the founders of Southern Baptist Theological Seminary, was then pastor of the Charlottesville Baptist Church. He baptized Lottie and years later claimed that she was the best educated and most cultured woman in the South.

Apparently a sense of calling to foreign missions came early in Lottie's life as a Christian. John Broadus was noted for his compelling appeals for college ministerial students to serve on foreign fields. Several of Lottie's Charlottesville friends agreed to go. Broadus would not have thought to direct the invitation to missions toward Lottie. Southern Baptists at the time had appointed only one unmarried woman as a missionary and had vowed never to do it again. To fulfill any such calling in the 1860s, she would have had to marry a missionary. But when Crawford Toy was ordained to go to Japan in 1860, he did not choose a wife to go with him.

Whatever Lottie's (or Toy's) dreams might have been, the Civil War interrupted. She rode out the war at Viewmont, teaching a beloved baby sister named Edmonia and occasionally assisting Dr. Orianna Moon as she tended wounded soldiers in Charlottesville. Lottie's wartime exploits were not as infamous as those of two glamorous cousins, Virginia and Charlotte Moon, who served as flirtatious Confederate spies in Ohio.

The Moon family's fortunes were forever lost, and the children scattered to earn their own living. For Lottie this situation perhaps afforded more opportunity than she would have enjoyed before the war. By September 1866 she was on the faculty of a school in Danville, Kentucky, which was a predecessor to Centre College.

There she made the closest friend of her life, Anna Cunningham ("A.C.") Safford, daughter of a Presbyterian missionary to the South. The two women were pious and attuned to missions. Each tolerated the other's denominational loyalty. They were eager to improve their earnings, for Lottie had to support her family at Viewmont, until her mother died in 1870. Also, Lottie wanted more money to give to missions. Together with her sister Edmonia, she had become one of the most notable, though anonymous, donors to SBC foreign missions.

Responding to a Higher Calling

Although highly regarded as a teacher and church worker, Lottie was struggling to answer a higher calling. She was apparently the author of articles suggesting deaconess jobs in which women could serve as city missionaries.[3]

Through connections with Lottie's cousins, Moon and Safford moved to Cartersville, Georgia, in 1871. For two years they operated a school for girls and took active leadership in their respective churches. At the same time, the woman's missionary movement was gaining momentum in the South. In 1871-72, a group of Baltimore Baptist women began to press the SBC Foreign Mission Board to appoint women missionaries and to encourage the organization of women support groups. The Baltimore women fostered branches in South Carolina and other states. The instant financial strength of new women's groups brought new life to the near-bankrupt Baptist mission board. The door suddenly opened for unmarried women to become missionaries.

With support from South Carolina women, Lula Whilden was permitted in 1872 to accompany her married sister and brother-in- law to China. Catching news of Whilden's plans, Edmonia Moon instantly volunteered to pay her own passage to China. Edmonia had become active in a student missionary society at the Richmond Female Institute (forerunner of Westhampton College of the University of Richmond). She corresponded with Martha Foster Crawford, a pioneer Baptist woman missionary in China. Martha and her irascible husband, Tarleton Perry Crawford, had invited Edmonia to come to China as their assistant. So in a two-week flurry in April 1872, Edmonia Moon had applied, been appointed, packed, and departed for China. Baptist women of Richmond had organized to guarantee her support.

From the moment Edmonia set foot in China, colleagues stamped her as too young, nervous, and spoiled to succeed as a missionary. Hearing of her older, accomplished sister, they joined in the chorus of pleas for Lottie Moon to come to China. A missionary sermon by the Baptist pastor in Cartersville decided the issue. In 1873, A.C. Safford was appointed by Southern Presbyterians and Lottie Moon was appointed by Southern Baptists to missionary service in China.

Moon and Safford parted company in Shanghai. Safford's field would be Soochow, where she had a distinguished career at the forefront of the "woman's work for woman" movement. She was the founding editor of the formative periodical *Woman's Work in China.*[4]

Moon sailed on to Shantung Province. Entering through the treaty port of Chefoo, she traveled overland by mule litter to Tengchow, where she made her home until her death in 1912.[5] Tengchow had been the headquarters of Southern Baptist missionary work in Shantung since 1861, but within the year of Lottie Moon's arrival it was still suffering active hostility from unwelcoming townspeople. Northern Presbyterians also had a mission there but were more strongly headquartered in Chefoo.

For the next forty years, Lottie seldom migrated far from Tengchow. There were rare trips to Shanghai. There was a happy period of sixteen months in 1900-1901 when she retreated to Fukuoka, Japan, during the Boxer Rebellion. In 1876 Edmonia suffered an alarming breakdown and had to be escorted back to Virginia. Lottie had only two other trips to the United States. During furloughs in 1892-93 and 1903-4, Lottie Moon spoke of Tengchow as home.

Moon's assignment in China was "women's work." This title denoted two philosophies that shaped her ministry and her world. First was the missionary strategy known as "woman's mission to woman." Second was the staunchly defended prohibition against women seeming to teach, preach, or exercise authority over men.

William Carey, the Baptist pioneer in India, recognized in 1796 that evangelization of women would require attention "different from, and far beyond, what men can or will bestow."[6] Baptists, however, were reluctant to send the unmarried female missionaries he requested.

Techniques of women's work had been advanced in North China by Martha Foster Crawford, who was married but had no children, and by Sallie Landrum Holmes, whose husband died in China, leaving her a baby son. Having gotten to China under protection of their husbands, Crawford and Holmes actively cultivated their own sphere of influence. These intrepid women won their way into homes, created essential literature, and carved out a women's ministry before the Moon sisters arrived.[7] While Edmonia clung sickly to schoolteaching in Tengchow, Lottie caught the courage and creativity of Crawford and Holmes.

The missionaries as a group were committed to the plan of conducting schools for girls. Under the guise of education, the missionaries fought against culture and custom to give women the freedom to become and live as Christians. While learning the Chinese language, Lottie was given supervision of a girls school associated with Holmes. She accepted schoolteaching as an avenue of ministry she could certainly manage, but schoolteaching was not her objective. Prior to sailing in 1873, she had written: "Could a Christian woman possibly desire higher honor than to be permitted to go from house to house and tell of a savior to those who have never heard his name? We could not conceive a life which would more thoroughly satisfy the mind and heart of a true follower of the Lord Jesus."[8]

So Lottie took every opportunity to learn the ropes of personal evangelism. Often the women left the schools in charge of Chinese teachers while they itinerated village to village. Trips sometimes brought them home to their own beds at night. With increasing frequency, however, the women took provisions for camping out along the way in the rude shelters for muleteers called "inns." Gradually they gained the hospitality of rough peasant homes. The women traveled by donkey or mule, often escorted by a Chinese Christian man or couple. The senior woman missionary would preach to women (and whatever men eavesdropped), and Lottie would drill children in Bible stories and hymns, teaching in the open air.

Colleagues quickly pronounced Lottie a true missionary and praised her grasp of language and custom. She proved herself wise enough to tiptoe between two warring colleagues: T.P. Crawford and James Boardman Hartwell. She kept up good correspondence with the Foreign Mission Board, participating in the slow dialogue that shaped mission policy. She maintained fruitful communication with a growing circuit of women's missionary societies that organized in support of her, especially in Georgia and Virginia.

During the years 1873-85, when her work was officially that of girls' schoolteacher, Lottie's greatest victories were personal. First, she gained an excellent command of Chinese that coworkers envied. She developed almost an obsession for honoring Chinese customs unless they were blatantly incompatible with Christianity.

Second, she disciplined herself to survive physically and emotionally while living in primitive circumstances with the lower-class Chinese people. She learned to endure scrutiny and commentary by curious people who did not consider her human and gave her no privacy. She conquered fears of people who continually reviled her as "Devil Woman," she stayed courageous in the face of death threats, and she kept her poise in confrontations with soldiers. She came to accept the "real drudgery" of mission life. She ennobled her view of the harsh realities by remembering that the Chinese peasants were living a simple existence with which the man Jesus would have been personally familiar.

She diligently exercised, sought a clean and balanced diet, and rested regularly. She obtained a steady supply of reading materials in French and English. She transformed her Tengchow house into a Virginia miniature where missionary guests loved to relax. She took cleanliness and all possible precautions along with her when living in vermin-infested, pigsty conditions as she traveled among the villages. When smallpox vaccinations and other vaccines became available, she was the first to take advantage of them.

Outlasting Colleagues and Controversy

Both Baptists and Presbyterians regarded Shantung as a killing place. Ability to survive was a major accomplishment when measured against the experience of most coworkers. Mrs. Holmes burned out by 1881 and returned to the United States to try to salvage a sane existence for her son. T.P. Crawford was subject to various fits and paralyses, which sorely tried his colleagues, and Martha Crawford several times was forced to retreat for health's sake. J.B. Hartwell outlived three wives and survived poor health himself by long sojourns elsewhere. Other early missionaries in Shantung, both Baptist and Presbyterian, suffered serious disabilities and death. Of those Baptists who arrived in Shantung during her first twenty years of service, only Lottie remained unbroken in body and spirit.

Another major development in Lottie's early China days surely contributed to her survival. This development occurred along spiritual fronts. She remembered that she had heard God's calling to China "as clear as a bell." After Edmonia's breakdown and departure, she filled her human loneliness with the Divine Presence. She daily studied the Bible in Hebrew and Greek. She read devotional materials from the Holiness movement and diligently read Thomas à Kempis's *On the Imitation of Christ*. Some called her a mystic, for her daily routines revealed that she was taking into account the personal presence of Christ. A favorite quotation was "Lord Jesus, thou art home and friend and fatherland to me."[9]

With emotional discipline she tried to live at peace with all – Chinese and missionary. This was difficult, since T.P. Crawford and J.B. Hartwell's feud grew into lawsuits and rumored murder plots that continued even after Hartwell left the field for a time. Then Crawford confronted the entire Southern Baptist mission system, making unauthorized trips through the homeland encouraging schism. Out of his own thwarted battles with the Foreign Mission Board, he adopted the belief that such boards were unscriptural. He began to promote the idea that Southern Baptist churches should send out their missionaries directly.

Controversy surrounding Crawford made Lottie consider and modify her own thoughts. She tended to agree with Crawford's contention that foreign mission money should not be paid out to Chinese assistants and should not be spent on church buildings. She never agreed with his opinion that the Baptist schools should be closed and vigorously opposed his plot to close down his wife's school while she was absent for medical treatment. However, she did come for a while to view schools as a waste of her own time and called them the greatest folly of missions.

As Crawford became more dictatorial about the methods of newly arrived young coworkers, she became more permissive, willing to allow each missionary to seek his or her own strategy and theology. In communication with A.C. Safford, she stayed abreast of the latest thinking about how best to evangelize women and improve their plight in society. She adopted the custom of wearing a form of native clothing.

Nothing in mission policy or strategy ruffled her equanimity except for threatened trespasses on her freedom and autonomy as an equal partner. An implied infringement on the dignity of unmarried women missionaries made her fire off a resignation to the Foreign Mission Board in 1885. Her anger was met by calming explanations, and she stayed on.

Her crisis in personal discipline came in 1881-85. Just past her fortieth birthday, she was said by T.P. Crawford to be planning to return to the States to marry Crawford Toy, who had been fired in 1879 from the Southern Baptist Theological Seminary because of his views about biblical inspiration. At the time, only T.P. Crawford and Moon were on the field, all other colleagues, including Martha Crawford, having been felled by illnesses. Seeing T.P. Crawford's irrational behavior, Lottie may have felt the necessity of sticking by her work. A wedding never took place. Some felt that Lottie had studied Toy's views and rejected him and them. However, she ardently tried to prevent the resignation of a young missionary colleague whose theological views matched Toy's. To a young person who once asked if she had ever been in love, she said, "Yes, but God had first claim on my life and since the two conflicted, there could be no question about the result."[10]

Lottie Moon entered a period of restlessness related to the growing controversy between Crawford and the Foreign Mission Board and also related to the growing agitation about the role of women in Southern Baptist life. Through letters, she and Martha Crawford encouraged the developments toward formation of the Southern Baptist Woman's Missionary Union from 1883 until formal organization occurred in 1888. As if to flee from unpleasantness, she gave herself with greater consecration to direct evangelism.

Pioneering in Inland China

A new leaf in her ministry was started in 1885, when she moved to Pingtu, approximately 120 miles from Tengchow. This area had been explored by some younger colleagues and was thought promising. While Crawford was making a controversial tour through the United States to expound his divisive views, she made her move. With only reluctant consent of coworkers, she took her own brief survey trip in autumn 1885, traveling for four grueling days into the interior. In December she moved to Pingtu with a caravan of provisions and settled into rented rooms in the city. She was thought in her own times to be the first woman of any mission to establish an inland mission station by herself.[11]

Lottie's tactic in Pingtu was to live quietly and acceptably among the people until they befriended her and invited her into their homes. She taught the women and children in the accustomed personal way. To placate any Americans who might criticize her for abandoning her assigned job as a schoolteacher, she wrote that she was still a teacher, but her school was mobile, following her from house to house.

For the next seven years, Pingtu was her primary base of work, although she maintained her home in Tengchow and retreated there occasionally. Not only did she work in Pingtu City, but also in surrounding villages, particularly one called Shaling. In Pingtu, she was beyond protection of treaty and foreign intervention on which coastal missionaries relied. In fact, when the American government tried to intervene in behalf of Americans during a 1887 skirmish in Tengchow, she fled not to the waiting warship but to Pingtu. She seldom heard any language spoken but Chinese and seldom had contacts with Westerners. Only rarely did a male colleague journey out to Pingtu to check on her well-being.

Her practice in Shaling village was repeated in a circuit of tiny rural outposts around Pingtu. She simply lived among the people as teacher and friend. She sat on a stone or pile of straw at the threshing floor of the village and chatted with the women as they came to prepare their grains. Or she crawled upon the warm brick bed with women who invited her to their homes. She taught rudimentary reading, Bible truths, and hymns.

As the only resident Christian in Pingtu, she found herself unavoidably teaching men as well as women and children. She reported this habit very casually but carefully in letters to America, knowing that she was committing a serious breach of Baptist etiquette. Her reports sought to shame American pastors for abdicating their duties to a woman. She reported that, while packing for her overdue furlough in the United States, a delegation of men from Shaling tracked her down in Tengchow to beg her to return to the village.

It was in the throes of isolated self-sacrifice in Pingtu that she wrote a letter that was to change the course of Southern Baptist history. The Pingtu field was too responsive to abandon and she decided not to leave it until more missionaries came to relieve her. She wrote to encourage Southern Baptist women to organize and end the hand-to-mouth patterns of mission support. Writing on September 16, 1887, she suggested that the women should take an offering at Christmastime, thus to obtain funds with which to send more women missionaries to Pingtu.

This letter helped to swing the tide in favor of organizing the Woman's Missionary Union, Auxiliary to Southern Baptist Convention, on May 11, 1888. By October the women had put Miss Moon's idea into operation. They issued offering envelopes calling for a Christmas offering for Pingtu, China. Hoping for $2,000 to send two helpers to Miss Moon, they in fact cleared more than $3,000, and three women were soon on their way to China.

Still Lottie would not leave until the new recruits were trained. After the arrival of Fannie Knight, the first new missionary, sufficient converts had been won to form the first Baptist church of Pingtu region, in Shaling village, and the third church in North China. A church was constituted in September 1889, with Miss Knight as one of the members. Knight moved into Moon's place as the resident missionary of Pingtu.

In the meantime, with the younger male missionaries suffering stress of adjustment, Moon became virtually the pastor of one of the earlier churches near Tengchow. A new outpost had been claimed in the city of Hwangsien (today Huangxien), but the young missionaries were frightened and sick, and she had to tend them. Though very busy in her role as senior missionary of the area, she continued to journey to Pingtu to encourage the new believers. A storm of persecution against the new church was so fierce that missionaries were forced out of the area. Refusing to call on the power of the United States government to protect the converts (as other missionaries often did), she could do little for the persecuted believers but send them messages of comfort.

Busy in productive work with converts and new missionary recruits, she tried to keep herself above the worsening conflict between T.P. Crawford and the Foreign Mission Board. In 1889 Crawford was taken off the board's missionary list, although Martha Crawford was retained until she sent in her own very reluctant resignation. Crawford's group by this time had taken on the name Gospel Mission Movement. Churches in the United States were beginning to drop their involvement in the Southern Baptist Convention's cooperative mission work. Crawford urged his colleagues in North China to join him in work that was not under control of the SBC. Many of the younger missionaries, including Fannie Knight, did resign. They moved off to the western end of Shantung, taking much home and field support with them.

Lottie Moon tried to make peace. She announced her intention to keep up friendly cooperation with the renegades. She expressed her agreement with some of the Gospel Mission group's field philosophies. In fact, she refused to use any mission money to build a church building for Shaling, instead helping the local believers to build their own.[12] But Lottie Moon remained loyal to the Foreign Mission Board.

It was in this state of severe controversy that the exhausted woman finally took her furlough, after sixteen unrelieved years in China. She arrived in Virginia with chronic headaches. She made very few public appearances but did consent to attend the WMU convention of 1893. The Gospel Mission controversy dogged her heels. H.A. Tupper, embattled secretary of the Foreign Mission Board, sought her consultation. She strongly objected when she learned of the board's plans to return J.B. Hartwell to the field, as senior man in the place of his old nemesis, Crawford. She begged to be transferred to Japan because "life would not be living" in China. One of Tupper's last acts before resigning in sorrow from the Foreign Mission Board's top post was to beg Lottie to return to China and to accept Hartwell. "I doubt if the Board has had a missionary more esteemed than yourself . . . If I had but one request in this world to make of you, my sister, it would be that, if possible, you keep in harmony as far as possible with the Board that honors you more than you know."[13]

She returned to Tengchow with a different status and different approach to work. Her seniority and her heroism were undisputed. She made up her mind to cooperate with Hartwell, but she did not break her communications with Martha Crawford and the young missionaries who had cast in their lot with the Gospel Mission group.

Reaping the Harvest

The early seed-sowing years were now yielding a great harvest. New missionaries constantly arrived. In answer to an appeal she made during furlough, the first Southern Baptist missionary hospital was opened in 1900, in Hwangsien, when the first practicing missionary nurse and doctor arrived. Other hospitals soon opened in Laichow and Pingtu. The humble schools of early years now grew into higher-level institutions. A theological seminary was begun.

Her daily duties as a missionary fell into three categories, with little change from 1894 until her death in 1912. She resumed management of schools, up to six at one time, for both boys and girls. She invested much time in guiding new missionaries, who relied heavily upon her. And she gave herself increasingly in personal ministries to the Chinese people.

Strangely, she never returned to Pingtu. Pingtu quickly became the most productive mission field of Southern Baptist experience until recent times. A young Confucian scholar whom Lottie had taught, named Li Show Ting, became the leading native evangelist. Baptisms in the area exceeded five hundred a year, and it was said years later that Pastor Li had baptized more than ten thousand people. Although Pastor Li and others never forgot Lottie's role in inaugurating the work in Pingtu, she never again spoke of it. Male missionaries came in to administer baptisms and perform pastoral roles. Lottie allowed them to take full credit. About the time of Lottie's death, there were thirty-two churches in the area.

She continued making day trips to nearby villages for evangelistic teaching until she was at last welcomed into the Tengchow city homes of the upper class, who had so long spurned the missionaries. Her converts and friends from Pingtu and other regions came to her. On her compound, called The Little Cross Roads house, she had extensive guest quarters. The rooms were constantly full, especially of women who came to her for personal training. At times the classes were more or less formalized, as she trained women for evangelistic work. But gradually, after her furlough in 1903-4, the students were replaced by the poor and homeless who needed basic human care.

While other missionaries fled, she weathered the Russo-Japanese War of 1904-5 at her home, despite being bombed. Her intention was to give courage to the Chinese. With the deaths of the Crawfords, most of the missionaries who had affiliated with the Gospel Mission group were coming back into the Foreign Mission Board's fold by 1909. Lottie urged the board to welcome them home and led her coworkers to make room for them.

In 1909, news came that sister Edmonia had committed suicide. She began to dread the specter of furlough or retirement in a land that was no longer home. The more she felt cut off from the United States, the more emotional investment she made in the neediest people of Tengchow. As the Chinese Revolution developed in 1911, she tried to maintain nonpartisan ministries to the wounded and was discovered in Hwangsien running the Baptist hospital while other missionaries joined a flood of refugees.

Despite the increased support fostered by the WMU, the Foreign Mission Board slipped into debt. Now instead of the personal, chatty letters she was accustomed to receive from the board headquarters, she was receiving mass-produced form letters threatening retrenchment. Lottie responded on a very personal level to the near-hysteria from the Southern Baptist homeland regarding the foreign mission debt. She began to give proceeds from the small annuity left at the death of Edmonia to the board's debt-payment fund. In China, drought and famine began to add human misery to the revolution. She heard reports of suffering among the Pingtu Christians. So she took her annuity proceeds to meet the needs closest to hand. Amid the gloom of 1911, she took a decisive step by gathering the leading Christian women of Shantung province. In her parlor, they organized the Woman's Missionary Union of North China, for support of women evangelists.

Paying the Price

By 1912, Lottie Moon was occupying Tengchow almost alone. J.B. Hartwell and family were in Hwangsien, with the theological seminary, when death claimed him. Younger missionaries were concentrating on Hwangsien, Chefoo, Pingtu, Laichow, and Tsingtao (Qingdao), where Baptists had extensive institutions and growing congregations. So her colleagues did not realize until late fall that Miss Moon had sunk into physical and emotional collapse. Nurse Jessie Pettigrew was called from Hwangsien to Tengchow. She found what was described as a carbuncle eating into the base of Moon's skull. She was horrified at the loss of weight and the depression she readily observed. Pettigrew bundled Moon off to Hwangsien. There the missionaries realized that she had ceased to eat, in order to assure food for her Chinese sisters in her compound. She was obsessed with the thought that the children of missionaries were starving to death. Malnutrition was advanced, and the young missionaries wanted to conceal Moon's mental state from the Chinese.

She was sent on to Laichow, but the doctor there, one of her favorites, could not turn back the horror Miss Moon was privately facing. He sent her on to the next station, Pingtu. There in a splendid medical compound near her old house, the missionaries decided that she must return to America. Keeping Moon's distress as quiet as possible, Dr.T.O. Hearn took her to the nearest port, Tsingtao. It was arranged that nurse Cynthia Miller would accompany her.

On Christmas Eve 1912, as the ship was in the harbor of Kobe, Japan, Lottie Moon died. In the hours before death, her mind had cleared. She had sipped some grape juice and expressed appreciation for her care. After prayer and hymns, she dozed, then smiled, lifted her hands in the customary form of Chinese greeting, and exhaled quietly.

The ship's captain, who attributed her death to melancholia and senility, arranged for her cremation in Yokohama. Her ashes were mailed to the Foreign Mission Board in Richmond, Virginia. The family ultimately buried them in Crewe, Virginia, home of her one remaining sister-in-law.

Then began the more famous phase of Lottie Moon's immortality. Cynthia Miller faithfully retold the circumstances of Lottie Moon's death. Leaders of the WMU were appalled as they heard how Miss Moon had weighed only fifty pounds at death. They conducted memorial services for her and pledged themselves to lift the debt of the Foreign Mission Board in the Christmas offering of 1913 as a memorial to Miss Moon. In various ways the women pledged to retell her story until indifference to missions was conquered.

Lottie's death brought forth many commendations and many lamentations from her friends. The young missionaries assessed her career not in terms of evangelization, women's work, or schoolteaching – all of which seemed incidental to them. They saw Lottie as one performing social or human needs ministries for the Chinese and diplomacy for the missionaries. She was called a statesman, a queen, and "the best man among our missionaries." One missionary wrote, "The most remarkable thing was that she was in the middle of a lifelong feud between two colleagues and throughout she remained the friend of both families."[14]

The Christmas Offering for Foreign Missions has been collected every year since the first one in 1888. Lottie herself had suggested that it be enlarged to include not only Pingtu, not only her work, not only China, but also Japan and all the world.

In 1918, the retired first executive secretary of WMU, Annie Armstrong, broke her silence on WMU matters with a proposal to strengthen the offering. Miss Armstrong proposed that the Christmas offering henceforth bear the name Lottie Moon Christmas Offering. In the mid-1920s, WMU leaders made an extensive investigative effort, asking eyewitnesses to write recollections of Lottie Moon, and they commissioned Una Roberts Lawrence to write a full biography, which was published in 1927. Ever since, the Lottie Moon story has been retold and rewritten to typify the sacrifice required of missionary and supporter. A contemporary missionary of another denomination, watching the growing fame of Lottie, is reputed to have said, "If I had known the old girl was going to become so famous, I would have paid more attention to her." Some of her coworkers cautioned that Miss Moon would not have approved of the adulation. The story has attracted not only funds but personnel to the mission cause. Beginning with Dr. T.W. Ayers in 1900, dozens of missionaries have testified that they responded to God's call to missions after reading about Lottie Moon.

The Lottie Moon story was retold in a different way in China. The Christians in Shantung immediately began collecting money to erect a monument in her honor. This was a form of appreciation accorded to few others. For instance, Martha Foster Crawford (but not her husband) was memorialized on a plaque inside the Tengchow Baptist Church. William H. Sears, first pastor of the Pingtu Baptist Church, was honored by a tablet detailing his biography.

The monument to Lottie Moon was different. It was set inside the walled yard of Tengchow Baptist Church in 1915. It was a simple shaft bearing her name in Chinese characters and a brief explanation that she was an American missionary. The inscription spoke not of her evangelistic work, not of her schoolteaching, and certainly not of her powers of persuasion in the United States. It simply said, "How she loved us."

In 1985-86, Baptists from the United States were able to return for the first time in thirty-five years to Tengchow. The first ones, visiting unofficially, could see that the Tengchow church building was still standing behind its locked wall. The second delegation was able to walk inside. Part of the building was in use as a clinic, but most of the auditorium was standing in dusty neglect. The visitors saw the plaque honoring Martha Foster Crawford inside. Outside, they found the monument of Lottie Moon lying on its side under a pile of rubble, as if buried for protection. One word of the inscription had been obliterated: "American." The word "missionary" and the words about her love for the Chinese remained.[15]

Notes

1. Records of the Lottie Moon Christmas Offering for Foreign Missions are maintained by Woman's Missionary Union, Auxiliary to Southern Baptist Convention, Birmingham, Alabama. The history of the offering and reports through 1985 are published in Catherine B. Allen, *A Century to Celebrate: History of Woman's Missionary Union* (Birmingham: Woman's Missionary Union, 1987). The 1992 offering totalled $80,980,881.

2. Unless otherwise noted, sources for this article may be found in Catherine B. Allen, *The New Lottie Moon Story* (Nashville: Broadman Press, 1980). A condensed version in Spanish was published in 1992 by the Woman's Missionary Union.

3. *Religious Herald,* newspaper of Virginia Baptists, March 23 and April 13, 1871.

4. See Irwin T. Hyatt, Jr., *Our Ordered Lives Confess* (Cambridge: Harvard Univ. Press, 1976). This book contains good biographies of Lottie Moon and two of her leading contemporaries in Shantung Province: Tarleton Perry Crawford and Calvin Wilson Mateer.

5. "Shantung" Province is today usually transliterated as "Shandong." "Chefoo" is known in modern Chinese nomenclature as "Yantai." "Tengchow" is now known as "Penglai."

6. Timothy George, *Faithful Witness: The Life and Mission of William Carey* (Birmingham, Ala.: New Hope: 1991), p. 114.

7. Hyatt, *Our Ordered Lives Confess.*

8. *Religious Herald,* August 28, 1873.

9. From St. Bernard, quoted in a letter to H.A. Tupper, November 11, 1878, Lottie Moon Letter File, Foreign Mission Board.

10. Quoted by Una Roberts Lawrence, *Lottie Moon* (Nashville: Sunday School Board of the Southern Baptist Convention, 1927).

11. Recent visits to Pingtu located the house and found it to be still in active use. Open meetings of the Pingtu city church were resumed in 1989.

12. The first Westerners to seek out the Shaling Christians in the post-Mao era visited the village in 1987. The grandson of the first convert, Dan Ho Bang, was visited. The church building, which had been a simple native-style shelter, had fallen down, but the benches had been preserved in local homes. Local Christians were maintaining worship in their homes.

13. H.A. Tupper to Lottie Moon, April(?) 28, 1893, Tupper's Copy Book, Foreign Mission Board Archives.

14. Notes of W.W. Adams, Woman's Missionary Union Archives.

15. By 1989, more than seven hundred Southern Baptist tourists had visited Penglai (as Tengchow was then called) and Pingtu in tours sponsored by the WMU. Because of interest shown by Americans, local authorities repaired the Penglai/Tengchow church building and reset the Lottie Moon monument. Christians from the community began to return to the church building, and the congregation was re-formed with a woman as pastor by early 1989. In Pingtu, the church building, which had been used as a meeting hall, was returned for use by the Christians. The hospital building, on the compound where Lottie was cared for at the end, was being reclaimed from overgrowth and was partially restored. Through a joint venture between U.S. Christians and the local authorities, a medical training program was begun in 1992. One of the researchers in the first WMU-sponsored tour returned to China in 1992 as a coworker to the Chinese Christians.

Bibliographic Notes

Lottie Moon wrote many letters, many of which were published in the *Foreign Mission Journal* of the Southern Baptist Foreign Mission Board. She was also often published in the Baptist newspapers of Virginia, Kentucky, Georgia, and occasionally other states. Despite real skill in written expressions, she wrote no books or pamphlets. A request from the WMU for a "bright little tract" drove her to adamant refusal. Her only formal article, published in *Woman's Work in China,* November 1881, concerned the rights and roles of unmarried women missionaries.

An amazing number of letters were saved by her correspondents – family, women's missionary circles, and others. These have been collected into two main repositories: the Jenkins Library and Archives of the Southern Baptist Foreign Mission Board, Richmond, Virginia, and another at the Hunt Library and Archives of Woman's Missionary Union, Auxiliary to Southern Baptist Convention, Birmingham, Alabama. Both of these archival collections contain much collateral data about Moon. The WMU collections focus on Christmas offering promotion, pamphlets, and biographical studies. Most of these retell the 1927 biography, *Lottie Moon,* by Una Roberts Lawrence. Also they draw on the eyewitness tracts produced by those who knew her: Mrs. J.M. Gaston, Dr.T.W. Ayers, Mrs. C.W. Pruitt, Mrs. W.W. Adams, and Dr.W.W. Adams. Another useful source is the pamphlet *Heavenly Book Visitor* by Eliza Broadus, a contemporary who was the daughter of the one who baptized Lottie. The complete research files for the *The New Lottie Moon Story* by Catherine B. Allen are held by the WMU Archives. The Foreign Mission Board archives are rich in extensive letter files from all North China missionaries during the Moon era. There are displays concerning Moon.

The original manuscript for *Lottie Moon* (1927) and some interview notes by Una Roberts Lawrence are at the Southern Baptist Theological Seminary Library, Louisville, Kentucky. The library also has a Lottie Moon historical room containing Moon's desk and a portrait.

Helpful references to Moon, her family, and her coworkers are found at the Historical Foundation of the Presbyterian and Reformed Churches, Montreat, North Carolina; at the Presbyterian Historical Society, Philadelphia, Pennsylvania; and at the Disciples of Christ Historical Society, Nashville, Tennessee.

Karl Ludvig Reichelt
1877–1952

Christian Pilgrim of Tao Fong Shan

Notto R. Thelle

One of the famous pictures of Karl Ludvig Reichelt (1877-1952) shows him on his beloved mountain, Tao Fong Shan, outside Hong Kong, ready to begin one of his numerous travels: a small, rather corpulent man in dark suit, flat felt hat, and with a pilgrim's walking stick in his hand. Several other walking sticks, brought back from his travels, were placed around the desk in his office. Through many decades of missionary work Reichelt traveled to all the famous Buddhist temples and pilgrim centers, not only in central China, but even to the borders of Tibet and Mongolia, to Taiwan and Japan, to Malaya, Burma, Thailand, Indochina, and Ceylon (Sri Lanka). Reichelt was a Christian pilgrim. Let us keep in mind the image of the missionary pilgrim in order to hold together some of the central concerns in his life as a missionary.

Reichelt's life was a pilgrimage with many dimensions. It was a pilgrimage into Buddhism. He was observing, seeking, and listening in order to discover the Buddhist insight into the Way, the Logos, the Tao. At the same time it was a lifelong inner pilgrimage, a continuous effort to penetrate to the sources of his own Christian faith. He was challenged by his unprotected encounter with Buddhist brothers, and guided by the vision of the Christ he had seen partially in the pietistic Christianity of his childhood and discovered more fully as the cosmic Christ, working in the lives of all people. Finally, it was a pilgrimage into the lives of his Buddhist friends and brothers. He entered their lives with the consciousness of being on holy ground, wanting to share with them the Way that was his life, the Tao who had become human in Christ and was the undiscovered guide of their lives.

Reichelt's missionary work is not conceivable without his pilgrim spirit. And his pilgrimage loses its meaning if it is not seen as a part of his missionary concern.

The Life of K.L. Reichelt

Reichelt was born on September 1, 1877, in the parish of Barbu, near Arendal, a small city on the south coast of Norway. The home was characterized by "godliness with contentment." His father died when he was a baby, but his mother was a remarkable personality who opened the home for visiting preachers and house meetings. Thus Reichelt grew up in an atmosphere of warm, somewhat strict, revivalist Pietism. Later, when he had discovered the limitations of his childhood Pietism, he recalled the atmosphere of the numerous meetings in home and "prayer houses":

> In these meetings I also met God, but mostly the God of Sinai. The atmosphere was serious and gloomy, or one-sidedly emotional. Everything was accompanied by an inexpressible oppressive feeling. I realized that this was not *the totality of God.* Mighty aspects of the idea of God were not revealed under the roof of the prayer house.[1]

His teachers, however, introduced him to other dimensions of Christian faith, and also helped him to clarify his missionary calling. In addition to such influences, Reichelt often referred to the quiet beauty and grandeur of the surrounding mountains, which gave him an overwhelming experience of divine presence. In this way his childhood Christianity was "consecrated and gradually elevated to a higher level." In spite of his somewhat negative evaluation of the pietistic tradition, there is no doubt that throughout his life it remained one of the vital elements of his faith.

Entering the Teachers' Training College in Notodden in 1895, he encountered a more open, broad-minded Christianity, which combined a sound faith with a deep appreciation of humanity, nature, national traditions, and the culture of the people. Such attitudes certainly helped him later when he had to meet other cultures and learn to appreciate the national and religious traditions of another people.

In 1897 he entered the Missionary Training College of the Norwegian Missionary Society in Stavanger. He was ordained in 1903 and sent to China the same year. After language studies he was sent to Ninghsiang[2] in Hunan where he worked until 1911, when he returned to Norway. In this period he made his first stumbling contact with the Buddhist world during an unforgettable visit to the famous Weishan monastery in 1905.

> I got a glimpse of a peculiar and exclusive world, permeated with deep religious mysticism, a world full of superstition and despair, but also wondrously rich in points of contact and sacred religious material. There arose in my soul an inexpressible urge to be enabled to reach just these circles with the eternal gospel of life.[3]

Reichelt realized, however, that his effort to tell the monks about Christ was in vain. They belonged to a world he did not know, and true communication was impossible. According to Reichelt this challenge determined his future course. He decided to devote his life to a "special work" among the Buddhists, and to prepare himself "through studies and observations, through friendly contact with Buddhist monks and learned Buddhist lay people." The years between 1905 and 1922, when he finally started his "special work," can be seen as a period of preparation.

When he returned to Norway in 1911 he had already a considerable knowledge about Chinese religions. His lectures during his furlough were published in 1913 under the title *Kinas Religioner* (The Religions of China), later translated as *Religion in Chinese Garment.*

During the second period in China (1911-20) he was assigned to the newly established Lutheran Theological Seminary in Shekow, where he taught the New Testament and wrote several commentaries in Chinese. But he was also able to deepen his study of Chinese Buddhism and to make valuable contacts. In the vacations he traveled to monasteries and temples in several provinces, and engaged in the study of the extensive Buddhist and Taoist literature he had collected. The quality of his studies can be seen in the book he published in 1922, *Fra Østens Religiøse Liv* (Religious Life in the East), translated as *Truth and Tradition in Chinese Buddhism.* The book was based on lectures at Scandinavian universities during his furlough in 1920-22. In spite of inaccuracies and a rather one-sided "Christian interpretation" of Buddhism, it demonstrated Reichelt's firsthand knowledge of Buddhist piety and thought.

In the summer of 1919 he also "providentially" met the Buddhist monk Kwantu, a deep religious spirit, with whom he made the outlines for the long-cherished "special work" for Buddhist monks. The plans were accepted by the Norwegian mission board, which released Reichelt for the work. The mission promised to pay his salary and to serve as the home base for the work, and additional support was supposed to come from interested groups and individuals in the Scandinavian countries.

Returning in 1922, this time to Nanking, Reichelt began to realize his dream, which had matured for more than fifteen years: a Christian community, organized as a sort of monastery, and serving as a "Brother Home" for religious seekers, notably for wandering Buddhist monks. The monks usually stayed for a couple of days, but could extend their stay if they wanted to continue the study of Christianity. Every year an average of one thousand monks visited the Brother Home in Nanking. Here they could encounter Christianity in an atmosphere adapted to their own traditions, and talk about religious problems with Christians who were familiar with their religion and moreover, regarded them as spiritual brothers, and "friends in the Way," or "friends in Tao." The place became famous not only in religious circles in China, but was also favorably reported in Japan by no less a person than D.T. Suzuki.[4]

Because of practical difficulties with finance and support in Scandinavia, and because of theological controversies, Reichelt's work was separated from the Norwegian Missionary Society and established as an independent missionary society in 1926, under the name Christian Mission to Buddhists.

Meanwhile the work in Nanking continued until 1927 when the so-called Nanking incident put an end to it. Looking for a more stable location for the work, Reichelt and his colleagues finally decided on a beautiful mountain in the New Territories of Hong Kong, and called it Tao Fong Shan, "The Mountain of the Logos [Tao] Spirit." Beginning in 1931 a beautiful institute was built in traditional Chinese Buddhist architecture: an octagonal church in the center surrounded by guest hall, pilgrims' hall, school, library, and other houses. The years before the Japanese occupation of Hong Kong in 1941 became the classical decade in Reichelt's life, the time when the "dream was realized."[5] Tao Fong Shan became known all over China and attracted monks from all provinces. At one time monks from more than fifteen different provinces were present. Reichelt himself claimed that Tao Fong Shan had become a center of religion in South China.[6] Apart from the activities at Tao Fong Shan, Reichelt continued his travels, and also established branch institutes in Nanking, Hangchow, Shanghai, Tali, and Omei, where former Buddhists, trained at Tao Fong Shan, tried to propagate his ideas.

The war with Japan and the occupation of Hong Kong in 1941 effectively put an end to the contact with Buddhist communities. Reichelt had health problems but managed to complete the three volumes, *Fromhetstyper og Helligdommer i Østasia* (Men of Religion and Sanctuaries in the Far East), the outcome of his lifelong pilgrimage into the Buddhist world. He returned to Norway after the war and retired. However, in 1951 he came back to Tao Fong Shan, where he died on March 13, 1952.

Reichelt married Anna Gerhardsen in 1905. Because of the political instability in the Far East and the special character of the work, she stayed for long periods in Norway, separated from her husband. It was not until after 1934 that she could be permanently with her husband and maintain a normal family life, either in Hong Kong or in Norway. When he returned to complete his "last mission" and died in Hong Kong in 1952, his wife remained in Norway. Thus it certainly involved great sacrifice on both sides to enable Reichelt to realize his vision. Their son, Gerhard Reichelt, also served as missionary for several periods.

With the death of Karl Ludvig Reichelt an epoch in the Christian Mission to Buddhists was over. The war and the Chinese revolution had created major changes in the political and religious situation. Reichelt's work was continued in various forms, adapted to new circumstances. However, it did not and could not function as in the golden days before the war.

The Challenge from Buddhism

The simple outline of K.L. Reichelt's life has indicated some of the aspects of his work that made him a unique missionary. Was he merely a shooting star that flashed over the firmament of Christian missions and then vanished without leaving any trace? A closer examination is necessary in order to see the lasting value of his work and vision.

Christian Mission to Buddhists

In his encounter with the Buddhist world, Reichelt discovered the great truth that God had been in China before the missionaries, preparing the way for the Gospel of Christ through glimpses of truth and points of contact. This was certainly unfamiliar to Norwegian missionary communities, but the ideas were not conceived by Reichelt himself.

Similar ideas were actually advocated in various forms in large sections of Protestant circles of his time. In some cases it was an expression of a characteristic nineteenth-century optimistic belief in spiritual progress combined with an emphasis on Christianity as the highest peak of religious development. Such a spirit permeated the World's Parliament of Religions in Chicago in 1893, which the leading Christian participants regarded as an expression of the fact that "the world moves, and on the whole moves Christward."[7] Similar trends were dominant in the great missionary conferences in Edinburgh in 1910 and Jerusalem in 1928. In India, China, and Japan there were numerous exponents of different sorts of fulfillment theologies. A typical representative from the missionary community in China was Timothy Richard, who advocated that Mahayana faith was "an Asiatic form" of the Christian Gospel.[8] Contemporary scholarship also tended to emphasize the influence of Eastern Christianity on Mahayana Buddhism.[9]

Reichelt's uniqueness thus did not consist in his ideas about Buddhist-Christian relations, which he shared with many others, but in his ability to transform the academic abstractions about missionary attitudes into a concrete "special work" among Buddhist devotees. The ideas about historical and ideological relationships between the two religions furnished him with a strategy for Buddhist mission, which he moreover managed to realize in a way that drew positive attention even from the Buddhist world. That was a remarkable contribution.

Reichelt's mission, which had the somewhat offensive name Christian Mission to Buddhists, was in China called the East Asia Christian Tao Yu Hui (Association of Friends in the Way). It was a thoroughly Christian community, but based upon a generous vision of God's work among all people who are seeking the truth. The Buddhists were not accustomed to such generosity from Christians and responded positively:

> The main reason for this success is the fact that all people who come there are met with as Tao-yu . . . that is, as friends in religion . . . The Christians acknowledge the fact that in spite of all differences there exists a strong and precious common platform, on which all enlightened and sincere religious people can meet and communicate.[10]

We shall see in some detail how Reichelt tried to overcome the religious and cultural barriers that separated Buddhists and Christians. The community life of the Brother Home was adapted to the traditions of Buddhist monasteries, following a rhythm of worship, study, and work. The meals were vegetarian. The Buddhist students and novices, often introduced by their Buddhist masters, lived in close fellowship with the Christian missionaries.

Reichelt regarded worship as the heartbeat of the community. The worship generally followed Lutheran traditions, but he also used what he regarded as the sacred material in Buddhism, prepared by God. The altar and the interior showed Buddhist influence. Incense was used until criticism forced him to abandon the practice. Beside the altar in the chapel there was, among biblical quotations, an inscription borrowed from the Pure Land tradition, expressing how the Great Vow guides mercifully across to the Other Shore. The Great Vow is the vow of Amida Buddha, but as Reichelt regarded the idea about Amida's grace as a Christian influence, he used Pure Land Buddhism as an important guide toward Christ. For him nothing but the cross was the real Great Vow, which encompassed the longings of Buddhist faith.

The liturgy was full of Buddhist expressions. It included a prayer taken almost directly from a Buddhist liturgy expressing the vow to reach the Pure Land (Heaven), as well as a threefold dedication to the Trinity, very similar to Buddhist patterns: "I take refuge in . . . " One example of Reichelt's boldness is found in a hymn to Christ included in the book of liturgy. Christ is there worshiped as "the Great Tao without beginning and end" (the eternal Word of God), and "the original face of all sentient beings" (the idea of *imago Dei*). He is the enlightened, the *"tathagata* [Buddha] of the West who came to the world" and "realized the Pure Land on earth." Christ is "constantly turning the great wheel of the Dharma" and is "teaching all according to their capacities." He is "saving all the people straying in the six paths of existence" and is "universally present in the one billion worlds" (the universe). Those familiar with Buddhism will immediately recognize the Buddhist background of the expressions. However, in the whole context of Christian worship the expressions changed character and became means of Christian worship. Christ's sacrificial death and atonement were central elements. There was never any doubt about the uniqueness of Christ, the One in whom the "Great Original Tao" had become man, "the great shepherd who draws people who love the Tao in all religions and gathers them to one flock."[11]

It is difficult to know what impact the worship made on the thousands of monks who came to Reichelt's institutes in Nanking and Hong Kong and other places. An indication is given in D.T. Suzuki's notes about the work where he referred to the worship with its "refined, religious atmosphere indigenous to the religious soul of China."[12] Anyway it was an example of a bold and unique effort to create an indigenous liturgy.

Also in Reichelt's teaching, preaching, and dialogues we see a similar combination of Christ-centered faith and radical openness to other faiths. His piety seemed to pave the way for what we now might call a "sharing of spirituality." One of his colleagues who traveled with him has described his exceptional ability to establish contact with all sorts of people. Again and again he was invited to preach in temples and religious associations. In many cases some of the monks in a temple had already visited the Brother Home, or the rumor about the Christian "Master" had reached the temple in advance. He was met as a brother and shared with deep conviction his Christian Way as a friend in the Way.[13]

Buddhist Studies

We have already referred to Reichelt's extensive studies of Buddhism, several of which have been translated into English and German. We will here limit ourselves to a few remarks.

There is no doubt about Reichelt's deep knowledge of Chinese Buddhism. However, modern scholarship may tend to emphasize the limitations of his studies due to numerous inaccuracies in his writings. His missionary concern never seemed to weaken his sympathy toward Buddhism, but sometimes it distorted the perspective. He tended to read too many Christian ideas into Buddhist piety. It is characteristic that he often translated Buddha with "God" and Amida with "the All-Father."[14] Whenever it seemed possible, he was likely to interpret similarities in doctrine or piety as a Christian influence. His evaluation of different types of Buddhism was characterized by a somewhat arbitrary judgment: he regarded Pure Land Buddhism as the highest peak of Buddhism because it seemed closest to Christianity and (according to Reichelt) had its deepest roots in Christianity.[15] His search for points of contact also naturally inclined him to emphasize the positive side of Buddhism. The negative aspects were usually described in dramatic generalizations about gloom, despair, darkness, and the like.[16] Finally, he never seemed to become really challenged by Buddhist philosophy. In his books there is no serious discussion of central philosophies such as the systems of Nagarjuna or Vasubandhu. Their "abstract ideas" seemed less important than their efforts to link Buddhist philosophy to personal faith in "the Great All-Father, Amitabha."[17]

On the other hand, Reichelt's missionary concern and his intuitive and sympathetic approach enabled him to convey some of the religious life behind the outward forms. His studies were often based on firsthand observations and offered new and fresh insights. Actually, his description of Buddhist piety has promoted a sympathetic understanding of Buddhism in Scandinavia, which a more objective analysis hardly could do. The second volume of his last work about holy men and sanctuaries in the Far East is totally devoted to a description of the spiritual pilgrimage of one Buddhist monk, and is a unique document.

Buddhist Influence?

Reichelt's effort to adapt his method to Buddhist traditions gained him many critics. He was accused of syncretism, and Tao Fong Shan was once described as a place where "one came in order to study Christianity, and was offered Buddhism instead."[18] This was certainly a narrow-minded or malicious interpretation.

On the other hand, it would be unnatural if several decades of intimate contact with Buddhist communities did not influence his understandings of Christianity. He was convinced that every generation, every culture, civilization, and religion that came in touch with the doctrine of Christ, would reveal "new colors and rays in the brilliant light emanating from God." So Buddhism would naturally add new insights to Christian piety.[19]

A recent study about Reichelt purported to demonstrate that his basic thinking was permeated with Buddhism, and that notably the philosophy of *sunyata* (emptiness) was a key to understanding Reichelt.[20] I think the conclusion is misleading, but the question about Buddhist influence is still valid. Numerous expressions and ideas about God, Christ, salvation, enlightenment, meditation, inner life, and so forth may indicate Buddhist influence. The problem is that his expressions are not only close to Buddhist terminology but are also familiar in Christianity, including Pietism and liberal theology, mystical traditions, and notably the Gospel of St. John. The problem needs further research. But ultimately it is a question of Reichelt's basic theological standpoint.

Reichelt's Theology: Christ-Centered and Christ-Open

As a missionary pilgrim Reichelt was engaged in a continuous struggle for theological clarification. What we have said about Buddhist influence would be misleading if we did not see how his theological world was centered in one point: the cosmic Christ.

The Johannine Approach

Reichelt often preferred to talk about his work as the "Johannine approach." His central creed was the Prologue of John with its proclamation about the Logos, the eternal truth incarnated in Christ. He found further support of his approach in the idea about *logos spermatikos,* characteristically developed by Justin Martyr and others. That is, the eternal Logos is spread in non-Christian religions and philosophies as grains of seed; whatever is true originates from the eternal Logos, Christ.

This was further deepened in the encounter with Chinese spirituality where the concept of Tao ingeniously expressed the implications of the Logos-idea. Tao means Way, that is, the spiritual

Way of humankind, the eternal truth. For a Buddhist, Tao was synonymous with the Dharma, the Buddhist law of life. With his profound faith in Christ as the incarnation of the eternal Logos or Tao, Reichelt was convinced that, ultimately, Christ would not be an offense or a stranger to the truth-seeking spirits of the East. He was the center they had been seeking all the time, the One who had been drawing them toward truth. It is characteristic that he wrote about one of those who had met Christ "from within," stating that his encounter with Christ was an "encounter with a friend. A deep joy of recognition filled his soul."[21] The true seekers would *re*-cognize Christ as the Tao they had been searching for all the time.

Christianity and Religion

The vision of Christ as the hidden center of Reichelt's missionary pilgrimage had implications for his view about the relation between Christianity and other faiths. This was developed in one of his great speeches, with the title "Christ – the Center of Religion." He described how the religions of humankind were like silver ore in the mountain. It might be impure and mixed with slag and stone. But further search would uncover veins of silver gradually leading down to the pure silver ore, the center and *telos* of religion, Christ. From this perspective it was difficult to express the essential difference between the general and the special revelation. Silver is silver even when it is mixed and impure, and is essentially identical with the pure silver in the center.[22]

As Reichelt's language was symbolic and lacked precision, he was inevitably attacked, especially in Norway where the front against liberal theology was strengthened in the 1920s. However, Reichelt's theology was rather conservative. He was pre-Barthian, but not liberal. It simply did not occur to him that his view on other religions could reduce the uniqueness of Christ. His whole thinking was so Christ-centered that the Barthian wave did not impress him. The antiliberal reaction was irrelevant for his thinking.

Under guidance from friends and colleagues he agreed to change his expressions and to emphasize the essential difference between general revelation and the revelation in Christ. This was certainly not an intellectual sacrifice, for he was himself totally aware of the limitations of other religions and was untiring in his emphasis of the uniqueness of Christ. However, it meant that he had to accept a theological model that was not his own and respond to questions that did not arise in his theological world. He was not interested in the lines of demarcation between Christianity and other faiths, but was concerned about the center, where Christ, the eternal Logos, was drawing all people to himself. The Barthian reaction and the numerous attacks from orthodox circles did not do justice to his Christ-centered theology. Symbolically expressed, Reichelt was seeking the center of the circle and was not so much concerned about drawing the periphery of the circle. He was Christ-centered and therefore Christ-open. He was both pre-Barthian and post-Barthian.

Reichelt is rightly celebrated as one of the greatest Norwegian missionaries, one of the few whose vision and work appealed far beyond the narrow borders of Norwegian missionary circles. Hendrik Kraemer, one of the most outspoken critics of Reichelt's theological ideas about Buddhism and Christianity, still maintained a deep admiration for the "great missionary" Reichelt, and recognized his plea for an understanding of the religious situation of Buddhism having to do with God.[23]

On the other hand, in missionary circles in his home country he was often denounced, and his name still evokes suspicion and anxiety about theological compromise and syncretism. One of the most influential Norwegian Christians in this century, Ole Hallesby, even said that Reichelt was preaching "an amputated gospel." It was difficult for these to see how a Christ-centered evangelical faith could be combined with a bold recognition of the truths of other religions.

The Norwegian critics had entrenched themselves in the fight against liberal theology and could not comprehend that even though Reichelt's theology did not fit into orthodox Lutheran Pietism, neither was he a liberal. Reichelt was rather *catholic* in the original sense of the word: belonging to the *universal* church. He was rooted in Pietism, influenced and challenged by theological currents and Buddhist ideas, but found his deepest inspiration in the old sources of the church: the thinkers of the early church, the New Testament, and, more than anything else, the Gospel of St. John.

Notes

1. Quoted from Filip Riisager, *Forventning og Opfyldelse* (Expectation and Fulfillment), pp. 12-13. See the bibliography for further bibliographical material.
2. We regret that in the present article we are not able to use the modern transcription of Chinese names and words.
3. The incident is reported several times in Reichelt's writings. Quoted from *Den Kristne Misjon blant Kinas Buddhister* (Oslo: Buddistmisjones Forlag, 1926), pp. 3-4.
4. In *The Eastern Buddhist* 4, no. 2 (1927): 195-97.
5. The title of the publication in connection with the 25th anniversary was *Drømmen som ølev Virkelighed* (The Dream That Was Realized), (Copenhagen: Gads Forlag, 1947).
6. See the monthly of the mission, *Den Kristne Buddhistmission* 12, no. 5 (May 1937): 73.
7. John Henry Barrows, *The World's Parliament of Religions* (Chicago: The Parliament Publishing Company, 1893), p. 1575.
8. Timothy Richard, trans., *The Awakening of Faith in the Mahayana Doctrine* (Shanghai: Christian Literature Society, 1907), p. iv.
9. See, e.g., P. Y. Sacki, *The Nestorian Monument in China* (London: Society for Promoting Christian Knowledge, 1928).
10. *The Eastern Buddhist*, 4 no. 2 (1927): 196.
11. There is no indication whether this was written by Reichelt himself or by his Chinese co-workers. The liturgy and the hymns were probably the result of close cooperation. We have used the Chinese text, and have not been able to compare it with translations. See also articles in *The Chinese Recorder*, mentioned in the bibliography.
12. *The Eastern Buddhist* 4, no. 2 (1927): 195-97.
13. Stig Hannerz, in Notto Normann Thelle, *Karl Ludvig Reichelt: En Kristen Banebryter i Øst-Asia*, pp. 140-54.
14. See, e.g., Reichelt, *Truth and Tradition in Chinese Buddhism*, pp. 112, 131, 136-40, 145-47, etc.
15. Ibid., pp. 6, 134, 145-46, 155-57, 163, etc.
16. Ibid., 134, 172, etc.
17. Ibid., p. 31.
18. N. N. Thelle, *Fra Begynnelsen til Nu*, p. 95.
19. Reichelt, *Fra Kristuslivets Helligdom*, pp. 95-105.
20. H. Eilert, *Boundlessness*.
21. Reichelt, *Kristus: Religionens Centrum* (Oslo/Copenhagen: Buddhistmisjones Forlag/ O. Lohse, 1927), pp. 26-27.
22. Ibid., pp. 7-8. Cf. also Reichelt's favorite expression, "the inner wellspring of religion."
23. H. Kraemer, *Religion and the Christian Faith* (London: Lutterworth Press, 1956), p. 225.

Selected Bibliography

Works by Karl Ludvig Reichelt

Books in Chinese on New Testament Scriptures include an introduction to the New Testament and commentaries on John, Galatians, Mark, James, and other books.

1913 *Kinas Religioner* (The Religions of China). Stavanger: Misjonsselskapet. German translation: *Der chinesische Buddhismus*. Basel Missionsbuchhandlung, 1926. English translation: *Religion in Chinese Garment*. London: Lutterworth Press, 1951.

1922 *Fra Østens Religiøse Liv*. Copenhagen: Gads Forlag. English translation: *Truth and Tradition in Chinese Buddhism*. Shanghai: Commercial Press, 1927.

Pamphlets and Articles

Reichelt wrote numerous articles in the monthly publication of his mission (*Den Kristne Buddhistmission*), *The Tao Fong Shan Magazine*, etc., and also published many pamphlets, which cannot be recorded here.

Some articles in *The Chinese Recorder* have special reference to material in this chapter on Reichelt's legacy: "Special Work Among Chinese Buddhists" 51 (1920): 491-97; "Indigenous Religious Phrases That May Be Used to Interpret the Christian Message" 58 (1927): 123-26; "Extracts from the Buddhist Ritual" 59 (1928): 160-70; "The Divine Seed in the Ethical System of Chinese Buddhism" 60 (1929): 287-94; etc.

Bibliographies

Myklebust, O.G. "Selected Bibliography." Appendix to Sverre Holth, *Karl Ludvig Reichelt and Tao Fong Shan* (see below).

Sommerfeldt, W.P. *Karl Ludvig Reichelt's Forfatterskap* (The Works of Karl Ludvig Reichelt). Oslo: Den Kristne Buddhistmisjon, 1947.

Fra Kristuslivets Helligdom (From the Sanctuary of Christlife). Copenhagen: Gads Forlag, 1931.

Fromhetstyper og Helligdommer i Øst-Asia (Men of Religion and Sanctuaries in the Far East). 3 vols. Oslo: Dreyers Forlag, 1947. English translation of vol. 1: *Meditation and Piety in the Far East* (London: Lutterworth Press, 1953), and vol. 2: *The Transformed Abbott* (London: Lutterworth Press, 1954).

Works about Karl Ludvig Reichelt

Eilert, Håkan. *Boundlessness: Studies in Karl Ludvig Reichelt's Missionary Thinking with Special Regard to the Buddhist-Christian Encounter.* Århus: Forlaget Aros, 1974.

Holth, Sverre. *Karl Ludvig Reichelt and Tao Fong Shan.* Hong Kong: Tao Fong Shan Christian Institute, n.d. Reprint of article in the *International Review of Missions,* October 1952.

Prenter, Regin. "Theologen Karl Ludvig Reichelt" (Karl Ludvig Reichelt, the Theologian). *Norsk Tidsskrift for Misjon* 32, no. 1 (1978).

Riisager, Filip. *Forventning og Opfyldelse* (Expectation and Fulfillment). Århus: Forlaget Aros, 1973.

Thelle, Notto Normann. *Fra Begynnelsen til Nu* (From the Beginning Until Now). Oslo: Den Kristne Buddhistmisjons Forlag, 1939.

_____. *Karl Ludvig Reichelt: En Kristen Banebryter i Øst-Asia* (Karl Ludvig Reichelt: A Christian Pioneer in East Asia). Oslo: Den Nordiske Kristne Buddhismisjon, 1954.

T.C. Chao

1888–1979

Scholar, Teacher, Gentle Mystic

Winfried Glüer

According to the official *pinyin* romanization recently adopted in China, Chao's name is to be spelled Zhao Zechen. However, as Chao himself used the older form for his name, it is given here in the familiar spelling. Had he lived longer he would, no doubt, have accepted the new romanization. He was never a traditionalist, but always remained flexible in responding to new developments, and this flexibility is an outstanding mark of his character. It must not be mistaken for a lack of stability. In looking at the legacy of T.C. Chao it is obvious that there is consistency amid the apparent changes of position. Although Chao's thinking, indeed, underwent far-reaching changes, his basic concern remained the same.

The various features of Chao's personality were well described when he received an honorary doctorate at Princeton University in 1947 together with thirty-five other persons (among them General Dwight Eisenhower and Cardinal Tisserant): "foremost interpreter of Christian faith to Oriental minds, scholar, inspiring teacher, distinguished poet, gentle mystic." To emphasize that Chao was a prolific writer would seem redundant, since it is implied in the eulogy. Yet, along with the diversity of his writing, it is important to note its truly Chinese character. Chao was deeply influenced by Chinese thought, and it was for the sake of China and its revolution that he struggled for most of his life to make the Christian church in China a *Chinese* church, and this not in a merely intellectual way but in the real life of the church in Chinese society.

Chao was known in China before liberation as one of the leading theologians of the Chinese church. As such he is still highly honored today by the church in the New China, even though he was extremely critical of the institutional church and, at the end of his life, moved away from Christianity itself, disclaiming the theological validity of all his former writings. Yet there is little doubt about his contributions to theology in a Chinese context, even if they leave many questions open. In his struggle for contextualization of the Gospel, both in Chinese traditional culture and in contemporary society, Chao clearly pointed to major problems the Chinese church will yet have to discuss in coming years.

Chao was well known in ecumenical circles beyond China. His theological reflection and experience are of importance even today in Asian, African, and Latin American countries where

225

similar questions are being raised in the search for an ecumenical theology, with which he dealt in his own quest for true practice of the Christian faith in a revolutionary setting.

A Biographical Sketch

Chao was born on February 14, 1888, in Deqing in the province of Jejiang. He died in Beijing on November 21, 1979. As he participated in the work of the Chinese National Christian Council from its very beginning in 1922, and had published a great number of theological articles and some monographs, he soon became widely known throughout China. He participated in the Jerusalem meeting of the International Missionary Council (IMC) in 1928 and made a major contribution to the Tambaram, Madras, meeting of the IMC in 1938. At the first Assembly of the World Council of Churches (WCC) at Amsterdam in 1948, he was elected as one of the six presidents of the WCC, representing the East Asian churches. Shortly afterward, in April 1951, at the height of the Korean conflict, Chao resigned from this office in a dramatic move, because of the "Statement on the Korean Situation and World Order," which the Central Committee of the WCC had issued at its meeting in Toronto the preceding year. In his letter to Dr. Visser 't Hooft he stated clearly that his resignation was of his own free will: "I have complete freedom to affirm my faith in, and my loyalty to Jesus Christ, my Lord and Savior." In 1956 Chao came under attack in China for his collaboration with the imperialism of the American mission boards. He lost his teaching position and had to resign his office as dean of the renowned School of Religion of Yenjing University at Beijing, the enlarged campus of which today houses Beijing University. Consequently, Chao had to experience bitter years, although he later participated in the Three-Self Movement. He suffered during the Cultural Revolution but experienced the joy of being rehabilitated officially shortly before his death at the advanced age of ninety-two (in the Chinese reckoning of years).

Chao taught theology at Yenjing beginning in 1926. Before that, he had been professor at the Methodist Dongwu University in Suzhou, his own alma mater. (In fact, he had attended school in Suzhou from the age of fourteen.) He wrote two detailed biographical accounts of his younger years, which reflect, among other things, the motivation for some of the important decisions that set the course for his later life. These accounts were both published in Chinese under the title "My Religious Experience." Stylized as they are, with the objective of personal witness to young Chinese intellectuals, they reveal to some degree Chao's intimate feelings and character.

Chao came from a family that had suffered economically from the upheavals of the Taiping Heavenly Kingdom in the middle of the nineteenth century, not very long before he was born. In his younger years, he had to struggle against financial difficulties. His father wanted to train him for a business career, but Chao had already set his mind on studying at a foreign school, even though the Bodhisattva Guanyin whom he consulted during a special visit to Juchai Monastery on Lingquanshan had advised him to attend a Chinese middle school in Hangzhou instead. At school he decided to join the church, a decision that gave rise to stern resistance at home. Even at the age of twenty-one Chao was beaten several times by his father for his betrayal of the old faith. Later, however, his parents also followed his example and became Christians. Chao remained critical of the mission school throughout his life because of its compulsory Christian education and, even worse, compulsory attendance at worship services. His decision to join the church was not influenced by the school as such but, rather, by personal encounters with Christian friends, and his conversion did not mean for him the abandonment of Chinese culture. At one time – these were the years of high national feeling, shortly after the Boxer uprising succumbed to Western arms – Chao joined anti-Western and anti-Christian activities. But in the long run the Christian influence was stronger. John Mott's visit to Suzhou left a deep impression on Chao. One year later, in 1908, he asked to be baptized.

For his theological education Chao went to the United States. From 1914 to 1917 he studied theology at Vanderbilt University in Nashville, Tennessee. He was a brilliant student who acquainted himself extensively, beyond the theological field, with Western philosophy. He also took some courses in sociology. In 1916 he obtained his M.A. degree, and concluded his studies at Vanderbilt in 1917. As the best student, surpassing his American classmates, he was honored with the Founder's Medal.

Chao's reflections on his development reveal a great sensitivity in the years of his childhood. At times he experienced visions and appearances. Also, at later times, he spoke of dreams that had some influence on him. But a strong rational trait superseded this mystical inclination, which expressed itself in his lyricism and aestheticism. The rational element remained dominant in his theology. But its extreme expression, in which Chao, sure of himself, ostracized other modes of Christian thought after his return from Vanderbilt University, was scorned by Chao himself a decade later when he renounced this "youthful immaturity."

Chao returned to China in 1917, bent on contributing to its national reconstruction as he had earlier decided to do at the age of sixteen, when he was a middle-school student at Suzhou. The missionary goal set by Mott at the Edinburgh Conference in 1910 had convinced Chao that China would be Christian in one generation. It was his hope, indeed, to renew China through the Christian spirit and a dedicated Christian life.

Most of Chao's writings have been published in the Chinese language, but there are about thirty articles in English. In these he addresses himself to theological problems arising in the context of China and of the church ecumenical. Many of these English publications were meant as a challenge to current Western theological thought from his Chinese vantage point. The themes of these writings focus around two emphases. One is the basic theological question of the authenticity of Christianity as expressed, for example, in his "Revelation" written for the Madras Conference of the International Missionary Council. The themes of two early articles indicate the other focus, expressed more extensively: "The Appeal of Christianity to the Chinese Mind" and, complementary to this, the more direct practical question "Can Christianity Be the Basis of Social Reconstruction in China?"

More than 100 articles in Chinese are available to us. Most of them were published in journals edited in Beijing by a group of Chinese and foreign Christians. The origins of this circle date back to the Apologetic Group, formed in 1918, under the influence of the May 4th movement, when the Chinese intellectuals discarded the traditional Chinese framework and brought about a "Chinese Renaissance." Some alert Christians saw the urgency of a Christian contribution for which this situation seemed to call.

Chen Duxiu, one of the group that in 1921 secretly founded the Chinese Communist party, published an article in February 1920 in which he pointed to the wonderful personality of Jesus as an inspiration to the Chinese in their national commitment. Chao contributed to the publication of the Apologetic Group and eagerly spelled out the main principles of Christian theology. He took great pains to show that religion, that is, Christian revelation and the reality of God, is easily accessible by philosophical reasoning. In these efforts, he readily joined forces with the philosophical-naturalist tradition, blended with the pragmatism of William James. Later, when Chao gradually became disenchanted with the growing anti-Christian and clearly secularist trends in intellectual China, traits of idealism and personalism came to the forefront of his thought and were never fully excluded from his thinking.

It is interesting to analyze the effects of Chao's student years at Vanderbilt in his early writings where we find a distinguished and somewhat strange consortium of Western, and particularly American, philosophers together with the liberal American theological school. Among the latter the prophets of the Social Gospel, whose thought Chao had imbibed with his daily food during the years in Nashville, hold a foremost place. The question, however, is whether Chao cites these Western thinkers merely to echo their views, or because their systems of thought reinforced an expression of his own Chinese understanding of the world and of Christian theology. The latter is obviously the case. Chao confirms this with his two monographs of the mid-1920s.

His *Christian Philosophy and Jesus' Philosophy of Life – On the Sermon on the Mount,* each written in a record time of about three weeks, expound Christian doctrine in Chinese vestments. The former work is written in the form of a dialogue, and its purpose is again apologetic. Among the participants in the dialogue, Chao includes some students of science who represent the thought of the intellectuals of his day in the wake of the May 4th movement. Chao takes up the whole range of theological themes already dealt with in his earlier writings, this time in systematic order. The main emphasis is to express Christian theology in the framework of Confucian thought, a most fascinating undertaking. He boldly paints a portrait of Jesus of Nazareth as presented by the New Testament Gospels. Similarly, in the second work, the Sermon on the Mount is interpreted basically from a viewpoint of the Confucian spirit. It is not so much a return to historic Confucianism, which at that time had already been rejected by China's intellectuals, but rather, an attempt at dialogue with Chinese humanism, be it traditional Confucian humanism or the humanism of the Chinese Renaissance. However, Chao had to learn soon that the two were not so closely related as he had believed. Brilliant as his approach appears – it might have been widely accepted had it been developed some decades earlier – Chao was nevertheless forced to abandon his attempts at coming to a full Christian-Confucian synthesis. He later spoke in a rather critical way of the theological premises underlying his theology during this period, particularly his *Christian Philosophy,* in which salvation in Christ is interpreted as an attainment to the perfection of humankind in Confucian terms.

A dialogue with China's youth was imperative for Chao. His many articles published in the Yenjing journal *Zhenli yu shengming* (Truth and Life) in which, among others, the tradition of the Apologetic Group is continued, show his incessant efforts at convincing young university students of the real power of the Christian spirit. Dedication and self-sacrifice are exemplified by Jesus. To follow Jesus in China would mean China's spiritual salvation and social renewal. Again and again the social situation of China is analyzed by Chao and confronted with the appeal to selfless sacrifice for the country. The tone of these writings becomes less apologetic. Although this element never disappears completely, it becomes more pastoral. The journal expresses the communal experience of the Life-Fellowship, a model for a Christian elite at Yenjing that Chao wished to see expanding over all of China, to reach its villages in far provinces and to transform the life of the peasants.

In this period of the mid-1930s Chao wrote *The Life of Jesus,* a work that also follows liberal theological thought patterns. The book is not intended as a historical investigation of the life of Jesus. Chao describes with much imagination and, sometimes, daring freedom the "eternal reality" of Jesus in the experience of faith. The book is written in masterly Chinese language and became a best-seller. By 1948 it had appeared in five reprints. Another reprint was published in 1965 in Hong Kong, although Chao's theological presuppositions of the 1930s are scarcely in accord with the requirements of contemporary Christianity. Chao looked back at this book with pride in its literary success, but he criticized the unbridled use of imagination, which impaired its theological quality.

His later theological monographs are of a different nature. In these he left the spirit of liberal theology far behind, although the traditional element of his younger years was not eliminated. A comprehensive study entitled *An Interpretation of Christianity, and The Life of Paul* were written during the war in Beijing. The former constitutes a more or less systematic theology written after his spectacular renunciation of liberal thought. After the prolegomena, the relationship between Christianity and Chinese culture is discussed extensively. Since practical application in the concrete life situation is inseparable from Christian faith, and also from the core of Chinese understanding, the book culminates in a chapter on Christian ethics. In its description of a just social and political order, it reflects Chao's dissatisfaction with the incompetent Guomindang regime, which he had already voiced in the late 1930s. *The Life of Paul* shows Chao's concern for the church and its mission.

The new discovery of Chao after the failure of liberalism was the church. This discovery coincides with his decision to join the Anglican Church in China, and he was ordained in 1941. Several treatises on the church spell out the mystery of the body of Christ and his saving act. The Christianization of the social order, which he wanted to attain directly in former times, now appears in an eschatological perspective. The kingdom of God, however, will be foreshadowed through the reality of the church.

In introducing the writings of Chao, a booklet that deals with his personal experience must be mentioned. *My Experience in Prison* (published 1947, in Chinese) gives a deep insight into his life. He was imprisoned by the Japanese, on the day of the Pearl Harbor attack, for a period of six months. During this time the theological recognition of the breakdown of liberalism, clearly experienced by Chao in preceding years, took final form. Chao's reflections on this change give valuable insights into the development of his thinking.

There is yet another category of Chao's writings to be mentioned: his poems. *My Experience in Prison* contains about 170 poems that Chao composed and memorized in prison and put on paper after his release. There are other volumes of poems, some of his poetry dealing with biblical themes. Chao also wrote church hymns in simple form for the Chinese congregations in their worship services. Other poems deal with the wonders of nature. Tao Yuanming, in his quest for life and meaning, and the great lyrics of the Tang Dynasty meant much to Chao and influenced his writings as well as his thinking.

Chinese Theology

How much Chao's lifework centered on the task of a Chinese Christian theology is evident from the preceding account. A presupposition for the positive task of developing a Chinese theology is a critique of Western theological thinking. Chao was not slow to apply his sharp criticism of the traditional doctrines, but bold rejection of elements of Western theology was for him no more than a first step in freeing the Chinese church from foreign bondage. Again and again he attempted to express the Gospel positively and authentically in the Chinese context, both by thorough and incessant reflection on the legitimacy of his venture and in the process of his theological expression itself.

Chao was a contextual theologian long before that term was coined. Context included for him the totality of life, in its cultural as well as sociopolitical dimensions. Challenged by the radical changes for China, the need of which was already clearly felt by him in his teens, and which continued through the Chinese Revolution from Sun Yat-sen to Mao Zedong, he constantly sought for an articulation of the relevance of the Gospel. He was deeply influenced by the earlier Social Gospel, although he never accepted its later development and often criticized "mere social action." The personalist approach of his Christian ethics, in accordance with the earlier Social Gospel and, as it were, Neo-Confucianism, proved a limitation to the viability of his hopes. Chao experienced a great disappointment for this reason, especially in the light of the minority situation of Christianity and the obvious shortcomings of a Chinese church, which for the most part was out of touch with the sociopolitical context of China.

New China

Like many other intellectuals, Chao was late to realize the real power of the Communist revolution. But already at Amsterdam in 1948 he pointed out that a meaningful life for Chinese society was to be found only by drastic changes. With expectation and fears he awaited the Communist troops to take Beijing and soon rejoiced in liberation and the opportunities for Christians to participate in building the motherland. In his personal experience, he was not spared bitter disappointments, however. Finally Christianity no longer held any relevance for him in view of the achievements of the New China. It is difficult for an outsider to understand this long intellectual journey. Its end, however, does not appear inconsistent with Chao's earlier thought, especially with his incessant calls for practice by which faith is to be realized. Chao saw the basis for it in the New Testament, and this with the eyes of a down-to-earth Confucianist. But in his situation he did not find sufficient evidence of this attitude in the actual performance of Christianity.

In his theology a number of questions about a theological anthropology, the understanding of God, church and society – all related to the Chinese context – remain open. That he was twice overwhelmed, as it were, by his context does not speak against the task of contextualization as such. Admission by Chao himself of his failure as a theologian in a letter only a few months before his death does not allow us to dismiss his work as meaningless. In fact, he has left a legacy for the Chinese church and ecumenical theology by the very fact of his personal aporia. And there is a Chinese church in China today eager to accept it and to continue where Chao was not able to carry on.

Selected Bibliography

Monographs by T.C. Chao in Chinese

1925 *Jidujiao jexue* (Chinese philosophy). Shanghai.
1926 *Yesudi rensheng jexue. Mingdengshan baoxun xinjie* (Jesus' philosophy of life – on the Sermon on the Mount). Shanghai.
1935 *Yesu zhuan* (The life of Jesus). Shanghai.
[1938] *Bolisheng* (poems). N.p.
1939 *Batedi zhongjiao sixiang* (The theology of Barth). Hong Kong.
1946 *Jiaohuidi tiyong yu qi biyaoxing* (The nature, purpose, and necessity of the church). Shanghai.
1947 *Jidujiao jinjie* (An interpretation of Christianity). Shanghai.
1947 *Sheng baoluo zhuan* (The life of Paul). Shanghai.
1948 *Jidujiaodi lunli* (Christian ethics). Shanghai.
1948 *Shenxue sixiang* (Four talks on theology). Shanghai.
1948 *Xiyuji* (My experience in prison). Shanghai.

Other Works by T.C. Chao in Western Languages

1928 "Christianity and Confucianism." *International Review of Missions* 17: 588-600.
1931 "Preface to the Moral and Social Problems of Chinese Youth." *Student World* 24: 206-14.
1932 "The Church." In *As It Looks to Young China*, ed. William Hung, pp. 143-77. New York: Friendship Press.
1938 *The Christian Movement in China in a Period of National Transition*. Ed. J. Merle Davis. Mysore City: Dept. of Social and Industrial Research of the International Missionary Council. Articles by T.C. Chao, R.O. Hall, and Roderick Scott.
1938 "Revelation." In *The Authority of the Faith*. The Madras Series, vol. 1, pp. 22-57. New York and London: International Missionary Council.
1939 "A Chinese Delegate Looks at Tambaram." *Christendom* 4: 197-204.
1947 "The Articulate Word: The Problem of Communication." *International Review of Missions* 36: 482-89.

1948 "Das Zeugnis der Christen in China." In *Amsterdamer Dokumente, Berichte und Reden auf der Weltkirchenkonferenz in Amsterdam 1948.* Ed. Focko Lüpsen. Bielefeld: Evangelischer Presseverband.
1949 "Amsterdam in the Perspective of the Younger Churches." *Ecumenical Review* 1, no. 2: 131-36.
1949 "Days of Rejoicing in China." *Christian Century*, March 2, pp. 265-67.
1949 "Christian Churches in Communist China." *Christianity and Crisis*, June 27, pp. 83-85.
1949 "Red Peiping after Six months." *Christian Century*, Sept. 14, pp. 1066-68.

Works about T.C. Chao

Glüer, Winfried, *Christlich Theologie in China: T. C. Chao, 1918-1956.* Gütersloh: Gütersloher Verlagshaus Gerd Mohn, 1979 (with detailed bibliography).
_____. "T.C. Chao and the Quest for Life and Meaning." *China Notes* 18, no. 4 (1980): 120-33.
Ng Lee-ming. "Christianity and Social Change. The Case of China, 1920-1950." Th.D. diss., Princeton Theological seminary, 1971. Published in part as "An Evaluation of T.C. Chao's Thought," *Ching Feng* 14 (1971): 5-59.
_____. "A Bibliography of T.C. Chao and Y.T. Wu." *Ching Feng* 16 (1973): 166-77.
_____. "The Promise and Limitations of Chinese Protestant Theologians, 1920-1950." *Ching Feng* 21, no 4.1 (1979): 175-82.

Francis X. Ford, M.M.

1892–1952

Maryknoll Pathfinder in China

Jean-Paul Wiest

Shortly after five o'clock one afternoon in January 1912, a priest entered the New York preparatory seminary on Madison Avenue to call upon the director of the New York branch of the Society for the Propagation of the Faith, located on the first floor of the same building. While he was rattling the door, a seminarian came down the stairs and told him the office had already closed. As they left the building together, the priest revealed he had come to discuss the details of the forthcoming opening of a new type of seminary – one for foreign missions.

The priest was Father James A. Walsh, co-founder of Maryknoll. The young man was Philip Furlong, future auxiliary bishop of New York. Furlong promptly excused himself and ran back to the preparatory seminary to bring the news to a friend who was deeply interested in foreign missions. Father Walsh had almost reached Grand Central Station, where he would catch a train home to Hawthorne, New York, when a slightly built young man with a gentle face and an attractive shyness caught up with him. Out of breath from hurrying, the young man said: "Father Walsh, I would like to go to your foreign mission seminary."

"That's good. What is your name?" asked Walsh.

"Frank Ford, Father," was the reply.[1]

Walsh had just recruited the first applicant to his new seminary. The next fall Ford was part of the first group of six Maryknoll seminarians who started their training on Sunset Hill in Ossining at the newly established center for the young Catholic Foreign Mission Society of America, the official name of Maryknoll. Six years later, in 1918, he was one of the first four Maryknoll missioners to leave for China.

In 1925, Ford became head of the newly created mission territory of Kaying (Jiaying) or Meihsien (Meixian) in the northeast corner of Kwangtung (Guangdong) Province in China. Ten years later he was made a bishop. For his episcopal motto, Ford chose the word *condolere*, meaning to have compassion, from the fifth chapter of the letter to the Hebrews. Better than anything else, perhaps, this motto exemplifies Bishop Ford's understanding of his missionary vocation and of his relationship to the Chinese. Although his great empathy for the Chinese of Kaying seemed natural, it was the result of an effort – the logical implementation of his missionary vocation. His compassion for the Chinese led to the ultimate sacrifice of his life in a Canton prison in February 1952. He had fulfilled Christ's saying that a man can have no greater love than to lay down his life for his friends (John 15:13).

Bishop Ford's accomplishments in China were acknowledged by the papal internuncio Antony Riberi, who called him "the most advanced missioner in China." Of course, this is an overstatement. By any measure, Francis Ford was extraordinary, but the names of other Catholic or Protestant missioners, who also deserved that compliment, come immediately to mind. My purpose is not to eulogize Ford but to consider his contributions as a member of that group of "most advanced missioners" in China.

Bishop Ford's Theology of Mission

Bishop Ford often told the Maryknoll priests and Sisters working for him in the territory of Kaying that "we missioners are here for a double purpose, first of all to found the Church, and secondly, to make converts."[2] These objectives per se were not original. They defined the overall purpose of the Roman Catholic Church as well as most Protestant churches working in China in the early part of the twentieth century. Yet the way Ford positioned these two objectives and enriched their meaning, as well as his methods of implementation, were innovative at the time and reveal his deep spirituality.

Ford put forth the establishment of the church as the missioner's primary objective; however, this did not mean – as it did for so many of his contemporaries – the construction of churches, schools, and hospitals. For him it meant the training and development of a living structure of native priests, Sisters, and lay leaders. He realized, of course, that without conversions there would be no Christian families to provide candidates for the priesthood, sisterhood, and lay leadership.

To ensure converts, Ford devised a special form of evangelization known as the Kaying method. He always denied, nonetheless, that the gathering of individual converts was the primary object of the missioner's apostolate. In an article written in 1932, he asked:

> Is the conversion of souls really the main immediate object of the Church? If so, why keep priests at home to minister to Catholics? Why send missioners to places that are hard to convert? Why not concentrate them among the simple savages where thousands instead of hundreds might be baptized each year? Evidently there is a reason for the Church's present system: The object of mission work is not primarily to convert pagans, it is to establish the Catholic Church in pagan lands. The purpose is to preach the Gospel and to build up as complete an organization as possible which will itself continue with better success the work of converting the native populations.[3]

In conclusion, he stated again, "Even were the whole mission field to prove a failure in respect to converts, it would still be worthwhile as following out our Savior's command to preach the Gospel to all nations."[4]

In pre-Vatican Council II times, the most important signs of the church's vitality were its size and its rate of expansion. Ford, however, was always bothered by statistical mission reports that calculated the church's success or failure in terms of building and numerical increases, because the spiritual dimension of the church, after all, cannot be measured. For him, the few hundreds who gathered around the altar represented the entire Chinese nation. This understanding of the church was shared, at first, only by a minority of foreign missioners but, during the late 1930s, began to receive more widespread recognition. In later years, it was one of many factors that led the fathers of Vatican II to redefine the church as "the sacrament or sign of salvation" (*Lumen Gentium* 1, 48). As Catholic theologian William Frazier wrote in 1967, this epoch-making advance in the Roman

Catholic Church's self-understanding was in sharp contrast with the image of the church projected by towering cathedrals, large schools, and imposing hospitals.

> The rule of expansion of the Church is simply the need to give the sign of salvation indigenous roots in every human situation. Beyond this it is useless to probe as to how little and how large the Church is meant to be. The important thing is that the Church understand and faithfully pursue its call to raise the sign of salvation in the world.[5]

Ford would have had no problem endorsing such an understanding of the church.

The Establishment of a Native Church

During the nineteenth century and the early part of the twentieth century, the movement toward the establishment of a native Chinese church within the Catholic Church made little progress. Foreign bishops held all the positions of leadership, and many missioners felt they belonged to a class superior to that of the Chinese priests. The excuse generally given was that the Chinese were not ready, at least for the foreseeable future, to assume the direction of the church in China.

This attitude was criticized in Rome when in 1919 Pope Benedict XV indirectly criticized the mission work in China. In his apostolic letter *Maximum Illud*, he declared how sad he was to think that there were still countries where the Catholic faith had been preached for several centuries and where civilization had produced people distinguished in most fields of arts and sciences, and yet these countries had no native bishops and the native clergy was still maintained in a position of inferiority (*Maximum Illud*, 13). He exhorted missioners to establish seminaries and to take particular care in training native priests and in turning over responsibility to them.

At the time, Ford had just arrived in China. The pope's letter was not well received by many seasoned missioners, who thought the pope had been influenced by rebel confreres such as Fathers Vincent Lebbe and Anthony Cotta. Ford, on the contrary, used the pope's words as the foundation for plans for the immediate implementation of a native church. His intention was to build a self-governing church not burdened by Western institutions and financially self-reliant. His plan called not only for well-trained Chinese clergy and sisterhoods but also for a well-educated lay leadership to take positions of responsibility in building a modern China.

Ford's Seminary

From his earliest days in China, Francis Ford was Maryknoll's main driving force for the establishment of seminaries. In 1921, while pastor in the mission territory of Kongmoon (Jiangmen), Maryknoll's first territory in China, he began preparing young teenagers for the priesthood. Two years later he started a formal program and the nucleus of a seminary by opening his rectory to eleven promising boys recruited from the territory of Kongmoon. In his activity report, he wrote:

> . . . the preparatory seminary is without doubt the strongest effect of the year's work, for the future Chinese priests will be the backbone of the Church in China. The seminary is really our motive for coming to China – to found a native Church – and the vocations so far presented to us argue well for the strength of the Catholicity in our section of China for years to come.[6]

In 1925, when he was transferred to eastern Kwangtung to direct the new mission territory of Kaying, Ford immediately started his own seminary with ten young boys. He transformed his rectory of five rooms into a seminary. By the next fall, he had twenty-one students and started building a permanent seminary. For a man supposedly committed to build a church known for its membership rather than for its buildings, this seemed quite a breach of resolution. But Ford felt forced to provide a training place for the future clergy: "We are building against our will." However, during the next twenty years, he did not engage in any other major construction: there was no imposing bishop's residence, nor any place worth calling a cathedral. As a visiting missioner wrote, "The Kaying mission has one building, the seminary, with the missioners living in odd corners."[7]

Bishop Ford paid special attention to the education of the seminarians. From experience during his early years in China, he realized that the Chinese priest, as he said, was seldom "a good mixer in the American sense of the term; he lived for the most part within the walls of the Church property and is rarely seen in the market place or at civil functions."[8]

Analyzing the cause of this attitude, Ford found that most Chinese priests were village boys who had been brought up in the shelter of Catholic homes, protected from pagan influences. This in itself could be overcome, but Ford also discovered that traditional seminary curriculum lacked preparation in the Chinese classics, history, and culture, and neglected the modern sciences. To correct these deficiencies in his Kaying seminary, Ford made a point of having most of the regular high school subjects taught by the best Chinese lay teachers he could afford. As a result, St. Joseph's Seminary became known not only as one of the best minor seminaries in South China but also as an outstanding high school.

The young men in the Kaying seminary were trained not only as pastors for the existing Catholics; they were also trained to be missioners themselves, alert to openings, alive to opportunities, exploring possibilities, reaching out to new villages for new converts. Ford reminded his Maryknollers that it was their responsibility to set the pattern: "The Chinese priest's idea of priestly work will be derived from our manner of thinking and talking and acting."[9]

At the same time, Ford sent some of his most promising seminarians to Rome for theology and graduate study. Upon returning, these priests were given important responsibilities. By 1948 Kaying's vicar general was Chinese and the seminary had its own Chinese rector heading an all-Chinese faculty of priests and laypersons. It seems practically certain that if the trend had not been interrupted, Kaying's next bishop would have been Chinese.

The legacy of Bishop Ford is recalled with much fondness by his Chinese priests:

I can say that because of his work we were instilled with a strong sense of loyalty to our diocese.

Bishop Ford had become so Chinese that we Chinese priests had to be careful of what we said in his presence about our people. Bishop Ford was there to defend them.

I took Father Cheung, the vicar general of Kaying, to the grave of Bishop Ford. There he began to cry. He missed Bishop Ford, who had a great influence on him.[10]

Ford's Novitiate

Just as Bishop Ford was convinced that the Kaying church had no permanent future if he did not prepare a native clergy to take over the duties of his Maryknoll priests, so was he convinced that Chinese Sisters must be trained for a successful apostolate among women and children. Because of the traditional Chinese segregation of the sexes and the absence of missionary sisters, the Catholic system of evangelization in China had long been defective. Missionary priests had concentrated on men without insisting that their wives and children be instructed and baptized at the same time. Ford thought he had found the reason for the shallow roots of the Catholic Church in China: "Had we won over the women to the true worship during the past three centuries, the Church would have had a far more glorious tale to tell."[11] Evangelization of women and children became the special apostolate of the Sisters.

Bishop Ford wanted his native sisters – he called them Sister Catechists of Our Lady – to be like Maryknoll Sisters, fully engaged in direct evangelization, but even more effective because they were Chinese. Consequently, he asked the Maryknoll Sisters to train them for that specific purpose.

The aspirants boarded at Rosary Hall where the Maryknoll Sisters oversaw their religious development.

In many ways his plan differed from the traditional formation of Sisters. Instead of rushing the aspirants into religious life, Ford required that they first complete their middle school studies in one of Kaying City's government middle schools. During these years the girls could weigh the pros and cons of unmarried life. By keeping in touch with the Chinese society, they learned how to manage ordinary human relationships. They gained poise, self-confidence, and a spirit of their own, which armed them against becoming second-rate submissive copies of Maryknoll Sisters.

Once they graduated, the aspirants were formally admitted as apprentices to sisterhood and followed a two-and-a-half-year period of formation common to most religious orders known as postulancy and novitiate. During their first year of training, Ford ensured that the native Sisters study more than the traditional courses on the obligations of religious life, religion, and apologetics. Courses in psychology, sociology, and economics were added to prepare the Chinese Sisters to be as self-reliant as possible. A wide range of manual skills were constantly practiced to make the novitiate self-supporting and to develop in each Sister the ability to improvise and to do rough work under less than propitious conditions. These courses and skills also taught the novices how to make effective contact with women by experiencing their daily work.

During the second year of the novitiate, emphasis was put on letting the native Sisters develop on their own. They were sent for short periods in twos or threes to outstations without being accompanied by Maryknoll Sisters. Living in two-Sister convents prepared them for their life as professed Sisters; they had to order their lives and their apostolates by themselves, guided by their Chineseness and their religious training. Such training did not give the native Sisters any sense of inferiority. They felt that they and the Maryknoll Sisters were sisters in the same big family; Sisters whose main role was to spread the good news by living among the people.

Like most of the Chinese priests who were usually not assigned to work under Maryknoll missioners, the professed Chinese Sisters never worked with the Maryknoll Sisters. The Maryknoll Sisters were sent to the east of the territory and the Chinese Sisters worked in the west. Bishop Ford seemed to have realized that the key to true indigenization was to let the Chinese take charge and to reduce as much as possible any outside – that is, Maryknoll – interference. In that transitional stage, the best way to maintain harmonious relationships was to keep responsibilities and places of work separate between his foreign and Chinese priests and Sisters.

The Laity

The Christian laity that Ford had in mind was primarily a responsible laity and, to the extent possible, a well-educated laity. Ford insisted that his Catholics not only witness to their faith on Sundays but continually live out their faith in the presence of their non-Christian friends and relatives. Rather than initiating and supporting all kinds of charitable works such as clinics and schools, Ford concentrated on establishing the church as a community of believers with the hope that the community would provide for its own needs.

To make up for the lack of Catholic schools, which he could not afford and which would absorb too many of his missionary personnel, Ford opted for hostels. In 1927, barely two years after he arrived, he opened the first dormitory for Catholic boys attending high schools in Kaying City. That same year he also sent eight young men to the Catholic university in Peking and the Jesuit normal school in Shanghai to be trained as teachers. Ten years later, Ford sponsored four high school dormitories for students attending government schools in the larger towns of his territory and a hostel for girls attending the government middle school in Kaying City. The role of the Maryknoll Fathers and Sisters in the hostels was to provide an atmosphere of quiet study and to enhance the development of the "natural and supernatural virtues" of their students. The Sisters, in particular, felt they had an important role to play in guiding middle-school-age girls:

> The middle-school girl in Hakka China was a pioneer in a new field: she lived a life that her elders had never lived; there were no traditions to guide her; she was a puzzle to her mother and the older women of the village . . . As a member of a new movement among Chinese girls the middle-school student needed understanding and direction. Therein lay our apostolate.[12]

Although these small hostels accommodated no more than thirty students each, they enabled Maryknollers to come in contact with a large number of students and teachers at the government schools:

> My purpose in coming to China [explained Ford to one student] is to preach the Gospel of God. Although these students are not Catholics, my objective is to help them know God; to help them feel the presence of God in their mind. I would not ask them to be baptized. What I want is that when they leave Kaying and go to some other place, they still feel the presence of God. The objective of preaching the Gospel is to save the soul. If a person finally can get close to God, the objective of preaching the Gospel is achieved.[13]

Direct Evangelization

Bringing the Chinese people close to God was the goal of Bishop Ford's use of "direct evangelization." Ford's methods in Kaying were particularly revolutionary when applied to the Maryknoll Sisters.

The nature of the Sisters' apostolate as envisioned by Ford was radically different from traditional practices. Their work was not to be institutional in character, as was the case with most Sisters in the United States and certainly in China; their purpose was not to supervise asylums, hospitals, or schools; they should not perform medical or charitable work, or engage in educational projects. Their sole aim was direct evangelization – leading non-Christian women to embrace Catholicism, instructing them for baptism, and watching over them during their first years as new Catholics. To qualify as a missionary Sister, said Bishop Ford, the Maryknoll Sisters had to become experts at making contacts:

> A contact Sister is expansive, expressive, exhilarating and exhibitive; in common language, a person large-hearted, ready-tongued, easily pleased and not dismayed by crowds . . . As a contact visitor to pagan women she literally penetrates into the inner courts where superstition has its firmest foothold; she attacks the enemy at his strongest fortress and until this has fallen, it is vain to hope for a solid Catholic family.[14]

When he invited the Maryknoll Sisters to Kaying in 1934 for the purpose of evangelizing the women, Sister Paul McKenna, the Sisters' superior in South China, saw an opportunity for the Sisters to realize their missionary vocation: "Monsignor Ford invites us to the Kaying mission as missioners – not only as Sisters for this or that work . . . Having the broader outline, more on the basis of the Maryknoll men, will give us the broader viewpoint which will make us *more truly missioners* – foreign missioners to a pagan people."[15]

Ford's approach to the evangelization of female non-Christians proved to be most innovative. In seeking the Sisters to spearhead this apostolate, the head of the Kaying territory tried something with no precedent in the mission history of the Catholic Church. This new approach, which responded to the young Maryknoll Sisters' deepest aspirations, was greeted enthusiastically at the home novitiate in the United States. The future of this type of apostolate, however, was still uncertain because it was only an experiment the Holy See could discontinue at any time. Finally, in March 1939, Cardinal Pietro Fumasoni-Biondi, prefect of the Sacred Congregation for the Propagation of the Faith, wrote a letter to Mother Mary Joseph (the Maryknoll Sisters' Mother General) telling her of Rome's approval:

> I wish you to know that I believe your greatest accomplishments lie before you through your direct cooperation in the conversion of non-Christian souls. I am aware of the courage and devotion which many Maryknoll Sisters have displayed in the work of conversion, particularly in the vicariate of Kaying, where they have gone from house to house among the people and they have proven valuable helpers to the Fathers in reaching the non-Christians.[16]

Upon learning the good news, Ford jubilantly told his missioners:

> *Roma locuta est.* Rome considers the greatest accomplishments of the Sisters will result, not from institutional work, but from direct cooperation in reaching non-Christians. This spontaneous approbation on the part of Rome has resolved whatever misgivings I may have had on the experiment. Rome has gone out of its way to orientate the work of the Maryknoll Sisters differentiating it from work hitherto considered the province of Sisters of older congregations. In short, Rome sets its approval on our thesis that foreign women can be missioners just as foreign men can; or rather it can be interpreted even more strongly as affirming that our Sisters should be direct missioners.[17]

Together with the Sisters, Ford refined what became known as the Kaying method. It was a multifaceted type of direct apostolic work which involved *(a)* making friendly contacts with non-Christian women until they spontaneously asked about the Sisters' Christian beliefs; *(b)* instructing women who were interested in pursuing the topic of Christian faith; *(c)* visiting and providing follow-up instruction for newly baptized Catholics, including courses toward confirmation and marriage; *(d)* visiting old Christians, faithful as well as lapsed or lax Catholics; *(e)* conducting Sunday school classes; and *(f)* training catechists through class and field work.

The distinctive feature of the Sisters' method of apostolate was that instead of residing in a large convent, they were sent two-by-two to live in a Chinese house that often was also used as the women's catechumenate. They visited and mingled with the women. Their small convents were not to provide enclosures but to serve as rallying points for old and new Catholics, non-Christians, and catechumens.

Every time Ford addressed the Sisters, he emphasized the link between contemplative prayer and mission activity by reminding them of their role as contact persons. He stressed that he had invited them to Kaying primarily to do visiting of non-Christian homes. Ford said, "Sisters, I want you to go out to the villages. I know you are going to miss mass but your presence there is going to mean much more than what you give up in regard to the mass for those people."[18]

His profound spirituality deeply influenced the Sisters. They learned to become living houses of prayer, so to speak, wherever their work took them, on the streets as well as over the mountain passes; they discovered how to visit with God, not in the chapel but as they walked along the trails or sat on buses or bicycles.[19]

Given the opportunity to become involved in the direct apostolate, the Maryknoll Sisters dispelled the objections that had prevented religious women from serving as missionaries. They proved, for example, that Sisters could endure as many physical hardships as priests, that they could handle dangerous situations, and that they could adapt their religious rules and schedules to fit an apostolate life outside convent walls.

The traditional organization of the mission was altered. The Sisters were no longer auxiliaries but full participants. The priest still assumed the overall direction of the parish, but the approach to the work, including the direct apostolate, was more that of a team. The Sisters were in charge of the women and children, while the priests concentrated on the apostolate among men. The Sisters were able to accomplish things that no male missioner had been able to do: mingle with the women in their own environment, speak their "kitchen" language, talk from a woman's point of view, and gear their instructions to the concrete daily life of Chinese peasant women.

As a result, the Chinese Catholic Church in Kaying territory began to change. Its membership, which had been prominently male, became more balanced: more children were baptized with their mothers and continued to receive education in Sunday school and during the summer vacation. Women converts joined the budding Catholic Action groups and became actively involved in the apostolate of other women.

As already mentioned, the Maryknoll Sisters imparted this same zeal for the direct apostolate to the native Sisters they were training. These Chinese Sisters focused primarily on direct contact with non-Christians and on catechumenates. They became the first of a new breed of women religious who would follow the same path in the 1950s and 1960s.

Because the lifestyle and apostolate pursued by the Maryknoll Sisters in China established a new pattern of Catholic apostolic work, it not only affected communities of Chinese Sisters, but also had repercussions on the role of women religious in the church. Out of their convents, on the roads, mixing with non-Christians, the Maryknoll Sisters provided a new model of mission activity for nuns and contributed to modernization in the Catholic Church. Other women's religious orders – many of which were not primarily aiming at foreign mission – adopted methods of direct apostolate similar to those of the Maryknoll Sisters. In 1957 Léon-Joseph Cardinal Suenens of Belgium wrote to Sister Thérèse Grondin of Maryknoll that, inspired by the Maryknoll Sisters, he had just launched an experiment in Europe involving forty convents of Sisters and twenty houses of Brothers who were stressing direct evangelization by apostolic teams. He further extolled the value of this program in his book *The Gospel to Every Creature*.[20]

In 1967, at the international meeting in Rome of superiors general of missionary organizations, Gregorio Petro Cardinal Agagianian, prefect of the Sacred Congregation for the Propagation of the Faith, stressed the primacy of evangelization and the direct participation by religious women in evangelizing. He singled out the "itinerant evangelical penetration" of the two-Sister convent system in Kaying and the type of mobile missionary apostolate as the model to emulate.[21] The small experiment started in 1934 by Francis X. Ford and a few Maryknoll Sisters had led to an important change in the role of women in the apostolate mission of the church.

Conclusion

Bishop Ford, Maryknoll's first seminarian, has left his imprint not only on Maryknoll but also on the whole church. In his theology and his methods, he was for the most part a ground-breaker who prepared the way for the transformation of the Catholic Church at Vatican II. But above all, he emerges as a spiritual man possessed by a vision, which today still remains meaningful:

> Never look down on the Chinese people . . . We have very little to offer them of our own American culture because we are only barely two hundred years old . . . When you introduce the people to Christianity, go back to the time when the Church was a fishing vessel along the Sea of Galilee.[22]

Bishop Ford was well ahead of his time; we may not have yet caught up with him.

Notes

1. This account is a faithful reconstruction of the meeting. It is based on recollections by Bishop Furlong and Bishop Walsh, which are preserved in the Maryknoll Fathers Archives. Previously published accounts of the same meeting differ, sometimes substantially, from this version; see in particular Glenn D. Kittler, *The Maryknoll Fathers* (Cleveland: World Publishing Company, 1961), p. 93.

2. Raymond Lane, *Stone in the King's Highway – The Life and Writings of Bishop Francis X. Ford* (New York: McMullen, 1953), p. 24.

3. Ford, in *The Field Afar*, September 1932, p. 236.

4. Ibid., p. 237.

5. William Frazier, "Guidelines for a New Theology of Mission," *World Mission* 18, no. 4 (Winter 1967-68): 20.

6. Maryknoll Sisters Archives, Box 48, Folder 03, Yeungkong Convent Diary, December 1924.

7. John Donovan, *The Pagoda and the Cross* (New York: Charles Scribner's Sons, 1967), p. 93.

8. Ibid., p. 95.

9. Ibid., p. 96

10. Maryknoll China History Project: Interviews of Chinese Priests.

11. Donovan, *Pagoda*, p. 99.

12. Thérèse Grondin (Sister Marcelline), *Sisters Carry the Gospel* (New York: Maryknoll Publications, 1956), p. 55.

13. Maryknoll China History Project: Interviews of Former Chinese Students in Maryknoll Hostels.

14. Maryknoll Sisters Archives, Sister Paulita Hoffman's Collection of Talks by Bishop Ford, "The Type of Sister for Direct Evangelization," p. 1.

15. Maryknoll Sisters Archives, CHP21F2A, Letter of Sister Paul McKenna to Mother Mary Joseph, April 5, 1934.

16. Maryknoll Sisters Archives, Sister Imelda Sheridan, "A Brief History of the South China Region, 1921-1958," pp. 30-31.

17. Maryknoll Sisters Archives, Sister Paulita Hoffman's Collection, June 29, 1939, "Foundation Day Report on Kaying Missions," p. 5.

18. Maryknoll China History Project: Interview of Father Dennis Slattery.

19. Sister Thérèse Grondin, "Contemplative Prayer and Mission Activity," in *Maryknoll-Taiwan, Mission Forum*, September 1982.

20. Letter of Cardinal Suenens to Sister Marcelline (Sister Thérèse Grondin), June 18, 1957, quoted in Sister Mary Ann Schintz, "An Investigation of the Modernization Role of the Maryknoll Sisters in China" (Ph.D. diss., Univ. of Wisconsin-Madison, 1978), p. 132. Léon-Joseph Suenens, *The Gospel to Every Creature* (Westminster, Md.: Newman Press, 1957), pp. 83-112; the original edition in French was entitled *L'Église en état de mission*.

21. Gregorio Petro Agagianian, "New Horizons on the Missionary Apostolate," *Christianity to the World* 13, no. 1 (1968): 63-64.

22. Maryknoll China History Project: Interview of Sisters Louise Kroeger and Madeleine Sophie Karlon.

Selected Bibliography

Works by Francis X. Ford

Bishop Ford wrote countless short pieces on missions. Many were published, and can be found in the following periodicals:

The American Ecclesiastical Review
China Missionary Bulletin
Maryknoll Mission Letters (1942-46)
Maryknoll – The Field Afar

Among Bishop Ford's spiritual conferences, one series on the Holy Spirit was published:

Come, Holy Spirit. Maryknoll, N.Y.: Orbis Books, 1976.

Works about Francis X. Ford

Donovan, John. *The Pagoda and the Cross: The Life of Bishop Ford of Maryknoll.* New York: Charles Scribner's Sons, 1967.

Grondin, Thérèse (Sister Marcelline). *Sisters Carry the Gospel.* Maryknoll, N.Y.: Maryknoll Publications, 1956.

Lane, Raymond A., ed. *Stone in the King's Highway: Selections from the Writings of Bishop Francis X. Ford (1892-1952)*. New York: McMullen Books, 1953.

Sheridan, Robert. *Compassion: The Spirit of Francis X. Ford, M.M.* Ossining, N.Y.: Maryknoll Publications, 1982.

"To Have Compassion." *The Anthonian* 50 (Fourth Quarter, 1985).

Tsai, Mark (Chai). "Bishop Ford, Apostle of South China." *American Ecclesiastical Review* 127 (October 1952): 241-47.

Part Four

SOUTHERN ASIA

William Carey

Claudius Buchanan

Henry Martyn

Alexander Duff

Thomas Valpy French

Lewis Bevan Jones

J.N. Farquhar

Lars Peter Larsen

Ida S. Scudder

C.F. Andrews

V.S. Azariah

A.G. Hogg

E. Stanley Jones

J. Waskom Pickett

Paul David Devanandan

D.T. Niles

William Carey

1761–1834

Protestant Pioneer of the Modern Mission Era

A. Christopher Smith

A scholarly quest for the "historical Carey" is long overdue. In spite of the fact that scores of biographies have been written about him, layers of popular mythology still remain to be cut through before the actual contours of his career as a pre-Victorian mission leader will be uncovered. His immediate brethren in the 1830s revered him as "the father of the Serampore Mission," while evangelical posterity went much further and saluted him rather inaccurately as "the father of modern missions." Since then, many attempts been have made to co-opt him as a heroic figurehead for the revitalization of missions in "the modern era."

One thing certain is that a wealth of primary missiological sources and of erudite, contextual studies still remains to be examined. This largely untapped deposit is enough to merit a new era in Carey scholarship. It has much to contribute to an analysis of the course of a very unassuming English Baptist, born August 17, 1761, died June 9, 1834, who ended up functioning as something of a missionary archetype.

Hermeneutical Considerations

The enigma of William Carey's life, historical significance, and missiological legacy is not easily resolved. What are we to make of this "consecrated cobbler" who invested so much of his life in a Calcutta college and then founded one of his own?

Let us begin by considering the epitaph he chose for his tombstone in Bengal. Far from being incongruous, it reflected the struggle that he and his close colleagues went through in life and the modesty with which they looked back on whatever they managed to achieve. The words were taken from the last verse of hymn 181 in John Rippon's *Arrangement of the Psalms, Hymns and Spiritual Songs of the Rev. Isaac Watts, D.D.* (1802, third edition). They were used by Joshua Marshman at William Ward's funeral, eleven years before our subject's demise. Carey felt they were particularly apt and chose the first couplet for himself:

A guilty weak and helpless worm,
On thy kind arms I fall.
Be thou my strength and righteousness
My Jesus – and my all.

Of course, this reflected Calvinistic conviction of personal unworthiness to stand alone before the Almighty; but there was, arguably, more to the inscription than that. Carey and his close colleagues were quite sure that they did not merit being decked with garlands or halos. Each was persuaded that it would be enough to be remembered simply as one who had sought to do his duty as a servant of Christ.

Ernest A. Payne was one of the few mission historians who realized that there was something profoundly enigmatic about Carey as a person. He asked in 1961: "How are we to reconcile his intense self-distrust with his great achievements, the range of his interests and his apparent [in]decision of character?" Of all Carey's biographers, only his nephew Eustace got close enough to him "on the mission field" to realize that there was something odd about the way in which Carey functioned and contributed to the running of "the Serampore Mission" (independently of the Baptist Missionary Society from the 1820s). His critique appeared in various publications and was given a more missiological turn by William Adam, a perceptive, young, Baptist missionary in Bengal of whom Carey once wrote very highly.

Just as relevant for our hermeneutical inquiry is evidence emerging from right within the inner circle of the Serampore mission operation. Along with Carey, William Ward and Joshua Marshman rose to fame in some British circles and became known as "the Serampore Trio." They were amazingly close-knit as a leadership team. For several decades they complemented one another in an intricate way. Indeed, very few people in Britain ever realized how dependent Carey was on his partners for insight and a wide range of initiatives. This in itself should alert us to the great need there is to refrain from assuming that Carey should be given the limelight, while his lesser-known colleagues fade into the background. To the contrary, historical integrity requires us to recognize that too much has been attributed to him at others' expense – as if he were a great, solitary figure who towered above his contemporaries. Carey would have been horrified to think, for example, that he was being credited with the wisdom of men such as Andrew Fuller, John Ryland, John Sutcliffe, or Charles Grant – not to mention his own partners and a host of other expatriates in Bengal. That is why a somewhat "trinitarian" approach is called for, which sees Carey as one member of a triumvirate, and which recognizes that he was greatly indebted to three immediate groups of people: the Baptist Missionary Society's home-base troika of Fuller, Ryland, and Sutcliffe; a sizable number of Orientalists and *pandits* (learned men) in Bengal; and his own close colleagues along with their dedicated wives. This does no despite to his person. Rather, it considers him in situ, recognizing what a huge difference others made to his life both before 1793 and after 1799. We therefore do well to distinguish carefully between his pre-1800 legacy and his post-1800 legacy.

Before 1800, Carey passed through three apprenticeships – as an artisan, a pastor, and a missionary. From then on, his career moved through several phases that mirrored the evolution of his metropolitan mission beside the Hoogli estuary of the Ganges delta. These phases also reflected developments in the fortunes of the East India Company and in the course of British rule in India. When such factors are taken into account, and special attention is given to the cultural dynamics of the Baptists' Serampore enterprise, it becomes natural to reevaluate some of the popular "pleasing dreams" that have accrued to his memory. These we will outline, believing that "truthfulness will be more of a contribution" than "heroic myths" to the cause of mission.[1]

Inspiration and Obligations

Carey's much-narrated years in England before 1793 certainly make a good story. His father, Edmund Carey, was a weaver who became "master of the small free-school" in Paulerspury, Northamptonshire, when William was about six years old. The boy's own grandfather, likewise, had once been the village's schoolmaster, so it comes as no great surprise that he himself turned to primary school teaching in another of his country's villages, when he was in his mid-twenties. His uncle, Peter Carey, was a local gardener who had once served as a soldier against the French in Canada. He stimulated his nephew's imagination greatly. Thus, although William was a poor country boy, living in a landlocked province far from London and the sea, he *was* able to count his blessings. These he turned to good use by applying himself to acquiring knowledge during spare time. He had two sisters and one brother who survived infancy. Brought up in an Anglican home, he married Dorothy Plackett, the daughter of a local Dissenter, in 1781, several years before he became a Baptist.

William Carey lived during a time of great change, when Europe's Enlightenment was beginning to make itself felt in English church and society. While a teenager, newspapers and mass-produced literature periodically came his way. As a young Midlands man, he became vividly aware of the outside world through reading about the American revolution and Captain Cook's voyages of discovery in the Pacific. He was most fortunate, during his shoemaking years, to live within reach of some noted Bible expositors. Anglican and Baptist pastors such as Thomas Scott, Andrew Fuller, Robert Hall, Sr., and John Sutcliffe provided him with guidance and a sense of church history that helped him break free from the straitjacket of hyper-Calvinism: namely, an exclusive type of Reformed theology that denied that sinners were duty-bound to exercise faith before they could be saved. A neo-Puritan theology much indebted to Jonathan Edwards thus was mediated to Carey without his having to pore over theological tomes. That freed him to focus on language-learning and to pursue his geographical interests during the little spare time he could find at day's end.

Six years (1787-1793) were spent pastoring Particular Baptist churches in Northamptonshire. That was when he became aware of early Protestant missionary work in North America during the previous 150 years. Given the evangelical-Calvinist convictions he had assimilated, he began to argue that *means* should be employed to propagate the Gospel throughout the world. By 1792, he finally prevailed on his provincial brethren to seriously consider founding a society to "preach the Gospel to every creature." With their support, he wrote an unpretentious booklet that has been popularly called "the charter of modern mission with its argument, review, survey and pro-gramme."[2] Entitled *An Enquiry into the Obligations of Christians, to Use Means for the Conversion of the Heathens,* it provided missionary apologetic and made practical suggestions in a forthright manner. His indebtedness to other authors for information was undoubtedly great. Distribution of the eighty-seven page pamphlet was very limited in Carey's day; however, it did contribute significantly to the formation of "the Particular Baptist Society for Propagating the Gospel amongst the Heathen" in October 1792. Humble and hesitant though that first step was, it surely represented a leap of faith on the part of the dozen or so Midland Baptists who first subscribed to the cause. This voluntary society was the prototype of what came to be known as the Baptist Missionary Society (BMS) by the end of the century.

Unusual Developments

Because times were so hard in Britain during the years after the French Revolution, late 1792 was a rather inauspicious time for "launching out into the deep." So many questions remained to be answered by the infant society, yet Carey forged ahead, declaring: "Expect great things. Attempt great things."[3] Little did they think how they would be overtaken by events. John Thomas, an eccentric, footloose, Baptist medic-cum-evangelist who had spent several years in Bengal, strangely turned up. After some rudimentary screening by the BMS's first leaders, his offer of service was accepted, as was Carey's. Thus by June 1793, after many embarrassing crises, Carey and his family, which included five young children, found themselves setting sail for India in a foreign ship that was engaged in clandestine trade for illegal English interest! "Providence" of a very unusual – even ominous? – sort was at work. Five months later, the largely unprepared mission party managed to slip into Bengal. Then six years of high drama began, in which Carey's wife was tragically driven insane. In order to survive, and to avoid deportation by the East India Company, Carey eventually accepted employment as superintendent of an ill-fated indigo works in the remote interior of Bengal. An "interloping" Dissenter who had recently displayed republican sympathies in Britain was a persona non grata. Thus Carey was under enormous pressure to "bend to the wind." As he did so, the BMS managed to put down its roots and make an impact in history.

During the first decade in Bengal, Carey discovered a surprising range of private enterprise and intellectual activity at work within the expatriate community. Precedents were to be found for almost every activity that his Serampore-based mission would engage in. For the most part, the Serampore Trio harnessed and adapted others' ideas, inventions, and procedures for use in an integrated missionary enterprise. Pragmatic, "Enlightenment" values operated within the framework of evangelical Calvinism, in the era of Britain's industrial and agricultural revolutions, to introduce something quite unusual into the stream of missionary history. Mission perspective thus broadened; but the aim was unchanged: to convert India's people and those who were part of the European occupation.

How different Carey's missionary career would have been had Marshman and Ward not arrived in the tiny Danish "colony," or entrepôt, of Serampore at the end of 1799! Their arrival upset all his mission plans, virtually forcing him to move to the coast, dangerously close to the British-controlled metropolis of Calcutta. However, he was soon to value his new colleagues highly. They rescued him from becoming a solitary missionary hero in contestation with heathen natives after the manner of David Brainerd. They provided the sort of skills needed for the creation of a team that could free him from most mission management and outreach responsibilities.

Here too we must add how much *shalom* was brought to his life by petite Charlotte Rumohr. Six months after his first wife died (1807) in a state of derangement in Serampore, he married this linguistically gifted, Danish lady-of-means whom he had baptized in the Danish enclave in 1802. With her, he enjoyed thirteen years of joy, until she passed away in 1821. Another gracious helpmeet came along two years later in the person of a British widow. Mrs. Grace Hughes had been part of colonial Bengal for many years; she was to survive him. With all their help over three decades, he consequently was able to devote his energies to a sedentary, though extremely demanding, ministry of Bible translation and college tutoring in secluded surroundings. It was a very unusual arrangement for one who was apparently a "mission pioneer," but it reflected the extraordinary and unrepeatable situation that the Serampore Mission managed to take advantage of between 1800 and 1837.

This sheds light on an innocuous-looking comment that Carey made in 1810 in a letter he wrote to Andrew Fuller, the secretary of the BMS in Britain whom he trusted so highly. In it he confessed: "In point of zeal he [Marshman] is Luther; I am Erasmus." This subtly pointed to the modus operandi of the Serampore triumvirate. It corroborates other evidence picturing Carey as a pious, irenic, hard-working, low-key leader who maintained a rather retiring, literary lifestyle, thanks to the complementary labors of two stalwart co-directors, and a large team of pandits. Unlike Marshman, who was an aggressive evangelical, ever ready to contend "up front" for the mission, Carey was a more meditative person who preferred to "sit on the fence" in times of strife. Perhaps that facilitated his surprising appointment by the British governor-general in 1801 to the post of tutor in Bengali – and later to the professorship in Bengali, Sanskrit, and Marathi – in what would now be called the "Civil Service" establishment of Calcutta's Fort William College. The *Enquiry* had never envisaged such a development. Such "subimperial" employment made all the difference to his career as a linguist and translator and dramatically affected his mission's prioritizing.[4] It meant that he functioned as a metropolitan official who never traveled beyond the twelve-mile stretch between Serampore and Calcutta after 1799. For more than thirty years, one of his major tasks was to earn huge amounts of money (many hundreds of thousands of pounds sterling, in today's value) and to secure printing contracts from the government for the Serampore Mission Press. By such means, the Trio sought to make themselves and the evangelization of northern India financially independent of the BMS. At the same time, they made themselves useful enough to Bengal's British rulers that they secured a significant measure of immunity from official opposition.

A Realistic View of Achievements

William Ward, Joshua Marshman, and Hannah Marshman each made a massive contribution to the Serampore Mission, severally running the large printing and publishing press, counseling Christian workers, managing the finances and public relations, developing mission strategy, running a boarding school and many day schools, as well as directing and caring for a large household including many orphans, missionary widows, and servants. Thanks to them, their wives and their protégés, Carey was able to beaver away in his study, being spared the rigors of furlough in Britain when serious disputes with the BMS had to be tackled. In fact, he never did leave Bengal. He went there "for life," and it was from that distant position that he emerged in the public mind as a mission catalyst. He was much more of a mission motivator and Bible translator than a pioneer in the heart of India – or a mission strategist. Thus it was the number of *languages* into which he carried out or superintended (rudimentary) translations of "the Holy Scriptures," rather than the small number of Hindus that he led to Christ, that impressed pre-Victorian and Victorian minds and made him a household name in evangelical circles. Direct evangelistic outreach generally fell into the hands of junior missionaries and people who were rather inaccurately termed "native" brethren by 1805. Much heart-searching was to follow.

In financial, literary, educational, and technological terms, there can be no doubt that Carey and his colleagues made their mark in Asia at the beginning of Protestantism's "modern missionary movement." Many in the Anglo-Saxon world sought to emulate them, and their accomplishments were chronicled religiously by scores of biographers. However, more than a century was to pass before perceptive scholars of Baptist history, such as Ernest A. Payne and Daniel E. Potts, stepped forward to further the business of accurate historical inquiry. Many secular historians did likewise. As a result, the field has been wide open since the 1960s for new investigation into Carey and his partners' lives, times, and work. Thus we turn now to identify some of the contours of his missiological legacy, hoping that interest in the legacies of Marshman and Ward will be revived in the process.

Many questions need to be answered on theological, ideological, cross-cultural, strategic, literary, and leadership aspects of the Serampore Baptists' grand enterprise. For example, one might ask whether it is valid to view Carey's *Enquiry* as a paradigm for his and his colleagues' missionary career. Here the evidence suggests in notable ways that it is very difficult to respond in the affirmative. So often, the triumvirate made decisions at variance with the tentative guidelines set forth in the pamphlet, which was written before Carey ever left the English Midlands. During his lifetime, much more was probably made of his original catalytic watchword – "Expect great things. Attempt great things" – which was later embellished by British Baptists.

It can be argued that the six-word dictum provides criteria that are more appropriate for evaluating the course and outcome of his life and mission. This motto was coined in keeping with postmillennial expectations that God would do great things throughout the world during their lifetime, and in certain respects the BMS men were not disappointed. Carey and his colleagues certainly attempted great things in God's name and were thrilled to see a whole swathe of missionary societies come to life around the turn of the century. But great accomplishments, in Western terms, depended on herculean efforts being made, most often at the expense of almost overwhelming personal cost. Carey's plentiful correspondence bears ample testimony to that. Providence had a way of earthing inclinations to a "theology of grandeur" in lifelong experience of a *theologia crucis*. As a result, Carey had no time for glib enthusiasm. He was too aware of personal and corporate failure – not to mention serious limitations – in many areas of his mission's operation and witness to entertain eulogies or attempts to set him up on a pedestal. A call for biblical realism therefore needs to be taken very seriously by future researchers into the actual scope of his team's achievements, particularly in the cross-cultural sphere.

A Tale of Two Models

There is no need to minimize what Carey and his cohorts achieved in the areas of philology, Bible translation, Orientalism, literacy, education, publishing, technology, relief work, social reform, botany, evangelization, and mission promotion. Our concern is simply to identify the unadorned, demythologized parameters and essentials of their capital-intensive, pre-Victorian missionary enterprise. Thus we turn to consider the two models from which they may be said to have operated: the "primitive" and the "professional."

In the 1790s, Carey began as a lonely pioneer, with little of this world's goods, living to some extent like a "faith missionary" of late Victorian times. He related to the pastoral BMS leaders back in Britain in a cordial, informal, and fairly intimate manner. All that changed as the BMS slowly institutionalized, as his position improved in the governor-general's prestigious college, after he married for the second time, and particularly after the death of Andrew Fuller in 1815. This "paradigm shift" was symbolized, first, by the creation of Serampore College on a grand scale emulating Brown College, Rhode Island, and Fort William College; and second, by the Trio's subsequent dispute with the BMS leadership under John Dyer over property rights and control of the mission estate at Serampore. In the second instance, Carey's team believed they could appeal to (what I have called) the "primitivist" model of relations that they had enjoyed for twenty years while Fuller headed British support. Their fundamental operational, and supposedly financial, "independence" of British direction had been taken for granted then. Such a model was an effective way of carrying out public relations in Britain and North America. For sincere theological reasons, key supporters such as Christopher Anderson (of Edinburgh, Scotland) advocated the Serampore cause by promoting a heroic image of embattled veterans "at the cutting edge" of mission.[5] However, none of those supporters ever managed to visit Bengal; thus they do not appear to have fully realized that Carey's enterprise had become more centralized than ever before. Was it becoming more of a burdensome "monument" than a lively movement? Few, if any, British Baptist leaders were clearly aware that Carey's team operated according to one model at their colonial base and yet appealed by means of another for practical expressions of solidarity from their mother-country. It was as if they functioned in two different worlds. No doubt that helps to explain why Marshman had such a turbulent furlough in England between 1825 and the rupture with the BMS in 1827.

During Carey's last twenty years, tensions increased rather than decreased in the Serampore Mission. Its identity as a Dissenting operation was rather ambiguous at times, and great problems were experienced in trying to accommodate a second generation of mission personnel. Institution-alization of the mission and maintenance of a large establishment resulted in the leaders increasingly losing touch with grassroots Indian life – notwithstanding their huge investment of time in linguistics and translation. Thus they became *sahibs* rather than *sadhus*. Even though they tried to put on a brave face in public, it caused them no end of sorrow that the real number of converts and homegrown churches resulting from decades of their (and their associates') ministry was so low, by many standards. That is why they admitted in an important report in 1817: "relative to the work of conversion in India, perhaps all our expectations have been far wide of the mark."[6] Perhaps they would have had far more indigenous "disciples," perhaps Baptist life in India would have been much more vibrant, perhaps the Serampore Mission would not have collapsed once the last of the veterans died (Marshman in 1837), if the resolute troika had focused on incarnating the Gospel directly in the midst of India's rural society rather than investing so heavily in professional, metropolitan means.

Tradition in the Balance

It is a commonplace that Carey "did more than any other man to awaken the conscience of Protestant Christians to the spiritual need of millions worldwide who had never heard of Jesus Christ."[7] But such a generalization may be far too sweeping. At least it needs to be examined carefully and restated with a sense of historical discrimination. To do this, we need to discover "the historical Carey" beyond the periphery of the Victorian era.

We will consider him as a Victorian and post-Victorian rallying point for Protestant mission shortly. Here, we would return to basics, noting that heroic imagery could be applied to him properly between 1793 and 1799. That imagery stuck to him in the popular mind during the next ten to fifteen years, especially during moments of high enthusiasm in Britain over the dramatic exploits of the Three. Certainly, he had enormous potential for stickability, and for submission to the inscrutable ways of Providence. He rose up the social scale in remarkable fashion in Bengal. In harness with Marshman and Ward, and with the help of scores of employed assistants, he was able to perform wonders, until 1818. Then the building of Serampore College took over, and Ward tragically succumbed to cholera. After that, it was hard going to keep the mission afloat. Strife with the BMS on various fronts sapped away at precious energy and stymied or retarded missiological progress. Then the East India Company got into serious financial difficulties. Thus his old age was a time of tears and strenuous labor to protect his mission enterprise from collapsing.

Some commentators have declared that Carey was "a forerunner whose missionary vision displayed a breadth and boldness which frequently embarrassed his contemporaries and immediate successors."[8] Perhaps that was so. Certainly, he appeared at times to be quite radical, holistic, and ingenious in his efforts to advance "the Redeemer's cause" in southern Asia, in the estimation of British evangelicals. To be sure, he played a major role in diffusing Christian principles throughout the subcontinent, and in encouraging Anglo-Saxon Christians of many denominations to cooperate voluntarily for the sake of propagating the Gospel overseas. But let us not hastily dismiss all the penetrating observations made of the Serampore project by the young British Baptist missioners who parted company from Carey and his colleagues. Of course, much can be said on both sides, but those observers did have a unique opportunity to grasp how the Serampore mission functioned in reality. Their published critiques therefore must be considered as firsthand testimony that has important implications for study of the Trio's legacy.

To obtain the sort of light that will disperse some of the murky mist surrounding Serampore mission history, we would be well advised to tackle questions such as the following: How did India respond to the Western, Christian overtures made to it by Carey and his cohort? Could she distinguish them clearly from the framework and values of British rule? Were India's people pleased to accept "benefits" from the occupiers' "civilization" only so long as they could avoid making way for "the Kingdom of God"? In Carey's day, did Protestant Christianity truly become owned by full-blooded Indians, or was it mostly "Asiatics" (the mestizo offspring of European men and Indian women) who heard the Baptists gladly and then formed churches? It is also worth asking whether the Serampore mission was subverted by the very forces of Western "modernity" and subimperialism that did so much to change the face of India. Such inquiry, of course, must be carried out in further studies.[9] Because of that, we will now draw to a close by focusing on Carey's missiological significance.

Legacy and Legend

From 1826 onward, Carey and his Serampore colleagues receded into the background of British Baptist approval. For a decade or more, official mission promotion referred very little to the lead they had set after 1800, except when funds needed to be raised for Bible translation and publishing. Publications and statements from the Trio's pens – from the 1792 *Enquiry* to the significant 1827 Edinburgh edition of *Thoughts on Propagating Christianity More Effectually among the Heathen* – were allowed to fall by the wayside or were consigned to oblivion.[10] By the 1830s, Serampore College, the crown of their mission, began to look as if it were "a white elephant." Thus we search in vain for evidence that Carey and his partners had much of an explicitly *missiological* impact on North Atlantic mission leaders – except perhaps among Baptists? – during the last two or three quarters of the nineteenth century. Their legacy was of a different kind.

The Baptist Trio in Bengal, and Carey in particular, were transitional figures in "modern missionary history." They paved the way for conservative Dissenters to launch forth into an era of pragmatic, evangelical mission outreach. They represented the meeting of American and British Protestant concerns for evangelizing "the heathen" at a time when missions were promoted only by a very small, zealous minority in the churches. Their cross-cultural evangelistic efforts probably had more in common with Puritan missions in North America than with mainstream Victorian evangelization in Asia. Their methods of Bible translation became a matter of considerable debate in their own day and needed to be overhauled. To be sure, they anticipated some Victorian and post-Victorian missio-theological reflection, but as evangelically reformed Baptists they were far more doctrinaire as Calvinists than were successive missionary generations. Their task was to make the most of the tense time when Britain's role in the East Indies evolved from being purely commercial to fully imperial.

Space does not allow us to reflect further on why Carey and his friends produced but a very small amount of missiological literature, by twentieth-century standards. Their hands were tied up with so many other responsibilities. Their concern was simply to provide basic tools for communicating the Gospel. They were filled with gratitude that the Lord spared their lives to do as much as they did for so long in Bengal, where the life expectancy of Europeans was extremely short. Carey, therefore, would not have stirred from his eternal rest if he had heard his dear friend Christopher Anderson declare in a special memorial sermon in Edinburgh in 1834 that his "labours, however great," were "chiefly preparatory or prospective."[11]

Surprisingly, extremely little has been done to investigate the extent (and nature) of whatever indigenous church growth did actually occur in Carey's mission domain throughout the nineteenth century. Yet many there have been during the last one hundred years or more who have held him high as a universal figure or missionary archetype. Symbols abound for him, as patriarch, apostle, prophet, or pioneer of modern Protestant missions, although some judge it wisest to see him as a convenient figurehead – who could not possibly have represented every aspect of the movement. All this calls for differentiation between "the Carey of tradition" and "the historical Carey." It leads us to identify some of the diverse streams that either converged in his life or came together in the pilgrimage of the Trio.

In Carey we have a person accessible both to the humble poor and the self-made middle-classes of the Anglo-Saxon world. A figure who embodied the ideals, values, and aspirations of British evangelicals during the pre-Victorian phase of their country's imperial history. A Nonconformist and a Dissenter who became a valued member of Britain's political establishments in Bengal. A self-educated young tradesman who rose to become a linguist and Orientalist – even a professor in a prestigious college. A penniless cottager who founded a grand scholarly institution of his own. A shoemaker who married an aristocratic lady. A rustic worker who used bare hands and improvised tools in an English backwater, who became a works foreman in the wilds of Bengal, only to end up at the cutting edge of European technology. A passionate village evangelist who spent precious years translating Hinduism's scriptures into English. Both a specialist and a generalist, he was an individualist and a trusty team-player who operated in creative tension between the poles of what are now labeled pragmatism and dogmatism, liberalism and conservativism, ecumenism and evangelicalism, imperialism and independency. He is revered as a world-oriented "man of vision," albeit from the European "Enlightenment." He was a catalyst extraordinary who operated during an unrepeatable and critical *kairos* in world history.

This was the man who has featured in popular tradition as a marvelous, if not mythical, ideal. A supposedly familiar figure in mission history, about whom much has remained hidden for far too long. One who has become legendary for arousing brave and purposeful notions of "good old days" in the pre-Victorian era. Yet that has happened in spite of the certainty that he would deplore such usage of his name and memory. Thus he would be fully justified if he chose to address us by means of the words of counsel that he and his brethren gave to two young missionaries in 1807. Serampore sent them to Burma on a pioneer, reconnaissance mission, with this sound advice:

> On every subject of research weigh well all you see, all you hear; take up nothing hastily. We are not so sanguine as to hope for satisfactory answers to all these questions . . . [in] a month or two. Get whatever real information you can . . . Satisfactory information on these points will much help . . . the cause to be begun there.[12]

Notes

1. Cf. Dorothy Friesen, *Critical Choices. A Journey with the Filipino People* (Grand Rapids, Mich.: Wm. B. Eerdmans Publishing Co., 1988), p. 106.

2. M. H. Khan, "History of Printing in Bengali Characters up to 1966," London: School of Oriental and African Studies (microfilm copy of a Ph.D. diss.), 1967, vol. 1, p. 218.

3. A. Christopher Smith, "The Spirit and Letter of Carey's Catalytic Watchword," *Baptist Quarterly* 33, no. 5 (January 1990): 226-37.

4. On the creeping capitalist "subimperialism" that occurred in Bengal from 1765, under the aegis of the British East India Company, see P. J. Marshall, *Bengal: The British Bridgehead, Eastern India 1740-1828*, vol. II.2 of *The New Cambridge History of India* (Cambridge: Cambridge Univ. Press, 1987), pp. 70-136. Bengal became "a largely autonomous British-Indian state that was rather loosely connected with imperial Britain and pursued its own purposes of 'safety' and consolidation" until the early 1830s.

5. Cf. A.C. Smith, "The Edinburgh Connection: Between the Serampore Mission and Western Missiology," *Missiology* 18, no. 2 (1990): 185-209. Also see the obituary on Carey by the BMS, in *Periodical Accounts* 9 (1835): 12.

6. On such confessions, see Smith, "The Spirit and Letter of Carey's Catalytic Watchword," pp. 23, 236f.

7. Cf. Brian Stanley, "Winning the World," in [anon.] *Heritage of Freedom*, Tring, England: Lion Publishing, 1984, pp. 78, 83. See Carey's letter "to the Society" from the Bay of Bengal, dated October 17, 1793, in *Periodical Accounts* 1 (1793): 63-64.

8. E.g., Stanley, "Winning the World," p. 81.

9. Such questions are explored in my forthcoming volume entitled *The Mission Enterprise of Carey and His Colleagues*, to be published by Mercer University Press, Macon, Ga.

10. Cf. Ernest A. Payne, "Carey's 'Enquiry,' " *International Review of Mission* 31 (1942): 185-86; and Smith, "Edinburgh Connection,": 185, 190-93, 199-200. The 1827 work was written primarily by Joshua Marshman, although Carey was privy to its contents before its first printing in 1825.

11. Christopher Anderson, "A Discourse Occasioned by the Death of the Rev. William Carey, D.D. of Serampore, Bengal," Edinburgh, 1834, p. 20 (delivered on November 30, 1834). Anderson called Carey "the Father of the Mission" at Serampore. When Carey thought that he himself was dying in 1823, he asked that Psalm 51:1-2 should be taken as the text for his funeral sermon.

12. These "Instructions to the Missionaries Going to Rangoon" were presented to Mardon and Chater in the form of a letter, dated January 13, 1807, signed by the Trio and three new missionary recruits. The quotation is from the last of twenty points drawn up by William Ward. The ms.is to be found in the BMS Archives, Oxford (box IN21) and in the BMS Archives microfilm reel no. 35. [The BMS is to be thanked for granting the present writer permission to quote from items in its archives.] For salutary hints on the dangers of myth-making (applicable to missionary biography), see Os Guinness, *The Gravedigger File* (London: Hodder and Stoughton, 1983), especially pp. 117-20.

Selected Bibliography

An extensive collection of Carey's letters, writings, and publications is now housed in the consolidated Baptist Archives in the Angus Library, Regent's Park College, Oxford. The Baptist Missionary Society Archives for 1792-1914 are otherwise available in microfilm form, published by the Historical Commission of the Southern Baptist Convention, Nashville, Tennessee 37234, USA.

Major Works by William Carey

1792 *An Enquiry into the Obligations of Christians, to Use Means for the Conversion of the Heathens,* in which the religious state of the different nations of the world, the success of former undertakings, and the practicability of further undertakings, are considered. Leicester, England. Further editions: 1818, 1892, 1934, 1961.

1801 *Dialogues Intended to Facilitate the Acquiring of the Bengalee Language.* Serampore (three editions in seventeen years; published in Bengali). Otherwise known as his *Colloquies.*

1800s *Itihasmala* (in Bengali), or *Garland of Stories.* Calcutta. A lively, earthy picture of the manners and notions of Bengali people.

1824 *Dictionary of the Bengali Language* [87,000 words]. Calcutta.

1828 *Letters from the Rev. Dr. Carey* (edited by Joshua Marshman). London. Three editions.

    For a listing of the Bible translations and Scripture portions (into many Indian languages) that he carried out or superintended, see Samuel Pearce Carey, *William Carey,* 8th ed. (London, 1934), p. 426. For the three dictionaries and six grammars he wrote for various Indian languages, see ibid., p. 214.

Works about William Carey

More than thirty biographies were written on Carey between 1836 and 1990, mostly in English, but also in Bengali, Danish, Dutch, German, Swedish, and perhaps other languages. An excellent essay was written on some of the better works in English by Ernest A. Payne some thirty years ago: "Carey and His Biographers," *Baptist Quarterly* 19 (1961): 4-12; see also his "A Postscript," *Baptist Quarterly* 21 (1966): 328-31; cf. 19 (1962): 156.

    Only the most noteworthy accounts and interpretations of his life are mentioned below; penetrating studies that make mention of him in his immediate context are identified elsewhere.

Carey, Eustace. *Memoir of William Carey, D.D.* London, 1836. 2d ed., 1837.

Carey, William Henry. *Oriental Christian Biography.* 3 vols. Calcutta, 1852.

Marshman, John Clark. *The Life and Times of Carey, Marshman, and Ward, Embracing the History of the Serampore Mission.* 2 vols. London, 1859.

Smith, George. *The Life of William Carey – Shoemaker and Missionary.* London, 1885.

Carey, Samuel Pearce. *William Carey, D.D., Fellow of Linnaean Society.* London: Hodder and Stoughton, 1923. 8th ed., 1934, by Carey Press.

Potts, E. Daniel. *British Baptist Missionaries in India, 1793-1837: The History of Serampore and Its Missions.* Cambridge: Cambridge Univ. Press, 1967.

Drewery, Mary. *William Carey: Shoemaker and Missionary.* London: Hodder and Stoughton, 1978.

    Dissertations dealing with Carey are not provided here because they are out-of-date and have been superseded by the works cited above.

Claudius Buchanan

1766–1815

Laying the Foundation for an Indian Church

Wilbert R. Shenk

Claudius Buchanan has been credited with playing the decisive role in opening India to Christian missions in the early years of the nineteenth century.[1] By the twentieth century, however, he was largely forgotten.[2] Never commissioned a missionary himself, Buchanan worked to break down the considerable barriers to missionary work that existed until 1813, and he contributed to the development of institutional infrastructures that would sustain missions. Buchanan is a worthy case study in evangelical activism.

Family and Education

Claudius Buchanan was born March 12, 1766, at Cambuslang, Scotland. His father, Alexander, was the local schoolmaster. His maternal grandfather, Claudius Somers, was an elder of the Cambuslang kirk when George Whitefield preached in the valley in 1742 and the family came under the sway of the Evangelical Revival. He was his grandfather's pride and joy, and the family early marked out Claudius for the ministry. In his teens, however, he turned away from the church. Between 1782 and 1787 he spent three years at the University of Glasgow and then left Scotland. By the time he reached London, he was in dire straits and had to abandon further travel. Eventually, he got work as a clerk in an attorney's office. In 1790 his inner turmoil reached a crisis. His mother wrote, advising that he seek out John Newton, rector of St. Mary Woolnoth. Newton not only led Buchanan to a satisfying spiritual experience but took a great personal interest in him.[3]

Two weeks later Claudius was arrested by the words from Isaiah: "How beautiful are the feet of them that preach the Gospel of peace!" This awakened in him the long-suppressed call to the ministry.[4] At age twenty-four he was beginning to find direction. Newton urged him to prepare for the ministry. As a member of the evangelical circle of movers and shakers, Newton introduced Buchanan to Henry Thornton, who immediately offered to support Buchanan while he pursued theological studies. It was decided that Buchanan should go to Cambridge to secure proper credentials for ministry in the Church of England. The autumn of 1791, at age twenty-five, he entered Queens' College, whose principal was Dr. Isaac Milner, a respected evangelical.

At Cambridge he became one of the "Sims," attending the Sunday evening event Charles Simeon held weekly for earnest students. Simeon also tutored him in public speaking. Because of his age and sense of obligation to Henry Thornton, Buchanan did little else than study. Later he would attribute his chronic poor health to overwork while at Cambridge.

The 1790s were a period of ferment and innovation. The Baptists organized a missionary society in 1792, followed by a string of new societies in Europe, Great Britain, and the United States. When the charter of the East India Company was renewed in 1793, William Wilberforce tried to get Parliament to amend it so as to allow missionaries to enter India. The antimissionary forces deflected this attempt, but the charter did require the company to continue to provide chaplains to the expatriate Indian civil service and military.

During his four years at Cambridge Buchanan corresponded regularly with John Newton. In 1792 he dined with Mr. and Mrs. Charles Grant in Cambridge and heard "various accounts of the apostolic spirit of some missionaries to the Indies."[5] In 1794 Newton pressed on him the possibility of the Indian chaplaincy, still the only legal basis for evangelical work in British India.[6]

A Passion for Mission

Upon graduation from Cambridge in 1795 Buchanan was ordained deacon and became Newton's curate. In early 1796 Charles Grant got Buchanan appointed a chaplain to the East India Company. That summer the bishop of London, Dr. Porteus, ordained Buchanan priest for the chaplaincy. Following a brief visit to his family in Scotland, he sailed for India in August, arriving March 10, 1797, two days before his thirty-first birthday.[7] At Calcutta the senior chaplain, the Reverend David Brown, who had been in India since 1786, received him cordially. The two men worked together harmoniously for the next ten years.

Buchanan was posted to the Barrackpur military garrison, sixteen miles upriver from Calcutta. His next two years were frustrating because the soldiers were totally indifferent to religion. He occupied himself with the study of the Persian and Hindustani languages. "Not knowing what may be the purpose of God concerning me," he wrote, "I have thought it my duty to attend early to the languages of the country."[8] Indeed, this gave impetus to much of his work during his years in India.

In April 1799, he married eighteen-year-old Mary Whish, who had come out to India with her older sister and aunt. She bore two daughters but soon became ill with consumption. On doctor's advice, accompanied by her two daughters, Mary Buchanan sailed for England in January 1805 to seek medical treatment. She died en route in June. The health of Buchanan himself, already at Barrackpur, was a constant concern. In addition to the usual attacks of malaria and dysentery, signs of a heart condition began to show.

Buchanan had come to India as a chaplain, but his passion was missions. Although the East India Company charter barred missionary work, Buchanan and his contemporaries refer freely in their writings to "missions" and "missionaries." His first conversation with William Carey focused on the best missionary approach to the people of India. Carey cautioned against the view of an early wholesale conversion of Hindus to the Christian faith. He said that he was "employed in laying the foundation of future usefulness . . . translating the Bible into the Bengal tongue."[9] In a phrase that was prophetic, Buchanan added: "This like Wickliffe's first translation, may prove 'the father of many versions.' "[10]

At the same time he was sensible of the fact that a less direct approach to evangelization, based on this sober estimate of the prospects, might make it more difficult to enlist support for missions. Buchanan struggled to find a formulation that was both realistic and compelling.[11] As an heir of the Evangelical Revival, he put a premium on wholehearted response to the call of Jesus Christ.[12]

The Buchanan legacy consists of four interlocking roles: promoter of Bible translation and distribution, architect of an ecclesiastical establishment for India, publicist and researcher, and ecumenical statesman.

Promoter of Bible Translation and Distribution

In 1799 Lord Wellesley, the forceful governor-general of the East India Company, appointed Buchanan a chaplain to the presidency, which meant that he moved from his Barrackpur exile to Calcutta. Shortly thereafter Wellesley enlisted Buchanan to draft plans for a college whose main purpose would be to train young Britons for the Indian civil service. This assignment gave full play to a Buchanan characteristic that was to show itself repeatedly: his flare for bold and visionary planning. The new college would offer a complete European curriculum plus the study of the Indian languages, history, customs and manners, Islam and Hinduism, with their respective codes of law. In addition, a department of Bible translation – a feature that must have appeared curious indeed to the Court of Directors in London – was to be established. In Buchanan's words, the object of the college was "to enlighten the Oriental world, to give science, religion, and pure morals to Asia, and to confirm in it the British power and dominion."[13] The College of Fort William opened in August 1800 with David Brown as provost and Claudius Buchanan as vice-provost. Buchanan was also professor of classical languages. By 1801 Brown and Buchanan had persuaded the governor-general to appoint the Baptist William Carey as instructor in Bengali and Sanskrit.

Buchanan took direct responsibility for the Bible translation department from the outset. During the first five years, the translation department worked on projects in five languages. Like the Baptist enterprise at nearby Serampore, this was a veritable translation factory, or "emporium . . . of Eastern Letters." To critics of this approach Buchanan replied in his immensely popular *Christian Researches in Asia:* "We have no hesitation in laying down this position: *the more translations, the better.* Even in their most imperfect state, like Wickliffe's version in a remote age, they will form a basis for gradual improvement by succeeding generations. Besides the very best translation must, in the lapse of ages, change with a changing language, like the leaves of a tree which fall in autumn and are renewed in spring" (p. 131).[14] This rationale contained linguistic insights that were not fully appropriated until the twentieth century.

Buchanan early became aware of limitations under which a self-taught Carey labored, but publicly he spoke of Carey and his associates with respect, crediting them with having revived "the spirit for promoting Christian knowledge, by translations of the Holy Scriptures."[15] Furthermore, he defended this "factory" approach as viable because the missionary was not the actual translator. This approach could be followed only when it was a team effort, and "it is to be understood, that the *natives* themselves are properly the translators" (p. 129), while the missionary supervised.[16] Of course, neither the missionary nor the native-speaker at that time had the tools of linguistic science, and much of the work of that generation has not stood up well.[17]

Buchanan shared the Serampore enthusiasm for producing as many translations in as many languages as possible. This tactic was buttressed by his almost boundless confidence in the power of the Christian Scriptures to "witness" to people, if only they were given access (see p. 70).

In 1806 the Court of Directors in London ordered the college curtailed, and the department of Bible translation was closed. Brown and Buchanan had seen this coming and arranged to have the various language projects taken over by missionary societies. Meanwhile the British and Foreign Bible Society (BFBS), founded in 1804, began providing support to groups like the Serampore Mission. At this time Buchanan's erstwhile cordial relations with the Baptists were breached when he took decisions without consultation and proposed a British "Propaganda" that would have put them under control of the established church.[18] Unsurprisingly, the Serampore Mission rejected the proposal out of hand.

Ecclesiastical Architect

In 1800 Church of England canon law had no provision for the extension of the church to territories beyond British political jurisdiction. This was fully consistent with a Christendom concept, which defined the church territorially as coextensive with the state rather than missionally.

Before Claudius Buchanan left for India in 1796, Bishop Porteus discussed with him the need for an ecclesiastical arrangement for India. In 1805 Buchanan submitted to Porteus a detailed proposal entitled *Memoir of the Expediency of an Ecclesiastical Establishment for India: both as the means of perpetuating the Christian religion among our own countrymen; and as a foundation for the ultimate civilizing of the natives,* a document that ran to 176 printed pages. The subtitle accurately states the thesis: the pastoral care of British subjects resident in India as well as the evangelization of the Indian peoples required a full-fledged ecclesiastical structure.

It is beyond our purposes here to discuss details of Buchanan's proposal. A few summary observations will suffice. First, Buchanan accurately anticipated future needs of the Anglican Church in India, and his aide-mémoire set the stage for the appointment of the first bishop for India in 1814. Second, he was sailing in stormy waters as far as his mission theory was concerned. The Church Missionary Society was founded in 1799 on the *church* principle rather than the High Church principle. Anglican evangelicals rejected the notion that a bishop should lead each mission, but the High Church view was similar to the Catholic. This long remained a contentious issue. Third, Buchanan was typical of evangelicals in his firm commitment to maintain the "church as by law established." Fourth, this means that Buchanan's rationale called for transplanting Christendom to India, even while he enthusiastically promoted vernacular translations and study of vernacular languages and cultures that would eventually lead to its breakup.[19]

Buchanan's proposal was received enthusiastically in London, and in 1806 the archbishop of Canterbury sounded out Buchanan concerning his willingness to be consecrated as the first bishop for India. This honor and responsibility he declined because of his own precarious health. In 1806 Buchanan had been so ill he expected to die and had made arrangements with David Brown for his funeral and the administration of estate.

Publicist and Researcher

If one were to single out Buchanan's most important contribution to the cause of missions in his time, it would undoubtedly be that of publicist. He both wrote and found ways of stimulating others to write in support of the cause of missions. Pearson summarized Buchanan's interests succinctly: "Publicity and inquiry were therefore his great objects."[20] Buchanan was always intent on awakening the British public to "the duty and the opportunity of promoting the moral and political welfare of our fellow subjects in India."[21] To do this required fresh and accurate information, and he had a journalist's feel for issues.

In 1803, with the backing of Lord Wellesley, Buchanan proposed a prize competition to the universities of Oxford, Cambridge, Edinburgh, Glasgow, Aberdeen, St. Andrews, and Trinity College, Dublin, for essays on "the best means of extending the blessing of civilization and true religion among the sixty millions, inhabitants of Hindostan, subject to British authority."[22] Buchanan paid out more than £1,650 from his personal resources in prizes during the several years of the competition. More than twenty of these prize essays and poems were published.

In recognition of Buchanan's work the University of Glasgow in 1805 conferred on him the degree of doctor in divinity. In March 1806 the governor-general authorized a leave of absence so that Buchanan could engage in research. From Fort William College, Brown and Buchanan had corresponded with people throughout India and elsewhere in Asia soliciting information about religious and social conditions, but they found that the reports were often contradictory. This convinced them that reliable information needed to be assembled. They wanted to know the state of Christianity and of other religions. In addition, Buchanan was eager to take an inventory of scriptures of various religions in the vernacular languages.

In spite of his precarious health, Buchanan traveled by elephant and horse overland from Calcutta to Madras, and then by ship as far as Cape Comorin. On a second trip he went to Malabar and Travancore, and he visited Ceylon three times. He experienced firsthand the importance of on-site observation. Buchanan visited major Hindu temples along his route, including the great Juggernaut in Orissa, and Protestant, Roman Catholic, and Syrian churches. He also made special inquiry into the Jewish communities in Asia. Wherever he went, he gathered samples of whatever scriptures were available in the various languages.

Buchanan's findings were published in 1811 as *Christian Researches in Asia*. The book was an immediate success. It went through twelve editions in two years and was republished as late as 1858.[23] In it he gave graphic accounts of Hindu religious ceremonies and brought to the attention of Christians in the West the existence of the ancient Syrian churches. Particularly compelling was the account of his visit to the dreaded inquisition at Goa, which he visited when en route to Great Britain in January 1808.[24]

His return to Great Britain opened a new phase in Buchanan's career as promoter of missions. He was in demand as a speaker and writer. His sermon "The Star in the East," preached in February 1809, went through repeated printings and aroused wide interest. As a speaker, Buchanan was solid but not flamboyant. Cambridge University made him a doctor in divinity in 1809 and appointed him to preach the two commencement sermons that year. In the appendix to his Cambridge sermons he made a vigorous statement about the importance of an "increased cultivation of the female mind" (p. 59, also p. 154), stimulated by what he observed of the status of women in Asian society. Buchanan is thus one of the earliest advocates for increased scope for women in ministry.

Those who had been involved in the 1793 campaign to amend the East India Company charter to allow missions to enter India knew their next opportunity would come in 1813. In connection with the successful antislave trade campaign in 1807 evangelicals had forged an effective system for enlisting public support for their causes in Parliament.[25] The basic instrument was the public petition signed by thousands of citizens. Publicity based on authoritative information was essential. Buchanan's ten years in India, his extensive knowledge growing out of his firsthand observations, and his ability to formulate ideas in accessible form made him an important ally in this new campaign. Unfortunately, every step he took was dogged by his declining health.

William Wilberforce tried to protect Buchanan from too much direct public exposure, which led to inevitable personal attacks, but he relied heavily on *Christian Researches* and other Buchanan pamphlets for his information as he led the fight to change the company charter. In 1813 Parliament did change the charter to allow missionaries to work in British India and to allow the founding of an ecclesiastical establishment. Without Buchanan's research, writing, and bold proposals, the outcome might have been as it was in 1793.

Ecumenical Statesman

The crisis in 1806 caused by the Court of Directors' order to curtail operations at Fort William College threatened the Bible translations scheme so dear to Brown, Buchanan, their Serampore colleagues, and others. Faced with demand either to close down or take an alternative route, Buchanan and Brown chose an alternative. Now that the centralized approach they had promoted through Fort William College had to be abandoned, they hived off the various language projects to denominational mission bodies: Society for Promoting Christian Knowledge, Baptists, Lutherans, Scottish, and Roman Catholics. The main criterion seemed to be a commitment to producing Bible translations in the vernaculars.[26] Always the promoter, Buchanan, with Brown's collaboration, wrote an appeal for financial support that went to potential subscribers in Great Britain and Asia. And he proposed expansion of Bible translation into still other Asian languages. To some extent the difficulties he had run into with the Baptists over his "propaganda" proposal were mitigated by his continuing efforts on their behalf in the Bible cause.

Reference has already been made to Buchanan's visits to the Syrian Christians at Malabar. These churches traced their origins to the Apostle Thomas. In the sixteenth century Catholic missionaries encountered the Malabar churches and took steps to incorporate them into the Roman Catholic Church. A minority of some 40,000 Syrians refused to accept the authority of the Roman pope. This was the group Buchanan met in 1807.[27] He easily established rapport with Metropolitan Dionysius, who agreed that a translation of the Bible into Malayalam, the language of the people, was urgently needed.[28] As a token of friendship, the metropolitan gave Buchanan an old manuscript copy of the Syrian Bible, which he later deposited in the Cambridge University library. Buchanan also broached the sensitive subject of possible relationship between the Syrians and the Anglicans.

Buchanan himself did little more in relation to the Syrian Church than to assist them with their Bible translation project. But the way in which he publicized the Syrians in India through *Christian Researches* created a precedent. At the time of his death Buchanan was planning a trip to the Middle East for the purpose of visiting the ancient churches there. As a result Anglican missions from that time showed a sympathetic interest in the historic churches in Ethiopia, Egypt, the Arabian peninsula, and Persia, on the basis of Buchanan's contention that these ancient churches had the potential to evangelize their own people much more effectively than could foreigners,[29] provided they were revived and purified. This would be done by making the Scriptures widely available in the vernaculars and by providing adequate theological training. Later it became apparent that Buchanan did not have an adequate grasp of the history and tradition of the Syrians and, consequently, was misled in some of his conclusions. Yet he showed exemplary sensitivity in insisting that the starting point in such a relationship is one of mutual respect and patient listening to one another.[30]

Buchanan's Last Years

After Buchanan returned to Great Britain in 1808, he hoped he might sufficiently recover his health to return to India. Alas, his health did not improve, and he decided he must give up any thought of going out to India again. In 1810 he met and married Mary Thompson. Within the next three years two sons were born to them, neither of whom lived; Mary died in 1813.

In 1811 Buchanan suffered the first of several strokes, which left him partially paralyzed. Never flagging in his passion, he continued to write on behalf of the opening of India to missions and to plan a visit to the Middle East.

In January 1815 he attended the funeral of Henry Thornton in London. On February 9 Buchanan died, a month before his forty-ninth birthday, and was buried in Yorkshire beside his second wife. He was survived by daughters Charlotte and Augusta. At the time of his death he was reading the proofs for the Syriac New Testament, which he spent several years editing and preparing for the printer.[31]

Notes

1. This is Stock's judgment (*History of the Church Missionary Society*, 1:97), which may seem overdrawn; but see Neill's appreciation (*History*, p. 256).

2. I have not been able to consult A.K. Davidson's Aberdeen Ph.D. dissertation, "The Development and Influence of the British Missionary Movement's Attitudes Towards India, 1786-1813" (1973), which studies Buchanan's role as publicist in particular.

3. Buchanan read Newton's *Life* at this time and saw in Newton's wasted youth a parallel with his own.

4. "It occurred to me, that that enviable office was once designed for *me*; that I was called to the ministry, as it were, from my infancy. For my pious grandfather chose me from among my mother's children to live with himself. He adopted me as his own child, and took great pleasure in forming my young mind to the love of God" (Pearson, *Memoirs*, 1:33).

5. Ibid., p. 77. Since at least 1787, schemes had been put forward for establishing missions to India for the purpose of evangelizing the whole population. Charles Grant, along with William Chambers, George Udny, and David Brown, in 1787 circulated "A Proposal for Establishing a Protestant Mission in Bengal and Behar." Charles Hole noted: "The claim which the natives had upon the British Government was forcibly set forth" (*Early History*, p. 7). The proposal called for eight missionaries and various projects to translate the Scriptures into the vernacular languages.

6. The standard gloss on this account is that Buchanan got to India because of Simeon's influence (see Stock, *History;* Hole, *Early History;* Gibbs, *Anglican Church*). But see Smith, *Conversion of India*, p. 107. Pearson indicates John Newton was his "father in God."

7. Neill incorrectly reports that Buchanan reached India just before his thirtieth birthday (*History*, p. 256).

8. Pearson, *Memoirs*, 1:148. Cf. the description of Carey's work routine once he settled at Malda in 1794: "His time was systematically apportioned to the management of the factory, the study of the language, the translation of the New Testament and addresses to the heathen" (Marshman, *Life and Times*, p. 69). Carey and Buchanan assumed language study and Bible translation to be foundational.

9. Later Buchanan reported of Carey: "He considers himself sowing a seed, which haply may grow up and bear fruit. He is prosecuting his translation of the Scriptures" (Pearson, *Memoirs*, 1:184).

10. Ibid., p. 164.

11. When word came of the disastrous beginning of the London Missionary Society venture in Tahiti, Buchanan commented: "I hope this South Seas scheme will not discourage the missionary societies. They have done no harm: and if they send out their next mission with less carnal éclat, and more Moravian diffidence, they may perhaps do more good" (ibid., p. 183).

12. Buchanan wrote to a friend: "Nothing great since the beginning of the world has been done, it is said, without enthusiasm" (ibid., p. 165).

13. Ibid., p. 368.

14. All page citations in the text are from the 1812 London eighth edition of *Christian Researches*, which includes Buchanan's Cambridge commencement sermons.

15. In 1799 Buchanan reported: "I explained to him [i.e., Carey], from sources with which he seemed unacquainted, the plan and progress of the Tamulian Scriptures, and the circumstances attending the publication" (Pearson, *Memoirs*, 1:184). Henry Martyn arrived on the scene in 1806 and soon expressed serious reservations about the quality of translations produced at Serampore (Potts, *British Baptist Missionaries*, p. 54).

16. One can conjecture that this point about collaboration, which Buchanan makes so strongly, was largely lost sight of because of the pressures on the missions system to raise financial support, which, it was assumed, could be done only by keeping the missionary central to the operation. But this resulted in a distorted view that reinforced Western domination and falsified the whole story (see Sanneh, *Translating the Message*). Buchanan maintained this collaborative view of translation rather consistently. In the Introduction to *Christian Researches* he identifies the principal "Oriental" translators for the versions then recently published (p. 2). His views on the importance of such collaboration are expressed in a letter (Pearson, *Memoirs*, pp. 254-55).

17. Hooper and Culshaw, *Bible Translation*, pp. 15-20; Smalley, *Translation as Mission*, pp. 47-50.

18. Potts, *British Baptist Missionaries*, pp. 54-55; Owen, *History*, p. 99; Buchanan, *An Apology*, p. 67 n.

19. Pearson, *Memoirs*, 1:310, 366ff.

20. Ibid., p. 281.

21. Ibid.

22. Ibid., p. 280.

23. Stock, *History*, 1:216.

24. See Priolkar, *Goa Inquisition*.

25. See Howse, *Saints in Politics*.

26. Whether Buchanan was conversant with the basis of the new BFBS in unclear. This inclusive view of the work of Bible translation was consonant with that advocated by John Owen in the inaugural meeting and made the basis of the society (Canton, *History*, pp. 12-19).

27. Buchanan, *Christian Researches* (9th ed.), pp. 99-135; Neill, *History,* pp. 238-39.

28. Canton, *History,* p. 279.

29. Stock, *History,* 1:222-23, 232; Mathew and Thomas, *Indian Churches,* pp. 44-73.

30. This same stance has been adopted in the twentieth century by certain missions that have collaborated with African Independent Churches without any attempt to incorporate the AIC into a Western denominational structure.

31. Canton, *History,* p. 295.

Selected Bibliography

Works by Claudius Buchanan

1805 *Memoir of the Expediency of an Ecclesiastical Establishment for India; both as the means of perpetuating the Christian religion among our own countrymen; and as a foundation for the ultimate civilizing of the natives.* London.

1805 *The First Four Years of the College of Fort William in Bengal.* Calcutta and London. Reprinted, London, 1810.

1807 *An Apology for Promoting Christianity in India.* London. 2nd ed., 1813.

1809 *The Star in the East; a sermon preached in the Parish Church of St. James, Bristol, February 26, 1809, on the author's return from India.* London.

1810 *The Light of the World; a sermon preached at the Parish Church of St. Anne, Blackfriars, London, June 12, 1810, before the society for missions to Africa and the East.* London.

1810 *The Three Eras of Light; two discourses preached before the University of Cambridge, on Commencement Sunday, July 1st, 1810.* London.

1811 *Christian Researches in Asia.* London. Several printings appeared in 1811, including the second edition enlarged; 1811 (Boston 2d ed., enlarged with Melvill Horne's sermon of June 4, 1811); 1812 (London, 8th ed., with two sermons preached at Cambridge); 1812 (Edinburgh, 3rd ed.); 1819 (11th ed.); 1840 (new ed.); 1849; 1858 (new ed. prepared by Rev. W.H. Foy).

1811 *Two Discourses preached before the University of Cambridge, July 1, 1810. And a sermon preached before the Society for Missions to Africa and the East, June 12, 1810. To which are added Christian Researches in Asia.* London. 5th ed., 1812.

1811 *The Healing Waters of Bethesda; a sermon preached at Buxton Wells, June 2nd, 1811.* London.

1812 *Eight Sermons.* London.

1812 *Sermons on Interesting Subjects.* (London.)

1812 *The Works of the Rev. Claudius Buchanan . . . Comprising his Christian Researches in Asia . . . His Memoir on the Expediency of An Ecclesiastical Establishment for British India, and his Star in the East, with three new sermons.* New York.

1812 *Collation of an Indian Copy of the Hebrew Pentateuch, with preliminary remarks: containing an exact description of the manuscript, and a notice of some other (Hebrew and Syriac), collected by the Rev. Claudius Buchanan, D.D., in the year 1806, and now deposited in the public library, Cambridge; also a collation and description of a MS. Roll of the Book of Esther; and the Megillah of Ahasuerus, from the Hebrew copy, originally extant in Brazen Tablets at Goa, on the Malabar Coast.* With an English translation, by Thomas Yeates, late of the University of Oxford. Cambridge.

1813 *Colonial Ecclesiastical Establishment: being a brief view of the state of the colonies of Great Britain and of her Asiatic empire in respect of religious instructions. To which is added, A sketch of an Ecclesiastical Establishment for British India.* London.

1814 An Address delivered before the Church Missionary Society for Africa and the East (Revd Messrs Scharre and Rhenius . . . missionaries to the Coast of Coromandel). London.

Works about Claudius Buchanan

Pearson, Hugh N. *Memoir of Rev. Claudius Buchanan, D.D. In Some Parts Abridged, and Enlarged from Dr. Buchanan's "Christian Researches in Asia."* New York: American Tract Society, n.d.

_____. *Memoirs of the Life and Writings of the Rev. Claudius Buchanan, D.D., late vice-provost of the College of Fort William in Bengal.* 2 vols. Oxford Univ. Press, 1817.

Other Works Cited

Canton, William. *The History of the British and Foreign Bible Society.* Vol. 1. London: John Murray, 1904.

Davidson, A. K. "The Development and Influence of the British Missionary Movement's Attitudes Toward India, 1786-1813." Ph.D. diss., Aberdeen University, 1973. This work now published as *Evangelicals and Attitudes to India 1786-1813: Missionary Publicity and Claudius Buchanan*. Abingdon, Oxford: Sutton Courtenay Press, 1990.

Gibbs, M.E. *The Anglican Church of India, 1600-1970*. Delhi: ISPCK, 1972.

Hole, Charles. *The Early History of the Church Missionary Society*. London: Church Missionary Society, 1896.

Hooper, J.S.M., and W.M. Culshaw. *Bible Translation in India, Pakistan, and Ceylon*. London: Oxford Univ. Press, 1963.

Howse, Ernest Marshall. *Saints in Politics: The "Clapham Sect" and the Growth of Freedom*. London: George Allen and Unwin, 1952; repr. 1971.

Marshman, John C. *The Life and Times of Carey, Marshman, and Ward*. Vol. 1. London: Longman, Brown, Green, Longman and Roberts, 1859.

Mathew, C.P., and M.M. Thomas. *The Indian Churches of Saint Thomas*. Delhi: ISPCK, 1967.

Neill, Stephen. *A History of Christianity in India, 1706-1858*. Cambridge: Cambridge Univ. Press, 1985.

Owen, John. *The History of the Origin and First Ten Years of the British and Foreign Bible Society*. London, 1816.

Potts, E. Daniel. *British Baptist Missionaries in India, 1793-1837. The History of Serampore and Its Missions*. Cambridge: Cambridge Univ. Press, 1967.

Priolkar, Anant Kakba. *The Goa Inquisition: Being a Quartercentenary Commemoration Study of the Inquisition in India*. Bombay, 1961.

Sanneh, Lamin. *Translating the Message: The Missionary Impact on Culture*. Maryknoll, N.Y.: Orbis Books, 1989.

Smalley, William A. *Translation as Mission*. Macon, Ga.: Mercer Univ. Press, 1991.

Smith, George. *The Conversion of India: From Pantaenus to the Present Time, A.D. 193-1893*. London: John Murray, 1893.

Stock, Eugene. *History of the Church Missionary Society: Its Environment, Its Men and Its Work*. London: Church Missionary Society, 1899-1916.

Henry Martyn

1781–1812

Scholarship in the Service of Mission

Clinton Bennett

Henry Martyn, says the *Oxford Dictionary of the Christian Church* and the *Dictionary of National Biography,* was a "missionary." Samuel Zwemer, Temple Gairdner, and numerous other writers also refer to Martyn as a "missionary." Frequently, he is called "the pioneer Protestant missionary to Muslims" or even "the first modern missionary" to Islam.

Technically, however, Martyn was not a missionary; he was neither sent to India by a missionary society nor commissioned by his church for missionary work. This raises the question whether his legacy should be included in this volume. The present writer believes it is correct to include Martyn's legacy, since undoubtedly he was a missionary in terms of his self-understanding and modus operandi.

Himself influenced by missionaries, especially by David Brainerd (1718-47) and William Carey (1761-1834), Martyn in turn influenced countless others, too numerous to mention, and, as Eugene Stock wrote in the *History of the Church Missionary Society:*

> Though his name does not actually honour the CMS roll of missionaries, it is a recollection to be cherished that he was really the society's first English candidate; and though his career was brief, and he was never technically a missionary, yet his un-reserved devotion to Christ's cause and the influence of his name and character upon succeeding generations, entitle him to be forever regarded as in reality one of the greatest missionaries.[1]

Having offered himself to the Church Missionary Society (CMS), Martyn was unable to proceed as a candidate because the sudden loss of his patrimony left his sister, Sally, dependent on him. This made it impossible for him to accept "the subsistence allowance of a missionary."[2] Instead, he accepted the post of chaplain in the East India Company's service – a post secured for him by Charles Grant (1746-1823), the influential, evangelical East India Company director who believed it his duty to "improve" the moral and spiritual welfare of India. He began by recruiting chaplains of higher caliber than the majority, who devoted more time to acquiring money than they did to the "cure of souls." Martyn gratefully accepted the appointment, though he would have been "infinitely better pleased to have gone out as a missionary, as poor as the Lord and his apostles."[3] He saw his task in India as primarily to further the cause of Christian mission. He recorded in his journal, "Walked by moonlight, reflecting on the mission . . . even if I never should see a native converted, God may design, by my patience and continuance in the work, to encourage future missionaries."[4]

The following appraisal of Martyn's legacy will outline his life and career, and then examine four areas in which Martyn's missionary thinking, strategy, and method are particularly noteworthy.

Childhood

Henry Martyn was born February 18, 1781, in Truro, Cornwall, where his father, John – an amateur mathematician and a former tin miner – had gained promotion as head clerk of a Truro merchant house. Henry, who suffered from tuberculosis from infancy, attended Truro Grammar School, from where he entered St. John's College, Cambridge, in 1797, after applying unsuccessfully to Corpus Christi, Oxford. At St. John's he had the advantage of following his friend John Kempthorne (1775-1838), whose graduation as Senior Wrangler in 1797 had already set Martyn a goal to emulate. It was at Cambridge, too, that Charles Simeon (1759-1836), fellow of King's and vicar of Holy Trinity, was leading the Evangelical Revival within the Church of England, much stimulated by the theology of the Wesley brothers, whose Methodists now formed a corporate body distinct from the Established Church. In Cornwall, where the Wesleys had numerous followers, Sally Martyn had already experienced a spiritual awakening, and she encouraged her brother to give thought to his own spiritual condition. Shortly, he joined her in expressing deep Christian conviction. Their correspondence from this period suggests Methodist influence; a group meeting for Bible study was termed a "society," while private devotions were a "secret duty."[5] Indeed, at Cambridge, anyone who took religion seriously was nicknamed a "a Methodist" whether they were followers of the Wesleys or not. By far the greatest influence, however, was Charles Simeon, whose church Martyn regularly attended from 1799.

At Cambridge

Martyn excelled as a student, gaining his B.A. as Senior Wrangler and First Smith's Prizeman in 1801, a College Fellowship, and the Member's prize for a Latin Essay in 1802, his M.A. in 1804, and his B.D. in 1805. It was obvious to his seniors that a brilliant teaching career (or perhaps a legal career – he planned to read for the bar) lay ahead. Indeed, Henry himself had, initially, no intention of taking a different course. He wrote, "I could not consent to be poor for Christ's sake."[6] However, Simeon, who was already scouting for evangelical chaplains for his friend, Charles Grant, and who was also involved in organizing the then embryonic Church Missionary Society, encouraged Martyn to think seriously about entering the ministry. In 1803, he finally accepted Simeon's offer of a curacy and was ordained deacon at Ely Cathedral.

By 1804, Martyn had read Jonathan Edward's *Life of David Brainerd* and Carey's *Periodical Accounts* and reached the conclusion that God was calling him to the work of overseas mission. Against the advice of his teachers, who "thought it a most improper step for him to leave the University to preach to ignorant heathen, which any person might do," he offered himself to the CMS as their first English candidate.[7] The circumstances already referred to above conspired to prevent this, and he sailed as a company chaplain instead. On his final visit to Truro, he was excluded from the pulpit of his home parish because of his "Methodist contamination." Other pulpits, though, welcomed him. He also left behind a sweetheart, Lydia Grenfell, with whom he corresponded regularly during his time in India.

In Calcutta

After a 305-day voyage, Martyn reached Calcutta in April 1806. He was welcomed, not by the senior Anglican chaplains – David Brown (1763-1812) and Claudius Buchanan (1766-1815), who were out of town – but by the Baptist, William Carey. They breakfasted together, and prayed, *in*

Bengali! Martyn had used the voyage to study his Bengali, Urdu, Persian, and Arabic grammars. For several months, he impatiently awaited appointment to an inland chaplaincy. He wanted to be stationed "at one of the great centers of Indian population," since he regarded ministry to Indians as well as to company personnel as integral to the job he had come to do.[8]

Meanwhile, he continued his language study and regularly visited the Baptists at Serampore, where he began to assist in the work of Bible translation. Stephen Neill has commented that Martyn's approach differed from that of the older, self-taught men. Martyn, he says, set himself "a standard of scholarship beyond their reach" and was sometimes critical of them.[9] Nonetheless, Carey reported, "We take sweet counsel together and go to the house of God as friends." He added that wherever Martyn went "the church need not send a missionary," and there is no evidence of a breach in their relationship.[10] Perhaps ironically, once in India (where missionaries were not legally allowed until 1813), Martyn found some advantage in being a chaplain. He wrote that "a missionary not in the service is liable to be stopped by every subaltern but there is no man who can touch me."[11]

As Chaplain

Subsequently, Martyn was stationed in Dinapore (from October 1806 to 1809), followed by Cawnpore (1809-1810). Previously, he had thought Hinduism his best field of endeavor. "I feel," he wrote as early as 1804, "the utmost encouragement and even desire to go and preach to the Hindus. My talents seem to me to be peculiarly suited to them."[12] In Calcutta, when he thought that his first posting would be to Varanasi, he wrote, "God will employ me to strike at the heart of Hinduism; may the Lord make bare his holy arm, and cause his worm to behold the downfall of Satan."[13]

But almost immediately after his arrival in Dinapore he began his Urdu translation of the Bible, assisted by a Muslim convert to Christianity, Nathaniel Sabat, with whose help he also embarked on Persian and Arabic versions. He began to read "everything I can pick up about the Mohammedans."[14] He sought out the Muslim ulama, whom he engaged in discussion and debate.

At Cawnpore, he translated the Book of Common Prayer into Urdu. His health, however, quickly declined and after just four full years in India he was granted unlimited leave of absence. In requesting leave, he had two purposes in mind. He intended to return to England to persuade Lydia Grenfell to return with him as his wife; and en route he proposed to visit Arabia and Iran, whose drier climates he thought might improve his health. There, he wanted to test the Persian and Arabic translations and, if possible, to gain for the former the shah's own commendation. Thomas Thomason (1774-1829), formerly Martyn's co-curate at Holy Trinity and now a company chaplain, wrote to Simeon: "He is on his way to Arabia, in pursuit of health and knowledge. You know his genius, and what gigantic strides he takes in everything. He has some great plan in his mind of which I am not competent to judge [but it is] much beyond his feeble and exhausted frame. In all other respects, he is the same as he was; he shines in all the dignity of love, and seems to carry about him such a heavenly majesty as impress the mind beyond description."[15] Sick, but as ambitious as ever, Martyn set sail, visiting Bombay and Goa and Muscat en route, as far as Bushire acting as chaplain of the ship *Benares*.

In Arabia, Persia, and Turkey

At Bushire, Martyn showed his Persian and Arabic translations to local scholars, who approved of the Persian but thought the Arabic defective. Then began Martyn's arduous and difficult journey through Iran, first to Shiraz, where his friend Sir John Malcolm (1769-1837) had commended him to the governor, then on to Tehran, where he was unsuccessful in gaining an audience with the shah.

It was at Shiraz that he wrote his *Controversial Tracts,* in reply to Muslim scholars (Mirza Ibrahim, "preceptor of all the Mullahs," and Muhammad Ruza Ibn Muhammad Amin of Hamadan) with whom he was invited to debate. There, too, he revised the Persian translation, since scholars there reversed the earlier opinion, rating the Arabic version higher than the Persian. It was at Teheran that, remarkably (or perhaps, miraculously), he survived the vizier's challenge to recite the Kalimah, and instead recited, "God is God and Jesus is the Son of God." It is impossible to tell whether the volatile crowd, which yelled "God is neither begotten nor begets," was held back by fear of reprisal or because they were impressed by Martyn's courage.[16] Certainly, there is evidence that Muslims, especially Sufis, recognized in Martyn a "spiritual drunkenness" and a piety (Thomason's "heavenly majesty") that led them to dub him "merdi Khodai" (a man of God).[17]

Next, Martyn visited Sir Gore Ouseley (1779-1844), the British ambassador at Tabriz, who, fearing confrontation if Martyn presented the translation to the shah, did so himself. It was well received: "In truth," said the shah, "through the learned and unremitted exertions of the Reverend Henry Martyn, it has been translated in a style most befitting sacred books, that is in an easy and simple dictum . . . The whole of the New Testament is complete in a most excellent manner, a source of pleasure to our enlightened and august mind."[18] The translation was subsequently published at St. Petersburg under Ouseley's personal supervision (1815) and at Calcutta (1816).

Martyn, now racked by tuberculosis, turned toward Istanbul en route for home. He survived as far as Tokat, where he died on October 16, 1812, and was buried by Armenian clergy, of whose "ancient and desolate church he was always a lover."[19] He had indeed "burned himself out for God," fulfilling the pledge he had made on first reaching India.[20] That example alone has inspired many to devote their lives to missionary service, and numerous books, both popular and scholarly (including at least one novel), have been written about him.

However, Martyn's legacy consists of much more than the inspirational value of his life.

Ecumenical Collaboration

Martyn's approach to mission was never narrowly sectarian. He knew that when he faced a Muslim he did so primarily not as an Anglican but as a believer in the Lord Jesus Christ. Also, in addition to his early collaboration with the Baptists, he regularly communicated, in Latin, with the Fathers of the Propaganda Fide and "more than once . . . protected the [Catholic] priests at Patna from the persecution of the military authorities." Biographer George Smith observes (1892), "At the beginning of this century, Anglican, Baptist and Romanist missionaries all over the East co-operated with each other in translation work and social intercourse."[21] Visiting Goa, Martyn commented, "Perhaps many of these poor people, with all the incumberances of Popery, are moving towards the Kingdom of God."[22] He also developed what proved to be a vital friendship with the Armenians, whose Calcutta clergy commended him to their brethren in Persia, whose patriarch he visited at Etchmiadzin, whose churches he visited at Teheran, and whose clergy finally honored him with the burial rite normally reserved for an archbishop.

Martyn and many of his colleagues, who formed what was known as "The Associated Clergy" to facilitate exchange of news and research, knew that rivalry between churches could only damage the cause of Christian mission. As mission to Islam developed, ecumenical collaboration became an important priority. When in 1906, Protestant missionaries to Muslims gathered at Cairo to think and plan together, their ecumenical impulse testified to the continuing power of Martyn's legacy.

Enlightened Attitude

Although the British in India displayed some respect for Indian institutions, the general attitude was one of disdain and superiority. Martyn quickly became aware of this: "They seem to hate to see me associating at all with the natives."[23] His Cambridge friend and biographer, John Sargent (1780-1833), wrote that if Martyn "so much as spoke to a native, it was enough to create wonder and alarm."[24] He soon earned the nickname "The Black Clergyman" because he received Indians in his home.[25] "Our Countrymen," Martyn wrote, "when speaking of the natives said . . . that they cannot be converted and, if they could, they would be worse than they are." He observed how annoyed the general in charge at Dinapore was because he dared to suggest that Indians "were not all fools, and that ingenuity and clearness of reasoning were not confined to England and Europe."[26]

It is indeed a tribute to Martyn that when attitudes toward Indians were becoming increasingly negative, he rejected that view. Arguably, Martyn, like Carey, went to India early enough to be free from the later, more imperialistic attitudes from which subsequent missionaries found it difficult to disassociate themselves. While mission historians are correct to censure those missionaries who devalued other cultures and imposed European culture, they can also argue, based on Martyn's legacy, among others, that imperialistic attitudes are neither inevitable nor intrinsic to the missionary mind-set.

Missionary Scholarship

Martyn qualifies as an early exemplar of a "missionary scholar." Although he sailed for India "without having first read a single word of the Koran, even in its English dress," he soon realized that knowledge of Islam was as necessary as knowledge of Christianity.[27] Nor was he too proud to confess his ignorance. As late as 1811, while en route to Iran, he recorded in his journal, "Making extracts from Maracci's Refutation of the Koran. Felt much shame at being obliged to confess much ignorance of many things which I ought to know."[28] Hearing of a book being written in Cambridge for Muslims, he wrote (1812), "Let it not go to press until it has been approved by men who know the East and know eastern ways of seeing, imagining and reasoning."[29] This emphasis on scholarship, on the need to study Islam, its history, authoritative texts, faith and practice, was later echoed by many who succeeded him as missionaries to Muslims. Perhaps many still rushed in with too little preparation, but Martyn's early example can be said to have contributed directly to an ongoing tradition of missionary scholarship. His *Tracts* were edited in 1824 by Samuel Lee (1782-1852) who, as a professor at Cambridge (1819-31) and at the CMS College (from 1825), did much to promote the training and orientation of missionaries.

Missionary Method

Martyn pioneered several models of missionary work. He was, for example, an early advocate of education, not in exchange for "conversion" but as an expression of Christian concern for the total person. He established a school at Dinapore in which he eschewed proselytization: "I told them that what they understand by making people Christians was not my intention. I wished children to be taught to fear God and to become good men."[30]

However, he is best remembered for his use of "controversy," especially in his *Controversial Tracts.* In these, he rehearsed all the old arguments against Islam: Muhammad was foretold by no prophet, worked no miracles, spread his religion by means utterly human, framed his precepts to gratify human sensuality.[31] This confrontational method was taken up by, among others, Karl Pfander (1803-65), whose work, says Christian Troll, "sowed the seeds of enmity and hatred in the hearts of Indian Muslims" who "started to suspect the missionary efforts of the Christians as a plot to destroy Islam." Since Martyn was one of Pfander's role models, his legacy here must, sadly, be recognized as having contributed to fostering Muslim animosity, a fact he would himself regret, because although he employed controversy, he had serious reservations about his effectiveness. This is suggested by his conclusion to his second *Tract:* "If you [Muslim ulama] do not see the evidence to be sufficient, my prayer is that God may guide you so that you, who have been a guide to men in the way you thought right, may now both see the truth, and call men to God through Jesus Christ."[32] This represents Martyn's real position; he knew that argument and debate would not win converts. They are won by God's love, when human souls are touched by that love.

In one journal entry he commented, "How impossible it is to convince the people of the world, whether Christian or Mohammedan, that what they call religion is merely an invention of their own, having no connection with God."[33] Consequently, though he thought that debate could usefully "entice a spirit of enquiry," he did not lay "much stress upon clear argument; the work of God," he said, "is seldom wrought in this way."[34]

A Soul-Centered Approach

Instead, Martyn preferred "personal talks" with "a small circle of interested Muslims," which he believed could produce "mutually responsive notes."[35] "Zeal in making proselytes they are used to," he wrote, "but a tender concern manifested for their souls is certainly new to them, and seemingly produces corresponding seriousness in their minds."[36] Martyn, writes Christian Troll, "saw it as his main endeavor to share the religious experiences of the forgiveness and peace of God attained through Jesus Christ. He purposefully set out to appreciate whatever was best in his Muslim acquaintances and ascribed such to the activity of God." He also knew (hence his single-minded approach) that the task of witnessing to Muslims was time-demanding and best pursued within the context of genuine friendship. Thus "he insisted on the need for fostering lasting friendships with the enquirer."[37]

How, then, did he regard Islam? There are frequent references in his work to Muhammad as an "imposter" and to Islam as Satan's child. Undoubtedly, this accurately represents his estimate of Islam. However, he believed that God could touch Muslims' souls despite Islam; therefore he revered and respected Muslims for the souls within them. He tried to see beyond a person's religion to the soul's spiritual condition. Also, like Carey, he thought Indian literature (and in his case, Persian, which he had admired from his Cambridge days) to be of at least "human interest." He saw profit in trying to understand not only the languages "but also the thought-world of those to whom the Gospel is preached."[38]

Though sometimes obscured by his *Controversial Tracts*, this soul-centered approach represents Martyn's most positive contribution to missionary method. In his *Tracts*, he identified an important stumbling block between Christians and Muslims – disagreement about "the genuineness and integrity of the Christian scriptures,"[39] which again suggests that "book based" approaches are of limited value; only when soul meets soul can progress be hoped for. Some of his successors, Thomas Valpy French (1825-1891) among them,[40] expressed a similar respect for Muslim souls and regarded them less as opponents to be defeated, more as "souls" to be won.

Conclusion

In addition, therefore, to the inspirational value of Martyn's life, his legacy in the areas of ecumenical collaboration, respect for Indian culture, scholarship, and missionary method, warrants him a place in mission annals as one whose life and work anticipated some of the best aspects of missionary endeavor as that enterprise developed in the years following Martyn's own premature death.

Notes

1. Eugene Stock, *History of the Church Missionary Society* (London: CMS, 1899), p. 82.
2. Constance Padwick, *Henry Martyn: Confessor of the Faith* (London: Student Christian Movement, 1922; rev. 1953), p. 56.
3. Ibid., p. 61.
4. J. Sargent, *Memoir of the Rev. Henry Martyn, BD* (London: J. Hatchard & Son, 1819), p. 177, citing Martyn's Journal, April 30, 1806.
5. Padwick, *Henry Martyn*, p. 35.
6. Ibid., p. 43.
7. Ibid., p. 51.
8. Ibid., p. 87.

9. Stephen Neill, *A History of Christian Missions* (London: Hodder and Stoughton, 1964), p. 266.

10. Cited by G. Smith, *Henry Martyn* (London: Religious Tract Society, 1892), pp. iv-v.

11. Ibid., p. 241.

12. S. Wilberforce, ed., *Journals and Letters of Henry Martyn* (London: R.B. Seeley and W. Burnside, 1837), 1:163. Wilberforce omits passages cited by Sargent.

13. Ibid., p. 478.

14. Padwick, *Henry Martyn*, p. 106.

15. Ibid., p. 128.

16. See Martyn's own account in Wilberforce, *Journals and Letters*, 2:450-52.

17. Smith, *Henry Martyn*, p. 373.

18. Padwick, *Henry Martyn*, p. 158.

19. Ibid., p. 152.

20. Wilberforce, *Journal and Letters*, 1:447 (May 17, 1806).

21. Smith, *Henry Martyn*, pp. 218-19.

22. Ibid., p. 318, and see Wilberforce, *Journals and Letters*, 2:86: "All the RC priests are lawful ministers, according to the word of God" (July 6, 1807).

23. Wilberforce, *Journals and Letters*, 2:1.

24. Sargent, *Henry Martyn*, p. 231.

25. Padwick, *Henry Martyn*, p. 98.

26. Ibid., p. 95.

27. Sargent, *Henry Martyn*, pp. 177, 225.

28. Wilberforce, *Journals and Letters*, 2:331.

29. Padwick, *Henry Martyn*, p. 159.

30. Wilberforce, *Journals and letters*, 2:30.

31. See summary in Sargent, *Henry Martyn*, pp. 388-89.

32. S. Lee, ed., *Controversial Tracts* (Cambridge: J. Smith, 1824), p. 123.

33. Smith, *Henry Martyn*, p. 412.

34. Wilberforce, *Journals and Letters*, 2:55 (April 28, 1807). See also 2:57: "I am preparing for assault of this great Mohammedan Imaun. I have read the Koran and notes twice for this purpose . . . but alas! What little hope have I of doing him or any of them good in this way" (May 4, 1807).

35. Christian Troll, *Christian Muslim Relations in India: A Critical Survey* (Bangalore: Association for Islamic Studies, 1980), p. 9.

36. Wilberforce, *Journal and Letters*, 2:46, letter to Associated Clergy, April 6, 1807.

37. Troll, *Christian Muslim Relations in India*, p. 9.

38. Neill, *A History of Christian Missions*, p. 264.

39. Smith, *Henry Martyn*, p. 416: "All controversy, from St. Xavier's time to Martyn's, Wilson and Pfander's shows that the key of the position is not the doctrine of the Trinity . . . but the genuiness and integrity of the scriptures."

40. See Samuel W. Zwemer, *Arabia: The Cradle of Islam* (New York: Fleming H. Revell, 1900), p. 357, citing French: "In memory of Henry Martyn's pleadings for Arabia . . . I seem . . . to follow more directly in his footsteps and under his guidance."

Selected Bibliography

Works by Henry Martyn

1824 *Controversial Tracts on Christianity and Mohammedanism.* Ed. Samuel Lee. Cambridge: J. Smith.
1837 *Journals and Letters.* Ed. S. Wilberforce. London: R.B. Seeley and W. Burnside.

Works about Henry Martyn

Butler, Howard T. *The Life and Work of Henry Martyn.* Madras: Christian Literature Society, 1921.
Frame, Hugh F. *Temperature 126!* London: Edinburgh House Press, 1937.
Padwick, Constance. *Henry Martyn: Confessor of the Faith.* London: IVF, 1922; revised 1953.
Page, Jesse. *Henry Martyn of India and Persia.* London: Pickering & Inglis, 1930.
Sargent, John. *Memoir of The Revd Henry Martyn BD.* London: J. Hatchard & Son, 1819.
Smith, George. *Henry Martyn.* London: Religious Tract Society, 1892.

Alexander Duff

1806–1878

Western Education as Preparation for the Gospel

Michael A. Laird

Alexander Duff was born at Moulin in the Perthshire Highlands of Scotland on April 25, 1806; his father was a tenant farmer and a fervent evangelical. He attended Perth grammar school and then proceeded to the University of St. Andrews, where he completed both the general and the divinity courses, and was greatly impressed by the teaching of Thomas Chalmers. He married Anne Scott Drysdale in 1829, shortly before setting out for India. He died on February 12, 1878, at Sidmouth in Devon, England.

Duff is best known for his work in establishing the system of Christian higher education in India, which had a major influence both on missionary policy and on the general development of education in that country. But before analyzing his work in India, one should say a little about his place in the modern Scottish missionary movement.

The Church of Scotland did not begin to undertake overseas missions until the mid-1820s, about a generation after the outburst of missionary activity that marked the start of the modern missionary movement in England. From the outset, however, the Scots laid a particular emphasis on education, as can be seen in the recommendations of Dr. John Inglis, the first convener of the church's foreign missions committee and more than any other individual the founder of the mission, in 1825-26. This special concern with education was in part a reflection of the Scottish situation at that time – it was much more widely available than in England; partly, also, a result of the insistence of the dominant moderate party in the church, to which Inglis belonged, that education – Western education – would be a *praeparatio evangelica:* that Indians who received it would be more receptive to the Gospel. Duff was an evangelical, but he emphatically shared this view, and indeed the successful establishment of the Indian mission was considerably due to the willingness of moderates and evangelicals to cooperate in the enterprise.[1]

"Pioneer" of Christian Education in India

On his arrival in Calcutta in 1830, Duff initially devoted all his energies to establishing and building up one school. His concentration of effort is noteworthy: the missionaries of the various English societies who had been working in the area since the 1790s had undertaken vernacular preaching, the preparation of tracts, the translation of the Scriptures, and other activities besides education; and in that department they had not concentrated on one school but had established a large number, which they had found difficult to supervise. Duff's policy of concentration was one reason for the greater success of his educational effort; but before assessing its significance one should note that he was not, strictly speaking, a pioneer: the English missionaries had already experimented in their schools with the main features of the policy with which he is particularly associated. They had all sought to combine Christian teaching with a broad range of secular subjects; they had recognized the importance of the English language for education, also of training Indian teachers and missionaries; and they were anxious to teach in such a way as to awaken the intellectual potential of their students. Indeed for a few years they had apparently attained a considerable degree of success; but by 1830, for a variety of reasons, the educational work of the English societies had declined, and there was some doubt among their missionaries as to its value. Duff's role was therefore not that of the pioneer; what he did was to approach the question of education with new energy, skill, and vision, which was rewarded with rapid and unprecedented success, with the result that the importance of education for missions in India was never seriously in doubt subsequently.

The school that Duff founded in 1830 developed eventually into the Scottish Church College of the present day; the college department was established at the end of the first decade, and in due course this was affiliated to Calcutta University. Almost from the start it had a broad curriculum, including in particular a wide range of science subjects; but of even more fundamental importance was the Christian religious teaching. Duff saw Hinduism as the root of India's problems, but he was hardly less implacably opposed to Western secularism, in which by the time of his arrival a group of young educated Bengalis was becoming interested. Duff's overriding concern was to present the claims of Christianity as the alternative to both of these, at the intellectual as well as the spiritual level. In his school Christianity was not simply one subject to be taught among others, it was an influence that permeated its whole life and work. The daily routine started with prayer, and parts of the Bible were read and explained every day in the higher classes; Duff regarded science as "the record and interpretation of God's visible handiworks" and expected that it would help to confirm the truth of Christianity and undermine Hinduism; he adjured a new missionary recruit to the staff to convert "every fact, every event, every truth, every discovery, into a means, and an occasion of illustrating or corroborating sacred verities."[2] One of his pupils, Lal Behari Day, commented that in fact "there was an interpenetration, or rather a chemical union, of the religious element with the whole system of teaching."[3] And it certainly had its effect on the pupils. There were relatively few actual converts, but many came to take a sympathetic interest in Christianity and a critical attitude toward at least the traditional forms of Hinduism. In addition to Christian teaching within his school, Duff gave public lectures on Christianity, which were attended by young men from other institutions.

As a graduate of the University of St. Andrews and pupil of Thomas Chalmers, Duff was better qualified to present this kind of challenge to Hinduism and secularism than the English missionaries, whose educational attainments had been somewhat modest – though this reflected the relatively limited scope in England as compared with Scotland for higher education for those not of upper- or affluent-middle-class parentage, rather than a lack of potential. Some of the English Baptists, in particular, had become major Oriental scholars despite their lack of formal education. But Duff aimed high socially as well as intellectually. He wrote: "It was our studied endeavor to court the society of those natives belonging to the more wealthy, influential, and learned classes."[4] In terms of caste, Brahmins constituted a quarter to a third of the pupils in his school. This kind of proportion had indeed been found in some of the English missionaries' schools before 1830, but probably only the Serampore Baptists, in the rather different circumstances of the first quarter of the century, equaled the impact that Duff made on the leadership of Bengali society. His desire to maximize it also explains his disregard of part of the initial instructions of the Church of Scotland's missions committee, that he should establish his school outside Calcutta. Duff quickly realized that the city was the focus of the intellectual and social life of Bengal, and therefore the appropriate center for his work.

An important reason for the rapid success of Duff's school was his concern for good educational method; indeed, he adopted a very professional approach to his work. Again, he was not the first missionary to show an awareness of its importance, but the English missionaries in the generation before him had placed what proved to be excessive faith in the monitorial system, which enjoyed a great vogue in early nineteenth-century England, before its limitations became clear. Duff's model, however, was the Edinburgh sessional school, from about 1820 under the direction of the educational reformer John Wood. In contrast to the traditional system of rote-learning, he stressed the vital importance of engaging the interest and understanding of the pupil in his studies, and Duff applied this principle to his school in Calcutta. Lal Behari Day subsequently recalled that Duff "did communicate knowledge; but before communicating, he brought out of his pupils whatever knowledge they had by a process of close questioning, subjected that knowledge to the crucible of investigation, and thus purified it, and last of all, added to its stores." Through this system, "The ideas of the pupils were enlarged; their power of thinking was developed; they were encouraged to observe; they were taught to express their ideas in words; and as learning was made pleasant to them, their affections were drawn towards the acquisition of learning."[5] Elsewhere Day makes it clear that in the classroom Duff could be not only stimulating but entertaining; in fact it is clear that he was an excellent teacher. His own talents in this respect were supplemented by those of his missionary colleagues in the school, notably W.S. Mackay, David Ewart, and Thomas Smith; and he also devoted considerable attention to the training of Indian teachers. And Duff's concern for a good and well-balanced education was not limited to the classroom; he made provision for the boys to take regular exercise and play games, and the annual examination of 1844 was enlivened by a gymnastics display. Duff seems to have been the first to introduce this kind of activity into schools in Bengal. One may discern here the influence of David Stow, another Scottish educational reformer whose ideas had impressed Duff.

Duff is, however, remembered above all perhaps for the impetus that he gave to English education in India. In his school this involved first teaching the boys English, then using it as the medium for an education in contemporary British learning, religious, scientific, and – though more selectively – literary. Duff was a leading protagonist of English because he saw it as by far the most suitable means for his ultimate aim, the Christianizing of India. Much of contemporary British learning and culture was steeped in Christian ideas; indeed, Duff argued, "in the very act of acquiring English, the mind, in grasping the import of *new terms,* is perpetually brought in contact with the *new ideas,* the *new truths,* . . . so that, by the time that the language has been mastered, the student must be *tenfold* less the child of Pantheism, idolatry and superstition than before."[6] Indians, he complained, were not impressed by the "evidences" invoked by the missionaries of that period in support of the claims of the Gospel, and the most promising solution to the problem was in effect to Anglicize their patterns of thinking, their basic terms of reference: then they would understand. Duff thus provided a powerful restatement of the concept of Western education as a *praeparatio evangelica.*

Duff supported his insistence of English-language education with the negative arguments that the only alternatives – the local vernacular and Sanskrit – were both impracticable, though for different reasons. Bengali, he argued, was not sufficiently developed for use as the medium of higher education. Duff, himself a Highlander who had had an English education, compared its role to that of Gaelic in the Scottish Highlands. As for Sanskrit, it was inseparably associated with Hinduism – that "stupendous system of error."[7] And he was fortunate in that his arrival in Calcutta in 1830 coincided with a growing movement in favor of English among Indians, the other missionaries, and government officials. By then small but influential groups of Indians, including the young radical secularists and an older group led by reformer Ram Mohan Roy, were strongly in favor of English education. They had a genuine interest in British culture, which they believed would help to regenerate India from what they saw as its "medieval" backwardness, combined with a recognition of its growing value as a qualification for employment by private firms and above all in government service. The English missionaries had hitherto used the vernacular as the medium in their schools, while the Serampore Baptists had at first laid particular stress on Sanskrit in the college that they had founded in 1818; but by the end of the 1820s they were all showing signs of a new appreciation of the importance of English. And the government, which until then had given its patronage primarily to institutions of a traditional Oriental pattern, in 1835 took the momentous step of decreeing that henceforth its funds should be devoted to English education. This decision was reinforced by others, which in effect made English the official language of British India. Duff's enthusiasm for English education was thus aptly timed. But he did not merely swim with the tide: he made important contributions to the development of the new policy in the period of controversy that preceded its adoption. The example of his school, as an English-medium institution that attained rapid success, was one of the factors that influenced Bentinck's administration to make the change of 1835 – and not only for general education but also for the establishment of an English-medium medical college in Calcutta.

The success of Duff's methods in fact earned him an extraordinary prestige within a very few years of his arrival in Calcutta, all the more remarkable as he was only twenty-four in 1830, and he went into a situation where missionaries and government had been wrestling with the problems of education for a generation and more. After some initial criticism, other missionaries, particularly of the London and the Church Missionary societies, hastened to establish English schools or reorganize their existing educational work on the lines of the General Assembly's institution. And Duff's influence was by no means confined to Bengal: his example was important in persuading his fellow Scot John Wilson to establish an English school in Bombay in 1832 – indeed it was crucial, as Wilson showed no interest in English education and little enthusiasm for schools of any kind before he started receiving reports of Duff's success. Duff's example was therefore significant for the establishment of the institution that was to develop into the celebrated Wilson College, Bombay.[8] Other ways in which Duff's influence spread was through his former pupils' going out to teach in missionary and government schools throughout India.

Duff's Legacy Evaluated

Duff made further contributions to the general development of education policy in India, most notably in that *magna carta* of the system known as Wood's Despatch (1854).[9] Among the proposals for which he argued and which were adopted was the principle of grants-in-aid by government for all schools, by whomsoever conducted, which provided a good education as attested by government inspectors. This education was to be essentially in Western learning, through the medium of English and the vernaculars – by this time Duff's original concentration on English education for an elite had been complemented by a recognition of the importance of vernacular elementary education for the mass of the population. Duff did not entirely have his way when it came to religious education, however. While he conceded the principle of government neutrality in its oversight of education, he proposed voluntary Bible classes for government schools and colleges, which the government, however, felt would compromise that neutrality. But on the need to establish universities his views were in accord with government's, and when the University of Calcutta was founded in 1857 Duff played an active role in its development prior to his final departure from India in 1863.

Duff was above all a missionary *educationist,* and his main legacy was the network of Christian colleges, using English as their medium and combining Christian religious teaching with a wide range of secular subjects, which by the end of the nineteenth century were to be found in every part of the Indian subcontinent. Although not strictly the pioneer, it was he probably more than any other individual who ensured that the missions would play a major role in the secondary and higher education of India. The result of this endeavor was not, as he had hoped and expected, a mass of converts into the visible church, followed by the collapse of Hinduism – though his converts did include several noteworthy individuals whose careers had a significance beyond their actual number. What mainly occurred was a considerable permeation of the Indian intelligentsia with Christian values and attitudes, not only through the intellectual encounter with Christianity that took place in the colleges but through the innumerable personal contacts with Christian staff members who in a variety of ways made an impression on their students. One should also not forget the part that the Christian colleges played, together with other institutions of higher education, in familiarizing Indians with general Western (especially British) concepts and institutions – for example, parliamentary democracy and nationalism,[10] with such momentous consequences for the modern history of the country.

Having said this, one must also note that certain aspects of Duff's policy came to be regarded very critically by subsequent generations. In the first place, he not only shared to the full the attitude of wholesale condemnation of the non-Christian religions that virtually all missionaries at that period expressed, but he had none of the scholarly interest in Indian culture that some of them – especially the Serampore Baptists and John Wilson – nevertheless displayed. Although Duff allowed Sanskrit and Persian to be taught in his school, and agreed that they must have a place in the University of Calcutta, his insistence that Western learning was superior and Eastern inferior – indeed intrinsically pernicious – was no help toward the necessary synthesis of the two cultures, and as far as the Indian church was concerned contributed to the sense of alienation from its Indian environment that was subsequently felt to be a major problem. Related to this was his overstressing of the importance of English, particularly in his early years. Although he subsequently admitted the educational value of the vernaculars, at least for elementary education, his initial dismissal of them – at a time when promising efforts were being made by others to develop them – must have contributed to keeping them in a relatively lowly position for a long period. And these criticisms were not made only with the benefit of years of hindsight; Duff was trenchantly criticized in the mid-1830s by, among others, John Wilson and John Clark Marshman of Serampore. Wilson criticized, among other things, Duff's policy on language and went on to work out a relationship between English, Sanskrit, and the vernaculars that recognized the value and significance of each. Marshman provided a radical critique of Duff's argument for the virtual necessity of an intellectual Anglicization to facilitate conversion; he both denied the necessity and pointed out that if it was carried through, Indians would become "unnaturalised in their own country."[11] At one level, therefore, Duff may be seen as a heroic figure who revitalized missionary education in India; at another, as one whose very success bequeathed a somewhat ambiguous legacy to India and its church.

Notes

1. This article is largely based on the author's *Missionaries and Education in Bengal, 1793-1837* (London: Clarendon Press, 1972), esp. chapters 7 and 8.

2. A. Duff, *Missions the Chief End of the Christian Church;* also, *The Qualifications, Duties, and Trials of an Indian Missionary* (Edinburgh: J. Johnstone, 1839), pp. 86-87.

3. L.B. Day, *Recollections of Alexander Duff, D.D., LL.D.* (London: T. Nelson, 1879), p. 125.

4. A. Duff, *India, and India Missions* (Edinburgh: J. Johnstone, 1839), pp. 500-501.

5. Day, *Recollections,* pp. 120-22.

6. Duff, *India and India Missions,* p. 520.

7. Ibid., p. 519.

8. M.A. Laird, "John Wilson: Aspects of His Educational Work," paper contributed to the Sixth European Conference on Modern South Asian Studies, Paris, 1978, in *Asie du Sud: Traditions et Changements* (Paris: Editions du Centre Nationale de la Recherche Scientifique, 1979).

9. R.J. Moore, "The Composition of 'Wood's Education Despatch,' " *English Historical Review* 80 (January 1965); A. Duff, "Brief Memorandum on the Subject of Government Education in India," Edinburgh, Jan. 25, 1854, India Office Records MSS. Eur. F.78/25.

10. D.B. Forrester, "Christianity and Early Indian Nationalism," Sixth European Conference, Paris, 1978, in *Asie du Sud: Traditions et Changements.* Professor Forrester shows that the missionaries made a peculiar contribution to the development of a sense of nationalism in India by arguing that only Christianity could provide a proper foundation for it.

11. *The Friend of India,* Serampore, Dec. 3, 1835.

Selected Bibliography

Works by Alexander Duff

A large number of Duff's addresses etc. were published. Following is a selection of the more important ones.

1835 *The Church of Scotland's India Missions; or, a Brief Exposition of the Principles on Which That Mission Has Been Conducted in Calcutta, Being the Substance of an Address Delivered Before the General Assembly of the Church, 25 May 1835.* Edinburgh.

1836 *The Church of Scotland's Mission to India.* Edinburgh.

1837 *New Era of the English Language and English Literature in India; or, an Exposition of the Late Governor-General of India's Last Act.* Edinburgh.

1837 *Speech Delivered in Exeter Hall, 3 May 1837.* Edinburgh.

1837 *A Vindication of the Church of Scotland's India Mission: Being the Substance of an Address Delivered Before the General Assembly of the Church, 24 May 1837.* Edinburgh.

1839 *Farewell Address, on the Subject of the Church of Scotland's India Missions; Being the Substance of a Speech Delivered Before the General Assembly of the Church, 23 May 1839.* Edinburgh.

1839 *Female Education in India: An Address.* Edinburgh.

1840 *Bombay in April 1840, with Special Reference to the Church of Scotland's Mission There.* Edinburgh.

1843 *The Cause of Christ and the Cause of Satan: An Address at the First Meeting for Public Worship in Connexion with the Free Protesting Church of Scotland.* London.

1848 *The Jesuits: Their Origin and Order, Morality and Practices, Suppression and Restoration.* Edinburgh.

1851 *India and Its Evangelization.* London.

1858 *The Indian Rebellion: Its Causes and Results.* London.

1866 *Foreign Missions.* Edinburgh.

Works about Alexander Duff

Duff, W.P. *Memoirs of Alexander Duff.* London: Nisbet Co., 1890.

Paton, W. *Alexander Duff.* London: SVM, 1923.

Smith, G. *The Life of Alexander Duff, D.D., L.D.* 2 vols. London: Hodder & Stoughton, 1879.

Smith, T. *Alexander Duff, D.D., L.D.* London: Hodder & Stoughton, 1883.

Thomas Valpy French

1825–1891

Intrepid Adventurer for Christ among Muslims

Vivienne Stacey

F ew seem to have heard of this self-effacing man, Thomas Valpy French. However, Bishop Stephen Neill described him as the most distinguished missionary who has ever served the Church Missionary Society (CMS).[1] For those concerned with communicating the Gospel to Muslims, his legacy is especially precious.

The Life of French (1825-1891)

Thomas Valpy French was born on New Year's Day 1825, the first child of an evangelical Anglican clergyman, Peter French, who worked in the English Midlands town of Burton-on-Trent for forty-seven years. In those days before the Industrial Revolution, Burton-on-Trent was a small county town. Thomas liked walking with his father to the surrounding villages where Peter French inspected church schools. Visiting missionaries stimulated Thomas's interest in other lands and, together with his four brothers and two sisters, he learned to pray for them. Thomas was sent to Rugby, one of England's most famous boarding schools, where Dr. Arnold, the distinguished educationalist, was headmaster. Thomas was better at his studies than at sport. He took teasing good-naturedly and helped his classfellows with their Latin homework. After Arnold's death, Dr. Tait became headmaster. Tait as archbishop of Canterbury later consecrated Thomas French after his appointment as the first Anglican bishop of Lahore.

Thomas won a scholarship to University College, Oxford, in 1843. He gained a first-class degree in classics. Two years later he won the Chancellor's Prize for a Latin essay and also obtained a fellowship in his own college. He was ordained deacon, becoming curate to his father in Burton. In 1849 he was ordained to the priesthood. During the university term he used to help at St. Ebbe's Church in Oxford, while in the vacations he worked with his father.

Both parents shared their deep faith with their children and taught them of the Savior whom they loved and served. One decisive spiritual influence on Thomas was the death of his eighteen-year-old younger brother Peter. Later one of Thomas's fellow students wrote that nobody would have predicted that the quiet scholar, undoubtedly clever and able, would one day develop into the heroic and apostolic character that he became. His aloofness and seriousness were perhaps an unconscious forecast of that devotion, which carried him through so many risks and ordeals to a death that resembled that of his hero Henry Martyn. In a way he was too serious, finding it hard to relax.

H.W. Fox, pioneer of the Telugu Mission in South India, urged Thomas French to come to India. French's growing influence at Oxford University and the staffing needs of the Church of England at home held him back, but Fox's premature death in 1848 made him rethink the question. An address by Bishop Samuel Wilberforce clinched the matter. French and his friend Arthur Lea talked and prayed together and dedicated themselves for service abroad. Soon after this Lea was fatally injured in a railway accident. Their mutual decision bound French even more and he applied to the CMS.

There was one other matter to be resolved before he and his companion, Edward Stuart, sailed in 1850 for India. Thomas was attracted to M.A. Janson, daughter of Alfred Janson of Oxford. Twice her parents refused permission to Thomas to pursue his suit even by correspondence. According to the custom of the day, he accepted this, though very reluctantly.[2] Then suddenly Alfred Janson withdrew his objections and Thomas was welcomed by the family. He became engaged to the young woman shortly before he sailed.[3] A year later she sailed to India to be married to him. Throughout his life, she was a strong, quiet support to him. The health and educational needs of their eight children sometimes necessitated long periods of separation for the parents.

French's Five Pioneer Works

Along with Edward Stuart, CMS appointed Thomas French to found an educational institution for the upper classes in the northern Indian city of Agra. Accordingly they established St. John's College in 1851. However busy he was with his administration and teaching duties, French always found time for evangelistic tours in the district around Agra.

French's next pioneer effort was the founding, with Robert Bruce, of the Derajat Mission in what is now the North-West Frontier Province of Pakistan. This new work included Dera Ismail Khan and Bannu. Sir Robert Montgomery, an able Christian administrator in India, wrote: "We are now at peace with all the tribes. Now is the time to hold out the hand of friendship and to offer through the missionaries the bread of life . . . I rejoice to see missions spreading." Inspired by Christian government officers who also contributed generous financial and prayer backing, the Derajat Mission got underway in 1862. French first visited Bannu that year but there was no resident missionary until 1873 when Rev. T. Mayer arrived. French's health could not stand the rigors of this new work and he was soon compelled to return to England to recover his health. Some thought that he would never be able to return to India. Some years later, speaking of this work, he wrote: "I felt a pang of deep regret at being withdrawn from that work. It has been begun in great weakness, but prayerfully, and on scriptural principles. None can say how important a bearing its future may have on the entrance of the light of the glorious gospel of Christ into the regions of Central Asia."[4] Since French's pioneer efforts the work continued at Bannu and Dera Ismail Khan and in other, newer centers, although always hampered by lack of personnel.

French's third pioneer work was the founding of St. John's Divinity School, Lahore, for the training of men for the ministry and as workers in secular spheres. He taught there for several years. Then in 1877 when the Diocese of Lahore was created out of the Diocese of Calcutta, French was chosen as its first bishop. In fact he was the first missionary to become a bishop in the subcontinent. This appointment gave him many opportunities of adventuring with God. In being approved by the queen, the secretary of state for India, and the archbishop of Canterbury, French was the appointee of the British Raj and had to resign from the CMS. He had the warm support of many individual Christian soldiers and administrators as well as mission leaders. A new diocese could develop new patterns; here lay the hopes for the emergence of an Indian church in which Christians of all races could join. French had his responsibilities to the British troops, to the government and the establishment, but he was above all an evangelist and church planter – a "missionary bishop" in the widest sense of those words. French has left us four volumes of sermons. They are biblically based and not too long. However, one senses that French was better as a personal evangelist than as a public preacher. He was a scholar-bishop with the heart of an evangelist. His method was conventional.

Founding and establishing a new diocese was French's fourth pioneer work, but ten years later, in 1887, broken in health and having found a suitable successor, he resigned his bishopric and retired to England. However, when in 1891 CMS appealed for volunteers for Arabia and no one responded, Bishop French, at the age of sixty-six, volunteered. He wrote to his successor in Lahore: "My present object countenanced by CMS, but timidly and indecisively, is to spend a few weeks or months at Muscat and the adjoining parts to discover and report upon present openings and possibilities of entrance for our missions." French thus entered on the fifth and last phase of his colorful career. After three months he died of exhaustion and fever at Muscat and lies buried on the seashore in a cove near Muscat in the Sultanate of Oman. On his tombstone is inscribed: "Thomas Valpy French, First Bishop of Lahore and First Missionary to Muscat." Then follow the words of John 12:24 in English and in Arabic.

French's Legacy: Lessons from His Life

Knowledge of Indian Languages, Indian Literature, and Islam

French from the outset was keen to learn local languages so that he could communicate freely. He spoke seven Indian languages and was known as "the seven-tongued man." He was not entirely academic in his approach to language-learning. One of his uncles questioned whether his preoccupation with evangelism did not hinder his language study. He replied: "I always spend from three to four hours in the direct study of the language daily, besides what I gain in teaching others and in conversation in the bazaars. It is essential for a thorough knowledge of the languages that they should be learned in this practical way."[5] He appreciated the wide range and wealth of Indian literature – unlike many of his contemporaries. He wrote: "Is it more profitable to Christianity . . . that this store should be thrown away as valueless for the purpose of Gospel extension?" He quoted Micah 4:13: "I will consecrate their gain unto the Lord, and their substance unto the Lord of the whole earth," and asked, "Is the wealth of India's literary treasures less available, less capable of consecration to the highest and holiest purposes than the merchant spoil of Tyre? . . . Is not the attempt to use it for the Lord's service worth making?"[6]

French was well versed in Muslim religious literature and in Islam. He declared: "I was reading a hymn of theirs a few days ago, in which were abasing confessions of sin but the meaning of the last stanza was, whatever our shortcomings, we have this to fall back upon, we are ahl-i-Islam [Muslims]."[7] During the first phase of his career he engaged in public debate. Such debate between Muslim and Christian religious leaders may not be popular or appropriate today, but in the 1850s Karl Gottlieb Pfander, a German missionary then serving under the CMS, with his chosen assistant French, engaged in such debate in Agra. It was Pfander's forte rather than French's. French preferred a more conversational and private type of evangelism. The Bible, the divinity of Christ, the Holy Trinity, Muhammad's mission and the Qur'an were the subjects discussed. That French could participate in such public debating illustrates his knowledge and competence. It is interesting to note that two minor assistants on the Muslim side became outstanding Christians – Saftar Ali, a highly placed government official, and Imad-ud-Din, who became a well-known Christian theologian and writer.

Use of Popular Literary Forms

Recitation. Muslims are particularly familiar with the recitation of the Qur'an. French realized that they might listen with almost equal reverence to the recitation of the Bible. His companion on an evangelistic tour described how he "found him sitting on the boundary wall of a mosque, reading some Scripture aloud, though not a soul was visible. I waited on and on in surprise for more than an hour before he stopped. Then on our way back he told me how he had gathered a great crowd of eager listeners, and how a passing mullah had given the word, and in a very few minutes it vanished away, but that there were very many still listening, though concealed from view."[8]

Poetry. French realized the value of poetry as a way of communicating Christian truth. While traveling and preaching in the state of Bahawalpur, he found an inquirer who had memorized a poem about the Christian faith. French noted: "Most of the knowledge these poor people have of anything bearing on religion is couched in poetical couplets and I long to see some good Christian poet arise who can represent Christian voice in song. Few things under God would carry the gospel wider and fix it deeper."[9]

Use of the Bible and Christian Literature

French always took parts of the Bible, Christian literature, and tracts with him. He recalled how, in the mountains of Kashmir while on an evangelistic trek, he met an inquirer. The man had read one of Pfander's books and wanted a Gospel, or the Law, or the Psalms. After testing him, French gave him his last Persian-language Gospel. He paid tribute many times to the help and cooperation of the Bible societies. Realizing the value of Christian literature, French became a member of the Agra Tract Committee and published his first Urdu tract in 1856. It was entitled "The Mirror of the Character of Jesus Christ." It was an attempt to illustrate the character, offices, and disposition of our Lord, from the prophecies about him, the titles ascribed to him, and the nature of his teaching and his works. At the end of his life, French was still distributing Bibles. Writing to his wife about his visit to Jiddah in Arabia, he said: "I put an Arabic Bible in each of my large pockets, and ventured forth. I got two occasions to give short Arabic addresses within the city, one in a learned mullah's house, whom I induced to invite me in and listen to the story of God's plan of salvation. The other opportunity was in a more open space, sitting on the door-step of an old blind man, whose friends gathered round to listen . . . The mullah wished to have a Bible, so left it with him . . . I seldom leave the New Testament without the Psalms and the Prophets."[10]

Evangelizing of Key People

One day when French was traveling alone on a evangelistic tour in northern India, a tailor came running to him in the wood, saying, "Oh, Sir, I know who you are; you are the Lord's servant." French inquired, "Whom do you mean by the Lord?" "I mean the Lord Jesus Christ," the man replied. French then asked him how he came to know the Lord Jesus Christ. The man said that some time ago an Indian preacher had visited his village and told him about the Lord Jesus Christ. At the close of the message he gave a tract to a man who immediately tore it up and threw it on the ground. The tailor picked it up, pieced it together, and learned to read it. He talked to his friends about it and a number of them became his disciples. The tailor requested French to visit his home. He found the tailor's courtyard filled with inquirers. Every time he traveled that way French visited the tailor, who also came several times to Agra for teaching. Finally, French baptized him.[11]

French had a continual stream of individual inquirers coming to him for various reasons. He received them all with patience and courtesy. During his last year at Agra, French recorded:

> I have baptized seven adult converts myself . . . Two of the converts are teachers of considerable ability and attainments, and are entrusted with the leading of Persian and Arabic classes in the college. It may please God eventually to make use of both of them as evangelists or pastors in His Church. They have paid very great attention to the vernacular theological and scriptural lectures which I held twice a week through the greater part of the year, and are now sharing in the daily instruction which Paul (a convert from Meerut) is

receiving from me preparatory to ordination. The regularity of their attendance at all Christian ordinances and intelligent appreciation of the Word preached is really edifying . . . all of them have forsaken all for Christ, and have suffered very bitter reproaches for His Name's sake.[12]

French identified and often approached key people and leaders. Writing of some of his evangelistic tours, he said: "I found no plan so successful for gathering a good and attentive audience as making straight for the mosque and enquiring for the mullah . . . Instead of hanging about the village and having one's object suspected, this was a definite and straightforward object; and besides often meeting in this way on equal terms with the mullah, the chiefs and other respectable villagers would congregate in the mosque."[13]

At the very end of his life French continued this policy of seeking out the leaders, but he neglected no one. He wrote to his wife at their home in England a few months before he died:

I am pushing on very hard with Arabic, copying out verses to give hopeful enquirers to carry home, and preparing a tract on the leading articles of the creed . . . the work is a great effort, and one has to hang upon God hourly for strength . . . I sat an hour in what is evidently the Chief mosque of this suburb of Muttrah [in Oman] . . . The dresses of the sheikh and head imam were all to match, tasteful and handsome. I told then that I was come to see the head teacher and I loved all lovers of God and those who sought the true knowledge of Him. I also said that as this was our great festival time and I had no brother in Christ to read his services with me, I was come to read the lessons for the season or some of them with him and his friends (Luke chapters 23 and 24) . . . it was the most learned and aristocratic audience I have yet come across, and to be allowed to read and comment on such chapters in a chief mosque speaks hopefully for the prospect of a mission here being now or eventually opened: but one must speak humbly and softly.[14]

Training of Others

French put a high priority on training others to do the work of evangelism and teaching. His proposals for the founding of the Lahore Divinity School and his establishment of it are sufficient proof of this. Even so French was not keen that every able Christian young man should enter the ministry. He felt that the future growth of the church depended on people of high caliber being active for Christ in every department of secular life. Writing of those who became students he said: "As regards the character of our students, I think we have cause to feel cheered and encouraged. Intellectually, the average excellence is far superior to what I expected . . .. We have promise of two or three excellent linguists as far as original languages of the Bible go . . . On the whole, their religious growth and advance in knowledge and love and obedience of the truth has been gratifying and edifying to us."[15] The students came from different racial groups – Pathans, Rajputs, Persians, Punjabis, and Kashmiris. Most had been brought up as Muslims, some as Hindus, and at least one as a Sikh. They came from different social ranks. Some had come to Christ through much suffering, others had been influenced gradually in Christian schools, while others were children of Indian Christians.

The training was practical as well as theoretical. French wrote:

I am trying to perfect more our arrangements for giving a *practical* training in preaching and other ministerial work to our students. Mr. Clark and I take one or more in turns out with us to preach at the gates and in the bazaars, letting them preach a little also. I encourage them on Saturday to go out two and two by themselves into the villages around Lahore, and to distribute books, converse with the people, bring in enquirers if possible, and learn the state of things as regards the preparation of the people for the gospel. One or two are very zealous in this matter, others will be so, I believe. On Sunday morning, before our bazaar service, they stand at the doors and gather the people together by preaching. It will be bad for them to be too exclusively occupied in learning and reading without exercise and practice.[16]

Thomas Valpy French evangelized, taught, preached, wrote, and exhorted a century ago. We can all learn from his life and example. Might we not also learn from his method? He worked in hard soil. He had many trials and sufferings. God gave him some fruit.

Notes

1. Stephen Neill, *Anglicanism,* 4th ed. (Oxford: Mobray, 1982), p. 354.
2. Lambeth Palace Library, MS. 1085, French to Rev. C.P. Golightly, Jan. 13, 1850.
3. Ibid., Aug, 9, 1850.
4. Henry Briks, *Life and Correspondence of Thomas Valpy French* (London: John Murray, 1895), 1:148.
5. Ibid., p. 74.
6. Ibid., p. 163.
7. Ibid., p. 145.
8. Ibid., p. 187.
9. Ibid., p. 202.
10. Ibid., 2:350.
11. Ibid., 1:79.
12. Ibid., pp. 82-83.
13. Ibid., p. 107.
14. Ibid., 2:372, 379.
15. Ibid., 1:234.
16. Ibid., p. 256.

Selected Bibliography

Works by Thomas Valpy French

1853 *Sermon preached . . . on Occasion of the Death of the Hon'ble James Thomason, Esq., etc. Lt. Governor of the N.W. Provinces, October 2, 1853.* Agra: Secundra Press.

1859 *The Lord's Voice into the City. Sermons commemorative of the war, the pestilence, and the mutiny, preached in the years 1852-1858, chiefly to the Civil and Military congregation in Agra.* Calcutta: Bishop's College Press.

1862 *Remember How Thou Hast Heard. Selections from the pulpit addresses of a brief ministerial course at Clifton, Bristol, chiefly adapted to the "Times and Seasons."* London, Edinburgh.

1890 *Missionary Addresses . . . Reprinted from "The Clergyman's Magazine."* London: Hazell, Watson and Viney.

1890 *Notes on Travel. By a (late) Missionary Bishop* [i.e. Thomas Valpy French], *with special reference to the Greek Orthodox and Anglican Churches, and some recent invitations to closer intercommunication and fellowship both of witness and service.* London: David Nutt.

N.d. *Taqrir dil-e-pazir.* The account of Thomas Valpy French's discussions with the ulama of Agra on Islam and Christianity. A nineteen-page Urdu pamphlet among the "Hindustani Texts" at the India Office Library, London.

Works about Thomas Valpy French

Briks, H.A. *The Life and Correspondence of Thomas Valpy French, First Bishop of Lahore.* 2 vols. London: John Murray, 1895.

Stacey, Vivenne. *Thomas Valpy French, First Bishop of Lahore.* Rawalpindi: The Christian Study Centre, 1982.

Stock Eugene. *An Heroic Bishop: The Life Story of French of Lahore.* London: Hodder & Stoughton, 1913.

Lewis Bevan Jones
1880–1960

Striving to Touch Muslim Hearts

Clinton Bennett

Lewis Bevan Jones (1880-1960), missionary scholar and Baptist pioneer in Christian-Muslim relations, was born at Agra, India, where his father, Daniel Jones (1852-1911), served with the Baptist Missionary Society (BMS).[1] "Bevan Jones," as he was known, was sent to England in 1888 to attend the School for the Sons of Missionaries, now Eltham College. While there, he was baptized at Heath Street Baptist Church, Hamstead. Between 1896 and 1900 he worked for Edward Jackson, magistrate and former mayor of Reading. Bevan Jones taught Sunday school at the King Street Church, where Jackson was a deacon.

In 1900 Bevan Jones entered University College, Cardiff, in his father's native Wales, where he graduated with a degree in Semitic languages in 1904. This was followed by the B.D. from the University of London, which he gained as a student at Regents Park College. As a candidate for the Baptist ministry, he shared in the pioneer work of R. Rowntree Clifford in the West Ham Central Mission, where evangelical zeal was effectively combined with social action.[2] Not until 1941 did he receive the M.A. from Cardiff for his thesis "The Status of Women in Islam."

In 1907 he was accepted for service in India by the BMS and sailed out as his father retired because of ill health. Thereafter, Bevan Jones was conscious of continuing where Daniel had started.

Bevan Jones spent the first two years of his missionary career in Agra, mastering Hindi and teaching in the school. In 1909 he was transferred to Dhaka (Dacca) in predominantly Muslim East Bengal, to work with Hindu and Muslim residents in the Baptist Students Hostel. A gifted linguist, he added Urdu and Bengali to his knowledge of languages. By 1911, when the second international missionary conference on behalf of the Mohammedan world met at Lucknow, India, Bevan had turned his attention almost exclusively to Islam.[3] In 1914 this specialist vocation was recognized by the BMS when the Triennial Conference (India and Ceylon) set him aside for Muslim work. This novel and pioneer move by the BMS determined the future direction of Bevan Jones's career.

To equip himself more adequately, he devoted a full year (1917) to further study, learning Arabic at Temple Gairdner's Cairo Study Center and spending six months researching at Oxford. In 1915 he had married Miss Violet Rhoda Stanford, a nurse at Berhampur Hospital, and she accompanied him to Egypt and England. Bevan Jones's marriage has been described as "an ideal partnership which laid the foundation for much of his future success."[4] Violet Jones worked with Muslim women and collaborated with her husband to write *Woman in Islam* (1941). Returning to Dhaka in 1918, they established a reading room in the Muslim bazaar, where they themselves made their home in 1922. In 1920, on a part-time basis, Bevan Jones began to lecture on Islam at Serampore College (this was later followed by lectures at Bishop's College, Calcutta) and assumed the editorship of *News and Notes*, the organ of the Missionaries to Muslims League, which fellow Baptist John Tackle had founded in 1911 as a response to the Lucknow Conference. The league coordinated missionary work among Muslims by sharing information and initiating training programs. Involvement in the work of the league introduced Bevan Jones to many distinguished colleagues in this field, including Edward Sell, Murray Titus, and Samuel Zwemer.

In 1924 Bevan Jones and his wife attended the third international conference of missionaries to Muslims at Jerusalem, which called for the establishment of Islamic study centers, modeled after the Cairo Center, in all major Muslim mission fields. In India a school of Islamics, funded by several Protestant societies, eventually opened at Lahore in 1930, the result of an initiative of the National Christian Council's Committee on Muslim Work, of which Bevan Jones was a member. The committee unanimously chose him to be the school's first principal, which office he held until 1941. "Henry Martyn School" was his personal choice of a name for the new school, honoring the man who is regarded as the first modern missionary to Muslims.[5]

Bevan Jones's two academic degrees, his editorship of *News and Notes*, and his several *Muslim World* articles were excellent qualifications for this challenging position. He headed a distinguished team drawn together to study contemporary movements in Indian Islam and to prepare appropriate Christian literature as well as to train personnel, expatriate and national, residentially and by extension. His colleagues were L.E. Browne, later professor of theology at Leeds; J.W. Sweetman, later professor of Islam at the Selly Oak Colleges, Birmingham; and John Subhan, later a bishop of the Methodist Episcopal Church. All produced major scholarly works within a few years of the school's opening. Violet Jones also lectured in the school – on the religious life of Muslim women – and edited a series of tracts for Muslim women.

Between 1941 and 1944 Bevan Jones pastored a church in Delhi, after which, returning to England, he pastored a church in Burgess Hill, Surrey (1944-47). Until his death, he remained active in ecumenical circles. From 1950 until 1959 he chaired the London-based Fellowship of Faith for Muslims, for which he wrote several booklets, still available today. From 1950 until his death in 1960, he served as a non-Anglican assessor on the Council for the Muslim World of the Church Assembly, alongside other eminent scholars of Islam.[6]

His Writings – Interpreting Islam

As principal of the Henry Martyn School, Bevan Jones contributed three books: *The People of the Mosque* (1932), *Christianity Explained to Muslims* (1938), and, coauthored by his wife, *Woman in Islam* (1941). His first two books were translated into several Indian languages as his earlier best-seller, *The Best Friend: A Life of Our Lord* (1925), had been translated into sixteen languages. This was written as a response to his own call for a new genre of literature, suitable for educated Muslim readers, an idea he borrowed from J.N. Farquhar.[7]

The People of the Mosque, based on his Serampore College lectures, introduced readers to Islam generally and to Indian Islam in particular, but it also suggested how Christians should approach Muslims. The book's title indicates its tenor; it was concerned with people, how they thought and lived, and what they believed. Bevan Jones's own career was people-focused, reflecting his father's influence. Daniel Jones had been renowned for his contact with ordinary Indians, especially with lepers. In his candidature to the BMS, Bevan Jones had spoken of "rendering obedience" to the needs of the people for whom he "hoped to live," and of his childhood knowledge of India, together with "the intercourse he once had with the people," giving India a double claim on him.[8]

The People of the Mosque draws heavily on such works as Sir William Muir's Life of Mahomet (1858), Edward Sell's Faith of Islam (1880), and Stanley Lane Poole's Studies in a Mosque (1883) and on the writings of Samuel Zwemer and Temple Gairdner and of fellow Baptists John Tackle and William Goldsack. Bevan Jones was also familiar with the work of T. Noldeke, I. Goldziher, Snouke Hurgronze, and Henri Lammens, a Belgian Jesuit. In addition, he corresponded with Duncan Black Macdonald.

Perhaps the most important element of his study of Islam was that it was set in the context of his personal experience among its practitioners. His knowledge of Islam was the fruit of direct observation as well as of academic study. He also knew that Muslim authorities must ultimately be the test of any appraisal of Islam. He therefore studied the Qur'an, the Hadith (Traditions), especially the Mishkatu' l Masabih, and the writings of Sir Sayyid Ahmad Khan, Sayyid Ameer Ali, Sir Ahmad Hussain, Khudha Baksh, and Cheragh Ali.[9]

Bevan Jones's work on Islamic faith and practice introduced little, if any, original material. Its value lies in the sheer skill with which the author succeeded in reducing almost the whole of Islam's basic system into one concise, readable volume. Bevan Jones endeavored to see Islam through Muslim eyes, to portray Islam accurately and sympathetically so that in what was written Muslims might recognize their own faith. He wanted to penetrate Islam's inner meaning and was fully aware that Christian writers, including some of his own sources, had all too often allowed bias and prejudice to color their work. He tried to move beyond traditional argument and debate to the sharing of spiritual experience and insight, to what he called the "rarer atmosphere of the things of the spirit."[10]

He was not wholly successful in this task, and his final estimate of Muhammad was negative: "We cannot escape the obligation to compare Muhammad with Jesus Christ, and, in that light seriously-minded and unprejudiced people all the world over, whose only concern is to follow the highest, have found in Muhammad what can only be described as grave moral defects."[11]

It must be noted, first, that very few Muslims have found "grave moral defects" in Muhammad. Therefore, the "unprejudiced" people referred to are almost undoubtedly Christians, prejudiced by their Christianity. Second, in comparing Christ and Muhammad, Bevan Jones knew full well that he was not comparing like with like, from either a Christian or a Muslim viewpoint.

However, in another passage, citing approvingly a Muslim friend, Bevan Jones writes with a more positive attitude about the Prophet: "A Muslim who respects the name of Jesus is more likely to form a right judgement about Christianity than is a Christian about Islam who enters his study with the conviction that Muhammad was an impostor."[12]

Although he dealt more sympathetically with Islam than had most previous writers, no Muslim would actually accept his account as unbiased. Arguably the value of The People of the Mosque lies more in its intent than in its content.

His Writings – Interpreting Christianity

Christianity Explained to Muslims aimed to interpret Christian faith for Muslims, though a secondary object was to "bring about better understanding between people of the two faiths."[13] In this book, Bevan Jones's Christian theology was brought into creative engagement with his study of Islam. He drew on a large number of Christian scholars, from a wide range of churchmanship and theological opinion. He was especially indebted to A.M. Fairbairn, H.R. Mackintosh, William

Temple, A.G. Hogg, and Nathaniel Micklem. Themes such as incarnation and kenotic theology, and a desire to reinterpret traditional thinking for new situations, were central. His own theological stance was described thus by John Subhan: "Bevan Jones was uncompromising in the fundamentals of the Christian faith. He could not be classified as an extreme liberal or a narrow fundamentalist. He might be termed orthodox in his belief, though he would wear no label."[14] Another writer has described his "dominating purpose" as "the placing of scholarship within the field of evangelical purposefulness."[15] If, in the present writer's opinion, Bevan Jones may fairly be regarded as a liberal, this must be balanced by the fact that he never lost the ability to communicate within his evangelical Baptist constituency.

Christianity Explained is an example of theological brokerage at its best. In it, Bevan Jones took the ideas and emphases of his theological mentors and applied them to Islam. He attempted to glean from an examination of Christian doctrine what he deemed essential for faith in Christ. Then, in the light of Muslim prejudice and objections, he sought to reexpress Christian faith so that, without compromising essentials, causes of misunderstanding were removed. Fundamental to his thinking was his concept of "essential Christianity." In the past, he believed, missionaries had too often stressed by-products of Christianity rather than the Christian message as such. His own Christianity was rooted in "spiritual experience," not in "intellectual statement." For example, in discussing the Trinity, he subordinated its "intellectual abstraction" to the experience that it describes: "If a Muslim can be brought to understand that in the doctrine of the Trinity an attempt is made to explain our apprehension of the redemptive operation of God's Holy Spirit within us — then, though it may still appear unacceptable to him, he will see it as no longer unreasonable and certainly not blasphemous."[16]

Bevan Jones suggested that Muslims often object not to what Christians actually believe but to what Muslims think they believe. He therefore emphasized the "why" rather than the "what" of belief and contended that beliefs or doctrines were essentially postexperiential attempts to describe, within the poverty and limitations of human language, what people believed to be true about their experience of God. He did not "demand from anyone, least of all Muslims, . . . acquiescence in particular dogmas of the church as a condition of discipleship or as necessary to faith in Christ."[17]

Freedom of conscience has always been central to Baptist tradition, which defends individual liberty to work out one's salvation before God free from doctrinal tyranny. Bevan Jones knew that Muslims would find it difficult to grasp accepted definitions of God and suggested that Christians should not be overly distressed by this. "What is really important," he said, "is to know God and to do His will"; citing Henry Drummond, of whom he thought highly, he summarized, "To become Christ-like is the only thing in the world worth caring for."[18]

His concept of Christlikeness and his distinction between belief and faith anticipate the work of Wilfred Cantwell Smith, who studied at the Henry Martyn School in 1940 and was later an associate staff member. The most significant and permanently valuable aspect of *Christianity Explained* is that in it Bevan Jones was prepared to take the challenge of Muslim theology into his understanding of Christian faith, which was both challenged and changed by his engagement with Islam. Perhaps not surprisingly, he regarded conversion as an ongoing process, summed up by the old term "sanctification."[19]

He did not hesitate to declare that mystery had a part to play, which enabled him to recognize spiritual truth and the presence of God's Spirit in other traditions. He spoke of Muslims and Christians exploring together the phenomena of spiritual experience, for "in [their] heart[s], as in ours, the spirit of God is usually at work."[20] He rejoiced in "whatever evidence we find of the presence of God's spirit in Islam and in every witness it makes to His Being and Majesty."[21] Referring to J.N. Farquhar's attitude toward Hinduism, Bevan called for "faith to believe that other nations and peoples of other religions do have a real contribution to make in the fulfillment of God's purposes for the world through Jesus Christ."[22]

He clearly did not accept Hendrik Kraemer's total divide between the revelation in Christ and religions, as though the latter were altogether futile attempts to bridge the gap between the human and the divine. Rather, he spoke of the revelation in Christ being "absolute" though not "exhaustive":

> We need not and indeed cannot claim that God is, in Jesus, exhaustively revealed . . . Let it not seem strange that we are forced to confess that our faith holds fast to contradictions – God is known, and yet not known. After all, in the Revelation of Himself in Jesus we stand face to face with a profound mystery; it is not surprising that we do not fully understand.[23]

His concept of revelation, however, was radically different from the Islamic concept of *wahi*. He believed that "real kinship" exists between God and humankind, making possible the translation of "eternal thought" into "the language of time."[24] Anticipating process theology, he spoke of the natural created world as "the plastic expression of God's will."[25] Consequently, he knew that the Bible and the Qur'an are regarded quite differently by those who possess them and that, "while to the Muslim the true revelation is to be found in a book, the Qur'an, to the Christian it is not to be found in the Bible, but in the Person of Christ."[26]

He also commented that, since the Gospels contain not what God said to Jesus but what their authors "had to say about what Jesus said and did," they qualify, for Muslims, as Hadith, not Scripture.[27] He identified this as one of the most fundamental stumbling blocks between Christians and Muslims. He believed, too, that due to Gnostic and Docetic tendencies in early Arabian Christianity, Muslims were victims of an ancient misunderstanding about the nature of the incarnation and passion of Jesus. As a result, they saw no beauty in the crucified Christ.

His Missiology

Bevan Jones's missiology was characterized by his rejection of controversy. While he had learned much from earlier missionaries and Christian apologists such as Karl Pfander and William Muir, he rejected their confrontational tactics. Pfander's writings, he suggested, "served best as a guide to something better." Written to touch Muslim minds, they failed to touch Muslim hearts. Showing "insufficient regard for the sensitive spirits of devout Muslims," they provoked counterattacks on Christian faith, as in the vehemently anti-Christian Ahmadiyya movement.[28] Bevan Jones's own work stands in the tradition of Thomas Valpy French and W. St. Clair-Tisdall, who, while both disciples of Pfander, did much to develop a more irenic approach.

Bevan Jones's modus operandi was people centered. One reason for his initial interest in Muslim work was the conviction that Christians had neglected Muslims in favor of Hindus.[29] He made practical action a plank of his missionary program; "substantial bridges of understanding, sympathy and friendship," he maintained, could be built "out of little acts of simple, ungrudging kindness."[30] He placed great value on forming friendships with Muslims and himself enjoyed lifelong relationships with two leading Ahmadis – Maulana Muhammad Ali and Yakub Khan. After Bevan Jones's death in 1960, Yakub wrote that Bevan Jones had made him "respect Christianity in its real sense of love and charity of heart." He described Bevan Jones as an exponent of "the new approach between the two great sister religions," which, he said, was then "coming to the forefront."[31] (He may well have had in mind as examples such books as Kenneth Cragg's *Call of the Minaret* [1956] and *Sandals at the Mosque* [1959].)

Also important in Bevan Jones's missiology were spirituality and prayer. Although he knew how to laugh and have fun, he was driven to his knees by his engagement with Islam. "We must know," he said, "what it is to agonize in prayer on behalf of these people."[32] His encounter with Islam involved internal as well as external discovery; the closer he came to Islam as practiced by devout, sincere souls, the harder and more painful he found it to assess the spiritual status of his Muslim friends. Ultimately, his aim remained traditional, to "trace out" and "lead back" Christ's "other sheep."[33] At the same time, he knew that Muslims might approach Christ in a different way than those brought up in Christian societies. Consequently, he was deeply concerned with the pastoral care of converts and regretted that the Indian church too often failed to meet their needs.

His Legacy – A Brief Assessment

Bevan Jones's most influential and popular book remains *The People of the Mosque*. A fifth edition, edited and revised by Dwight Baker (1980), with an updated historical section, bears eloquent testimony to the lasting value and quality of the author's work, though the present writer regrets that the editor chose not to include the sections on Christianity and Islam.

The Henry Martyn School (now Institute) continues to owe much to the legacy of its first principal. Links, for example, with the Muslim community remain vital to its programs. Now based in Hyderabad, it continually adjusts its program to the changing milieu in which it finds itself, a trend wholly consistent with the spirit of Bevan Jones. His approach is best described as open-ended – open to the Spirit's prompting, open to the challenge of Muslim religious thought, open to the idea that the religious life is an ongoing experience.

Also of significance today is Bevan Jones's commitment to Christian unity. He knew that a divided church could never win Islam for Christ and therefore tried, in Bishop Subhan's words, to be friend and brother to "men of all denominations."[34]

Finally, Bevan Jones's life and work is testimony to the value of building bridges between faith communities. To walk such a bridge-building road was not easy then, nor is it easy today. It requires courage and involves risk – courage to experience genuine anguish, the risk inherent in rethinking received beliefs and adapting them in the light of new experience. It is, Bevan Jones said, "a hard task," "an arduous enterprise," "the way of sacrifice and tears and un-requited love."[35]

Notes

1. See "Daniel Jones of Agra: A Great Heart of Our India Mission," *Baptist Missionary Herald* 94 (1911): 143, and D. Jones, "Memoirs" (in Welsh), *Yr Herald Cenhadol* (London: BMS, 1911).

2. See Paul R. Clifford, *Venture in Faith* (London: Carey Kingsgate, 1955). Reference to Bevan Jones is on p. 51.

3. For the three international conferences on mission to Muslims, see *Methods of Mission among Muslims: Cairo, 1906* (London: Fleming H. Revell, 1906), *Lucknow Conference Report* (London: CLS, 1911), and *Conference of Christian Workers among Muslims* (New York: IMC, 1924).

4. H.W. Pike, "Lewis Bevan Jones" (unpublished tribute, Oxford, Regents Park College).

5. See Constance E. Padwick, *Henry Martyn: Confessor of the Faith* (London: SCM, 1922).

6. The FFM was founded in 1915 following Zwemer's visit to England. For the CMW, see General Synod Archives. Kenneth Cragg and W.M. Watt were members.

7. See *India Report* (London: BMS, 1916), p. 48.

8. See Candidates Records File No. 393 (London, BMS Archives).

9. For a critique of these writers (except Hussain), see W.C. Smith, *Modern Islam in India* (Lahore: Minerva, 1943); for Hussain, see A. Hussein, *Notes on Islam* (Lahore, 1922).

10. L.B. Jones, *Christ's Ambassador to the Muslim* (London: FFM, reprinted 1972), p. 11.

11. L.B. Jones, *The People of the Mosque* (London: SCM, 1932), p. 265.

12. Ibid., p. 253.

13. L.B. Jones, *Christianity Explained to Muslims* (Calcutta: YMCA, 1938), p. xi.

14. J. Subhan, "The Reverend Lewis Bevan Jones," *Muslim World* 51 (1961): 129.

15 E.F.F. Bishop, "Tribute to Lewis Bevan Jones," *Muslim World* 51 (1961): 303.

16. Jones, *Christianity Explained*, p. 93.

17. Ibid., p. ix.
18. Jones, *The People of the Mosque*, p. 321, citing H. Drummond's *Changed Life*.
19. Jones, *Christianity Explained*, p. 149.
20. Ibid., p. 93.
21. Jones, *The People of the Mosque*, p. 253.
22. Ibid., p. 254.
23. Jones, *Christianity Explained*, p. 76. See also "Our Special Message to Muslims," *Moslem World* 10 (1930): 335a.
24. Jones, *Christianity Explained*, p. 52.
25. Ibid., p. 180.
26. Ibid., p. 53.
27. Ibid., p. 42.
28. Jones, *The People of the Mosque*, p. 248; see also p. 289.
29. L.B.Jones, "Some Educated Moslems in Bengal," *Moslem World* 6 (1916): 234.
30. Jones, *The People of the Mosque*, p. 316.
31. Cited in "Remarkable Tributes to a Great Missionary to Muslims," *Baptist Missionary Herald*, November 1960, p. 171.
32. Jones, *Christ's Ambassador*, p. 11.
33. Ibid., p. 12.
34. Subhan, "Jones," p. 128.
35. Jones, *Christ's Ambassador*, p. 12.

Selected Bibliography

Books by L. Bevan Jones

1925 *The Best Friend: A Life of Our Lord*. Madras: CLS.
1932 *The People of the Mosque*. London: SCM. 5th ed. (ed. D. Baker), New Delhi: ISPCK/CLS, 1980.
1938 *Christianity Explained to Muslims*. Calcutta: YMCA.
1941 (with V.R. Jones) *Woman in Islam*. London: Carey Press.

Articles in Moslem World *(1911-60; name changed to* Muslim World *in 1961)*

1916 "Some Educated Moslems in Bengal," 6:228-35.
1917 "Correspondence with D.B. Macdonald," 7:420-23.
1920 "The Paraclete or Muhammad?" 10:112-15.
1930 "Our Special Message to Moslems," 20:331-35.
1940 "How Not to Use the Qur'an: An Urdu Tract Explained," 30:280-91.
1952 "Christ's Ambassador to the Muslim," 42:80-81.
1953 "A Love That Persists," 43:3-6.

Pamphlets Published by FFM *(Fellowship of Faith for Muslims, London)*

The Ahmadiyya Movement (formerly *A False Messiah*).
Christ's Ambassador to the Muslim. 1952, reprinted 1972.
Five Pillars of Islam (no. 3). Rev. 1981.
Focus on Islam series. 1952.
From Islam to Christ: How a Sufi Found His Lord (Life of Bishop J. Subhan) (no. 6).

Works about L. Bevan Jones

Bennett, Clinton. "A Theological Appreciation of Lewis Bevan Jones: Baptist Pioneer in Christian-Muslim Relations." M.A. thesis, University of Birmingham, 1985.
_____. "A Theological Appreciation of Lewis Bevan Jones." *Baptist Quarterly* 32, no. 5 (January 1988): 237-52.
Bishop, E.F.F. "Tribute to the Memory of Lewis Bevan Jones." *Muslim World* 51 (1961): 302-3.
Subhan, J. "Lewis Bevan Jones." *Muslim World* 51 (1961): 128-31.

J.N. Farquhar

1861–1929

Presenting Christ as the Crown of Hinduism

Eric J. Sharpe

Arguably the most serious problem facing the Christian mission in our day centers on the two concepts of "religion" and "culture." How is what we call religion related to what we call culture? Are those (and there are many) who look with suspicion on Christianity because it appears to be related, perhaps to the point of bondage, to Western cultural patterns, justified in their belief? Are they right when they say that each cultural group must find and affirm its own religious roots, and that outside its own area, Christianity has nothing to offer?

Because these are today's questions, it is easy to assume that they were formulated only yesterday. This is a false assumption, and in the work of the Scottish lay missionary John Nicol Farquhar (1861-1929), who served in India from 1891 to 1923, we can find ample evidence of their urgency in an earlier period. Farquhar was perhaps the first Protestant missionary in India to base a missionary theology, not on Christian assumptions only, but on a close and sympathetic study of Hinduism, and to gain acceptance as an Orientalist in his own right. In his insistence that the Indian cultural heritage must be recognized, understood, and made one foundation of a Christian attitude, he anticipated some of the concerns of what we know as "interreligious dialogue."

The facts of Farquhar's life are soon told. Born in Aberdeen in 1861, he was early apprenticed to a draper and returned to school only at twenty-one. He passed rapidly through Aberdeen Grammar School and Aberdeen University, before completing his studies at Oxford – the Oxford of A.M. Fairbairn, Max Müller, and Monier-Williams, from all of whom he began to learn how to study India and things Indian. In 1891 he arrived in India, and taught for a decade at the London Missionary Society's college at Bhowanipur, Calcutta. In 1902, thanks to the intervention of the tireless John R. Mott, he was set free from college teaching to devote himself to evangelism and writing under the auspices of the YMCA.

From 1907 to 1911 he served as National Student Secretary of the Indian YMCA, representing the organization at World Student Christian Federation Conferences in Tokyo (1907), Oxford (1909), and Constantinople (1911), and making important contributions to all three. He was not actually present at the Edinburgh World Missionary Conference of 1910, though he was a correspondent, and his influence is clearly seen in the Report of Commission IV. In October 1913 he delivered the Hartford-Lamson Lectures at Hartford Theological Seminary, Hartford, Connecticut, on "Modern Religious Movements in India," by which time he had become literary secretary of the Indian YMCA, on a roving commission which allowed him to spend half of each year in Oxford, and half in India. This arrangement continued even during the 1914-1918 war, in the course of which he was also instrumental in bringing out to India T.R. Glover (author of *The Jesus of History*) and the New Testament and Zoroastrian scholar J.H. Moulton as visiting YMCA lecturers (Moulton lost his life on the return journey when his ship was torpedoed in the Mediterranean). In 1923 increasing ill health forced Farquhar to leave India. For the last six years of his life he was professor of comparative religion in the University of Manchester, England. He received honorary doctorates from the universities of Oxford and Aberdeen, was elected Wilde Lecturer at Oxford, and was a much-valued speaker in many other parts of the country. He died on July 17, 1929.

Farquhar married in 1891 his childhood friend Euphemia (Effie) Watson, the daughter of his former employer; they had two children, one of whom (Marjorie) later served as a CMS missionary in India.

Career as Writer and Editor

Farquhar's career as a writer began in his Bhowanipur days, but it was not until his emancipation from the routine of college work that he became more generally known. In 1903 he published *Gita and Gospel*, in which he considered the teachings of the *Bhagavad Gita* from a Christian point of view; in 1911 there appeared *A Primer of Hinduism*, and in 1913 his best-known work, *The Crown of Hinduism*, and in the following year his *Modern Religious Movements of India*, still a standard work. In 1920 he published *An Outline of the Religious Literature in India*, which at once assumed a place it has never lost as an invaluable scholar's work of reference.

Scarcely less important were the books that he persuaded other Christian scholars in India to write, and for which he assumed editorial responsibility. "The Religious Quest of India Series" included such titles as Nicol Macnicol, *Indian Theism* (1915), J.H. Moulton, *The Treasure of the Magi* (1917), and Margaret Stevenson, *The Rites of the Twice-born* (1920). "The Heritage of India Series" contained sixteen titles, among them A.B. Keith, *The Samkhya System* (1918), F. Kingsbury and G.E. Phillips, *Hymns of the Tamil Saivite Saints* (1921), and A.A. Macdonnel, *Hymns from the Rigveda* (1922). "The Religious Life of India Series" included Bishop H. Whitehead's study *The Village Gods of South India* (1916) and H.A. Walter, *The Ahmadiya Movement* (1918). It has sometimes been objected that these series were written entirely by Western missionaries, and that the authentic Indian voice is not to be heard in them. In point of fact, although Farquhar did his utmost to persuade Indian Christians to write, and at one time had more than a dozen books by Indian Christians on the stocks, none materialized – due almost entirely to the exacting scholarly standards demanded by the editor. Perhaps we might say, however, that the Protestant missionary corps in India during the first quarter of this century made its most distinctive and lasting contribution in the field of literature, and that Farquhar more than any other individual was its director, its inspiration, and its conscience.

When Farquhar arrived in India in 1891, India was just beginning to feel the impact of the national movement, though its zenith was not to be reached for some years. In face of India's new consciousness of national identity and national pride, Protestant missions had depressingly little to offer by way of understanding and affirmation. Missionary proclamation, where it noticed Hindu beliefs at all, reacted only to their darker side; missionaries as a rule knew no Sanskrit and were not trained in the field of Indian religions. The developing "science of religion," associated particularly with the name of Friedrich Max Müller, had touched them hardly at all. There were few "liberal" missionaries who were aware of the sea change that was coming over Christianity as a result of the intellectual ferment of the late nineteenth century. "Preach the gospel and confound the heathen" was the only approach that most knew – even those (and there were many) who found themselves involved in Christian higher education. This Farquhar found painful in the extreme. On the one hand he could see that the traditional missionary approach was serving only to alienate India – and particularly young India – from the Christian Gospel; on the other, he could not believe that it did justice to the emerging facts of the religious history of mankind. The need was for a new missionary approach to Hinduism, and to Indian life generally.

In one of his early articles, from 1901, we find Farquhar stating bluntly that "we want a criticism that will set Christianity clearly and distinctly in its relations with other faiths."[1] Missionary criticism of Hinduism may have been of some limited value in the past, but has seldom been scientific enough to be of permanent value. The rise of the science of religion might change radically the missionary's presuppositions, showing him how every form of religion has its place in the vast sweep of human evolution, and giving him a key for sympathetic and positive evaluation, while still demonstrating the superiority of Christianity.

> The main use . . . of the science, it seems to me, will be that, with the cold irresistible logic of facts, it will set forth the essentials of religion, and will exhibit historically the development of religion and religions. A scientific statement of the essentials of religion will at once show how exceedingly weak Hinduism and Muhammadanism are in comparison with Christianity.[2]

And he sums up: "The more knowledge missionaries have of the general progress of the science the better."[3]

But how could he make the claim that the scientific approach would inevitably demonstrate that Christianity is superior to Hinduism? Is there not a serious contradiction here? This is the claim that lies at the heart of the *Crown of Hinduism,* and it is necessary that we look at it a little more closely.

The dominant liberal intellectual theory of Farquhar's day was the theory of evolution, in the light of which all social institutions (as well as all biological organisms) find their place on an ascending scale of value and effectiveness. What is lower is not false, merely incomplete and undeveloped. The late nineteenth and early twentieth centuries saw this theory applied very extensively to the study of religion, and indeed it forms the theoretical heart of what was then called "the science of religion."[4] Religion, like every other organism, has grown from modest beginnings to the heights of ethical monotheism (or perhaps no less ethical agnosticism). Now from the point of view of the liberal missionary, it seemed not only feasible, but inevitable, that the relative positions of Hinduism and Christianity on the evolutionary scale should be recognized and evaluated. Hinduism, in this light, might then appear to be a less "developed" form of universal religion, to be recognized for what it is, but ultimately to be supplanted by Christianity as a "higher" form. This was certainly Farquhar's belief.

Standards of the Missionary Scientist

But the missionary scientist, whose calling is to help the evolution process along, so to speak, must actually be a scientist. He must know his sources, gather his material with meticulous accuracy, and apply to them the best thinking of which he is capable; but for the most part he must keep his knowledge in the background, and not use it as a weapon. In another early article we find Farquhar saying that

> while every missionary ought to study Hinduism as much as he possibly can, yet in ninety-nine hundredths of his work he ought to keep his knowledge strictly in the background. Our task is to preach the Gospel of Christ and to woo souls to Him; and to

that great end every element in our work should be made strictly subordinate and subservient.[5]

From this same article there emerges another vital point, that it is impossible to do accurate work in such a sensitive area as the encounter of religions without genuine sympathy.

All our study of Hinduism and everything we write and say on the subject should be sympathetic. I believe incalculable harm has been done to the Christian cause in India in times past through unsympathetic denunciation of Hinduism. Even if the severe condemnations passed on certain aspects of the religion be quite justifiable, it is bad policy to introduce these things into our addresses and our tracts; for the invariable result is that our audience is alienated . . . Our aim is to convince the mind and conscience of those who hear us, and we shall do that far more effectively if we eschew the traditional habit of denunciation, and try to lead Hindus to the truth by other paths.[6]

Scholarly accuracy and genuine sympathy, then, are the first two missionary requirements in face of the challenge of Hindu faith, in Farquhar's view. To these he was compelled to add a third – faithfulness to Christ. We may if we wish call Farquhar a "liberal," though for the most part his Christian stance was that of the evangelical – a simple and straightforward faith in Jesus Christ, from which he never deviated. In fact the focus of his faith might well be characterized as "the religion of Jesus."

This was not irrelevant to his development as a missionary theologian, for the simple presentation of Jesus as a religious teacher had long proved more acceptable to the Hindu mind than the attempt to expound an intricate system of theology. Again from the early part of his career, we find him asking "the thinking men of Calcutta":

Will you not try to see the real Jesus? Will you not study the Gospels, and try to understand the secret of his extraordinary influence? Will you not try to get a glimpse of this face that is loved as no other son of man is loved?[7]

Fulfillment – Cornerstone of Farquhar's Approach

These various trends come to a focus in the theological concept of *fulfillment,* which formed the cornerstone of Farquhar's missionary thinking, and which he advocated with such energy and eloquence that it became an item of Christian orthodoxy for a whole generation of Indian missionaries. It had already taken shape in his mind at the time of his recruitment by the YMCA; it reached its fullest expressions in his book *The Crown of Hinduism;* and it was an ideal Farquhar was never to relinquish. It contained two separate elements. First, from the perspective of the history of religions, the belief that universal religious elements reach their fullest and most complete form in Christianity – or rather, in Jesus Christ. And second, the belief that in Jesus Christ, all people everywhere can find resolution and goal of their religious quests. Thus from India's point of view, Hinduism poses questions – about human nature and destiny, community, renunciation and salvation – to which it is able to return either unsatisfactory answers, or no answers at all. India, further, is seeking for a form of religion that will fit her for life in the modern world; again Hinduism is unfitted to meet that need, but Christianity is. Christ, in Farquhar's view, stands for such ideals as progress, freedom, the search for truth, and the loftiest morality – all of which ideals India was striving to embrace, but all of which (again in Farquhar's view) were destined to prove very elusive indeed without the motive power that only Christian faith could provide. To say that Christ was the fulfillment of Hinduism was, therefore, a statement with social and political, as well as religious, overtones. In respect of caste, for instance, after noting that "the religious basis of caste is fading out of men's minds," Farquhar goes on to state that, nevertheless, religion and society are closely interwoven:

For the purpose of creating a living social order, a living religion is needed. It alone provides moral conceptions of strength and reach sufficient to lay hold of man's conscience and intellect and to compel him to live in society in accordance with them . . . Where [he goes on] . . . shall we find a religion whose governing conceptions, when they take organized form in society, will incarnate the great principles of the essential equality of all men, the rectitude and high value of complete social freedom, and the obligation of moralizing all social relations?[8]

What Farquhar was trying to say in *The Crown of Hinduism* was not always too well understood, either by Hindus or by other Christians. Although he was offering the "fulfillment hypothesis" as an item of private equipment to the missionary who needed to have some working theory of the theological relationship between Hinduism and Christianity, there were those who saw it more as either a peg on which to hang sermons or a gratuitous insult delivered at the heart of India. Some conservatives felt that in introducing the evolutionary theory, which they had been brought up to despise, as an element in missionary apologetics, Farquhar had virtually sold his soul to the devil. Others felt that in insisting on the final supremacy of Christ in the world of religions, he was undoing whatever good his protestations of sympathy might initially have achieved. To all of which Farquhar replied: "I have no desire to represent the fulfillment hypothesis as a revelation from heaven . . . It is to my mind merely the best hypothesis which has yet been suggested, a hypothesis to be tested and tried by all the relevant facts."[9]

Today perhaps one might be permitted to doubt whether the fulfillment hypothesis itself should be looked on as Farquhar's main achievement in missionary thought. It has proved fairly tenacious and, since Vatican II, has been unwittingly copied by not a few Roman Catholic missiologists. But as the much more acute theological mind of A.G. Hogg was not slow to point out, it may be tantamount to forcing on the Hindu answers to questions he has not asked, while the questions he *does* ask remain unanswered. It may also be the case that to speak of "fulfillment" in this way implies an unintentional condescension; Hindus are not only seekers, they are also finders, though what they find may not be easy for the Christian to recognize and accept.[10]

I tend to think that the true measure of Farquhar's missionary achievement lies not in his (alas dated) theories of encounter but in his solid scholarship. Scholarly achievement, particularly when it is based on firsthand observations, does not date. When theoretical constructions have retreated into that special limbo reserved for yesterday's insights, solid firsthand scholarship will remain for coming generations to use as best they can. In a sense, Farquhar knew more about Hinduism than he knew of Christianity. His Christianity, though intense and radiant, was of a particular kind; his knowledge of Hinduism was broad and catholic. He saw, as few missionaries before (or since) had seen, that Hinduism was an exquisitely complex organism, requiring for its understanding a full-time scholarly commitment. Most missionaries had neither the ability nor the time to acquire such knowledge. Farquhar had both. His mastery of the written sources is seen most clearly in his *Outline of the Religious Literature of India,* which is so much more than a bloodless catalogue; his capacity for patient observation gave rise to *Modern Religious Movements.*[11] I have already spoken of his exacting personal scholarly standards. In 1916, writing to the Reverend Joseph Passmore of Madras, he had this to say about two of his books:

Even if there were a call at once for the republication of the *Primer of Hinduism* and *The Crown of Hinduism* I could not agree to it without largely rewriting them. I have not changed in the slightest in my convictions as to the supremacy of Christ and the inadequacy of the religions of India. What I feel is that my work in the past has not been sufficiently scholarly and accurate.[12]

During virtually the whole of his career in India, Farquhar was in touch, not only with the Hindus he so much respected (even when he was unable to agree with them), and with his fellow missionaries, but also with the most prominent Western Orientalists of his day, among whom he held a leading position. He was also a significant figure in the international missionary movement, and his work on the borders of Hinduism and Christianity inspired workers on other, no less important, frontiers. With John R. Mott in particular he enjoyed close friendship, and along this channel there passed much mutual support and inspiration, as may be seen from their lengthy correspondence. It was Mott who had made it possible for Farquhar to devote most of his missionary career to writing and research, and for this he was always grateful. A letter written to Mott in 1923 includes the words:

> I should also like to say that it is to your emancipation of me for literature that I owe the opportunity these years have given me to study widely and to publish my books. Apart from all this, I should not have been appointed to Manchester. I thank you with all my heart. The work throughout has been a continuous joy, and I have constantly thought of you.[13]

Not all of Farquhar's personal attitudes would now win the unqualified approval of the Christian world. Christian ideas have moved on, and presuppositions have changed. For much of what now passes for "interreligious dialogue" he would have had little time, less on account of its warmhearted comprehensiveness than for its superficiality and its tendency to shy away from difficult issues of belief. He was not enamored of Indian nationalism, and believed wholeheartedly in India's need of the best that the West could offer. Those Christians, whether European, American, or Indian, who too readily adopted the Hindu nationalist point of view – among them C.F. Andrews on the European side and K.T. Paul on the Indian – disappointed him greatly, again not because of the warmth or sincerity of their beliefs, but because of the way in which they had permitted the heart to rule the head. This caused him real distress, and in one letter from late in his Indian career we find him saying, "I have been afraid some of my friends would think I was growing extremely self-confident and very harsh."[14] The cause of this anticipated judgment was, it should be added, his refusal to publish books of inferior scholarship – many of which today's publishers would probably accept without much ado.

I have already said that in my opinion Farquhar's lasting contribution was made as a scholar. This is not to devalue his very great importance as a missionary leader; after all, he taught the missionary corps virtually single-handedly the need for sympathetic and positive evaluation of the Indian cultural and religious heritage. But he did so under conditions which no longer obtain in today's world, and which it would be idle to attempt to re-create. Every generation must work out for itself its own understanding of both religion and culture – and this brings us back to our starting point. To Farquhar, with his fundamentally historical mind, the key to India's present was to be found in the proud record of India's past. But a modern nation, he believed, could not live on the mere memory of the past, however noble. Hinduism, whatever its achievements, remained in his view deficient in the area of morality, caused ultimately by its failure to recognize the moral nature of God and the force of the divine imperative. Living Hindu spirituality (for which he perhaps had little real feeling) he saw as a retreat from the world, not a commission to service. For this reason he was unable to contemplate any halfway meeting between Christian and Hindu traditions. He called himself a "Liberal Evangelical": today it would appear that his evangelicalism always had the upper hand.

But I am personally convinced nevertheless that he read the Hinduism of his day more sympathetically and more accurately than many of us as Christians read the Hinduism of ours. We need to rediscover his exacting standards of sympathy, accuracy, and Christian centrality, not with a view to applying yesterday's solutions to today's problems, but in order to bring our best thinking, as well as our deepest feeling, to bear on today's interreligious and intercultural encounters. He will not give us the answers; but he will at least show us how to ask the questions responsibly.

Notes

Books and articles are by Farquhar unless otherwise stated.
1. "The Science of Religion as an Aid to Apologetics," in *The Harvest Field* (1901), p. 369.
2. Ibid., p. 370.
3. Ibid., p. 374.
4. Sharpe, *Comparative Religion: A History* (London: Duckworth, 1975), esp. pp. 26ff.
5. "Missionary Study of Hinduism" (Calcutta Missionary Conference paper, May 1905), offprint, p. 3.
6. Ibid., p. 5.
7. *Christ and the Gospels* (Calcutta: Christian Tract and Book Society, 1901), p. 27.
8. *The Crown of Hinduism* (1913), pp. 191f.
9. *The Harvest Field* (1915), p. 317.
10. Hogg's manuscript answer to Edinburgh 1910 questionnaire (Commission IV); see also Sharpe, *Not to Destroy* (Lund: Gleerup, 1965), pp. 289ff., 350ff.
11. Reprinted by Munshiram Manoharlal, Delhi, 1967.
12. J.N. Farquhar to J. Passmore, June 1, 1916 (YMCA Historical Library, New York City).
13. J.N. Farquhar to J.R. Mott, October 25, 1923 (Farquhar Collection).
14. J.N. Farquhar to E.C. Jenkins, March 14, 1923 (YMCA Historical Library, New York City).

Selected Bibliography

Works by J.N. Farquhar

1903 (under pseudonym of Neil Alexander) *Gita and Gospel*. Calcutta: Thacker, Spink & Co.
   Second and third editions under own name: 1906 (London) and 1917 (Madras: Christian Literature Society).
1911 *A Primer of Hinduism*. London, Madras, and Colombo: The Christian Literature Society for India.
1912 *A Primer of Hinduism*. 2nd ed. revised and enlarged. London: Oxford Univ. Press. Reprinted 1914.
1913 *The Approach of Christ to Modern India*. Calcutta: The Association Press.
1913 *The Crown of Hinduism*. Oxford Univ. Press.
1915 *Modern Religious Movements in India*. New York: Macmillan Company. 1967 reprint, ed. Delhi: Munshiram Manoharlal.
1920 *An Outline of the Religious Literature of India*. London: Oxford Univ. Press.

Works about J.N. Farquhar

Macnicol, Nicol. Article on Farquhar, in *Dictionary of National Biography, 1922-1930*. London: Oxford Univ. Press, 1937. P. 296.
Sharpe, Eric J. *J.N. Farquhar: A Memoir*. Calcutta: YMCA Publishing House, 1963.
_____. *Not to Destroy but to Fulfil: The Contribution of J.N. Farquhar to Protestant Missionary Thought in India before 1914*. Studia Missionalia Upsaliensia V. Lund: C.W.K. Gleerup, 1965.
_____. *Comparative Religion: A History*. London: Gerald Duckworth, 1975. Pp. 151-54.
_____. *Faith Meets Faith: Some Christian Attitudes to Hinduism in the Nineteenth and Twentieth Centuries*. London: SCM Press, 1977. Pp. 19-32.

Lars Peter Larsen
1862–1940

India's Enduring "Great Dane"

Eric J. Sharpe

Denmark's contribution to the history of Christianity in India has not been large, measured by the size of the Danish missionary community. It has not, however, been insignificant. No one is likely to forget that two important steps in the establishment of Protestant missions in India could not have been taken when they were taken, had it not been for the existence of two tiny Danish trading posts – Tranquebar in the south at the beginning of the eighteenth century, and Serampore in Bengal at the century's end. Both settlements were sold to the East India Company in 1845. Both names, however, kept their place on the Indian Christian roll of honor – Serampore as an educational center, Tranquebar as the point from which a determined and controversial attempt was made in the middle years of the nineteenth century by missionaries of the Leipzig Society to claim India for the tradition of Martin Luther.[1] But by now the Danish involvement had begun to flow into other channels, and it was not until 1888 that the Danish Missionary Society (founded in 1812) sent its first ordained missionary, N.P. Hansen (1854-1919), to India. A year later there followed the second, Lars Peter Larsen (1862-1940), who served in India for no less than forty-four years, from 1889-1933. The affectionate label "the Great Dane" has at various times been bestowed on Kierkegaard, Grundtvig, the composer Carl Nielsen, and no doubt others. In the annals of the Indian church, however, there has been only one "Great Dane": L.P. Larsen.

Larsen brought together in his own mature and balanced personality qualities not often found in combination. He was an intellectual and a pietist, a liberal evangelical and a Lutheran holiness Christian. A Danish Lutheran by origin and affection, after a decade with the Danish Missionary Society he left for wider fields of service, first with the YMCA, then with the United Theological College in Bangalore, and finally under Bible Society auspices. Being neither British nor German, he was able to move with some freedom through the political minefield of the war years and the 1920s. Being in a sense undenominational, he had no need to toe anyone's party line. He could be highly critical of missions and their ways, but that did not make him ever want to masquerade as an Indian; most photographs taken during his years in India (at least those that have been published) show him dressing almost ostentatiously in European suits, with collar and tie and obligatory *sola-topi*. He was on record to the effect that the Westernness of Christianity in India was deplorable and needed to be corrected; to serve up Christianity with curry sauce, however, was not the way to set about it.[2] Race relations among Christians in India was a subject that troubled him greatly, to which he returned on many occasions, but he was never one to opt for band-aid solutions to problems of such multilayered complexity. Another untypical trait in Larsen's work was that, internationalist as he was, he was not as a rule an international conference-goer.[3] His legacy is therefore not to be found parceled out at strategic intervals along the conference trail.

From a Blacksmith's Home to India

Lars Peter Larsen was twenty-seven years old, newly ordained and newly married to Anna Elisabeth (Lise) Seidelin, when he arrived in South India in December 1889. He might never have arrived at all. A few months earlier, a catastrophe had almost taken place, as the young and undoubtedly intense Larsen had crossed theological swords at dinner table with the redoubtable Vilhelm Beck (1829-1901), at that time the leader of the evangelical faction (the Inner Mission) in the Danish church and the chairman of its missionary society.[4] Beck, deeply hurt at the young man's arrogance (as he saw it), had demanded an apology. Without it, Beck refused to ratify the young man's appointment as a missionary. Fortunately for the future of the church in India, Larsen went to see Beck and was warmly received. No apology needed to be given.[5] But the possibility of further friction between Larsen and church officialdom remained.

To begin at the beginning: Larsen was born on November 8, 1862, at Baarse, Denmark (some forty miles from Copenhagen), the eldest son of a blacksmith, Jens Larsen, and his wife, Ellen (née Nielsen).[6] Blacksmiths did not as a rule grow rich, and L.P. would probably have become just one more country artisan had it not been for the help of a local landowner, P.F. Fabricius, to whose estate the family moved in 1868. Lars Peter was obviously gifted and wanted to be a teacher; Fabricius, recognizing his abilities, not only financed his education but practically adopted him into his family.[7] Larsen entered the University of Copenhagen at the age of nineteen in 1882, just as the international student missionary movement was making its presence felt in the Scandinavian countries. A missionary hero was Lars Olsen Skrefsrud (1840-1910), a Norwegian worker among the Santals of northern India and an enthusiastic advocate of the so-called Gossner principle of employing wherever possible practical missionaries who in their education had not lost their passion for souls.[8] Had Skrefsrud done nothing but enthuse Larsen and Nathan Söderblom in the 1880s – as he undoubtedly did – his life could have been deemed well spent.[9] For a time, Larsen planned to accompany Skrefsrud back to India there and then. Fortunately, wiser counsels prevailed: Larsen could not have been the missionary he was had he not been educated as he was.

As the nineteenth century wound down, evangelical theology in Denmark, as elsewhere, stood at a parting of the ways, and which direction each individual took was largely determined by the kind of education each had received. On the one side, there was the conservative, confessional pietism of the Inner Mission; on the other, the cultural nationalism of the followers of N.F.S. Grundtvig. A third force was just beginning to emerge, in the shape of a moderate liberalism seeking to reconcile the old and the new, faith and scholarship.[10] This was eventually the position in which Larsen found himself, albeit less by choice than by necessity.

In the 1890s, working in Madras, the Larsens lived the serious and at times solemn life of any young missionary couple of the time. They agonized over their affluent lifestyle and began to ask questions about the relations between Indians and Europeans. Of course they spent much time studying Tamil. If any Indian city could be called a Christian center in the 1890s, it was Madras, not least thanks to the presence of the Madras Christian College, still at that time presided over by the great Dr. William Miller and serving as an example of practical cooperation in the service of the Gospel. As though to keep the Christians on their toes, out at the suburb of Adyar there was the Theosophical Society, with its curious mixture of Hindu, occultist, and rationalist ingredients. And as though in response, there was in Madras the most articulate group of Indian Christians to be found anywhere in the country.[11]

Larsen's first theological problems, however, came with him to India from Denmark. They concerned the sacrament of baptism. Before leaving his home base, Larsen had become involved in a dispute about whether an infant actually receives anything in baptism.[12] The Grundtvigian position was that baptism confers grace, irrespective of the state of mind of the one upon whom the ritual is performed. All well and good; others of us hold that position, while reserving a place for the ritual of confirmation. Larsen's difficulty came at the point in the Danish baptismal ritual where a question asked *of the child* is answered on the child's behalf *by a sponsor* (parent or godparent).[13] When Larsen's second child (his first daughter) was born in January 1893 and he proposed to baptize her, he simply altered the wording of the ritual to fit what he believed to be a matter of spiritual common sense. His difficulties with the Danish Missionary Society had begun.

Over the next few years, Larsen's relations with his Danish Lutheran colleagues, and with his home base, became strained. In his own life of faith, he was moving more and more in the direction of the Holiness movement, the natural roots of which were essentially Wesleyan Methodist, and Lutheran only at several removes. "It is quite clear to me," he wrote to his wife at this time, "that I think very differently about Christianity and the Christian life than do good Lutherans at home. My views on baptism and eucharist are definitely neither Lutheran nor Danish-Lutheran."[14]

Matters came to a head in 1898. Larsen was in Denmark on furlough. There, tensions between the Inner Mission and the Grundtvigians were more evident than ever before. Again the old warrior Vilhelm Beck, almost seventy years old in that year, provoked an outburst from Larsen by suggesting that the *numbers* of baptisms on the mission field ought to be increased. Larsen did not mince his words, accusing Beck of a total lack of understanding of conditions in India; adding insult to injury (especially where an evangelical was concerned), he labeled Beck's attitude "catholic."[15] Playing the numbers game was indeed irrelevant to the future of Christianity in India. Larsen's concern was that at home in Denmark, too few people could tell the difference between proclaiming the Gospel and proclaiming Lutheranism. In discussion at the Aalborg meeting of 1898, Larsen is reported to have said, "I would regret the day when the Danish missionaries wanted to win people for Christ so that they would become Evangelical-Lutheran. Although we [might] try to, we would not succeed." "It would be a disaster," he went on, if all Indian Christians "had strong confessional feelings . . . We do not need it in India."[16]

Enter John R. Mott

The time would come when the idea of German and Scandinavian Lutherans taking part in ecumenical projects would be unremarkable. At the turn of the century, however, the lack of understanding between Lutheran and Calvinist, German and Anglo-Saxon Christians (to use the crude labels then in vogue), made cooperation difficult. Early in 1899, however, Larsen was approached with a view to his taking up a YMCA position in Madras, to work in the new but increasingly important field of student evangelism.[17] It is hardly likely that he would even have been approached had he been thought to be a Lutheran of the hard-line confessional school. But this clearly he was not. Furthermore, in the spring of 1899 he had accompanied and interpreted for John R. Mott in Scandinavia, an arrangement made "partly to ascertain Larsen's fitness for a YMCA-related post back in India."[18] Next, Larsen went to America, visiting a number of major universities and the Northfield Conference. Returning to Europe in July, he went straight from Liverpool to the Keswick Convention – and loved it.[19] It was clear from this point on that his spiritual home was to be in or close to the Holiness movement, while intellectually he remained very much a liberal. Herman Jensen summed up the paradox: "Theologically he is a complete rationalist, but as a Christian he is power and devotion itself."[20]

Taking leave of the Danish Missionary Society in 1899, Larsen had stressed that he was not departing with bitterness as a result of irreconcilable theological differences. It is clear, however, that theology had something to do with his decision, alongside the Madras offer.[21]

Larsen found his YMCA work hectic but congenial; along with contact with students, he led study groups, taught occasionally at the Christian College, and monitored the rising political blood-pressure of "young India." In 1902, J.N. Farquhar, another scholar recruited by Mott, began doing very similar work in Calcutta.[22] As a Dane, Larsen was able to see, perhaps more clearly than the average British missionary, that all was not well between the missionary and the Indian Christian communities. The burden of his message was that "the Indian Christian has come to look upon the missionary as one to whom he cannot come with all the freedom and confidence with which you want to approach a friend."[23] Larsen was to return to this theme often. An identical note was sounded by V.S. Azariah in his "give us friends!" appeal to the Edinburgh Conference of 1910.[24]

In November 1903, tragedy struck. Larsen's wife died of appendicitis, leaving him with four small children, the oldest twelve and the youngest only three. He remarried seven years later.

John Wesley's instruction to his preachers never to be unemployed, and never to be triflingly employed, might well have served Larsen as a motto in these years. He traveled, spoke, and wrote incessantly, his writings covering a bewildering variety of topics. Two purposes dominated, however. To the Indian Christian community, he interpreted the Bible and the life of faith. Among colleagues and for Christians at home in Denmark, he was more the scholarly investigative reporter. His book-length writings listed in 1978 amount to thirty-six in all, though some are not more than pamphlets, and very few fall into the category of scholarly monograph.

One that does is a series of twelve lectures delivered in the University of Copenhagen in 1906 and published in the following years as *Hindu-Aandsliv og Kristendommen* (Hindu spirituality and Christianity). For some reason, these lectures were never translated into English. Had they been more widely read, it would have been very evident that Larsen was on a par with the best of the missionary writers of the time, including Farquhar, Hogg, Macnicol, and Andrews.

An episode in the previous year is worth a brief mention. In 1905 Larsen visited Pandita Ramabai's *Mukti* center at Kedgaon, where a semipentecostal revival had been in progress for some time, and attended an evening prayer meeting at which visions were seen and tongues were spoken. He was made very uneasy by all this. No doubt he admired Pandita Ramabai herself (it would have been hard not to), but in his world of religion he wanted things to be done decently and in order. On this occasion, disorder appeared to be breaking in.[25] For this same reason, Larsen was never much attracted to the mystical element in either Eastern or Western religion.[26]

The United Theological College

In 1909, after some years of discussion and planning, a scheme was finalized for setting up in Bangalore a United Theological College (UTC), on the very sensible principle that what single churches and missions did not have the resources to do on their own was possible through cooperative effort.[27] Behind the scheme stood the South India United Church, and at its inception in 1910 it had the support of the United Free Church of Scotland, the Arcot Mission and the American Board. Neither the Danish Missionary Society nor the YMCA was greatly interested at this stage. That Larsen was so soon involved, therefore, was due to his personal standing and not to his institutional affiliations. He joined the faculty in 1910 and became principal in March 1911, a post that he filled until 1924.

Also in August 1910, Larsen married Gertrud Andersen, a missionary of the Danish Missionary Society. There were two children from this marriage: a girl, who sadly died at the age of only five, and a boy.

In mission history, 1910 inevitably is associated with Edinburgh. We have already said that Larsen was not a conference-goer. Why he was not even an Edinburgh correspondent, bearing in mind his YMCA position and his relationship to Mott, is harder to explain. He did, however, review the report of Commission Five (Preparation of Missionaries/Training of Teachers) for the journal *Harvest Field*. Coming as it did on the threshold of his UTC career, this review may perhaps be seen as a statement of intention for the discharge of his future responsibilities.[28] It makes no attempt to gloss over the deficiencies of much (perhaps most) missionary education as it was at this time. Larsen allows himself to emphasize the point made in the report, that some missionaries are "far less proficient in languages than their Societies believe them to be"[29] – a sensitive subject, since no missionary has ever been known to admit to being an indifferent linguist! Larsen for his part wished to stress, further, the importance of comparative religion, ethnology, sociology, pedagogy, and the science of mission (missiology) in training, as well as the provision of adequate uninterrupted time for language work.[30]

The Bangalore initiative, however, was concerned with the training of *Indian* Christian ministers. The work proved to be difficult. Few Indian Christians at this time were well enough educated in the basics to benefit from regular theological training. The work of the Christian ministry was poorly paid and not highly regarded socially. As though this were not enough, an articulate minority among Indian Christian laymen had already fallen into the habit of criticizing theology at every turn as, in effect, the antithesis of spirituality and a typical Western substitute of Eastern "insight." In 1946 C.W. Ranson called the church's effort to train an ordained ministry for India "almost appallingly feeble."[31] Larsen's work was in no sense feeble. Often, however, it must have been discouraging. In the early years there were never more than a handful of students; finances were dismal; Larsen had many other demands on his time. Still, he seems never to have expressed in public the disappointment he must often have felt at the poor response to what the college had to offer. At times he wondered whether it might not have been better if the college had been located in Madras, rather than in Bangalore. In Madras, though, he would have been under the shadow of the mighty Christian College.

Larsen's principle while at Bangalore, where he taught Old Testament and comparative religion in addition to holding the principalship, was that his students should not so much *learn* theology (i.e., by rote) as *study* theology. One former student later testified that nowhere was there such a training as Larsen gave: "so thorough in the preparation of his lectures, so profound in understanding, and withal so humble and simple in the presentation of truth."[32] Even the bishop of Madras thought the UTC staff at this time excellent, and their teaching exceptionally good, with Larsen and his colleague Godfrey Phillips being singled out for special mention.[33] Bishop Whitehead was worried, however, that at some time in the future the college might fall into the hands of extreme liberals, some of whom he thought were little better than crypto-Unitarians.[34]

The outbreak of war in August 1914 made things desperately difficult for anyone in India having connections of any kind with Germany. German nationals, missionaries included, were interned or deported. Scandinavians were not, though their movements could be curtailed. Being Lutheran was now a liability, for was not Luther the father of the German nation? In South India, the Church of Sweden Mission found itself in charge of the whole of the former Leipzig field – a responsibility entirely beyond its resources at the time.[35]

Moves were being made to bring Larsen back to Scandinavia permanently. In 1912 he might have become professor of missions at the University of Lund in Sweden, an offer he had declined on account of his new Bangalore commitments. In 1918, however, he accepted an honorary doctorate from the same university.

In November 1922, Larsen celebrated his sixtieth birthday; at that point he had been working in India for more than thirty years, the last twelve of them as UTC principal. Mahatma Gandhi had been imprisoned for the past eight months; he was released from a six-year sentence in February 1924 after emergency surgery. Since the end of the war, life for the Christian community in India had been growing more and more difficult as the political temperature had risen, and no one would have begrudged Larsen the well-deserved retirement of an elder missionary statesman. But he showed no signs of wishing to retire, and his life went on at undiminished pace. Godfrey Phillips wrote in his reminiscences of Larsen that when his colleagues saw how crowded were his days, they wondered how he could ever write at all.[36] Teaching, lecturing, and conducting interviews made incessant demands on him. One work that many regretted that he was never able to write was (to quote Phillips again) "a coherent, full and systematic statement of the relation between Christianity and other great world religions."[37] Such works are, however (as some of us know to our cost) far more easily planned than executed. In the event, Larsen's last years in India were spent on a task of a far different kind: revising the Tamil translation of the Bible.

Servant of the Word

Late in 1923 Larsen was first approached by Godfrey Phillips and Bishop Waller of Madras as a possible reviser of the Tamil Bible. Already there were two Tamil versions in use – the Fabricius version of 1796 and the Union version 1869 – and it was felt, understandably, than an up-to-date translation would be a unifying factor for the churches. That Larsen was asked to assume this responsibility was a further sign both of his scholarship and his all-round acceptability to the churches. He would work under the auspices of the British and Foreign Bible Society and the National Missionary Council and would have G.S. Duraiswamy as his coworker, and it was hoped that the revision could be done within the space of three years (in the event, it was not). Larsen would certainly have preferred to have worked on a retranslation, rather than merely a revision; for one thing, he wished to produce a version whose language would be fully comprehensible to Hindus, which apparently the older versions were not. Apparently, too, Larsen and Duraiswamy had different approaches to the task and did not always pull together. The local committee was not always helpful, either, especially where the question of Hindu comprehensibility was concerned. On more than one occasion, Larsen was on the point of abandoning the enterprise altogether. However, he still had his wider contacts. In 1926, for instance, the year in which the revision work started, he had no less than 112 speaking engagements. He also attended Stanley Jones's "round table conferences," the basis of which was not doctrine or encounter but shared religious experience, an approach that Larsen must have found congenial.[38] The New Testament revision was complete early in 1927.

Larsen, liberal as he was, had never renounced his Lutheran heritage, and now, with his missionary career almost at an end, there seemed to be some chance of his spending his final years in India as a professor at Gurukul, the new Lutheran theological college in Madras, which opened in July 1927. But there was never really any chance of realizing this arrangement. Earlier, when Larsen had taught some Lutheran students in Bangalore, the more conservative missionaries had thrown up their hands in horror.[39] Not surprisingly, the strongest objections now came from the direction of the Leipzig mission, some of whose people seem to have feared that Lutheranism's days would be numbered if Larsen were allowed to corrupt their students![40]

One reads the record of Larsen's last few years in India with a certain feeling of sadness that so little seems to have been done to make them less stressful. Returning to India from Denmark in January 1928, he and his wife were shunted from one temporary lodging to another. In April 1929 he moved to Madura, where for a year he had the dismal experience of being a schoolmaster to children who wanted neither to be taught nor to learn. His assistant in the work of Bible revision, Duraiswamy, declined to live in Madura and, in any case, had lined up behind Gandhi. Not before October 1930 was the work of revising the Tamil Old Testament able to begin in earnest – in Bangalore – with Duraiswamy once more restored to the partnership.

In October-November 1932 the Old Testament revision committee held its last meeting, and on November 8, a day before the work of revision was officially concluded, Larsen celebrated his seventieth birthday. Whether the revision was in the end a successful one, this writer is in no way competent to say. But Bror Tiliander is lukewarm about it, saying only that "it was a step forward and induced further efforts."[41] Whether it had therefore been worth Larsen's time and energies, others will have to decide. Sherwood Eddy thought the Larsen version comparable to that of Moffatt in the English-speaking world; it was welcomed and enjoyed by liberals but ignored by practically everyone else.[42] In evangelical Tinnevelly, the Larsen-Duraiswamy New Testament was dismissed on account of its "Catholic" and "modernist" tendencies. Though some may not have even read it, they knew Larsen's liberal reputation.[43]

Larsen gave his last address to the United Theological College on February 7, 1933, and left India to return to Denmark for the last time six weeks later, on March 20. He had a little more than seven years left to him, his last two months darkened by the German invasion of Denmark on April 9, 1940. He died on June 23, at the age of seventy-seven.[44]

"The greatest missionary I have ever known"

All his life, Larsen was reticent about the details of his own experience, impenetrably so where spirituality was concerned. No one ever knew how, where, or when he had begun to live the life of faith, how he became a missionary, or how he had reacted personally to public events and private trials. (His diaries have not been accessible to me as I write this.) Never, it seems, could he have written an autobiography.

His missionary career had passed through four phases: DMS missionary, YMCA secretary, UTC principal, and Bible reviser/translator. This list by itself shows the breadth of his interests and his abilities. Other missionaries in India were at various times doing all these things, and doing them well; one imagines that only a Larsen could have done all of them. His voluminous writings, whether in English or Danish (on other languages, I am unable to pronounce), were invariably written to inform and enlighten, clearly and concisely and without any outward show. Again, many other missionaries were producing similar work; perhaps none covered such a wide range of topics or returned so naturally to the true missionary's commendation of the Lord and Savior.

There was, though, one concern to which he returned again and again: the un-Indianness of so much having the name of Indian Christianity. Indian Christians he felt to have been influenced more than was healthy by their connection with foreign missionaries; missionaries, he wrote in 1928, "bear a considerable part of the blame for the un-Indian character in the Christians."[45] Indian Christians, he insisted, must not become Europeanized, though perhaps in some ways it was already too late. At the end of his time in India, Larsen was still sounding this note of warning, stating drastically that "as yet nothing exists properly deserving to be called Indian Christianity" and admitting that most missionaries were hopelessly alien to Indian culture and thought.[46] The implication was obvious that the missionary's time was drawing to an end and should not be prolonged.

Larsen's understanding of the Christian message was ethical through and through. In 1905 he wrote that "the perfect personality is an absolutely ethical being. And where critical principles obtain, there is no more room for the idea of arbitrariness than in the realm of mechanical laws."[47]

Perhaps his secret was that he was always and everywhere fully himself, without pretense (and therefore entirely humble), and above all without ever playing to any real or imagined gallery. H.C. Balasundaram wrote in 1941: "Dr. Larsen did not believe in that very subtle form of condescension which exhibits itself in many ways, as for instance, the person from abroad assuming the garb of an Indian. He lived, as he should, a European: and yet made everyone, were he a Hindu or a Mohammedan or a Christian, feel perfectly at home in his good home – which was a center of culture. He was incapable of racial feeling."[48]

It may, though, be left to George Sherwood Eddy to pay the last tribute. Larsen, he wrote, was "perhaps the greatest missionary I have ever known. In Larsen's presence I felt like a crude, uneducated high school youth, yet he was so humble that he was an elder brother to us all."[49] Perhaps, Eddy admitted, there was an element of hero worship in his estimate of Larsen. Occasionally, though, one reflects, the missionary movement has produced real heroes, unassuming men and women who, while setting about their Master's business to the utmost of their capacity, have managed to remain free from the touch of fanaticism that so often stains the second-best. One can only regret having been too young to have known God's tireless blacksmith. To give Sherwood Eddy the last word, "Our world is richer for Larsen's having lived in it awhile. I would like to dream of someday being a little more like this winsome man – this great Dane, Larsen!"[50]

Notes

1. Relations between the Leipzig Lutherans and other Protestant missions in India were strained throughout the period 1830-1914, generally over the caste question, but also because of the Lutherans' reluctance to work according to the comity principle. See Sharpe, "'Patience with the Weak.' Leipzig Lutherans and the Caste Question in Nineteenth-Century India," in *Indo-British Review* 19, no. 1 (1993): 117-29.

2. James M. Gibbs, ed., *L.P. Larsen: A Theology for Mission* (Bangalore: United Theological College, 1978), p. 312.

3. The only exception of which I am aware was a WSCF conference in Basel, Switzerland, in 1935, for which Larsen wrote a paper entitled "Syncretism and Evangelisation." See Gibbs, *Larsen*, p. 28.

4. On Beck, see *Nordisk Teologisk Uppslagsbok* I (Lund: Gleerup; Copenhagen: Munksgaard, 1952), cols. 289-92. Cf. Hal Koch, *Danmarks kyrka genom tiderna* (Swedish translation) (Stockholm: SKDB, 1942), pp. 181ff.

5. Carl Bindslev, *L.P. Larsen: Hans liv og gerning* (Copenhagen: Dansk Missions Selskab, 1945), pp. 36-37; Gibbs, *Larsen*, pp. 69-70.

6. In the eyes of Herman Jensen, Larsen "was born a blacksmith with a big hammer in his hand." Quoted in Bindslev, *Larsen: Hans liv*, p. 54.

7. Bindslev writes that in his young days, Larsen was "tung og mørk" (*Larsen: Hans liv*, p. 316), which we may perhaps interpret as meaning "serious and introverted," and that all his life he found it hard to initiate a pastoral conversation. He was uninterested in even his own family history. Insights into his inner development are therefore hard to come by.

8. See Olav Hodne, *L.O. Skrefsrud* (Oslo: Forlaget Land og Kirke, 1966).

9. See Sharpe, *Nathan Söderblom and the Study of Religion* (Chapel Hill: Univ. of North Carolina Press, 1990), p. 19.

10. Koch, *Danmarks kyrka*, pp. 204-50.

11. The Madras Native Christian Association, established in 1888, among other things started the journal the *Christian Patriot* in 1890. It was out of this nucleus that the National Missionary Society developed. In 1891 there were 865,528 Christians in the Madras Presidency, and 1,027,071 in 1901.

12. Gibbs, *Larsen*, pp. 71-72.

13. Ibid., p. 44. The Danish baptismal ritual still retains this feature.

14. Quoted in Bindslev, *Larsen: Hans liv*, p. 72.

15. Ibid., pp. 88-89.

16. Gibbs, *Larsen*, p. 63.

17. The pioneer in this regard was Thomas Ebenezer Slater (1840-1912) who had been working as an evangelist to the educated classes in Madras under London Missionary Society auspices since 1871. See Sharpe, *Not to Destroy but to Fulfil* (Uppsala: Studia Missionalia Upsaliensia, 1965), pp. 95ff.

18. C. Howard Hopkins, *John R. Mott, 1865-1955: A Biography* (Geneva: WCC; Grand Rapids, Mich: Wm. B. Eerdmans Publishing Co., 1979), pp. 236, 249.

19. On the 1899 Keswick Convention, see Walter B. Sloan, *These Sixty Years: The Story of the Keswick Convention* (London: Pickering and Inglis, 1933), pp. 50-51.

20. Bindslev, *Larsen: Hans liv*, p. 54.

21. Gibbs, *Larsen*, pp. 53ff.

22. Sharpe, *Not to Destroy*, pp. 172ff.

23. Gibbs, *Larsen*, p. 160.

24. Cf. J.Z. Hodge, *Bishop Azariah of Dornakal* (Madras: CLS, 1946), pp. 1-7; Carol Graham, *Azariah of Dornakal* (London: SCM Press, 1946), pp. 38-39.

25. Bindslev, *Larsen: Hans liv*, p. 158. On the revival at Mukti, see Helen S. Dyer, *Pandita Ramabai: Her Vision, Her Mission and Triumph of Faith* (London; Pickering and Inglis, [ca.1924]), pp. 101-2; Nicol Macnicol, *Pandita Ramabai* (Madras: CLS, 1929), pp. 216ff.

26. Cf. Larsen, "The Interest of Mystical Christianity to Indian Missionaries," in Gibbs, *Larsen*, pp. 246-72 (originally in the *Harvest Field*, 1905), in which he calls mystical Christianity "a peculiar temptation to the minds of the people of this country" (p. 247). The same reservations were to be seen in the 1920s in respect of his estimate of Sadhu Sundar Singh. See Larsen, "Sadhu Sundar Singh," in *Kirke og Kultur* (1922), pp. 12-33. But at least he could see that Sundar Singh was genuinely Indian, which in his view could not often be said of Christians in India (p. 26).

27. Bengt Sundkler, *Church of South India* (London: Lutterworth, 1954), pp. 36ff.

28. Gibbs, *Larsen*, pp. 292-305.

29. World Missionary Conference, 1910: *Report of Commission V*, p. 60.

30. Gibbs, *Larsen*, pp. 279-86.

31. C.W. Ranson, *The Christian Minister in India: His Vocation and Training* (London: Lutterworth, 1946), p. 167; cf. pp. 13-33.

32. *Young Men of India*, July 1939, p. 164.

33. Sundkler, *Church of South India*, p. 75.

34. Ibid. At this time the meaning of "Unitarian" in this context was "Theist."

35. See Sigfried Estborn, *Fran Taberg till Tranquebar: Bishop David Bexell* (Stockholm: SKDB, 1940), pp. 100ff.

36. Gibbs, *Larsen*, p. 27.

37. Ibid., p. 28.

38. E. Stanley Jones, *Christ at the Round Table* (London: Hodder and Stoughton, 1928), pp. 125ff.

39. Sigfrid Estborn, *Johannes Sandegren och hans insats in Indiens Kristenhet* (Uppsala: Studia Missionalia Upsaliensia X, 1968), pp. 92, 133.

40. Ibid., p. 142.

41. Bror Tiliander, *Christian and Hindu Terminology* (Uppsala: Almqvist and Wiksell, 1947), p. 38.

42. G. Sherwood Eddy, *Pathfinders of the World Missionary Crusade* (New York: Abingdon-Cokesbury, 1945), p. 109.

43. Bindslev, *Larsen: Hans liv*, pp. 290-91.

44. Eddy (*Pathfinders*, p. 110) was wrong in supposing that Larsen had passed away *before* the German invasion.

45. Gibbs, *Larsen*, pp. 363, 365.

46. Ibid., p. 372.

47. Ibid., p. 271.

48. "Dr. L. P. Larsen – An Appreciation," in *Young Men of India* 53, no. 4 (April 1941): 90.

49. Eddy, *Pathfinders*, p. 104.

50. Ibid., p. 111. Stephen Neill also called Larsen "the greatest of all South India missionaries." Neill (ed. E.M. Jackson), *God's Apprentice* (London: Hodder and Stoughton, 1991), p. 69.

Selected Bibliography

Works by L.P. Larsen

1904 *Oneness with God: Four Lectures to Educated Hindus.* Madras: CLS.

1905 *Studies in the Two Epistles of Paul the Apostle to the Corinthians.* Madras: CLS.

1907 *Hindu-Aandsliv og Kristendommen* (Hindu Spirituality and Christianity). Copenhagen: Gad.

1915 *Prayer: A Course of Bible Studies.* Calcutta: Association Press.

1927 *Christ's Way and Ours.* Calcutta: Association Press.

A fairly full Larsen bibliography appears in James M. Gibbs, ed., *L.P. Larsen: A Theology for Mission* (Madras: CLS for United Theological College, Bangalore, 1978), pp. 33-43. This includes titles in Danish, as well as in English. As well as his books, during his years in India Larsen produced a vast output of articles and reviews for the English-language periodical press, which are not listed here.

Works about L.P. Larsen

Bindslev, Carl. *L.P. Larsen: Evangelist and Theologian.* Bangalore: UTC; Calcutta: YMCA Publishing House, 1962.

_____. *Larsen: Hans liv og gerning.* Copenhagen: Dansk Missions Selskab, 1945.

Eddy, George Sherwood. "Larsen, the Great Dane." In *Pathfinders of the World Missionary Crusade,* pp. 104-11. New York: Abingdon-Cokesbury, 1945.

Gibbs, James M., ed. *L.P. Larsen: A Theology for Mission.* Bangalore: UTC and Madras: CLS, 1978. An invaluable work containing some 350 pages of Larsen's own writings on a large range of subjects.

Ida S. Scudder

1870–1960

Life and Health for Women of India

Dorothy Clarke Wilson

The year was 1957. I had come to Vellore, a city in South India, to gather material for a biography of Dr. Ida Scudder, founder of the great international and interdenominational medical center. In the heart of that teeming city there was a gate. A Gate Beautiful, I called it, conceived in a flowing pattern of lotus leaves and opening buds and wrought in silvered iron. Each day at least 1,000 persons passed through its portals, a cross-section of 400 million people.

I watched them come and go. Young Indian doctors in crisp uniforms. Patriarchs in long skirts. Student nurses in blue-and-white saris. Villagers wearing only a strip of cloth about head and loins, yet possessing the peculiar dignity that is endowed by centuries of burden-bearing. Women with patient eyes and hard bare feet. Children clean and dirty, dressed and undressed, laughing, crying, faces bright with health and pinched with misery and disease.

A car drove up to the gate, and an old woman, leaning heavily on a cane, moved awkwardly out of it. Her face was crinkled with lines, but her eyes were a clean bright blue, and the mass of soft white hair above them was still faintly aglow with its youthful sheen of gold.

Instantly a dozen hands were outstretched to help her. "Thank you, thank you." She smiled gratefully, even while muttering rebelliously, "Oh, dear, terrible having to be helped like this. How I hate it!"

As she moved through the crowded room of the dispensary and onto the corridors of the great and busy hospital, crouching figures straightened. Sad eyes brightened. Hands sprang palm to palm into the welcoming gesture of *namaskar*. Lips tensed with pain of futility burst into smiles. Unnoticed, a brown hand reached to touch the hem of her blue-sprigged cotton dress. To her dismay a villager in dingy white *vaishti* sank to his knees, eyes aglow with unmistakable worship, and prostrated himself full length at her feet.

India has a word for it, the sudden radiance of well-being elicited by the appearance of such a person: *darshan,* the blessing, or benediction, imparted by the mere sight or physical presence of a *mahatma,* a great soul.

Pausing for a moment on one of the long, high, open corridors, she and I looked out over the hospital area: courtyards, sprawling wings, crowded verandahs, a vast network of veins and arteries pulsing with ceaseless activity. A mile from where we stood, beyond crowded streets and teeming bazaars, was a modest red-brick building, now an eye hospital, which was the core from which all these multiplying structures had sprung. Four miles to the south was a green valley housing a great college, a rural hospital, a leprosy rehabilitation unit, and a mental health centre. On and outward flowed the healing energy into a fifty-mile radius of towns and villages where some 200,000 persons were ministered to each year.

And it was this smiling, white-haired woman who had created this greatest medical center in all of Asia. I looked at her in wonder.

"Doesn't it make you feel a great satisfaction," I asked, "seeing all this and remembering how it all started?"

"Oh, yes, yes," she replied fervently. "God has been very good to me."

My wonder sharpened. What! Only this to sum up one of the most extraordinary successes of the century? *God has been very good to me.* No pride, only gratitude. [The preceding paragraphs are adapted from the introduction to the book *Dr. Ida,* by Dorothy Clarke Wilson.]

Three Knocks in the Night

Ida Scudder came from a remarkable missionary family. Her grandfather, the first Dr. John Scudder, was the first medical missionary ever to go out from the United States. He went out under the American Board of Commissioners for Foreign Missions in 1819. He had seven sons, every one of whom became at some time a missionary to India. In subsequent years forty-three members of the Scudder family gave over 1,100 years to missionary service.

Ida was born in India in 1870. She came to the United States for her education and graduated from Northfield Seminary in Massachusetts. Then she returned to India because her mother was ill. But she went with just one idea in her mind, that she was never, *never* going to be one of those missionary Scudders! She would come back to America, go to Wellesley College, and no doubt marry a rich man, a distinct possibility because she was very beautiful with sparkling blue eyes and a halo of blonde hair, and all her life men would be falling in love with her.

But something happened to her one night as she sat writing letters in the little bungalow in Tindivanum where her missionary parents were living. I myself heard her tell the story when I attended a missionary conference at Northfield in 1922. Like all the other teenage delegates, I felt captive to her beauty, her vivid charm, her contagious enthusiasm for Christian service, little suspecting that thirty-five years later I would be journeying halfway around the world to write her story. Though she was then over fifty, she seemed more radiantly youthful than some half her age who panted after her swift serves on the tennis court or struggled breathlessly to match her pace on the steep hillside paths. And no wonder! A woman who at eighty would still be whizzing tennis balls across the net and at eighty-five would be taking her first ride on an elephant, a four-hour jaunt through the jungle, was at fifty barely approaching her prime.

The story she told has often been called "three knocks in the night." While she sat writing letters three men came to her door, each, strangely enough, with the same request, that she come to his house and try to save the life of his very young wife who was dying in childbirth.

"But I know nothing about doctoring," she told each one. "It's my father who is the doctor. I'll be glad to go with him."

"Oh, no," each one replied, the Brahmin, the Muslim, and another high-caste Hindu. It was not in accordance with his religion to allow any man outside the family to enter the woman's quarters of his home. Better that his wife should die than that the laws governing her soul's salvation should be broken.

Three times this happened, and Ida was much troubled. She spent a sleepless night. In the morning she sent a servant to find out what had happened to the three young women. Even before he returned she heard the sound of funeral tom-toms as processions made their way to the riverbank. Each one of the three wives had died because there was no woman doctor to go to them. That was her call. All other ambitions were swept aside. She came back to the United States and graduated from Cornell University Medical College in the first class it opened to women.

A Hospital for Women

She returned to India, to Vellore (where her father was then a missionary), a city teeming with life, with its crowded bazaar section, its population of 60,000, its concentration of poverty, disease, and ignorance. She had no place to work but she could not bear to wait. She opened a little dispensary in a ten-by-twelve room in her father's bungalow and handed out medicines to an ever lengthening queue of patients who came to her window. Soon she was using not only the small room but her mother's guest room, big enough for three beds. Then she built a mud house on the compound with rooms for six beds. But, though she treated over 5,000 patients during the first two years, she was only marking time until her new hospital for women should be completed.

She had raised the money for it herself in America. Permitted by her mission board of the Reformed Church in America to solicit $8,000, she had tackled the job with her usual gusto, but her hopes had been sadly dashed. Then – a near miracle! A wealthy New Yorker, overhearing her impassioned recital of the needs of India's women, had donated $10,000 for a hospital in memory of his wife, Mary Taber Schell.

This building, dedicated in 1902, provided a full outlet for Ida's tremendous energy and purpose. Soon she was not only utilizing its original twenty-eight beds but putting patients on mats under the beds and in every available corner of verandahs and corridors. During the first months she had no professional help whatever, performing her first operation with only an untrained butler's wife, Salome, to help her. Even the acquisition of a pharmacist and a few nurses did not lessen her labors, for Schell Hospital offered the only medical service available to women in an area of at least a million people. In the first year she treated over 12,000 patients. By 1906 more beds had been added, and the number of patients treated annually had risen to 40,000.

But, of course, being Ida, she was not satisfied. Even training nurses for her own hospital was not enough. She must train dozens, hundreds, to staff other hospitals, to go out into remote villages and prevent disease as well as cure it, boldly facing the challenge of a country which had less than one nurse to 50,000 people. In 1909 she started the small nursing school that was to grow through the years until, in 1946, after awarding over 400 nursing certificates, it became the first graduate school of nursing in all India, affiliated with Madras University and giving a B.Sc. degree. Here, literally, Dr. Ida became a "lady with a lamp" as, year after year on the evening of her nurses' graduation, she stood in the darkened chapel of the great medical center holding the little lamp shaped like a teapot, a replica of Florence Nightingale's, and watched it kindle into flame.

Also in 1909, using a tiny French Peugeot, the first motor car seen in that part of India, she started her "Roadside" clinics, which were to become such a dramatic feature of the work at Vellore. Making weekly trips to a small dispensary in a churchyard twenty-five miles away and finding people all along the way who needed help, she appointed stations where she would stop each week – at the edge of the village, under a tamarind or banyan tree – and give treatments to all who wished to come. The little French car was succeeded by a Ford, a small ambulance, by well-equipped modern buses, until mobile clinics were going out on several "Roadsides" each week, taking teams of doctors, nurses, students, pharmacists, public health workers, a leprosy specialist, an evangelist.

It was a revelation to accompany one of these teams on "Roadside." I myself did it several times, once in 1957 with Dr. Ida B. Scudder, Dr. Ida's niece and namesake. I tried to describe some of the experience in a pamphlet entitled *Christ Rides the Indian Road.*

I follow Dr. Ida B. to the table under the trees where she takes her place with the two young Indian doctors, seating myself on a folding stool by her side. Now I am no longer a foreigner, aloof. With the crowd pressing around me, dark anxious faces close to mine, ragged saris brushing my shoulders, I am suddenly engulfed in all the poverty and sickness and suffering which still enslave so much of India. I feel an intense involvement. The baby with its knees painfully swollen and its little buttocks covered with red rash ("Congenital syphilis," explains Dr. Ida with brevity) . . . The young man with the inside of his arm one mass of ugly cancerous flesh . . . The blind man who used to be the village musician but lost favor with the coming of the radio, and whose wife had twins twice during the last times of famine . . . The little girl with the sweet face who discloses the fact that she has coughed blood. ("Oh, no!" wails Dr. Ida B. softly, taking the thin little face between her hands. "Don't, please don't have tuberculosis!" She turns to me in distress. "She's one of my own little girls. I've followed her family through so many years. I'd be just sick if I found she had TB.")

It was dark when we finished, the last treatments given by lantern light. In all, 787 patients had been treated. A small day, for it often ran above 1,000. In the year ending June 30, 1959, the year my book came out, treatments were given on "Roadside" to 92,756 patients.

By 1913 the hospital was getting far too small. Ida ventured to ask permission of her mission board for $3,000 to make additions. But her dreams were soaring high above the heads of plodding boards. It wasn't just an addition she needed. It was a new hospital! And – most daring of all – it wasn't just a new hospital. It was a *medical college for women!* Finally at a Missionary Medical Conference she exploded her bombshell.

Next, a Medical College!

"I propose that this body approve the founding of a medical school for women and that we begin to make plans for it immediately."

The bombshell elicited a startled volley of comment. "Impossible!" "My dear young woman, do you know what such a thing would cost?" "Government would never consent!" "Wonderful if it could be done! But–"

The words "but" and "if" were not in Dr. Ida's vocabulary. Already she had supporters in two denominations, Dr. McPhail of the Church of Scotland, and Dr. Anna Kugler, a Lutheran missionary. In 1913 two Baptist women came touring, Mrs. Lucy Peabody and Mrs. Helen B. Montgomery. They were interested in a women's Union Christian college in India, yes, but one for arts, not medicine. Ida took them first to a village, one of India's 700,000, craftily pointing out the tremendous needs.

"Are they all like that one?" asked the shocked Mrs. Montgomery.

"No," said Ida. "Most of them have never seen a doctor."

"And such a lot of women," commented Mrs. Montgomery thoughtfully.

"A hundred and fifty million," said Ida, hoping she would ask more right questions.

She did. "And how many women doctors?"

"About a hundred and fifty."

"But why don't they train Indian women to be doctors?"

Bless the woman! Ida chose her words carefully. "There is one Christian medical school for women in the north. But it's a thousand miles away, and Indian parents, even Christians, would not send their daughters so far."

She took the woman to a beautiful valley outside of town where she visioned, not the wild expanse where goats were grazing but the site of her medical college.

"Two hundred acres, you say?" said Mrs. Peabody. "Hm! Practically wasteland."

Ida was bleakly disappointed, but she was in for a surprise. "I have an idea!" Lucy Peabody came suddenly alive, her blue eyes glowing. "That medical college we were talking about. You must be the one to start it, Dr. Scudder. You are going to build a college, and – *you are going to build it here, in this valley!*"

Ida drew a long breath. She felt like Moses looking into the Promised Land.

Lucy Peabody was another dynamo, like Ida. She set to work immediately, enlisting women of many denominations, raising money, kindling interest in the project all over America and Britain.

In spite of government skepticism – "No buildings, no money, no staff!" – Ida opened her medical school in a rented building in 1918 with seventeen girls, fourteen of whom graduated in 1922, six of them, to the amazement of the British Medical Department, taking prizes for the Madras Presidency and one winning a gold medal in anatomy in competition with men from six medical schools! The growth of the pioneer institution was phenomenal. Soon the rented quarters were discarded for rooms in the new large hospital area in the bazaar section of the city, another of Dr. Ida's dreams fulfilled when the new impressive hospital building was dedicated in 1924. Then in 1932 the student body, then numbering 105, was moved again, this time into the beautiful white stone quadrangle of college buildings in the wide mountain-girt valley four miles from town, the "wasteland" where she and Lucy Peabody had caught a glimpse of the vision splendid.

Both the new hospital and the college continued to grow, thanks to the dedication of hundreds of Christians of diverse faiths and nationality and to the courage and zeal of one indomitable woman whose credo and goal were embodied in the words of her favorite marching song, "Be Thou My Vision, O Lord of My Heart." But in 1938, close to the medical school's twentieth anniversary, came a crisis that almost sounded the death-knell to her dreams, when the government of Madras Presidency at one stroke abolished the Medical Practitioner's certificate course, which was all she had been able to achieve for her students. Any less intrepid spirit would have bowed to the inevitable, for the task of upgrading to university status meant innumerable new departments, nearly a million dollars' worth of new buildings both at hospital and at college, 600 hospital beds instead of 300, at least a dozen new professors with higher degrees than those possessed by any member of her staff.

Surmounting a Crisis, at Age Seventy-two

The inevitable? Not to Ida. At age seventy-two she began her three-year fund-raising trek of the North American continent which, together with the bold decision to open the school to men, not only saved the project but gave it the broad strength of international and interdenominational support that made it one of the leading institutions of its kind in the world. Eighty years after the founding of Dr. Ida's work in India, the organizations supporting the Christian Medical College and Hospital would number seventy-five, two in Australia, four in Canada, two international, one in Taiwan-Hong Kong, one in Singapore, one in Germany, seven in the United Kingdom, twelve in the United States of America, one in New Zealand, and forty-four in India itself.

Dr. Ida died in 1960, in her ninetieth year. It was May. Vellore broiled in suffocating heat, yet crowds by the hundreds moved en masse into the center of town; others poured in streams from the surrounding countryside. Stores were closed, shops shuttered, bazaars deserted. An awed hush pervaded the crowds. Hindus, Muslims, Christians – all were fused into one by a heat of emotion stronger than India's blazing sun.

"Aunt Ida has gone!"

To do her honor they came in such crowds as only India can muster, following in dense masses after the flower-decked open carriage, lining the streets as the beloved figure, face visible to all after the Indian custom, made its last slow journey in pony cart, jutka, ancient Peugeot, modern ambulance, or on its own tireless swift feet.

An Enduring Legacy

The dream she brought to such glorious fulfillment – what has happened to it since? Has it kept growing like that banyan tree it so resembled, constantly thrusting down new roots until one can hardly tell where the first small tree emerged? And in spite of its vastness of size, is it still permeated with that life-giving spiritual force that was the essence of Dr. Ida's Christian concern and commitment?

I myself have been involved in a small part of that continued growth. I had heard about Dr. Mary Verghese when I was gathering material for *Dr. Ida*. In 1954, just after graduating from her residency in gynecology, Dr. Mary was involved in a terrible bus accident, which paralyzed her from the waist down. She showed incredible faith and courage, learning to perform surgery on leprosy patients because she could do that seated. Then she was inspired to help all the disabled for whom Vellore – and India – had almost no rehabilitation facilities. She came to New York in her wheelchair, studied in Dr. Howard Rusk's Physical Medicine and Rehabilitation Center. And so was born my second book about Vellore, *Take My Hands*.

How Dr. Ida would have rejoiced in the outgrowth of Dr. Mary's faith and courage! For she returned to become head of a new Department of Physical Medicine and Rehabilitation at Vellore, one of the first services of its kind in all India, with a building on the hospital grounds for outpatients, and a new Rehabilitation Institute for inpatients up on the college campus.

Dr. Ida had seen and rejoiced in the early work of Dr. Paul Brand, pioneer in surgery and rehabilitation for leprosy, marveled at the operation he had devised that re-created good mobile hands out of stiff claws, fully approved the world's first leprosy rehabilitation center on the college campus and Vellore's cooperation with the British and American Leprosy missions in building a Leprosy Research Sanatorium at Karigiri, ten miles from the hospital. But she never could have visioned the outreach of this work through coming years, the trainees who would come from all over the world to learn Dr. Brand's techniques, the worldwide impact of the discoveries made in her hospital.

It was the story of Dr. Paul Brand that I was privileged to write in my *Ten Fingers for God*.

Dr. Ida went out on one morning of her retirement, as I did, to see one of the "eye camps" pioneered by Dr. Victor Rambo, head of the eye department at Vellore. Like me, she was thrilled to see another sixty or more people out of India's curable blind being operated on for cataract and given their sight, a movement started at Vellore, which has continued to be carried into hundreds of villages and has brought sight to hundreds of thousands of India's blind. Coincidence, it seemed, that during the month of publication of my story of Dr. Rambo, *Apostle of Sight,* he was in India turning the soil for a new eye hospital on the grounds of the old Schell Hospital, where Dr. Ida's work had started. One could almost imagine her there wielding a shovel and urging them to hurry on with the building. For like the life-giving sap flowing from the original stock and activating every fresh shoot of the spreading banyan, the spirit of Dr. Ida is intensively alive, permeating this vast organism that she helped create.

She was an adventurer. The list of "firsts" in India instigated at Vellore during her lifetime is tremendous: mobile dispensary, medical college for women, college of nursing with B.Sc. course, mobile eye camps, neurology and neurosurgery department, cardio-thoracic department, "New Life Center" for rehabilitation of leprosy patients, heart surgery, mental health center pioneered by Dr. Florence Nichols, rural hospital. And her successors have been equally daring.

In 1961 Dr. Gopinath, an Indian physician trained by Dr. Reeve Betts who, with the cooperation of Dr. Kamala Vytilingam, developed the Department of Thoracic Surgery, performed the first successful open-heart surgery in all of India. In 1968 Dr. Stanley John, trained by Dr. Gopinath, performed the first calf's valve transplantation in a human heart. By 1975, some 5,000 heart operations, including 1,000 open-heart surgeries, had been performed at Vellore.

There were other "firsts." Returning from study in America, Dr. P. Koshy helped create a Department of Nephrology, establishing the first artificial-kidney unit in India. In 1971 a surgeon trained at Vellore performed the first kidney transplant. Other transplants soon followed. Progress was made possible by an artificial kidney machine, gift of a wealthy Indian publisher and banker. In 1976 Prime Minister Indira Gandhi officiated at the dedication of a new Nephrology Block.

An even more exciting innovation was the first betatron in India for the treatment of cancer patients, arriving in Vellore in 1976. Happily Dr. Ida B. Scudder, head of the Department of Radiology and Radiotherapy until her retirement, was back in India in time to dedicate this remarkable 42-million-electron-volt machine, a gift from the people of Denmark.

Dr. Ida saw her beloved "Roadside," started with her little chugging Peugeot in 1909, grow into an efficient mobile dispensary serving a wide network along four different roads each week, ministering each year to thousands of villagers. She rejoiced over the building of a rural hospital on her college campus in 1957, over the starting of public health training for nurses under the leadership of Pauline King, public health specialist, and would have delighted to see the further developments of this training under the leadership of Dr. Kasturi Sundar Rao, a graduate of her college of nursing. But she would have exulted even more over a development in rural outreach that took place in 1977.

With the Community, for the Community

RUHSA, they call it – Rural Unit for Health and Social Affairs, a team approach to rural development *with* the community *for* the community. It began by covering a population of about 100,000, with some 20,000 families in over eighty villages grouped about Kavanur, twenty-five miles from Vellore, where the Christian Medical College and Hospital had long conducted a Rural Health Center.

It is an ambitious program of total care and education for this vast area in cooperation with government, both local and national, involving not only medical and public health service but education in literacy, agriculture, family planning ante-natal and family welfare, immunization, cottage industries, women's clubs, young farmers' groups, school and road building, a ministry to the whole human being.

As Dr. Daleep Mukarji, its founder and director, said, "RUHSA is an extension and reemphasis of Vellore's commitment in service, training, and research for the needs of India," a commitment that Dr. Ida initiated when she stopped her Peugeot and gave birth to "Roadside."

Dr. Ida would rejoice over new facilities designed not only to heal but to prevent disease among the most needy, such as the beautiful big Williams Research Block built by the Williams-Waterman Foundation, its mission to wage war on nutritional problems like kwashiorkor, the protein-deficiency disease that wreaks such a havoc among children. She would heartily approve of the work done in the Department of Microbiology, where Dr. Ruth Myers, a Lutheran missionary, and her successor, Dr. Grace Koshi, have isolated many of the viruses causing such diseases as plague, rheumatic fever, and encephalitis.

Dr. Ida pioneered in developing Indian leadership. She saw Vellore staffed by a team of doctors from many countries and from all parts of India. How thrilled she would be to see it now, run by a dedicated group of Indian professors, most of whom were at one time Vellore students! For the head of every one of the multiplicity of departments is now a highly trained and dedicated Indian. At Vellore, as in many other mission projects, the missionary has fulfilled the ideal evolution of this function: first, walking ahead, leading; then, walking beside, cooperating; finally, walking behind, following.

There are many personalities, both missionaries and nationals, deserving of biographies, other than the four whose lives I have chronicled. One could write books about them all. At least we can mention a few.

Dr. Robert Cochrane, world-renowned leprologist, who was its first principal, coming to the aid of the college in its great crisis.

Dr. Hilda Lazarus, revered throughout India, who followed Dr. Cochrane as principal of the college during this critical era, when India became independent.

Sister Delia Houghton, first nursing superintendent, and Sister Vera Putnam, who saw the school of nursing advance into ever higher standards.

Dr. Jacob Chandy, India's great neurosurgeon, a devout Syrian Christian, trained in India, the United States, and Canada, who developed Vellore's Department of Neurology and Neurosurgery into one of the most advanced facilities in the country.

Dr. Carol Jameson, one of Dr. Ida's early staff, whose experiences in obstetrics and gynecology read like an exciting saga.

Treva Marshall, another early devotee, always available for every need and emergency, beloved mother-sister-friend of thousands of Vellore alumni.

Dr. Kamala Vytilingam, first of Dr. Ida's students to become a professor at Vellore, serving brilliantly as head of cardiology.

Dr. John Carman, Baptist missionary, urologist and surgeon, long the efficient director of the institution, and his many-talented wife, Naomi.

Dr. John Webb, pediatric specialist, trained at Oxford, responsible for the Department of Child Health and living exemplar of Vellore's dramatic film, *To Children with Love.*

Dr. K.G. Koshi, director, professor of community health, and college principal, and his sparkling wife, Susie, who made the Big Bungalow a haven of hospitality. How well I remember the trip we took together up the mountains of South India when I was gathering material for my biography of Granny Brand, Dr. Paul's mother!

And of course Dr. Ida B. Scudder, bearer of the immortal name, which she has worn with far more than reflected glory, building the Department of Radiology into the finest in India, training radiologists of high caliber, developing "Roadside," always fulfilling the nobility and high purpose associated with the name of Dr. Ida Scudder.

On December 9, 1966, which would have been Dr. Ida's ninety-sixth birthday, I was privileged to be in Vellore with Dr. Ida B. for the dedication of a beautiful auditorium erected in Dr. Ida's memory on the college campus. Dr. Ida would have approved of this memorial, for it is a source of rich blessing to her beloved students. Her beauty-loving gaze would have reveled in the spacious foyer with its lofty vistas, in the lovely gray-blue meeting hall with 1,000 seats, its white stage curtained with gold-colored jute, in the open-air theater extending into the large garden. But, oh, how she would have hated the plaster bust, later to be made into bronze, a poor likeness, hard, shining, metallic, which Dr. Ida B., with fully as profound distaste, unveiled in the foyer! Fortunately, this was later replaced by a much more attractive and lifelike marble bust fashioned by Mrs. Quien, a fine Swiss artist.

But Dr. Ida would have found this lovely work distasteful, too. As she had done when the city of Vellore proposed to erect a statue of her, I could almost hear her sputter, "Mercy, no! Cover up the drain instead!" Or, more likely at this later date, "Get a better water supply for the college!"

Before the day was over I saw a more beautiful tribute to her memory than a bronze or marble bust. In a bazaar shop across from the hospital the humble proprietor had hung a crude picture of her above his wares and circled it with a garland of marigolds. So greatly is she beloved, long after her death, that the humblest of people for miles around cherish her memory, revere her as a *mahatma*.

Dr. Ida lived her ninety years to the tune of trumpet calls, and they always sounded reveille, never taps. The last and clearest, for which she had waited long with faith and expectancy, was no exception. For never has she been more alive. Her skilled hands and brisk feet are multiplied by thousands, all dedicated to the sublime task of healing. Her energy flows through the pulsing arteries of a great subcontinent, creating new life, both physical and spiritual.

Almost ninety years have passed since she returned to India to meet the challenge of those three knocks in the night. The one bed for healing in her father's bungalow has become more than 1,000. Instead of the class of fourteen girls there is now a student body of more than 1,100 men and women each year. The staff of two, herself and the butler's wife, Salome, has multiplied to include some 380 doctors, 400 nurses, 270 paramedical workers, serving nearly 2,500 patients each single day. Dr. Ida lighted a small candle. In her hands it became a blazing torch. Her successors have taken up that torch of life, passed it from hand to hand, multiplied it by thousands until its light illumines not only the land of India but many other countries of the world.

Bibliography

Jameson, Carol E. *Be Thou My Vision.* New York: Vellore Christian Medical College Board (USA), 1983.
Jeffrey, Mary Pauline. *Dr. Ida, India: The Life Story of Ida S. Scudder.* New York: Revell, 1930.
Scudder, Dorothy Jealous. *A Thousand Years in Thy Sight: The Story of the Scudder Missionaries of India.* New York: Vantage Press, 1984.
Smith, Sheila. *Dr. Ida.* New York: Friendship Press, 1953. (Pamphlet: Eagle Book no. 63.)
Wilson, Dorothy Clarke. *Dr. Ida: The Story of Dr. Ida Scudder of Vellore.* New York: McGraw-Hill, 1959.

C.F. Andrews

1871–1940

The Most Trusted Englishman in India

Eric J. Sharpe

Among western Christians working in India during the struggle for national independence, a unique position was occupied by Charles Freer Andrews. At a time when British missionaries, often through no fault of their own, had come to be identified with those seeking to keep India under subjection, even the most vociferous of nationalists were prepared to make an exception in Andrews's case. Everyone knew of his friendship with Rabindranath Tagore and Mahatma Gandhi, with S.K. Rudra and Sudhu Sundar Singh, and with Maulvi Zaka Ullah. Everyone knew, too, of the depth of his concern for the poor and the disinherited. The Indian Christian nationalist K.T. Paul wrote of Andrews as a man "than whom no foreigner has a deeper knowledge of the Indian."[1] But it was not merely knowledge: many other missionaries and administrators had that; equally it was love and respect. Tissington Tatlow was scarcely exaggerating when he said that in the 1930s Andrews was "known all over the world as the Englishman who is more trusted than any other by the people of India."[2] And in the 1920s and 1930s the greater part of religious and political India concurred. Tagore thought of him as a Christian *sadhu,* and he was widely known as "Deen-abandhu" – friend of the poor. Someone, somewhere in India, once said that his initials really stood for "Christ's Faithful Apostle" – a little sentimental, perhaps, but then Andrews himself was no stranger to sentiment. His life was a life in which unremitting activity was prompted and supported by a long series of emotional attachments: "a catalogue of friendships," it has been called.[3] This Andrews himself was more than ready to admit. In his autobiography he wrote that "it is as if I saw Christ in the faces of those I met or felt His presence in the midst."[4] The more reticent spoke critically of Andrews's habit of "hero-worship." But if this was in some measure his weakness it was also his strength, since he was able by this means to reach the hearts of the Indian people as few Europeans, either before or since, have been permitted to do.

The Life and Work of Andrews

Charles Freer Andrews was one of the fourteen children, born on February 12, 1871, to John Edwin Andrews and Mary Charlotte Andrews (née Cartwright) in Newcastle-upon-Tyne in the northeast of England. Most of his youth was, however, spent in Birmingham; he attended King Edward VI School there, proceeding in 1890 to Pembroke College, Cambridge, where he graduated with a degree in classics three years later. The Andrews family belonged to the Catholic Apostolic Church, founded on the precept and example of the charismatic Scottish preacher Edward Irving (1792-1834), and Andrews's boyhood was spent in that church's "strange, emotional atmosphere of prophesying and speaking with tongues and ecstasy in the Spirit."[5] However, on coming to Cambridge, Andrews fell under the influence of a moderately High Church type of Anglicanism, which was associated with the names of B.F. Westcott and Charles Gore (whose manifesto *Lux Mundi* had appeared in 1889). Indeed, his closest friend was Westcott's youngest son, Basil. At this critical stage in his life Westcott provided him with a new theology, Platonic, Johannine, and socially activist. Unable to sustain his allegiance to his father's church, in 1895 Andrews became an Anglican; in the same year he took up lay parish work at Monkwearmouth, in Westcott's Diocese of Durham. There he became "an out-and-out opponent of the capitalist system."[6] He was made a deacon in 1896 and was "priested" in 1897, working during this time among the urban poor in the Pembroke College Mission in Walworth, South London (1896-99). Already Andrews was a "Christian socialist," and already he had published his first book, a prize essay entitled *The Relation of Christianity to the Conflict between Capital and Labour* (1896). But he had not yet begun to contemplate work in India.

In 1899 Andrews returned to teach at his old college in Cambridge, and there he remained until 1903. At that point he offered himself to the Society for the Propagation of the Gospel in Foreign Parts for missionary work in India. It seems that this decision was precipitated by the premature death in India of Basil Westcott, whom he hoped in some way to replace. He arrived in India early in 1904, and for the next ten years taught as a member of the brotherhood of the Cambridge Mission to Delhi at St. Stephen's College. For a time he was associated with S.E. Stokes, F.J. Western, and Sundar Singh in the quasi-Franciscan Brotherhood of the Imitation, but the experiment was short-lived. Despite his socialism, Andrews came to India a moderate imperialist. This phase did not last, however, and very soon he had identified himself completely with the Indian national movement. In 1907 he was instrumental in securing the appointment of S.K. Rudra as the first Indian principal of St. Stephen's College. Andrews became more and more critical of traditional missionary policy and practice in India, chiefly because of the distance that it placed between Europeans and Indians. Also in these years he broke away from the mainstream of Christian theology, moving gradually further in a liberal direction, until finally, in 1914, he felt himself unable to continue to serve as an Anglican priest.

Two years earlier, in 1912, Andrews had met the Bengali poet Rabindranath Tagore in London; and in 1914 he shocked and dismayed the missionary corps by abandoning his Delhi teaching post and joining Tagore at Shantiniketan. In 1914 he also met Gandhi for the first time, and for years his life was to be closely linked with the two Hindus. He traveled incessantly, often in the interests of Indian minorities, the products of the "indenture" system in South and East Africa and in Fiji. All his weight was thrown behind the cause of the poor and underprivileged, both inside and outside India. He wrote, spoke, lobbied, and negotiated on their behalf, producing a constant stream of books and articles in the attempt to interpret India to, and arouse the conscience of the West. He wrote books about his heroes – Gandhi, Tagore, Sundar Singh, Zaka Ullah – and works of Christian devotion, most notably *Christ in the Silence* (1933), *Christ and Prayer* (1937), *Christ and Human Need* (also 1937), and *The Inner Life* (1939). Everywhere he made friends. Only one type of friendship he never found, since he never married. He died in Calcutta on April 5, 1940, in his sixty-ninth year.

A Different Kind of Missionary

Andrews's vision of Christianity was simple, profound, all-embracing and, above all, practical. But he was hardly an innovator in terms of missionary theology. His uniqueness lay chiefly in the intensity with which, having attained a vision of Christian wholeness, he labored to translate that vision into a life of practical service.

From his Cambridge mentors, particularly Westcott, Andrews had learned to place particular emphasis on the Gospel of John in the Christian scheme of things. At the turn of the century, the commonest missionary alternatives were still the "Pauline" approach, with its emphasis on the categories of sin and forgiveness, and the "Synoptic" approach among liberals, where the emphasis was, rather, on the ethical teaching of Jesus and on the kingdom of God as an ideal earthly society. Both of these the Christian Neoplatonists found not wrong, but too narrow; the Gospel of John (and particularly the prologue, 1:1-14) placed the incarnation in a cosmic context and set the Christian message – or so they believed – largely free from cultural imprisonment. As early as 1909 (though the impulse was much earlier), we find Andrews writing that the result, as far as he was concerned, had been "to leave behind the narrower Judaic conceptions, and [to] dwell more and more on the thought of Christ as the Eternal Word, the Light and Life of all mankind."[7]

As in the case of Westcott, this approach was translated by Andrews into a program of social action. Andrews was certainly a socialist, though Marxism he considered to have acquired a "hard ungracious revolutionary spirit,"[8] which as a Christian he found repugnant. Capitalism was the chief enemy to be confronted. As he expressed it in 1937: "But how to change human society from within, so that capitalism, with its money-greed, becomes a hateful thing to a Christian, just as usury was in the Middle Ages, and slavery was in the nineteenth century, and war is becoming to-day! This is perhaps the greatest of all questions that the Christian who follows Christ has to face and answer in our own age."[9]

At this time, incidentally, Andrews had already come somewhat under the influence of the Oxford Group Movement (subsequently Moral Rearmament), which was not notably anticapitalist in its emphases. But perhaps in the late 1930s this discrepancy was not so obvious as it was later to become. At all events, in his very last book Andrews was to write of the incompatibility of "the modern industrial system" with "the standard of truth, purity and honesty required by the Sermon on the Mount"[10] (truth, purity, and honesty being, of course, three of the four Oxford "absolutes").

From Westcott, too, Andrews learned to look to India less as a mission field to be overrun than as a source of light and truth. To the West, India and Greece were "the two great *thinking* nations" that had influenced the course of world history. Again it was at the point of the Gospel of John that the two might some day meet: "One of his [Westcott's] great hopes was that Indian thinkers would be able to interpret fully the Gospel of St. John."[11] But the Bible as a whole Andrews always – again in terms of turn-of-the-century religio-cultural theory – believed to be "a truly Eastern book . . . It is positive; it is written by Easterners; it contains the universal truths."[12]

Nevertheless, the implications of this approach were not at once apparent in Andrews's missionary career. At one time he had refused to work with the Student Volunteer Movement on account of its "dissenting" element, and could be seen as a "narrow-minded High Churchman."[13] India was to cure him of that habit. Of course, there remained within him something of the High Churchman; but in later years he was to move more in the direction of the Quakers, thanks not least to their simplicity and their pacifism. But perhaps in this case the impulse came as much from Gandhi as from any specifically missionary source.

Another early vision that Andrews never lost was the Franciscan ideal of service to the poor; his happiest moments, he wrote, were found "not in university centres, or among the rich, or even among the middle classes, but among the suffering poor."[14] It was here, he believed, that the roots of "first-century Christianity" were to be found – in the life of heroic renunciation and service in the name of Christ. This life he found exemplified in the witness of such men as Albert Schweitzer and Sadhu Sundar Singh.

Andrews afterward claimed that his decision in 1914 to cease to be a conventional missionary had been precipitated by doubts about the virgin birth and the resurrection, and by the bête noire of all liberals, the Athanasian Creed. Several years earlier, however, he had written that Indian Christians needed to be set free from "the engrossing Western tradition" in order that the Oriental in them might live.[15] How far can Christianity, he asked, "be divested of its foreign accretions in order to appeal directly to the peoples of the East?"[16] The 1914 decision might have been triggered by creedal doubt, but it represented the last step in a long process of adjustment to that form of Christianity that Andrews passionately believed India had already accepted at heart – a form experiential, ethical, and theologically minimal. From being cast in the role of an active evangelist, potentially mistrusted by Indians (which he found distressing), he became an evangelist by precept and example. Most of all he became India's servant. Even his closest colleagues found it hard to appreciate his decision, much less to follow him. J.N. Farquhar thought him "grievously mistaken" and felt it unlikely that he would be able to do "any serious service" from within Tagore's ashram.[17] The break was all the more surprising, since at that time Andrews's position seemed to be close to Farquhar's own.[18] But Andrews's theology was already veering away from the mainstream of moderate liberal thought, and his personality was much more volatile and impressionable than was Farquhar's. With the romantic example of Sadhu Sundar Singh in mind, he might have tried to become a *sadhu* himself, had his health permitted it. But it did not, and in after years, though constantly on the move, he was seldom or never solitary.

As we have said, the story of Andrews's life was the story of his friendships. We shall return to some of these in a moment. But first a word about another, less specific focus of attraction – "youth" in general.

In the early years of the century, "Young India" was a motto to be conjured with. The Indian national movement recruited (despite its attempts to "mobilize the proletariat")[19] chiefly among the young of India's universities and colleges, as did so many Christian organizations, notably the YMCA. Living so much of his life among the young, Andrews longed for their respect and love and sought to make – and keep – their ideals his own. Christ, Andrews wrote in his autobiography, "represents for all time, in a classical and perfect form, the religion of youth."[20] This "religion" is active, facing obstacles the better to overcome them, placing little emphasis on tradition for its own sake, bent on "building the kingdom" in its own unstable image. The "generous indignation" of the young, Andrews wrote, is that of Christ himself.[21] The boys of Shantiniketan preserved his own youthful spirit. And at times – particularly in his later years – his enthusiasm for youth could lead him to rhapsodize: "In the Spirit of Youth, a joyous confidence perpetually rises afresh which laughs at dangers and overcomes them. Death itself is looked full in the face and conquered . . . How can we explain the deathless beauty in the heart of Youth except in terms of Him who is ever young?"[22] Doubtless it was this, the youthful element, that attracted Andrews to the Oxford Group Movement.

However, the greatest influences on Andrews were of another kind. His biographers Chaturvedi and Sykes wrote that "his whole temperament predisposed him to worship his ideals incarnate in human heroes, in symbolic situations."[23] These heroes, for India's part, included Rudra, Sundar Singh, and of course Tagore and Gandhi. To each he gave devotion; Tagore and Gandhi he served, much as a *chela* would serve a *guru*. To be sure, unlike the Hindu *chela*, he could be critical; some of Gandhi's enthusiasms – for instance for the restoration of the caliphate to Turkey – Andrews disliked intensely, and said so.[24] But Gandhi accepted such criticisms as these in the spirit of concern with which they were made, and clearly always thought of Andrews as his ideal of what a Christian missionary ought to be, not proselytizing but serving the Indian people in the name of Christ. As Gandhi put it in 1927: "It is better to allow our lives to speak for us than our words. C.F. Andrews never preaches. He is incessantly doing his work. He finds enough work and stays where he finds it and takes no credit for bearing the Cross. I have the honor to know hundreds of honest Christians, but I have not known one better than Andrews."[25]

Of course, Gandhi's standards were not those of the Christian missionary community at large, many of whose members hardly knew what to make of either him or Andrews, while being puzzled by the connection between them. And even Andrews himself confessed at one stage that he was in danger of being labeled as "a Gandhi enthusiast and nothing else."[26] A "Gandhi enthusiast" he certainly was; but he was many other things, and had many other friends.

Andrews appeared to have had few reservations about Tagore's work, either at Shantiniketan or internationally. He spoke of Tagore's having been sent to the world as "a messenger and revealer of peace and good will to mankind,"[27] and as a man who "had clothed his own deepest religious thought with a raiment of simplicity and beauty."[28] Tagore for his part was warmly appreciative, writing on Andrews's death that "he did not pay his respects to India from a distance, with detached and calculating prudence: he threw in his lot without reserve in gracious courtesy, with the ordinary folk of this land . . . His attitude was absolutely free from any suspicion of that self-satisfied patronage which condescends from its own eminence to help the poor."[29]

Concerning the enigmatic figure of Sadhu Sundar Singh, who passed like a meteor across the Christian world of the early 1920s, we must be brief.[30] Sundar Singh was a visionary. Andrews, thanks to his early years in the Catholic Apostolic Church, was well enough aware of the ecstatic dimension of religion. Indeed, there may have been something of the visionary in his own makeup. Clearly, though, ecstatic religion as such did not greatly appeal to him, and in the end he was to question whether Sundar Singh, all his virtues and all his Christian integrity notwithstanding, had been able to distinguish in the spiritual life between fact and fancy.[31] Added to this, Sundar Singh was interested neither in politics nor in direct social action. For the Sadhu's spirituality (insofar as he understood it) Andrews had the warmest respect; in the end, though, he was able to approach both Tagore and Gandhi with more genuine appreciation.

A Friend of India

In 1935 Andrews wrote of the daunting task confronting Christianity in India in these words: "The first thing to be done is to meet the psychology of India rather than impose upon India what we in India think is good for her . . . We have never yet touched India's heart, and therefore, in spite of all our good intentions, we have blundered."[32] But what was it necessary to do in order to "touch India's heart"? At Edinburgh in 1910 V.S. Azariah had answered the question by calling for friendship as the one thing needful: "You have given your goods to feed the poor. You have given your bodies to be burned. We also ask for *love*. Give us FRIENDS!"[33]

Friendship was the element in which Andrews moved. He at least did not need to be reminded of the centrality of interracial friendship in the life of the Christian church in India. Its marked absence from so much of the church's life he found as distressing as Azariah had, and did what he could to redress the balance. He was not alone in so acting, though characteristically he carried each of his friendships to its absolute limit. In a measure, this may initially have involved an act of will. In a peculiarly revealing passage in his autobiography, Andrews wrote: "I know full well that, apart from the presence of Christ with me in daily life, I should have gone farther than others in racial contempt and selfishness, for I had the seeds of these evils within me."[34] It is not entirely clear what this confession may have implied, except perhaps that Andrews had been brought up to believe in "the white man's burden," and found this attitude of mind difficult to discard. But it at least suggests that, at times, the very intensity of Andrews's open affection may have contained some element of overcompensation.

Emotional Andrews certainly was, but at the same time he was clearly also possessed of great stores of will power, which drove him constantly to the very limits of his strength in the pursuit of those causes in which he believed. His decisions may have been arrived at intuitively, but once made, he threw himself without reservation into the serious task of working out their implications. And this required much more than merely the impulse of the moment.

It is simply not possible in an essay of this kind to catalogue either Andrews's travels or the social and spiritual issues in which he involved himself between 1914 and the end of his life. There were simply too many of both. Everywhere he went, he carried a message of reconciliation, among individuals and communities and nations. And always his great principle of reconciliation was the cross of Christ. In 1938 he attended the Tambaram Conference of the International Missionary Council (IMC), where he gave the following testimony: "I have learned one lesson in all these nearly forty years I have been out here in the East, and that is, that one has to go beyond the bitterness, beyond the bitterness on both sides, beyond the controversy on both sides, beyond the rising hatred in one's heart on both sides, beyond the burning indignation in one's heart on both sides. One has to go farther – to the cross itself."[35]

Two years earlier Andrews had resumed his Anglican ministry after an interval of twenty-two years, writing in the register of the church in which he had once celebrated the Eucharist, "Charles Freer Andrews desires to return thanks to Almighty God for being allowed to renew his ministry after many years."[36] This was a private matter. It rather suggests that his liberalism notwithstanding, the church's sacramental life had always been important to him, and that without it he had long felt himself to be lacking something. At all events, the last years of his life were spent once more as an Anglican priest.

A Friend of the Poor

Despite the time that he spent among the leaders of Indian and world opinion, Andrews's greatest compassion was always shown for the suffering poor. In the mid-1930s George Sherwood Eddy recorded:

> Whenever a great catastrophe occurs in nature or at the hands of man, whether by famine or flood, by slaughter or as the result of race prejudice, there Andrews goes and ministers to human suffering, and there he makes his appeal for distressed humanity . . . He has barely escaped prison several times. He moves freely and fearlessly, equally with oppressed Indians or Negroes and with viceroys and prime ministers. In his combined gentleness and boldness he is not altogether unlike Francis of Assisi or Gandhi, whose closest friend he is, but he is more a man of sorrows than the gay troubadour of Assisi.[37]

Testimonies of this order might be multiplied many times. Most, however, came from the liberal wing of Christian opinion. To the more cautiously conservative, Andrews was much more of a controversial figure. Some spoke and wrote, in reference to his early days as a Christian freelancer, of "the Andrews school of compromise." But as the 1920s and 1930s advanced, it became more and more apparent that his intensely personal approach had taken him far closer to the heart and mind of India than would have been possible by any other means. He was happy that that approach should take place on India's own terms – not on those imposed on India from without. And therein lay his uniqueness. To be sure, since independence, Christians in India have come more and more to realize that India itself must be allowed to state the terms on which it will receive the Christian message, and how it will interpret that message. But in the interwar years few Christians in India, whether missionaries or not, had begun to take this possibility at all seriously. Among those who did, Andrews must occupy pride of place.

Andrews, though, never formed a "school," whether of "compromise" or anything else. His contribution was of such an intensely personal kind as to be scarcely capable of being imitated. In general terms he belonged within the fold of "Christian socialism," and argued for social action on the "Johannine" principle that he had learned from Westcott. He was, of course, in theological terms "liberal." But he had no real "method," in the sense in which missiologists commonly use that word. To India he was simply a servant – an unusually active and effective servant of powerful and obscure alike. To be sure, his enthusiasms could on occasion carry him away, and he was not always fair to those whose principles differed from his own. But had his convictions been less deeply felt, less insistently acted upon, less impelled by the desire truly to serve India in the name of Christ and in the spirit of *nishkama karma,* the "selfless endeavor" of which the *Bhagavad Gita* speaks, then he would not have been Charlie Andrews. And no one would have called him "Christ's Faithful Apostle."

Notes

1. K.T. Paul, *The British Connection with India* (London: SCM Press 1927), p. 156.
2. Tissington Tatlow, *The Story of the Student Christian Movement of Great Britain and Ireland* (London: SCM Press, 1933), p. 140.
3. T.G.P. Spear, quoted by D. O'Connor, *The Testimony of C.F. Andrews* (Bangalore: CISRS, 1974), p. 23.
4. Andrews, *What I Owe to Christ* (1932), p. 162.
5. Andrews, "A Pilgrim's Progress," in V. Ferm (ed.) *Religion in Transition* (1937), p. 64; cf. Andrews, *What I Owe to Christ,* chap. 4. On Irving and the Catholic Apostolic Church generally, see A.L. Drummond, *Edward Irving and His Circle* (London: James Clarke, n.d.); H.C. Whitley, *Blinded Eagle* (London: SCM Press, 1955).
6. From a 1915 article in *The Modern Review,* quoted by B. Chaturvedi and M. Sykes, *Charles Freer Andrews: A Narrative* (London: Allen & Unwin, 1949), p. 22.
7. Andrews, "A Missionary's Experience," in *Indian Interpreter* 4, no. 3 (October 1909): 103. The question of the role of the Fourth Gospel in shaping missionary thought has not, to the best of my knowledge, ever been fully investigated. But see Sharpe, "The 'Johannine' approach to the Question of Religious Plurality," in *Ching Feng* 22, no. 3-4 (1980): 117ff.
8. Chaturvedi and Sykes, *Charles Freer Andrews,* p. 28.
9. Andrews, "A Pilgrim's Progress," *Religion,* pp. 87f.
10. Andrews, *The Sermon on the Mount* (1942), p. 151. The influence of the Oxford Group Movement (Moral Rearmament) on the Christian and missionary world, particularly in the 1930s, is another subject much in need of scholarly investigation. I believe that influence to have been very considerable, but it is almost impossible to find any account that is not seriously partisan.
11. Unpublished reminiscences, quoted in Chaturvedi and Sykes, *Charles Freer Andrews,* p. 18. Again, the reasons behind Westcott's statement would bear further investigation, particularly since few Indian Christian theologians appear ever to have attempted the task. But see A.J. Appasamy, *Christianity as Bhakti Marga: A Study in the Mysticism of the Johannine Writings* (London: Macmillan, 1927).
12. Andrews, "Ordination Study in India," published as "Occasional Papers no. 33" (Delhi: Cambridge Mission to Delhi, 1910), p. 8.
13. Tissington Tatlow, letter quoted in Chaturvedi and Sykes, *Charles Freer Andrews,* p. 31.
14. Andrews, "A Pilgrim's Progress," *Religion,* p. 66.
15. Andrews, "Ordination Study in India," p. 4.
16. Andrews, *The Renaissance in India* (1912), p. 225.
17. E.J. Sharpe, *Not to Destroy but to Fulfil* (Lund: Gleerup, 1956), p. 237.
18. Andrews had assisted Farquhar in the preparation of *The Crown of Hinduism* (1913), and in these years often expressed himself in "fulfilment" terms; cf. *The Renaissance in India* (1912), p. 144.
19. On this subject generally, see Sharpe, "Avatara and Sakti: Traditional Symbols in the Hindu Renaissance," in H. Biezais, ed., *New Religions* (Stockholm: Almqvist and Wiksell, 1975), pp. 56-69.
20. Andrews, *What I Owe to Christ* (1932), p. 228.
21. Ibid., p. 229.
22. Andrews, *Sadhu Sundar Singh* (1934), p. 10.
23. Chaturvedi and Sykes, *Charles Freer Andrews,* p. 248.

24. Ibid., p. 155: "I hate the Khilafat doctrine of a Turkish Empire which was too sacred to be touched and which involves the refusal of independence to another race."

25. From *Young India*, Aug. 11, 1927. Quoted in Gandhi (ed. Hingorani), *The Message of Jesus Christ* (Bombay: Bharatiya Vidya Bhavan, 1963), p. 38.

26. Chaturvedi and Sykes, *Charles Freer Andrews*, p. 268.

27. Andrews, *Letters to a Friend* (London: Allen & Unwin, 1928), p. 332.

28. Ibid., p. 19.

29. Tagore's Foreword to Andrews, *The Sermon on the Mount* (1942), pp. vii-ix.

30. The literature on Sadhu Sundar Singh, most of it written in the 1920s, is enormous. The only reasonably comprehensive modern biography is A.J. Appasamy, *Sundar Singh: A Biography* (Madras: CLS, 1966), which is still incomplete and generally uncritical. Cf. Sharpe, "Sadhu Sundar Singh and His Critics," *Religion* 6 (Spring 1976): 48-66.

31. Cf. Andrews, *Sadhu Sundar Singh* (1934), p. 157: "Sundar Singh had, from the very first, powers of imagination and mystical vision far beyond those people. He could see things that others could not see, and lived in a world of his own." And on p. 167: "The Sadhu evidently crossed and recrossed, times without number, the border between the dream-life and the waking life, until the margin itself became blurred."

32. Quoted in Chaturvedi and Sykes, *Charles Freer Andrews*, pp. 278f.

33. *World Missionary Conference*, Edinburgh 1910, vol. 9 (Edinburgh and London: Oliphant, 1910), p. 315.

34. Andrews, *What I Owe to Christ* (1932), p. 282.

35. *Tambaram 1938, The Madras Series*, vol. 7 (New York and London: IMC, 1939), p. 94.

36. Chaturvedi and Sykes, *Charles Freer Andrews*, p. 298.

37. G.S. Eddy, *A Pilgrimage of Ideas* (London: Allen & Unwin, 1935), p. 217.

Selected Bibliography

Works by C.F. Andrews
Autobiographical

1932 *What I Owe to Christ*. London: Hodder & Stoughton.
1937 "A Pilgrim's Progress." In Ferm, ed., *Religion in Transition*. London: Allen & Unwin.

General

1896 *The Relation of Christianity to the Conflict between Capital and Labour*. London: Methuen.
1908 *North India*. London: Mowbray.
1912 *The Renaissance in India*. London: Young People's Missionary Movement.
1921 *The Indian Problem*. Madras: Natesan.
1923 *Christ and Labour*. London: SCM Press.
1929 *Mahatma Gandhi's Ideas*. London: Allen & Unwin.
1933 *Christ in the Silence*. London: Hodder & stoughton.
1934 *Sadhu Sundar Singh: A Personal Memoir*. London: Hodder & Stoughton.
1942 *The Sermon on the Mount*. London: Allen & Unwin.

Works about C.F. Andrews

Chaturvedi, Benarsidas, and Marjorie Sykes. *Charles Freer Andrews: A Narrative*. London: Allen & Unwin, 1949.
Hoyland, John S. *The Man India Loves: C. F. Andrews*. London: Lutterworth, 1944.
Macnicol, Nicol. *C.F. Andrews: Friend of India*. London: James Clark, 1944.
O'Connor, Daniel. *The Testimony of C.F. Andrews*. Bangalore: CISRS, and Madras: CLS, 1974.
Tinker, Hugh. *The Ordeal of Love: C.F. Andrews and India*. London: Oxford Univ. Press, 1980.

V.S. Azariah

1874–1945

Exponent of Indigenous Mission and Church Unity

Carol Graham

Vedanayakam Samuel Azariah, evangelist, apostle of India, and prophet of the worldwide church, could not have come from a humbler background. He was born in 1874 in a small village in the depths of South India, a child of many prayers in a home of deep evangelical piety. He attended the village school, learned to read from palmyra-leaf books and to write with his finger in the sand. His father died early, so he was reared by a widowed mother who neither spared the rod nor spoiled the child but was a paramount influence in his life.

Those were the days of missionary paternalism, and as Azariah pursued his way through various mission institutions he came under the influence of some very remarkable men until he finally reached the B.A. class of the Madras Christian College, which owed its origin to the Church of Scotland but was famous for its ecumenical outlook. Owing to illness he was unable to take his degree but emerged as a deeply dedicated young man with obvious gifts of leadership and a genius for friendship.

Azariah was immediately offered the post of secretary to the YMCA of South India, which he occupied for thirteen years and which brought him to the center of a group of young enthusiasts, Indian, British, and American. Here was a generation of Christian leaders sharing in the dawn of the newly awakening national consciousness of India, with whom he came under the influence of two outstanding American evangelists, John R. Mott and Sherwood Eddy. They opened for him new vistas of biblical scholarship, so that old truths were flood-lit by new interpretations. He interpreted for them the awakening of new Indian aspirations beginning to fret under Victorian dominance. Above all, the experience opened the possibility of a degree of interracial friendship that had hitherto seemed out of the question.

So it was that in the year 1902, at dead of night on a lonely beach beside a brilliantly moonlit sea, in a remote corner of Ceylon (now Sri Lanka), Azariah found himself kneeling in an agony of prayer. He had come on a mission to Jaffna, where he had found a completely indigenous missionary society, worked and supported entirely by Tamil Christians, and for the first time faced the bitter truth that India, with all its religious heritage, had allowed the spread of the Gospel to be undertaken by foreigners. This lonely midnight vigil gradually became a deep personal struggle. Was God calling him away from an ever widening sphere of exhilarating service? And for what? To lead a crusade against Western supremacy in the "younger churches"? But out of the travail of his soul that night was conceived and dedicated to God a purpose that never wavered and was to bear fruit a hundredfold.

Envisioning a Truly National Church

Back in India, Azariah imparted his vision to a few kindred spirits, including his beloved and devoted wife. For in 1898 he had married Ambu Mariammal Samuel, one of the first Christian women in South India to take a college course, whom he described as "the most spiritually minded girl in Tirunelveli." From the first it was a true partnership and all through life they grew together, she keeping pace with him, sharing his inward growth and outward responsibilities. She once showed me an entry in an old diary: "Started to pray for an Indian Missionary Society," and it was literally prayed into being. No public appeal was made but both workers and money were forthcoming. Within a very few years the National Missionary Society of India, with its special offshoot in Tirunelveli, became a living fact. Its avowed principles were Indian workers, Indian money, and Indian management, but its greatest difficulty was to find an area in which to work out these new ideals. The Tamil Nadu was already overflowing with missions from the West, and the little Indian group had to push its way northward until, in a corner of the old Hyderabad State, they found sixty miles of jungle into which Christianity had never penetrated.

It was, however, within the far-flung limits of the then Madras Diocese that Azariah made yet another vitally important friendship. Hitherto he had been something of a free-lance within an ecumenical and international environment, and his meeting with the bishop of Madras was a revelation to both of them. Azariah found in Henry Whitehead a deep sympathy with the urge for greater freedom within the Indian church, and the bishop saw in Azariah the possible answer to his dearest wish. Whitehead was in charge of a hopelessly unwieldy diocese and desperately in need of an assistant bishop, who, he was convinced, should be an Indian national. When Azariah appeared with his plan for a purely Indian mission, it seemed as if their two dreams might come true.

The choice of Dornakal as the center of the new venture was a happy accident. It was a small railway junction where there happened to be a disused brewery in which they established a chapel, a school, and living space for two missionaries, all under one roof; and in due course Azariah and Ambu took up their abode there. It must have demanded heroic courage on her part, for Dornakal was a far cry from her family surroundings, and to transport a young family to what was virtually a distant country, among primitive people speaking a foreign language, was a risky business, especially with a husband continually on tour. But for Azariah his home was always the center of his life to which he returned for deep personal refreshment. To his six children he was a revered if somewhat strict father. It was their mother who provided the solid background to life in their early years, but the perfect partnership of the parents was always the secure foundation of their home.

Meanwhile Azariah's growing contact with Bishop Whitehead was ripening into a lifelong friendship and also opening his eyes to the value of true catholicity and tradition in order and worship, which led him to offer himself for ordination to the Anglican ministry. A period of preparation spent largely in the bishop's house in Madras convinced Henry Whitehead that he had indeed found the first Indian bishop of the Anglican Communion and to begin the process of convincing other people. The ordination took place in 1909, and in 1910 came Azariah's first introduction to the world at large when he attended the great missionary conference at Edinburgh where his passionate plea for greater freedom in the relation between missionaries from the West and Indian church leaders has become a classic: "The Indian church will rise up in gratitude to attest the self-denying labours of the missionary body . . . You have given your goods to feed the poor, your bodies to be burned . . . We ask also for love. *Give us Friends."* This was indeed the cat among the pigeons, especially in view of the proposed bishopric; but by 1912 most of the opposition had melted away. It was wisely decided that the first Indian bishop should rule over a diocese of his own with Dornakal as its center. The consecration took place in Calcutta in the presence of both church and state dignitaries. An eminent member of the Church of Scotland wrote at the time: "The Anglican Church has done some big and brave things in India but among the biggest and bravest I would rank the appointment of Vedanayakam Samuel Azariah as Bishop of Dornakal."

The new diocese was roughly the size of Wales, with no town of any importance but with a rapidly growing church in the villages. There were only six ordained Indian clergy with a number of lay workers, and the obvious need was for an adequate ministry. The bishop began by gathering together a small group of men with outstanding gifts of leadership, who responded enthusiastically to his vision of an indigenous church. Several gave up good jobs to come to Dornakal with their wives, living in great simplicity and in intimate fellowship with the bishop and Mrs. Azariah, who took a leading part in training the women. This was to grow into the famous Divinity School, which concentrated on a family ministry at every stage in the life of the church. The mass movement was taking place entirely among the outcastes, or "untouchables," who were wholly illiterate, living in unbelievable squalor and desperate poverty. The coming of a Christian teacher and his wife to live among them was usually their first contact with any form of uplift, and a great deal depended on their joint witness as well as their teaching.

Meanwhile the movement as a whole was spreading throughout Andhra Desh, and two other big Anglican missions began to look to Azariah for leadership. By 1920 all racial feeling had disappeared and there was a unanimous request for these, too, to be included in the Diocese of Dornakal. In that year Azariah went to his first Lambeth Conference, knowing that he would return to administer a diocese roughly the size of England with about 90,000 Christians, most of whom were living under very backward conditions. He also foresaw that he would have to face the transfer of authority from the overseas mission to the local church. The desire for independence and freedom of expression in political life was finding its counterpart in the religious world, and on this Azariah delivered his own balanced judgment: "Our young theologians want autonomy at one step; sober minds are willing to work more slowly but legitimate aspirations must be met." These he defined as follows: the curtailment of missionary power; the training of Indian leadership in the government of their own church; the preparation of the whole Christian community for indigenous leadership and self-support. This was his clarion call to both East and West: "Do not fear to take risks. Believe in the Holy Spirit and trust men."

The scene was now set for the growth of a church truly indigenous in life and worship, for which Dornakal, although geographically remote, was the obvious center, since it had known no other tradition. The village population, spread over what had now become a vast area, varied considerably, from the primitive jungle dwellers of the north to the comparatively sophisticated cultivators of the southeast, but the social pattern of the village life remained rooted in the rigidly kept Hindu caste system. This meant that every individual lived and worked, married and died, as a member of the particular group into which he or she had been born. Against this background Azariah saw the mass movement as the natural and inevitable outcome of a way of life. He realized the risk of such an enormous intake into a comparatively young church in so short a time, and tried to minimize the danger by his insistence on the witness they must give through a transformed life · and a zeal for evangelism. The preparation for baptism was long and testing. Gone were the days when a more-or-less repetitive knowledge of the catechism might be sufficient. Azariah's vivid application of Christian truth to Christian life gradually produced wonders, and his special slogan to the newly baptized, "Woe unto me if I preach not the Gospel," solemnly repeated by them with their hands on their heads, was far more than lip service.

Azariah was convinced that there did exist a culture, specifically Indian but not necessarily Hindu, which must be brought into the life of the church. Illiterate people learn best through singing, and the Karnatica school of music, very rhythmic and tuneful, produced a fine collection of Telugu Christian lyrics, common to all the different traditions. The love of drama also was natural and spontaneous. Above all, the love of festivals, particularly those connected with rural life, provided opportunities for big gatherings. Thirty-six hours of glorious, crowded life, with processions and worship, drama and singing, often crowned with a baptism by immersion in a nearby river, emphasized a truly Christian fellowship, which filled a great need in the lives of a hitherto despised people.

Church Unity – A Matter of Life and Death

The legacy of Bishop Azariah to his own country was, first and foremost, the vision of an indigenous church, rooted in the soil of India, finding its expression through Indian culture and its leadership among its own sons and daughters. With its very modest beginnings in South India, it soon became widely recognized as the missionary strategy of the future. At this distance it is hard to realize what a gulf Azariah had to bridge, so far ahead of his time, for the changes that have come so rapidly in Christian thought and action have inevitably made him a pioneer in what is now a commonly accepted worldwide movement.

The Edinburgh Conference of 1910 was a great crisis in the history of Christendom because it marked the beginning of a new era in ecumenical understanding and cooperation. Today it seems incredible that, out of well over 1,000 delegates from all five continents, fewer than twenty were nationals from their own churches, but the breath of fresh air from that northern city stirred into being a whole series of national Christian councils all over the world. One of the first of these was in India, of which Azariah was chairman for many years. By the time the International Missionary Council met in Jerusalem in 1928, over 25 percent of the delegates were nationals sent by their own councils, for whom the chief interest was no longer the "foreign missionary enterprise" but the Christian message of the indigenous church. Could Azariah be anywhere but in the forefront of such a movement?

The road to union in South India began at Tranquebar in 1919 when a group of Indian Christian leaders of what was the forerunner of the United Reform Church met at the invitation of Azariah and the Rev. V. Santiago. These men were convinced that only their connections with the various churches of the West were responsible for their unhappy divisions, and their express purpose was to discuss the possibility of church union without the presence of naturally prejudiced foreign missionaries. As a result they discovered so much common ground that they issued an appeal to all the denominations they represented to consider the whole question of Christian unity in the Indian setting. From this grassroots beginning sprang the whole train of events that finally resulted in the inauguration of the Church of South India.

Azariah believed that certain conditions in South India made Christian unity both more practicable and more demanding than in other parts of the world. First, there was the background of a common Dravidian racial stock with a common social and cultural life, although sadly divided into four language areas. Second, there was a very rich Christian heritage ranging back to the first century with the apostle Thomas, through the established church of the Middle Ages, and on to the Reformed traditions of the modern evangelistic movement. That all this richness of belief and worship should have imposed upon Indian Christians a bewildering number of separate churches seemed to him an outrageous denial of the one true Lord whom they had come to know and love.

Therefore Azariah laid upon the worldwide church on every possible occasion his burning conviction: "We must have *one church,* a Church of India, in which Indian religious genius can find the natural expression of visible unity . . . Divisions may be a source of weakness in Christian countries; in non-Christian countries they are a sin and a scandal." He made it abundantly clear that, beyond the evil of a divided Christendom in a sinful world, he estimated the bitter hurt to Christ himself. "The cost of union is penitence, with agonizing prayer that the high-priestly prayer of Our Lord himself may be answered through the dedication of all our knowledge, possessions and prejudices to this great cause. Are we ready to pay the cost?" Perhaps his hardest task was to convince his own brother bishops of the Anglican Communion. At the Lambeth Conference of 1930 he challenged them straight out: "Have you sufficiently contemplated the grievous sin of perpetuating your denominational bitterness in your daughter Churches? We want you to take us seriously when we know the problem of Union is a matter of life and death to us. Do not, we plead, give your aid to keep us separate but lead us forward together to fulfill the prayer 'that they all may be one.' "

The different strands of Azariah's life came together in a wonderful climax at Christmastide 1938 when the World Missionary Conference met in Madras. Fifty percent of the delegates were sent by self-governing churches, and one-third of those delegates were under thirty-five. The theme of the conference was "The Church, Its Life, Witness and Environment," showing how the whole emphasis had been transformed in the past thirty years. Here Azariah was indeed on his native heath. His name had long since become a legend; he was regarded as one of the architects of the worldwide church, an elder statesman, yet completely accessible to all. He celebrated the Eucharist on Christmas Day, when surely there had seldom if ever been such a gathering of so many races and traditions at the Lord's own table on the Lord's own day. Then he hastened back to Dornakal to prepare for the consecration of the Cathedral Church of the Epiphany.

Dornakal had grown into what was virtually a homemade cathedral village. There were still no roads, but land had been cleared and one after another the necessary buildings had sprung up, all very simply built of homebaked bricks and tiles with whitewashed walls. The only stone building, standing right in the center, was the famous cathedral. Since this, too, must be purely Indian both in architecture and in cost, it had taken a quarter of a century to build while the growing congregation had continued to worship in the little old church beside the old brewery. Now at last, by a supreme effort, the cathedral was finished and the consecration took place amid a large gathering from the surrounding villages plus friends and fellow Christians from all over the world.

> Lift up your heads, O ye gates; and be ye lift up, ye everlasting doors; and the King of glory shall come in

rang out as the knock came on the great west door, and surely He did come in when 2,000 people joined in the Eucharist where forty years earlier there had not been a single Christian. On that Epiphany day, under the snowy towers reaching up into heaven, were surely manifested three things that sum up the life and work of Vedanayakam Samuel Azariah: the evangelical fervor of a witnessing church; the beauty of the catholic heritage in faith and worship; and the glory that India can bring to the unsearchable riches of Christ.

Within a few months the world was at war and India became threatened with a Japanese invasion. Azariah observed his birthday in 1944, surrounded by his closely knit family. His eldest daughter had long since been at his right hand; his two elder sons were both serving in his diocese, one as a doctor and the other as a priest, and his youngest daughter, a true follower of her mother, was married to a Tamil missionary priest working in the original Indian mission area. Two younger sons and eight lively grandchildren now completed the family. Azariah spent his last Christmas in a remote village area, walking from place to place, but after his return to Dornakal the end came suddenly, his marvelous constitution completely worn out by the pace at which he had lived and worked. Never wherever he was had he failed to keep his tryst with God at 4:30 A.M. Now on New

Year's Day, 1945, he slipped away into the nearer Presence with such a radiance in his face as to forbid all clamorous mourning. At sunset they laid him to rest in his beloved cathedral garden as they sang very softly the Telugu Easter lyric.

Like many a pioneer Azariah died in faith, not having obtained the promise but having seen it from afar. He himself said there are mountaintops in every religion, but it is when common people are changed that we see Christ. The secret of his power was that he believed in ordinary men and women until he made them believe in themselves. The Church of South India and the World Council of Churches have long since become solid realities; the Church of North India and Vatican II would have been to him a crowning joy. All through his life, deep in his heart, Azariah held fast to his favorite text: "By the grace of God I am what I am, yet not I but the grace of God in me."

Selected Bibliography

Works by V.S. Azariah

1936 *The Church and Evangelism.* Madras: Christian Literature Society for India (hereafter, CLSFI).
1936 *India and the Christian Movement.* Madras: CLSFI.
1938 *Christian Marriage.* Madras: CLSFI.
1940 *Christian Giving.* Madras: CLSFI. Reprinted, New York: Association Press, 1955.

Works about V.S. Azariah

Eddy, G. Sherwood. *Pathfinders of the World Missionary Crusade.* New York: Abingdon-Cokesbury, 1945.
Emmet, P.B. *Apostle of India: Azariah, Bishop of Dornakal.* London: SCM Press, 1949.
Graham, Carol, *Azariah of Dornakal.* London: SCM Press, 1946. Revised and reprinted, Madras: CLSFI, 1973.
Grimes, Cecil John. *Towards an Indian Church.* London: SPCK, 1946.
Heiberg, Knud. *V.S. Azariah of Dornakal.* Copenhagen: Det Danske Missionsselskab, 1950.
Hodge, J.Z. *Bishop Azariah of Dornakal.* Madras: CLSFI, 1946.
Sundkler, Bengt G.M. *The Church of South India.* London: Lutterworth Press, 1954.

A.G. Hogg

1875–1954

The Christian Message to the Hindu

Eric J. Sharpe

During the first half of the twentieth century, great numbers of Christian missionaries served in India, faithfully if not always wisely. It was a difficult time. India was changing, rapidly and sometimes violently, in the wake of the growing national movement, while India's ancient faith was finding new forms of expression and a new impetus; at the same time the Christian faith was being shaken to its very foundations by critical scholarship, by the international impact of war and social upheaval, and by growing uncertainty as to the final justification for the work of Christian missions amid India's ancient faiths and cultures. Many missionaries were not unnaturally forced onto the defensive, while having to sustain many and varied duties. The literature of the period attempted to interpret what was going on, but often pragmatically and with a half-hidden sense of bewilderment. Few missionaries had the time or the ability to reflect deeply on cardinal issues. There were exceptions, of course (and far be it from me to suggest that the Indian missionary corps as a whole was forced into a state of mental paralysis by the challenge of the hour), but these were few, and became fewer as the period progressed.

Between 1903 and 1938 Alfred George Hogg (1875-1954) was a professor on the staff of the Madras Christian College. In a sense it might be argued that in missionary terms, he led something of a sheltered life, bound up as he was in the round of the classroom, the study, and (particularly after 1928, when he became principal) the administration of the college. At times even some of his colleagues may have thought him remote from the "real" problems of the new India. But all the while he was thinking and writing incessantly about these very problems; and in the end the quality and depth of his thought was such as to set him apart from most of his missionary colleagues. He in fact won an acceptance (which he never sought) as the "theological conscience" of at least the British part of the Indian missionary community; he also came to be acknowledged as a man of the Spirit as well as of the intellect, and as a man to whom to defer.

Educational and Spiritual Formation

Hogg was in many ways an unusual missionary, who scarcely fitted into any of the conventional categories of preparation and training. In one respect, though, his credentials were impeccable. Both his parents, John Hogg and Bessie Hogg (née Kay), came of deeply devout evangelical stock;

his father was an outstanding pioneer missionary in Egypt, and A.G. Hogg was himself born on a mission field, at Ramleh (near Alexandria) in Egypt.[1] He was one of thirteen children, eight of whom survived infancy, and several of his brothers and sisters also became missionaries. In 1893 he entered Edinburgh University to prepare himself for the ministry of the United Free Church of Scotland, naturally with a view to missionary work. He completed his M.A. with honors in philosophy,[2] began the study of theology – and then his faith fell apart in one of those shattering crises that were common in the 1890s, as the life of faith and the demands of the scientific worldview came into head-on conflict. In time the crisis was resolved (thanks not least to his friendship with another outstanding Scottish theologian of his generation, David S. Cairns), but gone were many of the old evangelical affirmations. In effect Hogg emerged from his time of trial a Ritschlian – and Ritschlians did not normally become missionaries (if for no other reason than that their "liberalism" made them suspect in the eyes of most missionary societies, who would therefore not accept them).[3]

In 1902, however, Hogg was appointed to teach on the staff of the Madras Christian College. He arrived in India early in 1903 still a layman, and was in fact not ordained until 1915. His teaching responsibilities were initially in the area of ethics and economics, but soon he became professor of mental and moral science (philosophy), a position he held until his elevation to the principalship in 1928. A great deal of his most creative theological and philosophical work was therefore done from a position of relative freedom, as a lay missionary who was not bound by creeds and confessions. But instead he felt himself bound by a much more serious moral obligation. In Edinburgh he had learned to think; and since that time, as he put it in 1935,

> to track out all unconscious preconceptions, and to examine with ruthless honesty their title to acceptance, has appeared to me to be one part of the serious business of life. It is not, indeed, by any means the duty of every one; but for him who has the metaphysical bent of mind and leisure to exercise that bent, it is a sacred obligation which he owes to humanity and to his own soul.[4]

Three years after his ordination, he had spoken, in an article, of the Scottish ministry as embodying "the ideal combination of genuine piety with intellectual fearlessness and sound scholarship."[5] These were very much Hogg's own characteristics.

Perhaps because he remained in one teaching post for thirty-five years, the outward circumstances of Hogg's missionary career were unspectacular. He was never at the forefront of controversy, except in minor matters, which need not detain us. In 1907 he married Mary M. Patterson, a missionary teacher, but there were no children of the marriage. He did not attend either the Edinburgh 1910 or the Jerusalem 1928 conferences of the International Missionary Council (IMC), though he played some part as a correspondent in shaping the Edinburgh Commission IV Report (not least since Cairns chaired that commission, and Hogg answered the original questionnaire at great length).[6] Not until 1938 did he actually appear on the international missionary scene in person, when the IMC met on the new campus of the Madras Christian College at Tambaram. There he stood out as one of the most astute critics of Hendrik Kraemer – for reasons we shall examine shortly.

Hogg's intellectual career was marked by his various publications, which were actually quite extensive, though often in the pages of journals rather than in book form. His major writings included *Karma and Redemption*, which first appeared as a series of articles in the *Madras Christian College Magazine,* and in book form first in 1909;[7] *Christ's Message of the Kingdom* (1911), a course of Bible studies on the question of the kingdom of God, and by far the most widely read of Hogg's writings; *Redemption from This World* (1922), his weightiest theological work, delivered as lectures in Edinburgh; and after his retirement, *The Christian Message to the Hindu* (1947). It is perhaps worth noting that on his return to Scotland in 1939, Hogg took up routine parish work in obscure corners of the country. After the end of the war he was finally able to retire to the village of Elie, on the Fife coast, though by this time crippled by rheumatoid arthritis; there he died on the last day of 1954.

It is difficult to write succinctly about Hogg's contribution to missionary thought, if for no other reason than that his own personal Christian world of ideas was made up of intricately and tightly interwoven strands that are not always easily unraveled.

It is necessary first to bear in mind that Hogg always drew a clear distinction between *faith* and *beliefs* in matters of religion.[8] Faith is immediate trust in God, the existential dimension of religion; beliefs are the intellectual and culturally conditioned formulations to which people resort in attempting to delimit and explain faith. Faith is absolute; beliefs are relative, though frequently taken in error to be themselves absolute. This is a matter of the utmost importance in the Christian encounter with Hinduism. Writing in his early article "The Christian Interpretation of Mediation," he put it this way:

> Is it possible to state the Christian estimate of Jesus as the one unique Mediator between God and man in a way which shall not repel sympathetic and thoughtful Hindus? In the formulation of this estimate preserved in the Creeds of Christendom there is much that appears hopelessly foreign to Indian ways of thinking, and it may not be rash to conjecture that, if Christianity had made its first abiding conquest in India instead of in Europe, its Creeds would have been couched in a terminology singularly different.[9]

Christ and the Moral Nature of the Universe

The beliefs of even the "higher Hinduism" Hogg admitted to finding "strange and rather dismal."[10] Nevertheless they had to be understood, as a means of access to the one unifying faith that underlay them. In the preface to *Karma and Redemption* he confessed to a belief "that the innermost faith of all religions which are still, at any time, worthy of the name must be one and the same" – though he went on at once to record his conviction that he considered "the divergences between the intellectual beliefs by which men seek to preserve this common spirit of faith to be nevertheless an immensely important matter."[11] In his early years in India he was therefore working, not toward any lessening of belief in the uniqueness of Christ, but toward a restatement of that belief in terms that India (or rather, that part of India with which he was most intimately concerned) could comprehend and accept. The root of the matter, he believed, lay in the area of ethics – and Hogg's theology was always of a strikingly ethical kind, consistent with his Kantian philosophy. It was this that drove him to an examination of the antithetical doctrines of karma and redemption, and to his conclusion that the former, while it may be judicial, is not truly moral, since in true morality there is a reciprocity of rewards and punishments, which karma cannot embrace without losing its character. "The doctrine of karma [he wrote] fits beautifully into a system which recognizes no purpose in life other than expiation, but there is no room for it in a universe the purpose of which is moral not judicial."[12] The weakness of karma, in Hogg's view, was that it was maintained wholly apart from a corresponding belief in the moral nature of God, and thus took the form of a judicial system without a judge, and therefore without the possibility of mercy. This resulted in a quasi-moral belief in the isolation of every person, ethically speaking, from one's fellows; whereas in Christian belief, we may – indeed must – bear one another's burdens. Hogg also pointed out that if the karma doctrine be true, then not only are we prevented by it from harming our fellows: equally we are prevented from helping them, and love becomes an impossibility. On this view, then, one root difference between Hindu and Christian views of life has to do with the nature of the universe (judicial or moral), and there can be no deeper contrast than that. It was on reading this book that Cairns wrote of its author: "The Christian Church in India is fortunate in having not a few thinkers of exceptional gifts of heart and mind, and this little treatise makes plain that in its author the Church has one worthy to rank with the ablest of these, a constructive religious thinker of the best type."[13]

One further (and perhaps unintended) result of Hogg's *Karma and Redemption* was that it inspired some Hindu thinkers to meet Hogg's criticism that karma operates only on the judicial, and not on the moral, level, partly by reinterpreting the doctrine itself. Among Hogg's students at this time was Sarvepalli Radhakrishnan, and it was not least in Radhakrishnan's subsequent work that a new and more flexible pattern of Hindu ethics came to light, partly if not wholly as a result of the stimulus provided by Hogg's thinking.[14]

From the problem of finding a fundamental contrast of theological principle between Christian and Hindu modes of belief, Hogg next turned his attention to the question of the nature of faith. Intellectual beliefs are important, and Hogg was too much of an intellectual himself not to take them fully into account; but underlying the diversity of belief there is the oneness of faith. What *is* faith, though? Clearly it is absolute and unquestioning trust in a God who reveals himself; so much is clear. Hinduism is by no means without revelation; but to Hogg, God's revelation of himself in Jesus Christ is final and normative. Although this position is in some ways not unlike that of the "fulfillment school" led by J.N. Farquhar, Hogg was strongly opposed to the suggestion that *Christianity* fulfills *Hinduism* (a claim made by Farquhar only in the sense that Christ *is* Christianity – an extreme liberal point of view that Hogg found somewhat naive). The claim that the fulfillment relationship subsists between religions Hogg therefore found unacceptable; he found this claim both unintentionally condescending and theologically inadequate: "We feel [he wrote] that the claim that Christ is the crown of Hinduism is little more than a debating-point . . . What Christ directly fulfills is not Hinduism but the need of which India has begun to be conscious, the need, by making her feel conscious of which, he has made her no longer quite Hindu."[15] Hindu faith, in other words, must find a new point of reference, rather than merely a smooth organic (or evolutionary) transition into a closely related, though theologically minimal, Christianity. Again, though, one is forced back to the question of the nature of faith.

Hogg's second and third books (as well as numerous articles) deal with this question. *Christ's Message of the Kingdom* (1911) dismisses both the activist ethical notion that the kingdom of God is to be "brought in" by humankind's moral effort and the more passive notion that God will bring in the kingdom in his own good time irrespective of what human beings may or may not do; and it points to the importance of *faith* as the missing factor in the argument.[16] There is no question of God's *unwillingness* to bring the kingdom into being, merely of the human lack of faith *preventing* its coming. Hogg was to return to this question again and again in his subsequent writing, though in greatly refined forms. In practical terms, however, what it meant was that the Christian missionary in India (or elsewhere) was called, not to a life of more and more feverish activity, but first of all to a life of prayer and devotion – a life of faith. Without this firm spiritual foundation, in which the life of the intellect was brought into accord with the life of the Spirit, in which faith received fuller and more adequate expression in terms of belief, the missionary's task would be a hopeless one. It was in Hogg's book *Redemption from This World, or the Supernatural in Christianity* (1922) that the "faith" question received its fullest treatment. This book centers on the problem of miracles; but in the end it is a full and impressive statement of Christian belief in a God who is in no way bounded by the cause-and-effect categories associated with a mechanistic worldview. Again it was India that had taught Hogg the weakness of what was at that time the common liberal Christian assumption that "natural law" was, so to speak, God's only method of working in this world.[17] In 1910 he wrote:

> We have become obsessed by the idea of natural law to the point of tying down the infinite
> God to that single system of which science is spelling out the laws. But at the same time

our sensibilities have been aroused to the ruthlessness of natural, social, and economic law. India's question has come to us. *Can* such a tragedy, even if just, worthily sum up God?[18]

India denies that, provided that we can spell out *all* the laws of the system in operation around us, we shall have succeeded in searching out the ultimate Reality which is God. Hogg, too, denied it, believing the world instead to be, not *maya*, but "plastic, in an incalculable degree, to a will that transcends our fullest acquaintance."[19] Of this belief, *Redemption from This World* was Hogg's fullest and most mature statement. This book is a work of missiology only by implication; but we would do well to remember that although delivered in lecture form in Edinburgh, it was the product of a Christian theological mind at work in an Indian context, and a book the argument of which was organically related to the earlier *Karma and Redemption* articles.

It is not easy to divide up Hogg's career as a missionary by referring it to external events, or even to dramatic internal developments; there were few enough of either. He left no diaries, and not many letters have survived. Only his published works show an incisive mind grappling with interrelated problems, occasionally entering into polite discussion with an intellectual partner, but after 1928 being forced to concern itself more and more with the daily round and common task of Christian higher education in Madras and in India generally. He tackled some quite formidable opponents – most notably Albert Schweitzer, whom he accused of doing outstandingly right things for the most inadequate intellectual reasons.[20] In a politically hyperactive India he lectured on the same need for a solid basis for a belief in social progress, in his monograph *The Challenge of the Temporal Process* (1933). He opened a brief but important correspondence with Lesslie Newbigin, in which he discussed, among other things, the new "Barthianism": "I rejoice to see the Barthian lay low the Modernist, but I am rather appalled at the cost at which it seems to me to be done. I feel as if the Barthian bull had pursued the matador (Modernism) into the china shop and were disposing of him there, at a destructive cost to many precious things."[21] A couple of years previously on a slightly different and more practical level, he had been much involved behind the scenes in the work of the "Lindsay Commission" on Christian Higher Education in India.[22]

Challenging Kraemer on the Basis of God's Self-Revelation

There remain two further events to be recorded. In the late 1920s and the early 1930s Hogg's thought had undergone something of a revolution, in that he had been forced for the first time to take seriously the fact of the church. Previously, he felt, his interpretation of the Christian faith had been far too individualistic, and accordingly he jettisoned much of his pre-1928 theology.[23] And in 1938, at the Tambaram Conference of the IMC, he entered into a direct confrontation with Hendrik Kraemer over the presuppositions of the latter's massive book *The Christian Message in a Non-Christian World,* which he found impressive on a number of important points.[24] The trouble with Kraemer, he felt, was that while the noted Dutch missionary scholar had wanted to leave open the possibility of a positive affirmation of God's revealing work in religions other than Christianity, he had been unable to reconcile this possibility with a narrower view of revelation, in which *all* religion (empirical Christianity included) is merely an expression of human self-assertion, and as such antithetical to divine revelation. Kraemer would not have been in such difficulties, Hogg maintained,

> if he had held the conviction (grounded on faith in the Divine Love revealed in Christ) that God is *always* seeking to reveal Himself to *every* man, and that the limited measure (or the no-measure) in which the revelation succeeds in breaking through is man's fault and not God's decree.[25]

And why had Kraemer restricted to Christianity his separation between the ideal and the actual in religion? The distinction between faith and beliefs is everywhere apparent; and in Hogg's view it simply would not do to refer the latter to a human "religious consciousness" ("An abstract concept belonging to the psychologist's stock in trade")[26] and restrict the former to a Christian gospel having only an enigmatic and indistinct content.

The Christian must not merely announce to his Hindu or Muslim brother that a certain revelation has taken place; he must be explicit as to the *content* of the revelation of God in Christ. And for Hogg that content was perfectly summed up in the phrase "The Word was made flesh":

> Without some divine self-revelation there can be no real religion anywhere or of any kind. For God is subject, not object, and so cannot be known except He expresses Himself. God really speaks; He has spoken in sundry places and by diverse manners.[27]

It is perhaps also worth noting that several of the group of Indian lay theologians who at the time of the Tambaram Conference produced that notable manifesto *Rethinking Christianity in India* had formerly been pupils of Hogg's at the Madras Christian College. That Kraemer's book was in greater accord with the thinking of the European delegates to the conference is clear; and yet one cannot escape the impression, forty years on, that Kraemer was unable either to answer Hogg's objections or to comprehend the position taken by the *Rethinking Christianity* group.

Shortly after the end of this conference, Hogg left India for the last time, to become an obscure parish minister in obscure corners of wartime Scotland. But what had he left behind?

Most obviously, he had left a series of books and articles almost unique in twentieth-century missionary literature – unique for their elegance of style and their refusal to opt for easy pragmatic solutions to complex problems, unique for the tenacity with which their author pursued cardinal issues and the firmness with which he rejected the facile and the fashionable. As an educationist, Hogg left generations of devoted (if occasionally somewhat bewildered) students, both Christians (like P.D. Devanandan and D.G. Moses) and Hindus (like Radhakrishnan and C.T.K. Chari); he also left the new Tambaram campus as the visible sign of his unfulfilled dream of a Christian university in India.[28] On the spiritual level, his contribution is impossible to evaluate, but one is left with the impression that whether or not his colleagues fully understood him, very many looked up to him as a *karmayogin*, a man of depth and burning sincerity of purpose who had looked more into the secret place of the Most High, but whose devotion was never divorced from the practicalities of life in the India he loved.

Hogg's last book, *The Christian Message to the Hindu* (1947), summed up the whole of the missionary thinking of his thirty-five years in India. To some extent a recapitulation, this is still a book of freshness and insight, and a notable contribution both to missionary debate and to the wider field of Christian theology. It shows a man who all his life had learned the lessons of sympathy of approach, accuracy of thought, and courtesy of dialogue, and was prepared to compromise on none of them. It contains this exhortation to the missionary:

> Let us make the offer of our gift, the vision of the glory of God in the face of Jesus Christ; and let us leave it, as far as may be, to the Hindu himself to assess the worth of the life which that vision inspires as compared with what may be otherwise attained. In any case he [the Hindu] will accept no assessment but his own; and rightly so, for only he to whom God has drawn near through Hinduism can tell how far within "the secret of His tabernacle" God may set one whose thoughts and forms of worship are still Hindu.[29]

In writing thus briefly about Hogg, I have become more than usually aware of the danger of scaling down the contribution of such a man to the dimensions of one brief article. He was an intellectual giant, and a man whose writings can still inspire something of the same awe that his contemporaries, whether fellow missionaries or students, so evidently felt in his presence. Briefly forgotten, there are encouraging signs that Hogg may be well on the way to rediscovery, not only as a missionary alongside Farquhar, Macnicol, Andrews, and Larsen, but equally (and perhaps still more) as a theologian alongside Forsyth, Mackintosh, and the Baillies. In the last resort, though, it is perhaps best to try to sum up his life and legacy not in philosophical or theological terms, but as an example of Christian devotion. In 1933 Hogg spoke these words as part of an ordination address:

> Christian preaching is the effort to put into words the distinctive spiritual secret of the life of the Church . . . and it possesses ready appeal only for those who have watched that life being lived . . . In a non-Christian land this predisposing cause of attentiveness to the Christian message is absent. So everywhere the foreign missionary organization has to exhibit the Christian life in operation before there can be much effective preaching . . . Preaching is interpretation; and in order to be effectual, the missionary's preaching has to be the interpretation of a life which he is living with the people and for the people, directed to ends of which they appreciate the value. And this life must be of a distinctive quality which will make men wish to discover its spiritual secret. Only then will they give interested heed to the missionary's effort to interpret, in words and ideas which they can understand, that the Gospel is his inspiration.[30]

Hogg's life was of such quality; and that is why to some of us at least, both in India and beyond, the name of Alfred George Hogg is more than just another name in the history books, a representative of the missionary ideals and strategies of a bygone age. We need the witness of his wholeness, the example of his devotion, and the exhilaration of following his disciplined mind today more than ever. We need his theological realism and the courage with which he rejected spurious simplicity, slogans, and clichés. Surely the time is ripe for the rediscovery, not only of Hogg, but of the generation of which he was a part. Perhaps their problems are not the precise prototypes of our problems; but we are not so rich that we can afford to ignore them, nor so wise that we can do without them.

Sarvepalli Radhakrishnan, a Hindu who generally did not like missionaries, wrote on Hogg's death – and with this testimony we may end –

> He was undoubtedly one of the greatest Christian teachers of his generation. His books are known for their philosophical penetration and religious sensitivity. He has left a permanent mark on the minds of those who came under his influence.[31]

Notes

(Books and articles by Hogg unless otherwise stated)

1. For background and family details, see Rena L. Hogg, *A Master-Builder on the Nile* (New York: Fleming H. Revell, 1914).

2. His most influential teacher was Andrew Seth [Pringle-Pattison]. See Sharpe, *The Theology of A.G. Hogg* (Bangalore and Madras: CISRS and CLS, 1971), pp. 8ff.

3. For Hogg's estimate of Ritschlian principle, see "The Christian Interpretation of Mediation" (1904), p. 5.

4. "The Claim of Society on the Metaphysically-Minded," *Philosophical Quarterly*, 1936, p. 298.

5. "The Authority of the Bible," in *Madras Christian College Magazine* (1918), offprint pagination p. 2.

6. Two copies are extant. One is in the Missionary Research Library, New York; the other is in the possession of Rev. Prof. David Cairns, Aberdeen.

7. Reprinted in 1970, with an introduction by the present writer.

8. Recent writers who have drawn attention to the same fundamental distinction include Raimundo Panikkar, *The Intra-Religious Dialogue* (New York: Paulist Press, 1978), pp. 17ff; and Wilfred Cantwell Smith, *Faith and Belief* (Princeton: Princeton Univ. Press, 1979).

9. "The Christian Interpretation of Mediation," p. 1.

10. *Karma and Redemption* (1923 ed.), p. vii.

11. Ibid., p. 5.

12. Ibid., p. 49.

13. This quotation is from a 1909 book review, preserved in the Hogg Collection, Edinburgh. I have not been able to trace its original source.

14. Radhakrishnan wrote his first book, *Ethics of the Vedanta* (1908), partly as an answer to *Karma and Redemption*. It was highly commended by Hogg for its "remarkable understanding of the main aspects of the philosophical problem." See Radhakrishnan, "My Search for Truth," in V. Ferm, ed., *Religion in Transition* (London: Allen and Unwin, 1937), pp. 19f.

15. Review in *International Review of Missions*, 1914, p. 171.

16. In view of the importance to missiology of the kingdom-of-God idea, not least in the wake of the "Your Kingdom Come" conference (Melbourne 1980), it is a little surprising that earlier levels of the debate have aroused practically no attention. Would detailed examination show that the kingdom idea has been repeatedly pressed into service in support of a wide variety of conflicting missionary ideals?

17. The influence of Henry Drummond's book *Natural Law in the Spiritual World* (1883) should be borne in mind. Within a decade this book had passed through some thirty editions – adequate testimony to the force of its impact.

18. World Missionary Conference, *Monthly News Sheet* 4 (January 1910): 74.

19. "Christianity as Emancipation from This World" (1909), offprint, p. 22.

20. In his critique of Schweitzer, Hogg's question was: "With what right does the man of moral earnestness in the West reckon it a duty to toil for the betterment of the world, when more probably he would, had he only been bred in the East, have counted it almost his only ethical obligation to maintain a collected poise of soul and to further his own spiritual development?" "The Ethical Teaching of Dr. Schweitzer," in *International Review of Missions*, 1925, p. 239.

21. Letter, Hogg to Newbigin, June 13, 1937.

22. A.D. Lindsay, ed., *Report of the Commission on Christian Higher Education in India* (1931).

23. Characteristically, Hogg told the story of his "change of heart" in a letter to a student, Mr. (later Professor) C.T.K. Chari, dated January 27, 1939. See also *The Christian Message to the Hindu* (1947), pp. 45ff.

24. See "The Christian Attitude to Non-Christian Faith," in *The Authority of the Faith*, Tambaram Series I (1939), pp. 102ff. Later Hogg elaborated his views in a pamphlet, *Towards Clarifying My Reactions to Dr. Kraemer's Book* (privately printed, 1939). See also *The Christian Message to the Hindu*, pp. 37f.

25. *Towards Clarifying My Reactions*, p. 3.

26. Ibid., p. 5.

27. Ibid., pp. 7f. Cf. Hogg's Christmas Day sermon to the Tambaram Conference delegates, reprinted in *Addresses and Other Records*, Tambaram Series VII (1939), pp. 131ff.

28. *The Challenge of the Hour for the Madras Christian College* (1930), p. 12.

29. *The Christian Message to the Hindu*, pp. 29f.

30. The charges at the ordination of the Rev. R.S. Macnicol, M.A. (May 21, 1933). Manuscript in the Hogg Collection.

31. *Madras Guardian*, February 3, 1955.

Selected Bibliography

Works by A.G. Hogg

1903 "Agnosticism and Faith." *Madras Christian College Magazine (MCCM)*, August, pp. 75-84.

1904 "The Christian Interpretation of Mediation." *MCCM*, January, pp. 357-69. Also printed separately as *Papers on the Great Truths of Christianity*, no. 10. Madras.

1904 "Mr. S. Subrahmanya Sastri on Hindu Philosophy." *MCCM*, September, pp. 121-28.

1904-5 "Karma and Redemption." *MCCM*, December 1904, pp. 281-92; January 1905, pp. 359-73; February 1905, pp. 393-409; March 1905, pp. 449-62; April 1905, pp. 505-22. In book form, Madras: The Christian Literature Society, 1909. Reprinted 1923 and 1970.

1909 *Christianity as Emancipation from This World*. Reprinted from *MCCM*, July and August.

1911 *Christ's Message of the Kingdom*. Madras: Christian Literature Society. Numerous later editions under this and other imprints.

1917 "The God That Must Needs Be Christ Jesus." *International Review of Missions*, pp. 62-73, 221-32, 383-94, 521-33.

1922 *Redemption from This World, or the Supernatural in Christianity* (Cunningham Lectures). Edinburgh: T. and T. Clark.

1930 *The Challenge of the Hour for the Madras Christian College*. Madras: M.C.C.

1936 "The Claim of Society on the Metaphysically-Minded." *Philosophical Quarterly*, January, pp. 295-310.

1939 "The Christian Attitude to Non-Christian Faith." *The Authority of the Faith* (Tambaram Series I), pp. 102-25.
1947 *The Christian Message to the Hindu* (Duff Missionary Lectures, 1945). London: SCM Press.

Works about A.G. Hogg

Chari, C.T.K. "Alfred George Hogg as a Teacher of Philosophy." In *Souvenir Volume: 38th Session of the Indian Philosophical Congress,* pp. 61-64. Madras, 1964.
Cox, James L. "The Development of A.G. Hogg's Theology in Relation to Non-Christian Faith: Its Significance for the Tambaram Meeting of the International Missionary Council 1938." Ph.D. diss., University of Aberdeen, Scotland, 1977.
_____. "Faith and Faiths: The Significance of A.G. Hogg's Missionary Thought for a Theology of Dialogue." *Scottish Journal of Theology,* 1979, pp. 241-56.
Reid, John K.S. "Under-estimated Theological Books: A.G. Hogg's 'Christ's Message of the Kingdom.'" *Expository Times,* July 1961, pp. 300-302.
Sharpe, Eric J. *The Theology of A.G. Hogg.* Bangalore: CISRS; and Madras: CLS, 1971.

E. Stanley Jones

1884–1973

Following the Christ of the Indian Road

Richard W. Taylor

The world's greatest missionary" is what *Time* magazine called E. Stanley Jones.[1] The *Christian Century* called him "the most trusted exponent of evangelism in the American Church,"[2] and later said that "perhaps no Christian leader in America commands a wider popular following than he."[3] A spokesman of the government of India, when Jones was awarded the Gandhi Peace Prize, called him "the greatest interpreter of Indian affairs in our time," and went on to declare that he had done more than any other person to bring India and the United States together.[4] Stephen Neill maintains that "in his great days Jones was probably (second to C.F. Andrews alone) the best-known western Christian in the whole of India."[5] Some legacy!

Missionary, evangelist, India, America, trusted, interpreter, pacifist – these are the major dimensions of the Jones legacy. Perhaps the most admirable aspect of the legacy is that Jones was able to keep all these dimensions together – each enriching the others. And he was remarkably creative in interrelating these dimensions. He had an awesomely synthetic mind, and the ability to gather people around him who had fresh and timely ideas to contribute. There are not many missionaries like that any more. Times have changed. But there is still much that we can learn from him.

Eli Stanley Jones was born in Maryland in 1884. He went to Asbury College, felt called to be a missionary and evangelist, and arrived in India in 1907 as a Methodist missionary. In 1911 Jones married a colleague, Mabel Lossing, in Lucknow where they were both stationed. She had been teaching in Isabella Thoburn College. Soon after their marriage they moved to Sitapur where she continued to serve as an educational missionary until their retirement. He died at Bareilly in northern India in 1973. Their only child is Eunice Jones Mathews, whose husband is United Methodist Bishop James K. Mathews.

In the early years of his residence in India, Jones had a physical breakdown and a difficult emotional time along with it. Then he had a fresh religious experience and commitment – and never looked back. In 1928 he was elected a bishop by the Methodist General Conference in the U.S.A., but resigned the next morning before his consecration – feeling called to continue as a missionary evangelist. By 1930 his Methodist appointment was "Evangelist-at-large for India and the world."[6]

Stanley Jones was above all a brilliantly innovative evangelist. He was innovative principally in relation to culture and context. His legacy to us is both his style and approach, on the one hand, and his remarkable innovations, on the other. His style was Indianizing and de-Westernizing in the cultural, social, economic, and political spheres – all treated evangelically. It was timely – he usually dealt with current questions and problems. This style was based on deep and extensive immersion in many aspects of contemporary Indian culture – much of it outside the confines of the church. And it was based on great sympathy for and empathy with those he met in this immersion. In this way Jones's style differs crucially from that of some other evangelicals[7] who call for the same sort of innovation and who see clearly the instrumental need for indigenization, as Jones did, but who lack both specific cultural understanding and sympathy, and who tend therefore to make judgments about particulars of indigenization that are in danger of being bound by a very *Western* orthodoxy. Perhaps this sort of understanding of and friendship for a people and their culture can come only from years of labor – when it comes at all. I venture that it is a measure of the fruitfulness of Jones's style that many Indian Christian theologians continue to be stimulated by him – whereas many foreign indigenizers lecture these same theologians on the limits they must not transgress rather than stimulating them.

Let us look at some of his innovations – both as examples of his style and approach and because they still have a fruitful suggestiveness. I shall take mainly the Indian contributions because I am inclined to hope that I understand their significance better.

The Indian Christ

Stanley Jones's first book, written out of his wide experience as an evangelist to educated Indians, was *The Christ of the Indian Road,*[8] published in 1925. It developed out of articles he had written and his many public talks throughout India and North America.[9] Here, at a time when Indian nationalism was on the rise, he wrote:

> Christianity must be defined as Christ, not the Old Testament, not Western civilization, not even the system built around him in the West, but Christ himself, and to be a Christian is to follow him . . . Christ must be in an Indian setting. It must be the Christ of the Indian Road . . . Christ must not seem a Western Partisan . . . but a Brother of Men. We would welcome to our fellowship the modern equivalent of the Zealot, the nationalist, even as our Master did.[10]

The fact is, most missionaries and Indian Christians in the churches still led by them were supporting the British Empire and opposing the Indian national movement.

About theology, he wrote:

> We want the East to keep its own soul – only thus can it be creative. We are not there to plaster Western civilization upon the East, to make it a pale copy of ourselves . . . We are not there to give its people a blocked-off, rigid, ecclesiastical and theological system, saying to them, "Take that in its entirety or nothing." Jesus is the gospel – he himself is the good news. Men went out in those early days and preached Jesus and the resurrection – a risen Jesus . . . We have added a good deal to the central message – Jesus . . . Jesus is universal. He can stand the shock of transplantation. He appeals to the universal heart . . . We will give them Christ, and urge them to interpret him through their own genius and life. Then the interpretation will be first-hand and vital.[11]

Further on Jones writes of Christ: "He and the facts not only command us to go, but he, standing in the East, beckons us to come. He is there – deeply there, before us. We not only take him; we go to him . . . We take them Christ – we go to him."[12] While this sounds like something Roland

Allen wrote earlier,[13] Jones had the wit and courage to make it specific to his field of work and thought. In this passage Jones quotes much of the second half of Matthew 25 too. So he is seeing Christ already there in the hungry, thirsty, naked, and sick. I am inclined to see here a seed of what became a major South Asian contribution to ecumenical theological thinking in the late 1950s and early 1960s by thinkers who had been reared on Jones's thinking and preaching – heard most clearly, perhaps, in the New Delhi Assembly of the World Council of Churches in 1961,[14] where the importance of seeing Christ at work in the world was stressed.

In the heart of the following paragraph Jones has buried a remarkable picture of his Christ of the Indian Road:

> A friend of mine was talking to a Brahman gentleman when the Brahman turned to him and said, "I don't like the Christ of your creeds and the Christ of your churches." My friend quietly replied, "Then how would you like the Christ of the Indian Road?" The Brahman thought a moment, mentally picturing the Christ of the Indian Road – he saw him dressed in Sadhu's garments, seated by the wayside with the crowds about him, putting his hands upon the heads of the poor, unclean lepers who fell at his feet, announcing the good tidings of the Kingdom to stricken folks, staggering up a lone hill with a broken heart and dying upon a wayside cross for men, but rising triumphantly and walking on that road again. He suddenly turned to the friend and earnestly said, "I could love and follow the Christ of the Indian Road."[15]

This mental picture is both vivid and attractive. So attractive that within a few years two versions, one urban and one rural, entitled "Christ of the Indian Road" had been painted by the young Indian Christian painter A.D. Thomas – who went on to paint many events of Christ's life as Indian. Others also started to paint Christ as an Indian and/or in Indian settings at about the same time, and this trend has continued.[16] And a few years later, inspired by both Jones and Thomas, Chandran D.S. Devanesen, a descendant of two celebrated Tamil Christian poets who had himself become a recognized poet, wrote his poem "Christ of the Indian Road" while still a college student.[17]

Jones sought to "naturalize" Christ and Christianity. This is a lesson most of us have yet to learn thoroughly. In the final paragraphs of his book he puts it rather poetically:

> There is a beautiful Indian marriage custom that dimly illustrates our task in India, and where it ends. At the wedding ceremony the women friends of the bride accompany her with music to the home of the bridegroom. They usher her into the presence of the bridegroom – that is as far as they can go, then they retire and leave her with her husband. That is our joyous task in India; to know him, to introduce him, to retire – not necessarily geographically, but to trust India with the Christ and trust Christ with India. We can only go so far – and India must go the rest of the way.
>
> India is beginning to walk with the Christ of the Indian Road. What a walk it will be![18]

Round Table Dialogue

On P.D. Devanandan's first tour of North India as director of the Christian Institute for the Study of Religion and Society, in 1958, I took him to Rishikesh to meet my friend the late Swami Sivanandaji, the founder of the Divine Life Society, which became so open to interreligious dialogue. As Devanandan described our hopes for starting interreligious dialogue, Sivanandaji's face lit up and he said that of course he would cooperate, that he had been in such a meeting once before in Saharanpur and would welcome many more, and that it was a great pity that there had been none for so long. In Saharanpur, Sivanandaji had been in one of Jones's Round Table conferences for sharing religious experience and understanding. And Sivanandaji was right. There is much in common between the religious Round Table conferences originated by Jones and the interreligious dialogue of much more recent concern.

Jones got the idea for his Round Tables from a tea party hosted by a leading Hindu before one of his evangelistic lectures.[19] The other guests asked him various religious questions in that very civil social gathering. It became clear to Jones that *"they wanted to know about [the] Christ of experience."*[20] "Round Table conferences" must have been very much in the intellectual air. Jones was advocating them as a part of his concern for reconciliation in international affairs. The British government was proposing one on Indian constitutional reforms in response to Indian nationalism. With his remarkable sensitivity to people and times, Jones picked up this term for what it was clearly timely for him to do. The invited group of about fifteen members of other faiths and five or six Christians would sit in a circle. Jones would suggest that they use the then popular "scientific method" of experimentation, verification, and sharing of results. He really called for the sharing of religious experience in daily life. He suggested that no one argue and that no one talk abstractly. He also suggested that differences should not be suppressed to preserve the friendly atmosphere. Everyone should feel free, as in a family circle. Jones gives many pages of examples of such dialogue.[21]

I know of nothing like this previously in India. There must have been friendly conversations. But in public it was usually either monologue or debate. Even now that interreligious dialogue has become fashionable, not much of it is experience-based dialogue. More often it is about views and opinions and doctrines and practices – a point that Jones makes in his autobiography forty years later.[22] This is an important corrective for us in the dialogue business today. We must take religious experience seriously.

In Jones's recounting of various statements from the different Round Table conferences, there is a certain undertone of triumphalism – but a little triumphalism in 1928 is not really surprising. On the other hand, it is very refreshing to have Jones confess:

> The valuable thing for us as Christians in the Round Table Conferences with non-Christians lay in the fact that we were compelled to rethink our problems in the light of the religious experiences of non-Christians. So while these Conferences have been valuable in our approach to the non-Christian faiths, they have proved of even greater value to us in facing our own problems, spiritual and intellectual.[23]

Ashrams

Modern Indian ashrams have been an attempt to reclaim an ancient Indian social institution for contemporary, often nationalist, social, political, or religious purposes.[24] They originated in Bengal in the final decades of the nineteenth century within Hindu reform movements and spread widely. Then in the early decades of this century Gandhi brought his intentional communities from South Africa to India and soon decided that they too were ashrams. The first few Christian ashrams were founded in the early 1920s. Jones had been with Gandhi in the Sabarmati Ashram in the early 1920s.[25] He seems to have spent several months at Tagore's Santineketen Ashram in 1923. He wrote of it with great sympathy and appreciation.[26] I think it likely that his poem "I Took My Lamp"[27] was written during his stay there; it is certainly about that stay. How very like Jones to have written a poem as a result of his stay in the ashram of the Nobel laureate poet! Without ever losing his primary commitment, Jones seemed to try harder than most others I have known or studied to understand and fit in with people, both in groups and as individuals – and often to succeed in this remarkably well. I do not think he wrote many other poems. In fact, I know of none.

In 1930 Jones created his Christian ashram. In that period of national consciousness, in which missionary-founded Christianity seemed foreign in style and sympathy, the Christian ashram was to put the Christian movement into the center of national life and evangelize it. The ashram was to be truly Christian and truly Indian. As Jones thought about it, the ashram was to be an ongoing local community of living together.[28] But when he actually announced it a few months later, the ashram was to start out as a summer event at Sat Tal with the possibility of a permanent year-round community (which most ashrams were at their core).[29] The dress, the food, the style, and the simplicity of life would be Indian – very Gandhian, actually. There would be an attempt to make the Indian spirit creative in art, in music, and in Christian thinking. This would include the study of the Gospel, its implications, its relationship to India's heritage, and to India's present religions and to the national life of India. It was hoped that this would lead to publication. There would be absolutely no racial barriers or differentiation as between Indians and foreign missionaries – a giant step for those days. On the whole this is exactly what happened. The Indian clothes worn in the ashram were of homespun khaddar cloth – the very symbol of the nationalist movement. Once when Jones was in a meeting in the ashram he stood up, his dhoti (a sarong-like garment wrapped around the body and worn instead of trousers) became untied and, as it dropped, he grabbed it and ran from the room in confusion.[30]

In 1935, under Jones's leadership, the Lucknow Ashram grew out of the Sat Tal Ashram. This was a permanent, year-round community with much the same aims as the Sat Tal Ashram but with more emphasis on the community as being a model of the kingdom of God and with more outreach to college and university students of whom there were many in Lucknow, which was a provincial capital.[31] For Jones the ashram was more of a base than a residence.[32] He was much on the move throughout India and the world as a sought-after and effective evangelist. But other modern ashram leaders also roamed widely from their ashram base. Gandhi did. So did Tagore. So did leaders of other Christian ashrams from Jack Winslow of Pune to Murray Rogers of Jyotiniketan. Group thinking and publication, which had started at Sat Tal,[33] continued in Lucknow. This venture at Christian "group thinking" can be seen as a forerunner of the style of the Christian Institute for the Study of Religion and Society that was formed in Bangalore under the leadership of P.D. Devanandan and M.M. Thomas. The very success of the Lucknow Ashram led to its demise. Its Christian nationalist group thinking made it the center and base for the Kristagraha movement, a kind of Christian Gandhian nationalist freedom movement led by some members of the ashram. This led to the missionary deputy leader of the ashram, Jay Holmes Smith, being forced out of India by the British government, and the closing of the Lucknow Ashram.

A measure of the remarkableness of Jones's adaptation of the Indian ashram model to his evangelism is the institution contributed by his contemporary Asbury College-oriented fellow Methodist missionary E.A. Seamands, who was named "Missionary of the Century" by the South India Annual Conference during their 1976 session.[34] Seamands imported the Kentucky Camp Meeting into South India and called it a Jathra, which is a kind of Hindu religious fair. It works – to some extent. But it is not nearly so perceptive and effective as Stanley Jones was time and time again – starting always with something especially Indian and something especially timely. Jones even imported a couple of versions of his Christian ashrams into the United States and elsewhere, with considerable success. In the early 1940s the Harlem (New York City) Ashram was founded to bring reality to the kingdom of God and to work as a group for racial justice, Indian independence, Puerto Rican self-determination, and peace – all Jonesian themes. It was founded by some former members of the Lucknow Ashram and their friends.[35] Jones was a principal adviser. About the same time, Jones started his short-term ashrams in the United States. They began as week-long events, but many eventually became weekend only. Nevertheless they followed the general pattern of the Sat Tal Ashram.[36] These ashrams continue to look back to their Indian roots. They have served the growth of many. From Jones, here, we learn that missionary adaptation can indeed be a two-way street.

The Kingdom of God

Already in Jones's second book the kingdom of God is a social order to be achieved because of personal conversion and understood through Jesus, who is its illustration and meaning[37] – although its achievement might require the action of God as well as of human beings.[38] But after his visit to the Soviet Union in 1934, he spelled out the kingdom of God as an alternative social structure in considerable detail.[39] This was also in response to his keen awareness that Communism was attracting many intellectuals in India and elsewhere. As always, Jones was unusually sensitive to the concerns of those with whom he sought to share the Gospel. But it must be immediately added that Jones never neglected the social dimensions of the Gospel – as some other great evangelicals have tended to do.

This societal understanding of the kingdom of God was a part of Jones's understanding of his first ashrams. Of them he wrote:

It was this quest for a Kingdom-of-God order that drove some of us to adopt the Ashram as a possible mould in which this order might be expressed. This quest for the Kingdom-of-God order was not primary in the beginnings of the establishment of our Ashrams. That came out as we went along.[40]

And

We look forward to . . . the Kingdom-of-God order, which will gather up into itself all the good of individualism and socialism and fulfill each and add something lacking in each.[41]

And

what we try to be: A Family of God, a demonstration in miniature of the meaning of the Kingdom of God. People must not only hear about the Kingdom of God, but must see it in actual operation, on a small scale perhaps and in imperfect form but a real demonstration nevertheless.[42]

It also becomes clear, partly from the experience of the Lucknow Ashram, that an important aspect of the kingdom of God is economic.[43] They had a common purse and the group passed on individual "budgets" monthly in advance. So the ashram became a "model" for the kingdom of God, or at least a model for moving toward the kingdom of God.

Jones held up the kingdom of God as model for the community of Christian people. In this he was at one with P. Chenchia and other members of the Rethinking Christianity Group, who were the leading Indian theological thinkers of the time. They particularly emphasized the kingdom of God as against what they considered to be an overemphasis on the church at the meeting of the International Missionary Council, Tambaram, 1938. Their emphasis, like so many of the emphases of Jones, grew out of their Indian experience, in which the church appeared Western, imperialist, and communalistic – in the Indian sense of in-group oriented. Jones tried to carry this insight back to the West.[44] There were a number of establishment counterreactions to these reactions to Tambaram. The most critical was from Henry P. Van Dusen, a prominent professor at Union Theological Seminary, New York. Van Dusen aimed his guns at Jones – wholly turning his back on anything he might have learned from the Rethinking Christianity Group, whom he must have met at Tambaram.[45] I find it impossible to believe that Van Dusen had really read all that Jones had written on the kingdom. In his rejoinder to Van Dusen, Jones asserted that he was as much "pro-church and pro-ecumenical" as anyone. He observed that his own commitment to Christian community had been clearly shown by his founding and active participation in the Lucknow Ashram, which was a far deeper and more intimate fellowship than that found in most churches.

He then suggested that the church "gets its authority and function, its right to live, its discipline and judgment from a higher standard of reference, the Kingdom of God."[46] Finally he wrote:

> Stand before an intelligent non-Christian audience in India and begin from a church-centric position and work out and see how far you get. In a few minutes you will be floundering. For the church is deeply suspect in India as bound up with communalism, imperialism and the old order. But begin with the Kingdom God and work out to all the problems of life and you have a message that cuts through everything with incisiveness. Jesus, as the door to such a Kingdom, and the church as the chief means to the realization of that Kingdom, necessarily follow.[47]

I am inclined to think that his legacy is on target in a general way for the missionary movement of today precisely because it is still so very much on target in India today – where it was formed – as testified to by many Indian church leaders' references to Jones and his ideas even now. Maybe this is so because it was formed in context. I have elsewhere observed that today most Protestant missiologists are well-educated, male, former missionaries. Jones never became a "former missionary." He remained very much rooted in the Indian context. I venture that this may have contributed to the longer-lasting relevance of his ideas.

Notes

1. *Time,* Dec. 12, 1938, p. 47. I owe this and several other American citations to Martin Ross Johnson, "The Christian Vision of E. Stanley Jones: Missionary, Evangelist, Prophet, and Statesman," Ph.D. diss., Florida State University, Tallahassee, 1978.

2. *Christian Century* 54 (Apr. 21, 1937): 508.

3. Ibid. 58 (June 4, 1941): 743f.

4. Ibid. 81 (Feb. 12, 1964): 216.

5. Stephen Neill, *Salvation Tomorrow* (Nashville: Abingdon, 1976), p. 26.

6. Bishop Brenton Thoburn Badley, ed., *Indian Church Problems of Today* (Madras: Methodist Publishing House, 1930), p. 7.

7. Cf. John R.W. Stott, "The Biblical Basis of Evangelism" in J.D. Douglas, ed., *Let the Earth Hear His Voice* (Minneapolis: World Wide Publications, 1975); reprinted in Gerald H. Anderson and Thomas F. Stransky, eds., *Mission Trends No. 2* (New York: Paulist Press; and Grand Rapids, Mich.: Wm. B. Eerdmans, 1975); and expanded as John R.W. Stott, *Christian Missions in the Modern World* (London: Falcon, 1975).

8. E. Stanley Jones, *The Christ of the Indian Road* (Lucknow: Lucknow Publishing House, 1925; reprinted 1964; American edition, New York: Abingdon Press, 1925).

9. In this section and several of the sections below I follow largely Richard W. Taylor, *The Contribution of E. Stanley Jones* (Madras: CLS/CISRS, 1973).

10. Ibid., pp. 16f.

11. Ibid., pp. 28f.

12. Ibid., pp. 48f.

13. Cf. Roland Allen, *Missionary Principles* (London: Robert Scott, 1913), p. 98.

14. For this contention in fuller detail and documentation, cf. Richard W. Taylor, "Das Wirken Christi in unserer Gesellschaft," in Horst Burkle, ed., *Indische Beiträge zur Theologie der Gegenwart* (Stuttgart: Evangelisches Verlagswerke, 1966), pp. 205-17; translated as *Indian Voices in Today's Theological Debate* (Lucknow: Lucknow Publishing House, 1972). Chap. 5 on "What Is God Doing in India?" in Richard W. Taylor and M.M. Thomas, *Mud Walls and Steel Mills* (New York: Friendship Press, 1963), is an exposition of some aspects of this theme.

15. Jones, *The Christ of the Indian Road,* p. 23.

16. Cf. Richard W. Taylor, *Jesus in Indian Paintings* (Madras: CLS/CISRS, 1975).

17. Dr. Devanesen writes of this in his letter of Feb. 22, 1979, now in the archives of the United Theological College, Bangalore.

18. Jones, *The Christ of the Indian Road,* pp. 220f.

19. E. Stanley Jones, *Christ at the Round Table* (London: Hodder and Stoughton, 1928), p. 19.

20. Ibid.; italics are Jones's own.

21. Ibid., pp. 21ff.

22. E. Stanley Jones, *A Song of Ascents* (Nashville: Abingdon, 1968), p. 236.

23. Jones, *Christ at the Round Table*, p. 16.

24. Cf. Richard W. Taylor, *Modern Indian Ashrams* (Madras: CLS/CISRS, forthcoming).

25. E. Stanley Jones, *Mahatma Gandhi: An Interpretation* (Lucknow: Lucknow Publishing House, 1948; reprinted 1963), p. 36.

26. E. Stanley Jones, "My Stay at Santineketan," *Indian Witness,* Sept. 5, 1923, pp. 612f.

27. *Indian Witness,* Aug. 29, 1923, p. 601. The poem is also published in *The Christian Advocate,* March 13, 1924, p. 319, in the midst of an article "In Tagore's 'House of Peace' " by Jones, which is a rewritten version of "My Stay."

28. E. Stanley Jones, "The Ashram Ideal," in *Indian Church Problems of Today,* ed. Brenton Thoburn Badley, pp. 44-51.

29. "The Proposed Ashram at Sat Tal," *The Fellowship,* February 1930.

30. Described in detail in the typescript "Memoirs" of Boyd W. Tucker, in the archives of United Theological College, Bangalore.

31. Cf. "Our First Year," *The Fellowship,* August 1936, p. 30; cf. also "The Lucknow Ashram," *Indian Witness,* July 25, 1935, pp. 474f.

32. Cf. "The Acharya's Return," *The Fellowship,* January 1939, p. 3.

33. Typified by *The Message of Sat Tal Ashram 1931* (Calcutta: Association Press, 1932) and *The Message of the Kingdom of God: Sat Tal Essays 1932* (Calcutta: YMCA Publishing House, 1933).

34. Louisville Area edition of the *United Methodist Reporter* 5, no. 16 (Apr. 1, 1977).

35. "The Harlem Ashram," 8 pp., mimeographed, ca. 1944.

36. These are continued by the United Christian Ashrams, P.O. Box 97, Damascus, Maryland 20750.

37. Much of the material in this section is based on my contribution to a Bangalore Christian Theological Association study where its broader Indian setting was also stressed. For a somewhat garbled condensation, see "The Kingdom of God in the History of Christianity in India," *National Christian Council Review,* 100, no. 5 (May 1980): 238ff.

38. Jones, *Christ at the Round Table*, pp. 71, 90ff.

39. E. Stanley Jones, *Christ's Alternative to Communism* (New York: Abingdon Press, 1935), and E. Stanley Jones, *The Choice before Us* (New York: Abingdon Press, 1935).

40. Abridged from E. Stanley Jones, *Along the Indian Road* (London: Hodder and Stoughton, 1939), pp. 200-236, in Taylor, *The Contribution of E. Stanley Jones,* p. 83.

41. Ibid.

42. Ibid., p. 92.

43. Ibid., pp. 93f.

44. E. Stanley Jones,"Where Madras Missed Its Way," *Indian Witness,* Feb. 9, 1939, pp. 86f. Also published in *Guardian,* Feb. 23, 1939, pp. 101f., and in *Christian Century* 56 (March 15, 1939): 351f.

45. Henry P. Van Dusen, "What Stanley Jones Missed at Madras," *Christian Century* 56 (March 29, 1939): 411f.

46. E. Stanley Jones, "What I Missed at Madras," *Christian Century 56* (May 31, 1939): 705f.

47. Ibid.

Selected Bibliography

Major Works of E. Stanley Jones

1925 *The Christ of the Indian Road.* New York: Abingdon Press.

1928 *Christ at the Round Table.* New York: Abingdon Press.

1931 *The Christ of Every Road.* New York: Abingdon Press.

1935 *Christ's Alternative to Communism.* New York: Abingdon Press. British edition, *Christ and Communism.*

1937 *The Choice before Us.* New York: Abingdon Press. British edition, *Christ and Present World Issues.*

1939 *Along the Indian Road.* New York: Abingdon Press.

1946 *The Christ of the American Road.* Nashville: Abingdon-Cokesbury Press.

1949 *Mahatma Gandhi: An Interpretation.* Nashville: Abingdon-Cokesbury Press. Revised in 1984.

Works about E. Stanley Jones

Graham, James R., Jr. "The Need of a Twentieth Century Revival: The Cult of E. Stanley Jones and the Adulation of Kagawa." *Christian Beacon* 4 (Apr. 13, 1939).

Johnson, Martin Ross. "The Christian Vision of E. Stanley Jones: Missionary, Evangelist, Prophet, and Statesman." Ph.D. diss., Florida State University, Tallahassee, 1978.

Mark, Charles Wesley. "A Study in the Protestant Christian Approach to the 'Great Tradition' of Hinduism with Special Reference to E. Stanley Jones and P.D. Devanandan." Ph.D. diss., Princeton Theological Seminary, 1988.

Mathews, James K. "The Legacy of E. Stanley Jones." *Circuit Rider* (October, 1984): 8-9.

Taylor, Richard W. *The Contribution of E. Stanley Jones* (Madras: CLS/CISRS, 1973).

Thomas, C. Chacko. "The Work and Thought of Eli Stanley Jones with Special Reference to India." Ph.D. diss., University of Iowa, 1955.

J. Waskom Pickett

1890–1981

Social Activist and Evangelist of the Masses

John T. Seamands

Jarrel Waskom Pickett, son of a Methodist minister, was born on February 21, 1890, in northeast Texas. His father, L.L. Pickett, had attained considerable recognition as a hymn writer, editor, author, and controversial debater. After serving a few years in Texas and then in South Carolina, the Rev. Mr. Pickett moved with his family to Wilmore, Kentucky, where Asbury College had recently been established.

Waskom's childhood was, in many respects, unusual. His mother taught him to recognize the alphabet, both in capital and lower-case letters, before he was two years old. By the middle of his fourth year he began to read the morning newspapers and to report chief items of news at the breakfast table. Before he was six, he had read all of the New Testament and several books of the Old Testament.

On his first day at public school, Waskom was put in the kindergarten at nine o'clock, promoted to first grade an hour later, and to second grade in the afternoon. The next day he was promoted to third grade, and after a month was advanced to fourth grade. At eight years of age Waskom began to learn Greek, with his father as his teacher. So by the time he graduated from high school, he could read and translate the Greek New Testament with considerable proficiency. When he was thirteen, he enrolled as a student in Asbury College.

Two days after college opened, a young man called at the Pickett home, asking for a place to stay while he attended college. It was E. Stanley Jones. Waskom graciously accepted him as his roommate, and thus began a lifelong friendship between these two young men, both destined to be outstanding leaders of the church in India.

In May 1907 Waskom and Stanley graduated from Asbury College, both with academic honors. Stanley Jones went on to India as pastor of the English-speaking Methodist Church in Lucknow, while Waskom stayed on to teach at Asbury College and take a master's degree. He wanted to go to the School of Theology at Vanderbilt University, but his father objected strongly. He was prejudiced against seminaries and called them "cemeteries." So instead, Waskom accepted a position as instructor of Latin and Greek in a small college at Vilonia, Arkansas, and a year later became assistant professor of New Testament and Greek at Taylor University, Upland, Indiana.

In February 1910 Waskom received a cablegram from Stanley Jones, advising him to apply to the Board of Missions to be sent to India, to replace Jones in the Lucknow church. Waskom immediately applied, was accepted, and soon after began his journey to India. But he had been in India only about four years when he was ordered to return to America because he had contracted tuberculosis. The government expert in that disease said that his lungs were so badly affected that he would not live more than a year. But on board ship, during his second day at sea, Waskom spent a long time on his knees in prayer, and the Lord assured him that he would recover. Several weeks later when he arrived in San Francisco, he reported to a doctor on orders from the Mission Board. The doctor examined him and said, "Who told you that you had tuberculosis?"

Pickett showed him his X rays he had brought from India. The doctor said, "Well, you actually had advanced TB when these X rays were taken, but something wonderful has happened to you since then."[1]

During this first furlough, Waskom was married to Ruth Robinson, daughter of John Wesley Robinson, missionary bishop in India. For the next twenty-five years after the return to the field, Pickett served variously as pastor, superintendent, evangelist, and editor of the *Indian Witness*. In 1935 he was elected to the episcopacy and served in that capacity for twenty-one years, until his retirement in 1956. In the United States following his retirement, he served as visiting professor of missions at Boston University School of Theology.

Pickett, the Statesman

Waskom Pickett was especially gifted in meeting government officials and national leaders, and gaining their respect and confidence, not only for himself, but for the entire Christian movement in India. Though he had a wide range of such contacts, he made a great impact upon three persons in particular.

Bhim Raj Ambedkar was born into a low-caste Hindu family, but leaped into prominence after advanced study in England and America. He returned to India with an overpowering desire to free his people from agelong oppression. He traveled all across the country, holding mass meetings among members of the lower castes. He denounced Hindu gods as immoral and urged his people to renounce Hinduism, which, he claimed, was the cause of their poverty and social stigma. "I was born a Hindu," he shouted, "but I will not die a Hindu."[2]

Just at this time Waskom Pickett was elected bishop and appointed to the Bombay area, where Dr. Ambedkar served as president of the Law College. The two men became close friends and often prayed together. One day Ambedkar asked Bishop Pickett to baptize him as a Christian but, afraid it might ruin his political career, he wanted it done in secret. Bishop Pickett refused, and insisted that he should openly confess Christ as Lord and Savior. This, Ambedkar was not willing to do. Some time later, after he had become minister of law in Prime Minister Nehru's cabinet, he took the oath to Buddhism along with 75,000 of his followers.

During Ambedkar's last conversation with Bishop Pickett, he asked the bishop if he had lost hope for his acceptance of Christ. The bishop replied, "No, I am still praying for you." To this Ambedkar said, "Please keep it up. I am not yet satisfied, and may still ask you to baptize me and admit me to the Methodist Church." Shortly afterward, however, Ambedkar died of a heart attack.[3]

Early in his missionary career, Waskom Pickett met *Jawaharlal Nehru* and over the years a strong friendship developed between the two men. Nehru was by birth a Hindu, but he was fully committed to the Christian ideal. In one of their early conversations, Nehru said to Pickett, "Bishop, in the area of ethics I try to be completely Christian. If at any time you think I am doing wrong, please rebuke me, and I will be grateful."[4]

When Nehru was elected first prime minister of the new India in 1947, Pickett was resident bishop in Delhi. Immediately following independence, clashes between Hindus and Muslims took place in many parts of North India. Every day and night whole families were being murdered. Bishop Pickett felt concerned that he should organize a Relief Committee of Christians to help the Muslims who, in Delhi, were chief victims of the surging violence. When he approached the prime minister, Nehru asked Bishop Pickett to take charge of the Government Relief Station. The bishop told him he thought this would be unwise, so Nehru appointed a Christian official with the understanding that the bishop be his unofficial adviser. Messengers were sent out to the Christian community for volunteers, and within two or three days over 200 Christians were working in the Relief Center, seeking to stop the slaughter. Hindus and Sikhs threatened to kill Bishop Pickett and his wife, and one night actually fired a shot at them when he was in the upstairs bathroom of his home.

To care for the sick and wounded, Bishop Pickett prepared a list of needed medical supplies and tried to send it by cable to government friends in Washington. But Indian law-breakers had captured the telegraph offices and refused to accept the cablegram, saying, "You want medicine to save these damn Muslims. Let them die!" Bishop Pickett then went to the American ambassador, Dr. Henry Grady, who got the message through in a few hours. Within four days a plane landed in Delhi loaded with necessary supplies, donated by several pharmaceutical firms in the United States. In a few days these supplies were saving lives in every hospital in Delhi.

Mohandas K. Gandhi (Mahatma), father of India's independence, was another national leader with whom Waskom Pickett had close ties. Pickett was bold in his witness to Gandhi and often confronted him with the claims of Christ. In their very first interview, Gandhi made the statement that he was a Christian, as well as a Hindu, Muslim, Sikh, Buddhist, and Jew, and that he worshiped Christ along with the Hindu gods. Pickett then asked, "Mr. Gandhi, are you not aware of the teachings of Jesus that He is the one and only Savior?"

Gandhi said, "Yes, I know what He said, but I cannot accept that claim. It was, I'm sure, a mistake."

Pickett then asked, "Do you believe that Jesus was totally without sin in all His life?"

Gandhi answered, "No, I think He sinned like all others have done."

Pickett then asked, "Would you be willing to mention what you regard as His sins?"

To this Gandhi replied, "His greatest sin as I see Him was His apparent approval of the man who killed a calf to honor his repentant son. No man can hold my affection who approves killing a calf."[5]

Almost twenty years after this memorable personal contact with Gandhi, one of Gandhi's sons came to Bishop Pickett at his home in Bombay and asked him to baptize him. The bishop asked why he wished to be baptized. He said, "Because my father mistreats me and all my family. I hate him and want to hurt him. I know no possible way to hurt him more than to renounce Hinduism and become a Christian."

Gandhi's son was surprised when Bishop Pickett refused to accept him on these terms. A few weeks later, newspapers reported that young Gandhi had become a Muslim.

Shortly after independence, when the Hindu-Muslim conflict was at its height, Bishop Pickett was preparing to go to bed one night, when there was a sudden knock at the door. The Delhi commissioner informed Bishop Pickett that the police had uncovered a plot to assassinate Gandhi, and that his life was in danger. He requested Bishop Pickett to call on Prime Minister Nehru and explain the grave situation to him.

When the bishop explained his mission to Nehru over breakfast the next morning, Nehru said, "Bishop, I have done my best to persuade Mr. Gandhi to leave Delhi, but he will not listen. Why don't you go to see him? He has great respect for you."

Bishop Pickett went straight to Gandhi's residence, but found him adamant in his refusal to leave the city. "Why should I be afraid to die?" he asked. "I am a failure. I have pleaded for peace and we are having war. Hindus, Sikhs, and Muslims have forgotten their promise and are killing one another. All my hopes for a better India are being destroyed. Perhaps Gandhi dead will be more respected than Gandhi alive."

"Mr. Gandhi," Bishop Pickett replied earnestly, "I assure you that Indian Christians are working tirelessly for peace. In my opinion, you have never been fair to the Christians in India."

"That is true," Gandhi admitted. "I have failed at this point and I am planning to apologize to the Christian community."

"I am delighted to hear you say that," Pickett replied. "Now please *listen* to me and leave Delhi at once. India needs you and your life is in great danger."

The Mahatma looked thoughtful as their conversation ended.

Two days later an official in the prime minister's office phoned to tell Picket that Gandhi had been assassinated at a public prayer meeting.[6]

Pickett, the Churchman

Bishop Pickett loved the church and sought to serve it in every way possible. An evangelist at heart, he promoted the work of evangelism wherever he went and encouraged those who possessed the gift of preaching. He took keen interest in the institutional life of the church, particularly schools and hospitals. He established a Bible school at Bellia to train young couples for voluntary service in their villages and conduct worship services on Sunday. He encouraged the development of a new English-speaking department in Bareilly Theological Seminary, which was later moved to Jabalpur and became the well-known Leonard Theological College. Early in his career he volunteered to raise $150,000 to save Lucknow Christian College from bankruptcy.

Waskom Pickett took a special interest in the ministry of healing. He served on the board of Vellore Medical College in South India, and after retiring from the field in 1956, he undertook to raise funds for the Ludhiana Medical College in North India. When he told Prime Minister Nehru of the project, Nehru said to him, "If you raise a million dollars in America for Ludhiana, I'll give the college an additional million."

Bishop Pickett noted that there were very few church buildings in villages, and those few were built from the Christian community in the upper-caste section of town in order to attract the caste people. He began pleading with the village Christians to build churches near their own homes. He promised them if they would give suitable sites, lay the foundations, and build walls, he would raise money to put on the roofs. While in the Bombay area, Bishop Pickett saw twenty-six new churches constructed. As a result of the program, Christians grew spiritually, respect for them increased, and occasionally non-Christians came and joined in worship.

Waskom Pickett was a strong supporter of church union in India and actively worked for twenty-six years to achieve it. He was keenly disappointed when, after his retirement, a plan was submitted to form the Church of North India, but his own Methodist Church withdrew from negotiations at the last moment. Bishop Pickett felt that denominationalism was a great stumbling block to non-Christians in India and that a united church was necessary for the evangelization of the country.

In 1953 when the new king of Nepal decided to open up his country to the outside world and was seeking advice, Prime Minister Nehru said to him, "If you want your country to make progress, you will need the aid of Christian missionaries. I suggest that you contact Bishop Pickett of the Methodist Church. He will be able to help you."

The result was an invitation from the king to open up medical, educational, and agricultural work in Nepal. So Bishop Pickett wisely established the United Mission to Nepal, an interdenominational and international organization, which has served the Nepalese people with great effectiveness, and has helped to lay the foundations of the Christian church in that land.

One of the special contributions that Waskom Pickett made to the entire church in India was the research on mass movements, which he directed at the request of the National Christian Council. In the early 1930s many church leaders in India were questioning the validity of such group decisions for Christ, arguing that salvation is always an individual matter. Results of this investigation were published in a book written by Waskom Pickett, *Christian Mass Movements in India* (1933), which was read and studied avidly all over India. The research completely vindicated the integrity of group movements in the Indian context. Pickett pointed out that the practice of urging individuals to believe in Christ worked very well in the United States where Christianity was the major religion, and people could become Christians without separating from their families and friends. The one-by-one method, however, did not work in India among Hindus, because if only one person became a Christian he was thrown out of his family and caste, and suffered social dislocation.

One very significant result of the survey must be noted. A Disciple of Christ missionary, Donald McGavran, was greatly influenced by the findings of that research, and joined Bishop Pickett in subsequent studies on group movements. This later led to the publication of McGavran's two books, *The Bridges of God* and *How Churches Grow,* and eventually to the inauguration of the Church Growth movement, which has greatly influenced the strategy and teaching of Christian missions in the past two decades. Church Growth principles have been the driving force in establishing several departments and schools of World Mission and Evangelism in seminaries across the United States and around the world.

In a letter addressed to this writer, McGavran has expressed his debt to Bishop Pickett's influence in these words:

> Pickett limited his insight to India. He never hinted that this might be a universal principle applicable everywhere. During the years 1940 to 1952 I began to see that this principle applied everywhere. Between 1954 and 1961 I carried out extensive surveys in Puerto Rico, the Philippines, Formosa, Thailand, Belgian Congo, and Jamaica. What I had begun to see in the preceding decade was abundantly proved. In short, I universalized Pickett's findings concerning India . . . All this opening of vision I owe to Waskom Pickett.[7]

Pickett, the Social Activist

Waskom Pickett was not only concerned about the spiritual needs of the church in India, he was also concerned about the physical and material needs of Indian people, particularly in the villages. His interest in a variety of areas made a profound impact on life in India.

Discovering that the average Indian cow yielded little more than two quarts of milk a day, Waskom Pickett began to consider the possibility of importing first-class bulls from America and breeding them with the best cows in India. So he persuaded a successful dairyman in Merced, California, to ship four Jersey bulls to India, and arranged for the semen of the bulls to be artificially inseminated into several Punjabi cows. The result was a new breed of cows that produced considerably more and richer milk. Soon many Punjabi farmers were begging that their cows be inseminated so that they would have offspring equally productive and valuable. Finally the government imported over 800 Jersey bulls into India and started a full-scale program of inter-breeding. Consequently, the milk supply in that part of India increased greatly!

The worldwide influenza epidemic of 1918 and 1919 left a great many babies in India as orphans. Dozens were brought by their neighbors to Christian hospitals or schools. So Bishop Pickett raised Rs. 100,000 (then $30,000) and constructed an orphanage on land adjacent to Clara Swain Hospital in Bareilly. One baby was left on a winter morning in a basket on the verandah of the missionary in charge. Years later that baby became Bishop Pickett's secretary and sometime afterward came to America for advanced study. Today he is professor of Old Testament in Leonard Theological College in Jabalpur. Other orphanage wards hold responsible positions in church and state all over North India.

One of Bishop Pickett's chief public services was his campaign to promote prohibition in the country. He edited and published a biweekly *Temperance Clipsheet,* which contained articles on the evil effects of the liquor traffic in society, and was mailed to over 1,000 editors who were influencing public opinion across India. This effort acquired wide recognition and brought letters of support from every province in the country. Politicians and national leaders joined in the fight against liquor. The Right Honorable Chintamani Rajagopalacharia, chief minister of Madras and later acting governor general of India, developed a severe restrictive policy for dealing with the sale of intoxicants, which he called "a half-way to prohibition." He spoke of Bishop Pickett as "the father of Indian prohibition" and said that the *Temperance Clipsheet* had convinced him that it was his duty to support the struggle against alcohol, opium, and hemp drugs.[8]

This is the legacy of J. Waskom Pickett, evangelist and social activist, churchman and statesman, who untiringly and unselfishly served the people of India for forty-six years and made an impact upon both church and nation that continues to this day.

Bishop and Mrs. Pickett spent the last years of their lives in a retirement village in Columbus, Ohio. He passed away in the summer of 1981, at the age of ninety-one, and his wife, Ruth, followed just two years later. This writer had the honor of conducting a memorial service for the couple in July 1983, when their remains were interred in the cemetery at Wilmore, Kentucky.

Notes

1. Pickett, handwritten notes entitled "My Struggle with t.b.," Archives of Asbury College.
2. Narrated by Bishop Pickett while speaking in Dr. Seamands's class in Asbury Theological Seminary.
3. Pickett, *My Twentieth Century Odyssey,* p. 156.
4. Pickett, handwritten notes entitled "Indira Gandhi," Archives of Asbury College.
5. Pickett, *My Twentieth Century Odyssey,* p. 29.
6. Ibid., p. 151.
7. Letter from Donald McGavran to J.T. Seamands, dated Aug. 22, 1986.
8. Pickett, *My Twentieth Century Odyssey,* p. 57.

Selected Bibliography

The Archives of Asbury College, Wilmore, Kentucky, include an assortment of unclassified personal correspondence and handwritten materials left by Bishop Pickett.

Works by J. Waskom Pickett

1925 (ed.) *The Indian Witness.* January to December. Lucknow, India: Lucknow Publishing House.
1933 *Christian Mass Movements in India.* Nashville: Abingdon.
1938 *Christ's Way to India's Heart.* Lucknow, India: Lucknow Publishing House.
1938 (with Donald A. McGavran and G.H. Singh) *Christian Missions in Mid India.* Jabalpur, India: The Mission Press. A study of nine areas, with special reference to mass movements.
1956 (with A.L. Warnshuis, G.H. Singh, and Donald A. McGavran) *Church Growth and Group Conversion.* Lucknow, India: Lucknow Publishing House.

1963 *The Dynamics of Church Growth.* Nashville: Abingdon.
1980 *My Twentieth Century Odyssey.* Bombay, India: Gospel Literature Service.

Works about J. Waskom Pickett

"Bishop J.W. Pickett." *Indian Witness,* Sept. 15, 1981; pp. 8-9.
"Our Bishops Who Retire at the Central Conference This Year." *Indian Witness,* November 1, 1956, pp. 10-11.

Paul David Devanandan

1901–1962

The Church in Society and Nation Building

Creighton Lacy

Doc Devanandan – as his friends and associates called him – was above all an enabler, a facilitator, an encourager, an inspirer, a challenger, a friend. To be sure, he was – as farewell tributes reminded us – an outstanding preacher, pastor, scholar, prophet, evangelist, even practical joker. One colleague called him "a finder and builder of men."[1] Another wrote: "Gradually he built up a team of younger thinkers and writers who have the opportunity to move into larger areas of thought and witness which he suggested, but had no time to explore."[2] These are the marks of a gifted and humble teacher. Let me illustrate this in several areas.

In 1959 a relatively young, unknown American professor, totally ignorant of the Indian scene, arrived in New Delhi on an academic quest and a financial shoestring to undertake independent research on India's social ethics. Somehow Doc heard about it, and within a few weeks, on his next visit to the capital, he was literally on the doorstep (not merely offering an appointment), welcoming, advising, guiding, suggesting contacts, and inviting me to the next seminar/colloquium of the Christian Institute for the Study of Religion and Society (CISRS). (The group happened to be reviewing the World Council of Churches' Provisional Study Document on "Christians and the Prevention of War in an Atomic Age," but broadened its concerns to the controversial role of Christians in relation to India's foreign policy.[3])

At the "First Regular Meeting of the (Advisory) Council" of the CISRS in 1958 the directors presented an ostensibly joint report.[4] Devanandan's name appears only once in the annual review; he refers at least six times to his associate, giving M.M. Thomas credit for arranging seminars, supervising publications, editing the *Bulletin*, and so forth. At the memorial "Service of Thanksgiving" for P.D. Devanandan, E.V. Mathew, a distinguished Christian lawyer, recalled sitting beside Doc at the New Delhi Assembly of the World Council of Churches when Thomas read a paper. No mention of the fact that Devanandan also delivered a major address on Christian Witness. Said Mathew: "'Doc' was almost overcome by joy and pride at the achievement of his teammate. He gloried himself in the glory of his friends."[5] How much more he would have gloried – and probably did – when M.M. Thomas, years later, became chairman of the Central Committee of the World Council of Churches.

This trait of genuine modesty causes problems for biographers and interpreters. Few major books are directly and wholly attributed to P.D. Devanandan. Others he edited, without identifying the individual work of contributors; many CISRS publications were reports of seminars and conferences, in which Doc's hand – and mind and heart – played a key role as recorder and compiler, but cannot be isolated or "credited" as his personal input. Many of these collections or summaries are officially called "A Group Writing . . . ," "A Group Work . . . ," "A Symposium . . . "; Devanandan's name appears only as editor, usually along with that of M.M. Thomas.

His deference and self-effacement extended into all his relationships. Doc knew no boundaries of caste or class, race or rank; he "walked with kings" – or at least with presidents and sadhus and swamis and bishops – "nor lost the common touch." Frequently in his theological apologetics and his respectful study of Hinduism, Devanandan took issue with Sarvepalli Radhakrishnan, one of the great philosophers of the twentieth-century world. Yet Radhakrishnan, later the second president of independent India, contributed a foreword to Devanandan's book, *Christian Concern in Hinduism*, acknowledging that "it is written with learning and insight." In a final eulogy Russell Chandran, principal of United Theological College in Bangalore, neighbor and close associate of the CISRS, said of Devanandan: "No one in the Indian Church has had so many friends among non-Christian scholars and thinkers and few Indian Christians have been held in so high a regard by non-Christians."[6]

P.D. Devanandan was always on the move. It is appropriate – one resists such words as "fitting" – that he died at the railway station at Dehra Dun on his way to yet another conference at the Christian Retreat and Study Centre. He had averaged one such seminar/workshop/consultation a week for the preceding two hottest months, most of them in Kerala or Madras at the opposite end of the Indian subcontinent. Doc took his ideas and his challenges to all sorts of people where they were, never expecting them to come to him.

He was born on July 9, 1901, and graduated from Nizam College in Hyderabad. Stanley Samartha suggests[7] that the two paramount influences on Doc's life and thought were his mother and K.T. Paul, one of the first Indian Christian nationalists. *Christian Concern in Hinduism* is dedicated "to the memory of K.T. Paul in gratitude and affection." It was to K.T. Paul that Gandhi is reported to have written: "Pray help the Muslims to show a Christian attitude toward the Hindus." It was K.T. Paul who first took Devanandan to America as his personal secretary. Before that, however, Devanandan had taught briefly at Jaffna College in Ceylon and received an M.A. degree from Madras University.

In the United States the young Indian earned a B.D. from Pacific School of Religion and his first doctorate from Yale – though both American alma maters plus Serampore College in India were later to award him honorary D.D.s. His Yale dissertation was "The Concept of Maya," evidence of his determination to understand thoroughly the religious and philosophical concepts of Hinduism. His academic insights were recognized by distinguished engagements – notably, William Paton Lecturer at Selly Oak, England; Henry Luce Visiting Professor at Union Seminary, New York; Teape Lecturer at Cambridge University. At the time of his death (August 10, 1962) he was looking forward to a term of teaching at International Christian University in Tokyo. Commitment to the World Council of Churches, the East Asia Christian Conference, and other ecumenical agencies accounted further for his peripatetic life.

Back in India, however, he chose to "settle down" (a complete misnomer) at United Theological College, Bangalore, as professor of religions for seventeen years. This was a period, it should be noted, when serious and sympathetic study of other religions was neither common nor popular in many Christian seminaries around the world. Doc Devanandan contributed substantially to changing that outlook, not merely in his own country but by drawing other people and churches into his vision, thus laying foundations for later CISRS and World Council of Churches dialogues with persons of others faiths.

Two years he spent as head of the YMCA Department of Literature and Publications. But it was as director of the Christian Institute for the Study of Religion and Society, an appointment tragically cut short after only five years, that P.D. Devanandan traveled the length and breadth of India and shared more widely his mature social and theological reflections. The institute (when I saw it, at least) occupied a small, breezy, enormously cluttered bungalow immediately adjacent to the United Theological College in Bangalore. There the plain but pregnant *Bulletin*, later called *Religion and Society*, was published; there books and pamphlets were collected and edited; there plans were made for the seemingly endless succession of workshop consultations conducted all over the country.

For the CISRS was really at work, most truly carrying out its mission, wherever P.D. Devanandan and M.M. Thomas happened to be. From "The Urban Community and the Urban Church" to "The Pattern of Rural Community Development," from "Dynamic Democracy" to "The Communist Role in Kerala and Christian Responsibility," these seminars and study conferences focused the attention of Indian Christians on their essential involvements in "nation-building" (a favorite term). In writing on international affairs, for example, Devanandan asked: "Can foreign aid be so utilized as to realize cultural and social objectives as well" as economic and technological ones?[8]

But Doc knew – as many missionaries and church members did not – that a tiny minority of Christians could not make a significant contribution to their country or their community without understanding *and appreciating* the truths and values and insights of the dominant Hindu culture. Devanandan's final weeks of activity included a "dialogue on the Concept of Truth between Christian and Hindu friends held at the Christavasram" and a conference of theologians on the "Christian Doctrine of Creation," a conference to which he invited noted Hindu scholars to present "the Hindu view of purpose, society and history so that the theologians may do their thinking on the [Christian] Doctrine of Creation within the context of and in dialogue with Indian thought."[9]

Engaging Hinduism from Christian Foundations

Precisely because P.D. Devanandan was always so busy, so constantly "on the go," so involved in editing, organizing, and directing consultations, many contemporaries lost sight of the profound theology that undergirded and motivated these activities, as well as providing their substance and purpose. Looking back over the years since his death, rereading his most important works, one is struck by the clarity and directness with which he tackled most of the issues that still befuddle missiology, mission theology, and interreligious dialogue.

Doc was always building bridges, not erecting barricades. Without ever compromising his own faith, without ever denying or minimizing the differences, he sought for points on which Hinduism and Christianity might agree – or at least seek common goals. He declared that "the concept of man in society is a modern concept . . . [that] all rationalism tends toward individualism . . . [an individualism which has become] man against society." Yet at the heart of his thought and life lay the conviction that "essentially religion is concerned with the fulfillment of the human person, not in isolation of self but in community of being."[10]

As a Christian in "the world's largest democracy" Devanandan believed in religious pluralism, but also in the freedom to affirm an "exclusive," decisive, converting faith. In the perennial debate as to "whether the meeting of human need is a rightful function of the Church or is somehow only subservient to the evangelistic aim," he quotes Willem Visser 't Hooft with unqualified agreement: "Diakonia exists in its own right, and is a perfectly necessary and essential expression of the

Church's life."[11] With equal conviction Doc would place Christianity along with "Hindu secular-ism" (i.e., recognition of the reality and significance of the created world and human responsibility within it) over against the escapism, the world-and-life-denial, of traditional Hindu "spirituality." In these and other apparent dichotomies and tensions, for Paul David Devanandan, Jesus Christ is the ultimate "bridge."

Few if any Christians have demonstrated so deep and comprehensive an insight into Hinduism. Few if any Hindus have offered so clear and simple and fair a presentation of the strengths and weaknesses of contemporary Hindu thought as are to be found in the slim posthumous volume entitled *Preparation for Dialogue*. Hindu scholars may disagree with Devanandan's conclusions, but they seldom criticize his honesty or accuracy. On countless platforms in innumerable seminars, before all sorts of audiences, P.D. Devanandan probed the inconsistencies, the contradictions, the unanswered questions of ancient and modern Hinduism, not with a polemical, combative attitude, but to open channels of receptivity to Christian alternatives.

For example, "Hindu thinking will have to come to terms with the whole idea of personality as applied both to finite and infinite being."[12] A contemporary view of personality, Devanandan believed, is essential for the development of relationships, of true community, and of nationhood. Or again, "Hindu religious thought, in all its voluminous literature, takes no serious notice of history . . . The Hindu indifference to history is due to its characteristic theology, its conception of God and Reality."[13] This metaphysical view of reality and the absence of any doctrine of creation, Devanandan emphasized, produce a major dilemma for those modern "secular" Hindus who wish to stress social reform, economic development, and political responsibility.

Yet such lacunae in traditional Hinduism often pose more problems for Christians and Muslims than for Hindus and Buddhists, because Westerners are wedded to an either/or logic rather than both/and. One may argue that all faiths are but different paths to the same truth, that "the ultimate goal of all religions is beyond religion."[14] One may acknowledge that each faith is partially true, but that it is possible to "reconcile differences by setting them in the larger framework of an evolving world-religion."[15] Or one may reject all religion as false, unscientific, retrogressive – the charge of some Marxist-inspired materialists, even in traditionally spiritual India. But the Christian position espoused by Devanandan is that "each historic religion is an entity by itself . . . that there are differences which we should all be willing to accept, and to give all men of faith full freedom for religious self-expression."[16]

In this sincere invitation to dialogue in the midst of acknowledged pluralism, Devanandan never surrenders or blurs the central affirmation of the Gospel. There is no syncretism, no "Christo-paganism," not even the latent theological imperialism of claiming a hidden Christ, an "unknown Christ of Hinduism." For Devanandan the particularity, the admitted "exclusivism," of Christianity is out in the open, precisely because it is more inclusive than the claims of any single creed, confession, or church. "The Christian faith is that what God has done in Jesus Christ has been done for all men. So that the claim for uniqueness is only an affirmation of its universality."[17]

On the other hand, Devanandan – like his Lord! – reserves his harshest language for those orthodox pundits whose narrow, judgmental dogmatism alienates rather than attracts. He draws a sharp distinction between propagation and propaganda, between persuasion and coercion, as between conversion and proselytism. He acknowledges the regrettable frequency of "somewhat dubious methods" in the history of Christian missions, especially "the temptation of exaggerating the validity of Christian claims by deliberately minimizing the inherent worth of other faiths."[18]

"Conviction about one's religious beliefs does not necessarily involve condemnation of the faith of others," he reminds his Christian audiences.[19] In fact, "The claims made for the uniqueness of Jesus Christ, the reality of the Church, the urgency of the mission and the authority of the Bible, are claims addressed not to others but to those who profess the Christian faith."[20] In other words, the particularities, the distinctive elements that mark off Christianity from other faiths, are the *result* of the Gospel message, not the basis of it. "It is not Christianity that is preached as against other religions."[21]

What then, is the essential, irreducible Gospel message? Simply that "the Christian view is that revelation is of God Himself, not of truths about Him, and that it is the communication of Person to persons."[22] If that conviction cuts across many traditional Hindu doctrines, such as those cited above, so be it. According to Devanandan, "man reflects the nature of God, but . . . he is not of the same substance as God;[23] . . . he can share in the creative purpose of God *if* he is truly man, that is man-in-relation-with-God, and man-in-community-with-other men."[24] (Lest present-day readers denounce the sexist language, let it be added that Devanandan, writing in 1960 in a socially and religiously male society, affirmed "the essential equality of man and woman in the whole scheme of life and in the creative purpose of God . . . because Christian anthropology has always been concerned with mankind rather than with man as against women."[25])

Somewhat unexpectedly – at least to those who equate interreligious dialogue with liberal theology – Devanandan was biblically conservative, basically neo-orthodox. First exposed to the liberal currents of the twenties and thirties, he was profoundly influenced by Karl Barth and, according to M.M. Thomas, "found in Kraemer a basis of renewal of his theology." But in missiological terms Devanandan "has been in revolt against Kraemer, searching for the post-Kraemer approach to the relation between Christianity and other religions."[26]

That influence included a serious but nonlegalistic view of sin – another concept that has no ultimate meaning in traditional Hinduism. "Man individually and collectively chooses," Devanandan wrote, "to direct his affairs in accordance with his own will . . . The root-cause of all this disorder is the individual and collective selfishness of man."[27] But, he hastened to add at a Hindu-Christian colloquy: "The Christian faith does not stop with the conviction about the sinfulness of man in the here and now. It goes on to proclaim and testify to the fact of forgiveness of sin."[28]

Bearing Testimony to the Redemptive Work of Christ

Christian Concern in Hinduism was published in the spring of 1961. In the chapter entitled "Our Task Today" Devanandan declared: "We would now hesitate to talk of evangelism as what we do but [rather recognize it] as what God is doing through us."[29] In December of 1961 – to the surprise of some who tended to dismiss the speaker as a social activist, deeply involved in political and economic concerns – Paul David Devanandan delivered an address to the Third Assembly of the World Council of Churches meeting in New Delhi, on the theme "Called to Witness." "No one," he asserted in the opening paragraph, "can claim to be a Christian believer, unless he bears living testimony to the redemptive work of God in Christ Jesus as a present reality."[30]

In the earlier book Devanandan defined evangelism in "its fourfold character as a cosmic process, a historic reality, a divine undertaking and a people's movement."[31] At the New Delhi Assembly, where the International Missionary Council became the Division of World Mission and Evangelism within the World Council of Churches, he amplified these distinctions. First, basing his conviction on Ephesians 1 (and Colossians 1), he affirmed that "the whole creation, life in its totality, every aspect of . . . earthly existence, will be brought eventually under the direct sway of God."[32] Second, "the message of the Kingdom" as an experiential fact "is directed to the individual and collective conscience of humankind";[33] where it is thwarted, the cause is humanity's sinful rebellion. Third, "this work of redemption, made manifest in human history in the life, death, and resurrection of Jesus Christ, is in fact being carried out – now and everywhere in our world! It is a present occurrence." Finally, God has entrusted "the fulfillment of His purpose" to us, to be witnesses, fishers of men, missionaries, "members of a fellowship whose calling is to herald the Good News . . . In any locality the community of believers are in fact the Body of Christ, exercising Christ's continuing ministry of intercession, service and love in the concrete situation of contemporary life."[34]

Doc was committed to dialogue, not destructive debate, not demand for deserting community or denying genuine religious experience. Rather, dialogue that starts with persons, in the midst of their social heritage and spiritual pilgrimage. Dialogue that ends ultimately, in God's time and God's manner, with Jesus Christ. Dialogue, as essential for followers of the Way as for others. Said M.M. Thomas of his mentor and colleague: "His fundamental concern was to help the Indian Church to understand Jesus Christ as the final clue and fulfillment of God's work for the world of Indian religion, culture and society . . . Jesus Christ reinforced and clarified the common humanity of all men. On this basis all dialogues among men about man, his faith, his culture, or his society, become real conversations, conversations in Christ and conversations about Christ."[35]

Paul David Devanandan spent his life building bridges: between East and West, between Hindus and Christians, between religion and secular life, between church and society, between the individual and the group, between God and his people. In short, he undertook the work of Jesus Christ, and he did it as a labor of love. Furthermore, he did it in the *spirit* of Christ, a spirit too often lacking in today's world, where narrow dogmatism or political and theological conflict so often obscure the Light. Doc Devanandan, said Thomas, "always sought to look forward to new and emerging creative forces and ideas . . . He saw more clearly than anyone else I knew of his age that the new period was one, not of revolts, but of reconstruction, whether in theological endeavor, church-life, or nation-building."[36]

As long as Christians are concerned about a Christlike approach to social responsibilities or to other religious faiths, the legacy of Paul David Devanandan will be quietly, lovingly at work.

Notes

1. *In Memory of Devanandan,* p. 10.
2. *International Review of Mission,* 52 (April 1963): 185-90.
3. *Bulletin* (CISRS) 6, no.4 (December 1959).
4. *Annual Report* (CISRS), 1958, pp. 1-10.
5. *In Memory,* p. 10.
6. Ibid., p. 5.
7. *International Review of Mission,* 52 (April 1963): 185-90.
8. *Bulletin* 6, no.1 (July 1957): 10.
9. *In Memory,* pp. 14-15.
10. Devanandan, *Preparation,* pp. 28-30.
11. Devanandan, *Christian Concern,* p. 109.
12. Ibid., p. 112
13. Ibid., p. 111.
14. Devanandan, *Preparation,* p. 53.
15. Devanandan, *Christian Concern,* p. vi.
16. Ibid.; cf. *Preparation,* pp. 139-40.
17. Devanandan, *Preparation,* p. 137.
18. Devanandan, *Christian Concern,* p. 96.
19. Devanandan, *Preparation,* p. 134.
20. Ibid., p. 137.
21. Ibid., p. 114.
22. Ibid., p. 169.
23. Ibid., p. 146.
24. Ibid., p. 150.
25. Ibid., p. 148.
26. *In Memory,* p. 16.

27. Devanandan, *Preparation*, p. 153.
28. Ibid., p. 156.
29. Devanandan, *Christian Concern*, p. 117.
30. Devanandan, *Preparation*, p. 179.
31. Devanandan, *Christian Concern*, p. 118.
32. Devanandan, *Preparation*, pp. 181-82.
33. Ibid., p. 182.
34. Ibid., pp. 182-83.
35. *Frontier* 5 (Winter 1962-63): 560.
36. Ibid.

Selected Bibliography

Works by Paul David Devanandan

1950 *The Concept of Maya.* London: Lutterworth Press.
1957 "Foreign Aid and the Social and Cultural Life of India." *Christianity and Crisis* 17 (Aug. 5): 108.
1958 "Religion and National Unity in India." *Christianity and Crisis* 18 (Dec. 22): 179.
1959 *The Gospel and Renascent Hinduism.* London: SCM Press.
1961 *Christian Concern in Hinduism.* Bangalore: CISRS.
1963 *Christian Issues in Southern Asia.* New York: Friendship Press.
1963 *I Will Lift Up Mine Eyes unto the Hills.* Ed. Nalini Devanandan and Stanley J. Samartha. Bangalore: CISRS. Devanandan's sermons and Bible studies.
1964 *Preparation for Dialogue.* Ed. Nalini Devanandan and M.M. Thomas. Bangalore: CISRS.

Edited with M.M. Thomas

1953 *Communism and the Social Revolution in India.* Calcutta: YMCA.
1955 *Cultural Foundations of Indian Democracy.* Bangalore: Committee for Literature on Social Concerns.
1955 *India's Quest for Democracy.* Bangalore: CISRS.
1957 *Human Person, Society and State.* Bangalore: Committee for Literature on Social Concerns.
1958 *Community Development in India's Industrial Urban Areas.* Bangalore: CISRS.
1960 *The Changing Pattern of Family in India.* Bangalore: CISRS.
1960 *Christian Participation in Nation-Building.* Bangalore: CISRS.
1962 *Problems of Indian Democracy.* Bangalore: CISRS.

Writings about Paul David Devanandan

In Memory of Devanandan. Bangalore: CISRS, 1962. Reprinted from *N.C.C. Review*, National Christian Council of India, September and October, 1962.
Mark, Charles Wesley. "A Study in the Protestant Christian Approach to the 'Great Tradition' of Hinduism with Special Reference to E. Stanley Jones and P.D. Devanandan." Ph.D. diss., Princeton Theological Seminary, 1988.
Wietzke, Joachim. *Theologie im modernen Indien: P.D. Devanandan.* Bern: Herbert Lang, 1973.

D.T. Niles

1908–1970

Evangelism, the Work of Disrupting People's Lives

Creighton Lacy

Evangelism is witness. It is one beggar telling another beggar where to get food."[1] Few Christians who have heard that aphorism can identify its source; even fewer could identify, by time or nation or vocation or publication, the powerful evangelist D.T. Niles. In a sense it is not a representative figure of speech, for Niles's grateful obedience to Jesus Christ poured forth in a life of energetic service and joyous faith.

For all the ecumenical conferences and distinguished pulpits that kept D.T. Niles "on the go," he said very little about himself. "I am not important except to God," he once wrote, and a bit later, "We who speak about Jesus must learn to keep quiet about ourselves."[2] Nor did many friends and contemporaries say much about the man; they were too busy listening to the message of God he proclaimed in word and deed.

Niles's Life and Ministry

Daniel Thambyrajah Niles was born near Jaffna, Ceylon (now Sri Lanka), in 1908, a fourth-generation Christian. His great-grandfather had been the first Tamil baptized in the American Board Mission in 1821; his grandfather was a Methodist minister. His mother died when D.T. was only a year old, but his father's remarriage eventually brought eight younger siblings to be cared for. Largely on that account, his father wanted Daniel to become a lawyer. It was a Hindu mathematics teacher who, on the very day of law-school registration, persuaded the father that D.T. Niles should enter the Christian ministry, and that God would look after the family.

The year that he graduated from what is now United Theological College in Bangalore, South India, Niles attended the Quadrennial of the Student Christian Movement (SCM) for India, Burma, and Ceylon. Even then, in 1933, W.A. Visser 't Hooft, one of the principal speakers, took note of a young Ceylonese student who was concerned with how the SCM might become an effective evangelistic force. Five years later D.T. Niles was the youngest delegate at the Madras Conference of the International Missionary Council, paired with Henry P. Van Dusen in the workshop on "The Faith by Which the Church Lives." Ten years – and a world war – after that Niles delivered the keynote address at the founding of the World Council of Churches (WCC) in Amsterdam. He

362

addressed the Second Assembly at Evanston in 1954 and was chosen to replace the assassinated Martin Luther King, Jr., to address the Uppsala Assembly in 1968.

Meanwhile Niles had earned a doctorate from the University of London, served as general secretary of the National Christian Council of Ceylon and as first chairman of the Youth Department in the World Council of Churches, planning and organizing the World Youth conferences in Amsterdam and Oslo. From 1953 he occupied, concurrently, posts as executive secretary of the WCC Department of Evangelism, principal of Jaffna Central College, pastor of St. Peter's Church in Jaffna, and chairman of the World's Student Christian Federation. That link from local church to world Christian community was typical. At the time of his death in 1970, D.T. Niles was executive secretary (and chief founder) of the East Asia Christian Conference (EACC), president of the Methodist Church of Ceylon, and one of six presidents of the World Council of Churches.

In between these peripatetic commitments he shared a close partnership with his wife, Dulcie, helped to rear two sons, both of whom entered the ministry, was the first "younger churchman" to occupy the Harry Emerson Fosdick Visiting Professorship at Union Theological Seminary, New York, and published nearly a score of books. "God never gives gifts without seeking to give himself along with them," he wrote. "Those who minister . . . must judge their success not by how much service has been rendered but by how many have been led to God."[3] Niles would surely apply that measurement to his own activities.

The Work of an Evangelist

D.T. was above all an evangelist. "Evangelism is the proclamation of an event, it is also an invitation to an encounter."[4] "Evangelism is the impact of the Gospel on the world."[5] "Evangelism is not something we do, it is something God does."[6] "Evangelism happens when God uses anything we do in order to bring people to Him in Jesus Christ."[7] "The recovery of wholeness – that is the purpose of evangelism."[8] "In our part of the world, the preacher, the evangelist, is engaged in the work of disrupting people's lives."[9] If there is an ambivalence in these sentences between God's role and ours, it is inherent in the writer – and in theology. D.T. Niles was an Asian – and a Christian – who thought in terms of both/and rather than either/or.

One of Niles's major contributions was the blending, not the contrasting, of Eastern and Western thought, of "orthodoxy" and "liberalism." This can be seen in the diverse men who influenced him most profoundly. At the age of eleven Niles heard the great missionary of the Middle East, Samuel Zwemer. During his European studies, soon after meeting Visser 't Hooft, he became acquainted with Hendrik Kraemer and Karl Barth, who "befriends Niles" (as a son later wrote).[10] John R. Mott visited India in 1937. Even closer associates and ecumenical colleagues were Pierre Maury, one-time head of the Reformed Church in France, and John Baillie, whom Niles regarded as a "mediating bridge" between East and West.

In India Niles deeply appreciated C.F. Andrews, E.C. Dewick, and E. Stanley Jones, who tended to stress the immanence of God, and Paul David Devanandan and M.M. Thomas, committed to the social application of the Gospel. Niles himself acknowledged the contrasts insightfully:

> Hendrik Kraemer and Paul Devanandan are the two men to whom I am most indebted for the way in which I have learned to study other religions and to be in normal converse with adherents of these religions. Kraemer taught me to approach other faiths and to enter into them as a Christian; Devanandan taught me to see and understand the Christian faith from the vantage ground of other faiths.[11]

Add to these contemporary "gurus" the influences that Niles absorbed by osmosis from his Asian and Christian environment: worship in the Eastern Orthodox tradition, the hymns of Charles Wesley, the mysticism and devotion of Hindu *jnana marga and bhakti marga*. As his son Dayalan described him, "Niles was certainly no systematic theologian in the technical sense of the word."[12] Rather, he chose a pragmatic stance in dealing with both local and ecumenical issues, a kind of action/reflection model. "His overall frame of reference is Methodist as opposed to the early Barthian dialectical position."[13]

Interpreting the Bible and Christian Faith

D.T. Niles drew abundantly on Scripture, for illustrations as well as quotations. Many of his addresses and published works were frankly, deliberately Bible studies: for example, *Living with the Gospel* (1957), *Studies in Genesis* (1958), *As Seeing the Invisible* (1961; an interpretation of Revelation). "I cannot claim either adequate scholarship or accuracy of method," he modestly stated, "but [these essays] at least represent what happens when I read my Bible."[14] One of the earliest of such studies, *Reading the Bible Today* (1955), has been translated into at least fifteen languages. In it Niles revealed clearly his modern, open approach to Scriptures. Truth need not be taken literally, he said, as when his two-year-old son from a tropical clime described snow as "somebody throwing flowers."[15] The opening words of Genesis were written, he believed, "by a group of men belonging to the priestly families of Israel at that time in exile in Babylon with their people."[16] In his Beecher Lectures he declared that "the Genesis account of man's sin is an account which seeks to make plain the nature of sin and not its origin."[17]

"Some people treat every word in the Bible as equally true and inspired, and do not ask why and when it was spoken. This may lead to very wrong ideas about God."[18] For God is the hero of the Bible stories, the evangelist explained, not individual men and women; God speaks and people answer, rather than merely recording the human quest for the divine. The Bible, he continued, gives us the word of God as news, as law or demands, as faith.[19] In short, "the adventure of Bible reading is in praying the Holy Spirit to lead us to that point in the conversation between God and man at which we can hear what God is saying to us today."[20]

Central to the Scriptures, to all of Christian faith, for Niles, stood Christology. "Both the New Testament and the Old Testament," he wrote, "are about Jesus Christ and from Jesus Christ."[21] As important – nay, as imperative – as the obligation to love may be, he affirmed in reply to J.A.T. Robinson's *Honest to God,* "it is essential . . . to hold this command to love in conjunction with the command to believe in Jesus Christ."[22]

At the same time – and here emerges the paradox of all who engage in sincere interfaith dialogue – "the issues of Salvation and Damnation cannot be stated in terms of men's belief or unbelief in the special revelation of Christ: they can only be stated in terms of the outreach of the work and ministry of Christ himself."[23] "To speak about the finality of Christ is not to tie oneself to where his name is actually pronounced."[24] "There is no Saviour but Jesus and they who are saved are always saved by him. That is true without qualification."[25] "There is no salvation except in Jesus Christ, but who shall decide how and in what guise Jesus comes to men and claims their acceptance!"[26] To some this is the hidden or anonymous Christ; to others it is the universal word of God.

Doctrinal debates, which divided the early church and still produce fissures in the body of Christ, merited little concern for D.T. Niles. Intellectual arguments about the preexistent Son or the "two natures" dissolved for him into a personal experience of the Savior. The question, he wrote, is "not whether our understanding of God is illumined for us by the person, teaching, and work of Jesus Christ; nor whether in him is found a supreme illustration of God-consciousness; but whether our faith in God is such as to find its one possibility in him."[27] "The crux of the finality issue is whether or not in Jesus Christ men confront and are confronted by the transcendent God whose will they cannot manipulate, by whose judgment they are bound, and with whose intractable presence in their midst they must reckon."[28]

In like manner also Niles offered fresh, empirical insight into the true meaning of the Trinity. "The Christian faith is no simple Jesus-religion," he declared in the Lyman Beecher Lectures; "it is faith in God the Father, God the Son, and God the Holy Spirit, one God in three persons, Trinity in unity and unity in Trinity. But there is no way to the largeness of this faith except through faith in Jesus Christ."[29] In other addresses, however, Niles made very clear that the Trinity represented not a distinction within the Godhead, but a significant distinction for the work of salvation.[30] Converts were – and should be – asked not simply, Do you believe in Jesus Christ? but have you received the Holy Spirit? Citing Romans 8:26-27, the evangelist insisted that, while Jesus establishes us in relation to God, "it is only the Spirit who is able to maintain us therein."[31] Or again, the downward movement of God in creation and providence is revealed in Christ's incarnation, suffering, and death; the upward movement of the Holy Spirit (and the church) is manifest in his resurrection and ascension.[32] Finally, within the Trinity, "The Holy Spirit is the missionary of the gospel. It is he who makes the gospel explosive in men's lives and in human affairs."[33]

"This Jesus whereof we are witnesses" comes to us initially and personally in worship, in devotion. Niles's sermons drew copiously on hymns by Charles Wesley, on poems by Wordsworth, Donne, and many others, on devotional literature from the East. Would that we had collections of recorded prayers from this man of God, but they must have been profoundly private. The world church owes a lasting debt to D.T. Niles for conceiving and gathering the liturgical wealth of the Orient in the EACC *Hymnal* and writing the words for forty-five of the entries. "Even a hymnbook or a book of prayers is a form expressing a given unity," he once wrote.[34]

In one of his Lyman Beecher Lectures, Niles quoted a Christian student as declaring that devotion to Jesus brings deliverance from "seeking the good life," from "obedience to a moral ideal."[35] Yet in the same address he cautioned against substituting renunciation for real righteousness, piety for practice. Furthermore, he once warned, "There is a difference between offering beauty to God in his worship and worshipping beauty in the guise of worshipping God."[36]

Our fellowship with Christ can only be maintained, Niles would insist, within the fellowship of the church. This is not, as previously indicated, a condition for salvation, but it is for the Christian life. "The object of evangelism is conversion," Niles declared, "conversion to Christ and personal discipleship to him. But involved also in this conversion are conversion to the Christian community and conversion to Christian ideas and ideals."[37] In fact, he went on to explain, the normal order of mission priorities should be a welcome to the community (proselytization), an invitation to discipleship (evangelism), and a transformation of values (Christianization).

"I believe fully," Niles wrote on another occasion, "that a decision to follow Jesus Christ is inextricably linked with the decision to become a member of the Christian Church."[38] "Faith is the faith of a community,"[39] and he quoted approvingly Karl Barth's familiar pronouncement: "One cannot hold the Christian faith without holding it in the church and with the church."[40]

The Centrality of the Christian Church

Nevertheless this serving community, according to Niles, must never be mistaken for the institutional church. "Men can only be loved into God's kingdom, they cannot be organized into it," he said.[41] With a gentle dig at preachers he suggested, in the Warreck Lectures in Scotland, that the laity, the people of God, earn their right to preach by the daily lives they lead, whereas the ordained clergy does not have to renew its professional credentials.[42] Similarly Niles had little use for sectarian divisions. "The finality of Jesus Christ," he declared, "is a standing judgment on denominational separateness."[43] In *Upon the Earth* he told the devastating story of the immigration officer who inquired about a missionary's religion: "Yes, Madam, Christian – but what damnation?"[44]

The real test of the church's faithfulness to Christ is, of course, its activity in the world. "Those who accused Him of revolution put Him on a cross," Niles told an audience of "conservative evangelicals"; "those who accuse Him of nonsense put Him in a sanctuary."[45] Both individuals and the community are called to radical discipleship, Niles constantly affirmed. "This song of Mary (Luke 1:46-53) is still the song of the Christian revolution. This song we must sing, even though we are surprised that it is we who must sing it."[46]

For this quiet little man from Ceylon, the essential involvement of Christians in the world has abundant biblical sanction. Leaven does not function by itself apart from the flour; salt is not used to turn fish into salt but to keep fish fresh "as fish."[47] A hospital should never be "a stalking horse for evangelism,"[48] and presumably the same dictum applies to mission schools. The light of the world (Matt. 5:14) – both Christ and his disciples – meant "a lamp shining in the street and not one burning in the sanctuary."[49] This lamp, he wrote on another occasion, must be filled with oil, its wick trimmed, within the sanctuary, but not left there.[50] Most startling of all perhaps, most challenging to the complacent congregations of our day, Niles declared: "The answer to the problems of the world is not Jesus Christ. The answer to the problems of the world is the answer that Jesus Christ provided, which is the Church."[51] That bears reflection – and action!

With his own rich family heritage D.T. Niles was, of course, keenly aware of the missionary contribution. Many of his closest friends and mentors and colleagues were missionaries, from a broad ecumenical spectrum. He knew full well the importance of the foreign mission enterprise in the past, but also its ongoing imperative. Yet he did not base his commitment on the Great Commission or "in terms of what God has done for the evangelist but in terms of what God has done for the world; not in terms of a command to be obeyed but in terms of an inner necessity to be accepted."[52]

As a product of the missionary era, Niles was grateful and understanding. His son remarked on one occasion that there was "no critical and negative evaluation of the colonial age in his own immediate writings," and then went on to attribute his charitable outlook to "the optimism of grace."[53] Yet his address to the world Christian community at the Evanston Assembly of the WCC contained this loving rebuke: "There is a world of difference between the missionary who comes to proclaim the truth of the Gospel and the missionary who comes to care for a people with the care of Jesus Christ."[54] "To speak of a missionary is to speak of the world; to speak of a fraternal worker is to speak in terms of the Church."[55] One of his earliest, most popular volumes (for the Student Volunteer Movement in 1951) also chided gently: "There is a tendency for missionary agencies to be concerned exclusively with the Church in the missionary land rather than with the land itself."[56] "A missionary is primarily a person sent to a world and not to a church . . . not so much a person sent by a church as by its Lord."[57]

Proclaiming the Faith

The loving, caring, serving dimension has always been integral to Christian missions, along with proclamation. What has emerged as new during the lifetime of D.T. Niles has been the emphasis on dialogue with persons of other faiths. Here the influence of Asian colleagues and Asian cultures has merged with Niles's biblical, originally neo-orthodox theology. His Lyman Beecher Lectures at Yale in 1957 broke precedent, not only in being delivered by an Asian, but in tackling directly the Hindu, Buddhist, and Muslim "refusal" of the Christian proclamation – never an "apologetic" even in the technical sense. "The Christian Faith can be proclaimed," Niles insisted; "The other faiths can only be taught."[58]

The lecturer constructed his treatment of "the preacher's task" by asking three friends in other religious communities to identify their "stone of stumbling." For the Hindu this was the incarnation, for the Muslim the crucifixion, for the Buddhist the resurrection. Then Niles himself outlined five ways of proclaiming the Gospel "to unbelief and other belief": replacement by the use of polemics, fulfillment through comparative religion, transformation by conversation, judgment in dialectic (applied to Christianity as well as other faiths), reconception through cooperation (and sympathetic understanding). "There is true and essential discontinuity," he said; "the Christian message cannot be grafted upon other beliefs or added to them."[59] Yet in all of these, D.T. was convinced, "there are many who have not accepted him as their Lord and Saviour, and refuse so to accept him still; but even they are within the rule and saving work of Christ."[60]

Unlike his Indian friends and associates, Devanandan and Thomas, Niles said very little about specific social and political applications of the Gospel. For him sin was "an offense against God's sovereignty," not imperfection or disease or ignorance, but "an essential wrongness in man which only God's power and love can make right."[61] It is fallen man, he wrote in another context, who is constantly "searching for the laws of his being in the realm of sociology and economics."[62] He paid tribute to the Christian ethics of Reinhold Niebuhr as "more profound than that of any other because he maintains without wearying the tense dialectic between law and grace, justice and love."[63] Many years ago D.T. declared that "the gospel seed must be sown into the furrows of life."[64] "His salvation is no simple salvation of the soul. It is a salvation of the whole man. It is not a salvation of persons only. It is a salvation of the whole universe. It is not just a salvation of the Christian community. It is a salvation of human history."[65]

Thus Niles was naturally distressed by racism in any form and place. "In Africa," he wrote, "new wine is being put into the old bottles of racial attitudes between colored and white . . . and the day will not be far when they will be burst."[66] He was concerned with the impact of political systems on spiritual freedom. In an imaginary dialogue between Buddhist and Christian students he voiced his own conviction that "some, like the communists and the war-mongers, advocate further acts of injustice as a means of achieving justice."[67] On the other hand, he wrote, "the democracies of the world promise the maintenance of human rights; Jesus promises the maintenance of God's sovereignty . . . No human cause is identical with his cause."[68]

In the student dialogue, however, he expressed his own dissatisfaction with moral prescriptions in these words:

> Goodness demands that I do the lesser evil . . . No, goodness demands that I do no evil; and when circumstances force me to choose the lesser *evil* because I must be *good,* then it is that I am in the grip of moral tragedy . . . Don't you see that . . . a purely ethical formulation of religion leads to a sense of frustration.[69]

D.T. Niles clearly preferred theology to ethics. Yet only one slim volume was written as a deliberate theological treatise, a reply, or what Niles chose to call a "sequel," to Bishop J.A.T. Robinson's *Honest to God.* In that polite but indignant rebuttal Niles sharply rejected Robinson's claim of presenting the "substance of the Christian faith in more adequate terminology," though he conceded that it might appeal to some readers who would not otherwise listen. At the same time he categorically rejected the views of Tillich and Bultmann and even Robinson's interpretation of Bonhoeffer.

Niles's objections cannot be discussed at length here, but these might be briefly mentioned. The obligation of love is insufficient, for Niles, apart from the command to believe in Jesus Christ.[70] Universalism cannot be proved or disproved because it involves both God's love and the human being's answer to God in Jesus Christ.[71] The concept – and reality – of religionless humankind cannot be dealt with apart from the crucial decision in Jesus Christ.[72] Since all religious experience is dependent in some way on God's initiative, God's action, there must be some otherness, some distance, beyond the individual and beyond history. "Self-transcendence is dependence on transcendence itself."[73]

As previously stated, Niles was not a systematic theologian. If he was predominantly an evangelist, he was preeminently a preacher. Three of his most important books represented distinguished lecture series on preaching: *Preaching the Gospel of the Resurrection* (Bevan Memorial Lectures at Adelaide, Australia, 1952), *The Preacher's Calling to Be Servant* (Warreck Lectures in Scotland, 1959), and *The Preacher's Task and the Stone of Stumbling* (Lyman Beecher Lectures, Yale, 1957). Yet all of these – as previous quotations may indicate – were themselves sermons rather than lectures; they defined the homiletical task by doing it, by proclaiming the Gospel in its relationship to the world and to various cultures. In this they were indistinguishable from other books produced for other audiences. Indeed, as Niles himself affirmed in Adelaide, "To us who have been waylaid by God's call, preaching is power."[74]

Little has been said in this article about family life or travel, about ecumenical conferences and administrative office. To a unique degree the legacy of D.T. Niles remains in his spoken and written words. The effectiveness of those words in thousands of lives, Christians and others, lay in the fact that they reflected the word of God. That word was first received, accepted, proclaimed, and lived by Niles himself. "Often we are so concerned to tell the good news that we miss hearing it," he once wrote.[75] That was never true of D.T. Niles. "Essentially," he declared, "it is insight that is wanted, the sight within and from within, for the truest understanding of the Christian gospel comes only as one accepts and believes and enjoys."[76]

Equally important, he never failed to translate that word into the experience of his hearers. "It is not the meaning of Jesus Christ which must be stated in contemporary terms," he asserted; "Jesus himself, in his concreteness, must be seen as contemporary."[77] That contemporary Christ was affirmed by Niles as inclusive, decisive, redemptive precisely because he reveals for us an Eternal God. "I do not believe that God is because prayers are answered; prayers are answered because God is. I do not believe that God is because sorrows are healed; he is, even when sorrows go unhealed."[78]

"The basic fact on which everything depends is not whether I love God but whether He loves me, not whether I believe in God but whether He believes in me."[79] "Meaningful living, then, is to live *en rapport* with the purposes of God for us and for the world."[80] Measured by this standard, D.T. Niles had a meaningful life – and legacy.

Notes

1. *That They May Have Life* (hereafter *TTMHL*), p. 96.
2. *This Jesus . . . Whereof We Are Witnesses (TJWWAW)*, pp. 57, 58.
3. *TTMHL*, p. 77.
4. Ibid., p. 25; cf. p. 33.
5. Ibid., p. 66.
6. Ibid., p. 53.
7. *The Preacher's Calling to Be Servant (PCS)*, p. 28.
8. *TTMHL*, p. 57.
9. *PCS*, p. 31.
10. Dayalan Niles, "Search for Community," p. 3.
11. *Buddhism and the Claims of Christ (BCC)*, p. 10.
12. D. Niles, "Search, p. 8.
13. Ibid., p. 1.
14. *Studies in Genesis (SIG)*, p. 18.
15. *Reading the Bible Today (RBT)*, p. 49.
16. *SIG*, p. 54.

17. *The Preacher's Task and the Stone of Stumbling (PTSS)*, p. 44.
18. *RBT*, p. 54.
19. Ibid., pp. 17, 19, 37, 39, 43, and throughout.
20. Ibid., p. 55.
21. Ibid., p. 48.
22. *We Know in Part (WKIP)*, p. 21.
23. *PTSS*, p. 32.
24. *Who Is This Jesus? (WITJ)*, p. 104.
25. *PTSS*, p. 29.
26. "Work of the Holy Spirit," p. 101; cf. p. 100.
27. *WKIP*, pp. 13-14.
28. *WITJ*, p. 89.
29. *PTSS*, p. 15.
30. *Upon the Earth (UTE)*, p. 65.
31. "Work of the Holy Spirit," p. 93.
32. D. Niles, "Search," p. 6.
33. "Work of the Holy Spirit," p. 95.
34. *The Message and Its Messengers (MIM)*, p. 39.
35. *PTSS*, p. 61.
36. *MIM*, p. 71.
37. *TTMHL*, p. 82.
38. *WITJ*, p. 14.
39. *WKIP*, p. 21.
40. Ibid., p. 141, from Karl Barth, *The Knowledge of God and the Service of God* (New York: AMS Press repr. of 1939), p. 153.
41. *WITJ*, p. 18.
42. *PCS*, p. 18.
43. *WITJ*, p. 106.
44. *UTE*, p. 130.
45. *TJWWAW*, p. 13.
46. Ibid., p. 78.
47. Ibid., p. 32.
48. Ibid., p. 33.
49. Ibid., p. 63; cf. *UTE*, p. 74.
50. "Work of the Holy Spirit," p. 102.
51. *MIM*, p. 50; cf. *UTE*, p. 16.
52. *PCS*, p. 31; cf. *UTE*, throughout.
53. D. Niles, "Search," pp. 10-11.
54. *PCS*, p. 135.
55. *UTE*, p. 264.
56. *TTMHL*, p. 75.
57. *UTE*, p. 266.
58. *PTSS*, p. 98; cf. *UTE*, p. 242.
59. *PTSS*, p. 99; cf. *UTE*, p. 243.
60. *PTSS*, p. 90.
61. *BCC*, pp. 70, 72.
62. *SIG*, p. 78.
63. *WKIP*, p. 19.
64. *MIM*, p. 42.
65. Ibid.
66. *TTMHL*, p. 94.
67. *BCC*, p. 14.
68. *Living with the Gospel*, p. 20.
69. *BCC*, p. 15.
70. *WKIP*, p. 21.
71. Ibid., p. 19
72. Ibid., p. 17.

73. Ibid., p. 49 and throughout.
74. *Preaching the Gospel of the Resurrection*, p. 13.
75. *WITJ*, p. 138.
76. *BCC*, p. 80.
77. *WITJ*, p. 111.
78. *SIG*, p. 26.
79. *PCS*, p. 96.
80. *BCC*, p. 48.

Selected Bibliography

Works by D.T. Niles

1939 *Whose I Am and Whom I Serve*. London: SCM Press.
1939 *The World Mission Looks Ahead*. London: SCM Press.
1951 *That They May Have Life*. New York: Harper & Brothers.
1953 *Preaching the Gospel of the Resurrection*. London: Lutterworth Press.
1955 *Reading the Bible Today*. New York: Association Press.
1957 *Living with the Gospel*. New York: Association Press.
1958 *The Preacher's Task and the Stone of Stumbling*. New York: Harper & Brothers.
1958 *Studies in Genesis*. Philadelphia: Westminster Press.
1959 *The Preacher's Calling to Be Servant*. New York: Harper & Brothers.
1961 *As Seeing the Invisible: A Study of the Book of Revelation*. New York: Harper & Brothers.
1962 *Upon the Earth*. New York: McGraw-Hill.
1963 (gen.ed.) *EACC Hymnal*. Rangoon: East Asia Christian Conference.
1964 *We Know in Part*. Philadelphia: Westminster Press.
1965 *This Jesus . . . Whereof We Are Witnesses*. Philadelphia: Westminster Press.
1966 "The Christian Claim for the Finality of Christ." In Dow Kirkpatrick, ed., *The Finality of Christ*. Nashville: Abingdon.
1966 *The Message and Its Messengers*. Nashville: Abingdon.
1966 "To the Buddhists: 'All the Good That Is Ours in Christ.'" In Gerald H. Anderson, ed., *Sermons to Men of Other Faiths and Traditions*. Nashville: Abingdon.
1967 *Buddhism and the Claims of Christ*. Richmond, Va.: John Knox Press.
1967 *The Power at Work Among Us*. Philadelphia: Westminster Press.
1967 "The Work of the Holy Spirit in the World." In Gerald H. Anderson, ed., *Christian Mission in Theological Perspective*. Nashville: Abingdon.
1968 *Who Is This Jesus?* Nashville: Abingdon.
1972 Compiled by Dayalan Niles. *A Testament of Faith*. London: Epworth Press.

Works about D.T. Niles

Fleming, John R. "The Theology of D.T. Niles." *Trinity Theological College Annual* (Singapore) 4 (1967): 5-9. German trans. in *Tendenzen der Theologie im 20. Jahrhundert: Eine Geschichte in Porträts*. Hans Jürgen Schultz, ed. Stuttgart: Kreuz-Verlag, 1966.
Furtado, Christopher L. *The Contribution of Dr. D.T. Niles to the Church Universal and Local*. Madras: Christian Literature Society, 1978.
Nelson, J. Robert. "D.T. Niles, Evangelist and Ecumenist." *Ecumenical Trends* 9, no. 7 (July/August 1980): 100-104.
Niles, W. Dayalan. "Search for Community: A Preliminary Explanation of the Theology of Daniel T. Niles." Unpublished paper delivered at the Oxford Institute for Methodist Theological Studies at Lincoln College, Oxford, July 1977.
Schrading, Paul E. "D.T. Niles: Ecumenical Evangelical." *Christian Advocate*, April 29, 1971, pp. 13-15.
Snowden, Glen Wenger. "The Relationship of Christianity to non-Christian Religions in the Theologies of Daniel T. Niles and Paul Tillich." Th.D. diss., Boston University School of Theology, 1969.

Part Five

THEOLOGIANS
and
HISTORIANS

Gustav Warneck

Roland Allen

Robert Streit, O.M.I.

Johannes Dindinger, O.M.I.

Johannes Rommerskirchen, O.M.I.

Joseph Schmidlin

Pierre Charles, S.J.

Kenneth Scott Latourette

Johan Herman Bavinck

Walter Freytag

Stephen Neill

R. Pierce Beaver

Gustav Warneck

1834–1910

Founder of the Scholarly Study of Missions

Hans Kasdorf

Every age and generation has a variety of pilgrims. Some are pastors and some pedagogues, some are writers and some prophets, and some combine all in one person. Whatever their charisma may be, they themselves are a gift of the God of history to the times in which they live. Their legacy is what they inherited from their progenitors and what they in turn pass on to their progeny. Yet, unless used with prudence, such a legacy can become a burden rather than a blessing. Goethe's advice, as expressed in a Faust soliloquy, is noteworthy:

> Whatever you inherit from the past
> By usage does become a noble prize.
> But when neglected, never will it last.
> Your spirit, to creation, must arise.[1]

The legacy of Warneck deserves to be treated in that manner.

The Pilgrim

On March 6, 1834, Gustav Traugott Leberecht Warneck and his wife, Johanne Sophie, both of Naumburg near Halle (former East Germany) on the Saale River, became parents for the first time. Disregarding the orthodox tradition of the meaning of names, they simply called their son Gustav Adolf, a name which in mission circles of Protestant Europe has more historical than religious significance. The bearer of the name soon dropped the "Adolf" and went down in history as Gustav Warneck, the pioneer and father of Protestant missiology. His pilgrimage took him from a family needleshop in the present industrial city of Naumburg to a professorship in the intellectual circles of Halle.

As the oldest son of a master craftsman in needlemaking and in keeping with tradition, the vocation of Gustav Junior was predetermined; he too would become a needlemaker. The odds were against him for anything else. His parents were extremely poor. The outlook on life in the home was narrow; opportunities for education were scanty. In addition, Gustav was a delicate boy, suffering from a serious lung illness.

When still quite young, he entered his father's workshop, counting heaps of needles, thereby helping to eke out a living for a rapidly growing family. Inwardly, however, he possessed an insatiable yearning for knowledge and learning. By sheer self-determination and the reluctant consent of his parents he finally succeeded in entering the gymnasium (a grammar school) of the Francke Foundation at Halle. Without financial support from his father, Gustav left home with one taler (75¢) in his pocket. That was all his mother could spare for her oldest son.

A clear goal, hard work, the influence of several teachers, eventually a scholarship, and a "sound conversion experience" were a combination of factors that helped Warneck to graduate from the gymnasium with "shining honors" and to enter theological studies at Halle University (now Martin-Luther Universität) in 1855. In 1858 he passed his theological examinations – again with honors. In the same year he accepted a position as private tutor in a noble family at Elberfeld. Here he was introduced to the spiritual atmosphere of Lutheran Pietism in the Wuppertal-Rheinland region. He was also asked to serve as counselor to three hundred children in the local orphanage.

The year 1862 proved to be packed with events and decisions that changed the course of Warneck's life. For one thing, he became assistant pastor in Roitzsch, a small village in Saxony, within the Diocese of Bitterfeld. The place-name (literally "bitter field") was, indeed, indicative of his bitter experiences there. The people were crude compared to those in Wuppertal. Yet he got a taste of what it might mean to become a full-time pastor, should he move in that direction.

Moreover, this was also the year in which Warneck married Henriette Gerlach from his home village Naumburg. The Warnecks shared forty-six years of married life and became parents of nine children, of whom several died as infants. Here in Roitzsch, Warneck also met Reinhold Grundemann (1836-1924), his intimate colleague in later years. Their common interest was world mission and their friendship lasting and mutually enriching.

Finally, in Roitzsch Warneck came to grips with reality. Ever since his conversion in Halle he had entertained the thought of becoming a missionary. But a renewed attack from his besetting illness convinced him that he would never be able to pursue a missionary career overseas. He settled the matter by becoming a missionary to missionaries. But his joy was great when his son Johannes and one daughter went to serve overseas.

In 1863 Warneck followed a call to pastor a church in Dommitzsch, near Torgau in the Leipzig district. He stayed seven years. These were hard years, but fruitful for both the pastor and the people. It should be noted that with his *Pontius Pilate* (1867), Warneck began his literary career in Dommitzsch.

Meanwhile, however, Warneck continued his studies and eventually received a Ph.D. degree from the University of Jena in 1871, and an honorary doctorate (D.D.) from the University of Halle in 1883.

The following three years with the Rheinisch Mission Society in Barmen (1871-74) were the most formative years in terms of his mission philosophy. He taught at the seminary where mission candidates received their training; he traveled widely in churches where people prayed and paid for the mission enterprise; he interacted frequently with such eminent theologians and ecclesiastical leaders as Theodor Christlieb (1833-89) of Bonn and Johann Christoph Blumhard (1805-80) of Bad Boll; and he worked closely with administrators like Friedrich Fabri (1824-91) of the Barmen Mission. Warneck commented in later years that his experience in Barmen had been God's providential leading, exposing him to an area of service for which he had been searching all his life.

Barmen was not the last station of his pilgrimage. In 1874 he moved with his family to Rothenschirmbach (near Eisleben, Martin Luther's birthplace). Here he pastored a 700-member church for twenty-two years. With this move began his time of greatest productivity for the cause of world mission. He received and counseled missionaries and mission leaders from all continents, wrote hundreds of articles and over twenty books on mission. The hitherto remote village suddenly became famous throughout the world because of its famous pastor. Rothenschirmbach turned into such a busy place that the post office expanded its services from one mail delivery weekly to two daily. In all of this his church lent full support to its pastor in his endeavors as a world missionary spokesman, statesman, and penman. He became the apostle to apostles, the father of Protestant missiology, and the missionary educator par excellence.

Warneck often sensed a vacuum in his own spiritual pilgrimage. When the American revivalist Robert Pearsall Smith conducted meetings in Brighton, England, Warneck went to hear him. With the exception of brief visits to Switzerland and one to Sweden, this was his only trip to a foreign country.

In his book *Letters on the Meetings in Brighton* (1876), Warneck reflects on his own experience of renewal and *Heiligung,* or sanctification. Although not uncritical – that would have been against his nature – Warneck speaks of having found "freedom" and "true joy in Christ" at these meetings. In this fourth letter (July 31, 1875) he wrote his friend:

> Never in my whole life has the Majesty of the living God stood with such reality before my very eyes; never has this Majesty been so tangibly close; never did sin seem so exceedingly sinful as in the light of this holy Majesty; never has any object of shame appeared so despisably shameful as in these days.[2]

There was one more move for Warneck. In 1896 he occupied the first chair of mission studies in Germany, a position which he held for twelve years. Upon retirement in 1908 he remained active as a writer.

On December 26, 1910, the Halle newspaper headlines announced the passing of the greatest missiologist of the time. The pilgrim Gustav Warneck had reached the end of his terrestrial journey. He journeyed on to a celestial country while listening to the melody of the Christmas canticle:

> Lord, now lettest thou thy servant depart in peace,
> according to thy word;
> for mine eyes have seen thy salvation
> which thou hast prepared in the presence of all peoples,
> a light for revelation to the Gentiles,
> and for glory to thy people Israel.
>
> Luke 2:29-32 RSV

The Preacher

It is expected, even in our day, that the pastor be a preacher. But not always is it taken for granted that the preacher be a pastor. Warneck was both, but first a pastor/preacher, then a preacher/pastor.

The Pastor/Preacher

While studying at the Francke schools in Halle, Warneck manifested unique pastoral qualities. He was a member of the *Wingolf,* a nineteenth-century German model of the present Inter-Varsity Christian Fellowship. Students came to him for counsel, sought pastoral care, and requested prayer. He was always ready to help, even in times of sickness and poverty. But there were moments when he became very direct, almost to the point of being offensive. On one such occasion an older friend put his hand on Warneck and said, "Gustav, speak kindly with Jerusalem."

One time Warneck was again suffering from a severe lung hemorrhage, which "brought him to the brink of death and left little hope for future usefulness." But even then he encouraged those who came to see him and in turn was consoled by them. One day the Halle professor Friedrich August Gottreu Tholuck (1799-1877) came to his bedside, saying "Warneck, you will not die, but will proclaim the name of the Lord."[3] That was prophetic.

The Preacher/Pastor

The pastor became a great preacher. Although there were times when he agonized over his text, he was always a man with a message for the hour. When things were hard going, he followed the counsel of his teacher, Tholuck, who said, "When I prepare my sermons I throw myself on my knees and ask the Lord to unlock for me the door to the real life of the text."[4]

Warneck was a perfectionist both as pastor and as preacher. But he was as hard on himself as he was on young theologians and mission candidates. His son Johannes Warneck says that his father was frequent with criticism and infrequent with compliments. "I found father's criticism of my first sermons harder to bear than that of the examination committee. After what I thought had been a fair presentation he would calmly respond, 'That was nothing.' Or he would say, 'With such material you can't entice a dog to come out of his niche.' "[5] Conference speakers, particularly the younger ones, had to write out their speeches and sermons and hand them to Warneck for scrutiny. Whoever passed without having to revise or rewrite his paper was given a modest compliment in the third person: "He's a becomer."

But Warneck practiced what he preached. He himself was an outstanding orator. His sermons were well organized, rich in content, tastefully illustrated, rhetorically excellent, and spiced with humor. He despised boredom in preaching. Although he admitted that boredom is no "sin unto death," he maintained that "it is a sin that deadens."[6] Warneck's preaching focused on the church and the kingdom of God. "A healthy and actively fruitful missionary life," wrote Warneck on one occasion, "must be rooted in the local church." Convinced that the pastor is the key person to promote that kind of mission spirit and recruitment in his own congregation, Warneck labored tirelessly on mission sermons and lessons for the preacher's use. Such lessons, he contended, must be biblically sound, theologically stimulating, factually informative, scientifically accurate, homiletically useful, generally interesting and experientially practical. His three-volume *Missionsstunden* (1881; 1886; 1899) is a prime example of his creative mind in these areas. The kingdom parables of Jesus play a central role in his preaching.

The Pedagogue

Warneck had a desire to become a "teacher to the Gentiles," as his colleague Martin Kähler, his son Johannes, and others have pointed out. Although his physical weakness prevented him from becoming a teacher overseas, he did become a true pedagogue, molding thousands of lives. There are two dimensions to Warneck the pedagogue – one is philosophical, the other practical. Both are articulated in his major work, the *Evangelische Missionslehre*, or *Evangelical Theory of Mission* (1892-1905).

The Philosophical Pedagogue

Warneck's desire to become a teacher to the Gentiles was based on the assumption that life itself can be molded by external influences. In fact, the Finnish missiologist Seppo A. Teinonen calls Warneck's early theology a "theology of life." This is true. The life-principle can be traced through all his writings. Life is created by God, therefore precious. Though humankind has fallen and has become alienated, it is not entirely dead. Traces of the divine image remain, making human beings both redeemable and redeem-worthy.

According to Warneck it is possible for the natural person to know God, but only in part. Such partial knowledge of God gained by natural processes lays the foundation for a deeper religious experience to become a Christian. The fullness of life, however, is attainable only by grace through the Word of God. This life, in turn, helps humans understand the very Word they hear or read. He cautions, however, not to misinterpret the meaning of being Christian. The true Christian, he insists, is "a new creation" (2 Cor. 5:17), not merely an educated or a cultured manifestation of "natural man."

Just as there are two sources to bring fullness to life, so there are parallel currents from which emerge the fullness of history. One current evolves from the "kingdom of nature" and is seen as *Weltgeschichte,* or "world history"; the other evolves from the "kingdom of grace" and can be seen as *Reichsgeschichte,* or "kingdom history." As spiritual life is based on natural life, so is kingdom history based on world history. Thus he maintains that the developments in world history are in a sense prerequisite to kingdom history.

In his "Ethnological Foundations of Mission," Warneck expresses some rather modern ideas. He states that the Gospel in its very essence is "supraworldly"; it is simply not affected by social, cultural, and ethnic elements. Therefore, the Gospel has the capacity not only to transform every type of natural community and the culture of a people, but also to adapt to any kind of situation that is not in direct violation to the core of the divine message.

The Practical Pedagogue

I have already pointed out that Warneck the pilgrim accepted a private teaching assignment for a wealthy family in Elberfeld. This was a prestigious position for the time. Educators recognized in him the "young gifted pedagogue," and soon a more challenging opportunity presented itself to demonstrate his reputation.

In 1861 Warneck was called to an orphanage in Elberfeld where a religious revival of a rather emotional type had gone beyond control. It was making newspaper headlines throughout Germany. The record has it that Warneck's pedagogical efficiency soon normalized the unhealthy conditions among the young people of the orphanage. The seventy-five-page manuscript entitled "An Experimental In-Depth Evaluation of the 1861 Emerging Children's Revival in the Orphanage of Elberfeld" reveals Warneck's insight on religion and human nature sporadically surfacing in German Pietism at that time.

The third area in which Warneck practiced his gift of teaching was at the Barmen Mission. Here he dealt with seminary students who prepared to become overseas missionaries. He was an excellent teacher and knew how to create interest, enthusiasm, and love for world mission. Unlike most other teachers who relied on the lecture method, Warneck guided his students in reading and research to become independent thinkers. It was here in Barmen that he saw the need for a comprehensive mission theory. His vision turned into ideas, and his ideas into the most complete system of mission theory ever produced.

Warneck also became the first professor of missiology on the continent. "Warneck's life-work on behalf of the Christian world mission," writes the Norwegian missiologist Olav Myklebust, "was essentially an act of education, and that in the true and comprehensive sense of that term."[7] Warneck's goal was to make the study of mission an integral part of the university curriculum. His great phrase was that "mission as an academic discipline cannot remain a mere alien, but must attain the right and privilege of citizenship in the science of theology."[8] He realized his goal in his lifetime.

R. Zentgraf, a one-time student of Warneck, has called his teacher "the pedagogue of the church to world mission." Whether he wrote, lectured, or preached, says Zentgraf, he was always teaching world mission.

His mission seminar was such an introduction to the word and spirit of the Holy Scriptures that we simply became absorbed by the thought that the entire New Testament was part and parcel of mission literature. Indeed, we became so fascinated by this idea that henceforth we had to read the New Testament as *the* book of mission. Every paragraph and every line breathes mission and contains the key to interpret world history from a divine perspective.[9]

The Penman

Once Warneck had been captivated by the spirit of world mission, as he saw and experienced it in Barmen, he devoted himself unreservedly to that calling. Never was there a time in which he questioned his *Sendung,* his apostleship, or sense of sentness in that respect. That is why he has been called the "missionary to missionaries"; "the man of the hour for the mission of his time." His colleague Kähler, in a special tribute to Warneck, speaks of "Gustav Warneck's Sendung," or sentness.

In the very concept of sentness, Kähler points out, one recognizes an entirely new school founded by Warneck. It was a "school without walls" through which thousands of sent ones, according to Kähler, became aware of their own sentness and were sent into all the world to carry out the mandate of the Master to "make disciples of all nations."

The most effective means Warneck used to disseminate ideas and mission information was his writing. He wrote twenty-some books, at least ten times that many articles on mission, and hundreds of missionary letters – and all of that with a quill pen.

The Scientific Mission Journal

In 1873 Warneck attracted two of the most competent men – Grundemann, the cartographer-statistician, and Christlieb, the educator-theologian – and together with them founded the famous *Allgemeine Missions-Zeitschrift* (AMZ), whose chief editor he remained for thirty-seven years. In his dedicatory editorial, *"Dic cur hic? Unser Programm"* (Our Program), he fully recognized the various attempts made by others to bring the theory of mission to the level of an acceptable science. But he also pointed out the areas of failure. Thus he proposed and promised to provide for all levels a fundamental knowledge of mission history and discussions touching "geographical, linguistic, anthropological, ethnological, sociological, and religio-historical" dimensions as well as the theory of mission itself.

Those familiar with the *Zeitschrift* will be impressed not only with the wealth of accumulated knowledge contained in this "unique missionary encyclopedia," but also with the scientific thoroughness with which it has been treated. Warneck's exegetical treatment of Matthew 28:16-20, which he called "Christ's Magna Charta for the Church," is no less than a classic commentary on that text.

The Study of Mission History

Warneck contended that knowledge of world mission begins with acquaintance with world history. He produced a long essay entitled "An Abstract of a History of Protestant Missions," published in the *AMZ* and in *Herzogs Realenzyklopädie für protestantische Theologie und Kirche* (1882). Warneck does not treat mission history in isolation; every incident is treated in the context of world history, sociocultural history, and colonial history.

He constantly rewrote, revised, and expanded until his history of mission became "a classic masterpiece and the historical foundation for all future missionary histories," as Martin Schlunk puts it. "So surely had the master and the material grown together that after his death no single person was in a position to reedit his work; it took six of his ablest students to prepare the tenth edition."[10] It should be added that this history was translated into several foreign languages, including independent English editions in Europe and America.

The Field of Cultural Anthropology

Warneck was in many respects ahead of his time. He took the cultural implications for the communication of the Gospel remarkably seriously. This becomes even more striking when one thinks that cultural anthropology and ethnology as sciences were still in their infancy.

In 1879 Warneck published a monumental work on the reciprocal implications of world mission and culture. Four years later Professor Thomas Smith of New College, Edinburgh, translated this work under the title *Modern Missions and Culture: Their Mutual Relations.* Smith had intended to write his own book on the same subject. But, he says in the introduction, while reading the original, "I formed the opinion that, in respect to variety of research, and in respect of clear statement, Dr. Warneck's book is superior to any that I could expect to write."[11]

Considering the time in which Warneck wrote, one is amazed at the insights he expressed regarding the complexities of the sociocultural value systems of peoples and what bearing they have on the proclamation of the Gospel. He speaks of culture as being in itself "an entirely neutral concept," which is to be interpreted from the perspective of the insider. Only then, contends Warneck, can the missionary hope to understand the caste system in India and the polygamous marriages in African societies.

In principle, Warneck agreed with the ideals of the Western missionary to abolish the caste distinctions and to prohibit plural marriages. But, he cautioned, a measure of toleration must be exercised and the Gospel must be trusted as a transforming power to bring about the desired changes in due time.

On the basis of careful study, he insisted that Christians from various castes should be allowed to form their own church within the given social structure, and that men in polygynous marriages, when they become Christian, be admitted to baptism and church membership. He contended that consistent teaching of the Word was the key to achieve the ideal forms of the Christian way of life in any culture.

It cannot be overlooked, however, that Warneck was a "child of his time." This also applies to his view of culture. Despite his farsightedness in some areas, he was nearsighted in others. He says, for example, that Western culture is far superior to the cultures of Asia and Africa, even superior to the advanced Hindu and Chinese cultures. Cultural anthropologists of our day reject such views. Perhaps that is why his book – though without question a pioneer effort in missionary anthropology – is rarely referred to by scholars in that field.

Theory of Missionary Science

Warneck's five-volume *Evangelische Missionslehre* was his magnum opus. In 1955 Myklebust spoke of it as the unsurpassed treatment of "the Protestant theory of missions," and in 1978 Johannes Verkuyl called it "a trail-blazing in systematic missiology."[12]

This work more than any other has earned Warneck the title "Father of Protestant Missiology." During the last thirty years at least six major dissertations have been produced in which the *Missionslehre* received primary attention.

The five volumes are divided into three major parts, each dealing in great detail with the many dimensions of mission philosophy and principles. In part 1 Warneck attempts to build a broad foundation for his concept of mission from a dogmatic, ethical, biblical, ecclesiological, historical, and ethnological perspective. His thesis is that God has chosen to make himself known through Christianity as the full and final revelation of God for complete and universal salvation of humankind. This part contains valuable material and merits translation into English.

In part 2 Warneck discusses the various mission agencies. Because the church has failed, he maintains, the mission societies have been called into existence. He sees in this less the biblical model than the historical development. Thus he justifies the existence of the societies on the grounds of the church's failure.

The last part treats the mission fields of the world in all their complex geographic and religious diversities. The Great Commission, says Warneck, rests upon the Christians to Christianize all non-Christians by making disciples of peoples, not only of individuals. His key concept is *Volkschristianisierung*, the Christianization of entire peoples.

Because of this theological conviction, Warneck failed to see the legitimacy of the Student Volunteer Movement's slogan, "The evangelization of the world in this generation." He believed that this was not realistic optimism, but a statement of arrogance and the expression of sheer superficiality and naïveté.

John R. Mott (1865-1955), the international student leader and missionary statesman, discussed this matter with Warneck on several occasions. Although they respected each other, they never fully agreed. Warneck saw in his own concept of Christianization all that the evangelization theory contained and insisted that the task of mission goes far beyond mere proclamation of the Gospel throughout the world in a rapid and superficial manner.

In a critical review he categorically stated: "I cannot agree with the tone of triumphalism in which this new missionary movement is being signalized."[13] His reasons can be briefly summarized: (1) *There is unbiblical eschatology.* The evangelization of the world will not expedite the return of Christ, but it is his imminent return that motivates us to evangelize. (2) *There is weak ecclesiology.* The SVM slogan assumes the evangelization of the world in this generation by large groups of evangelists without giving due consideration either to a solid church base or to thorough preparation for the task. (3) *There is inadequate understanding of the task.* The evangelists confuse *kerússein* (proclamation) with *matheteúein* (making disciples). Disciplemaking, Warneck insisted, includes evangelization, baptism, church building, and continuing teaching. (4) *The goals are based on mechanical mathematics.* The apostolic missionary practice yielded not only quantitative, but also qualitative, fruit.[14]

Various attempts have been made to reconcile Warneck's theory with that of the Student Volunteer Movement. But no unanimity has thus far been achieved.

Warneck's *Missionslehre* was not only the standard work for Protestants; Catholics borrowed from him and developed their own theory of mission. Joseph Schmidlin (1876-1944) became a pioneer in this respect when he wrote his *Katholische Missionslehre im Grundriss* (1919), which was also published in translation as *Roman Catholic Mission Theory* (1931). In his foreword, Schmidlin acknowledges his indebtness to Warneck, calling him "the founder and pioneer-master of mission theory."

The Prophet

The pilgrim Warneck was more than preacher, pedagogue, and penman. He was also a prophet in his day. He was invited to speak at the London Missionary Conference of 1888. Circumstances at home prevented him from going. He did, however, submit a paper entitled "Missionary Comity," which was read by a representative.

In this paper Warneck delineated in detail the things that separated and those that united missionaries and mission organizations. He pointed out that the factors uniting the mission forces were more than those that divide. He also suggested ways to increase the positive and decrease the negative elements in the interest of sound ecumenism. In fact, he outlined a plan for decennial general missionary conferences. These conferences, he suggested, should be supported by a central committee that would continue to give counsel to agencies and coordinate all Protestant mission activities overseas.

The ideas Warneck expressed in this paper – and in part 3 of his *Missionslehre* – were so progressive and prophetic for his day that the London delegates listened to the reading, put the paper in the files, and never looked at it again. But several decades later Warneck's vision was realized at the 1910 Edinburgh Mission Conference and with the formation of the International Missionary Council in 1921.

Conclusion

Warneck could also be described as a philosopher or thinker. But that in itself deserves an entire article. So does his work as a promoter of mission. He was, indeed, a creative spirit, ever striving to improve on what he had inherited from the past in order to enrich the legacy for generations to come.

Some of the secondary literature, particularly that by Continental scholars, reflects a rather critical attitude toward his missiology. It is noted, however, that the majority of critics treat his work only in fragments. This means that the legacy of Gustav Warneck has never been fully dealt with and a biographical treatise of his life and work is long overdue.

Notes

1. *Goethe's Faust*, Part I: Text and Notes, ed. R.M.S. Heffner, Helmut Rehder, and W.F. Twaddell (Boston: D.C. Health, 1954), lines 682-85. This and all subsequent translations from German sources are the author's.
2. Gustav Warneck, *Briefe über die Versammlung zu Brighton* (Hamburg: Johannes Walther's deutsch-evangelische Buchhandlung, 1876), p. 38. A critical evaluation of Warneck's Brighton experience has been given by the Finnish missiologist Seppo A. Teinonen, "Gustav Warneck and Robert Pearsall Smith," *Studia Missiologica Fennica I* (Helsinki, 1957), pp. 39-57.
3. Martin Kähler, "Gustav Warnecks Sendung," in *Schriften zu Christologie und Mission*, Theologische Bücherei, Band 42, Hrsg. Heinzgünter Frohnes (Munich: Christian Kaiser Verlag, 1971), p. 266.
4. Ibid., p. 267.
5. Martin Kähler and Johannes Warneck, *D. Gustav Warneck 1834-1910: Blätter der Erinnerung* (Berlin: Verlag von Martin Warneck, 1911), p. 70.
6. Ibid., p. 75.
7. Olav G. Myklebust, *The Study of Missions in Theological Education*, 2 vols. (Oslo: Forlaget Land og Kirke, 1955), I: 281.
8. Of special significance is Warneck's essay entitled "Das Studium der Mission auf der Universität mit einem Anhang über akademische Missions-Vereine," *AMZ* 4 (1877): 145-64, 209-30.
9. R. Zentgraf, "Gustav Warneck als Erzieher der Kirche zur Mission," *Evangelisches Missionsmagazin* 78 (1934): 69.
10. Martin Schlunk, "Gustav Warneck," *International Review of Missions* 23 (1934): 398.
11. Gustav Warneck, *Modern Missions and Culture: Their Mutual Relations*, trans. Thomas Smith (Edinburgh: James Gemmell, 1883), p. xvi.
12. *Contemporary Missiology: An Introduction*, trans. and ed. Dale Cooper (Grand Rapids: Wm. B. Eerdmans, 1978), p. 27.
13. Gustav Warneck, "Missionschronik," *AMZ* 29 (1902): 530.
14. *Evangelische Missionslehre*, 2nd ed. vol. 3, pt. 1 (Gotha: Friedrich Andreas Perthes, 1902), pp. 235-36. Cf. "Die moderne Evangelisations-Theorie," *AMZ* 24 (1897): 306-8.

Selected Bibliography

Works by Gustav Warneck

In my dissertation I list nearly 400 titles by Warneck. From these I selected the following ten:

1872 *Pauli Bekehrung, eine Apologie des Christentums.* (Dissertation, Univ. of Jena, 1871.) Gütersloh: C. Bertelsmann.

1874 "Der Missionsbefehl als Missionsinstruction. Versuch einer missionsmethodischen Auslegung von Matth. 28, 16-20 in Verbindung mit Mark. 16, 15." *AMZ* 1: 41-49; 89-92; 137-51; 185-94; 233-39; 281-90; 377-92.

1876 *Die Apostelgeschichte und die Moderne Mission. Eine apologetische Parallele.* Gütersloh: C. Bertelsmann.

1876 *Briefe über die Versammlung zu Brighton.* Hamburg: Johannes Walther's deutsch-evangelische Buchhandlung. A series of ten letters addressed to a friend between July 7 and October 12, 1875, in which Warneck describes and evaluates the Brighton holiness meetings.

1877 *Das Studium der Mission auf der Universität.* Gütersloh: C. Bertelsmann. This essay appeared first in the *AMZ.* See note 8 above.

1879 *Die gegenseitigen Beziehungen zwischen der modernen Mission und Cultur. Auch eine Culturkampfstudie.* Gütersloh: C. Bertelsmann. For English translation, see note 11 above.

1880 *Warum ist das 19. Jahrhundert ein Missionsjahrhundert?* Halle: Julius Fricke.

1883-99 *Missionsstunden.* 3 vols. Vol. 1: *Die Mission im Lichte der Bibel.* 2nd ed. Vol. 2: *Die Mission in Bildern aus ihrer Geschichte.* 2nd ed. Vol. 3: (Same as 2). 3rd ed. Gütersloh: C. Bertelsmann.

1887-1905 *Evangelische Missionslehre.* 5 vols. 2nd ed. Gotha: Friedrich Andreas Perthes.

1913 *Abriss einer Geschichte der protestantischen Missionen von der Reformation bis auf die Gegenwart.* Berlin: Martin Warneck. Various independent translations appeared in England, Scotland, and America between 1901 and 1906.

Works about Gustav Warneck

Axenfeld, Karl. "Zum Gedächtnis Gustav Warnecks." *Evangelisches Missionsmagazin* 55 (1911): 49-58. See also article by Zentgraf, note 9, above.

Beyerhaus, Peter, and Henry Lefever. *The Responsible Church and the Foreign Mission.* Grand Rapids, Mich: Wm. B. Eerdmans, 1964. Chap. 2: "The German Concept of the National Church," pp. 45-53.

Dürr, Johannes. *Sendende und werdende Kirche in der Missionstheologie Gustav Warnecks.* Basel: Basler Missionsbuchhandlung, 1947.

Franke, Joachim. "Ausbreitungsmotive in der deutschen evangelischen Missionstheologie bei Gustav Warneck, Martin Kähler, Ernst Troeltsch." Inaugural-Dissertation, Martin-Luther-Universität, Halle-Wittenberg, 1962.

Hoekendijk, Johannes Christiaan. *Kerk en Volk in de Duitse Zendingswetenschap.* Bijdragen tot de Zendingswetenschap Deel I. Amsterdam: Drukkerij Kampert en Helm, 1948.

Kasdorf, Hans. "Gustav Warnecks missiologisches Erbe." D. Miss. diss., School of World Mission, Fuller Theological Seminary, Pasadena, Calif., 1976.

Richter, Julius, et al. *Missionswissenschaftliche Studien.Festschrift zum 70. Geburtstag des Herrn Professor Dr. Gustav Warneck.* Berlin: Martin Warneck, 1904.

Schlunk, Martin. "Gustav Warnecks bleibende Bedeutung." *Neue Allgemeime Missionszeitschrift* 11 (1934): 73-82. See also note 10, above.

Teinonen, Seppo A. *Warneck-Tutkielmia: Warneck-Studien.* Helsinki: Suomen Lahetystieteellisen Seuran Julkaisuja, FM 400, 1959. Summary in German. See also note 2, above.

Warneck, Johannes, and Martin Kähler. *D. Gustav Warneck, 1834-1910. Blätter der Erinnerung.* Berlin: Martin Warneck, 1911.

Roland Allen

1868–1947

"Missionary Methods: St. Paul's or Ours?"

Charles Henry Long and Anne Rowthorn

Roland Allen served briefly as an Anglican missionary in China at the turn of the century and even more briefly as a parish priest in England. He never held important office in church, mission, or academic institutions, yet few men have had such broad and lasting influence on movements for renewal and reform in Christian mission. His prophetic message was largely ignored in his own day, but subsequent generations have rediscovered the legacy of his writings on such themes as *Missionary Methods: St. Paul's or Ours?* and *Spontaneous Expansion of the Church and the Causes Which Hinder It.* These small books contain a radical criticism of missionary policy and practice current at that time and set forth an alternative vision of what might be done to establish truly indigenous, self-supporting churches.

A Sketch of Allen's Life

Roland Allen was born in Bristol, England, on December 29, 1868. He was the youngest of five children; his father was an Anglican priest who died when Allen was quite young. He attended St. John's College, Oxford, on a scholarship and came under the influence of F.E. Brightman, the great liturgist at Pusey House, whom Allen considered "my great father in God." After Oxford he was steeped in Anglo-Catholic tradition at Leeds Clergy Training School. He was described by the principal, Winfred Burrows, as being "a refined intellectual man, small, not vigorous, in no way burly or muscular. He is not the sort of man to impress settlers or savages by his physique."[1]

In 1892, while at Leeds, Allen had applied to the Society for the Propagation of the Gospel (SPG), because "I am simply thirsting to go to the foreign mission field, and I am ready to go wherever and whenever the Society has a vacancy . . . From my earliest years I was as firmly convinced of my vocation as I was of my existence."[2] After serving as a curate in Darlington, Allen's request was granted and he joined the North China Mission in 1895.

It was intended that he take charge of a small school in Peking "to train men for a native ministry." While preparing himself for the task and learning Chinese, he served as chaplain to the British Legation. In that capacity he had a firsthand view of the Boxer Rebellion of 1900 when the entire foreign community came under siege at the British compound until their rescue by foreign troops. Allen kept a diary, which he later published as *The Siege of the Peking Legations* (1901).

Following the defeat of the Boxers, Allen went home on furlough. He met and married Mary Beatrice Tarlton, daughter of an admiral and a keen supporter of the SPG. They later had a son and a daughter. In 1902 he returned to North China, as priest-in-charge of a rural mission in Yungching. This lasted only a few months as his health broke down and he had to return again to England with his wife and child.

Allen then took a parish in Buckinghamshire, Chalfont St. Peter, but resigned in 1907 on a matter of conscience. The rules of the Church of England required priests to baptize any infant from the community "on demand" without regard to the parents' Christian commitment or lack of it. He could not believe it to be right to extend the sacraments of the church to those who gave no evidence of faith. After this crisis he never again held any formal ecclesiastical office or missionary appointment but became a voluntary priest, earning his living by writing or in other ways until his death forty years later. In the last years of his life he exercised his priesthood only in the celebration of the Eucharist at home for his family and close friends.

A Literary Legacy

This brief missionary and parish experience led Allen to a radical reassessment of his vocation and theology, much as in the 1950s the Communist Revolution and the difficulties of reentry to ordinary church life at home changed the lives and thought of many young China missionaries. In 1930 Allen wrote:

> I have been a stipendiary missionary in China where I tried to prepare young men for the work of catechists with a view to Holy Orders; and there I learned that we cannot establish the Church widely by the method. Then I was in charge of a country district in China; and there I learned that the guidance of old experienced men in the Church, even if they were illiterate, was of immense value. Then I held a benefice in England and there I learnt the waste of spiritual power which our restrictions involve at home.[3]

In 1912, just two years after the celebrated World Missionary Conference at Edinburgh, Allen published his most enduring work, a brief but serious criticism of Western mission policy, *Missionary Methods: St. Paul's or Ours?* The year 1913 saw the publication of his *Missionary Principles.* In 1914 he met a wealthy congregationalist layman, Sidney J.W. Clark, who recruited him to work for a proposed Survey Application Trust and its publishing arm, World Dominion Press. Inspired perhaps by the detailed field surveys that preceded the Edinburgh Conference, Clark was keen to establish a continuing missionary research group, not tied to any one missionary society but dedicated to measuring the spread of Christianity and providing the facts upon which a more efficient deployment of missionary resources could be based. Although the start of the new venture was delayed by World War I, Clark became Roland Allen's patron and friend for most of Allen's remaining working life. Although he helped with some of the surveys, Allen had little enthusiasm for that side of the task. "What is the use of discovering and entering new fields to make the old mistakes?"[4] The trust attracted him first of all because it "was designed to be a perpetual challenge to the tendency of Missions to get into a rut and to follow conventional methods and principles."[5] Allen contributed to that challenge through a series of books and articles, including *Pentecost and the World: The Revelation of the Holy Spirit in "The Acts of the Apostles"* (1917), *Educational Principles and Missionary Methods (1919), The Spontaneous Expansion of the Church and the Causes Which Hinder It* (1927), and *The Case for Voluntary Clergy* (1930), a revision of two earlier books on the same theme published in 1923 and 1928.

Allen's ideas were far ahead of their time. He himself understood this and once predicted that his work would not be taken seriously until about 1960! Nevertheless he grew increasingly isolated and embittered. In 1932 he moved permanently to Kenya to be near his son, then working in Tanganyika. He learned Swahili and did some translations from English. Allen died in Nairobi on June 9, 1947.

The Major Themes of Allen's Teaching

David M. Paton, an authority on Roland Allen and editor of posthumous editions of his work, has summarized Allen's basic ideas as follows:

1. A Christian community which has come into existence as the result of the preaching of the Gospel should have *handed over to it* the Bible, the Creed, the ministry and the Sacraments.

2. It is then responsible, with the Bishop, for recognizing the spiritual gifts and needs in its membership and for calling into service from that membership priests or presbyters to preside at the Eucharist and to be responsible for the Word and for pastoral care.

3. It is also required to share the message and the Christian life with its neighboring communities not yet evangelized.

4. The Holy Spirit working on the human endowment of the community's leaders is sufficient for its life. Don't "train" these leaders too much. Don't import from the outside.

5. A Christian community that cannot do these things is not yet a *church,* it is a mission field.

6. The Bishop and his staff (cf. Timothy, Titus, etc.) are crucial, both for oversight and to serve as visible links with the rest of the Church.[6]

Each point represents a question Allen raised against the accepted policy and practice of his day. He did not intend to outline a complete theology of mission or a strategy for planting the church in every situation. On the contrary, Allen took seriously what we would call the cultural and historical context for the preaching of the Gospel and the priority that needed to be given to developing an indigenous and self-reliant church from its very beginning. This was a radical note in an era of missionary triumphalism and continuing colonial expansion, when the responsibilities of "Christendom" and the intrinsic moral superiority of Western culture were taken for granted. Missions were directed by the policies or actual presence of a generation of pioneers, tough-minded and dominating personalities as they were and had to be. They felt they had to maintain control of every aspect of the organization and development of a young church in order to preserve pure doctrine and also to prevent relapses into paganism and superstition. To such persons and to those with a strong sense of their accountability to supporters at home, Allen's ideas about "handing over" responsibility to new Christians and trusting the Holy Spirit seemed not only radical but irresponsible.

His attack on the structures and policies of churches and missionary societies was based on the distinction he made, with St. Paul, between law and Gospel. Under the law, Allen said, the letter is communicated. This means fixed rules for external obedience, numbers to measure achievement, and hierarchies of responsibility and accountability. Under the Gospel the Spirit is communicated, God takes command of one's heart, unites one to the whole community of believers locally and worldwide, and empowers the community with freedom, wisdom, and adaptability for the work of true evangelism.

The task of church leaders was, as Allen saw it, to help the church discern the Spirit and to submit *themselves* to the "administration of the Spirit" and not only to be administrators of the law. Allen would have appreciated the distinction between Tradition and traditions that developed later in the theological work of the World Council of Churches. He saw that the Tradition of the Gospel kerygma was often confused with or submerged in loyalty to the particular traditions of particular churches. Where the church was well established, as in the West, the preservation of the established order became an end in itself. In missionary work overseas, concern for "traditions" made missionaries reluctant to hand over real responsibility to indigenous leaders and often confused the Tradition of the Gospel with the particular traditions of the church and society from which the missionaries came.

Allen questioned the assumption that the church in its fullness had not been planted and was not ready for independence until there were professionally trained, salaried, full-time ministers, a faithful and literal translation of Western hymns and liturgies, and churches erected on Western architectural lines, not to speak of robed choirs, Mother's Unions, and other details of "normal" parish and diocesan organization. These were expressions of the law that might even be a hindrance to the Gospel.

Now that the myth of Christendom has been exposed and we begin to recognize that the church everywhere, including the West, is in a missionary situation, we need to reread Roland Allen in the light of our own experience and new opportunities. The discernment of the gifts of the Spirit, the renewal of lay ministry, reshaping theological education for laity and clergy alike, rethinking the meaning of baptism, the role of bishops and the structuring of congregations for mission – all are themes on which Allen had original and trenchant things to say. Above all, he challenged his readers to examine their assumptions concerning the relation of the Gospel to culture and tradition both in their own societies and among the people to whom they are sent.

By going back to the New Testament models of self-reliance, Allen sought to help the church escape from the economic straitjacket in which progress was dependent on money – mostly from abroad. There would never be enough money from abroad to support both expanding educational and medical work and the numbers of full-time pastors needed for a growing church. And what would happen if all funds were cut off, and the supply of missionaries as well? Allen's experiences of antiforeignism and the first stirrings of modern Chinese nationalism led him to predict that the day would come when all foreign missions would be excluded from China and perhaps from other parts of Asia and Africa. Thus he came to question the church's reliance on an unbiblical, peculiarly Western pattern of professionally trained full-time clergy. Again and again he tried to put the case for "voluntary clergy" who would be selected and trained in local congregations and continue to earn their own living in the community.

It was Allen's conviction that if Christianity were to spread, the faith would have to be carried by natural leaders, by missionaries among their own people. Using the example of St. Paul, he contended that every Christian community would develop the persons with the necessary gifts to sustain it and that clerical leadership could not be externally imposed (as by the importing of English or American priests). Leadership, Allen maintained, sprang up out of the midst of the religious community. Furthermore, such church leaders would also be leaders in the wider community. Allen described such "natural leaders" in this way:

> The man lives before our eyes. He is a man of mature age, the head of a family . . . His wife and children and household are well-governed and orderly. He is a man of some position in the community. Strangers and visitors . . . are naturally directed to his house . . . He is a man of certain gravity and dignity whose words carry weight. He can teach and rebuke those who would slight the exhortations of a lesser man . . . He is a man of moral character

. . . He is sober-minded and just. He is a Christian of some standing. He has learned the teaching of the apostles . . . He can teach what he has learned.[7]

Allen also questioned the priority given to schools and similar institutional work over evangelism. By establishing schools and hospitals and committing to them, rather than to the churches, the bulk of their budgets and personnel, missionary societies were not only trying to take "the best of the West" to backward peoples but to establish new cultural norms for them. In its extreme form this strategy led to the assumption that Western higher education was not only an expression of, but almost a precondition for, the life of the church.

A corollary of Allen's attempt to uncover the ancient understanding of clerical leadership arising from the faith community was his emphasis on the ministry of the laity. All the baptized are empowered and called to witness; evangelism is not the task of only the clergy or professional missionary. The clergy have in fact usurped the role of the laity:

In the beginning the local church was a society of men bound together by their faith in Christ and their communion with Him and with one another . . . But as time went on the professional spirit grew in the clerical order and the division became dangerous . . . Clericalism was the danger. It was [their] part to minister in holy things, it was the duty of the laity to hearken and receive.[8]

An even more radical suggestion was that the ministry of the laity would be nourished and expressed best when the center of worship was returned from church buildings to the homes of Christian families. Allen recalled that the first Christians had met in homes and shared the common Christian family meal but that hundreds of years of church tradition had corrupted Eucharistic practice and taken the common meal from the home and translated it into a "temple rite" to be presided over in great mystery by old men in decorous vestments.

During Allen's Kenya years he began both to simplify the Communion service and to celebrate it in his own home in the company of his family, friends, and neighbors. He explained this development as follows:

When I began to celebrate the Holy Communion at home with my wife as a regular thing . . . by degrees I felt instinctively that the vestments and ritual of a private chapel were out of place . . . so I began to drop them until I reached the point where I abandoned them altogether. Then I slowly realized more and more clearly that I had in fact returned to the family rite.[9]

The Rediscovery of Roland Allen

So far as is known, Allen's ideas had little influence on Anglican mission during his lifetime. His Spirit-centered ecclesiology seemed idealistic and impractical to the leadership of a highly institutionalized church closely associated with the British Empire. His exposure of conscious and unconscious paternalism, clericalism, and colonialism did not make friends for him either. His arguments from the New Testament must have been exasperating to those who saw themselves engaged in a far more complex enterprise than the original itineration of St. Paul. His stress on indigenization and the handing over of responsibility to new churches at an early stage implied a willingness to take risks and a respect for "pagan" cultures not shared by many of his contemporaries.

Because Allen was a prophetic and seminal thinker rather than a systematic theologian, his influence can be measured less by the actual applications of his ideas than by their power to inspire critical reflection on existing policies and theological systems. From the first, Pentecostal Christians, some of whom were associated with the Survey Application Trust, claimed him as their own, though he was in fact neither a Pentecostalist nor a radical Protestant. His principles were basically Anglo-Catholic. He believed in the necessity of episcopacy and the centrality of the Holy Eucharist in the life of the church as strongly as he believed in the Bible and in the Holy Spirit.[10]

As to the application of his ideas, the real difficulty seems to be that Allen set forth a model for beginning new work but gave little guidance for changing long-established policies and practices. For example, in the 1950s the Episcopal priest and sociologist Joseph Moore tried to apply the Roland Allen model to rural parishes in southern Indiana. In this and in later experiments in Nevada and Alaska, resistance to change came chiefly from the local congregations used to a dependency model of church life and from other clergy who saw traditional standards for training and ordination being reduced in the new plan.

Allen's ideas remained alive in seminaries and missionary training programs and influenced a wide variety of developments, from the Church Growth Movement led by Donald McGavran, to the pioneering work among the Masai in East Africa undertaken by the Roman Catholic missioner Vincent Donovan. Bishop R.O. Hall of Hong Kong successfully adapted Allen's vision to staff virtually his whole diocese with voluntary clergy who were also highly qualified in other professions and leaders of the community. Bishop K.H. Ting has stated that the Three-Self Movement in China owes much to the thinking of Roland Allen. In the United States the Student Volunteer Movement was nourished particularly by Allen's most popular books, *The Spontaneous Expansion of the Church* and *Missionary Methods: St. Paul's or Ours?*

Often the influence of Allen has been indirect and fortuitous but no less significant for that. The eminent Islamic scholar Kenneth Cragg once gave a series of lectures on Roland Allen to a group of missionaries in training. Among them was George Harris who was inspired to purchase and take with him to the Philippines all of Allen's books he could find. In 1960 another American Episcopal priest, Boone Porter, discovered the books while visiting Harris in Sagada. Porter in turn spread the word to David Cochran, a missionary to Native Americans in South Dakota, and to William Gordon, a priest in Alaska. Gordon, Cochran, and Harris later followed each other in becoming bishops of Alaska and were instrumental in establishing what was then a radical plan for the development of an indigenous ministry among native peoples in Alaska, following many of Allen's ideas.

With Porter and others they pressed the General Convention of the Episcopal Church to revise its canons, to provide far more flexible standards for the selection, training, and ordination of clergy to serve, often on a voluntary or part-time basis, isolated congregations and ethnic congregations, not only overseas but in the United States.

One consequence has been to make possible an intentional application of Roland Allen's ideas to Episcopal missions in Central and South America and a rapid development of indigenous churches where for many years there had been little growth. In Ecuador, for example, under the leadership of Bishop Adrian Cáceres, the Episcopal Church has grown from 394 members (and no local clergy) in 1971 to two dioceses, 240 congregations, and 20,000 baptized members served by 48 indigenous clergy in 1988. Bishop Cáceres says that this has happened because he took seriously the challenge in *The Spontaneous Expansion of the Church* to experiment with different forms of ministry, to put emphasis on "a flexible, locally contextualized and indigenous church," and to give priority to "the formation of Christians and their leaders."[11]

"Do You Deliver?" This, says David Paton, is the perennial question that Roland Allen addresses to the church. Paton writes:

St. Paul wrote to the Corinthians that he had delivered what he had received. When the postman hands over a parcel to me, he loses nothing and I am enriched. The museum curator or the librarian, on the other hand, hands over nothing. If I want to keep something from the museum I must learn it by heart or buy a copy. The postman delivers, the museum curator hangs on to what has been delivered to him. Both do their duty. But which is the image that symbolizes the missionary church? or the missionary? or ourselves? in theory and in practice?[12]

Notes

1. Alexander McLeish, "Biographical Memoir," in *The Ministry of the Spirit,* ed. David M. Paton (London: World Dominion Press, 1960), p. x.
2. Ibid.
3. Roland Allen, *The Case for Voluntary Clergy* (London: Eyre & Spottiswoode, 1930), preface.
4. Allen, quoted by McLeish, "Biographical Memoir."
5. Ibid.
6. David M. Paton, in *Setting Free the Ministry of the People of God,* ed. G.C. Davis et al. (Cincinnati: Forward Movement Publications, 1984), p. 21.
7. Allen, *Voluntary Clergy* (London: SPCK, 1923), pp. 48-49.
8. Allen, in *The Ministry of the Spirit,* ed. David Paton, pp. 183-84.
9. Allen, "The Family Rite," in *Reform of the Ministry,* ed. David Paton (London: Lutterworth Press, 1968), pp. 200-201.
10. For these and other insights the writers are indebted to an unpublished address by David M. Paton, "Roland Allen: Vision and Legacy," delivered at the Pacific Basin Conference 1984 and reported in *Setting Free the Ministry.*
11. From interview with Adrian Cáceres, July 6, 1988.
12. From unpublished address cited above, n. 10.

Selected Bibliography

Books and Articles by Roland Allen

1892 "Silvester II, Pope." *English Historical Review,* vol. 7. London.
1901 *The Siege of the Peking Legations.* London: Smith, Elder.
1912 *Missionary Methods: St. Paul's or Ours?* London: Robert Scott. Reprinted, London: World Dominion Press, 1930, 1949, 1956. Reset, with a memoir by Alexander McLeish, London: World Dominion Press; Grand Rapids, Mich.: Wm. B. Eerdmans Publishing Co., 1962.
1917 *Pentecost and the World: The Revelation of the Holy Spirit in "The Acts of the Apostles."* London: Oxford University Press.
1919 *Educational Principles and Missionary Methods: The Application of Educational Principles to Missionary Evangelism.* London: Robert Scott.
1920 (in collaboration with Thomas Cochrane) *Missionary Survey as an Aid to Intelligent Co-operation in Foreign Missions.* London: Longmans, Green.
1923 *Voluntary Clergy.* London: SPCK.
1923 "Christian Education in China: The Report of the China Educational Commission, 1921-1922." In *Theology,* vol. 6, London.
1927 *The Spontaneous Expansion of the Church and the Causes Which Hinder It.* London: World Dominion Press. Reprinted in 1949 and 1956. Reset with a memoir by Alexander McLeish, London: World Dominion Press; Grand Rapid, Mich.: Wm. B. Eerdmans Publishing Co., 1962.
1928 *Voluntary Clergy Overseas: An Answer to the Fifth World Call.* Privately printed at Beaconsfield.
1929 "The Provision of Services for Church People Overseas." In *Theology,* vol. 19. London.
1930 *The Case for Voluntary Clergy.* London: Eyre & Spottiswoode.
1932 *The Place of Medical Missions.* London and New York: World Dominion Press. A 14-page pamphlet.
1937 *S.J.W. Clark: A Vision of Foreign Missions.* London: World Dominion Press.

Posthumous Publications

1960 *The Ministry of the Spirit: Selected Writings of Roland Allen,* with a memoir by Alexander McLeish. Ed. David M. Paton. London: World Dominion Press, 1960; Grand Rapids, Mich.: Wm. B. Eerdmans Publishing Co., 1962. Rev. ed., 1965.

1968 *Reform of the Ministry: A Study in the Work of Roland Allen.* Ed. David M. Paton. London: Lutterworth Press. This book contains a "bibliographical and theological essay" by the editor, a history of the Survey Application Trust by Sir Kenneth Grubb, a list of the publications of the World Dominion Press, and an account of Allen's last years in East Africa by Noel D. King, together with previously unpublished writings of Allen and correspondence by him or to him.

1983 *The Compulsion of the Spirit,* selected writings of Roland Allen, with brief introductory material by the editors, David M. Paton and Charles H. Long. Grand Rapids, Mich.: Wm. B. Eerdmans Publishing Co.; and Cincinnati, Ohio: Forward Movement Publications.

Materials of Related Interest

Beyerhaus, Peter, and Henry Lefever. *The Responsible Church and the Foreign Mission.* London: World Dominion Press; Grand Rapids, Mich.: Wm. B. Eerdmans Publishing Co., 1964.

Davis, Gerald Charles, Eric Chong, and H. Boone Porter, eds. *Setting Free the Ministry of the People of God,* the report of a Pacific Basin Conference on the vision and legacy of Roland Allen, held in Hawaii in 1983. Cincinnati, Ohio: Forward Movement Publications, 1984.

Denniston, Robin, ed. *Part Time Priests: A Discussion.* London: Skeffington, 1960.

Donovan, Vincent. *Christianity Rediscovered: An Epistle for the Masai.* Maryknoll, N.Y.: Orbis Books; London: SCM Press, 1982.

McGavran, Donald A. *The Bridges of God: A Study in the Strategy of Missions.* London: World Dominion Press; New York: Friendship Press, 1955.

_____. *How Churches Grow: The New Frontier of Mission.* London: World Dominion Press; New York: Friendship Press, 1959.

Ministry Development Journal, no. 15. Irene Jackson-Brown, editor. Eighteen articles and reviews on the application of Roland Allen's principles today by an international group of contributors. New York: Episcopal Church Center, 1988.

Metzener, Hans Wolfgang. *Roland Allen: Sein Leben und Werk.* Gütersloh: Gütersloher Verlagshaus Gerd Mohn, 1970.

Paton, David M., ed. *New Forms of Ministry.* International Missionary Council Research Pamphlet no. 12. London: Edinburgh House Press, 1965.

Porter, H. Boone. "Roland Allen – Missionary Prophet." In *Living Church* magazine, July 17, 1983. Milwaukee, Wis.

Renouf, Robert W. "Anglicanism in Nicaragua, 1745-1985." In *Anglican and Episcopal History* 57, no. 4 (December 1988).

Talltorp, Åke. *Sacrament and Growth. A Study in the Sacramental Dimension of Expansion in the Life of the Local Church, as Reflected in the Theology of Roland Allen.* Uppsala: Swedish Institute of Missionary Research, 1989.

Thompson, Michael D. "The Holy Spirit and Human Instrumentality in the Training of New Converts: An Evaluation of the Missiological Thought of Roland Allen." Ph.D. diss., Golden Gate Baptist Theological Seminary, 1989.

Robert Streit, O.M.I., 1875–1930
Johannes Dindinger, O.M.I., 1881–1958
Johannes Rommerskirchen, O.M.I., 1899–1978

Bibliographers in the Service of Mission

Willi Henkel, O.M.I.

Robert Streit, O.M.I.

Roman Catholic missiology as such did not exist at the beginning of this century, and even the theological courses and textbooks included very little material about the missionary expansion of the church. Robert Streit, along with Joseph Schmidlin, pioneered in Catholic missiology, and it was Streit in particular who initiated the development of missionary bibliography through the publication of *Bibliotheca Missionum*.

Early Life and Education

Streit was born October 27, 1875, in Fraustadt (Posen), Germany, and grew up in Stendal (Sachsen), a town of 20,000 inhabitants.[1] His father, the president of the parish council, put special emphasis on the boy's early training in singing and music. Robert enjoyed religious pilgrimages with his pious mother, but it was the parish priest who discovered his priestly and missionary vocation, making the first contacts on his behalf with the Mission Secondary School in Valkenburg, Netherlands. A medical doctor refused to declare the boy healthy enough to undertake studies there, but the necessary certificate was finally obtained from another doctor. The school, directed by the Oblates, had about 120 students at that time and maintained a high standard of studies and religious discipline. Streit enrolled in the fall of 1889, and the teachers soon recognized his intellectual capacity and diligence.

After completing undergraduate studies, Streit began his novitiate at St. Gerlach, Netherlands, on August 14, 1895, and completed it on August 15, 1896. He then enrolled for philosophical and theological studies in Liège, along with students from Belgium, France and Ireland. He stayed in Liège very briefly, however, before going to Hünfeld in the fall of 1897, where the newly organized German Province of the Oblates was opening its own scholasticate. There, together with his fellow students, he helped in the construction of the new study center. Streit took final vows as a member of the Oblate order on August 15, 1897, and was ordained to the priesthood on April 28, 1901.

Streit's Early Writings

While still a student, Streit had published some poems under the penname "Bruder Eris."[2] His talent in composition was such that J. Classen, editor of *Maria Immaculata,* the monthly review of the German Oblate Province, asked the provincial to assign Streit to collaborate in that publication. He became a member of the editorial team in February 1902 and served as editor-in-chief from October 1905 to September 20, 1912.

Throughout those years Streit collected rich materials from all the Oblate missions: Canada, with the Eskimo and Indian missions, South Africa (Transvaal, Natal, Free State, South West Africa), and Ceylon. In many letters he encouraged the missionaries to write about their work, and he himself wrote numerous articles on the missions. He also published the following books: *Eine Opfer der Hottentotten* (Victim of the Hottentots), 1907; *Der letzte Franziskaner von Texas* (The last Franciscan from Texas), 1907; *Das Opfer: Eine historische Erzählung aus dem Zululand* (Victim: An historical account from Zululand), 1912; *Die Portugiesen als Pfadfinder nach Ostindien* (The Portugese as discoverers of East India), 1909; *Madhu* (a Marian shrine in Ceylon), 1911.

During this period, the Hereros of South Africa rebelled against the German colonists. Streit's interest in colonial matters was reflected in his writings and in the conferences he held. In the summer of 1912, for example, the Colonial Institute in Hamburg invited him to lecture on missions with particular reference to the German colonies.

Streit and the Development of Roman Catholic Missiology in Germany

His contacts with the missions enabled Streit to note the failure of Roman Catholic church historians to deal with missionary issues in more than a very limited and superficial way. Scholarly periodicals did not mention such issues, and Streit showed that the existing mission literature was quite disproportionately of a popular rather than scientific nature.[3] He developed his thought on that subject in a series of articles published from 1907 to 1910 in various journals. The articles dealt with exegetical, patristic, historical, and contemporary issues related to Roman Catholic missions, and also with Protestant missiological literature.[4] Catholics had largely ignored or even despised Protestant missions,[5] ever since Count de Maistre had described the nineteenth-century Protestant missionary enterprise as fruitless. Gustav Warneck's *Protestantische Beleuchtung der römischen Angriffe auf die evangelische Heidenmission* (Protestant view of Roman attacks on evangelical missions) had provoked no reaction on the part of Roman Catholics. However, Streit's articles deploring the lack of scientific mission studies found a considerable echo in German academic circles, thus preparing the way for a Catholic missiology. The primary need, he reasoned, was to provide an extensive bibliography of mission materials that lay buried in various libraries.

Following his inclination, Streit began collecting bibliographical notes, beginning with an examination of bibliographies of the old orders – Franciscans, Augustinians, Carmelites, Jesuits. He also studied classical bibliographical works by such people as Golubovich, García Icazbalceta, Beristain, and many others mentioned as sources in the later volumes of *Bibliotheca Missionum.*

The financial resources for such an undertaking had still to be found. In 1909 at the Katholiken-tag in Breslau, Fürst zu Löwenstein gave a memorable speech on "German Catholics and Foreign Missions." A mission committee was formed as a result, and a conference took place on January 22, 1910, in Berlin.[6] Streit was invited to speak at that conference on the duties and tasks of theology with regard to the missions. He declared the necessity of introducing missiology into seminaries and universities as a part of the curriculum,[7] and he made three concrete proposals: to deal with the missions in theological lectures and textbooks, to train missiologists, and to establish a chair of missiology at a university.

At the committee's request, Streit wrote a subsequent memorandum, emphasizing the importance of bibliographies for mission studies (a need ultimately met by the publication of *Bibliotheca Missionum*) and proposing the publication of a missiological journal. Professor Joseph Schmidlin at the University of Münster, in a further memorandum on the scholarly means of promoting mission studies,[8] suggested academic mission associations, lectures, and a missiological review. Both memoranda were submitted to all German bishops, missionary societies, and professors in the Catholic theological faculties and seminaries.

The matter was again considered at the Katholikentag in Augsburg in 1910, where the committee decided to launch a missiological journal, to ask Streit to present a plan for missionary bibliography, and to put Schmidlin in charge of developing guidelines for the publication of archival materials. More mission associations, academic lectures, and seminars, comparable to those Schmidlin had already begun in Münster, were recommended. In 1911 the first Roman Catholic chair of missiology was established in the Catholic Theological Faculty at the University of Münster, with Schmidlin as professor.[9] The International Institute for Missiological Research was founded at Mainz on August 11, 1911. On October 4 Schmidlin was elected president of the institute and Streit was named its secretary, a position he held until 1924 when he was called to Rome.

Streit Is Called to Rome

On May 3, 1923, Cardinal Van Rossum, prefect of the Sacred Congregation for the Propagation of Faith (Propaganda Fide), addressed a circular letter to the superiors of the missions, asking them to send books and objects of missionary interest for an exposition to be held in the Vatican during the 1925 Holy Year. Streit, together with other experts, was called to Rome in February 1924 for the preparatory work. On January 5, 1925, the prefect put him in charge of the literature section. Some 30,000 books, many of them in non-European languages, had been collected,[10] providing a unique opportunity for a survey of missionary literature. Pope Pius XI, himself a former librarian with special interest in missionary literature, encouraged continuation of the collection. It formed the nucleus of what was to become the Pontifical Missionary Library, entrusted to the care of the Propaganda Fide, and Streit was appointed the library's first director.

Streit's Character

Most of Streit's life until he went to Rome was spent in the Scholasticate of Hünfeld, where he participated actively in the religious and recreational life of the community. Although a recognized scholar, he remained at heart a modest priest, grateful to anyone who offered help in the bibliographical task. He regarded his learning as a means of service to missionaries and their colleagues, believing that the rich experience of the past could shed light on the present situation and aid in the solution of future problems. Throughout his life he was dedicated to pastoral activities, and in his homilies we see a pastor who knew how to arouse and communicate enthusiasm for the missions.

Streit's health was never robust, and from 1926 onward he suffered from an inflamed bladder that was helped by medical attention and surgery but never cured. He had hoped to return to Rome following holidays in Germany in 1929 to continue work on *Bibliotheca Missionum*. But that was not to be. He died in Frankfurt on July 31, 1930, at only fifty-five years of age,[11] leaving the completion of that monumental project to his successors, Dindinger and Rommerskirchen.

Johannes Dindinger, O.M.I.

Dindinger's name appears on the list of contributors in the first volume of *Bibliotheca Missionum*. In the following volumes he collaborated to an even greater extent, helping also to compile the indexes, and he was the logical successor to Streit in the task of continuing that publication.

Dindinger's Childhood and Studies

Dindinger was born at Heinrichsdorf in Lorraine on September 8, 1881. He learned both German and French at an early age. Like Streit, he did undergraduate studies at the St. Charles Mission Secondary School of the Oblates at Valkenburg, and took his novitiate at St. Gerlach. In 1902 he was sent to study philosophy and theology at the Gregorian University in Rome.[12] The atmosphere in Rome was conducive to learning other languages and to the study of history, two of Dindinger's major interests. In 1905 he received his doctorate in philosophy, and was ordained an Oblate priest in 1907.

Dindinger at Hünfeld, 1908-26

In 1908 the talented priest was assigned to teach philosophy at the Scholasticate in Hünfeld, where he met Streit. The latter continued to publish programmatic books and articles on Roman Catholic missiology, and Dindinger read them with enthusiasm. Streit, in turn, greatly appreciated Dindinger's linguistic abilities and wide knowledge, and introduced him to the art of compiling bibliographies. The two became increasingly close collaborators.

During the years he was at Hünfeld, Dindinger completed the three volumes of his *Institutiones Cosmologiae et Psychologicae*. And from the early years of his experience there, he became acquainted with such pioneers of missiology as J. Schmidlin, A. Huonder, S.J. (the editor of *Katholichen Missionen*), and F. Schwager, S.V.D.

Dindinger in Rome

When Streit moved to Rome he asked his superiors to assign Dindinger there also, so that the two men might continue to collaborate on *Bibliotheca Missionum* (originally planned as a four-volume work only) and in building up the Pontifical Missionary Library. After Streit's untimely death in 1930 Dindinger became the editor of that publication and director of the library. From 1932 to 1948 he served also as professor of mission history at the Missiological Institute of the Propaganda Fide Athenaeum. After 1948 he devoted major attention to the ongoing volumes of *Bibliotheca Missionum,* but also collaborated in the *Bibliografia Missionaria,* which had begun publication in 1935 under the direction of his assistant, Johannes Rommerskirchen.

Dindinger's Character

Dindinger, a kind and helpful person who would interrupt his own work to assist another with translation, had an unusual linguistic talent and an excellent memory. As a professor he was demanding, one who carefully weighed every word in his lectures and would not tolerate carelessness in the students' examinations. His students, in turn, were proud to be "disciples of old Dindinger."

Basically, he was an intellectual, whose piety was entirely unostentatious. He had great respect for scholarship, regarding intelligence and virtue as closely related. His judgment was prudent and sharp, but sometimes too critical and stubborn. Yet his readiness to help others was such that even the youngest student felt free to call upon him at any time.[13] The surest way to become his friend was to ask his advice.

Dindinger died on July 31, 1958, having been able to continue his work until only eight days before his death.

Johannes Rommerskirchen, O.M.I.

Rommerskirchen's Youth

Rommerskirchen, the son of a teacher, was born in Neuenhoven (Aachen) on January 5, 1899. Like Streit and Dindinger before him, he had his secondary schooling at the St. Charles Mission School of the Oblates in Valkenburg and took his novitiate (1915-16) at St. Gerlach. His studies in philosophy and theology at the Scholasticate in Hünfeld were interrupted by military service during World War I.

As a student Rommerskirchen lived in the community with Streit and Dindinger. He was ordained an Oblate priest on June 2, 1923. After completing his studies in 1924, his superiors assigned him to the editorial staff of the Oblate periodical *Monatsblätter der Unbefleckten Jungfrau Maria.* In the same year he began the study of missiology at the University of Münster, and missionary bibliography was to become for him also a lifelong vocation. From 1926 to 1933, under the guidance of Professor Schmidlin, his first bibliographical works were published in *Zeitschrift für Missionswissenschaft.* Under Schmidlin he completed his doctoral degree in 1930, with a dissertation on the Oblate missions in Ceylon.[14]

Rommerskirchen in Rome

Following Streit's death in 1930, Rommerskirchen was assigned to Rome to assist Dindinger in editing *Bibliotheca Missionum* and in strengthening the Pontifical Missionary Library. From 1933 to 1955 he also taught the history of missions at the Missiological Institute of the Propaganda Fide Athenaeum. It was in Rome that he established *Bibliografia Missionaria,* a working bibliography of current scholarly literature for mission studies. The first volume of the latter appeared in the 1935 issue of *Guida delle Missioni Cattoliche,* but it became an independent annual publication of which forty issues had been published by 1978, the year of Rommerskirchen's death.

Rommerskirchen's greatest achievement was the completion of *Bibliotheca Missionum,* to which he contributed increasingly from volumes 6 to 30. (His own bibliography indicates the extent to which he was preoccupied with missionary bibliography as such, a task that left him little time for writing other kinds of articles and books.[15]) It would be difficult to determine the precise extent of his collaboration throughout the history of that publication, but he became its editor-in-chief upon the death of Dindinger in 1958. He was assisted by N. Kowalsky, O.M.I., for volumes 13 and 14, and by J. Metzler, O.M.I., for volumes 22 to 30. From 1930 onward Rommerskirchen also made a considerable contribution to the development of the Pontifical Missionary Library, and was its director from 1958 to 1972. During the forty-two years of his association with that library, it became an increasingly important collection for missiological research.

Rommerskirchen, the Man

From the time of his doctoral dissertation and earliest publications, Rommerskirchen showed a real talent for writing. He was able to present the missionary cause in an attractive, understandable way to ordinary people. But in giving full attention to missionary bibliography, a task he regarded as his particular vocation, the mastery he achieved in that field was at the expense of time for more writing he might have done. He summarized the spirit of this self-dedication in the words of the Oblate rule: *Ferventi diletandi fidei desiderio* (rendered by English-speaking Oblates as "an ardent desire to spread the gospel of Christ"). A hard worker, he nonetheless enjoyed recreation and cultivating friendships among his confreres and other colleagues and students. Satisfied to have seen the completion of *Bibliotheca Missionum,* and the firm continuation of *Bibliografia Missionaria* in which he took active interest to the end of his life, Rommerskirchen died in Rome on February 24, 1978.

Nature of the Bibliographical Publications and Missionary Library

Bibliotheca Missionum

Robert Streit said, "The task of a bibliography of missions is to present mission literature according to the modern, scientific requirements of bibliography, in such a way as to provide all who study about the missions with a reliable, handy, and rapid orientation to the available documents, and to reflect the current situation with regard to missiological writings."[16] This is precisely what *Bibliotheca Missionum* does. The first volume lists a number of collaborators, along with the rules and procedures Streit had specified in the interest of uniformity.[17]

The publication as a whole includes African mission history from the tenth century, Asian from the twelfth, and that of the Americas from the European discovery of those continents. Volume 1 introduces the general literature on theory, pastoral concerns, and law with regard to the missions; volumes 2 and 3 are devoted to missions in the Americas; volumes 4 to 14 to Asian missions; volumes 15 to 20 to African missions; and volume 21 to the mission literature on Australia and Oceania. Streit had expected to terminate the series with volume 21 (1909), because that is the beginning date of *Zeitschrift für Missionswissenschaft,* a journal that adopted the publicaton of missionary bibliography as one of its aims. However, *Bibliotheca Missionum* was continued for nine more volumes (22 to 30) supplementing and updating the literature from 1909 to 1940 for Africa, 1950 for Australia and Oceania, 1960 for America, and 1970 for Asia.

This bibliography presents Roman Catholic mission literature in categories of various theological disciplines. First is material about the missionary objective among non-Christians, and missionary cooperation in achieving that objective. A second category involves catechisms, Bible translations, prayer books and other Catholic literature, dictionaries, grammars – all written by missionaries.[18] A third category has to do with missionary writings on geography, ethnology, and religions.

Streit did not want to produce a mere catalog of books. On the other hand, he considered it too expensive to reproduce lengthy abstracts from the books themselves. The "middle way" he chose was to add an annotation of a few lines to each title, enabling readers to understand its format and contents,[19] and listing whatever materials are known to have been written about it. Insofar as possible, the place in which each book may be found is also indicated. Where the compiler was unable to locate a given document, he gave the source of his information about it.

The contents of *Bibliotheca Missionum* are arranged chronologically through volume 18. In volumes 19 and 20 (Africa), Dindinger found the material so vast and complex that he arranged it in alphabetical order of the missionary institutes instead, listing anonymous works at the end. Rommerskirchen thereafter continued Dindinger's arrangement. Each volume has five indexes: authors; persons; subject matter; places, countries, and nations; and a linguistic index. The combined index in some of the volumes exceeds 100 pages.

Bibliotheca Missionum, from the first volume onward, has been widely appreciated. Schmidlin termed it the discovery of a new world, previously unknown to both Catholics and Protestants, and regarded it as an indispensable tool for the study of missions.[20] According to Johannes Beckmann, the volumes on the Americas and Asia have special importance, and Beckmann notes that many outstanding scholars such as Kenneth Scott Latourette, Charles R. Boxer, Antonio da Silva Rego, and others have made extensive use of the publication.[21] People doing research in such related fields as anthropology, history of religions, and linguistics have also profited from it. Thus Beckmann, in his review of volumes 19 and 20, says: "As one examines the long series of volumes of the now-completed bibliography of African missions, with its approximately 6,000 pages, one can be proud of a production for which the scholars in any other science may justifiably envy our young missiology. We express heartfelt thanks to the editor and his collaborators for the immense amount of detailed work, dedication and effort reflected in these pages."[22]

Bibliografia Missionaria

This publication may be described as the counterpart and complement of *Bibliotheca Missionum*. It has been published annually since 1935 by the librarians of the Pontifical Missionary Library as a current bibliography on the missions.

The material in each issue of *Bibliografia Missionaria* is divided into four parts, following an introduction that lists special bibliographies and new periodicals: articles and books about the different branches of missiology – theology, law, history, the current situation of the missions and pastoral concerns (sections 2-6); auxiliary studies, such as dialogue, anthropology, religions, atheism, development (sections 7-11); missionary personnel, institutions, cooperation, spirituality (sections 12-15); finally, the various mission lands (sections 16-25). The arrangement thus moves from general to particular, from the principles of mission theology to the implementation of those principles in actual practice.

Since Vatican II the material in *Bibliografia Missionaria* has become more ecumenically oriented. It now includes missionary literature in the major languages: English, French, German, Dutch, Italian, Spanish, Portuguese, the Scandinavian languages, and Polish. A glance at the index (in Italian) is sufficient to note the wide coverage of missionary experience, problems, and discussions. The linguistic publications of missionaries are still listed, but with the growing importance of the local churches, locally produced bibliographies have an increasing usefulness for missionary literature today. That is particularly true of materials written in the languages of the Third World.

The Pontifical Missionary Library

As indicated above, Pope Pius XI prompted the establishment of a mission library when he encouraged a missionary exhibit during the 1925 Holy Year.[23] The wealth of material collected on that occasion was placed under care of the Sacred Congregation for the Propagation of the Faith. It was located in the same building and in close proximity to the congregation's archives in order to make it readily available to mission scholars and to facilitate missionary research. We have already noted the succession of Streit, Dindinger, and Rommerskirchen as directors of this library, and it is largely through their efforts that it has become so useful an instrument for the study of missions.

In 1979 the library was moved to a new facility near the Urban University and merged with that university's library. It now houses 100,000 volumes, 3,416 periodicals that have ceased publication, and more than 500 periodicals that are still current. In addition to the author/subject catalogs, there is a catalog of books in 530 non-European languages (including some 270 African languages along with important collections in Chinese, Japanese, other Asian, and Native American languages). A microfiche section has been recently initiated, containing archival material on missions. Thus the Pontifical Missionary Library, building on the vision of Streit, Dindinger, and Rommerskirchen, seeks to promote and serve the study of missiology.

Notes

1. See J. Pietsch, O.M.I., *P. Robert Streit, O.M.I. Ein Pionier der katholischen Missionswissenschaft* (Schriftenreihe der Neue Zeitschrift für Missionswissenschaft, no. 11, 1952), pp. 7-8.
2. For the bibliography of R. Streit, see J. Pietsch, *P. Robert Streit*, pp. 50-55.
3. R. Streit, *Führer durch die katholische Missionsliteratur* (Freiburg: Herder, 1911).
4. See J. Pietsch, *P. Robert Streit*, p. 52.
5. See J. Schmidlin, "Chateaubriand und Maistre über die Missionen," *Zeitschrift für Missionswissenschaft* 21 (1931): 297.

6. See *Die Konferenz der Missionskommission des Zentralkomitees der Katholikenversammlungen Deutschlands am 22. Januar 1910,* Offizieller Bericht von Dr. Werthmann (Freiburg: Caritasdruckerei, 1910).

7. R. Streit, *Die Missionsgeschichte in ihrer gegenwärtigen Lage und der Plan einer Missionsbibliographie. Denkschrift im Auftrage des Missionsausschusses des Zentralkomitees der Generalversammlung der Katholiken Deutschlands* (Freiburg: Caritasdruckerei, 1910).

8. Zwei Denkschriften zur Missionsgeschichte: 1. *Über die Herausgabe missionswissenschaftlicher Quellen,* von Universitätsprofessor Dr. J. Schmidlin; 2. *Über die Herausgabe einer Missionsbibliographie,* von P. Rob. Streit (Freiburg: Caritasdruckerei, 1911).

9. See J. Glazik, M.S.C., *50 Jahre Katholische Missionswissenschaft in Münster, 1911-1961.* Festschrift herausgegeben von . . . (Münster: Aschendorff, 1961).

10. See R. Streit, "Die Eröffnung der Weltmissionsausstellung im Vatikan," *Die Katholischen Missionen* 53 (1924/25): 133-38; R. Streit, "Die Missionsbibliothek der vatikanischen Missionsausstellung," *Die Katholischen Missionen* 54 (1926): 165-68; R. Streit, *Catholic Missions in Figures and Symbols Based on the Vatican Missionary Exhibition* (New York: Society for the Propagation of the Faith, 1927).

11. See J. Pietsch, *P. Robert Streit,* pp. 43-46.

12. See R. Becker, O.M.I., "P. Dr. Johannes Dindinger, O.M.I. zum vollendeten 70. Lebensjahre," *Missionswissenschaftliche Studien,* Festschrift, J. Rommerskirchen und N. Kowalsky, eds. (Aachen: Verlag Metz, 1951), pp. 13-18. For Dindinger's bibliography, see ibid., pp. 16-18, also *Bibliografia Missionaria* 22 (1958): 4-6. *Sylloge,* a much-valued collection of documents of the Sacred Congregation of the Propagation of the Faith, was edited by Dindinger and G. Monticone (Vatican City: Typis Polyglottis Vaticanis, 1939).

13. See N. Kowalsky, "P. Johannes Dindinger," *Der Weinberg* 39 (1959): 349.

14. See A. Reuter, O.M.I., "Ein Leben im Dienste der Missionsbibliographie. Zum 70. Geburtstag von P. Johannes Rommerskirchen," in *De Archivis et Bibliothecis Missionibis atque Scientiae Missionum Inservientibus,* Festschrift, ed. by J. Metzler, and published as *Euntes Docete* 21 (1968): 11-21.

15. See W. Henkel, "The Bibliography of Fr. J. Rommerskirchen," *De Archives et Bibliothecis,* pp. 23-32; also in *Bibliografia Missionaria* 41 (1977): 5-12.

16. R. Streit, in *Bibliotheca Missionum* 1 (1916): v-vi.

17. R. Streit, in ibid., p. x.

18. J. Pietsch, *P. Robert Streit,* pp. 20-21.

19. R. Streit, *Bibliotheca Missionum* 1 (1916): xi.

20. J. Schmidlin, *Theologische Revue* (1917): 366-68. For further reviews, see J. Pietsch, "P. Robert Streit," pp. 24-30.

21. J. Beckmann, "Werden, Wachen und Bedeutung der *Bibliotheca Missionum,*" in *De Archivis et Bibliothecis,* pp. 33-57.

22. J. Beckmann, in *Neue Zeitschrift für Missionswissenschaft* 12 (1956): 74.

23. On this subject, see J. Metzler, "La Pontificia Biblioteca Missionaria 'de Propaganda Fide,'" *Bibliografia Missionaria* 25 (1962): 5-17, and "The Pontifical Missionary Library 'De Propaganda Fide,'" *De Archivis et Bibliothecis,* pp. 347-60.

Selected Bibliography of Robert Streit, O.M.I.

Streit's complete bibliography is published in *Bibliografia Missionaria* 2 (1934/35): 7-17.

Books

1907 *Der letzte Franziskaner von Texas. Ein geschichtliche Erzählung.* Dülmen: A. Laumannsche Buchhandlung.

1907 *Ein Opfer der Hottentoten. Dem Volk und der Jugend erzählt.* Dülmen: A. Laumannsche Buchhandlung.

1909 *Die Portugiesen als Pfadfinder nach Ostindien.* Regensburg: Manz.

1911 *Madhu. Die Geschichte eines Heiligfums in den Urwäldern von Ceylon.* Fulda: Parceller.

1912 *Das Opfer. Eine historiche Erzählung aus dem Zululande.* Cologne: Verlag von Bachem.

1928 *Die Weltmission der katholischen Kirche. Zahlen und Zeichen auf Grund der Vatikanischen Missionsausstellung, 1925.* Hünfeld: Verlag der Oblaten (with English, Italian, Spanish, and French editions).

Sermons on the Missions

1913 *Die Berufung der Heiden.* Freiburg: Herder.

1914 *Der Göttliche Wille.* Freiburg: Herder.

1914 *Das apostolische Werk.* Freiburg: Herder.

Articles and Brochures

1903 "Für Gott und König. Eine Episode aus der Eroberung Mexikos durch die Spanier." *Maria Immaculata* 10 (1902/3).

1909 "Die theologische-wissenschaftliche Missionskunde." *Der Katholische Seelsorger* 21:20-29, 79-77, 117-29. "Die Mission in Exegese und Patrologie." Ibid., pp. 296-306, 346-50, 400-407, 445-53.

1910 *Die Missionsgeschichte in ihrer gegenwärtigen Lage und der Plan einer Missions-Bibliographie.* Freiburg: Caritasdruckerei.

1910 "Die Missionsgeschichtliche Literatur der Katholiken." *Theologie und Glaube* 2:132-40.

1910 "Die Missionsgeschichtliche Literatur der Protestanten." Ibid., pp. 299-314.

1910 "Bemerkungen zu unserer wissenschaftlichen Missionsgeschichte." Ibid., pp. 466-79.

1911 "Der eschatologische Missionsbeweis. Eine Missionspredigt gehalten bei der akademischen Missionsfeier zu Münster, an 30 Nov. 1910." *Heiland* 3:50-59.

1913 "Focher, ein unbekannter Missionstheoretiker des XVI. Jahrhunderts." *Zeitschrift für Missionswissenschaft (ZM)* 3:275-84.

1917 "Der Missionsgedanke in seiner neuzeitlichen Entwicklung." *ZM* 7:1-20.

1919 "Der Missionsgedanke in den Homilien des Origenes." *ZM* 9:159-71.

1922 "Zur Vorgeschichte der ersten Junta von Burgos 1512." *ZM* 12:65-78.

1923 *Im Dienste der Mission. Der Missionsgedanke im Leben des Stifters der Oblaten von der Unbefleckten Jungfrau Maria, Karl Joseph Eugen von Mazenod, Bischof von Marseille.* Aachen: Xaveriusverlag.

1923 "Einige wichtige Quellen zur amerikanischen Missionsgeschichte vor der Gründung der Propaganda." *ZM* 13:110-14.

Bibliographical Works

1911 *Führer durch die katholische Missionsliteratur.* Freiburg: Herder.

1911 "Über die Herausgabe einer Missionsbibliographie." In *Zwei Denkschriften zur Missionsgeschichte.* Freiburg: Karitasverband für das Kath. Deutschland.

1911 "Missionsbibliographischer Bericht." *ZM* 1:92-104, 196-200, 275-80, 352-62. Streit continued this bibliographical contribution to the same journal until 1923.

1916-29 *Bibliotheca Missionum* publications: Vol. 1, *Grundlegender und allgemeiner Teil* (Veröffentlichungen des Internationalen Instituts für missionswissenschaftliche Forschung). Münster: Verlag der Aschendorff'schen Buchhandlung (1916). Vol. 2, *Amerikanische Missionsliteratur, 1493-1699.* Aachen: Xaveriusverlag (1924). Vol. 3, *Amerikanische Missionsliteratur, 1700-1909.* Aachen: Aachener Missionsdruckerei (1927). Vol. 4, *Asiatische Missionsliteratur, 1245-1599.* Aachen: Aachener Missionsdruckerei (1928).Vol. 5, *Asiatische Missionsliteratur, 1600-1699.* Aachen: Xaveriusverlag (1929).

1925 *Die katholische deutsche Missionsliteratur:* Part 1, "Die geschichtliche Entwicklung der katholischen Missionsliteratur in deutschen Landen von Beginn des 19. Jahrhunderts bis zur Gegenwart. Ein Beitrag zur Geschichte des heimatlichen Missionslebens." Part 2, "Bibliographie der katholischen deutschen Missionsliteratur, 1800-1924." Abhandlungen aus Missionskunde und Missionsgeschichte, Nr 50. Aachen: Xaveriusverlag.

Articles about Streit

Pietsch, Johannes. *P. Robert Streit, O.M.I. Ein Pionier der katholischen Missionswissenschaft.* Schriftenreihe der Neuen Zeitschrift für Missionswissenschaft, Les Cahiers de la Nouvelle Revue de Science Missionnaire. Schöneck/Beckenried: Administration der Neuen Zeitschrift für Missionswissenschaft, 1952.

Rommerskirchen, Johannes. "Im Dienste des Missionsgedankens: P. Robert Streit Obl. d. U.J.M." *Monatsblätter der Oblaten der Unbefleckten Jungfrau Maria* 37 (1930): 292-97.

Selected Bibliography of Johannes Dindinger, O.M.I.

Dindinger's complete biography is published in *Bibliografia Missionaria* 22 (1958):4-6.

Books

1934 *Guida delle Missioni Cattoliche.* Rome: Unione Missionaria del Clero in Italia.

1939 *Sylloge praecipuorum documentorum recentium Summorum Pontificum et S. Congregationis de Propaganda Fide necnon aliarum SS. Congregationum Romanorum.* Vatican City: Typis Polyglottis Vaticanis.

Articles

1929 "P. Thomas Stephens, S.J. und sein Purana." *Die Katholischen Missionen* 57:100-103, 133-36, 163-67.
1930 "Les Ordinations Goanaises de 1845. Note rectificative." *Revue d'Histoire des Missions* 7:439-41.
1937 "Bibliografia Missionaria." *Il Pensiero Missionario* 9:187-92.
1938 "Bibliografia sull'adattamento dell'arte indigena agli usi liturgici." Ibid. 10:164-85.
1939 "Die Sammlungen römischer Missionserlasse." *Missionswissenschaft und Religionswissenschaft* 2:125-41.
1943 "Il contributo dei Missionari cattolici alla conoscenza del Siam e dell'Indocina." In *Le Missioni Cattoliche e la Cultura dell'Oriente, pp. 293-338.* Rome: Instituto Italiano per il Medio ed Estremo Oriente.
1945 "Bemerkungen zu den ersten Missionsversuchen der Franziskaner in Aethiopien." *Antonianum* 20:97-126.
1947 "Missionsschrifttum von und über Kardinal Lavigerie." In *Miscellanea Pietro Fumascone-Biondi, pp. 105-91.* Rome: Edizione di Storia e Letteratura.

Articles about Dindinger

Becker, Robert. "P. Dr. Johannes Dindinger, O.M.I. zum vollendeten 70. Lebensjahre." *Missionswissenschaftliche Studien,* pp. 13-18. Aachen: Xaveriusverlag, 1951.
Beckmann, Johannes. "Hochwürden Herrn P. Dr. Johannes Dindinger O.M.I. zum 70. Geburtstag." *Neue Zeitschrift für Missionswissenschaft* 7 (1951):305-8.
Kowalsky, Nikolaus. "Ad piissimam memoriam R.P. Ioannis Dindinger O.M.I." *Priester und Mission* 1 (1959): 8-10.
_____. "Festakademie zu Ehren des hochw. Herrn P. Johannes Dindinger O.M.I. Direktor der Päpstlichen Missionsbibliothek." *ZMR* 35 (1951): 300-302.
Magyary, Julius. "Triplex Jubilaeum in Instituto Jubilanti (2) P. Johannes Dindinger O.M.I." *Euntes Docete* 10 (1957): 332-33.
Perbal, Albert. "Le Père Jean-Baptiste Dindinger O.M.I." *Études Oblates* 17 (1958): 370-74.
Schilling, Doroteo. "I 60 Anni di Padre Dindinger." *Il Pensiero Missionario* 14 (1942):136-41.

Selected Bibliography of Johannes Rommerskirchen, O.M.I.

Rommerskirchen's complete bibliography is published in *Bibliografia Missionaria* 41 (1977):6-12.

Books

1927 *Missionsbilder aus dem Basutoland.* Hünfeld: Verlag der Oblaten.
1931 *Die Oblatenmissionen auf der Insel Ceylon im 19. jahrhundert, 1847-1893.* Hünfeld: Verlag der Oblaten.
1951 *Missionswissenschaftliche Studien. Festgabe Prof. Dr. Johannes Dindinger O.M.I., Direktor der Päpstlichen Missionsbibliothek zum 70. Lebensjahr dargeboten von Freunden und Schülern.* Ed. with N. Kowalsky. Aachen: Xaveriusverlag.

Articles

1926 "Die Oblaten und der einheimische Klerus in Ceylon." *ZM* 16:318-21.
1951 "Afrikanische Bischofskonferenzen." *Missionswissenschaftliche Studien, pp. 393-407.* Aachen, Xaveriusverlag.
1952 "Die Fortschritte der Missionsarbeit, 1926-1951." *Euntes Docete* 5:11-34.
1956 "From Archive to Action. Do Missionaries Learn from History?" *Worldmission* 7:31-39.
1957 "L'Instituto Missionario scientifico di Propaganda Fide dopo 25 anni." *Euntes Docete* 10:315-29.
1961 "Die Afrikamission um das Jahr 1805." In *50 Jahre Katholische Missionswissenschaft in Münster 1911-1961,* ed. J. Glazik, pp. 147-62 (Münster: Aschendorff, 1961).

Bibliographical Works

1935 "Essai de Bibliographie Missionnaire de Langua Italienne (1924-1934)." *Etudes Missionnaires* 3:131-39, 314-20; continued in ibid. 4 (1936): 132-60.

1938 "Bibliografia sull'Adattamento dell'arte indigena agli usi liturgici" (with J. Dindinger). *Il Pensiero Missionario* 10:165-85.

1952 "Bibliographica. Litterae Encyclicae 'Evangelii Praecones.'" *Euntes Docete* 5:320-26.

1960 "Bibliographia in Litteras Encyclicas 'Princeps Pastorum.'" *Euntes Docete* 13:513-19.

Article about Rommerskirchen

Metzler, J., ed. "Miscellanea: De Archivis e Bibliothecis atque Scientiae Missionum inservientibus." Honoring J. Rommerskirchen, in a special issue of *Euntes Docete* 21 (1968).

Joseph Schmidlin
1876–1944

Pioneer of Catholic Missiology

Karl Müller, S.V.D.

When Professor Joseph Schmidlin celebrated the silver jubilee of his priesthood, his former student, Anton Freitag, S.V.D., wrote of him:

> The merits of this German missiologist are not to be found only in the scientific field; rather, through his very deepening of the idea of mission by means of missiological studies, he has made an impact on the entire Catholic world mission. The immense progress at home in work for the missions and the missionary drive itself, now undertaken with far more vision and understanding, are due to a very large extent to Schmidlin's pioneer work.[1]

Freitag wrote this appreciation while Schmidlin was still at the peak of his creativity, ten years before he began his tragic decline. The last ten years of his life were to be extremely bitter. Eventually he found himself incarcerated in a concentration camp. On the occasion of his brutal death, the Basel deanery newspaper wrote of him as follows:

> A few days ago, the parish priest of Hagenthal asked me to meet him at the border at Schönenbuch. There he told me how his unfortunate brother, Prof. Dr. J. Schmidlin, had been tortured to death in Schirmbeck concentration camp and had died like a martyr. How often had this thoroughly good, pious and learned priest visited the parish at Allschwiler. A deeply emotional man, he could never keep silent in the face of injustice. Zeal for God drove him on and he had to pay dearly for it. His dead body was burnt by his torturers and his ashes used as fertilizer.[2]

Chronology

Joseph Schmidlin was born on May 29, 1876, in Klein-Landau in Sundgau, Alsace. His father was a teacher in an elementary school, educated in the French tradition, but German at heart. Joseph describes him as a "genuinely good man, if at times a bit rough and vehement." His mother was a more intelligent person and was deeply religious; "she lived in a supernatural world, and we were never pious enough for her liking."[3] Of her five surviving children, three became priests. Schmidlin considers himself typical of the Alsace Sundgau people when he writes: "Whoever knows Sundgau and the sort of people who live there can use this knowledge to excuse many things which appear uncouth or temperamental in my character and even in my scientific and literary works: I have never been able to belie my Alsace and Sundgau origins, neither outwardly nor in my thoughts and feelings."[4]

Joseph was immensely talented and had an enormous capacity for work. When he finished his elementary schooling, he attended the minor seminary in Zillesheim for his high school studies. He graduated from St. Stephen's College, Strassburg, with the highest possible honors. Then he opted for theological studies. These he had to interrupt for some time because of pulmonary catarrh. The fruit of this break in his studies was a comprehensive history of Blotzheim and Sundgau (720 pages); a railway guide; a history of the pilgrimage center, Our Lady of the Oak; and a biography of the parish priest, Juif of Blotzheim. He was ordained priest at the age of twenty-three. In 1901 he became a doctor of philosophy, two years later, of theology, both degrees from the University of Freiburg in Breisgau. He was invited to Rome by Louis Pastor, whom he helped with his monumental *History of the Popes.* Over and above this work and the many articles he wrote, he published the following books during those years: *Papst Pius X., sein Vorleben und seine Erhebung* (1903), *Ein Kampf um das Deutschtum im Klosterleben Italiens, Farfa und Subiaco im 16. Jahrhundert* (1903), *Die Geschichte der deutschen Nationalkirche Santa Maria dell'Anima* (1906), *Die geschichtphilosophische und kirchenpolitische Weltanschauung Ottos Von Freising* (1906), *Die Restaurationstätigkeit der Breslauer Fürstbischöfe* (1907), *Die kirchlichen Zustände in Deutschland vor dem 30 jährigen Krieg nach den bischöflichen Diözesanberichten an den Heiligen Stuhl* (1908-10). In 1906 he became the first private lecturer in the newly founded Catholic theological faculty in Strassburg.

The relationship between Professor Albert Ehrhard, the inflexible professor of ecclesiastical history in Strassburg, and the equally obdurate Schmidlin was from the very start stormy. Thus it was that Schmidlin applied for a transfer to Münster. He was accepted, not without qualms, by the theological faculty in Münster, since "he had shown himself in the course of his studies to be an exceptionally talented man." Dean Hüls sent him a fatherly warning:

> After making conscientious enquiries we could not fail to recognize that the development of the Strassburg situation into what it actually became was due by and large to a certain imprudence in your own remarks and, even more, to the indiscreet way in which your friends backed your cause in public. You should, therefore, regard it as a sign of genuine goodwill if we express the wish that you do your very best to prevent your appointment as a lecturer here from being blazoned abroad in the press (especially in Strassburg), for should that happen, you could once more become the victim of the importunity of your own good friends.[5]

In Münster things went more smoothly and developed along normal lines. On April 27, 1907, he was appointed lecturer for church history of the Middle Ages and of modern times. In 1910 he took on the post of extraordinary lecturer for the history of dogma and for patrology. At the same time he was asked to teach scientific missionography, which in 1914 developed into a chair of missiology. From then on he devoted himself chiefly to missiology, although he continued to lecture in church history. One result of the latter activity was his four-volume history of the popes of modern times (1933-37).

His own publications in the field of missiology are legion. Besides his basic works – *Einführung in die Missionswissenschaft* (2nd ed., 1925), *Katholische Missionslehre im Grundriss* (2nd ed., 1923),[6] *Katholische Missionsgeschichte* (1925)[7] – he also published innumerable articles in *Zeitschrift für Missionswissenschaft; Historisch-politische Blätter; Philosophisch-Historisches Jahrbuch; Akademische Missionsblätter; Priester und Mission; Wissenschaftliche Beilage zur Germania; Allgemeine Rundschau; Zeitschrift für katholische Theologie; Schönere Zukunft;* etc.

In the first twenty-five years of *Zeitschrift für Missionswissenschaft,* there are no fewer than 165 lengthy contributions from Schmidlin's pen. In volumes 22 and 23 of *Bibliotheca Missionum,* 146 entries are his.

Schmidlin was nothing if not professional; his heart and soul lay in imparting his knowledge through teaching. One of his students in the early 1920s, Father John Thauren, S.V.D., speaks of his thorough preparation for his lectures in which he communicated a plethora of material; he traced the main themes and did not clutter up his presentation with a superfluity of details. His love for his subject and still more for the church and its mission came through all the time. In his seminars he presupposed a lot and demanded a great deal. Even in private conversation he spoke almost entirely about mission, scarcely ever about himself. He seldom went out but, rather, seemed wedded to his desk-work. Thauren also recognized the tough streak in Schmidlin's character and called him "a fighter for the fight's sake." But he adds: "Yet every fight affected him deeply. Those who knew him well know how much he suffered within himself: 'my greatest cross is myself.' " He himself was aware of how much of what he had built up with great effort and success he himself destroyed in the heat of battle.[8]

Schmidlin was not the kind of man to throw in his lot with the antidemocratic National Socialism. Because of his "opposition which brooked no bounds,"[9] he very soon ran up against reprimands and vexations; he even had to forfeit his passport. In a sharp letter to the minister of education on March 22, 1934, he broached the subject of an early retirement. It was immediately granted him. Since a return to his native Alsace had been officially forbidden because of his involvement in the Alsace Autonomy Process in 1928, he settled down in Neu-Breisach. Here he edited the *Zeitschrift für Missionswissenschaft* and continued his scientific work. In 1937 he was obliged to resign from the journal. Eventually he was condemned to seven months' imprisonment in Freiburg in Breisgau because of speeches he had made against the government. He was then put under house arrest in Rottenmünster Infirmary near Rottweil (Württemberg). As he did not observe this, he found himself again in prison, first in Offenburg and then in Struthof concentration camp near Schirmbeck (Breuschtal). But even here he could not hold his tongue. He was punished by being put into the "casemate," a small concrete dungeon in which it was impossible either to sit or to lie down – one could only stand. After some time here, he was beaten to death with rubber truncheons.[10] According to the official prison report, he died on January 10, 1944, as a result of "a stroke." Professor John Beckmann, S.M.B., wrote in his obituary: "Although both his personality and his written work are marred here and there by imperfections and mistakes, they are more than compensated for by the total dedication of his life to the great business of world mission and by the successes that were his in this field."[11]

Schmidlin and the Chair of Missiology in Münster

Long before there was any move in Catholic circles to approach the work of world mission scientifically, Protestant scholars were already attempting to lift it "out of the twilight of sentimental piosity into the bright noon of science enlightened by faith."[12] When Schmidlin in the winter semester 1909-10 commenced his lectures on the Catholic missions in the German protectorates, sixteen Protestant professors in twelve different German universities were giving one or more lectures on mission themes.[13] They also had to their credit Gustav Warneck's three-volume standard work, *Evangelische Missionslehre* (Gotha, 1892-1903); nothing comparable existed in Catholic circles. Schmidlin's first series of lectures in the 1909-10 winter semester were attended by 120 registered students.

The preparation of his lectures gave Schmidlin an insight into the deficiencies on the Catholic side and into the importance of a Catholic missiology. Very soon he was exerting himself to have a chair of missiology set up in Münster. The lectureship in missionography given him in 1910 partly met his request. He did not limit himself to missionography in the narrow sense, but took in at once the whole field of missiology. He himself lectured to 157 students in the winter semester of 1910-11 on the introduction to missiology. These lectures appeared in book form in 1917: *Einführung in die Missionswissenschaft*. He also held seminars on the bibliography and sources of mission history. Moreover, he succeeded in getting Professor Meinertz to lecture one semester on mission texts in Scripture. It was in response to his proposal that a chair for comparative religion was set up in 1912 to complement the lectures on missiology. From 1913 on, Professor Ebers in the faculty of law lectured on church law as obtaining in the missions, while Schmidlin himself spoke on normative and practical mission theory. A chair of missiology was formally established in 1914.

His aim, as explained in a memo to the faculty in 1911, was the setting up of a missiological institute at university level, which would comprehend the whole range of related missiological subjects: missionography and mission history, mission theory and mission methodology, comparative religion, ethnology, and linguistics. But such a university institute never materialized.

Already in the fall of 1909, Schmidlin was approached about the publication of a missiological journal by Father Friedrich Schwager, S.V.D., who had pursued this idea for many years and now believed that in Schmidlin he had found a suitable editor. Even Schmidlin hesitated: "What put me off was, on the one hand, the size and the difficulty of the proposed task, and, on the other, its novelty, which would impose on me the necessity of leaving the areas of church history well known to me and venturing into an almost unknown terrain whose extent could not be perceived."[14] But in the end he agreed to become editor-in-chief of the new journal, *Zeitschrift für Missionswissenschaft*. A team of colleagues was to help him in the work; for the first year this comprised seven university professors, Monsignor Baumgartner, and seven representatives of missionary congregations. Schmidlin's aim was a "harmonious wedding of mission and science, a synthesis on which the theorists and practitioners, the representatives of theology in the home countries and in the missions could easily agree."[15] Father Schwager moved to Münster to give him a hand. Cardinal Fischer of Cologne contributed the foreword to the first issue. The journal became in time a mine of missiological research and information. Besides book reviews and bibliographical reports, many of its essays were of lasting interest. Schmidlin himself provided sixty-two pages of text in the first year: his two articles "Die katholische Missionswissenschaft" (pp. 10-21) and "System und Zweige der Missionswissenschaft" (pp.106-22) were already very basic. His choice of themes and writers shows his openness and breadth of vision. His efforts found a great response from the very start. In order to support these missiological undertakings financially, especially the publications, the Internationale Institut für missionswissenschaftliche Forschungen was founded on August 10, 1911, as an autonomous institute, situated first in Münster, and later transferred to Aachen. Schmidlin became the director of the scientific commission of this institute. But the planned internationalization never really came about. The institute supported the publication of the *Zeitschrift für Missionswissenschaft* and the publication of the *Biblioteca Missionum*. It was the publisher of the two series of *Missionswissenschaftliche Abhandlungen und Texte* (14 tracts appeared before World War II); and of *Missionswissenschaftliche Studien* (9 tracts in all, discontinued after World War II). The series *Missionstudienwochen* was begun after World War II and likewise published by the institute. It is remarkable how quickly the missionary congregations responded and how many of their members decided to make a special study of missiology. Already on July 19, 1915, Father Anton Freitag, S.V.D., and Father Maurus Galm, O.S.B., obtained their doctorates in theology with dissertations on missiology. A year later, Father Laurence Kilger, O.S.B., did likewise. There were fourteen such doctorates awarded in Münster in Schmidlin's time and twenty-three in the first fifty years after the chair in missiology was established. All the recipients, with the exception of Jean Pierre Belche, who was a parish priest and national director of the pontifical mission works in Luxembourg, were members of religious congregations: five Divine Word missionaries, three Benedictines, three Capuchins, two Pallotines, two Oblates, two Sacred Heart missionaries, and one each from the Dominicans, Bethlehemites, Holy Spirit Fathers (Spiritans), Franciscans, and Marianhill missionaries.

Schmidlin is commonly regarded as the founder of a "school" of missiology – the Münster school. Is this really correct? Certainly he cannot be associated with the classic plantation theory of Pierre Charles, S.J. (Louvain). It seems to me, however, that one cannot identify Schmidlin with any school. Chronologically he was before them, and his ideas were of such general validity that they cannot be enclosed within the narrow confines of this or that school.

In his *Einführung in die Missionswissenschaft* (1917), Schmidlin deduces the mission of the church from the biblical text "As the Father has sent me, even so I send you," and so distinguishes a twofold task for the church: "1. to proclaim and spread the Christian faith and the Christian gospel and so, of necessity, propagate itself, and 2. to preserve and strengthen this faith and this church."[16] He distinguishes between "mission in the subjective sense" (missionary activity) and "mission in the objective sense" (missionary works). The first he defines as "that ecclesiastical activity whose aim it is to plant and spread the Christian religion and church,[17] and then to preserve it"; the second is "the totality of all ecclesiastical organizations which serve the spread of the faith."[18] He feels that there is also some sense in regarding Catholics as the "object" of mission, "especially those who outwardly count as church members but who, because of lack of faith or sin, are dead or estranged members, who stand in need of conversion anew."[19] For practical and historical reasons, however, he defines mission as "the spreading of the faith among non-Christians." While Warneck accepts three stages in the aim of mission – developing the mature Christian, the independent community, and the organized church – Schmidlin considers the "confession of Christian teaching" (with simultaneous reception of baptism) and the "grafting into the church" to be two aspects of the one mission, a "twofold function found inseparable in the aim of Catholic mission."[20] Later, in his *Missionslehre*, he distinguishes more clearly between the individual and social aims of mission, but he still holds firmly that "for the mission of the Catholic church the question doesn't arise in this absolute form, and the solution can only be individual conversion *and* the christianization of a people. Mission must strive for both and unite both, if not at the same time then in successive development; on the one hand, it should seek to convert the individual, or rather individuals, and on the other, to join these individuals together in community, that through it the whole people may be renewed in Christ."[21]

Schmidlin was hardly fifty-eight years old when he fell foul of the National Socialist system, which was to crush him mercilessly. He himself describes the end of his academic career in simple but moving words:

> The growth of the missiological faculty and seminar in Münster, which had given so much promise, was suddenly cut off, chiefly by my retirement in the summer semester 1934, at first at my own suggestion, but in the end by force. After I had begun a fifth series of lectures in that semester on ancient Christian and medieval mission history, I changed it into a seminar in which we treated the Indian missions of the past two years. Then, in the ensuing winter semester, I was forbidden by the rector to enter the university and a successor in the person of Prof. Lortz was appointed for the summer semester 1935.[22]

Schmidlin and Home Support for the Missions

Schmidlin, at his deepest level always a priest, pursued not only missiological but also practical missionary objectives. Already in March 1909 he urged his students in Münster to found an academic missionary association. His appeal fell on receptive ears, and on June 10, 1910, the first constituent meeting of the Akademischer Missionsverein was held with 100 students of Münster university and 175 from the Borromäum (seminary) taking part. After the solemn opening Mass, 600 students joined the association.[23] It turned out to be extraordinarily active, sending out invitations far and wide to the very best speakers.

Other colleges soon followed the example of Münster: the clerical seminary in Passau on February 26, 1911; Tübingen University (with 230 association members) on December 1, 1911; the seminary in Freising on February 6, 1912; St. Peter's Seminary in Baden on March 5, 1913; and soon afterward the house of studies for priests in Bonn, and many others. The Catholic Academic Association formed an Akademischer Missionsbund (missionary union) in 1920. From 1913 on, the academic missionary associations had their own paper, *Akademische Missionsblätter.*[24]

On January 22, 1912, Schmidlin, in the course of a lecture for the clergy of the city of Münster, called for a rise in contributions to the missions and for a discussion on the need for the clergy in the homeland to organize themselves into a mission association. Once more his proposal was readily accepted, and on May 7, the Missionsvereinigung des Münsterschen Diözensanklerus was inaugurated. There were 300 participants at the first meeting. The dioceses of Treves, Cologne, Paderborn, Strassburg, and others soon followed suit. All these diocesan units later merged in the Unio Cleri pro Missionibus founded in Italy in 1916 after the pattern begun in Münster.

Another of his great wishes was to found a missionary society of German diocesan priests. In 1930 he composed a memo on this theme, which was later published in the *Zeitschrift für Missionswissenschaft.*[25] In 1913-14 he made many a journey to the Far East. His intentions in doing so were concrete and specific, "not just a grandiose program of setting up mission universities and printing presses, but also the recommending of an international association to gather financial support, and a mission training society to prepare the necessary personnel."[26] Neither the missionary society of German diocesan priests nor the international association ever got off the ground. But they illustrate the breadth and vitality of Schmidlin's interest and imagination.

Schmidlin was also the organizer and animator of courses in missiology for the most diverse audiences: in 1916 there was a course for the clergy of Cologne, in 1917 for teachers in Münster, in 1919 for missionaries in Düsseldorf, in 1919-20 for missionaries home on leave in Münster, in 1925 for diocesan and religious priests in Steyl, in 1925 for academics in Siegburg, in 1926 and 1930 in St. Ottilien and Münster. He also played a decisive role in other congresses not organized by himself, for example, at Mödling/Vienna (1924 and 1929), Budapest (1925), Leitmeritz (1926), Poznań (1927), Würzburg (1928), Leibach (1930), and Freiburg, Switzerland (1932).

It must be added that the idea of having the theme of mission handled at the university level also caught on elsewhere. Thus in Munich missiological questions were treated by Königer in 1912, in Breslau by Seppelt in 1911, in Strassburg by Bastgen in 1912, in Hamburg by Schmidlin, Schwager, and Streit from 1911 to 1913, in Würzburg by Weber and Zahn in 1915. A lectureship in mission history and comparative religion (Professor Aufhauser) was set up in Munich in 1919. After World War I, the missiological movement passed on to other places too, especially to Rome, where the Urban College set up an institute and the Gregorian University established a chair for missiology. Professor Ohm, O.S.B., Schmidlin's successor in missiology on the faculty at Münster, was not exaggerating when he said, "It is impossible to think of missiology and mission history without Schmidlin. For a long time he was mistrusted or even rejected in many missiological circles. But he won through all the same. Catholic missiology gained a secure place in the curriculum of universities and developed into an independent, well-defined, clear-sighted and true science. It has, thanks to Schmidlin's exertions, reached a position that commands attention."[27]

Posterity has not really been fair to Schmidlin. His early forced retirement and, above all, his wild reactions to everything and everyone, whether pope or king or subject, were largely responsible for his being judged unfavorably. He said what he thought and was no respecter of persons. But, for all that, he deserves an honorable place in history. Not without reason has he been called the father of Catholic missiology. So much can be traced back to his inspiration and untiring zeal; so much is of permanent value. He maintained his own position clearly as distinct from the views of Protestant missiologists, notably Gustav Warneck. On the other hand, however, he is a great deal closer to them than is the "Louvain school." This, in these ecumenical days, is something positive. In Vatican Council II some central ideas of the "Louvain school" doubtless made an impact. But the "Münster school" was also represented and made its presence felt. Both were good and necessary.

If in some places today the idea of mission has been relegated to the background, one could only wish for another Schmidlin, one who would perhaps be calmer and more balanced, but who would add his weight to the missionary cause with the same clear-sightedness, energy, and love that were peculiarly his. Schmidlin was indeed a pioneer whose legacy has left its imprint on Catholic missiology.

Notes

1. *Zeitschrift für Missionswissenschaft* (ZM) 14 (1924):247. The chief sources of information on Schmidlin's life and work are the following articles: Schmidlin's own autobiography, found in E. Stange's *Die Religionswissenschaft der Gegenwart in Selbstdarstellungen* (Leipzig: Felix Meiner, 1927); L. Kilger, O.S.B., "Ein Lustrum katholischer Missionswissenschaft in Deutschland," *ZM* 6 (1916):1-15; J. Schmidlin, "Was wir wollen," ibid. 1 (1911): 5-10; "Wie unsere Missionswissenschaft entstand," *Zeitschrift für Missions und Religionswissenschaft (ZMR)* 21 (1931): 1-18; "Lehrstuhl und Seminar für Missionswissenschaft," ibid. 25 (1935): 226-34; obituaries by J. Beckmann, S.M.B., in *Bethlehem* 49 (1944): 442-45, and T. Ohm, O.S.B., in *Missions und Religionswissenschaft (MR)* 32 (1947): 3-11; K. Müller, S.V.D., "Joseph Schmidlin, Leben und Werk," in *50 Jahre katholischer Missionswissenschaft in Münster* ed. J. Glazik, M.S.C. (Münster: Verlag Aschendorff, 1961), pp. 22-23; E. Hegel, "Der Lehrstuhl für Missionswissenschaft und die missionswissenschaftlichen Studienrichtungen in der kath-theolog. Fakultät Münster," in ibid., pp. 3-21.

2. Dr. K. Gschwind, parish priest, Allschwil, in Basel deanery newspaper, 1944, p. 503.

3. Autobiography, *Josef Schmidlin,* p. 168.

4. Ibid., pp. 168-69.

5. Thus Hegel, "Der Lehrstuhl," p. 5, according to Schmidlin's personal file in the Cath. theol. faculty, Munster.

6. The mission bibliographer R. Streit, O.M.I., calls the *Missionshlehre* "epoch-making in German mission literature" (*Die katholische deutsche Missionsliteratur* [Aachen: Xavierusverlagsbuchhandlung, 1925], p. 127). Bishop Hennemann, P.S.M., called it "a literary event" and stressed its clear definitions, exact arrangement, all-round elucidation, brilliant mastery of the apposite literature, and splendid review of history (*ZM* 9, [1919]:204). It has been translated into English as *Catholic Mission Theory* (Techny, Ill.: Mission Press, 1931).

7. The *Missionsgeschichte* has been translated into Italian by G. Tragella, P.I.M.E. (Milan: Pontificio Institute Missioni Estere, 1927-29) and into English by M. Braun, S.V.D. (Techny, Ill.: Mission Press, 1933).

8. Notes for a conference on Schmidlin. To round off the picture of Schmidlin it must be added that before he took his degree he worked zealously as assistant priest in Gebweiler. As a young private lecturer, he also worked as a priest in the Antoniusstift, and later as chaplain to Count Hatzfeld in Dyckburg. During World War I, he organized the rescue of missions in the East endangered by the Turks. He also took spiritual care of those in a prisoner-of-war camp and gathered its French theology students together there into a wartime seminary. He worked a good deal for the poor (see Müller, "Schmidlin," pp. 23-24).

9. Hegel, "Der Lehrstuhl," p. 16.

10. According to information received from Dr. Clauss, archepiscopal archivist in Freiburg i.B. According to T. Ohm he was starved to death and his corpse left lying in the prison for days (*MR* 32 [1947]: 10.

11. Swiss church paper 112 (1944): 236.

12. Thus Karl Graul in his famous trial lecture at Erlangen, 1864. Cf. O. Myklebust, *The Study of Missions in Theological Education* vol. 1 (Oslo: Egede Instituttet, 1955), pp. 94-95.

13. From a conference of R. Streit at the Berlin Conference of the Mission Commission of the Katholiken-tag. Cf. *ZMR* 21 (1931): 8-9.

14. *ZM* 1 (1911): 5.

15. The name of the Münster journal changed through the years. Beginning in 1911 as *Zeitschrift für Missionswissenschaft* (ZM), the name changed to *Zeitschrift für Missionswissenschaft und Religionswissenschaft* (ZMR) in 1928. It returned briefly to *ZM* in 1936 and 1937, then changed to *Missionswissenschaft und Religionswissenschaft* (MR) for the years 1938 to 1949 (suspended 1942-46). From 1950 to the present it has been known by the earlier title *Zeitschrift für Missionswissenschaft und Religionswissenschaft*. During the *MR* period, volume numbers did not reflect the series as a whole. (*ZMR* should not be confused with a Protestant journal with a similar title published in Berlin.)

16. *Einführung in die Missionswissenschaft*, 1st ed. (Münster: Verlag Aschendorff, 1917), pp. 46-47. It is interesting that *Ad gentes* (AG) – Vatican II's document on the missions – speaks in its first five chapters of the "mission of the church" in general, and only in chap. 6 defines the specific term "missionary activity." Schmidlin had done likewise.

17. Ibid, p. 48. Cf. AG 6.

18. *Einführung*, p. 48. Schmidlin is thinking here of the house or group in which or from which mission proceeds, or again of a mission limited by place or specific personnel, such as the mission in Honduras or the Franciscan missions. AG stands by the geographical idea of mission. *Evangelii nuntiandi* (EN) – the apostolic exhortation of Paul VI on evangelization in the modern world (1975) – speaks of the missionary and of missionary activity but steers clear of the word "mission" as a geographical determination.

19. *Einführung*, p. 51. AG 6 is also aware of conditions which "demand a new onset of missionary activity." EN 56 speaks very fully of the "evangelization" of the nonpracticing but does not specifically make them the object of mission.

20. *Einführung*, p. 56.

21. *Katholische Missionslehre im Grundriss*, 2nd ed. (Münster: Verlag Aschendorff, 1923), pp. 243-44. For Schmidlin the word "conversion" means the profession of Christian teaching on the one hand, and baptism in the name of the Trinity, on the other (*Einführung*, p. 55).

22. *ZMR* 25 (1935): 232.

23. At the opening meeting speeches were made by Auxiliary Bishop Illigens, Prince Löwenstein, Abbot Weber, O.S.B., and Professors Mausbach and Schmidlin. Ulms, the general secretary, reported: "Within the next few days the young association could count about 1,000 members from all faculties and student groups. However skeptical the anticipations of some may have been as to how things would develop, this surprising outcome proved all doubts unfounded; it surpassed the greatest expectations" (*ZMR* 25 [1935]: 237).

24. See Ulms, "Fünf Lustren akademischer Missionsbewegung in Deutschland," *ZMR* 25 (1935): 234-42.

25. Schmidlin, "Deutsche Weltpriestermission und Priestermissionsvereinigung," *ZMR* 25 (1935): 51-53; see also Schmidlin, "Denkschrift über eine deutsche Weltpriestermission," *ZM* 26 (1936): 25-29.

26. Autobiography, p. 180.

27. *MR* 32 (1947): 7.

Pierre Charles, S.J.

1883–1954

Advocate of Acculturation

Joseph Masson, S.J.

Pierre Charles was born in Brussels on July 3, 1883. He became a Jesuit on September 23, 1899, and was ordained to the priesthood on August 24, 1910. He died at Louvain, the principal and final scene of his activities, on February 11, 1954.

Father Charles was of medium height, but solidly built and with broad shoulders. Throughout his entire life, and especially during the years of his priestly life, he resolutely arose before dawn and retired late at night, devoting all his time to study, prayer, and human associations. His understanding of the needs of both church and world grew within the context of wide scholarship, served by a prodigious memory and supported by a quick and subtle intelligence. He was a man who looked intently at people and things from under large, bushy eyebrows and through thick eyeglasses. That, however, was his only myopia.

A "Man Alive"

One who attempts to sketch the main characteristics of Pierre Charles's personality should begin by noting the expansiveness of his outlook and of his intellectual and religious horizons. He was wondrously interested in the world. Chesterton would have called him a "man alive," and indeed he shared some of Chesterton's own humorous and paradoxical nature. Born in a small country, he relished every opportunity throughout his life to travel beyond its borders.

The excitement of Pierre Charles about the missionary activities of his Belgian Jesuit mentors on the Zambezi dates to his high school days. From the beginning of his religious training he went beyond a perfunctory devotional life, combining the force of "catholic" doctrine and an interest in "worldly" realities into one and the same vigorous piety. His superiors contributed intelligently to that broad development by sending him to study philosophy with the German Jesuits who were then residing in Holland, and later to study theology with French Jesuits who were at that time refugees at Hastings in England (1907-1910).

The period of his religious formation was a time troubled by the problems of modernism, the synthesis of reason and revelation, science and faith, the Christ of faith and the historical Jesus, God and humankind, and so forth. Father Charles, a man of vigorous mind as well as a faithful

Christian, found the discussions about such matters an opportunity to deepen his own intellectual and spiritual life. One of his fundamental characteristics was a strong attachment to the essentials, mixed with freedom of thought. "Safe" people, he would say, are those who do not have ideas of their own. As for him, he was teeming with ideas; he verified and enriched them in Paris where he came into contact with widely contrasting viewpoints such as those found in the thought of Kant and Bergson. Later on, in America, Africa, India, and Ceylon, his hunger for human associations and experiences continued unabated. Thus his exceedingly open and well-informed mind was firmly established. He was, moreover, remarkably multilingual, mastering English, German, Portuguese, Spanish, and Italian in addition to French, Latin, and Greek.

Pierre Charles remained a faithful priest, and his concept of the priestly and apostolic life was heightened and broadened amid all these influences. Those who want to have an account of it, without spending the time necessary to examine his course notes in detail, will do well to read some of his hundred meditations given in *La Prière de Toutes les Heures,* of which more than 100,000 copies were printed, and others from *La Prière de Toutes les Choses.* Those titles are significant in themselves, introducing us to a second characteristic of Father Charles's personality.

For want of a better term, we may call it a mentality of *incarnation.* To so vital a man, religion, that is to say Christian faith and life, cannot be reduced to a simple compartment of existence, limited in time, space, and purpose. In each and every person, Christian and non-Christian alike, and in the entire cosmos, it is something experienced and wrought by grace. He wrote, "The earth is the only road by which we are led to heaven." For him all land is Holy Land, all history Sacred History – if not already in fact, at least in hope and potential. All humanity waits to become the people of God; the church is designed to take the world upon itself in its ascent.

Teilhardism before Teilhard? Yes and no. Around 1920, Pierre Charles had indeed expressed his opinion precisely on the manuscript of *Le Milieu Divin.* He evaluated it favorably, but added some comments of his own. In effect, despite his optimism, the reality of sin in a humanity that is incapable of redeeming itself, and the need for a Redeemer who (as *Ad Gentes* puts it) "cleanses, assumes and uplifts" the whole of creation, both human and subhuman, had always been clear to him. An indication of that conviction can be seen in the first proposition of a theological treatise entitled "The Incarnation of the Word," which he completed only fifteen days before his death and which is one of his most brilliant contributions. He says in it: "The object of the first divine decree was Christ as the head of the universe; the Incarnation would not have taken place if man had not sinned."

In his view of the world as a whole, he saw the richness of its spiritual character just as clearly as the lacunas. He also saw its absolute need of Christ – and the need for Christians, those who have received him, to bring this Christ to others.

If I am not mistaken, Pierre Charles's intense preoccupation with and activity on behalf of the missions grew out of all that has been described above: a deep and robust faith; an "appetite" for associations with people; a progressively wider international experience; a Christian view of the riches, needs, and aspirations of humanity as a whole; an almost prophetic eagerness to see the church become truly universal, rooted in all the world's diversity and cultural pluralism, as soon as possible.

In 1953 he wrote: "The mission is the bearer not only of doctrine and the means to eternal salvation, but also of a 'way of life.' This culture can and should reflect all the varieties to which its adaptation leads in the different human societies it penetrates" ("Mission et Acculturation," in *Nouvelle Revue Théologique,* 1953, p. 27). In substance, therefore, he was already contending for what, in today's terminology, we call incarnation, contextualization, and so forth.

Father Charles was, alas, too much in demand from all quarters and too incapable of refusing such requests, to have enough time left for minutely shaping his theological and missiological intuitions. By temperament, moreover, he was primarily an initiator of new and original ideas. He had a fondness for the research method of St. Thomas Aquinas in which one replies to whatever affirmation is made by saying: "It seems not to be so (*videtur quod non*)." It is an approach that irritates many orderly thinkers but, if applied to the hundreds of theological concepts that enjoy perfunctory acceptance, it can lead to often decisive refinements or insights. I may note in passing that the novel effects of this method were especially pleasing to the youthful audiences of religious and lay people whom the professor frequently addressed both in the line of duty and for his own enjoyment.

At the end of one of his meditations, Pierre Charles noted: "We have many professors, but what the world needs is seers!" Beginning in 1923-1924, after World War I and during the awakening of Asia and Africa, Father Charles developed the great issues now taken for granted but then much debated. These were discussed in lectures and in the Semaines de Missiologie that he directed at Louvain until 1950: the value of non-Christian cultures and religions; the spiritual competence of non-Christians, even the "primitives" as they were called; the missionary vocation of every Christian as a member of the body of Christ in growth toward its fullness; the need to have communities and local churches living in their own cultures and entrusted to local pastors; the role of the laity (in this matter he did not hesitate to use Protestant examples); and the advancement of women.

As typical example of this "foresight," much ahead of its time in the Roman Church at least, he advocated – as early as 1933 – the reestablishment of a permanent diaconate in the church. When objections were raised on the grounds that it was contrary to canon law, his reply seemed almost blasphemous in those days: Then let the canon law be changed if that is what it takes!

Incarnational Church Planting

Readers may ask what all the foregoing details have to do with a theology of mission. The answer is that they are enormously relevant, assuming that theology is not an intellectual game but a way of conceiving and living Christianity as leaven in the world. Those who knew Father Charles personally (and I had that privilege) can only smile or lose patience when intellectually myopic commentators interpret his favorite expression, "the planting of the church," as a "juridical" theory. It is, on the contrary, the liveliest and most dynamic of expressions, and it comes to us from long ago.

The Old Testament refers more than once to the people of God as a vine that their Lord plants or uproots. The same idea is reflected in *The Ascension of Isaiah* (3.3), a very old Hebrew document subject to Christian interpolations: "They will molest the planting that the apostles have planted." Jesus himself uses the words *tree* and *vine* in reference to the church; Paul employs the figure of the olive tree (Rom. 11:17, 24); Irenaeus, in *Adv. Haer.* (5.20, 22) has this phrase: "plantata est Ecclesia paradisus in hoc mundo"; and the Roman Breviary says that the apostles planted the church with their blood (not with laws – even those unquestionably legislated, beginning with the Council of Jerusalem).

For Pierre Charles, planting means a vital insertion into the human matrix, into a sociocultural whole, in such a way that the whole of the Gospel and of the church enters the whole life of a people. And the process is reciprocal. Father Charles underscored two aspects: mission *does* it, and mission *should* do it.

"The missionary activity of the Church is not at all identical with the [eventual] total conversion of a country; it involves not only religious and moral preaching, but the whole social and even material task: teaching, bricks and mortar, charitable works, professional services, and relief" (from the course given in Rome between 1932 and 1938). So much for the *deed*.

And now for the *duty*. It is based at the same time on a theology of the Redeemer and of those to be redeemed. "The Church is the divine form of the world, the only point of encounter by which the entire work of the Creator turns to the Redeemer; the only junction point in which the Redeemer himself enters into possession of his universal heritage" (from his course in Rome).

Further, "the Church accepts us as we are, and not as pure spirits" (*Prière missionnaire*, p. 8). "It is not merely with souls that the Church is concerned; it is the equilibrium of the world as a whole and its eternal value that it conserves and consecrates" (*Études missiologiques*, p. 37). Thus "the sanctification of the world is not only spiritual but also a very material task. Wherever the Church is propagated it should, by reason of its very structure and nature, promote the benefits of health, knowledge, social peace, decent life and holy joy, both for its own members and for those who are not yet members. Those responsibilities are not all outside the function of church planting but are very much included in it" (from his course in Rome).

Thus the goal is envisaged as "when the Church has become solidly established throughout the world, with her clergy locally recruited, her sacraments within reach of all sincere people of good will, her preaching available to all who are not willfully deaf, her laity disciplined and busy, her congregations both active and contemplative, with the salutary joy that she brings to her children" (*Études missiologiques*, p. 240). Those words were written in 1932. "The Church is not satisfied with saving people, but in bringing them to maturity in accordance with all their abilities" (from his course in Rome). Those words also date from 1932.

The missiology of Pierre Charles, as we have seen, is filled with his concept of the church, but it is a living church, a communion. Everything proceeds from the grace of Christ, the Head; and everything is directed to the whole of humanity, the environment of the church's life. In the power of the Trinity all that comes from God returns to God. And the church aids in it.

A Legacy Affirmed

Pierre Charles died in 1954. What has happened since then to his ideas and ideals? In substance they seem more current than ever. His books, reprinted more than once, are still used. Recently a university student who had just read the anthology entitled *Études missiologiques* declared, "That reads like a novel!" The living, imaginative style does, in fact, remain captivating. Whenever the present writer quotes from Father Charles in lectures or sermons, as he has often done and continues to do, invariably someone in the audience comes up to ask for the name of the author and the title of the book.

The major testimony to the lasting value of Pierre Charles's great contributions is, however, much more eloquent. It is seen by comparing them with the documents of Vatican Council II. The planting of the church, a phrase we all recognize as the key to his teaching, figures in the Council's definition of the aim of mission (*Ad Gentes*, no. 6). The mystical body of Christ as the dynamic motor of mission, a concept dear to Father Charles, is recaptured in the *Ad Gentes* expression "the life that Christ communicates to his members" (no. 5), and again as that which constitutes "the deep requirement of catholicity" (no. 1).

Another of Pierre Charles's favorite concepts, the church as the "divine form of the world" to lead all to the Redeemer, surfaced at the Council in numerous texts that recommend appropriating everything good in whatever religious and secular spheres the world offers. The entire constitution *Gaudium et Spes* is the implementation of that particular emphasis.

Some of the specific issues for which Father Charles fought, because in his day they were still challenged, have henceforth been taken for granted: the restoration of the diaconate, which he proposed in 1933, appears in *Lumen Gentium* (no. 29) and in *Ad Gentes* (no. 16); preference for local clergy, which he advocated from 1926, is the recommendation of *Ad Gentes* (no. 16); the acculturation process he foresaw from the outset, and systematized in 1953, is treated in various paragraphs of *Ad Gentes* and in an entire section of *Gaudium et Spes* (nos. 54-62); respect for and dialogue with the non-Christian religions, and the idea that certain aspects of Christianity are reinforced by them (a concept found in Pierre Charles's teaching from 1935 onward), comes to flower in the *Nostra Aetate* declaration and in the establishment of the Secretariat for the Non-Christian Religions.

Pierre Charles long and vigorously advocated a church visibly present and with established hierarchy, but he also emphasized the nature of that church as mystical body and communion (an emphasis some commentators have failed to note). All this is reflected in the appeal of *Lumen Gentium* (no. 8) for a necessary equilibrium.

There are two ways by which an author many become outdated. The first is by being so completely identified with and limited to his own era that he is destined for that very reason to disappear with it. Such, in fact, is the fate of all who attempt to be strictly "contemporary," and we may therefore be apprehensive about the future outcome of some very "contemporary" theories. The second way is to set forth ideas that can wait because they have permanent value. This can be done only by one who is ahead of his time or, to put it more precisely, one who is sensitive to issues of future and more universal appeal. Being durable, such ideas are absorbed little by little into the general, popular opinion. Thus the ideas that were earlier challenged become "the obvious," axioms so taken for granted that origin and author are forgotten, even when the substance is utilized and the formulas repeated.

In this second way Pierre Charles is becoming outdated. His concept of the church as body of Christ and sacrament of the world, with all the breadth of horizon and meaning implied in that, has now become part of our universal mentality. It is no small achievement to have contributed toward its coming to flower in the Christian and missionary mind.

Selected Bibliography

Major Works by Pierre Charles

1927-29 *Dossiers de l'action missionnaire.* Louvain: Editions de l'Aucam. 2nd ed., 1939.

1932 *Principes et méthodes de l'activité missionnaire en dehors du Catholicisme.* Louvain: Editions de l'Aucam.

1932-1938 "Cours de dogmatique missionnaire." Unpublished syllabus (in Latin) of course taught by Father Charles at the Gregorian University in Rome.

1935 *La prière missionnaire.* Louvain: Editions de l'Aucam. 3rd ed., 1947.

1939 *Missiologie* (an anthology). Louvain: Editions de l'Aucam.

1956 *Études missiologiques.* Bruges: Desclée de Brouwer. A comprehensive bibliography is found on pp. 423-32.

Works about Pierre Charles

Clarke, F.X. "The Purpose of Missions." Diss., Missionary Union of the Clergy, New York, 1948.

Levie, J. "In Memoriam: Le P.P. Charles." In *Nouvelle Revue Théologique*, pp. 254-73. Tournai: Casterman, 1954.

Masson, Joseph. "Fonction missionnaire, Fonction d'église." *Nouvelle Revue Théologique*, December, 1958 and January 1959.

_____. "Introduction." In *Études missiologiques*, pp. 7-11. Louvain: Desclé de Brouwer, 1956.

Paulon, J. "Plantatio Ecclesiae, il Fine Specifico delle Missioni." Diss., Unione Missionaria del Clero, Rome, 1948.

All Catholic historical works on missiological theory, up to the present, cite Pierre Charles, either to approve or to challenge. Some bits of information prior to 1955 are found in *Bibliografia Missionaria,* published annually in Rome. We learn, for example, that *La prière missionnaire* was again translated into Italian, Spanish, and Portuguese after the death of the author. Many articles were republished in different languages even without the knowledge of the author, who, as a matter of fact, was little concerned about what was done with his works.

Kenneth Scott Latourette
1884–1968

Interpreter of the Expansion of Christianity

William Richey Hogg

K enneth Scott Latourette (August 8, 1884-December 26, 1968) remains the twentieth century's towering figure in American missiology, and his worldwide influence continues. His adequate assessment requires a greater distance in time than is now available to place his contribution in proper historical perspective. A quarter of a century has passed since his death – only 100 feet from his Oregon home and at night when an automobile struck and killed him – so perhaps it is now possible to provide a brief and preliminary consideration of his legacy.

The Man

All who read these pages know Latourette's name and have benefited from his writings. Yet who was he? To answer that question one can turn to several sources that provide useful information. Fortunately, we have his 1967 autobiography[1] and also the Association of Professors of Missions' 1960 *Festschrift*.[2] The latter includes Latourette's taped address, "My Guided Life," E. Theodore Bachmann's splendid chapter on him, and the Yale Librarians' "Select Bibliography." Many memorial articles appeared in journals shortly after his death, but here only Searle Bates's "Christian Historian, Doer of Christian History: In Memory of Kenneth Scott Latourette, 1884-1968" in the *International Review of Mission*[3] can be included.

Much in what follows supplements the foregoing from personal recollection, and documentation will be kept to a minimum. Headed for China, I went to Yale (1943-1946 and 1947-1950) to study under Latourette. I lived in the same dormitory in which he did – from his arrival at Yale and as a bachelor, he had chosen to live on the campus to be near his office and the convenience of the dining hall and to provide in his suite with its living room a convenient meeting place for student groups – and our common interests provided a close bond. With the refectory closed on Sundays, for six years on that day "Uncle Ken," as many students addressed him, and I shared in my room a simple breakfast and supper. For two years (1944-1946) I served as his secretary and for several years participated in one of his weekly student groups. I also was privileged to spend parts of two summers – the first in 1947 writing *Tomorrow Is Here* – in his old Oregon family home. He officiated at our wedding when his niece and I were married in Oregon, and after our return from India in 1955, he visited our home annually. The foregoing suggests some of the background from which this is written, with close friendship needing to be weighed as it relates to perspective and judgment.

The Formative Years. Latourette's early years must be sketched briefly, but their elaboration appears in *Beyond the Ranges.* Each of his capable parents had earned an M.A. and had taught in college before their marriage – a rather remarkable background in the Pacific Northwest in the 1880s – but his father went on to become a lawyer and banker in the small town of Oregon City. The family was knit together in deep Christian faith, family worship, and pietistic Baptist church life. Young Ken worked for his father for two years, planned to follow in his footsteps, and was graduated as valedictorian with a B.S. in natural sciences from Linfield College (Baptist). Yet at a summer conference when he signed the Student Volunteer Movement (SVM) Declaration, he took a decisive step that would shape his life.

Already holding a degree, he crossed the continent and was allowed in one year to complete a B.A. in history at Yale in 1906. Then came a second decisive turning point. Asked to join Yale-in-China, he completed his M.A. and Ph.D. in history by 1909. Meanwhile, he had organized and guided a group of Bible study classes, each with its own leader, totaling some 350 students, and had attended Moody's Northfield Conferences each summer. In 1909-1910, at age twenty-five, he began his "missionary career" by traveling for the SVM. The following summer, just missing Edinburgh 1910 by days, he went by way of Europe and the Trans-Siberian Railway to China.

In September at Changsha, he began his responsibilities for the year, chief of which was Chinese language study, but the following summer he suffered a severe bout of amoebic dysentery. Through the fall, at the very time of Sun Yat-sen's revolution, although the prolonged, painful treatment seemed to be successful, he had suffered – unknown to him then, but with lifelong reminders – permanent colonic damage. His strength did not return, and so in March 1912 he returned to Oregon. He had been in China for twenty months and would never return, but in 1938 the Chinese government decorated him with the Order of Jade for his contribution to China through writing.

Two years of slow recovery followed in Oregon. During 1914-1916, he taught part-time at Reed College in Portland, developed Far Eastern courses, and wrote *The Development of China.* From 1916 to 1921 he served at Denison, a Baptist college in Granville, Ohio, as professor of history with courses in Far Eastern and Russian history. There he wrote *The Development of Japan,* also published his dissertation, launched a course on Christianity's missionary expansion, and began gathering materials for his *History of Christian Missions in China.* He declined a post in the Far Eastern section of the State Department, but was ordained in 1918 and thus also became chaplain at Denison. In 1921 at age thirty-seven and succeeding Harlan Page Beach, he became D. Willis James Professor of Missions ("and Oriental History" added in 1927) at Yale. From that university he retired in 1953.

The Latourette Era. Occasionally references appear to "the Mott Era" or "the Edinburgh [1910] Era" or "the Latourette Era." All three are related. The termini are not sharply drawn but usually begin with the 1886 founding of the SVM with its watchword, "The evangelization of the world in this generation." They end usually between 1948 and 1961, or even 1962-1965, the Vatican II years, when the ecumenical reality entered upon a decisive new stage.

Those years included the rise and decline of the Student Christian Movement (SCM) and the World's Student Christian Federation (WSCF), the peaking of the overseas sending mission of the major Western Protestant churches, the Social Gospel movement, the fundamentalist/modernist controversy in the United States, the two world wars, the Russian revolution and Maoist China, the rise of neo-orthodoxy, the West's growing pessimism beginning in the 1920s, and the growing belief in secularization, Christianity's decline, and the "post-Christian Age."

The era shaped Latourette, but he also left his imprint on it. From World War II onward, he sought to present a larger and, he believed, truer picture of Christianity than many Westerners with an increasingly pessimistic view could see. He wrote as a major era in mission and in Western European world hegemony was ending and also amid a massive political, technological, and cultural transition among the world's peoples. Published during World War II, his *Expansion* achieved a unique *kairos* amid the shifting dynamics of the Christian *oikoumene*.

Time Perspectives. To understand Latourette adequately, one needs to recall his long perspective on time. He began his study of geology at Linfield, continued it at Yale, and maintained it as a lifelong interest. As geologists do, he thought in aeons. To illustrate: if the 1,250-foot-high Empire State Building (on a scale in which 1 inch equals 313,333 years), represents this planet's geologic lifespan (ca. 4.7 billion years), then, if atop it one were to place two razor blades – one on the other – the first would represent two thousand years of Old Testament and the second two thousand years of Christian history. From such a perspective he often referred to Christianity's youth.

He had an equivalent interest in astronomy and knew that the universe is at least twice as old as our solar system. Like the psalmist, he saw in all this the glory of God's handiwork. It also enabled him to place human history in a magisterial perspective that most folk find difficult to comprehend. Geologic and astral time provided the time-matrix for his writing on the "brief span" of Christianity.

Biblical Understanding. Many have accused Latourette of naïve and uncritical – even literalistic – use of the Bible. Such judgments need to be assessed within the perspective noted above and placed in context. Latourette had a first-rate collection of works on critical biblical scholarship, and he had read them. He also had studied the history of biblical scholarship and saw in it the transient fads and "schools" that seemed often to negate one another. He recognized the problems that produced this situation, the difficulty of any ultimate resolution, and the constant need for reassessment. He utilized what he understood to be the best of critical biblical studies as an aid to faith's understanding.

He appreciated good biblical scholarship but believed that all too frequently the use of positivistic assumptions in its methodology produced sterile answers, not nourishment for Christian life. The early church had formed the New Testament canon. Its books reflected the remembered truth, and their message had sent the church on its amazing missionary course. God's truth inspired the Bible. In this he seems to have been rather like his great predecessor, Gustav Warneck.[4]

Like Barth, he believed the Great Commission to be the very words of the risen Lord. He also affirmed the virgin birth and the resurrection. He would, I believe, have agreed with J.V.L. Casserley's statement, "It is more urgent and important to be biblical about history than to be historical about the Bible."[5] Similarly, he would have understood and responded to the significance in Tillich's comment that in the Bible study Barth launched for the Confessing Church in the Third Reich, that body "returned to the original Christian message . . . and dismissed higher criticism not as false but as insignificant."[6]

Prayer and Devotion. From college days Latourette had observed the "Morning Watch." He had a deep devotional and prayer life and at minimum set aside special time for this each morning and evening. On the bookshelf beside his favorite chair were all the classics of prayer and devotion – Catholic, Orthodox, Anglican, and Protestant. William Temple's *Readings in St. John's Gospel* was a favorite and so were the three books on Christology (1942-1947) by John Knox, professor of New Testament at Union Theological Seminary, New York. Several times he had gone through the *Spiritual Exercise* of Ignatius Loyola. In his spiritual meditation, Latourette lived in the thought world of biblical reflection and reality.

Theological Perspectives. In the strict sense of the word, Latourette was not a theologian and never thought of himself as being one. He had read the classics – Athanasius, Augustine especially, some of Aquinas, Luther, and Calvin – and also Temple, John and Donald Baillie, and some Barth, Brunner, and Bultmann. Yet his mind was that of the fact-gathering historian whose data yield patterns and enable generalizations – not that of the theologian.

Latourette wrote as a convinced Christian and spoke theologically primarily through biblical phrases and images. In his writings on Christian themes his apologia for the faith is evident. Indeed, in his research findings for the *Expansion*, he believed that he was charting a mighty work of God expressed through human faith and obedience. Do not God's wonderful works constitute the primary data for theology? He was describing them. Implicit and explicit in his work is a theology of history informed by his own biblical understanding.

Theologically he declared himself to be Nicene and also affirmed the Chalcedonian Christology. Epistemologically, he viewed himself as Augustinian ("I believe in order to understand"), and with reference to natural and revealed theology he spoke of himself primarily as a Thomist. More than once in class he declared, "The older I grow, the more catholic I become," by which he meant embracing the worth of the central tradition of the church universal. Later years also brought the affirmation, "I am, frankly, an evangelical." Perhaps he can best be described as a catholic evangelical steeped in the Bible and of ecumenical conviction.

As a trained, critical historian he had learned to respect his data, and he prized historical "objectivity." For him that seemed to mean dispassionate impartiality with facts and balanced judgment with generalizations. Yet he recognized that pure objectivity is impossible and that the very selection of data involves nonobjective factors. Thus in each preface he indicated the Christian "bias" in his value-frame.[7] The Christian historian of Christianity or of the church must be skilled in the methods of his craft but must also be responsibly knowledgeable in theology, for the latter shapes data selection and interpretation. Precisely here his critics judged him to be weak. Reinhold Niebuhr referred to him as a layman in theology, a label widely repeated.

Critics, and Niebuhr was one of his constant and most trenchant, often scored him for an optimistic view of man and belief in evolutionary progress. To a Niebuhrian blast Latourette would quietly respond: "He knows thoroughly the meaning of Good Friday. I wish that he understood as fully the power of Easter." One notes also that between 1919 and 1968 Latourette's statements on progress and on man displayed wide variations – a not uncommon occurrence. From 1938 onward as reviews for each volume of the *Expansion* came in, he noted the theological critiques and sought to be responsible to them.

In his 1949 Presidential Address to the American Historical Association (AHA) Latourette made perhaps his most important statement on the faith of the Christian historiographer.[8] From that time there appears to be a growing consistency in his views on man and progress. In that address his comments on progress seem closely akin to the position expressed a year later by John Baillie in his *The Belief in Progress*. In that speech Latourette also scored Communism for seeking perfection in history. Moreover, he frequently pointed to its highly optimistic view of man as a major flaw in socialism – Marxian, Fabian, or other. Yet as a Christian he reflected steadily on the words "Be ye perfect, even as your father in heaven is perfect," and he favored the Eastern Fathers' view of man (e.g., Gregory of Nyssa's *teleosis,* "perfection") over that of Augustine.

In his 1949 address he also sought to deal briefly with criticisms of his inadequate eschatology. To convey a controlling perspective for his theology of history, he used the parable of the wheat and the weeds (Matt. 13:24-30, 36-40), which would grow side by side until the harvest. So, too, good *and* evil would grow on earth until history's consummation. Then, beyond history, God's full sovereignty would be revealed in its majesty. Again and again he returned to that parable to explain the problem of good and evil in history. God would deal with it in the end-time. Latourette would return to eschatology in later years but never in a fashion that fully satisfied his critics.

Latourette perceived a unitary, global history. Because the Gospel is for all, one must view its outreach and impact, that is, the history of Christianity, in the context of the whole world.[9] Moreover, because all history exists in God's hands, at the deepest level all history is one. He recognized the problem with which Augustine had dealt in his "two cities," but he rejected the contemporary dichotomy between world history and salvation history. Clearly, world history is under God's sovereign will and is what salvation is all about! Thus he wrote in 1962: "All history, could we but see it as God sees it, must be 'salvation history.' "[10] This seems remarkably close to Pannenberg's "universal history" and would seem to accord with Gutiérrez's rejection of the two histories to affirm instead that "history is one" and that God's salvific action underlies it. Yet Latourette would draw different inferences from that affirmation than does Gutiérrez.

Latourette's biblical faith also led him to affirm a cosmic redemption. As a historian he could not be confident of history's outcome. Yet as a Christian he believed that history would find its fulfillment in God. God "will triumph not only among human spirits but also in the entire universe."[11] Much with which the historian must deal is puzzling. Yet God's action in history – his *real presence* – and all that flows from it may provide to Christians evidence for their hope. That evidence is not the basis for faith but is history's window through which God's working may be seen. Beyond history lies the cosmic redemption.

His Missionary Vocation and Legacy

From the moment he signed the SVM Declaration, Latourette committed himself to mission – God's calling for his life – and he remained the missionary evangelist. He began as an SVM secretary, went to China, and regarded his teaching and writing career in the United States as continued labor within the missionary fellowship.

The Churchman. Accepting the Gospel, he gave himself to the church which grew from it and exists to make that Gospel known throughout the world. He reflected often on the small minority among Christians fully committed to the Gospel who, humanly speaking, have provided the church with its staying, reproductive, and outreaching power among humankind. Their unheralded and unrecorded lives, the very bedrock of the church, largely elude the historian's tools.

This may help to explain his dedication to local congregations and also, from college days onward, to the nearly continuous succession of Sunday school classes he taught – usually consisting of students. In later years he served an amazing array of boards and committees and occupied church posts of distinction, including the presidency of the American Baptist Convention (1951-1952) and for some years the presidency of the Japan International Christian University Foundation. Yet the Christian's basic allegiance caused him to invest the congregation and its groups of concerned Christians with major importance. That focus and example constitute part of his legacy.

The Ecumenist. Latourette was committed to the ecumenical movement with its concern for Christian mission and unity throughout the world for the sake of the world. In it he discerned an emerging new reality. He pointed to inaccurate use of the word "reunion" with its erroneous assumptions and backward-looking stance. Instead, he focused on that new obedience, springing from a church newly planted among *all* the world's peoples, which manifests its unity in Christ and in the growing oneness of the world Christian community. Involving the whole human family, this was a *new* work of God in history.

His ecumenism expressed itself in several ways. First, he served many bodies engaged in ecumenical work, and for him perhaps the most important of these was the International Missionary Council. He began attending its meetings in 1930, helped in 1934 to create, and became chairman of, its important Research Committee, and contributed to the shaping of IMC policies. Except for its editorial staff, beginning in 1918 he provided more articles by far (27) for the *International Review of Mission* than any other writer. For nearly four decades, from 1928, he served as American correspondent for the *IRM*. He also represented the American (Northern) Baptist Convention at Utrecht in 1938 in the gathering that drafted the Constitution for the World Council of Churches.

Second, he was a bridge-builder. Especially from the 1950s he was welcomed by evangelicals, spoke in their gatherings, and taught at the Winona Lake School of Theology for two weeks each summer from 1964 until his death. Perhaps less known are his close relations with Roman Catholics, including a warm and longtime friendship with John Considine, M.M. For some years he visited Maryknoll almost annually and was deeply touched that his *History of Christian Missions in China* was read aloud at mealtimes and in its entirety to the Maryknoll students. For a time he was a member of the Catholic Historical Association, participated in several Catholic mission gatherings, and maintained contacts with Catholic leaders in Europe.[12] He sought to bring together Christians of divergent views.

Third, an ecumenical perspective shaped all his writing. He was not the first historian to treat Roman Catholicism, Protestantism, and Orthodoxy together. Yet from the time when at Denison he began as a course what was to become his *Expansion* and also began preparations for his *History of Missions in China*, he followed a comprehensive, irenic, and worldwide treatment of the three groups. His global view and balanced appreciative openness toward each segment of the world Christian community became the hallmark of his writing. His 1953 *History* is the first comprehensive treatment of Christianity – as distinct from missionary expansion – written with ecumenical vision and intention. His ecumenical service and perspectives in writing constitute part of his legacy.

The Writer. Latourette's volume of writing impresses one immediately. The bibliography below lists only his books but omits some hundreds of chapters, journal articles, and book reviews. Obviously, he disciplined his life to produce in such volume. Each day he wrote 1,000 words and regularly made up any arrears. He saved book reviews for train trips to and from New York, sometimes managing one each way. He wrote whenever possible. He could stop in mid-sentence, teach a class and attend a committee, and then return and resume typing where he had ended. He penned the necessary corrections on each page – just one corrected draft – and sent it to his typist. His writing conveyed a certain refinement and was clear, smooth, and easy to read. It appeared at its best in a work such as his *History of Christianity* with vast coverage condensed into well-modulated sentences. Yet in the flat mosaic pattern of his more expansive works, his style produced solid but seldom inspiring prose.

Of necessity he utilized the carefully drawn bold stroke across broad canvas, the tool for his extensive rather than intensive scholarship. Relying heavily upon the studies of others, he saw his creativity and originality residing in the conception of his work – a broad field covered in pioneering fashion. He was a "trail-blazer." Monographic specialists could amplify or qualify many of Latourette's generalizations. Yet he pioneered vast murals of scenes never before painted. The norms for such art are different from those applying, for example, to the medical artist's depiction of the eye and its muscles.

Latourette lived on the campus in quarters only one minute from his office in the superb Day Missions Library, which provided a unique setting for his research and writing. The man and the library were meant for each other. Yet Latourette was no denizen of the stacks. He lived a well-balanced life. With no car in New Haven, he walked everywhere, and at least twice weekly took friends to dinner. He especially enjoyed Yale productions of Gilbert and Sullivan.

He was prudently careful in his personal expenditures, but was generous in his giving. Unbeknown to others, he provided timely aid, sometimes substantial, to theological students who might otherwise have had to leave seminary. Indeed, he divided his salary in four parts: he lived on one-fourth; he gave away or contributed one-forth; he saved one-fourth – fearing inflation and never wanting to be a burden on anyone in his old age; and he maintained inherited family responsibilities in Oregon with the remaining one-fourth.

He was a bachelor, and some argued that this enabled his prolific writing. In fact, at one time there had been a long and deep affair of the heart in which his proposal was rejected – she, too, went on to a distinguished academic career – and after which he accepted the unmarried state as a vocational enablement for the most productive missionary career. He sought always to know God's will for his life and believed that it had been guided. Without responsibility for an immediate family, he could do much that would otherwise have been impossible. Yet his disciplined commitment to writing – and with two or three exceptions, he did all his own research – sprang from his conviction that God's will for him was to use his obvious gifts this way.

Latourette wrote in four distinct fields. Although most are unaware of it, the first is Christian higher education, and in this area, from 1918 into the 1950s, he wrote only articles, no books.[13] His initial concern related to students and the meaning of faith for their problems. With eye-catching titles, his articles appeared chiefly in the student YMCA's *Intercollegian*. His other and longer-range interest focused on the Christian college and university and especially on its dechristianization or secularization – a phenomenon he had already noted in Christian institutions in Asia and Africa. He argued that a university can be Christian, while his colleague-opponents vigorously contested that by definition, and to be fully representative, a university cannot be exclusively Christian.

The other three major areas of his writings appear by section in the appended bibliography.

As the first section in the bibliography discloses, he built his reputation first as an expert on the Far East (his second area of writing). America was greatly lacking in Asian studies, and he wrote to dispel ignorance, create understanding, and enlist scholarly interest. He emphasized the cultural dimension and, unlike most European scholars, stressed the recent past, for it helped to explain the revolutionary encounter of Asia with the West. After all, he had lived through China's revolution of 1911! His books on China and Japan went through repeated editions, and *The Chinese: Their History and Culture* (1934) established his reputation as a sinologist.

His *History of Christian Missions in China* (1929) emerged from his dual interest in China and in missions, and until 1936 was his only real work in missions. Just as William Carey first established his reputation in Britain and on the Continent with his scientific botanical studies from India, so too Latourette emerged first as an expert in Asian studies.

The bibliography also indicates that he compacted his published Asian writing into two periods: the first from 1917 to 1934 (the dissertation had been written in 1909), and the second from 1946 to 1954 (*China* [1964] was basically a revised edition of its 1954 predecessor). The "sandwiching" is instructive. It left the years from 1934 to 1944 free for the *Expansion* and its related cluster of books. With that task completed, he produced his other major and best-selling Asian work (despite its title, it was a history of Asia), *A Short History of the Far East* (1946). The remaining ones were "summer books," that is, written in Oregon, which enabled him to give major attention to his forthcoming *History of Christianity*. Except for the YMCA's *World Service* (1957), with preliminary research work provided and sent to Oregon for summer writing, he devoted much of the 1950s to his second magnum opus, *Christianity in a Revolutionary Age*.

Missions constitute his third area of writing. Undoubtedly, he will be remembered best for his pioneering *History of the Expansion of Christianity* (7 vols., 1937-1945). It stands as the first major work to trace the missionary outreach of the entire church across nearly twenty centuries and blazed a trail for others to follow and develop. Its familiar schematization is notable: the first three volumes

(1,400 pp.) cover the first 1,800 years; the next three survey "The Great Century," the nineteenth (1,550 pp.); and the final volume examines the period 1914-1944 (550 pp.). In short, four volumes and 60 percent of the pages related to the most recent 130 years of the faith.

Many still debate Latourette's unique advance/recession pattern of missionary pulsations in the *Expansion,* with each advance, like the waves of the incoming tide, moving further ahead, and each recession becoming a shorter decline. Some have scorned it and profess to see in it the optimism of evolutionary progress. They dismiss it as naive and point to Latourette's inadequate reckoning with New Testament eschatology. He allows, as he must, for a reversal of the pattern and its collapse, but acknowledgment of this more sober New Testament eschatology hardly counterbalances the emphasis placed on the long-term pattern he discerns. On this critics concentrate their fire.[14]

Latourette proved that the Great Century had been unprecedented in Christianity's expansion. In this, and in all the vast panorama that lay behind it, he gave the history of missions, so long ignored in church history and the history of doctrine, status as an essential dimension of and indeed matrix for both. All else that he did was an outgrowth of the implications, themes, or issues present with the *Expansion.*

The fourth area of Latourette's writing relates to the history of Christianity – as distinct from missions. In it his *History of Christianity* represents his most notable work. It does not condense the *Expansion* but is indeed a new work – a departure from anything he had ever done before. In partial preparation for it he audited Robert L. Calhoun's Yale course in the history of doctrine and did enormous supplementary reading, including the doctrinal histories of Seeberg and Harnack.

Its unique contribution is to set the history of Christianity within the context of mission and of universal history. Accordingly, it follows the *Expansion'*s periodization. Within the original 1,500 pages, some 200 only are allocated to missionary outreach, but the Gospel is set within the *oikoumene.* Moreover, its proportions differ from those of the *Expansion.* The first fifteen centuries claim 45 percent and the period from 1500 to the present receives 55 percent of the text. Christianity's impact on the whole world since the sixteenth century becomes clear, including the emergence of the world Christian community. In coverage for the past two centuries, Latourette also introduces a subtle but powerful shift of emphasis. In Asia, Africa, and Latin America he focuses not upon the missionary incursion but upon the growth of Christianity in those areas. Christians in the Third World have warmly welcomed this work, but its price militated against wide use.

One confronts here another of Latourette's pioneering efforts. It emphasizes the universality of the Gospel and the unique world Christian community that has emerged from it. The latter now embraces the gifts, cultural treasures, and needs of all humankind. It also becomes the agent for religious and ideological encounter and for theological development in the period ahead. Latourette offers a post-Christendom, ecumenical, and global perspective. The writing of Christianity's history dare never again revert to provincialism. The Gospel's universality, once proclaimed in Palestine, appears here as a living reality.

The History of Christianity in a Revolutionary Age (5 vols., 1958-1962) chronicles the history of the church in the past 150 years. Ecumenical perspective, clarity of organization, and detailed coverage are all present, but interpretation is minimal in this volume; it repeats what was set forth earlier, and is not probing. Sustained reading becomes tedious, but brief reference use is helpful. Packed with factual detail and probably the outstanding instance of Latourette's effort to be comprehensive and objective, it will long serve as a reference to the period and to other resources. This is its strength.

In short, Latourette's legacy in writing is vast and includes several notable pioneering works of enduring worth.

The Professor. Latourette acknowledged that his classroom presentations were only average. He lectured as he wrote, with clarity and in factual detail. Students responded in proportion to their interest in the subject. He trusted the power and the sweeping vistas of his themes to help the majority enlarge their horizons and to prepare the minority for service overseas.

Far more important was his role as teacher-pastor to students, who were his chief interest.[15] He managed time for student groups and for conversations with the lonely, the confused, and the seeking. Daily in prayer he remembered his former students around the world and also maintained a correspondence with them that amazed and pleased all, even when only three penned sentences filled a full page. Moreover, in the morning of each class day he reviewed the rolls of those he would meet in class that day and remembered each in prayer. He was no scintillating lecturer, but the students who had him knew that he loved and cared for them, and they responded to him.

Some of his colleagues smiled patronizingly at Latourette's missionary evangelism, but they regarded him as a responsible and dependable member of the teaching guild. In the late 1930s when he was involved in his heaviest work in producing the *Expansion,* they asked him to become director of Graduate Studies in Religion. He agreed, and under the dean of the Graduate School coordinated all doctoral programs in religion at Yale. He assumed this administrative task in addition to all his other responsibilities and held it until retirement.

On occasion through bestowing one of its several Sterling Professorships, Yale University grants signal honor to its outstanding faculty persons. Only one ever had been given to the Divinity School faculty, and it was held by Dean Luther A. Weigle. On Weigle's retirement in 1949, Yale's president made Latourette a Sterling Professor of the University, and as such he retired in 1953. His legacy was that of edifying colleague, pastor to students, and the scholar-teacher-administrator.

The Scholar. Latourette was a productive, publishing scholar. The academic world first knew him as a sinologist and expert on the Far East. He sought always to encourage young academics to enter and develop the field and before 1920 had persuaded the AHA to provide the Far East a place in its annual programs. He steadily pushed development of the discipline. Yet he had early determined that his chief field would be mission. Thus as younger and better-trained scholars emerged, he gave less and less writing time to Asia, but with continuing keen interest produced scholarly articles into the 1960s. In tribute to his contribution, colleagues in the field elected him president for 1954-1955 of the Far Eastern Association (beginning in 1955, the Association for Asian Studies). Concern for a universal view of history and especially Asian studies was part of his legacy.

Second, in missions or missiology – a word he uttered with a tilt of the head and a wry smile – he was unique. His widely acclaimed writings alone greatly enhanced the field. Yet his worldwide reputation as sinologist, historian of Christianity, and ecumenical churchman gave the discipline a recognized stature it had never before enjoyed. Clearly the *Expansion* was his great contribution. It shaped all else that he did and will be a landmark for generations. Perhaps its greatest impact is yet to be in helping the church to understand its missional nature when, in an age of universal history and as a worldwide minority, it enters into dynamic engagement with all humankind and becomes, at least in part, a sacramental leaven for the whole. Dedicated scholarship in mission also constitutes part of his legacy.

Third, the guild of historians twice honored him: first, the American Society of Church History elected him president in 1945; and second, the American Historical Association elected him president in 1949. As a historian of Christianity, he used God's concern for the nations and his outreach to them through his covenanted people (cf. Gen. 10-12) as the context within which the history of Christianity and the church must be seen. That work began with Abraham's call, focused in the incarnation, and continues in encounter with cultures and faiths – and indeed with the very nature of humankind – until history's consummation. What lies beyond is not within the historian's province, but the historical record traced by Latourette of the Gospel's impact and spread cannot be dismissed. Its interpretation may be debated, but its documented reality also becomes part of his legacy.

From Europe came criticism of his theology. Yet also from Europe came response to the decisive importance of his contribution. Professor Ernst Benz of Marburg in 1961 in his *Kirchengeschichte in ökumenischer Sicht* (Christianity in Ecumenical Perspective)[16] probes Latourette carefully, notes his placing of church history within world history, and contrasts this with the usual provincial and narrow style of German and Continental church history. Latourette, he claims, frees church history from its previous regional blinders and offers it a new era. Indeed, in his comprehensiveness he provides an "Ecumenical Baedeker Guide" for the universal church.[17] Benz's key chapter on Latourette is entitled "Weltgeschichte – Kirchengeschichte – Missionsgeschichte" (World History – Church History – Missions History).

Thus are the lineaments of an unusual and rich legacy drawn – one created by faith and dedicated to the furtherance in life and understanding of God's mission.

Notes

1. K.S. Latourette, *Beyond the Ranges: An Autobiography* (Grand Rapids, Mich.: Wm. B. Eerdmans, 1967) (henceforth cited as *Ranges*).
2. Wilber C. Harr, ed., *Frontiers of the Christian World Mission Since 1938: Essays in Honor of Kenneth Scott Latourette* (New York: Harper & Row, 1962).
3. *IRM* 58, no. 231 (July 1969): 317-26.
4. O.G. Myklebust, *The Study of Missions in Theological Education*, 2 vols. (Oslo: Egede Instituttet, 1955), 1:281, 293.
5. J.V. Langmead Casserley, *Toward a Theology of History* (London: Mowbray, 1965), p. 97.
6. Paul Tillich, "The Meaning of the German Church Struggle for Christian Mission," in *Christian World Mission,* ed. W.K. Anderson (Nashville: Parthenon Press, 1946), p. 134.
7. Cf. *A History of the Expansion of Christianity*, 7 vols. (1937-45), 1:xvi-xviii, *A History of Christianity*, 2 vols. (1953; new ed., with foreword, final chapter, and bibliographic additions by Ralph D. Winter, 1975), 1:xx-xxi (henceforth cited as *History*); *Christianity in a Revolutionary Age: A History of Christianity in the Nineteenth and Twentieth Centuries*, 5 vols. (1958-62), 1:xiii (henceforth cited as *Revolutionary Age*); *Christianity Through the Ages* (1965), pp. xii-xiii (henceforth cited as *Ages*).
8. "The Christian Understanding of History," *American Historical Review* 54, no. 2 (January 1949): 259-76.
9. Cf. *History*, 1:xvi-xvii; *Ages*, pp. ix-x; *Ranges*, p. 114.
10. *Revolutionary Age*, 5:516.
11. Ibid., p. 534.
12. *Ranges*, pp. 69, 78-79, 104, 111, 113.
13. William Lee Pitts, Jr., "World Christianity: The Church History Writing of Kenneth Scott Latourette" (Ph.D. diss., Vanderbilt University, 1969), done under the direction of Wilhelm Pauck. Pitts deals with this area and provides some of the more important bibliography covering the years 1918-52. This is a most useful study of Latourette's historiography in the area of missions and the history of Christianity. The only other doctoral dissertations relating to Latourette and known to this writer are William Allen Speck, "The Role of the Christian Historian in the Twentieth Century As Seen in the Writings of K.S. Latourette, Christopher Dawson, and Herbert Butterfield" (Florida State University, 1965), and Juhani Lindgren, "Unity of all Christians in Love and Mission: The Ecumenical Method of Kenneth Scott Latourette" (University of Helsinki, 1990).
14. Cf. J.S. Whale, "A History of the Expansion of Christianity," *IRM* 34, no. 136 (October 1945):427-29; Ernst A. Payne, "The Modern Expansion of the Church: Some Reflections on Dr. Latourette's Conclusions," *Journal of Theological Studies* 47 (1946):143-55; Martin Wight, "Christianity in a World Perspective," *IRM* 38, no. 152 (October 1949):488-90; K.S. Latourette, Reinhold Neibuhr, and F.E. Stoeffler, "'Christ the Hope of the World': What Has History to Say?" *Religion in Life* 23, no. 3 (Summer 1954):323-51.
15. *Ranges*, pp. 133ff.

16. Leiden: Brill, 1961.
17. Ibid., p. 29.

A Latourette Bibliography

See "Select Bibliography of Kenneth Scott Latourette," in *Frontiers of the Christian World Mission Since 1938: Essays in Honor of Kenneth Scott Latourette*, ed. Wilber C. Harr (New York: Harper & Row, 1962). This detailed bibliography is complete through 1960 and includes Latourette's chapters in books, encyclopedia articles, many of his articles in periodicals, and also articles on him personally. The bibliography below includes titles after 1960 and is designed by category to indicate the pattern of Latourette's writings as disclosed by his books.

Asian and International

1917 *The History of Early Relations Between the United States and China, 1784-1844.* Originally, Latourette's Ph.D. diss, Yale University, 1909, which is a substantial monograph.

1917 *The Development of China.* Boston: Houghton Mifflin. Rev. eds. 1920, 1924, 1929, 1937, 1946.

1918 *The Development of Japan.* New York: Macmillan. Rev. eds. 1926, 1931, 1938. Issued as *The History of Japan* in 1947 and 1957.

1927 *Voyages of American Ships to China, 1784-1844.* New Haven: Connecticut Academy of Arts and Sciences. This work adds supplemental data to *The History of Early Relations Between the United Stats and China, 1784-1844.*

1934 *The Chinese: Their History and Culture.* 2 vols. New York: Macmillan. Rev. eds., 2 vols. in 1, 1934, 1946, 1964.

1946 *A Short History of the Far East.* New York: Macmillan. Rev. eds., 1951, 1957.

1946 *The United States Moves Across the Pacific.* New York: Harper.

1949 *The China That Is to Be.* Eugene, Oregon: Oregon State System of Higher Education.

1952 *The American Record in the Far East, 1945-51.* New York: Macmillan.

1954 *A History of Modern China.* London and Baltimore: Penguin Books.

1956 *Introducing Buddhism.* New York: Friendship Press.

1964 *China.* Englewood Cliffs, New Jersey: Prentice Hall

Missions

Expansion History

1937-45 *A History of the Expansion of Christianity.* 7 vols. New York: Harper. Latourette's magnum opus, shaping most of the works that follow.

1940 *Anno Domini: Jesus, History, and God.* New York: Harper.

1941 *The Unquenchable Light.* New York: Harper.

General and Ecumenical

1936 *Missions Tomorrow.* New York: Harper.

1946 (ed.) *The Gospel, the Church, and the World.* Interseminary Series, vol. 3. New York: Harper.

1947 (with W.R. Hogg) *Tomorrow Is Here.* New York: Friendship Press. IMC Whitby Meeting, 1947.

1948 *The Christian Outlook.* New York: Harper.

1949 *The Emergence of a World Christian Community.* New Haven: Yale Univ. Press.

1949 *Toward a World Christian Fellowship.* New York: Association Press.

1949 (with W.R. Hogg) *World Christian Community in Action: The Story of World War II and Orphaned Missions.* New York: International Missionary Council.

1950 *These Sought a Country.* New York: Harper.

1954 *The Christian World Mission in Our Day.* New York: Harper.

1957 *Desafío a los Protestantes* (Challenge to Protestants). Buenos Aires: Editorial "La Aurora." Cf. *Challenge and Response.*

Institutional

1957 *World Service: A History of the Foreign Work . . . of the YMCA's of the United States and Canada.* New York: Association Press.

1963-68 (in Prep.) *The History of the American Bible Society.* Completed after Latourette's death by Creighton Lacy. See the latter's *Word-Carrying Giant: The Growth of the American Bible Society.* Pasadena, Calif.: William Carey Library, 1977.

Other

1916 (co-editor) *Correspondence of the Reverend Ezra Fisher.* Portand, Oregon: privately printed.

1919 *The Christian Basis of World Democracy.* Bible studies and meditations.

1929 *A History of Christian Missions in China.* New York: Macmillan. Reprinted 1966, 1967.

1949 *Missions and the American Mind.* Indianapolis: National Foundation Press.

1967 *Beyond the Ranges: An Autobiography.* Grand Rapids, Mich.: Wm B. Eerdmans.

History of Christianity

1949 *The Christian Understanding of History.* Presidential address to American Historical Association; offprint from *American Historical Review* 54, no. 2 (January).

1953 *A History of Christianity.* 2 vols. New York: Harper. New ed., with foreword, final chapter, and bibliographic additions by Ralph D. Winter.

1955 *Challenge and Conformity: Studies in the Interaction of Christianity and the World of Today.* New York: Harper. A preface to the following large work:

1958-62 *Christianity in a Revolutionary Age: A History of Christianity in the Nineteenth and Twentieth Centuries.* 5 vols. New York: Harper.

1965 *Christianity Through the Ages.* New York: Harper. A popular condensation of *History of Christianity.*

1970 (with Hubert Jedin and Jochen Martin) *Atlas zur Kirchengeschichte.* Freiburg: Herder.

1967-68 (in prep.) "The Christian Factor in the Twentieth Century World in Historical Perspective." A partial manuscript was in the publisher's hands at the time of Latourette's death; it has not been published.

Johan Herman Bavinck

1895–1964

Understanding Religion in Light of God's Revelation

J. van den Berg

Johan Herman Bavinck, the son of Grietje Bouwes and Coenraad Bernard Bavinck, a minister of the Reformed Churches in the Netherlands (Gereformeerde Kerken in Nederland), was born at Rotterdam, the Netherlands, in 1895. The spiritual background of the Bavincks was in a church that had seceded from the Netherlands Reformed Church (Nederlandse Hervormde Kerk) in 1834. Jan Bavinck, Johan Herman's grandfather and a native of the German county of Bentheim near the Dutch frontier, had been a leading minister of the secession church, and it was perhaps only modesty that had prevented him from accepting a call in 1854 to a teaching function in the newly established theological college at Kampen. Jan's eldest son, Herman, did become a professor of dogmatics, first at the Kampen Theological College and later at the Free University in Amsterdam. Coenraad Bernard was also a theologian at heart (he was especially at home in the works of Augustine), although he left the writing of theological works to his elder brother.

The secession of 1834 originated in the protest of some Calvinistic ministers against the more liberal tendencies then prevalent in the Netherlands Reformed Church. With some of the seceders, however, the harsh contours of a strict and conservative Calvinism were softened by a milder evangelical spirit. The Bavincks were representatives of this more open-minded tendency within the church of the secession. In 1892 this church united with a church which, under the influence of Abraham Kuyper, had seceded from the Netherlands Reformed Church in 1886 to form the Reformed Churches in the Netherlands (Gereformeerde Kerken in Nederland). In the tradition of the Reformed Churches the name "Bavinck" is associated with the catholic and irenic form of Reformed thought that found its most succinct expression in a lecture by Herman Bavinck, published in 1888 under the title *The Catholicity of Christianity and Church.*[1]

Student Days

Johan Herman Bavinck grew up in an atmosphere of warm and mild piety, blended with a lively interest in theology and an open-minded attitude toward the world of culture. In 1912 he enrolled as a student of theology at the Free University in Amsterdam. The study of religious psychology became one of his major interests; in this he was possibly stimulated by his uncle, who was one of his professors. He was deeply influenced in this period of his life by his contacts with people in the

Netherlands Student Christian Movement – a circle in which a wider world of spiritual and theological interests was opened to a number of students who had grown up in the rather confined atmosphere of the Reformed Churches in the Netherlands.

After completion of his work at the Free University, Bavinck went for further studies to Germany (Giessen and Erlangen). In 1919 he was awarded the doctor of philosophy degree from the University of Erlangen, having written a dissertation on the medieval mystic Henry Suso, whose thought he approached from the viewpoint of the psychology of religion.[2]

Bavinck as Pastor

In the same year, 1919, Bavinck was called by a Dutch church at Medan in Sumatra, Indonesia, where he served for two years as assistant pastor. In 1921 he became the pastor of a Dutch church in Bandung, Java. This period in his life may be seen as a prelude to his later work as a missionary in Indonesia, although he did not yet have any intention of undertaking missionary service. In Bandung he found the time to pursue studies in psychology, and it was his psychological insight, combined with a natural ability to listen without intruding, that made him a good and sympathetic pastor. He was also a distinguished preacher whose sermons were marked by a combination of spiritual depth and lucid simplicity. Bavinck could not have been comfortable in the armor of dogmatic certainties, but he was deeply steeped in the biblical message through daily Bible study and reflection, and he had a special gift for relating that message to the great problems of his own times.

While in Bandung he was married to Trientje (Tine) Robers. More practical and matter-of-fact than her sometimes absent-minded husband, she brought much sunshine into a very happy marriage that lasted until her death in 1953. A daughter and two sons were born to this marriage.

The Bavincks returned to the Netherlands in 1926, where he became pastor in the village of Heemstede (near Haarlem), but for a briefer period than they had anticipated.

Bavinck as Missionary

In 1929 Bavinck was asked to become a missionary of his church in Solo (Surakarta), a town in central Java. There the old Javanese culture, influenced by Hinduism and Buddhism, was still very much alive under the surface of Muslim religious life. The call to missionary service conflicted with his plans for further activities in the field of religious psychology, but he responded to it in full confidence that it was God's will. He was particularly well qualified in both personality and education to penetrate the subtle and inscrutable world of Javanese mysticism. Bavinck had a rare gift for sharing other people's spiritual experiences, so much so that he was sometimes nicknamed "the white Javanese." He made contacts in the *kraton* (palace of the prince), one of the centers of old Javanese culture. Long talks with Javanese mystics on moonlit nights and an intimate knowledge of the *wajang* (play of light and shadows with puppets, representing heroes and demons of the old epic poems) gave him an even deeper understanding of the Javanese spirit. This writer has a lively memory of Bavinck's lectures on Javanese religious life; it was as though the bare lecture room in Kampen had become the courtyard of the *kraton* in Solo; as though a Javanese mystic, rather than a Dutch professor, were initiating his pupils into the mysteries of Javanese religion.

Bavinck's almost intuitive understanding of Eastern thought did not lead him, however, to any form of syncretism. His affinity with the Javanese mind in no way diminished his deep conviction that the God who has revealed himself in Jesus Christ is different from the "cosmological" God of Oriental mystical thought. He was a respectful missionary – but still a missionary – one who thought it important to confront the world of Eastern religious thought with the message of Christ.

In 1931 he became a lecturer at the theological college in Jogjakarta, also in central Java. There he was able to pursue his studies, especially in the field of Oriental mysticism, and at the same time help his pupils to relate the Christian message they were going to preach and teach with their Javanese heritage. His friend and colleague Abraham Pos once heard him say that the years spent at Jogjakarta were the most beautiful years of his life.

Bavinck as Professor

When the Reformed Churches in the Netherlands decided to establish a chair of missiology at their theological college, the choice of Bavinck as its first occupant was logical. He accepted the call and returned to the Netherlands in 1939, on the eve of World War II, to assume his post at Kampen Theological College. At the same time he was appointed professor extraordinary of missiology at the Free University, Amsterdam. Soon the Netherlands was caught up in the whirlpool of war. Academic teaching was still possible for only a few years; ultimately all universities and colleges were closed. For a man like Bavinck who, despite his apparent other-worldliness, reacted with deep intensity to the events of those years, the cessation of classroom activities could not be merely an opportunity for quiet and uninterrupted study. He gave spiritual guidance in various ways, among them the writing of books and pamphlets on a popular level, preparing the church for the resumption of its missionary task in the postwar period.

The outbreak of a long-smoldering conflict within the church on matters of doctrine and church order, in which he attempted vainly to mediate,[3] strengthened his aversion to doctrinal fanaticism and ecclesiastical self-centeredness. Neither aspiring nor attempting to become an ecclesiastical leader, he helped in his own quiet way to open a door to the future for a church that had been too concerned with the past to become sufficiently aware of the new-day challenges. In so doing, he remained true to the catholic ideal his uncle had already formulated in 1888.

When Bavinck was able to resume his professorial duties after the war, new problems demanded attention. The political and military conflict between the Netherlands and the new Republic of Indonesia created a cleavage between missionaries and missionary leaders, on the one hand, and church members who sympathized with the Dutch government's policies, on the other. Although not a radical by nature, Bavinck unhesitatingly sided with those who pleaded for more understanding of the motives and aspirations of the Indonesian nationalists. His wisdom and tact contributed to bridging the gap between those whose knowledge of Indonesian life led them to a more progressive stance, and those who still thought in categories that were to be invalidated by the winds of change.

A problem partly related to the former one was that of the changing relationship between the Dutch churches with their mission agencies and the Indonesian churches. The latter, during the period of Japanese occupation when Western assistance was totally absent, had shown that their institutional independence was more than a formal matter. After the war they were prepared to cooperate with the Dutch missions only if all vestiges of paternalism on the part of the missionary partners disappeared. Here again, Bavinck saw and accepted the challenge of a new phase in missionary history. In 1947 he shared in the discussions held in Djakarta between Indonesians and Dutch and, upon his return to the Netherlands, was able to convince his own church of the need for a new mission policy.

The new situation demanded new forms of mission organization. Under Bavinck's stimulating influence, a Missionary Center of the Reformed Churches in the Netherlands was established at Baarn. A Missionary Seminary was also established, to be united in the course of time with the Missionary College of the Netherlands Reformed Church to form the present Hendrick Kraemer Institute at Oegstgeest. Bavinck maintained his international contacts, lecturing in the United States (once at the invitation of Mircea Eliade) and in South Africa. He tried, in South Africa, to persuade his white fellow Christians of the evil of racial discrimination inherent in apartheid policies.[4]

Among the many obligations he assumed, the professorial task always dominated other interests. He was an inspiring teacher, one whose lectures left an unforgettable impression on his students. A number of those students, from the Netherlands and other countries as well, took their doctor's degree under his supervision. Ultimately, however, the work at Kampen and Amsterdam together became too heavy a burden; and, when the chair of practical theology at the Free University became vacant in 1955, Bavinck left Kampen to became full professor at the Free University. He was succeeded at Kampen by Dr. Hendrik Bergema, who also assumed a number of Bavinck's duties in the field of missionary organization. Bavinck's personality, his homiletical gifts, and his studies in psychology especially qualified him for his new position. At the Free University he retained his responsibilities in the field of missiology, although after some years he delegated the teaching of the history of missions to a former pupil who had become one of his younger colleagues.

Despite the realignment of his work, Bavinck's life remained busy, too busy for one whose physical strength was no longer equal to his great strength of mind and his multifarious tasks. His health began to fail and plans had to be unfulfilled. He died in 1964, a quarter of a century after first undertaking his professorial duties. During the last, difficult years he was lovingly supported by his second wife, Fennechien (Chien) Bavinck-van der Vegt.

Bavinck was a man of deep spirituality, with a warm personal interest in pupils and friends, a disarming sense of humor, and a subtle and respectful approach to life's great problems. His scholarly work reflects many traits of his personality.

The Scholarship of J.H. Bavinck

Variety and Continuity

Bavinck was a prolific and fluent writer. From 1923 onward there was scarcely a year in which he did not publish one or more books or articles. Within the confines of this essay it is impossible to do justice to the variety of those publications. I shall try, however, to summarize his broad range of interests, on the one hand, and to point out the element of continuity in his work, on the other. Some of his most important publications in the field of missiology will then be singled out for special mention. A preliminary remark is indicated: it is not always easy to make a clear-cut distinction between Bavinck's more popular works and his scholarly publications. Some, which to all intents and purposes belong in the first category, still reveal the scholar's mind and the fundamental pattern of his thought in an interesting way. And some of his typically scholarly publications were written with a lucidity and an almost deceptive simplicity that made them accessible to a much wider circle than that of the specialists. Bavinck himself was, in fact, not a specialist in the technical sense of the word. He was more a generalist, interested in all the great questions of his discipline. With fine intuition for discovering what is relevant, he approached those issues from the inside, as it were.

Bavinck's first publications were in the fields of psychology and philosophy. His doctoral dissertation on Suso (1919), mentioned above, dealt with the question of how far thinking in general, and religious thinking in particular, is influenced by feeling. This first work witnesses already to his understanding of and ambivalence toward the world of mystical thought. In 1926 he published *An Introduction to Psychology*, in the foreword of which he cited the words of Augustine that are so typical of his own approach: *Deum et animam scire cupio*, "I desire to know God and the soul."[5] To those words he added, "For one who has faith in God in his heart, in this world few things are more beautiful than to be allowed to penetrate into the depths of the soul." After returning to the

Netherlands he published a series of lectures on a number of great philosophers, concentrating on the relationship between personality and worldview.[6]

He would no doubt have pursued this line of psychological and philosophical studies had he not been called back to Indonesia. As indicated above, it was the mystical aspect of the Javanese world that became the center of his interests. This fascination is evident in a curious little book, written in Javanese, concerning the way Christ enters into the soul.[7] In this work, the *kraton* with its mysterious gateways and alleys stands as a model for the human soul. It appears that some of the more conservative missionaries rather frowned on that approach, the more so because much of the vocabulary of the book was derived from the mystic Al-Gazali. In any case it was an interesting and original attempt to relate the Christian message to the categories of Javanese mysticism. Bavinck dealt more fully with some of the underlying problems in what is undoubtedly one of his most important studies, *Christ and Eastern Mysticism*.[8]

During his missionary period as well as afterward, Bavinck wrote a number of works on biblical subjects. His earlier publications in this field – I refer especially to *People around Jesus* (1936),[9] and *History of God's Revelation*, vol. 2, *The New Testament* (1938)[10] – are indicative of his psychological approach. In his later biblical studies the historical dimension assumes a larger place; this is the case, for example, in his work on the spread of the Gospel in the days of Paul (1941), and even more so in that on the Book of Revelation (1952). His interest in the symbolic language of the Bible appears in his *Man and His World* (1946).[11] These and others he wrote in this field are not the contributions of a specialist in biblical studies, but they reflect in an original way his broad familiarity with the biblical message in its various aspects.

As a professor of missiology he wrote a number of studies in that particular field: a survey of the history of missions, studies on adaptation, communication, the "point of contact," and so forth. He wrote on the place of Christianity among the world religions, religious consciousness and Christian faith, the race problem, several topics of more incidental interest. In the last years of this life, he wrote a number of articles in the field of practical theology, but failing health made it impossible to realize his plans for a more comprehensive work in that field.

Bavinck's writings cover a wide, almost overwhelming and confusing, variety of subjects. Yet an element of continuity is clearly evident: his fascination with the problem of God and the human soul. Hence his interest was in both biblical theology and psychology, in the message of the Bible concerning people and their inner problems in the context of a changing world. It is the interrelationship of those two elements that flavors all his writings, a fact that will be evident from a closer look at his studies in the field of comparative religion and missiology.

Religion and the Christian Faith

The central problem, in Bavinck's thinking, was that of the relationship between religious experience and God's revelation in Jesus Christ. The tenor of his thought is reminiscent of Schleiermacher, who took the notion of religious experience as his starting point. The present writer has in his possession Bavinck's own marked copy of Schleiermacher's *Reden*, in which the underlinings show how much he was preoccupied with Schleiermacher's thought on this subject. However, at a later period he was also deeply impressed by Barth's emphasis on the critical character for revelation. One does not do justice to Bavinck by suggesting that his mind balanced between those two poles without reaching a decision. Rather, through a subtle and original approach, he tried to reach his own conclusion. In this there is a noticeable difference between Bavinck and his friend Hendrik Kraemer, though not of a fundamental nature. It is interesting to note that Kraemer, the opponent of a syncretistic approach, sympathetically advised and assisted Bavinck when he wrote his Javanese booklet on Christ's entrance into the human soul, mentioned above.[12]

That Javanese booklet was a prelude to Bavinck's larger work, *Christ and Eastern Mysticism.* At the very beginning of this book he states that the missionary task is one of striving to win people for Christ, but that it is also one of wrestling with a culture that has grown out of a different religion, and Bavinck indeed came to grips with Javanese culture. In many ways it attracted him, but at the same time in its fundamental presuppositions it was alien to the heart and core of his own beliefs. The result of this encounter was a book of great depth and beauty. In it Bavinck confronted Javanese thinking, influenced as it is by Hindu and Muslim mysticism, with the thought world of Augustine who, in his own day, had coped with the problems posed by Neoplatonic mysticism. On the one hand, Bavinck perceived many parallels between Javanese and Christian thought on deliverance from the power of darkness – parallels that led him to expect that once a living church had found its place in the Eastern world the message of Christ would be better understood there than in the secularized context of the Western world. On the other hand, one fundamental contrast remained: in the East, deliverance is primarily a psychological process; in the Christian message, it is a radical change in the relationship between God and human beings along the way of atonement and justification.

Bavinck stood as it were on the boundary between two worlds. *Christ and Eastern Mysticism* was written before the Tambaram Missionary Conference of 1938, and before Barth's theology (largely through Kraemer's mediation) had made its influence felt in missiological thinking. Yet this book pointed somehow toward the post-Tambaram stand missiology was to take with regard to the relationship between religion and the Christian faith. On some issues it is, of course, dated – especially in its evaluation of secularism. Yet perhaps its careful and understanding approach to the religious experience of the East may have a new relevance now that the emphasis on religious experience is more highly regarded than it was four or five decades ago.

The theme was taken up again in Bavinck's inaugural lecture of 1939, published as *The Proclamation of Christ in the World of Nations.*[13] In this he pointed to people such as Kanaharyan Paul and Vengal Chakkarai from India, Toyohiko Kagawa and Taisei Michihata from Japan, as examples of the way Christians in the East approach the mystery of the cross. In 1940 he published a summary in Dutch of Kraemer's *Christian Message in a Non-Christian World* (1938), in the course of which he remarked that Kraemer had made too sharp a distinction between Christianity and revelation.[14] But his most penetrating study on the subject, *Religious Consciousness and Christian Faith,*[15] appeared in 1949. In a masterly analysis of Romans 1, he showed that God in his general revelation is at work in this world, but that at the same time people replace God's revelation by images of their own making in a continuous process of substitution; as in a dream, sensations from outside are replaced by related yet different images. The originality of this study lies in the way Bavinck approached a central theological question within the context of his knowledge of religious psychology and the religious life of the East.

A summary of Bavinck's legacy is his great work *An Introduction to the Science of Missions.*[16] In it we meet with the various elements characteristic of his approach: his psychological interest traceable in many places (though not as explicitly present as in earlier publications), his biblical orientation (here very prominent), and the respectful way he dealt with other religions. From the vantage point of the several decades since the publication of that book, we are aware of a certain one-sidedness as a result of an almost exclusive attention to the confrontation between Christianity and the non-Christian religions. In that respect it reflects the major emphasis of a period in the history of missions when the non-Western world was not as deeply influenced by the modern secular climate as is the case today. Perhaps it is precisely that one-sidedness, inevitable in its time, that gives this book special flavor and lasting quality. It brings us into contact with a man who was not only a gifted missiologist but also a humble missionary – one who, just because of his belief in the unique meaning of God's revelation in Christ, could trace with an open mind and a respectful heart the vestiges of God's presence in the world of religions.

Notes

1. H. Bavinck, *De catholiciteit van Christendom en kerk* (Kampen: Zalsman, 1888).

2. *Der Einflus des Gefühls auf das Assoziationsleben bei Heinrich von Suso* (Erlangen: n.p., 1919).

3. For this, see his lecture *De toekomst van onze kerken* (The future of our churches) (Bruinisse: n.p., 1943).

4. A selection of his writings on South Africa is in J. van den Berg, *"Een geheel andere Waardemeter."* *Beschouwingen van Prof. dr. J.H. Bavinck over het rassenvraagstuk en over Zuid-Afrika* (Amsterdam: Bekking, 1971).

5. *Inleiding in de zielkunde* (Kampen: J.H. Kok, 1926), p. iii.

6. *Persoonlijkheid en wereldbeschouwing* (Kampen: J.H. Kok, 1928).

7. For this work (*Soeksma soepana*, written 1932 under the pseudonym Kjai Martawahana), see J. Verkuyl, *Inleiding in de nieuwere zendingswetenschap* (Kampen: J.H. Kok, 1975), p. 63.

8. *Christus en de mystiek van het Oosten* (Kampen: J.H. Kok, 1934).

9. *Menschen rondom Jezus* (Kampen: J.H. Kok, 1936).

10. *Geschiedenis der Godsopenbaring, vol. 2: Het Nieuwe Testament* (Kampen: J.H. Kok, 1938).

11. *Alzoo wies het Woord* (Baarn: Bosch en Keuning, 1941); *En voort wentelen de eeuwen* (Wageningen: Zomer en Keuning, 1952); *De mensch en zijn wereld* (Baarn: Bosch en Keuning, 1946).

12. Thus J.H. Banvick in his memorial article, "Kraemer als denker en medewerker," *De Heerbaan* 11 (1958): 87.

13. *Christusprediking in de volkerenwereld* (Kampen: J.H. Kok, 1939).

14. *De boodschap van Christus en de niet-christelijke religies* (Kampen: J.H. Kok, 1940).

15. *Religieus besef en christelijk geloof* (Kampen: J.H. Kok, 1949).

16. *Inleiding in de zendingswetenschap* (Kampen: J.H. Kok, 1954).

Selected Bibliography

Major Works by J.H. Bavinck

In J. van den Berg, ed., *Christusprediking in de wereld* (Kampen: J.H. Kok, 1965), a memorial volume published shortly after Bavinck's death, A. Wessels has provided a complete bibliography of J.H. Bavinck's writings. The following list is restricted to those that have appeared in English:

1948 *The Impact of Christianity on the Non-Christian World.* Grand Rapids, Mich: Wm. B. Eerdmans.
1949 "Four Stages in the Expansion of the Church." *Calvin Forum* 14:112-15.
1955 "General Revelation and the Non-Christian Religions." *Free University Quarterly* 4:43-55.
1956 "The Problem of Adaptation and Communication." *International Review of Missions* 45:307-13.
1956 "The Race Problem in South Africa." *Free University Quarterly* 4:85-98.
1960 "India in Transition." *Free Univerity Quarterly* 7:26-37.
1960 *An Introduction to the Science of Missions.* Trans. David H. Freeman. Grand Rapids, Mich.: Baker Book House.
1961 "Theology and Mission." *Free University Quarterly* 8:59-66.
1966 *The Church between Temple and Mosque.* 2nd ed. Grand Rapids, Mich.: Wm. B. Eerdmans, 1981.

Works about J.H. Bavinck

See "De wetenschappelijke arbeid van Prof. Dr. J.H. Bavinck," this writer's survey of Bavinck's work as a scholar, in J. van den Berg, ed., *Christusprediking in de wereld.* In the same volume is "Leven en werk van Dr. Johan Herman Bavinck," a short biography by Bavinck's friend and former colleague in Djokja, A. Pos, to whom this writer is indebted for some of the biographical details given in the present article.

Walter Freytag

1899–1959

The Miracle of the Church among the Nations

Hans-Werner Gensichen

Is there at all such a thing as a legacy of Walter Freytag? When Freytag died unexpectedly in 1959, in his sixty-first year, he left behind only one major book published in 1938, two or three pamphlets, and a number of scattered essays, sermons, and lectures, most of which were collected in two slim volumes two years after his death. He had been teaching missiology, history of religions, and ecumenical theology for thirty years. But he never produced a comprehensive scholarly survey of any of those fields. He had taught a large number of devoted students. As a teacher he was perhaps at his best, and he actually spent part of the last night of his life discussing with me how he could reduce his ecumenical obligations in order to gain more time for his students. But he never created a "school" of his own. He had never been a missionary or a mission board secretary, and neither a Third World church nor a mission society could claim to have been shaped by him.

He had indeed been holding a variety of leading positions in church, mission, and ecumenical bodies. Yet he cannot be said to have been one of the powerful strategists of the world church, either preservers or reformers, whose achievements have left indelible marks in the history of ecumenical Christianity. Nevertheless he is remembered, in the words of John A. Mackay, as "a pivotal figure in the life and thought of the Christian missionary movement."[1] And it is certainly not by chance that it was left to one of the great Christian laymen of his generation, Sir Kenneth Grubb, to explain even before Freytag's death why this was the case: Freytag's thought was "part of the man himself" who "conveyed certain precious attitudes" and not just "meaning."[2]

Freytag for his part, during his travels in India or his beloved New Guinea, in America or in China, had always been more keen on coming into contact with people than with systems of thought, cultural patterns, or church organizations. Because he never tried to dominate he was able to listen, sometimes for hours at a stretch. The highest tribute that a young African was able to pay to Freytag shortly after his death was that he remembered him as a man to whom he had been able to talk for a long time without having been interrupted. Another of Freytag's contemporaries, Max Warren, described it as perhaps the main source of Freytag's influence that he brought to all his companions in the missionary enterprise an understanding heart, which in turn admitted him to the heart of others in a unique way sharing particular experiences and drawing from them general applications.[3]

This approach occasionally led to doubts about the quality of Freytag's theological work, which, however, did not impress him unduly. "Maybe I am not a theologian at all," he would concede in a joking mood. He did not disregard theology as a scientific enterprise. But he knew, as the philosopher Martin Heidegger had said, that each science that claimed to be more than a mere technique rested on presuppositions that transcended scientific investigation. Theology, too, had to be more than an exercise in dialectics. It had to grow out of the individual and corporate experience of the redemptive purpose of God-in-Christ, and in that sense it could not but have a missionary perspective.

Background and Career

Freytag's father was a jeweler in Neudietendorf, a small town in Thuringia. Both he and his wife were members of the Moravian Brethren. Like Schleiermacher, Freytag might have considered himself a "Moravian of a higher order." Zinzendorf's *Unitas Fratrum* was and remained his spiritual home, even when he, a member of a "Herrnhuter" family in central Germany, became a minister in a German regional church. Later in his life in difficult situations he was sometimes heard to quote one or the other of Zinzendorf's hymns, which he had committed to memory as a youth. As a student of theology he was strongly influenced by Adolf Schlatter and Karl Heim at Tübingen, the leading representatives of biblical realism and a theology of *Heilsgeschichte*.

Shortly after ordination he received and accepted a call to work as a lecturer in religious education in Wuchang, China. In preparation for this task Freytag obtained a Ph.D. in Pedagogics, Psychology, and Chinese Religions at Hamburg University in 1925. However, developments in China forced him to cancel his plan. After a short period as a parish pastor he was appointed secretary and, two years later, director of a German agency for public relations and promotion of the missionary cause. In addition he was soon called as mission director of the churches of Hamburg, Bremen, and Lübeck as well as lecturer in missiology at the Philosophical Faculty of Hamburg University and the Theological Faculty at Kiel University. This unique combination of influential positions allowed Freytag, by teaching, writing, and lecturing, to lay the foundation for what was later to become the spiritual and administrative center of German Protestant missions. In 1925 he married Anne-Katherin Wohlfahrt. They had four children.

The Nazi regime succeeded in silencing Freytag for the last two years of the war. Yet in 1946 he not only resumed his activities but also became chairman of the German Missionary Council, which position he retained until he died in 1959. When in 1953 the University of Hamburg at last decided to establish a full-fledged theological faculty, Freytag was the obvious choice for the newly created chair of missiology and ecumenical relations. The Mission Academy, set up due to Freytag's initiative in 1954 as part of the university structure, became the institutional link between his activities as teacher, scholar, and missionary leader.

When ecumenical contacts with German churches had been reestablished, none other but Freytag could be thought of as the representative of German Protestant missions in the world church. He participated in all world missionary conferences from Jerusalem 1928 to Ghana 1957-58, became chairman of the Division of Studies of the World Council of Churches in 1954, a vice president of the International Missionary Council in 1958, and took an active part in numerous other ecumenical bodies. After 1945 Freytag paid repeated visits to the United States and Canada, mostly for participation in ecumenical events.

Far from being a mere "ecumaniac" or from considering missionary statesmanship as an end in itself, Freytag felt it to be part of his personal responsibility to make "the missionary dimension of the *whole* church and of *all* churches" manifest.[4] Identification with and participation in the world church called him to serve his German home church even more devotedly. He understood, as expressed in the title of his last address, "The Regional Church (*Landeskirche*) as Part of the World Mission." No less than three times he was urged to run for the vacant office of bishop in the regional church of Hamburg. Three times he declined. But as a member of the Hamburg church synod and various nationwide church committees he continued to exert considerable influence in German Protestantism as a whole.

It has quite rightly been said that Walter Freytag saw it as his task to lead both the church back to its mission and the mission back to the church. Whether he succeeded in doing so in Germany may be debatable. He certainly did achieve a degree of understanding and unity of purpose among German missionary agencies unheard of before, which seems almost incredible now as the polarization of so-called evangelical and ecumenical groups has been increasing at an alarming rate. Church leaders listened to Freytag's appeals and gave indications of their willingness to act accordingly. Yet when his charismatic persistence had disappeared, when his mediating skill was no longer in operation, things took a different turn. It is not only sobering but depressing to arrive at such a conclusion. Could it be that Freytag misjudged the situation? During the heated debates on the problems of integration of church and mission on the ecumenical level, in the years before the New Delhi Assembly of 1961, Freytag argued passionately in favor of integration, while some of his colleagues in Germany, no less insistently, maintained that the churches were not ready yet and that it was anybody's guess whether they ever would be. If the course of events after 1961 at least in Germany eventually proved them right, there is certainly no reason to acquiesce in a situation of which Freytag had been under apprehension more than most others.

"New Realities"

While Freytag respected the scholarly achievements of previous generations of missiologists, he had no use for mere repetition of theories of the past, hoary as they might be.[5] He was most seriously concerned to do justice to what he called the "new realities" or simply the "facts" of changed situations as he saw them. And was it not obvious that missions were deeply affected by such changes? "Then," at the time of the Jerusalem meeting of the International Missionary Council in 1928, "missions had problems, but they were not a problem themselves.[6] . . . Today we are uncertain about their patterns as they are and even more, the historic, basic conceptions of missions are being questioned."[7]

The questioning originated, in the first place, from new realities in national and international politics, in social and cultural affairs, in development and education, religion and spirituality. The age of colonial rule was patently in eclipse all over the world. A new longing for self-realization, although in many instances still unstable, made itself felt. Freytag together with others had sensed all this already in the twenties and early thirties. During his first extended journey in Asia on which he reported in 1938,[8] he had come to the conclusion that God was at work in the political, social, and cultural revolutions that stirred even the most backward peoples. How could traditional concepts of eternal return, of cyclic repetition of events persist when God himself provided new goals, a new kairos which created a new sense of direction and destiny?

Freytag knew that he was moving on dangerous ground. He had himself been in open conflict with German Christian theologians who, in a seemingly similar fashion, declared the new realities created by the Nazi regime to be unmistakable evidence of God's working in history. The personal experience of Hitler's tyranny and of the ensuing world war had led Freytag to a critical reappraisal of any facile identification of historical facts and the will of God. History could certainly not but be governed by God's own plan. Yet this was not evident on the surface of events. It had to be discerned by the eye of faith, more often than not in contrast to what the realities seemed to indicate. Insight into the meaning of history was not, as a generation later Wolfhart Pannenberg would maintain, the presupposition of faith but its consequence. *Heilsgeschichte* only would open up the depth dimension of all history. The "facts" as such proved to be ambivalent. As part of the old aeon, they had to be regarded as the linen cloths in the tomb of Jesus – serving a purpose in the world as the sphere of human life and action, yet in principle having been laid aside at the dawn of the new age of the resurrection.

Occasionally Freytag had been taken to task for what to some appeared to be a far too pessimistic view of history and the world. For example, was not Dietrich Bonhoeffer's concept of the modern world come of age, and man as its free agent, unencumbered by religious scruples, closer to the biblical view of what God had willed for his creation? Freytag might have replied that he was not primarily concerned about problems of anthropology or the interpretation of history in general. The focal point of his argument was an eminently practical one: the Christian mission in a changing world, and that not in a theoretical sense but as a challenge to the obedience of faith that God demanded at each particular historical juncture. It was as simple as that: "Without mission, history is nothing but human history, and its progress can lead nowhere except to a climax of its catastrophes."9 Or in more positive terms: "Mission is the real meaning of the interval in salvation history between Christ's resurrection and parousia. In mission the truly decisive things happen – those related to the end, irrespective of all human history and circumstances, in season and out of season."10 Yet from that angle even the things of this world could take on a new relevance.

Nothing could have been more important to Freytag than to trace the expressions that the obedience of faith would take among those who responded to the call under varying conditions. Those who knew him well have often remarked on his way of elaborating important points in his lectures and addresses with illustrations, sometimes attributing more weight to the latter than to the former. Mission had to do with the spontaneous, authentic response of faith, different in different contexts, but in any case embracing the total range of relationships in both society and environment, the organic life of the peoples, including culture and religion.

Freytag's concept of *Volk*, in his day a hotly debated issue, is an instructive case in question. While he spoke up against any pseudoreligious glorification of *Volk* as a natural point of contact for the Gospel, he insisted that such God-given societal patterns had to be respected and utilized in connection with the growth of the church precisely because in this age before the end they were not yet suspended, although in view of what was to come they could never claim ultimate loyalty. They might be dangerous wherever they appeared in *heidnischer Umklammerung*, that is, embraced by paganism, just as all other attempts at a synthesis of religions and social patterns had to be regarded with suspicion, not least the post-Christian and even the Christian ones. On the other hand, they, too, were part of the realities that had to be faced if, as Freytag liked to say, the mission was to become what it ought to be: "God's reality in this world."11 At an early stage of his career Freytag had a foretaste of the difficulties involved in maintaining so precarious a balance between positions that were indeed difficult to reconcile. He was one of the German delegates at the Tambaram Assembly of the International Missionary Council of 1938 who presented a statement of their own, trying to combine an eschatological emphasis with a defense of the "orders which God has established and ordained . . . for this period of transition between Christ's resurrection and His Second Advent," including nations and races.12 This was bound to be misunderstood as a veiled defense of the *Volk*-ideology of the Third Reich. Nobody could be further from such an intention than Freytag. But the experience helped him to clarify even more carefully the paradoxical character of the church's mission in this world, "witnessing by word and deed in real brotherhood and sacrificial service for the sake of mankind" and "so proclaiming the Lord's death till He comes."13

"Mission as God's Reality in This World"

Freytag's missiological approach has been described as inductive, in contrast to a deductive way of thinking that starts from Scriptures and then proceeds to the interpretation of contextual situations. It is not clear whether Freytag himself ever used this terminology. He certainly would never have consented to any philosophy or theology of mission that relied on the so-called realities of nature, world, and history more than on the explicit testimonies of Scripture. On that basis he would, however, attempt to make reality transparent, as it were, for the signs of God's eschatological work of salvation and redemption and thus to "find new openings towards the center secretly hidden" – openings that were not to be discovered except by attempting "to follow what God is doing step by step."[14]

This would, in the first place, imply a realignment of missions with reference to traditional patterns. The pietistic type, while rightly insisting on calling people to repentance and conversion, was one-sided in its individualistic emphasis. Church-centered missions were right in their concern for the gathering of believers into the church. But they often tended to identify the kingdom of God with the institutional church. Philanthropic missions were rightly concerned about obedience active in love. But not even the most devoted attempts to make the world a better place to live in would bring the coming kingdom any nearer. Finally, there was the one-sided emphasis on the "beyond" in apocalyptic missions, which believed they were called literally to speed up the return of Christ by their witness. In contrast to all these approaches, the relative merits of which he did not want to deny, Freytag advocated a view of mission as "taking part in the action of God, in fulfilling his plan for the coming of his kingdom by bringing about obedience of the faith in Jesus Christ our Lord among the nations."[15] Nowadays this may sound fairly conventional. But a generation ago Freytag's thought provided for many the kind of direction in mission whose loss had been widely deplored, not least by Freytag himself.

The World Missionary Conference of Willingen 1952 in this connection made the phrase *missio Dei*, God's own mission, internationally popular. Freytag himself had already ten years earlier described mission, with reference to Mark 13:10, as "part of God's own eschatological action," as "the sign of the coming end set up by Him."[16] To him this carried a dual emphasis. First, *missio Dei*, as the very term suggested, was meant to correct all undue indulgence in *missio hominum*. The signs of the times made it clear to everyone willing to see: the "loss of directness" in Western missions, their "endangered image,"[17] were more than a symptom of transitory weakness. Did they not rather point to a more permanent defect, a habitual overestimation of human missionary action and its achievements, perhaps even to the "spectre of panmissionism,"[18] and thus to a new and peculiar kind of active disobedience in the disguise of restless activity?

Second, *missio Dei* made sense only in view of the end, the *eschaton*, which alone gave mission the proper perspective. It has sometimes been said that Freytag had borrowed the eschatological emphasis from the Cullmann school of biblical exegesis. However he had learned it already from his teachers Adolf Schlatter and Karl Heim. Moreover he deliberately refrained from giving the mission its place in a comprehensive scheme of *Heilsgeschichte* whereby it might serve as an unfailing indicator of apocalyptic events to come, or even as a device of bringing those events nearer. The fact of the matter is that Freytag found the dialectic of mission and eschatology fulfilled in the continuing call to mission, "to take part in the responsibility of God's outgoing into the whole world," to such an extent that those "who live in the obedience of faith are part of His action."[19]

In this connection Freytag used to mention an experience he had in 1956 in China. He had been asked by Christians in Peking how the church in West Germany since 1945 had given witness to the lordship of Christ in this world. He had not been asked about the work of German missions – and was this not striking evidence that in the final analysis every Christian was supposed to be part of God's mission in the world, that "the decisions of God's action are made in our life with Christ"? Max Warren reported how Freytag summed this up in Christological terms at the Whitby conference of 1947: "The life of Christ has to do with the day of his return. Gospel is never glad tidings of solved problems but a summons to a fight in which victory is certain."[20]

Again, Freytag's strictly eschatological concept of mission has come in for questioning. Did he not perhaps, in order to maintain the perspective of the *eschaton*, play down the salvation that had already been achieved in Christ's cross and resurrection? Freytag might ask in return, as he did at Whitby: "Do not the acts of God which constitute the *kerygma* . . . contain the future acts of God – the future of history, the future of the Church – the end of the world?"[21] He probably would have cared little whether, in his outline of the *missio Dei*, reconciliation and redemption, presence and future, promise and fulfillment were perfectly in balance or not. What mattered most to him was, again, whether Christians in their whole life and existence were willing to become part of God's eschatological mission or whether they would stand in its way.

"The Miracle of the Church among the Nations"

It was this perspective with which, in Freytag's opinion, the church, too, would stand and fall: it has "its life towards that end, the goal of God in the coming again of Christ."[22] In saying this, Freytag steered a course between two extremes, neither of which seemed acceptable to him. On the one hand, there were those who regarded mission primarily as an operation from an existing church to a church to be, as it were, a device for the self-propagation of church bodies, their traditions and structures. Freytag would agree that the gathering into a visible community of those who came to believe was an indispensable part of the mission, just as mission in both the Old and New Testaments had a centripetal as well as a centrifugal aspect. Yet the mission as participation in the action of God could not possibly be domesticated within the limits of a confessional or regional church and its immediate outreach. On the other hand, the church was more than mission. Its total being was not to be reduced to its missionary action. J.C. Hoekendijk, otherwise on friendly terms with Freytag, could not help disagreeing violently with Freytag's rejection of "pan-missionism," which Hoekendijk quite rightly interpreted as an emphatic objection against Hoekendijk's favorite idea of "mission without church."[23] In fact in this respect some of Freytag's own disciples were more in sympathy with Hoekendijk than with him. But Freytag was not willing to yield because he was afraid of letting the church fall back from one captivity in human actionism into the other. Not mission but the grace of God, manifested in baptism and Eucharist, was the ground on which the church had to rely. There might be times of emergency and pressure when the church would have to survive by relying on that ground only, even without any outgoing mission. Was not China after 1949 a case in question – China, which had been the aim of Freytag's ambition in his younger days and had retained its special fascination for him ever since? And so he explained to the Ghana Assembly in a remarkably sober and cautious manner that in the varieties of "services" of the churches, mission was but one human form in which Christian obedience was to take shape, and that it might well become concrete in separate missionary organizations and institutions, which would send out witnesses in order to carry the Gospel from church to nonchurch. "This service of missions is human service, it cannot claim to be exclusively the mission of God" – which in its turn was of course more than such service, as Freytag never grew tired of emphasizing.[24] So he insisted that outdated patterns of mission should be overcome, that the missionary obedience of churches should find new forms in new contexts. But he was unwilling to abandon the idea of missions, foreign missions in particular, as a "special service" of the church, reaching out to what was yet to become a church.

His refusal to muster theological arguments for the integration of church and mission, as recorded above, fits into the picture. No wonder that Freytag seems to have had little trouble with the term *Äussere Mission*, foreign missions, as distinguished from *Volksmission*, home missions. God's outgoing into the whole world in which each church was to take part might happen in "nonchurch" areas as well as in countries in which the church had long been present – the task was essentially the same, "mission here and there,"[25] yet not simply to be identified with the conventional teaching and preaching of the church for its members.

There is a marked difference between Freytag's wrestling with the problem of calling saturated Western churches to missionary obedience, and his discovery of the "responding church" as he found it in Asia, the Pacific, and Africa. That was where the "miracle of the church among the nations" was really coming true, and where therefore, in Freytag's opinion, the criteria of what the mission was meant to achieve became manifest.[26]

It is neither possible nor necessary to analyze Freytag's concept of the "younger church" in detail – its special blessings and its special problems as he had observed and interpreted them in most of what he had said and written since his first comprehensive report of 1938. But there are emphases that are of more than historiographical interest, especially because they seem to provide clues to what, according to Freytag, established the obedience of faith in pursuit of the *missio Dei* and in relation to the new realities as they appeared in the various cultural contexts.

In 1925 Freytag had written his doctoral dissertation on "Patterns of Religious Formation and Education in A. Tholuck's Book on Sin." Here for the first time Freytag had concentrated on the role and function of human conscience in religious experience. Later he developed this further in his famous essay entitled "Psychology of Conversion among Primitive Peoples" and, finally, in one of his most mature treatises, written in the midst of isolation during the war, on "How Pagans Become Christians." The argument was as lucid as simple. There is a difference between the Gospel message as it is proclaimed and as it is received. The preaching is conditioned by the cultural and personal circumstances of the messenger as well as by those of the addressees. The Gospel message remains alien and ineffective unless it enters into the respective cultural and personal circumstances of those who hear, and thus appeals to their conscience. For there, and there only, in their very life center, both individuals and groups are able authentically to respond to the call of God's Word, either by opposition or by consent. There the struggle between the old and the new loyalties will be fought out. There alone the obedience of faith will be generated, which otherwise would remain superficial. "Conscience speaks the mother-tongue,"[27] and without its spontaneous response that Word would "return empty and not accomplish that which God purposes" (Isa. 55:11). Above all, the change of conscience under the impact of the Gospel is the decisive factor in the process of the genesis and growth of the younger church – a church which, as Freytag said frequently, comes into being and must be respected as "another and a different church."

Never before had Freytag expressed this as concisely and consistently as in a brief memorandum that he sent out to some contact people before his last major journey to Asia in 1956-57: "The decisive feature is that which we might call the 'responding church.' For what constitutes the life of a church, as seen from the human side, is that it is a responding one in the twofold meaning: responding to the Word, and in a given situation. It is in this twofold response that a given church has its identity as Church." It was Freytag's chief concern to discover the genuine response of the younger church "not only where we are used to do so according to the ideas which we derive from western churches, but perhaps most intensely at points where a church's reaction are different from those of western churches."[28]

It is remarkable that in this connection Freytag omits any reference to the confessional or denominational identity of the church. This may have been partly due to his upbringing as a member of the Moravian community which, while associating itself with the Lutheran family of churches in a broad sense, had traditionally placed loyalty to Christ as the Lord above any denominational affiliation. Even as an ordained minister in the Lutheran church of Hamburg, Freytag maintained membership in the local Moravian congregation. However, quite apart from biographical circumstances, Freytag was convinced that there was an organic relationship between the mission and the unity of the church, which the Moravian community in its history since the days of Zinzendorf had expressed in a specially convincing way. Generally speaking, only as divided churches agreed to go forth in mission could they be expected to make progress toward achieving a higher degree of unity. Here, too, Freytag could place the truth of the church, as he used to call it, above its historical appearance. "To ask for unity does not mean to ask for the sum total of empirical churches but for the true church,"[29] the church that is known precisely by its fruits beyond the borders of existing denominations. On the other hand, existing denominational churches should not be disregarded on that account only: "The fruits are there not in spite of people being members of an empirical church but because they are."[30]

This, incidentally, was the frame of reference in which Freytag considered the church's witness among people of non-Christian religions or no religious adherence whatever. There, too, Freytag would advocate waiting for a better proclamation of the Word, reaching deeper than hitherto experienced, searching for expressions of the faith that would do justice to the particular challenge presented by the encounter in a given situation. That challenge would never be met on the basis of a naïve assumption of Western-Christian superiority. "You have not really understood another religion unless you have been tempted by the insights of this other religion . . . There is no understanding of other religions which does not yield new biblical insights."[31] After all, the Christian religion itself was permanently in danger of falling victim to the assaults of demonic powers. And was it not at least partly due to the failure of the church's witness, its inadequate communication of the biblical message, that a phenomenon such as "post-Christian non-Christian" religion could at all come into being? Hence it was not any innate prerogative that Christianity could claim in the struggle. It was the living Lord alone to whom one had to resort in order to find the right approach – an approach that would eventually reach the conscience of those to whom the Gospel message of salvation in Christ was to be addressed, irrespective of any handy theological formulas like continuity and discontinuity, promise and fulfillment, question and answer.

Besides, while Freytag did give due attention to the general problems of the Christian approach to non-Christian religion,[32] he was prophetically aware of new developments that would require entirely new responses: "A new world religion is in process of formation which will embrace all religions, old and new, including the political ones in east and west, so that their traditional contradictions will appear merely like those of denominations within the same confession."[33]

In this respect as well as in others it would be tempting to determine how Freytag, the prophet of a past generation, would qualify as a judge of our own age, its achievements and failures. Even though not all of his contributions to the mission of the church and to a responsible science of mission will prove to have lasting effects, the fact remains that he stood out in his day as a teacher, preacher, and scholar, endowed not just with persuasive power but with authority in the sense of an *exousia* that drew its strength not from its own resources but from total submission to the guidance of God. Or as Freytag himself put it somewhat paradoxically a few months before the abrupt end of his life: "We ought to be much more conscious, should we not, of the danger implicit in wanting to see, here and now, the very things which we have only by faith and hope. It is only by this certain confidence in things *not* seen that we actually have them as our own."[34]

Notes

1. Mackay, *Basileia,* p. 13.
2. Grubb, ibid., p. 15.
3. Warren, ibid., p. 165.
4. Heinrich Meyer, quoted by J. Triebel, *Bekehrung,* p. 343 n. 49.
5. Freytag, "Changes," p. 139.

6. Ibid., p. 138. The official English translation of Freytag's speech at the Ghana Assembly missed the cutting edge of the original German wording: "Damals hatte die Mission Probleme, heute ist sie selbst zum Problem geworden" (*Reden und Aufsätze,* 1:111).

7. Ibid., pp. 138-39.

8. Freytag, *Die junge Christenheit im Umbruch des Ostens.*

9. Freytag, *Reden und Aufsätze,* 2:216.

10. Ibid., p. 214.

11. Ibid., p. 219.

12. *The Authority of the Faith,* Madras Series, International Missionary Council, vol. 1 (London: Oxford University Press, 1939), pp. 184-85.

13. Ibid., p. 185.

14. Freytag, "Changes," p. 145.

15. Ibid., p. 146.

16. Freytag, *Reden und Aufsätze,* 2:189.

17. Freytag, "Changes," p. 142.

18. Freytag, *Reden und Aufsätze,* 2:94.

19. Freytag, "Changes," p. 146.

20. Warren, "Thought and Practice," p. 161.

21. Ibid.

22. Freytag, "Changes," p. 146.

23. J.C. Hoekendijk, *Kirche und Volk in der deutschen Missionswissenschaft* (Munich: Chr. Kaiser Verlag, 1967), p. 334.

24. Freytag, "Changes," p. 146.

25. Freytag, *Reden und Aufsätze,* 2:208.

26. Translation of the title of the official German report on the Tambaram conference, 1938: *Das Wunder der kirche unter den Völkern der Erde,* ed. Martin Schlunk (Stuttgart/Basel: Evang. Missionsverlag). It was Freytag who suggested the wording of the title.

27. Freytag, *Reden und Aufsätze,* 2:72.

28. Ibid., 1:55. The English wording quoted here is Freytag's own.

29. Ibid., 2:120.

30. Ibid., p. 230.

31. From a speech on the research work of the International Missionary Council, delivered at Staten Island, New York, in 1954: quoted by Warren, "Thought and Practice," p. 164.

32. See in particular *Das Rätsel der Religionen und die biblische Antwort.*

33. Freytag, *Reden und Aufsätze,* 2:225.

34. Ibid., p. 97. "Sollten wir uns nicht der Gefahr viel bewusster sein, die darin liegt, dass wir jetzt und hier sehen wollen, was wir nur im Glauben und in der Hoffnung, nur in der gewissen Zuversicht dessen, das man *nicht* sieht, haben?"

Selected Bibliography

Works by Walter Freytag

For a complete bibliography covering the years 1926-58, see Ursula Ebert, "Bibliographie Walter Freyag," in *Basileia. Walter Freytag zum 60. Geburtstag,* ed. J. Hermelink and H.J. Margull, pp. 503-11. Stuttgart: Evang. Missionsverlag, 1959.

1938 *Die junge Christenheit im Umbruch des Ostens. Vom Gehorsam des Glaubens unter den Völkern.* Berlin: Furche-Verlag. 272 pp. English edition: *Spiritual Revolution in the East.* Trans. M.O. Stalker. London: United Societies for Christian Literature, 1940.

1952 "Die neue Stunde der Weltmission." In Walter Freytag and Karl Hartenstein, eds. *Die neue Stunde der Weltmission.* Stuttgart: Evang. Missionsverlag.

1956 *Das Rätsel der Religionen und die biblische Antwort.* Wuppertal-Barmen: Jugenddienst-Verlag. English edition: *The Gospel and the Religions. A Biblical Enquiry.* I.M.C. Research Pamphlets, no. 5. London: SCM Press, 1957.

1958 "Changes in the Patterns of Western Missions." In *The Ghana Assembly of the International Missionary Council,* ed. R.K. Orchard, pp. 138-47. London: Edinburgh House Press.

1958 *Kirchen im neuen Asien. Eindrücke einer Studienreise.* Weltmission heute, Heft 7/8 Stuttgart: Evang. Missionsverlag.

1961 *Reden und Aufsätze.* Ed. J. Hermelink and H.J. Margull. 2 vols. Munich: Chr. Kaiser Verlag.

Works about Walter Freytag

Beyerhaus, Peter. "Walter Freytags Begriff des Gewissens in der Sicht Südafrikanischer Missionsarbeit." In *Basileia. Walter Freytag zum 60. Geburtstag,* ed. J. Hermelink and H.J. Margull, pp. 146-57. Stuttgart: Evang. Missionsverlag, 1959.

Blauw, Johannes. "Dienst in gehóór-zaamheid." *De Heerban* (1961): 219-30.

_____. "Ik send U." *De Heerbaan,* 1961, pp. 235-48.

Grubb, Sir Kenneth. "Communication." In *Basileia,* pp. 13-14.

Mackay, John A. "A Tribute to Walter Freytag." *Basileia,* pp. 13-14.

Manecke, Dieter. *Mission als Zeugendienst,* pp. 64-106. Wuppertal: Theologischer Verlag Rolf Brockhaus, 1972.

Margull, Hans Jochen. "Walter Freytag als Lehrer." *Evangelische Missionszeitschrift* 16 (1959): 165-68.

Triebel, Johannes. *Bekehrung als Ziel der missionarischen Verkündigung. Die Theologie Walter Freytags und das ökumenische Gespräch.* Erlangen: Verlag der Ev.-luth. Mission, 1976.

Warren, Max A.C. "The Thought and Practice of Missions. Notes on Walter Freytag's Contribution." *Basileia,* pp. 158-65.

Stephen Neill

1900–1984

Unafraid to Ask Ultimate Questions

Christopher Lamb

Stephen Charles Neill (December 31, 1900–July 20, 1984) was a scholar, theologian, and missionary thinker of outstanding gifts and comparable influence. A man of unflagging intellectual energy, he published some fifty books, three of them in the last year of his life. A letter I received from him within a month of his death at the age of eighty-three hoped "that there may be some time left for things that I still want to be allowed to do." In particular he wanted to finish his projected three-volume *History of Christianity in India,* of which the first volume was published a few months before his death, and the second came out a year later.

The octogenarian ambition reflected perhaps a sense that he had never fulfilled the superlative promise of his youth. The reasons for that are not yet fully clear, though his autobiography speaks of internal struggles commensurate with the powers of mind that everyone recognized in him. The Neill family came originally from Ulster – "there were two kinds of Neill character, cautious and imprudent"[1] – while his maternal grandfather was successively distinguished in the Indian Civil Service, as the commissioner of the Metropolitan Police, and a missionary in Bengal. His father became a doctor and then a missionary, but during the years of Stephen's childhood his restless temperament kept the family home moving around southern England. Shyness, the son recalled, afflicted both his parents, and though he, as the third of six children, was less affected, he still experienced the temptation to contract out of society in a world of books and imagination. He was educated at Dean Close School, Cheltenham, a place that earned his affection for the quality of its teachers, and for providing him with the geographical roots of which his father's roving nature had deprived him. The precocious teenager, teaching himself Hebrew by torchlight under the bed-clothes, found it difficult to share what he was learning with his contemporaries, and may have taken early refuge in a kind of lonely stoicism. Religion, as well as nature and circumstance, may have conspired to mold him this way. Neill was converted during an attack of mumps, when he suddenly "just knew" the reality of the atonement. He wrote of his later, adult sense of isolation and deep despair: "It was good that I had been brought up in that austere form of Evangelicalism in which any mention of feelings was regarded as almost an indecency." But perhaps a less austere religion would have given the church a servant less deeply damaged.

Going on, in the Dark

His autobiography tells us of lifelong insomnia, leading to frequent irritability and loss of perspective, but much more seriously of a darkness that was no depression but despair; "it was as if all the lights went out." Beginning at Cambridge, after a spell of intensely hard work for his Prize Fellowship, he had several prolonged spells of "complete darkness," from 1926 to 1933 and later from 1946 for a decade. These, he recorded, "determined the major part of my career."[2] Characteristically he took refuge in the Psalms, especially 88:12: "Shall thy wondrous works be known in the dark . . . ? Unto thee have I cried, O Lord" (*Book of Common Prayer*); and also in the words of John Newton: "Don't tell of your feelings. A traveler would be glad of fine weather, but, if he be a man of business, he will go on." It is impossible to know what that "going on" cost him, and what might have been in his ministry had his problem been recognized earlier. A promising course of psychotherapy was cut short for reasons that he clearly resented but does not explain in his autobiography.[3] At times he contemplated suicide but was protected from it, he reckoned later, by an inherited Neill obstinacy and a deep-seated dislike of exhibiting such ingratitude to God.[4] He knew no complete freedom from this malady until 1965, after which, expect for a brief recurrence, it did not trouble him again.

Neill's academic career was spectacularly untroubled. From Dean Close he won a classical scholarship to Trinity College, Cambridge, followed by a string of university prizes. Later in life he received honorary doctorates from the Universities of Toronto, Culver-Stockton, Hamburg, Tokyo, Glasgow, and Uppsala, but perhaps nothing meant more to him than the award of a fellowship from his own college, the college of Bertrand Russell, G.M. Trevelyan, and so many others, founded by Henry VIII. For this he had to write a dissertation, and he chose to compare the writings of Plotinus with those of Gregory of Nyssa and Gregory of Nazianzen. The choice reveals perhaps the missionary in the making, for few subjects are more calculated to focus on the distinction between Hellenism and Christianity in the European intellectual tradition. The mysticism of Plotinus had many uses too as an introduction to Hindu monism, and served as a foundation and model for all Neill's writing on Christianity and other faiths. It reveals too the catholicity of mind that the study of the Greek and Latin classics had engendered in a personality molded by evangelicalism. The fact that it was the Fathers rather than the Reformers whom he chose to study indicated a more comprehensively Anglican spirit in this Englishman with his Scot and Irish forebears.

Comprehensiveness in Neill took other forms as well. He had become a member of the Cambridge Inter-Collegiate Christian Union (CICCU), the famous evangelical student body, early in his university career. As his student reputation grew, he was asked, to his great surprise, to be president of the university Student Christian Movement (SCM), the more liberal student body. Neither group, or those wider movements that they represented, gained his wholehearted loyalty. At the end of his life he wrote sadly: "For fifty years I have helplessly watched these two bodies corrupting one another." He saw an empty liberalism on one side, matched by an unthinking intransigence on the other.[5] These were days of bitter theological controversy as in 1922 the Church Missionary Society (CMS) split in two, giving birth to the more conservative Bible Churchmen's Missionary Society (BCMS). No detailed history of these events has ever been written, and the BCMS archives were destroyed by enemy bombing during the war of 1939-45, so perhaps the full story can never be told. It must have been personally as well as theologically painful for Neill, for in 1924, having only just gained his Trinity Fellowship, he became a CMS missionary in India, where his father was one of the few CMS missionaries to leave the parent body and serve with BCMS in Mirzapur. An uncle succeeded the BCMS founder and first general secretary, Daniel Bartlett, in the parish he had left near Bristol.[6] Perhaps such experience drove Neill to work for Christian reconciliation and unity with a lifelong intensity that theological motive alone could not have sustained. Certainly the combination of wide erudition, deep theological acumen, and passionate convictions about the co-inheritance of Gospel, mission, and church made him a formidable advocate of ecumenism.

At this stage, the resurrection was already the center of his faith, together with the atonement. Though he could write of Aeschylus' *Agamemnon* that it contained "religious utterances on the same level as that of the prophet Isaiah," he knew that "on certain levels of human distress Hellenism is not the answer," for it can only enable a reconception of the self. The resurrection, by contrast, is the rebirth of the universe. "What the Gospel offers is not a new understanding of self in an unchanged world but invitation to adventure in a world in which all things have become new."[7] It must have been such a conviction of adventure that led him to leave the security, and for him the immense attraction, of an academic life for missionary service in India. Few students of his age had achieved more, or, in consequence, had more to lose than Neill in "burying himself," as it must have appeared, in India. Perhaps the influence of CICCU was most evident here, but Neill does not stop to dwell on the matter in his autobiography as one might wish. He was accepted for work in the diocese of Tinnevelly (now Tirunelveli) at the southernmost tip of India, and plunged into learning Tamil and grappling with a literary culture as old as that of Greece.

Missionary Career in India

His missionary career lasted, with a few brief interruptions, for some twenty-two years. His early years were spent in evangelistic work and constant travel. For one spell he accompanied the pioneer in dialogue, E. Stanley Jones, as he sought out Hindu students and intellectuals for his "round table" discussions. As his gifts in teaching developed he was entrusted with the theological formation of Indian students, and in 1930 became warden of Tirumaraiyur's theological college. His own considerable learning must have made student life under his teaching exciting but also exacting, to judge from a casual footnote in his *Anglicanism* (1958, rev. ed. 1977), which reads: "All theological students should be compelled to read Butler [Bishop Joseph Butler, 1692-1752], not necessarily in order to think the same thoughts as Butler, but in order to learn how to think theologically. As a theological teacher in South India I used to make my students translate selections from Butler's Sermons into Tamil, a task which I think we all found difficult but profitable."[8] As an inevitable extension of his theological teaching Neill was drawn into the work of the joint committee that was preparing for church union in South India. Of his work there Bengt Sundkler has written: "He stated the Anglican stand-point with brilliant lucidity and had a capacity to understand other traditions which was of particular value."[9]

By his late thirties Neill's name was increasingly mentioned when a bishopric fell vacant. Among the possibilities canvassed were Western China, Rangoon, and Mombasa, in addition to Indian dioceses, but it was Tinnevelly, where he had been ordained deacon in 1926, that eventually received him as its bishop in 1939.[10] He remained bishop throughout the war, in circumstances of particular difficulty both social and personal, until in 1945 came the breakdown that altered his career. The full nature and consequences of this event cannot yet be known. Neill himself wrote that "for this period of my life alone I have difficulty in reconstructing the chronology."[11] His inner agony broke through to the surface in a way that, without the support of an assistant bishop, meant that he had to resign his bishopric and leave India for good. He never held high office in the Anglican Church again, nor was he given the academic responsibilities that his gifts deserved. He was made a Fellow of the British Academy in 1969, and served as professor of missions and ecumenical theology at the University of Hamburg (1962-67) and as professor of philosophy and religious studies at the University of Nairobi (1969-73), in addition to holding numerous visiting professorships. But after India, and a short time as chaplain to his old college in Cambridge, his principal contribution lay in writing and speaking.

From Teaching to Writing and Speaking

He was as lucid a speaker as he was a writer. He would give Bible studies and devotional addresses with nothing but the Greek testament in his hand, and people with no claim to learning themselves would listen eagerly as he developed his theme with color, vigor, and clarity. These gifts found their best expression in his work with the infant World Council of Churches and the International Missionary Council, which he served respectively as associate general secretary (1948-51) and as general editor of World Christian Books (1952-62). Up to this point his writing had been occasional, the writing up of Bible studies and addresses given at missionary conventions, and one or two books for committed missionary society supporters, like his very first publication *Out of Bondage: Christ and the Indian Villager* (1930). Now he was to embark on a much more serious attempt to reach and educate the English-speaking world church, with a particular concern for those churches still known at that time as the "younger churches," though he at least knew that "the old distinction between younger and older Churches no longer really holds. All Churches are faced by the same problems. In all countries the same questions are being asked." (These words were included in all the early volumes of the series, as part of the general editor's preface.) The World Christian Books, for which Neill was later joined as editor by John Goodwin, eventually numbered more than fifty, with an amazing range of international authors including third-world theologians like A.J. Appasamy (no. 13: *The Cross Is Heaven*), D.T. Niles (no. 17: *Living with the Gospel*), and Norimichi Ebizawa (no. 2: *Japanese Witnesses for Christ*), as well as Western scholars like Charles Raven (no. 4: *Christianity and Science*), Gerhard von Rad (no. 32: *Moses*), and Max Thurian (no. 46: *Modern Man and Spiritual Life*). Neill's particular fondness for patristic writers produced some translations from the early centuries: Justin Martyr, Chrysostom, and Augustine.[12] Six of the books he wrote himself, and at least two he translated.[13]

Neill's own books fall into three broad categories. He wrote many small books of biblical commentary, mostly on the New Testament and at a popular level. But he also wrote a solid history of biblical criticism in *The Interpretation of the New Testament 1861-1961* (1964). Second, he made considerable contributions to church history, or what he preferred to call "the church in history." His *Anglicanism* (1958, 1977) is primarily a study of the genesis and historical character of the Church of England. Other histories were *A History of the Ecumenical Movement 1517-1948* (with Ruth Rouse, 1954), *The Layman in Christian History* (with Hans Ruedi-Weber, 1963), and *A History of Christianity in India,* vol. 1 (1984). His two histories of mission, *A History of Christian Missions* (1964) and *Colonialism and Christian Missions* (1966), overlap with his third main area of interest, the unity and mission of the church, characterized by *The Unfinished Task* (1957) and *The Church and Christian Union* (1968). In this area too come his writings on other faiths and their relation to Christianity, in particular his *Christian Faith and Other Faiths* (1961), which was revised and reprinted in 1970, and further revised and retitled as *Crises of Belief* (1984) to appear just before his death. When his writings on personal discipleship and his editorial work (e.g., *Concise Dictionary of the Christian World Mission,* 1970) and his contributions to five separate English and German encyclopedias are considered, the range and significance of his written work begins to become apparent.

Usually the learning is worn lightly: "[These] lectures were delivered in Spanish," he explains in the preface to *Christian Holiness* (1960). Sometimes he feels it necessary to defend himself against a possible charge of academic inadequacy: "I felt with the historian of the Crusades that 'it may seem unwise for one British pen to compete with the massed typewriters of the United States.' But it seemed that the task ought to be attempted, though I can scarcely hope, like Mr. Runciman, to have succeeded in giving to my own work an integrated and even an epical quality that no composite volume can achieve."[14] At the end of his life there was some criticism that Neill should attempt a solo history of Christianity in India when a team of scholars would produce a more satisfactory result, but his defense was the same, coupled with the conviction that hardly anyone but himself could handle all the fourteen languages necessary for the task.

Neill's vocation, as we have seen, led a man magnificently equipped for academic work into Christian leadership. When he could not continue in that, and no British university post came his way, he was compelled to follow his calling through his pen, and through the numerous public lectures he gave that became further books. For such a man intellectual integrity is of more than usual importance, and it is not surprising to find that he had given the subject careful thought. The issue lies at the heart of the "evangelical"/"ecumenical" debate: just where long experience led Neill most to wish to be a reconciler. In his *Interpretation of the New Testament 1861-1961* he recounts the discussion between the New Testament scholars Westcott and Hort on the question of academic freedom. Westcott was worried in case the work of their commentary might endanger orthodox convictions about divine revelation. Neill, following Hort's response, insists that the conclusions of an investigation cannot be guaranteed in advance: "This is a position which cannot be taken up by the completely independent student. His position is 'dialectical.' . . . Hort was himself a man of profound Christian faith; he was convinced that the kind of investigation that he was carrying on could tend only to the strengthening and amplification of the faith . . . But this confidence in the general direction in which the evidence was moving was something quite different from the claim that the evidence must be made to conform to certain conclusions which had been reached independently of it." Hort would accept no collaboration on such a basis, and Neill entirely approved, recalling that "the late John Baillie once remarked to me of another great scholar, a friend of his and mine: 'The man was afraid to ask ultimate questions.' "[15]

It was this academic and intellectual integrity that made Neill acceptable to the "liberal," "ecumenical" mind. He had a confidence in "the general direction in which the evidence was moving," which came from a deeply held and broadly based faith in God as the creator of all available evidence. His faith was not immune to advances in human knowledge and he could not wish that it should be. He tried to ask ultimate questions. "It is often said," he wrote in reference to the famous saying of Lessing, "that the uncertain happenings of history cannot lead to faith. No, but they can destroy it; history is a great destroyer of myths. If it could be shown, as clear historical evidence, that the bones of Jesus of Nazareth had mouldered away in a Palestinian grave like the bones of any other man, I would cease to be a worshiping Christian."[16] The Gospels would still be good news, and Jesus our one hope in a wintry sea because of his teaching and example, but there would be no victory, no rejoicing, and no confidence in the "direction of the evidence." But as this quotation itself indicates, with Neill liberal methods reached conservative conclusions. For him a personal faith in Jesus crucified and risen, and the new world that results, was central, and nothing could replace conversion to that. This was what won the confidence of evangelicals, and made him so acceptable a speaker on their platforms. He often complained that no adequate study of conversion had been done since that of A.D. Nock, who had been one of his first acquaintances as a Cambridge student.[17] He reckoned personal conversion to be at the heart of mission and viewed the growing emphasis of the World Council of Churches on social justice with misgiving. "Those who start at the social end never seem to get to the Gospel, whereas those who start with the Gospel sometimes accomplish, without knowing or intending it, the social revolution."[18] Neill quotes with approval Hendrik Kraemer's words that "becoming a disciple of Christ means always a radical break with the past. Christ is, as we have repeatedly said, the *crisis* of all Religion (and philosophy, good or bad)."[19] It follows that "Christianity is a religion not easily fitted into the categories of natural human life . . . Is it possible that men have sought a synthesis where they could expect to find only a modus vivendi?"[20]

No doubt Neill can be faulted for his social conservatism and for occasional remarks of donnish prejudice. (" 'No Popery' is one of the few unchanging constituents of what the average Englishman calls his thoughts.")[21] But his gifts as communicator and his desire to communicate the Christian faith saved him from a sense of superiority. ("When I am in America I regularly read the comics, such of them, at least, as I can stand – and Blondie, Peanuts, and especially Dennis the Menace, are well-established dwellers in my inner world – with excellent theological results.")[22] A more serious criticism might lie in his comparative neglect of the Old Testament, and the kingdom theology that it might have stimulated in him. That in its turn might have given him a less Kraemerian attitude to other faiths, and led him to emulate as well as admire the work of scholars like Kenneth Cragg, with their more flexible doctrine of the Spirit. Neill's strength is in a mastery of detailed fact, logic, and inference. It is rare to notice in his writing about other faiths any feeling of the attractiveness of that other.

Complaints, however, are hardly in order. Some of Neill's last published words recall the implicit message of other faiths that "for the Christian, every study of his relationship to the other faiths and their adherents must end with the ancient words of the New Testament, 'What manner of persons ought you to be?' (2 Peter 3:11)."[23] In Neill's own life the question was answered in terms of faithfulness, honesty, and a sustained courageous "going on" that few of us are called to show.

Notes

1. Recorded in the manuscript (p. 3) of Neill's autobiography, which was substantially condensed in the published version.
2. Neill, autobiography, p. 92.
3. Ibid., p. 100.
4. Ibid., p. 98.
5. Ibid., p. 127.
6. Ibid., pp. 187f.
7. Ibid., pp. 150, 167f.
8. S.C. Neill, *Anglicanism* (London: Mowbrays, rev. ed., 1977), p. 186.
9. Bengt Sundkler, *Church of South India: The Movement Towards Union 1900-1947* (London: Lutterworth, 1954), p. 184.
10. Neill, autobiography, pp. 432f.
11. Ibid., p. 565.
12. No. 34, A.P. Carleton, *John Shines through Augustine*; no. 44, S.C. Neill, *Chrysostom and His Message*; no. 49, R.P.C. Hanson, *Justin Martyr's Dialogue with Trypho.*
13. See bibliography below.
14. S.C. Neill, *Towards Church Union (1937-1952)* (London: SCM Press, 1952), p. vii.
15. S.C. Neill, *The Interpretation of the New Testament 1861-1961* (London: Oxford Univ. Press, 1964), pp. 88-89.
16. Neill, autobiography, pp. 167-68.
17. A.D. Nock, *Conversion, the Old and the New in Religion from Alexander the Great to Augustine of Hippo* (Oxford: Clarendon Press, 1933). T.E. Yates recalls the same emphasis in Neill's personal conversation in his article "Anglican Evangelical Missiology 1922-1984," in *Mission Studies* II-2 (1985): 33.
18. Yates, "Anglican Evangelical Missiology," has two different references from Neill to the same effect.
19. S.C. Neill, *Crises of Belief: The Christian Dialogue with Faith and No Faith* (London: Hodder & Stoughton, 1984), p. 286.
20. T.M. Parker, *Christianity and the State in the Light of History* (London: A & C. Black, 1955), p. 172, quoted with unqualified approval by Neill in his *Unfinished Task* (London: Edinburgh House Press, 1957), p. 70.
21. S.C. Neill, *Anglicanism*, p. 140.
22. S.C. Neill, *The Eternal Dimension* (London: Epworth Press, 1963), p. 1.
23. S.C. Neill, *Crises of Belief*, p. 287.

Selected Bibliography: Books by Stephen Neill

World Christian Books (all published in London by Lutterworth)
1954 *The Christian's God.*
1955 *The Christian Character.*

1956 *Who Is Jesus Christ?*
1958 *Paul to the Galatians.*
1960 *What Is Man?*
1963 *Paul to the Colossians.*

Other Books

1952 *Towards Church Union (1937-1952).* London: SCM Press.
1957 *The Unfinished Task.* London: Edinburgh House Press.
1958 *Anglicanism.* London: Penguin Books; 2nd ed. London: Mowbrays, 1977.
1960 *Men of Unity.* London: SCM Press.
1961 *Christian Faith and Other Faiths.* London: Oxford University Press.
1964 *A History of Christian Missions.* London: Penguin Books.
1964 *The Interpretation of the New Testament 1861-1961.* London: Oxford University Press.
1966 *Colonialism and Christian Missions.* London: Lutterworth.
1968 *The Church and Christian Union.* London: Oxford University Press.
1974 *Bhakti: Hindu and Christian.* Mysore, India: CLS.
1976 *Jesus through Many Eyes: An Introduction to the Theology of the New Testament.* London: Lutterworth.
1984 *Crises of Belief: The Christian Dialogue with Faith and No Faith.* London: Hodder & Stoughton.
1984 *A History of Christianity in India:* vol. 1, *The Beginnings to A.D. 1707.* Cambridge: Cambridge University Press.
1984 *The Supremacy of Jesus.* London: Hodder & Stoughton.
1985 *A History of Christianity in India:* vol. 2, *1707-1858.* Cambridge: Cambridge University Press.
1991 *God's Apprentice: The Autobiography of Bishop Stephen Neill.* Edited by Eleanor Jackson. London: Hodder & Stoughton.

With Other Authors and Editors

1954 (with Ruth Rouse) *A History of the Ecumenical Movement, 1517-1948.* London: SPCK.
1961 (ed.) *Twentieth Century Christianity.* London: Collins.
1963 (with Hans Ruedi-Weber) *The Layman in Christian History.* London: SCM Press.
1966 (with Arthur Dowle and John Goodwin) *Concise Dictionary of the Bible.* 2 vols. London: Lutterworth.
1970 (with Gerald H. Anderson and John Goodwin) *Concise Dictionary of the Christian World Mission.* London: Lutterworth.

R. Pierce Beaver

1906–1987

Mission Historian and Builder of Bridges

F. Dean Lueking

If he were still with us it would surprise Robert Pierce Beaver to learn that his life is a legacy, both distinctive and distinguished, in the life of the church in the twentieth century. He was by nature a modest man, not given to wondering if his lifework was building a legacy as a scholarly teacher of the history of the Christian mission and tireless gatherer and preserver of the writings of those who made mission history.

All who knew him even superficially could sense an innate quality of reserve in the man, and all who knew him quite well can understand that he would be not a little impatient with attention to his life that stressed flattery but missed substance. Thus there is some risk in writing of the Beaver legacy. But I think he would be forgiving as well as approving, since my purpose is to portray his lifework as that which must be central and ongoing in the life of the church. Above all, he would be glad for whatever enhances the mission. In that confidence I am grateful to write of what he leaves us as a churchman, pastor, missionary, professor, scholar, librarian, and interpreter of the missiological data of the church's mission in the times past and present.

The legacy of Robert Pierce Beaver has varied strands. He knew and taught the history of the Christian mission. He contributed uniquely to its furtherance by gathering and preserving scattered and obscure documents of the more recent centuries of the Christian church in mission. He worked with imagination and diligence to find a proper repository for these documents. He fostered the idea of a mission research library and center. The uniting thread in all of these strands was to call the church to continued missionary obedience. This legacy took form through his labors during the middle decades of the twentieth century, when the nature and forms of missionary obedience went through nothing short of a seismic shift. The mission was no longer west to east, north to south: The mission was everywhere. His legacy was to help the church sense that and respond to it with a faithful spirit and a disciplined mind. From the 1930s to the 1970s, he not only saw these unexpected turns unfolding but experienced the disruption of these turbulent years in his own person and family. He trained a keen mind and a historically informed eye on the meaning of these things for the course of Christ's Gospel through the church for the world. He saw and performed tasks no one else undertook. He forged a legacy without ever bothering to notice if anyone was noticing.

At the heart of the Beaver legacy is, of course, a person with qualities that made him memorable as an individual as well as formidable as a scholar. All of us who were his students have our Beaver stories. Mine comes from an event from his early teaching years at the Divinity School of the University of Chicago in the mid-1950s. This happened during one of the evening meetings often held in the Beaver home. The entire class he was teaching that quarter was invited over for supper, since he was required to miss the regularly scheduled lecture due to an out-of-town lecture. Supper gatherings were his way of making up such required absences. As Wilma Beaver kept the food coming, Professor Beaver kept the table conversation lively. It was a typical Beaver gathering -- ecumenical, international, interfaith. His living room became the lecture room, no less demanding intellectually for its friendly, informal setting. On this occasion Beaver had invited Bishop Stephen Neill to join us. Neill was guest lecturer at the university through Beaver's arranging. It was an exceptional opportunity for us to hear two superb minds on the subject of the world mission of the church. I recall that Professor Beaver ended the evening with prayer, as he had also begun it by asking a blessing upon us and our food.

A modest, intellectually meticulous, warmly hospitable, academically demanding, genuinely spiritual man stood at the heart of the legacy which gave us far more than he himself would claim.

He was born on May 26, 1906, in Hamilton, Ohio. His father, James Beaver, worked with the Game and Fish Commission of Ohio. He was not active in the church. His mother, Caroline Nuesch Beaver, was a native Hamiltonian who exerted a positive spiritual influence upon her son. As a youngster, Pierce was even more influenced by the local pastor of the First Reformed Church of Hamilton. William Kissel was one of those gifted ministers who recognized unusual qualities in the youth of the congregation and planted seeds that were to mature in later years.

In his high school years Beaver met Wilma Manessier, a classmate he managed to sit next to in several classes. That high school romance ripened into a continuing romance during their college years at Oberlin, Ohio. Wilma Manessier became a kindergarten teacher, then she became Wilma Beaver for the next sixty years. They had three children: Ellen, who died in infancy, David, who went to China with them at age of three, and Stephen, who was born in China.

Pierce completed his baccalaureate studies at Oberlin College in Ohio and stayed on to take a master's degree in art history in 1928. During the next four years he moved toward the vocational direction that became his lifework. He entered Cornell University in Ithaca, New York, for graduate study in history and completed his doctorate there in 1933. His Ph.D. dissertation on the interaction of church and society in North Africa at the time of Augustine drew together key elements that interested him throughout his life: history, the Christian presence, and the societal environment. He took courses at the University of Munich in 1931-1932, no mean feat, considering that the depression years cut deeply into the pockets of graduate students as well as other segments of the American population.

Foundational Insights from Pastoral Ministry

While finishing his graduate studies at Cornell, he also completed his preparation for the ministry. He was made a minister of the Evangelical and Reformed Church in 1932, serving pastorates in Cincinnati, Ohio and Baltimore, Maryland, from 1932 to 1936. These were years of long-range importance, developing Beaver's strong sense of the place of the congregation in the life and mission of the church. Though brief, they gave him an unwavering conviction on this essential matter. Nearly forty years later, he expressed this bedrock belief in a speech to the Divinity School in 1971 on the occasion of his retirement from teaching. After reflecting on his frequent work with denominational executives, national and international judicatories, and interdenominational agencies of cooperation, he had this to say:

> The whole universal church, not excepting the Church Triumphant, is here in the local congregation with all its brokenness and sin. Through them it is that Christ still carries out his ministry of redemption and healing. I would stress the supreme importance of the local church despite the fact that so many in our country have written off the parish as an anachronism. Cells, house churches, communes are welcome developments, but being small groups of very likeminded disciples they are as likely to become bastions of spiritual pride and separatism as suburban parishes unless they are caught up in a larger community which manifests the reconciliation in Christ in the midst of human diversity and in outgoing service.[1]

His own parish ministry years are surely echoed in this claim, which was not by any means popular on seminary campuses and in university divinity schools in 1971.

The memories of serving men, women, and children in congregations gave him a critical perspective on the congregation-bashing prevalent in much of mainline Protestantism in the 1960s and after. He was too serious a historian to be taken in by trends that mirrored the culture. The disinclination to follow fads served him well all his life and brought a durability to his conviction about the inseparable connection between congregation, church, and mission.

His distaste for faddishness did not leave him without a perceptive awareness of the flaws in the church, however. In the same lecture cited above, Beaver applied his customary directness to his own ecclesiology and the tempering it had received over the years:

> When I came here to the divinity school sixteen years ago I thought of the church as the continuation of the Incarnation. Now I cannot say that. It is blasphemous. The church is too dismembered, lame, blind, deformed, ugly. The Incarnation is beautiful, perfect, and came once in history. When the church calls itself the continuation of the Incarnation it becomes puffed up with spiritual pride and tends to usurp the role of Christ himself. No, the church is not the extension of the Incarnation, but it is the body of Christ – only that. And that is saying a great deal. It is the organism through which the risen regnant Lord and Savior is at work in the world. A spirit communicates and acts through a body. Jesus Christ present in the church by the Holy Spirit acts through it, mediating God's reconciling love to men. Most of us know some magnificent personality who accomplishes great things through a miserable and decrepit body. So actually I have come to a much higher evaluation and appreciation of the church than when I thought of it in more pretentious terms, and this view better accords with Paul's teaching of the church as Christ's body.[2]

The memories of struggles and failures in his own pastoral ministry come through in these words, as well.

China – A Ministry Cut Short by War

The half-dozen years from 1938 through the end of World War II were a time of hopeful beginnings and unanticipated endings. Beaver went to China in 1938, just as the menace of Japanese pretensions to pan-Asian dominance became ominous. He went out under the auspices of the Evangelical and Reformed Church to teach at the Central China Union Theological Seminary in southern Hunan Province. No sooner had he and his family settled into their new locale than the Japanese invaders abruptly removed them. Wilma and the two little boys left China on orders from the American embassy and returned to the United States. Pierce, however, whose health had deteriorated from the rigor of the work in Hunan, was unable to make the long trip. Instead he was sent to Hong Kong, arriving there just one day before the Japanese bombed and occupied the city. His Hong Kong internment lasted for seven months. He was repatriated on the first Gripsholm exchange ship, and his eventual return to the United States ended a two-year separation from his wife and family.

After regaining his health, he served the Mission Board of the Evangelical and Reformed Church by taking speaking engagements. In 1943 he was loaned to Lancaster Theological Seminary, where he taught till 1948. The disruption he experienced was not time lost, although it must have seemed so at the time. He experienced firsthand the exigencies of war and the roughshod manner in which tender seeds planted in faith apparently disappear and die under the heel of those who bring death instead of life. The futility and chaotic turns of those years taught Beaver never to underestimate the fact of sin in every human being. It also showed him firsthand how discontinuities in mission can become an occasion for God to act in new and unexpected ways. He kept tracking this mysterious Providence, especially in the course of the mission in China, which seemed to die out after 1949 only to burst forth in unprecedented vitality after 1976. Beaver never regarded the church in China as dependent upon the missionary labors of Westerners such as himself. If that insight was more theoretical than actual when he arrived in 1938, it was indeed painfully real when he had to leave as a war refugee.

Precisely because he personally experienced the tenuousness of missionary labors and the fragility of the best human plans in the service of Christ, he was all the more mindful of the necessity to gather together the scattered testaments of missionary experience and preserve them for generations to come. Documents outlast people if they are saved from obscurity or oblivion. Beaver believed that mission libraries administered with scholarly excellence had to be established.

In 1948, at age 42, Pierce Beaver assumed leadership of the Missionary Research Library in New York City. In 1977 he wrote a brief reflection on how that library came into being as a firstfruit of the Ecumenical Missionary Conference of 1900 in New York City, with further help for its continuance given by the Edinburgh World Missionary Conference in 1910.[3] He cited the organizational genius of John R. Mott and the money of John D. Rockefeller as the key elements in the survival of the Missionary Research Library through three relocations in New York, followed by the inevitable financial pressure upon the existence of this lesser recognized tool of world mission through the 1930s.

With customary modesty, Beaver only indirectly hinted at the considerable expansion – both in breadth and depth – that he brought as director of the MRL. He increased the usefulness of the library by starting a new publication to disseminate survey data, research reports, and noteworthy articles on world mission in the years immediately following World War II. Working on a shoestring budget, he mimeographed the early issues. Furthermore, he established it as an occasional bulletin, thus providing the ongoing name for the publication. *Occasional* was an understatement; the bulletin appeared from ten to sixteen times a year during the seven years of Beaver's editorship.

The *Occasional Bulletin from the Missionary Research Library* – now the *International Bulletin of Missionary Research* – filled and continues to fill a critical gap in the English-speaking world of missiological research. Beaver supplied the quality of scholarship and theological depth that made it a respected and much-used publication by teachers, students, church administrators, missionaries, and clergy throughout the United States and the world.

Upon Beaver's leaving the position as director of the MRL in 1955, President John Bennett of Union Theological Seminary (where the MRL continues as part of the seminary library) paid tribute to Beaver's leadership in these words:

He was an extraordinary librarian, or rather, strategist in building a library. His scholarship was very remarkable in its breadth, and [in] the tenacity of his hold on facts. He was an imaginative and devoted worker, who made the library not merely a collection of books and materials, but a center of research.[4]

Beaver's work through the MRL is a paramount aspect of the legacy he leaves us. He scanned the rapidly changing world of global mission at the midpoint of the century, just as momentous shifts were beginning to take form. He called attention to promising new men and women from Africa, India, and the Far East. His own article in the *Occasional Bulletin* on single women missionaries, which appeared in 1953, became a book: *All Loves Excelling*. Well before the subject of women in the life of the church was widely recognized, Beaver was describing women of great gifts and faithfulness in the world mission. He also touched upon other often-neglected themes, among them issues of race and nationality in North American missions and the plight of the American Indian in the missionary enterprise. In 1953 he provided the first directory and statistical listing of Protestant mission agencies in the United States, keeping a running update in subsequent issues. No one else was attending to these varied strands in the field of missiological research. When he left, the work did not stop, which is what distinguishes a legacy from a personal dynasty.

University of Chicago, a New Mission Field?

In 1955 Beaver entered a new mission field, although the University of Chicago community may not have thought of itself as such. Nor did Pierce Beaver fail to honor the excellence of his gifted colleagues and students in and beyond his field. But he was clear and unapologetic about his distinctive vocation among his colleagues. He sensed that the West was in profound transition in respect to the mission of God in the world. For several centuries Europe and North America had been commonly assumed to be the established Christendom, the sending base of mission to the lands of the heathen. Beaver was among those who saw deeper. The sending lands needed to be receiving lands, as well. Within a decade of Beaver's going to Chicago, the Vietnam War and the bitter reactions to it became signs of a spiritual wasteland that Beaver recognized and pondered. It was no longer far-fetched to recognize Hyde Park as mission territory. The devastated houses, the grip of racism, the explosive rise of crime, and the advent of the drug culture made the matter plain: the redeeming power of the risen Lord was as needed in Chicago as in Zimbabwe or Nepal.

In 1953 Joseph Kitagawa and Jerald Brauer of the divinity school faculty had proposed that the long-standing Chicago tradition of rigorous academic theology be leavened by a scholar in the field of Christian mission. There was more daring in this proposal than one might think. The very concept of the Christian mission itself was viewed with condescension, if not disdain, by many in the university faculty and student body.

Beaver was a splendid choice. He had a sure grasp of what he came to teach. He was not given to stridency in asserting the significance of what he knew and believed. He was open to learning from all sources, remembering that God is not limited to the church. With a fascinating blend of self-deprecation, intellectual excellence, and tartness in confronting those who were insufferably ignorant of the Christian mission, he was quite willing to teach those willing to learn.

How well did it work, this Kitagawa-Brauer proposal to bring a mission historian to the divinity school faculty? Exceedingly well. Beaver found his way naturally and for the right reasons into the respect and affection of colleagues and students and he remained there throughout his sixteen years of service, being named professor emeritus upon retirement.

Perhaps my own experience can serve as a paradigm to suggest the extent of the Beaver legacy. I came to the divinity school as a doctoral candidate shortly before Beaver began teaching. I had recently returned from a two-year vicarage in Japan. My interest at the divinity school was to prepare myself for a return to the Far East with a more adequate grasp of Buddhism and other aspects of Asian religion and culture. Joachim Wach and Joseph Kitagawa were excellent mentors, and I thought I was on my way. Then Wach died suddenly in 1955 and Kitagawa was engulfed with other duties in the department. One spring afternoon in 1956, I sat down under a tree on the campus and explained my dilemma to Jaroslav Pelikan. He suggested that I consider switching my study focus from the Asian receiving side of the mission to the history of the American sending side. He then urged me to talk with a new member of the faculty about this – Robert Pierce Beaver. I did so. Within the first half-hour, I was struck by his immediate grasp of the possibilities of new direction and his astonishing knowledge of where to find the sources I needed for the study.

I learned why his students referred to him as a walking encyclopedia. In the seminaries, the research institutes, and clergy ranks around the world there are many who join me in regarding Robert Pierce Beaver as the ranking historian of missiological data in the middle decades of the twentieth century. We are all in his debt.

Following his retirement from the University of Chicago, he kept a steady pace of continued research and writing as well as serving as the director of the Overseas Ministries Study Center in Ventnor, New Jersey (now in New Haven, Connecticut). He filled this post from 1973 to 1976. Brief though they were, these three years contributed to the Beaver legacy. He brought the full maturity of his mission-teaching vocation to the task. The associate director at that time, Gerald H. Anderson, worked with Beaver and followed him as director. The fruitfulness of that association is evident in the continuing leaven of the OMSC and its publication, the *International Bulletin of Missionary Research.*

In 1976 Beaver edited a large volume of essays, *American Missions in Bicentennial Perspective,* which earned Robert Handy's tribute as one of the most important books in the field of religion to arise out of the bicentennial celebration.[5] Gerald Anderson calling Beaver a "bridge person," one who was trusted across the theological spectrum with his gifts, is another confirmation of Beaver's legacy.[6]

In 1976 he and his wife retired to Arizona. He continued his lively interest in the world mission, writing, lecturing, and taking short teaching assignments in various theological schools. In 1981 a stroke brought that to an end. Until his death on November 20, 1987, he lived quietly with Wilma in Arizona, appreciative of family and friends despite the limits of declining health. Several months before he died, he spoke of the final boundary over which the Gospel takes the people of God:

We know that our coming into this world must have been a tremendous adventure. And I am convinced that the greatest adventure of all still awaits us as we go to meet our Heavenly Father.[7]

That testimony is at the heart of the Beaver legacy. I'm glad we have it from him. It is his witness, right to the end of his life, to the empowering grace of Christ that calls the faithful of all the ages to the mission that will continue until its fulfillment in the final Day of Christ.

Notes

1. Robert Pierce Beaver, "Sixteen Years in the Divinity School: A Modest Change of Mind," in *Criterion* (Univ. of Chicago Divinity School) 10, no. 3 (Spring 1971): 7.
2. Ibid.
3. R. Pierce Beaver, "The Missionary Research Library and the Occasional Bulletin," *Occasional Bulletin of Missionary Research* 1, no. 1 (January 1977): 2-4.
4. Quoted by Wi Jo Kang, "A Tribute to a Teacher," *Criterion* 10, no. 3 (Spring 1971): 11.
5. Quoted by Gerald H. Anderson, "American Protestants in Pursuit of Mission: 1886-1986," *International Bulletin of Missionary Research* 12, no. 3 (July 1988): 112.
6. Ibid.
7. Personal communication from Wilma Beaver, Nov. 28, 1987, quoted in the Funeral Service Bulletin for Robert Pierce Beaver in Tuscon, Arizona, November 28, 1987.

Selected Bibliography

Works by R. Pierce Beaver

Beaver's personal library, papers, and unclassified documents are in the library of Memphis Theological Seminary of the Cumberland Presbyterian Church, Memphis, Tennessee.

1935 *The House of God.* St. Louis: Eden.

1946 *Below the Great Wall.* Philadelphia: Christian Education Press.

1957 *The Christian World Mission: A Reconsideration.* Calcutta: Baptist Mission Press.

1962 *Ecumenical Beginnings in Protestant World Mission: A History of Comity.* New York: Thomas Nelson & Sons.

1964 *Envoys of Peace: The Peace Witness in the Christian World Mission.* Grand Rapids, Mich.: Wm. B. Eerdmans Publishing Co.

1964 *From Missions to Mission.* New York: Association Press.

1966 *Church, State, and the American Indians.* St. Louis, Concordia Publishing House.

1966 (ed.) *Christianity and African Education.* Grand Rapids, Mich.: Wm. B. Eerdmans Publishing Co.

1966 (ed.) *Pioneers in Mission: A Source Book on the Rise of American Missions to the Heathen.* Grand Rapids, Mich.: Wm. B. Eerdmans Publishing Co.

1967 (ed.) *To Advance the Gospel: Selections from the Writings of Rufus Anderson.* Grand Rapids, Mich.: Wm. B. Eerdmans Publishing Co.

1968 *All Loves Excelling: American Protestant Women in World Mission.* Grand Rapids, Mich.: Wm. B. Eerdmans Publishing Co. Rev. ed., 1980.

1968 *The Missionary Between the Times.* Garden City, N.Y.: Doubleday.

1973 (ed.) *The Gospel and Frontier Peoples.* South Pasadena, Calif.: Wm. Carey Library.

1977 (ed.) *American Missions in Bicentennial Perspective.* South Pasadena, Calif.: Wm. Carey Library.

Tributes to R. Pierce Beaver

Danker, William, and Wi Jo Kang, eds. *The Future of the Christian World Mission: Studies in Honor of R. Pierce Beaver.* Grand Rapids, Mich.: Wm. B. Eerdmans Publishing Co., 1971. Includes bibliography of Beaver's publications.

Kang, Wi Jo. "A Tribute to a Teacher." *Criterion* 10, no. 3, Divinity School of the University of Chicago, Spring 1971, pp. 10-13. Includes bibliography of Beaver's publications.

Part Six

THEORISTS
and
STRATEGISTS

William Taylor

Duncan Black Macdonald

Wilhelm Schmidt

Daniel Johnson Fleming

Maurice Leenhardt

Frank Charles Laubach

Hendrik Kraemer

Donald A. McGavran

Jakób Jocz

Alan R. Tippett

William Taylor

1821–1902

Entrepreneurial Maverick for the Indigenous Church

David Bundy

Villiam Taylor (1821-1902) is a prominent figure in the history of Methodist missions. During his career as missionary, which began with his appointment as missionary to California in 1849 and ended with his retirement in 1896, Taylor was, more than any other, responsible for the extension of the Methodist Episcopal Church beyond the boundaries of Europe and North America. He personally worked on six continents and was instrumental in the establishment of Methodist churches in Peru, Chile, South India, Burma, Panama, Belize, Brazil, Angola, Mozambique, and Zaire. As well, he assisted the Wesleyan Methodists in Austria, New Zealand, Ceylon (Sri Lanka), South Africa, and throughout the Caribbean. During the Moody campaigns in England (1873-75) he preached as "Mr. Moody's Coadjutor" at Moody's invitation. As missionary bishop, he worked to establish the mission in Liberia as a viable and independent church and expanded that effort to indigenous peoples.

His travel and the expense of establishing churches were financed primarily through the sale of the seventeen books that came from his pen. The sales were encouraged by numerous periodicals that he edited, as well as by the weekly or monthly reports of his exploits, which he submitted to many Methodist and Holiness periodicals. These were read and provided models for ministry both within and outside of the Methodist tradition. Within the Wesleyan and Holiness traditions he became a crucial figure, but he was appreciated also by Baptists, Friends, Presbyterians, "Keswickian" evangelicals, and eventually Pentecostals both in North America and Europe.[1]

Despite this fame and influence, despite having spent the last twelve years of his career as missionary bishop (1884-96), and despite having established patterns for "self-supporting" missions, writers as diverse as official historians of Methodist missions and Robert Speer, secretary of the Presbyterian Board of Foreign Missions, sought to undercut the legacy of William Taylor.[2] As a result he disappeared from the historiography of mission; even Stephen Neill and William Hutchison are silent about him.[3] Who, then, was William Taylor and what is his legacy?

Taylor as Missionary, to 1875

Taylor's father, Stuart (married Martha E. Hickman in 1819), was converted in a Methodist camp meeting in the hills of Virginia and became an evangelist. William Taylor attended the local one-room school, where he received all of his formal education. Like his father, who belonged to the Methodist Episcopal Church, he also had a religious experience at the Panther Gap Camp Meeting (Virginia) and, after a few months of teaching school (1842), he entered the ministry of the Methodist Episcopal Church. He married Ann Kimberlin in 1846. She accompanied him on his early travels, but thereafter mostly stayed at home to care for their five children. The next seven years saw a slow, painful adaptation of a lower-class country youth to the demands of ministry. In 1845 he became a member of the Baltimore Conference. Under the influence of Walter and Phoebe Palmer, he became a lifelong advocate of "holiness." He pastored both in Georgetown and North Baltimore, where he attracted the attention of Bishop Beverly Waugh of the Baltimore area, who was the driving force of Methodist Episcopal missions to the West.

Waugh recruited Taylor as a missionary to California. With a portable church building and his family, Taylor sailed from Baltimore on April 19, 1849, rounded South America and arrived in San Francisco after a stressful voyage (a child died on route). There he avoided the easier and more prosperous sites of ministry to focus on the central "Plaza" area. Here he nursed the sick, aided the impoverished, defended native Americans, ministered in Chinese labor camps, and built a church complete with a bookroom and a temperance hotel for seamen in the port area. In order to build the complex, a loan was taken out by the Annual Conference of the Methodist Episcopal Church. In 1856, the uninsured facility burned; as he described it, "rents stopped; interest on money went on."

The disaster forced Taylor to return to the East, where he endeavored to raise money to repay the loan. He was successful as an evangelist, and his book describing his experiences in California sold well, but national financial crises worked against his purposes. After continuing his efforts in Canada, he went via England (where he wrote a treatise on the U.S. Civil War) to Australia (May 1863-March 1866). In Australia "California Taylor," as he was known, proved effective as an evangelist and raised significant funds for Australian Methodist schools but little for himself. His son's illness required a climatic change, and he had money only to move his family to South Africa (March-October 1866).

South African white Christians did not generally respond favorably to his American revivalist style and message, so he went to the black tribes, where he became an effective evangelist among the indigenous population. This success led to getting his family back to America and then to Ceylon (December 1866-October 1870). In each instance there were reports of thousands "saved and sanctified," mission efforts were transformed, persons were "called" to ministry, and institutions were established. We are never told whether the debt in California was repaid.

Taylor arrived in India, typically penniless, in November 1870, at the invitation of the Methodist Episcopal missionary and Holiness advocate James Thoburn. Here, however, there was no success among the Indians in the shadow of the mission compounds. At loose ends and still impoverished after months of fruitless efforts, the disappointed Taylor struck out on his own. He preached in the large cities of southern India and established Methodist Episcopal churches, thereby breaking the comity agreements. Churches were founded in Bombay, Calcutta, and dozens of other centers. Drawing on his experiences in California and Australia, Taylor established the churches not as missions but as self-supporting churches – equal, he argued, to any church in North America. He adapted Indian architecture, which, the entrepreneurial impoverished missionary noted, allowed churches to be built for a fraction of the price from available materials and also did not give offense to Indians. After the congregation was established, he appointed a pastor on site and moved onto another city.

This major expansion of Methodist Episcopal churches was not greeted with enthusiasm in the missionary community. The Methodist Episcopal mission was embarrassed by the breaking of the comity agreements with the (English) Wesleyan Methodists.[4] The mission board was angry that this expansion was done without permission and that the new churches, at Taylor's instruction, insisted on receiving no financial support. The board initiated a ten-year campaign to discredit the concept of self-supporting missions and to force the (eventual) South India Conference to accept American money and status structures as well as mission board control.

Taylor left India early in 1875 for England, where he was invited to preach in the Moody campaigns, often substituting for Moody himself in the main meetings. The British religious press gave him positive coverage, comparing his preaching favorably with that of Moody. After that brief sojourn, he was back in the swirl of controversy engendered by his concept of self-supporting mission. The Methodist Mission Board refused to send out the missionaries Taylor requested, and so he recruited volunteers, raised funds, and sent them himself, including the first Methodist Episcopal missionaries to Burma. This intensified the conflict over mission method. Taylor countered mission board claims of irresponsibility, wastefulness, and insubordination with his first foray as mission theorist.

The Pauline Method of Missions

In the midst of the controversy over his activities in South India, Taylor wrote his first missiological essay.[5] It was actually a revision of a diary kept during the years in India that described in detail the failures of the traditional approach to mission and Taylor's lack of success in the traditional mission context, and then chronicled the procedures and results in each city in which self-supporting churches were established. It was a powerful, passionate statement. Taylor universalized his claims, arguing that all mission should be done on a self-supporting model that gives immediate recognition to churches, irrespective of nationality, politics, or geography.

He lacked proof of the theory's viability in other arenas. South America became the site for his grand experiment. On October 16, 1877, Taylor sailed for South America in steerage to survey the situation. Economic, religious, legal, and political structures were studied. He secured pledges from South Americans to support missionaries he promised to send, found jobs for others as teachers of English and agricultural/industrial arts, and founded fledgling congregations. A Transit and Building Fund was established by Taylor and Holiness entrepreneurs in New York to provide for travel and initial capital expenses. Missionaries were recruited and sent.[6] This unauthorized mission effort again intensified the conflict with the Methodist Episcopal Mission Board. Holiness leaders and congregations, however, rallied to his support and fueled his South American missions (1878-84).

It was during this conflict that Taylor produced his remarkable volume on mission theory, *Pauline Methods of Missionary Work*. The book set forth the theoretical framework that undergirded Taylor's missionary enterprise, "a brief exhibit of Pauline methods of missionary work." The exposition of the mission theory is remarkably concise. Only the first six and one-half pages (about eight hundred words) are devoted to the "Pauline methods of planting the gospel in the heathen lands." This is followed by a short chapter arguing that the methods are "suited to the demands of this age." The third chapter, on the present outlook for Pauline self-supporting missions in foreign countries, draws an analogy between the mission opportunities afforded by the Roman and British empires. There are no recognizable sources other than the profuse citations of Pauline biblical texts. The rest of the volume describes the "practical tests" in India and South America before concluding with sixteen pages of lists of donors!

Taylor argued that the goal of Pauline mission is independent churches that are self-supporting, entrusted with their own governance, and committed to an evangelistic style that enables them to grow according to their own cultural patterns. Missionaries are to model and encourage that development. Paul's mission endeavors as reported in the Acts of the Apostles and the biblical Pauline literature were thereby construed as the paradigmatic basis for articulating a mission theory. Taylor presented the "Pauline plan" in the following list:

1. To plant nothing but pure gospel seed.

2. Paul laid the entire responsibility of Church work and Church government upon his native converts, under the immediate supervision of the Holy Spirit, just as fast as he and his tried and trusted fellow-missionaries could get them well organized, precluding foreign interference. His general administrative bishops were natives of the foreign countries in which he planted the gospel; such men as Timothy and Titus.

3. Paul "endeavored to keep the unity of the Spirit in the bond of peace" with the home Jerusalem Churches by all possibilities short of corrupting his gospel seed, or allowing the home Churches to put a yoke of bondage on his neck, or laying any restrictions on his foreign Churches.

4. He went and sent, according to the Master, "without purse or scrip," or an extra coat, or pair of shoes above the actual requirements of their health and comfort.

5. In utilizing for the advancement of Christ's kingdom, and for the support of its ministers and institutions, all available agencies and resources, he uniformly commenced in Jewish communities which had become indigenous in all the great centers of population throughout the Roman Empire . . . As fast as Paul and his fellow-missionaries could get those Jews to receive Christ . . . he organized them in the houses of their leading men and women, into self-supporting Churches and spiritually aggressive combinations of agency for the salvation of their heathen neighbors.

6. To give permanency and continued aggressive force to his organizing . . . he remained in each center of work long enough only to effect a complete organization . . . (and) to develop the Christian character of each member up to the standard of holiness.[7]

Despite his favorable comparison of the Anglo-Saxon empires to that of Paul's Rome, for Taylor the British and American presence did not have inherent value. It was merely a historical accident that should be used to the advantage of proclaiming the Gospel. He harbored no illusions about the Christian identity of Anglo-Saxon culture. He felt it was in the process of contaminating the native populations, thereby giving Christianity a bad name. Mission work that did not address the problem posed by heathen expatriates was doomed to failure. The great cities of Asia, Africa, and South America with concentrations of Anglo-Saxons and their descendants were the scenes in which this battle should be fought.

Taylor also argued that one should avoid a confrontational style when relating to other cultural or religious traditions:

The modern method of most of the learned advocates of Christianity in dealing with Buddhists, Mohammedans, Hindoos, and unbelievers at home and abroad, is to set forth their tenets of belief in the form of dogmatic propositions, and proceed with their arguments to prove that those religions of their opponents are all wrong, and that theirs are all right, but unfortunately, their opponents do not admit premises on which the attacking argument is based, hence the argument is worthless . . . The Apostles, as sound logicians, always laid the major premise of their arguments in the region of admitted truth.[8]

His respect for Asian, African, and South American cultures is evident in his writings, and his descriptions of peoples and places has enduring ethnographic value. Contrary to most mission publicity efforts, he did not seek to portray others in an unfavorable light, and he urged his missionaries to adapt to and adopt the host culture. Those who did so needed no furlough, and those who refused to do so should be sent home as soon as possible!

Experience in California, Australia, and India had also taught Taylor that when missionaries insisted on establishing structures that were expensive to maintain, they made it impossible for a church to achieve independence and vitality. He notes that the churches established by the apostles were "purely self-supporting from the start. It seems never to have entered the minds of the inspired apostles, nor of the people, that the great work of their high calling, the salvation of the world, required the construction of costly edifices, with their expensive appendages, to be called churches, involving a vast outlay of funds, making dependence on rich men a necessity."[9]

There are several recurring themes in Taylor's analysis. The desire for independence in the mission processes, both in recruitment and acculturation of converts, is primary. The missions are to be self-supporting with the efforts funded by resources raised among the target population. Missionary leadership is to be temporary but exacting, and missionaries are to model moderate asceticism. These issues were not new with Taylor. What gave these assertions a revolutionary ring in North American mission circles were the underlying assumptions. Perhaps the most provocative was the assumption of the centrality of indigenous economic resources to the mission process, and its corollary that North American or European resources have no advantage or priority over other resources and may even be counterproductive to the development of committed indigenous Christian communities in other cultures. His opponents claimed that the mission board structure was *the* modern approach to missions; they insisted that the mission agencies receive and channel all funds, maintain instructional control over converts, and directly supervise the missionaries. The American mission establishment was incapable of understanding the significance of Taylor's critique.

What was better understood was the shift in the reading of the biblical text. In Taylor's early writings, the biblical stories of Paul's exploits were used to illustrate concerns and techniques with special attention to theoretical content. In *Pauline Methods of Missionary Work* Paul's missionary activity is taken as a normative model for modern missions; the Pauline narratives become paradigmatic. Thus the biblical Paul became a battleground for competing mission theories.

Proving the Theory: William Taylor as Model

This small missiological essay by itself would not have made a long-term impact on mission theory. Taylor's *Pauline Method* achieved lasting significance because he was able to maintain a public discussion for nearly two decades. This discussion continued on two levels: (1) the dispute with the Methodist Mission Board and, more important, (2) the presentation of "scientific proof" that the method worked by narrating in detail his own experiences in many religious journals. The two foci were always closely related. Taylor, being unaware of the depth of the sociocultural gulf separating him and his supporters from the mission board and their nouveau riche urban constituency, naively thought that if he could only demonstrate that the method produced the results the mission board professed to seek, the board would legitimate and adopt the theory. The appeal to popular opinion kept those alienated by the embourgeoisement of American Methodism after the Civil War supportive of his cause.

In 1882 the General Missionary Committee, in support of the mission board, forced Taylor and his missionaries to "locate" in local churches.[10] Taylor responded by becoming a member of a local church in the South India conference, but stayed in South America where he pastored in Coquimbo, Chile, and loosely supervised his missionaries. While there, he was chosen as a lay delegate to the 1884 General Conference by the South India Conference, which was still struggling to resist mission board domination and funds. At the 1884 General Conference of the Methodist Episcopal Church in Philadelphia, Pennsylvania, Taylor was elected missionary bishop for Africa.[11] As part of a compromise arrangement, the mission board agreed to continue the "self-supporting" pattern of the new Methodist Episcopal churches in South America. This arrangement was continued until Taylor's retirement, when the board asserted more direct control of local mission activity and churches, a move that led to the development of Pentecostalism in Chile and Peru.

As missionary bishop (1884-96), Taylor had more visibility but no success in changing the ecclesiastical and mission board structures. He also had no success in weaning the Methodist Church in Liberia from the board's supervision and financial infusions. Always clear, often strident, he continued to argue for the "Pauline Method." His books and articles describing mission work in India, Latin America, and Africa continued the discussion long after his retirement and death.

It was the life of William Taylor as narrated and interpreted by himself that provided the base for mission theories in the Holiness churches and, eventually, the European Pentecostal churches.[12] Paul's model received for thousands of missionaries its definitive exegesis in the intense entrepreneurial style that remained unwavering in its conviction and that sacrificed all else for the cause of the propagation of the Gospel.

There are a myriad of examples of individuals who became missionaries on Taylor's example and sought to accomplish the same goals. These individuals became the theorists and practitioners of the next generation of revivalist mission, including most Holiness and Pentecostal efforts, both in North America and Europe and in the so-called Third World. For example, Taylor served as model for Free Methodist Vivian Dake, the Pentecost Bands, and A.B. Simpson.[13] William Sherman and Anna Abrams established the Vanguard Mission, a mission organization based on Taylor's principles in St. Louis that influenced the Wesleyan/Holiness and Pentecostal movements.[14] Lela McConnell, convinced of Taylor's program, developed a self-supporting mission in eastern Kentucky.[15] Fort Wayne College was moved to Upland, Indiana, and renamed Taylor University, by which the board and administrators affirmed their independence from denominational controls on the model of Taylor's program of missional self-reliance. Within European[16] and Chilean[17] Pentecostalism, Taylor provided a theoretical basis for local autonomy and a model for indigenous mission activity. In the present generation he is being rediscovered in Latin American Pentecostal missiology.[18] He thus had a formative influence on the Holiness and Pentecostal movements, the eleventh and third largest Christian communions respectively. He also inspired numerous Methodist missionaries. Among Methodist missionaries to India, for example, he was the inspiration of, among others, J. and I. Thoburn, E. Stanley Jones, J. Waskom Pickett, Frederick Bohn Fisher, and E.A. Seamands. In many ways it was Taylor who is primarily responsible for the rapid expansion of the Methodist Episcopal Church in the late nineteenth century. It was the theory of Pauline methods modeled by his life that achieved that legacy. As a theorist who wrote before Nevius and Allen, William Taylor deserves attention as an eminent mission thinker.

Notes

1. For a detailed analysis of Taylor's life, ministry, and publishing history, see D. Bundy, "Bishop William Taylor and Methodist Mission: A Study in Nineteenth Century Social History," *Methodist History* 27, no. 4 (July 1989): 197-210; 28, no. 1 (October 1989): 2-21. Taylor's papers have not been located and probably no longer exist. Most extant letters and other relevant unpublished works are mentioned in the above article.

2. W. Crawford Barclay, *The History of Methodist Missions*, vol. 3: *The Methodist Episcopal Church, 1845-1939: Widening Horizons* (New York: Board of Missions of the Methodist Church, 1957); Robert E. Speer, *Servants of the King* (New York: Young People's Movement of the United States and Canada, 1910).

3. Stephen Neill, *A History of Christian Missions*, Pelican History of the Church, 6 (Grand Rapids, Mich.: Wm. B. Eerdmans Publishing Co., 1964); William R. Hutchison, *Errand to the World: American Protestant Thought and Foreign Missions* (Chicago: Univ. of Chicago Press, 1987). The only biography, the quaintly titled work of the Holiness scholar John Paul, *The Soul Digger: or, The Life and Times of William Taylor* (Upland, Ind.: Taylor Univ. Press, 1928), adds little to the works of Taylor. William Taylor contributed many

autobiographical statements, the most comprehensive being *Story of My Life: An Account of what I have thought and said and done in my ministry of more than fifty-three years in Christian lands and among the heathen*, ed. John Redpath (New York: Eaton and Mains, 1895); British edition, *William Taylor of California, Bishop of Africa, an Autobiography* (London: Hodder and Stoughton, 1897).

4. Taylor's breaking of the comity agreements was a major issue at the first Methodist Ecumenical Conference, held in London in 1881.

5. William Taylor, *Four Years Campaign in India* (London: Hodder and Stoughton; New York: Nelson and Phillips, 1875).

6. Taylor's account was published as *Our South American Cousins* (New York: Nelson and Phillips; London: Hodder and Stoughton, 1878).

7. William Taylor, *Pauline Methods of Missionary Work*, (Philadelphia: National Association for the Promotion of Holiness, 1879), pp. 5-9.

8. Ibid., pp. 31-32.

9. Ibid., p. 33.

10. The hierarchy's intent was to reassert control over Methodist clergy, insisting that they would lose their Methodist ecclesiastical standing if they remained in missionary activity not approved, controlled, and funded by the Methodist Mission Board. This effort failed, as only one of the Taylor missionaries left the field of service to return to the United States. It is also worth noting that, contrary to the practice of the established mission boards, Taylor recruited women (including single women) without prejudice and appointed them to positions in which they were able to design, found, and direct their own mission programs.

11. The election of Taylor as missionary bishop was the result of a remarkable and unorganized coalition. The mission board attempted to control him with a salary and remove him from South America; Holiness advocates saw him as their representative; racist Methodist Episcopal clergy and laity used his election to avoid being forced to confront the idea of electing an African-American bishop. On this, see D. Bundy, "Bishop William Taylor," part 2, pp. 10-12. For the larger cultural context, see Victor B. Howard, *Religion and the Radical Republican Movement, 1860-1870* (Lexington: Univ. Press of Kentucky, 1990).

12. This is explored in detail in "Pauline Methods: The Mission Theory of William Taylor," in D. Bundy, "Holiness unto the Lord: The Cultural Structure of Wesleyan-Holiness Evangelicalism" (typescript).

13. T.H. Nelson, *The Life and Labors of Rev. Vivian A. Dake* (Chicago: T.B. Arnold, 1894); A.B. Simpson, *Larger Outlooks on Missionary Lands* (New York: Christian Alliance Publishing Co., 1893).

14. Detailed in the *Vanguard*, which is only partially preserved at the Missouri State Historical Society, Columbia, Missouri.

15. Lela G. McConnell, *The Pauline Ministry in the Kentucky Mountains* (Berne, Ind.: Economy Printing, 1972).

16. See, for example, T.B. Barratt, "Bishop William Taylor," *Kristelig tidende* 18, no. 23 (June 7, 1889): 179; O. Nilsen, *Ut i all verden* (Oslo: Filadelfiaforlaget, 1981); D. Bundy, "T.B. Barratt's Christiania (Oslo) City Mission: A Study in the Intercultural Adaptation of American and British Voluntary Association Structures," in *Crossing Borders*, Conference on Pentecostal and Charismatic Research in Europe (Zurich: n.p., 1991), pp. 1-15.

17. J.B.A. Kessler, Jr., *A Study of the Older Protestant Missions and Churches in Peru and Chile, with Special Reference to the Problems of Division, Nationalism, and Native Ministry* (Goes: Oosterbaan en Le Cointre, 1967).

18. Ruben Zavala Hidalgo, *Historia de la Asambleas de Dios del Peru* (Lima: Ediciones Dios es Amor, 1989). Much of the fabled Latin American Pentecostalism (as in China, India, and Africa) traces its origins back to European, especially Scandinavian and British, roots, the chief theorists and practitioners of which were influenced by Taylor through T.B. Barratt.

Selected Bibliography

Works by William Taylor

1856 *Seven Years Street Preaching in San Francisco, California: Embracing Indigents, Triumphant Death Scenes, etc.* Ed. W.P. Strickland. New York: Carlton and Porter.

1858 *California Life Illustrated.* New York: Carlton and Porter.

1862 *Cause and Probable Results of the Civil War in America: Facts for the People of Great Britain.* London: Simpkin, Marshall.

1868 *The Election of Grace.* London: Hodder and Stoughton; New York: Carlton and Lanahan.

1875 *Four Years Campaign in India.* London: Hodder and Stoughton; New York: Nelson and Phillips.

1878 *Our South American Cousins.* London: Hodder and Stoughton; New York: Nelson and Phillips.

1879 *Pauline Methods of Missionary Work*. Philadelphia: National Association for the Promotion of Holiness.

1882 *Ten Years of Self-Supporting Missions in India*. New York: Phillips and Hunt.

1885 *Africa Illustrated: Scenes from Daily Life on the Dark Continent, with Photographs Secured in Africa by Bishop William Taylor, Dr. Emil Holub, and the Missionary Superintendents*. New York: Illustrated Africa.

1895 *Story of My Life: An Account of what I have thought and said and done in my ministry of more than fifty-three years in Christian lands and among the heathen, written by myself*. Ed. John Clark Redpath, engravings by Frank Beard. New York: Eaton and Mains. British edition: *William Taylor of California, Bishop of Africa, an Autobiography*. Revised with a preface by C.G. Moore. London: Hodder and Stoughton, 1897.

1898 *The Flaming Torch in Darkest Africa*, with an introduction by Henry M. Stanley. New York: Eaton and Mains.

Taylor also edited a number of periodicals, the most important of which are *African News* (1889-94), *Illustrated Christian World* (1894-98), and *Illustrated Africa* (1891-96). There appears to be no significant collection of manuscript materials. Individual letters are scattered throughout the United States in the personal papers of his correspondents. However, much of his correspondence (together with appeals from his supporters) appears to have been published in various periodicals, including the *Christian Advocate* (various regional editions), the *Gospel in All lands*, the *Guide to Holiness*, *Zion's Herald*, *Divine Life*, the *Vanguard*, and *Indian Witness*, as well as his own publications.

Works about Taylor

Arms, Goodsil F. *History of the William Taylor Self-Supporting Missions in South America*, New York: Methodist Book Concern, 1921.

Barchwitz-Klauser, O. von. *Six Years with William Taylor in South America*. Boston: McDonald and Gill, 1885.

Bundy, David. "Bishop William Taylor and Methodist Mission: A Study in Nineteenth Century Social History." Part 1: "From Campmeeting Convert to International Evangelist"; part 2: "Social Structures in Collision." *Methodist History* 27, no. 4 (July 1989): 197-210; 28, no. 1 (October 1989): 2-21.

_____. "Pauline Methods: The Mission Theory of William Taylor." In "Holiness unto the Lord: The Cultural Structures of Wesleyan/Holiness Evangelicalism" (typescript).

_____. "Wesleyan Holiness Mission Theory." In "Holiness unto the Lord: The Cultural Structures of Wesleyan/Holiness Evangelicalism" (typescript).

Davies, E. *The Bishop of Africa; or, The Life of William Taylor, D.D., with an Account of the Congo Country and Mission*. Reading, Mass.: Holiness Book Concern, 1885.

Paul, John. *The Soul Digger: or, The Life and Times of William Taylor*. Upland, Ind.: Taylor Univ. Press, 1928.

Duncan Black Macdonald

1863–1943

Preparing Missionaries for the Muslim World

J. Jermain Bodine

Although he is primarily known as a scholar in the fields of Islamic theology and religious experience, Duncan Black Macdonald began his long career at the Hartford Theological Seminary as an instructor of Semitic languages in the Department of Exegetical Theology.[1] His appointment came as the result of a series of coincidences and tragedies, since he was appointed to replace an American student from Hartford who died while studying in Germany – as was Macdonald at the time.[2] While he is remembered as a scholar engaged in the training of missionaries for service in Muslim lands, he himself never served in the mission field. Indeed, there are grounds for seeing a certain ambiguity in his attitude toward the enterprise of missions to Islam.

In a review of Macdonald's three books on Islam,[3] *The Development of Muslim Theology, Jurisprudence and Constitutional Theory*,[4] *The Religious Attitude and Life in Islam*,[5] and *Aspects of Islam*,[6] W.H.T. Gairdner remarks:

> In the two former [books] he had written about Islam with complete objectivity. In writing them he had not its relation to Christianity in mind, and apparently, therefore, he had preferred to keep absolutely clear of all comparisons between the two faiths of whatever sort. This, combined with the sympathy that is inseparable from interest, may have led readers of the first two books to think that the author had no interest in the Christianization of Islam.

Private correspondence, now in the Archives of the Hartford Seminary Foundations's Case Memorial Library, suggests that this impression was not fully inaccurate. In a letter to George Sarton, American historian of science and founder-editor of the journal *Isis*, Macdonald says, "It is my greatest merit as an orientalist that I discovered that you could smuggle Muslim studies into a theological seminary under the guise of training missionaries."[7] Further, in a note written to his successor as chairman of the Muslim Lands Department of the Kennedy School of Missions, Dr. E.E. Calverley, he says, "[I] . . . was told there was no opening in this country for Arabic, but . . . did not believe it . . . saw a demand for missionaries in Arabia . . . jumped at this and therefore founded the first real school for Arabic in this country."[8] And to this we may add Macdonald's description of his involvement in the training of missionaries, found in a letter to Calverley from

1930: "Often, I am sorry to say, I get fed up with Mission news-sheets. You won't understand that but remember that I am a wild olive grafted in – an Arabist who has turned teacher of missionaries, which has its humorous side."[9]

From these statements we may gain the impression that, for Macdonald, the training of missionaries was a kind of backdoor means of introducing the study of Arabic and Islam to the United States. However, while the Orientalist himself may well have felt from time to time that his true calling was as "an Arabist," and not a missionary, his continuing commitment to quality training for mission workers, his deep Christian faith, and the care and attention that he devoted to missions to Islam throughout his life are clear. Gairdner, in the review earlier mentioned, goes on to say that the third book, *Aspects of Islam*, showed that the author was "wholehearted for missions to Islam, and only deeply concerned that missionaries should be adequately equipped for their work."[10]

Macdonald's Major Concern: Adequate Preparation for Mission

If there is one thread that runs through the story of Macdonald's involvement with missions to Islam, it is the quest for adequate preparation and equipment of workers in the field. This concern, observably deep through all his published articles and editorials dealing with the subject, evidently first arose during his only visit to the Near East, in 1907-8. In Cairo he found himself impressed with the lack of training characteristic of most missionaries and wrote to the seminary to ask about the possibility of Hartford's accepting some of the American Mission and Cairo Missionary Society personnel for an intensive period of study.[11] The touring scholar appears to have been scandalized at the missionaries' lack of acquaintance with a number of areas of Islam, beginning with the most rudimentary knowledge of colloquial languages and going through the Qur'an (in Arabic) as well as a more than passing acquaintance with Muslim theological systems. In addition, he felt quite strongly that a missionary must be well acquainted with the actual practices and life of those to whom he sought to minister and witness. It is in this deep concern for the adequate preparation of the missionary that the legacy of Duncan Black Macdonald lies.[12]

He was born in Glasgow, Scotland, on April 9, 1863. The youngest of six children, his early life shows a great contact with all sorts of literatures, including the *Arabian Nights* as well as other books and stories closely related to the Romantic school.[13] He prepared to enter the ministry of the Presbyterian Church of Scotland, matriculating at the University of Glasgow in 1880. While there he fell under the spell of Arabic studies through the teaching of James Robertson, professor of Hebrew. From Glasgow he went to Berlin to study under the great German scholar Eduard Sachau. It was during his years in Berlin that events transpired which brought him, in 1892, to the Hartford Theological Seminary – where he remained for the rest of his scholarly and teaching career, holding positions with the seminary and with the Kennedy School of Missions, as chairman and later consulting professor in the department of Muslim Lands.

He married the former Mary Leeds Bartlett, from his standpoint a most fortunate choice, since she provided all the support and encouragement he could have asked in his pursuit of a scholarly career. Mrs. Macdonald, who died in 1929, fourteen years before Duncan Black, combined graciousness in entertaining her husband's friends and students, a talent for poetry, musical researches, and a willingness to learn as much as she could of her husband's fields of study to be of what he characterizes as inestimable aid. In one other way she was of great help: she began to experiment with "automatic writing," as the result of his having once said he would like to meet such a "medium." Macdonald himself was deeply interested in psychic phenomena as a means of understanding religious inspiration, particularly that of prophets. A perusal of his *The Religious Attitude and Life in Islam* will make this apparent. Although the Macdonalds were childless, the marriage was an evidently happy one.[14]

He was succeeded in the Kennedy School of Missions by one of his own students, Dr. E.E. Calverley, in 1925. His retirement from active participation in the school was precipitated by the need to look more closely after his wife's failing health. In 1932 he retired from the Hartford Theological Seminary but remained in close contact with the school – particularly the Kennedy School as "Honorary Consulting Professor of Muhammadanism" until his death in 1943. It was during his retirement that the two books on the Hebrew Bible, *The Hebrew Literary Genius*[15] and *The Hebrew Philosophical Genius*,[16] appeared. A projected third volume dealing with the Hebrew religious genius exists in partial manuscript but was never completed. Throughout his life Macdonald maintained a voluminous correspondence with fellow Orientalists, students and former students, and missionaries in the field. He served on the editorial board of the *Moslem World*, founded by Samuel Zwemer in 1911 (now the *Muslim World*), contributing numerous articles and editorials to that journal. His bibliography includes, in addition to the five books, over eighty articles in the Leiden *Encyclopedia of Islam* (including those on "Allah," "Kalâm," "al-Ghazzâlî," and many other major theological entries as well as one on the *Arabian Nights* contributed to the Supplement), seventeen articles of the eleventh edition of the *Encyclopedia Britannica*, as well as numerous contributions to the *Jewish Encyclopedia*, Hastings's *Encyclopedia of Religion and Ethics*, and *A New Standard Bible Dictionary*.[17] He also contributed numerous signed and unsigned reviews and articles to the *Nation*, the *Review*, the *Constructive Quarterly*, and a host of scholarly journals as well as the *Moslem World*.[18] Macdonald's interest in the *Arabian Nights* led to the publication of still more articles,[19] as well as his unfinished task of a critical edition of the Galland manuscript of the *Nights*.[20]

In his time and after, Duncan Black Macdonald was seen as one of the most important contributors to the study of Islam, popular religion among Muslims, the *Arabian Nights*, and Muslim theology. He is still of importance, though the passage of time and the increase of scholarly knowledge has somewhat dimmed his glory. His articles on Muslim theology remain of value, as do his works on the *Arabian Nights* and al-Ghazzâlî. His students include a large number of outstanding figures both on the mission field and in scholarship; among them are Fred Field Goodsell, E.E. Calverley, Walter Skellie, W.H.T. Gairdner, Alford Carleton, Murray T. Titus, Earl E. Elder, and John K. Birge. He corresponded with the "greats" of European and English Orientalism on a regular and familiar basis, and was obviously considered a peer by them. The mere fact that he was entrusted with the major articles on Muslim theological subjects for the *Encyclopedia of Islam* provides one of the most convincing testimonies to his stature as a scholar. It is reported that one of the first acts of Louis Massignon, the great French scholar of Sufism, when he reached Hartford, was to pay homage to Macdonald at his grave.[21]

Macdonald's Principles for Effective Ministry among Muslims

We turn now to a consideration of the contributions of Macdonald to the training of missionaries for work in Muslim lands. As has been remarked earlier, his visit to the Near East convinced him of the need for more extensive and exhaustive preparation on the part of prospective workers in the field. His concern was that those who represented the Christian church be the best examples of learned concern and empathy for their peoples possible. Time and again, he would sound the note that missionaries must be willing to know their people from within, must be willing to understand the religion of their people as fully as possible, while holding to a fully owned and articulated Christian faith. The motto he gives his book on *Aspects of Islam* is indicative of this attitude:

> The paradox, in truth, of the missionary's life is that he must have a liking for his people and their queerest little ways even while he is trying to change them.[22]

His writings and teaching were devoted to helping the missionary gain both understanding and liking for the people as well as for points of contact between Christianity and Islam. Throughout his writing, Macdonald advocates approaching the Muslim as a person, as a human being who has his or her own value and religion, which must be understood and appreciated before any effort can be made to present Christianity to him or her. Ill-informed, unsympathetic, controversy-oriented persons would not serve the cause of Christ, he held; and he set about to provide such tools as would equip persons for an understanding mission.

He advocated patience, tolerance, participation, and understanding on the part of the missionary. He felt that the "wandering Arabist"[23] approach that he had taken in the Near East would be a good preparation for the missionary; enabling the missionary to gain insight into the life and personality of the people before entering into the task of witness and ministry. He sought to find points of contact between Muslims and Christians particularly in the areas of ideas, words, and human feelings. In an outline for a talk on missionary methods,[24] he notes the following "axioms":

Avoid controversy.
Seek points of contact.
Foster the idea that the Bible may be worth reading.
Assimilate yourself to Muslims in language as far as conscience will permit

[marginal note: "Good Muslim Arabic. Avoid Christian Arabic."]
Be perfectly clear that our notion of God [is] different.
Remember distinction of [between] Religion and Theology.

Many of his articles in response to questions directed to him from missionaries in the field sought to establish for the missionary the points of contact, or to define with greater understanding the particular point of information on Islam which would enable the missionary to enter into the life of the people among whom he or she served.[25]

In an earlier article of mine, I have dealt with his use of the *Arabian Nights* as an avenue for the missionary who seeks to understand Muslims.[26] This theme sounds constantly through his works for missionaries, especially the early ones. Misunderstanding of Macdonald may easily arise at this point – as if he perceived all Muslims, or at least all Arab Muslims, as having stepped out of the pages of the *Arabian Nights*. The point of his insistence on use of the *Nights* was that it could enable readers who spent extended and careful time with the tales to come to a deeper appreciation of the ways and mores of the people to whom they sought to minister. Macdonald used the *Arabian Nights* as a means of grasping and understanding the psychology of the Muslim Arab, as a way in to appreciating the life and civilization of Islam reflected in and by the *Arabian Nights*. He suffered no illusions that he would himself encounter all the events and characters found therein; nor that a total understanding of Islam could be gained by reading the tales. But he did understand the role of popular literature and particularly popular folk literature in shaping and informing the kinds of persons he encountered. So much was this true for him that he could say, at the conclusion of his trip to the Near East, that he needed in no particular to revise his impressions. W.H.T. Gairdner, in the review of his books mentioned above, seconds this opinion and suggests that others might well look to the use of extensive reading as a means of better preparation for the mission field.[27] Macdonald sought to catch and convey the spirit, the flavor as it were, of the Muslim world through the *Arabian Nights*. In view of the testimony of his success at penetrating that world, it would appear that his instincts were sound.

In an article as necessarily brief as this, it is manifestly impossible to present all of Macdonald's views or accomplishments. His interests and achievements were as broad as his understanding and scholarship were deep. One area in relation to missions remains to be dealt with: his insight into the continuing need for Christian missions from the West to the East. It has been related that he himself was never a missionary, nor so far as can be ascertained did he ever feel a call to be one. He perceived his role as that of scholar-teacher, enabling others to go out on the basis of such preparation and learning as he could provide them. He also counted on those in the field to provide him with further information for his own researches – enabling him to keep up with developments in the Muslim world on a firsthand basis. But he was convinced of the importance of a continuing Christian missionary presence in the Muslim world.

It is after World War I that we begin to find a deeper reason for missions, according to Macdonald. He was greatly concerned with the incursions of Western (European and North American) technological, scientific, and philosophical civilization into the world of Islam. His perception was that little of the moral or truly spiritual values of the West accompanied these invasions. He felt keenly the Muslim criticism of the materialism of the West, the spiritual drought that made itself apparent to the Muslim world – which at the same time accepted the technology and sciences of the West. Macdonald pleads for missions as a means of countering the value-poor, or at least spiritually value-poor, Western developments. He was deeply concerned that the best of Christian spirituality, represented in honest, convinced missionaries who were also in love with their Muslim brethren and sisters, not be surrendered, nor be changed simply into medical, agricultural, or scientific stations.[28]

In an editorial written for the *Moslem World* in 1933,[29] he sets the contemporary Muslim consciousness of Islam's past glories in contrast to the actual situation of Western superiority. Noting that in this the Muslim world looks to the West as an enemy, he goes on to say that the archenemy as perceived by the Muslim world is "Christendom," an anachronism to be sure, but nonetheless so perceived as *the* enemy, with Christian missionaries as the militant phase of the church. But he goes on to note that the attitude toward the missionary will vary in proportion to that person's respect, understanding, and approach to Islam. Courtesy, he says, will always meet with response; yet missionaries must be explicitly and exactly Christian lest they be thought "crypto-Muslims" and therefore less trusted. Missionaries must incarnate in their own lives and dealings the Christian message. What Macdonald is here arguing for is the presence of honest and earnest missionaries who will show in their lives that all from the West is not devoid of spiritual life and concern, that Christianity is not to be identified with the West, that there are those in the West who deny the ultimate value given by so many to the merely technological advances now sweeping over the entire world. He is deeply concerned that others of spiritual persuasion see that even in the materialistic and secularist West, there are those who strive to impart a different insight, a different value system; that the church, which is not the West, comes not to conquer, to crusade, but to love.

This is the task of Christian missions, the reason why Macdonald urges its continuation in response to the Great Commission: that the vacuum left by the incursions of a superior Western military, technological, and scientific presence not be ignored and left to fill itself with misunderstanding of Christianity, but that Christianity be found in its most explicit and open form. Let the church not be perceived as an enemy, but as a co-worker with Islam, striving against the problems raised by materialism, hedonism, and decreasing interest in the life of the spirit. He hopes to see Christianity presented as a viable option, as a real choice, not as the inevitable concomitant of Western decadence. To this task he calls those persons who are willing to undergo lengthy and intensive training to acquire the tools that will enable them to express their own faith intelligently and honestly, as well as to enter into a deep, human, and empathetic understanding of the life and religious experiences and beliefs of those to whom and with whom they seek to witness and minister.

Notes

1. *Hartford Theological Seminary Register* for 1892-93, "Faculty Listing."

2. Details of these circumstances may be found in "The Romanticism of Duncan Black Macdonald," by J. Jermain Bodine (Ph.D. diss., Hartford Seminary Foundation, Hartford, Connecticut, 1973).

3. W.H.T. Gairdner, "Professor D.B. Macdonald's Works on Islam," *Moslem World* 2 (1912): 313-17.

4. New York: Charles Scribner's Sons, 1903.

5. Chicago: University of Chicago Press, 1909. The book is the text of the Haskell Lectures on Comparative Religion, delivered by Macdonald in 1906.

6. New York: Macmillan Company, 1911. This book is the text of the Hartford-Lamson Lectures for 1909.

7. D.B. Macdonald to George Sarton, May 22, 1933.

8. D.B. Macdonald to Edwin E. Calverley, 1943 (undated, presumably summer).

9. D.B. Macdonald to E.E. Calverley, July 5, 1930.

10. Gairdner, "Macdonald's Works on Islam," p. 314.

11. D.B. Macdonald to M.W. Jacobus, March 15, 1908.

12. It is to be noted that the capitalization of Macdonald's last name, used in this article, is that employed by the scholar himself. Although it appears in numerous citations as "MacDonald," this latter usage is incorrect and should be avoided.

13. For details, consult the dissertation noted in n. 2 above.

14. Ibid., pp. 50-54.

15. Princeton: Princeton University Press, 1933.

16. Princeton: Princeton University Press, 1936.

17. Edited by M.W. Jacobus, E.E. Nourse, and E.C. Zenos.

18. See bibliography in dissertation cited in n. 2 above.

19. J. Jermain Bodine, "Magic Carpet to Islam: Duncan Black Macdonald and the Arabian Nights," *Muslim World* 67, no. 1 (1977).

20. Ibid.

21. Reported in the *Bulletin of the Hartford Seminary Foundation*, n.d. (evidence points to either late 1940s or early 1950s).

22. Title page of *Aspects of Islam*. This is a quotation from p. 359 of that book.

23. See Macdonald's description of his approach in *Aspects of Islam*, "Introduction" and "Lecture I."

24. Notes in Case Memorial Library Archives, n.d.

25. Examples of this may be found in the "Question Drawer" series appearing in the *Moslem World* on an occasional basis. See also Macdonald's "The Idea of Spirit in Islam," *Acta Orientalia* 9:307-51; and "From the Arabian Night to Spirit," *Moslem World* 9 (1919): 336-48.

26. Bodine, "Magic Carpet to Islam."

27. Gairdner, "Macdonald's Works on Islam," p. 313.

28. See D.B. Macdonald, "The Essence of Christian Missions," *Moslem World* 22 (1932):327-30.

29. D.B. Macdonald, "The Christian Message Is Peace," *Moslem World* 23 (1933):325-29.

Wilhelm Schmidt, S.V.D.

1868–1954

Priest, Linguist, Ethnologist

Louis J. Luzbetak, S.V.D.

The Society of the Divine Word is an international Roman Catholic missionary order founded in Steyl, Holland, in 1875, by Arnold Janssen, a German diocesan priest known for his extraordinary vision, persistence, and ability to recognize and utilize the enthusiasm, talent, and dedication of others. Today the society numbers approximately 5,000 professed members[1] and is established in thirty-five countries around the world. As one might expect, this new missionary society was not spared from the ethnocentrism, paternalism, and triumphalism that characterized European Christianity of the times. It was quite generally felt that "primitives," "savages," and "pagans" of mission lands had first to be "civilized," that is, Europeanized, before one could expect them to be genuinely Christianized. However, Arnold Janssen's missionaries, early in their history, began to react against this common attitude in a rather novel manner: they introduced a somewhat revolutionary dimension into the meaning of mission – *the scientific study of humankind as an integral part of the missionary task itself.*

Before long, serious study of non-Western cultures, especially linguistics, ethnology, and the study of religions (*Religionswissenschaft*), became a tradition with the Divine Word missionaries,[2] a tradition that was expressly incorporated into their constitutions, seminary curriculum,[3] budget, and personnel policies. As the *Osservatore Romano*[4] on the occasion of the seventy-fifth anniversary of the society put it: "From the Middle Ages to our present day, missionaries have constantly enriched our knowledge of unknown languages and cultures; but never has any missionary group so systematically – both theoretically as well as practically – devoted itself to this particular effort with such dedication as the Society of the Divine Word." It is of this legacy that the present article speaks.

The prime mover behind this new and broadened understanding of missionary work was a young talented seminary professor, Father Wilhelm Schmidt, S.V.D., a linguist turned ethnologist. The author of the present article knew Schmidt personally, having done graduate work in anthropology under his tutelage. The author had, in fact, the privilege of living with Schmidt in a small community of anthropologists for some three years (1947-50), thus being able to observe this great scholar and "missionary" at close range and to share, with him, in the spirit that underlies "the Wilhelm Schmidt Legacy."

Biographical Sketch

Wilhelm Schmidt was born in the industrial area of the Ruhr in Westfalen, Germany, on February 16, 1868.[5] His father, Heinrich Schmidt, a factory worker, was forty-seven when he married the twenty-four-year-old Anna Maria Mörs. Not long after their marriage, tragedy struck the Schmidt family: Heinrich Schmidt died when his first child, Wilhelm, was only four. With this family background in mind, it is easy to understand the closeness Wilhelm felt toward his mother and the deep respect he had for her throughout his life, attributing to her not only his physical features but many of his personality traits, religious values, and his extraordinary energy and stamina.

Wilhelm's boyhood dream of someday becoming a missionary led him at the early age of fifteen to Arnold Janssen's first mission training center in Holland, located across the German border to avoid the antireligious restrictions of the *Kulturkampf*. Here Wilhelm the seminarian was to spend nine years preparing himself for a missionary career that was never to be realized. He completed his secondary schooling in 1886, his philosophy course in 1888, and his four-year theology training in 1892, the year of his ordination to the priesthood.

After a brief initial assignment of less than a year as teacher at a preparatory seminary for missionary candidates in eastern Germany, Schmidt spent two years (1893-95) studying Middle Eastern languages at the Oriental Institute of the University of Berlin.[6] Behind this assignment was Arnold Janssen's plan – totally unknown to Schmidt at the time – to have his society assume activities in Palestine, a plan, however, that never materialized. Instead, Schmidt found himself teaching at St. Gabriel's Missionary Seminary in Mödling near Vienna, teaching at first a variety of subjects, then chiefly linguistics, ethnology, and the study of religions. For the next forty years, St. Gabriel's was to be Schmidt's home and Austria his adopted country.[7] (It should be noted that for thirty years Schmidt taught also on the university level: at the University of Vienna, 1921-38; at Fribourg, 1939-51.)

His university training as such had relatively little to do with the fields in which he was later to distinguish himself. Schmidt, it must be emphasized, was largely a self-taught scholar – a pioneer in many ways – rather than the product of formal and systematic university training in a well-defined discipline. It was especially during his first decade at St. Gabriel's (1896-1906) that this self-education took place. Perceptive and easily stimulated intellectually by others, the young seminary professor learned much through his involvement in the activities of various academic circles of Vienna, especially the Anthropological Society. Another asset was his natural enthusiasm as teacher, which greatly accelerated his personal professional growth as he taught others. With data provided him by missionaries, especially his former students, he began to publish the results of his studies, first on the languages of New Guinea and then on all of Oceania and Southeast Asia. In a matter of eight years (1899-1907) he had about forty publications to his credit, not counting his many book reviews.[8] The titles of these publications clearly reveal a steadily widening interest from purely linguistic issues to cultural and religio-historical problems. His ability came to public notice in his study of the Mon-Khmer peoples,[9] in which he established the relationship between the languages of Southeast Asia and those of Oceania, a major accomplishment that won for him an award from the prestigious French Académie des Inscriptions et Belles Lettres and membership in the Austrian Imperial Academy of Sciences, two distinctions that were to be for him only the beginning of a long succession of honors.[10]

Schmidt's research was, as a rule, culture-historical with a predilection for "primitive societies," that is, the simple peoples whom ethnologists of the Schmidt persuasion regarded as most closely reflecting the life of early humankind. The origin of religions and beliefs regarding the Supreme Being were his very special interest.

He was also a methodologist. The ethnological approach that seemed most promising to him was that of the best-known German anthropologist at the turn of the century, Fritz Graebner,[11] whose comparative method for reconstructing relationships between cultures and for establishing their relative age was not only applied by Schmidt but critically reexamined, refined, and further developed.[12]

But Schmidt was even more than a scholar, prolific writer, critic, systematizer: he was also a stimulator and organizer. His enthusiasm was contagious. He *promoted* research and writing as much as he himself was engaged in study and publishing. Fearing that invaluable observations of missionaries would be lost for lack of a suitable journal to publish their studies, he founded in 1906, with the full financial support of his missionary society, the *Anthropos International Review of Ethnology and Linguistics*. He also promoted field research by encouraging and guiding missionaries in their study of local languages and cultures and by assisting and organizing expeditions for his associates and collaborators. As the number of associates and collaborators grew and their activities multiplied, Schmidt felt the need for organization, and in response to this felt need he founded the Anthropos Institute in Mödling in 1932, where it was located until 1938 when, owing especially to Schmidt's opposition to Nazi racist theories, he and the institute had to seek refuge in neighboring Switzerland. Here in Switzerland, a few miles outside the city of Fribourg, Schmidt was to continue his research, writing, and teaching well into his eighties. It was not until he had reached his eightieth birthday that he voiced any desire to give up some of his many responsibilities,[13] not so much in order to retire but, rather, to be able to devote more time to such projects as the completion of his monumental work begun in 1912, *Der Ursprung der Gottesidee*,[14] and the revision of *Völker und Kulturen*.[15] Wilhelm Schmidt, working almost to his dying day, finally succumbed to his chronic bronchitis, diabetic condition, and heart problem in Fribourg, Switzerland, on February 10, 1954, at the age of eighty-six.

Schmidt's Personality

Schmidt was endowed with what seemed to be limitless energy. As Monsignor John Montgomery Cooper of the Catholic University of America so aptly expressed it, "The days of Mödling-bei-Wien must be more than twenty-four hours long."[16] Schmidt, the prolific writer, was a genius who somehow never cared to learn to use the typewriter because he was convinced that the fountain pen (a pen with a built-in inkwell) was the greatest of all modern inventions. His more than 600 publications, including his encyclopedic *Der Ursprung der Gottesidee*, were all first written out in longhand. Despite this almost superhuman activity, he always had time for a friendly conversation, especially at his regular coffee breaks with his associates. He particularly enjoyed routine strolls through the garden or woods and occasional outings.

Schmidt was a man of wide interests. As a young priest he was actively engaged in social work, at times leaving some of his own clothing behind for the needy he would visit. He was a popular marriage counselor and was fond of giving religious instructions to teenagers. He was involved in church unity efforts, first with the Orthodox and then with the Protestants. His immersion in anthropology never became so total as to keep him from such interests as the writing of a comprehensive popular life of Christ[17] and what turned out to be a widely accepted work on Christian marriage and family life.[18] He was also a musician. He regularly played the reed organ for services in the small chapel of the Anthropos Institute (and sometimes he played merely to relax); he was choir director and gave violin lessons at one time; on occasion he attended concerts, and he composed church music even in his declining years.[19] He was always interested in politics and the postwar economic development of Europe, and he never gave up his dream that someday a Catholic university would be established in Salzburg, a dream that over the years cost him considerable time and energy.[20]

Merciless in dealing with his critics, he nevertheless was a fatherly and very sympathetic person. Although insisting on having his way and irked when people disagreed with him, he would not lose his temper or hold a grudge against such persons or impose his views on them.[21] His many honorary degrees and state and church honors were humbly accepted without fanfare on his part or desire for publicity. Above all, Schmidt's scholarly involvement never made him lose sight of the fact that he was a member of a missionary society and that it was ultimately the mission cause to which he had dedicated his life.

Schmidt as Scholar and "Missionary"

Schmidt had a very definite understanding of "ethnology," a concept he as scholar would not sacrifice at any cost. While appreciating and promoting ethnology as a useful tool for missionary action, he felt that qua ethnologist he could not mix practical considerations with the discipline as such and still call it "ethnology." To him, ethnology was a pure *Geisteswissenschaft* and a strictly historical field.[22] As a scholar who believed in the purity of his discipline, he would not allow his journal or institute to depart from this concept, insisting that concentration on strictly scientific, rather than applied, ethnology would assure the needed respect of the world of science.[23]

For Schmidt there were three fundamental reasons that made ethnology a basic missionary concern. In his earlier days the first of these reasons was particularly strong – evolutionism. Although he saw no problem in the concept of evolution as such, he was adamantly opposed to the existing theories of evolutionism,[24] that is, the assumption that everything in the universe, including the origin of religion and the idea of God, was determined by the "law" of straight-line progression from the lower to the higher, from the more simple to the more complex, from the less perfect to the more perfect, from the less civilized to the more civilized. What seemed to excite Schmidt most of all was the conviction that both the missionary and ethnology were in a unique position for counteracting the fallacy of this "abomination," which was then rampant and which continued well into the second decade of the twentieth century.

Schmidt further argued that missionaries, if properly trained and given appropriate guidance in the field, could through ethnographic research and publication make invaluable contributions to humanity's understanding of itself.[25] In fact, in many ways, Schmidt argued, missionaries were even better equipped to gather useful ethnographic information than many professional anthropologists. Missionaries generally enjoyed the confidence of the local people; they usually spoke the local language; and, as a rule, they remained in the field over longer periods of time, rather than just a year or two as was the case with professional anthropologists on occasional field trips. Missionaries might, in fact, be able to provide important data that otherwise would be unattainable.

The third reason for missionary involvement in ethnology, according to Schmidt's thinking, was the very practical consideration now generally unquestioned but at the turn of the century considered novel, if not revolutionary: ethnological training could be a great asset to any church worker called upon to spread the Gospel outside his or her own cultural milieu. Early Divine Word missionaries, confronted with difficult language or culturological problems in the field, spontaneously turned to the most logical person for help – their former professor of linguistics and ethnology. Schmidt, as an "armchair missionary," thousands of miles removed from the scene, would try as best he could through correspondence to provide the professional guidance sought. It was especially with missionaries in mind that he initiated, with the assistance of F. Bouvier, S.J., the workshops known as Semaine d'Ethnologie religieuse in Louvain in 1912 and 1913, in Tilburg (Holland) in 1922, in Milan in 1925, and in Luxembourg in 1929. He welcomed the opportunity offered him by the pope to organize the international Vatican Mission Exhibit (1925) and to build the Missio-Ethnological Museum at the Lateran in Rome (1925-27), and then ten years to be its director, seeing as he did the educational value such projects would have for all Catholics, but especially the missionaries.

The Legacy

Schmidt's writings and influence are generally recognized in Europe, especially in the German-speaking countries. Unfortunately, such does not seem to be the case in America. Anthropologists, even some who are otherwise well versed in the history of their field, sometimes show only a limited knowledge of the nature and scope of Schmidt's contribution to anthropology and his rightful place in anthropological history. Two basic reasons might be attributed to this limited appreciation. Some American anthropologists seem to think that it is impossible for a committed Catholic, especially a priest, to be objective when dealing with religio-cultural matters.[26] Moreover, Schmidt and his early collaborators usually published their studies in non-English languages, especially German.[27] Consequently, some of Schmidt's critics seem not to have read Schmidt at all, only *about* Schmidt, seeing him primarily, if not exclusively, in the somewhat limited light of a die-hard *Kulturkreisler*, who championed the "Culture Circle Theory" even after his own collaborators had abandoned the theory or at least seriously questioned its premises and conclusions.[28] Like most anthropological theories, the *Kulturkreislehre* had its merits and its many deficiencies, and after it had made its contribution, it too was destined to be superseded by still other theories. What is being stressed here is the fact that Schmidt's significance goes far beyond any short-lived "culture circles." Besides his very notable personal accomplishments, which the historian of linguistics, ethnology, the study of religions, and missiology must recognize, there is the priceless and vast legacy which Schmidt left behind – the stimulus, which Raymond Firth, one of today's best-known British anthropologists, described as "difficult to measure because of its pervasiveness."[29] One might even say that Schmidt's *primary* significance lies in the stimulus he gave to others – scholars, field workers, and missionaries.

But first, an overview of his outstanding personal achievements.

Schmidt's Personal Accomplishments

a) It was Schmidt who disentangled the languages of Southeast Asia and Oceania and brought linguistic order to what had been sheer chaos.[30] He showed that the Mon-Khmer were a bridge between the people of Central Asia and Austronesia and that certain languages of Southeast Asia and Oceania were related. This discovery was not only important in itself but of importance for further research in comparative anthropology and comparative religion.[31]

b) Schmidt refined and further developed the *Kulturkreislehre*, the so-called Culture Circle Theory or Cultural-Historical Method of Ethnology, a theory and methodology that in its day had a major impact on much of European ethnological thought.[32]

c) Schmidt was able to synthesize in a way unequaled by anyone the available research data regarding the religious beliefs and practices of primitive peoples, especially their views regarding the Supreme Being. Whether one accepts Schmidt's conclusions or not, his masterful sifting and ordering of the vast amounts of data was in itself an important contribution to the study of religions.

d) His high regard for non-Christian cultures, clearly reflected in his teaching and writings, in his Semaine d'Ethnologie religieuse workshops, the Lateran mission museum, the Vatican Mission Exhibit, and the Anthropos Institute and its journal, served as important groundwork for the further development of the missiological concept of "accommodation" and "contextualization."

e) As missiologist J. Beckmann, S.M.B., rightly observed,[33] Schmidt paved the way for the acceptance of Catholic missiology as a reputable discipline worthy of serious scholars.

f) Schmidt founded, or was instrumental in founding, such milestones in anthropological history as the Anthropos Institute and the Missio-Ethnological Museum in Rome, and a number of professional journals, especially *Anthropos.*

g) It is also to Schmidt's credit that well ahead of his time he encouraged missionaries to undertake seriously and professionally the study of linguistics, ethnology, religions, and other related fields.

Schmidt the Stimulator

Today there are three distinct activities of the Divine Word missionaries that have been greatly influenced by Schmidt and might rightly be labeled "the Schmidt legacy."

a) There is, first of all, a contingent of Divine Word missionaries whose full-time task is not so much to preach and baptize as it is to continue and further develop the vision of Schmidt in such modern disciplines as ethnology, social anthropology, archaeology, physical anthropology, sinology, ethnomusicology, folklore, linguistics, sociology, and the study of religions. This contingent of trained social scientists, scattered around the globe, works either as individuals or as groups studying, doing fieldwork, writing, instructing, or simply striving to help human beings better understand themselves. The main Divine Word center for anthropology is, of course, Schmidt's Anthropos Institute, now located at St. Augustin near Bonn, Germany, with its research and publication facilities and one of the best anthropological libraries to be found anywhere on the Continent.[34] Adjoining the institute is a separate unit for sinological research, the headquarters of the *Monumenta Serica, Journal of Oriental Studies,*[35] with its excellent library of Chinese culture and its publication offices. Independent offshoots of the Anthropos Institute have been established in Switzerland, Japan, the Philippines, India, and Zaire.

b) A second contingent of experts is engaged in theoretical missiology, with their institute, the Steyler Missionswissenschaftliches Institut, located adjacent to the Anthropos center. Although missiology in the Society of the Divine Word developed independently of Wilhelm Schmidt, his influence on missiological thought, within as well as without the society, was considerable.[36] Schmidt's high regard for primitive religion and his respect for native social practices, art, philosophy, myth, ritual, and other aspects of primitive lifeways all entered into the very process of giving birth to what is known today as "Catholic missiology." A few decades ago, when the Divine Word missiological center was being established, it was the Anthropos Institute that served as model.

c) There is also a third group of mission specialists, whose activities might best be placed in a *practically oriented* category of missiology. For instance, there is the Melanesian Institute, in which the Divine Word missionaries play a major role. This institute focuses its attention on translating theoretical linguistic, ethnographic, psychological, and theological concepts and principles into the concrete mission situation of Papua New Guinea. The purpose of the Melanesian Institute is to develop culturally sensitive pastoral strategies for that part of the world. Another good example of this third category is Father George Proksch, who by means of music, dance, drama, and poetry has successfully combined the aesthetics, folklore, and religious feeling of India with the Christian message. Although himself not an Indian, he is looked upon as a guru and is highly respected as a teacher of Indian choreography.[37] The Society of the Divine Word, to offer another example, maintains an architectural center at Nemi outside Rome, the purpose of which is to encourage the development of mission architecture in accord with the modern times and local aesthetic values.[38] In this third, practically oriented category of missiology one might also include the author's own humble efforts toward the development of an "Applied Missiological Anthropology."[39] But the most notable example is perhaps the Center for Religion and Culture of Nanzan University in Nagoya, Japan. In a spirit of genuine openness and scholarship, the center, through joint research and dialogue with non-Christian scholars, seeks to bring together Christian and Oriental philosophy and theology with such divergent disciplines as psychology, folklore, sociology, ethnology, archaeology, pedagogy, linguistics, aesthetics, history of art, and history of religion – all in the hope of creating a better understanding between Eastern and Western minds.

The best developed and organized of these three groups is the first. As mentioned earlier, the founding of the *Anthropos* journal resulted from Schmidt's genuine fear that valuable scientific observations of missionaries would be lost. What was needed, he felt, was an "archives" in which the linguistic and culturological studies of missionaries might be published and preserved. The journal became one of the main interests of Schmidt and his early associates, and to this day it remains one of the chief concerns of the Anthropos Institute. The annual volume averages more than a thousand pages. As a point of editorial policy, *Anthropos* has been publishing articles in most of the important European languages.[40] Consistent with an old practice begun by Schmidt, a large portion of each issue comes from missionary authors.[41] It is interesting to note that the first twenty-six volumes of *Anthropos* expressly mention on the cover page, after the name of the editor, the fact that the journal is being published "with the collaboration of numerous missionaries." By "missionaries" was meant not only members of the Society of the Divine Word (although their articles may predominate) but also of many other Catholic, and some non-Catholic, missionary groups.

The amount of ethnographic and linguistic information for which Schmidt and his associates have been responsible is formidable indeed.[42] Besides the annual volumes of *Anthropos* there were two early monograph series, one ethnological and the other linguistic, which served as supplements to the journal.[43] Since then, several new series have been inaugurated. Thirty-six volumes have so far appeared as *Studia Instituti Anthropos*, dealing with such varied subjects as the religion of East Flores, the tonality of North Chinese dialects, marriage and the family in the Caucasus, the Supreme Being among the Manggarai, Nuer society and religion, the Negritos of Asia, the agricultural practices of Turkestan, the cross as a non-Christian symbol, and the structural analysis in anthropology. Another twenty-two volumes have appeared in *Collectanea Instituti Anthropos*, dealing with such topics as the Aharaibu Indians of Northwest Brazil, the passing scene of Northeast New Guinea, Ethiopian myths and rites, North Cameroon marriage customs, Taiwan headhunting, and shamanism in Northwest China. A large microfilm series, mostly linguistic studies of missionaries, which by their very nature cannot be expected to have more than a limited circulation, is published as *Micro-Bibliotheca Anthropos*. Many books and articles of the Divine Word missionaries have, of course, been published by outside publishers, including Schmidt's own *Der Ursprung der Gottesidee*. Schmidt and his early collaborators have been among the most productive researchers in anthropological history: Schmidt, as already indicated, authored more than 400 books and articles and about 200 book reviews; Wilhelm Koppers has 200 titles to his credit; Martin Gusinde, 150; Paul Schebesta, 130.[44]

When speaking of anthropological publications one must not overlook the important linguistic and culturological journals and series of publications which at least indirectly owe their existence to Schmidt and which are, or have been edited by Divine Word missionaries, especially *Monumenta Serica Journal of Oriental Studies* (32 volumes), *Asian Folklore Studies* (37), and such journals as *Annali Lateranensi and Wiener Beiträge zur Kulturgeschichte und Linguistik*. As the Australian anthropologist A.P. Elkin expressed it: "The establishment of an international anthropological journal, *Anthropos*, by a missionary order, the Society of the Divine Word, and its maintenance for the past forty-five years [since 1906], has itself been a remarkable contribution to anthropology and the foundation more recently (in 1937) of a similar journal, the *Annali Lateranensi*, by the Pontificio Museo is also very welcome. Through these media, the anthropological and linguistic studies of Roman Catholic missionaries are made available to the scientific world."[45] Or as Robert H. Lowie in his *History of Ethnological Theory* put it: "Ethnology owes much to Schmidt for the establishment of *Anthropos*, a journal second to none in the field. With unsurpassed energy Schmidt enlisted the services of missionaries scattered over the globe and thereby secured priceless descriptive reports."[46] Or in the words of Raymond Firth, partially cited earlier: "His [Schmidt's] foundation of the journal *Anthropos* was one of the milestones in the development of more systematic anthropological records from exotic cultures, and the stimulus that he gave the field-workers in cultural anthropology and linguistics is difficult to measure because of its pervasiveness."[47]

The intensity and volume of work of the Divine Word missiologists, although considerable and significant, has perhaps not been so great as that of the anthropologists. Not only were the missiologists organized much later than their colleagues in anthropology, but, unlike the latter, they have more often than not been assigned to full-time teaching or to important administrative positions rather than allowed the freedom for research that the anthropologists have enjoyed. The most important missiological publications today are their journal *Verbum SVD* and the series *Verbum Supplementum*, the Studia Instituti Missiologici Societatis Verbi Divini, and the *Veröffentlichungen des Missionspriesterseminars St. Augustin.*[48]

Divine Word missionaries were closely connected with the very birth of modern Catholic missiology,[49] especially Friedrich Schwager, Anton Freitag, Theodor Grentrup, Karl Streit, and Johannes Thauren, all students or collaborators of Joseph Schmidlin, the "Father of Modern Catholic Missiology." It was especially Schwager who convinced young Schmidlin, the church historian at Münster, to shift his scholarly focus from general church history to missiology. It is indeed regrettable and very unfortunate for Catholic missiology, however, that as early as 1912 a misunderstanding arose between the two great giants, Schmidt and Schmidlin, a misunderstanding that never was resolved.

What the laboratory is to the chemist and the physicist, fieldwork is to the anthropologist. Fieldwork, therefore, has always been a major concern of the Divine Word anthropologists. Although Schmidt personally never went on an expedition,[50] nor did he ever serve on a mission, he nevertheless was a firm believer in the importance of field research, relying heavily on the field data of others, especially those of missionaries and his collaborators. He helped to plan and organize the expeditions of such expert ethnographers as Gusinde, Koppers, Schebesta, Schumacher, Vanoverbergh, and Lebzelter. Gusinde's fieldwork among the Fuegians and Schebesta's expeditions to the African and Asian pygmies unquestionably rank among the most significant ethnographic achievements in anthropological history.[51]

Divine Word mission specialists have always placed a high value also on teaching their disciplines to others, especially to future missionaries and to veteran missioners interested in graduate training. Divine Word anthropologists and missiologists teach, or have taught, not only in their own seminaries and mission universities but also at such universities as Vienna, Fribourg, Bonn, Basel, Nijmegen, Catholic University of America, and Georgetown – to mention a few examples.

Conclusion

The impact of all this activity on modern mission thought has not been easy to describe and is even more difficult to measure.[52] Nor was it the intention to belittle the contributions of other individuals and missionary groups in their role in the development of the mission sciences. The present article has focused on a particular legacy, a precious heritage, which is perhaps not so well known to the English-speaking missiologists as it rightly deserves.

Notes

1. "Professed" members are those who have taken their religious vows in the society. Associated with this all-male missionary group, but independently structured, are the two congregations of women religious founded also by Arnold Janssen, numbering about 4,500 Sisters: the Servants of the Holy Spirit, whose primary task is active missionary work, and the Servants of the Holy Spirit of Perpetual Adoration, a congregation of cloistered nuns committed to a life of prayer and sacrifice for the missions.

2. Helmut Loiskandl, S.V.D., "Scholars among Us: Scientific Research Has Long Been a Hallmark of the Divine Word Missionaries," in J. Boberg, S.V.D., ed., *Word in the World* (Techny, Ill.: Divine Word, 1975), pp. 24-25.

3. General linguistics and phonetics became required courses for the society as early as 1900, ethnology and the study of religions in 1912. Missiology in an embryonic stage was taught as early as 1896.

4. December 30, 1950. The article, authored by Dr. Heine-Geldern, a Viennese anthropologist, originally appeared in *Furche* (Vienna), October 21, 1950.

5. The best biography of Schmidt is that by Joseph Henninger, "P. Wilhelm Schmidt, S.V.D., 1868-1954: Eine biographische Skizze," *Anthropos* 51 (1956): 19-60. Particularly useful are Henninger's bibliographical references, pp. 19-21.

6. Schmidt later took additional courses in the languages and cultures of the Middle East at the University of Vienna.

7. He became a naturalized citizen of Austria in 1902.

8. Fritz Bornemann, "Verzeichnis der Schriften von P.W. Schmidt (1868-1954)," *Anthropos* 49 (1954): 385-432, is the most complete list of Schmidt's writings.

9. *Die Mon-Khmer-Völker, ein Bindeglied zwischen Völkern Zentralasiens und Austronesiens* (Braunschweig: Vieweg, 1906).

10. For a lengthy but still incomplete list of Schmidt's degrees and other honors, see Henninger, "P. Wilhelm Schmidt, S.V.D., 1868-1954," pp. 41-42.

11. For an evaluation of Graebner, see Robert H. Lowie, *The History of Ethnological Theory* (New York: Rinehart, 1937), pp. 177-95. See also Paul Leser, "Fritz Graebner – Eine Würdigung: Zum 100. Geburtstag am 4. März 1977," *Anthropos* 72 (1977): 1-55; J. Henninger, "Fritz Graebner und die kulturhistorische Methode der Ethnologie: Zum Geburtstag von Fritz Graebner (4 Marz 1977)," *Ethnologica*, n.s. 8 (1979): 7-51.

12. Lowie, *History*, p. 191; Wilhelm Schmidt, *The Culture Historical Method of Ethnology: A Scientific Approach to the Racial Question* (New York: Fortuny, 1939), is a translation by S. Sieber of the original *Handbuch der Methode der kulturhistorischen Ethnologie* (Münster: Aschendorf, 1937).

13. He gave up his post as religious superior of the Anthropos community in 1949, the editorship of *Anthropos* some months later in 1949, the directorship of the Anthropos Institute in 1950, and his teaching at the University of Fribourg in 1951.

14. Münster: Aschendorf, 1912-55, 12 vols.

15. Coauthored with Wilhelm Koppers in 1924 (Regensburg: Habbelt, 1924). This is a large (740 pp.) compendium of the culture history of the world as interpreted according to the "Cultural Historical Method of Ethnology."

16. *American Anthropologist* 36 (1934): 599. For a more complete description of Schmidt's personality, see Henninger, "P.W. Schmidt, S.V.D., 1868-1954," pp. 57-60, and J. Henninger, "P. Wilhelm Schmidt: Zum Gedächtnis," *Furche* (Vienna), May 8, 1954.

17. *Ein Jesus-Leben* (Zurich-Altstetten: Göttschmann, 1944). The first edition appeared under the pseudonym Arnold Fabricius, Arnold being Schmidt's middle name, and Fabricius being the Latin translation of "Schmidt." The second edition appeared under his own name in two volumes (Vienna: Mayer, 1948).

18. *Liebe, Ehe, Familie* (Innsbruck, Vienna, Munich: Tyrolia, 1931; 2nd ed., Luzern: Stocker, 1945).

19. His published compositions are listed in Bornemann, "Verzeichnis," p. 430.

20. In 1936 he became president of the Episcopal Commission for the Establishment of the University of Salzburg.

21. Despite F. Bornemann's strong criticism of Schmidt's methodology in *Die Urkultur in der kulturhistorischen Ethnologie: Eine grundsätzliche Studie* (Mödling bei Wien: Sankt Gabriel, 1938), Schmidt chose Bornemann to be his successor as editor of *Anthropos* and director of the Anthropos Institute.

22. For Schmidt's change of attitude toward functionalism and personality studies in anthropology, see Arnold Burgmann, "Sechzig Jahre Anthropos," *Anthropos* 61 (1966): 6.

23. Ernst Brandewie, "The Anthropos and Our Missionary Apostolate," *Verbum SVD* 9 (1967): 22-24; Burgmann, "Sechzig Jahre Anthropos," pp. 1-8.

24. E. Brandewie, "Anthropos," pp. 24-26.

25. Wilhelm Schmidt, "Is Ethnological Information Coming from Missionaries Sufficiently Reliable?" *Anthropos* 6 (1911): 430-31. See also the very first article ever to appear in *Anthropos,* Alexandre Le Roy, "Le rôle scientifique des missionnaires," 1 (1906): 3-10.

26. See, for instance, Marvin Harris, *The Rise of Anthropological Theory* (New York: Thomas Y. Crowell., 1968), p. 390. An objective stance is taken by Lowie, *History,* p. 193.

27. Bornemann, "Verzeichnis," pp. 385-432; Rudolf Rahmann, "Vier Pioniere der Völkerkunde. Den Patres Paul Arndt Martin Gusinde, Wilhelm Koppers und Paul Schebesta zum siebzigsten Geburtstag," *Anthropos* 52 (1957): 263-76.

28. Fred W. Voget, "History of Cultural Anthropology," in John J. Honigmann, ed., *Handbook of Social and Cultural Anthropology* (Chicago: Rand McNally, 1973), pp. 34-35; Charles Hudson, "The Historical Approach in Anthropology," in ibid., pp. 115-16.

29. Citation from Henninger, "P.W. Schmidt, S.V.D., 1868-1954," p. 56.

30. *Anthropos* 49 (1954), frontispiece; Joseph Henninger, "P. Wilhelm Schmidt SVD (1868-1954), 25 Jahre nach seinem Tod," *Anthropos* 74 (1979): 1-5; Fritz Bornemann, "Urreligion und Uroffenbarung, bei P.W. Schmidt," *Anthropos* 74 (1979): 6-10; Arnold Burgmann, "P.W. Schmidt als Linguist," *Anthropos* 49 (1954): 627-58; Fritz Bornemann, "P. Wilhelm Schmidts Bedeutung für Theologie," *Schweizerische Kirchenzeitung* (Luzern), July 15, 1954, pp. 337-39; Sylvester Pajak, S.V.D., *Urreligion und Uroffenbarung bei P.W. Schmidt,* Studia Instituti Missiologici Societatis Verbi Divini, vol. 20 (St. Augustin: Steyler Verlag, 1978); M. Gusinde, "Wilhelm Schmidt, S.V.D., 1868-1954," *American Anthropologist* 56 (1954): 868-70; J. Beckmann, "Mission und Ethnologie. Zum Tode von P. Wilhelm Schmidt, S.V.D. (1868-1954)," *Neue Zeitschrift für Missionswissenschaft* (Beckenried) 10 (1954): 293-96; Ernest Brandewie, "Pater Wilhelm Schmidt, S.V.D.: Contribution to Comparative Religion," unpublished manuscript, 1976; J. Henninger, "P.W. Schmidt, Einiges über sein Leben und sein Werk," *Verbum SVD* 20 (1979): 345-62; J. Henninger, "Im Dienste der Mission: 60 Jahre Anthropos," *Zeitschrift für Missionswissenschaft* 23 (1967): 202-21.

31. Burgmann, "P.W. Schmidt als Linguist," pp. 627-58.

32. Lowie, *History,* pp. 177-95.

33. Beckmann, *Mission und Ethnologie.*

34. The membership of the institute is limited to Divine Word missionaries. It should be noted, however, that not all Divine Word ethnologists, linguists, and other specialists in related fields are members. A Ph.D. degree and election are required for membership.

35. Originally the *Monumenta Serica* was a publication of Fu Jen, the Divine Word university in Peking.

36. Beckmann, *Mission und Ethnologie.*

37. Herman Hagenmaier, S.V.D., "Dancing the Good News," in J. Boberg, ed., *Word in the World* (Techny, Ill.: Divine Word, 1973), pp. 125-27.

38. Brother Wilfrid Sammon, S.V.D., "Apostles and Architects: Divine Word Architectural Bureau, a Unique Missionary Idea," in P. Knitter and J. Boberg, eds., *Word in the World* (Techny, Ill.: Divine Word, 1967), pp. 178-82.

39. Louis J. Luzbetak, S.V.D., "Toward an Applied Missionary Anthropology," *Anthropological Quarterly* 34 (1961): 165-76; *The Church and Cultures: An Applied Anthropology for the Religious Worker* (Techny, Ill.: Divine Word, 1963), 4th printing (1977) now available from William Carey Library, Pasadena, California.

40. Currently, about half of the articles are in English, the rest mostly in German and French.

41. Burgmann, "Sechzig Jahre Anthropos," p. 3; Henninger, "P. Wilhelm Schmidt, S.V.D., 1868-1954," p. 60.

42. See note 27 above.

43. *Internationale Sammlung Ethnologischer Monographien,* 16 vols., first vol. 1909, and *Internationale Sammlung Linguistischer Monographien,* 14 vols., first vol. 1914.

44. Rahmann, "Vier Pioniere der Völkerkunde," p. 268. My figures have been slightly updated.

45. A.P. Elkin, *Social Anthropology of Melanesia* (London: Oxford Univ. Press, 1953), p. 8.

46. Lowie, *History,* p. 192.

47. Citation taken from Henninger, "P. Wilhelm Schmidt, S.V.D., 1868-1954," p. 56.

48. All four titles published by Steyler Verlag, St. Augustin bei Bonn, Germany. To date [1978], 24 volumes of the *Studia* and 28 volumes of the *Veröffentlichungen* have appeared.

49. Anton Freitag, S.V.D., "Der Anteil der Steyler Missionsgesellschaft am Zustandekommen und an der Weiterentwicklung der katholischen Missionswissenschaft," in *50 Jahre katholische Missionswissenschaft*

in Münster 1911-1961: Festschrift von Joseph Glazik MSC (Münster: Verlag Aschendorf, 1961), pp. 131-39. This is an excellent, personal account of one of the pioneers in modern Catholic missiology, in which he describes the important role played by Divine Word missionaries in the origin and further development of missiology.

50. Schmidt's many involvements and style of work made longer absences from his headquarters difficult, if not impossible. Moreover, Schmidt's personal research interests were global, while in-depth field studies are necessarily local. However, he did manage to go on a world lecture tour in 1935, a tour that took him to the United States (with lectures at Princeton, Pennsylvania, and Berkeley, among others) and to Japan, China, Korea, and the Philippines.

51. R. Rahmann, "Fünfzig Jahre Anthropos," *Anthropos* 51 (1956): 7-10; Rahmann, "Vier Pioniere der Völkerkunde," pp. 263-76.

52. It is especially difficult to measure the influence Schmidt exerted on mission-related policies of the Vatican. What is certain, however, is the fact that he was highly regarded at the Vatican, as is evidenced by his papal assignment to organize and direct the Lateran mission museum and to head the scientific section of the Vatican Mission Exhibit, and especially by his membership in the Pontifical Academy of Sciences. It was Pius XI whose intervention enabled Schmidt to leave Austria after the Nazi occupation of the country (Schmidt, it is said, had been offered a residence in the Vatican by the pope, but chose to move to Switzerland instead). In fact, Schmidt was so highly regarded at the Vatican that at one time there were rumors of his becoming a cardinal. In a special audience granted the members of the Eighth General Chapter of the Society of the Divine Word, Pius XII singled out the work of Schmidt and his associates as meriting special recognition, calling it "a most noble apostolate." It is difficult to imagine that this high regard for Schmidt would remain exclusively on the purely theoretical plane.

Daniel Johnson Fleming

1877–1969

A Large Heart in the Narrow Way

Lydia Huffman Hoyle

In the history of mainline Protestant missions, 1932 stands out as a watershed year. In that year, Ernest Hocking published and widely disseminated his conclusions regarding the missionary enterprise in a book entitled *Rethinking Missions*.[1] Though Hocking's work was embraced by few mission organizations or enthusiasts, it set the agenda for discussions of missions for the following decade as many began to rethink the pillars and practices of the enterprise.

For the most part, Hocking's arguments and ruminations were not original. A rethinking of the missionary endeavor had long been underway by persons for whom the missionary enterprise was more than a passing interest. Prominent among these was Daniel Johnson Fleming (1877-1969). A missionary and later a professor of missions at Union Theological Seminary in New York, Fleming was the most prolific, creative, and arguably the most influential of those prior to World War II who sought to articulate a missions theory to accompany modern thought.

Birth and Rebirth

Fleming's involvement in missions was not a natural outgrowth of his upbringing. Though his parents, Daniel and Josephine Fleming, were actively involved in the local Presbyterian church, neither was caught up in the missionary fervor of the period. By necessity and interest, their energies were committed to various business ventures in their Xenia, Ohio, hometown. The spiritual needs of the world were not in their line of vision.

When Fleming left home to attend the College of Wooster, Ohio, he was suddenly immersed in mission enthusiasm. He heard numerous missionary talks and saw the "red-hot YMCA men" signing on the dotted line, but remained unmoved. Since his youth, he had been enamored with business and money-making and had little interest in or intention of becoming a missionary.[2] As a college senior, however, he came into contact with J.C.R. Ewing, a furloughing Presbyterian missionary. After much conversation, Ewing was successful in convincing Fleming to serve with him at Forman Christian College in Lahore, India, as a short-term instructor in math and science.[3]

In 1898, Fleming set sail for India. Still bereft of any missionary zeal, he viewed the assignment as an opportunity to travel. His intent was to return to America in three years to study and practice

486

law. Thus, he arrived in India with "no intention whatever of becoming a missionary."[4] So much for the burning heart and visionary hope expected from a missions volunteer.

Fleming was enthralled by his new home. Lahore, though once described by Rudyard Kipling as "in as foul and as filthy a state as any city can be,"[5] was for Fleming a place full of charm and beauty. Indeed, as time passed, he came to love everything about India – the country, the college, and even missionary life. In many ways, India became a place of transformation for him. "I was rudely awakened from my religious lethargy," Fleming recalled; "I was shocked intellectually and spiritually. After being sheltered by the Killbuck and the hills of Wooster, I saw the world as it really was. Wooster was the garden, so to speak, of my soul, but India planted the seed of vision. India captivated me. It became my meat and drink. Really, I was *reincarnated*."[6]

Though Fleming had come to India with no message save that of science, he became a missionary even as he served as one. As symbol and strengthener of his new commitment to the cause of Christ, he burned his law books and began investigating the education he would need to spend his life in India as a career missionary. By the end of his three-year term, he had decided to study in New York, where he could take courses at Union Theological Seminary while simultaneously working toward a Master of Arts in physics at Columbia. From 1901 to 1903, Fleming worked to complete both courses of study.

The years in New York were difficult ones for him, "the late delayed *Sturm* and *Drang* period" of his life. His recently enlivened faith was so devasted by his studies, in fact, that he became unsure about missionary work and considered returning to India as a government official. As time passed, however, Fleming rebuilt his religious life and turned with renewed vigor to prepare for a career overseas.[7]

After completing his study in New York, Fleming was ordained by the Presbyterian Church and moved to Chicago for further training in chemistry at the University of Chicago.[8] There, he received a Master of Science and, more important, met Elizabeth Cole, who a year later became his wife. Shortly after the wedding, the Flemings returned to India. Lahore became their home for the next eight years and the birthplace of their three children – Elizabeth, McClung, and Helen.

As Fleming taught, evangelized, and discipled his Indian students, he built on two key principles. First, he held a firm belief that Christianity was true and that this truth could be demonstrated through experience. Citing examples from the research of prominent early scientists, he asserted that each investigator had been willing to act "as though they knew, for the sake of an end which they sought." Similarly, he told his students, "we need to act in order to know, to test by experience, to appeal to verification. 'Oh taste and see that the Lord is good.' "[9] There was no doubt in Fleming's mind that anyone who experienced Christ would choose him over any other.

Second, he argued that the value of any religion would be demonstrated through its self-expression in social service. This action-orientation took quite concrete forms. Students at the college were not simply instructed to do good – but rather were encouraged to chose a program of service for themselves. At each break, when the students returned to their homes, the majority, with Fleming's prompting, committed themselves to at least one form of service. The emphasis on Christian action remained central throughout Fleming's life.[10]

Mission Revision

Late in 1912, the family returned from India, anticipating a two-year furlough in the United States. Settling in Chicago, Fleming began work toward his doctorate at the University of Chicago Divinity School.[11] As the months passed, a return to India began to appear improbable. Both Fleming's wife and his children needed medical attention best received in the United States. Reluctantly, he decided to remain there, disappointed that God was leading him "to a sphere of less usefulness, than the one to which I had given my life."[12]

With this unhappy decision made, another more encouraging one confronted him. First Yale, then Union scrambled to offer Fleming a faculty position. The choice was a complicated one for Fleming, but it ended in his decision to join the Union faculty. Harlan Beach, hoping to build a stronger program of missions at Yale, responded graciously to the news but called it the "greatest disappointment" of his life.

In February 1915, Fleming taught his first course at Union. In the tradition of Rufus Anderson, he focused on the problems that arose in the establishment of self-governing, self-supporting, and self-propagating indigenous churches. His goal was to help prospective missionaries "get thoroughly into a point of view which makes the native Church of any Field absolutely centric in thought and service."[13] Fleming taught scores of courses built on this and related themes in the years that followed as he served first as director of the Department of Foreign Service (1915-18) and later as professor of missions (1918-44).

Judging by correspondence, Fleming received the support and encouragement of each of the seminary presidents under whom he worked.[14] With this undergirding he set out to build the missions program. He began by developing and coordinating a sound curriculum. By the fall of 1915, a total of thirteen courses were offered at Union alone, with an additional fifty-two courses in the related disciplines of languages, anthropology, and so forth taught at nearby institutions.

Fleming also took other measures to enhance the missions program at Union. Beginning with the 1917-18 academic year, several fellowships were provided to missionaries on furlough and to qualified nationals. In addition, a building was secured in 1927 that provided apartments for these missionary students. Most significantly, financial and space considerations caused the Missionary Research Library, begun in New York in 1914, to be moved to the seminary. The library, Fleming's "workshop and joy," was an added boon to the missions education program that Fleming was developing.

Fleming also contributed to missionary education and research outside of the seminary. When it was amenable to his schedule at Union, he taught at such schools as Boston University, the Hartford School of Missions, Columbia University, and Yale Divinity School. In addition, he provided many series of lectures in the United States, England, and Canada. Beyond his role as educator, Fleming contributed his expertise to various missionary and nonmissionary conferences and commissions. In 1919-20, he served as the sole American on the International Commission on Village Education in India sponsored by the British Missionary Societies. A decade later, he served on the staff of the Laymen's Foreign Missions Inquiry in India (headed by Hocking). Traveling five times to Europe and three times around the world, Fleming was a delegate to numerous missionary conferences and twice served as missionary representative to the Institute of Pacific Relations in Hawaii.

Though Fleming's work day was filled with teaching, conferences, and so forth, he spent his free time writing. Through this medium we understand best the nature of his contribution to missions theory. During his career, he published twenty books, at least fifteen booklets, and scores of articles. Four of his first five books reflected his continued involvement with India and education and had a limited readership. Beginning with *Marks of a World Christian,*[15] however, Fleming directed his writing toward a wider audience. Though he continued to focus on a constructive restructuring of the missionary endeavor, his work also held interest for any Christian seeking to learn how to adapt to an increasingly pluralistic society. Based on this wider foundation of interest and on the integrity and clarity of Fleming's style, scores of reviews from a variety of periodicals greeted each of his publications.[16]

One central goal dominated Fleming's writing – making missions ethical in the eyes of the world. For many Americans, such a revision of missionary theory was becoming a necessity. The questions raised by the sciences, historicism, and biblical higher criticism had begun to filter down to the average church member. Further, travel and increasing numbers of books about the non-Western world were bringing a new consciousness of the excellencies of Eastern civilizations while revealing the weaknesses of the West. This new knowledge led many to question the straightforward goal of world evangelization.[17]

Meanwhile, the awakening East was increasingly communicating its distaste for certain missionary attitudes and practices. Many factors fed this growing discontent. As in the West, World War I contributed to a general reduction of Western prestige. This decline in perceived Western superiority was accompanied by an increase in nationalism in the lands where missionaries primarily labored. As Westerners, missionaries often bore the brunt of nationalistic antiforeign sentiment.[18] As in the United States, science also struck a devastating blow. Educated Easterners reportedly knew "more about Darwin and Huxley and Dewey and Russell and all the ancients and moderns than an old missionary can ever hope to know."[19] Thus, many were critical of traditional ideas of all kinds, as well as those that propagated such "worn-out" ideas.

Fleming listened to the West and to the East and responded. In classroom lectures, conference presentations, and a constant stream of books and articles, he sought to encourage a new ideology and methodology for the missionary enterprise that took seriously the many issues being raised. Central to his theory was a firm belief in the equality of all persons. Meshing liberal Protestantism's affirmation of human goodness with anthropological evidence regarding basic racial equality, Fleming denied the traditional and lingering belief in Western superiority. He concluded, rather, that "just as we have given up the idea of the divine right of kings and are giving up the age-long conception of male superiority, we will very likely have to give up the flattering delusion of decided racial superiority."[20]

Fleming went a step further by embracing and even reveling in the unique contribution of individual cultures and religions. Just as Franz Boas, the dominant anthropologist of the period, called for an appreciation of cultural peculiarities, Fleming sought a Christianity that respected rather than denigrated or feared the best in other faiths. He based his appeal on the assumption that God was working universally in all races. Thus, Christians should be prepared to recognize all elements of truth and goodness even when they appeared in other religious systems.[21] It is important to note that while lessening the huge chasm believed to exist between Christianity and other religions, Fleming consistently upheld the superior revelation of Jesus Christ. For Fleming, though other religions had much to offer, no other "gift" of East or West equaled the gift of Christ.[22]

Building on this foundation that heralded the equality and integrity of all persons, Fleming called for a remapping of the world. Denouncing missionary maps that painted the West in white and the receiving countries in black, he argued that the West was actually a part of the non-Christian world. There was no portion of the world where Christianity prevailed. If anything, Fleming wrote, "the West is of a deeper black because it has had access to Christ so long."[23]

Recognizing the power of language over thought and practice, Fleming also fought for a change in missionary nomenclature. Terms of battle (e.g., "warfare against Islam," "conquest for Christ," etc.) needed to be eliminated. Such words were clearly offensive to the Easterner and self-deceptive for the Westerner. Likewise Fleming encouraged the elimination of once-acceptable terms like "heathen," "native," and "foreign," which had taken on derogatory meanings.

As a scientist, Fleming also saw the need for scientific integrity on the part of the Western missionary. For "it is only Christianity at its best – a Christianity that has freed itself from invalid accretions, conflicting dogmas and a mind that wars against science – that can compete with the best in reformed and purified ethnic faiths."[24] The missionary was to approach others as one who had been and still was seeking truth. He must make it plain "that he believes the truth as revealed in Jesus because he has found it to be the supreme truth, experimentally and practically: and that the Christianity he presents is itself scientific in the sense that it welcomes the most careful and exact experiment or the test of any seemingly contrary truth."[25] Though Fleming recognized the danger in such an attitude, he believed that Christianity could stand the test of logical and practical evaluation.

Most important, Fleming called for an attitude of humility. The arrogance of the past could not continue. The shameful attitudes and conditions of the West demanded "an indubitable and pervasive humility on the part of Christians . . . A deep sense of national and racial repentance should accompany any further missionary work that we do."[26]

In Fleming's theory, altered attitudes led to changes in missionary methodology. Like many earlier theorists, he encouraged the separation of Christianity from the West. This separation could be demonstrated through the encouragement and development of indigenous churches. For "it is not enough that the Church be Christian; it should be Indian, or Japanese, or African."[27] The missionary role was thus to become that of a helper or enabler, not a leader.

Fleming then encouraged these enablers to apply the Golden Rule on a global scale. Thus, they were to evangelize those of other faiths in the way that they would want to be evangelized. In one article, for example, Fleming sought to put the reader in the shoes of a Buddhist in America. Acceptable missionary practices for the Buddhist were discussed as a means of setting up a mirror in which American missionary practices in other countries could be examined.[28]

Though it was not Fleming's method to proclaim "ready-made solutions and categorical answers"[29] to ethical issues, he also spent much space addressing particular problems facing the "world Christian." These ranged from economic issues (e.g., Should Christian organizations accept money from donors who illegitimately secured their wealth?) and political questions (e.g., In troubled countries, should Christian missionaries align themselves with the forces of law and order or with those working for greater freedom?) to religious questions (e.g., Should Christians worship with those in other religious groups?). In each case, Fleming presented the problem and offered alternative responses without proclaiming his own opinion. The reader was then forced to work out his own position. Thus, while Fleming did not hesitate to demand specific changes in missionary attitudes and methods, he acknowledged the complex nature of the ethical issues facing world Christians.

World Unity

In the last third of Fleming's long life, he came to focus on one component of his theory – the unity of humankind. He elaborated on this theme in seven books and a plethora of articles. Through collections of international Christian art, architecture, symbols, and prayers, he denied the unethical bifurcation of people according to race, nationality, culture, or religious heritage. Several of these collections received a great deal of attention. This was particularly true of *Each with His Own Brush* (1938). This compilation of indigenous Christian art, printed eight times, was included in the Graphic Arts show presented in 1948 by the Grand Central Place in New York, was sent on tour through Latin America by the Institute of Graphic Arts, and was chosen by the Catholic Foreign Missionary Society of America to be used in a series of exhibits in some two hundred Catholic schools and colleges.[30]

World community remained the theme in Fleming's final two works. Written during World War II, *Bringing Our World Together* focused on the role of Christianity and the church in "bringing the nascent universal fellowship" to maturity. Fleming believed that many collaborators were together moving the world toward unity,[31] and that a world religion was a necessary partner in this endeavor. Christianity was deemed to be uniquely suited to be this faith because of its revelation of God through Jesus Christ, assurance of purposeful existence and relation to God, and vision of the brotherhood and equality of all. Further, Christianity, to a greater extent than any other religion, was already becoming the world religion. Thus, Fleming called the Christian community to permeate the world – "bringing Christianity to bear on continents of thought such as war, race, and industry."[32] In this way, Christians could fulfill their responsibility in the quest for unity.

Fleming's last book, *Living as Comrades*, was an effort toward bridging one of the great gulfs still separating the people of the earth – economic status. As in an earlier effort entitled *Ventures in Simpler Living*, Fleming led an inquiry into the question of what the Christian plane of living should be. Having spent his missionary years in a beautiful home filled with servants amid the poverty of India, the question ate at Fleming in a personal way. As with all his books, he offered no clear-cut answers but a multitude of possibilities. Using illustrations from the lives of many young Western Christians living in poverty-stricken Eastern countries, Fleming sought to deal with the problems that arose when one contemplated the simple life. While the examples were drawn largely from the lives and concerns of missionaries, the book clearly laid the question at the feet of all Christians. "The general principle is plain. High ethics impose upon one the moral responsibility to use wealth in the furtherance of God's purpose for mankind as a whole, not simply for one's private satisfaction."[33] Though the book did not demand that all Christians live in poverty, it made it difficult to ignore the issue of personal consumption.

Though Fleming published his last book in 1950 at the age of seventy-three, he continued to live a quite vital and full life for another nineteen years. With the end of his teaching career and the death of his wife of fifty-one years, he moved to Pilgrim Place, a community of retired missionaries in Claremont, California. There he married Helen Mack Howard and enjoyed "one of life's unexpected bonuses." In March 1969, Helen Fleming died suddenly. Within a month, Fleming, at the age of ninety-two, followed.

Conclusion

Early in his life Fleming quoted Sir Andrew Fraser, lieutenant governor of Bengal, who said: "Remember that Jesus Christ walked with a large heart in the narrow way."[34] In the space of a few words, this statement summarizes Fleming's life and work. His large heart enabled him to respect the religion and culture of others and to seek to serve them according to Christ's example. The narrow way, however, provided him motivation and direction. For though he longed for and encouraged a sympathetic attitude toward other religions, he consistently built on the belief that Jesus Christ was the clearest and best revelation of God. Perhaps a large heart and narrow way are together necessary to have an enterprise that is both ethical and missionary.

Notes

1. Though the book summarized the findings of laypeople who visited and evaluated various missionary sites, it was stamped with Hocking's personal theology and viewpoint.

2. Elmer E. Voelkel, "Woosterians Who Are Achieving: Daniel Johnson Fleming, '98," *Wooster Alumni Bulletin,* March 1927, 15. Between 1887 and 1914, the College of Wooster, a Presbyterian school in Ohio, was the alma mater of thirteen of the forty-three Presbyterian missionaries in the Punjab. See John C.B. Webster, *The Christian Community and Change in Nineteenth Century North India* (Delhi: Macmillan of India, 1976), p. 24.

3. Short-term appointment was a new idea at the time. Fleming was the first Presbyterian so designated. See Webster, *Christian Community*, p. 40. Forman College, named after its founder Charles Forman, was responsible for educating 20 percent of the men who received higher education in the Punjab.

4. Voelkel, "Woosterians," p. 15.

5. Rudyard Kipling, "A Week in Lahore," *Civil and Military Gazette*, May 20, 1887, in Pinney, ed. *Kipling's India: Uncollected Sketches, 1884-88* (New York: Schocken Books, 1986), p. 19.

6. Voelkel, "Woosterians," p. 15.

7. "Notes on Religious Life of D.J. Fleming." (Written for the Board of Foreign Missions, 1904; in author's possession.)

8. Because he was returning to India as a college instructor, appropriate education in his teaching field was a necessity.

9. D.J. Fleming, "The Scientific Method as a Means to Vital Religious Life," *Punjab Education Journal* (ca. 1909); p. 248. (Publication data unavailable – article in author's possession.)

10. Though Fleming stressed Christian service, he did not share the social gospelers' emphasis on structural reform.

11. Fleming's dissertation, "Devolution in Mission Administration," was completed in 1914, at which time he received his Ph.D. and graduated summa cum laude. In 1916, the dissertation was published. Fleming also received an honorary doctorate in 1925 from his alma mater, the College of Wooster.

12. D.J. Fleming to Francis Brown, November 13, 1914. (Copy in author's possession.)

13. D.J. Fleming to Francis Brown, November 13, 1914.

14. These included Francis Brown (1915-16), Arthur Cushman McGiffert (1917-26), and Henry Sloane Coffin (1926-45).

15. Frank Laubach pointed to this book as the one that gave him the "clue" that started him on his world literacy campaign.

16. Two of his books, *Attitudes Toward Other Faiths* (1928) and *Bringing Our World Together* (1945), were named as Book of the Month by the Religious Book Club.

17. See Kenneth Scott Latourette, "What Is Happening to Missions?" *Yale Review* 18 (September 1928): 76.

18. *Recent Social Trends in the United States* (New York: McGraw-Hill, 1933), p. 1046-47. This report, commissioned by the American government, listed nationalism as the dominant factor influencing foreign missions in the previous decade.

19. Pearl Buck, "New Difficulties for the Missionary," *Literary Digest* 82 (October 18, 1924): 36.

20. D.J. Fleming, *Whither Bound in Missions* (New York: Association Press, 1925), p. 15.

21. D.J. Fleming, *Attitudes Toward Other Faiths* (New York: Association Press, 1928), pp. 160-61.

22. Fleming, *Whither Bound*, p. 31.

23. Ibid., p. 47.

24. Fleming, "Open-minded Christianity," *Asia* 24 (1924): 472-75, 490-91.

25. Fleming, *Whither Bound*, pp. 106-7.

26. Ibid., p. 64.

27. Ibid., p. 155.

28. D.J. Fleming, "If Buddhists Came to Our Town," *Christian Century* (February 28, 1929), 293-94.

29. See review by Archibald Baker of *Ethical Issues Confronting World Christians*, in *Journal of Religions* 15, no. 4 (October 1935): 487-88.

30. Memorial notice, n.a. (in author's possession).

31. This included, in Fleming's view, adherents of non-Christian religions, social scientists, and others who were working socially and politically for a unified world.

32. D.J. Fleming, *Bringing Our World Together* (New York: Scribners', 1945), p. 128.

33. D.J. Fleming, *Living as Comrades* (New York: Agricultural Missions, 1950), p. 156.

34. D.J. Fleming to Friends-of-the-Lahore-Station, Lahore, January 13, 1908, India Letters, Punjab Mission, v. 166.

Selected Bibliography

Works by D.J. Fleming

1916 *Devolution in Mission Administration*. New York: Fleming H. Revell.

1919 *Marks of a World Christian*. New York: Association Press.

1921 *Schools with a Message in India*. London: Oxford University Press.

1923 *Contacts with Non-Christian Culture*. New York: George H. Doran.

1923 "Relative Racial Capacity." *International Review of Missions* 12, no. 45 (January): 112-21.

1924 "Open-minded Christianity." *Asia* 24: 472-75, 490-91.

1925 *Whither Bound in Missions*. New York: Association Press.

1928 *Attitudes toward Other Faiths*. New York: Association Press.

1928 "Degrees of Aggressiveness in Religion." *Journal of Religion* 8, no. 1 (January): 1-13.
1929 "A Code of Ethics for Missionaries." *Religious Education* 24, no. 12 (December): 967-70.
1929 "If Buddhists Came to Our Town." *Christian Century* 46, no. 9 (February 28): 293-94.
1933 *Ventures in Simpler Living.* New York: International Missionary Council.
1935 *Ethical Issues Confronting World Christians.* New York: International Missionary Council.
1938 *Each with His Own Brush: Contemporary Christian Art in Asia and Africa.* New York: Friendship Press.
1945 *Bringing Our World Together: A Study in World Community,* New York: Scribner's.
1950 *Living as Comrades.* New York: Agricultural Missions.

Works about D.J. Fleming

Hoyle, Lydia Huffman, "Making Mission Ethical: Daniel Johnson Fleming and the Rethinking of the Missionary Enterprise." M.A. thesis, University of North Carolina, Chapel Hill, 1987.
Hutchison, William R. *Errand to the World: American Protestant Thought and Foreign Missions.* Chicago: University of Chicago Press, 1987.
Stanfield, Claude E. "The Missionary Philosophy of Daniel Johnson Fleming." B.D. thesis, Duke Divinity School, 1946.

Maurice Leenhardt

1878–1954

Building Indigenous Leadership

Marc R. Spindler

We French Protestants call it a "tribe": the Leenhardts and their relatives have a sense of belonging together and know that in unity is strength. They have exerted a distinct influence in French Protestantism and in society at large. A daughter of Maurice Leenhardt remembers that the family counted twenty-four Reformed ministers in the 1930s.[1] The family is also active in university, politics, art, and industry. On occasion, they all meet at the ancestral castle at Fonfroide-le-Haut near Montpellier (Hérault, France), where sometime in the eighteenth century the first Leenhardt settled in France, coming from the "North" (Sweden?). Maurice Leenhardt was one of the most brilliant offspring of the family in the twentieth century.

He was born in Montauban in 1878. His father was professor of natural sciences at the Protestant faculty of theology; a distinguished geologist, he was also interested in the biological theories of Darwin. His influence on his son was considerable. Maurice Leenhardt felt called to become a missionary, so he studied theology in Montauban and wrote his bachelor's thesis in 1902 on "The Ethiopian Movement in Southern Africa from 1896 to 1899." It was a pioneering piece of scholarly research on what now is known as the African Independent Churches, and it is still widely quoted as a classic reference.

Maurice Leenhardt dedicated his thesis to Dr. F. Hermann Kruger, professor at the School of Missions of the Paris Evangelical Missionary Society, and a former missionary in Lesotho where he was involved in the efforts to set up a "self-governing" indigenous church. The concern for local initiative and leadership, which is so typical of Maurice Leenhardt, was certainly a legacy of Hermann Kruger.[2]

In the meantime the Paris Evangelical Missionary Society was planning to open a new mission field in New Caledonia, and had sent a missionary for an exploratory trip. The region, mainly the Loyalty Islands, had been evangelized by the London Missionary Society and by indigenous evangelists visiting the various islands spontaneously. The large island of New Caledonia, called Grande Terre, was reached by at least two Melanesian evangelists, Mathaia and Haxen. But a European missionary was requested for further evangelistic progress and church planting.

Maurice Leenhardt became that missionary. He arrived in November 1902 with his wife, Jeanne Michel, the daughter of a famous art historian in Paris, to take over the task of the Melanesian evangelist Haxen, who died shortly after Leenhardt's arrival.[3] Maurice Leenhardt and Philadelphe Delord – the missionary who prepared the way – immediately convened a conference of local evangelists. Two dozen came, all of them sent by Loyaltian churches.

Maurice Leenhardt established the base of his missionary activities at Houailou on the eastern coast, and named the station "Do Neva," meaning "the true country." He worked there and, from there, throughout the whole of Grande Terre, from 1902 to 1926.

A second career began for Leenhardt in Paris, although not exactly what he and his wife had expected. He could have been appointed director of the Paris Evangelical Missionary Society or of the School of Missions. However, there were already two members of the Leenhardt family in these positions. It is not necessary to imagine an intrigue against "the liberal missionary," as some biographers do, in order to understand why Maurice Leenhardt had to wait his turn.

Leenhardt's new base became a popular parish in a working-class district of Paris. And in the evenings he worked on his material from New Caledonia: linguistic and ethnographic notes and documents. Articles were written, books prepared. He renewed his friendship with the leading French anthropologists whom he had met during his furlough in 1921: Lucien Lévy-Bruhl, Marcel Mauss, Paul Rivet. He visited the newly established (1925) Institut d'Ethnologie, which eventually published his first great anthropological studies in 1930. He brought fresh air into the scholarly world of French anthropologists; most of them were theorists working on secondhand material. No one had performed "fieldwork" during twenty-four years, as Maurice Leenhardt had done. This field experience was the great strength of Leenhardt, but it was also his burden, because he remained committed to New Caledonia in a very special way; it contrasted with the so-called uncommitted or value-free attitude in cultural anthropology that was becoming the rule of the game.

Indeed, Leenhardt held fast to the missionary mandate he had received in the beginning. Even if he was no longer a missionary of the Paris Evangelical Missionary Society, he stayed with the "missionary fellowship," and what is more, he assumed an increasing responsibility in foreign missions with regard to the cultivation of missionary vocations, the training of missionaries and, above all, the furtherance of mission studies.

In 1927 Leenhardt launched a missiological bimonthly bulletin, *Les Propos missionnaires*, meant for private circulation among missionaries in the field, regardless of denomination, society, or nationality. In the long run the English-speaking subscribers got a regular supplement to the *Propos*, entitled *The Link* and prepared by the secretary of the Paris Missionary Fellowship, the Rev. M. Warren, from the North Africa Mission. Seventy-four issues were published until World War II disrupted everything; the last issue was dated April 1940. The *débâcle* in France took place in May.

Maurice Leenhardt was also the driving force behind the Youth Missionary Commission, a French resurgence of the Student Volunteer Movement with which Franz Leenhardt had been connected in 1900. He took an increasing share in the training of missionaries at the School of Missions of the Paris Evangelical Missionary Society. In 1936-37 he taught a course entitled "Prudence missionnaire" that dealt with history's lessons for today's missions, explained principles and methods of missions, introduced applied anthropology, and emphasized missionary spirituality.

In an excellent biography of Leenhardt, James Clifford, relying on family sources, insists that there were conflicts between his hero and the Paris Evangelical Missionary Society.[4] Of course, the board of the society was not happy with the frequent interference of the Leenhardts in the missionary policy in New Caledonia; clashes took place. However, on the whole, Leenhardt remained loyal to the Paris Mission, teaching a course at the School of Missions, writing a biography of Alfred Boegner, a former director of the society, and launching the missiological review *Le monde non chétien* (old and new series) with the moral and material support of the society.

Meanwhile Leenhardt's ethnographic reputation and anthropological skill were growing. Marcel Mauss associated him with his own teaching task at the École des Hautes Études, from 1935 onward, working to such good purpose that his protégé was appointed full professor in his chair in 1942. In 1944 Leenhardt started a course in Austronesian languages (as we call them today), helped the Société des Océanistes in its reorganization, and eventually was elected its president. In 1947 he was sent to New Caledonia by the French government in order to establish the French Institute of Scientific Research in Oceania, and served as its founding director. In 1948 he was elected a member of the Academy of Colonial Sciences (later renamed Academy of Overseas Sciences). He spent his last years in Paris as a respected patriarch of French cultural anthropology and of French Protestant missiology. He died in 1954.

In this article, I shall focus my attention on the missionary and missiological contributions of Maurice Leenhardt. His legacy in the fields of ethnography and applied anthropology has been exhaustively analyzed by James Clifford, who is a reliable guide for those needing more details in these fields.[5]

The Missionary Legacy

Maurice Leenhardt was, strictly speaking, a pioneer missionary, namely, the first white missionary among many tribes of New Caledonia. He was not, however, the very first messenger of the Christian Gospel in the region. The first messengers were Melanesian *natas* (a local word meaning "messengers," later "pastors"). Leenhardt respected, valued, and stimulated local initiative and leadership. He insisted again and again that a missionary should not do things that indigenous church members and leaders could do. But he did not believe that this ability to do things was innate or easily given. This ability has to be educated, improved – and tested. The heart of missionary activity in his view was the pastoral school, or the theological college, where the leaders of the nascent church were trained for their ministry. Again, he warned against a timorous recruitment and selection for the ministry. The easy way is to dismiss the rebels and strong-minded individuals; actually, the church needs these kinds of persons in order to be strong. Leenhardt was indeed very critical about missionary and ecclesiastical bureaucracy that tends to eliminate nonconformists and to produce narrow-minded pen-pushers and spineless personages (in French: *moules*). He wanted a virile indigenous leadership, and this very aim required strong missionary leadership. This implied that disciplinary measures could be taken against the *natas*. But, said Leenhardt, "Now disturbed and upset, these *natas* will be later, when their new congregation has conquered their mind, faithful friends of the missionary who has warned, encouraged and finally loved them."[6]

Leenhardt displayed an intense curiosity for everything belonging and pertaining to his mission field. He observed everything, he noted everything, and he related things to one another intelligently and lovingly. Observation was for him a missionary method. He taught it to his students at the School of Missions: "To learn how to observe is half of wisdom." He was an extraordinary observer, perceiving the commonly unperceivable. For instance, he observed the making of shell money and noted the name of shell dust, *kororo*, residue of the process, a neolithic technique already obsolete.[7] The psychology of conversion was considerably enriched by his acute perception of the slightest symptoms of a new Christian life.[8] He also knew how to infect others with his curiosity: his own family, his students, and the *natas* who contributed to the harvest of data. This collective-gathering technique was particularly applied to the local languages. Leenhardt once told how his missionary activity was mixed with research:

At Do Neva I used to preach on the same topic in all Sunday worship services. The day began with the Sunday school. Then, in the morning service, I took my text from the lesson that was just dealt with. In the afternoon the pupils brought their writing slates with their own summary of the sermon . . . and sometimes it happened that an expression, an image, a word I did not know formulated exactly what I wanted to say. I was delighted, everybody understood at once, began to talk, and in the second worship service the teaching of the day was summed up with a richer and clearer vocabulary. There are few greater encouragements for a missionary than to learn from his catechumens and to receive something from them.[9]

The Missiological Legacy

Maurice Leenhardt was not the man of a system; he was too much imbued with Melanesian, indeed, "Kanaka" ideas. (Kanaka is the name of a Melanesian people that is sometimes applied to all Melanesians.) He was doing theology with a "kanakized mind."[10] He accepted the validity of affective modes of knowledge, where life is the key concept. Two areas in Leenhardt's experience illustrate this.

The first is the theology of adoption. Mission is a continuing process of adoption.[11] Leenhardt told it in the form of a short story:

A Kanaka from New Caledonia, staying in the South of France, was once caught sitting in an empty church, copying in a notebook the names of martyred pastors from a commemorative tablet of marble, a moving list of a tight succession.

–What are you doing here?

–I am copying the names of my ancestors.

And seeing that he was not understood, he explained:

–You, Christian Whites, were adopted first; by means of you, we were too, afterwards.[12]

The second area is the ecclesiology of Leenhardt.[13] The "church" was not the primary concern of the young missionary when he left France in 1902. But his Melanesian experience with the young, newborn church, sustained by the theological renewal of the 1920s, led to a real discovery of the "church" as the living body of Christ, planted by the missionary, but shooting out by itself in the force of the Word and the Holy Spirit of God. Leenhardt has briefly sketched a theory of church genetics, what I have called an "ecclesiogenetics," perhaps in a positive sense a kind of ecclesiological Darwinism, which he did not work out. The important discovery was that the life of God should and could take a social shape in full authenticity.

Concluding Remarks

Space does not allow me to dwell on the anthropological legacy of Maurice Leenhardt. Suffice it to say, first, that he successfully introduced a way of understanding "Ethiopianism," that is, African Independent Churches, as movements of social protest against oppression and racism. Second, he successfully contributed to the rehabilitation of "mythic thought" as a mode of knowledge in the cultural anthropological discussion of his time. The originality of Leenhardt, however, lies in his refusal to translate the *mythe vécu* (living myth) into rational, clear, and distinct ideas, as Claude Lévi-Strauss, his successor at the École Pratique des Hautes Études, has tried to do.

At this time of history, the name of Maurice Leenhardt is still revered by the Kanakas, although their interest in the old traditions exposed in his book *Do Kamo* (1947a) has diminished. And his memory is still hated by those French settlers and colonialists who sometimes tend to think that Kanakas are unwanted in New Caledonia, mere nobodies. When Leenhardt arrived in Noumea in

1902, the mayor of the city asked him cynically: "So what have you come here for? In ten years there won't be one Kanaka left!"[14] Actually these Kanakas were resigned to die, but they came back to life, by the grace of God, by means of the Gospel. They experienced a cumulative transformation in the social order, in mentality, in the personal conscience of the believers, and in their relations to the living God. Leenhardt was privileged to be instrumental in this transformation, and to witness it, being aware that nobody is perfect and that the final harvest is still to come.

Notes

1. Roselène Dousset-Leenhardt, *La tête aux antipodes: Récit autobiographique* (Paris: Galilée, 1980), p. 75.
2. André Roux, *Missions des Églises: Mission de l'Église* (Paris: Cerf, 1984), p. 83.
3. James Clifford, *Person and Myth: Maurice Leenhardt in the Melanesian World* (Berkeley: Univ. of California Press, 1982), p. 42.
4. Ibid., pp. 74-77, 109-11, 115-21.
5. Ibid., pp. 124-224.
6. Maurice Leenhardt, unpublished memorandum on the situation in New Caledonia, December 1932, quoted in Jean Guiart, *Destin d'une Église et d'un peuple: Nouvelle-Calédonie 1900-1959* (Paris: Mouvement du Christianisme social, 1959), p. 82.
7. Jean Poirier, "Maurice Leenhardt, océaniste et sociologue," *Le monde non chrétien* 9 (1955): 94.
8. Raoul Allier, *La psychologie de la conversion chez les peuples non-civilisés* (Paris: Payot, 1925), quotes Maurice Leenhardt on fifty-four occasions.
9. Maurice Leenhardt, "Notes sur la traduction du Nouveau Testament en langue primitive," in *Protestantisme et missions* (Paris: Je Sers, 1951), p. 177, first published in 1922.
10. In French: "l'esprit tout enkanaké" (Roselène Dousset-Leenhardt, *La tête aux antipodes*, p. 23).
11. Romans 8:15-17. See Roux, *Missions des Églises: Mission de l'Église*, pp. 238-43.
12. Maurice Leenhardt, "Les missions protestantes françaises," in *Protestantisme français* (Paris: Plon, 1945), p. 395.
13. See Marc Spindler, "L'ecclésiologie de Maurice Leenhardt," *Journal de la Société des Océanistes* 36 (1980): 29-91.
14. Maurice Leenhardt, *De la mort à la vie: L'évangile en Nouvelle-Calédonie* (Paris: Société des Missions Évangéliques, 1953), p. 5.

Selected Bibliography

Works by Maurice Leenhardt

1902 *Le mouvement éthiopien au sud de l'Afrique de 1896 à 1899*. Cahors: Coueslant; reprinted, Paris: Académie des Sciences d'Outre-Mer, 1976, with contributions by Robert Delavignette and Robert Cornevin.
1921 "Expériences sociales en terre canaque." *Revue du christianisme social* 29:96-114; republished under the new title "De la gangue tribale à la conscience morale," *Le Monde non chrétien* 17, no. 66 (1963): 114-32.
1922 *Le catéchumène canaque*. Les Cahiers Missionaires, no. 1. Paris: Société des Missions Évangéliques.
1922 *De la mort à la vie: L'Évangile en Nouvelle-Calédonie*. Les Cahiers Missionaires, no. 3. Paris: Société des Missions Évangéliques. Republished, with some revisions, by same publisher, 1953.
1922 "Notes sur la traduction du Nouveau Testament en langue primitive." *Revue d'histoire et de philosophie religieuses* 2:193-218. Republished in *Protestantisme et missions*, Paris: Je Sers, 1951, pp. 149-78. Partly translated into English, "Notes on Translating the New Testament into New Caledonian," *Bible Translator* 2 (1951): 97-105, 145-52.
1922 *Peci arii, Vikibo ka dovo i lesu Keriso, e pugewe ro verea sce Ajie*. Paris: Société des Missions Évangéliques. (Translation of the New Testament into Houailou.)
1927 (ed.) *Les Propos missionnaires*, no. 1. This bulletin of missionary formation and intermissionary correspondence was edited by Maurice Leenhardt until April 1940, totaling 74 issues, many of them including notes and articles by him.
1930 *Notes d'ethnologie néo-calédonienne*. Travaux et mémoires de l'Institut d'ethnologie, vol. 8. Paris: Université de Paris.

1931 (ed.) *Le monde non chrétien.* Cahiers de Foi et Vie. Occasional supplement to the theological review *Foi et Vie*, Paris. Seven issues were published from Fall 1931 to April 1936, with many notes and comments by the editor, M. Leenhardt.

1932 *Documents néo-calédoniens.* Travaux et mémoires, vol. 9. Paris: Institut d'ethnologie.

1937 *Gens de la Grande Terre: Nouvelle Calédonie.* Paris: Gallimard. Revised, expanded edition, 1953.

1939 *Alfred Boegner (1851-1912) d'après son journal intime et sa correspondance.* Paris: Société des Missions Evangéliques.

1947 *Do Kamo: La personne et le mythe dans le monde mélanésien.* Paris: Gallimard. Republished, 1960, with a preface by M.I. Pereira de Queiroz. English translation: *Do Kamo: Person and Myth in the Melanesian World.* Chicago: Univ. of Chicago Press, 1979, with an introduction by Vincent Crapanzano.

1947 (ed.) *Le monde non chrétien.* Nouvelle série. A missiological quarterly review, founded and edited by Maurice Leenhardt. Most issues include leading notes, articles, and reviews from his pen.

1949 "Préface to Carnets de Lucien Lévy-Bruhl." Paris: Presses Universitaires de France. English translation in L. Lévy-Bruhl, *The Notebooks on Primitive Mentality.* Oxford: Blackwell, 1975.

1953 "Quelques éléments communs aux formes inférieures de la religion." In M. Brilliant and R. Aigrain, eds., *Histoire des religions* (Paris: Quillet), 1:83-110.

1970 *La structure de la personne en Mélanésie.* Milan: S.T.O.A. Edizioni. A revised edition of six essays, edited by H.J. Maxwell and C. Rugafiori.

Works about Maurice Leenhardt

Clifford, James. *Person and Myth: Maurice Leenhardt in the Melanesian World.* Berkeley: Univ. of California Press, 1982. (Ph.D. diss. Harvard University, 1977.) (Important bibliography, pp. 257-64).

Dousset-Leenhardt, Roselène. *A fleur de terre: Maurice Leenhardt en Nouvelle-Calédonie.* Paris: L'Harmattan, 1984.

_____. *La tête aux antipodes: Récit autobiographique.* Paris: Editions Galilée, 1980.

Guiard, Jean, *Destin d'une Église et d'un peuple, Nouvelle-Calédonie, 1900-1959: Étude monographique d'une oeuvre missionnaire protestante.* Paris: Mouvement du Christianisme social, 1959.

Gusdorf, Georges. "Situation de Maurice Leenhardt ou l'ethnologie française de Lévy-Bruhl en Lévi-Strauss." *Le monde non chrétien* 18 (1964): 139-92.

Hommage à Maurice Leenhardt, président de la Société des Océanistes. Paris: Société des Océanistes, 1954.

Hommage à Maurice Leenhardt. Special issue of *Le monde non chrétien* 9, no. 33 (1955).

Leenhardt, Raymond H. "Témoignage: Une tournant de l'histoire de la Nouvelle Calédonie, Maurice Leenhardt." *Revue française d'histoire d'outre-mer* 65 (1978): 236-52.

Massé, Jean. "Maurice Leenhardt: Une pédagogie libératrice." *Revue d'histoire et de philosophie religieuses* 60 (1980): 67-80.

Offprint from *Journal de la Société des Océanistes* 10 (1954). Paris: Société des Océanistes, 1955.

Spindler, Marc. "La découverte missiologique de l'Église chez Maurice Leenhardt." *Nederlands Theologisch Tijdschrift* 36 (1982): 223-37.

_____. "L'ecclésiologie de Maurice Leenhardt." *Journal de la Société des Océanistes* 36 (1980): 279-91.

_____. "Maurice Leenhardt et Madagascar." *Le monde non chrétien* 17 (1963): 39-59.

Teisserenc, Pierre. "Science sociales, politique coloniale, stratégies missionnaires: Maurice Leenhardt en Nouvelle Calédonie." *Recherches de science religieuse* 65 (1977): 389-442.

Frank Charles Laubach

1884–1970

Apostle to the Silent Billion

Peter G. Gowing

rank Laubach's bequest to the worldwide mission of the church was a zeal, motivated by the love of Christ, to bring the illiterate millions of the world's people to a richer experience of God through literacy education. His "Key Word" and "Each One Teach One" methods of literacy teaching have been credited with enabling over 100 million people to read.

After fourteen years of a more or less conventional missionary career of church planting and theological education in the Christian regions of the Philippines, Laubach arrived in 1929 to work among the Muslim Filipino (Moro) population of the Lake Lanao area of Mindanao. Convinced that the usual evangelistic and educational programs would be counterproductive as a means of touching Moro lives with the light and love of Christ, Laubach almost immediately determined that literacy teaching was potentially the more fruitful approach.

In the course of a dozen years of literacy work among the Moros – those of the Lanao area were called Maranao ("People of the Lake") – Laubach and his associates developed exciting new principles and techniques that caught the attention of government, missionary and private organizations around the world concerned with literacy. Early in 1935, on his way back to the United States for furlough, Laubach visited several countries in southern Asia, the Middle East, and Europe to explain his literacy methods. While still on furlough in the fall of 1935, he and interested friends formed the World Literacy Committee in Upper Montclair, New Jersey, which in 1941 merged with the Committee for Christian Literature of the Foreign Missions Conference of North America to form the Committee on World Literacy and Christian Literature.

From 1942 until his retirement at the age of seventy in 1954, Frank Laubach was on the staff of that committee – informally known as "Lit-Lit" – which in 1950 became a unit of the National Council of the Churches of Christ in the U.S.A. In that capacity, Laubach gave himself tirelessly to technical assistance and the promotion of literacy campaigns in many lands. After his retirement from Lit-Lit, he founded in 1955 a private, nonsectarian, nonprofit educational organization called Laubach Literacy, Inc. Now headquartered in Syracuse, New York, and headed by Frank's son, Robert, Laubach Literacy continues to challenge and assist individual volunteers and public and private agencies around the globe to undertake literacy education in a spirit of compassion for, and a deep sense of the worth and dignity of, the illiterate half of the world's population.

By the time Frank Laubach died on June 11, 1970, at the age of eighty-five, he had carried his literacy ministry to 103 countries and had been involved in developing literacy primers embodying his principles and methods in 313 languages. He had promoted both his spiritual and literacy causes in forty-three books, including *Toward a Literate World* (1938), *How to Teach One and Win One for Christ* (1964), and *Forty Years with the Silent Billion* (1970). He had given impetus to the opening of literacy and journalism courses at the Kennedy School of Missions at Hartford Seminary, Syracuse University, Asbury College, Baylor University, the University of California, and in more than twenty other centers in the United States. Popularly hailed as "Mr. Literacy," Laubach was featured in many religious and secular magazines. *Time* referred to him as "Founder of a world literacy drive." Newscaster Lowell Thomas called him "the foremost teacher of our times." *Newsweek* featured him as "one of the grand men of the missionary world." And Norman Vincent Peale in *Look* declared Laubach to be "one of the five greatest men in the world." Ten universities and colleges – among them Princeton and Columbia, Wooster, and Baldwin-Wallace – conferred honorary degrees on Frank Laubach in recognition of his enormous contribution to world literacy. A deeply spiritual Christian, Frank Laubach's religious faith was the inspiration of his great vision for the literacy of "the Silent Billion"; it was the wellspring of his eloquent preaching and teaching in that field; and it was the source of his boundless energy in that ministry until the day he died. He will be long remembered by a designation bestowed on him years ago and richly deserved: "Apostle to the Illiterates."

The Making of a Literacy Evangelist

For Frank Charles Laubach the journey toward his calling as an apostle to the illiterates began at Benton in rural Pennsylvania on September 2, 1884, where he was born into a devout Methodist family. His father, John Brittain Laubach, was the town dentist. Young Frank attended the local public schools, after which, at age eighteen, he taught in one of the grade schools for a year. He then attended a nearby normal school but soon decided to continue his further college preparation at the Perkiomen Preparatory School near Philadelphia. He graduated from Princeton University in 1909, majoring in sociology. In these years he was thrilled by the vivid accounts that two of his townmates, Harry Edwards and Joe Albertson, wrote of their experiences as young school teachers in the Philippines and particularly of the Moros of Mindanao and Sulu, "the worst troublemakers American soldiers had ever faced." Feeling called to missionary service, Laubach attended Union Theological Seminary in New York City, from which he graduated in 1913. The year before, he had married a Benton girl, Effa Seely, who was a cousin of Harry Edwards. As further preparation for missionary service, Laubach continued his studies at Columbia University, earning the Ph.D. degree in 1915 with a dissertation on vagrants in New York City. In their New York years, the Laubachs did settlement work and for a time held a student pastorate. He was ordained to the Congregational ministry in 1915 and that same year he and his wife left for the Philippines as missionaries of the American Board of Commissioners for Foreign Missions (now the United Church Board for World Ministries) to which the Evangelical Union in 1902 had committed northern and eastern Mindanao for mission work.

The Laubachs proceeded at once to Dansalan (now Marawi City) to begin evangelistic work among the Moros, believing that in the battle for Jesus Christ to conquer the world, that was one place in the Orient where "the ranks are thinnest and the battle hottest." At Dansalan, however, American officials told them in no uncertain terms that inexperienced missionaries talking religion to the Moros would only make matters worse in that troubled area. For three and a third centuries the Muslim Filipinos had fought ferociously against Spanish efforts to subjugate them and convert them from their Islamic religion and lifeways. When in 1898 the Americans succeeded the Spaniards as colonial rulers and sought to integrate the Moros into the political system they were shaping for the rest of the Philippines, the Moros likewise took up arms against the new invaders. The Maranao Muslims of the Lake Lanao area were among the most stubborn in their resistance to American rule even after they learned the futility of a military struggle against a disciplined, well-armed modern U.S. army. Officers of that army tactfully but firmly stressed to the Laubachs that the Moros would not be ready to listen to missionaries for some time to come.

Thus barred from working at Dansalan, Frank and Effa Laubach then proceeded to Cagayan de Oro on the north-central coast of Mindanao and engaged in evangelistic work among the Christian population, which then numbered very few Protestants. Later in life, the Laubachs were to become ecumenical Christians par excellence, working closely with Christians of all denominations and people of many different faiths. But as new Congregational missionaries in Mindanao in 1915 they had strong anti-Roman Catholic prejudices common to Protestants of that time, which were, of course, reciprocated by Catholics. For several years the Laubachs established and nurtured Protestant (evangelical) congregations in Cagayan and several other towns in northern Mindanao. For a month each year, however, they would take their vacation in the cool climes of Dansalan (2,300 feet above sea level, on the shores of Lake Lanao) where they would monitor the prospects for eventual work among the Moros.

In 1921 the Laubachs moved to Manila where Frank was invited to teach at Union Theological Seminary. There he not only taught but shared administrative and fund-raising responsibilities in the seminary and gave strong spiritual leadership in the city as well. He also found time to plunge into serious, scholarly research on the history, culture, and religion of the Philippines, which resulted in two popular books: *The People of the Philippines* (1925) and *Seven Thousand Emeralds* (1929). In these years he also revealed a strong social conscience and exhibited a sensitivity for crucial social issues that was way ahead of his time. In 1926, for example, he asked in the *Missionary Herald* (vol. 132, p. 309):

> Shall the public domain be homesteaded out to small Filipino landholders or shall it be given over to great American corporations? . . . The question in this country for missionaries is whether Christianity is chloroform poured on a feather, with which missionaries tickle the chins of the Filipinos, while America, big business, persuades Congress to pronounce upon the Philippines the same curse of landlordism that has paralyzed Ireland for a thousand years.

All the while the Laubachs were in Manila they did not abandon their dream of some day returning to take up a mission to the Lanao Moros. That Dr. Laubach maintained his interest in the Moros is demonstrated in his many articles about them (some published in the *Moslem World*) and references to them in his books during these years. Indeed, he had a grand, if rather naive, vision of the Moros being ripe for a Christian missionary campaign of such a success and magnitude that it would swoop down from Mindanao to engulf as well the Muslim peoples of Malaya, the East Indies, and even the subcontinent itself. In this vein (and in vain), he tried to recruit Frank Carpenter, newly retired governor of the Department of Mindanao and Sulu, to head a proposed nondenominational Christian mission to the Muslims of southern Asia, which would make use of Moro converts and would be financed in part by John D. Rockefeller. Carpenter replied, tactfully, that ill health prevented his considering such a proposition. Finally, Frank Laubach's chance to try his hand at mission work among the Moros came. Resigning his post at Union Theological Seminary, and leaving his wife, Effa, and son Robert briefly in the north, he arrived in Dansalan in December 1929 to open the Lanao Station of the American Board's mission in Mindanao. He was forty-five years old and he had been in the Philippines fourteen years.

Occupying a small cottage near the American military camp at Dansalan, Laubach soon concluded that any ideas he had about carrying out his mission to the Moros through the usual methods of preaching and teaching – he had a notion to found a normal school at Dansalan – simply would not work. He found the Moros unapproachable and resistant to all his overtures. Indeed, he confessed that his first month in Lanao was the hardest month of his life and he was discouraged and depressed. One evening, in that mood, he climbed Signal Hill, near Dansalan town, with his dog, Tip. According to his own report, as he sat overlooking the province that had him beaten, tears welled up in his eyes. His lips began to move and it seemed that God was speaking:

My child, you have failed because you do not really love these Moros. You feel superior to them because you are white. If you can forget you are an American and think only how I love them, they will respond.

To this, Laubach found himself replying:

God, I don't know whether you spoke to me through my lips, but if you did it was the truth. I hate myself. My plans have all gone to pieces. Drive me out of myself and come and take possession of me and think Thy thoughts in my mind.

Laubach reported that from that moment God had killed his racial prejudice and made him "color-blind." Again God spoke to him:

If you want the Moros to be fair to your religion, be fair to theirs. Study their Koran with them.

Coming down from his Signal Hill experience, Dr. Laubach contacted the *panditas* (Muslim religious teachers) at once and told them he wanted to study their Qur'an. The next day, with their enthusiastic help, he began a thoroughgoing study of the religion, culture, and language of the Maranao Muslims, which lasted many months. In the course of these studies Laubach drew closer to the Moros, and they to him.

About that time (January 1930) Laubach was joined in Dansalan by Donato Galia (M.A., Columbia University) and his wife, teachers from the Visayas who had come to help with the normal school that Laubach had had in mind to establish. Finding that the missionary had now abandoned the idea of a normal school as unsuited for Moro needs, Galia joined Laubach in the study of Maranao language. Together they adopted a Roman alphabet for that language, which up to then had been written in Arabic letters, in which only 3,000 to 4,000 out of 90,000 Maranaos were literate. They devised a perfectly phonetic system of using one Roman letter to a sound and one sound to a letter. As Laubach and Galia engaged in this work, which also included unraveling the mysteries of the language's complex grammar, it occurred to them that they were being drawn into a vitally important work. As the two Christians teachers sought to reduce the Maranao language to easy reading and writing in Roman letters for themselves, they were also making it possible for the largely illiterate Maranao population to learn easily the reading and writing of that language.

Laubach and Galia were excited at the prospects opening before them. The Maranaos were totally illiterate in Roman letters. Their language had never been written, let alone printed, in Roman letters. Would it not be a great service – a great Christian service – to teach them to read and write their language using the letters employed not only in English but in all the other major languages of the Philippines as well? The two teachers received much encouragement in this line of thinking from their new Moro friends.

By February 1930 Laubach had acquired a small secondhand printing press from friends in Cagayan – and with the press came a printer, Silvino Abaniano. With the help of their Maranao language teacher, Pambaya Bayabao, Laubach and Galia prepared copy for a two-page Maranao-language tabloid called *Totwl Ko Ranao* ("The Story of Lanao"). Their first number featured on page 1 material in Maranao language, set in type for the first time ever, while on page 2 the Maranao material was in Arabic script written (by a *pandita*) on stencils supplied by the superintendent of schools. This first issue, published on February 16, was not very handsome to Laubach's critical eye, but the Moros were delighted and the paper was a huge success. At once it stimulated much interest in learning to read, and the two teachers were deluged with requests from Moros wanting to be taught in the "new" letters.

At first the two men used the usual sentence method of teaching literacy, which seemed to them and to their Moro pupils unnecessarily long. Month after month they sought after a better method, and corresponded with literacy workers around the world. After some six months of experimenting they finally hit upon a revolutionary idea. They searched for three words that would contain all the sounds the Maranao language used, made up of twelve consonants and five vowels. (Laubach made use of the letter *w* to stand for the vowel sound *oo* as in "tool," while retaining *o* for the vowel sound as in "total." Thus the Maranao word for "story" was spelled *totwl*, pronounced *totool*. He received much criticism from this and eventually dropped the *w* and taught two sounds for *o*.) More months and at last they found three "key words," each containing four different consonants, the consonants followed by the letter *a* (as in "father"): *Malabanga* (a town in Lanao); *karatasa* ("paper"); and *paganada* ("to learn"). Every word in the Maranao language can be derived by varying the vowels with the consonants used in those three familiar words. Teaching the Maranao to read became an infinitely easier task when, with the aid of a large chart and simple primers, the aim became the teaching of the phonetic sound of easily recognized syllables and combinations of syllables. Now any Moro could be taught to read in a day – and he could also be easily taught to write.

As the course became easier, the number of Moros who desired to learn increased, until hundreds crowded into the old building that Laubach had purchased to house his family, the press, and the literacy classrooms. Laubach and Galia continued to publish their tabloid, which was soon expanded to a four-page fortnightly and distributed by the thousands in Lanao. This and their other publications were very important for the new literates, of course. Laubach and Galia also trained a corps of literacy teachers to help instruct classes not only in Dansalan but in communities throughout the lake area. Most of the teachers were themselves graduates of Laubach's literacy classes. From mission funds, they were paid wages ranging from $2.50 to $20.00 per month. In addition to the paid teachers, there were many volunteers who assisted in what became a major literacy movement in the province of Lanao. By late 1932 the movement was averaging 3,000 new literates a month and Frank Laubach's "literacy thermometer" showed that 45,000 Lanao Moros had at least begun to read and write in Roman letters.

Building upon the success of his literacy work, Frank Laubach found ways to maintain the interest and harness the energies of the new literates. *Totwl Ko Ranao* gave way to a fourteen-page newspaper called *Lanao Progress*, which was printed not only in Maranao but Cebuano Visayan and English as well. The press became the foundation for Lanao Press Publishers, which turned out various instructional primers, books, and pamphlets in addition to the newspaper. The literacy classes in various communities (including at Dansalan) developed into Maranao Folk Schools and taught not only literacy but health and hygiene, improved childcare, and farming methods. A library was set up in Dansalan, and friends in the Philippines and America contributed books to a collection that came to number over 5,000 volumes. Under Laubach's inspiration and leadership a Moro Book Store was established; also a kindergarten for Moro children, a dispensary with a trained nurse, and even a small experimental farm to promote new varieties of food crops among Maranao farmers. Laubach established dormitories for Moro students attending school in Dansalan, to provide them with a wholesome "home away from home." His wife and the wives of missionary colleagues who joined him in the ever-growing work assisted in organizing Moro women's clubs, which among other activities sought to promote literacy among Moro women. Early on, Dr. Laubach organized throughout Lanao some twenty-five Societies of English Speaking Youth (later called Societies of Educated Youth) to assist the literacy campaign in their own communities. The effort was to get everybody in every Moro house to become literate, and it became a matter of high prestige to have a tin sign posted on one's house declaring in Maranao: "Certificate of Honor, 100%" – meaning that the whole household (i.e., everyone over ten years old) could read and that it had subscribed to *Lanao Progress*.

The economic depression in the United States threatened Laubach's literacy work in Lanao for a time but it also had a significant methodological impact. Learning in December 1932 that his mission funds would be cut back so that he could no longer pay his literacy teachers, Dr. Laubach called the teachers together with some of the *datus* (Moro chiefs) to explain to them the sad news. Kakai Dagalangit, the leading *datu* of southern Lanao, a man with piercing eyes, arose and said: "This [literacy] campaign is the most important thing that ever came to Lanao. It shall not stop. Every person who learns must teach five others. I will see that they do." (This is Dr. Laubach's earliest account of the *datu's* words. With the passage of time, the account became somewhat embroidered to the point where the *datu* was reported to have said: "I'll make everybody who knows how to read teach somebody else, or I'll kill him.") According to Laubach, this was the origin of the "Each One Teach Five" idea, which, when implemented in Lanao, was very successful, and even more so when it was soon transformed into "Each One Teach One." The "Key Word" system combined with one-on-one instruction, which did away with the cost and inhibiting atmosphere of large classes, resulted in a methodology of literacy instruction that caught on like wildfire.

The concept of volunteer literacy teachers and their pupils who became volunteer literacy teachers in geometrically ever-expanding numbers quickly caught the imagination of the world. News of the literacy movement in Lanao spread all over the Philippines and visitors came down to see what was happening there among "the bloodthirsty Moros." In 1933 and 1934 Dr. Laubach was invited to go all over the islands and assist in preparing charts and primers in some twenty languages using the "Key Word" and "Each One Teach One" methods perfected in Lanao. This so-called Philippine Method attracted the attention of literacy experts in other lands, and before long Laubach's mail was flooded with inquiries and invitations to come and explain his techniques. In his office he posted a map of the world and from a tack marking the location of Dansalan, he stretched colored thread to other tacks marking locations from which the inquiries and invitations came. Moros visiting his office clucked their tongues in delight and said: "Just see how important we are getting in the world."

When Laubach left Dansalan for furlough early in 1935, a trip that would take him on his first visits to other lands to instruct literacy workers in the Philippine Method, he was accompanied to the boat in Iligan by several thousand Moros. As the boat was about to leave, the chief *pandita* of Lanao prayed for the safe journey of Laubach and his family and many Moros kissed "Dr. Frank's" hand and told him, "We will pray for you in every mosque in Lanao." Laubach returned to Lanao in 1936 and stayed for five more years during which he was sometimes off on literacy missions elsewhere in the Philippines and Asia. In June 1941 he presided at the opening of the Madrasa High School, which was the first private secondary school in the province and was designed to meet the special needs of Moro students. A few months later, in October 1941, he and his family were once more off on furlough. By then World War II was already over a year old in Europe and two months later it was to engulf Asia and the Pacific. Dr. Laubach did not know it at the time, but he was never again to work in Lanao. From October 1941 on, the literacy evangelist to the Moros of Lanao was to become an apostle to the illiterates of the world. He was fifty-seven years of age and had been in the Philippines twenty-six years.

The Romance of Opening Blind Eyes

Very early in his literacy work, Frank Laubach found a phrase that aptly described not only the work but the ethos of what he was about as a Christian missionary engaged in literacy education: "the romance of opening blind eyes." Laubach was nothing if not a romantic, in the best sense of that term. He thought large thoughts. He pursued his ideas with enthusiasm and fervor. He brought passion and idealism to everything he did. His motives were pure and continually subjected to searching introspection in a finely tuned life of prayer. Sometimes his ideas and actions could be judged naive and impractical, but he was always ready to dare great things for Christ. Mention was made of his notion in 1921 that the Muslim peoples of southern Asia were ripe for mass conversion to the Christian religion. On Armistice Day 1933 he launched a campaign to get people in every land to "pair off" with people in other lands of the same calling and in a "continuous plebiscite" repudiate war and pledge their nonparticipation in armed conflict. A letter addressed to the highest officials in the Philippines and the United States, to the heads of state and governments of all the nations of the world and to as many world figures (Einstein, Dewey, Gandhi, Mott, Kagawa, etc.) as could be thought of, was sent out from Dansalan backed by the signatures of twelve sultans, nearly two hundred sheiks, hadjis, imams *panditas*, and gurus as well as over 1,200 other Muslims, plus 200 Christian Filipinos, 20 Americans, 18 Chinese, and 4 Japanese – all residing in Lanao. Not content with preaching an Armistice Day sermon, Laubach set out "to do something" about the horror of human warfare. The campaign did not catch on and did little to avert World War II – but Laubach was never one to be discouraged from attempting to implement a romantically right idea.

World literacy was one romantically right idea that Laubach attempted to implement – and the results of his own contribution were very impressive indeed. Literacy for him was work that brought the Christian worker close to the estimated one billion people in the world who were "blind" and "unable to speak" because they could not read or write. Said Laubach in 1932: "They are the most backward, the most impoverished and the most oppressed of all classes of people, the kind for whom the heart of Christ bled most, the kind to whom one following Christ would naturally turn. They are in prison, hungry, thirsty and naked."

When Laubach came to work in Lanao he found the Moros hostile and unapproachable. Literacy provided the means not just to approach them but to approach them as one who wanted to share the love of Jesus Christ with them. In his early years in Lanao, Laubach was in the habit of writing his father in Benton a six-page letter each week, and these letters were published in the *Argus*, the local newspaper. Years later Constance Padwick, a missionary in Egypt, was able to excerpt passages from these letters that reflected the profoundly mystical quality of Frank Laubach's spirituality. These excerpts were eventually published in a book that became a spiritual classic: *Letters by a Modern Mystic* (1937). In the letter dated March 3, 1930, – four months after he had come to Lanao, three months after his Signal Hill experience, and at a time when he was well into his studies of Moro religion and culture and also into his new work in literacy – Laubach wrote:

> For the first time in my life I know what I must do off in lonesome Lanao. I know why God left this aching void, for himself to fill. Off on this mountain I must do three things:
>
> 1. I must pursue this voyage of discovery in quest of God's will. I *must* because the world needs me to do it.

2. I must plunge into mighty experiments in intercessory prayer, to test my hypothesis that God needs my help to do his will for others, and that my prayer releases his power. I *must* be his channel for the world needs me.

3. I must confront these Moros with a divine love which will speak Christ to them though I never use his name. They must see God in me, and I *must* see God in them. Not to change the name of their religion, but to take their hand and say, "Come, let us look for God."

What right then have I or any other person to come here and change the name of these people from Muslim to Christian, unless I lead them to a life fuller of God than they have now? Clearly, clearly my job here is not to go to the town plaza and make proselytes; it is to *live* wrapped in God, trembling to his thoughts, burning with his passion . . .

I look up at this page and it is not red hot as my soul is now. It is black ink. It ought to be written with the red ribbon. You will not see the tears that are falling on this typewriter, tears of a boundless joy broken loose.

For forty years more Frank Charles Laubach labored in literacy education in the spirit of a "boundless joy broken loose." He rightly belongs among that very select group of missionaries whose good work in Christ's name touched the lives of millions of people across the barriers of race, nationalities, tongues, and cultures.

Selected Bibliography

Works by Frank Laubach

1925 *The People of the Philippines*. New York: George H. Doran.
1929 *Seven Thousand Emeralds*. New York: Friendship Press.
1936 *Rizal, Man and Martyr*. Manila, Philippines: Community Publishers.
1937 *Letters by a Modern Mystic*. New York: Student Volunteer Movement.
1938 *Towards a Literate World*. New York: Columbia Univ. Press.
1947 *Teaching the World to Read: A Handbook for Literacy Missions*. New York: Friendship Press.
1954 *Channels of Spiritual Power*. Westwood, N.J.: Revell.
1960 (with Robert S. Laubach) *Toward World Literacy*. Syracuse, N.Y.: Syracuse Univ. Press.
1964 *How to Teach One and Win One for Christ*. Grand Rapids, Mich.: Zondervan.
1970 *Forty Years with the Silent Billion*. Old Tappan, N.J.: Revell.

Works about Frank Laubach

Chmaj, Deborah R., and Menbere Wolde (compilers). *The Laubach Collection: Personal Papers of Frank C. Laubach, Documents of Laubach Literacy Inc.* Syracuse, N.Y.: Syracuse Univ. Libraries, 1974.
Frenzke, Lucille Eleanor. "The Development of the Literacy Movement under Frank Laubach and Its Contribution to World Mission." M.R.E. thesis, Biblical Seminary in New York, 1952.
Horbach, Elizabeth. "An Analysis of the World Wide Literacy Program Developed by Frank C. Laubach." M.A. Thesis, Glassboro State College, N.J., 1967.
Mason, David E. *Frank C. Laubach, Teacher of Millions*. Minneapolis: Denison, 1967.
Medardy, Marjorie. *Each One Teach One*. New York: Longmans, Green, 1954.
Roberts, Helen M. *Champion of the Silent Billion*. St. Paul, Minn.: Macalester Park Publishing Co., 1961.
Scofield, Willard Arthur. "A Study of Frank C. Laubach's Methods of Communicating a Concern for Adult Literacy to the People of the United States." Ph.D. diss., Syracuse University, 1980.
Wiley, Ann L. (compiler). *Frank C. Laubach: A Comprehensive Bibliography*. Syracuse, N.Y.: New Readers Press, 1973.

Hendrik Kraemer

1888–1965

Biblical Realism Applied to Mission

Libertus A. Hoedemaker

Hendrik Kraemer was a pioneer with a vision, and for that he will be remembered, rather than for his role as a scholar. To be sure, he was a scholar, too, a man of great learning in the fields of Eastern languages, Islam, and history of religions (he held the chair of Comparative Religion at Leiden University from 1937 to 1947). But his legacy is the legacy of a missionary, and of a missionary theologian whose awareness of the problematic of the present and future of Christian missions was sharper than that of many of his contemporaries. Not a missiologist, perhaps, in the technical sense of the word, yet one who put his stamp on twentieth-century missiology by the force of his involvement and his personality. It is easier to undergo the influence of such a man than to analyze his thought and his relation to other thinkers.

Kraemer was born in 1888. He lost his father when he was six years old and his mother when he was twelve. In these years – that is, before he entered a Protestant orphanage with rather rigid conceptions and methods – he lived in an environment of socialist-anarchist influences. In the orphanage, in spite of its regime, he found his way to a personal conversion to Christ through independent Bible study. At sixteen he decided to become a missionary, and this remained the dominant passion of his life, even when the Dutch Bible Society enabled him to acquire a doctor's degree in Eastern Languages and Religions. It was in the service of this society that he first went to the Netherlands Indies (Indonesia), on a formula that he himself had designed: someone needed to go as a translations consultant for the work on the Javanese Bible who would have the additional task of studying the newer currents among Javanese intellectuals and among the Muslims. Kraemer's acute awareness of the need for such work had developed during World War I, when he learned to see the profound crisis of European culture and the changes that were to be expected in East-West relations.

Kraemer married Hyke van Gameren in 1919, a woman he had met in the Student Christian Movement as his opponent in a debate on the necessity of Christian witness. Two daughters and two sons were born in this marriage; one of the sons died in 1931 at the age of seven.

Kraemer's health was always precarious. Insomnia, probably caused by conflicting tendencies in his personality, was the basic problem, and it was never solved, not even by the famous Swiss psychiatrist Maeder. In Kraemer's active life, periods of depression alternated with periods of vigorous activity.

Kraemer worked in the Netherlands Indies from 1922 to 1937. After ten years as Professor of Comparative Religion at the University of Leiden in the Netherlands – a period during which he was very active in Dutch church life, to the point of being a hostage for some time under the German occupation – he became the first director of the Ecumenical Institute in Bossey near Geneva. After his retirement he was guest-lecturer at Union Theological Seminary in New York for a year (1956-1957). He died in 1965.

Those who are somewhat knowledgeable in the recent history of missions and missiology will undoubtedly connect Kraemer's name to his widely known work *The Christian Message in a Non-Christian World* (1938) – the book that became the focal point for the discussion on the relation of Christianity to other religions at the Tambaram conference of the International Missionary Council, and remained so for a long time afterward. Many interpreters still struggle with it because, here again, it is easier to undergo its influence than to determine its exact place among other contributions to the debate. A sketch of Kraemer's legacy should, therefore, at least include an attempt to deal with this book. But it should be more than that. In fact, it is the thesis of this article that Kraemer's position, even in his contribution to the international debate on missions and the theology of religions, can only be understood against the background of his basic concerns, both during his work in Asia and during his work in the Netherlands, and against the background of the major emphases in his other books. Asia and Europe: he saw them involved in what was basically one crisis, and in need of one thing: cells of conscious Christians who could find new forms for the ever-transcending Christian message in the human cultural struggle. In Asia he insisted on the development "from mission to church," in the Netherlands on the development "from church to mission," but in both situations he saw one basic need for church-with-mission, for a missionary church, which can be a signpost and a source of inspiration in the confusion of colliding peoples, cultures, and religions.

Involvement in Asia

Kraemer went to the Netherlands Indies with the special commission to study the new currents in Javanese spiritual life, in Islam, and in the incipient nationalist movement. His work made missionaries and indigenous Christians aware of the importance of these new currents. Kraemer became an adviser to missionary agencies and traveled widely to investigate the problems of the independence of the indigenous church.[1] His growing conviction was that only an indigenous Christian community, conscious of its independence and responsibility, could become a partner in the necessary dialogue with Islam and other ideological currents, and that a prolonged period of "education" by missionaries was not necessarily an adequate means to this end. An encounter of Christianity with other systems of life and thought presupposes an independent confessing church, Kraemer felt; gradually, therefore, the indigenization of the church became the major focus of his work.

In his report on the situation in East Java, to give only one example, Kraemer criticizes in the history of missions there both the trend of excessive Europeanization and the opposite trend of excessive Javanization: both trends keep the Christians isolated from what actually happens in their world. The most serious obstacle on the way to independence, however, is the deeply rooted sense of dependence among the Javanese, and the consequent lack of prophetic consciousness and church awareness.[2] Missionaries have not always worked on the level of these deep roots, and therefore they have not really managed to stimulate the desire for independence. A church will never be ripe for independence as long as its independence qualities are not consciously practiced. Only when this happens can the real confrontation between the Gospel and Asian culture take place, because only then does the Gospel have the opportunity to challenge the deepest spiritual attitudes of people, which, if left unchallenged, keep working toward maintaining the status quo of dependence. In his report on West Java, Kraemer writes: "Christianity must be rooted in the soul of the Sundanese, it must learn to express itself in Sundanese terms and forms, but it must also conquer the ancient view of the world and of life and transform it into spiritual life of an essentially different, Christian nature, instead of being submerged by or amalgamated with the old nations, as has been the case with Islam."[3]

Here is Kraemer's program for mission and dialogue in a nutshell. Its main points are that church consciousness is far more essential than church organization, and that "rootedness in the soul" is the only adequate point for a dialogical position in any culture. The problem of syncretism, therefore, is, in Kraemer's diagnosis, a problem for the indigenous church rather than for missions, and it is a problem that can only be dealt with on the level of practical prophetic Christian life, not on the level of dogmatics.[4] This is of course a burden for the indigenous church, but it is at the same time its great opportunity: for the end of the colonial era also signals the end of an unnatural position of Christianity in its surrounding world, which means that the church can finally show its real face and take its place in the crisis that involves both East and West. The analysis of the nature of this crisis remained an important part of Kraemer's program. In his last major work[5] he insists on the necessity to take it seriously and to refuse to take an easy way out in an attitude of relativism. When the objective force of secularization joins hands with the subjective force of religious desire, says Kraemer, the church is challenged in a radical way – and this situation and this challenge should be reflected in "indigenous theology," rather than testimonies about personal pilgrimages from non-Christian religious life to life in Christ.[6]

Involvement in the Netherlands

When World War II broke out, the Netherlands Reformed Church had for some time been involved in serious efforts to arrive at an authentic presbyterian church-structure, suitable to replace the bureaucratic form of organization imposed on it in the beginning of the nineteenth century. Several committees had started to work on patterns and models to overcome the situation of stalemate that existed among liberal, orthodox, confessional and nonconfessional organizations within the church, and to return to a church organization based on confession, in which a synod would have some authority to speak. Several attempts failed, but then the years of the German occupation opened up new possibilities and deepened the consciousness of the need for radical change among many people. At this point Kraemer entered the scene. In a committee for church consultation, established in 1940, he became the soul and the driving force of one of its working groups called "the building up of the congregation." Nowhere does Kraemer's emotional involvement in the life and mission of the church, in its authentic "indigenization," shine through as clearly as it does in his numerous activities, reports, articles, and speeches of the period between 1940 and 1947. The emphases of his student days on the necessity of a clear witness in the midst of crisis – between Pietism and relativism – return in full force here, matured by the Asian experience. The church needs to be awakened by a renewed consciousness of the source from which it lives; it must undergo the radical judgment and renewal of the revelation of the living God before it can deal with problems of confession and organization. There is a basic Christian faith-attitude, which precedes all theology and all confessional formulation, and it is on the basis of this attitude – an attitude of fear and trembling and longing for purification – that "strong and conscious Christians" should be brought together who can make all the "frozen assets" of the church come alive again.

Kraemer advocates strong leadership for the church, a leadership able to overcome the basic illness from which all problems of confession and organization spring: the blindness for the tremendous possibilities of living biblical witness in the midst of crisis. The church should again become the *militia Christi,* which learns to stand in the dimension of the apostolate. For the church exists in and for the sick world. "Mission" simply means "to have a healthy vigorous heart-beat of the church so that the life-blood of the revelation of God's will can be pumped through the body of the world."[7]

Theological Emphases

Our sketch so far has made clear that both the immediate problems of "missions" and the problem of the encounter between Christianity and other systems of life and thought are, for Kraemer, encompassed by a larger and deeper problem: the problem of the need of a world-in-crisis for clear and authentic forms of biblical witness, and for an awakening to God's will that is not self-defensive but creative and open to many new possibilities. This is the main line in all Kraemer's books. One cannot talk about "missions" and "religions" before the particular historical framework in which we live has clearly come into focus: Western secularization is uprooting the religious culture of the East, and the resulting defensiveness on both sides – "East" and "West" each having its own specific cultural design – has an atrophying influence on the religious life of humankind anywhere. Problems of nationalism and colonialism, of new ideologies and of racial tensions, are only the symptoms that guide us to the deeper layers of what is happening. For the church, the confrontation with this crisis must coincide with the ever new confrontation with its own nature and destiny: the revelation of the will of God for human life. It is mission, therefore, that will give new life to the church.

How does Kraemer speak about this "mission"? In early articles (1916 and 1921) he speaks of mission as pouring out the divine life that Christ has called forth in us, penetrating into the deepest and the best of human spirituality, and in so doing arriving at the deepest truth of the Gospel, which always includes its contradictions, its over-againstness to human life. Kraemer sticks to this basic approach in all his work, although his formulations undergo some change under the influence of men like Brunner and Barth. In the basic approach we can establish a link between Kraemer and the so-called Dutch ethical theology:[8] a mediating type of theology (between liberalism and fundamentalism), which sought to combine an emphasis on the existential nature of truth and on the value of the human personality, with an emphasis on the need for confrontation with the objective givenness of God's revelation in Christ. The human person is molded, as it were, in its own struggle with God, in its particular religious and cultural setting, but this struggle reaches its goal and arrives at truth only when it is confronted and directed by the challenging revelatory act of God in Jesus Christ. On this line of thinking, "mission" comes to mean the creation of autonomous persons through the powers of renewal inherent in Christianity.[9] The tension between the two sides of "ethical theology," the subjective and the objective, never left Kraemer, although increasingly he placed full weight on the necessity to speak objectively about God's dealings with humankind, which are discontinuous with all natural religious longings, rather than subjectively about human struggle and pilgrimage. This has led several interpreters to establish a certain link between Kraemer and Barth, and this again has tended to obscure the fact that Kraemer basically never departed from his original pattern of thinking about missions. For all his "Barthian" terminology, Kraemer – unlike Barth – kept thinking within the general framework of the divine-human encounter, the encounter of the challenging and overpowering will of God-in-Christ and the will of the religious or irreligious person who struggles to make sense out of life. The term "biblical realism," which dominates so much of *The Christian Message,* must be understood against this background. "Biblical realism" is the life in which God is allowed to be God and in which the human being forgets self in order to find self again in the light of revelation; it is a life, therefore, which transcends, contradicts, and appeals to all forms in which human beings seek to apprehend and shape reality.[10] This is why, for Kraemer, the only real point of contact between the Gospel and the human life is the missionary presence, from which many new points of contact between God's revelation and human culture can develop.

Kraemer's emphasis on objectivity and discontinuity remains, therefore, within the limits of the "ethical" approach and does not solve its basic ambiguity. This means also, that the tension between Christ-centrism, on the one hand, and appreciation of the significance of human cultural-religious life, on the other, is not solved in a systematically satisfying way, either.

Obviously related to the theological emphasis we have described is the specific way in which Kraemer speaks about the church. Here he shows himself to be indebted to the tradition of Pietism, revivalism, and perhaps also Methodism. Resisting a concept of truth that is intellectualistic (and therefore leads either to absolutism or to syncretism, both of which are dead-ends in the present crisis), he stresses "will" and "obedience." In Kraemer's thought the church almost becomes a militant order, a corporation of conscious Christians. A certain voluntaristic and deontological one-sidedness has been criticized by several of his contemporaries in Dutch theology, who took Kraemer to task for his supposed neglect of ontological elements in the revelation, of the work of the Holy Spirit in the church, and of the value of rational theological reflection. Kraemer always countered his critics by insisting on the importance of living confrontation with God's will as the precondition and presupposition of any theology and any constructive reflection on the church.

Christianity and Other Religions

The preceding descriptions of Kraemer's involvement and thought should enable us to assess his place in the discussions on the theology of religions, for which the Tambaram conference provided the setting. In the book that Kraemer wrote for the preparation of this conference, *The Christian Message in a Non-Christian World,* there are actually two lines of argument. On the first line, Kraemer distinguishes "radically" between "biblical realism" and the basic human "religious approach," which seeks to order reality according to the drive of religious self-expression. On the second line, he sets the great non-Christian systems of life and thought – except, in a certain sense, Islam and Judaism – off against the world of biblical realism, the former being outgrowths of the "religious approach." Empirical Christianity, though permanently in need of the same criticism and judgment as all other religions (the first line) is, by virtue of the fact that it "has stood and stands under continuous and direct influence and judgment of the revelation in Christ . . . in a different position from the other religions,"[11] and thus has, in a sense, a head start in the dialogue.

The entanglement of these two lines of argument presents certain difficulties. It might perhaps be possible to clarify Kraemer's intentions by a further analysis of the relations between theology (missiology) and comparative religion in the Dutch "ethical" tradition.[12] Yet even without such an analysis we should be able to understand Kraemer's position on the basis of our sketch of his background and major concerns. Kraemer rejects all approaches – whether they speak of fulfillment, continuity, or even of a radical break – which see the encounter between religions as an affair taking place within the realm of human religious self-expression, because these approaches preclude or at least restrict the possibility of a radical critical relation between God's will and human life. And he rejects the Barthian approach, which makes the distinction between revelation and religion the fundamental cornerstone of all theological reflection to the extent that – according to Kraemer – it precludes or at least restricts the possibility of speaking about the human struggle with God. It is his "ethical" background, systematically unsatisfying though it may be, which provides Kraemer with a mediating position, and it is the acute awareness of the intercultural and interreligious crisis which compels him to stick to it.

Kraemer's position was not always sufficiently appreciated and understood in the Tambaram debate. Generally speaking, the emphasis in the debate had shifted since the Jerusalem conference of 1928. In Jerusalem the values of the various religious systems, especially in comparison with secularism, formed the focus of the discussion; in Tambaram the main question concerned the revelatory activity of God in non-Christian systems in view of the church's obligation to proclaim the Gospel. A great variety of positions had been developed, centering around key words such as *fulfillment, continuity, uniqueness, universality, discontinuity* – key words that could be connected with one another in various mutually exclusive ways. Especially challenging for Kraemer were the views of W.E. Hocking on the necessity for each religion to reconceive its fundamentals in the light of the interreligious encounter. In the context of this debate, Kraemer's emphasis on discontinuity was understood by some to be a "Barthian" insistence on the absoluteness of Christianity, which precluded the possibility of a new creation of the unique Christ, for instance, in Hinduism (Chenchiah). And critics like A.G. Hogg still wanted to allow for the possibility of faith as genuine God-relatedness even in the context of other faiths.[13] Over against these criticisms, Kraemer stressed that one could simply not start on the basis of faith or religion without at least taking into account the unique character of God's revelation in Christ. For Kraemer, the basic choice is: Does one reason about the pilgrimage of the human soul, or about the acts of God? On the basis of a clear choice for the latter alternative, it remains quite possible to speak about fulfillment and continuity. But in that case the basic direction of reasoning is not from human religious reality toward Christ but from biblical realism toward human reality. There is always a formal continuity between religious systems and values; there is real and true continuity only inasfar as it makes room for the most fundamental discontinuity between God and humankind, which is part and parcel of his revelation in Christ. As long as one does not lose sight of the unique nature and content of this revelation, the concepts of uniqueness and universality, or even of discontinuity and continuity, need not be mutually exclusive.[14]

Concluding Remarks

The major concern in Kraemer's work is not the relation between Christianity and other religions, although he expressed himself on this issue and became widely known for it. The central questions that form part of his legacy are: How can we deal theologically with the deep crisis that is the result of the meeting between East and West and in which (Western) secularism and (Eastern) religiosity together raise unprecedented and complicated questions for humankind? and How can we arrive at authentic living forms of witness that provide for new contacts between the judging and redeeming acts of God, on the one hand, and human reality on the other? How can the church become "what it is in Christ"? It is striking that a book like *Religion and the Christian Faith* (1956) actually stands alone among Kraemer's works in that it focuses exclusively on the problem of religions, faith, and Christianity. In all his other works, the necessity of the coming dialogue fascinates Kraemer from beginning to end, even though "dialogue" is not his theological principle, as it is, for instance, for Kenneth Cragg. In view of the coming dialogue, his concern is the "incarnation" of the fundamental God-human discontinuity in the greatest possible openness to the struggles of humankind and the widest possible communication.

In discussing Kraemer's postwar publications, C.F. Hallencreutz notices certain changes or shifts of emphasis: Kraemer focuses more on discontinuity in its existential meaning, and simultaneously becomes more interested in communication than in controversy.[15] When one reviews Kraemer's work as a whole, however, it appears to be unnecessary or even an exaggeration to speak of significant changes. Rather, Kraemer's later works enable us to see more clearly what had been his concern all along: the confrontation of humanity with the will of God. In hindsight, one might even venture the thesis that it was the theology-of-religions debate – into which Kraemer was drawn in 1938 – that sidetracked him, or at least made him express himself in categories that did not really fit what he had to say.

It is not impossible that more light can be shed on this whole issue by an analysis of Kraemer's position and the reception of his work in the newer developments of the dialogue debate in which the need to reflect on the place of religions in the broader "economy of salvation" is stressed much more than in Kraemer's works. The Indian theologians P.D. Devanandan and M.M. Thomas combine this latter concern with an explicit indebtedness to Kraemer: a combination that is highly fascinating. Whereas, as we have seen, there are some Indian theologians who reject or misunderstand Kraemer's intentions and over against whom Kraemer keeps defending his major concern, the thought of men like Devanandan and Thomas – even though it introduces "un-Kraemerian" theological principles – represents an effort to build on his foundation and to establish closer contact between his concern and the reality of interreligious dialogue. Viewed from this angle, the emphases of Kramer's *Christian Message* are thrown into relief even more sharply. To be sure, M.M. Thomas has a basic criticism of Kraemer's theology: Kraemer's need to systematize the non-Christian religious life and to reduce it to basic religious attitudes prevents him from discriminating further what is human and inhuman in the resurgence of the non-Christian religions; Kraemer is stronger in questions of the "ultimate" than of the "penultimate."[16] There is, however, a very clear link: the fundamental dialogue between God and humankind must be kept alive by a church that is conscious of its missionary nature and constantly seeks to relate God's "discontinuous" will to the dynamics of crisis and development in the surrounding human world. In this respect, Kraemer's emphasis on the "missionary as the point of contact" connects his thoughts very fruitfully to later developments in the theology of religions and of dialogue. It is the central element of his legacy. With the aid of this element, we can learn to see the relation between Christianity and other religions as an aspect of the church-world relation, in the framework of an intercultural crisis that makes dialogue necessary and possible; and we can learn to understand "mission" once again as the coming to life of God's judging and redeeming word in a religiously pluralistic and secular world. This judging and redeeming word simultaneously liberates men and women from the need to cling defensively to any particular cultural or religious system.

Notes

1. The most important reports of that period have been collected and published in *From Missionfield to Independent Church* (London: SCM Press, 1958).

2. Ibid., pp. 86-87.

3. Ibid., p. 130.

4. "Syncretism as a Religious and a Missionary Problem," *International Review of Missions* 43 (1954): 253-73.

5. *World Cultures and World Religions, the Coming Dialogue* (London: Lutterworth Press, 1960).

6. A criticism with regard to some Indian theologians, voiced in an essay on the "theological problematic of the young churches" (1948 or 1949), published in Dutch in a posthumous collection, *Uit de nalatenschap van Hendrik Kraemer* (Kampen: Kok, 1970).

7. All Kraemer's publications on the themes discussed here are, obviously, in Dutch. However, many of the emphases recorded here may be found also in his *Theology of the Laity* (London: Lutterworth Press, 1958).

8. In his dissertation on Kraemer, Carl F. Hallencreutz analyzes this background, without, however, specifying how this background determines the problematic of Kraemer's position in the debate on religions. See *Kraemer Towards Tambaram* (Uppsala: Gleerup, 1966), chap. 3. Kraemer's indebtedness to P.D. Chantepie de la Saussaye (1848-1920), who held professorships in Comparative Religion and in Christian Ethics successively, becomes especially clear.

9. Chantepie de la Saussaye used this emphasis in connection with his study of non-Christian religions. He advocated empathetic analysis with the yardstick of the "free human person." Another teacher who influenced Kraemer on this issue, however, is Brede Kristensen, who insisted on the "objective relative absoluteness" of each religious system. See Hallencreutz, *Kraemer*, chap. 4.

10. It would be worthwhile to explore the affinities and the contradictions between Kraemer's "biblical realism" and the early Tillich's "beliefful realism," which means an attitude of apprehending reality "under the aspect of the Eternal." Kraemer's term, which he, incidentally, no longer uses in his later works, does not represent an effort to bypass reflection on the content of revelation by means of wholly subjective categories

as Sharpe seems to think (Eric J. Sharpe, *Faith Meets Faith* [London: SCM Press, 1977], pp. 92-98); it is, rather, the expression of the unique context of Christian revelation in the terms of life, challenge, conversion, and obedience.

11. *The Christian Message in a Non-Christian World* (London: Edinburgh House Press, 1938), p. 145.

12. See Hallencreutz, *Kraemer,* chap. 4, and above, n. 9. Kraemer felt that an approach of sympathetic understanding on the basis of one's own explicit believing position was the most adequate one. He speaks of comparative religion as "our intelligent and much appreciated informant" (in *The Authority of the Faith,* Tambaram Series, vol. 1 [Oxford-London: Oxford Univ. Press, 1939], p. 11), and elsewhere of a "theological science of religions" (*Religion and the Christian Faith* [London: Lutterworth Press, 1956], chap. 20).

13. See for these points *The Authority of the Faith* and *Religion and the Christian Faith.*

14. It should be noted that in the writings mentioned in n. 13, Kraemer in fact drops the concepts "continuity" and "discontinuity" as not very helpful.

15. C.F. Hallencreutz, *New Approaches to Men of Other Faiths* (Geneva: World Council of Churches, 1970), chap. 6. Hallencreutz thinks especially of *Religion and the Christian Faith* (London: Lutterworth Press, 1956), and of *The Communication of the Christian Faith* (Philadelphia: Westminster Press, 1956).

16. For the relation between Thomas and Kraemer now, see M.M. Thomas, *Some Theological Dialogues* (Madras: Christian Literature Society, 1977), pp. 22-33.

Bibliography

Some evaluations of Kraemer in the English language (from a bibliography compiled by E. Jansen Schoonhoven):

Kulandran, S. "Kraemer Then and Now." *International Review of Missions* 46 (1957): 171-81.

Latuihamallo., P.D. "Church and World: A Critical Study about the Relation of Church and World in the Writings of Hendrik Kraemer." Diss., Union Theological Seminary, New York, 1959.

Thomas M.M. "A Rewarding Correspondence with the late Dr. Hendrik Kraemer." *Religion and Society* 13 (1966): 5-14.

Various contributions in *Religion and Society* 5 (1958), in a special issue entitled "Religion and the Christian Faith."

Donald A. McGavran

1897–1990

Standing at the Sunrise of Missions

George G. Hunter III

Donald Anderson McGavran was born in Damoh, India, on December 15, 1897, the second child of missionaries John Grafton McGavran and Helen Anderson McGavran. He was raised in central India with two sisters, Joyce and Grace, and a brother, Edward. Joyce and Grace eventually pursued vocations in the United States, while the brothers remained in India – Edward as a physician and public health pioneer, and Donald as a third-generation missionary of the Christian Church (Disciples of Christ). Donald McGavran received his higher education in the United States, attending Butler University (B.A.), Yale Divinity School (B.D.), the former College of Mission, Indianapolis (M.A.), and, following two terms in India, Columbia University (Ph.D.).

McGavran invested his "first career" in India as an educator, field executive, evangelist, church planter, and researcher. In the early 1930s, McGavran began to wonder why some churches reached people and grew while others declined. He pointedly asked, "When a church is growing, *why* is it growing?" Discovering the answers to that question became his obsession. For twenty years, he studied growing and nongrowing churches in India, Mexico, the Philippines, Thailand, Jamaica, Puerto Rico, West Africa, North America, and other lands.

In 1955, publication of *The Bridges of God* made McGavran's name known in Christian mission, but his ideas did not greatly influence mission policy, strategy, or practice until he emerged from semiretirement in 1965 for a second career as founding dean of Fuller Theological Seminary's School of World Mission. In that role, his understanding deepened and widened through the research projects of his graduate students and through collaboration with Fuller colleagues such as Alan Tippett, Ralph Winter, Peter Wagner, and Arthur Glasser. *Understanding Church Growth* (in 1970, 1980, and 1990 editions) established McGavran as a premier foreign mission strategist. In the 1970s, as he perceived the validity of some of his insights for Europe and North America, he collaborated with Win Arn, George Hunter, and others to help inform evangelism and church growth in the West.

Much of Donald McGavran's enduring contribution and legacy can be described in three areas, perhaps in ascending order of importance.

The Church Growth Movement

The church growth movement represents one legacy from Donald McGavran. He identified four questions that were to preoccupy a generation of church growth scholars:

1. What are the *causes* of church growth?

2. What are the *barriers* to church growth?

3. What are the factors that can make the Christian faith a *movement* among some populations?

4. What *principles* of church growth are reproducible?

McGavran also developed a field research method for studying growing (and nongrowing) churches, employing historical analysis, observations, and interviews to collect data for analysis and case studies. From 1964 to 1980 McGavran published research findings and advanced church growth ideas in the *Church Growth Bulletin* and other publications. By the mid 1980s, the North American Society for Church Growth and several regional societies were established, publishing several journals, including *Global Church Growth.*

It is not clear whether "church growth" will survive indefinitely as a term and movement, but it is clear that church growth perspectives and methods will substantially inform mission strategy across cultures and effective evangelism within culture.[1] McGavran's church growth school developed a distinctive and enduring approach to evangelism and mission. Consider the following distinctive themes and claims:

1. The perennial and indispensable work within total mission is apostolic work, that is, continuing the work of the earliest apostles and their congregations in reaching lost people and peoples.

2. The key objective in evangelism is not to "get decisions" but to "make disciples."

3. The key objective in mission is to plant an indigenous evangelizing church among every people group.

4. There is no one method for evangelizing or church planting that will fit every population, but the church growth field research approach can help leaders discover the most reproducible methods for reaching any population.

5. The pragmatic test is useful in appraising mission and evangelism strategies and methods, so churches should employ the approaches that are most effective in the given population.

6. The Christian movement can be advanced by employing the insights and research tools of the behavioral sciences, including the gathering and graphing of relevant statistical data for mission analysis, planning, control, and critique.

7. The church growth movement affirms a high doctrine of the church: the church is Christ's body, all people have the inalienable right to have the opportunity to follow Christ through his body, and the living Christ has promised to build his church.

8. The supreme reason for engaging in evangelism and mission is summarized in Donald McGavran's most famous declaration: "It is God's will that his church grow, that his lost children be found."

Distinctives such as these – particularly those related to McGavran's field research methods for discovering the reproducible causes for the Christian faith's expansion – have shaped the church growth paradigm.[2]

Christian Mission: A Subject of Serious Research

McGavran's second legacy (though he is not its only source) is the restoration of Christian missions as a serious and viable subject of study and research. When McGavran was young, mission was taught in virtually every seminary curriculum, and there were schools of mission and prominent graduate programs. In the 1950s, 1960s, and much of the 1970s, under the impact of theological liberalism, religious tolerance, and other Enlightenment influences, schools of mission expired while, in seminaries, retiring missions professors were not replaced and mission dropped out of the curriculum. The School of World Mission at Fuller, which McGavran founded, has been very influential in reversing this trend. Fuller adopted the term "world mission"[3] to connote the school's vision, adopted the Roman Catholic term "missiology" to refer to the field of study, developed a doctor of missiology program, helped lead a movement within mission to shape a postcolonial agenda, and identified the several disciplines needed to inform that agenda. Fuller attracted a student body of nationals and missionaries from every continent, fostered a new era of missiological research through several degree programs, and facilitated the placement of graduates in field leadership roles, mission agencies, and colleges and seminaries. The success of the Fuller experiment has stimulated similar degree-granting schools or centers at Biola University, Trinity Evangelical Divinity School, Asbury Theological Seminary, Southwestern Baptist Theological Seminary, and other institutions in North America and most other continents. Mission has now been reinstated in the curricula of many colleges and seminaries, although the institutions still most committed to Enlightenment ideas and/or the graduate school of religion model have not yet participated in, or contributed to, the renaissance of missiological education.

McGavran's Mission Paradigms

Donald McGavran's third, and perhaps greatest, legacy is found in several very major constitutive ideas through which increasing numbers of mission leaders and personnel are perceiving and practicing mission and evangelism very differently than before McGavran. Some contemporary interpreters of mission have not yet understood McGavran's contribution at the paradigm level. For instance, David J. Bosch's 600-page *Transforming Mission: Paradigm Shifts in Theology of Mission*[4] appears to report all the major determinative ideas about mission from the early church to those most likely to shape Christian mission's future. Yet this volume perceives McGavran as merely a generic conservative evangelical with a preference for numbers, slogans, and church planting. However, history has already demonstrated McGavran's key paradigms to be much more significant (and pervasive!) than Bosch and some other missiologists have acknowledged.

To be sure, Donald McGavran did not invent his most important ideas ex nihilo, nor did he advance them alone. He stood on the shoulders of earlier theorists such as William Carey, John Nevius, Roland Allen, and Kenneth Scott Latourette. Acknowledging J. Wascom Pickett's pioneering church growth field research, McGavran was fond of saying, "I lit my candle at Pickett's fire."[5] McGavran, however, partly rediscovered strategic insights that shaped a number of historical Christian movements.[6] Some ideas were developed collaboratively with Alan Tippett and Ralph Winter; Winter and Peter Wagner in turn developed some ideas beyond McGavran's own thinking.[7] Wagner, Vergil Gerber, and Win Arn popularized much of McGavran's thought.[8] The ideas have been advanced, interpreted, and adapted to denominational traditions by Baptists such as Ebbie C. Smith, Wendell Belew, Charles Chaney, Elmer Towns, and John Vaughan; Methodists such as Lyle Schaller and George Hunter; Christian Church-Church of Christ leaders such as Paul Benjamin, Herb Miller, and Flavil Yeakley; and by Kent Hunter (Lutheran), Eddie Gibbs (Anglican), and Bill Sullivan (Nazarene). Yet Donald McGavran is the seminal mind of the church growth tradition, and his distinctive mission paradigms often challenged the status quo.

In *The Bridges of God* McGavran burst onto the missiological stage by challenging two entrenched paradigms behind prevailing missions practices. First, McGavran observed that most missionaries see the world through Western culture's paradigm of "individualism," which, by analogy, regards humanity as so many unconnected "atoms." Reflecting this paradigm, most missions won a few converts one by one and assumed that conversion against the wishes of one's kin was more faithful than conversion with kin support. Individual conversion was much preferred to group conversions within families, clans, tribes, or castes. But McGavran also observed that most (non-Western) cultures see humanity as "molecules" rather than atoms, that most people define themselves by a group identity, do their thinking in a group process, making important decisions together. He saw that the usual mission practice, based on the individualism paradigm rather than the group-consciousness paradigm, produced tragic social dislocation in the lives of many converts, as Christianized individuals were rejected by their people and cut off from them.

Second, McGavran challenged the "mission station" paradigm that prevailed in Christian mission's "Great Century" (1800 to 1914), and that still flourishes today. He observed the following pattern. Typically, after an exploratory period in which the pioneering missionaries learn the language, gain rapport with the nationals, and perhaps win a handful of converts, the missionaries organize their activities around a mission station or compound. They acquire land in a major transportation center and then build a chapel, residences for mission personnel and their families, and other living quarters for their national helpers, and perhaps a school, an orphanage, an agricultural center, a leprosy home, a clinic or hospital, and even a printing shop. The church at the compound is a "gathered colony" church, reflecting the missionaries' home culture, composed of the mission personnel and their families, and the first converts, who may also live and work at the mission compound, socially isolated from their people. Most activity takes place within the compound – teaching children, caring for sick people and so forth. In this model mission personnel also engage in forays into the hinterland within manageable travel distance from the compound, establishing casual and cordial contacts with the nationals – but not "living contacts" – and perhaps raise up a few small congregations.

McGavran concedes that, typically, mission stations were built as a first stage, with the hope of a later "great ingathering."[9] Wherever great ingatherings did not occur, however, the means became the end, and mission experienced a "diversion to secondary aims."[10] Mission was redefined as education, medicine, relief work, and so on, for which missionaries could see results and that involve the activities the missionaries were now used to; the next generation of missionaries were then recruited to perpetuate these activities. In such an arrangement, the activities of the mission station dominated the mission's agenda; the churches were peripheral.

McGavran saw this oft-repeated phenomenon as a tragic case of Christian mission's arrested development. The mission station should never have been regarded as an end in itself but as a stage leading to the nationalization of leadership and then to the much wider expansion of the national church. McGavran acknowledged that the mission-station approach once contributed to a remarkable period of nation building; the mission schools developed tomorrow's national leaders, and the mission stations "were seed-beds of revolutionary Christian ideas about justice, brotherhood, service and the place of womanhood."[11] But that colonial era in which mission stations had great national influence is now past. In any case, McGavran perceived – in a phenomenon already taking place among some peoples beyond the range of missions stations – the need for a revolutionary "people movement" paradigm for strategic mission thinking.

McGavran, following Pickett, became vitally interested in the people movements that were occurring in India by the 1930s – movements that sometimes brought to faith most members of a local caste or tribe within several years. He discovered that these movements were not unique, that such was the usual pattern of the faith's first-century expansion among Jews, then among the Gentile "God-fearers" that attended the synagogues, then among various culturally distant Gentile societies, and much later in the faith's spread among the peoples of Europe.[12] Furthermore, McGavran observed that the Gospel does not require converts to leave their people and join another people, and that "people like to become Christians without crossing racial, linguistic, or class barriers."[13]

McGavran first saw this principle as a strategic way past India's formidable caste barriers, but later he developed the "Homogeneous Unit" (HU) as a generic concept applicable to many fields. He defined a HU as any group of people with some characteristic in common who communicate and relate to each other more naturally than to other people. The principle is important for evangelism because "unbelievers understand the gospel better when expounded by their own kind of people."[14] So McGavran came to believe that the people movements that permitted "multi-individual, mutually interdependent conversion" were indigenous to the people and represented a very great way forward for Christian mission.[15] Not only did he see precedence for people movements in the apostolic era, he believed that the Great Commission to disciple *panta ta ethne* (Matt. 28:19) was a mandate to reach the families, clans, tribes, castes, and ethnic groups – that is, the "peoples" – of humanity. He reasoned that mission's objective, therefore, is to "reach" each cultural group by planting indigenous self-propagating churches in every population within the earth's rich mosaic of peoples.

Though McGavran's HU principle has been criticized, the equivalent concept of communication and movements within "affinity groups" has become an established principle of the behavioral sciences. In mission literature the HU term has largely been dropped, in favor of "people groups" or "peoples," and in these current forms the concept has experienced an extensive impact. For instance, the 1974 Lausanne Congress on World Evangelization projected that, of the world's approximately 30,000 known peoples, approximately 16,750 were "unreached." By the 1989 Lausanne II Congress in Manila, it was estimated that approximately 4,750 of these peoples had been "reached" in the intervening fifteen years. Many mission boards and agencies are now focusing their plans and efforts on planting indigenous churches in as many of the remaining 12,000 people groups as possible by A.D. 2000.

Another McGavran paradigm shift has become even more influential. McGavran saw that, contrary to prevailing evangelical myths, people do not usually become Christians when a stranger bears witness to them; indeed, most Christian strangers (including most missionaries) make few converts. Most people become Christians when reached by a Christian relative or friend in their intimate social network; these social networks of living Christians, especially those of new Christians, provide "the bridges of God" to undiscipled people. Today, virtually every enlightened evangelism program and ministry takes this relational paradigm for the Gospel's spread very seriously. Win and Charles Arn's *The Master's Plan for Making Disciples*[16] delineates an evangelism approach based upon this principle.

McGavran and His Critics

McGavran's work necessarily involved the critique of other points of view and schools of thought, and his work was also critiqued and challenged from several sides.[17] Leaders who especially desired dialogue and better relations with people of other religions, including those who accepted the Enlightenment teaching that all religions are essentially the same, were affronted by McGavran's emphasis on evangelism for conversion. Some Christians distrusted McGavran's use of field data, statistics, graphs, and behavioral science insights; the approach was insufficiently "biblical," "theological," or "spiritual." Some Christians, who especially want churches to transcend humanity's divisions and model reconciliation, contested McGavran's conviction that homogeneous unit congregations can be a faithful, though penultimate, expression of the universal church and its mission. To McGavran's credit, he valued his critics and used their feedback to reflect upon and refine his missiology, though they gave him no sufficient reasons to abandon his apostolic agenda.

McGavran and his critics especially disagreed on the role of mission in the future. As some mission boards and agencies reflected upon the abuses of mission's colonial period, resolved not to repeat the mistakes of the past, and heard the "missionary go home" appeal from some Third World Christians, they called for a moratorium on sending missionaries and announced the end of the missionary era. McGavran countered that "we stand in the sunrise of missions!" He challenged the agencies because he believed that "postcolonial" approaches to mission were possible and desirable.

His theological reflection and field research led him to the "receptivity" paradigm. He observed that there are always winnable people and whole fields ready for harvest because, in every season, God's prevenient grace is moving through the events and circumstances of some persons' lives and within whole peoples, generating receptivity. But, he observed, receptivity ebbs and flows in history; people and societies who are receptive this year may not be receptive next year, so the church is called to "win the winnable" while they are winnable. McGavran developed indicators of likely receptive people, and he advocated the revolutionary strategy of deploying mission personnel, in disproportionate numbers, where the Spirit is moving and the people are receptive.[18] This explains the apostolic confidence, blended with urgency, that characterizes Donald McGavran's missiological perspective: "Opportunity blazes today, but it may be a brief blaze. Certainly conditions which create the opportunity – as far as human wisdom can discern – are transient conditions. We have today. Let us move forward."[19]

Donald McGavran died July 10, 1990, about three months after the death of Mary, his wife of sixty-seven years. Donald and Mary McGavran are succeeded by five of their six children, sixteen grandchildren, and a host of colleagues in the Christian movement. McGavran wrote books, articles, and countless letters of counsel and encouragement and communicated with his characteristic precision, passion, and wit until the last week of his life in this world.

Notes

1. "Mission strategy" is now an indispensable subject with any informed contemporary mission curriculum. By 1988 McGavran was already providing another key term: "effective evangelism." (See *Effective Evangelism: A Theological Mandate* [Phillipsburg, N.J.: Presbyterian and Reformed Publishing Company, 1988].)

2. See C. Peter Wagner's article "Church Growth Research: The Paradigm and Its Applications," in *Understanding Church Growth and Decline: 1950-1978*, ed. Dean R. Hoge and David A. Roozen (New York, Pilgrim Press, 1979), pp. 270-87.

3. The term "world mission" was needed because many mistook "mission" for "everything the church does," thereby blurring the focus of classical apostolic mission. McGavran and his colleagues advocated evangelism and church planting as perennial and indispensable parts of mission.

4. Maryknoll, N.Y.: Orbis Books, 1991.

5. See Pickett's *Christian Mass Movements in India* (Lucknow, India: Lucknow Publishing House, 1933), *Christ's Way to India's Heart*, 3rd ed. (Lucknow, India: Lucknow Publishing House, 1960), and "J. Wascom Pickett" in the present volume.

6. John Wesley especially anticipated, and predicated Methodism's early expansion on the basis of several strategic insights later rediscovered by McGavran. See George G. Hunter III, *To Spread the Power: Church Growth in the Wesleyan Spirit* (Nashville: Abingdon, 1987), especially chap. 2.

7. See especially C. Peter Wagner's *Our Kind of People: The Ethical Dimensions of Church Growth in America* (Atlanta, Ga.: John Knox Press, 1979).

8. McGavran and Arn's *How to Grow a Church* (Glendale, Calif.: Regal Books, 1973), featuring a conversational format, is the most widely circulated church growth book, with over 200,000 copies sold.

9. Donald McGavran, *The Bridges of God: A Study in the Strategy of Missions*, rev. ed. (New York: Friendship Press, 1981), p. 49.

10. Ibid., pp. 51ff.

11. Ibid., p. 63.

12. See ibid., chaps. 3 and 4.

13. Donald A. McGavran, *Understanding Church Growth,* 3d ed. (Grand Rapids, Mich.: William B. Eerdmans Publishing Co., 1990), chap. 13.

14. Ibid., p. 167.

15. Ibid., pp. 227ff.

16. Pasadena, Calif.: Church Growth Press, 1981.

17. The most representative critical collection is Wilbert R. Shenk, ed. *Exploring Church Growth* (Grand Rapids, Mich.: Wm. B. Eerdmans, 1983).

18. See McGavran, *Understanding Church Growth,* 3d ed., chap. 14: "The Receptivity of Individuals and Societies"; and Hunter, *To Spread the Power,* chap. 3: "Identifying Receptive People."

19. Donald Anderson McGavran, *How Churches Grow* (New York: Friendship Press, 1959), p. 9.

Selected Bibliography

Works by Donald A. McGavran

1955 *The Bridges of God: A Study in the Strategy of Missions.* New York: Friendship Press.

1959 *How Churches Grow: The New Frontiers of Mission.* New York: Friendship Press; London: World Dominion Press.

1965 (ed.) *Church Growth and Christian Mission.* New York: Harper and Row.

1970 *Understanding Church Growth.* Grand Rapids: Wm. B. Eerdmans Publishing Co. Rev. eds. 1980 and 1990.

1972 (ed.) *Crucial Issues in Missions Tomorrow.* Chicago: Moody Press.

1972 (ed.) *The Eye of the Storm: The Great Debate in Mission.* Waco, Tex.: Word Books.

1973 (with Winfield Arn) *How to Grow a Church.* Glendale, Calif.: Regal Press.

1975 *The Clash Between Christianity and Cultures.* Grand Rapids, Mich.: Baker Book House.

1975 "The Dimensions of World Evangelization," In *Let the Earth Hear His Voice,* ed. J. Douglas. Minneapolis, Minn.: Worldwide Publications.

1977 (with Winfield Arn) *Ten Steps for Church Growth.* San Francisco: Harper and Row.

1979 *Ethnic Realities and the Church: Lessons from India.* Pasadena, Calif.: William Carey Library.

1980 (with George G. Hunter III) *Church Growth: Strategies That Work.* Nashville: Abingdon Press.

1980 (with James Montgomery) *The Discipling of a Nation.* Milpitas, Calif.: Overseas Crusades.

1983 (with Arthur F. Glasser) *Contemporary Theologies of Mission.* Grand Rapids: Baker Book House.

1984 *Momentous Decisions in Missions Today.* Grand Rapids: Baker Book House.

1986 "My Pilgrimage in Mission." *International Bulletin of Missionary Research* 10, no. 2 (April).

1988 *Effective Evangelism: A Theological Mandate.* Phillipsburg, N.J.: Presbyterian and Reformed Publishing Co.

1990 *The Satnami Story: A Thrilling Drama of Religious Change.* Pasadena, Calif.: William Carey Library.

Works about Donald A. McGavran

Tippett, Alan R., ed. *God, Man, and Church Growth: A Festschrift in Honor of Donald Anderson McGavran.* Grand Rapids: Wm. B. Eerdmans Publishing Co., 1973.

Jakób Jocz
1906–1983

"To the Jew First": First Principle of Mission

Arthur F. Glasser

Almost uniquely among theologians and missiologists of the twentieth century, Jakób Jocz approached the missionary task from the perspective of the church in encounter with the synagogue. Like the apostle Paul, he saw himself as "a Jewish Christian, standing between the Jewish people and the Church, belonging to both . . . and . . . owing a debt to both."[1] Only in this encounter, Jocz argues, does the church really become aware of its true nature, for it is thereby obliged to acknowledge its Jewish roots and face the acid test of its loyalty to its Lord. Will it in obedience to him seek to evangelize the Jewish people?

Jakób Jocz's long career involved a sequence of ministries that began in Eastern Europe before World War II, then took him to Jewish evangelism in England along with parish ministry in an Anglican congregation in London. The culmination was a professorship of systematic theology in Wycliffe College connected with the University of Toronto. He was a missionary, a theologian, and a missiologist – an outstanding Jewish Christian of the twentieth century.

His Life and Times

We would not know many of the details of Jocz's family history had he not written a somewhat disguised autobiography.[2] In it we find his Lithuanian Jewish roots clearly delineated along with the record of the family's first encounter with the Christian Gospel. This took place in 1900 in the isolated shtetl of Zelse near Vilnius, Lithuania, where his maternal grandfather, Johanan Don, was a local milkman, married to Sarah and blessed with Hannah, a fourteen-year-old daughter. It was while Johanan was seeking medical assistance for Hannah, who had earlier sustained a fall that threatened to leave her permanently crippled, that he reluctantly went to the Lutheran Medical Mission clinic in Vilnius for assistance. Reluctantly, because he had been warned that Dr. Paul Fröhwein, the doctor in charge, was "kind of a Jew, and yet not a Jew." Actually, he found Dr. Fröhwein's welcome most disarming. While waiting in the anteroom, Johanan's curiosity was aroused by a small black book on the table – a Hebrew New Testament. Upon opening it, he encountered almost immediately something that he had not heard before, that Jesus was "the son of David, the son of Abraham." When Dr. Fröhwein reappeared and noticed his interest, the doctor encouraged him to take the book with him.

In the weeks that followed, Johanan secretly studied the Gospels and eventually became a believer in Jesus. Baptism followed, to the disgust of his wife, Sarah. But Hannah believed soon afterward, to his great delight.

Johanan died while still relatively young. Sarah moved the family to Vilnius and to make ends meet rented a room to Bazyli Jocz, a young rabbinical student from the yeshiva of the Vilno Gaón. One day while Bazyli was reading the Book of Isaiah, questions arose that he could not answer. Upon asking his teacher, he was rebuked with such startling vehemence that he sought the help of the same physician who had earlier helped Hannah. It was through Dr. Fröhwein that Bazyli came to faith in Jesus. But he told no one. He continued his studies at the yeshiva and, as was the custom, learned a trade also. He became a rather successful cabinetmaker, but his deepening relationship with Jesus made him begin to ponder the future. When he shared his faith with Hannah, she disclosed her similar secret. Not unnaturally, their common faith in Jesus drew them together, and the way eventually opened for them to marry. Jakób, their first child, was born in 1906.

World War I brought great distress, particularly to Lithuanian Jews, caught as they were between Polish Catholic and Russian Orthodox anti-Semitism. The Jocz family did not escape, even though they were confessing Christians. On one occasion a nun denied young Jakób relief food, simply because he was Jewish – and she told him so in no uncertain terms.

During those difficult years Jakób did not receive much formal education, but through parental instruction he came to Christian faith. He early showed remarkable ability as a linguist. Over the years he became fluent in Russian, German, Polish, and English, in addition to his native Yiddish.

By 1920 Bazyli became associated with the Church's Mission to Jews (CMJ-Anglican) as an evangelist. Jakób was drafted for army service in postwar Poland. Following demobilization he also offered himself for evangelistic service with the CMJ and was enrolled in its newly formed training center in Warsaw. Three years of study coupled with missionary service in Poland were followed by two years of study at the German Methodist seminary in Frankfurt am Main. Because he showed unusual promise, the CMJ sent him to England, where he completed training for Anglican ordination at St. Aidan's College in Birkenhead. During this period he met his future wife, Joan Celia Gapp, an Anglican missionary volunteer. They were married in 1935 and assigned to CMJ ministry in Poland. This involved itinerant evangelism ranging into the Polish countryside and assuming responsibility for the Yiddish-speaking messianic congregation in Warsaw.

Ministry in Poland prior to the Nazi assault was very fruitful. Although opposition at times was quite intense, the reports Jocz and others submitted contained instances of unprecedented Jewish interest in their evangelical witness to Jesus. One report by Jocz states:

> Before we started, the church was filled and a bigger crowd was sent home than the one which was inside . . . We had before us a crowd of good-looking and well-behaved young men and women, who did not come out of curiosity, but who really sought something which could fill their lives. Mr. Wolfin addressed them in Yiddish, and I spoke in Polish on the text, "I am the way." It was indeed a very inspiring meeting; sometimes we forgot that we had Jews before us. The stillness and the attentive faces made us almost believe that we were speaking to Christian people.[3]

This unprecedented receptivity was confirmed by Nicholas Berdyaev: "We live in a time not only of bestial anti-Semitism, but of increasing Jewish conversions to Christ."[4] And Jocz added: "We missionaries know the full truth of these words – today when the cross is being twisted into a swastika. When thousands of gentiles refuse to acknowledge the sovereignty of Christ, Jewish men and women flock into the mission halls to hear and to learn about the wonderful Savior."[5]

Then came an unexpected deliverance. Joan had returned to England in late May 1939 to await the arrival of their first child and to ensure its British citizenship. Jakób remained in Warsaw. A minor crisis in England – the illness of the key speaker for the Church Missionary Society Summer Conference – resulted in an urgent phone call to leave Warsaw immediately and fill this assignment. How providential this proved to be! Had Jocz remained in Warsaw, he no doubt would have been destroyed along with the hundreds, even thousands of Jews who had believed, and the hundreds of thousands of other Jews whom the Nazis also liquidated. After the war he learned that his father had been betrayed to the Gestapo and shot, and that other members of the family had perished in Hitler's death camps.

Meanwhile Jocz had been appointed to head CMJ's work in London. Somehow he managed to include graduate studies at the University of Edinburgh. In 1947 his ministry was enlarged to include serving a small Anglican congregation in Hampstead. His literary career took on prophetic dimensions with the publication of his doctoral dissertation, *The Jewish People and Jesus Christ* (1949). This was the first of six major works and marked the beginning of his lifelong theological struggle for Jewish evangelism.

Ever since Warsaw days Jocz had been involved in the work of the International Hebrew Christian Alliance. In 1957 he became its president and in that capacity traveled widely. An earlier invitation to take charge of a rather large Jewish evangelism center in Toronto proved irresistible, and in 1956 the family left England. Strangely, his service at the Toronto Nathanael Institute proved frustrating. Fortunately, he was rescued by an invitation to join the faculty of Wycliffe College, the local Anglican theological seminary. From 1960 onward he occupied its chair of systematic theology.

It was in this post that Jocz truly came into his own. He was known for "taking the glibness out of theology by showing students how to think theologically, as well as how to preach and live theologically."[6] All spoke of his personal warmth and spiritual insight. Students who submitted papers to him encountered exacting standards. "Back the essays came, punctuation errors circled, spelling errors underlined, awkward syntax exposed, faulty argument disclosed, false information denounced (and, on occasion) a gentle request to rewrite the entire paper because 'You really are capable of much better work than this.' "[7]

Over the years Jocz accepted lectureships and conference engagements and wrote constantly. Following retirement in 1976, he continued at a heavy pace for seven more years. He died in 1983 after a brief illness.

Literary Work

Early in his missionary career in Poland, Jocz produced *The Essence of Faith* (1936). For some years he edited the Yiddish journal *Der Weg* and encouraged outstanding Hebrew Christians to contribute. This publication ceased to exist with the fall of Poland in September 1939. The suffering of his own people prompted a second book, an appeal to the churches: *Is It Nothing to You?* (1940). As the anguish of the European Jewry deepened, he revised and greatly enlarged this publication in 1941.

His essays and book reviews increasingly appeared in such journals as the *International Review of Missions, Jewish Missionary Intelligence, Life of Faith, Christian, World Christian Digest, Judaica, Hebrew Christian,* and *Church of England Newspaper.* He wrote as an advocate of the Jewish people but against Zionist ideology and always on behalf of missions to Jews. He was adamant in his conviction that there are not two ways to God, not two covenants – one for Jews (Sinai) and the other for Gentiles (Golgotha). "I see my people from within and also have the spiritual discernment of the Christian believer." Hence, with respect to his literary output he wrote:

"It has been my endeavor to treat a difficult subject in a scholarly manner, though I have not tried to hide my own convictions regarding Jesus Christ."[8]

Then came his second major book, *A Theology of Election* (1958), quickly followed by *The Spiritual History of Israel* (1961); in 1968 *The Covenant: A Theology of Human Destiny* appeared. The climax of his major writings was *The Jewish People and Jesus Christ After Auschwitz* (1981). This brought up to date his comprehensive grasp of the age-long controversy between church and synagogue. It is a tragedy that most of these books are currently out of print.

His most popular publication was *Christians and Jews: Encounter and Mission* (1966), originally delivered as three lectures at Princeton Theological Seminary (1964). This book was translated into German and Norwegian, but it was bitterly attacked because it dared to challenge the theological position that Jesus Christ is without salvific significance to the Jewish people.

Mention should be made of Jocz's unpublished titles: "Modern Judaism and Jesus Christ," "Religion and the Christian Faith," "Jews in the Bible," and "Evil and Sin." He also wrote "Guide to Family Worship," a libretto to a four-act opera entitled "David the King," "God's Quarrel with Religion," and a somewhat autobiographical novel, "War Without Peace: The Life and Times of Moishe Litvak."

Because of his knowledge of German, Jocz was able to introduce fellow theologians to the insights of Karl Barth's theological revolt long before Barth's writings had been translated into English. But he never uncritically adopted all the theses of the "biblical theology" movement that resulted from Barth's vigorous assault on philosophical and religious liberalism. Jocz was wary of Barth's overemphasis on election to the neglect of the need for personal repentance and faith. Just because Israel was an elect nation was no guarantee that all Israelites were salvifically related to God. Jocz unapologetically accepted the thesis of the apostle Paul: "Not all who are descended from Israel belong to Israel, and not all are children of Abraham" (Rom. 9:6-7).[9]

Jocz's Legacy: Its Distinctives

Many subjects dominated the thought of Jakób Jocz during his long years of missionary obedience, pastoral concern, and theological reflection. Admittedly, it is impossible to subject his literary legacy to brief statements, but what follows is an attempted distillation of his thought on themes very germane to missiological debate today.

Although Jocz's arguments are never forced or trivial, he tends to intimidate the reader by the incredible breadth of his learning. He writes as a systematic theologian, not as a biblical scholar although all his writings reflect the heart and mind of a devout Christian who had the utmost confidence in the integrity and authority of Scripture. He disavows "scientific detachment," stands squarely within the context of faith, is scrupulously fair in handling material with which he disagrees, but writes as a partisan with burning conviction.

The Synagogue

Jocz's lifelong concern was that synagogue and church should engage in continuing dialogue. Both have much to learn from the other. Stereotypes need to be reexamined as well as all aspects of their parting of the ways in the first century and the two thousand years of mutual hostility that have followed.

Jocz's constant theme is that only in Judaism does the church meet its equal. Both share the same ethical code, the same social vision, the same spiritual tradition, and the same cultural standards. As far as human religions go, Jocz contends that Judaism has no peer. Its unitarian monotheism is philosophically and metaphysically more palatable to modern men and women than Trinitarianism. Its ethics appear better adjusted to practical living. Its freedom from cumbersome dogma calls for no wrestling over the intellectual paradoxes one encounters in Christian theology. Judaism is this-worldly, but not overindulgent. It affirms human dignity and self-reliance and can boast high moral achievements in Jewish personal and family life. In Jocz's eyes Judaism has all the advantages of an intelligent religion, representing an integration between religion, race, and culture unequaled in history. And in this day of widespread religious pluralism, Judaism is tolerant, sensing no compunction to proselytize beyond its ethnic group.[10]

The Synagogue and Jesus Christ

Jocz frequently admits that synagogue and church possess no common denominator that could form the basis of a "bridge theology between them." Indeed, "the synagogue perpetuates her existence in the continued negation, and the church in her continued affirmation of the claims which Jesus made."[11] It is an offense to all forms of Judaism that the church persists in confessing his authority, uniqueness, and sinlessness. Biblically informed Christians have always believed that Jesus, declared to be the Son of God by his resurrection from the dead (Rom. 1:4), was able to do and say all that the Evangelists recorded. The New Testament bears no evidence of any debate on Christology; the apostle Paul taught nothing on the person and work of Jesus that is out of character with the way he is portrayed in the Gospels.

"Christian" Anti-Semitism

Inevitably, Jocz devoted much study to Christian origins and found himself repeatedly "driven to the conclusion that the church never tried to separate herself from the synagogue. She was forced out of the Jewish community for reasons which made coexistence impossible."[12] And yet, Jocz never forgets the long history of anti-Semitic hate and contempt that was nourished by the clergy. He repeatedly speaks of their inexcusable crimes against his people. For this reason, although he asks searching questions of the rabbis, he never allows a spirit of Christian triumphalism to dominate his encounter with them.[13]

The Rabbinic Conception of Humankind

What particularly troubled Jocz was that Jewish scholars had successfully persuaded most Christian writers of two things: first, that there is an unbroken line of development between the Old Testament and later rabbinism; second, that Pharisaic Judaism was the religion in which Jesus was reared and which was congenial to him. Jocz rejects these theses. Furthermore, he refuses to concede that the rabbinic conception of humankind has biblical support.

The synagogue, in Jocz's critique, misstates the divine image in people, promotes an idealistic and optimistic humanism, and downplays the Fall. It rejects human depravity and the consequent inability of people to make themselves fit for the presence and acceptance of God. For any person to claim relationship with God without the substitutionary atonement embodied in the cross is to overlook the mortal disease of sin. To Jocz, this is an act of supreme presumption. In contrast, the rabbis teach that, although people sin, they are not sinful in essence. People are not estranged from God by the Fall. Evil is but an acquired deficiency, not an inherent characteristic of human nature. Hence Judaism's confidence in human ability to approach God without the need for a mediator or savior.

Judaism and the Prophetic Tradition

Jocz frequently speaks of the tragedy of rabbinic Judaism. He evaluates in various ways the fateful efforts of the synagogue in the first and second centuries to cope with two awesome realities: the growing vigor of Hebrew Christianity in its midst, and the implications of the A.D. 70 destruction of the second temple. Jocz is at his best when he explores the manner in which the synagogue removed a central aspect of religious life from the Jewish people and reoriented its approach to God away from a sacrificial and substitutionary approach to something direct and immediate –

shifting from the sacrificial cult to a preoccupation with the study of the law. When the priestly dimension of Old Testament religion disappeared in rabbinic Judaism, the prophetic aspects of biblical faith also largely faded away. This meant that all Jews by virtue of their birth could automatically assume acceptance into convenantal relationship with God, whether or not they were religiously observant.

The prophets of ancient Israel spoke otherwise. The individual Jew was never free to take his or her Jewishness for granted. To be a Jew is not a static condition; it is a calling and a responsibility. This becomes clear when full weight is given to the prophetic tradition and the literally hundreds of occasions when the prophets called the descendants of Abraham to turn back to God and seek personal relationship with him (Hag. 2:17; Zech. 1:3; etc.).

An unbroken and intimate link exists between this prophetic tradition and the New Testament faith. Indeed, first-century Hebrew Christianity has its roots in the pious, prophetic circles within Jewry that derived inspiration from the prophetic message and put their hope not in the meticulous observance of the law – although they were a law-abiding people – but in the prophetic vision of the messianic age that Jesus had inaugurated. Both the priestly and prophetic aspects of Old Testament religion were fused into the redemptive work of Jesus the Christ, the Mediator between God and humankind in both the prophetic and priestly sense. Hence, Jocz asks why the synagogue elevates engrossment in the study of Torah as having precedence over every other segment of biblical revelation. In contrast, he notes that Jewish and Gentile followers of Jesus were concerned to develop a personal, spiritually energized relationship with God through him.

Hebrew Prophetism and the Nations

Furthermore, Jocz stands against the rabbis who seek to safeguard Israel's separate existence from the Gentiles. He follows the apostle Paul in contending that the messianic theme of the Old Testament not only points to God's ultimate triumph in Israel but that this triumph will extend to all the nations of the world. They too will join with Israel in the worship of the one true God. Hence, messianism in the Old Testament promises the vindication of God within history. Through the worldwide witness of Hebrew and Gentile Christians, Hebrew prophetism has already had a significant impact on world history. It promises yet greater things for Israel and the nations in the Last Day.

When Jocz writes of the prophetic vision of a new world and a united humanity, he can only lament what he called Judaism's penchant for tribalism, sensing no duty toward the nations and remaining passive with no message of salvation for the outside world. Nothing is more foreign to rabbinic Judaism than Isaiah's cry, "Turn to me and be saved, all the ends of the earth. For I am God, and there is no other" (Isa. 45:22). When the synagogue turned so completely from the universal character of the Old Testament prophetic message, it could not but alienate the followers of Jesus – Jews and Gentiles – who read the Scriptures so differently.

God's Quarrel with Religion

Some of Jocz's most controversial writings are concerned with what he calls God's quarrel with religion. He regards the Bible as a long historic record of the clash between human religions and the revelation of God's good news for sinful people. This clash reaches its climax in the crucifixion of Jesus Christ and reveals the Gospel as the opposite of religion – not of false religion, but of all religion. Seen in this light "religion reveals itself as man's word about God – whereas the Gospel is God's word to man."[14]

Jocz laments what is seldom recognized: "Religion is always the most bitter opponent to the Gospel."[15] It represents the self-assertive universal human impulse to secure protection from the unknown and to achieve harmony with the universe. "The religious man tries to take hold of God and use him for his own ends. Not God, but himself, is in the center; and everything else is subservient to his needs."[16] Religion rejects the biblical witness that all people are rebels: fugitives from God, defiled by sin, and given to evil. Hence, to Jocz the synagogue is the epitome of religion, since Judaism requires no salvation. Pious Jews are confident that forgiveness can be secured by earning it. Jocz concludes: "Had religion been able to save people, Christ need not have come. Had the most perfect religion been able to save the Jewish people, Christ need not have been born a Jew."[17]

Zionism and the State of Israel

It was inevitable that religious editors would turn to Jocz for commentary, both political and theological, upon events in the Middle East. Toward the end of 1948 he responded with a short article, "Jews and Palestine: The Background to the Struggle for a Jewish State." He began with a review of anti-Semitism in the twentieth century, then sought to evaluate the secular philosophy of the Zionist movement. When Zionists contended that the Jewish people would find freedom only in the context of a free, independent state, Jocz disagreed. Zionism, he argued, cannot solve Israel's underlying problems; rather, it only transfers them to the Middle East. True and lasting freedom for the Jewish people can be found only beneath the cross. It is only there that Jews and Gentiles can together attain the sort of unity that will transcend their cultural and ethnic diversity. Jocz grants that God can use Zionism for his own inscrutable purposes, but Jocz remains convinced that the nationalism promoted by Zionism will not enhance Israel's spiritual development.

Mission to Jews

Throughout his life Jocz was an indefatigable advocate of evangelizing the Jewish people. He wrote extensively on this theme, invariably beginning with the reminder that mission to the Jews began when Jesus preached the kingdom of God to his own people. The primitive church continued this witness out of loyalty to him and out of profound concern for the Jewish people. It is the acid test of the church's submission to Christ's lordship that it continues in efforts to call the Jewish people to Jesus Christ. For the church to leave them out of its evangelistic effort is tragic evidence that it has lost faith in the miracle of conversion to Christ by the Holy Spirit. Jews, as well as Gentiles, must experience rebirth by the Holy Spirit if they would enter the kingdom of God (John 3:1-10).

One of Jocz's memorable statements frequently quoted today bears repeating: "If the Church has no Gospel for the Jews, it has no Gospel for the world."[18] In this connection Jocz laments what had happened to the synagogue: "A faith which confines itself to one people is not the faith of the Old Testament prophets. By its lack of a world mission, Judaism separates itself from the rest of humanity, and also from the Bible."[19]

Hebrew Christianity

Jakób Jocz regarded the current emergence of Hebrew Christianity as the most remarkable sign of our times. He rejoiced that the Jewish people today are able to hear the message of Jesus Christ from Jewish lips in a Jewish idiom and in the context of Jewish life. To him Hebrew Christians stand as a reminder that there can be no collective decision for God, only a personal one. The Jewish community rejects them, for it makes no allowance for such a decision. This rejection indicates that its priorities have shifted from God to nationhood as the ultimate loyalty. As a result, Hebrew Christians (or Messianic Jews) find themselves in a prophetic role, not by choice but from necessity, even though this isolates them from their community and marks them as rebels. They pose profound questions to their fellow Jews: Why do you accept the rabbinic tradition about the crucifixion of Jesus? Why have you uncritically adopted the decision against Jesus made long ago by a minority of our people – the religious establishment? Should you not examine the Gospels personally, and not automatically follow the decision of those who have perpetuated this tragedy?

The only issue on which all Jews agree is their rejection of Jesus Christ. Some charge that for any Jews to speak otherwise is to destroy Jewry. When challenged, they invariably reply, "But isn't the survival of our people a good ultimate goal?" Jocz would answer that the higher scriptural goal is the unity of the human race in the Messiah.

Messianic Jews are also an anomaly to the average Christian, for they remind the church that God is still the God of Israel. The Jewish people still have a future role in the divine purpose. God will be faithful to the covenant and promises made with them. But Jewish believers are also a rebuke to the compromises many Gentile Christians continually make with the world. They challenge the church's nominality, its baptizing, marrying, and burying the unconverted in the name of Jesus. This follows because Messianic Jews have come to faith not by birth but by costly decision. They are a reminder that neither synagogues nor churches can take themselves for granted. If historic Israel failed, despite her privileges, so can the churches fail. Indeed, Messianic Jews are a sign of the utter spiritual need of the human race and the unsearchable riches of God's grace.

Conclusion

Out of loyalty to Jesus Christ, Jakób Jocz stood against the syncretistic tendencies both within the synagogue and the church. He could not endorse a rabbinic Judaism that saw fit to downplay the central event in ancient Israel's worship – represented by the temple – with its single focus on the need for expiation and atonement. He could not agree with the rabbinic denial of the need for any mediatorial priesthood between a holy God and sinful people, much less for the need of a prophetic order to call people to repentance and faith. Nor could Jocz endorse a largely Gentile church that tolerates "Christian" anti-Semitism, racism, and sentimental religiosity instead of the rigorous demands of historic, biblical Christianity. When the synagogue asks in all seriousness: "Yes, you Christians have Jesus, but where is the redeemed world, the kingdom he reputedly inaugurated?" Jocz then turns to the church and says, "You owe the synagogue an answer; where is the evidence of God's grace to be seen in this generation?"

Notes

1. Jocz, *The Jewish People and Jesus Christ* (1979 ed.), Preface. In writing this essay, I found very helpful the annotated bibliography in Elizabeth Louise Myers, "The Literary Legacy of Jakób Jocz" (M.A. thesis, Fuller Theological Seminary, 1989).

2. Jocz, "War Without Peace: The Life and Times of Moishe Litvak" (unpublished, 1973).

3. Jocz, "The Gospel in the Little Towns of Poland," *Jewish Missionary Intelligence* 28, no.8 (August 1937): 88.

4. Quoted by Jocz in "The People of the Cross," *Jewish Missionary Intelligence* 31, no. 2 (February 1940): 13.

5. Ibid.

6. *Cap and Gown*, no. 53 (1976): 7.

7. Ibid., p. 25.

8. Jocz, *Jewish People and Jesus Christ*, Preface.

9. Jocz, *The Jewish People and Jesus Christ After Auschwitz* (1981), p. 121.

10. Jocz, *Christians and Jews* (1966), pp. 36, 37.

11. Jocz, *The Jewish People and Jesus Christ* (1949), p. 264.

12. Jocz, *Christians and Jews*, p. 40.

13. Jocz, *Jewish People and Jesus Christ After Auschwitz*, pp. 186-92.

14. Jocz, "Religion and the Gospel," *Victoria Institute* 84 (1952): 79.

15. Ibid., p. 80.

16. Ibid., p. 86.

17. Ibid.

18. Jocz, *Christians and Jews*, p. 48.

19. Jocz, *Spiritual History of Israel* (1961), p. 160.

Selected Bibliography

Major Works by Jakób Jocz

1949 *The Jewish People and Jesus Christ.* London: SPCK.
1958 *A Theology of Election: Israel and the Church.* London: SPCK.
1961 *The Spiritual History of Israel.* London: Eyre and Spottiswoode.
1966 *Christians and Jews: Encounter and Mission.* London: SPCK.
1968 *The Covenant: A Theology of Human Destiny.* Grand Rapids, Mich.: Wm. B. Eerdmans Publishing Co.
1981 *The Jewish People and Jesus Christ After Auschwitz.* Grand Rapids, Mich.: Baker Book House.

Alan R. Tippett

1911–1988

Anthropology in the Service of Mission

Darrell L. Whiteman

A lan R. Tippett (1911-88) was a man who emerged from twenty years of missionary service with the Australian Methodist Mission in Fiji to become a significant missiologist contributing to the so-called church growth school of missiology. His passion was to enable the missionary enterprise to move more quickly from the colonial to the postcolonial era, and he came to believe that anthropological insights were indispensable in that endeavor. In this article we will consider several areas where Tippett has left his missiological legacy through his impeccable scholarship and wide range of publications.

Early Life

Alan Richard Tippett was the descendant of devout Wesleyan, lower-middle-class tin-miners who emigrated from Cornwall, England, in 1853 and settled in Victoria, Australia. Tippett frequently credited his Cornish background for his "defiant spirit which refused to admit defeat" when the going got tough, which it often did for him.[1] The elder of two sons of a Wesleyan pastor, Tippett's school days were filled with unpleasant experiences of being bullied by schoolmates, and on occasion being misunderstood and unappreciated by teachers. These memories haunted him all his life and often drove him to being a perfectionist in order to prove himself. Tippett was profoundly influenced by his father, who was an amateur naturalist of some renown in Victoria and passed on to his son Alan a scientific mind, a voracious curiosity about the world, and an innate ability to organize and classify data.

Tippett's "Aldersgate experience" of faith came one evening on the way home from work in 1929, passing by an open-air evangelistic meeting in the Victoria Market in Melbourne (p. 43). Shortly afterward he knew a vocation in missions was to be his calling. "I was ready there and then to go to China or New Guinea or wherever, just as I was" (p. 44). Reluctantly taking the advice of his father, however, he pursued the full ministerial training course (1931-34), earning his L.Th. at Queens College, Melbourne University. His training, however, had no cross-cultural dimension to it and "no course in Missions, either its Theology, Theory or History" (p. 52). He resented this lack of appropriate training and years later, when he encountered formal anthropological studies, realized what a tragedy it was to have been sent to Fiji without adequate preparation.

In 1938 he was ordained in the Methodist Church and also married Edna Deckert, to whom he had been engaged for several years. In the following three years they served two rural pastorates in Victoria, had their first of three daughters, and were accepted by their mission board to serve in Fiji.

Missionary Work in Fiji

After being denied even two or three weeks of specific missionary training before departing Australia, Tippett arrived in Fiji on May 6, 1941, walking right into what he perceived to be a thoroughly colonial mission.

In this situation he realized the importance of becoming a learner and so threw himself into the task of language and culture learning with great enthusiasm, setting aside a minimum of five hours a day for this purpose (p. 121). He was obviously serious about language, for within eight to nine weeks of his arrival he preached (or rather read) his first short sermon in Fijian without a translator (p. 123).

It did not take him long to recognize that it would be very easy to get sidetracked and swallowed up in administrative duties, noting that,

a man may become so involved with this kind of administration that it takes possession of his whole life and hinders his language learning and thereby his witness. A missionary at everyone's beck and call, however patient and loving his service, if he never learns the language to speak the things of the Spirit, is a pathetic figure. In my missionary research the wide world over I have met this person. How sad! (P. 123)

He soon discovered the worldview of the Fijians, recognizing that "more and more I became aware of the Hebrew character of it all and . . . I discovered what I had really never discovered in all my training – the Old Testament world" (p. 128). He felt his biggest missionary challenge in Fiji was "how to interpret a New Testament message to an Old Testament people" (p. 168). Early on in Fiji, Tippett began to question the picture of mission that had been given to him by his home promotion and deputationists. He remembers,

Our promotion had been built on the idea that the island people were "child races," that they were delightful children growing up, that some day with continuing mission, with more advanced education, they would mature and be able to stand on their two feet and be an independent church. I began to question the whole concept of the "primitive" and the "child mind" as a concept of western conceit and supposed superiority. (P. 131)

During Tippett's twenty years in Fiji (1941-61) he served in various capacities in five locations, but his pattern of missionary work always involved heavy itineration through Fijian villages in order to stay in close contact with the world in which Fijians lived. And he always went on these treks barefoot.

I had tried boots, shoes, sandshoes, and sandals, all of which damaged the feet. I found the Fijian way the best, once one had learned how to walk on coral. I continued with this until I left Fiji. It was the only way of crossing coconut trunk bridges in the rain. I also discovered why the good Lord had given us big toes. (P. 166)

During his first term Tippett was instrumental in helping to write a new constitution for the mission that would pave the way for the colonial mission to become an indigenous church, a goal he hoped would be accomplished within twenty years of the time the new constitution went into effect in 1946. Its manifest purpose was to bring an end to the long era of colonial paternalism that Tippett and other younger missionaries believed would never die of its own accord. "It had to be deliberately 'put to sleep,' and this is what we set out to do," he said. The major issue was where the decision making and ultimate authority lay. "We argued for the Fijian majority as over against the Board, or even the European Synod. We were convinced, that [European paternalism] had to go" (p. 169). And it did, with independence coming to the church in 1964, owing in no small measure to Tippett's tireless efforts to bring it about.

Although Tippett was thrust into positions of leadership in the mission's educational centers, he says, "I had not seen myself as an institutional man. It was in my itinerations, my preaching, evangelism and pastoral counselling that I found my most satisfying experiences. What spiritual gift God had given me seemed to lie in that direction" (p. 177). Nevertheless, he was given institutional responsibilities, including the editorship of the church paper *Ai Tukutuku Vakalotu* in 1951, and he served once as acting chairman of the mission. All of the administrative hassles dealing with a colonial structure Tippett saw retrospectively as "part of my preparation as a missiologist of post-colonial mission" (p. 294).

In 1955 Tippett went to American University in Washington, D.C., where he earned an M.A. focusing on social anthropology, history, and archives. He returned to Fiji in 1956 for what would be his last term of missionary service. Upon reflection, he saw these five years as the most manifestly rewarding years of his missionary life, but he felt it was now time to pass from the Fijian scene.

Tippett considered transferring to another field of mission or becoming involved in some aspect of training new missionaries in Australia, but his mission board provided no opportunity for either.

Alan Tippett and Donald McGavran Join Forces

In 1961 McGavran read an article published by Tippett the previous year in the *International Review of Missions* entitled "Probing Missionary Inadequacies at the Popular Level."[2] McGavran was fascinated by Tippett's perceptions, which were so similar to his own. McGavran had come out of India after thirty years' struggling against colonial paternalism and had recently established the Institute of Church Growth at Northwest Christian College in Eugene, Oregon. He wrote to Tippett in Fiji, inviting him to become one of the research fellows at the institute.[3] Tippett was familiar with McGavran's writing, including *Bridges of God*. "When I read it," he says, "I reflected and said to a friend in Fiji, 'This is absolutely right but this man will never sell it to the mission Boards.' So I was more than delighted when he wrote to me out of the blue. Our correspondence showed that we shared a great deal and had reacted to, and against, the same things in Christian mission" (p. 273).

Tippett settled his family in Australia and departed for the United States in late 1961 to accept McGavran's invitation, not for only nine months as he had intended, but for a long, painfully drawn out two and half years. He joined a handful of other men studying with McGavran, noting,

> We . . . shared convictions from our missionary experiences. We sought to modify colonial, paternalist mission strategy. We were aware of the fact that anthropological research had something important to say to Christian mission. We were aware that there were cases of growth and non-growth that called for scientific study. We all believed that in the world we faced days of unprecedented opportunity for Christian expansion. We were all drawn to Donald McGavran as the man who had most articulated these convictions, and was disposed to gather men together to study them. (P. 277)

Tippett had gone to Eugene expecting to earn an M.A. during his study, but neither the Institute of Church Growth nor Northwest Christian College could give one. He thus felt "hoodwinked" into doing a Ph.D. in anthropology at the University of Oregon, located across the street from Northwest Christian College in Eugene.

At the University of Oregon, Tippett's mentor was Homer Barnett, the leading applied anthropologist at the time. The two hit it off, as Barnett was pleased to have a mature student with such a rich resource of twenty years of "fieldwork" in Fiji, and Tippett was thrilled with Barnett's theories and models of culture change, which he found to be so illuminating for missiology. Of Barnett's book *Innovation: The Basis of Cultural Change* (1953), Tippett wrote, "Barnett's work on Innovation was the most influential book on my life, with the exception of the Bible . . . It was the most exciting thing I ever found in academia" (p. 288).

An important turning point for McGavran and Tippett came in 1963 with a consultation on church growth called by the Division of World Mission and Evangelism of the World Council of Churches to examine the two men's viewpoint, discuss the problems it raised, and make a statement for the world church.[4] Out of this consultation came a good statement on church growth that McGavran and Tippett used widely in subsequent years. Moreover, Tippett met Victor Hayward, who later invited him to participate in the "Churches in Mission" project, which sent him to the Solomon Islands in 1964. Tippett's research there led to what is probably his best-known book, *Solomon Islands Christianity* (1967).

The Solomon Islands research project (August-December 1964), in which he compared Methodist and Anglican mission work, seemed almost tailor-made for Tippett. He says, "Surely I could never have found a more suitable field for testing out the theoretical base of church growth missiology" (p. 300). It was an important "rite of passage" from the role of a missionary to Fiji to becoming a missiologist to the world. He summed up the experience, noting that

> after my term with McGavran I could look more critically at a situation with what he called "church growth eyes." After my tutelage under Homer Barnett I saw situations pulsating with innovations, natural and directed culture change, and found a new world of models and demonstrated anthropological principles. My terms of reference had been to look at everything critically, but helpfully. I thought I could see a whole area of application of anthropology for the sake of the Gospel . . . I felt now I could face my fellow anthropologists and McGavran himself as a peer. I was raring to go. (P. 316)

In 1965 McGavran was invited by Fuller Theological Seminary in Pasadena, California, to found a new School of World Mission. Tippett notes that "McGavran was not interested, unless they would consider taking over the whole project of the Institute of Church Growth, including both himself and myself" (p. 317). Although Tippett spent only twelve years of his life at Fuller (1965-77), it is within this relatively short time span that he made his mark on the wider missiological world.

The Legacies of Alan Tippett

Let us move now from the chronological development of his thought to the substantive areas where he has left a legacy. Beyond the legacy of being instrumental in ushering in the transition from colonial mission to indigenous church in Fiji, Tippett has contributed to missionary strategy, missiological theory, teaching, scholarship, and publications.

Contribution to Missionary Strategy

Although Tippett was not as prominent on the lecture circuit as his colleague Donald McGavran, there is no doubt that through his careful research, strong anthropological underpinnings, and theological soundness Tippett gave much-needed credence to the emerging church growth movement.[5] Tippett, more than his colleague, saw the necessity of using multiple models, methodologies, and approaches to the study of church growth. For example, he required his doctoral students to write their dissertations using as-yet unexplored anthropological models or ethnohistorical methods applied to missiology, and no two students ever used the same models and theories under Tippett.

This approach gave a richness and depth to church growth studies that was much needed. He was always open to employing new methods of critique and never shied away from self-examination.

To McGavran's church growth concepts of discipling (quantitative growth) and perfecting (qualitative growth), Tippett stressed the importance of organic growth. He summarized it thus:

> Those of us who have studied intensively the planting and growth of churches on the mission field have found that the churches that grow best and vibrate with indigenous life have paid attention to three things – a concern for winning large numbers of people from the world, a concern for effective nurture within the fellowship, and a concern for the development of functional roles and opportunities for service. Each of these stimulates a form of church growth, which we may call quantitative, qualitative and organic.[6]

The strategy of church growth owes much to Alan Tippett, although the name of Donald McGavran is most often associated with this movement.

Contribution to Missiological Theory

Tippett saw missiology as an interdisciplinary field of study and brought to that field competencies in anthropology, history, and theology. He was driven by the conviction that missiology must be holistic and interdisciplinary, always striving for synthesis out of analysis, and that one area of its development must not occur at the expense of another's neglect.

In addition to the anthropological contributions Tippett made to missiological theory, he also helped shape a number of key concepts that became popular in missiological discourse. Among these are the concepts of functional substitutes,[7] power encounter,[8] people movements, [9] and indigenous church.[10] Tippett also demonstrated over and over again in his research that missionaries might be the advocates of change, but it is the receptors who are the real innovators and bring change to their lives and culture.[11] There are many more we could highlight, and of course they are not all original with him, for he borrowed many from anthropology, but he gave them prominence because of his careful research and insightful missiological application.

I believe he was enthralled with anthropology because it opened up to him a whole new world of understanding mission, and he came to see it as indispensable for missionary training. It was this very dimension that he regretted so much having missed in his own preparation for missionary service in Fiji. "Anthropology does not bring individuals to Christ," he said, "but it shows missionaries how they may be more effective and less of a hindrance in doing so."[12] In his efforts to create a postcolonial missiology, he saw anthropology as fundamental, noting that "in the area of Christian education for mission, the inclusion of courses in anthropology [is] essential, and that for the post-colonial era of mission it is inconceivable that missionaries should be sent out without exposure to this discipline" (p. 339). His enthusiasm for anthropology in the service of mission was contagious, noting once that "I never found any aspect of social cultural anthropology which did not speak somehow to mission" (p. 333).

Contribution to Missiological Teaching and Scholarship

Tippett's strengths in teaching were evidenced more in the one-on-one mentoring mode than as a classroom lecturer. For those students who wanted to mine the depths of his insight and share from his reservoir of mission experience, any time spent with him, whether in class or out, was always worthwhile. I have vivid memories of meeting with him in his office surrounded by his marvelous library.[13] He would throw himself into the conversation, asking me if I had read this book or that one, if I was familiar with this author's perspective or that anthropological concept. And then he would pull from his shelves book after book to illustrate his points. It was all deliciously scintillating for an eager doctoral student.

He alerted students to the diachronic and historical dimension of mission by bringing to bear ethnohistorical methods on church growth studies. And he always insisted that events be interpreted in their proper context, not from the perspective of another time or place. He could get "picky," much to the annoyance of his colleagues, as for example, when he held up for six years the publication of *People Movements in Southern Polynesia* until he could check the accuracy of a single paragraph to make sure he interpreted it according to its proper context. And he was mighty glad he did!

Finally, we cannot conclude this section without acknowledging Alan Tippett's role as founding editor (1973-75) of the journal *Missiology*. In 1972 the American Society of Missiology was founded, and plans were laid for its journal *Missiology* to continue *Practical Anthropology*, which was being terminated by its sponsor, the American Bible Society. Tippett, who was absent at the organizing meeting, felt pushed into the editor's role, which he neither sought nor wanted. Nevertheless, he was ideally suited for this role because of his anthropological background and breadth of missiological acumen. He notes,

> In that three years we covered most of the aspects of missiology, published material from every Continent, by missionaries and nationals. I tried to maintain a balance. If an article was at one extreme I sought another to balance it. It was a middle of the road publication between Evangelical and Conciliar emphases, though we were specific about standing on the Great Commission and Scripture. (P. 444)

Conclusion

We have witnessed how through teaching, publishing, and editing Alan Tippett made so many important contributions to the field of missiology. Reflecting in his unpublished autobiography, he surmised,

> If I have made any worthwhile contributions to missiology for the post-colonial era, it has probably been in the area of the theoretical base, the development of research methodology, the application of anthropological principles positively to church growth, and the exploration of research models for pin-pointing matters for concentration of evangelistic thrust and pastoral care. (P. 446)

Alan Tippett was a remarkable and complex man, and only a fraction of his story has been told here. The missionary world is much richer today because of the legacies he has left us. He was that rare breed who combined the careful, meticulous eye of the scholar with the passion of a fiery evangelist. Few missiologists have blended so well the two worlds of ministry and scholarship. Perhaps it will be fitting to close with his own thoughts on how his scholarly pursuits were motivated by the drive for practical results. He says, "I have aimed at bringing anthropology as a science, the Bible as a record of God and humanity in relationship, and Christian mission as its medium for demonstration until the end of the age, together in a missiology adequate for the post-colonial era" (p. 447).

Notes

1. Alan R. Tippett, "No Continuing City" (unpublished autobiography, 1988), p. 32. Subsequent page citations in the text refer to this manuscript.
2. Tippett, "Probing Missionary Inadequacies at the Popular Level," *International Review of Missions* 49 (1960): 411-19.
3. McGavran, "Missiologist Alan R. Tippett, 1911 to 1988," *Missiology* 17, no.3 (1989): 262.
4. "The Growth of the Church: A Statement Drawn up by a Consultation Convened by the WCC Department of Missionary Studies at Iberville, Quebec, July 31-August 2, 1963," *Ecumenical Review* 16, no. 2 (1964): 195-99.
5. See Tippett, *Church Growth and the Word of God* (1970).

6. Ibid., p. 34.

7. Tippett, "The Functional Substitute in Church Planting," in *Introduction to Missiology* (1987), pp. 183-202.

8. Tippett, "Problems of Encounter," in *Solomon Islands Christianity* (1967), pp.100-118; "Universalism or Power Encounter," in *Verdict Theology in Missionary Theory* (1973), pp. 79-91.

9. Tippett, *People Movements in Southern Polynesia* (1971).

10. Tippett, *Solomon Islands Christianity;* "Indigenous Principles in Mission Today," in *Introduction to Missiology*, pp. 371-86.

11. Tippett, "Ethnic Cohesion and Acceptance of Cultural Change: An Indonesian Ethnohistorical Case Study," in *Introduction to Missiology*, pp. 285-301.

12. Tippett, *Introduction to Missiology*, p. 28.

13. Today this library of more than 16,000 books and documents is the Tippett Collection of St. Mark's Library in Canberra, Australia.

Selected Bibliography

Works by Alan R. Tippett

1954 *The Christian: Fiji 1835-67*. Auckland, New Zealand: Institute Printing and Publishing Society.

1967 *Solomon Islands Christianity: A Study in Growth and Obstruction*. London: Lutterworth Press. Reprinted in 1975 by William Carey Library, South Pasadena, Calif.

1969 *Verdict Theology in Missionary Theory*. Lincoln, Ill.: Lincoln Christian College Press. 2d ed. printed in 1973 by William Carey Library, South Pasadena, Calif.

1970 *Church Growth and the Word of God*. Grand Rapids, Mich.: Eerdmans.

1970 *Peoples of Southwest Ethiopia*. South Pasadena, Calif.: William Carey Library.

1971 *People Movements in Southern Polynesia: Studies in the Dynamics of Church-Planting and Growth in Tahiti, New Zealand, Tonga, and Samoa*. Chicago: Moody Press.

1973 *Aspects of Pacific Ethnohistory*. South Pasadena, Calif.: William Carey Library.

1973 *God, Man, and Church Growth: A Festschrift in Honor of Donald Anderson McGavran*. Ed. A.R. Tippett. Grand Rapids, Mich.: Eerdmans.

1977 *The Deep Sea Canoe: The Story of Third World Missionaries in the South Pacific*. South Pasadena, Calif.: William Carey Library.

1980 *Oral Tradition and Ethnohistory: The Transmission of Information and Social Values in Early Christian Fiji, 1835-1905*. Canberra, Australia: St. Mark's Library.

1987 *Introduction to Missiology*. Pasadena, Calif.: William Carey Library.

Works about Alan R. Tippett

Caldwell, Larry W. "Selected Missiological Works of Alan R. Tippett." *Missiology* 17, no. 3 (1989): 283-92.

Davis, Peter. "Portrait of a Pioneer: Alan Tippett, 1911-1988." *St. Mark's Review* 136 (Summer 1988): 29-31.

Dillman, Kathleen A.W. "Alan R. Tippett's Elaboration of Biblico-Classical Anthropologese for the Christian Mission and Its Significance for Missiology." Ph.D. diss. (research in process), Golden Gate Baptist Theological Seminary, Mill Valley, Calif.

Kraft, Charles H., and Douglas D. Priest, Jr. "Who Was This Man? A Tribute to Alan R. Tippett." *Missiology* 17, no. 3 (1989): 269-81.

McGavran, Donald. "Missiologist Alan R. Tippett, 1911 to 1988." *Missiology* 17, no. 3 (1989): 261-67.

Part Seven

ADMINISTRATORS

Henry Venn

Rufus Anderson

Arthur Judson Brown

Robert E. Speer

J.H. Oldham

William Paton

Karl Hartenstein

Norman Goodall

Charles W. Ranson

Max Warren

Henry Venn

1796–1873

Champion of Indigenous Church Principles

Wilbert R. Shenk

Henry Venn was one of the shapers and movers of the nineteenth-century missionary movement. Today he is known chiefly as a father of the "indigenous church" principle (self-supporting, self-governing, self-propagating). There was considerably more to the man and his long service than this. In addition to his missionary statesmanship, Venn influenced government policy and stood in the front ranks of nineteenth-century evangelicals.

Venn's background and training equipped him for the several roles he was to play. He was born on February 10, 1796, on London's outskirts at Clapham. His father, John (1759-1813), was rector of Clapham parish and pastor to William Wilberforce, Henry Thornton, James Stephen, and others who made up the famous coterie later called the "Clapham Sect."[1]

The "Clapham Sect" was the center of initiative among second-generation Evangelicals.[2] The first-generation Evangelical Revival had been dominated by the Wesleys and George Whitefield. Another prominent personality was Henry Venn (1725-1797), father of John and grandfather of Henry.[3] In a movement that was torn by doctrinal controversy between Whitefield and the Wesleys, Anglicans like Henry Venn took a mediate position. They rejected Whitefield's Calvinism and Wesley's perfectionism while affirming the need for conversion, genuine piety, warm fellowship, and evangelism.[4] Although it was often questioned by their critics, they maintained their fidelity to the Church of England. It was this theological position that informed the social and missionary activism of the second generation. The first Henry Venn was spiritual father of the Clapham Sect.

Whereas the first-generation Evangelicals were preoccupied with leading a revival, the second generation organized an almost endless series of philanthropic and religious societies. They helped the poor, taught children to read, wrote and published literature, combated the slave trade, and sent missionaries to other lands. Wilberforce led the antislave trade movement in Parliament with the full cooperation and support of his Clapham circle. John Venn presided at the meeting at which the Church Missionary Society (CMS) was organized in 1799 and wrote the original charter. The Clapham Sect had a major part in formation of the Religious Tract Society in 1799 and the British and Foreign Bible Society in 1804.

Evangelical Interpreter

The Venns had an unusually happy family life, but when Henry was seven his mother died and ten years later his father also passed away. At seventeen, with four sisters and a brother, he was left as family head. One of the duties that fell to him was to complete the work his father had begun on a biography of his venerated grandfather. *The Life and a Selection from the Letters of Henry Venn* was finally published in 1834 and subsequently went through at least five further editions. In the style of the day, this bulky volume consisted largely of his grandfather's letters. But in the preface Venn had tried to come to terms with and disentangle the origins of Evangelicalism. With the publication of this *Life* of his grandfather, Venn established himself as an interpreter of the Evangelical tradition. For the rest of his life he influenced the Evangelical course through his writing.

Venn did not possess the same outstanding preaching gifts as his namesake grandfather. He exerted leadership in the committee room and through administrative initiative. Already by 1825 the Church Missionary Society had risen to preeminence among Evangelical societies, and this fact was not lost on Venn. The third-generation Evangelicals extended the work begun by the second-generation leaders. Lord Shaftesbury and others pioneered legislative social reform as well as home missions from the 1830s onward. Annual meetings of these many religious societies took place during the spring. The "May meetings" held at Exeter Hall on the Strand were an annual celebration lasting for six weeks when the hearts of the faithful were warmed, new commitments were made, and enthusiasm for a plethora of evangelical causes was rekindled.

Evangelical leaders in Victorian Britain continued both to organize channels of ministry and to define and defend the Evangelical position. Controversy was never far away. Starting in the 1830s Evangelicalism had been affected by both the Tractarians (some of whom were of Evangelical background) and the Brethren and other elements on the right. As Evangelicals grew in strength and influence, they were also criticized by other parties in the church.

Venn sought to maintain the tradition handed down by his grandfather and father. This tradition was Evangelical in doctrine and spirit but loyal to the Anglican Church. It was moderate in outlook. Theological innovations or fads had little appeal. For example, Venn had no sympathy for the millennialism introduced by the Irvingites and Brethren. When the Evangelical Alliance was launched in 1846, Venn and many other Evangelicals remained aloof because of the alliance's attitude toward the established church. Although Venn was open-minded about the 1859 revival, he sought to steer people away from emotionalism toward a more balanced attitude and into constructive service.

An important vehicle for Evangelical leadership was the monthly *Christian Observer*. This was another venture founded by the Clapham Sect in 1802, and Venn's father had been a major contributor in its first years. The *Christian Observer* always remained a private publication but from the beginning won a respected role as an authoritative Evangelical voice. Venn was a longtime member of the *Observer*'s board and contributed regularly to its pages. Finally, in 1869, he "temporarily" assumed the editorship. From this position he pronounced vigorously on various theological issues before the church.

Venn's standing as an Evangelical leader can be measured by the fact that twice he was appointed by the Prime Minister to serve on Royal Commissions. In 1864 he was a member of the Commission on Clerical Subscriptions and in 1867 he was named to the Ritual Commission. Both commissions dealt with ecclesiastical questions on which Evangelical feeling was deep. Venn tried to represent these concerns in the work of the commissions in a way that advanced the welfare of the church as a whole.

Public Policy Proponent

The Clapham tradition combined personal piety with social activism. The members were men of wealth and social standing. A number of them were members of Parliament. They had access to the corridors of power and believed they should exert Christian influence on public policy.

The younger James Stephen, son of a prominent Clapham Sect member, became legal counsel to the Colonial Office. He married Henry Venn's older sister, Jane. Stephen rose to a top position in the civil service when he became Permanent Under-Secretary of the Colonial Office in 1836. Besides his considerable contribution to the development of the civil service system itself, Stephen exerted major influence on colonial policy for an entire generation. He argued that British colonies were a temporary responsibility. Eventually each of the colonies would sue for independence. Stephen urged that official policy should set the course for this development by encouraging each colony to evolve social, political, and legal institutions suited to its unique circumstances. Meanwhile it was the responsibility of Great Britain to guard the integrity of the peoples in the colonies and use her power to eradicate such evils as slavery.

The Stephen viewpoint was generally shared by missionary leaders. During the 1830s, for example, the Methodist Missionary Society and Church Missionary Society worked to prevent the colonization of New Zealand. Another Clapham son, the younger Charles Grant (by then Lord Glenelg), was Secretary for the Colonies and entirely sympathetic to these views. CMS Lay Secretary Dandeson Coates helped form a society for the protection of "native" rights. Commercial interests eventually won out but the Evangelicals had put up strong opposition.

Venn became CMS Secretary in 1841, less than eight years after Parliament passed the act abolishing slavery from all British territories. Yet the slave trade was flourishing. Sir Thomas Fowell Buxton popularized the concept that the "Bible and plow" would eradicate slavery by providing a legitimate alternative to this illicit commerce. When Buxton died in 1845, no one took up the cause more vigorously than Venn. He lobbied Parliament to maintain the British Squadron Patrol on the West African coast. When the Squadron issue came up for review in 1849, he led a delegation of some dozen persons to see Lord Palmerston, the Foreign Secretary, armed with a sixteen-page closely reasoned and well-documented memorandum. Palmerston was impressed and the Squadron was continued. Not until 1865 was the West African slave trade effectively ended. Without the vigilance and moral leadership of Venn and others, the outcome would have been different.

No sooner was the West African slave trade ended than Venn turned his attention to slavery on the East African coast. He did not live to see the back of the East African slave trade broken, but he had a hand in mapping out a strategy and mounting the first attack.

Education was the second focal point of Venn's public policy concern. Venn, Alexander Duff, and other missionary society leaders took an active part behind the scenes in influencing the drafting of the famous 1854 Education Despatch. This order committed the East India Company to a substantial enlargement of the Indian educational system and paved the way for grants-in-aid. This latter provision became the cornerstone for the extensive system of mission-sponsored schools throughout British India and, subsequently, other countries.

Venn urged that education should be conducted in the vernacular, a view opposite that of Duff. He recognized that education would remain the privilege of only a small elite if English were the medium of instruction. He organized the Christian Vernacular Education Society for India to promote such schools. At the same time he also argued that the government should authorize the use of the Bible in all public schools in India. Not even Venn's friends were persuaded that this was the right policy. Although it was never adopted by government, Venn always believed that a "Christian" government was obligated to provide for its citizens' religious welfare. This did not mean the people should be forced to accept the established religion but only that a "Christian" government should exert a Christian influence consistent with its character.

Educational developments in West Africa were even more dependent on the missions than in India. Venn believed education to be the foundation for political, economic, and social development. In 1864 he prepared a long brief urging a more enlightened government policy with regard to West Africa. He insisted that the Africans themselves should be trained to assume full responsibility for government and commerce. Years before, he had begun bringing young Africans to Great Britain for training. One of the first West Africans trained in Europe to be a medical doctor, Africanus Horton, was beneficiery of Venn's personal intervention.[5]

Venn also wanted the government to take a more aggressive role in economic development. Security was a major problem in West Africa because of the slave trade and lack of government services. Venn lobbied to get government support for shipping and exploration of the interior. He did not wait, however, for official action. He privately encouraged Manchester merchants to establish a cotton industry in Sierra Leone and Yorubaland. He invested his own capital in machinery, seeds, and the training of Africans for the cotton industry. This venture was ultimately doomed to failure because the soil was not suitable for cotton growing, but his confidence in Africa's human and natural resources was unbounded.

This interest in economic development, of course, stemmed from Venn's conviction that if people's economic needs were met through constructive and legitimate commerce, evils such as slavery would be eliminated.

In his thirty-one years as CMS Honorary Clerical Secretary, Venn met government representatives on many occasions. He was respected, even if his viewpoint did not always prevail, because he prepared thoroughly and articulated his case well. He often had superior sources of information and marshaled his facts with care. He also had influential friends to stand with him on the issues.

Missionary Statesman

Although missions were no longer a novelty by the time Venn became a missions administrator, he recognized that there were gaps in missionary theory and practice. The modern missionary movement operated without a special theoretical or theological framework. It was a movement based on pragmatic considerations. Venn frequently mentioned the need to identify and codify missionary principles. Toward the end of his life he spoke of the "science of missions." Throughout his career he encouraged an attitude of experimentation and exploration in order to discover "principles of missionary action" that he believed to be the basis of effective missionary work.

The nineteenth-century missionary movement received its major impulse from the eighteenth-century Evangelical Revival, but the eighteenth century was also the age of exploration and discovery. Captain Cook's *Journals* were influential. Some of the most important missionary literature during the first half of the nineteenth century was in the form of Christian "researches" and missionary travelogues. But theologies of mission were unknown during the first half of the nineteenth century. To remedy this lack Alexander Duff, Thomas Chalmers and others in Scotland sponsored by an essay contest in 1839 that resulted in the publication of several books, including John Harris, *The Great Commission, or The Christian Church Constituted and Charged to Convey the Gospel to the World* (London, 1842). Anthony Grant delivered the Bampton Lectures in 1843 in which he espoused a theory of mission based on High Church views on the episcopacy, an approach completely unacceptable to evangelicals like Venn.

Venn worked inductively at finding the principles of mission. He observed weaknesses in a missionary-founded, missionary-led church. What, he asked, gave a church integrity? A church had to feel self-worth. Over a period of fifteen years he identified three aspects of that self-worth. A church must be led by persons drawn from its own membership. So long as a group of people look to an outsider to furnish leadership, they will feel less than fully responsible. Similarly, if they do not bear the burden of supporting the life of the church financially, their membership will lack integrity. The final test of the integrity of the life of a church is the readiness to evangelize and extend itself. When a church has been founded through the work of an outsider, it is easy for it to become dependent on the missionary to continue this function. This is perhaps the most difficult aspect of self-responsibility to acquire. These three ingredients of a church's integrity were finally stated as self-support, self-government, and self-propagation.[6]

As already implied, Venn posited two conditions to be met in successful church development: a self-reliant church and a properly responsive mission structure. He likened the relationship between church and mission to that of edifice and scaffolding. From this he derived the oft-quoted phrase "the euthanasia of a mission." This was no foolhardy, simplistic slogan.[7] It presupposed that a vigorously mission-minded church had developed, that the mission structure was a temporary expedient to be removed as early as possible so as to allow the new church to express its own sense of mission freely, and that the purpose of mission structures was to be engaged in continuous advance into the "regions beyond." To help keep the mission of the new church in the foreground, he repeatedly arranged for the training and appointment of members of the younger churches to serve as missionaries. A notable example of this was the sending of Samuel Ajayi Crowther from Sierra Leone to Yorubaland in 1845 and later to the Niger Delta. Eventually Crowther presided over the Delta as bishop.

As an Evangelical, Venn assumed there was a fixed theological deposit on which mission was based. In his search for missionary principles, he did not draw on biblical or theological insights as much as on contemporary experience. The theological base was not negotiable, but the emerging principles were plastic. The integrity of the young church continued to be central to his system of thought, but Venn was less doctrinaire than some of his successors in the way he used his formulation. Furthermore, he never assumed that the formulation was the last word. He was constantly scanning the horizon for new insights that might lead to a reformulation of missionary practice.

In the last decade of his secretariat he was particularly intrigued with cases of "spontaneous" expansion that he studied. Anticipating Roland Allen's critique fifty years later, Venn wrestled with new questions about the role of the missionary and the work of the Holy Spirit in mission. His waning physical strength prevented him from investigating and developing his thought in this area.

In addition to keeping abreast of contemporary missions through reading missionary magazines and reports, Venn also devoted some time to the study of missionary history. For some fourteen years he studied the life and works of the great Roman Catholic missionary Francis Xavier. His book-length study was published in 1862. It was misunderstood by fellow Evangelicals and rejected by Roman Catholics. Yet it furnished Venn with a valuable historical reference point in his evaluation of "modern missions."[8]

Conclusion

A case can be made that the most powerful Anglican in the nineteenth century was Henry Venn, by virtue of a long CMS tenure, clear vision, and unusual gifts of leadership and administration. He played an unequaled role in revolutionizing the character and geographical dispersion of the Anglican communion in modern times.

Venn suffered a near-fatal heart condition in 1838-1839. Spurning medical advice to lead a quiet life, he learned to pace himself and took on appointment as CMS Honorary Clerical Secretary at age forty-five. His 6,000 official letters in the CMS archives and 230 items in the bibliography of his printed writings bear testimony to his capacity for disciplined work. Unlike his great American contemporary Rufus Anderson, Venn never visited any of the missions overseas. He early learned to make allowance for lack of perspective in missionary accounts and mistrusted the "romance of missions." He maintained a wide circle of friends among Africans and Asians and entertained them in his home when they came to London. These contacts had a definite influence on the development of Venn's policies.

Venn's wife, Martha, died in 1839 after eleven years of marriage, leaving him to rear their three young children. The Venns had had an unusually happy marriage, which, according to nephew Sir Leslie Stephen, was spoken of with awe by other family members. Venn's son John eventually became president of Gonville and Caius College, Cambridge, and son Henry was a parish priest.

When Henry Venn died on January 13, 1873, he was buried, according to his request, in Mortlake Parish Cemetery, West London, in a plain wooden coffin. The simple dignity of the service reflected the strength of the man. The missionary theme of the hymns sung on that occasion pointed to his lifelong commitment to world mission.

Notes

1. This was not a formally organized group. The name derives from the village of Clapham on London's outskirts. Not all were Anglicans, and not all were regular residents of Clapham. Approximately a dozen men composed the group, of which William Wilberforce was the best-known member. Nearly all were members of Parliament. The group was bound together by a social and political vision reinforced by religious convictions. Cf. E.M. Howse, *Saints in Politics* (London: George Allen and Unwin, 1973 repr.) for a vivid account of this influential group.

2. Following British convention, "Evangelical" here designates members of the Church of England who espoused the preaching of justification by faith, personal conversion, and warm and fervent piety. Early Evangelicals often used the term "experimental religion" to signify both an inwardly intense religious experience and practical actions through service and missions. (The term "evangelicals" denotes non-Anglican evangelicals.)

3. Historians sometimes confuse the Henrys and Johns of the Venn family since these names were used generation after generation. Thus, D.W. Bebbington, in his fine, comprehensive study of British evangelicals attributes an incident in the life of Henry Venn (1725-97) to his grandson Henry (1796-1873) when seeking to illustrate the growing social conservatism of nineteenth century evangelicals. See Bebbington, *Evangelicalism in Modern Britain: A History from the 1730s to the 1980s* (London: Unwin Hyman, 1989), p. 131.

4. Bebbington defines the troublesome term "evangelical" in the first chapter of his *Evangelism . . .* in terms of four emphases: conversionist, crucicentric, biblicist, activist.

5. Christopher Fyfe, *Africanus Horton: West African Scientist and Patriot* (New York: Oxford University Press, 1972), p. 32.

6. For a more complete account of Venn's contribution as a mission theorist, see Wilbert R. Shenk, *Henry Venn – Missionary Statesman* (Maryknoll, NY: Orbis Books, 1983), chap. 3. On the question who was the originator of the "three-selfs" formula, see my essays: "Rufus Anderson and Henry Venn: A Special Relationship?" *International Bulletin of Missionary Research* 5, no. 4 (Oct. 1981): 168-72, and "The Origins and Evolution of the Three-Selfs in Relation to China," *IBMR* 14, no. 1 (Oct. 1990): 28-35.

7. This was Stephen Neill's dismissive judgment on Venn. But see Shenk (1983), chap. 9.

8. See Shenk, "The Contribution of Henry Venn to Mission Thought," *Anvil* 2, no. 1 (1985): 25-42.

Selected Bibliography

Works by Henry Venn

Henry Venn's official letters numbering some 6,000 are preserved in the Church Missionary Society Archives deposited in the University of Birmingham Library. An index to all Venn letters, including a resume of the contents of each letter, is available. In addition, Venn family correspondence and manuscripts are also on deposit. A comprehensive Bibliography of Henry Venn's printed works is given in Wilbert R. Shenk, *Henry Venn – Missionary Statesman*. The majority of these 230 items are pamphlets, official statements, addresses, and articles.

1834 *The Life and A Selection from the Letters of Henry Venn.* London.

1862 *The Missionary Life and Labours of Francis Xavier taken from His Own Correspondence: with a Sketch of the General Results of Roman Catholic Missions among the Heathen.* London: Longman, Green, Longman, Robert and Green.

Works about Henry Venn

Knight, William. *Memoir of the Rev. H. Venn – the missionary secretariat of Henry Venn, B.D., Prebendary of St. Paul's and Honorary Secretary of the Church Missionary Society.* London, 1880.
_____. *Memoir of Henry Venn, B.D. – Prebendary of St. Paul's and Honorary Secretary of the Church Missionary Society.* London, 1882. This is a substantially reorganized and modified edition.

Shenk, Wilbert R. *Henry Venn – Missionary Statesman.* Maryknoll, NY: Orbis Books, 1983. Includes comprehensive bibliography of Venn's writings plus two of Venn's most influential policy statements not available elsewhere.

Venn, John. *Annals of A Clerical Family: Being Some Account of the Family of William Venn, Vicar of Otterton, Devon, 1600-1621.* London, 1904. For Henry Venn, see pp. 148-74.

Warren, Max, ed. *To Apply the Gospel – Selections from the Writings of Henry Venn.* Grand Rapids, Mich.: Wm. B. Eerdmans Publishing Co., 1971.

Williams, C. Peter. *The Ideal of the Self-Governing Church: A Study in Victorian Missionary Strategy.* Leiden: E.J. Brill, 1990.

Yates, T.E. *Venn and Victorian Bishops abroad: The missionary policies of Henry Venn and their repercussions upon the Anglican Episcopate of the colonial period, 1841-1872.* London: SPCK, 1978.

Rufus Anderson

1796–1880

To Evangelize, Not Civilize

R. Pierce Beaver

Rufus Anderson died more than a century ago, but his influence did not die with him. Scores of missionaries and mission board members who do not know his name will state that it is the aim of missions to plant and foster churches that will be self-governing, self-supporting, and self-propagating. There has never been another person in the American world mission who has rivaled Anderson in creativity, in shaping policy, and in uniting the roles of administrator and theoretician.

Anderson was born into a Congregationalist parsonage at North Yarmouth, Maine, on August 17, 1796, where the theological atmosphere was Hopkinsian. He was therefore immersed in concern for mission from infancy. His personal missionary vocation was confirmed when Pastor Anderson took his sixteen-year-old son to witness the ordination of the first group of American overseas missionaries in the Tabernacle at Salem, Massachusetts, in 1812. Rufus studied at Bradford Academy and Bowdoin College, where he took his A.B. degree in 1818. Then he enrolled in Andover Theological Seminary and, while studying, worked at the office of the American Board of Commissioners for Foreign Missions (ABCFM) in Boston as assistant to Jeremiah Evarts. When he graduated in 1822, Anderson formally applied for appointment to India, but was asked to work at headquarters during another year. Before that year ended, the officers decided that the board needed the young man more in Boston than in India, and appointed him assistant secretary. In 1826 he was ordained for secretarial service with the title of evangelist, one of the very earliest ordinations for denominational service in America. Anderson's entire ministry until retirement in 1866 was spent in administration in the American Board, forty-four years. On January 8, 1827, he married Miss Liza Hill, who survived him after fifty-three years of marriage.

It was a missionary that Rufus Anderson considered himself, and it was a missionary's field salary which he received, not that of a homeland pastor or denominational dignitary. He was made one of the three "corresponding secretaries" in 1832, and soon was given total responsibility for the overseas work, usually being called "the foreign secretary" or "the senior secretary." For thirty-five years he guided the Prudential Committee, which determined policy, carried on all business between annual meetings, and appointed missionaries.

The charge has been made that Dr. Anderson was a tyrant who ruled the American Board, the Prudential Committee, and the missionaries with an iron hand. He disclaimed that. When in the course of the famous deputation to the missions in India, Syria, and Constantinople in 1854-1855 the several missions adopted his recommendations to break up the large stations, found village churches, ordain native pastors for them, and give up English-language secondary schools in favor of vernacular-language schools, a few missionaries objected and said that he had been coercive. But the majority said he was persuasive because his logic was irrefutable. Nevertheless, Anderson was conservative on some matters and could resist change. Thus he asked Mrs. Sarah R. Doremus in 1834 not to organize a women's missionary sending society. Yet in 1866 when he retired, he told his successor, N.G. Clark, "I cannot recommend bringing the women into this work; but you are a young man, go and do it if you can." Anderson held rigidly to certain requirements, such as the prohibition of any missionary becoming engaged with a government or any kind of business. When Dr. Peter Parker became secretary and interpreter to the American Legation to China, Anderson terminated his employment with the board, even though it was the American government rather than a foreign one and despite the fact that Parker applied his salary to the support of his hospital in Canton.

When he retired Dr. Anderson was given an office at board headquarters and devoted several years to writing the histories of four of the board's missions. He was careful to avoid interference with his successor, but he did remain a member of the Prudential Committee until 1875, when he was made emeritus. He lectured on missions at Andover and other seminaries and colleges for a few years. During many years he delivered the lecture at the Monthly Concert of Prayer at Park Street Church, Boston.

Anderson's Writings

Apart from the *Memorial Volume of the First Fifty Years of the American Board of Commissioners* (1861) and four histories of the board's missions (Hawaiian Islands, India, and two volumes on Oriental Churches), Dr. Anderson published few books. They include *Foreign Missions: Their Relations and Claims* (1869), being a collection of lectures; a volume of reports of the 1854 deputation (1856); *Observations on the Peloponnesus and Greek Islands* (1830); and *Memoir of Catherine Brown, a Christian Indian of the Cherokee Nation* (1824). His voluminous writings were in the form of articles in the *Missionary Herald*, instructions to missionaries, pamphlets, and the *Missionary Tracts of the American Board*, all of which were written by him except No. 13, *The Grand Motive to Missionary Effort*, by Swan L. Pomroy, and No. 15, *Outline of Missionary Policy*, in which S.B. Treat in 1856 drew up a statement of Anderson's system for adoption by the board. A number of his articles are also in the board's *Annual Report*. There is a complete bibliography in *To Advance the Gospel*. Anderson never systematized his principles or practice of missions. His books, tracts and pamphlets are now extremely rare items. The author of this article has attempted to give today's students of missiology direct access to Anderson's thought by bringing together from the literature pertinent selections with an introduction and notes in the volume *To Advance the Gospel. Selections from the Writings of Rufus Anderson* (Grand Rapids, Mich.: Wm. B. Eerdmans, 1967).

The Practice of Missions

Anderson's fundamental thesis was that "missions are instituted for the spread of a scriptural, self-propagating Christianity. This is their only aim."[1] These factors are included in the aim: "(1) the conversion of lost men, (2) organizing them into churches, (3) giving these churches a competent native ministry, and (4) conducting them to the stage of independence and (in most cases) of self-propagation."[2] Anything additional is secondary, or even superfluous. Simplicity of operation and good stewardship are required. Comity, that is, mutual division of territory and cooperation among mission agencies, is necessary so that there be no waste of personnel and money and that all peoples everywhere be evangelized. "Civilization" or social transformation is not a legitimate aim but will come as the consequence of the impact of the Gospel. Apart from preaching, no method is prescribed, and every method is permissible if effective, that is, contributing to the upbuilding of the local church for aggressive mission. A truly mature local church is an evangelizing, missionary one, a growing church, a church going out to others. Bible translation, literature, schools, the press, and all other activities should be directed toward that end.[3] "The governing object to be always aimed at is self-reliant, effective churches – churches that are properly native."[4] The missionary is not to be a ruler or pastor, but an evangelist, who hastens on as soon as possible to another place, leaving the local church under a native pastor and in full Christian liberty to manage its own affairs. The school, seminary, and any other institution exist only to build up the local churches.[5]

This scheme of practice terminated the older "mission families" of ministers, teachers, farmers, carpenters, masons, and other artisans who aimed at first civilizing the American Indians and the Hawaiians so that they could then be evangelized. Social transformation would in due time result from the Gospel. However, seldom would a missionary move on to pioneering on new ground and leave a congregation to its own independent existence. It was hard to agree that one was dispensable and to leave the fruits of one's labor. Only in one instance during the nineteenth century was a whole mission terminated, that is, in the case of Hawaii, where the independent Hawaiian Evangelical Association was created.

Missionary Principles

Rufus Anderson found the norm and abiding model for missions in St. Paul's missionary action as revealed in the New Testament. He summarizes his findings there, which are to guide modern missionaries, in these sentences:

> Such were the apostolic missions. Such were the efforts made for propagating the Gospel among the heathen by missionaries under a special divine guidance. It was by gathering converts into churches at the centers of influence, and putting them under native pastoral inspection and care. The means employed were spiritual; namely, the Gospel of Christ. The power relied upon for giving efficacy to these means was divine; namely the promised aid of the Holy Spirit. The main success was among the members of the middle and lower classes of society; and the responsibilities for self-government, self-support, and self-propagation were thrown at once upon the several churches.[6]

Anderson found in the apostolic record no evidence of an aim to change and transform society and, therefore, he opposed the efforts and apparatus for furthering "civilization," which had prevailed until then. They were complicated and costly and in his view deflected concentration from the rightful objective.

The foremost motive for mission is obedience to Christ, since the Great Commission presents the church with "its standing work . . . for all ages of the world." But the obligation rests on the individual disciples rather than on the church collectively, because the Great Commission was given before the birthday of the church. Each person under the guidance of the Holy Spirit must decide whether to serve overseas or, at home, to support those who go. The mission board or society exists solely to help the missionary discharge his or her duty. The missionary is not a servant of the society. Few mission boards appeared to have treated the missionaries as employees. This obedience is not legalistic submission to authority but, rather, the glad obedience of love.

The Holy Spirit is God himself in missionary action. He prompts the church and the disciple, opens doors of opportunity, and gives power for witness. There will be a great outpouring of the Spirit, which will ensure the publication and the triumph of the Gospel throughout the earth.

The mission board or society may not be a denominational or confessional empire builder, but it sends persons to plant and foster churches that will join in the universal task of evangelization. Every action and program should be subordinate to the multiplication and upbuilding of missionary churches. The test of success with respect both to a congregation and to an individual disciple is the clear evidence of a religious life. Neither is to be judged by the behavior of New England Christianity, which is the result of many centuries of nurturing in the Gospel. They are to be judged by whether there has been a genuine change in the quality of life, a reorientation toward Christ.

Schools should be principally village vernacular ones, which provide evangelistic opportunities among the families of the children. Mission education aims at training the laity and educating national church workers. Schools that build up the church are essential, but those that primarily supply the government and commerce with trained employees are not.

Missionaries are ambassadors of Jesus Christ, beseeching people to be reconciled to God. Their business is not with believers, but unbelievers; they are not pastors or rulers, but evangelists. Their first duty is to gather a local congregation. They will be spiritual leaders to it but will leave it to a native minister and move on to preach the Gospel in some other place. The sole exception is when a church is organized and there is no suitable native pastor available. The missionary should raise up ministers and give them responsibility. Too many missionaries in any area will retard the development of the churches. Missionaries should be married, and their home will be a model of Christian family life.

The native church and ministry form the keystone of Anderson's theoretical system. That church is not to be an end in itself, a self-contained institution, but one more unit in an ever-growing and expanding worldwide mission. The end of mission is "a scriptural, self-propagating Christianity." A local church is to be leaven, and it cannot be mature until it engages in what to it is virtually a foreign mission. The missionary may initially establish any order of polity that seems to be compatible with the New Testament, but as soon as it has a national pastor it has the freedom to change. A church from the very first has full liberty in Jesus Christ, and it does not properly come under the jurisdiction of any foreign ecclesiastical body. Self-support will free any local church from missionary paternalism. Anderson provided only for adaptation in polity and church building, but in his insistence on full liberty he gave the indigenous church a charter to be itself.

Rufus Anderson and Henry Venn of the Church Missionary Society each came independently to the three-self formula. Together they provided a guiding principle for the whole Protestant-world mission. Too few held all three terms in proper unity and tension. Mission board executives usually stressed self-support; national church leaders emphasized self-government; and too few put self-propagation in the first place that Anderson awarded it.

Criticism of Anderson

Rufus Anderson and the three-self formula have been sometimes criticized in this century. The Chinese Communist government-sponsored "Three-Self Movement" inspired much of the criticism. That was a travesty of the concept. There was widespread disapproval of any local or national church that tried to live to itself in a self-centered existence, because the church is to live for others. Anderson, too, would have disapproved. The church that he sought was to be part of a world mission, ongoing, self-propagating, sharing its treasure with others.

Anderson's concept of mission is too simplistic. He overreacted to the earlier creation of those Siamese twins, "civilization" and "evangelization." His discernment that evangelization is the central purpose of the mission is right, but he was too narrow in his definition. He did not make sufficient place for the social service and justice aspects of the Gospel. While he warned that new Christians should not be expected to conform to the behavior patterns and standards of European-American Christians, he did not question the superiority of Western civilization and failed to see the need for thoroughgoing cultural adaptation in the young churches.

The Influence of Rufus Anderson

Dr. N.G. Clark, successor to Dr. Anderson as foreign secretary of the American Board, stated at the funeral service: "There can be no hesitation in saying that the world owes to Dr. Anderson the reviving of the true method of missionary effort as illustrated most fully in the Acts of the Apostles by the Apostle Paul . . . This method and the principles involved are now the common possession of all missionary societies the world over. They are recognized in the plans adopted and the tributes paid to Dr. Anderson in this country, in Great Britain, in Germany, and wherever missions are known."[7] He also had impact in the Netherlands.[8] Certainly all American church missions followed the American Board theoretician in their general policy and practice down to World War II. They departed from him in particulars but at least gave his principles lip service. During his active career the secretaries and officers of other boards read his tracts, articles, and the *Missionary Herald*; exchanged letters with him; and consulted him personally. The American Baptist Board of Foreign Missions had its headquarters in Boston, too, and the secretaries were in constant consultation with their American Board counterparts; so much so, that Isaac McCoy, Baptist missionary to the American Indians, complained about their domination by the Congregationalists.

However, the long endurance of Anderson's influence was due largely to the fact that he had an extremely able posthumous disciple, Robert E. Speer (1867-1947), general secretary of the Board of Foreign Missions of the Presbyterian Church in the USA, through whose views, lectures, books, articles, and administrative policy the heritage of Anderson was transmitted. Speer wrote of Anderson that he was "the most original, the most constructive, and the most courageous student of missionary policy whom this country has produced, and one of the two most aggressive and creative administrators of missionary work"[9] (Walter Lowrie was the other). Speer also was both administrator and theoretician. He restated and updated the older statesman's principles in his *Missionary Principles and Practice*,[10] *What Constitutes a Missionary Call*,[11] and other works. Speer was the dominant American theologian and philosopher of missions from 1900 to his death in 1947 and was therefore especially powerful in the transmission of the Andersonian theory and policy, and in applying them to new situations. He was more concerned than Anderson with social issues and had a scholarly concern for world religions and cultural adaptation of Christianity, which his mentor had lacked. When this writer returned from China in 1942 and began attending the Foreign Missions Conference of North America, Anderson was still very much a living force through Speer.

Anderson's insistence on the personal nature of the missionary vocation and the focus of the Great Commission on each and every disciple bore superabundant fruit in the Student Volunteer Movement, including the notion that the call was first of all to overseas service and that a decision to remain in the homeland had to be specially justified. These views were directly transmitted by Robert E. Speer and broadcast through the amazing circulation of the pamphlet *What Constitutes a Missionary Call?*

The American Board did not long continue Anderson's limitation of English-language secondary and higher schools, nor did the other boards. Yet Anderson would have approved the high schools and colleges in China and Japan, because they were potent agencies of conversion as well as effective means of leavening a nation with Christian principles and idealism.

John L. Nevius, in devising his "method," was obviously influenced by Rufus Anderson. Roland Allen probably never heard of him, but his principles and his insistence on native ministry and freedom of the new church is consistent with Anderson even more than with Venn.

It is always extremely difficult to tell in later times where and when the influence of any older molder of thought and action is being exerted unless there is explicit acknowledgment. Certainly the emphasis of American evangelicals on evangelism and rejection of social concerns in the quarter century after World War II was a return to Anderson's viewpoint. The leaders of the church growth school have recovered a fundamental principle of Anderson's in the stress on the necessity of each church growing and reaching out in evangelization, and they honor his memory. All contemporary missiologists follow the nineteenth-century statesman in seeking a biblical basis and guidance for the missions of a new day.

Notes

1. Tract 15, *Outline of Missionary Policy* (Boston: ABCFM, 1956), p. 3.
2. Ibid., p. 5.
3. Anderson, *Foreign Missions: Their Relations and Claims* (New York: Scribners, 1869), p. 5.
4. Ibid.
5. Refer to *To Advance the Gospel* for full documentation.
6. Anderson, *Foreign Missions: Their Relations and Claims*, p. 61.
7. N.G. Clark, Funeral Sermon, included with *Discourse Commemorative of Rev. Rufus Anderson* (Boston: ABCFM, 1880), pp. 57-58.
8. J. Verkuyl, *Contemporary Missiology* (Grand Rapids, Mich.: Wm. B. Eerdmans, 1978), p. 187.
9. Speer, *Studies of Missionary Leadership* (Philadelphia: Westminster Press, 1914), p. 187.
10. New York: Revell, 1902.
11. New York: Association Press, reprinted many times, including 1918.

Arthur Judson Brown

1856–1963

Believing in the Power of the Sovereign Lord

R. Park Johnson

Arthur Judson Brown was an outstanding "board secretary" – he never had another title, although he and his colleague Robert E. Speer were designated as joint supervisors of the executive staff during his last few years in office. He was a secretary of the Board of Foreign Missions of the Presbyterian Church in the U.S.A. from 1895 until his retirement at the age of seventy-two in 1929. It is perhaps unfortunate that his name in later years has generally evoked, not first of all an appreciation of his skillful administrative abilities, his wise influence on evolving mission policy, and his major contribution to the growth of the ecumenical movement, but simply an awareness of his unusual longevity!

He was born in Holliston, Massachusetts, on December 3, 1856, and died in New York at the age of 106 on January 12, 1963. A centennial dinner in New York was held on his 100th birthday in 1956, sponsored by the Presbyterian Board of Foreign Missions and the Church Peace Union. After several addresses and presentations, Dr. Brown responded: "The first time I faced an audience was at the age of six. I was required to speak a piece in school. The opening lines of that piece are as appropriate this evening as they were ninety-four years ago:

You would scarce expect one of my age
To speak in public on the stage.[1]

There continued to be annual luncheon celebrations of Brown's birthday for several more years, and he spoke in vigorous and prophetic tones at each of them.

Early Life Spanning the American Continent

Arthur Brown's father was a factory worker who volunteered for the Union Army and was killed in action at the battle of Petersburg in the Civil War on July 23, 1864. His mother then moved from Massachusetts to live with a sister in Neenah, Wisconsin. He graduated from Wabash College in 1880, and from Lane Seminary in Cincinnati in 1883. His next twelve years were spent in three pastorates: Ripon, Wisconsin, for a year and a half; Oak Park, Illinois, for three and a half years; and Portland, Oregon, for seven years. He was an eloquent preacher, sometimes criticized for sermons exposing abuses in state welfare institutions and sweatshop conditions in the local clothing industry. Many years later he commented, "In all my ministry I held firmly to the conviction so clearly expressed in the New Testament that the Gospel of Christ is for the whole man in his whole life and all its relationships."[2] He also specialized in popular sermons on church history.

On July 10, 1883, Arthur Brown was married to Jennie E. Thomas. They had five children, three sons and two daughters. His wife accompanied him on many of his overseas tours. She died in December 1945.

First Presbyterian Church, Portland, entertained the annual General Assembly in 1892, and in 1894 Arthur Brown was nominated for moderator of the General Assembly. When he lost by three votes, he was asked what he felt was the reason for his defeat. He answered, with his characteristic dry humor, "The other man got more votes." At this assembly he was chairman of a committee considering a move of the Home and the Foreign Mission boards from their old building at 53 Fifth Avenue, New York, to a new headquarters building at 156 Fifth Avenue. In 1895 he was, to his surprise, called to work in this building as an administrative secretary of the Presbyterian Board of Foreign Missions.

Main Career Encompassing the World

Arthur Judson Brown's career of thirty-four years in the capacity of a board secretary spanned the growing, exciting, formative years in the history of the world Christian mission and the nascent ecumenical movement. He soon became, not just an efficient administrative officer, but an active participant and respected leader in both the developing strategy of the world-mission enterprise, especially in the region of his assigned portfolio, the Far East, and in the gradual emergence of organized ecumenical cooperation on the whole world Christian scene.

An early landmark in the history of international Christian cooperation was the gathering in New York in April 1900, which bore the significant title Ecumenical Missionary Conference. Brown was a member of the executive committee and chairman of the hospitality committee. In 1907 he was named chairman of the Committee of Reference and Counsel, which speeded the formation, out of an informal group representing several denominational mission boards, of the Foreign Missions Conference of North America.

When plans were initiated for the great Edinburgh World Missionary Conference that took place in 1910, Brown was chosen as chairman of the American Section of the International Committee on Arrangements, and of the executive committee of the Conference. The Edinburgh Conference appointed a Continuation Committee, of which Brown served as a member for eighteen years. Out of this committee emerged the International Missionary Council in 1921.

These developments paved the way for the memorable Universal Christian Conference on Life and Work in Stockholm in August 1925. At the outset of planning for this conference, Arthur Brown was elected chairman of the American Section of the International Committee on Arrangements. In the wake of World War I the first meeting of the international group was held in Geneva in the summer of 1920. As chairman of this session, faced by bitterness left over from the war and the Versailles Treaty and a tense atmosphere, Brown succeeded in drawing the members together in support of a decision to proceed with plans for the conference. At a meeting of this group in 1922, four joint presidents for the Stockholm Conference were appointed: the Archbishop of Canterbury, the Archbishop of Uppsala, the Patriarch of Constantinople, and the American Board secretary, Arthur Judson Brown. When the conference met in Stockholm, Brown shared in presiding at the sessions and was the Sunday preacher, provided for the occasion with a gleaming white robe. He recalls that "an incorrigible American remarked that it was the first time I had been arrayed in white, and he hoped it wouldn't be the last."[3]

The four presidents of the conference were elected presidents of the Continuation Committee. Brown, on becoming seventy years of age in 1926, resigned as president but served as a member of the committee until the age of eighty.

It was not only as a church representative in international Christian cooperative movements that Brown took an active part. He was one of twenty-nine religious leaders invited by Andrew Carnegie to organize the Church Peace Union, and was a member of the executive committee, and later treasurer, and was for many years the only surviving member of the original organizing group. It was a mark of the singular esteem in which he was held by his colleagues in the Church Peace Union that this organization shared with the Presbyterian Board of Foreign Missions in sponsoring the centennial dinner in honor of Arthur Judson Brown on his 100th birthday on December 3, 1956.

Brown was a member of the Hoover relief committee for Europe (1915), a trustee of Near East Relief (1915), a trustee of the Rockefeller-sponsored medical college in Peking (1917), a member of a national committee for famine relief in China (1920), and chairman of the American Committee on Religious Rights and Minorities (1920) and chairman of its delegation to Hungary (1920).

Brown was born too early for direct involvement in the later development of the World Council of Churches in 1948, and the merger with it of the International Missionary Council in 1961, but from an early period he helped build the consensus that mission and unity are indissolubly connected features of the Christian church in the world. In the foreword of his book *Unity and Missions* (1915) he wrote, "Amid the solemnities of the closing weeks of the life of our Lord on earth, two desires for his disciples stand preeminent, Unity and Mission . . . Some experience in missionary administration has convinced me that the two subjects are indissolubly connected. In proportion as the Church becomes missionary, it feels the need of unity, for it is futile to expect a divided Church to evangelize the world."[4] When, following the Boxer Rebellion in China in 1900, there were voices counseling a suspension of mission work in those unsettled conditions until there would be a "settlement of political negotiations," Brown almost scornfully opposed such suggestions, and asked, "Does any sane man imagine that the Church could cease to be missionary and remain the Church?"[5]

Books Interpreting the World Mission

Arthur Brown's creative leadership in the development of mission policy was reinforced through the years of his career as a board secretary by the prolific production of significant books issuing from his personal experience, wise judgment, and scholarly research. The two books of greatest influence and importance, retaining a remarkable vitality through the years, are *The Foreign Missionary*, published in 1907, with repeated printings and with later revisions in 1932 and 1950, and *One Hundred Years*, a comprehensive history of 1,084 pages, published in 1936. The preparation of this work, in observance of the 1937 centennial of the Presbyterian Board of Foreign Missions, was Brown's major post-retirement assignment in the years 1929-36 and constituted a fitting capstone to the administrative and literary achievements of his active career.

However, perhaps more influential, in both the development of mission policy among church leaders and the education of church members and the general public, was the succession of descriptive books about the countries of the Far East and the development and progress of mission work in these lands, which were then far less known than today. The themes of these books are, of course, dated, and now belong to the archives of history, but they were timely and relevant when published, and helped stir the understanding and enthusiasm of readers in a day when the expansion of the missionary enterprise required an informed constituency in the churches. The list of Brown's publications appended to this article shows the broad span of his interests and labors.

Many of these "country briefing papers" rest on Brown's personal observations and experiences during two fruitful trips of visitation to the Far East in 1901-2 and 1909. Immediately upon his return, he produced detailed reports of his visits in each country, and many of his following books were an amalgam of his personal experiences on those visitation trips, his continuing day-by-day administrative wrestling with immediate decisions of mission policy, and further careful historical research.

Vision Reaching to the Future

An important element in Arthur Judson Brown's legacy lies in the influence he brought to bear, not only in the counsels of his own denomination, but on the wider world stage, on the evolving answers to two basic questions of missionary policy: (1) How does a denominational mission board or an independent missionary society, and its workers (missionaries), relate to bodies of Christians (national churches) in the country or region of its work? (2) How do different Christian churches in any country or region, or in the world, relate to each other?

In 1895, when Brown began his service as a board secretary, these questions were in some places not yet a real issue, but in other places they had begun to raise their head or were already matters of serious debate. The situation in each country was different. In 1901-2 Brown found himself in a China dominated by the rivalries of European colonial powers and still reeling from the violence of the previous year's Boxer Rebellion; in a Philippines just trying to find its feet anew as an American possession, after the end of centuries as a colony of Spain; in a Korea threatened by Japanese hegemony in the period between the China-Japan (1894-95) and Russo-Japanese (1904-5) wars; and, in 1909, in a Japan already flexing the biceps of nationalism and regional imperialistic expansion. Mission is never prosecuted in a vacuum, and mission policy was confronted with a host of changing conditions in the countries where missionaries were at work.

In reviewing the records of these years, one is struck by the degree to which Brown, in his judgment on policy, honored both the past and the future. Even in the early years of his service, as one studies his 1901-2 and 1909 travel reports and his convictions set forth in *The Foreign Missionary*, it is nothing short of amazing to find that many of the sweeping changes of the following decades, and of the fifty years of missionary history after his retirement, were adumbrated in Brown's thinking, his active counsel, and his written judgments. He possessed no crystal ball, but in dealing with current issues he discerned the shape of the evolving future and planted seeds that only in later years came to full flower. He anticipated many of the changes to come, and he welcomed, was ready for, and sought to make the church ready for the developments of succeeding years.

Brown would not have been surprised by the title of a book published in 1982, reviewing the history of developments of the Christian world mission in the fifty years following his retirement. *From Colonialism to World Community* was written by a worthy successor as a Presbyterian board secretary, the late John Coventry Smith. Well before the post-World War II end of the colonial era, marked by the independence of nations all over Asia, Africa, and Oceania, with the concomitant rise of nationalistic consciousness and power and the inevitable effects on mission organization, policy and practice, Arthur Brown foresaw the trends of change and set in motion the ideas of flexible adaptation and response.

Principles Guiding Thought and Action

Before touching in detail on Brown's views in the areas of mission-church relations, and of cooperative organization and church union, it is possible to identify a number of axiomatic principles that underlay his judgments and actions. These were principles that he found embedded in the very bedrock of the Christian Gospel, and they served as steadfast and creative guidelines for practical decision on issues of many sorts. Brown believed:

1. in the imperative character of the missionary obligation for the Church of Christ. In his centennial history Brown says by way of summary, "The numerous changes in the political, economic and intellectual life of the world, in the attitude of 'Christian' nations toward the non-Christian and their attitude in return toward us, do not impair in the slightest degree the imperative character of the missionary obligation."[6]

2. that human beings everywhere, no matter what the accidents of geography, color, language, degree of advancement, or other superficial differences, are people like ourselves and are worthy of respect. In his farewell address to the General Assembly in 1929, he spoke of better understanding of non-Christian peoples: "These closer contacts have enabled us to see that they are men and women of like passions with ourselves, capable of development, responsive to friendship, worthy of respect . . . We now know that there is only one race and that is the human race."[7]

3. that in making decisions the most important factor is the main aim, the primary purpose, the desired long-term end, not any lesser factors of habit or tradition, or forms of organization, or prerogatives of persons. In his 1909 Report he comments on arguments against a plan of cooperation proposed by the Japanese church: "They emphasize secondary considerations rather than primary ones. One misses a large view of the question as it concerns the cause of Christ irrespective of local difficulties."[8] In another place he wrote, "It is often necessary to remind ourselves of fundamental principles, lest we allow sporadic and exceptional cases to drift us into policies which are antagonistic to our true aims."[9]

4. that Christians can and should cooperate without having to agree on everything. Brown wrote at retirement in 1929: "If a man believes in God as Sovereign and Father, in the Bible as the revelation of the will of God, in Jesus Christ as the propitiation for our sins and for the sins of the whole world, I am willing to unite with that man or to cooperate with him on any practicable terms, whether I agree with him in other matters or not. Face to face with the tremendous issues of the non-Christian world, the question is not whether Asia or Africa or Latin America shall be Presbyterian, or Episcopalian, or Methodist, but whether they shall be Christian."[10]

5. that the Gospel of Christ can be communicated, and must be expressed, by word and deed together. "Appointees for medical missionary service are charged to regard themselves not merely as ambulance surgeons at the bottom of a precipice to care for those who have fallen over, but as health officers active in preventive measures at the top . . . All this is deemed not simply an adjunct or a by-product of missionary work, but an integral part of it, a work inspired by a conviction that the Gospel should be expressed as Christ himself expressed it, in humanitarian deeds as well as in spoken words."[11]

These axioms, derived from the Gospel, simple as they are, would doubtless win the immediate verbal assent of most Christians, but all too often they are forgotten or give way to the pressures of self-seeking, or the immediate zeal of controversy, or the pall of inertia. Brown acted on them with unswerving loyalty, and in so doing provided us with a legacy that we would do well to claim and use.

Policies Responding to Change

As early as 1907 Brown had written, in reference to Japan, China, and India, "The growth of the native Church in numbers and power has developed within it a strong nationalistic feeling, a conviction that the natives should be independent of foreign control in religion as in government."[12] (In the foreword to the 1950 revision of *The Foreign Missionary*, Brown remarks, "If I were re-writing the entire book I would probably substitute 'national' for 'native' and 'non-Christian' for 'heathen.' " But he explains the original unpejorative meanings of these terms and considers it unnecessary to incur the expense of changing plates for merely verbal alterations. In his later books Brown uses the more modern terminology.) The prophetic note in Brown's thinking is seen in these further words written in 1907: "If there is ever to be a self-supporting, self-governing, and self-propagating native Church, the missionary must anticipate the time when it will be in entire control . . . The mission has been paramount and expected to run everything . . . But a native Church has now been created, and from now on we must concede its due share of responsibility for making the gospel known and for directing the general work . . . The mission is a temporary and diminishingly authoritative body, and the native Church is a permanent and increasingly authoritative body . . . A policy which builds up a big, all-powerful and all-embracing foreign mission is inherently and radically unsound."[13]

In the additional pages of the 1950 revision, Brown does not go essentially beyond the positions stated in the original edition, but simply reinforces them. "Most of these National Churches still need, and plainly say they do, the assistance of the older churches . . . But they rightly want this assistance given in a spirit of brotherhood and with due recognition of their primary responsibility in their own country . . . The modern missionary in most mission fields is no longer the supreme authority responsible only to his Board in America or Europe, and 'native' pastors and evangelists are no longer his 'helpers.' He is a helper himself, working under a National Church."[14]

The report of Brown's 1909 visit to Japan deals at length with the relation of the mission to the "Native Church." Indeed the subtitle of the report is "The Problem of Missionary Relationship to an Imperial Nation and a Self-Governing Church." The following sentences, we need to remember, were not written in 1949 or 1959, but in 1909.

Hitherto, throughout the non-Christian world, the Mission and the Board have been virtually supreme. Questions on the field have been decided by the organized body of missionaries, subject only to the approval of the Board. This is inevitable during the early stages of the work when there is no Native Church . . . As the Native Church grows in number and power, it is equally natural that this state of things should be disturbed. Now in Japan, a self-governing, self-propagating, self-supporting Native Church has developed . . . Manifestly the Mission and the Board can no longer do as they please without reference to the judgment of such a Church.[15]

Our responsibility for a people continues after the Church is in the field, but it continues through and in cooperation with the Church and not independently of it.[16]

If we are going to work for the Native Church, we must work with the Native Church.[17]

Our policy in its practical operation has not sufficiently taken into account the development of the Native Church and the recognition of its rights and privileges. We have built up Missions emphasizing their authority and dignity, and kept them separate from the Native Church, until, in some regions at least, the Mission has become such an independent centralized body, so entrenched in its station compounds and with all powers so absolutely in its hands, that the Native Church feels helpless and irritated in its presence.[18]

It seems to me indisputable that the time has already come, in some places, and is swiftly coming in others, when the Native Church is reaching self-consciousness, when it is restive under the domination of the foreigner, and when it is desirous of managing fully its own affairs.[19]

Although in the 1950s and early 1960s Arthur Judson Brown was no longer at the center of action, he lived to see the fulfillment of many of the policies that his earlier words had prophetically expressed, as "mission" organizations were abolished, and the full responsibility for mission was transferred to national churches.

Brown in similar fashion anticipated many of the achievements of Christian cooperation and unity that emerged in the years following his retirement. He was an indefatigable champion of union churches. In the report of his 1901 visit to China, he quotes an 1889 policy statement of the Presbyterian Board of Foreign Missions: "The object of the foreign missionary enterprise is not to perpetuate on the mission field the denominational distinctions of Christendom, but to build up on Scriptural lines and according to Scriptural principles and methods the Kingdom of our Lord Jesus Christ." He goes on to cite a 1900 board action approved by the General Assembly: "We encourage as far as practicable the formation of union churches in which the results of the mission work of all allied evangelical churches should be gathered, and that the missions observe everywhere the most generous principles of missionary comity."[20]

Brown frequently took aim at the objection to church union, in the United States or in the lands of the developing national churches, embodied in what he calls "the familiar refrain": "The time is not ripe." He wrote in his *Memoirs*: "The first time I heard that was seventy-three years ago at the Presbyterian General Assembly in 1884."[21] At the meeting of the World Council of Churches in Evanston in 1954 a revered bishop thanked God for the evident spirit of unity but added, "The time is not ripe. We should await the Will of God. We cannot hurry Him." Brown comments, "Fortunately, I was not present, or I would have been tempted to shout: 'The time has been ripe for fifty years. The will of God is written across the sky.' " Back in 1915 Brown wrote, "We are told that 'conditions are not ripe' for organic union. This objection confuses men with Providence. Conditions have been ripe for a dozen years." And he then delivers a delightful final jab: "It is the objectors that are unripe."[22]

"Morning Is in My Heart"

Throughout Arthur Judson Brown's life, perhaps because he was always ready to adapt to changing conditions, and certainly because he was convinced of the eternal truth and the enduring power of the Gospel of Christ, he was an optimist. After explaining the discouraging obstacles to comity in the newly opened Philippines in 1901, Brown says, "But I am not ready to admit that comity is a failure. I cannot admit that it is our duty to perpetuate on the foreign field the blunder which has crowded our American towns with rival congregations. Comity is right. Comity is coming. Let us not be discouraged by obstacles."[23] After enumerating the difficulties facing the Christian mission by reason of the chaotic conditions created by the Chinese Revolution in 1911, Brown wrote in 1912, "It would not be fair, as it would not be Christian, to discover the difficulties of the future apart from the influence which the Gospel of Christ has in modifying these difficulties."[24]

At his 100th birthday dinner, Brown proclaimed, "Under the troubled surface of our material world and through all the vicissitudes of mortal time runs the majestic current of the Divine purpose of righteousness and peace. I know that there are pessimists abroad, but I am an incorrigible optimist, not because I underestimate the power of evil, but because I believe in the transcendent power of the sovereign Lord."[25]

In one of his last interviews Brown remarked, "Though my clock of time points to an evening hour, morning is in my heart."[26]

Very few of us are given the length of years accorded to Arthur Judson Brown – the thirty-four years of his main career as a board secretary from 1895 to 1929 (age 38 to 72) were matched by an additional thirty-four years of retirement from 1929 to 1963 (age 72 to 106!) – but we can make the most of our given span of years, early and late, as we share the attitude of faith-inspired optimism that galvanized his tireless obedience to the Gospel's imperatives of mission and unity.

Notes

Where there is no author attribution, references are to works by Brown.

1. *Memoirs*, p. 167.
2. Ibid., p. 16.
3. Ibid., p. 41.
4. *Unity and Missions*, p. 7.
5. *1902 Report, China*, p. 161.
6. *One Hundred Years*, p. 1082.
7. *The Trend of the Kingdom*, p. 7.
8. *1909 Report*, p. 46.
9. *The Foreign Missionary* (rev. ed., 1950), p. 310.
10. Wysham interview, *Presbyterian Life*, Nov. 24, 1956, p. 24.
11. *Memoirs*, pp. 46-47.
12. *The Foreign Missionary* (rev. ed., 1950), pp. 295-96.
13. Ibid., pp. 296-97.
14. Ibid. (rev. ed., 1950), pp. 318a-318b.
15. *1909 Report*, pp. 31-32.
16. Ibid., p. 34.
17. Ibid., p. 47.
18. Ibid., p. 56.
19. Ibid., p. 58.
20. *1902 Report, China*, p. 99.
21. *Memoirs*, p. 43.
22. *Unity and Missions*, p. 84.
23. *1902 Report, Philippines*, p. 35.
24. *The Chinese Revolution*, p. 207.
25. *Memoirs*, p. 171.
26. Wysham interview, *Presbyterian Life*, Nov. 24, 1956, p. 22.

Selected Bibliography

Books by Arthur Judson Brown

1902 *Reports on Tour of Asia: China, Korea, Philippines, Siam, Syria*. New York: Presbyterian Board of Foreign Missions.
1903 *The New Era in the Philippines*. Old Tappan, N.J.: Revell.
1904 *New Forces in Old China*. Old Tappan, N.J.: Revell.
1907 *The Foreign Missionary*. Old Tappan, N.J.: Revell. Rev. eds. 1932, 1950.
1908 (with Samuel M. Zwemer) *The Nearer and Farther East*. New York: Macmillan.
1909 *Report on Second Visit to China, Japan and Korea*. New York: Presbyterian Board of Foreign Missions.
1909 *The Why and How of Foreign Missions*. New York: Missionary Education.
1912 *The Chinese Revolution*. New York: Student Volunteer Movement.
1915 *Rising Churches in Non-Christian Lands*. New York: Missionary Education.
1915 *Unity and Missions*. Old Tappan, N.J.: Revell.
1917 *Russia in Transformation*. Old Tappan, N.J.: Revell.
1919 *The Mastery of the Far East*. New York: Scribners. Rev. ed. 1921.
1925 *The Expectation of Siam*. New York: Presbyterian Board of Foreign Missions.
1928 *Japan in the World of Today*. Old Tappan, N.J.: Revell.
1936 *One Hundred Years*. Old Tappan, N.J.: Revell.
1957 *Memoirs of a Centenarian*. Ed. William N. Wysham. New York: World Horizons.

Pamphlets (all published by the Presbyterian Board of Foreign Missions, New York)

1905 *The Lien-Chou Martyrdom*.
1912 *The Korean Conspiracy Case*.

1914 *Why Foreign Missions Cannot Retrench Because of the War.*
1918 *Foreign Missions and the War – General Assembly Address.*
1924 *The World-wide Work of the Presbyterian Church – General Assembly Address.*
1929 *The Trend of the Kingdom – General Assembly Address.*
1956 (interview with William N. Wysham) *Presbyterian Life*, Nov. 24.

Note re Arthur Judson Brown Papers

By Martha Lund Smalley, Archivist, Yale Divinity School Library

A substantial collection of papers documenting the life and work of Arthur Judson Brown was donated to the Yale Divinity School Library by his daughter in 1967. These papers include nine linear feet of correspondence, diaries, writings, printed material, photographs, and memorabilia. The varied aspects of Brown's career are reflected in extensive correspondence with prominent religious, political, and social leaders such as William Jennings Bryan, John R. Mott, Nathan Söderblom, and Robert E. Speer. Numerous letters document Brown's connections with missionaries and Christian leaders overseas, particularly in China. Valuable and unique information is provided by the diaries that Brown kept while on trips abroad in 1901-2 and 1909. The seventeen diary volumes recording his experiences in Asia during a fifteen-month tour beginning in February 1901 include descriptions of professional conferences and meetings; visits to hospitals, schools, and churches; personal impressions and travel adventures in Japan, Korea, China, the Philippine Islands, Siam, India, Arabia, Palestine, and Syria. The record of his time in Peking, for example, documents meetings with missionaries of various Protestant denominations, a visit with the Roman Catholic bishop, and an interview with Sir Robert Hart, inspector general of Imperial Maritime Customs. The Boxer Rebellion and subsequent indemnity questions figure prominently in these volumes. Few researchers have delved into the resources available in the Arthur Judson Brown papers at Yale, a fact reflected in the dearth of published writings about Brown. The Brown papers contain one typescript draft of an article about Brown (for publication in the *Phi Gamma Delta*). The Yale catalog does not list any published writings or dissertations about Brown. A seventy-page register describing the Arthur Judson Brown papers is available upon request to the Archivist, Yale Divinity School Library, 409 Prospect Street, New Haven, CT 06510.

Robert E. Speer
1867–1947

Affirming the Finality of Christ

H. McKennie Goodpasture

The missionary movement has been deeply indebted to many of its lay leaders over the years. One of them was Robert Elliott Speer (1867-1947), evangelist, mission theorist, administrator, spokesman, and historian in the first half of this century.[1] Luther Weigle, former dean of Yale Divinity School, wrote, "Let no one think . . . that Robert E. Speer was simply a great missionary leader of the generation that is past; he was a prophet for the present day and for those that are to come."[2] John A. Mackay, president of Princeton Seminary for many years, former missionary in South America and a close associate of Speer, referred to him as "one of the greatest figures in American Christianity. Judged by any standard intellectual or spiritual, Dr. Speer was incomparably the greatest man I have ever known."[3] Many of our elders remember hearing Speer speak. They often refer to his "majestic presence" on the platform and to the unusual spiritual power in his addresses.

An outline of Speer's life is easy to make. He was a Pennsylvanian and was educated at Phillips Academy in Massachusetts and at Princeton University. After graduation, he spent a year itinerating for the Student Volunteer Movement and then studied a year at Princeton Seminary. Without finishing seminary and without ordination, he accepted in 1891 a position on the staff of the Presbyterian Board of Foreign Missions in New York and stayed there until retirement in 1937. In 1893 he married Emma Doll Bailey, who had a Quaker background and was also a Pennsylvanian. She was a graduate of Bryn Mawr and came to be a prominent leader in the church. For many years she was president of the National Board of the Young Women's Christian Association. She accompanied her husband on many of his travels, and her intellectual and spiritual companionship deepened his thought. Among other things, her interests encouraged him to be an early advocate of women's rights. Speer's books, lectureships, travels, memberships on boards of trustees, chairman and moderatorships, and presidencies were all taken on while he was secretary of the Board of Foreign Missions. He died in 1947 after an active retirement. During his life, he wrote sixty-seven books and numerous articles; many of the books were collections of his addresses. They read well today, and their publication gives evidence of his care in preparing them. As I studied these, I found that his volume entitled *The Unfinished Task in Foreign Missions*, a series of lectures delivered at Union Seminary in Virginia in 1926, gives a convenient introduction to his thought as a whole.[4] Moreover, it provides us insight into his legacy to missiologists and mission studies. It can be examined under four headings.

Interpreter of the Purpose of "Foreign Missions"

Speer was, perhaps first of all, an interpreter of the purpose of foreign missions. In a period of exuberant expansionism of Western powers in which the missionary movement was a participant, this mission board secretary emphasized the proclamation of the Gospel above all else. As we read what Speer wrote in the 1890s and early 1900s, we see that he was to some extent a child of his age and culture. He shared the optimism over Western democracy and progress; he attributed much of it to its Christian heritage.[5] He was at the same time critical of much in American life. He knew there was paganism and immorality here and he pointed it out. However, relative to what seemed to be grim, retarded conditions in places like Puerto Rico, Cuba, the Philippines, or Shanghai, Speer considered the intervention of American power to be liberating and civilizing. He was influenced by the times in which he lived but not captive to them, because he was committed to one whose claims took priority over all others. That one was "the man Christ Jesus."[6] The purpose of foreign missions, he said, speaking in 1900, had to do with "implanting the life of Christ in the hearts of men." In a time of uncritical optimism about the benefits of Western civilization he made his position clear. The aim of missions was not "the total reorganization of the whole social fabric. I had rather plant one seed of the life of Christ under the crust of heathen life than cover that whole crust over with the veneer of our social habits, or the vesture of Western civilization."[7]

How did proclamation relate to social justice? This leads to a second observation. Speer interwove evangelism with his concern for social uplift and all along insisted that faith was primary. In 1902 he wrote, "It is impossible that any human tyranny should live where Jesus Christ is King."[8] From our perspective, many wars and injustices later, that sounds naive, but in a time when Western culture was accepted as king, his calling attention to the ultimate King was crucial. In 1919 he wrote:

> The Board I serve has 1,721 schools and colleges and 191 hospitals and dispensaries. It has asylums for orphans, lepers and the insane, schools for the blind and the deaf and dumb, printing presses, homes for tuberculosis patients; and men and women are needed for these and truly serve Christ in these; and rightly conducted these are not only agencies of evangelization, they are evangelization.[9]

Yet Speer went on to make the point that in spite of all these services he was convinced that the Gospel was central, and the direct, unencumbered approach of the apostle Paul inviting listeners to faith was still primary.

In his lectures in Richmond in 1926, he raised the question about the way in which the kingdom of God was to be made visible. It shall come, he said,

> By many forces wielded by the purpose of God, – good government and honorable trade and true education, care for human health, the production and conservation and just distribution of wealth, man's fuller knowledge of himself and of his brothers and of the world. The mission enterprise does not speak slightingly of these or of any of the unnumbered ways in which God is advancing His purpose of righteousness and unity upon the earth. But it believes that it is doing His work in the most central and fundamental way of all. "How do you plan to help Persia?" we asked a young Christian man in Tabriz. In his own English he replied, "By preaching Christ in the crucified style." That is the one supreme business of missions, "Preaching Christ in the crucified style, – Crucified and Risen."[10]

One of Speer's legacies was this firm union of the practical demonstration of God's love with the proclamation of the Gospel, giving priority to the latter.

Historian of Mission

While Speer was an interpreter of the purpose of mission, he was also one of its historians. His books and articles in this area drew on various sources. For example, he had the interesting lifetime habit of reading, on the average, two books a week. He read large amounts in the areas of history, biography, world religions, and political science, with special interest in Asia and Latin America. He was a frequent traveler in those areas and always combined the trips with consultations and board meetings. His reading knowledge was supplemented and corrected by those encounters and by the study documents that inevitably preceded them. Turning to his writings, we find a series of essays on nineteenth-century subjects such as the Taiping and Boxer rebellions in China, the midcentury mutiny in India, the transformation of Japan in the Meiji era, and the emancipation of the Latin American republics in the 1820s. In later books he returns to these geographic areas for twentieth-century subjects. Interspersed were biographies and a history of Presbyterian missions.

Reading over these, one finds that Speer was a historian with a double purpose. He wished to describe a particular area and period in such a way as to reveal the resources and needs of the people about whom he was writing. And second, he wished to show the healing effect of Christian witness and the continued challenge before it. One of his lectures in Richmond in 1926 illustrates his approach. He called it "The Present Situation in South America."[11] He was not a beginner in this field; he had written extensively on it in 1909 and 1912.[12] In 1913 he was an organizer of the Committee on Cooperation in Latin America, which continues today as an area unit in the National Council of Churches (NCC/USA). He chaired that committee for many years and saw it through two landmark congresses, one in Panama in 1916 and the other in Montevideo in 1925. He was an editor of the two-volume report which emerged from the second of these.[13]

His Richmond lecture on South America was based on this accumulation of study. The intellectual climate across the southern republics was changing, he said. In earlier decades Latin prophets had spoken of theirs as a "sick continent" with an impoverished inner life, but in 1925 there was new hope for a cultural and moral renaissance. The evidence for this was in the new concern for public education and public health, for the rights of women, and for the right of labor to organize.[14] He documented each of these and then turned to inter-American relations, which he saw deteriorating. He quoted Julius Klein, who at the time was director of the United States Bureau of Foreign and Domestic Commerce:

Our total trade with Latin America, exports and imports, has increased two and a half times in the last ten years, rising from a pre-war average of about $730,000,000 to $1,800,000,000 in 1924 . . . American capital has a dominant position in such basic industries as mining on the West Coast and in Mexico, meat packing in the River Plate region, petroleum in Mexico, Colombia and Peru, and sugar and tobacco in Cuba. Significant advances are also probable along certain lines in Brazil.[15]

These facts, Speer told his audience, had led to a widespread fear among Latin Americans, a fear, he said, of what Manuel Ugarte called "the imperialistic tendencies of the United States," and which an Argentine scholar called "the egotistic motive . . . that guides the United States . . . [that is] the conquest of our markets."[16] This growing alienation of the continent disturbed Robert E. Speer. A basic part of the answer, he said, was spiritual. He informed the Richmond seminary community of this history with a view toward their helping to restrain North American acquisitiveness. As for the Latin Americans, who suffered injustices both from without and from within and who historically had lacked an effective social conscience, the problem lay in the inadequate Christology inherited from Spain and Portugal. The image of Christ that was deeply embedded in the culture was anemic and docetic. For Speer the answer to the problem lay not in proselytism by Protestants but in irenic, persistent evangelical witness. A "prophetic spirit" and an "adequate embodiment" of it are, he said, the best contribution Protestants could make to the Latin American peoples, to their traditional church, and to inter-American relations.[17]

Ecumenical Pioneer

Robert E. Speer was an interpreter and historian of mission. He was also an ecumenical pioneer. Several illustrations of this dimension of his work have already been mentioned. We can add his presidency of the Federal Council of Churches in 1920 and his responsibilities in the International Missionary Council, a parent body of the World Council of Churches. The point is that Speer was committed to unity in Christian witness and service. In several ways he implemented his commitment in the "mission fields." First, he worked for the emergence of genuine national churches. The aim, he said, was "to plant and set in the way to autonomy and self-maintenance the Christian Church in nations where it did not exist."[18] Second, he worked for church union. He put it this way in 1910:

> The churches, which it is the aim of foreign missions to found . . . ought . . . to be united churches. They are not a set of imported denominations or western churches orientalized. For we are not trying to spread over the world any particular view of Christian truth or any particular form of Christian organization. I belong to the Presbyterian Church, but I have not the slightest zeal in seeking to have the Presbyterian Church extended over the non-Christian world. I believe in one church of Christ in each land, and that it is far more important that the Presbyterians of Japan should be related to the Methodists of Japan than that either of these bodies should possess any connection whatever with any ecclesiastical organization in the United States.[19]

The third concern of Speer was to avoid prolonged paternal care of younger churches. "The aim of the foreign missionary is like the doctor's – to make himself unnecessary." Missionaries are "to plant Christianity in each nation . . . foster its growth . . . and then withdraw . . . They are not the church. They are simply the founders and helpers of it." Speer then went on to make the point that this planting had "not yet been adequately done."[20] Thus the title of his lecture series in 1926: "The Unfinished Task of Foreign Missions." Speer's sharp distinction between mission and church has had to be modified in recent decades, but his fear of paternalism is still valid.

It is interesting to note that in the conclusion of his lectures in 1926 he alluded to what our generation has witnessed, the demise of the colonial era, at least its political phase. For the missionary implications of this, Speer quoted K.T. Paul, a church leader in India:

> If the day of the British "Ruler" is done, so is the day of the foreign "Teacher." It is in no spirit of arrogance, but in honest difficulty that India desires its friends from abroad to come in the attitude of fellow-students and fellow-workers.[21]

This issue has, of course, come into full bloom over the past two decades or so. Speer saw it clearly on the horizon. From Speer's legacy we can be sure that he would have welcomed the six-continent approach to mission and the ecumenical exchange of personnel that goes on in our day.

Witness amid the Religions

Another aspect of this Pennsylvania layman's work is of particular interest today. Speer was a consistent champion of the finality of Christ amid the religions of the world. It was a theme he touched repeatedly in his books. Two experiences give us insights into his theological position. The first was the fundamentalist-modernist controversy in the 1920s in the Presbyterian Church in the U.S.A. This is not the place for details, except to say that the contest was fought on three battlegrounds: the Board of Foreign Missions, the General Assembly, and Princeton Seminary.[22]

Speer was executive secretary of the one, moderator of the other (1927-28), and on the Board of Directors of the third. The basic issue was whether those institutions would be characterized by "a broad and warm evangelicalism on the one hand" or a "highly rational orthodoxy and extreme literalism on the other." All three opted decisively for the former and broader position. According to a leading historian on the period, it was Robert E. Speer who did "more in forming the theological policy of the Presbyterian Church than perhaps any other individual."[23] His theology gave him convictions and a generosity of spirit which would brook no inquisition within the church.

The second experience grew out of the report which W.E. Hocking and others published in 1932 called *Re-thinking Missions: A Laymen's Inquiry after One Hundred Years*.[24] Speer appreciated many of the recommendations of the report, which aimed at the improvement of educational, medical, and other mission services. In the matter of the interreligious encounter, however, he felt that the report left an uncertain place for the person of Jesus; it implied that Christian truth was not absolute but relative. Speer soundly rejected that part of the report and wrote extensively to make his position clear.[25]

His position in regard to the other religions contained two major thrusts, and the first was more important than the second. The first had to do with the finality and incomparability of Christ, and the second with the consequent superiority of Christianity over the other religions. In the first place, he sought to set forth Jesus Christ as absolutely unique and as the full revelation of God.

It is not enough to say that the central thing in Christianity is Christ. Christ is not only the centre. He is also the beginning and the end. He is all in all . . . If there were any words that one could use or any mode of approach to this one supreme issue which would more highly exalt Jesus Christ or make more clear and vivid the faith that He is God and the Son of God, not to be classified in any human category, and the One Saviour from sin and the One Answer to all the need of the world, the writer would use those words and pursue that approach.[26]

This was his main theme; he drew his support for it from Scripture and from an array of witnesses out of church history.

In the second place, he insisted upon the superiority of Christianity. To the Richmond seminarians in 1926 he outlined his consistent position.[27] Christianity is universal; its conception of God is superior. It is "the only religion . . . which clearly diagnoses the disease of humanity . . . and . . . attempts . . . radically to deal with it." Further, Christianity is "historical, progressive and spiritually free." It possesses an ethical uniqueness and "contains all the good and truth . . . found in any other religion, and is free from the evils" which they contain. On the basis of these arguments, he concluded that Christianity was "absolute" and "must displace all that is partial or false. It must conquer the world." Its attitude to other religions is "not one of compromise, but one of conflict and conquest. It proposes to displace the other religions."[28] In his readable and influential work *The Finality of Christ* (1933), Speer continually equated the Christian religion, or sometimes the "ideal Christianity," with Jesus Christ. Therefore, the ideas of "conquest" and "displacement" referred to Christ's owns conquering and were no problem for him; indeed, he saw them as necessary.[29]

What do we say with regard to this part of Speer's legacy? Many will agree with him. Others will wish to preserve his high Christology, yet modify his view of the religious traditions of others and demur to his stating that Christianity was superior. The latter involves semantics, since by Christianity Speer meant the ideal content of the faith, whereas today it is usually used to refer to both the faith and practice of Christians, and neither has been ideal. The issue is important. Speer's missiology tended to be church-centered; many today would wish to hold differently. Perhaps it is the prevenience of the triune God and his participation in the meeting with people of other faiths that some will miss. However, Speer's straightforward insistence that God abhors and works to overcome that which is evil, destructive, and false, and his clear affirmation that the true and full life God intended for people comes only in Jesus Christ are both legacies that many today will wish in turn to pass on to their heirs.

Robert E. Speer was a towering figure in American and world Christianity in the first half of this century. We have named at least four elements of his large bequest, which missiologists today will recall with gratitude: (1) his clarity about the purpose of mission, (2) his careful exposition of the history and contemporary condition of various people and churches, (3) his resolve to promote ecumenical consultation and action, and (4) amid religious pluralism his unequivocal confession of Jesus Christ as the King of kings and the Lord of lords and therefore the ultimate standard for moral and religious judgments.

Notes

1. Much of the material in this article appeared first in *Affirmation* 1, no. 5 (September 1973): 25-34. This is an occasional publication of Union Theological Seminary in Virginia.

2. Quoted in W. Reginald Wheeler, *A Man Sent from God: A Biography of Robert E. Speer* (New York: Fleming H. Revell Co., 1956), p. 270.

3. John A. Mackay, "Robert Elliot Speer," *Princeton Seminary Bulletin* 60, no. 3 (June 1967): 11, and 41, no. 3 (Winter 1948): 26.

4. New York: Fleming H. Revell Co., 1926.

5. See R.E. Speer, *Missionary Principles and Practice* (New York: Fleming H. Revell Co., 1902), chaps. 12, 36. See also his *Missions and Modern History*, 2 vols. (New York: Fleming H. Revell Co., 1904), chaps. 2, 4; vol. 2, chap. 10.

6. See R.E. Speer, *Studies of the Man Christ Jesus* (New York: The International Committee of Young Men's Christian Association, 1896).

7. Speer, *Missionary Principles*, pp. 34, 35, 37.

8. Ibid., p. 34.

9. R.E. Speer, *The Gospel and the New World* (New York: Fleming H. Revell Co., 1919), p. 164.

10. Speer, *The Unfinished Task of Foreign Missions* (New York: Fleming H. Revell Co., 1926), pp. 347-48.

11. Ibid., pp. 218-69.

12. R.E. Speer, *Missions in South America* (New York: Board of Foreign Missions, Presbyterian Church in the USA, 1909); *South American Problems* (New York: Student Volunteer Movement for Foreign Missions, 1912).

13. R.E. Speer, Samuel G. Inmann, and F.K. Sanders, eds., *Christian Work in South America: Official Report of the Congress on Christian Work in South America, at Montevideo, Uruguay, April, 1925*, 2 vols. (New York: Fleming H. Revell Co., 1925).

14. Speer, *The Unfinished Task*, pp. 220, 237-38.

15. Ibid., p. 233.

16. Ibid., pp. 262-64.

17. Ibid., pp. 255, 261-67.

18. Ibid., p. 272. It had long been his aim; cf. R.E. Speer, *Christianity and the Nations* (New York: Fleming H. Revell Co., 1910), p. 330.

19. Speer, *Christianity and the Nations*, p. 331.

20. Speer, *The Unfinished Task*, pp. 273, 307.

21. Ibid., p. 310.

22. See Lefferts A. Loetscher, *The Broadening Church: A Study of Theological Issues in the Presbyterian Church since 1869* (Philadelphia: University of Pennsylvania Press, 1954), pp. 90-156.

23. Ibid., pp. 105, 147.

24. W.E. Hocking, Chairman, The Commission of Appraisal, *Rethinking Missions: A Laymen's Enquiry after One Hundred Years* (New York: Harper Bros., 1932).

25. R.E. Speer, *The Finality of Jesus Christ* (New York: Fleming H. Revell Co., 1933). See also his "An Appraisal of the Appraisal," *Missionary Review of the World* 55 (January 1933): 7-27.

26. Speer, *The Finality of Christ*, p. 5.

27. For what follows, see Speer, *The Unfinished Task*, pp. 43-54. Also see his *The Finality of Christ*, chap. 5.

28. W.N. Clark, quoted with approval in Speer, *The Unfinished Task*, p. 54.

29. See *The Finality of Christ*, pp. 130, 137, 275-76, 277-78, 287-88, 372-76.

Selected Bibliography

Works by Speer

1898 *Missions and Politics in Asia.* New York: Fleming H. Revell Co.

1901 *Presbyterian Foreign Missions.* Philadelphia: Presbyterian Board of Publication.

1902 *Missionary Principles and Practice.* New York: Fleming H. Revell Co.

1904 *Missions and Modern History.* 2 vols. New York: Fleming H. Revell Co.

1910 *Christianity and the Nations.* New York: Fleming H. Revell Co.

1912 *South American Problems.* New York: Student Volunteer Movement for Foreign Missions.

1926 *The Unfinished Task of Foreign Missions.* New York: Fleming H. Revell Co.

1933 *The Finality of Jesus Christ.* New York: Fleming H. Revell Co.

1933 *"Re-thinking Missions" Examined: An Attempt at a Just Review of the Report of the Appraisal Commission of the Laymen's Foreign Mission Inquiry.* New York: Fleming H. Revell Co.

Works about Speer

Buchanan, John G., et al. "Robert E. Speer." In *Princeton Seminary Bulletin* 42, no. 1 (Summer 1948): 5-17.

Eddy, Sherwood. "Robert E. Speer." In *Pathfinders of the World Missionary Crusade*, pp. 259-70. New York: Abingdon Cokesbury Press, 1945.

Mackay, John A. "Robert Elliott Speer: A Man of Yesterday Today." *Princeton Seminary Bulletin* 60, no. 3 (June 1967): 11-21.

Wheeler, Wm. Reginald. *A Man Sent from God: A Biography of Robert E. Speer.* New York: Fleming H. Revell Co., 1956.

J.H. Oldham

1874–1969

From "Edinburgh 1910" to the World Council of Churches

Kathleen Bliss

Joe Oldham (as he was almost universally called, even in an age of sparse use of Christian names) was the organizing secretary of the World Missionary Conference, usually spoken of as "Edinburgh 1910." Thereafter he was secretary of its Continuation Committee and, from 1921 to 1938, a secretary of the International Missionary Council. Cooperating with the Life and Work Movement, he organized the Oxford Conference on Church, Community and State (1937) and then took the crucial steps that led to the emergence of the World Council of Churches, of which he became, in his last years, honorary president. Throughout his long career he worked for fruitful cooperation among missions, fought battles for their freedom, opened new doors for their service, found them new resources of materials and people. Yet this more-than-busy life was underpinned by a constant reflection on the meaning of the Christian Gospel, the nature of the missionary task, looking always beyond the succession of problems and duties presented by each day to the unfolding of God's mercy and his beckoning call to his church.

Oldham was a prophet, looking out on the world with a keen eye for the acceptable moment at which a blow could be struck against oppression and for justice. "A wily saint" and "the arch-intriguer for good," he was called. Yet well on in his eighties he wrote to a friend, "I think that really I am still the missionary at heart that I used to be in practice in my youth." As his biographer, I can regret that he never wrote a diary or kept letters; he did not want to justify or explain his actions, even the most controversial of them. When I expostulated that a bonfire at the bottom of the garden might be consuming several Ph.D. theses, he replied, "Thank God for that; young men should be thinking about the future." He thought of himself as an enabler. And so he was – on the grand scale.

The Educating of a Missionary Internationalist

Joseph Houldsworth Oldham was born in India on October 20, 1874. He was the eldest son of Colonel George Oldham of the Royal Engineers, whose work in Bombay was the building of the railways that did so much to alleviate the scourge of recurrent famine. George Oldham's conversion led him to leave the fashionable suburb of Bombay, where his position entitled him to an excellent house, and to move to a poor part of the city where he shared a mission bungalow with an Indian family. Joe Oldham thus spent the first years of his life with Indian children as playmates. His schooling was in Scotland; he passed from Edinburgh Academy as "dux" of the school (1892) to Trinity College, Oxford. He was attracted to the idea of the Indian Civil Service as a career, but two events changed his course: his conversion at an evangelistic meeting conducted in Oxford by the American evangelist Dwight L. Moody, and his signing of the pledge of the Student Volunteer Missionary Union. Through the latter he met John R. Mott on his first visit to Oxford. Mott made a note of him as a "likely lad."

After a year as the first full-time secretary of the Student Christian Movement, Joe Oldham sailed for India in 1897 under the Scottish YMCA, to work in Lahore among students and young Indians employed in government offices. In Lahore Cathedral he was married (October 1898) to Mary Fraser, daughter of the future governor of Bengal Province and sister of Oldham's Oxford friend, Alek Fraser, one of the greatest of all missionary educationists.

Thus began a partnership of sixty years. Childless, they made their home a place of welcome for nephews, children of colleagues abroad (such as the Patons), and for overseas students. Mary, with her fluency in languages and her self-taught shorthand and typing, was an equal partner in much of the personal side of Oldham's work.

Early in 1901 both the Oldhams contracted typhoid. He hovered for days at the point of death, and she, less ill, struggled to nurse him. The medical verdict was absolute: immediate return home to Scotland and no return to India. To Oldham the blow was bitter. He was intensely happy in his work, living all the time with Indians, learning Urdu and thinking deeply about the future of Christianity in India. His letters show his early conviction that only an Indian church could win India for Christ. Sherwood Eddy, an American fellow secretary in the Indian YMCA, and associated with Oldham in the founding of the Student Christian Movement in India, wrote that anyone who sat with him in committee knew "his spiritual consecration and the drive of his strong will." S.K. Datta, who knew him in Lahore, wrote of his brief period there: "He left no buildings or institutions, but he builded mightily in the hearts of a few men," men who, like Datta himself, became dedicated servants of their country and of the Christian church.

Since much of this article will be concerned with Oldham's relations with institutions, it is important to stress this personal side of his legacy. Hundreds of men and women have treasured some conversation with him that set them thinking or persuaded them toward a new job. Comparative strangers would find themselves invited to lunch; overseas visitors to a weekend at the Oldhams' home. He had "read your book or article or letter in the press and would like to have a talk." It is greatly to the credit of the Phelps-Stokes Fund of New York that, realizing the crippling disadvantage of Oldham's severe deafness, they provided him with a hospitality allowance. This enabled Oldham to entertain visitors in private settings where successful discussion was possible.

"As always, it was a memorable thing to meet you. You say a lot without saying it. I have chewed the cud since." That is from one of England's foremost educationists, Sir Michael Sadler. But it could have been a young YMCA secretary, or a young man in industry whose headmaster had pointed him out as a promising fellow.

Back from India in 1901, Oldham entered New College, Edinburgh, to study for the ministry of the United Free Church of Scotland. His academic record includes prizes in Hebrew, Greek, and New Testament. During the duller lectures he worked at German vocabulary (Mary was a fluent German speaker), and after his course he went to Germany, to the University of Halle to study under the foremost professor of missions, Gustav Warneck. Several of the guiding principles of his life in the service of missionary cooperation derive from this period of study.

Oldham was never ordained as a minister, but he held an important assistantship at Free St. George's Edinburgh. (He remained an elder in the church until he moved to England in 1921, when he became an Anglican layman.) He had renewed his contacts with the Student Christian Movement while studying and became, and continued as, chairman of its theological college department. With its secretary, Tissington Tatlow, Oldham started a movement for mission study among the theological colleges and organized a number of joint missions to leading Scottish towns. Even more important for the future was the work he did as organizer of mission study in Scottish churches. From a small office on the Mound in Edinburgh, hundreds of study groups were registered and supplied with materials (written or edited by Oldham), and training schools for lay leadership were organized. The novelty and scale of this work attracted visitors from England, Europe, and America.

All this helps to explain why there was in Scotland not only the enthusiasm for inviting a World Missionary Conference into their midst but the large number of dedicated volunteers willing to do the work needed. It also explains why Oldham was chosen in 1908 to become its secretary.

Steering a New Course

Much has been written about "Edinburgh 1910"; its role as the starting point of the modern ecumenical movement has perhaps been overwritten. It was after all a missionary conference, and it stood firmly in the tradition of the evangelical revival that had done so much to kindle among Protestants the zeal for evangelism to the ends of the earth. So it ought to be assessed as a mission-event, and Oldham's role is set within that event and its outcome. At the end of the conference, when he rose to give out a few notices (he played no part in the debate), the whole company gave him a standing ovation. This was a tribute to the immense thoroughness that he had put into the preparation of the conference, and the skill with which he had brought the mass of preparatory material to ordered form in printed volumes by working closely with the chairmen and secretaries of the commissions, crossing the Atlantic by sea, moving from one continental country and language to another. Certainly one of Oldham's legacies was this pattern of thorough preparation for any world conference of the future.

A more solid tribute to Oldham's achievement as the secretary of the Edinburgh Conference was his appointment to an entirely new post. The conference decided – and it was by no means an easy decision – to set up a continuation committee. The Germans had been pressing for some time for a permanent organ of cooperation. The Americans were won over; the British took more convincing. Once the decision was taken, however, Oldham was the unanimous choice as secretary. But he did not accept with any alacrity. There were no precedents for such an appointment, no United Nations or League of Nations secretariats. Later he said, "I was thrown out on an uncharted sea and told to steer a course."

Temperamentally Oldham was not a man to jump into a situation and hope for the best. Careful preparation was always his watchword. So he prepared meticulously for the first meeting of the Continuation Committee in 1911. The conference report was published and its nine volumes (thanks to the widespread publicity the conference had received, and the amazingly low price) sold like hotcakes. The profit provided a small balance on which to start work until mission boards could decide on permanent financing. Many of the commissions continued the work they had begun at Edinburgh, and there were some lasting achievements, notably in missionary training, in the cooperative production of literature, and in education.

The most important memorandum the first meeting of the committee received was a proposal from the secretary himself. He was concerned with keeping communication alive, and with broadening its scope to include discussion of the interaction between missions and their environment. He proposed "an international review of missions," to be published quarterly. His idea was based partly on the journal that Warneck had started in Germany, and partly on the *Hibbert Journal*, a prestigious British publication characterized by substantial articles of considerable length. The memorandum was an early example of that capacity for what he called "thinking things together," which he possessed himself and looked for in others. His idea was accepted as it stood: the title was to be *The International Review of Missions*, issued quarterly. The committee only added that Oldham must edit it himself. Thus in 1912 began the *IRM* with its well-informed contributed articles and book reviews and the notable annual "review of the year" based on the large amount of information that flowed into Oldham's Edinburgh office. Assisted from an early stage by Georgina Gollock ("Georgie," one of the unsung builders of the ecumenical movement) and with Kenneth Maclennan as business manager, the *IRM* survived World War I, honored on both sides of the struggle for its fair treatment of difficult issues. Oldham continued as editor until 1927.

Those who set up the Continuation Committee of the Edinburgh Conference knew that it would have to give way to some more representative body. It was a rump. There was no financial provision for the two Asian members to attend, and the committee became a meeting of American, Continental, and British members of the home boards of missions. In spite of Oldham's continuous pressure, the Continuation Committee never managed to solve the problem of renewing and extending its membership beyond the Western mission-sending bodies. Behind the apparent difficulties were the hidden fears of alienating their supporters or surrendering their powers. And mission boards were powerful bodies! On the mission field instances of cooperation were on the increase, but mission boards, like their parent churches, were deeply divided by the legacy of the Reformation. To work with them, bringing their leaders into personal knowledge and trust of one another, encouraging them in cooperative projects in literature, missionary training, education, and the study of certain intransigent problems faced by missions (the approach to Muslims, for example), was important work. Oldham threw himself into it with characteristic energy and that gift as a catalyst with which he was so generously endowed. But he knew all the time that there was no future in the Continuation Committee as such. The war only gave the coup de grace to what was bound to be a dying institution.

Steering through the Storms of War

When war broke out in 1914, Oldham and Maclennan transferred their services to the Conference of British Missionary Societies (CBMS) "for the duration." Every accessible member of the Continuation Committee agreed with this step, for the main action on behalf of missions had to be taken in London. All missions suffered shortages and restrictions, but none suffered as did the German missions. German colonies rapidly became theaters of war. In British colonies and India – and the majority of German missions had most of their work in those territories – nearly all German missionaries were repatriated or interned; their mission properties were commandeered by government. It was Oldham's role, as the convener of the Committee on Missions and Governments, to back up the efforts of local missionaries to mitigate the sufferings of German missionaries, to get them released from internment, and (within their limited resources) to carry on some of their work. In India they had considerable success in using the National Missionary Council for a joint approach to the government in Delhi. Oldham did the same in London. Officials at the India Office, the Colonial Office, and even the Foreign Office greeted with astonished relief his mandate to speak on behalf of all the main Protestant missions. He was a frequent visitor and established himself as one who always knew his facts and never went beyond them, who would listen as well as present a case.

William Richey Hogg, in his history of the International Missionary Council, reckons that the principles on which the council always acted in relation to governments were laid down and exemplified by Oldham in these critical war and postwar years, before the council itself had come into being. It is worth saying what they were: Have as little to do with government as is strictly necessary and keep the distinctions clear. Missions have a spiritual task but, as he often used to say "the first duty of government is to govern," a maxim often ignored by protesters, to their own disadvantage. If you *have* to negotiate, act together, prepare and know your facts, be consistent in what you are asking, listen to how the government's spokespersons see things (and it will be a help if, in general, missions have been appreciative of any government actions that have been on the side of justice and the welfare of the governed). Lastly, know your officials and let those who have an underlying sympathy with the Christian cause do some of your work for you!

Late in 1917 everything blew up into a crisis. The Colonial Office informed the Basel Mission, through the British ambassador in Bern, that its properties in West Africa, already in government hands, were to be sold by auction to the highest bidder. Fortunately Oldham already had an unwritten understanding with officials that he would be told of any government moves toward missions. He managed to get a stay of execution; but the real trial would come over the making of a peace treaty. By the time that operation got under way there was a new alignment of missionary forces: American, British, and neutral countries' missionary representatives formed the War Emergency Committee to deal with all matters affecting missions as the result of war and its aftermath. Mott was chairman; Oldham and Maclennan were secretaries.

There were two main issues for the committee's endeavors. One was the German mission properties. Painstakingly the Americans conducted a country-by-country survey of these, and went armed with the results to Versailles, only to discover that the clause confiscating German properties as part of "war debts" was already drafted and they were too late. However, "the wily saint" had been there before them, and clause 438 included an exemption for German mission properties. Far more dangerous than the possible loss of properties was the threatened loss of missionary freedom in British dependencies and in former German colonies that became mandated territories under the League of Nations. Not just the India Office and the Colonial Office were involved. Their policy was dictated by the all-powerful Foreign Office. The British government was adamant that German missions with their large stake in education and their famed knowledge of native languages, should be kept out, probably forever, certainly for the foreseeable future, and all other foreign missionaries should be let in by licence. This was an issue demanding high-level treatment. The British foreign secretary would recognize in the archbishop of Canterbury (Randall Davidson) his equal in a different realm of affairs of state. Davidson happened also to be a man sincerely committed to the missionary cause and a warm admirer of both Oldham and Mott. He presented Oldham's brief to enormous effect, putting into the official mind considerations that had not occurred. How would Americans (with whom the British government was particularly anxious to keep on good terms) react to having their missionaries "vetted" by British officials? How about retaliation against British nationals by other powers? How could they justify letting in traders without limit, who could scarcely be said to be there in the disinterested service of local peoples, and exclude missionaries? As the result of these endeavors the preliminary licensing of missionaries passed to those cooperative bodies that had proved their value in wartime. The system later became a nuisance, but it tided over a difficult period. In the long run German missions recovered almost all their property, and missionaries gradually returned.

Into the picture of the busy activist in the corridors of power let me insert the following from a letter from the Swedish Mission leader Karl Fries, to Frederick Wurz of the Basel Mission. He visited Oldham and others in London in February 1919:

It may seem to you that the results are meagre, but the difficulties he had to overcome were quite enormous. He has sacrificed himself to the point of affecting his health. When we joined in prayer for the Mission, I realized how deeply he has taken the matter of the German missions to heart.

Henry Hodgkin, Quaker member of the Continuation Committee, wrote in the same vein. Prayer runs like a thread through Oldham's life, and W.A. Visser 't Hooft opened his address at the memorial service for Oldham, held in London in June 1969, by referring to the evening prayers in the Oldham household as they met on the eve of the outbreak of World War II. At the busiest period of his life in the mid-1920s, Oldham compiled and published his *Devotional Diary*, and revised and enlarged it two years later. It broke new ground in manuals of devotion and was by far his most popular book. "What did I learn from Joe Oldham?" asked a prominent headmaster. "How to pray in a new way."

Missionary freedom is, of course, a part of the wider issue of religious freedom. It was greatly in peril at the end of World War I, and several groups were concerned to get it established in the peace treaty. Oldham took one highly significantly step. He realized that resolutions even from weighty bodies are liable to bounce off the official mind without leaving a dent, while the quotation of a legal precedent will be fastened on as an acceptable way out of a difficulty. So, on his own initiative, Oldham asked the question, "Why not take the provisions of the Berlin Act of 1885 [by which the colonizing powers in Africa guaranteed, in a central strip of the continent, from the Atlantic to the Indian oceans, free trade, freedom of religion and worship, and protection for traders, scientists, and missionaries] and apply them to all colonial dependencies and former Germany colonies mandated under the League of Nations?" Why not, indeed? It made an essential point of departure. Others completed what Oldham, by this simple action, began.

During the war Oldham thought constantly about the future. What should be the pattern of missionary cooperation? And toward what goals should the missionary effort be directed in what would be, he was sure, a different world?

The first question Oldham answered in a series of exchanges with American colleagues culminating in a proposal drafted by him for an ad hoc advisory conference, subsequently held at Crans, Switzerland (June 1920). Here the International Missionary Council was born, designed to be a council of national or regional councils. Only three such existed: the Auschuss in Germany, the Conference of British Missionary Societies, and the Foreign Missions Conference of North America. All three represented boards and societies sending missionaries, not missions or churches in the field. In a remarkable tour of the Far East in 1912, John R. Mott had gone a long way toward the establishment of such councils when he held follow-up meetings to the Edinburgh Conference and insisted on at least one-third indigenous leaders in their membership. Oldham went out to build on this foundation in India, spending four months in 1922 partly in visiting former German missions, but mainly in sounding out Indian Christian opinion, which was fretting under the tight control that many missionaries and home boards kept on overseas missions and churches. He presented to the national Missionary Council, meeting at Poona, a scheme for a national Christian council, including a proposal that the young and inexperienced YMCA secretary, William Paton, should head a staff that he hoped would be mainly Indian. He saw urgency. Home boards saw precipitate action and unmeetable financial obligations. Oldham went to Canada to follow up promises of support and back again to India in the following year, with a visit to China crowded into the same period. No one who knew the National Christian Council of India would doubt its importance to the Christian churches in India in the ensuing years. Oldham paid a heavy price in health for his travel.

The second question, that of the goals of Christian mission in the changed world of the postwar period, Oldham tackled in his book *The World and the Gospel*. Published in 1916 at the darkest period of World War I, it had the effect of lifting the sights of Christians beyond the horrors of the present to a renewed faith in God's call to mission. Twenty thousand copies were sold in Britain alone. Soberly he reflected that so-called Christian nations had lost all credibility. The church was standing beneath the cross sorely in need of pardon and renewal. That renewal would not come by self-absorption but, as in the past (and he has striking examples), by responding to some new challenge of the Gospel. His whole emphasis was that there is *one* Gospel, and it is entrusted to Christ's *one* church, broken though it may be. There was also emerging *one* world, whose problems, though having different local manifestations, were in essence the same. Oldham held to these views to the end of his life. Wherever the church preaches and exemplifies its Gospel and offers its worship, there it stands for the whole church.

Oldham took his understanding of "one world" from a book by Graham Wallas called *The Great Society*, in which the author spoke of the inexorable grasp on individual lives of worldwide economic and political forces. Today we take for granted that the causes of local poverty or oppression may be half a world away and that the local church needs the wide church. We have institutionalized these insights in organizations for aid. But still we ask, as Oldham did, "Is this not part of mission? Of doing the Gospel we preach?" Like, let us say, any priest organizing a trade union or a boycott, Oldham too went through the hoops of criticism. The battle, he believed, must be engaged where and when the challenge presented itself. From this conviction arose his long concern with Africa. In *The World and the Gospel* he wrote:

> The problem with which we are confronted in Africa is one of the great issues of history. Have we eyes to see its immense significance? Shall the African peoples be enabled to develop their latent powers, to cultivate their peculiar gifts and so enrich the life of humanity by their distinctive contributions? Or shall they be depressed and degraded and made the tool of others, the instrument of their gain, the victim of their greed and lust?

The first encounter came in 1919 when the government in Kenya authorized what amounted to forced labor by African men, women, and children on the private estates of European settlers. District officers were ordered to put on "every legal pressure"; one or two actually refused to comply. Missionaries on the spot said that no more could be done than to ask for some safeguards for women and children. But Oldham (closely in touch with the Anti-Slavery League) thought the issue demanded a sharp challenge to the British government. He therefore wrote a strong letter to the secretary of state for the colonies, but he first had it read and assented to by every member of the Conference of British Missionary Societies. He then published it in the *Times* (London) and orchestrated a massive press campaign. The order was rescinded; the governor was recalled. Oldham knew that humiliated adversaries live to fight again even more bitterly – as Kenya settlers would, and did.

The next encounter took place shortly after Oldham's second visit to India (1923), where he had seen something of the agitation on behalf of the demands of Indians living in Kenya for equal voting rights with whites. He suddenly became a mediator, and the British government got itself off the hook by accepting from him the statement that "the interests of Africans must be paramount." This was endorsed by Parliament in an official statement of policy (July 1923). Thus Oldham was the source of this concept of *paramountcy*, used most recently by British Prime Minister Margaret Thatcher in relation to the Falkland Islanders. As the price for that is "Fortress Falklands," so for Oldham the price for the paramountcy of African interests was constant vigilance.

Far more characteristic of Oldham was his long, patient approach to the British government to persuade it to accept responsibility for providing an educational system for the people of its colonies, and for developing a consistent policy. In fact, he was the anonymous writer of the first statement of that policy. Hand in hand with this went the delicate persuasion needed to get missions to face *together* the opportunities and snares of cooperation with government. Missions cannot possibly provide an educational system, he argued, but they have a vital contribution to make, which should be a contribution of quality. He did not mean by that the large prestigious school;

"the rural school beside the rural church" was also in his thoughts. Oldham got missionary educators to meet with pioneer thinkers and experimenters in education, and with government officials who would have to implement the policies. He visited centers for education of blacks in the United States, sent out a commission on rural education as part of community development, and threw his support behind Florence Allshorn, whose genius was shaping a new form of missionary training and whose biography he later wrote.

Oldham was greatly influenced by the writings of the American philosopher William Ernest Hocking. He took the title of Hocking's book *Human Nature and Its Re-making* and reshaped it for a book that he wrote with Betty Gibson as *The Remaking of Man in Africa*. Later this title was misunderstood. Had he been trying to remake Africans in the Western image? Certainly not. Oldham understood the effects on African traditional life of the incursion of the white person, the breakdown of the tribes and the loss of their land. He wanted to equip Africans, through education, with the tools of a new life, without which they were ripe for exploitation.

What Oldham's critics perhaps did not know was that at the same time he was working to get a proper system of education established by government, he was putting an equal effort into organizing for the study and preservation of African languages and cultures. Alerted in the first instance by American missionaries working in French and Belgian colonies where government policies made French the medium of instruction in schools at so early an age that native language was rapidly lost, Oldham and his German colleague Hans Westermann took the lead in creating the International Institute of African Languages and Cultures. Oldham secured large grants from Rockefeller. The important journal *Africa* started its distinguished course; monographs on aspects of African culture began to appear; researchers were helped. Perhaps most important were the seminars, conducted by the distinguished anthropologist Bronislaw Malinowski, for young anthropologists. Almost all of these students later filled important professorial chairs. With them in the same seminars were missionaries, hand-picked by Oldham to share a unique experience of learning and contributing. When funds ran low in the recession of the early 1930s, Oldham took on the post of administrative director, and the institute contributed a quarter of his salary to the International Missionary Council (1931-38).

In 1924 Oldham published his most influential book, *Christianity and the Race Problem*. A whole generation of Christian students – not to mention many of their elders – had their eyes opened to the challenge of racism by this book. He was invited to South Africa and met church and political leaders. He was present in the Cape Parliament as the first stages of the apartheid policy passed into law with the Colour Bar Act. He was appalled by what he foresaw. On a sheet of paper now in this writer's possession, Oldham wrote: "Agenda for a possible return visit: (1) Race discrimination – the greatest enemy of a humane society." He never returned but went to fight the same battle in East Africa and to serve on the Hilton Young Commission on Closer Union. When the chairman and the government rejected the report, Oldham was left alone to try to rouse public opinion to the issues at stake. He wrote, at the request of the Conference of British Missionary Societies, *What Is at Stake in East Africa: An Appeal to the Christian People of Great Britain* (1930). But Britain was deep in the recession, and the old will to fight injustice, so much alive in 1919, seemed now asleep. Some of Oldham's American colleagues grew sharp in their criticism; what business was it of an officer of the International Missionary Council to rescue the British Empire from its follies? He was ready to resign, if that was their wish.

Oldham's task in Africa was now over except for one punching blow. In 1930 the South African premier and popular World War I hero General Christian Smuts delivered the Rhodes Lectures in Oxford and repeated the gist of them on what was then called "the wireless." This writer can still hear that mellifluous voice coming through the crackling of the old crystal set. There was a new task for white Christian civilization, to spread it from Cape to Cairo up the broad highway of the East African Highlands. Stirrings of an old imperial dream! Oldham slammed back with *White and Black in Africa*. Fifty years later the opening of government papers revealed Smuts in close contact with L.S. Amery, the colonial secretary, urging the necessity to counter moves toward the establishment of native states on the route of his projected civilizing march, and referring to paramountcy as "stupid."

Still the Missionary, but in a New Field

Oldham did not resign – Mott would not let him, for Mott saw that, although Oldham had not been present at the meeting of the International Missionary Council in Jerusalem in 1928, he was already thinking how to make a start on its most important finding. The council identified the growth of a secular view of the world, based largely on science and technology, as a worldwide phenomenon. People's hopes were being directed towards new possibilities of life; religion – all religions – seemed increasingly irrelevant. Oldham saw in these developments a new challenge to evangelism. When he addressed the next meeting of the International Missionary Council in 1929 on "The New Christian Adventure," he commented that more books worth reading were written from the standpoint of scientific humanism than by Christians taking account of the realities of the modern world. This was a new task that ought to be taken up by a rising generation of theologians. He called together a first conference of young theologians from Britain and the Continent, held at York, England (this included the young Visser 't Hooft and Michael Ramsey, future archbishop of Canterbury). Oldham then went to the United States where eager young theologians readily set up for him the sort of groups he could so ably chair and guide.

What then was his missionary message? Emphatically it was not antiscientific. He welcomed the ability of science to lift from people's backs the burdens of poverty, ignorance and disease. But insofar as science tended to present a view of the world as a series of problems that could be mastered by knowledge, it was inadequate. Life does not consist of achieving power over things and people; it is fundamentally *relational*. A person meets another person not as an object but as another autonomous self. One has to learn or relearn what this means. God can never be the object of scientific inquiry or technical manipulation; He is the Other, with whom we have to do. Oldham drew on his rich store of reading and his personal friendship with Swiss and German philosophers. He expounded to students Martin Buber's little classic *Ich und Du* long before it was translated into English as *I and Thou*. Around Oldham there grew a group of intellectuals who called themselves "the Moot" – among them, T.S. Eliot, Karl Mannheim, and Michael Polanyi. All of them acknowledged Oldham's influence.

Besides the intellectual task of mission, aimed at bringing Christianity into encounter with the currents of modern thought, there was another task that occupied Oldham. This was the relation of the church to the contemporary lives of people in society and to the modern state. It has two strands; one is concerned with the problems of the Christian lay man or woman trying (to quote his words) "to find out how the Christian faith bears on the questions which they have to deal with in their daily occupations"; the other is concerned with the far larger questions of the church as an institution in relation to other institutions. For the first, he established the Christian Frontier Council; for the second he accepted the chairmanship of the research department of the Life and Work Movement and carried out the preparations for the Oxford Conference on Church, Community and State (1937). As a follow-up to the latter he launched in 1939 the weekly *Christian News Letter,* which he edited till 1945; it was owned by the Christian Frontier Council.

Thus Oldham had what would have been for other men a life's work after he left the sphere of overseas mission, and it is impossible to do full justice to it here. His books are witnesses to that work. In 1952 he retired to the YMCA college at Dunford near Midhurst in Sussex, where he continued his writing and his friendships. There was a brief African postscript when he wrote, for his friends in the Capricorn Africa Society who were trying to reconcile black and white in central Africa by creating a common citizenship, his last book, *New Hope in Africa*. He was over eighty but his intellectual vigor was unimpaired and his capacity for making new friendships with younger men and women flourished in the atmosphere of this beautiful house (home of the famous nineteenth-century social reformer Richard Cobden). Always a man for walking, he grew to love the Sussex countryside. As physical strength began to fail, he and Mary moved to a nursing home in St. Leonards on sea where he built up yet another library and Mary plied her typewriter, sending letters and memoranda to friends, helping to sort out their ideas and write their books. Predeceased by Mary, he died on May 16, 1969.

Selected Bibliography

Books and Pamphlets by J.H. Oldham

1912 *The Possibilities of Prayer*. London and Edinburgh: T. N. Foulis.
1913 *The Progress of the Movement for Co-operation in Missions*. Swanwick: Conference of Missionary Societies in Great Britain and Ireland.
1916 *The World and the Gospel*. London: United Council of Missionary Education.
1918 *The Comprehensiveness of the Evangelistic Aim*. New York: Association Press.
1920 *The Missionary Situation after the War*. London: Edinburgh House.
1923 *A Devotional Diary*. London: SCM Press.
1924 *Education and Evangelism*. London: The Auxiliary Movement.
1929 *The New Christian Adventure*. London: International Missionary Council.
1930 *The C.M.S. and the Adventure of To-day*. London: Church Missionary Society.
1930 *White and Black in Africa*. London: Longmans, Green.
1931 (with B.D. Gibson) *The Remaking of Man in Africa*. London: Oxford Univ. Press.
1932 *The Christian Message in the Modern World*. London: International Missionary Council.
1935 *Church, Community and State: A World Issue*. London: SCM Press.
1936 *The Question of the Church in the World of To-day*. London: Edinburgh House Press.
1937 *The Oxford Conference (Official Report)*. Chicago: Willett, Clark.
1940 *The Resurrection of Christendom*. London: Sheldon Press.
1942 *Real Life Is Meeting*. London: Sheldon Press.
1950 *Work in Modern Society*. London: SCM Press.
1951 *Florence Allshorn and the Story of St. Julian's*. London: SCM Press.
1953 *Life Is Commitment*. New York: Harper & Row.
1955 *New Hope in Africa*. London: Longmans, Green.

Articles by J.H. Oldham

(*IRM = International Review of Missions*)
1919 "Co-operation – Its Necessity and Cost." *IRM*, April, pp. 173-92.
1919 "German Missions." *IRM*, October, pp. 459-78.
1920 "Christian Education." *IRM*, January, pp. 3-18.
1920 "The Interchurch World Movement: Its Possibilities and Problems." *IRM*, April, pp. 182-99.
1920 "Nationality and Missions." *IRM*, July, pp. 372-83.
1920 "A New Beginning of International Missionary Co-operation." *IRM*, October, pp. 481-94.
1921 "Christian Missions and African Labour." *IRM*, April, pp. 183-95.
1921 "A Philosophical Interpretation of the Missionary Idea." *IRM*, January, pp. 63-76.
1922 "Aim and Function of the National Christian Council Viewed in the Light of Experience in Other Lands: Conference Address." *Chinese Recorder*, June, pp. 399-409.
1922 "New Spiritual Adventures in the Mission Field." *IRM*, October, pp. 526-50.
1923 "Five Conferences in India." *IRM*, April, pp. 262-76.
1923 "Missions and the Supernatural." *IRM*, January, pp. 59-71.
1924 "Christian Education in Africa." *Church Missionary Review*, December, pp. 305-14.
1924 "Religious Education in the Mission Field." *IRM*, October, pp. 500-517.
1925 "The Christian Opportunity in Africa." *IRM*, April, pp. 173-87.

1925 "Educational Policy of the British Government in Africa." *IRM*, July, pp. 421-27.

1926 "Population and Health in India." *IRM*, July, pp. 402-17.

1926 "The Success and Failure of Western Education in India." *IRM*, October, pp. 692-703.

1927 "The Christian Mission in Africa." *IRM*, January, pp. 24-35.

1933 "Professor Brunner on the Christian Ethic." *IRM*, January, pp. 3-16; April, pp. 201-14; July, pp. 331-44; October, pp. 500-509.

1934 "The Educational Work of Missionary Societies." *Africa*, January, pp. 47-59.

1935 "After Twenty-five Years." *IRM*, July, pp. 297-313.

Works about J.H. Oldham

Bliss, Kathleen. "J.H. Oldham." Article in *Dictionary of National Biography*. London: Oxford Univ. Press, 1981.

Clatworthy, Frederick James. *The Formulation of British Colonial Education Policy*. Ann Arbor, Mich.: Univ. of Michigan Press, 1971.

Eddy, George Sherwood. *Pathfinders of the World Missionary Crusade*, pp. 277-86. New York: Abingdon-Cokesbury, 1945, pp. 277-86.

Hogg, William Richey. *Ecumenical Foundations*. New York: Harper, 1952.

Hopkins, C. Howard. *John R. Mott, 1865-1955*. Grand Rapids, Mich.: Wm. B. Eerdmans, 1979.

Martin, W. Lance. "Joseph Houldsworth Oldham: His Thought and Its Development." Ph.D. diss., University of St. Andrews, Scotland, 1968.

Rouse, Ruth, and Stephen Charles Neill, eds. *A History of the Ecumenical Movement, 1517-1948*. Philadelphia: Westminster Press, 1954.

Visser 't Hooft, Willem A. "Oldham Takes the Lead." Chapter 8 in *The Genesis and Formation of the World Council of Churches*. Geneva: World Council of Churches, 1982.

William Paton

1886–1943

A Finger in Every Godly Pie

Eleanor M. Jackson

William Paton (1886-1943) once complained to his son during World War II, "I seem to have a finger in every godly pie there is,"[1] and it was hardly an exaggeration. He was involved at that time with the Religion and Life weeks in Britain and the founding of the British Council of Churches; with the spiritual and physical welfare of thousands of interned aliens and prisoners of war in Britain; with the high-level transatlantic discussions on the creation of a new society after the war (the Peace Aims Group); with the training of pastors and lay workers for the Confessing Church in Britain; fighting to free foreign missionaries from internment camps wherever possible, and to get the ban lifted on American Lutheran missionaries proceeding to India; generally working for religious liberty in colonial countries; raising money for the infant World Council of Churches and its refugee work; receiving clandestine messages from Bonhoeffer and his friends; struggling to rescue Jews whom he knew to be doomed when few others knew or cared; encouraging the formation of the Church of South India and the development of Christian unity everywhere.

A Doer of the Word

Paton's work was catholic and ecumenical in the fullest sense of the words. Paton has been accused of being involved, like William Temple, in too many things at once and of thus spreading himself too thinly, whereas it would have been better if, like J.H. Oldham or W.A. Visser 't Hooft, he had concentrated fully on one task at a time. There was, however, nothing shallow about Paton's work or thought, but rather, it was his genius to bring together differing ideas, people, movements, and institutions and weld them together into a whole. He would make things cohere, whether he was organizing support for stranded missionaries at opposite ends of the globe or holding students or soldiers or townsfolk spellbound with his vision of the worldwide church – the church not as some distant ecumenical ideal but as it really is. As Screwtape says in the *Screwtape Letters* of C.S. Lewis: ". . . the Church as we see her spread out through all time and space and rooted in eternity, terrible as an army with banners. That, I confess, is a spectacle which makes our boldest tempers uneasy. But fortunately it is quite invisible to these humans."[2] Paton did see. Although his sense of history and *Heilsgeschichte* was very weak, he saw the universal challenge in provoking a response to it, and flung himself into the frays. He was essentially a doer of the Word.

Alan Booth, sometime director of Christian Aid, gave one of the best descriptions of Paton's character as it struck him in his student days:

> There was nothing sentimental or "pious" in the bad sense about him, but one of his most attractive features was a certain sort of adolescent mischievous delight which he took in moving about the corridors of power, and, he felt, influencing events. He had some of this responsibility always as a missionary statesman and more particularly of course in the war years when his responsibilities to the I.M.C. [International Missionary Council] in relation to governments was very considerable. He was not above a certain boyish boastfulness and name-dropping but at the same time he was a man of very great wisdom and far-sightedness. He combined a certain evangelical simplicity of faith with a real appetite for handling events and people and manoevering committees.

A student contemporary of his, the Rev. A.J. Haile, remembers his "buoyant and eager personality; his deep base voice and broad grin and hearty laugh marked him in any company. . . his self confidence was never offensive." Like William Temple, he was the source of endless practical jokes, and his four sons and two daughters kept him from any incipient tendency to pomposity in middle age by relentless teasing. His closest friend, Bishop L.S. Hunter, recalls, "William Paton's contemporaries forgave him his forcefulness because he was so obviously first class and worked hard, but there were occasions when he was a little too ruthless and at meetings sometimes a little too compelling, but he was right at the heart of the early days of the ecumenical movement." Sir Kenneth Grubb, who worked with both men, compared him with Churchill (whom Paton could not stand), and said he did not suffer fools gladly,[3] but in fact he had the knack of making fools laugh with him and he had few if any enemies.

He certainly enjoyed the influence he had with politicians, civil servants, journalists and archbishops, but this derived from his wisdom and his extensive knowledge of India and the Far East. Being a lower-middle-class scholarship boy from a minor public school and a small Oxford college, he had no immediate access to the Establishment, and being a member of a small Free Church denomination, the Presbyterian Church of England, no natural platform, such as Temple and Bell had as bishops. He described himself as having a "good second class brain" and would never have claimed to be a theologian. The significance of his life lies in that a man with no social or intellectual advantages was able by sheer faith, vision, and hard work to do great things for God.

Paton was very reticent about his conversion, which seems to have taken place in 1905 in the spring of his first year at Oxford. His parents, who were Scottish but moved to London shortly before his birth in 1886, observed the conventions of Victorian piety, though one of Paton's surviving "unconverted" sisters recollects that the servants had to work on Sunday and there was no grace before meals. An article Paton wrote in 1902 for his school magazine justifies foreign missions on rationalistic but not theological grounds. His conversion was due to the influence of Frank Lenwood of Mansfield College, the chaplain of the Free Church students, who kept at him until he came to a decision, and then set him to work preaching in country churches around Oxford and drew him into the Student Christian Movement. The Student Christian Movement (SCM) of Great Britain was reaching its zenith (10,000 out of a total student population of 44,000 in Great Britain were members in 1910). Paton found himself drawn into mission study, Bible study, and the famous SCM summer camps. D.S. Cairns recalls the way he threw himself into everything, on one occasion singing his head off in a boat on Lake Coniston in order to put the students who were new to SCM camps at their ease. Cairns apparently did not realize that Paton was a newcomer himself![4] Some time about 1908 he signed the famous Student Volunteer Mission Union (SVMU) Declaration: "It is my desire, if God permit, to be a foreign missionary." He was later instrumental in getting the wording changed to: "It is my purpose, if God permit, to undertake foreign missionary service abroad," the change partly due to a desire to emphasize lifelong service to God abroad. When he completed his theological studies at Westminster College, Cambridge, he was asked to become Men's Volunteer Secretary of the SCM (since the SVMU had been integrated into the younger body). Throughout the period of his service in the SCM (1911-21) he was responsible for mission studies, and thereby came to write his best-known book: *Jesus Christ and the World's Religions* (1916, last reprinted in 1956).

While Paton was a student, he was assigned to preach at a Presbyterian church in London. Entering the manse, he fell in love with the minister's daughter, Grace MacKenzie MacDonald (a cousin of Mrs. Henry Pitney Van Dusen), as she came down the stairs to greet him, and she with him. Their turbulent romance, as both sets of parents tried to thwart the match, could have been taken from a Brontë novel. Their great love for each other endured throughout their marriage despite the long separations, the difficulties in raising a family in India (1921-26), and the inevitable tensions when Grace Paton became first an Anglican (1918) and then a Roman Catholic (1936). For Paton, therefore, Christian unity was not something abstract or just part of his job. He had to work it out at home in his family. He let the children be brought up as Anglicans, worshiped at St. Albans Abbey himself (but communicating only four times a year in the Presbyterian manner), and insisted on the validity of his orders.

The family always displayed great solidarity in the face of criticism. They loyally defended Mrs. Paton, whose decision to become a Catholic was in keeping with her mystical temperament and socialist views. (During their furlough in 1926 the Patons helped the railway workers – Paton organized lectures and talks, Mrs. Paton a subsidized canteen – during the General Strike.) When Paton died, a fellow parishioner tried to comfort Mrs. Paton. She stoutly replied that it was all right, that her consolation was in knowing that her husband had gone straight to heaven. The astounded Catholic lady said, since she considered Paton a "heretic," "What? Not even a little bit of Purgatory?"

Grace Paton wrote an excellent book, *The Child and the Nation*, in 1916 about child poverty and the nation's responsibility, anticipating the welfare state with her ideas. She was undoubtedly responsible for bringing Paton to a socialist viewpoint, introducing him to Ramsey MacDonald and Keir Hardie. (Later he was friendly with Tawney.) But he never comprehended Marxism, his son David says, a statement that is borne out by a letter from a friend at Chatham House, the Foreign Office's "Think Tank," who rebuked him for thinking that military victory or political defeat would extinguish Communism, which had to be fought on ideological grounds. He supported independence for India, and came to appreciate Nehru's stand following a meeting with him in 1936. But after the Patons had met Gandhi, it was Grace whom Gandhi wanted to see again, probably because he could see the mystical depths in her.

Paton's Faith

Paton's faith was of a more simple and direct kind, though no less deep. He kept up the SVMU practice of the "morning watch" all his life, and studied his Greek New Testament daily. This faith was particularly necessary to sustain him when he first went out to India in 1917 on secondment to the YMCA of India after a hasty ordination, the result of an anomalous situation whereby Anglican SCM secretaries were ordained before or during SCM service, but Presbyterians were not. Thus Paton before ordination was liable for conscription in 1916. He was a convinced pacifist and a founding member of the Fellowship of Reconciliation, and was in imminent danger of imprisonment and mistreatment (at least seventy pacifists died under such brutality, including those who were forcibly enrolled and then later shot as "deserters").[5] In World War II he was no longer a pacifist, but fought for the right of pacifists to make broadcasts on nonpolitical subjects. (His friend Charles Raven, scientist, ornithologist, and theologian, was banned from giving his popular talks on bird watching.) This was changed when Vaughan Williams said he would not allow the BBC to broadcast his latest symphony unless they revised this policy.[6]

Some words from a broadcast relayed posthumously convey Paton's faith and vision:

> As we look at all these gigantic tasks [of postwar reconstruction] we need to remember that God has set us in this particular historic moment, and that we are in the hands of his providence. What nations can do for good or evil in modern conditions of organized power, is greater than past ages, but we are not in a world of chance, we're in our Father's House, and we need to rise to the height of this historic moment in which we are set, not trusting only in our own cleverness and skill in devising, but far more to His love and guidance.[7]

Paton was entrusted with the final address at the SCM summer conference in Cheltenham in 1943, but to the surprise of his old friends listening, he did not speak about peace aims, or reconstruction of the world mission of the universal church, or any of his usual world-embracing themes. Instead he spoke very quietly of prayer and how one lives the Christian life, though he was normally reticent about his personal faith. His closing statement was, "If you put your life into the hands of God, he will never let you go." These words, spoken a few days before his death, also sum up his faith.

On his visits to America in 1940 and 1942, Paton had once contracted pneumonia. He might have died then, had not a new drug been available in the United States. Weakened by this illness and by the strain of war, as he worked himself to death to assuage worry and grief about his sons – Christopher, who twice survived the sinking of his ship in Kendal in the Lake District; Michael, who was in a tank regiment on the frontier in India; and David, who was in Chungking working for the YMCA of China – he succumbed after an emergency operation in Kendall for a perforated stomach ulcer. Just like Archbishop William Temple's death, the result of a condition acerbated by overwork in 1944, and just like William Elmslie, a Presbyterian church leader, and Father Tribe, S.S.M., an Anglo-Catholic theologian and a member of the British Faith and Order Commission who were both killed by enemy bombs in 1945, so also Paton died as a result of trying to maintain Christian witness and fellowship in the universal church in wartime.

Much of Paton's work that had to do with coordination and organization ended with his death. Norman Goodall, who took over his IMC work, and Oliver Tomkins, who assumed the WCC duties, had to start again from scratch, without Paton's contacts in government and the churches overseas. Bishop G.K.A. Bell took over his work coordinating help for refugees, aliens, and prisoners of war, and his work in establishing a Confessing Church college. In 1942, in the face of all sorts of ecclesiastical difficulties and obstruction from older founding members of the ecumenical movement,[8] Paton and Temple finally got the British Council of Churches organized, thus giving impetus to that peculiarly British kind of ecumenical organization, the local council of churches. Paton traveled throughout the country, preaching at the Religion and Life weeks – described as civic SCM camps, but actually more like the German *Kirchentage*, and based in towns and cities in an effort to evangelize, to stimulate renewal of the church, and to involve as many people as possible in the thinking about postwar reconstruction.

It would make this article far too long to describe his role in the creation of the World Council of Churches and his work as part-time general secretary of the WCC in Process of Formation, in liaison with W.A. Visser 't Hooft, the general secretary based in Geneva.[9] A friend described Paton's efforts to get the IMC to accept integration with the WCC as an attempted shotgun marriage. Being also secretary of the IMC (1927-43), he could integrate his own work, but after his death, the two organizations parted and were not formally merged until 1961, though some departments such as the Churches' Commission on International Affairs worked jointly from 1948. The IMC meetings at Jerusalem (1928) and Tambaram (1938) stand as monuments to his efforts, industry, vision, and powers of persuasion, not to mention the conference material that he edited and sometimes wrote himself.[10] From 1927 to 1943 he was editor of the *International Review of Missions*. He provided logistical support for the IMC's department of Industrial and Social Research (founded in 1930), whose fieldwork brought the problems of industrialization in the Third World and social change home to the missionary societies, and to the International Christian Council for the Approach to the Jews. He got a dynamic young American, Conrad Hoffman, a World's Student Christian Federation (WSCF) worker, appointed as secretary to this body, which was composed mainly of septuagenarian representatives of missions to Jews. Paton considered it anti-Semitism not to preach to Jews, because they deserve the offer of salvation as much as anyone. He would not have understood modern ideas on dialogue, but he rejected charges of deicide against the Jews, saying he was an old-fashioned evangelical who believed that Christ died for his sins and those of all humanity.[11] He also got on very well with his daughter's future parents-in-law, the Montefiores, who were Orthodox Jews of a well-known family.

Paton became convinced by 1938 that Hitler was bent on the extermination of the Jews, though he could not conceive how this would be technically possible. He fought to get Jews admitted to Britain and strove to get help for refugees, but he was acutely aware of how inadequate it was to admit only 38,000 to Britain (even so, considerably more than the United States admitted). In working for the WCC, he raised money for the CIMADE (Comité Inter-Mouvements auprès des Evacuées), a group of courageous French students who were smuggling Jews into Switzerland with the support of Marc Boegner and Visser 't Hooft. His comparative failure to mobilize and raise international opinion makes this the saddest chapter of his life. However his dialogue with Dietrich Bonhoeffer in 1940-41, and his effort for Adam von Trott zu Solz at the same time, as well as his "peace move" in 1939, remain among the most significant things he did.[12] He was determined that, however grim the situation militarily, there should be proper planning for reconstruction in Europe and that the government should develop "peace aims" which, while destroying fascism, would not be vindictive or destructive of Germany.[13]

Paton's Indian Legacy

In India his "monuments" are indeed those of brick, concrete, and stone because of the financial support he organized for the rebuilding and reorganizing of Christian higher education in that country following the Lindsay Report. When a request was made by the National Christian Council of India in 1929 for a survey, he assembled a team of experts including two Indians, under the leadership of A.D. Lindsay of Balliol (later, 1949, vice-chancellor of a new-style university of Keele). The defects the commission highlighted, after a thorough examination of the colleges in India, sadly remain today. Vast numbers of Indians wanting higher education in a Christian college still cannot be accommodated, and examinations still dominate the Indian educational system. But other recommendations of the commission, such as education by extension, control of the colleges by Indians themselves, education designed for an India independent rather than under colonial authorities, and increased cooperation and sharing of facilities, were implemented and extended. The support Paton and the Lindsay commission gave to women's education was particularly important at this juncture in Indian history. Kinnaird College, Lahore, fittingly has Paton's name on the foundation stone.

In India, first as a YMCA secretary, then as first secretary of the National Christian Council of India, and later in the IMC, Paton's aim was not only to make evangelism more effective but also to facilitate the transition from evangelism as a specialized activity, organized by foreign missionary societies and foreign personnel, to evangelism as an integral part of the Indian church's own life. Today this transition from mission to church seems obvious. Paton, however, lived in an age of paternalism and colonialism (which have not wholly disappeared, even now), and one of the most imaginative things he organized was a "Mission of Fellowship" – bringing Chinese, India, and African leaders as evangelists to Britain in 1932. In his important work to help "orphaned missions" during World War II, and to succor the interned "enemy alien" missionaries in the British Empire, he encouraged the participation of African and Indian Christians to help their own missionaries and churches.

At first Paton fought many battles against bureaucracy, urging governments to ease restrictions on missionaries, and part of the declaration concerning political neutrality of missionaries that he drafted for the India Office is still used by the government of India. But in the 1930s he came to see that this was less important than the fundamental right of Christians as religious minorities to practice their religion and communicate it to their fellow citizens. His thoughts on this matter are basic to some of the later work of the WCC on religious freedom.

Paton's Theology

Paton's theology, as it can be traced through more than twenty-one books and sixty-nine articles, letters, book reviews, and memories of his conversations, also developed and changed greatly, especially with regard to the content and implications of Christian mission. Changes are especially notable with respect to social ethics and ecclesiology. Often he was articulating the beliefs of his generation, but the fact that he was a Presbyterian with thorough theological training meant that he was less susceptible to "liberal" theology, and his ecumenical contacts brought him to an early and sympathetic understanding of Karl Barth. While one can speak of a unique eclecticism in his orthodox theology, Paton selected what was meaningful to his own religious experience, not what was merely fashionable. In the last year of his life he, like Bonhoeffer, embarked on a radical new departure. Unfortunately, however, he left behind only sketches for future books.

Paton enjoyed theology and would spend entire evenings discussing Karl Barth with a friend. On one occasion he took great pains to arrange three hours between trains in the Zurich station waiting room in order to talk to Emil Brunner who, he said, needed Moral Rearmament to discover religion (although Paton himself was very critical of Moral Rearmament). He once told Dr. Archie Craig, "The recipe for my books is: (a) scissors and paste, (b) being content with a seventy percent mark, and (c) a dash of bluff now and then." Craig commented that Paton had "the kind of blithe insouciance of a man who knows that he will never make anything if he is afraid of making a mistake, and who will therefore push along with a given piece of work without a sidelong glance." Yet this should not disguise the fact that what were basically impressionistic works painted on a broad canvas with sweeping brush strokes were reinforced by great knowledge of the world situation, including specialized aspects of world religions.

His purpose was generally to provide a Christian apologetic for the interested inquirer who has a perceived need of the sacred, and to educate the average, ill-informed Christian. As he wrote at the beginning of *Jesus Christ and the World's Religions:* "A diffused knowledge of the subject combined with some misapprehension as to the nature of Christianity has produced in many quarters a kind of nebulous tolerance of everything which calls itself religion, which is different from the attitude of Christian scholars who treat other religions sympathetically but remain convinced of the supremacy of the revelation of God in Christ." In the second edition (1927) he added that in the upheaval and social change in the East, Christians owe to the world the supreme duty of faithfulness to the truth, studied and grasped with sincerity and honesty, and preached in love.

In an unpublished manuscript dated 1911, "St. Paul's Missionary Methods," Paton wrote,

It many fairly be said to be a condition of success in modern missions among the civilized peoples of the East, that missionaries shall begin with native ideas of God and lead thence to the true God whom they are groping after in ignorance. We must seize upon national thought and tradition and atmosphere, and develop these so that they blend with the Christian revelation. It will be a practical point to educate Indian and Chinese children in their own sacred books, and bid them dig deep into the lore of their national sages and seers. It is a thought which should reduce us to deep humility that the fullness of Christ is to be apprehended not by the Jew alone, nor by the Englishman nor by the American, but by the whole race of the sons of men. We need to be wary of how we thrust upon our Eastern converts anything that is solely of ourselves and not of Christ, for it is their own Christ whom they must find.

Paton wrote those words before he came to know J.N. Farquhar well, and to be so much influenced by his idea of Christianity as the fulfillment of all that is good in other religions.[14] From a very positive assessment of Hinduism written in 1916 without any personal experience of India, he came to write in 1922, from Calcutta, after traveling throughout India (1917-19): "He [Alexander Duff] is not the only man in whom huge shrines, memorials as they are to the religious quest of mankind, have aroused horror and loathing."[15] He criticized Duff's conclusion that modern science and philosophy would undermine Hinduism so that it would rot away, but it was not until he confronted the nihilistic philosophy of national socialism that he doubted Christianity's ultimate triumph. Instead he came to agree with Hendrik Kraemer that the traditional Christian religion would also perish, but nothing would extinguish the claims of Christ. Initially he was very sympathetic to Buddhism because of its pacifism and because of the character of the Buddha as he understood it. Then, after a visit to Ceylon, he wrote, "I have no use for Buddhism in practice. The national movement in Ceylon is galvanizing Buddhism with a kind of life . . . but it has not got the necessary guts. It is fatalistic and anti-western."[16] Paton required of religion a strong ethical sense and equality for women (he was critical of the way women are treated in Hinduism and Islam), and as the father of six children, he showed little interest in asceticism or celibacy!

Although Paton regarded a sense of sin as essential, he did not come to grips with the problem of evil. Hence, particularly in relation to Buddhism, he did not succeed in asking the right questions concerning non-Christian religions, and not always the right questions about the Christian faith. Gradually he came, via criticism of Barth, to the Kraemer position of the radical discontinuity of the Christian faith. While Christian religiosity stands condemned along with other religions, Christianity is not a rival religion in the sense that Hinduism and Islam are: "On God's side it is the revelation of Himself in the sublime act which is the giving of Himself by Christ: on man's side it is the humble acceptance of forgiveness and sonship in a fellowship of those who believe in God!"[17] No longer did Paton emphasize people's need of God, whatever their religion, but God's love, which should inspire all mission. In a similar way he appreciated what science can achieve, but insisted that a scientific explanation of the world is no substitute for a spiritual one.

Paton was in fact responsible for getting Kraemer to write *The Christian Message in a Non-Christian World*. Like Kraemer he did not consider religion to be theology and worship in isolation, but in its political and social context. Like Kraemer too, he condemned any hint of superiority on the part of missionaries. Only Christ is the ultimate standard, and in him can all be found – ethics with guts, the humanity of women, the condemnation of racism and other social evils – with the love of God transcending all. From his first student work in 1911, Paton always insisted that mission is the work of God, and not of human devising. Faith in God is required, not conferences about missionary methods and calculations of manpower in human terms (this is criticism of John R. Mott). This is reminiscent of Roland Allen, but there is no evidence that Paton was directly or even indirectly influenced by Allen.[18]

For Paton, it was intolerable that one should speak of the love of God in Christ without finding in the Gospel a concommitant challenge to action. Hence some of his best writings are on social questions, though he was never seduced by the "Social Gospel." In challenging secularism he made an original contribution to the debate that has continued ever since the Jerusalem conference of 1928. Starting with a letter written in 1927, Paton anticipated Rufus Jones's essay for the Jerusalem meeting. At first Paton simply identified the spirit of the age with secular regimes in Turkey and Russia, the fin-de-siècle feeling, the reliance on science and modern art, the striving for a better humanity. He could see positive values in all that, as he did in Hinduism. Then he evolved a second way of understanding secularism:

> It is the separation of the departments of life from the centre to which they belong, so that they become kingdoms in their own right, self-dependent, acknowledging no suzerainty. Business will then be business, art will be art for art's sake, education will solve the mystery of human life in its own strength, the chemist's crucible will be a sufficient test of all reality, and then religion becomes a little department of life with its own petty interests, its own peculiarly odious separations, its own professional jargon. The heart of secularism is the divorce of religion from its proper task, and it is here that some of us have come to look for the centre of the world's evil.[19]

Paton was right to call for a worldview in which everything – politics, economics, ethics, art – can be integrated. However, it was J.H. Oldham who developed Paton's insight, while Paton addressed himself to specific dehumanizing evils: racism, anti-Semitism, and totalitarianism of both right and left.

Paton developed an ecclesiology relatively late, and as the result of his missionary and ecumenical experience. When he was converted, the church seemed to him an enabling body of friends, but only in 1929 do we see any understanding of the church as a divine community emerging in his thought. Even then he tended to limit it to an instrument for mission, albeit one that transcends all human divisions because it is the body of Christ, comprising all who are called by God in Christ. His theology, and that of others as well, was strengthened by the need to counter the attacks against the church in Germany and the Far East. He developed an understanding of the church as the army of saints in heaven and on earth, and of the sacraments. It is, he said, a hopeless failure in many circumstances; but it is the hope of the world, because in it forgiveness is experienced – and the understanding that in the cross of Christ the very life of God breaks into the world. The church is not a welfare organization, a political power, or a social club. Nor is it only a corporate body of clergy. It is based on the Easter Gospel and the message of reconciliation of all to God.

When David Paton heard of his father's death, he wrote to his brother William: "Daddy was a very human person underneath the international big shot covering, and I deeply hope that this won't be covered up if a memoir is written, partly on personal grounds and also because I think it is rather irreligious to present the leaders of the church or any other human beings for that matter as inhuman and sinless."[20] Sinless Paton was not. When he made a mistake he did it on a big scale, but one of his most attractive features was his readiness to admit his mistakes and also to shoulder the blame for mistakes made by subordinates. All in all he was on the side of the angels, and this very human "pocket battleship," as he once was called, showed in his life what can be done if one really believes that all things are possible with God.

Notes

(Fuller documentation is supplied in Eleanor M. Jackson, *Red Tape and the Gospel.*)

1. Unpublished letters to David Paton, Nov. 22, 1942, and March 28, 1943, in the possession of Mrs. Elizabeth Montefiore. Paton's family kindly allowed the writer to make full use of their family papers.
2. C.S. Lewis, *The Screwtape Letters* (London: Fontana Books, 1962,) p. 15.

3. All these comments are from letters to the writer in 1973, and from her interview with Sir Kenneth Grubb, September 1973. See Grubb's autobiography, *Crypts of Power* (London: Hodder and Stoughton, 1971).
4. Unpublished letter of condolence to Grace Paton, Montefiore Papers.
5. John Graham, *Conscription and Conscience* (London: George Allen & Unwin, 1964); John Rae, *Conscience and Politics: The British Government and the Conscientious Objectors to Military Service, 1916-1919* (London: Oxford Univ. Press, 1970).
6. F.W. Dillistone, *Charles Raven, Naturalist, Historian, Theologian* (London: Hodder and Stoughton, 1975). See also references to Raven in Eleanor M. Jackson, *Red Tape and the Gospel* (Birmingham, England: Phlogiston Publishing in association with Selly Oak Colleges, 1980).
7. From "Some Principles of Reconstruction: The Proposals of the American Churches," published in William Temple et al., *The Crisis of the Western World* (London: George Allen & Unwin, 1944).
8. Jackson, *Red Tape and the Gospel*, pp. 272f.; interview with A.G. Craig; J.H. Oldham file, British Council of Churches archives at Selly Oak Colleges, Birmingham; Visser 't Hooft/Elmslie and Visser 't Hooft/Craig correspondence, WCC general correspondence, World Council of Churches, Geneva.
9. Jackson, *Red Tape and the Gospel*, p. 240; Visser 't Hooft, *Memoirs* (London: SCM Press, 1973), p. 82; F.A. Iremonger, *William Temple, Archbishop of Canterbury: His Life and Letters* (London and New York: Oxford Univ. Press, 1948), p. 411.
10. E.g., vol. 5 of *The Jerusalem Meeting of the International Missionary Council, 1928* entitled *The Christian Mission in Relation to Industrial Problems* (New York and London: IMC, 1928).
11. Paton, *World Community* (London: SCM Press, 1938), pp. 126, 149. Paton did not accept the way in which he was excluded from the Council of Christians and Jews because he was a missionary. See papers of International Christian Council on the Approach to the Jews, WCC archives, Geneva; also Paton *The Church and the New Order* (London: SCM Press, 1941).
12. Armin Boyens, *Kirchenkampf und Oekumene*, vol. 2, 1939-45 (Munich: Chr. Kaiser Verlag, 1974).
13. See Jackson, *Red Tape and the Gospel*, pp. 367-68, for full "Peace Aims" bibliography. The papers are in WCC archives, Geneva, with copies in Selly Oak Colleges archives.
14. Compare Paton's *Jesus Christ and the World's Religions* with J.N. Farquhar, *The Crown of Hinduism* (London: SCM Press, 1915). For Farquhar's influence, see Eric Sharpe, *J.N. Farquhar* (Calcutta: YMCA Press, 1963).
15. Paton, *Alexander Duff: Pioneer of Missionary Education* (London: SCM Press, 1922). Mrs. Paton echoed the same sentiments in a letter to her mother, Mrs. MacDonald (in Montefiore Papers).
16. Paton's letter to Grace Paton, Montefiore Papers.
17. Paton, *The Faiths of Mankind* (London: SCM Press, 1932), p. 157.
18. This is the belief of David Paton, William Paton's son and an authority on Roland Allen. See David Paton, *The Ministry of the Spirit: Selected Writings of Roland Allen* (London: World Dominion Press, 1960).
19. Paton, "What Is Secularism?" *International Review of Missions* 18 (1929): 354. This article is discussed by David Gill in *IRM* 57 (1968): 347. The essay of Rufus M. Jones, "Secular Civilization and the Christian Task," is in *Jerusalem Meeting of the International Missionary Council, 1928*, vol. 1 (New York and London: IMC, 1928), pp. 230-37.
20. Margaret Sinclair, associate editor of the *International Review of Missions*, wrote a biography at Mrs. Paton's request: *William Paton* (London: SCM Press, 1949), but the author herself called it a "hopeless task" because of limited time and no access to archives or private papers outside the Paton family.

Selected Bibliography

1911 "St. Paul's Missionary Methods." 12-page handwritten essay, preserved by Elizabeth Montefiore. Discussed in Jackson, *Red Tape and the Gospel*.
1916 *Jesus Christ and the World's Religions*. London: United Council of Missionary Education. Ten printings, 1916-26; rev. ed., London: Edinburgh House Press, 1927.
1919 *Social Ideals in India*. London: United Council for Missionary Education.
1921 *The Highway of God*. Jointly with Kathleen Harnett. London: SCM.
1925 "India and Opium." *International Review of Missions* 14: 161-76.
1927 "Eastern Industrialism and Christian Missions." *IRM* 16:542-55.
1929 "What Is Secularism?" *IRM* 18:346-54.
1929 *A Faith for the World*. London: Cargate Press.
1932 *The Faiths of Mankind*. London: SCM Press.
1934 *The New Era in Missionary Work: Next Steps*. London: Conference of British Missionary Societies.
1937 *Christianity in the Eastern Conflicts*. London: Edinburgh House Press. German trans., *Das Christentum im Ringen des Ostens* (Frauenfeld und Leipzig: Verlag von Huber, 1938) under the IMC imprint, and

Forschungsabteilung des Ökumenishes Rat für Praktisches Christentum Kirche und Welt Studien und Dokumente, vol. 2.
1939 *The White Man's Burden: The Beckly Social Service Lecture.* London: Epworth Press.
1940 "The World-wide Christian Society." *The Christian Newsletter,* supplement no. 10, March 1.
1941 *The Church and the New Order.* London: SCM Press.
1942 Preface to *The Jew in the Christian World,* by Hans Kosmala and Robert Smith. London: SCM Press.
1942 "The Churches Help Each Other." 800 words, mimeographed, in WCC archives, discussed in Jackson, *Red Tape and the Gospel.*

These are selected from among some 100 titles, some of which are no longer extant. Paton also edited many collections of essays and documents of the IMC meetings, of which the most important are the preparatory studies and conference reports of the IMC meetings at Jerusalem (1928) and Tambaram (1938).

Except for the one mentioned in note 20, above, there are no biographies of Paton. For a critical study of his career, see Eleanor M. Jackson, *Red Tape and the Gospel: A Study of the Significance of the Ecumenical Missionary Struggle of William Paton (1886-1943)* (Birmingham: Phlogiston Publishing in association with Selly Oak Colleges, 1980). A tribute to Paton by John R. Mott was published in the *International Review of Missions* 33 (1944): 3-9. Mention of Paton in ecumenical biographies is brief and sometimes inaccurate, but there are short articles about him in the *Concise Dictionary of the Christian World Mission,* Stephen Neill, Gerald H. Anderson, and John Goodwin, eds. (Nashville: Abingdon; and London: Lutterworth, 1971), and in the latest edition of the *Oxford Dictionary of the Christian Church* (London and New York: Oxford Univ. Press, 1977).

Karl Hartenstein

1894–1952

Missions with a Focus on "The End"

Gerold Schwarz

L ord God, who has so conspicuously blessed my life, let me, as in the past five years, rise to ever greater knowledge and grant me Thy strength to become a good theologian." The young man about to enter university who wrote this prayer in his diary was Karl Hartenstein, the son of a businessman, born in Bad Cannstatt near Stuttgart on January 25, 1894. To the surprise of his parents, he began to study theology in 1913. He did not complete his studies at the University of Tübingen, however, until 1921, having spent the years from 1914 until 1918 in military service at the western front. After lecturing at the Tübingen Stift, he assumed a pastorate. The course of his life would lead from the church into missions and from missions back into the church. Thus, in a special way, he realized in his life and thinking the unity of church and missions. In 1923 he married Margarete Umfried; the marriage was blessed with three sons.

In 1926 the Basel Mission appointed the Swabian theologian, then only thirty-two years old, as its director. His new position in missions was for Hartenstein not a change in vocation but, rather, a God-given opportunity to fulfill his missionary calling on an ecumenical scale. In 1928-29, Hartenstein was in India and China, in 1931 in Africa, and in 1938-39 again in India. Besides his theological missionary work, he also dealt with a multitude of practical tasks during these visits to the field, including tasks of an organizational and business nature. Through many discussions on the mission field he promoted the growth toward independence of the young churches, especially in terms of their apostolic-missionary responsibility. Hartenstein's participation, especially on the level of theological deliberation, in the world missionary conferences in Tambaram near Madras, India (1938), in Whitby, Canada (1947), and in Willingen, Germany (1952), contributed materially to the ecumenical shaping and recognition of German missiology. Walter Freytag wrote: "At each of these conferences he was part of the small group that decisively influenced the course and results of the conference, either as the editorial committee that influenced the formulation of especially controversial documents (e.g., in Madras, the statement concerning the Message in relation to the religions, and in Willingen, the effort concerning theological reflection), or, in Whitby, as the steering committee."[1]

When World War II broke out, Hartenstein resigned his position in Basel, lest as a German he jeopardize the work in the mission fields. The board of the Basel Mission sent him as plenipotentiary to Stuttgart to assume the leadership of the Basel Mission Church in Germany.

In 1941 he was appointed prelate of the *Landeskirche* of Würtemberg in Stuttgart. From 1949 onward, Karl Hartenstein was a member of the Assembly of the Evangelical Church in Germany, which represented all evangelical Christians in Germany. In addition, a series of important diaconal tasks accrued to him.

With the exception of his commentary on Revelation, the results of his mental labor, which spanned approximately three decades, are no longer in print. A large portion of his theological legacy lies unpublished in countless files in Basel and Stuttgart. Both the turbulence of the political events in the Third Reich, which he experienced at first hand, burdened by heavy responsibility in an exposed position on the cutting edge of the issue of church and state, and his early death on October 1, 1952, prevented him from presenting his thinking in a unified, systematic theological form. Furthermore, the true locus and wellspring of his theology was not so much the lectern of the scholarly theologian as the pulpit of the preacher and pastor. For Hartenstein, all theology led to proclamation in the full apostolic breadth of missionary thought and action. Many people still remember the sermons and meditations he gave in Stuttgart, which, born from the passion of faith, were able to provide true consolation and direction in the chaotic events of the war and the years after the war.

The "Yes" to Karl Barth

An attempt to define Hartenstein's theological position more precisely must first distinguish several antecedent lines in the history of theology of church and missions. Throughout his life, Hartenstein's theological thinking was deeply rooted in the native soil of Swabian Pietism. He continually struggled to make the theological legacy of Johann Albrecht Bengel (1687-1752), Friedrich Christoph Oetinger (1702-82), Michael Hahn (1758-1819), and many others fruitful in the establishing of a basis and objective of missions.

In Tübingen he studied intensively under Adolf Schlatter and Karl Heim; especially with Heim he established a lifelong and close personal friendship, which enriched his missiological thinking with ever new and crucial stimuli. When in 1919 Karl Barth sounded the signal for attack against the bastion of idealistic, neo-Protestant religion with his *Commentary on Romans,* Karl Hartenstein joined the front ranks. He saw Barth's crisis theology as a purifying fire that would subdue the liberal-humanistic principles, and passionately defended Barth's dialectical theses while lecturing at the Tübingen Stift. His two expositions of 1926, on Ecclesiastes and Amos, unmistakably show the marks of this "dialectical" Sturm-und-Drang period.

Hartenstein follows the Barthian critique in a three-pronged attack: against the historicism in the interpretation of the Scriptures, against the moral-religious optimism in ethics, and against religion as the presumptuous human effort at self-redemption.

By studying Kierkegaard on his own, he deepened the dialectical-theological principle of an infinite, qualitative distance between God and man, reason and faith, heaven and earth, time and eternity. After assuming his position as director in Basel in 1926, his occupation with dialectical theology acquired a truly missionary dimension. His publication "What Does Karl Barth's Theology Have to Say to Missions?" (1928) initiated the dialogue between missions and dialectical theology, and thereby pointed German missiology as a whole in a new direction. His doctoral dissertation for the theological faculty at Tübingen, "Missions as a Theological Problem" (1933), also documents this effort to link missions and dialectical theology and shows how much Hartenstein saw himself as the advocate of dialectical theology who defended its essential tenets in the realm of missions. This encounter with dialectical theology resulted in a new and purifying awakening for missions.

The concept of *missio Dei,* which gained currency after Willingen (1952), was already coined by Hartenstein in 1934. Its locus in the history of theology is the dialectical theology of Karl Barth with its radical emphasis on the *actio Dei,* which precedes all human action and severs missions from any contemporary secular rationale by characterizing missions as participation in the redemptive work of God. "Thus, missions are fundamentally removed from the sphere of purely human activity, characterized and understood as God's will and act, an inalienable indication of God's revelation."[2] The mission of the church finds the ground of its existence and its limits in God's mission. The proclamation of the sovereignty of God and the emphasis on his exclusive initiative in his liberating and saving dealings with this world, independent of any subjective experience or effort, places church and missions always anew under the crisis of God's Word. This stress on the crisis of church and missions later became considerably more pronounced in Hartenstein's thinking in the context of the salvation-historical basis of missions. The dialectical-theological starting point retains permanent significance for Hartenstein through the fall of the "walls of Jericho" in the form of the rapprochement between God and world, religion and culture in secularized cultural Protestant liberalism. Karl Barth has liberated the concept of God from the ghetto of the human understanding of self and reality, and has allowed God to appear once again as the confronting Judge and Savior who confronts of his own accord.

The "No" to Karl Barth

As early as 1933 Hartenstein veered away more sharply from Barth, back toward the heritage of his native church and above all toward the eschatological thinking of the Pietism of Württemberg. The "unfinished questions" of dialectical theology increasingly troubled him. Hartenstein felt that in the long run the sharply antithetical position of the early Barth toward anthropocentric thinking was too barren and one-dimensional. The rigid form of the "either-or" of Barthian logic insupportably curtailed the "historical and experiential [*geschichtliche und seelische*] reality" of faith so frequently disparaged by Barth. Barth's ethical nihilism, which largely abandoned a material ethic, became a problem in the day-to-day reality of the mission field, where the question "What must we do?" in each new situation pressed for an answer. Also, Hartenstein's eschatological perspective with its emphasis on the future aspects of salvation history came to stand in increasingly sharp contrast to the nonhistorical and transhistorical eschatology of Barth's *Commentary on Romans.*

Hartenstein's most important interlocutors now became Karl Heim and Emil Brunner, whose theology showed the same missionary inclination. Emil Brunner also separated himself during this time from the ranks of early dialectical theology. It was necessary for Hartenstein to develop beyond Barth if the salvation-historical elements of his Swabian heritage were to bear fruit.

It was Oscar Cullmann who enabled Hartenstein to develop his salvation-historical position in an exegetically responsible manner. In turning to biblical theology and to the prophetic word, he attempted to renew the tradition of salvation-historical thought that stretches from Irenaeus via Bengel to the salvation-historical theologians of the nineteenth century and to make this tradition missiologically operative. Hartenstein essentially provided the impetus for a basis of missions from a salvation-historical eschatological perspective with "a focus on the End" (*im Blick auf das Ende*), which had a deep impact on an entire era in German missiology and introduced an almost Copernican revolution in the traditional, "organic people's" (*volksorganic*) approach systematized by Gustav Warneck. In contrast to the more noneschatological, Lutheran-romantic theology of missions of Warneck, Hartenstein's strictly biblicist and pietistic-eschatological basis of missions marked a significant new approach. His exegetical works "The Prophet Daniel" (1936) and "The Returning Lord" (1940), as well as numerous studies and sermons on apocalyptic New Testament texts, witness to his ever-growing occupation with the relationship between missions and eschatology during the last fifteen years of his life.

Hartenstein incessantly reminded the church of its prophetic word and complained in view of Matthew 25:6 that too little of the "cry at midnight" could be heard in the church. He sought to understand the world and history from a universal salvation-historical cosmic view of Christian faith. The doctrines of the last things were for Hartenstein not merely a final chapter of dogmatics, a no-man's-land where generally fanatics and ideologists of all persuasions settle, but the indisputable and peculiar territory of the church, which the church must claim and defend against the manifold forms of "degenerate eschatology."

Focus on the End

Like Bengel, Hartenstein was convinced of the need for the *cognitio oeconomiae divinae universalis* (cognition of the all-inclusive plan of salvation of God) and drew from it the conclusion that the interpretation of the Book of Revelation should enjoy the same rights as that of the Epistle to the Romans, or, stated differently, that Pauline theology should again be understood more in its salvation-historical context.

The central perspective that governs life and doctrine was for Hartenstein the returning Lord. Ever since World War I, his wristwatch was always fifteen minutes fast, a symbol of the fact that his whole thinking was motivated and dominated by the dynamics of the hope of the future of the returning Christ and thus geared toward tomorrow and the day after tomorrow. He concludes a sermon on 2 Corinthians 5:15 by looking at the certainty that undergirds our existence, the return of Christ: "This certainty is the strongest consolation in the darkest nights, but it is also the highest responsibility for each day, because on 'today' rests the weight of the eternal decision for which we must prepare ourselves ever again anew . . . And to be prepared for that hour when our Lord comes is worth the sacrifice and suffering of an arduous Christian life. Yes, come Lord Jesus. Amen."

The return of Christ also gives missions their ultimate basis and urgency. Missions take place within the salvation-historical ordinates of the resurrection and return of Jesus Christ. In the framework of these ordinates the nature, course, and goal of missions are clearly defined:

> The central salvation-historical meaning of the interim period between the Ascension and the return of the Lord lies in missions. As Gospel witness, missions are the continuation in the present of the line of salvation that leads toward the Parousia. Missions are the Lord's tool, in and through which He carries out His plan of salvation. The missionary task requires one's whole life, and even martyrdom. Is it perhaps the greatest weakness of the church and of missions that they no longer see themselves in this salvation-historical context as being the Lord's tool for the execution of His plan of salvation? . . . But this is certain: the moment the church again recognizes these salvation-historical correlations, she will wake up to an entirely new, joyful attitude toward missions.[3]

Hartenstein's establishing the basis of missions by means of placing missions in their proper position in the historical theological context of the resurrection and return of Jesus Christ can, on the one hand, be traced to his intensive study of Bengel's writings through which the fundamental recognition of the hope of the kingdom was revived in Germany. On the other hand, Hartenstein adopted Karl Heim's basic contrast between the reconciliation of the world (the solution to the problem of guilt) and the consummation of the world (the solution to the problem of authority).

The temporal and salvation-historical break between redemption and consummation creates an interim period, "in which the anti-God power has been deprived of its right, but not yet of its control."[4] This eschatological interim, or pause, as Karl Heim could also say, is the milieu of the church of Jesus. The Great Commission is during this interim consequently the lifework and raison d'être of the church. The church exists "between the times." It lives in the "already now" of the accomplished redemption and orients itself in all its manifestations toward the "not yet" of the coming consummation. "The cross and the Kingdom are the two acts of God between which the Lord ultimately wants nothing else and expects nothing else from His church than the obedient service of His servants, their unconditional faithfulness in calling and loving until the End."[5]

Hartenstein's basis of missions with "a focus on the End" was materially supported by Oscar Cullmann's New Testament study *Christ and Time,* in which the temporal dualism, the tension between the "already fulfilled" and the "not yet consummated," is seen as the real key to the understanding of the entire New Testament.[6]

"Missions with a focus on the End" also means always missions and church under God's judgment. The ultimate goal of missions is not the church but the kingdom of God. The church is not the final purpose of God's dealings. "Missions must realize that the crucial elements in God's plan of salvation is not the church but the kingdom, not an institution but the witness of the believing church, not the formation of an independent, indigenous or ecumenical church, not the temple, but the unassuming and humble tabernacle, which Israel carries through the wilderness as the sign of and witness to God's presence in the world."[7] Hartenstein's eschatological, salvation-historical basis of missions averts in principle any church-centered motivation for missions. The empirical-sociological form of the church, all that is institutional and legitimately organized in the church, is temporary, "a provisional, transitory entity, that derives its meaning and legitimacy only from the consummation."[8]

The only function of the church is the Johannine one of preparing the way for the returning Lord through its witness vis-à-vis all principalities and powers. The church loses its life and is submerged in the kingdom of God.[9]

Church and missions, on their journey from the first to the second coming, go through three stages of salvation-historical development: (1) the powerlessness of the early church in its struggle with the powers of this world; (2) the merger of state and church under Constantine: the church in league with the ways and powers of this world; (3) the dissolution of this synthesis, which began with the Reformation.

Under the influence of Carl August Auberlen (1824-64), Hartenstein sought to provide an exegetical basis for this historical division of the interim by means of a historico-theological interpretation of the apocalyptic symbols of Revelation 13; to the extent that the church becomes politically stronger, the diabolical vitality of the world powers is weakened. According to Revelation 13: 3, 12, 14, the beast, apparently in its seventh and final development, receives a fatal wound, which changes the character of the beast. This wound symbolizes the decisive historical caesura and the change of the pagan nations into Christian nations, although their Christianity is not real but merely facade and veneer. The Christian centuries are characterized by, on the one hand, a secularized Christianity and, on the other hand, a Christianized world. Correspondingly, the healing of the wound symbolizes that the Christian state becomes again an anti-Christian power, which tries to expel the church as an alien element. In the apocalyptically viewed present, Hartenstein sees, in the dissociation of the church from state and nation, the church in retreat, a retreat that is at the same time a return to the situation of the early church. The church becomes again a "free church" by its exclusive commitment to its Lord, independent and precisely for that reason excluded and persecuted by the powers of this world.

The interim between the "times" of God is according to 1 Peter 1:5 "the last time," and according to 1 Peter 1:17 the time of living "as strangers" (NIV). The church is in the process of regaining its identity, its essence, and of becoming a minority church, a sojourning church, a witnessing church, a church under the cross. Thus comes about, in Hartenstein's perspective, the "miracle of the church" as the body of Christ among the nations.

From this view of the salvation-historical interim also follows the definition of the church's commission, which, according to Hartenstein, has the triadic structure *missio-unio-passio*. The first aspect of this commission, *missio,* has God as its subject, so that all missionary activity of the church is grounded in God's sending. But the *missio Dei* is also always a countermovement to the missionary endeavor of the church. The Spirit of God does not only blow powerfully into the sails of the ship that calls itself "church" – he can also be a head wind that blows the ship off a self-chosen course. Nor are missions a monopoly of missionary societies; missions do not belong in the realm of human governance and competence at all. God alone sustains missions, rather than any missionary or ecclesiastical institution. All believers, the whole church, are sent into the world and the missionary societies serve only vicariously.

Over all missions is written the "must" of the eschatological determinism of Mark 13:10, according to which missions are the last task of the church in the world and a sign of the coming End. Missions are the church in motion, while a church without missions is a church of rigid formalization. The "must" of the proclamation of the Gospel before the End, the categorical imperative of missions, is grounded in the will of God itself. Thus, while the focus on the final consummation is the decisive motive of missionary activity, the End itself is God's concern.

Mark 13:10 should set us free from an unbiblical, activistic, strained optimism in the evaluation of missionary results. Hartenstein wrote:

As the nation of Israel in Abraham was called and chosen out of the nations in order to intercede vicariously for the nations before God, so also has the church been called out and chosen from among the nations of the end time to intercede vicariously before God on their behalf as a believing remnant, to believe and hope on behalf of the world, to proclaim God's salvation to the world – until the returning Lord establishes his rule on a renewed earth in which all redeemed humanity and the whole renewed creation make manifest the final purpose of God's dealings.[10]

The growth of the church toward its Head is by no means unconditional or always a quantitative expansion, and the victory of Christianity is not the result of an immanent development but the result of the sovereign act of God, who comes to judge and who resolves the history of the world by lifting it up into its conclusion.

The second aspect is the *unio*, the unity of the church of Jesus among all nations. The interim period is also the time of the ingathering of the church. This *unio,* viewed in the context of salvation history, is the reason why Hartenstein almost enthusiastically welcomed the founding of the World Council of Churches as a sign of the end-time. The end-time finds its climax in the third aspect, the *passio* (suffering), which ultimately will intensify into persecution.

These then are the essential features of Hartenstein's view of salvation history, which is not limited to the time from Christ's birth until A.D. 33, but comprises the "mighty event of God from Creation through Redemption to consummation."

The Missionary Encounter with the Religions

Since the early 1930s Hartenstein called more strongly for an "evangelical science of religion" as an inalienable task of the theology of missions. By an evangelical science of religion he means the attempt "to determine properly the relationship between the Gospel and, on the one hand, Christianity, and on the other hand the non-Christian religions."[11] With this call for the theological determination of the interrelationship between the three crucial concepts – gospel, church (Christendom), and non-Christian religions – Hartenstein turns against a relativistic and speculative study of comparative religions, which reduces and levels religion's claim to revelation on the basis of a "theologically and scientifically questionable concept of the nature of religion and of Christianity."[12] "All religions, when taken seriously in terms of their true spirit [*Seele*] and outward form, are distorted and misrepresented when stretched on the Procrustean bed of a general notion of religion."[13]

In the wake of Karl Barth, Emil Brunner, and Hendrik Kraemer, Hartenstein strove for a biblical-theological interpretation of the religions from the standpoint of the Gospel and used for this theological departure the formula "a critique of all religions from the standpoint of the Gospel." A Christian theology of the religions can be determined only by "the application of the doctrine of justification by faith alone to the world of the religions. The sweeping concept of pagandom outside Christ can become clear again only if revelation is taken as the starting point, and only through revelation can we receive definite criteria for pagandom from Christ's perspective. An 'evangelical science of the religions' can therefore only be a concrete critique of all religions with Christ as its principle."[14]

Theology must grasp anew the essence of pagandom "in all its various forms standing under the drastic judgment on the deification of the creature and the humanization of God."[15] In the perspective of biblical realism, the

> dreadfulness and the demonic aspect of the religions must be perceived more distinctly; at the same time, the signs and evidences that witness, in the perspective of revelation, to the active patience of God at work among the religions must also be perceived more clearly.[16]

> Yet in this rebellion and apostasy the nations prove that they cannot get away from God and the entire world of the religions, the "idolatry of the nations" (Brunner), becomes a testimony to a relationship with God, even if this is a wrong relationship. In all falsehood they ask for truth, in their flight they flee toward the "unknown God." This twofold statement makes it clear that the mystery of the revelation of Christ contains both the end and the judgment on all religions and the offer of grace to the world of the religions, which signifies its end as much as it signifies the beginning of the church, the rule of the true God, pointing to the fulfillment in the coming kingdom of God.[17]

In terms of Hendrik Kraemer's polar concepts "continuity/discontinuity," Hartenstein's position on the question of the encounter with the religions falls on the side of discontinuity; the line of discontinuity can be traced from Tertullian via the Reformers Luther and Calvin to Karl Barth and Emil Brunner. Hartenstein sees the entire Reformation movement as a critique of all religions from the standpoint of the Gospel. Through the intensive concentration of the word of the Bible alone, the Reformation, for the first time in the history of the Christian church, led to a theology of religion and the religions that was sharply distinct from the Christian philosophy of religion of the medieval Scholastics. For Hartenstein, the reformational contrast between *religio vera* (the theocentric form of religion of grace and salvation) and *religio falsa* (the anthropocentric form of religion of work-righteousness and self-redemption) remains fundamental to a theological interpretation of the religions.

With Luther, Hartenstein distinguishes between "work-religion," the "attempt of man to reach up and grasp the eternal, to understand it, to earn it, to invent it," and "arbitrary religion," the attempt to "consciously detach that which is human from the eternal, to take human creations such as culture, science, and technology as ultimate and thus to deify them."[18]

From this Reformation position, Hartenstein understands paganism as "ill-gotten continuity between God and man, the sacrilege of the human being who believes himself to be standing before

God and to be able to live in the certainty that somewhere and somehow the ultimate unity between God and man is given."[19] This "ill-gotten continuity" is the deepest expression of the human seeking after and longing for God, while the flight from and rebellion against God, on the other hand, express themselves in the "imagined discontinuity," the illusion of secularism that it is possible to detach human beings and their world from God.

In the exclusively theological assessment of religion and the religions on the part of Karl Barth and Emil Brunner, Hartenstein saw the Reformation position realized again for the first time in the history of theology. Barth's strict distinction between religion and revelation, between the futile human activity aimed at self-liberation from below and the *actio Dei,* the salvation of the world from above, had erected a dam against the relativization of Christianity in the current of historicism, against any religious a priori, against religious metaphysics and the mere interiority of acculturated Protestant religiosity.

Hartenstein shares Barth's theological concern to inquire after the meaning of religion and the religions in the light of the Christian revelation. Christ as the "crisis of all religion" from the perspective of the justification of the sinner and revelation as the "dissolution of religion" form the central reference point in the theology of Barth, Brunner, and Hartenstein. The theological fork in the road where Hartenstein, Brunner, and Barth would later part ways was the view of the concrete historical reality of the religions.

In spite of Barth's emphatic claim that his severe verdict on religion did not mean a blind condemnation of religion and that the "divine judgment" on religion should not lead to human condemnation and devaluation of that which is true, good, and beautiful in the religions, it is nevertheless evident that Karl Barth never came to a correct assessment of the concrete reality of the religions. Barth established a restricted zone around religion where theology henceforth was not allowed to enter. Through forcible simplification and the subtlety and constraint of systematic logic, which made all religions appear as merely the concern of godless people and as unbelief, he crippled the interest of evangelical theology in the concrete religions. But especially in view of the actual missionary situation of preaching the Gospel to pagans, Hartenstein could not but experience this exclusively negative fixation of the concept "religion" increasingly as a burden and impediment in the effort toward an understanding of and coming to grips with other religions. The harsh dualism between religion and revelation was theologically problematic from the standpoint of the incarnation.

With Emil Brunner and Hendrik Kraemer, Hartenstein now placed more emphasis on the revelatory quality in all religions, the proofs of God's revelatory activity in the realm of the religions. In the religions, people actually deal with God. That which is specifically religious in the religions, what makes the religions religion, is the hidden reality of the living God. Hartenstein attempted to revive in missiology the question of the missionary encounter with pagandom, and hoped that this effort would spread to theology. The revelation of God as the *proprium,* the characteristic mark, of the Christian faith, so clearly attested by Karl Barth, should not be lost again; at the same time, the elements of truth in the non-Christian religions should be recognized more clearly. Thus, Christ means both fulfillment of all religions and judgment on them, inasmuch as they are the organized effort of both searching for God and fleeing from God.

This double critique of paganism from the standpoint of biblical realism corresponds to the understanding of humankind in the conflict between Creation and sin: "created by God, incessantly busy asking for God, and at the same time fleeing from God, in rebellion and defiance against God. Only thus can we understand Genesis 3, Romans 1:18ff., and Romans 11:16ff."[20] An evangelical science of religion that takes its direction from biblical anthropology and epistemology must hold fast to this dialectical truth concerning human beings and must not minimize the ambivalent character of the divine and the demonic in all religions.

With Eduard Thurneysen, Hartenstein compares the world of the religions with a circle whose hidden center is identical with the living God. According to Genesis 3-11, the connection between the Center and the circumference (the religions) has been broken. Christianity also lies somewhere on the circumference, a religion among the religions, an "also-religion," in its empirical form subject to ambiguity, relativity, and transience. But in the case of Christianity there is a living connection, the way of Christ, between Center and circumference.[21]

According to Hartenstein, the Christian faith as a religion among, and in solidarity with, the religions can serve, penitently and humbly, only by obediently heeding the voice of the non-Christian religions. In this penitent and humble attitude toward the religions, missionary service, standing under the "critique of all religions," sees itself ever anew as failure and weakness of the Christian proclamation. Yet this service may be done in the unconditional, transcendent certainty that the unknown God has revealed himself, that Love has appeared, that the kingdom of God has begun in him who is the salvation of the world. Thus Christianity cannot lay claim to absoluteness, but can only be absolutely loyal and faithful to Jesus Christ.

The message of missions, the prophetic-apostolic witness of Jesus Christ, can "only occur in boundless love, in deepest solidarity, and in humility, which excludes any personal sense of superiority, just as it excludes a relativistic tolerance with respect to the truth of the message."[22] In the light of the biblical revelation seen as the crisis of *all* religions, including Christianity in the various forms of its historical manifestation, tolerance can have nothing in common with relativism, syncretism, or indifference. Tolerance exercised at the expense of the truth must sooner or later lead to the loss of the spiritual identity and legitimacy of the Christian faith.

Hartenstein's missiological thinking moves on the plane of discontinuity. His theological struggle is guided by the intent to preserve for the church, in the face of the challenge of historicism, relativism, and secularism, its prophetic-apostolic authority, that it may be able to maintain the position of the early church also with respect to the religions.[23]

It is for Hartenstein, so to speak, a missiological axiom that revelation is the only criterion of truth and "that revelation can never be ultimately interpreted from the standpoint of religion, but the religions only from the standpoint of revelation."[24]

Nevertheless, Hartenstein has already clearly taken the step beyond Barth toward an attitude toward the religions that is more open to dialogue and more willing to understand; the religions are no longer seen as pure abstractions in the perspective of demonic self-assertion of human beings without God, but as realities with their own value and values. Only in the tension between Yes and No can missions do justice to the reality of revelation and of the religions. The dialogue, that is, the missionary encounter with the religions, derives life from the missionary intent to save. Missions are more than a sympathetic and friendly, but in the final analysis noncommittal, rapprochement. Missions must not only be the world's advocate, but also an advocate and trustee of the inalienable soteriological claim of the Christian faith. The vertical dimension of faith must not be excluded from the theological-dialogical effort.

Church and State in the Third Reich

Hartenstein's theological determination of the unity of church and missions and his ecumenical missionary attitude caused him to recognize as early as 1933 the threat to the missionary societies posed by the effort to integrate church and missions in the planned *Reichskirche,* an effort based on a nationalistically motivated ideology of unity. It is in a real sense due to the determined stand of Karl Hartenstein, Johannes Warneck, and Walter Freytag that the German evangelical missions in 1933 remained largely resistant to the pragmatic organizational integration of missions into the *Reichskirche* that was demanded by the Glaubensbewegung Deutscher Christen (the Faith Movement of German Christians, a group of pro-Nazi churchmen), and aligned themselves rather with the Confessing Church. At conferences in Barmen (October 1933), Bethel (June 1934), and Tübingen (October 1934), the National Socialist strategy of assimilation was courageously resisted; thus was averted in good time the threatening danger of ideological infiltration and political abuse of missions as a National Socialist propaganda tool abroad.

Immediately after the war, Hartenstein was instrumental in the adoption of the Stuttgart Confession at the plenary session of the missionary convention in Herborn in September 1946. With this, the door that had for so long been closed to missions, the door to the ecumenical fellowship of the International Missionary Council, was reopened. Hartenstein participated in the first assembly of the World Council of Churches in Amsterdam (1948) as a church representative.

It is to be hoped that missions will not evade an encounter with Karl Hartenstein, one of their prominent representatives of the most recent past, but will, rather, come to grips with Hartenstein's position in a critical and self-critical discussion, in which both the weaknesses and the enduring significance of his theology of missions could be established. His was a theology of missions that grew out of a lifelong struggle for the recognition of missions as the unconditional obligation of the church into an inalienable act of witness to Jesus Christ before the world.

Notes

1. Walter Freytag, "Karl Hartenstein: Zum Gedenken," *Evangelische Missions-Zeitschrift* (hereafter, *EMZ*) 10 (1953): 4.
2. Karl Hartenstein, "Die trinitarische Verkündigung in der Welt der Religionen," in *Die Deutsche Evangelische Heidenmission (Jahrbuch)* (Hamburg: Selbstverlag de Missions Konferenz, 1939), p. 6.
3. Karl Hartenstein, "Zur Neubesinnung über das Wesen der Mission," in *Die Deutsche Evangelische Weltmission (Jahrbuch)* (Hamburg: Verlag der deutschen evang. Missionshilfe, 1951), pp. 18f.
4. Karl Heim, *Jesus der Weltvollender* (Berlin: Furche-Verlag, 1937), p. 229.
5. Karl Hartenstein, "Krisis der Mission?" *Die Furche* 17 (1931): 207.
6. Oscar Cullmann, *Christus und die Zeit,* 3rd rev. ed. (Zollikon-Zurich: Evang. Verlag A.G., 1962), p. 180.
7. Karl Hartenstein, "Was bedeutet das Werden der Jungen Kirchen für die Mission heute?" in *Die neue Stunde der Weltmission* (Stuttgart: Evang. Missionsverlag, 1952), p. 27.
8. Karl Hartenstein, "Verwilderte Eschatologie," *Die Neue Furche* 6 (1952): 26.
9. Karl Hartenstein, *Der wiederkommende Herr* (Stuttgart: Evang. Missionsverlag, 1940), p. 29.
10. Karl Hartenstein, "Zur Neubesinnung," p. 24.
11. Karl Hartenstein, *Die Mission als theologisches Problem,* Furche-Studien, vol. 10 (Berlin: Furche-Verlag, 1933), p. 23.
12. Ibid., p. 17.
13. Hendrik Kraemer, *Religion und christlicher Glaube* (Göttingen: Vandenhoeck und Rupprecht, 1959), p. 77.
14. Karl Hartenstein, "Religion and Offenbarung," in *Calwer Kirchenlexikon,* vol. 2 (Stuttgart: Calwer Verlag, 1941), p. 709.
15. Ibid., p. 710.
16. Ibid.
17. Karl Hartenstein, "Die Kirche und die Religionen," *EMZ* 1 (1940): 16.
18. Karl Hartenstein, "Säkularismus und Mission," *Mitteilungen des DCSV* 5 (Winter 1929/30): 108.
19. Ibid., pp. 106f.
20. Karl Hartenstein, "Die missionarische Begegnung mit dem Heidentum," *Evangelisches Missions-Magazin* 82 (1938): 314.
21. Karl Hartenstein, *Die Mission als theologisches Problem,* p. 23.
22. Karl Hartenstein, "Die missionarische Begegnung," pp. 310ff.
23. Karl Hartenstein, "Die Kirche und die Religionen," p. 12.
24. Ibid., p. 14.

Selected Bibliography

Works by Karl Hartenstein

1928 *Was hat die Theologie Karl Barth's der Mission zu sagen?* Munich: Chr. Kaiser Verlag.

1929 *Auf Gottes Spuren in Indien.* Stuttgart, Basel: Evang. Missionsverlag.

1930 *Gandhi: Eine Auseinandersetzung zwischen Evangelium und indischer Geisteswelt.* Basler Missionsstudien N.F.H. 7. Stuttgart, Basel: Evang. Missionsverlag. See also *Evangelisches Missions-Magazin* 74 (1930): 289-303, 338-45 (hereafter *EMM*).

1931 "The Theology of the Word and Missions." *International Review of Missions* 20: 210-27 (hereafter *IRM*).

1932 *Anibue: Die "Neue Zeit" auf der Goldküste und unsere Missionsaufgabe.* Stuttgardt, Basel: Evang. Missionsverlag.

1932 "Die Goldküste-Mission in ihrer Bedeutung für unsere gengenwärtige Missionsaufgabe." *Gott ist unsere Zuversicht: Vom Jahrefest der Basler Mission* 117: 6-14. Basel: Evang. Missionsverlag.

1933 *Die Missions als theologisches Problem: Beiträge zum grundsätzlichen Verständnis der Mission.* Furche-Studien, vol. 7. Berlin: Furche Verlag.

1934 "Wort und Wandel im Leben des Missionars." In *Wort und Gist: Festgabe für Karl Heim zum 60. Geburtstag am 20. Januar 1934,* ed. Adolf Köberle and Otto Schmitz, pp. 229-45. Berlin: Furche Verlag.

1935 "Versuch einer missionarischen Ethik." *EMM* 79: 1-10, 33-44, 65-72.

1938 "Pflicht und Weg evangelischer Kirchenzucht." In *Rechtgläubigkeit und Frommigkeit.* Berlin: Furche Verlag.

1939 "The Biblical View of Religion." In *The Authority of the Faith,* pp. 117-36. Vol. 1 in the Tambaram-Madras Series, 7 vols. London: Oxford Univ. Press.

1948 "Die Botschaft." In *Der gross Auftrag: Weltkrise und Weltmission im Spiegel der Whitby-Konferenz Internationalen Missionstrats. Bericht der deutschen Tielnehmer,* ed. Walter Freytag, assisted by Karl Hartenstein and Carl Ihmels, pp. 32-51. Stuttgart: Quell Verlag.

1951 "Zur Neubesinnung über das Wesen der Mission." In *Deutsche Evangelische Weltmission (Jahrbuch),* pp. 5-24. Hamburg: Verlag der deutschen evang. Missionshilfe.

1952 *Entrückung oder bewahrung.* Kronbüchlein, no. 9. Stuttgart: Evang. Missionsverlag.

1952 "Der gekreuzigte Herr – die Hoffnung für die Welt." Introduction in "Ersten Bericht der beratenden Kommission für das Theme der 2. Vollversammlung des Ökumenischen Rates." *Ökumenische Fundschau* 1: 43-52. Stuttgart: Evang. Missionsverlag.

1952 *Israel im Heilsplan Gottes: Eine biblische Besinnung.* Stuttgart: Evang. Missionsverlag.

1952 "Theologische Besinnung." In *Mission zwischen Gestern und Morgen. Vom Gestaltwandel der Weltmission der Christenheit im Licht der Konferenz des Internationalen Missionsrats in Willingen,* ed. Walter Freytag, pp. 51-72. Stuttgart: Evang. Missionsverlag.

1952 "Übergang und Neubeginn: Zur Tagung des Internationalen Missionsrats in Willingen." *Zeitwende* 24: 334-45. Stuttgart: Evang. Verlagswerk.

1952 "Verwilderte Eschatologie." *Die neue Furche* 6: 18-28. Stuttgart: Verlag die Neue Furche.

1952 "Was bedeutet das Werden der Jungen Kirchen für die Mission heute?" In *Die neue Stunde der Weltmission,* Weltmission heute, no. 2, ed. Walter Freytag and Karl Hartenstein, pp. 22-32. Stuttgart: Evang. Missionsverlag.

1954 *Der wiederkommende Herr: Eine Auslegung der Offenbarung des Johannes.* 3d rev. ed. Stuttgart: Evang. Missionsverlag.

Works about Karl Hartenstein

Maier, Friedrich. "Das missionstheologische Erbe Karl Hartensteins." *Für Arbeit und Besinnung* 8 (1954): 258-68, 278-85. (Kirchlichtheologische Halbmonatsschrift.) Stuttgart: Quell Verlag.

Metzger, Wolfgang, ed. *Karl Hartenstein: Ein Leben für Kirche und Mission.* Stuttgart: Evang. Missionsverlag, 1953.

Schwarz, Gerold. *Mission, Gemeinde und Ökumene in der Theologie Karl Hartensteins.* Stuttgart: Calwer Verlag, 1980.

Thomä, Hedwig. "Karl Hartenstein: Ein Leben in weltweitem Dienst." In *Ökumenische Profile,* vol. 2, ed. Gunter Gloede, pp. 85-94. Stuttgart: Evang. Missionsverlag, 1963.

Wiedenmann, Ludwig. *Mission und Eschatologie: Eine Analyse der neueren deutschen Missionstheologie,* pp. 67-72, 132-44. Padderborn: Bonifacius-Druckerei, 1965.

Norman Goodall

1896–1985

Pilgrim in Missions and Ecumenism

Paul Rowntree Clifford

Norman Goodall was one of the most influential personalities in the missionary and ecumenical movements of the twentieth century. The adjective has been chosen deliberately. To have called him outstanding would have given entirely the wrong impression. In spite of the high offices he held in the International Missionary Council and in the British Free Churches, and his service as moderator of the International Congregational Council, his worldwide ministry was chiefly exercised behind the scenes and out of the limelight – an assessment pointedly emphasized by his own choice of *Second Fiddle* as the title of his delightful autobiography published toward the end of his life.[1] But his influence was wide-ranging, not only on the development of international structures of cooperation, but more particularly on individual people of many races and cultures who were grateful to be able to call him their friend.

The Christian Disciple

All those who knew and loved Norman would want to speak more of the impact of the man himself than of the considerable achievements of his long and varied career. In *One Man's Testimony*,[2] a little gem written shortly after the end of World War II, he set out in clear and simple terms the faith that had held him throughout the years. By that he lived, and the graciousness of his personality was a reflection of the grace of God in Jesus Christ, which had shaped his character from his earliest days. I first came to know him when he was nearly seventy years of age, ostensibly retired, but still full of vigor, lecturing, writing, counseling, supporting – sharing with the younger and less experienced the treasures of a richly stored mind and a profound faith. To see him striding up the path to a meeting over which I was to preside at the Selly Oak Colleges in Birmingham was to know that, whatever the difficulties of the agenda, his wisdom would keep us from making any serious mistake.

Norman had extraordinary clarity of mind and a capacity for expression, both in speech and in writing, which rivaled the best of English prose. This was all the more remarkable in that in his youth he had lacked any formal education beyond the age of fourteen. Leonard Wilson, the bishop of Hong Kong interned by the Japanese and later bishop of Birmingham, once said of him, "He is my mentor for English style," and after a particularly elegant speech of welcome to a conference of church leaders, a bystander was heard to remark, "Don't you long for that man to split an infinitive!"

This pellucid clarity of thought and expression was a reflection of the high standards and self-discipline that were among the most striking characteristics of Norman's whole life. But they did not make him, as they might have done, a formidable person in whose company others felt diminished and ill at ease. He was essentially a gentle soul, sensitive to the feelings of others and with a compassionate understanding of human foibles and faults. It is dangerous to describe anyone as Christlike, and Norman would have found it acutely embarrassing to have had this ascription applied to him. But there can be no doubt that he mirrored the Lord in whose presence he lived and whom he rejoiced to serve. The impact of this on countless people of all ages and races was his principal legacy.

The Foundation of Goodall's Career

Norman was born in Birmingham at the industrial heart of England on August 30, 1896, the twelfth of thirteen children of Thomas Goodall and Amelia Ingram. The family lived in cramped conditions over their father's sweet shop in Handsworth and poverty was never far from their door. Thomas Goodall was the son of "an amiable drunkard," to use Norman's own description, and in his youth belonged to a gang that secured notoriety by breaking up political meetings. Intent on a similar venture one Sunday evening, they entered Wesley Chapel. While his companions slunk out, Thomas stayed and was soundly converted. Some years later he shared a hymnbook there with a young servant girl whom he courted and subsequently married. Together they made a home that became the formative influence on Norman's life.

Thomas had no schooling, began work at eight years of age, and was taught to read by a local barber. Amelia was illiterate and remained so to the end of her days. But their deep Christian faith and their standards of excellence were the matrix in which Norman developed his love for literature and music. A young violin teacher was given the use of the Goodalls' little parlor and in exchange Norman was offered free lessons. His tribute to this unnamed musician, but above all to his father and mother, constitute the most moving passages in his autobiography. The young teacher opened up a world of beauty and delight in the midst of ugly surroundings. Norman's father was a sterling example of the combination of resolute faith and radical politics, informed by an inquiring mind and a remarkably developed sense of literary style. But it was obviously his mother's influence that shaped Norman's character. "There was a moment at the end of her days," he wrote, "when a brother and I were looking at her hands, lined and worn with the years of labour in the service of those she loved. Touching one of her hands my brother said, 'They remind me of the words "I bear on my body the marks of the Lord Jesus." ' He was right. In the whole realm of human relationships I have known no love greater than hers."[3] Norman would undoubtedly have said that the legacy of his own life should properly be ascribed to these three people.

Formal education beyond the age of fourteen was not an option for any boy with Norman's background. The straitened circumstances of his parents made it necessary for him to take a job as an office boy to supplement the marginal family income. However, the routine duties of a junior clerk in the South Staffordshire Water Authority quickly failed to satisfy the ambitions and abilities of a youth who was taking every advantage he could of evening classes, and he was encouraged by an older employee to apply for a clerical post in the Birmingham City Treasurer's Department. He was interviewed and appointed by the treasurer himself, a circumstance that might well have opened up a distinguished career in governmental service, for Norman was brought to the notice of someone who was to play a prominent role in the Civil Service during World War I. That is to anticipate, however. In the meantime Norman had to work his passage in the junior ranks of local government.

In 1915 Norman enlisted in the Royal Army Medical Corps, and after a short spell of service was seconded for clerical duties to the Ministry of Munitions, to which Arthur Collins, the Birmingham City treasurer, had been lent as financial adviser. Encountering his former employee as he was leaving the ministry, Collins handed Norman a note to take to St. Ermin's Hotel, Westminster, adding, "You are the first member of the staff of the Department of National Service. The hotel has been commandeered by the Office of Works and the residents are beginning to move out. I shall be joining you there before long and Neville Chamberlain will arrive as soon as he can free himself from Birmingham."[4] Thus began Norman's wartime service in what was to become a major government department in which he rapidly assumed increasing responsibilities as Arthur Collins's private secretary. This brought him into close contact with ministers of the Crown and high-ranking officials, giving him the opportunity to display the administrative gifts that in later years were to be placed at the service of the world church.

When the war ended, Norman was urged to enter the permanent Civil Service, in which he would doubtless have had a distinguished career. But he felt an irresistible call to the Congregational ministry. The problem was that he had no educational qualifications for admission to training and his heart was set on entering Mansfield College at Oxford, which was open only to postgraduates with a first degree in another discipline. Norman had not even a school-leaving certificate.

He was encouraged to seek out the principal, the renowned Dr. Selbie, to whom he explained his predicament. This wise man obviously spotted the latent gifts of the young civil servant and promised that he could sit an entrance examination if he would prepare for it over the next six months by learning some Greek and Latin, reading the Bible, and practicing essay writing. Thus it came about that Norman entered Mansfield in 1919 to reach the Honours School of Theology under a distinguished faculty, which included C.H. Dodd, G. Buchanan Gray, and Vernon Bartlett. He secured a respectable degree, which was underwritten thirty years later by an Oxford award of a D.Phil. for a thesis entitled "The Principles and Characteristics of Missionary Policy during the Last Fifty Years Illustrated by the History of the LMS." To the end of his life he was a devoted son of the college that had given him such an unexpected opportunity, serving for many years as a member of its governing body.

Ministry and Mission

In 1920 Norman married Doris Stanton, a medical doctor and the daughter of a barrister. They would have two sons and one daughter in the years ahead. On completion of his Oxford course, they offered for service abroad with the London Missionary Society, but the regulations in force prevented them from being accepted because wives were not allowed to take appointments alongside their husbands. So Norman was ordained to the ministry in 1922 at Trinity Congregational Church, Walthamstow, where he remained in pastoral charge for six years until he moved, for another eight years, to a church in the London suburb of New Barnet. In both these congregations he came to value the meaning of Christian fellowship, which, while internally mutually supportive, was outward-looking to mission throughout the world. His people in their turn experienced his sensitive conduct of worship and the quality of his pastoral care, which were to be placed at the service of so many others in the years that followed.

The summons to ministry to the churches overseas was only to be postponed, for in 1936 Norman was invited to become a staff member of the London Missionary Society with secretarial responsibility for India and the South Pacific. This led to extensive travel throughout these regions and a widening circle of personal contacts with missionaries and government officials. His account of visits to 140 Indian villages, his close ties with Dr. Howard Somervell, the Everest explorer and renowned surgeon in charge of the South Travancore Medical Mission at Neyyoor, and his meetings with Mahatma Gandhi, Subhas Chandra Bose, Rabindranath Tagore, and Dr. Ambedkar illustrate the depth and range of his involvement in the service to which he was committed. Clearly he also fell in love with the islands and people of the South Pacific; many of the people became his personal friends. All this prepared him for the wider responsibilities that before long he was asked to shoulder.[5]

In 1944 Norman was appointed to succeed Dr. William Paton as London secretary of the International Missionary Council (IMC), and this was to place him at the center of the developing ecumenical movement. The office was based at Edinburgh House where the Conference of British Missionary Societies had its headquarters. As a member of its committees Norman had come into intimate contact with its formidable secretariat: J.H. Oldham, Kenneth Maclennan, and William Paton himself. He was therefore no stranger to the tasks that now confronted him.

The ending of World War II necessitated IMC's facing the future of the German missions, which, together with those of the occupied countries of Europe cut off from their home bases, had become the responsibility of the IMC during hostilities. The complex problems of dealing with a changed situation landed on Norman's desk, involving establishing relations of confidence with missionary leaders in Europe for which his diplomatic skills and sensitivity were admirably fitted. Furthermore, there was the challenge of reassessing the entire missionary strategy in the confusion of the postwar world.

Plans were afoot for bringing into being the World Council of Churches (WCC), but the missionary organizations felt that the problems confronting them were so urgent that they had to take immediate steps to call an international conference under the auspices of the IMC. Norman was not convinced. He thought that it was better to wait until the WCC had been inaugurated. However, he was overruled and in 1947 a conference was convened at Whitby, Ontario, to review the whole strategy of mission. Norman played a significant part in its preparation and conduct. Writing about it many years later he said, "It is never possible to measure the results of such a meeting as Whitby. If some of its hopes and expectations were never fulfilled this is another reminder both of the agelong mystery of iniquity and the need for a universal Church equipped for a world-wide task and with wisdom and spiritual resources equal to it."[6]

However, the keynote of the conference was the conviction that henceforth the missionary task could be undertaken only in full partnership between the younger and older churches, a conviction that was to take time to be established among those upon whom the missionary societies relied for support and who found it hard to recognize and break with the past assumptions of imperialism. Nevertheless, Norman was convinced that thinking must go much further. A new theology of mission had to be worked out in the radically changed situation of the postwar world. This led to the planning of a further conference of the IMC, held in Willingen, Germany, July 5-17, 1952.

Those who were involved maintain that its conception and conduct were very largely Norman's work. Strangely enough, however, he does not even mention it in his autobiography. The explanation may be that he was disappointed with its outcome. Some of those who knew him best go so far as to say that he thought it was a failure. That is hardly borne out by the introductory chapter he wrote to his edited report of the conference in which he argued that Willingen was a milestone on the road to a theology of mission and not a terminus.[7]

At all events it is clear that Norman believed that the missionary organizations had to come to understand that they were agencies of the world church, and for the next decade he persistently worked to bring about the full integration of the IMC and the WCC. The opportunity to do so was opened up by his appointment in 1954 as secretary of a joint committee to explore ways and means of achieving this end. In the face of a good deal of resistance from those, like Max Warren, who felt that the freedom of missionary societies would be imperiled by integration with ecclesiastical structures, Norman's conviction that church and mission were indivisible won the day. He saw his endeavors finally consummated at the Third Assembly of the World Council at New Delhi in 1961, when integration was finally adopted and Lesslie Newbigin, "representative of the world mission at its best,"[8] was appointed an associate general secretary of the WCC.

On any estimate this was a historic milestone in the evolution of the world church, and with his retirement due at the end of the New Delhi Assembly, Norman's career might well have been thought to have reached its climax. But it is arguable that the last phase of his life not only added to the legacy he left to the ecumenical movement but actually may prove to have been of even greater significance. His contribution to the WCC continued with the invitation to serve for another two to three years as assistant general secretary to Dr. W.A. Visser 't Hooft, and he was later to edit the report of the Fourth Assembly at Uppsala in 1968. Other important publications came from his pen. Following his definitive history of the London Missionary Society in 1954, the Oxford University Press published what have become two standard works on the ecumenical movement: *The Ecumenical Movement: What It Is and What It Does* in 1961, and *Ecumenical Progress: A Decade of Change in the Ecumenical Movement,* eleven years later.

Retirement gave Norman the opportunity to devote himself to interchurch relations in a variety of ways. He was moderator of the International Congregational Council from 1962 to 1966, and moderator of the Free Church Federal Council in the following year – and he played an influential part in bringing together the English Presbyterians and Congregationalists and later the Churches of Christ in the United Reformed Church. He lectured extensively as visiting professor of mission at the Selly Oak Colleges in Birmingham, at the Irish School of Ecumenics in Dublin, at the Jesuit Heythrop College, and at the Pontifical Gregorian University in Rome.

The awakened interest of Roman Catholics in the ecumenical movement following Vatican Council II meant that many were concerned to enter into serious dialogue with leading Protestants. Who was better informed or more sensitively equipped for this than Norman? Hence the invitations that came to him to lecture in Dublin and at Heythrop, where he made many friends. But it was what he called his "Roman Pilgrimage"[9] that in perspective may be judged the climax of his contribution to ecumenism. The way had been paved in Dublin and at Heythrop as well as in many personal friendships. But there can be little doubt that his two visits (when he was nearly eighty years of age) to the English College in Rome, in 1975 and 1976, were fruitful beyond any immediately apparent result. He established relations of confidence with both faculty and students, who appreciated the integrity of his Protestant convictions as well as his openness to all that was best in Roman Catholicism. In particular, a firm friendship was forged with the rector of the English College, Mgr. Murphy O'Connor, later bishop of Arundel, who visited Norman in Oxford in the last stages of Norman's life and who paid a moving tribute to him at his memorial service in London.

Norman sums up his Roman Pilgrimage by saying that he is not sure whether it "has made me a Catholic Protestant or a Protestant Catholic. I hope it has made me a better Christian."[10] If that was true for him, it was certainly true for those who sat at his feet. The influence of such an encounter is impossible to measure, though it is likely to have had more lasting results than many of the more formal conferences that are an increasing feature of Roman Catholic/Protestant relations. At any rate, among those taking the lead in open commitment to ecumenical pilgrimage in Britain are some who shared in the eventful weeks of Norman's own pilgrimage to Rome.

At the end of his life, Norman was cared for by an old friend, Dr. Elizabeth Welford, whom he engaged to marry after the death of his wife. On January 1, 1985, two days before the wedding, he died from a heart attack at her house in Oxford.

Norman was no facile ecumenist. He spent his life wrestling with the obstacles to understanding among Christians and the difficulties inherent in working together with those of differing backgrounds and convictions. But he brought to everything he did not only patience and perseverance but the readiness to listen to and learn from others, which won their respect and affection. While he was too honest to evade or minimize problems, he never allowed them to weaken his vision of One Church United for Mission. That is Norman Goodall's abiding legacy.

Notes

1. Goodall, *Second Fiddle* (London: SPCK, 1979).
2. Goodall, *One Man's Testimony* (London: Independent Press, 1949).
3. Goodall, *Second Fiddle,* p. 9.
4. Ibid., p. 14.
5. Ibid., pp. 42-67.
6. Ibid., p. 93.
7. In *Missions under the Cross* (London: Edinburgh House Press, 1953).
8. Goodall, *Second Fiddle,* p. 107.
9. Ibid., pp. 133-47.
10. Ibid., p. 147.

Selected Bibliography

Works by Norman Goodall

1933 *With All Thy Mind.* London: SCM Press.
1949 *One Man's Testimony.* London: Independent Press. Reprinted with a memoir by Kenneth Slack (SCM Press, 1985).
1953 *Missions under the Cross.* London: Edinburgh House Press.
1954 *History of the London Missionary Society: 1895-1945.* London: Oxford Univ. Press.
1961 *The Sacraments: What We Believe.* London: Independent Press.
1961 *The Ecumenical Movement: What It Is and What It Does.* London: Oxford Univ. Press.
1963 *Christian Ambassador: A Life of Livingstone Warnshuis.* New York: Channel Press.
1966 *The Local Church: Its Resources and Responsibilities.* London: Hodder & Stoughton.
1972 *Ecumenical Progress: A Decade of Change in the Ecumenical Movement.* London: Oxford Univ. Press.
1979 *Second Fiddle.* London: SPCK.

Norman Goodall also wrote numerous articles and pamphlets on mission and theology, a comprehensive collection of which are included in the archives of the London Missionary Society, held at Dr. Williams's Library, Gordon Square, London.

Charles W. Ranson
1903–1988

Missionary, Administrator, Mentor – with a Global View

James K. Mathews

Death came to Charles W. Ranson on January 23, 1988, in Delray Beach, Florida, soon after he had completed his autobiography, *A Missionary Pilgrimage.* We may say that, having lived a full and meaningful life, he died a significant death, for "whether we live or whether we die, we are the Lord's."

Ranson's legacy is manifold: to his family and to a vast network of friends all over the world, to the ecumenical movement, to missionaries and mission-minded persons, and to the church and its ministry in the Third World. He has bequeathed to all who knew him a rich memory of one who combined qualities of Christian statesperson with eloquent preacher, inspiring teacher, sound administrator, scholar, writer, innovator, pastor, friend. I suspect that, most of all, he would want to be remembered as missionary, a thread running through his entire life. In fact, during the last year of his life, in the final conversation I had with Ranson, he expressed the view that the churches at present have not kept faith with the pronounced missionary vision of the nineteenth and early twentieth centuries – to the point of betrayal of that mission.

Charles W. Ranson was born on June 15, 1903, in Ballyclare, County Antrim, Northern Ireland. The middle initial in his name stood for Wesley, and that very fact may have shaped something in him. He was born in an Irish Methodist manse, the third of four children of Henry J.F. and Elizabeth Clarke Ranson. Both parents came from farming families.

Ranson's father trained for the Methodist ministry in Belfast and was ordained in 1895. Ranson remembers his father as a devoted and efficient minister content with mostly rural and small appointments. He was a "good man and a good parent." His mother was brought up in the Church of Ireland, where she acquired a lasting love of the Book of Common Prayer, an enthusiasm she passed on to her son. She also lent laughter, a lighthearted dimension to life, that never left her son. He spoke of a strictly disciplined but kindly upbringing that contributed in every way to his adult life.

The itinerant system of Methodism meant that the family moved at least once every three years. Thus by young manhood he had lived in seven towns. This did tend to his sense of rootlessness. Nevertheless, no serious consequences resulted from this feeling. In fact, it brought enrichment to

Charles Ranson and not a bad training for missionary work. Compensation for Methodist ministers was very modest, assuring a simple existence, likewise familiar to the average missionary.

Early schooling was in the village schools, but at age twelve Ranson departed for Methodist College, Belfast, a good school that was mostly for the children of Methodist manses. He records that his achievements in the classroom and on the playing fields were modest. His years at this school coincided with World War I and so were marked by strictures of many kinds. Nevertheless, his five years at this institution gave him solid learning and lifelong friendships.

There followed a period of about two years during which young Ranson ventured into the business world as an apprentice in the wholesale textile business. This was accompanied by a venture into worldliness in the form of practices and diversions not in keeping with his rather strict Wesleyan upbringing. As he himself states it, he "drifted away from the faith" into a "gloomy nihilism." This took place during a period of considerable unrest in both parts of postwar Ireland.

Call to a Missionary Vocation

This depressing period did not last long. His spirit awakened during evangelistic services in his father's church in 1921. Charles tells the story of his conversion in a simple, straightforward way. He came under conviction, confessed to his father, who did not condemn him but rather prayed with him. His burden lifted, new life began, and his life was redirected. Moreover, his mind was set aflame with a renewed passion for learning. At the same time his sense of vocation was clarified: he was called to be a missionary.

Ranson began to study in earnest for the ministry. He entered Cliff College in Derbyshire, an institution established for the training of lay ministers. A part of the curriculum was practical in nature, contributing toward self-support. Once again, this helped in no small measure to later missionary effectiveness. Cliff also afforded sound grounding in theological studies.

Irish Methodism required of ministers a probationary period of service under the direction of an experienced minister. Ranson was fortunate in having as his mentor a rather colorful and stalwart minister in Belfast, T.J. Allen.

After two years of experience, further formal theological study, and due examination, a successful candidate could be admitted into what was termed *full connexion,* ordained, and a conference member – that is, a member of a preaching order and subject to appointment to a pastoral charge by the Methodist conference. This nomenclature may seem a little quaint to those unfamiliar with Methodist parlance, but it is well understood by members of the Wesleyan family of whatever particular persuasion.

The aspiring young missionary, having completed his probationary period, studied theology at Edgehill Theological College in Belfast. At the same time he pursued studies in philosophy at Queens University in the same city, where he received a diploma in education – also much needed for his future work.

Meanwhile, having offered himself for missionary service, Charles Ranson was accepted by the Methodist Missionary Society in London, first of all for Africa (Gold Coast, later Ghana) and then for India. This involved directed reading in fields related to these areas.

After the manner of many other future ecumenical leaders, he became involved in the Student Christian Movement. He speaks of attending two SCM conferences in 1929. One was a Quadrennial Missionary Conference held at Liverpool and attended by more than two thousand persons. There he met and came under the influence of some of the outstanding missionary and ecumenical figures of the time, among them T.Z. Koo, C.F. Andrews, William Temple, Joseph H. Oldham, and S.K. Datta. He would see more of them and others like them through the years and throughout the world.

The second conference was of the World's Student Christian Federation at Glion above Montreux, Switzerland. This experience broadened Ranson's horizons and was the occasion for his first meeting with the young Dutchman Willem A. Visser 't Hooft, later to become first general secretary of the World Council of Churches. Their paths would cross repeatedly in the years ahead.

The year 1929 was also marked by Ranson's ordination as a minister in the Irish Conference of the Methodist Church and his departure for missionary service in India. As in the case of many missionaries he was not without a sense of pouring his life down the drain of history – "ministerial oblivion." But not so! It opened up the whole world to him and provided the wide stage upon which he would make his most solid contributions. It was a handsome and eager young missionary who was met at the bottom of the gangplank in Madras some weeks later.

The India Years

It was another missionary, David Livingstone, who used to say that after the exploration was the beginning of the enterprise. That enterprise, for Charles Ranson, began at Madras, an often hot and sticky city. Actually, the setting was at the village of Ikkadu, west of Madras. There, as a neophyte missionary must, he confronted the formidable task of learning the language. In his case it was Tamil. It was not all work, however, for it was punctuated with tennis, teas, some other socializing, and the beginning of some direct involvement in the missionary enterprise and engaging in village church services. Some relief from the "hot weather" was a period each year spent in a hill station, beautiful Kodaikanal.

Unfortunately, the young missionary's study of the language was to be interrupted by his being transferred back to the city of Madras proper, to Triplicane, to fill a sudden vacancy. At Triplicane there was a threefold evangelistic, educational, and social-service institute all named after a famous predecessor, F.W. Kellett. Since the principal medium used was English, Ranson admits that he never really attained full mastery of Tamil, a great disappointment for him. He suddenly found himself principal of a school and a teacher of religious studies and English in the same. He had to do general coordination of the whole complex, including the securing of Sunday-evening lectures for Kellett Hall. Frequently these were outstanding figures, and the lectures contributed to the cultural life of the whole city.

Ranson also engaged in other useful activities, notably the addressing of a succession of social problems of Madras. He helped motivate like-minded persons in social change through an organization called the Triplicane Sociological Brotherhood. He mentions the building of sewers, working toward a minimum-wage law, opposing child labor, and later working toward the improvement of housing. He also helped establish the first radio station in India, later to become a part of All-India Radio. During this period, Gandhi was at the height of his activity and influence; Ranson became acquainted with his thought and nationalist program.

Most important for him personally was that he met the woman who was to become his wife, Grace Gibb, a professor of history at Women's Christian College, Madras. She was of Quaker background and Scottish. They were married in 1932. Grace was a lovely lady, a person of spirit, as this writer can testify, having known her for the last dozen years of her life. In 1935 they returned to England on furlough.

Their two years in the homeland were well-spent at Oxford University. While at Triplicane the multifaceted institution was visited by the famous Lindsay Commission, which was studying the future of education in India. They were particularly taken by the rather unique approach of the Kellett complex. Moreover, the chairman, A.D. Lindsay, master of Balliol College, Oxford, seems to have been taken by young Ranson and especially by the social outreach of the institution.

Accordingly, he encouraged the missionary to undertake studies at Balliol College during his forthcoming furlough.

Charles was actually enrolled as a student at Oriel College rather than Balliol. This proved to be a very successful venture, extending to two years. Years later while in England, Ranson proudly showed me around his college; clearly, it had been significant in his career. It afforded him once again a very wide circle of new friends. It served to mature his theological understanding and commitment. Almost by accident it afforded him an opportunity for an unusual visit to Nazi Germany with a group of concerned British churchmen. It saw the birth of the Ransons' first child, Mary. (There was later a son, John, and a daughter, Anne.)

Charles earned an Oxford degree and published in book form his dissertation entitled *A City in Transition: Studies in the Social Life of Madras.* Lindsay wrote a foreword to it. The work had to do with the social outreach program of Kellett. Thus it arose out of missionary activity and proved of further value in the later development of Christian work in that great city, a part of Ranson's legacy.

I have referred above to a maturing of his theology. This was influenced in part by Barth; in part by Kraemer's emphasis on biblical realism; in part by British reflection as diverse as William Temple, C.H. Dodd, John Baillie; together with the practical missiological wisdom of J.H. Oldham, Walter Freytag, and Max Warren; and not forgetting the insights of such Indian theologians as Paul Devanandan, M.M. Thomas, and P. Chenchiah. He became a passionate believer in the meaning and relevance of Christ's mission in the world today. Ranson was nothing if not Christ-centered, thoroughly committed to the mandate: "As the Father has sent me, even so send I you." Hear him state his perspective directly:

> The Christian world mission is rooted in the Christian revelation. That revelation, though it is preserved and communicated in the written record of the Bible, is essentially a revelation through action. For the Bible is the record of God's mighty acts. God's action in history – in His dealings with men – is a disclosure both of His sovereign purpose and of the way in which that purpose is fulfilled.[1]

Upon returning to India in 1937 Ranson soon took up his erstwhile field of labor at Ikkadu. Medical, agricultural, and educational work was extended also to an industrial emphasis under the leadership of Blanche Tweddle, a perfect genius in this field and a person who was to become another close, lifelong friend. Ikkadu was also the base of an extensive village evangelistic program in a mass-movement area. There Charles Ranson gained experience over a broad range of work that made up the missionary endeavor.

Ranson was an observer and minor participant at the famous World Conference of the International Missionary Council held in Tambaram at Madras Christian College, which brought together nearly five hundred Christian leaders from all over the world. Here again he was enabled to extend his already wide circle of acquaintances. It was also an opportunity to observe the state of the world church on the eve of World War II. The "Younger Churches," as they came to be known in that setting, were already manifesting a mounting self-consciousness. Heated debates took place on relationships among the world religions, prompted by Hendrik Kraemer's great and controversial book *The Christian Message in a Non-Christian World.* Likewise a discussion of church versus kingdom of God was carried on. One might almost say that the theological and missionary agenda was effectively set for the rest of Ranson's life. Once again he was in the right place at the right time.

During World War II, Ranson made a self-conscious decision not to volunteer for military service. Probably he was right. The early war years found him a pastor in the hill station of Simla,

India's summer capital in the Himalayas. This appointment to a union congregation in that city was partly owing to his poor health. It meant that he did frequently preach to the viceroy, Lord Linlithgow, an elder in the Church of Scotland. Here he had occasion to become acquainted with some of India's national leaders.

In 1943 Ranson joined the staff of the National Christian Council of India, Burma, and Ceylon, with headquarters in Nagpur. While there he shared responsibility as an editor of the *National Christian Council Review,* quite influential in its day. The council work enabled him to travel all over India. His major responsibility was for theological education, and he became thoroughly familiar firsthand with the then-existing facilities in the region. This, in turn, led to the publishing of a report on this subject, his second and widely influential book entitled *The Christian Minister in India.* Soon after its completion he returned to England for a well-deserved furlough, which began in 1945 and from which the Ransons were not to return to India.

It must be acknowledged that *The Christian Minister in India* is an authentic part of Ranson's legacy to India. Though the survey itself was the work of scores of people over many years, the report was his own. It was well received, widely used to guide theological education in India, and is not without continuing value to this day. Here are two samples from its pages, emphasizing that "the paramount need of the Church in India" is the recruitment and training of an adequate ministry:

> The example of our Lord and the experience, through the centuries, of His Church sustains the conviction that the strategic point in the missionary task is the preparation of Christian pastors and teachers. The concentration of adequate resources at this point is, humanly speaking, the only guarantee both of the Church's stability and of its power to meet widening opportunities.[2]

> There is no task in the whole Christian enterprise in India which calls more clearly for the close and continued partnership of the older churches with the Church in India than the education of the indigenous ministry. There is no task on which the future well-being of the Church in India so greatly depends. The resolve to make the training of the ministry the pivot of Christian strategy may well be for churches and missions in post-war India, "the one great choice, which . . . carries all the rest in the end and carries them high."[3]

Secretary of the International Missionary Council

The year 1946 saw a further turn in Ranson's career. He became research secretary of the International Missionary Council (IMC), founded in 1921 largely on the initiative of John R. Mott. For the next several years the Ransons shuttled their residence between the New York region and the London region. It was in 1946 that this writer came first to know Charles Ranson in what was to be a growing and enduring friendship extending almost exactly over the last half of his life.

July 1947 saw the assembling of a smaller meeting of the IMC in Whitby near Toronto, Ontario. It picked up the missionary strands severed by the agony of World War II. In addition to his research duties, Charles was asked to organize this meeting. Moreover, he edited its proceedings in *Renewal and Advance,* published in 1948. The chief business was to receive an update on the missionary movement and to plan with regard to the new situation that lay ahead for the churches. Several phrases lifted out of the Whitby gathering reveal its emphases: "Partnership in Obedience," "Supranationality of the Church," "Expectant Evangelism." All have remained in the parlance of the worldwide church. The meeting decided that the IMC should not then be a part of but "in association with" the World Council of Churches (WCC), which was founded in Amsterdam the next summer. Finally, Whitby unanimously elected Charles W. Ranson to the newly created post of general secretary of the IMC. He served in that capacity for ten years. It might be said that a principal contribution he made was simply to show over a decade what "partnership in obedience" really means in a global sense.

Ranson did not administer the IMC from a swivel chair in New York or London. He was very much a field person, and his field was the world, visiting the member councils. Those of us who were fortunate enough to receive his travel diaries were highly favored. He rendered a fascinating and illuminating account of his labors in what might be regarded as obscure corners of the world. A part of his contribution was thus on a person-to-person basis.

His tenure was punctuated also by two other IMC gatherings. One was at Willingen in West Germany, July 5-17, 1952. This was for the writer and for a number of other young mission executives a first ecumenical experience – a thrilling one. The theme was "The Missionary Obligation of the Church." For some this phrasing was regarded a "disastrous prejudgment"; for others a simple acknowledgment of the fundamental mandate of the church. The churches were beginning to renew their pace in global witness following World War II. Strangely enough and in contrast to Whitby's "Partnership in Obedience," Willingen produced no slogans. Still, the influence of Willingen continues until the present. Notable at this meeting were the remarkable Bible studies on 1 Corinthians by Hendrik Kraemer. Of significance also was the statement on behalf of Pentecostal churches offered by David J. du Plessis. Ranson's firm hand was evident throughout the sessions.

The second major meeting was held from December 28, 1957 to January 8, 1958 at University College, Accra, Ghana, and is known simply as "the Ghana Assembly." In contrast to its predecessor, sharper questions were raised concerning the legitimacy of the missionary movement. Its discussions presaged many of the more drastic changes that have characterized the enterprise since that time such as the rapid reduction in Western missionary personnel of mainline denominational mission agencies. A statement entitled "The Christian Mission at This Hour" set forth the tenor of the meeting. This is found in *The Ghana Assembly of the International Missionary Council*, edited by Ronald K. Orchard. The integrating of IMC with the World Council of Churches was hotly debated but generally approved. Thus in 1961 the IMC became the Commission of World Mission and Evangelism (CWME) of the WCC.

A pall was cast upon this meeting with the word that Grace Ranson had been killed in an automobile accident on New Year's Eve 1957. This tragedy occurred at about the time the assembly was celebrating John Wesley's Watchnight Covenant Service. A part of this service includes the words: "put me to doing, put me to suffering; . . . let me be brought low; . . . let me be empty." By God's mercy Ranson was given the power to endure this tragic loss. Tragedy was to strike again in the death by cancer of his second wife, Barbara, in 1971; and yet again in the death of his eldest daughter, Mary, of a brain tumor in 1984. Again, sustained of God, Charles endured.

Theological Education Fund

In spite of all that has been recounted, what was to be in many respects Charles Ranson's major contribution lay ahead of him. At its last meeting before "integration" the IMC approved in Ghana the Theological Education Fund (TEF). This initiative was consistent with Ranson's interest in theological education in India, now enlarged to the world scene. The universal need was evident enough. Charles sought financial resources from John D. Rockefeller, Jr. He was very cautious and circumspect. Indeed, Yorke Allen of Sealantic Fund (a Rockefeller enterprise) was assigned to gathering facts on theological education around the world. He did this, amassing his facts in a massive volume, *A Seminary Survey*. The result was a conditional Rockefeller offer of $2 million, provided this was matched by mission boards. This was done in two weeks' time.

The total sum was expended within five years. The Mexico City meeting of CWME (1963) then authorized raising another $4 million. It should be noted that Europeans were at first suspicious of these American proposals, but this was overcome and they too supported the continuing program. Charles Ranson was invited to administer the TEF and did so from 1958 to 1962. (He served also in 1961-62 as president of the Irish Conference of the Methodist Church.) Buildings, libraries, and textbooks were provided, but chiefly people benefited through more adequate ministerial training. This contribution of Ranson to church life and work in third-world countries is beyond calculation.

From 1962 to 1968 Ranson was professor of Ecumenical Theology at Drew University, Madison, New Jersey, serving in 1964-66 also as dean. This was followed by teaching theology and ecumenics at Hartford Seminary Foundation (1968-72). Finally, he was minister from 1969 to 1975 of the Congregational Church in Salisbury, Connecticut, where he had settled. Thus, toward the end of his active career his contribution was again as teacher and pastor, roles in which he was highly effective.

As the story has unfolded various aspects of Ranson's legacy have been noted. Allow me to add two more. First, he had a talent for making and keeping friends in every setting and across every national and denominational boundary. He made each and all of his friends seem special. In the United States he was part of at least two small discussion groups, one of which was "Lux Mundi," a circle of distinguished missiologists and mission administrators.

Another was a smaller and less-formal group that met for some years at Drew. He was the mentor of this group. Not the least of his contributions was to suggest to others the reading of books he had found particularly helpful. Among many others were these: *The Apostolic Preaching and Its Developments,* by C.H. Dodd; *The Lower Levels of Prayer,* by George S. Stewart; and *The Fourth Gospel,* by Sir Edwyn Hoskyns. This sort of thing was immensely helpful to the younger members of this group. He loved books. On the occasion of one of his several retirements, our little group, having made a tactful inquiry of his preferences, presented him with the complete *Oxford English Dictionary,* which I later noted was well used. This was vintage Charles W. Ranson.

A further contribution, and an enormous one, is surely Ranson's record as one of the ablest interpreters of and apologists for the world mission of the church in his day. This was accomplished in literally hundreds of forums, including many university lectureships, across the world. He had an attractive mode of speech and the hint of an Irish accent did not harm at all. He was thoughtful, evangelical, and always possessed of good common sense and great good humor. He had about him a touch of the poet. It was always a joy and a profit to hear him. Fortunately some of these utterances are preserved for us in such books as *The Things That Abide; That the World May Know;* and finally in his autobiography. He remained a committed missionary to the very end. In one sentence his view was that which was underscored at Willingen: the missionary movement is the mission of the triune God. For all of which we say, Thanks be unto God for the life and work of Charles W. Ranson.

Notes

1. Address in *"Adam, Where Art Thou?"* (New York, Interdivision Committee on Foreign Work, Methodist Board of Missions, 1956), pp. 65-66.
2. Charles W. Ranson, *The Christian Minister in India* (London: Lutterworth Press, 1947), p. 271.
3. Ibid., p. 274.

Selected Bibliography

Works of Charles W. Ranson

1938 *A City in Transition: Studies in the Social Life of Madras.* Madras: The Christian Literature Society for India.

1940 *The Things That Abide.* Madras: The Christian Literature Society for India.

1947 *The Christian Minister in India.* London: Lutterworth Press. (First published in India in 1945.)

1948 (ed.) *Renewal and Advance.* London: Edinburgh House Press.

1952 *Three Addresses,* Sixteenth Quadrennial Conference of the SVM. New York: Student Volunteer Movement.

1953 *That the World May Know.* New York: Friendship Press.

1956 Address in *"Adam, Where Art Thou?"* Ed. Creighton Lacy. New York: Interdivision Committee on Foreign Work, Board of Missions of the Methodist Church.

1988 *A Missionary Pilgrimage.* Grand Rapids, Mich.: Wm. B. Eerdmans.

Max Warren

1904–1977

Disciplined Intercession That Embraced the World

F.W. Dillistone

Max Warren (August 13, 1904-August 22, 1977) was the outstanding missionary leader in Britain in the midtwentieth century. He became general secretary of the Church Missionary Society in 1942 and served in that position for twenty-one years. During the last fourteen years of his life he continued to remain in close touch with overseas missionaries and to think and write and speak about many aspects of the missionary cause. As leader in the theology of mission, as well as in the policies and organization of a great missionary society, he occupies an unparalleled position in the history of overseas missions from Britain in the twentieth century.

Early Years

Max was of Irish parentage. His father and mother had each responded to the missionary challenge and were on furlough when Max was born. He went out with them to India and during most of the first eight years of his life absorbed the sounds and sights of a great Eastern civilization. A sister had died of bubonic plague and his two bothers were at school in the homeland. In consequence, he was in many ways a lonely child but maintained in his autobiography that the effect of this on his imagination and love of reading had been altogether beneficial. At length it was necessary for him to take up school life in England. This brought him eventually to one of the famous English public schools, Marlborough, where he showed promise on the hockey field and gained a love of the study of history through the influence of an enthusiastic master.

This love of history never faded from schooldays onward. He won highest honors at Cambridge in this discipline and could have taken up an academic career. But he had already been seized by a more intense devotion – a devotion to Jesus Christ and his service. This meant that the study of history was to be dominantly focused upon *God's* activity in history and in particular in the Christ-event and the succeeding history of the Christian church. The sending of the Son, and the consequent sending of his disciples to continue his mission, became to Max the theme of supreme interest, though this did not prevent him from stretching out through books in all directions in order to learn about the customs and histories and cultures of people the world over. He read voraciously and constantly did his utmost to pass on to others the insights gained thereby.

The dedication to discipleship was made within the context of evangelical Christianity. The Church Missionary Society (CMS) drew its support from the evangelical wing of Anglicanism in the British Isles and in some of the Dominions. Max took a share in seaside missions in which his brother was leader; at Cambridge he became a vigorous member of the evangelical Christian Union. Even before he entered university he had become convinced that his calling was to missionary service, and in his very first term an appeal for recruits to go out to begin new work in northern Nigeria led him to a firm commitment. Throughout his period at Cambridge, however fully occupied he might be with academic work, athletic pursuits, and personal witness, he never lost the burning enthusiasm to make the Gospel of Christ known among Muslims in the borderland between Nigeria and the Sudan.

He was accepted as a layman by the CMS and sailed for Nigeria in 1927, hoping to be married on his first furlough to Mary Collett, to whom he had become engaged some months before leaving England. He threw himself into the work at the mission station in Zaria, learning the language, teaching in the school, helping in the dispensary. But before a year had passed his health collapsed, he was sent home to England critically ill and for three years struggled to survive the ravages of tuberculosis, which had infected his body. In hospital he passed through travail of soul as well as of body, but ultimately came forth a new man, with scars still on him but ready now to begin his life's work. He was married and shortly afterward ordained into the Christian ministry. After a comparatively brief period spent mainly in youth work, he was appointed to the incumbency of the strategically important parish of Holy Trinity, Cambridge.

The Church Missionary Society

Holy Trinity became famous in the nineteenth century by reason of the outstanding ministry of Charles Simeon, one of the most distinguished of Anglican evangelicals and a wholehearted supporter of CMS in its early days. The church, situated in a central position in Cambridge, provided rich opportunities for a ministry of preaching and leadership in worship and at the same time made possible the outreach in personal evangelism and counseling in which Max excelled. He built up the congregation and prepared them for the crisis of war, seeking to strengthen their confidence in the unceasing providence of the living God. At the same time he kept steadily before his people the call from the wider world and soon was appointed to serve on the Executive Committee of the CMS in London. When the general secretary of the CMS resigned in 1942, the young man of thirty-eight had already made so marked an impression by his obvious ability and promise of leadership that he was chosen to fill the post.

It is hard now to imagine a more daunting task in Christian leadership for any man to have been called to undertake at that particular time. There were more than a thousand CMS missionaries scattered over Africa and the East, some in prison camps, some prevented from returning to England for furlough, many cut off from any regular communication with headquarters, many uncertain regarding the possibilities of war in their own territory. In addition there was widespread disruption among those parishes in England that supported the CMS, and the financial outlook was therefore precarious. Finally, the air raids on London were making work in the city, where CMS headquarters was situated, dangerous and exhausting for the society's staff. Yet Max had little hesitation in responding to the call to responsibility for the society whose members had been a supportive community for him since childhood and in whose particular function in the calling of God he most firmly believed.

He set to work at once to renew the vision and energies of the home staff by establishing personal relationships with them and by recalling in his writings the history of the CMS in the purpose of God. The work of mission had never been easy. Heroic men and women had labored in the nineteenth century, often against fearful odds. However difficult the present situation might be through the shaking of the nations, the call to evangelize still sounded insistently in the ears of all who honored Christ as Lord. Max tried to build up a dedicated team in Britain of those willing to consecrate their varying gifts to the one task of communicating the Gospel.

Only once during his five years as secretary was he able to travel abroad, though to visit overseas and see mission stations at firsthand was his ambition as soon as conditions allowed. In 1943 he faced the hazards of a transatlantic crossing in order to attend the Jubilee meeting of the Foreign Missions Conference of North America in Chicago in January 1944. By so doing he began to establish the links with American missionary leaders that were to prove so valuable in days to come. He saw, as few others in Britain did at the time, how vitally important the contribution of America within the total missionary enterprise was going to be in the postwar world. The old concept of empire was on its way out, and yet that was the context within which so much of Anglican missionary activity had been carried on. Within the new world order, it was supremely desirable that cooperation among the missionary societies – and many of those were American-based – should be fostered in every possible way. Questions of denomination were secondary. The all-important matter was to promote intelligent interchange within the common task of world evangelization.

Such an attitude would have gained general approval within the Church of England but there was still too strong a tradition of seeking to plant Anglicanism within the countries united within the British Commonwealth. Max was a keen patriot and a loyal Anglican, but he knew that transcending all particular loyalties was the universal obligation to be faithful to the Lord of the Gospel. So he rejoiced whenever an opportunity occurred to make friends with those who owed their primary obedience to the Lord and to his commission. From 1947 onward Max visited America frequently, and friendships, for example, made at one of the great Meadville conferences, remained with him to the end of his life.

A Legacy of Writing

By 1947 the way was open for Max to begin his long series of visitations (I use this term because they were much more than casual or even merely friendly visits) to different parts of the world. On each of his journeys he kept a careful and yet lively travel diary. However exhausted he might be at the end of a day, he still found strength to write down his impressions, his memories of significant interviews, his comments on important issues raised. When he returned to London, the whole diary for the particular trip was typed and circulated to his fellow secretaries for information, and ultimately all the diaries were bound into separate volumes. There are nearly forty of these volumes in existence and in some respects they constitute Max's most distinctive legacy. I do not know of any comparable record of developments international, political, ecclesiastical, and missiological between the years 1944 and 1970.

Max had a deep concern for accuracy of reporting and believed that one way to achieve this was to accept the discipline of a *daily* recall of events. He possessed an unusual command of language, which enabled him to transmit vivid impressions of social intercourse, lively descriptions of scenery, and pen-portraits of those whom he met on his journeys. He knew well the value of such records to a trained historian, and he was determined to do everything in his power to make the future historian's task easier. But this was not the only use to which the diaries could be put. Not long before Max assumed his responsibilities at CMS the general secretary had launched a monthly *News-Letter* as a way of keeping home members of the society in touch with significant developments on the field. Max quickly saw the potentialities of this medium and decided to make it a major instrument in his strategy of communication. He was convinced that it was necessary for people at large to become aware of the realities of the world situation. It was not enough for the *News-Letter* to record statistics of conversions or stories of the successful establishment of new Christian institutions. Rather, it was of the first importance that those concerned with the missionary enterprise should come to realize what great changes were taking place in the world, the emergent problems of race, the burgeoning of nationalistic aspirations, the decline of European influence, the resurgence of non-Christian faiths – in short, the wholly new context within which the missionary enterprise must be carried on.

Gradually, not only CMS supporters but also a wider body of missionary sympathizers recognized that here was a balanced, informed, farsighted commentary on what was happening in the world, based on careful reading of up-to-date books and on a constant flow of letters coming in from different parts of the mission field. There was nothing quite like it. Every issue was carefully planned, sometimes months ahead, and every issue dealt with an important feature affecting the spread of the Gospel. Often events proved that Max's insights regarding likely developments were better informed than those of many politicians or journalists. Yet he had no desire to establish himself as an authority on world affairs. He wanted, rather, to discern the signs of the times and to summon those obeying the Great Commission to face the realities of the movements of peoples and to work out appropriate policies accordingly.

For Max was convinced that no individual can survive in a closed shop, secular or sacred. We are all subject to the influences that surround us, social, economic, cultural, and religious. The Gospel must be proclaimed to the individual in his particular setting, and that means in his language, in his social context, in his aspirations, in his fears. To help readers grasp the nature of these varying settings, Max spared no pains. He engaged research assistants, but still never recommended a book that he had not read himself. He kept the CMS *News-Letter* as his own personal medium and in twenty-one years produced an invaluable series reflecting world events and what he believed to be the courageous Christian reaction to them.

In addition he found time to write an impressive array of relatively small books and pamphlets and articles, dealing with such subjects as the missionary imperative, partnership, and the pastoral care of missionaries. A special interest, to which he devoted time and attention, was that of the recruitment and training of missionaries; his insights he freely shared with American leaders, and much thought has been given to the subject in the past twenty-five years. It was only after his retirement from the general secretaryship that he could attempt to write larger books, and not until the last three years of his life did two major volumes appear: his autobiography, entitled *Crowded Canvas,* and his apologia for his missionary calling, *I Believe in the Great Commission.* In and through these two books he gathered up his life experiences and his understanding of the Christian mission. They can be regarded as a major part of his legacy to the future.

The Voluntary Principle

If there was one issue in missionary policy about which Max felt more deeply and expressed himself more forcefully than about any other, it was that to which he constantly referred as the "voluntary principle." In some respects it has a particular relevance, historical and organizational, to the situation within the Church of England, but he was convinced that other churches and denominations needed to remind themselves of its importance. In the laudable desire of many Christians to view the missionary calling as addressed to *the whole church,* there was ever the danger that missions would become just one among many other interests and would cease to be the major, even consuming, interest for a particular band of devoted disciples. He did not dispute the fact that every church in its corporate life must make provision for worship, for relief work, for care of the aged and sick, for youth organizations, and so on. But he was ever jealous for priority to be given to the commission from the One who has said, "As my Father hath sent me, even so send I you." And he believed that this sense of priority could be preserved only if there were bands of volunteers, dedicated specifically to this task, on behalf of and as a continuing example to, the whole church.

A task force, a band of pioneers, a reconnaissance team was, he believed, essential if the missionary response to the divine calling was to receive its rightful expression.

The insistence on the voluntary principle involved him in two famous encounters. In the Church of England, since the end of World War I, there had been a strong movement toward a fuller independence of the church in relation to the state. In consequence the Church Assembly, the church's "parliament," was set up with its sectional committees. Not unnaturally a Missionary Council of the Assembly was established to keep in touch with the varying activities of the missionary societies within the Church of England. By the time Max assumed his responsibilities as general secretary, questions were arising: Could not all the societies be integrated and become a single department of the Church Assembly under its control? Was not the missionary call a challenge to the *whole church?* Would there not be significant economies and increased efficiency if all could work together under one strategic control? An authoritative book was written, surveying all the overseas commitments of the Church of England, and a commission was appointed to consider how these might be brought under more unified control.

But Max saw immediately that the voluntary principle, on which he set so much store, was at stake. He sensed the dangers of standardization and remote control. In a brilliant pamphlet entitled *Iona or Rome,* he looked back on the history of Christianity in England and drew attention to the *two* strands that had characterized it from the beginning. There was the Celtic strand, the result of heroic efforts by bands of monastic missionaries from Ireland, held together within their order by a common loyalty; there was the Roman strand, the result of the extension of Roman Christianity by more authoritarian means. Max did not deny that there was a place for both concepts of mission but deplored the possibility of the first being nullified by being swallowed up in the second.

Few men, I suspect, have ever gloried in the history and character of the Church Missionary Society in the way that Max did. He wanted it to make a major contribution to the establishment of the church in other lands but also, at the same time, to be ever pressing forward into the regions beyond. He was convinced that a voluntary society, whose members shared one dominant purpose, and who were linked together by one common loyalty, constituted an essential element within the strategy of world evangelization. So far as the Church of England was concerned, the commission to which I have referred reported in favor of the continuance of missionary societies, and the CMS (though smaller today in its number of overseas workers) survives as a vital part of the life of the Church of England.

The second encounter took place in Ghana on the occasion of the meeting of the International Missionary Council (IMC) in December 1957-January 1958. Here the issue at stake was the possibility of the IMC becoming a division or department of the World Council of Churches (WCC). At first sight this seemed an eminently desirable development. Since 1948 the WCC had fostered ecumenical relationships and coordinated Christian witness in various spheres. The IMC had a long and distinguished history in the field of mission. Could it not become even more effective if it acted under the umbrella of the WCC? And could not its representatives at Geneva ensure a proper place for mission within the many and varied activities of the WCC?

Max, however, was not convinced. Again he saw the danger of the damping down, if not of the extinguishing, of the voluntary principle. It was not the case for a moment that he was cool on ecumenism. He had crusaded in favor of the united Church of South India being recognized in England, and the CMS had continued to give it full support. Moreover, he had rejoiced in his links with members of other denominations and had welcomed possibilities of cooperation with other missionary societies. But again he feared that the great and free fellowship of missionary societies within the IMC could easily lose its drive and enthusiasm if regarded simply as a department of the WCC. He was too well aware of the history of officialdom and institutionalism and believed that the proposal as presented at Ghana was premature and could lead to the withdrawal of certain valued societies that had hitherto been glad to be associated with the IMC.

On this occasion Max's protest, though treated with respect, did not prevent the proposed integration taking place at New Delhi in 1961. One of the last essays he wrote was a contribution to the Festschrift for Professor Dr. J. Verkuyl. In this he looked back on the decade and a half that had passed since the fusion. It is a fair, careful, and wide-ranging survey, which does not seek simply to justify his own doubts and apprehensions. Nevertheless, it is impossible not to feel the throb of his never-ceasing concern for world mission and his conviction that this can best be implemented by voluntary societies fostering that "spiritual energy" to which he alludes and directing their efforts toward that goal of world evangelization that was so near to his own heart.

A Deepening Theology of Mission

Bearing all the responsibilities of administration, correspondence, personal counseling, travel, authorship of books and newsletters, Max might surely have been justified in concluding that he could give little time to wide reading and deep thinking. On the contrary, however, this was the part of his ministry that he regarded as so important that only by paying constant attention to it could he adequately fulfill his other duties. In spite of all that there was to be proud of in the history of evangelical missionary activity, it could not be claimed that the *theology* of mission had received the attention it deserved.

He determined, therefore, to spare no effort in working at the subject himself and in encouraging young scholars in particular to devote themselves to it. Missionaries had always responded to the call to bear witness to the good news of God's saving activity through Christ. But it is not sufficient, he held, simply to utter a form of words, however orthodox the form may seem to be. It is necessary, rather, to relate the Gospel to all that we can discern of God's activity in history both before and after the Christ-event.

Ever since the earliest years of his own Christian discipleship, he had been fascinated by the prophetic books of the Old Testament. Here were the utterances of men who looked out toward the horizon of their world scene and discerned signs of God's working, not only in the experiences of the covenant people, but also in the movements of other nations. His favorite was the prophet Habakkuk, a noble watchman, who faced the reality of events in the world around, yet declared that those who maintained a true reliance upon God would live. Max saw a developing pattern emerging, the result of God's controlling hand in world affairs, a pattern that was to receive its definitive shape in and through the sending of the Christ. Here was the first stage in a theology of mission.

But this was not enough. What had been happening in the world since the great events of the first century? What had God been doing through his servants in the church? What had God been doing, what was God still doing, *outside* the obvious borders of Christian communities? These were questions that pressed in upon Max with increasing insistence. In part they could be tackled academically, but he himself was deeply involved in the actual missionary enterprise, and these questions were intimately related to it.

While trying in every way possible to watch world developments and to discern signs of God's providence, he read, in the late 1950s, a book that made a profound impression upon him. It was Kenneth Cragg's *Call of the Minaret*. Can we with all honesty affirm that God is at work in the world of Islam as well as within the Christian community? If so, what does this mean for the task of communicating the Gospel? In the history of Christian missions there have been shining examples of men and women who have become exceedingly proficient in Arabic and thereby able to bear witness to their faith among Muslims. But has there been a sufficient willingness to enter into the actual worldview of the Muslim, his outlook on God, humankind, and the world, and to discern signs of the divine presence in areas hitherto regarded as pagan?

Max resigned his post as general secretary in 1963 but this did not imply any relaxing of his concern for missiology. During the last period of his life the new emphases in his theology, which began to find expression around 1960, occupied his thinking and writing more and more. He edited The Christian Presence series of books. These were written by men who had labored as missionaries among Muslims, Hindus, Buddhists, and devotees of primitive religions. In these books they attempted to understand how God was at work in the hearts of those committed to other faiths. In addition, Max sought to explore more comprehensively the doctrine of the Holy Spirit, trying to discern evidences of the Spirit operating within non-Christian cultures. At the same time he tried to penetrate more deeply into the central Christian affirmation concerning the *uniqueness* of Jesus Christ and into the meaning of the cross as the power of God unto salvation for *all* people.

Nothing, however, brought him greater joy and satisfaction than the opportunity in the last twelve years of his life to enter vicariously into the actual work of mission in India. In the course of her training for missionary service, his daughter met Roger Hooker, himself in training for work in north India. They were married and went out to work, first in theological training, and then in a pioneering adventure in evangelism in the city of Varanasi. Roger entered the university as a student and gained proficiency in Hindi and Sanskrit languages and literature. Meanwhile he and his wife were seeking to carry on their evangelistic mission through *dialogue*, a word that has gained increasing attention in missionary circles in recent years.

In his characteristically imaginative way, Max allied himself enthusiastically with this new venture. Whatever other demands there might be on his energies (and often toward the end of his life his bodily energy was severely limited), the weekly letter went out, conveying news and comments and responding to the equally regular letters coming from the field. The exchange of correspondence became, as it were, a primal dialogue giving continuing inspiration to Roger in his dialogues with Hindus and Muslims, and to Max in his dialogues through personal conversation and correspondence and writing. "Dialogue" was no mere gimmick or catchword. It described a process of establishing real friendship and of obtaining, through that process, a deepening understanding of the faith by which each other lived.

All this, Max believed, could be theologically grounded in the nature of God's activity through his prophets, through his Son, and through his Holy Spirit. The Gospel could not be forced upon human consciousnesses. Nor could it be broadcast as a mere item of information. God's way had always been the way of self-involvement in a situation leading to understanding, sacrifice, and love. "As my Father hath sent me, even so send I you."

In the year of his seventieth birthday, Max, in his autobiography, looked back on his experiences of divine goodness and guidance, and two years later gave his final extended testimony in the book *I Believe in the Great Commission.* He never ceased to be an evangelist. He believed that the supremely important method of evangelism was through friendship. He and his wife opened their home and maintained a program of boundless hospitality to make friendships possible. And behind all outward engagements there was the firm discipline of disciplined intercession which, as one of his closest friends wrote, "embraced the world."

Let me conclude with words of his written in a *News-Letter* in 1962. They reveal the nature of the "dialogue" with God that inspired and undergirded all his self-giving in "dialogue" to his fellow men and women.

If we are to pray "without ceasing" to pray: if we are to pray expecting the answer which we know to be God's will: then we need all the time to be deepening our understanding of those for whom we pray. Only through understanding, itself nourished by the exercise of imagination which places us within the spiritual circumstance of those for whom we are praying, can we know the full meaning of intercession, its discipline, its pain, its joy.

Selected Bibliography

An extensive collection of Max Warren's letters, articles, and books is now housed in the CMS Archives at 157 Waterloo Road, London SE1. The *CMS News-Letters* (1942-63) constitute his chief legacy in the field of missionary literature. Though written to deal with issues of importance at the time of writing, they set forth insights and principles of abiding value.

Major Books of Max Warren

1951 *The Christian Mission.* London: SCM Press.
1955 *Caesar, the Beloved Enemy: Three Studies in the Relation of Church and State.* London: SCM Press.
1955 *The Christian Imperative.* New York: Charles Scribner's Sons.
1956 *Partnership: The Study of an Idea.* London: SCM Press.
1964 *Perspective in Mission.* London: Hodder and Stoughton.
1965 *The Missionary Movement from Britain in Modern History.* London: SCM Press.
1966 *Interpreting the Cross.* London: SCM Press.
1967 *Social History and Christian Mission.* London: SCM Press.
1974 *Crowded Canvas: Some Experiences of a Lifetime.* London: Hodder and Stoughton.
1976 *I Believe in the Great Commission.* Grand Rapids, Mich.: Wm. B. Eerdmans.

Works about Max Warren

Dillistone, F.W. *Into All the World: A Biography of Max Warren.* London: Hodder and Stoughton, 1980.
Haaramäki, Ossi. Max A.C. *Warrenin Missionaarinen Ekklesiologia: Systemaattinen selvitys vuosien 1942-1963 Warren-tuotannosta.* (With summary in English: "The Missionary Ecclesiology of Max A.C. Warren: A Systematic Research on the Warren Production of 1942-1963.") Helsinki: Finnish Society for Missiology and Ecumenics, 1982.
Kings, Graham. "Max Warren: Candid Comments on Mission from His Personal Letters." *International Bulletin of Missionary Research* 17 (1993): 54-58.
Yates, T.E. "Anglican Evangelical Missiology, 1922-1984." *Missiology* 14 (1986): 147-57; also in *Mission Studies* 2/2 (1985): 32-38.
_____. "Unhyphenated Evangelicalism: Max Warren, the Tradition and Theology of Mission." *Anvil* 2, no. 3, pp. 231-45.
"The Theology of Mission in the Writings of Max Warren," was written by Francis Eamon Furey in partial fulfillment of requirements for the Licentiate in Sacred Theology from Louvain University in 1974.

Index of Personal Names and Authors

Abrams, Anna, 466
Adaï, 162
Adam, William, 246
Ahui, Jonas, 160, 162
Agagianian, Gregorio Petro, 239
Aké, 160, 162
Albertson, Joe, 501
Al-Gazali, 432
Ali, Cheragh, 285
Ali, Maulana Muhammad, 287
Ali, Saftar, 279
Ali, Sayyid Ameer, 285
Allen, Mary Beatrice Tarlton, 384
Allen, Roland, 170, 383-90, 466, 518, 545, 553, 587; and culture, 387; contextualizer, 385, 387; denominational participation, 383-84; early life of, 383; family, 385, 387; influence, 385, 387-88; innovator, 383, 384-85, 387; minister, 384; mission participation, 383-84; spiritual pilgrimage, 383-84; theory of, 383, 385-87; visionary, 384; writer/editor, 383, 384-85
Allen, Yorke, 613
Allshorn, Florence, 110-18, 577; disciple, 112, 114-16; early life of, 110-11; educator, 111, 112-14; innovator, 113, 114; missionary, 111-12; mission participation, 111-12, 113, 114; spiritual pilgrimage, 111-12, 115; theology of, 112
Ambedkar, Bhim Raj, 349, 604
Anderson, Christopher, 250, 252
Anderson, Gerald H., 457
Anderson, Rufus, 71, 488, 546, 548-53; administrator, 548-49; early life of, 548; educator, 549; family, 548; influence, 548, 552-53; innovator, 549; mission participation, 548, 549; theory of, 549-51; writer/editor, 549
Andrews, C.F., 295, 300, 316-23, 336, 339, 363, 609; contextualizer, 319, 321; denominational participation, 317, 321; early life of, 316, 317; methodology of, 319; ministry to poor, 316, 317, 321; relations

with local people, 316, 319-20; social activist, 317, 317-19; spiritual pilgrimage, 317, 318, 319; student worker, 319; theology of, 317-19, 321; theory of, 318, 320; writer/editor, 317
Anthony, Susan B., 63
Appasamy, A.J., 448
Armstrong, Annie, 214
Arn, Charles, 520
Arn, Win, 516, 518, 520
Ashmore, William, 30, 65
Atcho, Albert, 162
Aufhauser, Johann Baptist, 407
Ayers, T.W., 214
Azariah, Ambu Mariammal Samuel, 325, 326
Azariah, V.S., 300, 320, 324-29; administrator, 326; contextualizer, 327; denominational participation, 325-26, 328; early life of, 324; ecumenism, 325, 327-28; evangelist, 324; family, 325, 328; independence activist, 325-27; innovator, 325-28; mission participation, 324-25; spiritual pilgrimage, 324-25; theory of, 324-25, 327; visionary, 324, 325, 327

Bachmann, E. Theodore, 416
Baillie, John, 88, 336, 363, 419, 449, 611
Baker, Archibald Gillies, 89
Baksh, Khudha, 285
Balasundaram, H.C., 304
Baller, F.W., 200
Barclay, James, 205
Barnett, Homer, 535
Barrett, Adoniram Judson, 62-63
Barth, Karl, 117, 363, 365, 418, 432, 433, 513, 526, 586, 592, 593, 597, 598, 611
Bartlett, Daniel, 446
Bartlett, Mary Leeds, 470
Bastgen, Hubert, 407
Bates, Searle, 416
Bavinck, Johan Herman, 428-34; and culture, 429, 432, 433-34; denominational participation, 429, 430; early life of, 428-29;

Index of Subjects and Places

Oxford Conference on Church, Community and State (1937), 578

Oxford Group Movement, 318, 319

Pakistan, 278

Palestine, 51

Pan-African church, 157

Panama, 461

Papua New Guinea, 480

Paris Evangelical Missionary Society, 126, 129, 494-95

Paris Missionary Fellowship, 495

Parsees (India), 95

Particular Baptist Church, 247

Particular Baptist Society for Propagating the Gospel amongst the Heathen, 247

Peabody-Montgomery Homes, 66

Peace Aims Group, 581

Penal code reform, 11

Pentecostalism, 466

People groups, 520

People movements, 519

Persecution, 226, 229, 233, 402, 404, 406

Persian, 256, 266, 267, 269, 275

Personality: J.H. Bavinck, 429, 431; R.P. Beaver, 452-53; W. Carey, 245-46, 248; T.C. Chao, 225; P. Charles, 410; P.D. Devanandan, 355-56; J. Dindinger, 394; T.V. French, 277-78; W. Freytag, 435; N. Goodall, 602-3; W.W. Harris, 158, 159; L.P. Larsen, 297, 298, 304; K.S. Latourette, 418; S. Neill, 445, 446, 449, 450; J.H. Oldham, 571; W. Paton, 582, 588; C.W. Ranson, 614; J. Rommerskirchen, 395; J. Schmidlin, 403-6, 408; W. Schmidt, 477-78; H.P.S. Schreuder, 150; I.S. Scudder, 308, 315; R.E. Speer, 563; R. Streit, 393; J.H. Taylor, 198, 199, 202; G. Warneck, 375, 376; M. Warren, 618

Personal ministry, 98, 212, 267, 279, 280-81, 284-85, 287, 420

Peru, 461, 466

Phelps-Stokes commissions, 170

Phelps-Stokes Report, 111

Philadelphia, 30-31

Philippines, 500, 501-6

Pietism, 591, 592, 593

Piety, 429, 501, 503, 506-7, 570, 575, 583, 584

Pingtu (China), 210-11

Planters, colonial, 13

Pluralism, 120

Poland, 524

Polygamy, 160

Pontifical Gregorian University (Rome), 606

Pontifical Missionary Library, 57, 393, 395, 397

Pontificio Museo, 482

Poona (India), 73

Poor. *See* Poverty

Postmillennialism. *See* Millennialism and mission theory

Poverty, 212, 316, 317, 321, 462, 541

Pre-imperial missionary period, 140, 143, 145

Premillennialism. *See* Millennialism and mission theory

Presbyterian Church, 28-30, 33, 34, 35, 37, 38, 41, 50, 72, 487, 555, 563, 566-67. *See also* Board of Foreign Missions; Southern Presbyterian Church

Presbyterian Church of England, 582, 583, 606

Princeton Foreign Mission Society, 72

Promotion of mission: C. Buchanan, 256, 257, 258-59, 260; S. A. Crowther, 135; F. Franson, 52, 53; W. Freytag, 436; A.J. Gordon, 18, 19, 20, 21; F.C. Laubach, 500, 501, 502, 505, 506; H.B. Montgomery, 64, 65, 66; C. Moon, 206, 207, 208, 213; J.R. Mott, 79, 80, 82, 83 ; J. H. Oldham, 575; W. Paton, 584, 585; L.W. Peabody, 64, 65, 66, 67; J. Philip, 129; J.W. Pickett, 351, 353; A.T. Pierson, 28, 30, 31, 33; Pius XI, 56-57, 58-59; R. Rouse, 94-95, 96; J. Schmidlin, 406-7; F. Schwager, 103, 104, 105, 106; C. Simeon, 5-6, 7; A.B. Simpson, 37, 40, 42; R.P. Wilder, 72, 74, 74

Propaganda Fide, 56, 57, 59, 106, 267. *See also* Sacred Congregation for the Propagation of the Faith

Propaganda Fide Athenaeum, 394, 395

Prostitution, 20

Prussia, East, 51

Pune (India), 343

Quaker, 11

Qur'an, 136, 268, 279

Racism, 129 , 577, 588

Reinische Mission Society, 374, 377

Reformed Churches in the Netherlands, 429, 430

Refugees, 581

Relations with colleagues: C.F. Andrews, 317, 320, 321; C. Buchanan, 257-58; W. Carey, 248, 250; L.P. Larsen, 299, 302; M. Leenhardt, 495; W. Taylor, 462-63, 465

Relations with local people: C.F. Andrews, 316, 319-20; J.H. Bavinck, 429; C. Buchanan, 260; W. Carey, 250; D. Fraser, 166, 169; B. Gutmann, 179; E.S. Jones, 339, 340, 342, 343; L.B. Jones, 284-85; L.P. Larsen, 300, 304; F.C. Laubach, 503, 505, 506; M. Leenhardt, 496, 497; H. Martyn, 267-68; H.P.S. Schreuder, 149, 150; I.S. Scudder, 307, 308-9, 312

Relief work, 43, 97, 127, 193, 350, 556, 584